Human Geography

For the AP® Course

Human Geography

For the AP® Course

ERIN H. FOUBERG
Northern State University

ALEXANDER B. MURPHY
University of Oregon

PAUL GRAY
Russellville High School

GREG SHERWIN
Adlai E. Stevenson High School

with contributions from **H. J. DE BLIJ**

WILEY

Vice President & Director	Veronica Visentin
Executive Editor	Glenn Wilson
Assistant Editor	Monica Rogers
Instructional Design Lead	Karen Staudinger
Assistant Instructional Designer	Megan Garvin
Senior Content Manager	Svetlana Barskaya
Marketing Manager	Carolyn Wells
Production Services	Lumina Datamatics
Cover & Interior Design	Wendy Lai
Front Cover Photo	Photo by A. B. Murphy. © 2020 John Wiley & Sons, Inc.

This book was set in Lumina Datamatics, Inc. and printed and bound by Quad Graphics. The cover was printed by Quad Graphics.

Founded in 1807, John Wiley & Sons, Inc. has been a valued source of knowledge and understanding for more than 200 years, helping people around the world meet their needs and fulfill their aspirations. Our company is built on a foundation of principles that include responsibility to the communities we serve and where we live and work. In 2008, we launched a Corporate Citizenship Initiative, a global effort to address the environmental, social, economic, and ethical challenges we face in our business. Among the issues we are addressing are carbon impact, paper specifications and procurement, ethical conduct within our business and among our vendors, and community and charitable support. For more information, please visit our website: www.wiley.com/go/citizenship.

ePub ISBN 9781119623489
The inside back cover will contain printing identification and country of origin if omitted from this page.

In addition, if the ISBN on the back cover differs from the ISBN on this page, the one on the back cover is correct.

Printed in the United States of America

VD46C99AD-4BD0-457F-B9FF-E89E449349D4_022720

Preface to Human Geography: People, Place and Culture

The noted geographer Yi-Fu Tuan once said, "People make places." People create cultures, values, aesthetics, politics, economics, and more, and each of these affects and shapes places. Places do not exist in a vacuum, as places are constantly being changed from within and in the context of the broader world. The study of human geography constantly reminds us of how people shape their worlds and of how people and places vary across space.

People build homes and buildings, establish economic and political systems, interact with one other, construct cultures, and shape physical environments. In the process, they create and transform places. On the front cover, the street scene in China reflects the growth of the country that sees itself as a continuation of a 4000-year-old civilization. Throughout history, the majority of Chinese lived in rural areas, but since 2015, most Chinese live in cities. Since 1979, China has focused the majority of its infrastructure projects on megacities like Shanghai and Beijing, but now the country is investing more than $4 trillion in roads, bridges, dams, ports, and airports in around 100 countries through its Belt and Road Initiative. To understand the past and present and think about the future of China, you need to think geographically. In this course, you will learn to apply geographic concepts, including context, scale, diffusion, and networks, to analyze places and people that are constantly changing.

In the AP® edition of *Human Geography: People, Place, and Culture*, you will learn to appreciate the pace of change in the world. You will also understand the causes and consequences of the deepening interconnections among places. Globalization factors heavily into the many ways people influence places. Globalization is a set of processes that flow and pulsate across and through country boundaries with uneven outcomes. Improvements in transportation and communication allow ideas and people to move quickly, creating an environment suitable for change. Through this course in human geography, you will learn to think geographically about what they see, read, and hear about their world.

In writing the twelfth edition of *Human Geography: People, Place, and Culture*, our goals are to teach students to think geographically and critically, to help students understand the role people play in shaping the world, to provide geographic context to the issues we discuss, and to explain how the processes of globalization continue to change and imprint the world. We draw from our own field experiences as well as the research and fieldwork of hundreds of other geographers in an effort to enrich the text.

The AP® edition of *Human Geography* includes significant revision to and reorganization of nearly every chapter. We reorganized chapters to better build student knowledge over the arc of each chapter. Drawing from research in threshold concepts, we spiral approximately 30 threshold concepts across the chapters so that you have multiple opportunities to engage with geographic concepts that, once known, help you see the world as geographers do.

In our writing, we meet you, the students, where you are. As active teachers in geography, we recognize the varying base knowledge of students across the country and in any single classroom. We carefully wrote each caption to help you see the pattern or understand the significance of the image. We also incorporated case studies, including music festivals like Coachella and Governors' Ball (see Chapter 4), to help you understand geography through events that are significant to your generation.

In this edition, we integrated threshold concepts into every Thinking Geographically question found at the end of each chapter section. In each Thinking Geographically question, the threshold concepts in geography are in **bold**. We ask you to get in the habit early on of reading the definitions of each threshold concept in a Thinking Geographically question first. Then, use the concepts to answer each question. Research in geography education confirms that students learn concepts when they apply them. Each Thinking Geographically question gives you an opportunity to apply concepts – use the concepts to make sense of the case study or to connect the ideas in the question.

Threshold concepts are pivotal concepts in geography that, once you know and can successfully apply, will change the way you see the world. By learning, applying, and understanding threshold concepts, you will learn to think geographically. You will ask your own geographic questions and apply threshold concepts to answer them. "A threshold concept can be considered as akin to a portal, opening up a new and previously inaccessible way of thinking about something" (Meyer and Land 2003). Threshold concepts have five traits: They are transformative, probably irreversible, integrative, bounded, and troublesome. They are transformative because they shift the way you see something; irreversible because once you see a threshold concept, like cultural landscapes, you cannot stop seeing them. They are integrative because you can use threshold concepts to organize information and connect with other concepts to deepen learning. They are bounded because threshold concepts are generally important in one discipline more than another (though that is not true of concepts like race and gender). And they are troublesome because it takes effort and uncertainty to go from a basic definition to truly understanding the concept.

We draw from threshold concept research in geography and the threshold concepts in *Understanding World Regional Geography* (Fouberg and Moseley, 2018) to identify around 30 threshold concepts that are spiraled across chapters to improve student learning. Threshold concepts can be found in the Thinking Geographically questions and also in the text as a whole. You will notice that unlike some disciplines, where a concept is confined to one chapter, in geography, we repeatedly apply threshold concepts like cultural landscape, scale, identity, and place. Whether specifically stated or implied, geographers use threshold concepts in our discipline to study the world.

In each Thinking Geographically question, a threshold concept icon appears **TC**, and the threshold concepts in the question are highlighted to ensure you concentrate on the concepts in your answer. The more Thinking Geographically questions you answer, even if not for a grade in your course, the more you will learn to think geographically. Research in threshold concepts recognizes that learning to think geographically will take time—you will need to be uncertain before you are certain. We want you to enter the liminal space, the area of knowing and unknowing—of mimicry and uncertainty—in your thinking. Being uncertain is a healthy part of learning. Struggling to understand a concept or think through a case study of a place you have never been is not easy, but it leads to learning. You will leave this course with a better understanding of the world, and you will also leave with the ability to think geographically. That ability will serve you throughout your life.

When you truly think geographically, you see patterns, you read cultural landscapes, you question how places are connected, you consider how one process can have different outcomes in different places, and you think about scale from local to global in ways others do not. Put in the work to learn—not just memorize—concepts. Work to actually understand and apply concepts, and you will surprise yourself with how much you learn in this course.

We recognize the important role we play in shaping the way students learn and understand human geography. We approach our writing as we do our teaching and research. We draw from the foundational research geographers have done in the field, we look through the lens of major theories in our discipline, and we read current research of geographers who are doing fieldwork on the topic. We apply geographic concepts and select case studies to present how geographers think about language, religion, development, culture, industry, agriculture, and more. We work extensively with our cartographers at Mapping Specialists to find data and imagine the best way to tell a story with each map. We draw from our own field research and collection of photographs to show you what we are saying. We even sketch diagrams by hand, like we would on a SMART Board in the classroom, and ask our cartographers to draw new diagrams. We worked with our colleague Harm de Blij, the sole author of the first edition of this book, on several editions before he passed away. With each revision, we recognize the imprint he made on human geography. Harm drew the map of European colonization. He sketched the sub-Saharan Africa city model, and he helped us draw the map of world religions. Harm was a wonderful teacher and he brought his excitement for the discipline of geography to every page of this book. As we take the mantle with this edition, we brought our own sense of excitement for our discipline to each page.

We established an ArcGIS Online mapping program to support this course through partnerships with Esri and Maps. com. Maps.com used ArcGIS to create thematic maps for print and digital that are found in the book and in your online course materials. Clicking on the ArcGIS Online webmaps opens the maps in ArcGIS Online, making maps dynamic and interactive. The demographic data table found in Appendix B is mapped in ArcGIS Online. Each column of data in the table is a layer in ArcGIS Online. You can turn on and off layers and manipulate their appearance instantly on ArcGIS Online.

The field notes in this edition provide context and will help you learn to think geographically. Each chapter opens with an author field note, and in this edition, we wrote new opening field notes that are short hooks into thinking about the topic of the chapter. We want you to understand right away why the material in a chapter is significant. For example, the growth of Airbnbs and the sharing economy is changing the nature of residential neighborhoods in cities (see Chapter 9). The replacement of people with robots on the BMW assembly line in Germany reveals the changing nature of manufacturing and asks you to think about the nature of work and the kinds of jobs you will have (Chapter 12).

Each chapter also includes one or more author field notes, in addition to the opening field note. The author field notes serve as models of how to think geographically. We took a significant number of the photographs in this edition. In addition to the author field notes, we include a number of guest field notes written by geographers who have spent time in the field, researching the places that they profile. All guest field notes include a photograph and a paragraph focusing on how the guest field note author's observations in the field influenced their research.

The AP® edition of *Human Geography: People, Place, and Culture* is supported by a comprehensive supplements package that includes an extensive selection of print, visual, and electronic materials.

Online Resources

This course includes numerous resources to help you enhance your current presentations, create new presentations, and employ our premade PowerPoint presentations. Resources include:

- Looking Closer Videos are curated to give students a first-hand look at life in other parts of the world.

- Practice Questions provide students a chance to check their understanding of the concepts discussed in each section.

- Image Gallery. We provide online electronic files for the illustrations and maps in the book, which you can customize for presenting in class.

- Area and Demographic Data are provided for every country and world region along with an interactive ArcGIS Online map that automatically maps each column of data in the table.
- PowerPoint presentations are available to instructors for classroom discussions and lectures.
- ArcGIS Online maps designed for this book and question sets written by professional geographers are available as automatically graded assignments in each chapter's online activities.

A comprehensive Test Bank includes multiple-choice, fill-in-the-blank, matching, and essay questions. The Test Bank is available in the Instructor's Resources as electronic files and can be saved into all major word-processing programs.

Acknowledgments

In preparing the twelfth edition of *Human Geography*, we benefited immensely from the advice and assistance of many of our colleagues in geography. We thank human geography teachers, professors, instructors, and students from around the country who emailed us questions and gave us suggestions. Some told us of their experiences teaching the material, and others provided insightful comments on individual chapters. The list that follows acknowledges their support, but it cannot begin to measure our gratitude for all of the ways they helped shape this book:

Ian Ackroyd-Kelly, *East Stroudsburg University*
Frank Ainsley, *University of North Carolina, Wilmington*
Victoria Alapo, *Metropolitan Community College*
Jennifer Altenhofel, *California State University, Bakersfield*
Charles Amissah, *Hampton University*
Alan Arbogast, *Michigan State University*
James Ashley, *University of Toledo*
Scharmaistha Bagchi-Sen, *SUNY Buffalo*
Nancy Bain, *Ohio University*
Jeff Baldwin, *Sonoma State University*
Brad Bays, *Oklahoma State University*
Sarah W. Bednarz, *Texas A&M University*
Sari Bennett, *University of Maryland, Baltimore County*
T. Bertossi, *Northern Michigan University*
J. Best, *Frostburg State University*
Brian Blouet, *College of William & Mary*
Mark Bockenhauer, *St. Norbert College*
Margaret Boorstein, *C.W. Post College of Long Island University*
Patricia Boudinot, *George Mason University*
Michael Broadway, *Northern Michigan University*
Michaele Ann Buell, *Northwest Arkansas Community College*
Patrick Buckley, *Western Washington University*
Scott Carlin, *Long Island University*
Carolyn Coulter, *Atlantic Cape Community College*
Fiona M. Davidson, *University of Arkansas*
L. Scott Deaner, *Owens Community College*
Evan Denney, *University of Montana*
Ramesha Dhussa, *Drake University*
Dimitar Dimitrov, *Virginia Commonwealth University*
Dawn Drake, *University of Tennessee, Knoxville*
Steve Driever, *University of Missouri, Kansas City*
Anna Dvorak, *West Los Angeles College*
James Dyer, *Mount St. Mary's College*
Adrian X. Esparza, *University of Arizona*

Stephen Frenkel, *University of Washington, Seattle*
Juanita Gaston, *Florida A&M University*
Matthew J. Gerike, *Kansas State University*
Lay James Gibson, *University of Arizona*
Sarah Goggin, *Santa Ana College*
Abe Goldman, *University of Florida*
Richard Grant, *University of Miami*
Alyson Greiner, *Oklahoma State University*
Jeffrey A. Gritzner, *University of Montana*
Qian Guo, *Northern Michigan University*
Nicole Harner, *Souderton Area High School*
Joseph P. Henderson, *Georgia Gwinnet College*
John Heppen, *University of Wisconsin, River Falls*
John Hickey, *Inver Hills Community College*
Miriam Helen Hill, *Jacksonville State University*
Peter R. Hoffmann, *Loyola Marymount University*
Peter Hugill, *Texas A&M University*
Francis Hutchins, *Bellarmine University*
Jay Johnson, *University of Nebraska, Lincoln*
Tarek A. Joseph, *Central Michigan University*
Rajrani Kalra, *California State University, San Bernardino*
Melinda Kashuba, *Shasta College*
Artimus Keiffer, *Wittenberg University*
Les King, *McMaster University*
Paul Kingsbury, *Miami University, Ohio*
Frances Kostarelos, *Governors State University*
Darrell P. Kruger, *Illinois State University*
Paul Larson, *Southern Utah University*
Jess A. Le Vine, *Brookdale Community College*
Ann Legreid, *Central Missouri State University*
Todd Lindley, *Georgia Gwinnett College*
Jose Lopez, *Minnesota State University*
David Lyons, *University of Minnesota, Duluth*
Patricia Matthews-Salazar, *Borough of Manhattan Community College*
Darrell McDonald, *Stephen F. Austin State University*
Wayne McKim, *Towson University*
Neusah McWilliams, *University of Toledo, Ohio*
Ian MacLachlan, *University of Lethbridge*
Glenn Miller, *Bridgewater State College*
Katharyne Mitchell, *University of Washington, Seattle*
Terri Mitchell, *University of South Alabama*
Katera Moore, *Camden County College*
John M. Morris, *University of Texas, San Antonio*
Garth A. Myers, *University of Kansas*
Darrell Norris, *SUNY Geneseo*

Ann Oberhauser, *West Virginia University*
Kenji Oshiro, *Wright State University*
Bimal K. Paul, *Kansas State University*
Gene Paull, *University of Texas at Brownsville*
Daniel R. Pavese, *Wor-Wic Community College*
Walter Peace, *McMaster University*
Sonja Porter, *Central Oregon Community College*
Virginia Ragan, *Maple Woods Community College*
Jeffrey Richetto, *University of Alabama*
Rob Ritchie, *Liberty University*
Mika Roinila, *State University of New York, New Paltz*
Karl Ryavec, *University of Wisconsin*
James Saku, *Frostburg State University*
Richard Alan Sambrook, *Eastern Kentucky University*
Joseph E. Schwartzberg, *University of Minnesota*
Allen Scott, *University of California Los Angeles*
Gary W. Shannon, *University of Kentucky*
Betty Shimshak, *Towson University*
Nancy Shirley, *Southern Connecticut State University*
Susan Slowey, *Blinn College*
Andrew Sluyter, *Pennsylvania State University*
Janet Smith, *Shippensberg University*
Herschel Stern, *Mira Costa College*
Neva Duncan Tabb, *University of South Florida*
Thomas Terich, *Western Washington University*
Donald Thieme, *Georgia Southern University*
James A. Tyner, *University of Southern California*
David Unterman, *Sierra and Yuba Community Colleges*
Barry Wauldron, *University of Michigan, Dearborn*
David Wishart, *University of Nebraska, Lincoln*
George W. White, *South Dakota State University*
Leon Yacher, *Southern Connecticut State University*
Donald Zeigler, *Old Dominion University*
Robert C. Ziegenfus, *Kutztown University*

In the twelfth edition, several of our colleagues in geography provided guest field notes. The stories these colleagues tell and the brilliant photos they provide will help you better appreciate the role of fieldwork in geographic research:

Jonathan Leib, *Old Dominion University*
Korine Kolivras, *Virginia Tech*
Elsbeth Robson, *Keele University*
Carol Farbotko, *Commonwealth Scientific and Industrial Research*
Simon M. Evans and Peter Peller, *University of Calgary*
Steven M. Schnell, *Kutztown University of Pennsylvania*
Richard Francaviglia, *Geo. Graphic Designs*
Ines Miyares, *Hunter College of the City University of New York*
Sarah Halvorson, *University of Montana*
Derek Alderman, *University of Tennessee*
Mary Lee Nolan, *Oregon State University*
Paul Gray, *Russellville High School*
George White, *South Dakota State University*
Johnathan Walker, *James Madison University*
Rachel Silvey, *University of Toronto*
Judith Carney, *University of California, Los Angeles*
Fiona M. Davidson, *University of Arkansas*
William Moseley, *Macalester College*
Kenneth E. Foote, *University of Connecticut*

On a day-to-day basis, many people in the extended John Wiley & Sons family provided support and guidance. We thank Vice President and Director Veronica Visentin for her support of this edition of *Human Geography*. Glenn Wilson, executive editor for geography, brought energy, vision, and focus to this edition, and we are incredibly thankful for his support and friendship. Development Editor Meg Garvin handled our excitement and frustration equally with grace. From giving feedback on writing to problem solving behind the scenes, Meg was integral to the success of this edition. Sundar Ananthapadmanabhan, permissions specialist, tracked down sources around the world to obtain permissions for the twelfth edition, enabling us to create dozens of new maps and diagrams for this edition. Sundar and his team also found photos that helped bring to life the words we described on the page. Monica Rogers, assistant editor, organized reviews and helped get the revisions started for this edition. Don Larson and Terry Bush, our cartographers at Mapping Specialists, are outstanding professionals who used their design aesthetic and skills in cartography and GIS to update or create at least 100 maps and figures in this edition. We benefited from an exceptional production editor on this edition. Trish McFadden gracefully kept us on track with a tight schedule. Marketing Manager Carolyn Wells worked with the author team to translate our vision for *Human Geography: People, Place, and Culture* into an effective marketing message.

We thank Erin's writing mentor, David Wishart of the University of Nebraska-Lincoln, whose suggestions are found in many new topics discussed in the twelfth edition. Erin appreciates ideas shared by geography educators at the AAG, the NCGE, the NCSS, and on the Human Geography Teachers Facebook page. Their passion for teaching students and their excitement for the field of human geography inspired her to find new ways to explain several complicated geographic concepts in the twelfth edition.

We are grateful to our family and friends who supported us faithfully through this edition. Special thanks from Erin to Maggie and Henry for tolerating the constant presence of her laptop, giving feedback on photo options and captions, and reading edits to explain what they took from different passages. We are grateful to our mentor, Harm de Blij, who was generous and kind to both of us. Harm shared his insights, gave feedback, and made us think. He set the tone for how we continue to work together in his absence. As always, our greatest thanks go to our spouses, Robert Fouberg and Susan Gary, who through their support, understanding, and patience make us better people and better authors.

ERIN H. FOUBERG
Aberdeen, South Dakota

ALEXANDER B. MURPHY
Eugene, Oregon

PAUL GRAY
Russellville High School

GREG SHERWIN
Adlai E. Stevenson High School

Welcome to The World of AP® Human Geography

Every important journey should start with a map. The purpose of this introduction is to help students begin to navigate their way around the AP® Human Geography course. The introduction is a road map to the organization and goals of the course. It should help provide direction for students before they begin their exploration into AP® Human Geography.

For many students, AP® Human Geography will be their first venture into a college experience and the AP® environment. In addition to this challenge, AP® Human Geography may also be their first full yearlong course focused solely on geography. Therefore, it is imperative for students to have an idea of what to anticipate before the year starts.

This preface explores the following topics:

1. What does AP® mean?
2. What is AP® Human Geography?
3. How are content and skills organized for AP® Human Geography?
4. How is the AP® Human Geography Exam administered?
5. How are students assessed on the AP® Human Geography Exam?
6. How do students prepare for the AP® exam?

1) What Does AP® Mean?

To understand AP® Human Geography, one must first understand what AP® means and how this course is connected to possible credit at numerous colleges and universities. AP® is shorthand for Advanced Placement, and there are currently 38 Advanced Placement subjects organized and overseen by the College Board.[1]

The College Board's mission started in the 1950s and its goal was to create college-level courses for high school students. Teams of college professors and high school teachers design the curriculum to ensure the course meets the content and goals of a first-year college course. Students who take AP® classes are evaluated in May by taking the Advanced Placement exam for their course.

Currently, AP® exams cost $94. In 2019, the College Board moved registration for AP® exams to early fall. This means that students enrolled in AP® Human Geography classes must make the decision earlier than before to take the exam. Taking the AP®

exam is not necessarily a requirement for taking AP® Human Geography, but early registration makes it challenging not to sign up for the test. Regardless, it is strongly encouraged to sign up for the exam because it is the only way for students to receive potential credit at colleges and universities.

The College Board uses a 5-point system for all AP® exams as a way to recommend whether or not a student should receive credit at a college or university.

AP® Exam Score[2]	Recommendation	College Grade Equivalent
5	Extremely well qualified	A+ or A
4	Very well qualified	A−, B+, or B
3	Qualified	B−, C+, or C
2	Possibly qualified	
1	No recommendation	

According to the College Board, scoring a 3 or higher on the AP® Human Geography Exam is considered a passing grade. However, please note that colleges and universities establish their own specific rules and policies on what is accepted for credit at their schools. Therefore, the best advice for students is to search the AP® credit policy for colleges and universities on their own. Thankfully, the College Board has provided this resource for students online in the section "AP® Credit Policy."

Please note that many state governments across the United States have put into law that any student receiving a 3 or higher on an AP® exam will receive credit at the public institutions in those states regardless of where students currently live. For example, a student from Russellville, Arkansas, who receives a 3 on the AP® Human Geography Exam would receive 3 credit hours of course work at the University of Illinois if he or she was accepted and chose to attend the school. However, if a student wished to attend DePaul University in Chicago, Illinois, the standards would be different. DePaul University is a private institution and thus sets its own standards for AP® Human Geography credit. DePaul will not give credit for a 3 on the AP® exam, but it gives 4 credit hours for a 4 and 8 credit hours for a 5 on the AP® exam.

Further, some elite universities, notable the Ivy League schools, will not accept AP® Human Geography credit regardless of the score. Yet at the same time, these same universities demand that students take a challenging curriculum in high school to demonstrate their readiness for these top schools.

---

[1]https://apstudents.collegeboard.org/course-index-page

[2]https://apstudents.collegeboard.org/about-ap-scores/ap-score-scale-table

Therefore, taking AP® Human Geography and receiving a 5 on the exam may provide a student with one example to highlight in their application portfolio.

Finally, it is worth mentioning that there is no penalty for students who score poorly on the exam. Scores on AP® exams do not have to be shared with colleges or universities. Therefore, taking the exam can be beneficial for students because it will give them a sample of a challenging examination under a strict time limit, which should help prepare them for standardized tests in the future.

Regardless of the score on the AP® exam, most universities and colleges want to see students challenge themselves in high school. Taking the AP® Human Geography Exam serves notice to colleges and universities that a student is serious about future success. Therefore, it is recommended that all students enrolled in AP® Human Geography take the exam.

2) What is AP® Human Geography?

Oftentimes, students and parents struggle with understanding what the "human" part of AP® Human Geography is. Students feel like they have an elementary understanding of geography and geography skills. Therefore, it is important to break down each part of the course title to help students understand what they will be learning in class. Thus far, we have covered the "AP®" part of the title. Let's move to the final word, "Geography," next.

Geography is the systematic study of the spatial patterns of all phenomena on or near the Earth's surface. Its primary methodology is spatial analysis, which asks two basic questions: *Where* are things located? (spatial), and Why are they located where they are? (analysis—*why there*). Historians use time as their foundation, think chronologically, and ask "when" and "why"; geographers use space as their foundation, think spatially, and ask "where" and "why there."

Geography is not history, though both courses are related to each other and historical information "serves to enrich analysis of the impacts of phenomena such as globalization, colonialism, and human–environment relationships on places, regions, cultural landscapes, and patterns of interaction."[3]

The primary tools of geography are maps, charts, and photographs due to geography's focus on "where" and "why there." However, geography is truly a twenty-first-century discipline, with geospatial technologies including geographic information systems (GIS), satellite navigation systems, remote sensing, and online mapping and visualization playing a major role in presenting data and displaying information. Remember, geography is a spatial discipline, which means it will look at different variables and how they are organized in space. Then geographers ask, "Where is it?" and "Why is it there?"

Human geography is one of the major divisions of geography; the spatial analysis of human population and its cultures, activities, and landscapes. Instead of presenting geography through a regional perspective, human geography covers thematic topics such as population growth, migration patterns, language distribution, and economic differences. Therefore, students in AP® Human Geography will analyze a theme such as population growth in the world and ask the two fundamental questions of the course "where is it" and "why is it there".

According to the College Board, "The content is presented thematically rather than regionally and is organized around the discipline's main subfields: economic geography, cultural geography, political geography, and urban geography. The approach is spatial and problem oriented. Case studies are drawn from all world regions, with an emphasis on understanding the world in which we live today."[4]

Human geography thus provides the foundation for understanding fundamental similarities and differences between people culturally, politically, economically, and socially through a spatial perspective. Human geographers look at *where* something occurs, search for patterns, and span most of the other social studies disciplines to answer the *why there* question.

Questions of Human Geography

- *Where* is population growing? *Where* are people migrating? *Why there*?

- *Where* are different languages spoken? *Why* are they spoken there?

- *Where* are different religions practiced? *Where* is there religious conflict? *Why there*?

- *Where* do people live in the United States? *Why* do so many people live in the suburbs? *Why* do more people live on the coasts throughout the world?

- *Where* are textile mills (clothing manufacturers) located in the world today? *Why* are they *there*? *Where* were textile mills in the United States? *Why* did they leave the United States? *Where* are new factories locating in the United States? *Why there*?

According to the College Board,

The goal for the course is for students to become more geoliterate, more engaged in contemporary global issues, and more informed about multicultural

---

viewpoints. They will develop skills in approaching problems geographically, using maps and geospatial technologies, thinking critically about texts and graphic images, interpreting cultural landscapes, and applying geographic concepts such as scale, region, diffusion, interdependence, and spatial interaction, among others. Students will see geography as a discipline relevant to the world in which they live; as a source of ideas for identifying, clarifying, and solving problems at various scales; and as a key component of building global citizenship and environmental stewardship.[5]

3) How are Content and Skills Organized For AP® Human Geography?

There are two different areas students must focus on in AP® Human Geography: content and skills. To be good at geography, students need to understand specific geography. Further, they need to know how to apply that knowledge by developing geography skills at the same time.

The Content   AP® Human Geography covers seven major topics throughout the year. The following lists the topics in the order assigned by the College Board (please note that teachers sometimes will cover these topics in a different order):

	Content Area (Topic)	Percentage Goals for Exam
I.	Thinking Geographically	8–10%
II.	Population and Migration Patterns and Processes	12–17%
III.	Cultural Patterns and Processes	12–17%
IV.	Political Patterns and Processes	12–17%
V.	Agriculture and Rural Land-Use Patterns and Processes	12–17%
VI.	Cities and Urban Land-Use Patterns and Processes	12–17%
VII.	Industrialization and Economic Development Patterns and Processes	12–17%

The percentages mark the range of multiple-choice questions that will be on the AP® exam from each section.

[5]College Board AP® Human Geography Course and Exam Description, p. 11

This textbook covers the content in the following chapters:

Content Area (Topic)	Chapters in the Text
Thinking Geographically	Ch. 1
Population and Migration Patterns and Processes	Ch. 2–3
Cultural Patterns and Processes	Ch. 4–7
Political Patterns and Processes	Ch. 8
Agriculture and Rural Land-Use Patterns and Processes	Ch. 11
Cities and Urban Land-Use Patterns and Processes	Ch. 9
Industrialization and Economic Development Patterns and Processes	Ch. 10 and 12

Chapters 13 and 14 of the textbook cover important topics such as the environment and globalization that tie all the units neatly together.

In addition to the seven major topics, the College Board expects students to be able to weave in three big ideas into every unit. These three ideas are:

1. *Patterns and Spatial Organization*
   This course asks students to understand the patterns and spatial organization of people, places, and environments—where are they similar and where are they different, and why.

2. *Impacts and Interactions*
   This course asks students to look at the impacts of human decisions on the Earth's surface and the impacts of how different groups of humans have interacted over space and time—where are they similar and where are they different, and how have they changed over time, and why.

3. *Spatial Processes and Societal Change*
   This course asks students to explain the spatial movement of people and the impact of this movement while also looking at how change has occurred over time and space—where are they similar and where are they different, and why.

The Course Skills   Finally, in addition to understanding the content and the big ideas, the College Board expects students to develop the following skills over the course of the school year:

1. Concepts and Processes
2. Spatial Relationships
3. Data Analysis
4. Source Analysis
5. Scale Analysis

The following chart from the College Board details these skills more specifically.

AP® Human Geography Course Skill⁶

Skill Category 1	Skill Category 2	Skill Category 3	Skill Category 4	Skill Category 5
Concepts and Processes 1	**Spatial Relationships** 2	**Data Analysis** 3	**Source Analysis** 4	**Scale Analysis** 5
Analyze geographic theories, approaches, concepts, processes, or models in theoretical and applied contexts.	Analyze geographic patterns, relationships, and outcomes in applied contexts.	Analyze and interpret quantitative geographic data represented in maps, tables, charts, graphs, satellite images, and infographics.	Analyze and interpret qualitative geographic information represented in maps, images (e.g., satellite, photographs, cartoons), and landscapes.	Analyze geographic theories, approaches, concepts, processes, and models across geographic scales to explain spatial relationships.

Skills

1.A Describe geographic concepts, processes, models, and theories.	**2.A** Describe spatial patterns, networks, and relationships.	**3.A** Identify the different types of data presented in maps and in quantitative and geospatial data.	**4.A** Identify the different types of information presented in visual sources.	**5.A** Identify the scales of analysis presented by maps, quantitative and geospatial data, images, and landscapes.
1.B Explain geographic concepts, processes, models, and theories.	**2.B** Explain spatial relationships in a specified context or region of the world, using geographic concepts, processes, models, or theories.	**3.B** Describe spatial patterns presented in maps and in quantitative and geospatial data.	**4.B** Describe the spatial patterns presented in visual sources.	**5.B** Explain spatial relationships across various geographic scales using geographic concepts, processes, models, or theories.
1.C Compare geographic concepts, processes, models, and theories.	**2.C** Explain a likely outcome in a geographic scenario using geographic concepts, processes, models, or theories.	**3.C** Explain patterns and trends in maps and in quantitative and geospatial data to draw conclusions.	**4.C** Explain patterns and trends in visual sources to draw conclusions.	**5.C** Compare geographic characteristics and processes at various scales.
1.D Describe a relevant geographic concept, process, model, or theory in a specified context.	**2.D** Explain the significance of geographic similarities and differences among different locations and/or at different times.	**3.D** Compare patterns and trends in maps and in quantitative and geospatial data to draw conclusions.	**4.D** Compare patterns and trends in sources to draw conclusions.	**5.D** Explain the degree to which a geographic concept, process, model, or theory effectively explains geographic effects across various geographic scales.
1.E Explain the strengths, weaknesses, and limitations of different geographic models and theories in a specified context.	**2.E** Explain the degree to which a geographic concept, process, model, or theory effectively explains geographic effects in different contexts and regions of the world.	**3.E** Explain what maps or data imply or illustrate about geographic principles, processes, and outcomes.	**4.E** Explain how maps, images, and landscapes illustrate or relate to geographic principles, processes, and outcomes.	
		3.F Explain possible limitations of the data provided.	**4.F** Explain possible limitations of visual sources provided.	

Summary Because this is a college-level course, there is a lot expected, and all the previous lists can appear overwhelming at first. However, it is best to think of each of three parts (content, big ideas, skills) as working together throughout the course and not necessarily all at the same time. For instance, a student might be studying a topic like population distribution. Clearly, the student will be studying geographic content. Further, in order to truly understand population distribution, one must work through each of the three big ideas to master the content. However, it might not be necessary to go through all five skills directly to work with population distribution. The five skills are developed holistically over the course of the school year. The best advice for students is to learn the content and practice the skills as one goes along.

4) How is the AP® Human Geography Exam Administered?

The AP® Human Geography Exam is administered to students across the world on the same day, sometime during the first two weeks of May. The day changes from year to year; therefore, it is essential to check the College Board's website (AP® Central) for information about the dates and times for the AP® Human Geography Exam.

The purpose of the AP® Human Geography Exam is to assess how well the student has mastered the content, big ideas, and

⁶College Board AP® Human Geography Course and Exam Description

skills addressed in the previous section. The exam is 2 hours and 15 minutes and has two main components: 60 multiple-choice questions followed by 3 free-response questions.

Section	Question Type	Number of Questions	Exam Weight	Time
1	Multiple-choice	60	50%	60 minutes
2	Free-response	3	50%	75 minutes

It is important to note that each portion of the exam is administered fully with a break in between for students. Students are not allowed to start the free-response section until after the break.

Here are some basic facts about the multiple-choice questions on the AP® exam:

- All multiple-choice questions will have five choices (A–E).
- Fifty percent of the multiple-choice questions will have a stimulus (map, chart, data table, etc.) with the question.
- There will be six to eight item sets with two to three questions included using the same stimulus.

Here are some basic facts about the free-response questions (FRQs) on the AP® exam:

- Each free-response question will be scored as a 7-point question.
- Each free-response question will have five to seven task verbs for the student to answer (A–G).
- The first free-response question will NOT have a stimulus.
- The second free-response question will have one stimulus (map, chart, data table, etc.) with the question.
- The final free-response question will have two stimuli (map, chart, data table, etc.) with the question.
- Below are the task verbs that will be used on the AP® exam:

FRQ Task Verbs	Meaning
Compare	Provide a description or explanation of similarities and/or differences.
Define	Provide a specific meaning for a word or concept.
Describe	Provide the relevant characteristics of a specified topic.
Explain	Provide information about how or why a relationship, process, pattern, position, or outcome occurs, using evidence and/or reasoning.
Identify	Indicate or provide information about a specified topic, without elaboration or explanation.

5) How are Students Assessed on the AP® Human Geography Exam?

SECTION 1: Multiple-choice questions (60 questions in 60 minutes)
The AP® exam will assess student learning in the multiple-choice portion with the following weighting in content areas:

Content Area (Topic)	Percentage Goals for Exam
I. Thinking Geographically	8–10%
II. Population and Migration Patterns and Processes	12–17%
III. Cultural Patterns and Processes	12–17%
IV. Political Patterns and Processes	12–17%
V. Agriculture and Rural Land-Use Patterns and Processes	12–17%
VI. Cities and Urban Land-Use Patterns and Processes	12–17%
VII. Industrialization and Economic Development Patterns and Processes	12–17%

In addition, students will also be assessed on the following skills in the multiple-choice portion with the following weighting:

Skill Category	Weighting
1. Concepts and Processes	25–36%
2. Spatial Relationships	16–25%
3. Data Analysis	13–20%
4. Source Analysis	13–20%
5. Scale Analysis	13–20%

SECTION 2: Free-response questions (3 questions in 75 minutes)
The AP® exam will assess student learning in content areas in the free-response portion by including at least two different units in each question. These combinations will vary from year to year and question to question.

There is no way to predict which units the FRQs will cover in any year. Below are the 7 units for potential questions.

Content Area (Topic)

I. Thinking Geographically

II. Population and Migration Patterns and Processes

III. Cultural Patterns and Processes

IV. Political Patterns and Processes

V. Agriculture and Rural Land-Use Patterns and Processes

VI. Cities and Urban Land-Use Patterns and Processes

VII. Industrialization and Economic Development Patterns and Processes

In addition, students will also be assessed on the following skills in the free-response portion with the following weighting:

Skill Category	Weighting
1. Concepts and Processes	23–29%
2. Spatial Relationships	33–43%
3. Data Analysis	10–19%
4. Source Analysis	10–19%
5. Scale Analysis	10–14%

6) How Do Students Prepare for the AP® Exam?

The goal in this introduction is to make sure students understand how AP® classes like AP® Human Geography work. In the appendix to this book, students will find access to strategies on how to prepare for the AP® exam. The strategies will focus on how to prepare for both the multiple-choice and free-response portions of the exam. In addition, there are online resources for this book such as an AP® practice exam available to students.

Finally, there is a test prep app designed by AP® Human Geography teachers called iScore5. The app is available for both Apple and Google devices and costs $4.99. The app includes hundreds of practice multiple-choice questions for each specific unit, designed from easy to hard. In addition, it has free-response questions and a full practice exam for students.

Photograph by Robert Fouberg

ERIN HOGAN FOUBERG grew up in eastern South Dakota. She moved to Washington, D.C., to attend Georgetown University's School of Foreign Service, where she took a class in Human Geography from Harm de Blij. At Georgetown, Erin found her international relations classes lacking in context and discovered a keen interest in political geography. She earned her master's and Ph.D. at the University of Nebraska-Lincoln (1997). After graduating, Dr. Fouberg taught for several years at the University of Mary Washington in Fredericksburg, Virginia, where the graduating class of 2001 bestowed on her the Mary Pinschmidt Award, given to the faculty member who made the biggest impact on their lives.

Dr. Fouberg is professor of geography and director of the honors program at Northern State University in Aberdeen, South Dakota, where she won the Outstanding Faculty Award in 2011. She has expertise in political geography and geography education. Her research on threshold concepts and student learning won the Biennial Award for Teaching and Learning from the *Journal of Geography in Higher Education*. Professor Fouberg served on the board of the National Council for Geographic Education. Dr. Fouberg co-authors *Understanding World Regional Geography* with William G. Moseley, also published by Wiley. She is active in her community, serving in leadership roles on fundraising campaigns for children's charities. She enjoys traveling, reading, golfing, and watching athletic and theater events at Northern State.

Photograph by Jack Liu

ALEC MURPHY grew up in the western United States, but he spent several of his early years in Europe and Japan. He obtained his undergraduate degree at Yale University, studied law at the Columbia University School of Law, practiced law for a short time in Chicago, and then pursued a doctoral degree in geography (Ph.D. University of Chicago, 1987). After graduating, Dr. Murphy joined the faculty of the University of Oregon, where he became professor of geography and was named the James F. and Shirley K. Rippey Chair in Liberal Arts and Sciences. Professor Murphy is a widely published scholar in the fields of political, cultural, and environmental geography. His work has been supported by the National Science Foundation, the National Endowment for the Humanities, the Rockefeller Foundation, and the Fulbright-Hays foreign fellowship program.

Professor Murphy served as the president of the Association of American Geographers in 2003–2004. He is currently senior vice president of the American Geographical Society. In the late 1990s, he led the effort to add geography to the College Board's Advanced Placement Program. He chaired a National Academy of Sciences study charged with identifying strategic directions for the geographical sciences. In 2014, he received the Association of American Geographers' highest honor, its Lifetime Achievement Award. His interests include hiking, skiing, camping, music, and of course exploring the diverse places that make up our planet.

Paul Gray

Greg Sherwin

PAUL GRAY grew up in western Arkansas very near the Oklahoma border. He loved maps and globes as a child and spent a lot of time studying them in hopes of going to all seven continents one day. Paul served in United States Army intelligence for four years, where he spent most of his service in Germany as a Morse Intercept Operator. Paul holds a B.A. and M.Ed. from Arkansas Tech University and an Ed.D. from Walden University. Paul has been teaching at Russellville High School in Arkansas since 1993 and has been the social sciences and humanities department chair there since 2000. Paul has been active in many facets of geography education including the AP® Human Geography Test Development Committee from 2002-2007 and was one of 17 original readers at the 2001 AP® Human Geography Reading. Paul was the 2008 National Geographic Society Grosvenor Teacher Fellow and the 2013 president of the National Council for Geographic Education. Paul was named the 2008 Arkansas Teacher of the Year by the Arkansas Department of Education and received the Distinguished Teaching Award from NCGE in 2003. Paul has authored several publications on geography education and has presented at numerous geographic conferences throughout the United States, Europe, and Australia. He has been active on many geography education committees and writing teams, including the 2nd edition of *Geography for Life*. He co-authored the 10th and 11th editions of Advanced Placement Study Guide for *Human Geography: People, Place and Culture* with Greg Sherwin (Wiley Publishing). Paul is also a co-founding partner of iScore5® which produces AP® exam prep mobile phone apps for AP® human geography and other AP® subjects. He lives in Arkansas with his wife Beth and is the father of Jenny, Zach, and Ariston and a grandfather to Grayden and Emma. In 2010, Paul realized his childhood dream by visiting his seventh continent.

GREG SHERWIN grew up in the suburbs of Chicago. His love of geography began in the sixth grade when he was selected to go on a student exchange program to Egypt, Israel and Vatican City shortly after the Camp David Accords in 1978. He attended DePaul University and took Human Geography as a freshman using the third edition of *Human Geography: People, Place and Culture*. He currently teaches AP® Human Geography at Adlai E. Stevenson High School in Lincolnshire, Illinois. He has served in a variety of leadership capacities at the annual AP® Human Geography reading and within the AP® Human Geography community. He served on the AP® Human Geography Test Development Committee (2002-2006). In 2007, he co-authored the AP® Human Geography Teacher's Guide with Paul Gray and published by the College Board. He has presented topics for the College Board on AP® Human Geography at conferences and workshops throughout the country and in Scotland and Australia.

Most recently, he co-authored the 10th and 11th editions of Advanced Placement Study Guide for Human Geography: People, Place and Culture with Paul Gray (Wiley Publishing). In 2015, Mr. Sherwin received a Distinguished Teaching Award from the National Council for Geography Education (NCGE). He also has teamed up with 30 other AP® Human Geography teachers who value technology to create an app (iScore5) to prepare students for the exam. His cultural landscape field study assignment was recognized by the College Board and is available on the AP® Central Website. He lives in the Chicago area with his wife Heather and is the proud father of Carter and Dylan. He enjoys spending time with his family at music and sporting events.

To Generation Z

may understanding
human geography help
you create solutions that
can improve our world

Brief Contents

Appendix D can be found in WileyPLUS

xviii

Contents

7 Religion **186**

8 Political Geography **225**

*Appendix D can be found in WileyPLUS

CHAPTER 1

Introduction to Human Geography

Daily Mirror Gulf coverage/3rd Party - Misc/Getty Images

FIGURE 1.1 **Baghdad, Iraq.** U.S. Marines pulled down the statue of Saddam Hussein in Firdos Square in the center of Baghdad on April 9, 2003.

Troops from the United States, the United Kingdom, Poland, and Australia invaded Iraq in March 2003 with the primary goal of bringing peace and stability to Iraq by removing the dictator Saddam Hussein. By April 2003, American Marines toppled a statue of Hussein from a central square in Baghdad (**Fig. 1.1**), but the conflict continues. Why? Leaders of the campaign failed to think geographically.

Nationally, Iraq has arbitrary borders drawn by France and Great Britain that put together diverse ethnic, religious, and cultural groups. Critical resources, especially oil, are unevenly distributed among the ethnic regions. One political party controlled the country for four decades. A dictator created his own security forces and used an iron fist to run the country for 24 years. Iraqis detested the idea of external rule, dating back to the country's rule by the Ottoman Empire for centuries and colonization by Great Britain for 17 years. Regionally, Iraq invaded its neighbor Iran in 1980 and deployed chemical weapons in a war that lasted for 8 years. Tensions between Iraq and Iran remained after the war ended, in part because both countries wanted to lead the Persian Gulf region and because southern Iraq has many sacred sites holy to Shi'ite Muslims, a sect of Islam prominent in Iran. Globally, Iraq has a shaky past with the United States, including the Persian Gulf War, when American troops helped push Iraqi troops out of Kuwait. The United States also plays a balancing act in the region between its alliances with Jewish Israel and Muslim Saudi Arabia.

The ongoing conflict in Iraq stems from a failure to think geographically. Any significant consideration of the geographic complexities of Iraq would have challenged the idea that removing the dictator in Iraq would automatically lead to a more peaceful Middle East. It would have directed more attention to the importance of internal divisions and the relationship between ethnic distributions and access to resources.

Iraq is a reminder that geographical understanding is not an exercise in memorizing trivia. Thinking geographically is fundamentally important to any effort to make sense of people, places, and cultures. The goal of this chapter is to teach you to think geographically and see the many interconnections and complexities of our world.

CHAPTER OUTLINE

1.1 Define human geography and describe the value of thinking geographically.

- How People Make Geography
- The Spatial Perspective
- The Value of Thinking Geographically

1.2 Identify and explain geography's core concepts.

- Location
- Human–Environment Interactions
- Regions
- Place
- Movement
- Expansion Diffusion
- Relocation Diffusion
- Cultural Landscape
- Scale
- Context
- Why Thinking Geographically Matters

1.3 Identify types of maps and examine the role maps play in understanding the world.

- Mental Maps
- Generalization in Maps
- Remote Sensing and GIS

1.4 Describe how culture influences patterns and processes in human geography.

1.1 Define Human Geography and Describe the Value of Thinking Geographically.

Geography is the study of the spaces and places people create on the ground and in their minds, and the ways in which people use and shape the environment. The field of **human geography** focuses on how we organize ourselves and our activities in space; how we are connected to one another and the environment; how we make places and how those places in turn shape our lives; and how we think about and organize ourselves locally and globally.

Human geography includes the subdisciplines of political geography, economic geography, population geography, and urban geography. Human geography also includes cultural geography, which is both part of human geography and also its own approach to all aspects of human geography. Cultural geography looks at the ways culture, including religion, language, and ethnicity are distributed and affect human geography. Cultural geography also examines how culture affects our understanding of topics addressed in human geography. Cultural geography can be thought of both as a component of human geography and a perspective on human geography.

How People Make Geography

People have a bigger impact on the world now than at any point in history. In 1900, the world had 1 billion people. The fastest ways to travel were steamships, railroads, and horse and buggy. Now, nearly 8 billion people can cross the globe in a matter of days, with most having easy access to automobiles, high-speed railroads, airplanes, and ships.

Traveling long distances in short times and communicating instantly have globalized the world. An idea can spread across the world and connect people from different places within minutes. **Globalization** is a set of processes that are increasing interactions, deepening relationships, and accelerating connectedness across country borders. It includes the movement of money, the migration of people, the flow of ideas, and the making and trading of goods. You might think of globalization as a blanket covering the world and making every place the same, but that is not the case. Differences from place to place matter. An idea or innovation may spread around the world, but people will interpret or change that idea depending on their own experiences and the particular characteristics of individual places. Globalization creates connections when 2 billion people can read the same tweet at the same time, but it also creates divisions because those 2 billion people can interpret the tweet hundreds of different ways, and many other billions will never see the tweet.

This book devotes considerable attention to globalization and its impacts. We recognize that a globalized process has different impacts in different places because no two places are

the same. Moreover, whenever we look at something at one *scale*, we always try to think about how processes that exist at other scales may affect what we are studying (see the discussion of scale later in this chapter).

We come back again and again to globalization because of the profound impacts it has had on the human geography. As geographers Ron Johnston, Peter Taylor, and Michael Watts (2002) explain, "Whatever your opinion may be, any intellectual engagement with social change in the twenty-first century has to address this concept seriously, and assess its capacity to explain the world we currently inhabit." We integrate the concept of globalization into our discussion of human geography because processes at the global scale, processes that are not unique to local places or confined by national borders, are clearly changing people, places, and cultures.

Consider the issue of hunger. On its face, the world's hunger problem might seem easily solvable. Take the total annual food production in the world, divide it by the world's population, and you have enough food for everyone. Yet 11 percent of the world's population is hungry or chronically undernourished. Of the 815 million undernourished people globally, the vast majority are women and children, who have little money and even less power.

Figure 1.2 shows how food consumption is currently distributed—unevenly. Comparing Figure 1.2 with **Figure 1.3** shows that the wealthier countries also are the best fed, whereas Africa has numerous countries in the highest categories of hunger and undernourishment.

Is solving hunger as simple as each country growing enough food to feed its people? Do the best-fed countries have the most farmable (arable) land? Only 4 percent of the land in Norway is suitable for farming, while more than 70 percent of Bangladesh is farmable (**Fig. 1.4**). Yet Norway is a wealthy, well-fed country, while Bangladesh is lower income and undernourished. Norway overcomes its inadequate food production by importing food. Bangladesh depends on rice as its staple crop, and the monsoon rains that flood two-thirds of the country each year between June and October are good for rice production, but they make survival a daily challenge for some. Explaining these differences is impossible without considering the geographical characteristics of individual places and how they are positioned in relation to other peoples, places, and things.

Take the case of the east African country of Kenya. It has enough farmable land to feed its population, but the most productive land in the western highlands is used to produce coffee and tea instead of foods for local consumption. Foreign corporations own the coffee and tea plantations, and they sell the crops abroad. While the foreign income from selling coffee and tea helps the trade balance and economy of Kenya as a whole, small farmers in Kenya face challenges. Small farms in the

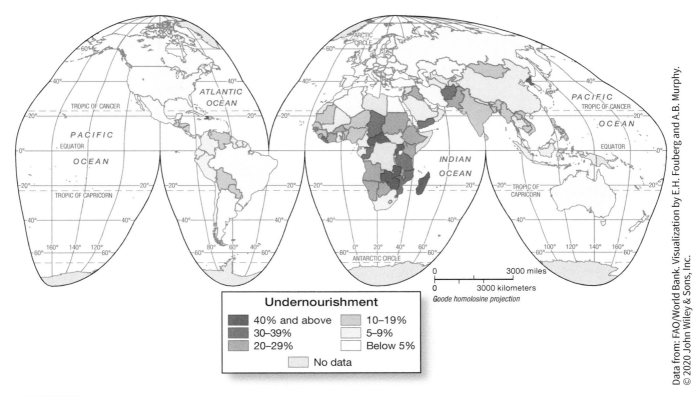

FIGURE 1.2 **World Undernourishment.** Undernourishment rates are higher in Africa and Asia than in North America and Europe. The World Food Program estimates that just under one billion people worldwide are malnourished, with the highest rates in Africa, South America, and Asia.

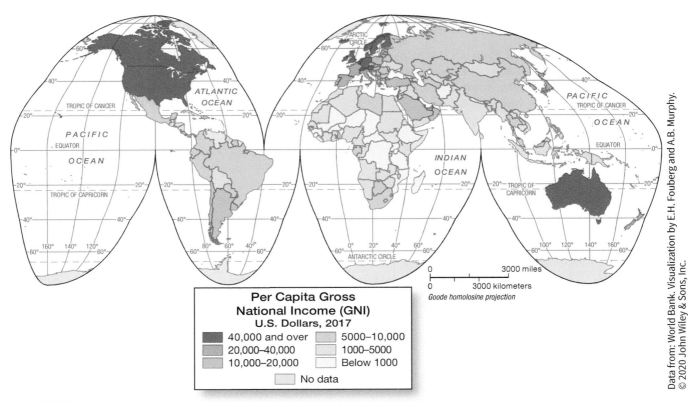

FIGURE 1.3 **Per Capita Gross National Income (in U.S. Dollars).** Wealth is distributed unevenly, with countries in the global north having higher incomes than countries in the global south. Maps that report data by country like this one do not tell us about differences within countries.

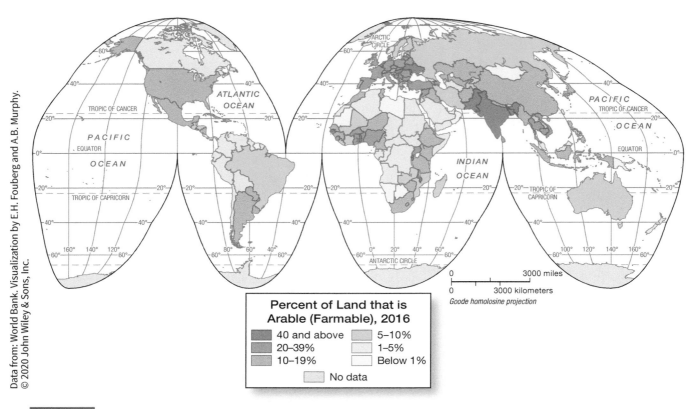

Data from: World Bank. Visualization by E.H. Fouberg and A.B. Murphy. © 2020 John Wiley & Sons, Inc.

Percent of Land that is Arable (Farmable), 2016

- 40 and above
- 20–39%
- 10–19%
- 5–10%
- 1–5%
- Below 1%
- No data

Goode homolosine projection

FIGURE 1.4 **Arable (Farmable) Land.** The percent of arable (farmable) land varies by country. South Asia and eastern Europe have the highest rates. Arable land tells us potential for agriculture, but it does not necessarily correlate with nourishment or undernourishment. Countries with limited arable land and higher incomes, like Japan and Norway, import the food needed to feed their population.

lowlands have been subdivided to the point that many are too small to be productive farms. Kenya has a gendered legal system that disempowers women, who make up most of the country's agricultural labor force, which makes it nearly impossible for small farmers who are women to create, invest in land and technology and grow their production. In the northeast, Kenyan farmers have suffered through severe droughts, diseases attacking their herds, and conflict in neighboring Somalia.

Solving one of the Kenya's problems often raises another. If Kenyans converted the most productive farmlands to growing crops for local markets and local consumption, how would lower income families afford the crops that were grown? What would happen to the rest of Kenya's economy and the government itself if there were significantly less export revenue from tea and coffee? If Kenya lost its export revenue, how could the country pay the loans it owes to global financial and development institutions?

Answering each of these questions requires thinking geographically because the answers are rooted in the characteristics of places and the connections those places have to other places. Geographers often use on-the-ground **fieldwork** to gain insights into such questions. Geographers have a long tradition of fieldwork. We go out in the field and see what people are doing, we talk to people and observe how their actions and reactions vary across space, and we

develop maps and other visualizations that help us situate and analyze what we learn. We, the authors, have countless field experiences, and we share many with you to help you understand the diversity of people and the influences shaping the development of places.

Addressing major global problems such as hunger or inequality is complicated in our interconnected world. Any solution will play out differently from place to place, and how things play out will have regional and global consequences over time. Our goals in this book are to help you make connections among people and places, enable you to recognize **patterns** and processes in human geography, give you an appreciation for the uniqueness of place, and teach you to think geographically.

AP® Exam Taker's Tip

Basic map reading skills are essential to success in geography. Use the world maps throughout the text to divide the world into two groups—generally wealthy countries and generally poorer countries. As you read a map, divide the world into regions and look for patterns in each region: North America, Latin America, Europe, North Africa and Southwest Asia, sub-Saharan Africa, South Asia, Southeast Asia, East Asia, and Oceania.

The Spatial Perspective

Geographers study human phenomena, including language, religion, identity, settlement patterns, and land use. They also examine the interactions between people and the physical environment. Human geography is the study of the spatial and material characteristics of human-made places and people, and **physical geography** is the study of the spatial and material characteristics of the physical environment. Human and physical geographers may study different things, but they adopt a similar perspective.

Geographer Marvin Mikesell once gave a shorthand definition of geography as the "why of where." How does *where* something happens affect *what* happens? Why and how do things come together in certain places to produce particular outcomes? Why are some things found in certain places but not in others? To what extent do developments in one place create unintended consequences in another place? To these questions, we add "so what?" Why do differences across geographic space matter, and what do those differences mean for people there and elsewhere? Questions like these are at the core of thinking geographically, and they are of critical importance if we are to make sense of our world.

Since geography covers so many things, from people and places to migration and climates, you might be wondering what everything geographers study has in common. Geographers study the world with a spatial perspective. Geographers are interested in the spatial arrangement of places and phenomena, how they are laid out, organized, and arranged; how they appear on the landscape; and how the various characteristics of individual places—physical and human—influence one another.

Mapping the **spatial distribution** of a phenomenon can be an important first step to understanding it. Maps raise questions about how arrangements come about, what processes create and sustain them, and what relationships exist among different places and things. Mapping the distribution of a disease, for example, is often the first step to finding its cause.

Understanding the Causes and Spread of Cholera

In 1854, Dr. John Snow, an anesthesiologist in London, mapped cases of cholera in a neighborhood of London called Soho. Cholera is a disease that causes diarrhea and dehydration, and it was found mainly in India until the beginning of the nineteenth century. Between 1816 and 1823, cholera diffused to China, Japan, East Africa, and Mediterranean Europe in the first of several **pandemics**, worldwide outbreaks of the disease. Death by cholera was horribly convulsive and would come in a matter of days, perhaps a week, and no one knew what caused the disease or how to avoid it.

A second cholera pandemic struck between 1826 to 1837 when cholera crossed the Atlantic and arrived in North America. During the third pandemic, from 1842 to 1862, England was severely hit. When cholera swept through Soho, Dr. Snow made a map. He marked the home of each person who died from cholera with a dot, and he also marked the water pumps where people went to get fresh water for their homes (**Fig. 1.5**). Approximately 500 deaths occurred in Soho, and as the map took shape, it showed that an especially large number of those deaths clustered around the water pump on Broad Street. At the doctor's request, city authorities removed the handle from the Broad Street pump, making it impossible to get water from it. The result was dramatic. Almost immediately the number of reported new cases fell to nearly zero, confirming Snow's theory that cholera is spread through contaminated water.

Cholera bacteria are carried in feces of people who have the disease. Cholera is still common in places where water is not adequately treated or sewage seeps into water supplies. People ingest cholera bacteria by eating contaminated food or water. In places without a sanitary sewer system, human feces can easily contaminate the water supply. Even in places with sanitary sewer systems, cholera contamination can occur when rivers, which are typically the water supply, flood the sanitary sewer system.

Cholera remains a threat in urban slums (see Chapter 9) where access to sanitation and clean water are lacking. Cholera outbreaks also occur in places with armed conflict and in places with natural hazards, including earthquakes and hurricanes. Cholera spreads quickly, so an outbreak can easily diffuse regionally and turn into an **epidemic**, a regional outbreak of a disease. Starting in 2016, a cholera outbreak in Yemen, on the Arabian Peninsula, became the fastest-spreading outbreak in modern history. More than 1 million people were quickly infected because an estimated 16 million of the 29 million people in Yemen do not have access to clean water and basic sanitation as the result of a civil war and bombing of infrastructure from neighbor Saudi Arabia (who supports the government in exile).

In January 2010, an earthquake that registered 7.0 on the Richter scale hit Haiti, near the capital of Port-au-Prince. Months later, there was a cholera outbreak in the Artibonite region of Haiti (**Fig. 1.6**). The United Nations (UN) acknowledges that peacekeepers from Nepal who were sent to help Haiti after the earthquake brought cholera with them. The UN camp that hosted the peacekeepers was located on a small river that flowed into the Artibonite River, and the sewage from the camp's residents was discharged into the river. Cholera broke out among the thousands of Haitians who used the Artibonite River for their water supply. The disease spread quickly, reaching the capital city of Port-au-Prince. More than 9200 Haitians died in an outbreak that infected 770,000 people.

Boiling water before consumption and thorough washing of hands prevent the spread of cholera, but water contaminated with cholera and a lack of access to soap are commonplace problems in many parts of world cities. A vaccine exists, but its effectiveness is limited, and it is costly. Dr. Snow achieved a victory by thinking geographically, but the war against cholera is not yet won.

The Value of Thinking Geographically

The Snow example shows that thinking geographically involves much more than memorizing places on a map. Place locations are to geography what dates are to history. History is not merely about memorizing dates. To understand history

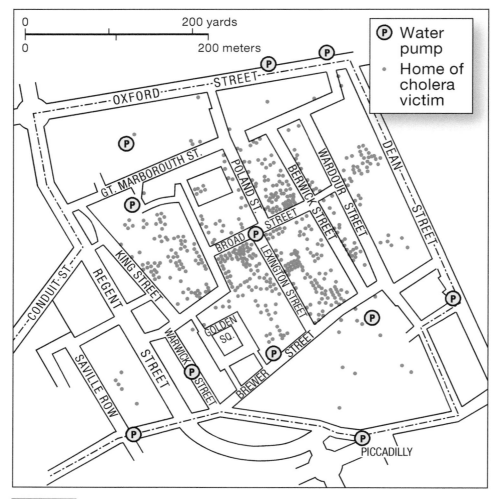

FIGURE 1.5 **Deaths from Cholera in the Soho Neighborhood of London, England, 1854.**
Dr. Snow mapped the deaths caused by cholera in the Soho neighborhood of London along with the locations of the water pumps and noticed a spatial correlation. Most of the deaths were clustered around a single water pump. As Dr. Snow's experience showed, maps are not just attractive or interesting representations of the world. Maps also help us understand and confront problems.

is to appreciate how events, circumstances, and ideas came together at particular times to produce certain outcomes. Knowledge of history, of how different people created and experienced events that have developed over time, is critical to understanding who we are and where we are going.

Understanding change across space is equally important to understanding change over time. The great German philosopher Immanuel Kant argued that we need disciplines focused not only on particular concrete attributes of the world around us (such as economics and sociology), but also on time (history) and space (geography). The disciplines of history and geography have intellectual cores defined by their perspectives as opposed to a particular subject of study. The **spatial perspective** that human geographers bring to studying the world offers a particular way of looking at a multitude of phenomena, ranging from political elections and urban slums to race and migration.

Because the spatial perspective gives insight across a broad range of topics, human geographers have careers as location

analysts, urban planners, diplomats, remote sensing analysts, geographic information scientists, area specialists, travel consultants, political analysts, intelligence officers, cartographers, educators, soil scientists, transportation planners, park rangers, and environmental consultants. All of these careers and more are open to geographers because each of these fields requires a spatial perspective to understand people and places.

TC Thinking Geographically

Imagine you are studying the 2010 outbreak of cholera in Haiti before the United Nations admitted the role of their peacekeeping camp in the outbreak. Knowing cholera **diffuses** from bacteria in human waste that gets into the water supply, and thinking geographically like Dr. Snow did, determine what layers of data you would need to add to Figure 1.6 to find the **hearth**, the origin, of the outbreak in Haiti.

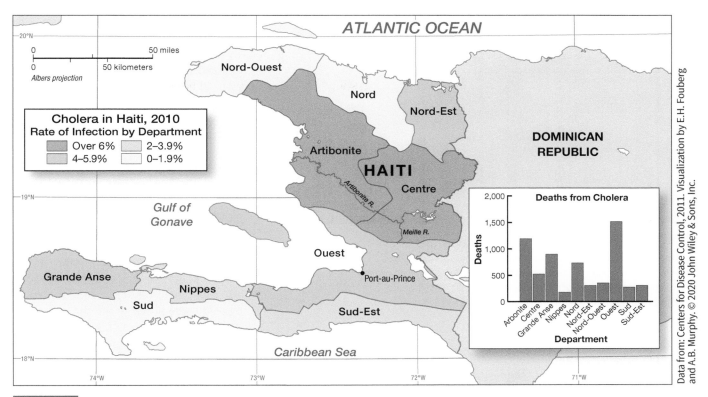

FIGURE 1.6 **Cholera in Haiti, 2010.** Artibonite and Centre departments were hit hard by a cholera outbreak in Haiti just after the 2010 earthquake. Sewage from a UN peacekeepers camp contaminated the Artibonite River with cholera bacteria. The cholera outbreak was amplified because a large number of Haitians displaced from Port-au-Prince fled to camps in Artibonite and Centre.

1.2 Identify and Explain Geography's Core Concepts.

Geographic concepts help us think geographically, make connections, and understand case studies. Eight major concepts in geography that both human geographers and physical geographers use to study the world include location (absolute and relative), human–environment interactions, region, place, movement, cultural landscape, scale, and context.[1]

Location

Location refers to the geographical position of people and things on Earth's surface. A concern with location underlies almost all geographical work. If we are studying a place or a specific hazard, we need to know the **absolute location**, the precise location of a place, usually defined by locational coordinates

(latitude and longitude). Geographers prefer to go to the location to do field work to see the place and meet the people. But location is not only about coordinates; it is about considering how the place plays a role in the larger region and how that affects what happens in the location and why. **Relative location** is the location of a place or attribute relative to another place or attribute. Absolute and relative location provide starting points for context. To understand what happened and why, you first need to know where—both in absolute and relative terms.

> **AP® Exam Taker's Tip**
>
> Using **absolute location** is not as helpful in daily life as **relative location**. When asked what city you are from or how to get to a restaurant, you would not provide latitude and longitude coordinates. Relative location is descriptive, or qualitative, while absolute location is empirical, or quantitative. Think about using prepositions when answering questions about where the city is that you are from or for directions to a restaurant. What is the restaurant *near, between, beside,* or *by*? These kinds of descriptive (relative location) answers will help you learn to think like a geographer.

[1]Four geography organizations in the United States formed the Geography Educational National Implementation Project in the 1980s with the goal of improving geography education in the United States. They identified five themes of geography: location, human–environment interactions, region, place, and movement. The other 3 concepts we incorporate in Chapter 1 are based on research on threshold concepts in geography conducted by Dr. Erin H. Fouberg. She found students identified four geographic concepts as threshold concepts, helping them think like expert geographers: scale, cultural landscape, context, and region (also one of the five themes).

pisaphotography/Shutterstock.com

FIGURE 1.7 **Florida Everglades.** The Florida Everglades are part of the watershed of Lake Okeechobee. When the lake overflows its banks, water drains downhill and south toward the tip of Florida, forming the Everglades, a tropical wetland that once covered the southern third of Florida. As early as 1881, developers and the U.S. Army Corps of Engineers built a series of dikes and canals to drain much of the Everglades to develop agriculture and urbanism on the land.

Geographers develop models describing the locational properties of particular phenomena—even predicting where things are likely to occur. Geographers, especially economic geographers, use **location theory** to answer theoretical and practical locations about where something should be located or why it is located where it is. An economic geographer who knows location theory might ask whether a Whole Foods should be built downtown or in a suburb. Using geographic information systems (GIS), the economic geographer would consider characteristics of existing neighborhoods and new developments, median incomes, locations of other shopping areas and grocery stores, and existing and future road systems. Similarly, a geographer could determine the best location for a wildlife refuge by analyzing existing wildlife habitats and migration patterns, human settlement patterns, land use, and road networks.

Human–Environment Interactions

Thinking geographically requires understanding the reciprocal (mutually affecting each other) relationship between humans and the physical world, a relationship geographers call **human–environment interactions**. People change environments and changing environments place pressure on people to react. For example, the U.S. Army Corps of Engineers drained part of the Florida Everglades, which changed the physical environment (**Fig. 1.7**). Changes in Florida's environment, including draining wetlands, flattening coastal sand dunes, building on barrier islands, and removing mangrove trees make an easier path of destruction for hurricanes. People respond by building up seawalls and infrastructure, creating new paths for water to flow, and erecting taller homes on stilts. Each human action will create new environmental impacts, which will spur another iteration of human-environment interaction.

Thinking geographically often requires looking at the reciprocal relationship between humans and environments.

To understand how contemporary geographers look at human–environment interactions, it is easiest to start by defining what we do not do. The ancient Greeks noticed that some of the people who came within their expanding empire were relatively peaceful while others were rebellious, and they attributed such differences to differences in climate. Over 2000 years ago, Aristotle described northern European people as "full of spirit . . . but incapable of ruling others," and he characterized Asian people (by which he meant the inhabitants of modern-day Turkey) as "intelligent and inventive . . . [but] always in a state of subjection and slavery." Aristotle attributed peoples' response to being taken over by an outside power to the climates of the regions where they lived. In his mind, the cold northern European environment encouraged people to rebel and the warmer climate of Southwest Asia forced people to become enslaved.

Aristotle's views on this topic had a long lasting impact. As recently as the first half of the twentieth century, similar notions still had strong support. In 1940, in the *Principles of Human Geography*, Ellsworth Huntington and C. W. Cushing wrote: "The well-known contrast between the energetic people of the most progressive parts of the temperate zone and the inert inhabitants of the tropics and even of intermediate regions, such as Persia, is largely due to climate . . . the people of the cyclonic regions rank so far above those of the other parts of the world that they are the natural leaders."

Huntington and Cushing claim that climate is the critical factor in how people behave. Yet what constitutes an "ideal" climate lies in the eyes of the beholder. For Aristotle, it was the Mediterranean climate of Greece. Through the eyes of more recent commentators from western Europe and North America, the climates most suited to progress and productiveness in culture, politics, and technology are (you guessed it) those of western Europe and the northeastern United States. These theories are examples of **environmental determinism**—the idea that individual and collective human behavior is fundamentally affected by, or even controlled by, the physical environment.

Environmentally deterministic theories that explain Europe as "superior" to the rest of the world because of its climate and location ignore the fact that for thousands of years, the most technologically advanced civilizations were not in Europe. The places where the agricultural and urban revolutions originally took place—their **hearths**, the area or place where an idea, innovation, or technology originates—were in North Africa, Southwest Asia, Southeast Asia, and East Asia, not Europe. The same can be said for the hearths of the world's major religions.

Chipping away at environmentally deterministic explanations helped move the human-environment interactions in more insightful directions. Everyone agrees that the natural environment affects human activity in some ways, but people are the decision makers and the modifiers—not just the slaves of environmental forces. People shape environments, constantly altering the landscape and altering environmental systems.

In response to environmental determinism, geographers argued that the natural environment merely serves to limit the range of choices available to a culture. The choices that a society makes depend on what its members need and on what technology is available to them. Geographers called this doctrine **possibilism**.

Even possibilism has its limitations, partly because it encourages a line of inquiry that starts with the physical environment and asks what it allows. Human cultures, however, frequently push the boundaries of what is "environmentally possible" through their own ideas and advances in technology. For example, one theory in sustainable development is **carrying capacity**, which holds that an area of land can support a certain number of people and species. While carrying capacity makes intuitive sense, it is not easy to identify a particular area of land's carrying capacity. Also, in the interconnected, technologically dependent world, it is possible to transcend many of the limitations imposed by the natural environment.

Today, much research in human geography focuses on how and why people have altered their environment and on the sustainability of their practices. In the process, two overlapping fields of study have developed: cultural ecology and political ecology. **Cultural ecology** is concerned with culture as a system of adaptation to and alteration of the environment. **Political ecology** is fundamentally concerned with the environmental consequences of dominant political-economic arrangements and assumptions (see Chapter 13). The fundamental point is that human societies are diverse and the human will is too powerful to be determined by environment.

Regions

Regions are another central concept in geography. A **region** is an area of Earth with a degree of similarity that differentiates it from surrounding areas. Human phenomena (e.g., languages and religions) and physical phenomena (e.g., tornadoes and earthquakes) are not evenly distributed across Earth. Instead, they tend to be concentrated in regions. A region can be an area dominated by an individual feature, such as the Corn Belt in the United States or the French-language region in Canada. Regions can also be products of political developments (the European Union) or people's perceptions (the Midwest).

Geographers use fieldwork and both quantitative and qualitative methods to develop descriptions of different regions of the world. Novelist James Michener once wrote that whenever he started writing a new book, he first prepared

FIGURE 1.8 **Guilin, China.** The South China karst region, bisected here by the Li River outside Guilin, is a UNESCO World Heritage Site. The landforms of the region clearly distinguish it from surrounding areas.

Barcroft Media/Getty Images

himself by turning to books written by regional geographers about the area where his book would be set. Understanding the regional geography of a place allows us to make sense of much of the information we have about it.

Formal Regions Geographers identify three kinds of regions: formal, functional, and perceptual. A **formal region** has a shared trait, either physical or cultural. A formal physical region shares a certain geographic feature, such as the karst region of China (**Fig. 1.8**). In a formal cultural region, people might share one or more **cultural traits**. For example, the region of Europe where French is spoken by a majority of the people is a formal region. Whether physical or cultural, when we change the scale of analysis, the formal region changes. If we move up to the global scale, the karst region globally includes limestone regions along coastlines and in interiors of continents that were historically under water. At the global scale, the French-speaking formal region expands beyond France to include former French colonies of Africa, French Quebec, and overseas territories that are still under control of the French government.

Functional Regions A **functional region** is an area that shares a common purpose. Functional regions have **nodes**, places that function as central connecting points for a functional region. Functional regions have a shared political, social, or economic purpose. For example, a city has a commuter flow region (see **Fig. 9.18**) that can also be considered a trade regions. People drive into the major city to work, shop, or visit doctors. Trade regions or commuter flow regions are functional regions. The function is shopping or work, and the major city to which people flow is the node.

Functional regions are often culturally diverse. A functional region is not defined by similar cultural traits, but rather by the fact that the people within the region function together politically, socially, or economically. Connections to the node help define the boundaries of a functional region. For example, the city of Chicago is a functional region because the people within the city's limits pay city taxes, look to the city for services, and vote in city elections. Once you start thinking about functional regions, you will realize that at this moment you are in hundreds or thousands of functional regions at the same time. A neighborhood in Chicago is part of the city, a delivery zone for a restaurant, a school district, a trade region, the state of Illinois, the seventh Federal Reserve district, and hundreds (maybe thousands) more. Each functional region the neighborhood is in has a purpose or a function—whether political, social, or economic.

Perceptual Regions

Perceptual regions are images people carry in their minds based on accumulated knowledge of peoples, places, and things (**Fig. 1.9**). Perceptual regions can include people and their cultural traits (dress, food, language, and religion), places and their physical traits (mountains, plains, or coasts), and built environments (windmills, barns, skyscrapers, or beach houses). For example, Cajun country in the U.S. Southeast is associated with particular foods like étoufée and jambalaya and also a joie de vivre (joy of life)—a positive disposition people share that is centered on families and communities.

Whether we are conscious of it or not, we use perceptual regions to make sense of the world. When a news report says something happened "in the Middle East," we have perceptions of where the Middle East is and what the region looks like. Our perceptual regions can change over time. Before September 11, 2001, most Americans thought the Middle East region included Iraq and Iran, but stretched no farther east. As the hunt for Osama bin Laden began and the media focused attention on the harsh rule of the Taliban in Afghanistan, perceptions of the Middle East changed. For many Americans, their perceptions of the Middle East stretched east to include Afghanistan and Pakistan. Scholars who specialize in this part of the globe had long studied the relationship among parts of Central Asia, South Asia, and the traditional "Middle East," but prior to 9/11 the connections between Afghanistan and Pakistan and the rest of the Middle East were almost invisible to most Americans.

Perceptual regions are also called vernacular regions. A vernacular is a local language people use to communicate. A **vernacular region** is a perceptual region that has such strong significance to the people in the perceptual region that it becomes the lens through which they see their world and a way people identify themselves. For example, if Cajun people identify strongly with a Cajun region in Louisiana, they may see things happening at the scale of Louisiana or the scale of the U.S. in terms of how the happenings impact Cajun country. Driving through the Cajun region, you may see signs saying things like "This is Cajun country!" or "Welcome to Cajun country." By calling themselves a region and identifying strongly with that region, the perceptual region of Cajun country has become vernacular—part of the language used to make sense of the people and the place.

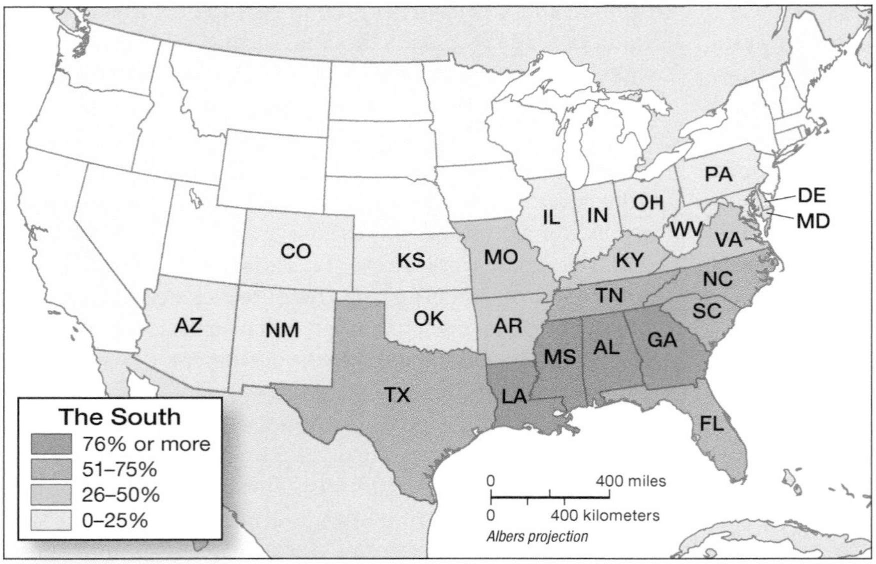

Perceptual Regions in the United States

Cultural geographer Wilbur Zelinsky analyzed the names businesses chose in major cities to identify 12 perceptual regions in the United States and southern Canada. To make his regional map of the United States, Zelinsky analyzed telephone directories of 276 metropolitan areas in the United States and Canada, noting the frequency with which businesses and other enterprises use regional or locational terms (such as *Southern Printing Company* or *Western Printing*) in their listings.

The resulting map of Zelinsky's perceptual regions (**Fig. 1.10**) may align well with formal cultural regions based on ethnicity, race, settlement patterns, and shared history identified by geographers. When you examine Zelinsky's map, you will notice that some of the regions overlap in certain places. For example, the more general term *the West* incorporates part of the Northwest and part of the Southwest. Like formal regions, perceptual regions often overlap and do not have clear-cut boundaries.

Perceptual regions are not static. How we identify different regions and how people in the perceptual regions see themselves and their region changes over time. The perceptual region of the South has changed since the civil rights movement of

FIGURE 1.9 **The South.** The boundaries of perceptual regions are difficult to define precisely. Nate Silver's blog FiveThirtyEight (owned by ESPN) teamed up with SurveyMonkey to poll people on the web who identified themselves as a Midwesterner or Southerner "a lot" or "some," and generated maps of the perceptual regions of those who identify with the regions. Lifestyle editor Walt Hickey analyzed the data and found Midwesterners have less agreement on what states are in the region (Illinois was chosen most frequently, with 80 percent agreeing it's part of the Midwest), whereas Southerners have a clearer idea of the states definitively in the South (about 90 percent agreed Georgia and Alabama are in the South and more than 80 percent put Louisiana and Mississippi in the South).

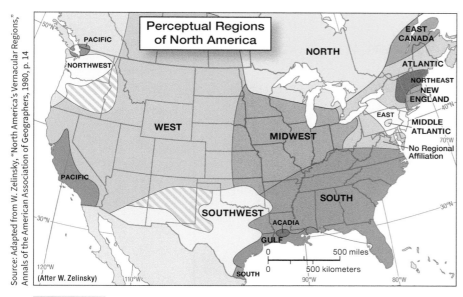

Source: Adapted from W. Zelinsky, "North America's Vernacular Regions," Annals of the American Association of Geographers, 1980, p. 14

FIGURE 1.10 **Perceptual Regions of North America.**   This map represents geographer Wilbur Zelinsky's research on perceptual regions in the United States and southern Canada.

be associated with the South (such as Waffle House restaurants), and at some stage of the trip these features will begin to dominate the landscape to such a degree that you will say, "I am really in the South now." This may result from a combination of features in the culture: the style of houses and their porches, items on a roadside restaurant menu (grits, for example), a local radio station's music, the sound of accents that you perceive to be Southern, a number of Baptist churches in a town along the way. These combined impressions become part of your overall perception of the South as a region.

Regions, whether formal, functional, or perceptual, are ways of organizing people and places geographically. Regions are a form of spatial classification, a kind of shorthand used to handle large amounts of information so we can make sense of people and places.

the 1960s (**Fig. 1.11**). A "New South" has emerged, forged by immigration from other countries, urbanization, and the movement of people from other parts of the United States to the South. At the same time, the South continues to carry imprints of a culture with deep historical roots through language, religion, music, food preferences, and other traditions and customs.

If you drive southward from, say, Pittsburgh or Detroit, you will not pass a specific place where you enter the South. You will note features in the cultural landscape that you perceive to

Guest Field Note   Standing at the Corner of Rosa Parks and Jefferson Davis in Montgomery, Alabama

Jonathan Leib
Old Dominion University

Located in a predominantly African American neighborhood in Montgomery, Alabama, the street intersection of Jefferson (Jeff) Davis and Rosa Parks is symbolic of the debates and disputes in the American South over how the past is to be commemorated on the region's landscape. The Civil War and civil rights movement are the two most important events in the history of the region. The street names commemorate Montgomery's central role in both eras, and they do so in the same public space. Montgomery was the site of the first capital of the Confederacy in 1861 while Jefferson Davis was president. The Alabama capital was also the site of the 1955-1956 Montgomery bus boycott that launched the civil rights movement. The boycott was sparked by Rosa Parks's arrest after she refused to give up her seat on a city bus when ordered to do so by a white person. Most of my research examines the politics of how the region's white and African Americans portray these separate heroic eras within the region's public spaces, ranging from support for and against flying the Confederate flag to disputes over placing statues and murals honoring the Civil War and the civil rights movement in the South's landscape.

© Jonathan Leib

FIGURE 1.11 **Montgomery, Alabama.**

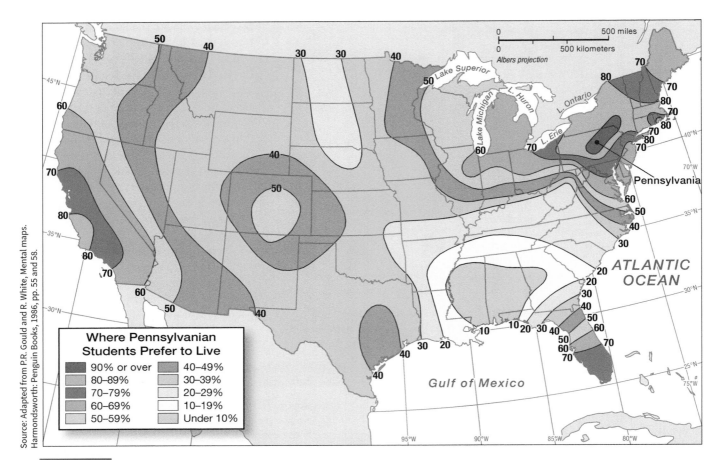

Source: Adapted from P.R. Gould and R. White, Mental maps. Harmondsworth: Penguin Books, 1986, pp. 55 and 58.

FIGURE 1.12 **Desirable Places to Live.** Proximity affects the impressions students have of other places—but so do stereotypes about certain parts of the country. How would this map look if we took a survey of Pennsylvania and Californian college students now? Would the South be more desirable with the growth of the Sun Belt?

Place

A fourth major geographical concept is captured by the seemingly simple word **place**, the uniqueness of a location. All places have unique human and physical characteristics, and one of the purposes of geography is to study the special character and meaning of places. Geographers pay attention to the attributes that create places and consider how the complex of attributes in a place shapes what happens and why. One of geography's core ideas is that *what* happens is often influenced by *where* it happens. Place matters. Since no two places are the same, a similar issue, like whether to allow a Walmart to be built in a residential neighborhood, will play out in different ways.

Through experiences we have in places, we assign meaning and emotion to places. People develop a **sense of place** by infusing a place with meaning and emotion, by remembering important events that occurred in a place, or by labeling a place with a certain character. Because we experience and give meaning to places, we can have a feeling of "home" when we are in a certain place. We can also infuse negative memories or experiences in a place and develop a negative sense of place.

We also develop **perceptions of places** where we have never been through reading books, watching movies,

hearing stories, and seeing pictures. Geographers Peter Gould and Rodney White asked college students in California and Pennsylvania: "If you could move to any place of your choice, without any of the usual financial and other obstacles, where would you like to live?" Student responses showed a strong bias for their home region and revealed that students from both regions had negative perceptions of the South, Appalachia, the Great Plains, and Utah (**Fig. 1.12**). Experiences we have had in places, lack of experience in other places, and images we get from books, movies, and even video games shape our perceptions of places.

Movement

Movement refers to the mobility of people, goods, and ideas. Movement is an expression of the interconnectedness of places. Movement is so important in geography that several other geographic concepts can be considered part of movement. Two of the most important concepts in geography, migration and diffusion, are part of the larger theme of movement. We dedicate Chapter 3 to migration, so, in this section of the chapter, we focus primarily on diffusion. Geographic

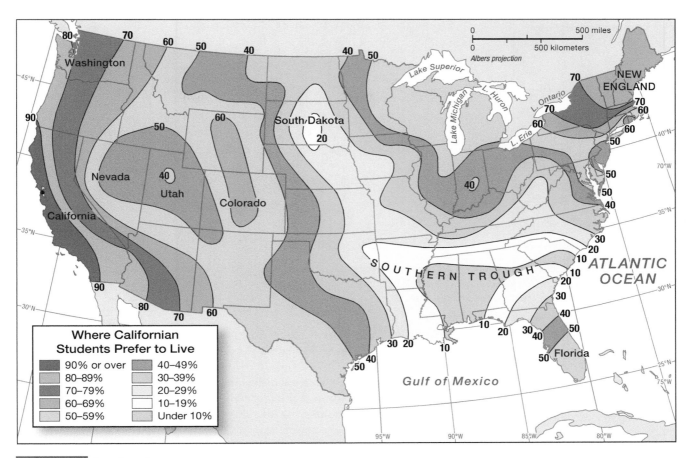

FIGURE 1.12   (continued)

concepts are often interconnected and can be used together to think geographically. As you read about the concepts in this section, think about how each ties into the larger idea of movement and how each is connected to the others.

Diffusion is the spread of an idea, innovation, or technology from its hearth (origin) to other people and places. Whether and how something diffuses depends on the amount of interaction between and among places. If people in two places interact frequently through trade, cultural traits like language, religion, and clothing styles are more likely to diffuse between the two places. **Spatial interaction** between places depends on the **distances** between places (the measured physical space), the **accessibility** of places (the ease of reaching one location from another), and the transportation and communication **connectivity** among places (the degree of linkage between locations in a network).

The diffusion process depends, in part, on the time and distance from a hearth. In 1970, Swedish geographer Torsten Hägerstrand published pioneering research on the role of time in diffusion. Hägerstrand's research revealed how time, as well as distance, affects individual human behavior and the spread of people and ideas. Hägerstrand's fascinating research attracted many geographers to the study of diffusion. As a general rule, the farther a place is from a hearth, the less likely an innovation will spread there and be adopted. Similarly, the acceptance of an innovation becomes less likely

the longer it takes to reach its potential adopters. In combination, time and distance cause **time–distance decay** in the diffusion process.

> ### AP® Exam Taker's Tip
>
> An easy way to understand the concept of **time–distance decay** is by using spatial skills. The farther you are away from something or the longer it takes for you to get there, the less it is likely you know about what is there. For example, if you live in south Texas, you are much more likely to speak Spanish than someone living in northern Minnesota. And if you live in Georgia, you are more likely to go on vacation in Florida than to California due to time and distance.

Not all traits or innovations diffuse. Existing cultural preferences or taboos in a place can make it less likely for certain innovations, ideas, or practices to diffuse. Religious beliefs may work against the adoption of certain practices or ideas, such as divorce, abortion, or contraceptive use, on theological or moral grounds. Some cultures or religions prohibit consumption of alcoholic beverages, and others prohibit consuming certain kinds of meat or other foods. A new food product that includes pork will not diffuse into predominantly

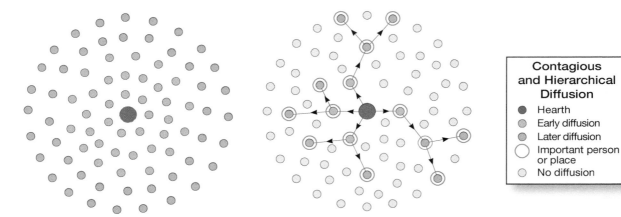

A. Contagious Diffusion   B. Hierarchical Diffusion

FIGURE 1.13 **Contagious and Hierarchical Diffusion.** In contagious diffusion, the trait spreads from the hearth outward contiguously and evenly. In hierarchical diffusion, the trait spreads from the hearth to the most linked or most important people or places first.

Muslim or Jewish regions because followers of these religions are expected not to consume pork.

Geographers distinguish between two major types of diffusion: expansion and relocation. Within expansion diffusion, geographers identify three types of expansion diffusion: contagious, hierarchical, and stimulus.

Expansion Diffusion

Expansion diffusion describes an innovation or idea that develops in a hearth and remains strong there while also spreading outward (**Fig. 1.13**). An example is the expansion of Islam. Islam's hearth was on the Arabian Peninsula. From there, Islam diffused to Egypt and North Africa, through Southwest Asia, into West Africa, and later to the east, even as it remained strong on the Arabian Peninsula.

When expansion diffusion occurs primarily as result of person-to-person contact, it is called **contagious diffusion** (see Fig. 1.13). The clearest example is the diffusion of a disease through a community. For example, a student comes to class with a case of the flu and will infect those seated nearby, who then interact with and infect others close to them. Cultural traits can also diffuse through contagious diffusion. An example might be someone coming to school wearing a new style of shoes, which then classmates see and adopt, and then fashion choice spreads from there.

When a trend or innovation diffuses quickly, it sometimes seems to come out of nowhere and then suddenly "explode" and be seen virtually everywhere. Kevin Plank, a graduate of the University of Maryland who played football as a walk-on for the Terrapins, invented a heat gear shirt that wicked away sweat and functioned as a cooling layer under football gear. Plank called his new body-hugging gear Under Armour. He gave samples of heat gear Under Armour shirts to his friends at the University of Maryland and to friends at other football teams in the East Coast Conference (**Fig. 1.14**). The first "knowers" of

the new Under Armour brand were football players connected to Kevin Plank or to college teams on the east coast.

The spread of Under Armour heat gear is a case of **hierarchical diffusion** (see Fig. 1.13), a type of expansion diffusion that starts with the knowers, those who have already adopted the idea or innovation, and then diffuses through a hierarchy of most linked people or most linked places. Fashion houses in Paris, Milan, and New York create new styles, which then diffuse hierarchically first among the people most connected to the fashion industry, then to major companies that make affordable fashion sold in malls and online, and eventually to shoppers.

When an innovation, trait, or technology diffuses hierarchically, it reflects how power is distributed in the underlying political, social, or economic system. In our fashion example, those with the greatest power in the industry are the first "knowers," and then the next to become adopters are the next most

FIGURE 1.14 **College Park, Maryland.** Under Armour designs the uniforms for their flagship university partner, the University of Maryland. Since 2013, Under Armour has incorporated elements of the state of Maryland's red, black, gold, and white flag into jerseys, helmets, and gloves.

Mitchell Layton/Getty Images

powerful. The diffusion of cultural traits like religion and language also occurs hierarchically and follows the underlying distribution of power. For example, during the Roman Empire, the Latin language diffused from Rome through military and political hierarchies. When the empire conquered lands, young people were required to join the army, and to move up through the ranks, they had to learn Latin. Latin also diffused through the political hierarchy. Roman senators spoke Latin, and Rome issued laws in Latin. In the empire's provinces, judges ruled using Latin.

Rarely do ideas, innovations, or technologies diffuse only contagiously or only hierarchically. At first, Under Armour diffused contagiously from the founder to his friends on different football teams to their friends. The first adopters were college football athletes who were trying to stay cool and keep their clothing light while practicing in the hot sun twice a day. Friends of football athletes, such as lacrosse and soccer players who also practiced their sports in the sun, saw Under Armour and also adopted it. Under Armour also diffused hierarchically. The company's heat gear diffused from college and professional football players to young athletes who, as fans, took note of the Under Armour logo on their favorite players' sportswear and wanted to wear what their idols were wearing. Eventually, Under Armour diffused to non-athletes who saw people they knew wearing Under Armour clothing and bought the gear as a fashion trend—expanding Under Armour's revenue base from $200 million in 2004 to $5 billion in 2017.

When an innovation, trait, or technology gains popularity through diffusion, it often spurs spin-off ideas and new products. For example, college and professional athletes whose teams had contracts with Nike or Adidas wanted to wear heat gear clothing, and some wore Under Armour beneath their Nike and Adidas uniforms. This prompted Nike, Adidas, and other athletic companies to offer their own performance gear, including compression shirts, compression shorts, and sports bras bearing their logo. Under Armour acted as a stimulus to

Nike's Pro Performance line and Adidas's Clima Ultimate line. Under Armour's performance line prompted stimulus diffusion or local experimentation and change in the Nike and Adidas brands. **Stimulus diffusion** is the third type of expansion diffusion and is the process of diffusion where two cultural traits blend to create a distinct trait.

Cultural traits or practices that are already held by a people in a place can encourage stimulus diffusion. Not all ideas can be readily and directly adopted by a receiving population; some are simply too vague, unattainable, different, or impractical for immediate adoption. Nonetheless, a new idea may indirectly promote local experimentation and eventual changes in ways of doing things. For example, the diffusion of fast, mass-produced food in the late twentieth century led to the introduction of hamburgers to India. Approximately 80 percent of India's 1.3 billion people are Hindu. In Hinduism, cows are considered holy and followers of the religion are expected to not consume beef. The prohibition of beef consumption is a major cultural obstacle to adoption of the hamburger (**Fig. 1.15**). In India, retailers like McDonald's began selling burgers made of vegetable products. Thus the diffusion of the hamburger stimulated a new form in the cultural context of India.

AP® Exam Taker's Tip

Diffusion is another core concept in AP Human Geography and is also critical to map reading, as well as understanding and applying concepts in every chapter of this text. First, learn to use the word **adopt** when thinking about diffusion. People *adopt* ideas, tools, religions, languages. This is diffusion. **Hearths** are where these ideas, tools, languages, religions, and other human innovations begin. Think about a hearth in your home. The heat from the fire *diffuses* out into the room and around the house.

Agence France Presse/Douglas E. Curran/Hulton Archive/Getty Images

Photo by A.B. Murphy. © 2020 John Wiley & Sons, Inc.

FIGURE 1.15 **New Delhi, India (A) and Jodhpur, India (B).** Hindus believe cows are holy, and in India, evidence of that can be seen everywhere from cows roaming the streets to the menu at McDonald's. In 1996, the first McDonald's restaurant opened in New Delhi, India, serving Maharaja Macs and Vegetable Burgers with Cheese. In Indian towns, such as Jodhpur, cows are protected and share the streets with pedestrians, bicyclists, and motorists.

Relocation Diffusion

With expansion diffusion, whether contagious, hierarchical, or stimulus, people stay in place and the innovation, idea, trait, or disease moves. **Relocation diffusion** occurs when an idea or innovation spreads from its hearth by the action of people moving and taking the idea or innovation with them. Relocation diffusion primarily happens through migration. When migrants move from one place to another, they take their culture traits with them. Developing an ethnic neighborhood in a new country helps migrants maintain their culture in the midst of an unfamiliar one (see Chapter 4). Relocation diffusion involves the actual movement of individuals who have already adopted the idea or innovation and who carry it to a new, perhaps distant, locale, where they proceed to disseminate it (**Fig. 1.16**). Relocation diffusion can even help maintain cultural traits and customs. If the homeland of migrants loses enough of its population, cultural traits and customs may fade in the hearth while gaining strength in the ethnic neighborhoods abroad.

AP® Exam Taker's Tip

Simplifying the two types of diffusion is helpful. **Expansion diffusion** occurs when human *ideas*, *innovations*, and *tools* move among people. **Relocation diffusion** occurs when *people* move from one place to another and then the diffusion of ideas, innovations, and tools begins.

Photo by E.H. Fouberg. © 2020 John Wiley & Sons, Inc.

FIGURE 1.16 **San Francisco, California.** Migrants from China started coming to North America in the mid- to late nineteenth century. They played an important role in developing the economy. Many ended up in neighborhoods called Chinatowns—not simply because they wanted to live together, but because discrimination made it difficult for them to live elsewhere. The San Francisco Chinatown was one of the largest. Those who settled there brought with them customs and practices that are still very much in evidence today.

Cultural Landscape

Geographers use the term *landscape* to refer to the material character of a place, the complex of natural features, human structures, and other tangible objects that give a place a particular form. Human geographers are particularly concerned with the **cultural landscape**, the visible imprint of human activity on the land. Reading cultural landscapes provides insights into the practices and priorities of those who shaped the landscape over time. Former University of California at Berkeley professor Carl Sauer explains cultural landscapes are composed of the "forms superimposed on the physical landscape" by human activity.

No place on Earth is untouched. People have made an imprint on every place on Earth (**Fig. 1.17**). Physical environments like mountains and glaciers have the imprint of people and are part of the cultural landscape. Built environments like buildings, roads, memorials, churches, fields, and homes are also part of the cultural landscape. Each culture makes its own imprint on the landscape, which creates layers of cultural landscapes in one place.

Cultural landscapes can reflect long periods of human activity. As each group of people arrives and occupies a place, they carry their own technological and cultural traditions and transform the landscape in their own way. In 1929 Derwent Whittlesey used the term **sequent occupance** to describe the imprint made by a series of people living on a landscape—each creating a layer on top of the one that came before. The Tanzanian city of Dar es Salaam provides an interesting example of sequent occupance. Arabs from Zanzibar first chose the site for the African city in 1866 as a summer retreat. Next, German colonizers imprinted a new layout and architectural style for homes and government buildings (half-timbered Teutonic) when they chose the city as the center of their East African colonies in 1891.

After World War I, when the Germans were ousted, a British administration took over the city and began yet another period of transformation. The British encouraged immigration from their colony in India to Tanzania. The new migrant Asian population created a zone of three- and four-story apartment houses, which look as if they were transplanted from Bombay (now Mumbai), India (**Fig. 1.18A and B**). Then, in the early 1960s, Dar es Salaam became the capital of newly independent Tanzania. The city experienced four stages of cultural dominance in less than one century, and each stage of the sequence remains imprinted on the cultural landscape.

A cultural landscape offers clues to the cultural practices, values, and priorities of its layers of occupants. As geographer Peirce Lewis explained in *Axioms for Reading the Landscape* (1979), "Our human landscape is our unwitting autobiography, reflecting our tastes, our values, our aspirations, and even our fears, in tangible, visible form." Like Whittlesey, Lewis recommended looking for layers of history and cultural practice in cultural landscapes, adding that most major changes in the cultural landscape occur after a major event, such as a war, a technological revolution, or an economic depression.

Author Field Note   Hiking through Glacier National Park, Montana

"Hiking to the famed Grinnell Glacier in Glacier National Park brings you close to nature, but even in this remote location people have made an imprint on the landscape. The parking lot at the start of the six-mile trail, the trail itself, and the small signs en route are only part of the human imprint. When I hiked around the turn in this valley and arrived at the foot of the glacier, I found myself looking at a sheet of ice and snow that was less than a third the size of what it had been in 1850. Human-induced climate change is changing glaciated areas around the world. If the melt at Glacier National Park continues at present rates, scientists predict this glacier will be gone by 2030."

– A.B. Murphy

Photo by A.B. Murphy. © 2020 John Wiley & Sons, Inc.

FIGURE 1.17   **Glacier National Park, Montana.**

Scale

Geographers study places and patterns across scales, including local, regional, national, and global. **Scale** has two meanings in geography: The first refers to the distance on a map compared to the distance on Earth, and the second is the spatial extent of something—the scale of an individual, a family, city, a state, a watershed, a continent, a region, or the world. When we refer to scale, we are typically using the second definition because this way of thinking about scale impacts how we interpret patterns and factors of both human and physical phenomena.

Geographers' interest in the second type of scale derives from the fact that something found at one scale is usually influenced by what is happening at other scales. The growth of a city, for example, may well be the product of economic forces unfolding at the scale of a state, a region, or the world. Explaining a geographic pattern or process requires looking across scales. The scale of research or analysis matters because we can make different observations at different scales. We can study a single phenomenon across different scales to see how what is happening at the global scale affects what is happening at the local scale and vice versa. Or we can study something at one scale and then ask how processes at other scales affect what we are studying. For example, if you want to understand the conflict between Arabs and Kurds in Syria, you cannot look solely at Syria. Developments at a variety of different scales, including histories of relations among people at the local scale, regional patterns of migration, economic and political relations between Syria and its neighbors, and global involvement by the United States and Russia in the region all affect the conflict.

The scale at which we study a geographic phenomenon influences what we see. When we study the distribution of material wealth at the global scale (see Fig. 1.3), we see that the countries in western Europe, Canada, the United States, Japan, and Australia have the highest GNI per capita, and the countries of sub-Saharan Africa and Southeast Asia have the lowest GNI per capita. Does that mean that everyone in the United States has higher incomes while everyone in Indonesia has lower incomes? Certainly not, but at the global scale, that is how it looks.

When you shift scales to North America and examine median household income for the states of the United States and the provinces of Canada (**Fig. 1.19**), you see that the highest income areas are on the coasts and the lowest incomes are in northeastern Canada and the South. The state of Alaska and the Northwest Territories have high median household incomes, supplemented by oil revenues shared among residents.

Photo by A.B. Murphy. © 2020 John Wiley & Sons, Inc.

Photo by A.B. Murphy. © 2020 John Wiley & Sons, Inc.

FIGURE 1.18A AND B **Mumbai, India (A) and Dar-es-Salaam, Tanzania (B).** Apartment buildings throughout Mumbai (formerly Bombay), India, are typically four stories with balconies. In Dar-es-Salaam, Tanzania, this four-story walkup with balconies (right) stands where single-family African dwellings once stood, reflecting the sequent occupance of the city, as migrants from India left their imprint on Dar-es-Salaam.

By shifting scales again to a single city, such as metropolitan Washington, D.C. (**Fig. 1.20**), you observe that suburbs west, northwest, and southwest of the city have the highest incomes and that suburbs to the east and southeast have lower income levels. In the city itself, a clear dichotomy of wealth divides the northwest neighborhoods from the rest of the city. Shifting scales again to households or individuals, if you interviewed people who live below the poverty line in Washington, D.C., you would quickly find that each person's experience of poverty and reasons for being in poverty are unique. You might find some trends between groups—women, for example, might have different experiences than men—but no two individual cases are exactly the same.

Because the level of detail and the patterns observed change as the scale changes, geographers must think about the scale of analysis they use. We must also be wary of generalizations about people or places that fail to consider how the scale of analysis affects the generalization.

Jumping Scales
Geographers are also interested in how people use scale politically. Locally based political movements, like the Zapatistas in southern Mexico, have learned to **rescale** their actions to involve players at other scales and to create global support for their position. Zapatistas gained attention from the global media by broadening their protests against international trade agreements to the national scale and using the Internet to develop a global campaign. Relatively few political movements achieve that kind of exposure.

Geographer Victoria Lawson uses the term *jumping scale* to describe such rescaling activities. She compares the ways in which Western countries, multinational corporations, and the World Trade Organization take products and ideas created in Western places by Western corporations and globalize all rights to profits from them through intellectual property law. Efforts to push Western views of intellectual property challenge other

local and regional views of products and ideas. To the West, rice is a product that can be owned, privatized, and bought and sold. To many East Asians, rice is integral to culture, and new rice strains and new ideas about growing rice can help build community, not just profit. Taking the view of a single region (the West) and globalizing it (i.e., jumping scales) can serve to make that globalized view seem legitimate and appropriate for all places, while undercutting regional and local views.

AP® Exam Taker's Tip

Scale is perhaps the most important spatial skill to be able to effectively and accurately deploy in this course and text. The use of scale is absolutely critical to effective map reading and applying the concepts in every chapter of this text. With regard to scale, always think about this statement: "What is true at one scale is not necessarily true at another scale."

Context

Context is the bigger picture in which a human or physical geography phenomenon takes place. It is the physical and human geographies that give meaning to the place, environment, and space in which events occur and people act. When you think about relative location, the historical geography of the people and place, or analyzing a geographic phenomenon across scales, you are thinking in terms of context.

Geographers do not see the world as a static stage upon which actions take place. Rather, geographers think about context. We consider how the bigger picture, including the human and physical geographies of a place, create a dynamic, ever-changing world. And we think about context in order to appreciate that cultural traits and meanings of symbols are not the

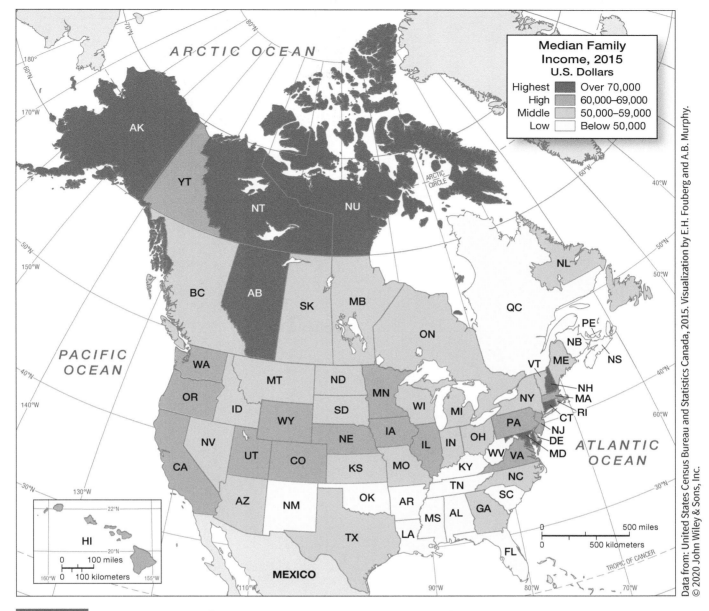

FIGURE 1.19 **Median Family Income (in U.S. Dollars).** The relatively higher incomes of Canadian provinces and the East Coast of the United States stand out. The relatively lower incomes of the American South also stand out on the map.

same in different places or among different people. For example, Rosa Parks Street (see Fig. 1.11) has a different meaning in Montgomery, Alabama, where segregation was entrenched and where Parks launched the Montgomery bus boycott began, than the Rosa Parks Street on the campus of Ohio State University in Columbus, Ohio. Montgomery and Columbus provide different contexts, which create different meanings to the presence of a street sign commemorating Rosa Parks.

Why Thinking Geographically Matters

Our world consists of nearly 200 countries, a diversity of religions, thousands of languages, and a wide variety of settlement types, ranging from small villages to enormous world cities. All of these attributes come together in different ways around the globe to create a world of endlessly diverse people, places, and cultures. Understanding and explaining this diversity are the mission of human geography.

To think geographically, start by asking a geographic question, one with a spatial or landscape component (e.g., how patterns of inequality or the types of housing found in different neighborhoods in Houston have changed). Alternatively, ask a question that focuses attention on how the character or geographic situation of a place affects what happens (e.g., how the physical and cultural character of Shanghai influences the growth of the city). In doing this, you'll see that raising a geographic question opens up new and

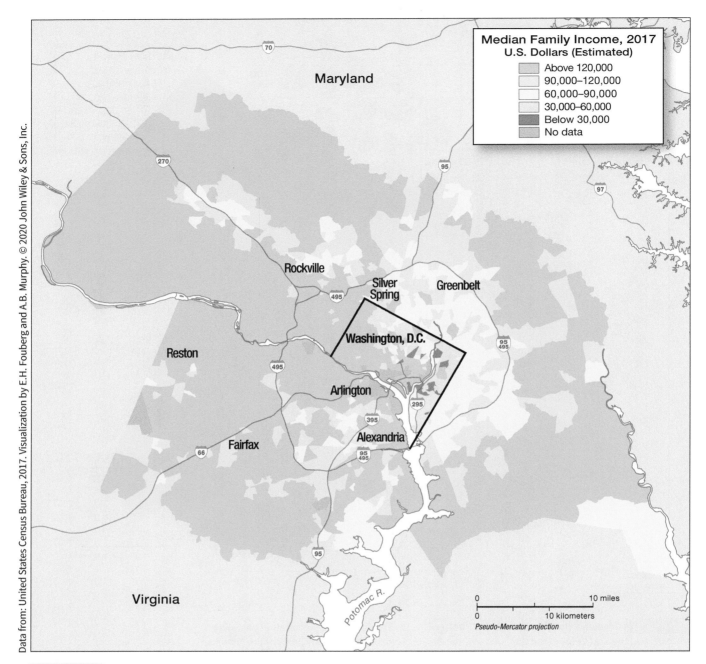

FIGURE 1.20 **Median Family Income (in U.S. Dollars) in Washington, DC.**   Washington, D.C. is a diamond shape with the Potomac River as its southwest border in the middle of the map. Notice the sharp contrast in income between western and eastern D.C. The surrounding suburbs in Maryland and Virginia are also mapped with the same general trend: The western suburbs have higher incomes than the eastern suburbs.

important ways of thinking about what is going on in the world around you.

Learning and applying geographic concepts and making links among concepts in your mind is the next step to thinking geographically. Once you have a geographic question, as simple as why are there so many one-way streets in a certain neighborhood or as complex as why do people in the oil-producing region of Nigeria have relatively low incomes, you can use geographic concepts to start to discover answers.

TC **Thinking** Geographically

Study the **cultural landscape** of San Francisco's Chinatown in Figure 1.14. Using the geographic concept **scale**, consider what role San Francisco's Chinatown plays at three different scales: locally (in San Francisco), nationally (along the west coast of the U.S.), and regionally (as part of the larger Pacific Ocean region). Bonus: If you were to walk around San Francisco's Chinatown, what might you see in the cultural landscape that reflected this Chinatown's **identity** locally, nationally, and regionally?

1.3 Identify types of maps and examine the role maps play in understanding the world.

Maps are incredibly powerful tools in geography. **Cartography**—the art and science of making maps—is as old as geography itself. (For details on maps and map projections, see Appendix A.) People use maps for countless purposes, including bringing relief to refugees, waging war, promoting political positions, solving medical problems, locating stores, and warning of natural hazards. **Reference maps** show locations of places and geographic features. **Thematic maps** tell stories, typically showing the spatial distribution (clustering or dispersal) or movement of people and things.

Reference maps accurately show the **absolute locations** of places, using a coordinate system that precisely plots where on Earth something is found. Imagine taking an orange, drawing a dot on it with a marker, and then describing the exact location of that dot to someone who wants to mark the same spot on her orange. If you each draw and number the same coordinate system, the task of drawing the absolute location on each orange is not only doable but simple. The coordinate system most frequently used on maps is based on latitude and longitude. For example, the absolute location of Chicago is 41°, 53' north latitude and 87°, 37' west longitude. Using these coordinates, you can plot Chicago on any globe or map that is marked with latitude and longitude lines.

A satellite-based **global positioning system** (GPS) enables us to locate features on Earth with extraordinary accuracy. We not only know the absolute locations of places; we also know the *absolute distance* and *absolute direction* between them, which means we can use maps for wayfinding. Researchers collect data quickly and easily in the field, and low-priced units make it possible for drivers, fishers, hunters, runners, and hikers to use GPS to find absolute direction and absolute distance between places, and track paths. Cars are equipped with GPS units, and dashboard map displays help commuters navigate traffic and travelers find their way. Smartphones are equipped with GPS, helping spread the use of GPS even further. Geocaching is a popular hobby based on GPS. Geocachers use their GPS units to play a treasure hunt game all over the world. People leave the treasures ("caches") somewhere, mark the coordinates on their GPS, and post clues on the Internet. If you find the cache, you take the treasure and leave a new one.

Relative location describes the location of a place in relation to other human and physical features. Descriptors such as "Chicago is on Lake Michigan, south of Milwaukee" or "Chicago is located where the cross-country railroads met in the 1800s" or "Chicago is the hub of the corn and soybean markets in the Midwest" are all descriptors of Chicago relative to other features. In the southern Wisconsin, northern Illinois, and western Indiana region, all major roads lead to Chicago (**Fig. 1.21**). Within this region, people define much of their lives relative to Chicago because of the tight interconnectedness between Chicago and the region. Northwest Indiana is so connected to Chicago that it has a time zone separate from the rest of Indiana, allowing people in northwestern Indiana to stay in the same time zone as Chicago.

Absolute locations do not change, but relative locations change over time. Fredericksburg, Virginia, is located halfway between Washington, D.C., and Richmond, Virginia. Today, it is a suburb of Washington, D.C., with commuter trains, van pools, buses, and cars moving commuters between their homes in Fredericksburg and their workplaces in metropolitan

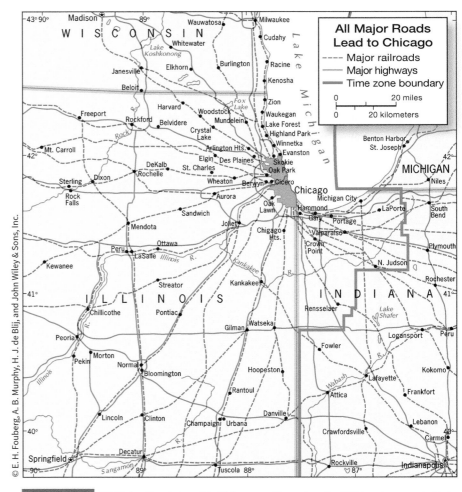

© E. H. Fouberg, A. B. Murphy, H. J. de Blij, and John Wiley & Sons, Inc.

FIGURE 1.21 **All Major Roads Lead to Chicago.** The network of Midwestern roads that lead to Chicago reflects the dominance of the city in the region.

Washington. During the Civil War, several bloody battles took place in Fredericksburg as the North and South fought halfway between their wartime capitals. The absolute location of Fredericksburg has not changed, but its place in relation to surrounding places certainly has.

Mental Maps

We all carry maps in our minds of places we have been and places we have merely heard of; these are called **mental maps**. If you have never been to the Great Plains of the United States, you likely imagine a region encompassing some or all of North Dakota, South Dakota, Nebraska, Kansas, Oklahoma, and northern Texas. Even if your mental map is not accurate, you still use it to process information about the Great Plains. If you hear on the news that a tornado damaged a town in Oklahoma, you use your mental map of the Great Plains region and Oklahoma to make sense of where the tornado occurred and who was affected by it.

Our mental maps of local places often reflect our **activity spaces**, the spaces we move through routinely. Our mental maps of places we travel through routinely are much more accurate and detailed than our mental maps of places we have never been. If your friend calls and asks you to meet her at the movie theater you go to frequently, your mental map will engage automatically and your brain will start planning routes to get to the theater. You will envision the hallway, the front door, the walk to your car, the lane to choose in order to be prepared for the left turn you must make, where you will park your car, and your path into the theater and up to the popcorn stand.

Geographers who study human–environment behavior have made extensive studies of how people develop mental maps. Early nomadic humans had incredibly accurate mental maps of where to find food and seek shelter. Today, city

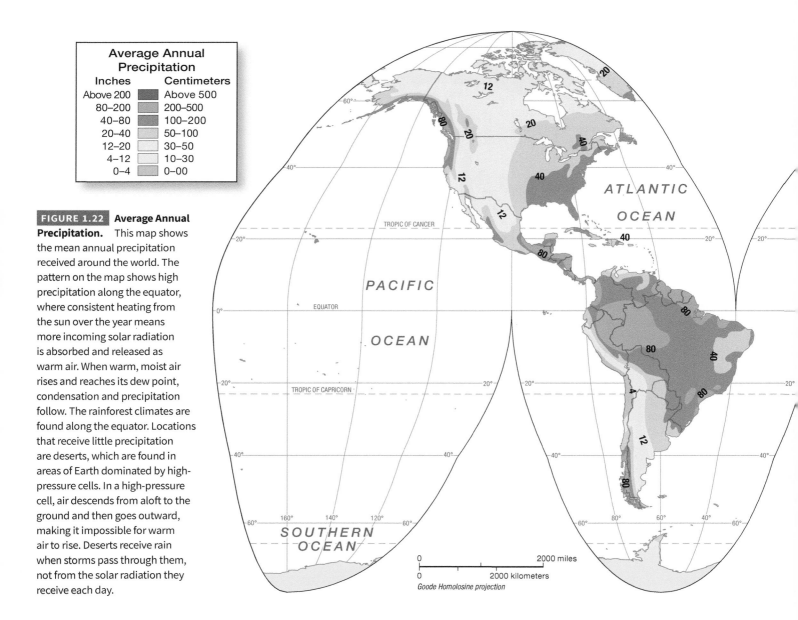

FIGURE 1.22 **Average Annual Precipitation.** This map shows the mean annual precipitation received around the world. The pattern on the map shows high precipitation along the equator, where consistent heating from the sun over the year means more incoming solar radiation is absorbed and released as warm air. When warm, moist air rises and reaches its dew point, condensation and precipitation follow. The rainforest climates are found along the equator. Locations that receive little precipitation are deserts, which are found in areas of Earth dominated by high-pressure cells. In a high-pressure cell, air descends from aloft to the ground and then goes outward, making it impossible for warm air to rise. Deserts receive rain when storms pass through them, not from the solar radiation they receive each day.

dwellers use mental maps to find their way through the concrete jungles of cities and suburbs.

Geographers have also studied the mental map formation of children, the blind, new residents to cities, men, and women. Researchers observed differences in how each group forms mental maps. For example, to learn new places, women tend to use landmarks, whereas men tend to use paths. Mental maps of children show smaller areas because their activity spaces are smaller.

Mental maps include **terra incognita**, unknown lands that are sometimes off-limits. If your path to the movie theater includes driving past a school that you do not attend, your map on paper may label the school, but no details will be shown regarding the place. However, if you have access to the school and you are instead drawing a mental map of how to get to the school's cafeteria, your mental map of the school will be quite detailed. Thus mental maps reflect a person's activity space, including what is accessible to the person in his or her rounds of daily activity, and what is not.

Generalization in Maps

All maps simplify the world (see discussion of projections in Appendix A). A reference map of the world cannot show every place in the world, and a thematic map of hurricane tracks in the Atlantic Ocean cannot pinpoint the precise path of every hurricane for the last 50 years. When mapping human or physical data, cartographers (the geographers who make maps) generalize the information they present on maps. Many of the maps in this book are thematic maps of the world. Shadings show how much or how little of a phenomenon is present, and symbols show where specific phenomena are located.

Generalized maps help us see trends because we cannot see all cases of a given phenomenon. The map of world precipitation (**Fig. 1.22**) is a generalized map of mean annual precipitation received around the world. The areas shaded in blue and dark green are places that receive the most rain, and those shaded in orange receive the least rain on average. Take a pen and trace along the equator on the map. Notice how

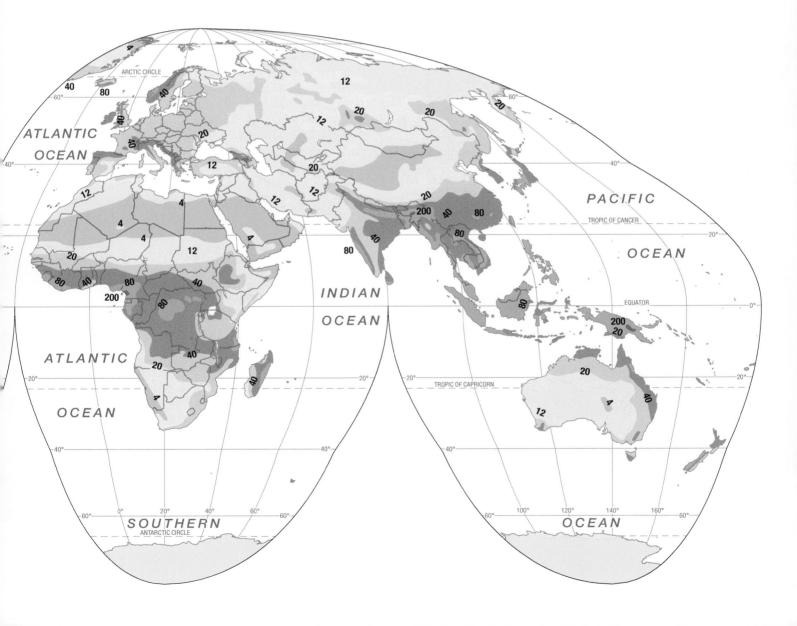

many of the high-precipitation areas on the map are along the equator and in the tropics, between 23.5° north and 23.5° south. The direct rays of the sun consistently heat the equator and tropics over the course of the year, which means more warm air is rising along and around the equator relative to the rest of Earth. Warm air rising is a condition for precipitation, so the tropics receive more annual precipitation than other latitude zones like the mid-latitudes or polar regions.

Using Figure 1.22, we can describe the spatial distribution of precipitation as clustered or dispersed. Bands of high precipitation are clustered in the tropics, and low precipitation areas are dispersed between polar regions and bands at around 30 degrees north and south. Studying Figure 1.22 is a good reminder that the **patterns** we see on a map are limited to the data presented on the map. This map only shows data at the global scale. We can see general trends in precipitation and compare large regions like the tropics to other regions like the polar region. At this scale and using the data in Figure 1.22, we cannot see, nor do we know anything about, summer rainstorms that bring areas of intense precipitation and flooding. To see individual storms, we would need a weather map for a smaller area.

Remote Sensing and GIS

Geographers study long- and short-term environmental change. To monitor short-term environmental change, geographers use remote sensing technology. **Remote sensing** is a method of collecting data or information through instruments that are physically distant from the area of study. Satellites, aircrafts, and drones collect remotely sensed data, which are often instantaneously available. After a major weather or hazard event, remotely sensed data show us the areas most impacted (**Fig. 1.23**). For example, satellites, aircraft, and drones help monitor wildfires in California or hurricanes in the Bahamas to help first responders and assess damage (**Fig. 1.24**).

Geographers integrate remotely sensed images into geographic information systems, which enable us to study change to a specific place or region over time. **Geographic information systems** (GIS) combine computer hardware and software to show, analyze, and represent geographic data. Anytime you use Apple Maps, Google Maps, or your

August 16, 2019

September 5, 2019

Claudia Weinmann/Alamy Stock Photo

FIGURE 1.23A **Great Abaco, Bahamas.** The top image shows Great Abaco before Hurricane Dorian passed by, and the bottom photo shows after. The before photo has vegetation covering the islands, and the land in the bottom photo is brown where the hurricane wiped vegetation and houses. The bottom photo also shows much more sediment in streaks in the water, from the tons of material Hurricane Dorian moved off the islands and into the harbors and sea.

Jose Jimenez/Getty Images

FIGURE 1.23B **Great Abaco, Bahamas.** Aerial view of the damage Hurricane Dorian caused. The hurricane hit Grand Abaco as a Category 5 storm. Its 20 foot storm surges leveled much of the northern Bahamas.

elections. In this case, a geographer can draw a line around a group of people and ask the computer program to tally how many voters are inside the region, determine the racial composition of the district, and show how many of the current political representatives live within the new district's boundaries.

Students who earn undergraduate degrees in geography with a minor or certificate in GIS are employed by software companies, government agencies, and businesses to use GIS to survey wildlife, map soils, analyze natural disasters, track diseases, assist first responders, plan cities, plot transportation improvements, and follow weather systems. Intelligence agencies including the Central Intelligence Agency (CIA) and the Office of Naval Intelligence integrate the data they gather into GIS and use spatial analysis tools to discover patterns and

Miami Herald/Tribune News Service/Getty Images

FIGURE 1.24 **Great Abaco, Bahamas** Hurricane Dorian destroyed a neighborhood at Marsh Harbour. The hurricane sat over the Bahamas for two days before moving north.

Garmin running watch to find or track your way, you are using GIS. Geographers use GIS, including Esri's ArcGIS and ArcGIS Online, to analyze spatial relationships among different mappable phenomena. Professional geographers use GIS to compare spatial data by creating digitized representations of the environment (**Fig. 1.25**), combining layers of spatial data, and creating maps that superimpose patterns and processes. Once spatial data are entered, geographers use GIS to analyze data, and these analyses offer new insights into geographic patterns and relationships.

Geographers use GIS in both human and physical geographic research. For example, political geographers use GIS to map layers showing voters, party registration, race and ethnicity, likelihood of voting, and income to determine how to draw voting districts in congressional and state legislative

make predictions. Geographers who work in the intelligence field can use GIS to see local patterns, and they can also think geographically, using scale, to see how processes happening at other scales impact and shape local patterns.

Geographers can answer complicated questions using spatial analysis tools in ArcGIS to analyze enormous amounts of data. For example, geographer Korine Kolivras analyzed the probability of dengue fever outbreaks in Hawai'i using GIS (**Fig. 1.26**). The maps Kolivras produced may look as simple and straightforward as the cholera maps produced by Dr. John Snow in the 1800s, but the amount of data that went into Kolivras's analysis is staggering in comparison. Dengue fever is carried by a particular kind of mosquito called the *Aedes* mosquito. Kolivras analyzed the breeding conditions needed for this mosquito, including precipitation, topography, and

USGS/NASA

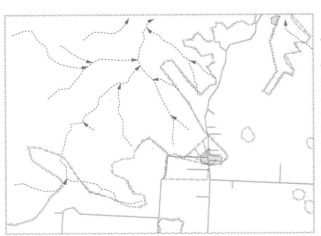

Courtesy of: Joseph J. Kerski using ArcGIS software from Environmental Systems Research Institute, Inc.

FIGURE 1.25 **Two Representations of St. Francis, South Dakota.** Left is a panchromatic raster satellite image collected in 2002 at 10 m resolution during a grassland wildfire, and the right displays vector data—rivers, roads, cities, and land use/land cover—digitalized from the image on the left.

Guest Field Note Predicting Dengue Outbreak in Maui, Hawai'i

Korine N. Kolivras
Virginia Tech

The diffusion of diseases carried by vectors, such as the *Aedes* mosquito that transmits dengue, is not solely a result of the environmental factors in a place. I use disease ecology to understand the ways environmental, social, and cultural factors interact to produce disease. Through a combination of fieldwork and GIS modeling, I studied the environmental habitat of the *Aedes* mosquito in Hawai'i and the social and cultural factors that stimulated the outbreak of dengue in Hawai'i.

When I went into the field, I observed the diversity of the physical geography, from deserts to rainforests. I saw the specific local environments of the dengue outbreak area, and I examined the puddles in streams (**Fig. 1.26A**) where mosquitoes likely bred during the dengue outbreak. I talked to public health officials who worked hard to control the dengue outbreak so that I better understood the local environmental factors contributing to the disease. I visited a family that had been heavily affected by dengue, and I saw their home, which, by their choice, lacked walls or screens on all sides. In talking with the family, I came to understand the social and cultural factors that affected the outbreak of dengue in Hawai'i.

I created a GIS model of mosquito habitat that considered total precipitation in Hawai'i (**Fig. 1.26B**), seasonal variations in precipitation (**Fig. 1.26C**) and temperature (**Fig. 1.26D**), to help explain where the *Aedes* mosquito is able to breed and survive. I also studied seasonal fluctuations in streams and population distributions to create my model of dengue potential areas (**Fig. 1.26E**).

My GIS model can now be altered by public officials to reflect precipitation and temperature variations each year or to incorporate new layers of data. Officials will be able to better predict locations of dengue outbreaks so they can focus their efforts to combat the spread of disease.

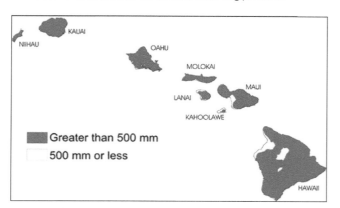

FIGURE 1.26A **Maui, Hawai'i.** *Aedes* mosquitoes breed in artificial and natural water containers, including puddles.

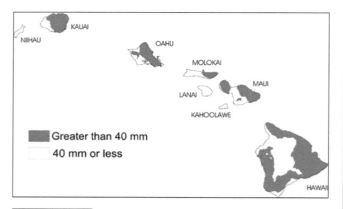

FIGURE 1.26C Average June Precipitation.

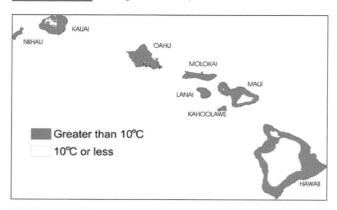

FIGURE 1.26D Average February minimum temperature.

FIGURE 1.26B Total annual precipitation.

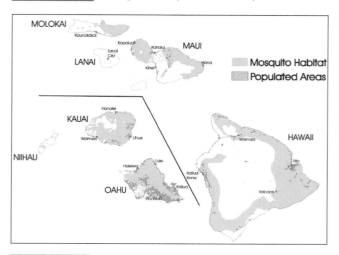

FIGURE 1.26E Dengue potential areas.

several other variables, to predict what places in Hawai'i are most likely to experience an outbreak of dengue fever.

The power of GIS continues to evolve with advances in data storage and retrieval technologies. Real-time data collection and analysis in GIS has enabled companies like Uber to match you with a driver and show you where the driver is and when the driver will reach you. Waze, an app designed to help drivers find safe and fast routes, integrates crowd-sourced data from all app users in real-time to warn drivers of accidents and re-route them around construction or traffic jams. Real-time GIS also enables crowd-sourcing data, which is valuable to organizers protesting in Hong Kong or Moscow and to governments of China and Russia who are monitoring protesters. Crowd-sourcing data helps first responders to wildfires in California or floods in Houston. Emergency management systems use real-time data in GIS to respond to every 911 call.

In addition to helping in crises, geographic data are more accessible to consumers, which may help them make better decisions. Real estate apps show buyers and sellers recent sales prices and assessed values of houses in neighborhoods, enabling consumers to assess the value of one house relative to the neighborhood and the city as a whole. Large companies like Target and Costco use GIS to build more efficient supply chains. GIS makes just-in-time delivery (see Chapter 12) possible. GIS is also part of the growing field of Artificial Intelligence (AI). The Chinese government uses

real-time facial recognition-AI integrated with GIS to track movements of Chinese citizens, especially minority Uighurs and people living in cities (see Chapter 9), and visitors.

The field of advancing GIS is called Geographic Information Science (GISci). Your school may have a program in GISci that incorporates multiple disciplines, bringing together computer scientists who write programs, engineers who create sensors that gather data about Earth, and geographers who combine layers of data and interpret them to make sense of the world.

TC Thinking Geographically

Look at the map pattern in Figure 1.26E. Note that this map is more "zoomed in" than 1.26 B, C, and D, and the three Hawai'ian islands to the farthest north, Nihau, Kauai, and Oahu, are placed to the west of the other four islands so that you can see more detail on the map of each island. Describe the **pattern** of likely mosquito habitats on the map. Then, describe the relationship between mosquito habitats and populated areas. Finally, imagine you are advising the government of Hawai'i who wants to conduct a pilot study on the island where dengue will have the biggest impact on people. Which island should Hawai'i use for its pilot study and why?

1.4 Describe How Culture Influences Patterns and Processes in Human Geography.

Culture influences music, literature, and arts as well as prevailing modes of dress; routine living habits; food preferences; attitudes toward gender and racial differences; the architecture of houses and public buildings; the layout of fields and farms; and systems of education, government, and law. **Culture** is a group of belief systems, norms, and values practiced by a people. Culture is an all-encompassing term that identifies not only people's tangible lifestyles, but also their prevailing values and beliefs. Culture lies at the heart of human geography.

While we offer one definition of culture, academics from human geographers to anthropologists have defined culture in many different ways over time. Some have stressed the contributions of humans to the environment; others have emphasized learned behaviors and ways of thinking. Several decades ago the noted anthropologist E. Adamson Hoebel defined culture as "[the] integrated system of learned behavior patterns which are characteristic of the members of a society and which are not the result of biological inheritance . . . culture is not genetically predetermined; it is noninstinctive . . . [Culture] is wholly the result of social invention and

is transmitted and maintained solely through communication and learning."

Hoebel's emphasis on communication and learning anticipated the current view of culture as a system of meaning, not just a set of acts, customs, or material products. Clifford Geertz advanced this view in his classic work, *The Interpretation of Cultures* (1973), which influenced much work in human geography. Human geographers are interested not just in the different patterns and landscapes associated with different culture groups, but also in how cultural understandings affect both the creation and significance of those patterns and landscapes.

A **culture trait** is a single attribute of a culture that can be identified and described. For example, wearing a turban is a culture trait in certain societies. Many men in the semiarid and desert areas of North Africa, Southwest Asia, and South Asia wore turbans before the birth of Islam. Turbans protected the wearers from sunlight and also helped distinguish tribes (**Fig. 1.27**). Not all Muslim men wear turbans, but in some Muslim countries, including Oman, wearing turbans is popular because either religious or political leaders prescribe it for

Author Field Note   Dressing for the Climate in Nizwa, Oman

"Witnessing the scene at the morning animal market in Nizwa, the old interior capital of Oman, reminded me of the adaptations people have made to the natural environment. The clothing and turbans were practical for the hot, dry climate there, and the early morning timing of the market ensured that the market would be over by the time the hottest hours of the day arrived."

– A.B. Murphy

Photo by A.B. Murphy. © 2020 John Wiley & Sons, Inc.

FIGURE 1.27 Nizwa, Oman.

men. Today, turbans often distinguish a man's status in society or represent faithfulness to God.

In some Muslim countries, including Egypt and Turkey, men rarely wear turbans. When men in other Muslim countries do wear turbans, the appearance of the turban varies a great deal. For instance, in Yemen, men who cover their heads typically wear kalansuwa, which are caps wrapped in fabric. In Palestine, Jordan, and Saudi Arabia, men who cover their heads typically wear kaffiyeh, which are rectangular pieces of cloth draped and secured on the head.

Wearing turbans is not a cultural trait limited to Muslims. In the United States, most men who cover their heads with turbans are Sikhs, followers of Sikhism, which is a different religion from Islam. In Sikhism, men are required to keep their hair uncut. The common practice is to twist the hair, knot it on top of one's head, and then cover it with a turban. Sikhism began in the 1500s; in the late 1600s, the tenth guru of the religion taught that wearing a turban was a way to demonstrate one's faithfulness to God.

As the turban example shows, a culture trait is not always confined to a single culture, nor does it carry the same meaning across cultures. More than one culture may exhibit a particular culture trait, such as turbans. A distinct combination of culture traits is a **culture complex**. Herding of cattle is a culture trait shared by many cultures, but different cultures regard and use cattle in different ways. The Maasai of East Africa, for example, follow their herds along seasonal migration paths, consuming blood and milk as important ingredients of a unique diet.

Cattle occupy a central place in Maasai existence; they are the essence of survival, security, and prestige. Although the Maasai culture complex is only one of many cattle-keeping complexes, no other culture complex exhibits exactly the same combination of traits. In Europe, cattle are milked, and dairy products, such as butter, yogurt, and cheese, are consumed as part of a diet very different from the Maasai diet.

A cultural **hearth** is an area where culture traits develop and from which they diffuse. For example, the religion of Islam emerged in a single place and time. Muhammad founded Islam in the 600s CE (common era) in and around the cities of Mecca and Medina on the Arabian Peninsula. Other culture traits, such as agriculture, spread from several hearths thousands of years apart. When such a trait develops in more than one hearth without being influenced by its development elsewhere, each hearth operates as a case of **independent invention**.

TC Thinking Geographically

Geographers who undertake fieldwork keep their eyes open to the world around them and, through practice, become adept at reading the **cultural landscape**. Take a walk around your campus or town and try reading the cultural landscape. Choose something that you see and ask yourself, "What is that and why it is there?" Take the time to find out the answers!

Summary

1.1 Define Human Geography and Describe the Value of Thinking Geographically.

1. Human geography is concerned with how we organize ourselves and our activities in space; how we are connected to one another and the environment; how we make places and how those places in turn shape our lives; and how we think about and organize ourselves on the planet.

2. A geographic perspective focuses on the spatial arrangement of places and phenomena: how they are laid out, organized, and arranged on Earth; how they appear on the landscape; and how the various characteristics of individual places—physical and human—influence one another. Geographical thinking also involves thinking about place-based interactions between humans and the environment.

1.2 Identify and Explain Geography's Core Concepts.

1. Looking at the world geographically means focusing particular attention on location, human–environment interactions, regions, places, movement, landscape, and scale.

2. There are different types of regions: formal regions (areas with a shared trait), functional regions (an area defined by a pattern of interaction), and perceptual regions (an area that exists in people's minds).

3. Traits and innovations diffuse through expansion diffusion (developing in a place and spreading out from there), contagious diffusion (spreading through interpersonal contact), hierarchical diffusion (spreading through a hierarchy), stimulus diffusion (spreading to a new location, followed by a change that occurs in that location), and relocation diffusion (spreading as the result of people moving from one place to another).

1.3 Identify Types of Maps and Examine the Role Maps Play in Understanding the World.

1. Maps are fundamental tools that geographers use to make sense of the world. They show patterns and the relationships that exist among things in geographic space. Satellite-based global positioning systems make it possible to produce highly accurate maps.

2. Geographers draw a distinction between absolute location (the precise specification of a location based on a coordinate system) and relative location (the location of something in relation to a human or physical feature or process).

3. People construct mental maps to make sense of the world. Mental maps at the local scale are influenced by people's activity spaces (the spaces people move through routinely).

4. Remote sensing and geographic information systems have revolutionized mapmaking. They have made it possible to address complex problems using powerful computer-generated location analysis tools.

1.4 Describe How Culture Influences Patterns and Processes in Human Geography.

1. *Culture* is an all-encompassing term that identifies not only people's tangible lifestyles, but also their prevailing values and beliefs.

2. Geographers identify, map, and examine the impacts of culture traits (individual attributes of a culture that can be identified and described). They also seek to understand where those traits first developed (culture hearths), as well as how and why they diffused from those places.

Self-Test

1.1 Define human geography and describe the value of thinking geographically.

1. Human geographers study:
   a. language patterns
   b. land use.
   c. human–environment relations.
   d. the political organization of space.
   e. all of the above.

2. In the study of geography, memorizing place names is equivalent to:
   a. developing theorems when studying mathematics.
   b. discovering new stars when studying astronomy.
   c. learning dates when studying history.
   d. explaining meanings when studying philosophy.
   e. testing hypothesis using the scientific method.

3. Understanding human geography requires focusing attention on globalization because what happens at the local scale no longer plays much of a role in shaping the human geography of the planet.
   a. true
   b. false

1.2 Identify and explain geography's core concepts.

4. The now discredited idea that human behavior is dictated by the natural environment is known as:
   a. environmental determinism.
   b. environmental possibilism.
   c. cultural ecology.
   d. political ecology.
   e. cultural relativism.

5. A region that is defined by interactions across space is a:

  a. formal region.

  b. functional region.

  c. perceptual region.

  d. vernacular region.

  e. cultural region.

6. When a senior church leader adopts a particular ritual, and that ritual is then adopted and followed by widely scattered congregations, which of the following types of diffusion has occurred?

  a. expansion diffusion

  b. contagious diffusion

  c. hierarchical diffusion

  d. relocation diffusion

  e. stimulus diffusion

1.3 Identify types of maps and examine the role maps play in understanding the world.

7. The term *cartography* refers to:

  a. the collection of locational data through surveying.

  b. the art and science of mapmaking.

  c. the creation of written accounts of a geographic practice.

  d. the making of photographs that capture a geographic phenomenon.

  e. the practice of describing site and situation.

8. The concept of relative location refers to:

  a. how location changes with mobility

  b. the position of a place on a latitude-longitude grid system.

  c. the north-south-east-west orientation of a place.

  d. the elevation of a place above sea level.

  e. the location of a place in relation to other human and physical features.

9. A geographer who uses map layers showing the distribution of voters, party registration, race and ethnicity, likelihood of voting, and income to figure out how to draw voting districts is taking advantage of:

  a. a geographic positioning system.

  b. a geographic information system.

  c. information from mental maps.

  d. remote sensing analysis.

  e. social scientific research.

1.4 Describe how culture influences patterns and processes in human geography.

10. Each of the following is a cultural trait except:

  a. a person's skin color.

  b. a person's food preferences.

  c. a person's language.

  d. a person's mode of dress.

  e. a person's style of housing.

11. A cultural hearth is an area to which cultural traits diffuse after they have emerged elsewhere.

  a. true

  b. false

12. Geographers use the term *culture complex* to refer to:

  a. independent invention that results from people interacting in a place.

  b. the tendency for cultural baggage to inhibit innovation.

  c. the relationships that develop among peoples living in different cultural realms.

  d. the distinct combination of cultural traits found in a place.

  e. the way different cultures interact across space.

CHAPTER 2

Population and Health

Photo by A.B. Murphy. © 2020 John Wiley & Sons, Inc.

FIGURE 2.1 **Shanghai, China.** The Shanghai tower is over 2000 feet (600 m) tall. The view from the observation deck is dramatic, but murky at best.

AP® Exam Taker's Tip

One of the most important concepts to understand about population is the impact humans have on the environment. The opening focuses on China's development and its impact on the environment, but think about where you live. How has your country, region, city, or town altered the environment in the name of development? What are some advantages of China's development? What are some disadvantages of China's development?

I have been coming to Shanghai for years and have seen the rapid transformation of the city on the ground. Small houses have been leveled by the thousands and replaced with thousands of apartment buildings, each a dozen or more stories tall. The opening of the observation deck atop the recently built 128-story Shanghai Tower gave me the chance to get a bird's eye view of the city. It's a sunny day, but the view is obscured by air pollution (**Fig. 2.1**). The explosive growth of Shanghai and other Chinese cities has come with costs, and one of them is significant air pollution.

China's population of 1.4 billion people has been migrating to cities in droves. China has more than 100 cities with more than 1 million people. Shanghai is the largest, with an estimated 22 million people. Rapid urbanization, stemming from a combination of rapid economic and population growth, has taken its toll on the environment and people's health. Coal is the biggest source of fuel in China. Burning coal emits PM-2.5, a small (fine particle) air pollutant that is particularly dangerous to human health because when it is inhaled, it damages the lungs. Unlike larger particles that may simply irritate your eyes or throat, PM-2.5 particles are so fine they can even get into the bloodstream. One study found that Chinese life expectancies in the north, where air pollution rates are higher, are 5.5 years shorter than life expectancies in the south. To reduce air pollution, China limited coal burning, banned imports on plastics for incineration (see Chapter 13), and restricted the number of cars on roads in major cities.

In this chapter, we examine population trends across the world and at different scales. We also look at how population growth is tied to global health because health, well-being, and population growth are closely related, in China and around the world.

CHAPTER OUTLINE

2.1 Describe the patterns of population distribution.
- Population Density
- Population Distribution
- Reliability of Population Data

2.2 Identify and explain influences on population growth over time.
- Malthus
- Natural Increase Rate
- The Demographic Transition

2.3 Explain how health and disease affect peoples' well-being.
- Health of Women and Children
- Life Expectancy
- Infectious Disease vs. Chronic Disease

2.4 Identify why and how governments influence population growth.
- Expansive
- Eugenic
- Restrictive

2.1 Describe the Patterns of Population Distribution.

Geographers examine patterns of population distribution. We ask why population densities are higher in some places than in others, and why population growth rates differ from place to place. **Demography** is the study of general population trends. Population geographers work together with demographers, seeking answers to how and why population trends vary across space (**Fig. 2.2**). Scale (see Chapter 1) is crucial to studies of population because population dynamics that are evident at small scales (local or state) cannot necessarily be seen when one looks at the country, region, or global scales. For example, people may migrate from the central city to the suburbs in one city, but that trend is not evident globally.

Population Density

Population density is a measure of total population relative to land area. Population density assumes an even distribution of people over an area. The United States, for example, with a territory of 5,692,815 sq miles or 9,161,966 sq km,[1] has a population of 326 million. This yields an average population density for the United States of just over 86 people per sq mile (33 per sq km). This density figure is also known as the country's **arithmetic population density**, and in a very general way it emphasizes the contrasts between the United States and much more densely populated countries, including Bangladesh at 2962 people per sq mile (1144 per sq km), the Netherlands with 1068 people per sq mile (412 per sq km), or Japan at 869 people per sq mile (335 per sq km).

No country has an evenly distributed population. Arithmetic population densities do not reflect the emptiness of parts of Alaska or the sparseness of population in much of the West. Arithmetic population figures can actually be quite misleading. Egypt, with a population of 97.6 million, has a seemingly moderate arithmetic population density of 252 people per sq mile (97 per sq km). Egypt's territory of 384,345 sq miles (995,450 sq km), however, is mostly desert, and the vast majority of people are crowded into the valley and delta of the Nile River. Nearly 98 percent of all Egyptians live on just 3 percent of the country's land; so, the arithmetic population density figure is meaningless in this case (**Fig. 2.3A and B**).

Physiologic Population Density

Physiologic population density relates the total population of a country to the area of arable (farmable) land. Like arithmetic population density, physiologic population density is expressed in number of people per sq mile (sq km), but the only land counted in the area is agriculturally productive land. Take Egypt as an example again. The population density of Egypt is 252 people per sq mile, but if we only count arable land in the calculation, the population density is much higher. Egypt's physiologic density is 6995 people per sq mile (2701 per sq km). The higher density expressed in the physiological population density better reflects Egypt's population pressure, and it continues to rise rapidly despite Egypt's efforts to expand its irrigated farmlands.

AP® Exam Taker's Tip

Understanding the different types of density is important in AP Human Geography. Two densities mentioned in the chapter are **arithmetic density** and **physiological density**. There is another density that is important to AP Human Geography, and that is **agricultural density**. Agricultural density is the number of farmers per unit of arable land. Agricultural density gives geographers a sense of who is farming the land and what is being farmed. If agricultural density is high, then people are farming the land and the region is not as developed. If agricultural density is low, then machines (like tractors) are farming the land.

[1]Territory excludes the surfaces of lakes and ponds and coastal waters up to three nautical miles from shore.

Author Field Note   Taking in the Busy Streets of Yangon, Myanmar

"An overpass across one of Yangon's busy streets provided a good perspective on the press of humanity in Southeast Asia. Whether in urban areas or on small back roads in the countryside, people are everywhere – young and old, fit and infirm. When population densities are high in areas of poverty and unsophisticated infrastructure, vulnerabilities to natural hazards can be particularly great. This phenomenon became stunningly evident in 2008 when a tropical cyclone devastated a significant swath of the Irrawaddy delta south of Yangon, killing some 100,000 people and leaving millions homeless."

– A. B. Murphy

Photo by A.B. Murphy. © 2020 John Wiley & Sons, Inc.

FIGURE 2.2 Yangon, Myanmar (Burma).

Author Field Note	Traveling from Lush Fields to Desert Sands in Luxor, Egypt

"The contrasting character of the Egyptian landscape could not be more striking. Along the Nile River, the landscape is one of green fields, scattered trees, and modest houses, like along this stretch of the river's west bank near Luxor (**Fig. 2.3A**). But anytime I wander away from the river, brown, wind-sculpted sand dominates the scene as far as the eye can see (**Fig. 2.3B**). Where people live and what they do is not just a product of culture; it is shaped by the physical environment as well."

– A. B. Murphy

Photo by A.B. Murphy. © 2020 John Wiley & Sons, Inc.

FIGURE 2.3A AND B   **Luxor, Egypt.**

Appendix B provides complete data on both arithmetic and physiologic population densities, and some of the data are striking. Mountainous Switzerland's physiologic density is 10 times as high as its arithmetic density because only 1 out of every 10 acres in Switzerland is arable. Ukraine's population is 44,800,000, and its arithmetic population density is 192 per sq mile (74 per sq km). Ukraine has vast farmlands, which make its physiologic density 281 people per sq mile of arable land (109 per sq km). The difference in arithmetic density and physiologic density for a single country reveals the proportion of arable land to all land. In the case of Ukraine, the physiologic density is 1.46 times as high as the arithmetic density because 1 out of every 1.46 acres of land in Ukraine is arable.

In Appendix B, the countries and territories of Middle America and the Caribbean stand out as having high physiologic densities compared to the moderate physiologic densities for South America. India's physiologic density is the lowest in South Asia despite its huge population. Both China and India have populations well over 1 billion, but according to the physiologic density, India has much more arable land per person than China.

Population Distribution

Globally, people are not distributed evenly, and within world regions or countries, people are not distributed evenly, either. One-third of the world's population lives in China and India. Yet each country has large expanses of land (the Himalayas in India and a vast interior desert in China) where people are very sparsely distributed. In addition to studying population densities, geographers study population distribution. A **population distribution** is the description of the pattern in the spatial arrangement of people, including where large numbers of people live closely together (*clustering*) and where few people live (*dispersed*).

Historically, people lived in places where they could grow food—making for a high correlation between arable land and population density. Cities generally began in agricultural areas, and for most of history, people lived closest to the most agriculturally productive areas. In recent times, advances in agricultural technology and in the transportation of agricultural goods have begun to change this pattern. Population distribution maps reflect this change, as people cluster more closely together in urban areas and are more dispersed across rural areas.

Geographers represent population distributions on thematic maps using **dot maps**, with each dot representing a certain number of people. At the local scale, a dot map of population can show each individual farm in a sparsely populated rural area. At the global scale, the data are much more generalized (**Fig. 2.4**).

At the global scale, where one dot on a map represents 100,000 people, three major clusters of population stand out. The three largest clusters are East Asia, South Asia, and Europe. North America is fourth.

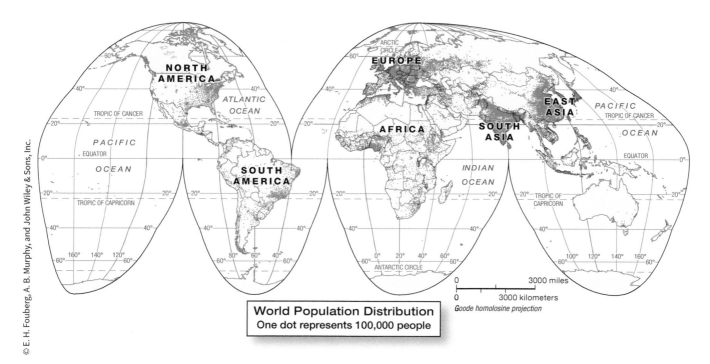

FIGURE 2.4 **World Population Distribution.** The largest clusters of people globally are in East Asia, South Asia, and Europe. Throughout the world, people are concentrated along coastlines, near major rivers, and in cities. Extreme climates, including polar regions and deserts, are sparsely populated as are mountainous areas.

East Asia **Figure 2.5** is a dasymetric map of population. It takes into account underlying landscape and topography to better estimate where people are clustered and where they are sparsely distributed. The largest population concentration lies in East Asia, primarily in China but also in Korea and Japan. Almost one-quarter of the world's population is clustered here—1.4 billion people in China alone. In addition to high population density in China's large cities, ribbons of high population density extend into the interior along the Huang He and Yangtze valleys. Farmers along China's major river valleys produce crops of wheat and rice to feed not only themselves but also the population of major Chinese cities such as Shanghai and Beijing.

AP® Exam Taker's Tip

Figures 2.4 and 2.5 are good maps to learn the skill of taking "mental snapshots." These population distribution and density maps show you where people do and do not live. Study these maps and take "mental snapshots" of them. It is important to know where areas of high and low population distribution are for exam preparation and success.

South Asia The second major population cluster also lies in Asia. At the heart of the South Asian cluster of 1.5 billion people is India, and the cluster extends into Pakistan and

Bangladesh and onto the island of Sri Lanka. On the map, the South Asian cluster looks more concentrated than the East Asian cluster because the region is surrounded by physical barriers where population density abruptly declines. South Asia is surrounded physically by the Himalaya Mountains to the north, mountain chains in Afghanistan and Pakistan on the west, and the Indian Ocean around the south and east.

As in East Asia, people in South Asia cluster in major cities, on the coasts, and in major river basins, including the Ganges, Indus, and Brahmaputra. The South Asian population cluster is growing more rapidly than East Asia because India's growth rate of 1.17 is higher than China's at 0.56. Demographers predict that by 2030, India will be the most populated country in the world, and 1 out of 6 people in the world will live in India.

Population density is so high in South Asia that even rural areas of the region have high population densities. In Bangladesh, over 156 million people, almost all of them small farmers, are crowded into an area about the size of Iowa. Over large parts of Bangladesh, the rural population density is between 3000 and 5000 people per sq mile. By comparison, in 2017 the population of Iowa was just about 3.15 million people, and the rural population density was 55 people per sq mile.

Europe The European population cluster contains over 725 million inhabitants, less than half the population of the South Asia cluster. A comparison of the population and physical maps indicates that in Europe, terrain and environment are not as closely related to population distribution as they are in

East and South Asia. In Asia, high population densities follow coastlines and rivers more clearly than in Europe. Europe is densely populated even in mountainous, rugged country.

Europe was the hearth of the Industrial Revolution and the second urban revolution. That means Europe industrialized and had a second urban revolution (see Chapters 9 and 12) before Asia. European cities and towns grew through the 1800s and 1900s, especially in industrial areas, including northern France, western Germany, northern Italy, and east into Russia. In Germany, 77 percent of the people live in urban places; in the United Kingdom, 83 percent; and in France, 80 percent. With so many people concentrated in the cities, the rural countryside is more open and sparsely populated than in East and South Asia.

The three major population concentrations we have discussed—East Asia, South Asia, and Europe—account for approximately 4 billion of the world population of 7.7 billion people. Nowhere else on the globe is there a population cluster even half as great as any of these. The populations of South America and Africa combined barely exceed the population of India alone.

North America   The fourth largest population cluster is North America, and we describe it here for a reference point for students living in or familiar with the U.S. and Canada. North America has one quite densely populated region, stretching along the urban areas of the east coast, from Boston in the north to Washington, D.C. in the U.S. and from Quebec City to Montreal, Ottawa, Toronto, and Windsor in Canada. Areas of dense population extend from one city in the region to the next, as shown in **Figure 2.6**. Urban geographers use the term **megalopolis** to refer to a huge urban agglomeration like this one. The cities of this megalopolis are home to more than 70 million people. Half of Canada's population lives in the Quebec City to Windsor corridor, and about 20 percent of Americans live in the Boston to Washington, D.C. corridor.

The combined North American megalopolises in the northeast U.S. and southeast Canada create a population cluster that is about one-quarter the size of Europe's population cluster. If you have lived or traveled in this megalopolis, you can think about traffic and comprehend what dense population means. However, the total population of this megalopolis is small in comparison with the East Asian population cluster, and the 28,717 people per sq mile density of New York City (11,000 per sq km) does not rival the density in world cities such as Mumbai, India, with a population density of 68,400 per sq mile (26,400 per sq km), or Dhaka, Bangladesh, with a population density of 122,700 per sq mile (47,400 per sq km).

Reliability of Population Data

When the United States plans and conducts its **census** every 10 years, the government runs a marketing campaign encouraging every person in the country to be counted. Because much federal government funding depends on population data, state and city governments also recognize the importance of having their citizens counted in order to gain more federal dollars per capita. If the population is undercounted, that translates into a loss of dollars for city governments.

Research confirms that migrants, racial minorities, families who double up in rentals or do not have homes, and low-income families are less likely to complete a census form. Advocates for disadvantaged groups encourage people to fill out their census forms. They are concerned that the people in disadvantaged groups suffer further from lack of additional funding for services when they are undercounted in the census. Being undercounted also translates into less government representation because the number of congressional seats allotted to each state is based on the census counts.

For recent censuses, advocacy groups have urged the Census Bureau to sample the population and derive population statistics from the samples. They argue that this approach would more accurately reflect the number of people in the United States. However, the United States Census Bureau has continued to conduct its census as it always has, trying to count each individual in its borders. Controversies have also arisen over asking citizenship questions on the census. Advocates of such questions point to the importance of drawing distinctions between citizens and unauthorized or undocumented immigrants. Opponents argue that a citizenship question will discourage anyone with any legal concerns about citizenship from filling out census forms, which will produce an inaccurate count of the population in the U.S.

The debates over how to conduct a census and the cost involved in counting every person in a country make getting accurate counts difficult. Nonetheless, several agencies collect data on population by country. The United Nations assembles and reports official statistics from governments of countries. The World Bank and the Population Reference Bureau also gather and generate data and report on the population of the world and of individual countries. If you compare the population data reported by each of these sources, you will find inconsistencies in the data. Data on population, growth rates, food availability, health conditions, and incomes are often informed estimates rather than actual counts.

TC Thinking Geographically

How does reading about the 3 largest population clusters in the world (East Asia, South Asia, and Europe) and studying Figures 2.4 and 2.5 change your **mental map** of where people live in the world and why people are clustered in certain regions? Compare Figures 2.4 and 2.5 with Figure 9.41. Explain the role **world cities** play in the distribution of people.

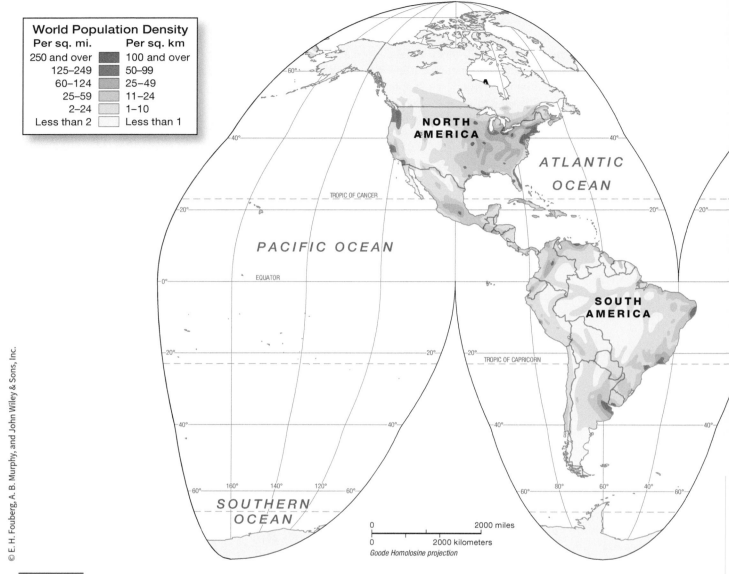

FIGURE 2.5 **World Population Density.** This dasymetric map of population takes the underlying landscape, land cover, and topography into account when distributing people on the map. You can see where people cluster and which areas are sparsely populated. The common color among East Asia, South Asia, and Europe shows that these regions have similar population densities.

2.2 Identify and Explain Influences on Population Growth over Time.

In the late 1960s, alarms sounded throughout the world with the publication of Paul Ehrlich's *The Population Bomb*. Ehrlich and others warned that the world's population was outpacing food production. We can trace alarms over the rapidly increasing world population back to 1798, when a British economist published an essay warning that the world's population was growing at a rate faster than food supplies and that famine and war would be the result.

Malthus

The British economist Thomas Malthus published *An Essay on the Principles of Population* in 1798. He warned that the world's population was increasing faster than the food supplies needed to sustain it. Malthus reasoned that food supplies grow linearly, adding acreage and crops incrementally by year, but population grows exponentially, compounding on the year

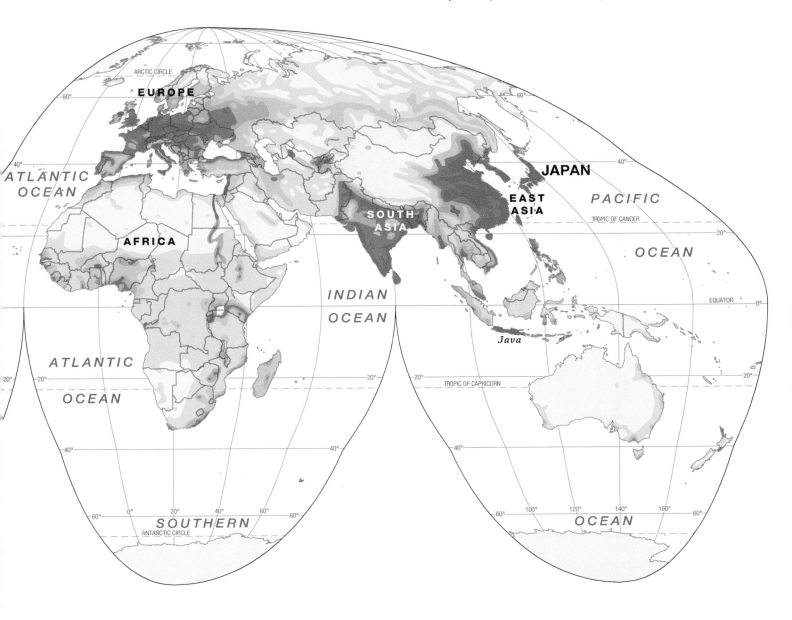

before. From 1803 to 1826, Malthus issued revised editions of his essay and responded vigorously to criticism. Malthus's predictions assumed that what people can eat within a country depends on what is grown in the country.

We now know his assumption that countries depend completely on what is grown inside their borders does not hold true. Countries are not closed systems. Malthus did not foresee how agricultural goods would be exchanged across the world through globalization. Mercantilism, colonialism, and capitalism brought global interaction among the Americas, Europe, Africa, Asia, and the Pacific. Through global interaction, new agricultural methods developed, and commodities and livestock diffused across oceans. Crops well suited for certain climates and soils arrived in new locations. For example, while the potato is associated with Ireland, Irish farmers did not grow potatoes until the 1700s, when the crop arrived from South

America. Countries with little arable land were increasingly able to import a wide variety of crops. Only 2 percent of the land in Norway is arable, but they can import the majority of their food, circumventing the limitations on food production there.

In recent decades, food production has grown rapidly because the amount of cultivated land has expanded. Improved seed strains, pesticides, fertilizers, irrigation systems, and constant innovation have remarkably increased yields per acre (see Chapter 11). In the twenty-first century, bioengineering continues to bring new hybrids, genetically modified organisms, and new fertilizers that have continually expanded food production.

The environmental costs of modern farming techniques raise serious questions about future limitations on the exponential expansion of agriculture. Neo-Malthusians who are reviving Malthus's ideas focus much more on the growing

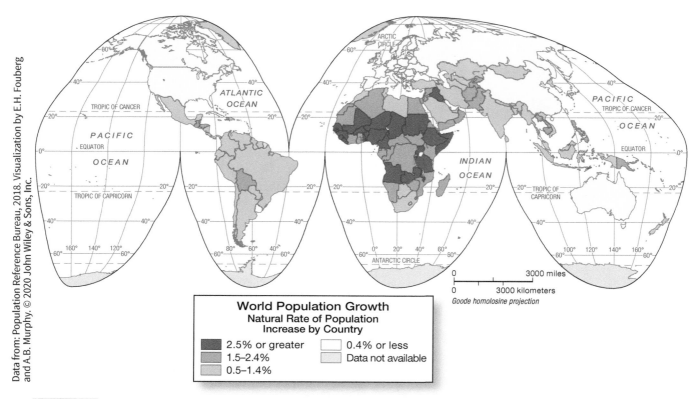

Data from: Population Reference Bureau, 2018. Visualization by E.H. Fouberg and A.B. Murphy. © 2020 John Wiley & Sons, Inc.

FIGURE 2.6 **Natural Increase Rate.** The natural increase rate subtracts crude death rates from crude birth rates and does not include immigration or emigration. Natural increase rates are high in Africa and low in North America, Europe, Russia, China, Japan, and Australia.

population of the world than on food production. Although many demographers predict that the world's population will stabilize later in the twenty-first century, neo-Malthusians argue that overpopulation is a real problem and will cause human suffering. Neo-Malthusians are pessimistic that Earth can sustain a larger population and believe population will be checked when we reach the limits of resources including not just food, but also energy and water.

Natural Increase Rate

Geographers and demographers measure population change and composition to compare relative differences among countries, study outcomes of population change, and make predictions. Two statistics are used to calculate the **natural increase rate** of a population: the crude birth rate and the crude death rate (**Fig. 2.6**). The **crude birth rate** (CBR) is the number of live births per year per thousand people (**Fig. 2.7**). The **crude death rate** (CDR) is the number of deaths per year per thousand people (**Fig. 2.8**). Subtracting the crude death rate from the crude birth rate gives us the rate of natural increase. The natural increase rate shows how a country's population is changing without migration, because immigration (in) and emigration (out) are not included in the natural increase rate. Europe and Russia have negative natural increase rates, meaning that without immigration, their populations are declining.

> **AP® Exam Taker's Tip**
>
> **Crude birth rate − crude death rate = natural increase rate:** These numbers show the growth of a population without regard to migration. If the natural increase rate is low, then fertility is low.

The world map (Fig. 2.6) shows a wide range of natural increase rates across world regions. Countries and regions go through stages of expansion and decline. In the mid-twentieth century, the population of the former Soviet Union was growing vigorously, but the country's growth rates fell quickly when the Soviet Union dissolved in 1991. Thirty years ago, India's population was growing at nearly 3 percent, more than most African countries; then India's growth rate fell below Africa's. Today, Africa's rate of natural increase still is higher than India's (2.43 percent to 1.17 percent), but parts of sub-Saharan Africa are still being impacted by the HIV/AIDS epidemic, which killed millions, produced orphaned children, reduced life expectancies, and curtailed growth rates.

The map also reveals continuing high growth rates in Muslim countries of North Africa and Southwest Asia, including Sudan (2.55 percent), Yemen (2.52 percent), Afghanistan (2.65 percent) and the Palestinian territories (2.83 percent). For much of the second half of the twentieth century, countries in this region saw their growth rates increase even as those in most of the rest of the world were declining. But more recently

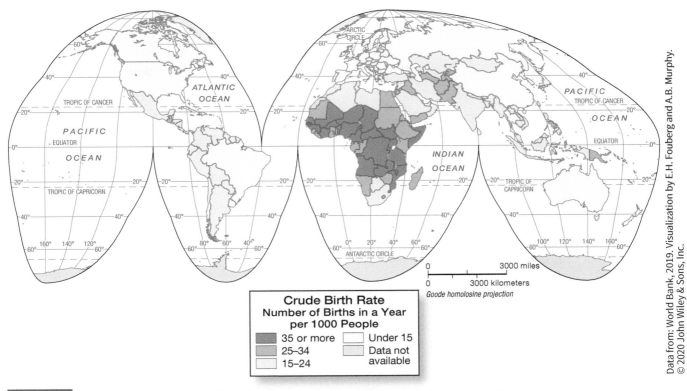

Data from: World Bank, 2019. Visualization by E.H. Fouberg and A.B. Murphy.
© 2020 John Wiley & Sons, Inc.

FIGURE 2.7 **Crude Birth Rate. Number of Births in a Year per 1000 People.** A fairly distinct north–south pattern is evident, as northern countries have lower crude birth rates than southern countries. Africa has higher crude birth rates than South America, South Asia, and Southeast Asia.

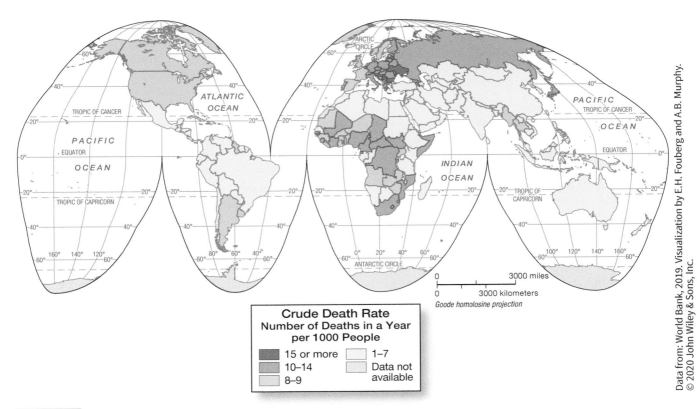

Data from: World Bank, 2019. Visualization by E.H. Fouberg and A.B. Murphy.
© 2020 John Wiley & Sons, Inc.

FIGURE 2.8 **Crude Death Rate: Number of Deaths in a Year per 1000 People.** The death rate has declined globally as countries have transitioned into the third stage of the demographic transition and beyond. A few countries in the global north have relatively high death rates, including Russia and a number of eastern European countries.

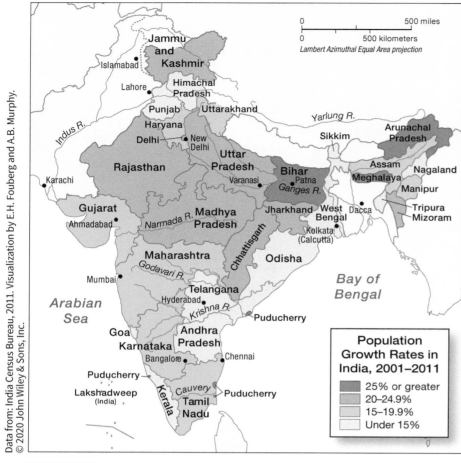

FIGURE 2.9 **Population Growth Rates in India, 2001–2011.** Northern India continues to have the highest growth rates. Population growth rates are lower in southern India, where women have higher literacy rates, better access to health care and birth control, and higher land ownership rates than in northern India.

several countries with fast-growing populations, such as Iran, Oman, and Morocco, have shown significant declines. Demographers point to the correlation between high growth rates and opportunities for women. Where cultural traditions restrict educational and professional prospects for women, and men dominate family dynamics as a matter of custom, rates of natural increase tend to be high.

South Asia is a particularly important geographic region in the population growth rate picture. The region includes India. India's growth rate has slowed significantly in recent years—even falling a little below the global average, but it remains higher than China's. The situation in East Asia, the world's most populous region, is different. China's official rate of natural growth has fallen well below the global average, and Japan's population is shrinking. Southeast Asia's natural growth rates remain higher, but this region's total population is much lower than that of either East or South Asia. Moreover, key countries, such as Indonesia and Vietnam, have declining growth rates, and in Thailand's case, the growth rate is negative.

South America, whose natural population growth rates were quite high just a generation ago, is experiencing significant reductions in growth rates. The region as a whole is still

growing at a little over 1 percent, but Brazil's population growth rate, for example, has declined from 2.9 percent in the mid-1960s to 0.8 percent today. And the populations of Argentina, Chile, and Uruguay are growing at rates well below the world average.

As **Figure 2.6** shows, the countries with the lowest growth rates—including those with declining rates of natural population increase—lie in the global economic core, extending from the United States and Canada across Europe to Japan. Australia and Uruguay are in this category. Wealth is not the only reason for negative population growth rates. After the Soviet Union dissolved in 1991, deteriorating health conditions, high rates of alcoholism and drug use, a rise in male suicide rates, and economic problems led to negative population growth in Russia and several of the other countries that were once part of the Soviet Union. In recent years, Russia's economy has improved, but its birth rate has remained low. The same is true in Ukraine (also once part of the Soviet Union), which shows negative growth.

Between 1900 and 2000, the world's population rose from 1.6 billion people to 6.1 billion, and in 2019, it rose above 7.7 billion. Population growth is not simply a result of women having more children. It is also a result of expanded life expectancies. In 1900, global life expectancy was 30 years; by 2016, it was 72 years. Demographers now predict that world population may well level off at 10 to 11 billion people somewhere between 2050 and 2100. The global composition of younger to older people in 2050 will be markedly different than the global composition in 1900 because of declining birth rates and rising life expectancies.

India The world map of growth rates is a good overview, but it does not show us differences within countries. India is a federation of 29 states and 7 union territories, and the individual states differ greatly both culturally and politically. In India, states in the north record population growth rates far above the national average (**Fig. 2.9**). In southern and western India, populations are growing much more slowly. Women in southern and western India have higher literacy rates (**Fig. 2.10**), greater land ownership rates, better access to health care, and more access to birth control methods. All of these factors keep growth rates lower in southern and western India than in northern and eastern India.

In 1952, India became the first country in the world to institute a population planning program. The goals were to lower fertility rates and slow the population growth rate. In 1976, the Indian government led a mass sterilization drive. The

government focus was forced sterilization of any man with three or more children. Zealous government agents, some
working under quotas, brought men
without children into clinics to be sterilized. One doctor reported that he let
men without children out the back door
of the clinic without sterilizing them
during the 1976 sterilization campaign.
In 1976, the state of Maharashtra sterilized 3.7 million men and women before
public opposition led to rioting, and the
government abandoned the program
(**Fig. 2.11**). Other states also engaged in
compulsory sterilization programs, with
heavy social and political costs. The
1976 program sterilized 6 million men.

India shifted its family planning
focus from sterilizing men to distributing birth control to women. The Indian
government makes injectable contraceptives available to women across the
country. Most Indian state governments
are using advertising and persuasion to
encourage families to have fewer children. Posters urging people to have small
families are everywhere, and the government supports a network of family planning clinics even in the remotest villages.

An increasing number of women,
especially in southern and western
India, are using modern contraceptives.
The **contraceptive prevalence rate** is
the percentage of women ages 15 to 49
who are currently using or whose part-
ner is currently using at least one contraceptive method. In
India, the contraceptive prevalence rate for the country is 55.1
percent. Southern states like Andhra Pradesh (69.8 percent)
and Maharashtra (63.5 percent) have higher rates of contraceptive prevalence than northern states, including Bihar (26.0 percent) and Meghalaya (21.1 percent) (**Fig. 2.12**).

A world map of growth rates is a global overview, a mere
introduction to the complexities of the geography of population. The India example demonstrates that what we see at the
scale of a world map does not give us the complete story of
what is happening within each country or world region.

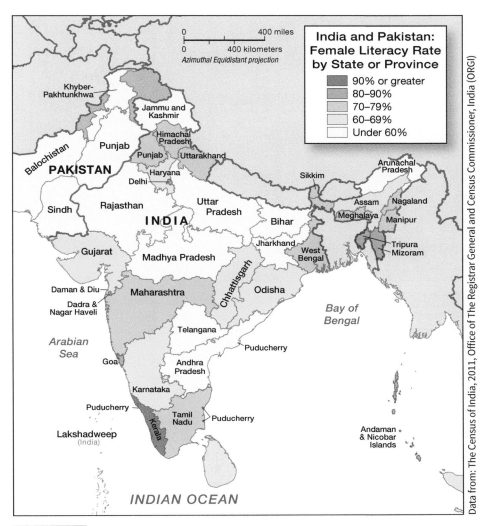

Data from: The Census of India, 2011, Office of The Registrar General and Census Commissioner, India (ORGI)

FIGURE 2.10   **Literacy Rates by State in South Asia.**   The lowest literacy rates are in
Pakistan, and the highest literacy rates are generally in southern India.

another seven years to become $800. A growth rate of 10 per-
cent has a doubling time of around seven years.

> ### AP® Exam Taker's Tip
>
> Geographers may explain global and regional population growth
> rates by **doubling time**. It is an easy calculation to make. Doubling
> time (DT) equals the natural increase rate (NIR) divided by 70, or
> DT = NIR/70. If a population grows at 10 percent, the doubling
> time is seven years. That is very fast growth—and usually unsus-
> tainable. Look at the map on p. 38. Why are rates of 2.5 percent or
> greater considered high natural increase rates? What would the
> doubling time be for these countries compared to a country that
> is increasing at 0.4 percent?

Doubling Time

One way to explain the growth rate in world population is to
compare the population's rate of growth to its **doubling time**.
Every rate of growth has a doubling time. For example, if you
invested $100 at 10 percent, compounded annually (expo-
nentially), it would take about seven years to double to $200.
It would take another seven years to become $400, and then

Two thousand years ago, the world's population was an
estimated 250 million. More than 16 centuries passed before this
total doubled to 500 million, the estimated population in 1650.
Just 170 years later, in 1820 (when Malthus was still writing), the
population doubled again, to 1 billion (**Fig. 2.13**). And barely

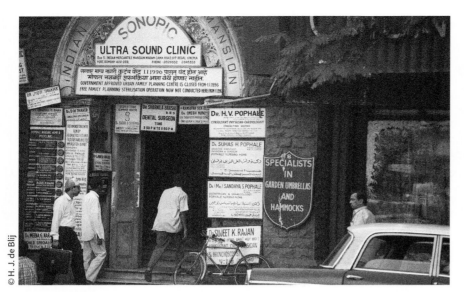

© H. J. de Blij

FIGURE 2.11 **Maharashtra, India.** Above the entrance to a suite of medical offices is a sign announcing that the "free family planning sterilization operation" closed in 1996. The Indian government ended forced sterilization programs after protests and now simply sets goals of lowering birth rates. States in India are at liberty to create their own population control policies. For example, the state of Maharashtra has a policy of paying cash to newly married couples who delay having their first child until two years after marriage.

more than a century after this, in 1930, it reached 2 billion. The doubling time was down to 100 years and dropping fast. The population explosion was in full gear. Only 45 years elapsed for the next doubling to take place, to 4 billion (1975). In the mid-1980s, doubling time was only 39 years. Since then, population policies designed to slow growth, including China's one-child policy, have lengthened the world population's doubling time to 54 years.

For demographers and population geographers who study global population growth today, the concept of doubling time is losing much of its punch. With populations falling in many places, fears of global population doubling quickly are subsiding. Many indicators, such as the slowing of the doubling time, suggest that the explosive population growth of the twentieth century will be followed by a slowdown during the twenty-first century.

No single factor can explain the variations shown in Figure 2.6. Economic prosperity as well as social dislocation reduce natural population growth rates. Economic well-being, which is associated with urbanization, higher levels of education, later marriage, and family planning, lowers population growth. In the table presented in Appendix B, compare the indices for natural population increase and the percentage of the population that is urbanized. In general, the higher the population's level of urbanization, the lower its natural increase.

Total Fertility Rates

Demographers who predict growth in world population will eventually taper off and stabilize base their predictions on a combination of longer life expectancies coupled with lower total fertility rates. Demographers measure whether a population can replace its deaths with births by looking at total

fertility rates. The **total fertility rate** (TFR) is the average number of children born to women of childbearing age (between 15 and 49). To stay at replacement levels and keep a population stable over time without immigration, a country needs a TFR of 2.1. More than 95 countries, containing 41 percent of the world's population, have fallen below replacement level (**Fig. 2.14**).

Demographers at the United Nations predict that the TFR of the combined world will fall to less than 2.2 by 2050. The world TFR combines regions including Europe, where TFRs are low, and regions including Africa, where TFRs are high. In 2016, the worldwide TFR was 2.4, ranging from 1.2 in South Korea to 7.2 in Niger.

Predicting population growth is difficult because so much depends on the decisions made by women of childbearing age. In wealthier countries, more women are choosing to continue education, develop careers, and marry later, delaying childbirth. This results in an aging population, which in turn affects the **old-age dependency ratio**—the relationship between the number of people over the age of 65 and the working-age population between 15 and 64. Europe has 29.9 old-age dependents for every 100 working-age people, and that figure is expected to rise to 47 by 2050. The old-age dependency ratio for sub-Saharan Africa, by contrast, is 5.7. For Africa, the challenge is a high **child dependency ratio** (74 compared to just 23 in Europe).

AP® Exam Taker's Tip

Dependency ratio is the ratio of people under the age of 15 and those 65 and older compared to those 15–64 in a population. Basically, the 15–64 age group are those working jobs, producing incomes, and generating tax revenues. The under 15 group is too young to produce and the 65 and older group is retired/not working and is no longer generating work and revenue.

What are the consequences of dependency ratios that are skewed? Identify reasons a country could produce an overly large, aging population. What does the 65 and older group require that the other groups may not?

An aging population requires substantial social adjustments. Older people retire and eventually suffer health problems, so they need pensions and medical care. Younger workers in the population provide tax revenues that enable governments to pay for services for older people. As the proportion of older people in a country increases, the proportion of younger people decreases. Aging countries have relatively fewer young workers to provide tax revenues and support programs for a growing number of retired people.

To change the age distribution of an aging country and provide more tax-payers, a country can either increase its TFR or enable immigration. Immigration yields an influx of younger workers who pay taxes on their wages, homes, and purchases. What happens if a country resists immigration despite an aging population? Japan is an interesting case study. Japan's population is no longer growing, and demographers project the Japanese population will continue to decline. The population fell from a peak of 128.06 million in 2008 to 126.8 million in 2017. Japan predicts that its population will fall to around 100 million by 2050, a loss of 20 percent of its current population. However, Japan was a closed society for hundreds of years, and even today the Japanese government discourages immigration. More than 98 percent of the country's population is Japanese, according to government statistics.

Today, TFRs are falling in almost every country, in large part because of family planning. In some lower income countries, a combination of government and nongovernment organizational programs encourage women to have fewer children. Some women are also choosing to have fewer children because of economic and social uncertainty. In some countries, TFRs are declining dramatically. Kenya's TFR was down to 3.85 in 2016; China's fell from 6.1 to 1.75 in just 35 years and in 2010 dropped to 1.5, though it hit 1.62 in 2016. Once the government of Iran began to allow family planning, the TFR fell from 6.8 in 1980 to 1.7 in 2016.

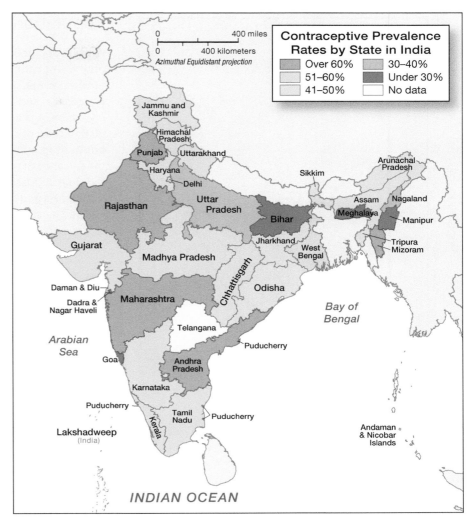

FIGURE 2.12 **Contraceptive Prevalence Rates by State in India.** The lowest contraceptive prevalence rates are in northern India, and the highest contraceptive prevalence rates are generally in southern India.

Data from: New et al., "Levels and trends in contraceptive prevalence, unmet need, and demand for family planning for 29 states and union territories in India: a modelling study using the Family Planning Estimation Tool", Lancet Glob Health. 2017 Mar;5(3):e350-e358. Visualization by E.H. Fouberg and A.B. Murphy. © 2020 John Wiley & Sons, Inc.

At one time a low TFR was a goal that demographers generally agreed all governments would surely want. However, long-term economic implications and demographic projections have given many governments pause. Countries need a young, vigorous, working-age population to work and pay taxes to grow a country's economy and support the long-term needs of an aging population.

In the face of declining population growth rates, some governments have taken countermeasures. Sweden, Russia, and other European countries provide financial incentives such as long maternity leaves and state-paid daycare to prospective mothers. Japan has public service campaigns encouraging men to do more housework. Such programs and debates have had only limited success in encouraging sustained population growth.

How can the worldwide population continue to increase when so many countries are experiencing low TFRs and population decline? Despite declining population growth rates and even negative growth rates in a number of the world's countries, the global population continues to rise. The worldwide TFR was 2.43 in 2016, above the replacement level of 2.1. Although the population bomb Ehrlich warned of is no longer ticking at the same rapid pace, the worldwide population continues to grow. The low TFRs and low population growth rates described in this chapter continue to be offset to a degree by additions to the population in countries where growth rates are still relatively high, including India, Indonesia, Bangladesh, Pakistan, and Nigeria.

AP® Exam Taker's Tip

The ability to recognize, understand, and apply population data in AP Human Geography is important. Applying population data to real-world situations is critical to success in this course.

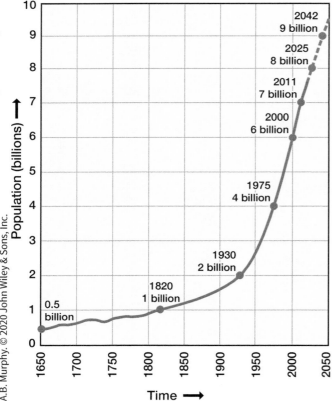

Data from: United States Census Bureau and World Bank. Visualization by E.H. Fouberg and A.B. Murphy. © 2020 John Wiley & Sons, Inc.

FIGURE 2.13 **Population Growth, 1650–2050.** The dashed line indicates one estimate of global population growth until 2050.

Population Pyramids

When geographers study populations, they are concerned not only with distribution and growth rates, but also with **population composition**: the structure of a population in terms of age, sex, and other properties such as marital status and education. Age and sex are particularly key indicators of population composition, and demographers and geographers use **population pyramids**, which are graphic representations of the age and sex composition of a population (**Fig. 2.15**).

To read a population pyramid, start by looking at the horizontal axis and notice males are on the left side of the pyramid and females are on the right side. Then, look at the vertical axis and note that the age composition of the country is broken into age groups, normally five-year increments. The youngest age groups, starting at birth (age 0) are at the bottom and the oldest age groups are at the top. All population pyramids start at age 0, but not all end at the same age at the top. Countries with higher life expectancies have higher numbers in their top age bracket than countries with lower life expectancies. So, it's always a good idea to look at the numbers in the top age bracket on a population pyramid.

A population pyramid can instantly convey the demographic situation in a country. In lower income countries, where birth and death rates generally remain high, the population pyramid looks like a pyramid or an evergreen tree, with wide branches at the base and short ones near the top. The youngest age groups have the largest share of the population. In the pyramid for most lower income countries, the three groups up to age 14 account for more than 40 percent of the population. From age group 15 to 19 upward, each group is smaller than

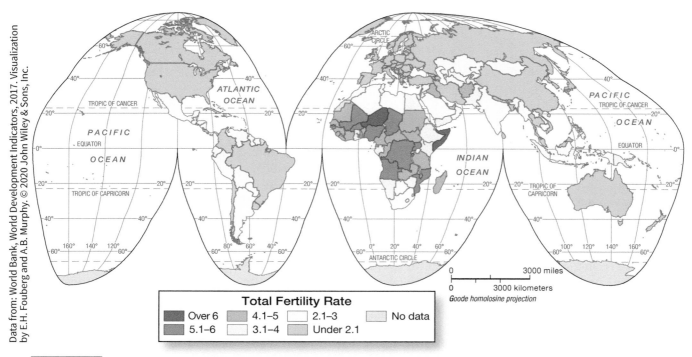

Data from: World Bank, World Development Indicators, 2017. Visualization by E.H. Fouberg and A.B. Murphy. © 2020 John Wiley & Sons, Inc.

Total Fertility Rate

Over 6	4.1–5	2.1–3	No data
5.1–6	3.1–4	Under 2.1	

FIGURE 2.14 **Total Fertility Rate (TFR).** TFRs are lowest in Europe, North America, Japan, Australia and New Zealand. TFRs remain relatively high in Africa and Southwest Asia.

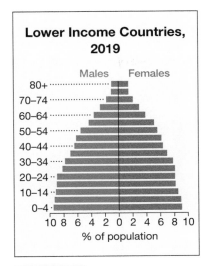

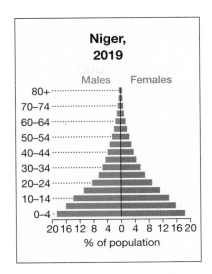

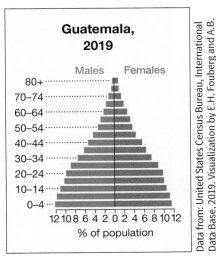

Data from: United States Census Bureau, International Data Base, 2019. Visualization by E.H. Fouberg and A.B. Murphy. © 2020 John Wiley & Sons, Inc.

FIGURE 2.15 **Age–Sex Population Pyramids for Countries with High Population Growth Rates.** Countries with high total fertility rates, high infant mortality rates, and low life expectancies will have population pyramids with wide bases and narrow tops.

the one below it. Older people, in the three highest age groups, represent less than 10 percent of the total. Slight variations on this pyramid mark the population structures of such countries as Pakistan, Yemen, Guatemala, Cameroon, and Laos.

Higher income countries have population pyramids that do not look like pyramids at all. Families become smaller, children fewer. The "pyramid" looks like a slightly lopsided chimney, with the largest components of the population not at the bottom but in the middle. The middle-age bulge moves upward, reflecting the aging of the population (**Fig. 2.16**) and the declining TFR. Countries with low TFR and high wealth, such as Italy, France, and Sweden, fit into this pyramid model.

The religious composition of a population can influence growth rates, and by extension the look of the pyramid. The Roman Catholic Church does not support contraception, and

some conservative branches of Islam frown on the use of contraceptives as well. In countries such as Nigeria, for example, conservative Islam is practiced in the north, and northern Nigeria has notably higher population growth rates than southern Nigeria.

There are, however, many places where dominant religious traditions do not tell us much about population trends. Some areas of the world with low population growth rates are in the very heart of the Roman Catholic world, even though Roman Catholic doctrine opposes birth control and abortion (**Fig. 2.17**). Curiously, adherence to this doctrine appears to be stronger in areas farther from the Vatican (headquarters of the Catholic Church). The Philippines, for example, has a relatively high population growth rate.

The situation is different in the case of Islam. Saudi Arabia, home to Mecca (the hearth of Islam), has a relatively high

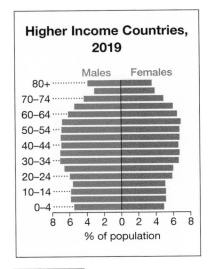

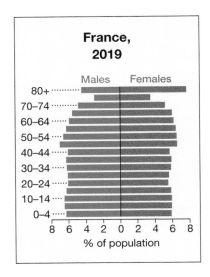

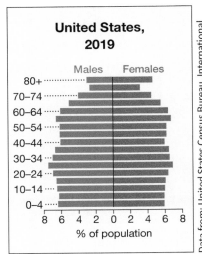

Data from: United States Census Bureau, International Data Base, 2019. Visualization by E.H. Fouberg and A.B. Murphy. © 2020 John Wiley & Sons, Inc.

FIGURE 2.16 **Age–Sex Population Pyramids for Countries with Low Population Growth Rates.** Countries with lower total fertility rates and longer life expectancies have population pyramids shaped more uniformly throughout.

population growth rate, with the population increasing at 2 percent each year. Yet in Indonesia, thousands of miles from Mecca, the government began a nationwide family planning program in 1970 when the population growth rate was high. Conservative Muslim leaders objected, but the government used a combination of coercion and inducement to continue its program. By 2000, Indonesia's family planning program had lowered the growth rate to 1.6 percent, and in 2016 it stood at 1.1 percent.

The Demographic Transition

The **demographic transition** is a model suggesting that a country's birth rate and death rate change in predictable ways over stages of economic development (**Fig. 2.18**). The model is based on population change in western Europe after the Industrial Revolution.

Stage 1: Low Growth   The world population rose from 250 million people 2000 years ago to 500 million people in 1650. Charts may show that growth as a line sloping upward gently. However, in reality, population did not trend steadily upward. Populations rose and fell with fluctuating birth rates and death rates, reflecting the impacts of disease, crop failures, and wars. Stage 1 is the initial low-growth phase, where all places stayed for most of human history. This stage is marked by uncertainty, including high birth rates and equally high death rates. In this phase, epidemics and plagues keep the death rates high. At times, death rates exceeded birth rates.

For Great Britain and western Europe, death rates exceeded birth rates during the bubonic plague (the Black Death) of the 1300s, which hit in waves. The bubonic plague began in Crimea on the Black Sea, diffused through trade to Sicily and other Mediterranean islands, and moved through contagious diffusion and the travel of rats (which hosted the flea, the insect responsible for spreading the plague) north from the Mediterranean.

Once the plague hit a region, it was likely to return within a few years, creating another wave of human suffering. Estimates of plague deaths vary between one-quarter and one-half of the population, with the highest death rates recorded in western Europe (where trade among regions was the greatest) and the lowest in the east (where cooler climates and less connected populations delayed diffusion). Across Europe, cities and towns were left decimated. Historians estimate that the population of Great Britain fell from nearly 4 million when the plague began to just over 2 million when it ended.

Famines also limited population growth. A famine in Europe just prior to the plague likely facilitated the diffusion of the disease by weakening people's immune systems. Famines in India and China during the eighteenth and nineteenth centuries resulted in the deaths of millions of people. At other times, destructive wars have largely wiped out population gains.

Stage 2: High Growth

Stage 2 of the demographic transition had high birth rates, rapidly declining death rates, and very high natural increase rates. Stage 2 came after the Industrial Revolution (around 1750) in Europe when access to food, sanitation, and health care improved, resulting in much lower death rates. Improvements in agriculture that preceded the Industrial Revolution created a more stable food supply (see Chapter 11). Sanitation facilities made towns and cities safer from epidemics, soap became more widely used, and modern medical practices began to take hold.

Data from church records in Great Britain (the hearth of the Industrial Revolution) reveals that after industrialization began, death rates in Great Britain began to fall. Before 1750, death rates in Europe may well have averaged 35 per 1000 (birth rates averaged under 40), but by 1850 the death rate was down to about 16 per 1000. With a rapidly falling death rate and a birth rate that remained high, Britain's population explosion took place.

Countries in stage 2 today are much lower income countries with relatively high birth rates and natural increase rates, along with slowly falling death rates. Lower income countries that already went through stage 2, as well as countries like Palestine and Afghanistan that are going through stage 2 now, have been helped by the diffusion of western medicine, including vaccinations against common childhood diseases.

Stage 3: Moderate Growth

Stage 3 of the demographic transition has rapidly declining birth rates, continually declining death rates, and a low natural increase rate. In stage 3, death rates continued to decline and birth rates began to fall but stayed higher than death rates, resulting in continued growth in natural increase rate, but at a slower pace. For Great Britain, this was after the Industrial Revolution, from around 1870 through two world wars in the 1900s. New opportunities—especially for women— were not always compatible with large families. Women delayed marriage and childbearing. Medical advances lowered infant and child mortality rates, lessening the sense that multiple children were necessary to sustain a family. Young adults began marrying at later ages, leading to a natural decrease in TFR and crude birth rates.

Stage 3 of the demographic transition happens when a country's birth rate begins to fall. Countries in stage 3 today include middle-income countries like Brazil. Brazil's lower birth rates came about through increasing access to modern contraceptives, rather than a change in the age of marriage.

Improving educational opportunities for women correlates with declining birth rates. Studies in Mali have shown that girls who go to school end up having just over half as many

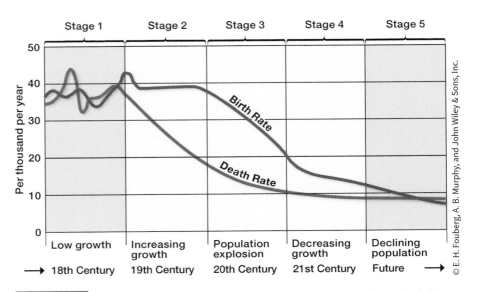

FIGURE 2.18 **The Demographic Transition Model.** Population growth is particularly high between the middle of stage 2 and the middle of stage 4, when death rates have declined due to better food supply and access to medicine, but birth rates have stayed relatively high before later declining.

children as women with no access to education. Expanding educational opportunities for girls and women in countries such as Mali, then, will likely have a significant impact on future population growth.

Stage 4: Low Growth

Stage 4 of the demographic transition has low birth rates, low death rates, and stable or slowing rates of natural increase. In Great Britain after 1950, both the birth rate and death rates declined to low levels, resulting in slow or stabilized population growth. Advances in modern contraceptives and access to legal abortion expanded after the 1950s, which also helped keep birth rates quite low in Great Britain and other higher income countries.

Countries in stage 4 today include higher income countries like the United States and the United Kingdom. The diffusion of contraceptives, access to abortion, and conscious decisions by many women to have fewer or no children, or to start having children at a later age, have lowered birth rates.

Stage 5: Negative Growth

Stage 5 of the demographic transition has very low birth rates, increasing death rates, and declining natural increase rates. Countries in stage 5 include Japan and Russia. The global growth rate is now down to 1.2 percent, perhaps slightly lower, even though the increase in world population still exceeds 80 million annually. With women having fewer children, many demographers are predicting that as more countries reach stage 5 of the demographic transition, the world will reach **zero population growth** in the next 50 years. The result would be a planet that has achieved what is called a *stationary population level* (SPL).

Predictions about future population growth require frequent revision, and anticipated dates for population stabilization are often moved back. In the late 1980s, for example, the World Bank predicted that the United States would reach SPL in 2035 with 276 million inhabitants. Brazil's population would stabilize at 353 million in 2070, Mexico's at 254 million in 2075, and China's at 1.4 billion in 2090. India, destined to become the world's most populous country, would reach SPL at 1.6 billion in 2150. These figures have proven unrealistic. China's population passed the 1.2 billion mark in 1994, and India's reached 1 billion in 1998. Recent reports predict that China's population will "stabilize" at 1.45 billion in 2030 and India's at 1.7 billion in 2060.

> **TC** **Thinking Geographically**
>
> Pick two countries with high growth rates. Determine the state of the demographic transition for each country. Sketch what you imagine their **population pyramids** look like. Hypothesize what may lead them to the next stage of the demographic transition.

2.3 Explain How Health and Disease Affect Peoples' Well-Being.

Medical geographers increasingly study not just disease patterns, but issues such as access to medical care and the ways in which inequalities and place-based social norms affect disease transmission. How healthy a population is depends on geographical differences in sanitation and access to health care. For many people, access to medical care is fundamentally a geographic matter, because access is a function of *absolute distance* to medical facilities and the available transportation infrastructure. Infrastructure can impede or facilitate access to health care.

Access to medical clinics and hospitals, fully certified medical staff, and prescription medicines is greater in higher income countries. Europe, North America, Japan, and Australia and New Zealand spend much more money on health care per person than other world regions (**Fig. 2.19**). Patients with greater access to health care have lower infant mortality rates

and longer life expectancies. Higher rates of health expenditures per capita occur in countries where medical hospitals put forth great effort in terms of procedures, technologies, medicines, and care to the most vulnerable populations, including premature babies and frail elderly (defined as those over age 85).Social norms and circumstances matter as well. The transmission of HIV/AIDS is partly a product of attitudes toward the use of condoms, mobility patterns, socioeconomic status, and other place-specific social variables. Social context also matters in chronic obesity, which is associated with higher rates of heart disease and diabetes. In places where heavily processed foods become popular or are the cheapest and most available food options, chronic obesity is reaching epidemic levels. As these examples illustrate, understanding global health requires taking into account the geographic context within which diseases are embedded.

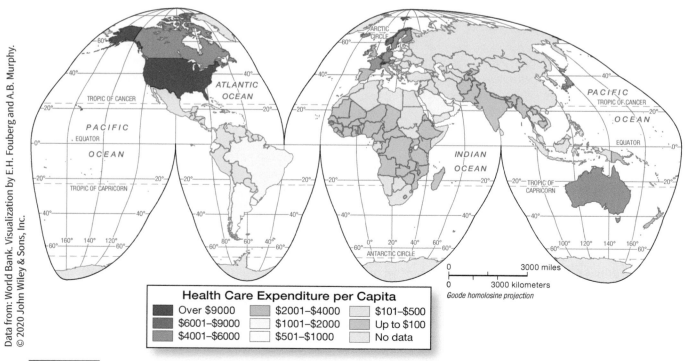

Data from: World Bank. Visualization by E.H. Fouberg and A.B. Murphy. © 2020 John Wiley & Sons, Inc.

Health Care Expenditure per Capita

- Over $9000
- $6001–$9000
- $4001–$6000
- $2001–$4000
- $1001–$2000
- $501–$1000
- $101–$500
- Up to $100
- No data

Goode homolosine projection

FIGURE 2.19 **Health Care Expenditures per Capita.** Health care expenditures per capita are highest in North America, Europe, Japan, and Australia.

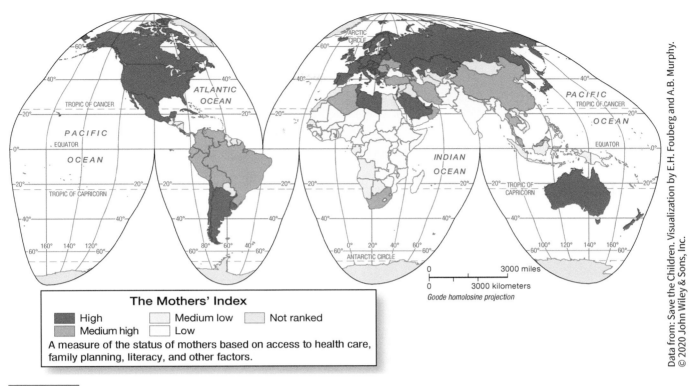

The Mothers' Index

- ■ High
- ■ Medium high
- □ Medium low
- □ Low
- □ Not ranked

A measure of the status of mothers based on access to health care, family planning, literacy, and other factors.

FIGURE 2.20 **The Mothers' Index.** Save the Children annually calculates the Mothers' Index, based on 13 indicators, to gauge the overall well-being of mothers and their children by country.

Data from: Save the Children. Visualization by E.H. Fouberg and A.B. Murphy. © 2020 John Wiley & Sons, Inc.

Health of Women and Children

Figure 2.20 maps the Mothers' Index from the *State of the World's Mothers* report. The Mothers' Index measures barometers of well-being for mothers and children. The Mothers' Index confirms that income and access to medical care are major factors in the health of women and children. Specifically, 99 percent of newborn deaths and 98 percent of maternal deaths (deaths from giving birth) occur in lower income countries globally.

For the countries in the world experiencing violent conflict, the Mothers' Index plunges and the chances of newborn survival fall. Examine Figure 2.19 again and note the position of countries that have violent conflict or a recent history of conflict: Iraq, Afghanistan, Syria, and Sierra Leone.

Infant Mortality Whether a baby lives to its first birthday is one measurement of mortality. Differences in infant mortality rates vary depending on access to health care, sanitation, and education. **Infant mortality rate** (IMR) is the probability that a child will die before reaching the age of 1 year. The child mortality rate (CMR) records the probability a child will die before reaching the age of 5 years. Both infant mortality and child mortality rates are given as the number of cases per 1000 live births.

Another measurement of children's health early in life is the newborn death rate—a measurement of the number of children who die in the first month of life out of every 1000 live births. Save the Children's annual *State of the World's Mothers* report explains that the high newborn death rate in the United States

and in other higher income countries is typically from premature births and low-birthweight babies. In lower income countries, diarrhea and infections cause half of newborn deaths.

Infant and child mortality reflect the overall health of a society. High infant mortality rates have a variety of causes. The physical health of the mother, which includes access to prenatal care and access to sanitation and hygiene, are major factors. In societies where most women bear a large number of babies, women also tend to be inadequately nourished and poorly educated. Diarrhea and malnutrition are the leading killers of infants and children throughout the world. Save the Children's annual *State of the World's Mothers* reports that in lower income countries, diarrhea and infections cause half of newborn deaths (mortality under age 1 month).

In lower income countries, women, even pregnant women, often feed themselves last by family tradition. This means the mother may not consume enough calories during pregnancy for the baby to grow to a healthy weight or during nursing to produce nutritious breast milk. Pregnant women with low education may have health-care providers who explain the importance of sanitation and hand washing to avoid diarrheal disease, but they may ignore the advice of medical staff over the advice given at home by their mothers-in-law. Roughly 30 percent of the world lacks ready access to clean drinking water, 6 out of 10 lack access to hygienic human waste-disposal facilities, and as many as 4 billion people live without basic sanitation (including toilets).

Figure 2.21 shows the variability of the infant mortality rate by country and world region. The lowest infant mortality rate among larger populations has long been reported by

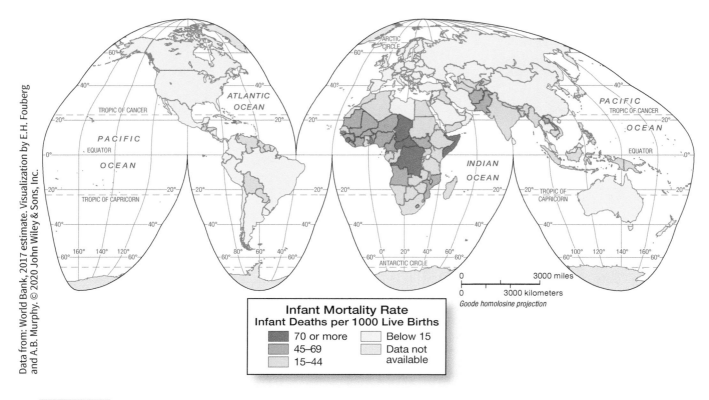

Data from: World Bank, 2017 estimate. Visualization by E.H. Fouberg and A.B. Murphy. © 2020 John Wiley & Sons, Inc.

Infant Mortality Rate
Infant Deaths per 1000 Live Births

- 70 or more
- 45–69
- 15–44
- Below 15
- Data not available

FIGURE 2.21 **Infant Mortality Rate.** The map shows infant mortality patterns at five levels ranging from 70 or more per 1000 to fewer than 15. Compare this map to that of the overall crude birth rate (CBR) in Figure 2.7, and the correlation between high infant mortality rates and high birth rates is evident.

Japan, with 1.9 deaths per 1000 live births in a country of over 126 million people. Singapore has over 5.4 million people and a low IMR of 2.2, and Sweden's 9.6 million people record an IMR of 2.3.

In 2017, five countries still reported an IMR of 70 or more—the Central African Republic, Sierra Leone, Somalia, Chad, and the Democratic Republic of the Congo. The Central African Republic's IMR of 87.6, the highest in the world, reflects one death or more among every eight newborns. Dreadful as these figures are, they are a substantial improvement over the situation in 2012, when 11 countries reported IMRs of 70 or more. Globally, infant mortality has been declining, even in low income world regions.

Each of these observations about infant mortality rates considers what is happening, on average, in a country. IMR varies within countries and gives us insight into variations in access to health care and health education depending on region, ethnicity, social class, or other criteria. The IMR of South Africa is 48 per 1000, an average of all the people within the country's borders. The IMR for South African whites is near the European average; for black Africans it is nearer the African average; and for "coloured" (multiracial) and Asian population sectors it lies between these two figures.

IMR in the United States The IMR in the United States varies by region, with the highest IMR in the South and the lowest in the Northeast (**Fig. 2.22**). Race, ethnicity, social

class, education levels, and access to health care also vary by region in the United States. In 2015 the IMR for African Americans was 11.7 in the United States, above the country-wide average of 6. The IMR for non-Hispanic whites was 4.8, below the U.S. average. According to the Centers for Disease Control, in 2016, 82.3 percent of non-Hispanic whites, but only 66.5 percent of African Americans, received prenatal care starting in the first trimester of their pregnancy. Lower education levels for African American women also contributed to the higher IMR. However, one risk factor that contributes to high IMR, smoking during pregnancy, was higher for non-Hispanic whites than for African Americans. The Centers for Disease Control found that 10.5 percent of non-Hispanic whites smoked cigarettes during pregnancy in 2016, and 6 percent of African American women smoked during pregnancy.

According to the Department of Health and Human Services, "the leading causes of infant death include congenital abnormalities, pre-term/low birth weight, Sudden Infant Death Syndrome (SIDS), problems related to complications of pregnancy, and respiratory distress syndrome. SIDS deaths among American Indian and Alaska Natives is 2.3 times the rate for non-Hispanic white mothers."

Child Mortality Infants who survive their first year of life have lower life expectancies in lower income world regions. The child mortality rate, which records the deaths of children

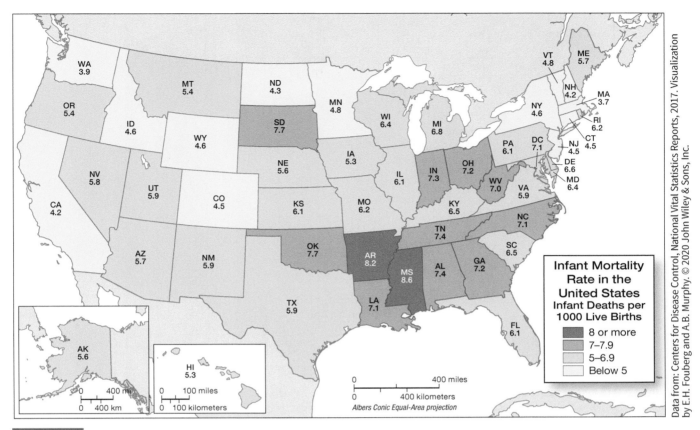

Data from: Centers for Disease Control, National Vital Statistics Reports, 2017. Visualization by E.H. Fouberg and A.B. Murphy. © 2020 John Wiley & Sons, Inc.

FIGURE 2.22   Infant Mortality Rate in the United States.   This map shows infant deaths per 1000 live births. In Figure 2.21, the entire United States is in the lowest class on the map. Shifting scales to states within the United States, the infant mortality rate shows variation, with high infant mortality rates in the South and low infant mortality rates in the states of Washington and Massachusetts.

between the ages of 1 and 5, remains disturbingly high in significant parts of Africa and Asia, notably in protein-deficient regions. *Kwashiorkor* (also known as protein malnutrition), a malady resulting from a lack of protein early in life, afflicts millions of children. *Marasmus*, a condition that results from inadequate protein and insufficient calories, causes the deaths of millions more. In some countries, more than one in five children still die between their first and fifth birthdays, a terrible record in the twenty-first century.

Life Expectancy

Life expectancy is the average number of years a person is expected to live. **Figure 2.23** shows life expectancies by country. Japan's life expectancies are the highest in the world. With its low infant and child mortality rates and low fertility rates, Japan's life expectancy may rise to 106 by the year 2300. African countries have the lowest life expectancies. The spread of HIV/AIDS over the past four decades has lowered life expectancies in some countries below age 40. Lowest life expectancies in Africa are now just over 50 due to improved access to antiretroviral treatments and programs to prevent mother-to-child transmission of HIV/AIDS.

Life expectancies of men and women are grouped together into one statistic by country in Figure 2.23. At the start of the twenty-first century, world average life expectancy was 68 for women and 64 for men. You can get a sense of differences in life expectancy between men and women by looking at population pyramids. If the oldest generation on a country's population pyramid has much wider bands for women than for men, it indicates women have longer life expectancies than men in that country. Women commonly outlive men. Women outlive men by about four years in Europe and East Asia, by three years in sub-Saharan Africa, by six years in North America, and by seven years in South America. In Russia, women are expected to outlive men by 11 years.

The map reveals significant regional contrasts. In the former Soviet Union, and especially in Russia, the life expectancies of men dropped quickly following the collapse of communism, from 68 to 60 in 2008. Life expectancies for men in Russia remain lower than for women. In 2014, the BBC, citing an article in a medical journal, reported that 25 percent of Russian men die before they reach the age of 55. Russia's men experience much higher rates of alcoholism and suicide than women.

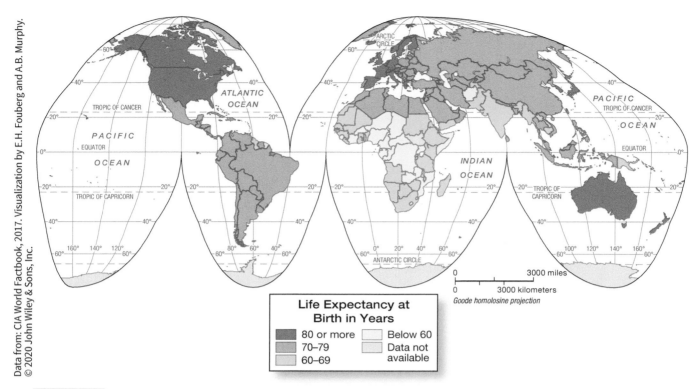

Data from: CIA World Factbook, 2017. Visualization by E.H. Fouberg and A.B. Murphy.
© 2020 John Wiley & Sons, Inc.

Life Expectancy at Birth in Years

- 80 or more
- 70–79
- 60–69
- Below 60
- Data not available

FIGURE 2.23 **Life Expectancy at Birth in Years.** This map highlights global inequalities in life expectancies. Someone born in Japan has a life expectancy that is three decades longer than someone born in Afghanistan or Nigeria.

Life expectancy figures do not mean that everyone lives to a certain age. The figure is an average that takes account of the children who die young and the people who survive well beyond the average. The dramatically lower figures for the world's lower income countries primarily reflect high infant mortality rates. The low life expectancy figures for countries where malnourishment is a challenge remind us again how hard hit children are in parts of the world.

Infectious Disease vs. Chronic Disease

Most of the world maps in this chapter show differences in population and health between higher income world regions and lower income world regions. Whether we look at population growth rates, TFR, infant mortality, or life expectancy, we see North America, Europe, Japan, Australia and New Zealand in one camp, and Latin America, Africa, and much of Asia in another camp. Demographers report that differences in income also impact the types of disease to which people are susceptible. The **epidemiological transition** holds that as a country moves from high population growth rates to stable population growth rates, the causes of death and the age at which people are afflicted by disease change. Countries with high birth rates and high population growth rates tend to have more infectious diseases that afflict younger populations. Countries with stable growth rates, including low birth rates and low death rates, tend to have more chronic diseases that afflict older populations.

AP® Exam Taker's Tip

The **epidemiological transition** explains the causes of changing death rates. Can you explain the changes in how people die as countries go through the demographic transition?

Scientists estimate 65 percent of all diseases are **infectious diseases**, resulting from an invasion of parasites and their multiplication in the body. The remainder can be divided into the **chronic** or **degenerative diseases** that come with old age, such as heart disease, prostate cancer, and diabetes, and **genetic** or **inherited diseases** we can trace to our genetic makeup. Genetic diseases, including sickle-cell anemia, hemophilia, and cystic fibrosis, are of interest to medical geographers because they tend to appear in specific places and in particular populations.

Three geographic terms are used to describe the spatial extent of a disease. A disease is **endemic** when it prevails over a small area. A disease is **epidemic** when it spreads over a large region. A **pandemic** disease is global in scope.

Infectious Diseases
Battling infectious disease is far from a thing of the past. In early 2019, Washington and Oregon struggled to contain a measles outbreak that infected more than 50 children. Although measles was fully eradicated in the United States decades ago, anti-vaccination campaigns in the Pacific Northwest led to particularly low vaccination rates in the region. Nearly a quarter of kindergartners in Washington are

not vaccinated against measles, making the outbreak especially difficult to manage. The challenge of such a case is place specific. The outbreak was made possible and exacerbated by the fact that vaccinations are seen with suspicion in Washington and Oregon.

Infectious diseases continue to sicken and kill millions of people annually. Malaria, a tropical disease, still takes more than a million lives annually and infects between 300 and 600 million people today. HIV/AIDS, an virus that erupted in Africa four decades ago, has killed about 35 million people globally. These two maladies illustrate two kinds of infectious disease: *vectored* and *nonvectored*.

Malaria and Other Vectored Infectious Diseases   A vectored infectious disease such as **malaria** is transmitted by an intermediary vector—in malaria's case, a mosquito. What happens is that the mosquito stings an already infected person or animal, called a host, and sucks up some blood carrying the parasites. These parasites then reproduce and multiply in the mosquito's body and reach its saliva. The next time that mosquito stings someone, some of the parasites are injected into that person's bloodstream. Now that person develops malaria as the parasites multiply in his or her body, and the infected person becomes a host.

Malaria manifests itself through recurrent fever and chills, with associated symptoms such as anemia and an enlarged spleen. Malaria is a major factor in infant and child mortality, as most of the victims are children age 5 or younger. If a person survives the disease, he or she will develop a certain degree of immunity. However, many infected by malaria are weak, lack energy, and face an increased risk of other diseases taking hold.

Malaria occurs throughout the world, except in higher latitudes and elevations and in drier environments. Although people in the tropical portions of Africa suffer most from the disease, malaria is also prevalent in parts of India, Southeast Asia, and the tropical Americas (**Fig. 2.24**). No disease in human history has taken more lives than malaria, and the battle against this scourge is not yet won.

There are signs of progress, however. Infection rates have been falling in sub-Saharan Africa because of the increasingly wide distribution of insecticide-laden mosquito nets that are used to surround sleeping quarters and protect people from malaria-carrying mosquitoes, which are most active at night. Efforts are also under way to introduce genetically engineered mosquitoes that do not have the capacity to transmit the malaria parasite. The hope is that the genetic mutation of these mosquitoes will diffuse through the offspring of the current mosquito population.

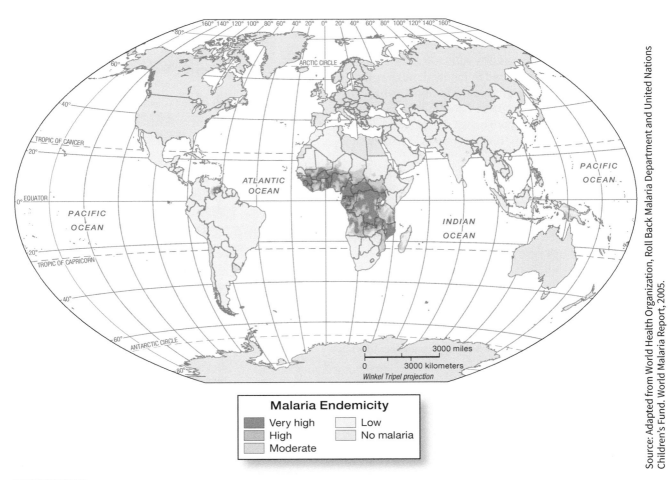

Source: Adapted from World Health Organization, Roll Back Malaria Department and United Nations Children's Fund. World Malaria Report, 2005.

FIGURE 2.24   **Global Distribution of Malaria Transmission Risk.**   Malaria was once more widespread, but it is now concentrated primarily in the tropics, where moisture allows higher breeding rates for mosquitoes.

Mosquitoes are especially effective vectors of several other infectious diseases, ranging from yellow fever to dengue. Yellow fever killed vast numbers of people in the past. It is being driven back by a vaccine, which can provide immunity for 10 years, but it is still prevalent in tropical Africa and South America, where it has long been endemic.

In addition to mosquitoes, other vectors, including fleas, flies, worms, and snails, transmit infectious diseases including river blindness, guinea worm, and elephantiasis. Sleeping sickness, which is transmitted by the tsetse fly, is a particular menace. The fly sucks the blood from an infected animal or individual and then infects others with its bite. Sleeping sickness began around 1400 in West Africa, but it spread throughout much of sub-Saharan Africa in the succeeding centuries. Both people and animals infected by the disease come down with a fever, followed by the swelling of lymph nodes and inflammation of the brain. Death is not uncommon. Progress has been made in combating the disease through tsetse fly eradication campaigns, but much of sub-Saharan Africa is still affected. Tropical climates, where warm, moist conditions allow vectors to thrive, are the worst afflicted areas of the world, but vectored infectious diseases are a global phenomenon.

HIV/AIDS and Other Nonvectored Diseases

Nonvectored infectious diseases are transmitted by direct contact between host and victim. A kiss, a handshake, or even contact with someone's breath can transmit influenza, a cold, or some other nonvectored diseases. HIV/AIDS is a nonvectored infectious disease that is transmitted primarily through sexual contact and secondarily through needle sharing. The hearth of the HIV/AIDS pandemic is in Africa. After four decades of rapid diffusion, HIV/AIDS has created one of the greatest health catastrophes in modern history. Nowhere has its impact been greater than in Africa itself.

Medical geographers estimate that in 1980 about 200,000 people were infected with HIV (Human Immunodeficiency Virus, which causes AIDS, Acquired Immune Deficiency Syndrome), all of them Africans. By 2018, the number worldwide exceeded 36.9 million and totaled 77.3 million since the start of the epidemic, according to the United Nations AIDS Program. The majority of all cases of HIV/AIDS are concentrated in sub-Saharan Africa. The infection rate worldwide has fallen dramatically since 2001 and is continuing to slow, but eastern Europe and Central Asia have recently seen a surge in HIV/AIDS.

The impact of HIV/AIDS on sub-Saharan Africa is striking. In 2017, 27 percent of people aged 15 to 49 were infected in Eswanti, 23.8 percent in Lesotho, almost 23 percent in Botswana, and 18.8 percent in South Africa. These are the official data; medical geographers estimate that as much as 20 percent of the entire population of several African countries may be infected. The United Nations AIDS program reports that nearly a million people died of AIDS in 2017 alone. Geographer Peter Gould, in his book *The Slow Plague* (1993), said HIV/AIDS had made Africa a "continent in catastrophe," and the demographic statistics support his viewpoint. In a continent already ravaged by tropical diseases (see discussion above), AIDS is still the leading cause of

death for adults. It has reshaped the population structure of the countries hardest hit by the disease. Demographers look at the projected population pyramids for countries with high rates of infection and no longer see population pyramids. They see population chimneys—reflecting the major impact of AIDS on the younger population in the country (**Fig. 2.25**).

Over the past four decades, the AIDS pandemic has reached virtually all parts of the world. China reported at least 820,000 infected in 2018, with 40,000 new cases in a single quarter of 2018 alone, and the number in India may well exceed 2 million living with HIV. Estimates of the number of cases in the United States surpass 1 million; in Middle and South America, nearly 2 million are infected. Southeast Asia now has as many as 5.2 million cases.

People infected by HIV do not immediately display visible symptoms of the disease; they can carry the virus for years without being aware of it, and during that period they can unwittingly transmit it to others. Add to this the social stigma many people attach to the disease, and it is evident that official statistics on AIDS do not give a full picture of the toll the disease takes.

Fieldwork conducted by geographers is shedding light on the human toll of HIV/AIDS locally and within families. Geographer Elsbeth Robson has studied the impact of HIV/AIDS in hard-hit Zimbabwe. She found that the diffusion of HIV/AIDS and reductions in spending on health care, often mandated by structural adjustment programs, "shape young people's home lives

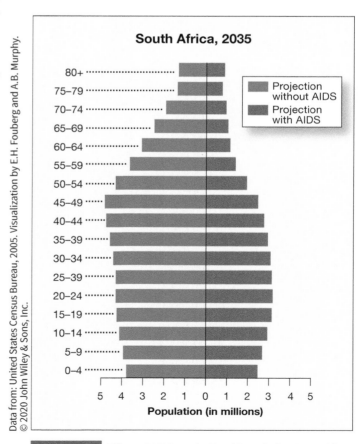

Data from: United States Census Bureau, 2005. Visualization by E.H. Fouberg and A.B. Murphy.
© 2020 John Wiley & Sons, Inc.

FIGURE 2.25 **Effect of AIDS on the Total Population Pyramid for South Africa, Predicted 2035.** This graph shows the estimated population, male and female, with AIDS and without AIDS.

and structure their wider experiences." In sub-Saharan Africa, the number of children orphaned when parents die from AIDS is growing rapidly (**Fig. 2.26**). In 2004, UNICEF reported that in just two years, between 2001 and 2003, the number of global AIDS orphans (children who have lost a parent to AIDS) rose from 11.5 million to 15 million. As of 2015, 13.4 million children had lost one or both parents to AIDS, and 80 percent of those were found in sub-Saharan Africa. Robson found that in addition to the rising number of AIDS orphans, many young children, especially girls, are taken out of school to serve as caregivers for their relatives with AIDS (**Fig. 2.27**). In her words, "more children are becoming young carers as households struggle to cope with income and labor losses through illness and mortality."

Despite the magnitude of the HIV/AIDS pandemic, enormous strides have been made in the past decade in the fight against the disease. Medical advancements have allowed people infected with HIV to live longer with antiretroviral treatments, which work to suppress the virus and halt the progression of the disease. In 2016, 17 million people living with HIV had access to antiretrovirals, and AIDS-related deaths had decreased more than 50 percent from their peak in 2005. Uganda, once Africa's worst-afflicted country, has slowed the growth of HIV/AIDS through an intensive, government-sponsored campaign of propaganda and action—notably the distribution of condoms in even the remotest part of the country. Life expectancy in Botswana and Swaziland, at 34 during the worst of the epidemic, has risen to 67. In Zimbabwe, life expectancy rose from 36 in 2007 to 61 in 2016. In addition to treatment, reproductive education programs have helped stem the transmission of the virus. Since 2010, the number of children with HIV/AIDS worldwide dropped 47 percent, largely as a result of programs aimed at preventing mother-to-child transmission.

Turning to other nonvectored infectious diseases, ebola is a serious disease that starts when humans come into contact with the bodily fluids of infected monkeys or fruit bats, and it is then spread from person to person through bodily fluids. Outbreaks in sub-Saharan Africa are deadly; the outbreak in West Africa in 2014 killed more than 11,000 people. Although the international health community mobilized to help stop the spread of ebola in West Africa, outbreaks continue. Almost every year, another outbreak occurs in the Democratic Republic of the Congo.

The origin of Middle East respiratory syndrome (MERS) is suggested by the name. A more recent disease, and less deadly than ebola, MERS has spread well beyond its source region, with cases appearing as far away as the United States by 2014. A particularly large outbreak took place in the Republic of Korea in 2015.

The most common nonvectored infectious disease is influenza, or the flu, which affects millions of people every year. Most infected individuals recover, but hundreds of thousands do not. Influenza epidemics often start when humans come into contact with infected pigs, which in turn contract the virus from birds and waterfowl. Southeastern China is a particularly common source region. In some years the spread of the virus reaches pandemic proportions. The most famous pandemic occurred in 1918–1919, leading to some 50 to 100 million deaths around the world. More recent pandemics have been less serious, but approximately 500,000 people succumbed to one strain of influenza in 2009–2010 (the so-called swine flu pandemic). Vaccines have slowed the spread of influenza, but staying ahead of virus mutations is an ongoing challenge.

Chronic and Genetic Diseases
Chronic diseases (also called degenerative diseases) are primarily afflictions of middle and old age. Among the chronic diseases, heart disease, cancer, and stroke rank as the leading diseases in this category, but pneumonia, diabetes, and liver diseases also take their toll. In the United States 100 years ago, tuberculosis, pneumonia, diarrheal diseases, and heart diseases (in that order) were the chief killers. Today, heart disease and cancer head the list, with

---

Author Field Note Visiting an AIDS Hospice Village in Johannesburg, South Africa

"The day was so beautiful, and the children's faces so expressive I could hardly believe I was visiting an AIDS hospice village set up for children. The Sparrow Rainbow Village on the edges of Johannesburg, South Africa, is the product of an internationally funded effort to provide children with HIV/AIDS the opportunity to live in a clean, safe environment. Playing with the children brought home the fragility of human life and the extraordinary impacts of a modern plague that has spread relentlessly across significant parts of sub-Saharan Africa."

– A. B. Murphy

Photo by A.B. Murphy. © 2020 John Wiley & Sons, Inc.

FIGURE 2.26 **Johannesburg, South Africa.**

TABLE 2.1	Leading Causes of Death in the United States, 2017
Cause	**Percent of Total Deaths**
1. Heart Disease	23.0
2. Cancer	21.3
3. Accidents	6.0
4. Chronic Lower Respiratory Disease	5.7
5. Stroke	5.2
6. Alzheimer's Disease	4.3
7. Diabetes	3.0
8. Influenza and Pneumonia	2.0

Source: "Deaths: Leading Causes for 2017", National Vital Statistics Report, Vol. 68, No. 6, 2019.

accidents next (**Table 2.1**). In the early 1900s, tuberculosis and pneumonia caused 20 percent of all deaths; today, they cause around 2 percent of all deaths. Diarrheal diseases, which were so high on the old list, are now primarily children's maladies. Today, diarrheal diseases are not even on the list of the leading causes of death in the United States.

At the global scale, cancer and heart disease take a high toll. Recent decades have brought new lifestyles, new pressures, new consumption patterns, and exposure to new chemicals, and we do not yet know how these are affecting our health. The health impacts of the preservatives that are added to many foods are not fully understood. We substitute artificial flavoring for sugar and other calorie-rich substances, but some of those substitutes have been proven to be dangerous. Even the treatment of drinking water with chemicals is rather recent in the scheme of global population change, and we do not know its long-term effects. Future chronic diseases may come from practices we now take for granted.

Diseases of Addiction   Alcohol and drug addiction are also chronic diseases that are hazards of the modern world. The World Health Organization estimates that well over 200 million people worldwide are addicted to alcohol, with the highest rates of addiction found in eastern Europe and Russia. The disease is also prevalent in other parts of Europe, North America, and East Asia, with serious negative consequences for mental health and life expectancy. In contrast, the Middle East and sub-Saharan Africa exhibit some of the lowest rates of alcohol addiction.

As for drugs, the addiction pattern depends in part on the particular drug in question. Cocaine addiction is highest in parts of the United Kingdom, Spain, and the United States, whereas amphetamine-based stimulants are particularly prevalent in the Philippines, El Salvador, and Australia. What is clear is that

Guest Field Note   Learning the Perspectives of Young AIDS Caregivers in Marich Village, Kenya

Elsbeth Robson
Keele University

This drawing was done by a Pokot boy in a remote primary school in northwestern Kenya. He agreed to take part in my fieldwork some years after I had started researching young carers (caregivers) in sub-Saharan Africa. Since those early interviews in Zimbabwe, I have been acutely aware of young carers' invisibility – you can't tell who are young carers just by looking at them. Indeed, invisibility is a characteristic of many aspects of the social impacts of HIV/AIDS. This young person drew himself working in the fields and taking care of cattle. African young people help with farming and herding for many reasons, but for young caregivers, assisting their sick family members in this way is especially important.

© Elsbeth Robson

FIGURE 2.27   **Marich Village, Kenya.**

the region where drugs are produced does not necessarily correspond with the region of the greatest consumption. Europe and North America lead the world in the consumption of many drugs, but the vast majority of them come from elsewhere.

Opioid addiction is a growing epidemic impacting every socio economic class within primarily higher income countries. Pharmaceutical companies pitched prescription opioids to medical doctors, claiming the drugs had low addiction rates. Doctors wrote prescriptions for high-dose pills and recommended patients take them for long periods after surgeries and injuries. Observant doctors, nurses, and community members recognized the addictive properties of opioids, while pharmaceutical companies continued to deny it. The opioid epidemic took root **(Fig. 2.28)**.

Both prescription and nonprescription opioids flooded the market, leading to medical complications and death for tens of thousands of people in the United States alone. In 2016, opioid overdoses accounted for more than 42,000 deaths, and in 2017 the U.S. Department of Health and Human Services declared the opioid problem to be a public health emergency. Some states began limiting the length of opioid prescriptions, and the medical community is moving to adopt alternative approaches to pain management. The opioid crisis includes prescription pain relievers, heroin, and synthetic opioids such as fentanyl. Addicts who cannot access or afford prescription opioids turn to the equally addictive but less expensive heroin. The National Institute on Drug Abuse reports that "about 80 percent of people who use heroin first misused prescription opioids." Most deaths are from overdose or tainted fentanyl, and non-Hispanic whites have the highest rates of overdose death in the U.S.

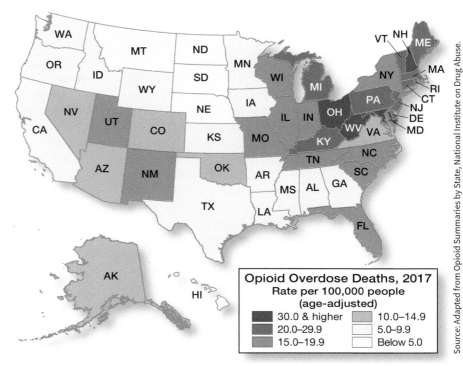

Source: Adapted from Opioid Summaries by State, National Institute on Drug Abuse.

FIGURE 2.28 **Opioid Deaths.**   The hearth of the opioid epidemic in the United States is West Virginia and the surrounding states. The crisis is spreading across the country at an alarming rate.

TC **Thinking Geographically**

Study Figure 2.22, the infant mortality rate (IMR) by state in the United States. Hypothesize reasons that would explain why the IMR is low in some **regions** of the country and high in others. Shift **scales** in your mind, and choose one state to consider: How do you think IMR varies within this state? At the scale of the state, what other factors might explain the pattern of IMR?

2.4   Identify Why and How Governments Influence Population Growth.

Governments have enacted policies to influence population growth rates or the ethnic composition of their countries. Government policies may lower birth rates through subsidized abortions or forced sterilization. Policies may also work to promote higher birth rates through tax incentives and marketing campaigns. Government population policies fall into three categories: expansive, eugenic, and restrictive.

Expansive

The former Soviet Union and China under Mao Zedong led other communist societies in **expansive population policies**, which encourage large families and raise the rate of natural increase. Although such policies have been abandoned in China, countries in stages 4 and 5 of the demographic transition are pursuing expansive population policies because their populations are aging and their growth rates are declining. Countries in the former Soviet Union and Europe are encouraging families to have more children through tax incentives and the expansion of family-friendly social services.

In response to concerns over Russia's aging population, the government of Ulyanovsk Province has held a National Day of Conception each September 12 since 2005. In 2007, government and businesses in Ulyanovsk offered the afternoon off for people to participate in the National Day of Conception. The government planned to award a free car to the proud parents of one of the children born 9 months later, on June 12— the Russian National Day. On June 12, 2008, 87 children were born in the province, about four times its average daily birth rate. Between 2005 and 2011, the number of births in the province rose by 19.5 percent. Although Russia's birth rate has rebounded somewhat, its ability to sustain a higher TFR will depend on many factors, including alleviating social problems, stabilizing incomes, and having continued government support.

In the 1980s, the governments of several European countries, including France and Sweden, adopted family-friendly policies designed to promote gender equality and boost fertility rates. The programs focused on alleviating much of the cost of having and raising children. In Sweden, couples who work and have small children receive cash payments, tax incentives, job leaves, and work flexibility that lasts up to eight years after the birth of a child. The policies led to a mini-birth-rate boom by the beginning of the 1990s.When the Swedish economy slowed in the early 1990s, so did the birth rate. The children born in 1991 made up a class of 130,000 students in the Swedish education system. But the children born three years later, in 1994, made up a class of only 75,000 students. The birth rate fell to 1.5 children by the end of the 1990s, and the country had to think anew about how to support families and promote fertility.

One imaginative approach was suggested by a spokeswoman for the Christian Democrat Party, who urged Swedish television to show racier programming at night in hopes of returning the population to a higher birth rate! Over the last 20 years, increases in child allowances and parental benefits have helped to produce a natural rate of increase that is a little higher than that in many other European countries and a TFR of 1.9, the third highest in Europe behind Iceland and the United Kingdom. In 2015 the Swedish population saw its largest annual increase in 70 years, a result of family-friendly policies but also record-high immigration.

Even China is realizing the low birth rates that came from nearly four decades of the one-child policy are problematic for the country's continued growth. The Chinese government is now offering incentives for highly educated Chinese women to have more children.

Eugenic

Eugenic population policies are designed to favor one racial or cultural group by discouraging ostracized groups from having children. Nazi Germany was a drastic case in point, but other countries also have pursued eugenic strategies, though in more subtle ways. Until the time of the civil rights movement in the 1960s, some observers accused the United States of pursuing social policies tinged with eugenics that worked against the interests of African Americans.

Many countries have a history of forced sterilization of lesbian, gay, transgender, and bisexual individuals; some even maintain those policies today. In January 2019, Japan's Supreme Court upheld a lower-court ruling that anyone officially registering a change in gender has to be sterilized. In other places eugenic population policies are practiced covertly through discriminatory taxation, biased allocation of resources, and other forms of racial favoritism.

Restrictive

Restrictive population policies are designed to reduce a population's natural increase rate. Policies range from tolerating unapproved means of birth control to outright prohibition of large families. One of the most famous restrictive population policies was China's one-child policy. Instituted in 1979, the **one-child policy** financially penalized families (other than minorities) who had more than one child and kept educational opportunities and housing privileges from families who broke the one-child mandate.

The one-child policy drastically reduced China's growth rate from one of the world's fastest to one of the world's slowest (**Fig. 2.29**). In the 1970s, China's growth rate was 3 percent; in the mid-1980s it was 1.2 percent; and today it is 0.5 percent (**Fig. 2.30**).

YOU'D BETTER HAVE ONE CHILD ONLY

只生一个孩子好

© H. J. de Blij

FIGURE 2.29 **Chengdu, China.** A large billboard from the 1990s warned readers to follow China's one-child policy.

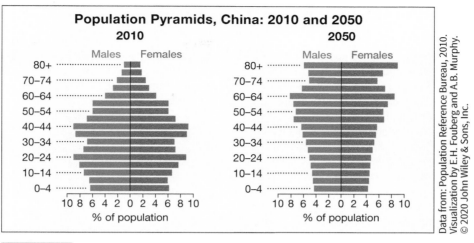

FIGURE 2.30 **Population Pyramids, China: 2010 and 2050.** The 2050 pyramid assumes that present growth rates continue into the future.

The main goal of the one-child policy was achieved, but the policy had several unintended consequences, including an increased abortion rate, an increase in female infanticide, and a high rate of abandoned girls (many of whom were adopted in the United States and Canada).

During the 1990s, under pressure to improve its human rights records and also with the realization that the population was quickly becoming gender and age imbalanced, China relaxed its one-child policy. Several exemptions allowed families to have more than one child. Rural families whose first child was a girl could have a second child. If both parents of the child are only children, they could have a second child.

In late 2013, China officially amended the one-child policy to allow all couples to have two children provided one parent is an only child. Despite the changes in policy, China's birth rate has not rebounded as much as the government anticipated. The Chinese government is realizing the impacts of its one-child policy could last for decades to come.

AP® Exam Taker's Tip

Know the different types of **population policies** that governments use to promote (**expansive**) or discourage (**restrictive**) population growth in a country. **Expansive** and **restrictive** population policies are also called *pronatalist* and *antinatalist,* respectively. The most well-known population policy was China's **restrictive** one-child policy (see Figs. 2.29 and 2.30). Why did China institute such a strident policy? What are some impacts of this one-child policy 30 years after its inception? One impact is a future one. How will China cope with a large, aging population compared to a smaller workforce of younger people? Another impact is how China is dealing with its skewed gender ratio. That is, China has large numbers of men (most are poor, living in rural areas) who likely will never marry. This is due to gender ratios as high as 118:100 in some parts of China.

TC Thinking Geographically

Recognizing that China's one-child policy left a significant impact on its **population pyramid** (Fig. 2.30), and thinking about China's expansion into Southeast Asia and Central Asia through the Belt and Road Initiative (Chapters 8 and 10), imagine how the Chinese government may use **migration** as a strategy to remedy its low birth rates and provide the population growth they want. Consider how **gender** was impacted through the one-child policy and how it could be impacted through your hypothetical, new migration policy.

Summary

2.1 Describe the Patterns of Population Distribution.

1. There are two common ways of calculating population density: arithmetic population density (average density in a unit area) and physiologic population density (average density in relation to the amount of arable land in a unit area).

2. Population distribution across Earth's surface is highly uneven. The areas of highest density correspond with places where the growing and harvesting of food are easiest. The largest population concentrations are found in the most agriculturally productive parts of East and South Asia, Europe, and North America.

2.2 Identify and Explain Influences on Population Growth over Time.

1. In the late 1700s, Thomas Malthus warned that Britain faced massive famine because of rapid population growth. A great famine did not happen, but the rapidly growing worldwide population of more recent times has led many to embrace Malthusian ideas. A stronger case can be made for these ideas at the global scale than at smaller scales because the interconnections among places undermine the significance of the population–food production ratio in any one place. Even at the global scale, increases in agricultural production complicate the relationship Malthus emphasized.

2. Total fertility rates (TFRs—the average number of children born to a woman of childbearing age) tell us how fast populations are growing. Places with TFRs below 2.1 are not growing. More and more countries, particularly high-income countries, are not growing, making it challenging for the working-age population to support children and the elderly.

3. Population pyramids show the age and sex structure of a population. They are called pyramids because, when first developed, most countries had a population structure in which children represented the highest proportion of the population, followed by young adults, followed by older adults, followed by the elderly. The result was a diagram that looked like a pyramid. The population pyramids of more prosperous countries today do not look like pyramids because the largest components of the population are not children, but middle-aged people.

4. The overall size of the human population has grown dramatically over the past few centuries. The demographic transition model shows that this happens when death rates decline but birth rates remain high. Population growth slows when birth rates also decline. Birth rates declined first in countries with greater urbanization and wealth. Birth rates are now declining in most places, but they still remain relatively high in poorer, less urbanized parts of the world.

5. There is a strong correlation between areas with improving educational opportunities for women and declining rates of natural population increase. The educational and economic opportunities afforded to women will play a central role in the population picture in the decades to come.

2.3 Explain how Health and Disease Affect Peoples' Well-Being.

1. Rates of infant mortality, child mortality, and life expectancy reflect the overall health of a society. The lowest rates of infant and child mortality are found in countries such as Sweden, Japan, and Singapore.

2. There are three basic types of diseases studied by geographers and others: infectious diseases, chronic or degenerative diseases, and genetic or inherited diseases. An infectious disease is epidemic when it spreads over a large region. A pandemic disease is global in scope.

3. Malaria and HIV/AIDS are two of the most deadly infectious diseases plaguing the planet over the past half-century. Some progress is being made in combating both diseases through education, the development of new drugs (in the case of HIV/AIDS), and the distribution of nets plus the introduction of genetically engineered mosquitoes (in the case of malaria).

4. Chronic diseases such as heart disease and cancer are afflictions of middle and old age. Recent decades have brought new lifestyles, new pressures, new consumption patterns, and exposure to new chemicals. We do not yet know how these are affecting our health.

5. Mapping diseases and the access of communities to medical facilities can tell us much about the health issues and challenges facing different populations.

2.4 Identify Why and How Governments Influence Population Growth.

1. Governments sometimes adopt policies that are designed to increase or reduce population growth rates. A number of states with low TFRs have adopted expansive population policies (e.g., tax incentives for having more children and generous maternal leave policies).

2. The most influential restrictive population policy of the last few decades is China's one-child policy. That policy has now been relaxed out of concern that China's population is aging.

Self-Test

2.1 Describe the patterns of population distribution.

1. In the study of demography, an advantage of looking at physiologic population density as opposed to arithmetic population density is that:

   a. you learn more about the health of a population.

   b. you learn more about the wealth of a population.

   c. you learn more about the agricultural base that can support a population.

   d. you learn more about the industrial base that can support a population.

   e. you learn more about population density per total land area.

2. Throughout most of human history, population density has been highest:

   a. in areas where food can be grown.

   b. in areas where average temperatures are high.

   c. in areas with high levels of biodiversity.

   d. in areas where few or no dangerous animals can be found.

   e. in areas where average temperatures are low.

3. Which world regions have the highest population densities?

   a. East Asia, sub-Saharan Africa, and Europe

   b. East Asia, Europe, and North America

   c. South America, sub-Saharan Africa, and North America

   d. East Asia, South Asia, and sub-Saharan Africa

   e. East Asia, South Asia, and Europe

2.2 Identify and explain influences on population growth over time.

4. Thomas Malthus is famous for arguing that:

    a. population growth would have serious environmental consequences.

    b. population growth would outstrip food supply.

    c. population growth would lead to industrialization.

    d. population growth would slow with greater urbanization.

    e. population growth would be sustainable.

5. If immigration is not a factor, a population needs a total fertility rate of _____ to reach replacement level.

    a. 1.5

    b. 2.1

    c. 2.5

    d. 3.1

    e. 1.0

6. In which of the following countries is the old-age dependency ratio a significant concern?

    a. Nigeria

    b. Mexico

    c. Indonesia

    d. United States

    e. Japan

7. A population pyramid for which of the following countries would most likely have the shape of an actual pyramid (a broad base that then tapers upward to a point)?

    a. France

    b. Russia

    c. Bangladesh

    d. Canada

    e. China

8. The demographic transition model charts the relationship over time between:

    a. birth rates and death rates.

    b. death rates and disease.

    c. birth rates and average family size.

    d. death rates and the child dependency ratio.

    e. fertility rates and disease.

2.3 Explain how health and disease affect peoples' well-being.

9. Life expectancy at birth in the United States is the highest in the world.

    a. true   b. false

10. Malaria is an example of:

    a. a chronic disease.

    b. a genetic disease.

    c. a vectored infectious disease.

    d. a nonvectored infectious disease.

    e. a food-borne illness.

11. Which of the following terms describes a disease that spreads around the globe?

    a. vectored

    b. endemic

    c. epidemic

    d. pandemic

    e. global

12. Which of the following statements about HIV/AIDS is correct?

    a. The disease started in North America and then spread around the world from there.

    b. The disease started in Europe and then spread to North America, but not elsewhere.

    c. The disease started in sub-Saharan Africa and then spread around the world from there.

    d. The disease started in East Asia and then spread to sub-Saharan Africa and North America.

    e. The disease started in Southeast Asia and then spread to mainland Asia and Europe.

2.4 Identify why and how governments influence population growth.

13. China's one-child policy, which has now been relaxed, is an example of:

    a. an expansive population policy.

    b. a restrictive population policy.

    c. a eugenic population policy.

    d. an anti-infant-mortality population policy.

    e. a health-based policy.

14. Each of the following countries has made efforts to increase population growth rates except:

    a. Russia.

    b. Denmark.

    c. India.

    d. France.

    e. Iceland.

15. Government initiatives designed to boost the population growth rate in Sweden have produced a modest uptick in the growth rate.

    a. true   b. false

CHAPTER 3

Migration

A patchwork of tarps, some dirty with the grit of the city and some new and still bright blue, covers the tent settlements of migrants. I wondered what rural village the migrants came from and how they chose this spot, tucked between high-rise developments in the middle of the city (**Fig. 3.1**).

Migrants leave rural villages and move to cities, and in India, they keep a connection to their village by their choice of where to live. Through interviews with migrants living in tent settlements, Indian researchers have found that migrants who live in a tent settlement like this one tend to come from the same village and stay connected with their family and friends in the village.

At the global scale, rural-to-urban migration represents one of the most dramatic shifts in human geography over the last century. In 1900, only 13 percent of people worldwide lived in cities; now more than 50 percent of people live in cities worldwide. Rapid migration from rural to urban helped Mumbai's population double from 5.9 million in 1971 to 12.73 million in 2019. The greater urban area of Mumbai now has more than 22 million people.

Informal settlements are found tucked between buildings in the central city like this one and also along railroad tracks in the eastern and western suburbs of Mumbai. Migrants living in slums and tent settlements have little security in terms of personal safety or control of land. Most lack access to drinkable water or sanitary sewers. The Census of India includes a survey of people living in slums in Mumbai. The vast majority of residents reported working in the service sector, including construction, or working in hutment factories located inside slums. Most are migrants who reported average salaries of less than $150 a month.

This chapter explores why people migrate, whether by force or voluntarily. We discuss where people migrate, both within countries and across country borders, and how governments impact migration.

Photo by A.B. Murphy. © 2020 John Wiley & Sons, Inc.

FIGURE 3.1 **Mumbai, India.** A view from the top of a high-rise in the central city, looking at one of the slums found tucked between buildings throughout the city. The Census of India reports that more than 50 percent of the Mumbai's residents live in slums.

CHAPTER OUTLINE

3.1 **Explain migration as a type of movement.**
- Cyclic Movement
- Migration

3.2 **Explain Historic and Modern Forced Migration.**
- Historic Forced Migration
- Modern Slavery and Human Trafficking

3.3 **Explain the Theories of Migration and Understand the Motivations for Migration.**
- Laws of Migration and the Gravity Model
- Push and Pull Factors

3.4 **Identify why refugees are a distinct group of migrants and describe where most refugees migrate.**
- Distribution of Refugees
- Areas of Dislocation

3.5 **Determine how government policies impact migration.**
- Waves of Immigration in the United States
- Legal Restrictions

Explain Migration as a Type of Movement.

Migration is a type of movement that changes both the places migrants leave and the places they go. The movement of people along paths of migration creates connections and networks among places. Migration changes how people see themselves and others. It also increases spatial interaction and speeds the diffusion of ideas and innovations among places connected through migration.

Geographers identify two basic types of movement. Leaving home for a defined amount of time and returning home is called **cyclic movement**. Migration changes the location of home and has a degree of permanence not found in cyclic movement. **Migration** is movement from a home location to a new place with an intent to stay in the new place permanently.

Cyclic Movement

Cyclic movement describes a regular journey that begins at a home base and returns to the same home base in a relatively short period of time. One form of cyclic movement is

daily, routine movement. People have daily routines that take them through a series of short moves within a local area, such as home to work, work to errands, and errands to home. These moves create what geographers call **activity spaces**, places in which people move in the rounds of everyday activity. The scale of activity space varies by age, gender, and income.

Commuting within a person's activity space is a cyclic movement. Commuting, the journey from home to work and home again, takes from minutes to hours and can involve several modes of transportation. The average American commuter travels 26.2 minutes one way each day (52.4 minutes round trip). South Dakotans have the shortest one-way commute at 16.6 minutes, and New Yorkers double that average with an average commute of 33.6 minutes. New York City and Long Island, New York have the top two longest commutes, with 34.7 and 33.3 minutes, respectively (**Fig. 3.2**).

Another form of cyclic movement is seasonal movement. **Snowbirds** are retired or semiretired people who live in cold states and Canada for most of the year and move to warm

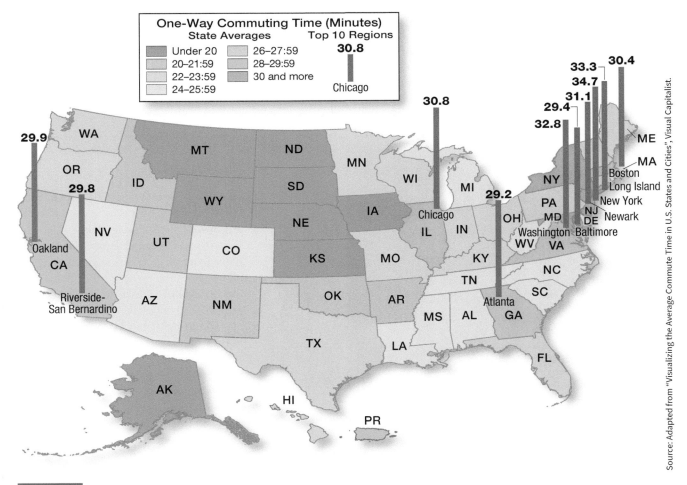

Source: Adapted from "Visualizing the Average Commute Time in U.S. States and Cities", Visual Capitalist.

FIGURE 3.2 **One-Way Commuting Time by City.** Coastal states have longer commute times than states in the interior. Much of the Great Plains, Midwest, and West have relatively short commute times. Among the 10 cities with the longest commute times, New York and Long Island have the longest commute time.

states like Florida, California, and Arizona for the winter. This seasonal movement enables them to avoid snow and have warmer weather year-round. By spending part of the year in each state, snowbirds economically impact both their home state and their winter state. The Canadian Snowbird Association estimates that 450,000 Canadians spend between one and six months in Florida each winter. Eight out of 10 own a property in Florida and pay taxes there. While in Florida, snowbirds boost local economies, filling restaurants, grocery stores, pharmacies, beauty shops, and clinics, and paying local and state taxes on each item or service they purchase. Snowbird movement is cyclical because snowbirds return home in the spring.

The seasonal transfer of snowbirds from north to south also impacts the temporarily depopulated northern states. Businesses like restaurants have fewer customers, and organizations like churches that depend on monthly donations may have lower financial support in winter months. This temporary depopulation of northern states even impacts the census every 10 years. The U.S. Census asks you to enter the number of people living in the home on April 1. After the 2000 census, the state of Michigan estimated that Michigan snowbirds who were still in the South on April 1 and counted themselves in their winter state instead of their home state cost the state of Michigan a congressional seat and approximately $200 million in federal funds.

Another type of cyclic movement, **pastoralism**, happens when herders move livestock throughout the year to continually find freshwater and green pastures. Instead of feeding livestock on agriculturally produced feed, pastoralists move livestock seasonally to find naturally growing pastures. Pastoralism is an effective and sustainable form of agriculture in dry lands with limited rainfall. To find water, food, and shelter in their cyclic movements, pastoralists must know their territory well.

Their movement is purposeful and takes place along long-familiar routes that are passed down through generations.

The savanna climate in Africa, which has well-defined rainy and dry seasons, is well suited for sustainable pastoralism, and an estimated 200 million Africans make a living as pastoralists. Pastoralists in northern Uganda, including Jei and Karamoja, move cyclically with thousands of head of cattle across semiarid and savanna lands, following rainfall patterns so that the cattle can graze on fields after they have grown during rainy periods (**Fig. 3.3**). Government policies in Uganda that discourage movement, as well as rainfall patterns that are changing as a result of climate change, threaten the livelihoods of pastoralists in Africa.

Transhumance is a specialized form of pastoralism practiced in mountain areas when ranchers move livestock vertically to graze on highlands during summer months and lowlands during winter months. In Switzerland, for example, farmers drive cattle up mountain slopes to high, fresh pastures during the summer, and farm families follow the herds, staying in cottages that are left empty during cold winters. Among the 200 million pastoralists in Africa, about 25 million pastoralists live in the Horn of Africa (Northeast Africa, in and around Somalia and Ethiopia). Ethiopian pastoralists who live near the mountains practice transhumance, herding their livestock from highland to lowland and back in search of pastures renewed by seasonal rainfall.

Migration

Whereas cyclic movement begins and ends at home, migration begins at one home and ends at a new home. Migration happens when persons, families, or larger groups leave home and move to a new location with the intent of permanently changing where they live. Migrants move a significant distance within a country or across country borders.

Migration is the major source of **relocation diffusion**. Migrants take their cultural values and practices with them to their new location, thus making an imprint on the cultural landscape. For example, Little Havana in Miami, Florida (**Fig. 3.4**), has the visible human imprint of generations of Cubans migrating to and living in Dade County, Florida. Even before Cuba became a communist state, 60,000 Cubans lived in the United States, primarily in New York. Between 1959, when Fidel Castro led the Cuban Revolution, and 1961, when Castro made Cuba officially

Alan Gignoux/Alamy Stock Photo

FIGURE 3.3 **Eastern Uganda.** Karamoja pastoralists in Uganda rely on their livestock in this region with a short rainy season in April, a longer rainy season in July, and a dry climate the rest of the year. The pastoralists move their livestock to freshwater and vegetation during the long dry season.

communist, 248,000 Cuban refugees fled to the United States, settling mainly in and around Miami, Florida.

The U.S. government legally allowed Cuban migration because it saw the migrants as refugees escaping a communist government. Cuban migrants arrived and shaped neighborhoods in the greater Miami area (Dade County). Within a generation, Cuban Americans developed businesses, settled in neighborhoods, and became a political force in Dade County. In 1973, Dade County officially became bicultural and bilingual. Then in 1980, when the Cuban economy crashed, 125,000 Cubans fled to the United States by boat in a six-month period. Cuban Americans in the United States helped organize the refugee flow, hiring boats to transport Cubans to the country. As the Cuban economy continued to falter, migration to the United States persisted throughout the 1980s. In 1994, the government enacted the wet feet, dry feet policy (since ended in 2017). Under wet feet, dry feet, the United States returned Cuban migrants intercepted on water (wet feet) to Cuba or a third country, and allowed Cuban migrants who made it to shore (dry feet) to apply for permanent residency a year after arrival. The 1994 reforms also set a quota that allowed the United States to admit a minimum of 20,000 Cubans a year, plus family reunifications. Since 1994, more than 650,000 Cubans have migrated to the United States.

FIGURE 3.4 **Little Havana, Miami.** A Cuban restaurant advertises mojitos and Cuban foods to passers-by on a corner of Little Havana. Cuban cafes and restaurants, cigar stores, mosaic tile work, statues of famous Cubans, Catholic churches, and vibrant facades and murals are all part of the cultural landscape of the ethnic neighborhood. The neighborhood dates to the 1960s and the first major migration of Cubans to Miami.

Karel Miragaya/123 RF

AP® Exam Taker's Tip

Migration is the major source of **relocation diffusion** (see pp. 12–15 to review). Relocation diffusion occurs when people move and take their cultural values, practices, innovations, and so forth to their new locations. These values and practices show up on the new landscape. Look around your own community. Can you see imprints on your landscape that show evidence of migration and relocation diffusion?

International Migration   **International migration** is movement across country borders. When migrants leave their home country, they are classified as **emigrants**, those who migrate out of a country. When the same migrants enter a new country, they are classified as **immigrants**, those who migrate into a country. Emigration subtracts from the total population of a country, and immigration adds to it. For example, during the Potato Famine, Ireland's population fell from 8.2 million in 1841 to 6.5 million in 1851 (*Irish Times,* 2018). The nearly 2 million

people Ireland lost in 10 years either died of famine or migrated. The famine in Ireland made the Irish sick, desperate, and hopeful about opportunity across the Atlantic Ocean. In 1847 alone, 250,000 Irish migrated, mainly to North America. Not all who fled famine made it to shore, as those who were sick or weak from famine died in transit. At ports in New York, Boston, New Orleans, and Quebec, authorities often quarantined sickly Irish migrants. In the same year that 250,000 Irish emigrated (1847), the United States accepted approximately 150,000 Irish immigrants, and the ports of Montreal and Quebec in Canada accepted 70,065 Irish immigrants.

Ireland remained a country of emigration until 1996, when Ireland's economy boomed, experiencing a 30 percent increase in employment opportunities between 1996 and 2001. In 1996, more immigrants arrived in Ireland than emigrants departed. When the European Union (EU), which includes Ireland, added 10 new countries in 2004, mostly in eastern Europe, Irish and EU migration policies allowed immigration from the new EU countries. Responding to the availability of jobs in Ireland, 306,000 people from the newest member countries of the EU have immigrated to Ireland since 2006. From 2010 to 2014, Ireland's economy weakened after the 2008 global recession and the number of immigrants to Ireland declined. Since 2015, however, immigration has again been higher than emigration. In 2018, 90,300 immigrants moved to Ireland, and fewer emigrants, 56,300, left Ireland, primarily for opportunities in other parts of the EU (*Irish Examiner,* 2018).

The difference between immigration and emigration is **net migration**. Before 1996, Ireland had more emigrants (people

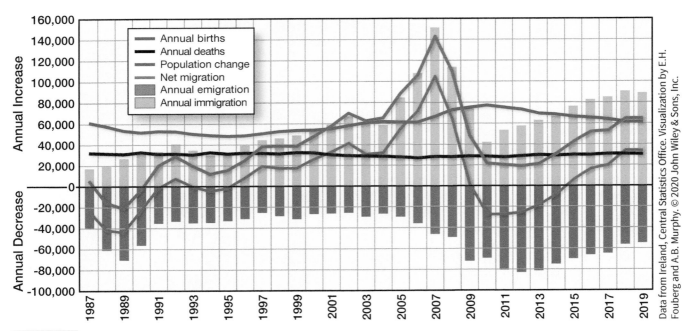

FIGURE 3.5 Ireland's annual emigration is shown in purple bars as a negative because it subtracts from the total population. Annual immigration is shown in orange bars as a positive because it adds to the population. The combination of those two bars is shown in the line for net migration. Adding annual births and deaths gives us the total population change each year.

leaving Ireland) than immigrants (people coming to Ireland), so it had a negative net migration. From 1996 to 2009 and again since 2015, Ireland has had more immigrants than emigrants, giving it a positive net migration (**Fig. 3.5**). Net migration can be added to births and deaths (see Chapter 2) to understand whether a country's population is growing or declining.

Major Migration Paths Major migration paths at the global scale since 1500 are shown in **Figure 3.6**. The migration flows include movements from Europe, including (1) from northern and western Europe to North America; (2) from southern Europe (Spain and Portugal) to South and Central America; and (3) from Britain and Ireland to Africa and Australia. The migration flows also include involuntary (forced) migration caused by Europeans, including (4) enslaved Africans from Africa to the Americas; and (5) indentured laborers from South Asia to eastern Africa, Southeast Asia, and Caribbean America.

Among the greatest human migrations in recent centuries has been the flow from Europe to the Americas (arrows 1 and 2 in Fig. 3.6). Before the 1830s, 2.75 million Europeans migrated overseas. British migrants went to North America, Australia, New Zealand, and South Africa (arrow 3 in Fig. 3.6). Spanish and Portuguese migrants settled in South America (arrow 2 in Fig. 3.6). Across the Americas, Africa, and Asia, Europeans, especially colonizers, built up port cities with ethnic neighborhoods. The rate of European migration increased sharply between 1835 and 1935, with perhaps as many as 75 million departing for colonies in Africa and Asia and for economic opportunities in the Americas. Although millions of Europeans eventually returned to their homelands, the net outflow from Europe was enormous, as evidenced by the large number of

Canadians and Americans who identify themselves as being of European ancestry.

In the seventeenth and eighteenth centuries, Europeans rationalized the forced migration of enslaved Africans (arrow 4 in Fig. 3.6) as economically essential to European colonization and plantation agriculture. After the slave trade ended, the British, who colonized South Asia, transported tens of thousands of indentured laborers (also called debt laborers) from present-day India, Pakistan, and Sri Lanka to Southeast Asia (especially Malaysia) and to East Africa to labor on plantations and in mines (arrow 5 in Fig. 3.6). Descendants of South Asian migrants in eastern and southern Africa now control a large share of businesses in South Africa, Kenya, and Tanzania.

Chinese migration in the 1800s flowed into North America and Southeast Asia (arrow 6 in Fig. 3.6). In North America, Chinese migrants primarily became indentured laborers (debt laborers) who built railroads and worked in mines in the United States. In Southeast Asia, Chinese migrants settled in major cities, especially ports, and became business leaders and owners. After several generations of having been born in Southeast Asia, people of Chinese descent in Southeast Asia are still called Overseas Chinese (see section "Overseas Chinese"). The seventh arrow in Figure 3.6 is for internal migration from the east coast to the interior with the westward expansion of the United States as well as forced migration of Native Americans (see also Fig. 3.10). Finally, the eastward migration of Russians into Central Asia and Siberia (arrow 8 in Fig. 3.6) dates to tsarist policies to move Russians into the outer parts of the empire in the 1800s and Soviet policies to forcibly move political opposition to Siberia.

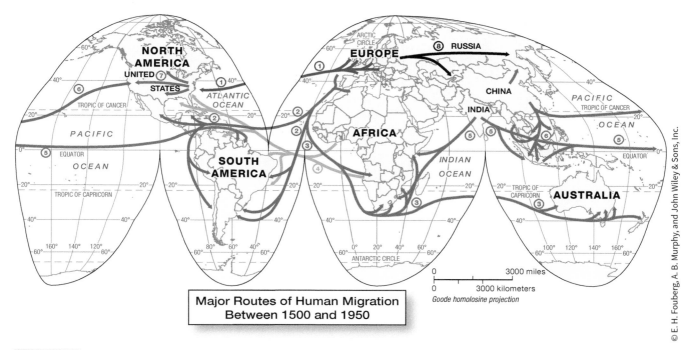

Major Routes of Human Migration Between 1500 and 1950

FIGURE 3.6 **Major Routes of Human Migration Between 1500 and 1950.** **1.** Migration of Europeans to North America. **2.** Migration of southern Europeans to South and Central America. **3.** Migration of British and Irish to Africa and Australia. **4.** Forced migration of enslaved Africans to the Americas. **5.** Migration of South Asians to other British colonies as indentured servants and to serve administrative roles. **6.** Migration of Chinese to Southeast Asia and the Americas in the nineteenth and twentieth centuries. **7.** Westward migration and forced migration of Native Americans in the United States. **8.** Forced migration of Russians and eastern Europeans into Siberia and Central Asia.

Remittances   The biggest incentives for international migration are safety and economic opportunities. Migrants fleeing violence and persecution to find safety are **refugees** and typically come from lower income countries and migrate to neighboring lower income countries. Non-refugee migrants who come from lower income regions and countries searching for better economic opportunities in the semiperiphery and core often do so in hopes of earning enough to send money back to their families in their home countries. These funds are called **remittances**. Migrants (refugees and non-refugees) sent $574 billion to family and friends in their home countries from all around the world in 2017, which is about twice the amount of remittances migrants sent in 2006. In the same year, migrants living in the United States sent $148 billion in remittances to home countries, including $30 billion to Mexico, $16 billion to China, and $11.7 billion to India (**Fig. 3.7**). American migrants living in other countries also send remittances back to the United States. In 2017, families and friends in the United States received $6.6 billion in remittances from abroad.

Remittances sent back to a lower income country can account for a significant amount of that country's economy. For example, Haitians living in the United States sent $1.4 billion in remittances back to Haiti, the country with the lowest gross domestic product (GDP) in the Americas. Haitians living in the United Kingdom, Canada, and other countries also send remittances home. Remittances received in Haiti account for 32.37 percent of the country's GDP. An estimated one in five Haitian families receive remittances from abroad.

The downturn in the U.S. economy after 2008 generated a new flow of money called **reverse remittances**: money flowing from other countries to the United States. Of the $6.5 billion in reverse remittances received in the United States in 2016, 26 percent ($1.75 billion) came from Mexico.

> **AP® Exam Taker's Tip**
>
> **Net migration** can show political, economic, and cultural causes and effects. What *causes* are there in a country that has high numbers of **emigrants** or **immigrants**? What *effects* are there on a country that has high numbers of **emigrants** or **immigrants**? What role do **remittances** play for both the country of origin and the destination country?

Guest Workers   Migrants, both internationally and internally, are attracted to growing economies where jobs are available. After World War II, European countries recognized that they had a shortage of labor because of the massive military and civilian deaths during the war. Between the loss of 18 million people and extensive bombing, Europeans needed to find funds and people to rebuild their cities and their economies.

The United States invested in rebuilding Europe through a post–World War II initiative called the Marshall Plan. To find labor to work in farms and factories, France, Germany, the Netherlands, and the United Kingdom looked first to workers from lower income countries in Europe. In need of still more workers,

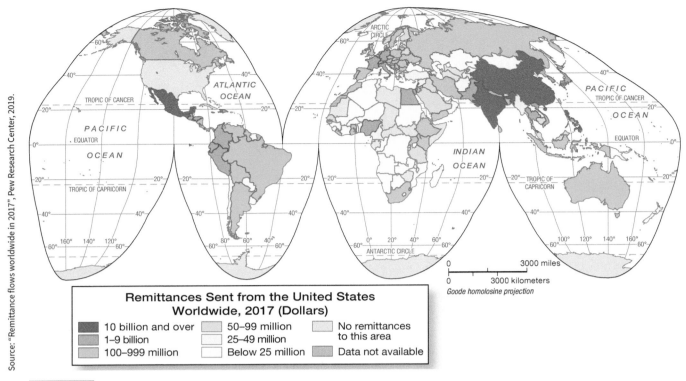

Source: "Remittance flows worldwide in 2017", Pew Research Center, 2019.

Remittances Sent from the United States Worldwide, 2017 (Dollars)

- 10 billion and over
- 1–9 billion
- 100–999 million
- 50–99 million
- 25–49 million
- Below 25 million
- No remittances to this area
- Data not available

FIGURE 3.7 **Remittances Sent from the United States Worldwide in 2017.** After Mexico, China, and India, most remittances from workers in the United States were sent to the Philippines ($11 billion), Vietnam ($7.7 billion), Guatemala ($7.2 billion), and Nigeria ($6.1 billion).

Europe then looked outside the region and invited guest workers from North Africa (to France and the Netherlands), Turkey (to Germany), and former colonies of Great Britain in the Caribbean, India, and Pakistan (to the United Kingdom).

European governments called the labor migrants **guest workers**, migrants who were invited into a country to work temporarily, were granted work visa status, and were expected to return to their home country at the end of the visa. The laws allowing guest workers in Europe assumed that the workers would fill the void left by those who died during World War II, and then they would return to their home countries. Instead, most guest workers stayed, both because they wanted to and because they were needed. Three to four generations of Turks have been born in Germany since World War II, making them far more than guests. In 2005 the German government, which had for decades defined German citizens as those of German descent, changed the law so that Turks could become citizens of the country.

Guest workers often work in agriculture or service industries, including hotels, restaurants, and tourist attractions. Countries invite guest workers when labor is in short supply. The economy may be booming, and more labor may be needed. For example, Germany continues to invite guest workers because its economy is the fastest growing in Europe. A country may also have a small labor supply for cultural reasons; for example, only 56.4 percent of Saudi Arabia's population is in the workforce. Finally, a country may have a low total fertility rate (TFR) and not enough citizens in the working-age population. For example, Japan's TFR of 1.43 and a declining population led the government in 2018

to commit to inviting 500,000 guest workers into Japan by 2025, mainly to work in manufacturing and construction.

Despite the legal status of guest workers and the work of governments and international organizations to protect them, employers may abuse guest workers who are unaware of their rights. Long hours and low pay are common, but guest workers continue to work because the money is better than they would ordinarily receive and because they are supporting families at home.

In many instances, the economies of the home countries come to rely on remittances, and the home governments may work with destination countries and with international labor organizations to protect the rights of their citizens abroad. Governments of home countries can pull their guest workers out of countries and or stop the legal migration flow when conditions in the destination region become dangerous. For example, around 1 million Indonesians, mostly women, work as domestic servants in Southwest Asia and North Africa (the Middle East). Indonesian women are often abused physically and sexually in the homes where they work, and the laborers have little recourse in the country where they work. Saudi Arabia has executed several Indonesian domestic workers who killed their Saudi abusers. In 2015, Indonesia banned their citizens from migrating to 21 countries in the region. Despite the ban, recruiters still operate in Indonesia, especially in rural areas, and Indonesian women who are unaware of the ban or motivated by economic opportunity continue to migrate to the 21 banned countries.

Sending governments can attempt to stop guest worker flows, but receiving governments can increase the number of guest worker visas they grant or extend guest worker visas if demand for labor remains. Whether short or long term, guest workers make an imprint on the cultural landscapes of the communities and neighborhoods where they live. They open restaurants and retail shops, build mosques and churches, create demand for new ethnic foods in grocery stores, require certain beauty products and shops, and establish businesses such as wire transfer services and travel agencies for support.

AP® Exam Taker's Tip

Guest workers are migrants who come to a country for a specific purpose. Guest workers are generally legal immigrants who work. Many times a country will invite people to do jobs such as agriculture, construction, hospitality, and so forth. Sometimes they might be professionals like teachers or nurses. How are **guest workers** and **remittances** possibly connected, and what roles do remittances play in the local political culture and economy?

Islands of Development   Cities in lower income countries are typically where most foreign investment goes, where the vast majority of paying jobs are located, and where infrastructure is concentrated. Migrants are drawn to port cities in lower-income countries because investments and job prospects are concentrated in port cities. Geographers describe cities in developing countries where foreign and domestic investment and job prospects are concentrated as **islands of development**. The term conveys a place where infrastructure, housing, jobs, and businesses thrive in the middle of a more rural and less developed countryside. Migrants from rural areas and neighboring countries are pulled toward these cities to find work. Commodities produced in islands of development are typically exported.

Figure 3.8 maps islands of development in Africa. Within the region of West Africa, the cities in the oil-producing areas of Nigeria are islands of development. In the mid-1970s, people in Togo, Benin, Ghana, and the northern regions of Nigeria,

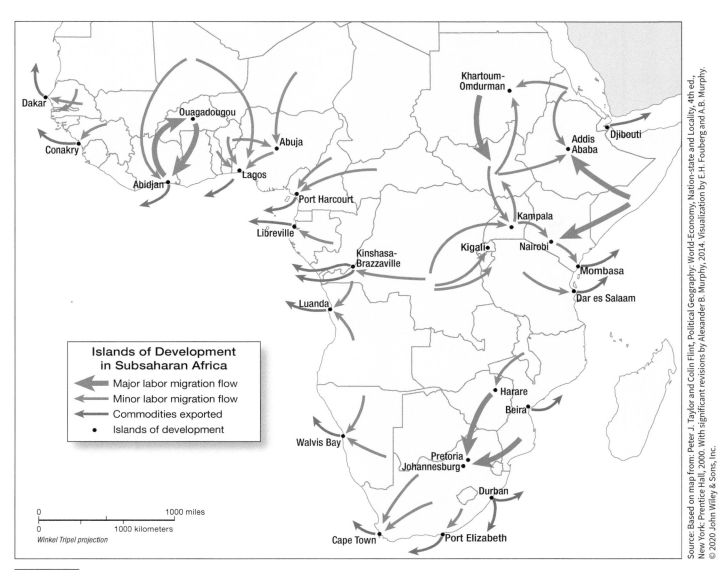

Source: Based on map from: Peter J. Taylor and Colin Flint, Political Geography: World-Economy, Nation-state and Locality, 4th ed., New York: Prentice Hall, 2000. With significant revisions by Alexander B. Murphy, 2014. Visualization by E.H. Fouberg and A.B. Murphy. © 2020 John Wiley & Sons, Inc.

FIGURE 3.8 **Islands of Development in sub-Saharan Africa.**   Major cities in Africa function as islands of development. These cities receive foreign and domestic investment and are a major pull for migrants from rural areas and neighboring countries. Migrants are drawn to the prospect of work in the formal or informal economies of the cities. Port cities and heavily populated interior cities are the major islands of development in Africa.

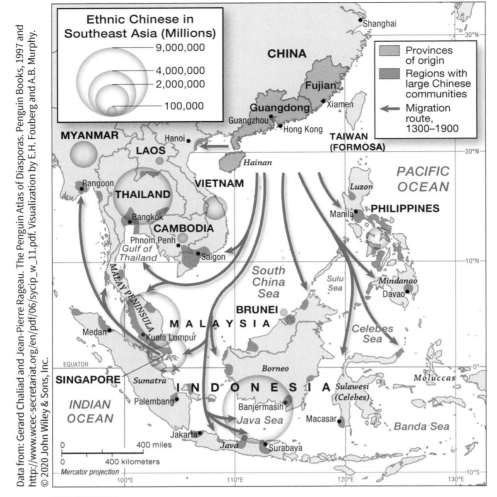

FIGURE 3.9 **Chinese in Southeast Asia.** Most Chinese who live in Southeast Asia are descendants of Chinese who migrated from southeastern China in the 1800s. Chinese migrated primarily to port cities and along coastlines.

perceiving that economic life was better in coastal Nigeria, were lured to the coast for short-term jobs while the oil economy was good. The migrants, usually young men, worked as much as they could and sent almost all the money they earned home as remittances to support their families. They worked until the oil economy declined in the early 1980s. At that point, the Nigerian government decided the foreign workers were no longer needed, and 2 million foreign workers were forcibly pushed out.

Overseas Chinese
European colonialism also had an impact on regional migration flows in Southeast Asia. Europe's colonial occupation of Southeast Asia presented economic opportunities for the Chinese. During the late 1800s and early 1900s, millions of Chinese laborers fled famine and political strife in southern China to work as contract laborers in Southeast Asia (**Fig. 3.9**). Many remained, and today their descendants constitute a Chinese minority in Southeast Asian countries that accounts for a substantial part of the population: 14 percent in Thailand, 23 percent in Malaysia, and 74 percent in Singapore.

Over time, Overseas Chinese in Southeast Asia became leaders in trade, commerce, and finance in the region, taking an economic position much like that of South Asians in eastern and southern Africa. Overseas Chinese heavily invest in Hong Kong and in growth industries in mainland China. The difference in wealth between Overseas Chinese and locals from the majority population can cause political and economic problems. In May 2014, tensions erupted into violent protests after China announced plans to build an oil rig in an area in the South China Sea that is also claimed by Vietnam. Rioters attacked Overseas Chinese settlements, where 21 died, and set fire to Chinese businesses (many of which were owned by Taiwanese migrants).

Internal Migration
Countries also experience **internal migration** when migrants stay in the same country but move to a different part of the country. Internal migration can be a rapid response, such as the flow of 250,000 residents of New Orleans to Houston, Texas, after Hurricane Katrina flooded 80 percent of New Orleans in 2005, or a slow shift over a country's history. The United States began with 13 colonies along the east coast and expanded west over time, taking over Indian lands, entering treaties with other countries, and eventually adding Alaska and Hawaii in 1947. As the United States expanded

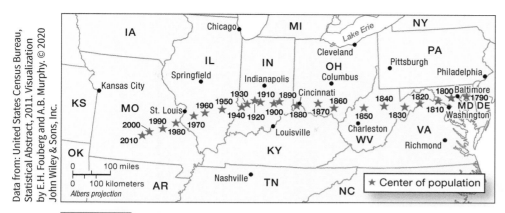

Data from: United States Census Bureau, Statistical Abstract, 2011. Visualization by E.H. Fouberg and A.B. Murphy. © 2020 John Wiley & Sons, Inc.

FIGURE 3.10 **Changing Center of Population.** The center of population in the United States has moved west and south, reflecting an internal migration westward and southward in the time period of the map. The center of population shows the average population distribution. If every person and where he or she lives are weighted the same way, the center of population is the fulcrum, the balance point of all the people.

The Great Migration The Great Migration, from about 1900 to 1970, marks a significant period of internal migration in the United States. After the Civil War, Southern states passed racist Jim Crow laws, segregating blacks and whites in schools, hospitals, public spaces, public transportation, and even cemeteries. Even though the Fourteenth Amendment extended voting rights to African Americans, governments in the South refused to allow African Americans to vote. At the same time civil and political opportunities were restricted, economic opportunities for African Americans in the South declined. The widespread use of mechanical cotton pickers in the 1940s meant fewer jobs in agriculture.

west, so did the center of population. **Figure 3.10** shows how the center of population in the United States has changed since the 1790s, reflecting the internal migration west and south that followed the expansion of the country.

In response to these conditions and the growth of manufacturing in the Northeast and Midwest, between 5 and 8 million African Americans left the South for opportunities in the north and west (**Fig. 3.11**). The car industry in Detroit, manufacturing, textile, and meat processing in Chicago,

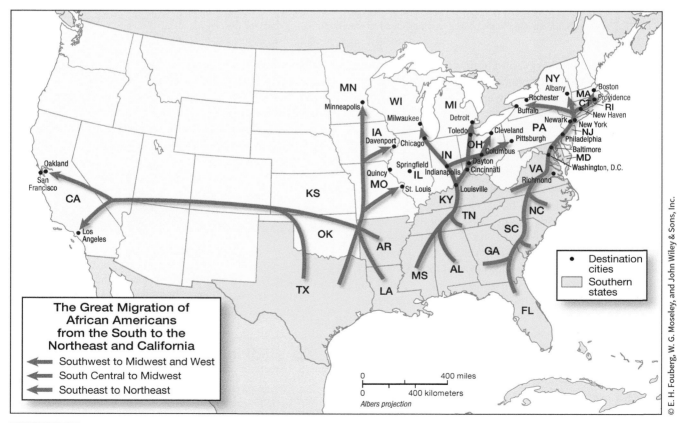

© E. H. Fouberg, W. G. Moseley, and John Wiley & Sons, Inc.

FIGURE 3.11 **The Great Migration of African Americans from the South to the Northeast and California.** Between 1900 and 1970, African American migrants followed three migration paths into cities in the Northeast and in California. The three clear paths are a great example of chain migration. Migrants who found work in the north or California sent word of economic opportunity to family and friends in the South, who in turn followed the same path of migration.

Luke Sharrett/Bloomberg/Getty Images

FIGURE 3.12 **Youngstown, Ohio.** This industrial zone in Youngstown, Ohio used to be a bustling place. The city recently closed 4 miles of streets where homes of people who once worked in this industrial zone have been abandoned. The closed neighborhood once had a streetcar line that ran from the homes to the industrial zones. The mayor stated that closing the streets was a recognition that the city's population is shrinking and a way to reduce street maintenance costs for the city.

steel production in Pittsburgh, and agriculture in California boomed in the early 1900s. The promise of good jobs, like making $5 a day at the Ford factory in Detroit, and relative freedom from oppressive laws pulled African Americans north and west.

Rust Belt to Sun Belt Job opportunities are a major motivation for voluntary migration. When the economy shifts and a region loses jobs, people migrate to growing regions of the country. In 1948, 131,700 people worked in coal mining in West Virginia, and in 2018, fewer than 18,000 West Virginians worked in coal mining. Manufacturing jobs declined in the United States from 19 million in 1980 to between 12 and 13 million today.

The location of manufacturing jobs shifted, too. In 1980, 41 percent of people in the Midwest (Ohio, Michigan, Indiana, Illinois, and Wisconsin) were employed in manufacturing, and in 2015, only 13.1 percent of Midwesterners worked in manufacturing. What was once a booming industrial and coal-mining region rusted out as companies abandoned factories (**Fig. 3.12**). Americans started to call the Midwest and Northeast the **Rust Belt**, defining it as a region that once had a vibrant manufacturing sector but is now deindustrialized (see **Fig. 12.23**).

People move from areas in economic decline to areas that are growing. Manufacturing jobs in the United States shifted south to states with low union rates, employees who did not demand higher wages, climates that were warmer and air-conditioned year-round, and states with low tax rates for businesses. The decline of the Rust Belt happened at the same time as the growth of the **Sun Belt**, a region of economic growth with an expanding technology-based service sector and a stable manufacturing sector that stretches along the southern United States from Virginia to California. The widespread use of air conditioning to cool homes, businesses, schools, and factories made it possible for the Sun Belt to grow since the 1970s. **Figure 3.13** shows population change by state since 1990, confirming the slow growth of the Midwest and rapid rise of the Sun Belt and the West in the U.S. economy.

AP® Exam Taker's Tip

Examples of **internal migration**: **Great Migration**—African Americans from the South to the Northeast and California; **Rust Belt to Sun Belt**—Economic shifts brought northern factory workers from the northern United States to the southern states.

TC Thinking Geographically

Study the picture of Little Havana in Miami (Fig. 3.4) and read the caption again. Now, examine Figure 3.9. Imagine how **migration** of Chinese to Southeast Asia changes the **cultural landscapes** of the **region**. Focus on Kuala Lumpur, Malaysia and hypothesize whether the city has a Chinatown and how it has changed over time as Overseas Chinese have gained economic power in the region.

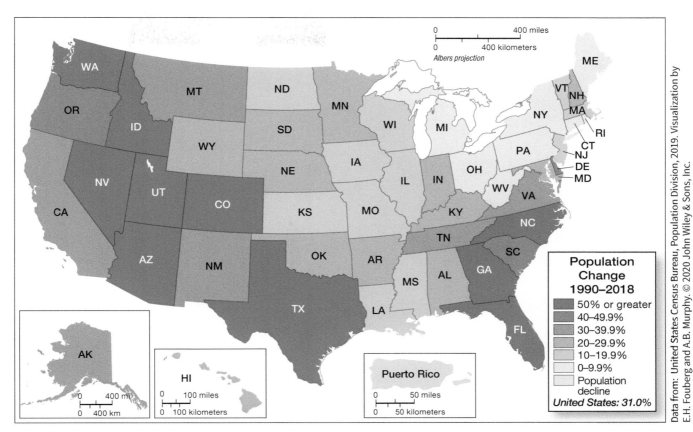

FIGURE 3.13 **Population Change 1990–2018 by State and Puerto Rico.**   States with growing
economies experienced the highest population growth. Midwestern and Northeastern states along
the Great Lakes, grew at a much slower rate, as the manufacturing sector continued to decline in the
region. States in the Sunbelt, especially North Carolina, Georgia, Florida, and Texas, and states in the
West grew fastest.

3.2 Explain Historic and Modern Forced Migration.

Migration can be voluntary, a conscious decision to move
from your home to a new destination, or it can be forced,
a movement imposed on a group of people. The distinction
between forced and voluntary migration is not always clear-
cut. In the nineteenth and twentieth centuries, millions of
Europeans migrated to the United States, and this European
migration is typically cited as a prime example of voluntary migration. However, some European migration can be
seen as forced. When Great Britain colonized Ireland, it took
nearly all Irish Catholic lands and enacted Penal Laws to try
to stop Catholics from practicing their religion. The Penal
Laws fined and imprisoned Catholics who participated in
Mass and rendered more severe punishments, including
execution, on Catholic priests who performed the Mass or
other sacraments. Until 1829, the British enforced laws preventing Irish Catholics from buying land, voting, or carrying weapons. The British treatment of the Irish during their
colonial rule was political persecution. Moreover, British

persecution of the Irish led to widespread famine in the
1840s and 1850s. As a result, Irish migration can be seen
as forced.

At the scale of an individual region or country, we can
question whether a decision to migrate is forced or voluntary.
The neutral title *migrant* hides how complex decision making
is and the agency, or decision-making ability, the migrant
has within the family, where power is divided by gender and
age. Studies of gender and migration find that, as a group,
men are more mobile than women and migrate farther than
women. Men have more choices of employment than women,
and women earn less than men in the jobs they find. One
study of migration in Mexican households found that strongly
patriarchal households tend to shield young women from
migrating, sending young men to migrate for work. Mexican
households without a strong patriarchy more commonly send
young, unmarried women to the city or another country to
gain employment.

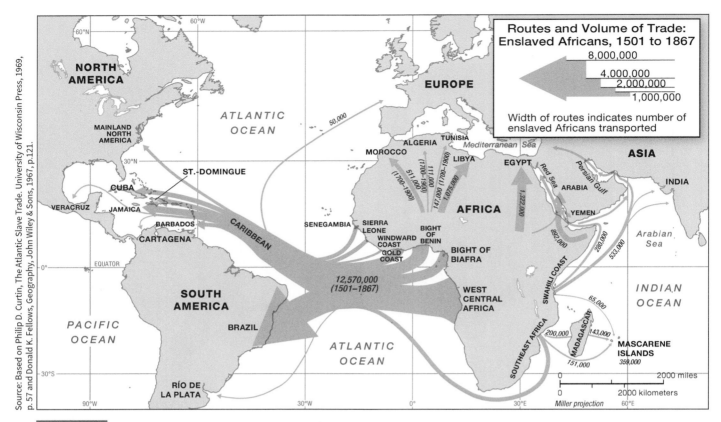

Source: Based on Philip D. Curtin, The Atlantic Slave Trade. University of Wisconsin Press, 1969, p. 57 and Donald K. Fellows, Geography, John Wiley & Sons, 1967, p.121.

FIGURE 3.14 **The Atlantic Slave Trade.** The majority of enslaved Africans who were forcibly migrated from Africa to the Americas in the 1700s went to the Caribbean, where Europeans were intensively growing sugar on plantations. For every enslaved African forcibly migrated to the United States, eight or more were brought to the Caribbean and Central and South America.

Ultimately, the decision or directive to migrate happens to an individual migrant within a household, place, country, region, and world, each of which has its own dynamics. The key difference between voluntary and forced migration, however, is that voluntary migrants have an option—at the very least, where to go or what to do once there; forced migrants do not.

Historic Forced Migration

The history of global migration is filled with stories of people choosing to leave home for the hope of a better life somewhere else. Stories like these are told of voluntary migration. In forced migration, people have no choice. Forced migrants do not weigh push and pull factors. They do not have a say in whether they leave or where they go. Forced migration changes both the place the migrants leave and their destination. The absence of the migrants is felt in the home country, and their presence becomes part of the fabric of the place where they land.

The Atlantic Slave Trade
The Atlantic slave trade from 1503 to 1867 was a devastating period of forced migration. During this period, Europeans enslaved and forcibly migrated approximately 12 million Africans across the Atlantic to South America, the Caribbean, and North America.[1] The slave trade

created an African **diaspora**, or dispersal, of Africans through forced migration. **Figure 3.14** maps the destination countries of enslaved Africans who survived the Middle Passage, the treacherous voyage across the Atlantic in slave ships, during which an estimated 20 percent (more than 2 million people) died on board.

Slavery plays such a central role in U.S. history that many American students assume that most enslaved Africans were taken to the southeastern United States. However, as **Figure 3.14** shows, most enslaved Africans were forced across the Atlantic to the Caribbean and Brazil. Descendants of enslaved Africans constitute the majority population of several Caribbean countries today, including more than 90 percent of the population in Saint Kitts and Nevis, Haiti, Jamaica, the Bahamas, Barbados, Turks and Caicos, and Antigua and Barbuda.

Money was the motivation for the Atlantic slave trade. Before the trade evolved, Europeans bought sugar produced in North Africa on the Mediterranean Sea. But after Europeans experimented with plantation agriculture in the Caribbean, they realized they could outcompete Mediterranean sugar by producing as much sugar more cheaply using slave labor on plantations.

[1]Europeans also operated a slave trade on the east coast of Africa, where they enslaved and forcibly migrated between 9.4 and 14 million Africans to the region in and around the Arabian Peninsula.

The profits from sugar production in the Caribbean and Brazil were astronomical. Brazil was the first sugar colony in the region. By 1600, the annual profit from sugar production in Brazil was 2 million pounds sterling (Blaut, 1989). In 1627, Great Britain established its first sugar colony in Barbados with the help of Dutch sugar producers from Brazil (**Fig. 3.15**). British plantation owners deforested the entire island of Barbados to plant sugarcane. Between 1627 and 1807, 387,000 enslaved Africans were taken to Barbados alone, primarily to labor in sugar production.

Sugarcane production diffused from Barbados to the neighboring island Antigua in 1674. British plantation owners drove out indigenous farmers who were also susceptible to European diseases. British brought enslaved Africans to their colony to labor on sugarcane plantations and in sugarcane processing. Sugarcane processing was grueling. Antigua had 150 windmills in the middle of the 18th century. Each powered a mill. Enslaved Africans cut sugarcane and fed it into the mill, where they ran the canes back and forth in rollers to be crushed. Juice flowed into pipes that ran to a boiler tank, where it was heated and stirred. The work was dangerous and time was tight, because the sugarcane had to be processed before it went bad. Colonizers forced enslaved Africans to work in 12-hour shifts, 24 hours a day during processing.

The growing demand for sugar, which was used both as a sweetener and to distill rum, drove the slave trade. As sugar production in the Caribbean rose, so too did the number of Africans who were enslaved and taken to the Americas. Spain, Denmark, France, and the Netherlands colonized islands in the Caribbean, established sugar plantations, and purchased enslaved Africans to labor on the sugarcane fields.

Slavery also extended beyond sugar plantations in the Caribbean. The Portuguese used enslaved Africans for labor on coffee and banana plantations in Brazil, and the British used enslaved Africans for labor on cotton and tobacco plantations in what became the United States.

The Atlantic slave trade seriously impacted both Africa and the Americas. Enslaved Africans used their indigenous knowledge of agriculture to successfully cultivate crops in the Americas, including rice production in the Yazoo River delta in the American South. Slave labor brought millions of pounds of gold and wealth into Europe in the seventeenth and eighteenth centuries, and this wealth helped Europe start the Industrial Revolution. While Europe accumulated wealth, Africa lost millions of people and pounds of gold. African civilizations also lost the contributions enslaved Africans would have made to societies and economies at home. Thus slavery established an unequal power relationship between Africa and Europe that continued into the nineteenth and twentieth centuries, when Europe colonized Africa. Slavery also made racism an entrenched part of the unequal power relationships in the Americas and Europe.

The Forced Removal of American Indians   The Trail of Tears is the most well-known forcible migration of Native Americans from their lands. Between 1838 and 1839, the U.S. government marched Cherokees from the American South to Indian Territory (what became Oklahoma). Tens of thousands of Cherokees died in the forced removal from their lands. But the Trail of Tears is not the only case of the U.S. government removing Native Americans. From 1864 to 1866, the U.S. government removed Navajos from their homeland in a series of 53 forced marches called the Long Walk of the Navajo. The marches took Navajos from their homeland in what is now eastern Arizona across present-day New Mexico and held approximately 10,000 Navajos captive in an internment camp for four years. Navajos demanded to be returned to their homeland, and eventually the U.S. government entered a treaty to establish the Navajo reservation in 1868.

Beginning in the 1870s, the U.S. government also forcibly removed Native American children from their homes as part of the country's **assimilation** policy. Richard Pratt founded the first Native boarding school and operated under the philosophy "Kill the Indian in him and save the man." Government school employees were emboldened to bathe

William Clark/British Library

FIGURE 3.15 **Antigua.**   Enslaved Africans cut sugarcane along the coast of Antigua while a British colonialist sits on horseback. This is one of 10 images showing the steps in sugarcane production, painted by British artist William Clark in Antigua in 1823. The artists painted the images to show productivity and positive working conditions for enslaved Africans. The reality for enslaved Africans was much more negative than this image displays. See: https://runaways.gla.ac.uk/minecraft/index.php/slaves-work-on-sugar-plantations/ for discussion.

Native children in kerosene to try to lighten their skin color, to forcibly cut their hair, to change their names, and to punish them for speaking their language. Schools were rife with abuse. Teachers and staff physically, mentally, and sexually intimidated, threatened, and abused American Indian children. Being taken from home, abused in schools, and "civilized" into behaving "like the white man" left generations of trauma in Native American tribes. The U.S. government maintained the practice of removing Native children from their homes and placing them in boarding schools until Congress passed the Indian Child Welfare Act in 1978.

Modern Slavery and Human Trafficking

Sex trafficking of children and adults, forced labor, bonded or debt bondage labor, involuntary domestic servitude, forced child labor, and the recruitment of child soldiers all fall under the broad umbrella of modern slavery. The International Labour Organization (ILO) describes *modern slavery* as an umbrella term that essentially "refers to situations of exploitation that a person cannot refuse or leave because of threats, violence, coercion, deception, and/or abuse of power." Modern forms of slavery affect 40.3 million people worldwide, with 24.9 million people in forced labor in private sectors, 4.8 million in forced sexual exploitation, and another 4 million in forced labor under governments such as China and North Korea, according to the ILO. Each form of modern slavery often involves **human trafficking**, the recruitment of people by force, coercion, deception, or abduction with the aim of controlling and exploiting the person for labor or sexual exploitation.

Forced Labor in Private Industry
Forced labor is common in the hotel industry in the United States and Europe. Recruiters charge would-be migrants fees that average $6150 to get a legal, temporary visa to work in a hotel in the United States. This H-2B visa is tied to a specific employer. The migrant with the H-2B visa is in debt to the recruiter already and, once in the United States, is at the mercy of the hotel owner listed on the visa. This level of control makes it easy to exploit and abuse migrant workers. Hotel owners can pay low wages, ignore safety protocols, and require extra hours of work, even push workers into sexual exploitation. Migrants have no agency that can change their situation when their visa is tied to a specific job, the hotel owner controls their papers, and they are in debt to a recruiter.

Hotel worker exploitation is not only an urban issue. In 2008, the owners of a Comfort Inn Suites on the east-west interstate in South Dakota were convicted of peonage, or "involuntary servitude imposed to extract repayment of an indebtedness." The court found that the husband and wife owners enslaved four Philippine workers to clean and work at their hotel, controlling "every aspect of the victims' lives, including what they ate, where they lived, and the hours they worked." The owners forced the migrants to work up to 18 hours a day at their hotel and at fast-food restaurants. They issued the migrants paychecks, made them endorse the paychecks, and then cashed them and kept the funds for themselves.

Forced Labor by Government
Governments, including North Korea and China, sponsor forced labor within their countries and across borders. A government may intend to control a segment of the population, such as with China's forced labor of Muslims in the southwest, or may intend to provide labor in a country under a dictator, such as forced labor in North Korean gulags. A cash-strapped country like North Korea may export its citizens as forced labor and take a cut of their checks to bring cash into its economy.

The North Korean government sponsors forced labor of its citizens, both inside the country in gulags and in 20 countries outside of North Korea. Kim Jong-Un, dictator of the most repressive country in the world, denies that his North Korean government sponsors state-forced labor in gulags. But satellite images and defector accounts confirm that the North Korean government sponsors forced labor in four huge **gulags**, or prison labor camps, where up to 130,000 North Koreans suffer. North Koreans are sentenced to gulags for speaking out against the government or having a family member speak against the government. The International Bar Association reported in 2017 that citizens are sentenced either to "total control zones" in gulags, where they are to labor until they die, or to "revolutionizing zones" in gulags, where they are reeducated to support the government and have a chance of being released. The report states, "In actuality, many prisoners in revolutionizing zones perish as a result of overwork, starvation, torture, or disease. Some are simply executed outright" (2017).

In a globalized world, any policy can have unintended consequences, as change in one place causes change in another. The North Korean government has sponsored forced labor of its own citizens abroad since the inception of the country, and one unintended consequence of United Nations and U.S. sanctions against the North Korean government has been an increased number of North Koreans in forced labor abroad. In October 2006, the United Nations passed sanctions on North Korea in response to its first nuclear test, and it has continually increased sanctions for this reason.[2] Without income from selling its goods abroad, North Korea has used forced labor to generate cash.

In 2017, analysts estimated that the North Korean government had at least 60,000 forced laborers working in 20 different countries. The laborers generated between $200 million and $2 billion a year for the government of North Korea. North Koreans labor in the oil and gas fields of Russia, work in the estimated 1200 Korean restaurants the North Korean government owns abroad, and build soccer stadiums in Qatar to prepare for the 2020 World Cup. Recent sanctions sought to crack down on the overseas forced labor market, but what effect they will have on the North Korean government remains to be seen. The situation of North Korean laborers at home and abroad remains dire.

AP® Exam Taker's Tip

Forced migrations include slavery and events that produce **refugees**, **internally displaced persons**, and **asylum seekers**.

---

[2] For a timeline, see Albert 2018: https://www.cfr.org/backgrounder/what-know-about-sanctions-north-korea.

Human Trafficking for Sexual Exploitation

Human trafficking for sexual exploitation of women and girls accounts for at least 95 percent of victims of human trafficking for sexual exploitation globally. The lack of power, agency, or value of women and girls in many countries makes them susceptible to abuse and violence. Accurate numbers of victims of human trafficking for sexual exploitation are difficult to verify, but reports of registered victims, those counted by governments through criminal cases or through self-report, are widespread. One report of registered victims in the European Union found that 67 percent of all human trafficking in the EU is for sexual exploitation, and women and girls constituted 95 percent of victims.

Women and children are forced into sexual trafficking through coercion and manipulation. As in forced labor, debt bondage is common in human trafficking for sexual exploitation. Traffickers take women and girls to another country with the promise of jobs, marriage, or citizenship. Once in the new country, females are in debt to traffickers and forced into sexual exploitation to repay the debt. The exploitative relationship has similarities to domestic abuse in that the victims of sexual exploitation may feel either indebted to or afraid of the trafficker or pimp, depending on how they are manipulated. Traffickers may take control of victims' identity papers, making escape nearly impossible.

In 2018, seven members of a sex trafficking gang in the United Kingdom (UK) were sentenced to jail for trafficking at least 13 Romanian women by manipulating the victims to believe they were in a relationship with them or that they had legitimate jobs secured for them in the UK. The perpetrators advertised the victims as "fresh stock" on porn websites and forced the women into prostitution in brothels. A police sergeant from Lancashire explained that the women were treated as commodities and were moved around to different brothel owners. One of the women, who was lured to the UK because she thought she was in a relationship with one of the gang members, kept a diary during her captivity. She wrote, "I thought that the sun will eventually shine in my life but I was wrong and the mist doesn't seem to want to go away. I feel sad and tired, ill and fragile. It's like I'm suffocating" (BBC, 2018).

> **TC Thinking Geographically**
>
> **Migration** impacts both the people who migrate and the places they go. Because it is illegal, sex trafficking is hidden from view. Reading the quote from a victim at the end of the last paragraph in this section, consider how the **identities** of trafficked women and children are impacted through trafficking.

3.3 Explain the Theories of Migration and Understand the Motivations for Migration.

Why do people choose to migrate? Researchers have been intrigued by this question for more than a century. Studies of voluntary migration flows indicate that the intensity of a migration flow varies based on similarities between the source and the destination, the effectiveness of the flow of information from the destination back to the source, and the physical distance between the source and the destination.

Laws of Migration and the Gravity Model

Over a century ago, British demographer Ernst Ravenstein sought an answer to the question of why people voluntarily migrate. He studied data on internal migration in England and proposed several laws of migration, many of which are still relevant today, including:

1. Every migration flow generates a return or countermigration.
2. Most migrants move a short distance.
3. Migrants who move longer distances tend to choose big-city destinations.
4. Urban residents are less migratory than people in rural areas.
5. Families are less likely to make international moves than young adults.

Ravenstein also believed that the volume of a migration flow was a function of **distance decay**, the idea that the likelihood of a trait or innovation diffusing decreases the farther away in time or distance it moves from its origin (hearth). (**Fig. 3.16**). That is, the number of migrants who go to a destination declines as the distance they must travel increases. Another way of saying it is that more migrants travel short distances and fewer migrants travel longer distances.

Ravenstein's law on volume is an early observation of the **gravity model**, a mathematical prediction of the degree of interaction and probability of migration (and other flows) between two places is based on population size and the distance between them. The gravity model assumes that spatial interaction (such as migration) increases as the size and importance of places become greater and decreases as the distance between them grows. The balance between population size and distance predicts the likelihood of migration. In mathematical terms, the gravity model holds that migration potential can be calculated by multiplying the size of the populations of two places and then dividing the product by the distance between them. That calculation had more meaning in an age before airplane travel and the Internet, when physical distance meant something different from what it means today. But even now more migrants move shorter rather than longer distances, suggesting that the model still has some relevance.

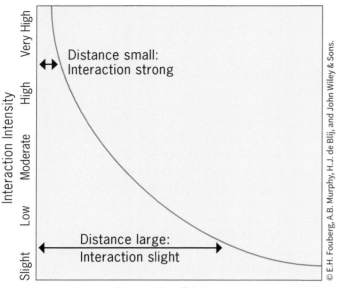

© E.H. Fouberg, A.B. Murphy, H.J. de Blij, and John Wiley & Sons.

FIGURE 3.16 **Distance Decay.** The farther from the hearth in time and distance, the less likely a trait or innovation will diffuse. In migration, distance decay means that more migrants will move short distances and fewer migrants will move long distances.

Push and Pull Factors

Although the gravity model gives us a guide to expected migration, migration is not as simple as a mathematical equation. **Push factors** are the conditions and perceptions that help a migrant decide to leave a place. **Pull factors** are what attracts a migrant to a certain destination, the factors that help the migrant decide where to go. A migrant's decision to emigrate from the home country and immigrate to a new country results from a combination of push and pull factors.

Push factors include work or retirement conditions, cost of living, personal safety and security, environmental catastrophes and hazards, or even issues such as weather and climate. Pull factors tend to be more vague and may depend solely on perceptions gathered from things heard and read rather than on experiences in the destination place. Migrants may have unrealistically positive images and expectations regarding their destinations, which create a large pull force and motivation for migration.

Since interaction with faraway places generally decreases as distance increases, prospective migrants are likely to feel much less certain about distant destinations than about nearer ones. This prompts many migrants to move to a place closer to home than they originally planned when an **intervening opportunity** arises: an opportunity near a migrant's current location that greatly diminishes the attractiveness of migrating to a site farther away. According to Ravenstein's laws of migration, a migrant from a family in rural Brazil is likely to move first to a village, then to a nearby town, later to a city, and finally to a metropolis such as São Paulo or Rio de Janeiro. At each stage a new set of pull factors comes into play. The migrant may decide that the prospects at one of the steps in the process create an intervening opportunity

that provides a greater reason to stay than an uncertain pull to the intended destination.

Types of Push and Pull Factors   Any single factor can be either a push for migrants to leave their home countries or a pull to destination countries. Migrants weigh their decisions of whether to leave and where to go based on experiences at home and perceptions of their intended destination.

Legal Status   Migrants can arrive in a country with or without the legal approval of the host country. Every country decides who can legally enter and under what circumstances. If you apply for and receive a work visa from another country, you are legally allowed to live in the country and work there for the time on the visa, usually a period of months or years. Having a visa makes you an authorized or documented migrant, because you have the formal right to be in the country. If you do not have a visa, you are an **unauthorized** or undocumented migrant in the country. Unauthorized migrants can be those who enter a country legally, as authorized migrants with a visa, and then stay when the visa expires. They can also enter a country without permission by crossing a border without legal approval.

Immigration contributes to population growth in the United States. Foreign-born nationals contribute to the positive net migration in the United States and supplement the U.S. total fertility rate (TFR) of 1.8 (see Chapter 2) to help the country's population continue to grow; they also provide a labor supply and tax base. **Figure 3.17** shows the proportion of population who were foreign born from 1990 to 2017 by county.

Of the estimated 43.7 million migrants in the United States today, 10.7 million are unauthorized, which is the lowest amount since the prerecession spike of 12.2 million. Among all migrants in the United States, authorized and unauthorized, migrants from Mexico are 26 percent, and migrants from South Asia and East Asia are 27 percent. Two-thirds of the unauthorized adult migrants (7 million) have lived in the United States for more than 10 years.

The United States recognizes where migrant labor is needed in the economy and has policies allowing, indeed encouraging, legal, authorized migrants to work under temporary visas to fill various needs, whether as medical doctors, computer engineers, construction workers, or hotel cleaners and restaurant waitstaff (**Fig. 3.18**). Authorized migrants working in the United States and Canada also have temporary visas to fill seasonal jobs in agriculture and forestry. In the United States, over 45,000 agricultural workers enter the country with documents that allow unskilled laborers in economic sectors with domestic labor shortages. Canada has recruited temporary agricultural workers under a similar

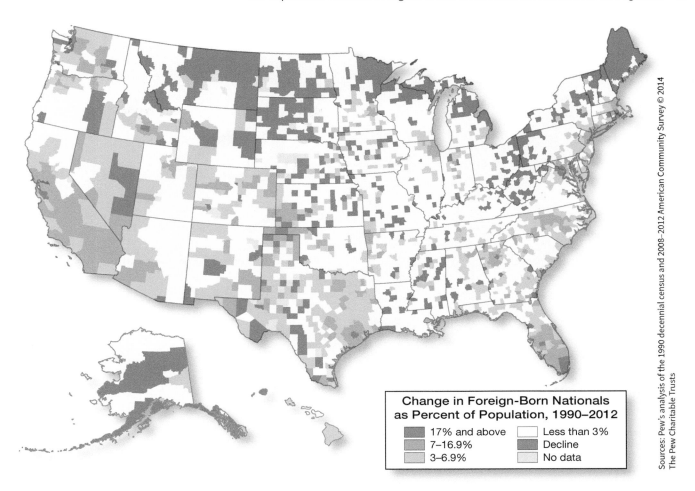

Sources: Pew's analysis of the 1990 decennial census and 2008–2012 American Community Survey © 2014 The Pew Charitable Trusts

FIGURE 3.17 **Change in Foreign-Born Nationals as Percent of Population 1990–2012.** Data from the U.S. Census shows the percent of people by county who were born in another country (foreign-born is the term the Census uses). A cluster of counties in the north, from Idaho east to Maine, have seen declines in the proportion of the population that was born in another country. Counties along the coasts have seen the greatest increase in the proportion of the population who are foreign-born.

program since 1966. In both the United States and Canada, agricultural workers come mainly from Mexico and Central America.

The United States has earmarked significant sums for building fences along its border with Mexico, hiring additional border patrol agents and installing new technology to intercept unauthorized migrants. As a result, the cultural landscape of the border region is changing. The government is erecting specially designed fences that are difficult to climb, though there are openings in the fences where people across the border can speak with one another. The new fences and security south of San Diego, California, are pushing those seeking to cross the border without documentation farther east into the desert. Unauthorized migrants also employ **coyotes**, who smuggle people across the border for a sizable fee. Fences there are marked by empty water bottles and memorials to Mexicans who have died trying to cross the border (**Fig. 3.19**).

Even though globalization has promoted a freer flow of goods across the world, the free flow of people is far from realized. The flow of unauthorized migrants has slowed in recent years, but that may well have more to do with

changing economic circumstances than with walls and fences. Unauthorized immigrants go to great lengths to find their way into the United States; similarly, the U.S. government goes to great lengths to deter an influx of unauthorized migrants.

Gender, Ethnicity, and Race Opportunities for jobs and personal safety in a destination country depend on gender, ethnicity, and race. Hiring for positions based on gender, race, or ethnicity makes power relationships visible and reinforces stereotypes or the roles that members of each group are expected to play.

Women with high economic status often hire female domestic helpers from a different ethnic group to differentiate themselves from those who work for them. A woman's ethnicity thus becomes a visible signal of who is in power in the home and region. In their study of placement agencies that help people hire domestic workers, Stiell and England found that placement agencies in Toronto, Canada, used scripted stereotypes to describe women of different ethnicities. For instance, agencies at first described migrant workers from the Caribbean as "docile,

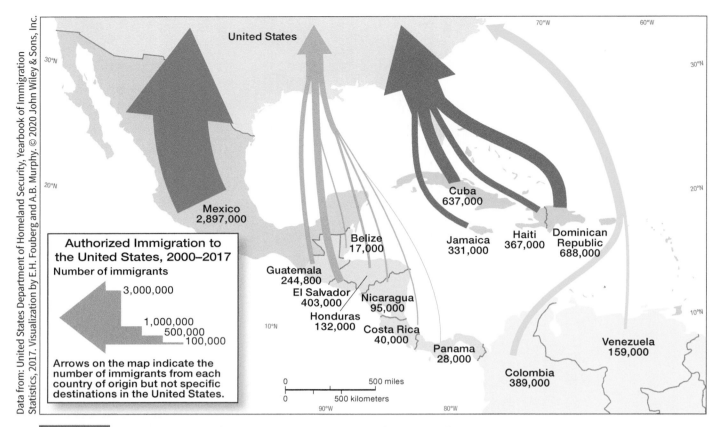

Data from: United States Department of Homeland Security, Yearbook of Immigration Statistics, 2017. Visualization by E.H. Fouberg and A.B. Murphy. © 2020 John Wiley & Sons, Inc.

FIGURE 3.18 **Authorized Immigration from Central and South America to the United States.**
This map shows the total number of authorized immigrants to the United States from Mexico and countries in Central and South America and the Caribbean between 2000 and 2017. Arrows show the number of migrants from each country but not their specific destinations.

FIGURE 3.19 **Tijuana, Mexico** Tijuana and San Diego, California, are separated by a highly guarded border infrastructure that in this section includes two walls to discourage crossing by those who do not have visas. Human rights activists placed crosses on the wall to memorialize people who died while attempting to cross into the United States.

jolly and good with children," and later depicted the same group as "difficult, aggressive and selfish." Placement agencies portrayed women from the Philippines as "naturally docile, subservient, hardworking, good natured, domesticated, and willing to endure long hours of housework and child-care with little complaint."

Environmental Conditions Environmental crises also stimulate migrations, including earthquakes, hurricanes, volcanic eruptions, tsunamis, floods, fires, and climate change. Migration flows generated by environmental crises can be temporary, as many migrants return home after the crisis improves.

The devastation from Hurricane Katrina in New Orleans, Louisiana, in 2005 was amplified by human changes to the environment. Decades of government-sponsored flood-control projects and resource extraction activities have marked the landscape of the Gulf Coast. The Army Corps of Engineers and private industries, including oil companies and developers, have dramatically altered the physical environment and particularly Louisiana's coastline, destroying natural barriers provided by wetlands, increasing erosion rates, and effectively bringing the Gulf of Mexico to New Orleans's doorstep. The many ways people have changed the physical environment of New Orleans made the damage from Hurricane Katrina much worse.

More than 85 percent of the city of New Orleans flooded, and residents fled to family or larger cities where work and shelter could be secured. Between the 2000 and 2010 censuses, the population of New Orleans fell by 11 percent as a result of the devastation of Hurricane Katrina in 2005 and the economic recession in 2008 (**Fig. 3.20**). The proportion of children in New Orleans's population also fell, from 27 percent in 2000 to 23 percent in 2007. Mapping of where children live in New Orleans reflects another trend in post-Katrina New Orleans: Families with children in the New Orleans region moved out of the city center and close-in suburbs and into the farther-out suburbs.

Increasingly erratic weather events spurred by climate change are projected to contribute to future migration flows as people use migration as an adaptive response to climate change. So-called climate refugees from low-lying areas seek refuge elsewhere (**Fig. 3.21**). One report suggests that the world will see 150 to 300 million climate refugees from 40 countries by 2050. Countries in the Pacific, from small (Tuvalu with 12,000 people) to large (Australia with 24.1 million people), are already experiencing shortages of freshwater, a rise in wildfires in drought-ridden areas, and increasingly intensive storms. Tuvalu is a small group of atoll islands barely 2 meters (6.5 ft) above sea level. Climate change, which starts with carbon dioxide produced by industry and cars in high income countries half a world away, is already impacting Tuvalu. Tuvaluans have developed environmental adaptation strategies to sustain the islands and the people. Migrating is one strategy Tuvaluans use in response to climate change.

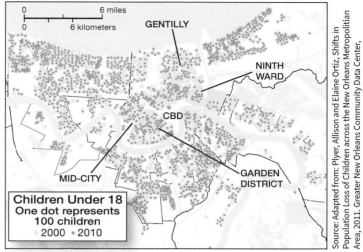

FIGURE 3.20 **Population Density of Children Under Age 18 in New Orleans, 2000 and 2010.**   Families with children were less likely to return to New Orleans to reside after Hurricane Katrina. The CBD is the central business district, where few homes are located. A dramatic drop in the number of young people in the city, especially in Mid-City, Gentilly, the Garden District, and the Ninth Ward, has led to the need for fewer schools and has changed the feeling of neighborhoods.

Political Conflict   Political conflict and war can generate major refugee flows (see section "Distribution of Refugees"). Changing or establishing political borders also generates migration flows. People may fear that their culture and traditions will not survive a major political change, and they may migrate to a nearby place where more people are like them and they can be safe.

Guest Field Note   Interviewing Locals about Climate Change in Funafuti, Tuvalu

Carol Farbotko
Commonwealth Scientific and Industrial Research Organisation, Australia

Tuvalu is an independent country of 12,000 people in the central Pacific. Comprised of low-lying islands, its land territory in its entirety is at risk from rising sea levels associated with climate change. My work in Tuvalu involved interviewing Tuvaluan people about climate change and the concept of climate refugees. I also observed the activities of journalists and environmentalists who came to the islands from around the world during seasonal king tide flooding to witness climate change impacts.

While Tuvaluan people have serious concerns about climate, they reject the label 'climate refugee' because it positions them as passive victims and does not address the responsibility of industrialised countries to reduce greenhouse gas emissions. Tuvaluans see international migration as a solution of last resort to climate change. However, international media and environmental organisations are prematurely depicting Tuvalu as a place in environmental crisis, often suggesting migration as refugees is the only option for Tuvaluans. These representations marginalize authentic Tuvaluan voices and yet ventriloquise them for environmental purposes: to present international climate change migration as a problem and to convince climate skeptics in business and politics that climate change is occurring.

FIGURE 3.21 **Funafuti, Tuvalu.**

AP Images

FIGURE 3.22 **Punjab, India.** More than 14 million migrants moved across the newly defined border when Britain partitioned South Asia into India and Pakistan in 1947. This image shows hundreds of people carrying their belongings on any space they could find on a train. Muslims who lived in the newly defined state of India fled to Pakistan and Hindus who lived in the newly defined state of Pakistan fled to India. The British border split Punjab, homeland of Sikhs, between India and Pakistan.

The British government colonized South Asia, what is now Pakistan, India, and Bangladesh, from 1857 to 1947. When the British left in 1947, they partitioned the colony into two countries: a Hindu-majority India and a Muslim-majority Pakistan. They carved out borders for a divided Pakistan with two parts to the country: a western section (present-day Pakistan) separated by 800 miles from the eastern section (present-day Bangladesh). The British drew the borders of the new countries in secrecy and then held ceremonies to convey independence to Pakistan on August 14, 1947, and then to India on August 15, 1947. After formally granting each country independence, the British revealed the new borders and corresponding maps. Fear and uncertainty prevailed, and on August 17, a mass migration of 14 million began (**Fig. 3.22**). Seven million Muslims living on the newly named Indian side of the border migrated to the new majority-Muslim state of Pakistan. An additional 7 million Hindus and Sikhs living on the newly named Pakistan side of the border migrated to the majority-Hindu state of India. In the chaotic migration, 1 million people died. Partition and the mass migration that followed are a traumatic memory for generations of South Asians and began the split between India and Pakistan that festers today.

Family Links and Chain Migration When deciding where to go, migrants are pulled to places where family and friends have already found success. When a migrant chooses a destination and texts, calls, or communicates through others to tell family and friends at home about the new place, the migrant helps create a positive perception of the destination for family and friends and may promise help by providing housing and assistance obtaining a job. Geographers call these flows along and through kinship links **chain migration**. When a migrant reassures family and friends that a new community has been formed, a place where they can feel at home, further migration often occurs along the same path, creating a chain. Chains of migration build upon each other to create immigration waves connecting the home country to the destination.

TC **Thinking Geographically**

Think about a **migration** flow within your family, whether internal, international, voluntary, or forced. The flow can be one you experienced or one you only heard about through family. List the push and pull factors. Then, hypothesize how the migration flow of your family was tied to larger migration flows at the time. Does your family's migration flow fit into the global map in Figure 3.6? Was your family's migration at a different **scale** - nationally or locally? Determine both the scale of your family's migration flow and identity how the scale of the flow impacted your family - did they find others like themselves at their destination? How would finding or not finding others like themselves impact the **identities** of your family members who migrated?

3.4 Identify Why Refugees Are a Distinct Group of Migrants and Describe Where Most Refugees Migrate.

Refugees are migrants who are fleeing political persecution and violence in their home country. They travel by foot or boat with few possessions. Most refugees walk to a neighboring country, seeking protection from the violence in their home country.

The 1951 Refugee Convention established an international law specifying who is a refugee and what legal rights refugees have. The main goal of the convention was to help European refugees following the end of World War II. The office of the United Nations High Commissioner for Refugees (UNHCR) helped to repatriate (return home) most of the refugees in Europe after World War II. The 1951 Refugee Convention defines a refugee as "a person who has a well-founded fear of being persecuted for reasons of race, religion, nationality, membership of a particular social group, or political opinion."

The UNHCR, the International Red Cross, and the World Food Program work with several other organizations and governments, especially in destination countries, to protect the safety of refugees and provide relief. The UNHCR organizes and funds international relief efforts and negotiates with governments and political groups on behalf of refugees.

Refugees have legal status under international law, which protects refugees because their governments are threatening their basic human rights. The United Nations Declaration of Human Rights guarantees the right to *asylum* for refugees, which means that refugees have the right to be protected and the right to temporarily stay in a country other than their home country. The UNHCR, the International Red Cross, and the World Food Program provide shelter and food, typically in refugee camps, for refugees in the countries where they have asylum. In camps across the world, millions of refugees simply want to go home, to repatriate. But instability in some regions and countries has led to generations of families living their lives in refugee camps.

The United Nations helps ensure that refugees are not forcibly returned to their home country when persecution is ongoing. Once violence and persecution decrease and the conditions of the home country improve, the UNHCR helps return refugees to their homelands, a process called **repatriation**.

Sometimes countries other than the country of asylum can choose to welcome refugees for permanent resettlement. For example, the United States welcomed 160,000 Karen refugees from Burma (Myanmar) who lived in refugee camps in Thailand between 2007 and 2017. When the United States accepts a certain number of Karen refugees, it is agreeing that each one has the legal right to live and work in the United States. Each refugee is vetted and receives help from a nongovernmental organization to find housing and acclimate to the United States.

Asylum seekers are people who have left their home country where they are experiencing persecution and human rights violations and are seeking protection in another country, but have not been legally recognized as refugees. They arrive at a port or land border in the country where they want asylum, and then make a claim for asylum upon arrival. Countries typically keep asylum seekers in a holding facility until their asylum claim can be decided upon. When they meet with a judge or government official, asylum seekers need to explain the persecution they experienced in their home country and provide evidence supporting their claims. It takes time for asylum cases to be heard, and in the meantime, some asylum seekers are held in detention centers and others live in temporary housing. The government can choose whether to grant them asylum, which would give the asylum seekers refugee status. If asylum is denied, countries can send asylum seekers back to their home countries.

> **AP® Exam Taker's Tip**
>
> How is a **refugee** different from a **migrant**? Are refugees entitled to **asylum**?

Distribution of Refugees

Most refugees move by foot, without any more goods than they can carry. The UNHCR estimates that 83 percent of refugees flee to a country in the same region as their home country. The countries that generate the most refugees and the countries that receive the most refugees are near each other. In 2018, ongoing wars in Syria (6.3 million), Afghanistan (2.6 million), and South Sudan (2.4 million) produced the most refugees. The three countries that received the most refugees, Turkey (3.5 million), Pakistan (1.4 million), and Uganda (1.4 million), are next door to Syria, Afghanistan, and Sudan, respectively.

Most refugees make their first "step" on foot or by bicycle, wagon, open boat, or crowded caravan (**Fig. 3.23**). Refugees are

Xinhua/Alamy Stock Photo

FIGURE 3.23 Zaatari, Jordan. Syrian refugees walk to the Zaatari refugee camp on the Jordanian side of the border in 2016. The Syrian civil war started in 2011, and refugees continue to leave the country as conflict continues. Most refugees worldwide flee by foot to the closest safe country. The women and men in this photo are carrying their belongings across the border in hopes of finding safety in Jordan.

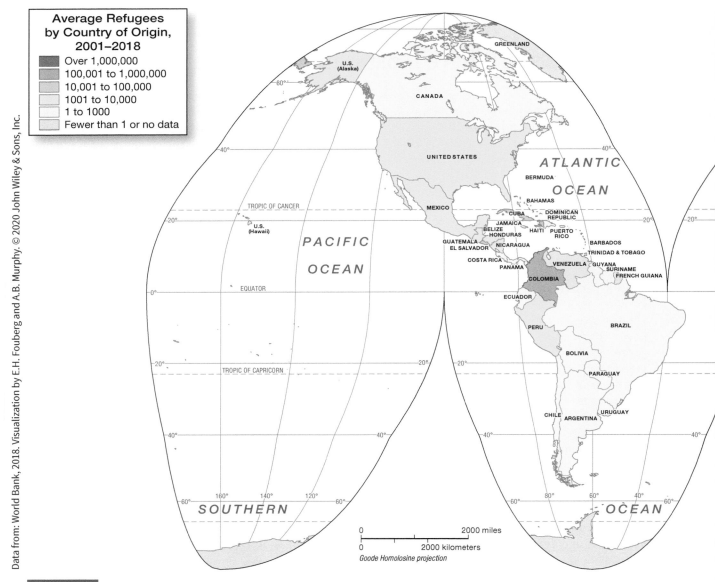

Data from: World Bank, 2018. Visualization by E.H. Fouberg and A.B. Murphy. © 2020 John Wiley & Sons, Inc.

FIGURE 3.24 **Average Number of Refugees by Country of Origin, 2001–2018.**   This map highlights the home countries of the world's refugees. Refugees are defined as migrants fleeing political persecution or who have a well-founded fear of political persecution. That is why areas with major political conflict, including Syria and Afghanistan, stand out on the map.

suddenly displaced and have limited options, and most have few resources to invest in their journey. As a result, the vast majority of the world's refugees come from relatively low income countries and travel to neighboring countries that are also lower income. The impact of refugee flows is certainly felt most in the lowest income countries of the world.

In 1970, the United Nations reported 2.9 million refugees worldwide; the majority were Palestinian Arabs dislocated by the creation of the state of Israel and the armed conflicts that followed. In 1980, the global refugee total had nearly tripled, to over 8 million. By 2018, the UNHCR reported 25.4 million refugees worldwide, with 5.4 million being Palestinian Arab refugees who have lived in camps since UNHCR first collected statistics in 1970 (**Fig. 3.24**).

> **AP® Exam Taker's Tip**
>
> Use Figure 3.24 to explain why countries such as Colombia, Iraq, Afghanistan, Sudan, Myanmar, and others have so many refugees leaving their countries of origin.

The United Nations and international law distinguish between refugees, who have crossed one or more international borders during their move and encamped in a country other than their own, and **internally displaced persons (IDPs)**, people who must leave their homes but remain in their own countries. Under the 1951 Refugee Convention, IDPs are not refugees. Their lives

can be even more unstable than life for refugees because IDPs stay in the country where a crisis, whether political violence, flooding, or famine, is taking place. IDPs are often uncounted because they do not cross international borders. In 2018, UNHCR estimated that 40 million people were IDPs who were remaining in their home countries but not in their homes. With 40 million IDPs, 25.4 million refugees, and 3.1 million asylum seekers, 8.6 percent of the world's population is displaced.

Areas of Dislocation

North Africa and Southwest Asia and sub-Saharan Africa continue to generate more than half of all refugees worldwide. Most refugees under UNHCR's responsibility today, some 60 percent, fled conflicts in Afghanistan, Syria, Sudan, South Sudan, Somalia, and the Democratic Republic of the Congo.

Syria Since the outbreak of the Syrian civil war in 2011, 5.6 million Syrians have fled to neighboring Turkey, Lebanon, Jordan, and Iraq, countries that already had substantial refugee populations from other regional conflicts or had their own conflicts. The UNHCR built the temporary Zaatari refugee camp in Jordan near the Syrian border. The camp, only 3 sq mile (7.8 sq km), has become a more permanent living space for over 100,000 refugees living in harsh conditions and cramped quarters. Another 50,000 to 80,000 Syrian refugees have fled across the border to the tiny town of Arsal, Lebanon (**Fig. 3.25**). The refugees now outnumber the local population in Arsal, and the "town's electrical grid, waste management system and water supply are struggling to serve a population almost three times its original size" (Gebeily and Haines-Young, 2014). An additional 6.6 million Syrians are internally displaced, meaning they still live in Syria but have had to leave their homes.

FIGURE 3.25 Arsal, Lebanon. Syrian women and children are among the 65,000 refugees in the small border town of Arsal, which became a refugee camp after the Syrian civil war broke out in 2011. The small, remote town suffered fighting and bombing when ISIS controlled it from 2014 to 2017. While ISIS has been pushed out, conditions remain unsafe.

Rwanda

During the mid-1990s, a civil war engulfed Rwanda in equatorial Africa, a conflict that pitted militant Hutu against the minority Tutsi and "moderate" Hutu. The carnage claimed an estimated 800,000 to 1 million lives and produced huge migration flows into neighboring Zaïre (now the Democratic Republic of Congo) and Tanzania. More than 2 million Rwandans fled their homeland. The Tutsi–Hutu strife in Rwanda spread to neighboring Burundi and dislocated tens of thousands. After the civil war in Rwanda calmed down in 1996, the UNHCR and the World Health Organization watched and aided 500,000 Rwandans repatriate, or return home.

Israel/Palestine

The history of one of the most contentious places in the world today is a story of migration. The land between the Jordan River and Mediterranean Sea is sacred to Jews, who lived there for centuries until persecution during the Roman Empire spurred a Jewish diaspora to Europe around 70 CE. Six hundred years later, the land became sacred to Muslims because Muhammad ascended into heaven next to the most sacred site in Judaism (see Chapter 7). After this, the local tribes and people in the region converted to Islam. From 700 to the 1900s, Muslims, Christians, and Jews lived on this small sliver of land in relative peace with the notable exception of the crusades.

In 1910, fewer than 50,000 Jewish residents lived in what is now Israel/Palestine. Then Jews, whose ancestors had fled to Europe more than a thousand years earlier, began to migrate back to the region as part of a growing Zionist movement. **Zionism** is the movement for the establishment of a national homeland for Jews in the land between the Mediterranean Sea and the Jordan River. The movement grew in the late 1800s because of increasingly common persecution, control, and fear of Jews in Europe. This persecution was the roots of the Holocaust, where Nazis who came to power in 1933 killed 6 million Jews in concentration camps.

From 1919 to 1948, the United Kingdom formally controlled Palestine as a League of Nations mandate (like a colony). The 1917 Balfour Declaration, a letter written by a British official to a prominent Jewish family, promised the establishment of a Jewish homeland in Palestine and encouraged Jewish migration. By 1948, as many as 750,000 Jews had migrated to Palestine. Britain handed over control of the simmering Palestinian mandate to the United Nations, an organization that began in 1945. The United Nations decided to partition the Palestinian mandate into two countries: Palestine and Israel.

The 1948 boundaries of Israel are shown in orange in **Figure 3.26**. Drawing these new state borders generated a migration stream in which 600,000 Palestinian Arabs fled or were pushed out of new Israeli territories. Palestinians became refugees in neighboring Jordan, Egypt, Syria, and beyond. Their plight illustrates that refugee status can extend over decades and become a way of life. In Jordan, Palestinian refugees have become so integrated into the host country's

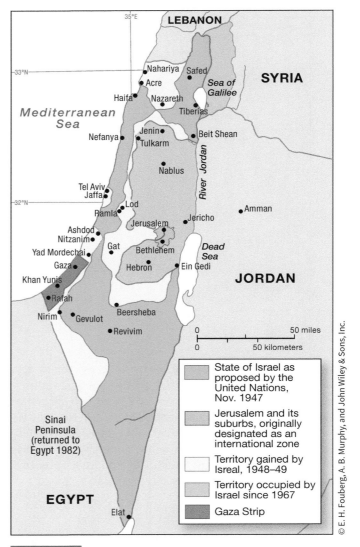

FIGURE 3.26 Changing Boundaries of Palestine and Israel. The areas in green on the map were the territory of Palestine under the 1947 United Nations plan. After partition, Palestine quickly lost the areas in light green to Israel. Israel returned the Gaza Strip to Palestine in 2005. The areas in medium green on the map are the "Occupied Territories," including the West Bank and the Golan Heights.

Author Field Note   Claiming Land through Settlements in the West Bank

"Just a few miles into the West Bank, not far from Jerusalem, the expanding Israeli presence could not be missed. New settlements dot the landscape, often occupying strategic sites that are also easily defensible. These 'facts on the ground' will certainly complicate the effort to carve out a stable territorial order in this much-contested region. That, of course, is the goal of the settlers and their supporters, but it is salt on the wound for those who contest the Israeli right to be there in the first place."

– A.B. Murphy

Photo by A.B. Murphy. © 2020 John Wiley & Sons, Inc.

FIGURE 3.27 **West Bank.**

---

national life that they are regarded as permanent refugees, but in Lebanon, Palestinians wait in refugee camps for resettlement and still qualify as temporary refugees.

After the Six-Day War in 1967, Israel expanded its territorial control (Fig. 3.26) and actively built settlements for new Jewish immigrants in Palestinian territories (**Fig. 3.27**). When the Soviet Union dissolved in 1991, 2 million Jews who had been unable to practice their religion in the Soviet Union migrated to Israel. Today Israel's population of 7.8 million, including almost 2 million Arab Israelis, continues to grow through immigration as well as relatively high birth rates.

North Africa and Southwest Asia
The region stretching from Morocco in the west to Afghanistan in the east contains some of the world's longest-lasting and most deeply entrenched conflicts that generate refugees. Conflict in Afghanistan has lasted more than 40 years, generating the largest refugee flow in the world today, with a quarter of the refugees worldwide coming from Afghanistan alone.

The Gulf War of 1991 and the Iraq War of 2003 produced millions of refugees in the region. In 1991, in the aftermath of the Gulf War that followed Iraq's invasion of Kuwait, a significant percentage of the Kurdish population of northern Iraq was threatened by the surviving military apparatus and under Baghdad's control. They abandoned their villages and towns and streamed toward and across the Turkish and Iranian borders. The refugee movement of Iraq's Kurds involved as many as 1.85 million people. It led the United States and its allies to create a secure zone for Kurds in northern Iraq in the hope of persuading displaced Kurds in Turkey and Iran to return to their country. But this effort was only partially successful, and many remain refugees in Turkey as well as Iran.

The war in Iraq in 2003 generated over 2 million refugees, most of whom are living in neighboring Syria and Jordan, and 2.8 million IDPs. Following the outbreak of civil war in Syria in 2011, hundreds of thousands of Kurds, some of whom had sought refuge in Syria only a few years earlier, were forced to flee. Some 200,000 Syrian Kurds became refugees in Iraq, where a 1971 Iraqi law gives refugees the legal right to stay and grants them protection. To make matters even more complex, there is still a sizable population of Iranian refugees in Iraq stemming from the Iran–Iraq conflict over three decades ago, including members of the exiled People's Mujahedin of Iran, or MEK, a political opposition group from Iran that was exiled in 1980.

During the 1980s, Afghanistan was caught in the Soviets' last imperialist campaign and paid an enormous price for it. The Soviet invasion of Afghanistan at the end of 1979, in support of a puppet government, as well as Afghan resistance, generated a double migration stream that carried millions westward into Iran and eastward into Pakistan. At the height of the exodus, 2.5 million Afghans were estimated to be living in camps in Iran, and some 3.7 million gathered in tent camps in Pakistan's northwestern province and in southern Baluchistan (**Fig. 3.28**). The Soviet invasion seemed destined to succeed quickly, but the Russian generals underestimated the strength of Afghan opposition. U.S. support for the Afghan rebel forces in the form of weapons supplies helped produce a stalemate and eventual Soviet withdrawal, but this was followed by a power struggle among Afghan factions. As a result, most of the more than 6 million refugees in Iran and Pakistan, about one-quarter of the country's population, stayed where they were.

In 1996, the Taliban, an Islamic fundamentalist movement that began in northwest Pakistan, emerged in Afghanistan and took control of most of the country, imposing strict Islamic rule

AP Images/BULLIT MARQUEZ

FIGURE 3.28 **Pakistan.** Refugees from Afghanistan cross the border into Pakistan in crowded caravans after the U.S. military action began in Afghanistan in 2001. Conflict in Afghanistan is ongoing, and an estimated 1.3 million Afghan refugees still live in Pakistan, according to the United Nations High Commissioner on Refugees.

and suppressing the factional conflicts that had prevailed since Soviet withdrawal in 1989. Although several hundred thousand refugees moved back to Afghanistan from Pakistan, the harsh Taliban rule created a counter-migration and led to further refugee movement into neighboring Iran, where their number reached 2.5 million. Eventually, Afghanistan became a base for anti-Western terrorist operations, which reached a climax in the attack on the United States on September 11, 2001. Even before the inevitable military retaliation began, and despite efforts by both Pakistan and Iran to close their borders, tens of thousands of Afghan refugees flooded across, intensifying a refugee crisis that is now more than a quarter-century old. Amidst the crises in Israel/Palestine, Iraq, Syria, and Afghanistan, nearly every country in Southwest Asia is currently experiencing the impact of refugees.

Sub-Saharan Africa
Despite ongoing problems with political instability in the region, the refugee situation is improved in some parts of sub-Saharan Africa. In 1997, civil wars in West Africa, particularly in Liberia and Sierra Leone, sent 1.5 million refugees streaming into Guinea and the Ivory Coast. In 2013, the number of refugees in West Africa fell to under 270,000 as a result of improved political stability and repatriation. The largest refugee flows in sub-Saharan Africa now come out of Central and East Africa, including the Democratic Republic of the Congo, Sudan, South Sudan, and Somalia.

Sudan, which began a second civil war in 1983, demonstrates the complexities of refugee crises in sub-Saharan Africa today. The conflict in Sudan was originally between the north, which is largely Arab and Muslim, and the south, which is majority black African and Christian or animist. Sudan, a country whose borders exist because of European colonialism, was home to traditional religions as well as Christianity brought by

Western missionaries in the south, and Islam brought by North African traders in the north.

During the north–south civil war, which lasted from 1983 to 2005, the government in Khartoum, located in the largely Muslim north, waged a campaign of genocide aimed at ethnic groups in the Christian and animist south. The Janjaweed militia practiced a scorched earth campaign, burning villages throughout the south, and the civil war caused immense damage. Over 2.2 million people died in the fighting or starved as a result of the war. More than 5 million people were displaced, with over 1.6 million fleeing to neighboring Uganda alone. Both sides of the Sudanese civil war interfered with the efforts of international agencies to help the refugees.

In 1999, Sudan began exporting oil, which is extracted from southern Sudan. Global attention to the humanitarian crisis of the Sudanese civil war prompted the northern government to agree to a compromise. In 2002, the north and south brokered a temporary peace deal, but shortly thereafter, violence began in the Darfur region in western Sudan. Although the entire north of Sudan is largely Muslim, only two-thirds of the northerners speak Arabic as their native language. The other one-third are Muslim, but are not ethnically Arab. The non-Arab Muslims are part of at least 30 different ethnic groups in the Darfur region of western Sudan. The Arab Muslim government (located in the north) began a campaign of genocide against the non-Arab Muslims in Darfur. The Janjaweed has waged a genocide campaign against the non-Arab, Muslim, darker-skinned Africans in Darfur—a campaign that includes killing over 400,000 people, raping women and girls, taking lands and homes from Africans, and displacing 2.5 million people (**Fig. 3.29**).

Scott Nelson/Getty Images

FIGURE 3.29 **Bredjing, Chad.** Refugees from the Darfur region of Sudan bake bread near their tent in Chad's largest refugee camp. The tents are stamped with UNHCR, which stands for the United Nations High Commissioner for Refugees. The UNCHR estimates that worldwide, 6.6 million refugees live in camps, and 4.6 million are in camps like this, which are planned and managed by the UNHCR and other non-governmental organizations. The other 2 million refugees live in camps they created themselves and receive little to no support from agencies like the UNHCR.

In 2004, U.S. Secretary of State Colin Powell labeled the Janjaweed's actions in Darfur a genocide. The 1948 Convention on Genocide defines genocide as "acts committed with intent to destroy, in whole or in part, a national, ethnical, racial, or religious group." The international community is trying to negotiate an end to the government-backed campaign in Darfur, with mixed success. In the meantime, South Sudan in 2011 voted to secede from Sudan. Ironically, the new border, which was created as a solution to a civil war and refugee crisis, has already generated new refugee flows in the region. Many people living in the borderlands between Sudan and South Sudan are unhappy with the placement of the international boundary. In 2012, the countries fought a six-month-long border war, displacing thousands, and violence in South Sudan has resumed as different groups vie for power. In a country of 12 million, recent violence has displaced 1.3 million people, with over 300,000 South Sudanese fleeing across the border. The long-lasting refugee and IDP crisis in Sudan and South Sudan helps us understand the complexity of political conflict and migration flows in sub-Saharan Africa, while the Muslim-against-Muslim conflict in Darfur demonstrates that political conflict is not just religious; it is also ethnic and political.

Neighboring countries have not helped create stability in the region. Since 1998, just under 6 million people have died in violence in the neighboring Democratic Republic of the Congo, where violence was partially spurred by the instability created as a result of refugee flows from the 1994 war in neighboring Rwanda. In 2009, attacks by the rebel group Lord's Resistance Army in the northeastern portion of the Democratic Republic of the Congo generated over 1 million refugees.

South Asia
In terms of refugee numbers, South Asia is the third-ranking geographic realm, mainly because of Pakistan's role in accommodating Afghanistan's refugees. During the Soviet intrusion in the 1980s, the UNHCR counted more than 3 million refugees; during the 1990s, the total averaged between 1.2 and 1.5 million. That number rose when U.S.-led forces began retaliating against terrorist bases in October 2001. Today, Afghanistan has an enormous refugee crisis, with more than 2 million refugees living outside of Afghanistan, mostly in Pakistan and Iran.

The other major refugee problem in South Asia stems from a civil war in Sri Lanka. This conflict, which formally ended in 2009, arose from demands by minority Tamils for an independent state on the Sinhalese-dominated and -controlled island. The conflict cost tens of thousands of lives and severely damaged the economy. The United Nations reports that about 200,000 people are internally displaced. The United Nations, the European Union, and the Canadian government are working to repatriate the IDPs, particularly in the northern provinces of Sri Lanka, but an estimated 90,000 internally displaced persons are uprooted in Sri Lanka today.

Climate change will likely have a significant impact on the refugee picture in South Asia in the decades to come. While the effects of climate change will be felt worldwide, scientists believe that Bangladesh will be "ground zero" for climate refugees. The country's 156.6 million citizens live in a river delta one-fifth the size of France, most of which is no more than 6.1 meters (20 ft) above sea level and through which 230 major rivers and streams

flow. The country is thus unusually vulnerable to flooding and typhoons. The situation is made worse by human alterations of the environment; extensive groundwater pumping is causing cities to sink, and mangrove deforestation has increased erosion rates and removed natural barriers against storm surges. By 2050, 17 percent of the country may well be inundated. For years, so-called environmental refugees have been moving from Bangladesh into neighboring India, but India is building a border wall to ward off further migration. In a country already facing significant demographic challenges, climate change puts Bangladesh in an even more precarious position.

Southeast Asia
Southeast Asia is a reminder that refugee problems can change quickly. Indochina was the scene of one of the twentieth century's most desperate refugee crises when a stream of between 1 and 2 million people fled Vietnam in the aftermath of the long war that ended in 1975. During the Vietnam war, the U.S. bombed Cambodia and worked to bring a pro-West leader to power. After the U.S. left Vietnam in 1975, Pol Pot came to power in Cambodia on an anti-U.S. and anti-Soviet wave. From 1975 to 1979 Pol Pot and the Khmer Rouge controlled Cambodia and inflicted a genocide, killing 1.7 million Cambodians (about one-quarter of the country's people). The Khmer Rouge focused the genocide mainly in cities, seeking to persecute. re-educate, or kill the educated class and those most influenced by the West. Cambodians who fled went to refugee camps in Thailand and from there to the West, including the United States. Today, the largest camps in this region are for IDPs in Myanmar (formerly Burma), who are victims of the 2004 tsunami, the 2008 cyclone, and the repressive rule of generals who are seeking to subdue the country's minorities.

Europe
In the 1990s, the collapse of Yugoslavia and its associated conflicts created the largest refugee crisis in Europe since the end of World War II. In 1995, the UNHCR reported the staggering total of 6,056,600 refugees, a number that some observers felt was inflated by the Europeans' unusually liberal interpretations of the United Nations' rules for refugee recognition. Nevertheless, even after the cessation of armed conflict and the implementation of a peace agreement known as the Dayton Accords, the UNHCR still reports over 100,000 IDPs in the area.

The Americas
In the Western Hemisphere, Colombia has around 5.7 million IDPs, caused by political violence tied to narcotics production. Colombia's IDP numbers were the largest in the world until 2013, when Syria's civil war generated 2 million more IDPs than Colombia. Significant areas of Colombia's countryside are vulnerable to armed attack by "narcoterrorists" and paramilitary units; these rural areas are essentially beyond government control, and thousands of villagers have died in the crossfire. Hundreds of thousands more have left their homes to seek protection.

Elsewhere in the Western Hemisphere, recent earthquakes have displaced millions. A 2010 earthquake in Chile killed hundreds and displaced 2 million Chileans. Six weeks before the Chilean quake, an earthquake in Haiti killed 200,000 people and displaced 1.5 million. Haiti had not recovered from the 2010 earthquake when Hurricane Matthew hit in 2016 and Hurricane Irma followed in 2017. Hurricane Matthew caused 546 fatalities and impacted 2.1 million people in Haiti. Refugee agencies report that in the region impacted by Hurricane Matthew, 140,000 households "still do not have access to minimum earthquake and seismic-resistant homes and shelters, thus remaining highly vulnerable to future shocks" (Relief Web 2018).

People who abandon their familiar surroundings because conditions have become unlivable perform an ultimate act of desperation. In the process, they often face unimaginable challenges and hardships. Refugee and internally displaced person populations are a barometer of the world's political strife.

> ### 🖳 Thinking **Geographically**
>
> Imagine you are from a very low income country, and you earn less than $1 a day. Choose a country to be from, and analyze its **site** and **situation** on a map. Assume you are a potential refugee— your ethnic group is being persecuted by your own government. Analyze your access to transportation and the opportunities you have to go elsewhere. Be realistic, and describe the larger **context** of your decision—how you determine where you will go, how you will get there, and what you will do once you get there.

3.5 Determine How Government Policies Impact Migration.

With 8.6 percent of the world in a state of displacement, including refugees, IDPs, and asylum seekers, migration makes news daily around the world. Political parties use anti-immigration stances to encourage their base to vote. Border areas within countries experience migration differently than the rest of the country, and perceptions of migration, in many ways, depend on where you stand and how often you interact with migrants at work and school and in social situations.

Media coverage, political debates, and political wrangling make us think that politicization of migration is new. But in the fourteenth century, China built the Great Wall in part as a defensive measure, but also as a barrier to keep Chinese in and Mongols out. Governments have an unfortunate history of embedding racism in migration policies. In 1901, Australia approved the Immigration Restriction Act, which ended all nonwhite immigration. The policy targeted Japanese, Chinese, and South Asian migrants. The act also prohibited South Pacific Islanders who worked on Australia's large sugar plantations from immigrating. Australia's immigration policies created what is known as the White Australia Policy, which remained in effect until the 1970s.

Waves of Immigration in the United States

Changes in a country's migration policies can be seen in the number of immigrants and the origin of the immigrants over time. Push factors for immigrants to the United States are reflected in **Figure 3.30**, as people in different regions experienced similar reasons to leave their home and migrate.

Between 1820 and 1900, Europeans constituted nearly all the immigrants entering the United States (see Fig. 3.30). After the Great Depression, European migration slowed, and Europe became a region that received more migrants than it sent (see section "Guest Workers" on pages 67–68). A steady stream of migrants into the United States continued after World War II, but the source of immigrants changed

in the 1960s when new migration legislation was passed. Since the 1960s, migrants in the United States have come mainly from Latin America and Asia.

Legal Restrictions

Typically, the obstacles placed in the way of potential migrants are legal, not physical. In the United States, restrictive legislation on immigration can be traced to 1882, when Congress approved the Oriental Exclusion Acts (1882–1907) to prevent the immigration of Chinese people to California.

With the exception of this legislation excluding Chinese people, during the 1800s the United States opened its doors to immigration. Most of the migrants arrived from Europe, especially northern Europe (Scandinavia) and western Europe (including Ireland, Great Britain, Germany, and France). In the later part of the 1800s, a greater proportion of Europeans who immigrated to the United States came from southern and eastern Europe (including Italy, Spain, Portugal, Russia, and Poland).

Following World War I, political tides in the United States turned toward isolationism—a policy that favors staying out of entanglements abroad. In addition, at that time, Congress feared the growing migration from eastern and southern Europe. Many whites in the United States saw migrants from southern Europe as darker skinned and therefore inferior. In this context, Congress passed restrictive legislation in 1921, deterring immigration from southern and eastern Europe. Specifically, it set immigration quotas to 3 percent of the number of a given European country's nationals living in the United States in 1910. Since the greatest proportion of migrants in the United States in 1910 came from northern and western Europe, the quotas allowed much more migration from northern and western Europe than from southern and eastern Europe (**Fig. 3.31**).

In 1924, Congress altered the Immigration Act by lowering the quota to 2 percent and making 1890 the base year, further

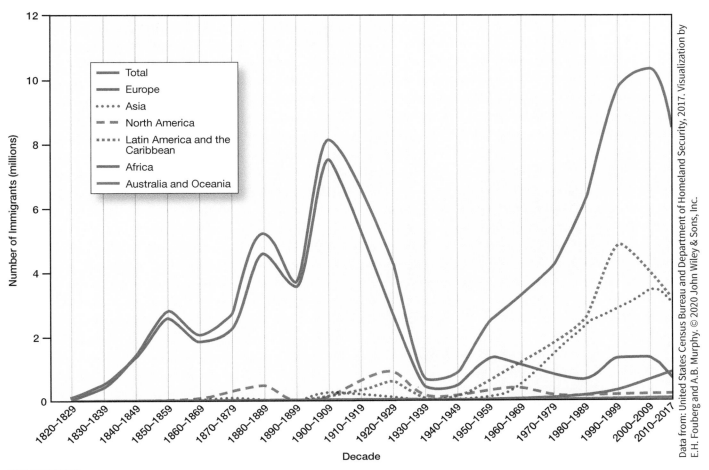

Data from: United States Census Bureau and Department of Homeland Security, 2017. Visualization by E.H. Fouberg and A.B. Murphy. © 2020 John Wiley & Sons, Inc.

FIGURE 3.30   **Immigration to the United States by Region, 1820–2017.**   During the first wave of migration to the United States, from 1820 to 1930, most migrants to the United States came from Europe. During the second wave of migration, from 1930 to the present, a shift occurred, and migrants to the United States now mainly come from Latin America and Asia. The number of migrants to the United States fell after the 2008 financial crisis.

reducing the annual total to 150,000 migrants and further discouraging eastern and southern European migration. The rapid fall in total immigration to the United States is clearly shown in Figure 3.30. Just prior to the Great Depression, Congress passed the National Origins Law in 1929, which limited immigration to 150,000 persons per year. Congress also tied immigration quotas to the national origins of the U.S. population in 1920. As a result, Congress in effect prevented substantial immigration from Asia. With these laws in effect and the Great Depression in full swing, immigration slowed to a trickle during the 1930s.

After 1940, Congress modified the restrictions on immigration. When the United States needed labor during World War II, the **Bracero Program**, passed by Congress and signed by the president in 1942, invited Mexicans to come to the United States to work in agriculture. Between 1942 and the end of the Bracero Program in 1965, Mexicans migrated mainly to the American Southwest and Florida. This Mexican migration was often **cyclical**, as migrants left Mexico for agriculture jobs in the United States during planting and harvest season, and then returned home to Mexico. In 1965, Congress ended the Bracero Program and passed the Immigration and Nationality Act, which began a major shift in Mexican migration to the United States. Mexican migrants now crossed into the United States and stayed instead of cyclically returning home (**Fig. 3.32**).

In 1943, Congress gave China equal status to European countries and in 1952 granted Japan a similar status. In 1952, immigration began to rise again (Fig. 3.30) after Congress passed a new Immigration and Nationality Act. Designed to incorporate all preceding legislation, the act established quotas for all countries and limited total immigration numbers to 160,000. However, far more than 160,000 migrants entered the country as refugees, thereby filling quotas for years ahead. Estimates vary, but more than 7 million migrants may have entered the United States as refugees between 1945 and 1970.

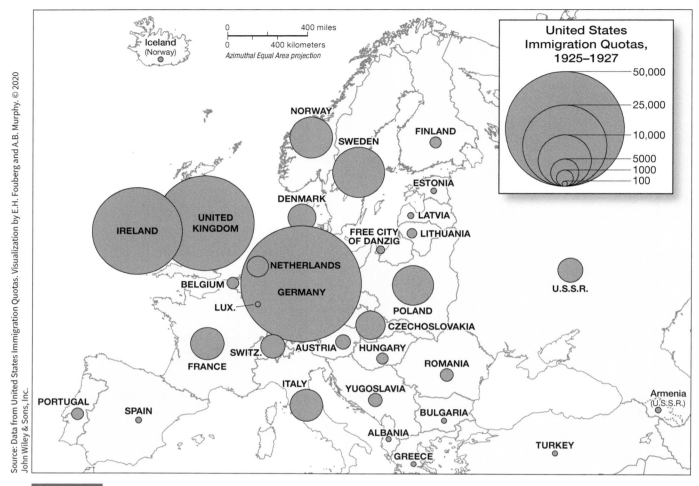

FIGURE 3.31 **United States Immigration Quotas 1925-1927.** The U.S. government set quotas on the number of migrants allowed from each country in Europe between 1925 and 1927. The United States let in the most migrants from western (Ireland, United Kingdom, Germany) and northern (Norway, Sweden, Denmark) Europe. At this point in United States history, the government had a bias against southern (Portugal, Spain, Greece) and eastern Europeans, and the quotas reflect that.

By 1965, Congress recognized the 1952 act as a failure and abolished the quota system. Congress set new limits, which are also reflected in Figure 3.30. The United States allowed 170,000 migrants per year from countries outside the western hemisphere and 120,000 from countries in the Americas. Refugee policies and guest worker policies over the succeeding decades allowed many more migrants to come into the country than these limitations would suggest.

In 1986, the U.S. government passed the Immigration Reform and Control Act (IRCA), which gave permanent residence and a path to citizenship for 2.6 million unauthorized migrants living in the United States. A significant recent example of regional migration is the migration from Mexico and Central America into the United States, which rapidly accelerated in the 1970s and 1980s—peaking around the year 2000 with close to 1 million migrants arriving each year. The number of migrants fell off sharply after the economic downturn of 2008, but the imprint of this decades-long migration is still very much in evidence. Mexican migrants alone now constitute close to 4 percent of the U.S. population, and they play a fundamentally important economic role in many states and cities.

Post–September 11 Since September 11, 2001, U.S. government immigration policies have focused on security concerns. Prior to 9/11, the U.S. border patrol was concerned primarily with drug trafficking and human smuggling. The new government policies affect asylum seekers and both authorized and unauthorized migrants.

After September 11, the U.S. government designated 33 countries as places where al-Qaeda or other terrorist groups operate, and under a policy called Operation Liberty Shield, the government automatically detained anyone from any of these 33 countries who entered the United States looking for asylum. On March 25, 2003, Human Rights Watch criticized the policy, contending that it created "a blanket suspicion of links to terrorism based on nationality alone." On April 17, 2003, the

Source: Data from United States Immigration Quotas. Visualization by E.H. Fouberg and A.B. Murphy. © 2020 John Wiley & Sons, Inc.

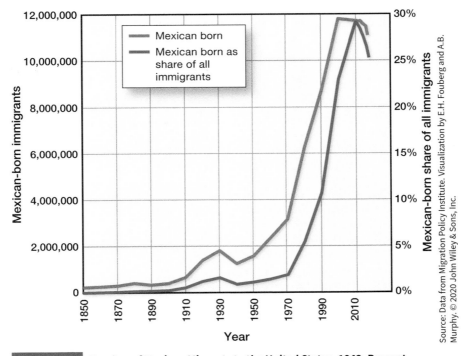

Source: Data from Migration Policy Institute. Visualization by E.H. Fouberg and A.B. Murphy. © 2020 John Wiley & Sons, Inc.

FIGURE 3.32 **Number of Mexican Migrants to the United States, 1942–Present.** The number of migrants from Mexico to the United States rose in the second wave of immigration (see Fig. 3.30) and has declined since the 2008 financial crisis. The proportion of Mexican migrants is also declining. Before the financial crisis, Mexicans made up almost 30 percent of all migrants to the United States, and since 2008, that number has fallen closer to 25 percent.

Department of Homeland Security quietly terminated Operation Liberty Shield. Nonetheless, controls along the U.S. border are much tighter than they were prior to 9/11, with implications not just for the flow of migrants but for business and commerce in border regions as well.

In the wake of terrorist attacks in Europe—including major bombings in Madrid in 2004 and London in 2005—European governments have also focused more attention on immigration. Whereas the U.S. government pursued a "hard" approach, expanding immigration controls after 9/11, the free movement of peoples among most European countries has led state governments to seek to limit unauthorized migration into the larger European space while promoting internal policies aimed at fostering migrant buy-in to the host society. In some cases, migrants must complete an "integration agreement" before receiving permanent status and access to social welfare programs. Austria's integration package, for example, includes 300 hours of language training and a civic education course—which is often challenging for recently arrived migrants who need the financial support provided by social welfare programs.

People and organizations opposed to the U.S. and European policies adopted in response to terrorist incidences argue that these policies may do more harm than good because they can intensify misunderstanding and hatred. Whether or not that is true, it seems that concerns about the migration–terrorism link will continue to shape security policy in the United States, Europe, and beyond for some time to come.

TC Thinking Geographically

Analyze Figure 3.30, **migration** to the United States by region. Choose one **region** and one time. Research an example of a migration flow to the United States from that region at that time (e.g. east European migration in 1900). Describe where migrants from that region primarily settled in the United States. Explain relocation **diffusion**. Imagine how the migration flow you chose can be seen in the **cultural landscape** of the destination region in the United States both at the time of migration and today.

Summary

3.1 Explain Migration as a Type of Movement.

1. Migration is a type of movement that changes people and places. It is movement from a home location to a new place with an intent to stay in the new place permanently. Migration changes the location of home and has a degree of permanence.

2. Cyclic movement is different from migration. With cyclic movement, people leave home for a defined amount of time and return home. Examples of cyclic movement include snowbirds who winter somewhere warmer than their permanent home; commuters who leave home in the morning and return at night; and pastoral farmers who herd animals to fresh vegetation seasonally. Pastoral farmers may herd animals to higher elevations in summer and lower elevations in winter (transhumance) or may follow seasonal rains, moving into areas once the rains have passed and vegetation has regrown.

3. Migration drives relocation diffusion, which happens when people carry their ideas and cultural traits with them as they move. Migrants often settle in the same neighborhoods in cities or the same towns in rural areas. They carry their ideas and cultural traits, and imprint them on the cultural landscape, creating ethnic neighborhoods and small towns.

4. Migration includes both international migration and internal migration. Significant flows of international migration since 1500 have shaped globalization. Remittances, money sent to family and friends at home, are a major motivation for migration.

3.2 Explain Historic and Modern Forced Migration.

1. Migration can be forced or voluntary. In forced migration, the migrants do not have a choice whether to migrate and do not weigh push and pull factors. They do not have a say in whether and when they leave or where they go. Forced migration changes the place the migrants leave and the destination. The absence of the migrants is felt at home, and the migrants become part of the fabric of the place where they land. The Atlantic slave trade and the forced removal of American Indians are examples of forced migration.

2. Forced migration can be part of a larger policy of assimilation. Through assimilation policies, a government institutes programs and systems of penalties and rewards to force a minority group to lose distinct cultural traits, such as dress, food, or speech, and to adopt the customs of the dominant culture. The U.S. government forcibly removed Native American children from their homes and placed them in boarding schools as part of its assimilation policy. Canada, Australia, and New Zealand also had assimilation policies and forcibly removed indigenous children to boarding schools.

3. Sex trafficking, child sex trafficking, forced labor, bonded or debt bondage labor, involuntary domestic servitude, forced child labor, and the recruitment of child soldiers all fall within the broad umbrella of modern slavery. Women and girls account for at least 95 percent of victims of human trafficking for sexual exploitation globally. The lack of power, agency, or value of women and girls in many countries makes them susceptible to abuse and violence.

3.3 Explain the Theories of Migration and Understand the Motivations for Migration.

1. How much migration occurs between two places varies based on similarities between the source and the destination, the effectiveness of the flow of information from the destination back to the source, and the physical distance between the source and the destination.

2. Ravenstein's gravity model predicts that the degree of interaction or amount of migration flow between two places varies based on population size and distance between the two places. It states that the number of migrants who go to a destination declines as the distance they must travel increases, or that more migrants travel short distances and fewer migrants travel longer distances.

3. Voluntary migrants weigh push and pull factors to decide whether to migrate and where to migrate to. Push factors are the conditions and perceptions that help a migrant decide to leave a place. Pull factors are what attract a migrant to a certain destination, the factors that help the migrant decide where to go.

3.4 Identify Why Refugees Are a Distinct Group of Migrants and Describe Where Most Refugees Migrate.

1. Refugees are migrants who are fleeing political persecution and violence in their home country. They typically travel by foot to neighboring countries. Organizations such as the United Nations High Commissioner on Refugees provide shelter and food to refugees in camps in the countries where they land. Entire generations have been born and raised in refugee camps because of continued violence in certain countries and regions.

2. Refugees have legal status under international law. If a country recognizes a migrant as a refugee, the migrant has the legal right to live and work there. Countries can determine how many refugees to accept and from where. Governments and nongovernmental organizations work together to help refugees acclimate to their new country and find housing and work.

3. Asylum seekers are migrants who are asking for refugee status. They are experiencing persecution in their home country and do not see themselves as safe there. An asylum seeker enters a country at a port, airport, or border crossing and claims the right to asylum. It takes time for governments to hear the cases of asylum seekers, and during that time governments may detain them in holding facilities or may house them in temporary housing. A government may decide that asylum seekers are suffering persecution and grant them the right to asylum, which gives them refugee status. Or a government may decide to send them back to their home country.

3.5 Determine How Government Policies Impact Migration.

1. Governments impact migration through policies that allow certain groups into the country at certain times. Governments can use quotas and specify how many migrants are allowed into the country legally. The origins of migrants coming to the United States have changed over time. Before the 1930s, most migrants to the United States were voluntary migrants from Europe and

forcibly migrated enslaved Africans. Since the passage of immigration legislation in 1965, most migrants to the United States have come from Latin America and Asia.

2. The United States has changed its policies over time, sometimes making it easier for migrants to come into the United States and sometimes making it more difficult. During and after World War II, the United States needed farm laborers. The Bracero Program, passed by Congress and signed by the president in 1942, invited Mexicans to come to the United States to work in agriculture. Between 1942 and the end of the Bracero Program in 1965, Mexicans migrated mainly to the American Southwest and Florida. Migration from Mexico during this time was cyclical: Migrants would come to the United States during planting and harvest seasons and go home to Mexico much of the rest of the year.

Self-Test

3.1 Explain migration as a type of movement.

1. Migration is a form of movement that does all of the following except:

   a. change both the places migrants leave and the places migrants go.

   b. change how people see themselves and others.

   c. slow the diffusion of ideas and innovations.

   d. increase spatial interaction.

   e. enable the diffusion of cultural practices.

2. For a person's movement to be cyclic, the person must:

   a. move permanently.

   b. return home.

   c. be prompted to move by dates on the calendar.

   d. be moving as part of a larger group, like an ethnic group or class.

   e. be moving to join family members.

3. Activity spaces are the places where people move in the rounds of everyday activity. If you conducted a study of the activity spaces of snowbirds in Michigan and Florida, you would most likely notice that snowbirds have one set of activity spaces in summer and a different set of activity spaces in winter.

   a. true

   b. false

4. Migration always creates _____ diffusion.

   a. stimulus

   b. contagious

   c. hierarchical

   d. nodal

   e. relocation

3.2 Explain Historic and Modern Forced Migration.

5. Through the Atlantic slave trade, millions of Africans were forcibly enslaved and forcibly migrated to the Americas. In the Caribbean, enslaved Africans labored mainly in the _____ industry:

   a. coffee

   b. cotton

   c. corn

   d. sugar

   e. shipping

6. The U.S. government forcibly removed Native American children from their homes and removed them to boarding schools as part of its official policy of:

   a. acculturation.

   b. enslavement.

   c. assimilation.

   d. vernacularization.

   e. liberation.

7. In modern forced labor and human trafficking, business owners and traffickers control victims by controlling their identification papers and also their movement. In doing this, traffickers are controlling the _____ of the victims.

   a. assimilation

   b. activity spaces

   c. ethnic neighborhoods

   d. language

   e. social media space

3.3 Explain the theories of migration and understand the motivations for migration.

8. Migrants who look at the conditions of their hometown, including the lack of jobs and lack of affordable housing, and decide to move are weighing the:

   a. chain factors.

   b. ethnic factors.

   c. push factors.

   d. pull factors.

   e. risk factors.

9. Ravenstein's gravity model says that migration between two places will vary based on the:

   a. relative population size and distance between the two places.

   b. relative wealth and distance between the two places.

   c. relative population and connectedness between the two places.

   d. relative wealth and connectedness between the two places.

   e. relative health and wealth of the population in the two places.

10. If migrants have chosen a destination, but stop along the path between the home and the destination because they find a place with favorable conditions to live, that stop is a(n):

    a. chain migration.

    b. intervening opportunity.

    c. world city.

    d. refugee camp.

    e. cyclic point.

3.4 Identify why refugees are a distinct group of migrants and describe where most refugees migrate.

11. Under international law, refugees have the right to asylum, which means they can live:

    a. in a detention center until their case is adjudicated.

    b. in any country in the world they want to move to.

    c. in a refugee camp or a detention center.

    d. in any country in the European Union.

    e. in another country until the political persecution in their home country ends.

12. The countries that generate the most refugees and the countries that receive the most refugees are near each other.

    a. true

    b. false

13. Internally displaced people are similar to refugees in all of the following ways except they:

    a. come from lower income countries.

    b. are fleeing violence.

    c. travel by foot into another country.

    d. may spend many years away from home before they can return.

    e. fear for their lives.

3.5 Determine how government policies impact migration.

14. Between 1820 and 1900, most migrants to the United States came from _____, and between 1900 and the 1930s, most migrants to the United States came from _____.

    a. southern and eastern Europe/northern and western Europe

    b. northern Africa/eastern Asia

    c. eastern Asia/northern Africa

    d. northern and western Europe/southern and eastern Europe

    e. eastern Asia/southern Asia

15. During and after World War II, the United States needed farm laborers, so the government created a policy and opened the country to legal migration from:

    a. Canada.

    b. South Africa.

    c. Mexico.

    d. China.

    e. India.

16. Since Congress passed new legislation in 1965, most migrants to the United States have come from:

    a. Africa and Latin America.

    b. Asia and Latin America.

    c. Europe and Africa.

    d. Asia and Africa.

    e. Europe and India.

CHAPTER 4

Local Culture, Popular Culture, and Cultural Landscapes

Photo by E.H. Fouberg. © 2020 John Wiley & Sons, Inc.

FIGURE 4.1 New York, New York. An Asian woman and child walk past the closed Italian eatery Positano in Little Italy. Little Italy is getting pressure from all sides. Chinatown is expanding from the south, and real estate developers are creating trendy, expensive neighborhoods that are pushing in from the west and north. The *New York Post* reported that eight Italian eateries closed within a year's time, when new landlords doubled rents on Mulberry Street.

A young man with a thick New York accent offered a few expletives as he looked at me and said, "This used to be an Italian restaurant. Not anymore." Pointing up at the Positano sign, he predicted, "It's probably gonna be a Chinese restaurant next."

Positano once stood next to dozens of other Italian restaurants on Mulberry Street, at the heart of Little Italy, an ethnic neighborhood in New York City that dates to 1880 (**Fig. 4.1**). In 1900, 10,000 Italian immigrants lived in Little Italy, which covered 50 square blocks of Manhattan. Little Italy now covers 3 square blocks of Mulberry Street, and only 5 percent of the 8600 people living in the area identify as Italian American.

Migrants develop ethnic neighborhoods in world cities as a home base, a place where they build restaurants, churches (or mosques or temples), stores, and schools to support and maintain their culture. Ethnic neighborhoods change when new migrants move in and reshape the cultural landscape. In the early 1900s, Chinese migrants developed Chinatown next to Little Italy, and it keeps growing even as Little Italy shrinks. But today Chinatown is not only Chinese: Many of the Asians living in Chinatown are newer migrants from Vietnam and Malaysia.

This chapter explores how people develop and maintain cultures and shape cultural landscapes in both cities and rural areas. It also discusses how local cultures use traditions and customs to strengthen identities and how global, popular culture is constructed and diffused.

CHAPTER OUTLINE

4.1   Explain Local Cultures and Popular Culture.

A **culture** is a group of belief systems, norms, and values practiced by a people. Although this definition of culture sounds simple, culture is complex. People who share common beliefs can be recognized as a culture in one of two ways: (1) They may call themselves a culture or (2) Other people (including academics) can label them as a culture. Traditionally, academics label cultural groups as either folk cultures or as part of popular culture. The idea is that a **folk culture** is small, incorporates a homogeneous population, is typically rural, and maintains cultural traits by passing them down through generations. **Popular culture** is large, incorporates heterogeneous populations, is typically urban, and quickly changes cultural traits.

Folk culture is a limiting and arbitrary concept because it requires us to create a list of characteristics and look for cultures that meet the list. This methodology leaves much to be desired. Once we have our list of characteristics, we have to test each culture, whether Amish or Navajo, to decide if it is a folk culture—a frustrating and relatively futile process. It is not how academics define a culture that counts; it is how the people define themselves that matters.

We would rather ask how the Amish create and maintain cultural practices and navigate through the onslaught of shifting popular culture. We want to understand why a group of Americans in a small town identify themselves as Swedish Americans and hold festivals to commemorate important Swedish holidays, while other Swedish Americans in other parts of the country function completely unaware of the Swedish holidays. We are curious why ethnic holidays like St. Patrick's Day transcend ethnicity to be celebrated as a part of popular culture.

Instead of classifying cultures as either folk or popular, we recognize that people create and maintain cultures both locally and globally, so we chose to use the concept of local culture rather than folk culture. A **local culture** is a group of people in a certain place who see themselves as a collective or a community, who share experiences and traits, and who work to preserve distinct customs in order to claim uniqueness and to distinguish themselves from others.

Local Culture

Local and popular cultures operate in the same places and spaces, manifest in different ways, and are constantly being shaped. In an era of globalization, popular culture diffuses around the globe instantly, being embraced by some and rejected by others. Local cultures persist, and in many places the communities thrive, but they face constant pressure from the enveloping popular culture. Local cultures choose to accept, reject, or alter the diffusion of popular culture. Local cultures may rely on religion, community celebrations, family structures, or a lack of interaction with other cultures to maintain their culture.

Local cultures are constantly redefining or refining themselves based on interactions with other cultures and the diffusion

of cultural practices. Local cultures also affect places by establishing neighborhoods, building churches or community centers to celebrate important days, and expressing their material and nonmaterial cultures in certain ways. **Material culture** includes things people construct, such as art, houses, clothing, sports, dance, and foods. **Nonmaterial culture** includes beliefs, practices, aesthetics (what is seen as attractive), and values. What members of a local culture produce in their material culture reflects the beliefs and values of their nonmaterial culture.

Popular Culture

Unlike local cultures, which are found in relatively small areas, popular culture is everywhere and can change in a matter of days or hours (**Fig. 4.2**). Popular culture is practiced by a

FIGURE 4.2   **Los Angeles, California.**   Kylie Jenner celebrates her 21st birthday wearing a fuchsia satin dress designed by Peter Dundas. Fashion Nova sold a knock off version online within 24 hours.

heterogeneous group of people—people of different races, ethnicities, genders, and ages. Like local culture, popular culture includes music, dance, clothing, food preferences, religious practices, and aesthetic values. The main paths of diffusion of popular culture are the transportation, marketing, and communication networks (including social networks) that interlink vast parts of the world.

Fashion, a form of popular culture, diffuses incredibly quickly today. On her to her 21st birthday party on a Friday night, Kylie Jenner wore two outfits: a fuchsia dress designed by Peter Dundas that she wore to her birthday dinner (see Fig. 4.2) and an $8000 pink romper encrusted with Swarovski crystals that she wore later in the night. By Saturday, Fashion Nova posted a look-alike model wearing a knock-off dubbed "Birthday Bash Sequin Romper" on Instagram with a price point of $34.99. Fashion Nova advertises the romper on its website with its own look-alike model, customer photos, and the original Instagram photo Jenner posted of herself in the LaBourjoisie original. Fashion Nova's "Birthday Behavior" collection included knock-offs of Jenner's romper, her fuchsia dress, and the pink cutout dress Kim Kardashian wore to her party.

In popular culture, fashion trends spread very quickly through fast fashion; it is a classic case of **hierarchical diffusion**. Hierarchical diffusion can occur through a hierarchy of people. In this case, a designer is the **hearth**, celebrities and influencers are the first adopters, fast fashion companies such as Zara, H&M, Primark, and Fashion Nova create knock-offs, and followers and customers adopt the fashion.

Hierarchical diffusion can also occur through a hierarchy of places. The hierarchy in the fashion world typically begins with the runways of major fashion houses in world cities, including London, Milan, Paris, and New York, which act as the **hearth**, the place of origin. The next tier of places includes flagship stores for the fashion house and editorial headquarters of fashion magazines, also located in world cities. Department store brands interpret the runway fashions for consumption by a larger audience, and the suburban mall receives the innovation.

Local and Popular Culture Together

Local and popular culture are not separated physically. You may go to a major department store such as Target or Walmart and see Hutterites or Mennonites dressed in distinctive local clothing in the midst of the ultimate in popular culture: a major international department store. Traditions such as painting henna on one's hands or practicing mystical Kabbalah beliefs are carried from centuries-old customs of local cultures to the global popular culture through a popular culture icon or through the corporations (such as marketing firms) that work to construct popular culture (**Fig. 4.3**).

Both local and popular cultures are constantly navigating through customs diffused from each other and across scales,

Josiah Kamau/BuzzFoto/Getty Images

FIGURE 4.3 **New York.**   In a truly global fashion, New York City tattoo artist Keith McCurdy flew to the Dominican Republic to ink a design based on traditional Indian henna over an existing tattoo based on a traditional New Zealand design on the hand of Barbados-born singer Rihanna.

through a complex of political and economic forces that shape and limit their practices, and through global communications and transportation networks that closely link certain parts of the world and distance others. Local and popular culture impact each other. Local cultures are sustained despite the onslaught of popular culture, and popular culture diffuses and is practiced in unique ways around the world.

TC **Thinking Geographically**

The fast fashion industry takes runway looks and turns them into low-cost, disposable clothing immediately available to consumers. The fashion industry accounts for $1.2 trillion globally, and the amount of clothing being produced has doubled since 2005. How has **time-space compression** enabled fast fashion to knock off a celebrity look and make it available to consumers in 24 hours?

Follow-up: In 1960, the United States generated 1.7 million tons of textile waste (mostly clothing), and in 2015, it generated 16 million tons of textile waste (15 percent of the 16 million was recycled, 9 percent burned, and the rest placed in landfills). Thinking about waste, fabrics used, and factories, how is fast fashion evidence of the **Anthropocene**?

4.2 Understand How People Sustain Local Cultures in Rural and Urban Areas.

Local cultures are sustained through **customs**, practices that a group of people routinely follow. People have customs regarding all parts of their lives, from eating and drinking to dancing and sports. To sustain a local culture, people must retain or regenerate their customs. Customs change in small ways over time, but they are maintained despite the onslaught of popular culture.

Local cultures desire to keep popular culture out, keep their culture intact, and maintain control over customs and knowledge. Geographers also recognize that through these actions, places become increasingly important. In rural communities or urban ethnic neighborhoods, local cultures can sustain their customs, see and interact with each other, and access goods and services important to their local cultures through shops and restaurants. Living together helps members of a local culture reinforce their culture and resist both assimilation and cultural appropriation by the dominant culture.

Withstanding Efforts at Assimilation

During the 1800s and into the 1900s, the U.S. government had an official policy of **assimilation**, forcibly suppressing Native American customs and replacing them with customs of the dominant culture. The federal government wanted to assimilate indigenous peoples into the dominant culture in order to make Native Americans into "Americans" rather than "Natives" or "Indians." Canadians, Australians, Russians, and other colonial powers adopted similar policies toward indigenous peoples, using schools, churches, and government agents to discourage Native customs and undermine local culture.

Following this policy, the United States forced tribal members to settle in one place and farm rather than hunt or fish. Government agents rewarded the Natives they deemed most "American" with citizenship and jobs in the formal economy. The U.S. government also took Native American children from their homes and placed them in boarding schools, where teachers punished children for using their Native language and forcibly cut their hair. The federal government employed east coast women from 1888 until 1938 to live on reservations and show the Native women how to be "good housewives" by teaching them Victorian ways of cooking, cleaning, and sewing.

Several churches and governments have apologized for these assimilation policies. The government of Australia officially apologized to the Aboriginals in Australia. The Australian Parliament unanimously passed a motion stating: "We apologize for the laws and policies of successive parliaments and governments that have inflicted profound grief, suffering and loss on these our fellow Australians." Former Australian prime minister Kevin Rudd apologized specifically for the government's policy of taking Aboriginal children from their homes

and placing them in residential schools—a policy that lasted from the 1800s until the late 1960s.

Canadian prime minister Stephen Harper also cited the disastrous outcomes of assimilation policies in his apology to Canada's 1.3 million indigenous people—the First Nations and the Inuit. He apologized for the abuse and the lasting negative effects of Canada's residential schools, stating: "We now recognize that it was wrong to separate children from rich and vibrant cultures and traditions, that it created a void in many lives and communities, and we apologize for having done this. We now recognize that, in separating children from their families, we undermined the ability of many to adequately parent their own children and sowed the seeds for generations to follow." Speaking to the indigenous people seated in the House of Commons, he continued, "Not only did you suffer these abuses as children, but as you became parents, you were powerless to protect your own children from suffering the same experience, and for this we are sorry."

AP® Exam Taker's Tip

In order to succeed on the AP exam, you will need to know what **assimilation**, **acculturation**, **syncretism**, and **multiculturalism** are. **Assimilation** is mentioned in the text. Look up the other terms and see how they relate to cultures interacting with one another.

Persisting: Regenerating Local Culture Through Customs

Official assimilation policies were practiced by American, Canadian, Russian, Australian, and New Zealand governments and were designed for the express purpose of disrupting and changing **indigenous local cultures**. Western, democratic governments no longer have official policies of assimilation. Yet, for people in many local cultures and in regions that are not hearths of popular culture, popular culture itself can feel like assimilation.

Historically, the economic activities of Native American tribes were the focal point of daily life. Numerous customs and festivals revolved around activities like whale or bison hunting, salmon fishing, or wild rice growing. In the early 1800s in North America, Plains Indians tribes migrated during the year based on the bison. They made tools, shelter, and clothing out of the bison, and they held dances and ceremonies that surrounded the bison hunt.

When a Native American local culture discontinued its major economic activities of hunting bison and whales, it faced the challenge of maintaining the customs built around those economic activities. This, in turn, made it difficult to sustain the local culture. Nevertheless, Native Americans across the

FIGURE 4.4 **Thunder Valley.** Thunder Valley community in Pine Ridge, South Dakota, is a regenerative community created by young Native leaders. It includes a Lakota-language immersion childcare center and elementary school. Nick Tillson, Thunder Valley's founder, shows the front porch of the first home under construction in the community. Watch the story of Thunder Valley at https://thundervalley.org/learn-more/our-story.

United States persisted through a century of assimilation. To regenerate and sustain their local cultures, tribes such as the Oglala Lakotas and Makahs are embracing traditional customs.

Thunder Valley: Oglala Lakotas

Native American tribes now fund programs and set up schools to teach children Native languages. On the Pine Ridge Reservation, Oglala Lakota families are creating a planned community centered on traditional spiritual ceremonies, sustainable building techniques, and food production and consumption (**Fig. 4.4**). The Thunder Valley community is using green building practices, helping families build their own homes, and creating community gardens. Through this grassroots development, Thunder Valley is creating a place centered on customs that also help Oglala Lakota combat endemic poverty.

The vision for Thunder Valley came to a group of young Oglala Lakota, including founder Nick Tilsen, who wanted to regenerate spiritual ceremonies, including the sun dance. Nick Tilsen explained in the community's video why the families who began the Thunder Valley community chose to raise their children on a reservation where 80 percent of the people lived below the poverty line: "It's important for us to raise our kids amongst our own people." Living with each other, practicing ceremonies, revitalizing the Lakota language through immersion childcare and schools, building homes and workforce skills, producing food as a community, and developing economic opportunities sustains, revitalizes, and empowers indigenous local culture.

Whale Hunts: Makah

In the late 1990s, the Makah Native Americans of Neah Bay, Washington, did what environmentalists considered unthinkable: reinstated the whale hunt. Makah had hunted whales for 2000 years. When the Makah tribe entered a treaty with the U.S. government that ceded land, it specifically and explicitly preserved whaling rights. However, the U.S. government stopped the whale hunt in the 1920s because the gray whale had become endangered. In 1994, the National Oceanic and Atmospheric Association (NOAA) removed the eastern North Pacific gray whale from the endangered list.

In 1999, when Makah reinstated the whale hunt, tribal members interviewed by journalists spoke of their traditional culture as their reason for returning to the hunt (**Fig. 4.5**). They needed to return to their past, they said, to understand their ancestors, to recreate and solidify their local culture. Amid a popular culture onslaught, Makah sought refuge in customs and ceremonies around the whale hunt that the tribe describes as "deeply spiritual."

Although Makah wanted to hunt whales as their ancestors did, the 1999 hunts took place in a completely different **context** from that of a century before. This time, Makah hunted whales under the watchful eye of the International Whaling Commission. They faced numerous protests by Greenpeace and local environmentalists, and they found themselves in federal court with the George W. Bush administration on their side supporting the reinstatement of the whale hunt.

Makah wanted to hunt with traditional canoes and harpoons because they wanted to hunt as the tribe's elders and ancestors did. However, in the context of the twentieth and twenty-first centuries, the choice of tools for the Makahs' hunt was not up to them alone. Actors at the regional, national,

FIGURE 4.5 **Neah Bay, Washington.** The whale hunt is a traditional Makah custom. Support for maintaining the custom is a way of resisting the forces of assimilation.

and global scale influenced not only whether Makah could hunt whales, but also the methods they used. The International Whaling Commission dictated that Makah hunt gray whales with a .50 caliber rifle, arguing that the rifle would kill the whale more quickly and humanely than harpoons. In May 1999, Makah hunters killed a gray whale using a .50 caliber rifle.

Makah have not been legally allowed to harvest a gray whale since 1999. The Makah hunt is currently held up by environmental impact studies in the U.S. government. The Makah tribe continues to pursue legal permission to hunt whales because "for the Makah Tribe, whale hunting provides a purpose and a discipline which benefits their entire community" (Makah).

Rural Local Cultures

Members of local cultures in rural areas often have an easier time maintaining customs because of their isolation. By living together in a rural area, members of a local culture can more easily keep external influences on the outside. Rurality enables local cultures to define their own space, to create a place, town, or rural landscape that reflects their values, and to practice customs relatively unfettered.

Rural local cultures have something in common: Each is surrounded by a popular culture that challenges its place in the world, and each has chosen to maintain or reconnect with its local culture. Central concerns for indigenous cultures discussed in the last section include thinking in their own language, defining and writing their history, and coming to know who they are despite what others have done to subvert their identity. For some rural local cultures, the goal is to maintain what they have, to adopt only those technologies that advance their agricultural pursuits, and to limit those that challenge their religion. Other local cultures may use festivals to celebrate the immigrants who made the place unique and connect with their community.

Hutterites Hutterites are an Anabaptist ethnic group who migrated to North America from Ukraine in 1874 (Evans and Peller 2018). During the Protestant Reformation, Anabaptists broke from both the Catholic Church and the new Protestant churches. Followers of the new religion were called Anabaptists, meaning baptized again, because of their belief in adult baptism, despite having been baptized as infants in the Catholic or Protestant churches.

Anabaptists broke from the state as well as the church and stressed pacifism, and they soon suffered persecution. They migrated from German-speaking areas of western Europe east to Moravia and Austria, and then to Russia and the Ukraine. Continually moving to rural areas to live apart and avoid persecution, a group of Anabaptists eventually migrated to North America in the second half of the 1800s. This group was called Hutterites, named after leader Jacob Hutter.

Old Order Anabaptist groups are often shown in stereotypical ways in the popular media, but major differences exist across Old Order Amish, Mennonites, Hutterites, and Brethren. Hutterites are the only Anabaptist group who live communally (**Fig. 4.6**). Rather than living with immediate family on a farmstead, Hutterites live in colonies of about 100 people, with individuals ranging in ages from infant to elderly. Hutterites have more than 520 colonies in North America, with the majority in South Dakota, North Dakota, Montana, Alberta, Saskatchewan, and Manitoba (**Fig. 4.7**). They locate colonies in rural states and provinces to "set themselves apart, as far as they are able, from contagion and all that is 'worldly'" (Evans and Peller 2018, 360).

In their book *On the Backroad to Heaven,* Donald Kraybill and Carl Bowman explain that the linchpin of each colony is the Hutterite religion. Members of the colony join for a 30-minute service every night as well as on Sundays. The most prominent position in a colony is held by the minister, who speaks in archaic German, reading sermons written in the sixteenth century.

Unlike Amish, Hutterites readily accept technologies that help them in their agricultural pursuits. However,

FIGURE 4.6 **Stratford, South Dakota.** A Hutterite boy who lives in the Hutterville Farm colony near Stratford, South Dakota. Distinctive dress and ways of living help to sustain group identity.

Photo by E.H. Fouberg. © 2020 John Wiley & Sons, Inc.

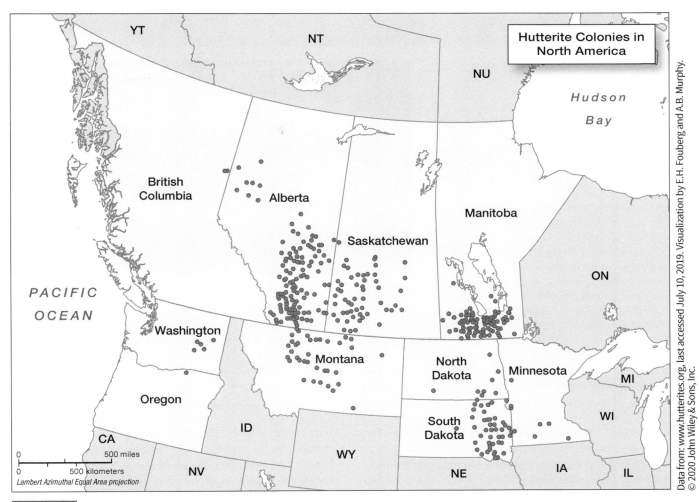

Data from: www.hutterites.org, last accessed July 10, 2019. Visualization by E.H. Fouberg and A.B. Murphy.
© 2020 John Wiley & Sons, Inc.

FIGURE 4.7 **Hutterite Colonies in North America.**   The first Hutterites who migrated to North America came from Ukraine and settled in three colonies in eastern South Dakota. When a colony's population reaches a certain size, its members purchase new land, split the population, and form a daughter colony. Hutterite colonies are clustered, with large concentrations in eastern South Dakota, southern Manitoba, and Alberta.

their colonies were generally slow to accept technologies such as cameras and cell phones out of concern that they would encourage individualistic behaviors or undermine Hutterite religion. Today, it is common for young adult Hutterites to use cell phones and Hutterite dating sites to find suitable marriage partners in colonies in other states or provinces.

Colonies assign separate jobs and tasks to men and women, which reinforces a patriarchal social structure. Kraybill and Bowman explain that marriages happen across colonies, and women move to their husband's colony after marrying. If a Hutterite woman from Alberta meets a Hutterite man from North Dakota through a Hutterite dating site, and they eventually decide to marry, the Canadian woman will move to the United States. As a result, a single colony is usually composed of only one or two surnames. Moving to their husband's colony perpetuates women's weaker political position in the colony. Women are expected to rear many children, currently averaging five or six, but the colony as a whole is responsible for raising and disciplining the child.

Hutterite colonies specialize in diversified agriculture, raising feed, food, and livestock on up to 10,000 acres. Hutterite men often barter with neighboring farmers to fix machinery, trade goods, and lend help. The minister and other male leaders in the colony work with lawyers and bankers to keep the colony corporation operating smoothly and profitably. The most economically successful colonies have created products used in agriculture that they produce in their shops and sell to other farmers. One colony produces stainless steel animal feeders, and another colony markets its own animal feed. Some colonies also invest hundreds of thousands of dollars in computerized milking systems for their dairy operations, in computerized systems for feeding and raising hogs, or even in livestock processing plants.

The spatial layout of a Hutterite colony reflects the importance of community, church, education, and agriculture (**Fig. 4.8**). When the population of a colony reaches between 120 and 150 people, Hutterites start the process of dividing the colony. Colony leaders purchase farmland and erect buildings

Guest Field Note Living Communally on a Hutterite Colony in Alberta, Canada

Simon M. Evans and Peter Peller
University of Calgary

The Hutterites are a German-speaking ethnic group who can boast of 400 years of history. Arriving in North America from the Ukraine as forced migrants in 1874, they established three colonies in Dakota Territory. It is their religion which binds them together. Like the early Christian church they "hold all things common." It is the colony – not the individuals who make it up – that owns the land and the tools of production, and provides for each member from birth to death.

The Hutterites are fascinating to geographers because when a community reaches a threshold size of about 150 people, it divides into two, and a daughter colony is established. This has resulted in a regular diffusion pattern as the original three colonies have grown to number more than 500, spread over four Canadian provinces and six states.

As shown in the photograph, Hutterite colonies have a distinctive layout. The residential area is set apart from the barns and ringed with trees and bushes. On the left side of the photo, communal housing

FIGURE 4.8 **Crossfield, Alberta, Canada.**

© Simon Evans

units (3 residential units each housing 6 families) are grouped next to the kitchen-dining room complex (far left in the photo) where the Brethren meet for meals three times a day. Barns, corrals, and grain storage are in the background. The growing number of colonies adds a significant element to the cultural landscape of the Great Plains.

over a period of about five years (Evans and Peller 2018). Each colony has a common industrial kitchen and dining room where the community eats. Housing for 15 to 20 families is built around or near the kitchen, and a chapel space for daily services is built near the housing and kitchen. Some colonies have schools, and all colonies have farm buildings.

AP® Exam Taker's Tip

There are many case studies of local cultures, including Hutterites, Lakotas, and Makahs. Think about what traits make them unique on the cultural landscape. Are they indigenous or a product of relocation diffusion? How do they seek to protect their traditions?

Little Sweden, U.S.A. Throughout the rural United States, immigrants from Europe built small towns, and many local cultures have defined entire small towns as places to maintain their culture and to teach others about their customs and beliefs. Residents of Lindsborg, Kansas, proclaim their town Little Sweden, U.S.A. Geographer Steven Schnell asked why a town of 3300, which a few decades ago had little or no sign of Swedishness on its landscape, transformed itself into a place where Swedish culture is celebrated every day in gift stores on Main Street and in restaurant buffets (**Fig. 4.9**).

Cynics would argue that the reason is purely economic. But Lindsborg residents benefit from promoting a sense of a shared history and a common place. In the 1930s, the townspeople shared stories about the roles of Swedes in American history and the importance of their Swedishness to Lindsborg. From that

base, the townspeople began to celebrate their Swedish heritage in the 1950s, highlighting the "everyday existence" (the local culture) of the Swedes who immigrated to Lindsborg. During festivals today, the townspeople, whether Swedish or not, dress up in peasant clothes modeled after those worn by Swedish immigrants in the 1800s. Geographer James Shortridge (1996) refers to this as **neolocalism**, seeking out the regional culture and reinvigorating it in response to the uncertainty of the modern world.

Urban Local Cultures

Some local cultures have successfully built a world apart, a place to practice their customs, by constructing tight-knit **ethnic neighborhoods** within a major city. For example, Hasidic Jews in Brooklyn, New York, and Italian Americans in the North End of Boston, Massachusetts, maintain their distinct local cultures in urban environments.

Runners of the New York City marathon can see the ethnic neighborhoods of New York City's boroughs firsthand. Running through Brooklyn, they pass through a predominantly Mexican neighborhood full of Mexican flags and mariachi bands, followed in sharp contrast by a Hasidic Jewish neighborhood with streets lined with men and boys on one side and women and girls on another, all dressed in clothes modeled after eighteenth-century Russian and Polish fashions (**Fig. 4.10**).

In the North End of Boston, the Italian community still celebrates the feast days of Italian saints. Twelve religious societies, each focusing on an Italian saint, hold festivals between June and September. Members of the societies march through the North End holding a statue of their saint, collecting money,

Guest Field Note   Shaping a Swedish Identity in Lindsborg, Kansas

Steven M. Schnell
Kutztown University of Pennsylvania

Lindsborg, Kansas, founded by Swedish Lutherans in 1869, has remade itself in recent decades as "Little Sweden, U.S.A." Swedish gift shops, restaurants, and ethnic festivals, along with faux-Swedish storefronts, all attract visitors interested in the Swedish American heritage. Here you see a Dala horse, a traditional Swedish folk craft that has been adopted as the town symbol. Note, too, the Swedish and American flags flying in the background. Most visitors to the town assume one of two things: Either the town is an island of nineteenth-century culture passed on unchanged for generations, or it is a crock of Disneyesque fakery cooked up to draw in gullible tourists. The fascination of fieldwork is that it undermines any such simplifications. I found ethnicity here to be complex, quirky, ever-changing, and very much a part of the people's lives. Swedishness in Lindsborg has been invented and reinvented time and time again through the decades, as people constantly look for answers to that most basic of questions: Who am I?

FIGURE 4.9 **Lindsborg, Kansas.**

© Steven Schnell

Author Field Note   Running through Ethnic Neighborhoods in New York, New York

"One of the most amazing aspects of running the New York City marathon is seeing the residents of New York's many ethnic neighborhoods lining the streets of the race. Running through the Hasidic Jewish neighborhood in Williamsburg, Brooklyn, was striking. Even before noticing the traditional dress of the neighborhood's residents, I noticed that the crowd was much quieter—the people were not yelling, but they were clapping and quietly cheering."

– E.H. Fouberg

FIGURE 4.10 **Williamsburg, Brooklyn, New York.**

M. David Leeds/Getty Images

Martin Thomas Photography/Alamy Stock Photo

FIGURE 4.11 **Boston, Massachusetts.** North End residents and Italians from around Boston and the region gather during festivals to honor Italian saints, including Saint Anthony, every summer.

and adorning the saint with it (**Fig. 4.11**). The Roma Band, an Italian band that has been in existence since 1919, leads each society through the streets of the North End. Each march ends with a street celebration, including vendors selling everything from fried calamari to hot dogs.

Having their own ethnic neighborhood enables members of a local culture in an urban area to set themselves apart and practice their customs. Schools, houses of worship, food stores, and clothing stores all support the aesthetics and meet the needs of members of the local culture. The greatest challenge to local cultures in cities is the migration of members of other local cultures or ethnic groups into the neighborhood. Local cultures in Brooklyn and the North End work to maintain their culture and customs as young professionals move into their respective neighborhoods. Rents and housing costs are climbing, and cultural landscapes are starting to reflect the neighborhood's new residents. For example, a young, urban, hipster community has inundated the traditionally Hasidic neighborhood of Brooklyn called Williamsburg.

Brooklyn became a destination neighborhood for migrants after the Brooklyn Bridge opened in 1883. The Williamsburg Bridge opened in 1903, and Jewish migrants who lived in Manhattan walked across the bridge, attracted to the much lower rents in Williamsburg. The subway connected Manhattan and Williamsburg in 1908. In the 1980s, artists and students in Manhattan crossed into Williamsburg also looking for lower rents and converted warehouses into studios and apartments.

Since the 1990s, Williamsburg has undergone more **gentrification**, the renewal or rebuilding of a lower-income neighborhood, than any other neighborhood in New York's five boroughs. It became a neighborhood of art galleries, coffee shops, breweries, restaurants. Warehouses converted into condominiums have filled blocks radiating from subway stations

and Bedford Avenue. Rents have risen by 78.8 percent since 1990 (compared to 22.1 percent for the entire city).

In Boston, young professionals gentrified the North End starting in the 1970s. The Big Dig, a 10-year project finished in 2007, moved an elevated interstate between the North End and the rest of Boston underground. The North End is connected by pedestrian-friendly boulevards to Boston. The roads are now at ground level and are surface roads designed for much lighter traffic than the interstate below ground. Drawn to the North End's increasingly favorable location and the quaintness of Italian restaurants, shops, and wine stores, young professionals continue to flock to the North End, choosing apartments that give them a walking commute to jobs in the financial district and city center.

Cultural Appropriation, Commodification, and Authenticity

A local culture may set itself apart in rural and urban areas not only to maintain customs, but also to avoid **cultural appropriation**, the process by which other cultures adopt customs and knowledge and use them for their own benefit. Cultural appropriation is a major concern for local cultures because people from outside often privatize the knowledge of a local culture, including natural pharmaceuticals or musical expression, to accumulate wealth or prestige. Local cultures work to keep their customs and knowledge to themselves to avoid cultural appropriation and to prevent others from appropriating their customs for economic benefit. Anthropologists and geographers have studied how others are using local cultural knowledge, customs, and even names. For example, the estate of Crazy Horse (a Lakota Indian leader) sued a brewery that produced Crazy Horse beer.

The process through which something (a name, a good, an idea, or even a person) that previously was not regarded as an object to be bought or sold becomes an object that can be bought, sold, and traded in the world market is called **commodification**. Commodification affects local cultures in numerous ways. First, their material culture—their jewelry and clothing, their food and games—can be commodified by themselves or by nonmembers. Similarly, their nonmaterial culture—their religion, language, and beliefs—can be commodified, often by nonmembers selling local spiritual and herbal cures for ailments. Local cultures may also be commodified as a whole—think of tourist buses "observing" the Amish culture of Lancaster, Pennsylvania, or travel agencies

FIGURE 4.12 **Sun City, South Africa.** The Lost City resort in Sun City evokes the mystical images of Africa described in a legend. Landscapes such as this blur what is "authentic" and what is not.

offering trekking trips with "traditional" Nepalese guides on spiritual journeys through the Himalayas.

When commodification occurs, the question of **authenticity** follows. When a local culture or custom is commodified, usually one image or experience is typecast as the "authentic" image or experience of that culture, and it is that image or experience that the tourist or buyer desires. However, local cultures are dynamic, and places and people change over time. To gain an "authentic" sense of place, people need to experience the complexity of a place directly rather than its stereotype. An "authentic" local culture does not fit into a single experience or image; rather, an "authentic" local culture is one that is complex and not stereotyped.

The act of stereotyping local culture is quite confusing for the members of the local culture because rarely is there consensus that all things must be done in one traditional way. Tourists in Lancaster County, for example, may be disappointed to see some Amish driving tractors across their fields. European, Canadian, American, or Australian trekkers in Nepal desire the same "authentic" experience that a travel website promotes. However, the "authentic" experience may be one the travel company constructed for tourist consumption.

Authenticity of Places
During the process of colonization, Europeans tagged many cultures they encountered as savage or mystic. "Authentic" tourist destinations are often designed to exploit the mystical in local cultures. A South

African theme park, the Lost City (built on the site of the resort Sun City), capitalizes on mystical images of Africa described in a legend, thereby "freezing" the continent to a time that never existed (**Fig. 4.12**).

In tourism, authenticity of local culture is constructed. The city of Branson, Missouri, is capitalizing on a local culture in the Ozarks, melding several perceptions in one place for tourists to consume. Geographer Johnathan Bascom studied the processes by which the city of Branson has effectively tapped its local customs, such as food preferences, history, and music, to create an "authentic" identity for Branson that sets it apart from neighboring towns. Branson becomes "authentic," and surrounding towns that try to capitalize on their rural, country heritage become "copies."

AP® Exam Taker's Tip

Test your ability to spot **cultural appropriation**, **commodification**, and **authenticity** in your own location or when you are traveling. You will need to have a keen eye and a willingness to ask questions and do some research.

Guinness and the Irish Pub Company
Theme parks and entertainment venues overtly choose a stereotype and perpetuate it, but a discerning tourist or consumer may be aware of what is occurring. The act of corporations commodifying the

LensCapp/Alamy Stock Photo

FIGURE 4.13 **Dubai, United Arab Emirates.** An old Irish truck marks the entrance to an Irish Pub Company pub in Dubai.

mystique of local cultures to drive profits can, however, be less obvious to the consumer. The Guinness Brewing Company of Dublin, Ireland, created a business plan in 1991 aimed at capitalizing on the global mystique of the traditional Irish pub. Guinness saw the sales of its stout beer declining in Ireland and the United Kingdom and decided to go global.

Guinness formed a partnership with the Irish Pub Company, which has offices in Dublin, Atlanta, the United Arab Emirates, and Australia. The Irish Pub Company studied traditional Irish pubs and created five Irish pub prototypes—shop, country, Victorian, Celtic, and brewery. A hotel owner in Naples, Florida, or a businessperson in Dubai, United Arab Emirates (**Fig. 4.13**), to cite two examples, might work with the Irish Pub Company to choose a good site and to choose the pub type. The specifications are sent to Ireland, and the pub itself is built in Ireland and shipped abroad. Along with the pub, the Irish Pub Company provides food recommendations, training, music suggestions, and, notably, Irish bartenders trained in their Dublin "pub school." The Irish Pub Company also sells bricabrac (Irish antiques and reproductions) to give the place the feel of an Irish pub. Of course, every pub has Guinness on tap. All of these components create what the Irish Pub Company refers to as ambience that leads to *craic* (an Irish term for fun). Guinness and the Irish Pub Company have built over 1000 pubs in 40 countries around the world (**Fig. 4.14**).

Remarkably, dozens of the pubs are in Ireland proper. The most enigmatic of the pubs is in Las Vegas, Nevada. The Irish Pub Company designed and built a pub called Nine Fine Irishmen that spans 9000 square feet in the New York-New York Hotel & Casino and spills an additional 20,000 square feet onto Las Vegas Boulevard. The "authentic" Irish pub in "authentic" New York in the "Disney-fied" Las Vegas is one mashup we can chew on for a while.

The commodification of local customs freezes customs in place and time for consumption, with claims of "authenticity" abounding. The search for "authentic" local cultures implies

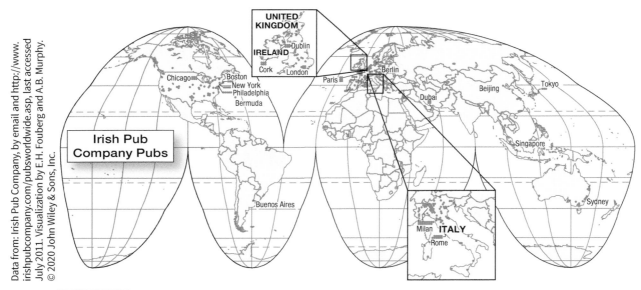

Data from: Irish Pub Company, by email and http://www. irishpubcompany.com/pubsworldwide.asp, last accessed July 2011. Visualization by E.H. Fouberg and A.B. Murphy. © 2020 John Wiley & Sons, Inc.

FIGURE 4.14 **Irish Pubs Designed by the Irish Pub Company.** The distance decay principle is evident here, with the greatest number of pubs located in Europe and North America, where the Irish Pub Company headquarters are. The map also highlights the diffusion of popular culture to world cities, including Buenos Aires and Singapore.

Author Field Note   Enjoying Live Music in Dingle, Ireland

"The tip of the Dingle Peninsula and the Basket Islands off its shore are the westernmost points in all of Ireland. During British control, Irish on the remote Dingle Peninsula maintained the Irish language, song, and dance more so than many other places in the paths of the British. Dingle, a town about three-quarters of the way down the peninsula, was once a fishing village and is now a frequently visited tourist destination on Ireland's west coast. Shops and pubs on the main road through town are painted different, bright colors. An Droichead Beag means "The Little Bridge," and this pub is known for its mighty sessions of traditional Irish music and its small dance floor that attracts revelers nightly. The building dates back to the 1700s but only became a pub in 1986. The pub is owned by a local family and is the kind of pub that the Irish Pub Company replicates."

– E.H. Fouberg

Photo by A.B. Murphy. © 2020 John Wiley & Sons, Inc.

FIGURE 4.15   **Dingle, Ireland.**

an effort to identify peoples who are seemingly untouched by change or external influence. However, all local cultures (rural and urban) are dynamic, and all have been impacted by external influences throughout their existence (**Fig. 4.15**). The search for an "authentic" local culture merely perpetuates myths about local cultures. Members of local cultures are constantly renegotiating their place in this world and making sense of who they are in the midst of the popular culture onslaught.

TC Thinking Geographically

What are cultural traits, and what role do cultural traits play in maintaining and reinvigorating local culture? Examine the website for Thunder Valley, the Ogallala Lakota community (http://thundervalley.org/#). How do the **site** and **situation** of the community help support cultural traits and values?

4.3   Explain How Global, Popular Culture Is Created and Diffused.

Popular culture was once created in hearths and diffused in clear paths around the world. During the twentieth century, the United States and United Kingdom influenced movies, television, music, sports, and fast food. Japan influenced electronic games, new technologies, and children's television. Western Europe functioned as a hearth for fashion, television, art, and philosophy. South Korea has been a hearth for television dramas, movies, and music, and India has been a hearth for movies.

Paths of diffusion and hearths of popular culture have changed radically in the twenty first century with the growth of the Internet, social media, and streaming. YouTube has made it possible for a singer's basement to be a hearth, and streaming platforms like Twitch have made it possible for viewers to interact directly and in real time with celebrities of popular culture. Social networking and YouTube have shortened the distance and accelerated the diffusion of popular culture by intensifying time-space compression. Popular culture is constantly being constructed, consumed, commodified, and reterritorialized around the world.

Social Networking

Social networking cuts the distance between knower and follower, enabling instant sharing across the globe through messaging and postings. Social networking site Facebook has the largest number of monthly active users globally, followed by YouTube and Instagram. Mark Zuckerberg launched Facebook, which had 500 million subscribers worldwide in 2010 and reported 2.23 billion monthly users at the end of 2018.

The map of Facebook users (**Fig. 4.16**) highlights the interconnectedness of individuals around the world, and it also points out the lack of interconnection between individuals in China with the rest of the world via this social media tool. In 2009, China banned Facebook, Twitter, and Google. Chinese who want to use Facebook have to use proxy servers to get around the government's ban. Chinese social networks have grown in place of Facebook. The top social media networks in

Data from: Alexa.com September 2014. Visualization by E.H. Fouberg and A.B. Murphy.
© 2020 John Wiley & Sons, Inc.

Social Networks Worldwide
Most Frequently Accessed
Social Media Sites by Country

Top Ranked Site
Facebook
VKontakte
Qzone
Cloob
No data

Other Ranked Sites
● Draugiem
○ Facebook
■ Instagram
● LinkedIn
○ Qzone
▲ Twitter
◉ VKontakte

FIGURE 4.16   Social Networks Worldwide.   The most popular social networks vary across the world, with Facebook having the largest imprint in terms of territory. Qzone in China is monitored and censored by the Chinese government. Cloob battled Iranian censors for 12 years until officially closing in 2017.

China are WeChat, which is seen as the Facebook of China, and SinaWeibo, the equivalent of Twitter in China.

WeChat is described by *New York Times* writer Yuan Ren as "all your phone apps" rolled into one. WeChat's 1 billion monthly users can hail cabs, book doctor's appointments, chat with friends, and purchase goods and pay for them, all within the app. Weibo has a bit less than half the monthly users of WeChat, but is China's most popular microblogging app. The information shared on Weibo is highly censored and controlled by the Chinese government. "Official news channels have large followings" on Weibo, "but there is little political content that is user-generated because censors quickly remove anything that is deemed sensitive" (Ren 2018).

China's Social Credit System Controlling information flow is a primary goal of China's government. WeChat can activate microphones and cameras at any time and collect and use the data. It has censors that monitor all postings for topics the Chinese government does not want discussed online. In 2019, censors removed WeChat posts with #MeToo, posts that mentioned the China-U.S. trade dispute, and posts about a concern over a vaccine scandal in China (**Fig. 4.17**).

In addition to Chinese government censors, Chinese citizens tend to self-censor Internet posts and receive pressure from family and supervisors to voluntarily remove posts that could be censored. Widespread monitoring goes into a social credit system the Chinese government enacted that gives each Chinese

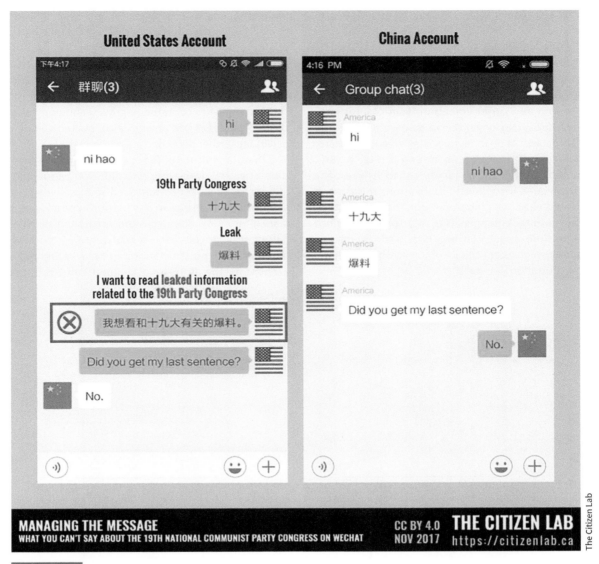

FIGURE 4.17 **Beijing, China.** Citizenlab used three phones, one in China, one in the United States, and one in Canada, to test how Chinese censors handled incoming and outgoing messages about political leaders and issues in China. In this exchange, the Chinese account on the left is receiving texts from the U.S. account on the right. Individual words did not trip the censors, but the string of words asking about leaked information from the 19th Party Congress tripped the censor, and the Chinese phone did not receive that message.

citizen a score for his or her social behavior and compliance with the government, like a financial credit score in the United States. The Chinese social credit score is designed to encourage Chinese to follow the government line; those with low social credit scores are denied freedoms like travel by air or rail, have slower Internet speed, are prohibited access to the best schools, and are denied opportunities for the best jobs (Ma 2018).

Time–Space Compression

Extraordinary changes have occurred since 1900 in the time it takes for people, innovations, and ideas to diffuse around the world. The innovation of agriculture took nearly 10,000 years to diffuse globally. In much more recent times, the diffusion of developments such as the printing press or the Industrial Revolution took 100 years or more. During the twentieth century and now into the twenty-first century, however, the time period for diffusion has shrunk to months, weeks, days, and in some cases even hours or minutes. Simultaneously, the spatial extent of diffusion has expanded, so that more and more places and people are affected by ideas and innovations from far away.

Transportation and communication technologies have altered **distance decay**. No longer does a map with a bull's-eye surrounding the hearth of an innovation describe how quickly the innovation will diffuse to areas around it (**Fig. 4.18A**). Rather, what geographer David Harvey called **time–space compression** explains how quickly innovations diffuse and refers to how interlinked two places are through transportation and communication technologies (**Fig. 4.18B**). Time–space compression, or time–space convergence, is the increasing connectedness between world cities from improved communication and transportation networks.

AP® Exam Taker's Tip

Figure 4.18A represents how diffusion occurred up until the late twentieth century. Figure 4.18B represents how diffusion occurs since the advent of the personal computer, the Internet, and social media. Explain what the dysmorphic parts of Figure 4.18B mean. Hint: The top of the diagram may mean high levels of Internet connectivity and transportation routes that allow the information to quickly diffuse from the hearth.

In the past few decades, major world cities have become much closer to one another as a result of modern technologies, including jet planes, high-speed trains, expressways, cellular phones, broadband wireless, email, and social media. All the new technologies create the infrastructure through which innovations diffuse. Because technologies link some places more closely than others, ideas diffuse through interconnected places rapidly rather than diffusing at constant rates across similar distances. Places that lack technologies are now more removed from interconnected places than ever. When disconnected places grow technologically at a slow rate and the most connected places continue to grow technology at a fast pace, connected places become more connected and disconnected places lag farther behind.

Popular culture diffuses hierarchically in the context of time–space compression, with diffusion happening most rapidly across the most compressed spaces. Even local customs practiced for centuries in one place can be swept up into popular culture. How does a custom, idea, song, or object become part of popular culture? It is relatively easy to follow the communications, transportation, and marketing networks that account for the diffusion of popular culture, but how do we

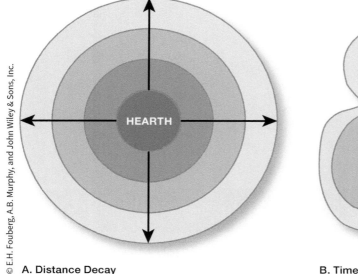

A. Distance Decay

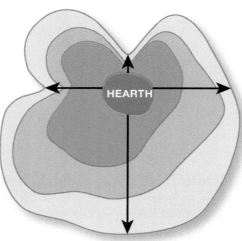

B. Time-Space Compression

© E.H. Fouberg, A.B. Murphy, and John Wiley & Sons, Inc.

FIGURE 4.18A and B   **Distance Decay and Time–Space Compression.**   With distance decay, the likelihood of diffusion decreases as time and distance from the hearth increases. With time–space compression, the likelihood of diffusion depends on connectedness, the degree of communication, and ease of transportation among places.

find the hearths of popular culture, and how do certain places establish themselves as those hearths?

Creating Popular Culture

All aspects of popular culture—music, sports, television, food, and dance—have a **hearth**, a place of origin. Typically, an idea first begins to diffuse from a hearth through contagious diffusion. Developers of an idea or innovation may find they have followers who dress as they do or listen to the music they play. In the 1980s and 1990s, bands such REM, Hootie and the Blowfish, and the Dave Matthews Band began as college bands or in college towns. They played a few sets in a campus bar or at a campus party and gained followers. They then started to play for bars and campuses in nearby college towns, and soon they produced their own music and sold it at their concerts. Bands that begin on college campuses or in college towns and build from their base typically establish a hearth for their sound, which diffuses first through contagious diffusion rooted in a place and then through hierarchical diffusion among connected places and people. College towns such as Athens, Georgia; Burlington, Vermont; and Charlottesville, Virginia, are the perfect nesting spaces for new bands.

Since 2000, accelerated use of the Internet, proliferation of music streaming services, and social media have changed how and where new music is produced and consumed. Certain places, including Los Angeles, Nashville, New York, and Las Vegas remain important music production centers and attract musicians in large numbers. Musicians are attracted to the live music venues, potential collaboration with songwriters, creativity fueled by performing with other talented musicians, and the music production companies housed in these cities.

With social media, performers can make their basements or local clubs the hearth of their music and gain followers through YouTube and other platforms. Singer-songwriter Billie Eilish was homeschooled in suburban Los Angeles and began writing songs at age 11. At 15, she released her first single to SoundCloud and attracted a following that led to record label contracts. Eilish's story is not unique, as physically starting in a major label's recording studio or in bars in a college town is no longer essential to making it in music.

Music Festivals
How music is diffused has fundamentally changed as well. Streaming services made chain record stores obsolete. Record stores were once the hub of music sales. At its peak in the late 1990s, Tower Records had around 200 stores in 15 countries. The company filed bankruptcy in 2004, and it closed in 2006. Independent record stores, like independent bookstores, still have followers, but making a profit in either music sales or book sales is increasingly difficult with online and digital competition. As music stores declined, music consumers turned to live music festivals as important places to discover new music, see artists perform live, connect with other music followers, and shape their identities.

While much of music diffusion and consumption takes place in digital space, music festivals demonstrate that physical spaces are still important. The first **music festival** in the United States was the Newport Jazz Festival in 1953, but the hearth of the culture around the modern music festival is Woodstock, which was held in rural upstate New York in 1969. Woodstock drew 500,000 people to see acts including The Who, the Grateful Dead, and Jimi Hendrix perform live in a three-day event. Festivals including South by Southwest, Lilith Fair, and Lollapalooza grew followers in the 1980s and 1990s (Florida 2019). The music festival took off after 2000. Coachella was founded in 1993 after Pearl Jam played a concert at a polo field outside of Los Angeles to protest Ticketmaster, which charged high fees and controlled access to tickets in arenas around the country. Pearl Jam proved the polo field could be used for a concert (Desert Sun 2016).

The first Coachella Music Festival was a one-day festival held on the same polo grounds in 1999, and it's still the venue for one of the largest music festivals in the United States. (**Fig. 4.19**). The Coachella Music and Arts Festival is held annually each spring over two consecutive weekends and is one of the highest earning festivals held annually. Tickets in 1999 were $50 and today are around $500 for regular admission

FIGURE 4.19 **Indio, California.** Coachella kicks off festival season in the United States each spring. Fans, celebrities, and social media influencers attend the event that has become a hub for brand promotions. Festival goers and social media influencers post hundreds of thousands of photos like this one on social media during a single festival.

Matt Winkelmeyer/Getty Images

and $1000 for VIP admission for one weekend pass. Coachella attendees are there for the music and experience and to see and be seen. Among the festival goers at the well-publicized event are celebrities and social media influencers, all of whom take and post photos. The first weekend of the 2018 festival led to over 460,000 social media posts and had a total Media Impact Value of $116 million (*Insider* 2019). Coachella also generates revenue online by livestreaming the festival on YouTube. Coachella generates profit for the concert promoters, sales tax for local governments, and revenue for hotels, airlines, food trucks, alcohol distributers, influencers, and brands.

Coachella's epic rise in popularity and revenue inspired hundreds of other festivals, large and small. Each spring, Coachella marks the beginning of festival season in the United States (**Fig. 4.20**). The majority of major festivals are held in major cities. Governor's Ball in New York launched in 2011 and is held in early June on an island off Manhattan in the East River. Among the top music festivals in the United States, only Bonnaroo, Exit 111, and WE Fest are held in rural areas. Los Angeles hosts the largest number of major music festivals annually, with nine festivals attracting at least 25,000 fans each. New York, Chicago, San Jose/San Francisco, and Las Vegas follow in numbers of festivals hosted annually.

Music festivals are a global phenomenon that generates billions in revenue annually. Live music events, including festivals and concerts, generate more revenue in the music industry than download sales and subscriptions from streaming music. Globally, festivals attract audiences much larger than Coachella or the Governors Ball in the United States. The largest music festival is in Austria on an island in the Danube River. The three-day Danube Island Festival (Donauinselfest) hit the Guinness World Record for attendance in 2015 with 3.3 million people. The festival grounds hold 350,000 fans, but the event is free and fans walk onto and off the grounds periodically over the three days, generating an annual attendance of over 2 million and a world record in 2015.

YouTube YouTube launched in 2005 and started its partner program in 2007, which pays YouTubers for the content they post. Instant online access to content has radically changed how musical artists launch, as a video can get millions of followers in a short time. In this sense, YouTube serves as a hearth of popular culture, where artists post clips and find followers. YouTube is also a site of diffusion, which can be seen in the list of top YouTube videos of all time. Music videos are 15 of the top 15 most viewed videos on YouTube, and 85 percent of Generation Z reports using YouTube daily. The intensity and frequency of interaction on YouTube enable videos to go viral, reaching millions of viewers in hours.

Generation Z is almost always online telling everyone what they like and why, interacting with others of similar interests or fandoms, and tracking what their favorite social media

© E. H. Fouberg, A. B. Murphy, and John Wiley & Sons, Inc.

FIGURE 4.20 Major Music Festivals. Each of the music festivals on this map had at least 25,000 people in daily attendance. While music festivals like Woodstock create the perception that festivals are held in remote locations, all but three of the music festivals on this map were held in major urban areas.

influencers and celebrities are posting. Using big data mined from users' social media behavior and likes, media companies can analyze celebrities' followers and gauge commonalities among their fans in order to carefully plan marketing campaigns for new products, movies, and music.

Influencers cross platforms from Instagram to Twitter to YouTube and use their large fan base or fandom to leverage corporate sponsors and advertising opportunities. An influencer's fame is an online currency used in media campaigns to create what is worthy of following or thinking about in popular culture (Koughan Rushkoff).

Social networks create opportunities for constant contagious and hierarchical diffusion. Teens become knowers of new trends both contagiously through friends' posts and hierarchically by social media influencers.

Finding a Niche in Popular Culture: South Korean Hallyu

South Korea has made a mark on popular culture from television to popular music. In 1995, Chinese television stations began broadcasting South Korean television dramas. The dramas typically aired late at night, often after midnight, but they quickly gained a large following in China. After the Chinese government changed a law that restricted Korean content on television to 15 percent of airtime, South Korean popular television dramas took off in China. An entire wave of South Korean popular culture, including television shows, movies, fashions, and music, diffused throughout China, Japan, and Southeast Asia. **Hallyu** (also called Hanryu) are waves of South Korean popular culture that move quickly through Asia and that have resulted in significant growth in the South Korean entertainment and tourism industries (**Fig. 4.21**).

Beginning with television dramas and movies, Hallyu expanded to music in the early part of this century. South Korean popular music, known as K-pop, has followed the same path of diffusion. The Chinese government allowed the Korean band H.O.T. to play in a stadium in Beijing in 2002. Today, K-pop bands, including Super Junior (called SuJu) and Girls Generation; K-pop recording artists, including Psy, Rain, and BoA; and Korean movie stars, including Bae Yong Joon, have fans throughout East Asia, Southeast Asia, and increasingly in the Middle East.

Ironically, South Korea was quite protective of its entertainment industry in the post–World War II era for fear that Japan, which formerly colonized South Korea, would export its entertainment industry and overpower South Korea's entertainment industry.

Hallyu has diffused not only to China but also to Japan. In turn, millions of Japanese and Chinese are taking Korean language classes, traveling and studying abroad in South Korea, and adopting South Korean fashions. Hallyu, especially television, has diffused throughout "East and Southeast of Asia, including Japan, Hong Kong, Taiwan, Singapore, Malaysia, Thailand, Vietnam, Philippines and later even to the Middle East and East Europe" (Kim et al. 2009). Interest in South Korean celebrities has crossed over into interest in South Korean fashion, food, and even plastic surgery throughout Asia.

Reterritorialization of Popular Culture

With viral videos that can criss cross the world in hours, we might expect popular culture to act as a blanket, evenly covering the globe. But even as popular culture diffuses throughout the world,

---

Author Field Note   Consuming Popular Culture in Seoul, South Korea

"Just days before the Japanese tsunami in 2011, I walked out of the enormous Lotte department store in Seoul, South Korea, and asked a local where to find a marketplace with hand-crafted goods. She pointed me in the direction of the Insa-dong traditional market street. When I noticed a Starbucks sign written in Korean instead of English, I knew I must be getting close to the traditional market. A block later, I arrived on Insa-dong. I found quaint tea shops and boutiques with handcrafted goods, but the market still sold plenty of bulk-made goods, including souvenirs like Korean drums, chopsticks, and items sporting Hallyu stars. Posters, mugs, and even socks adorned with the faces of members of Super Junior smiled at the shoppers along Insa-dong."

– E.H. Fouberg

FIGURE 4.21 Seoul, South Korea.

Photo by E.H. Fouberg. © 2020 John Wiley & Sons, Inc.

it does not blanket it, hiding all existing local cultures underneath it. Rather, one aspect of popular culture (such as music or food) will take on new forms when it encounters a new locality and the people and local culture in that place. Geographers and anthropologists call this the **reterritorialization** of popular culture, a process in which people start to produce an aspect of popular culture themselves, doing so in the context of their local culture and place and making it their own.

An example of reterritorialization is a popular culture restaurant, such as McDonald's or Starbucks taking on a local culture feel in each country it enters. McDonald's has more than 36,000 locations in more than 100 countries. It offers menu items unique to each country, merging local culture tastes with global food production. For example, it produces a Nutella burger in Italy, poutine in Canada, a white burger made of fish in Hong Kong, and a matcha Oreo McFlurry in Japan. Combining local foods with global restaurant chains is a form of **stimulus diffusion** (see Chapter 1).

Another form of reterritorialization happens when migrants take their local food to a new place and redesign it to make it appealing to masses even if it no longer resembles the food of its cultural origin. The local food spreads through **relocation diffusion** and a new, unique form is created and commodified in the new place.

In the United States, Chinese food was the first local cuisine to be "highly commodified" and served in restaurants across the country (Chen 2017). In the 1800s, Chinese migrants brought local cuisine from the Canton province of China through relocation diffusion, and by 1856 migrants who had arrived in California to work in the gold mines had developed 33 grocery stores and 5 restaurants in San Francisco's Chinatown, producing food mainly for consumption by Chinese migrants. As anti-Chinese violence increased in the late 1800s,

culminating in the Chinese Exclusion Act in 1882, Chinese Americans and Chinese migrants moved from rural to urban areas for safety in numbers and opened laundries in non-Chinese neighborhoods. Then, in the early twentieth century, Chinese entrepreneurs opened Chinese restaurants in neighborhoods near established laundries and tweaked recipes to make foods sweeter and more attractive to working-class Americans.

With the Immigration Reform Act of 1965 (see Chapter 3), the United States changed the quota system to be based on skills and worker needs instead of race. As a result, Chinese migration rapidly increased. Between 1970 and 2000, the number of people who identified as Chinese in the United States rose from under 500,000 to over 2,400,000 (Chen 2017). A steady supply of Chinese migrant workers enabled Chinese restaurants to expand to nearly every city and even rural towns. Migrants in this period came from throughout China, and offerings of Chinese cuisine changed to incorporate additional local Chinese foods. Chinese food in the United States today varies from more expensive, destination Chinese restaurants, including P. F. Chang's, to inexpensive Chinese buffets. Chinese food has been commodified for American tastes. One of the most popular, orange chicken, has no equivalent in China proper.

Hearth and Reterritorialization of Hip-Hop

Hip-hop and rap grew out of a hearth in the Bronx (New York) in 1973, when DJ Kool Herc hosted a back-to-school party in the first-floor community room of his apartment building at 1520 Sedgwick Avenue in the Bronx (**Fig. 4.22**), charging a small entrance fee to raise money for his sister to buy back-to-school clothes. Here DJ Herc originated and popularized an extended dance break. During the extended dance break, DJ Herc emceed, which helped launch break dancing. The apartment building at 1520 Sedgwick Avenue is recognized as the birthplace of hip-hop and is eligible for a place to be listed on the National Register of Historic Places.

Hip-hop diffused from the Bronx to include Compton (Los Angeles) in the 1980s, memorialized by N.W.A.'s album *Straight Outta Compton*, released in 1988. A third coast emerged in the South, centered on Atlanta, around the same time a distinct Midwest sound came out of Detroit (Eminem), Chicago (Kanye West and Chance the Rapper), and St. Louis (Nelly). The hearth in the Bronx and the three secondary hearths on the west coast and in the South and Midwest developed into the authentic spaces of hip-hop and rap. Neighborhood venues became the best place to enjoy an authentic performance, and the lyrics reflected the importance of local places.

In the 1990s and 2000s, hip-hop from the east coast, west coast, South, and Midwest diffused abroad, especially to major cities in Europe. MC Solaar, Die Fantastischen Vier, and Jovanotti each made hip-hop their own by writing music that connected with the youth of their country

Al Pereira/Getty Images Entertainment/Getty Images

FIGURE 4.22 **Bronx, New York.** 1520 Sedgwick Avenue in the Bronx, New York, is the hearth of hip-hop and rap.

(France, Germany, and Italy, respectively). As hip-hop diffused throughout Europe, it mixed with existing local cultures, experiences, and places, reterritorializing the music to each locale.

As hip-hop has diffused and grown, artists have addressed major concerns of their local cultures in their lyrics. Hip-hop and rap artists in the United States wrote about social issues in the 1970s and 1980s, and some wrote about violence, crime, and surviving urban life in the gangsta rap of the 1980s and 1990s. Other artists write more about having fun and partying. In France and Germany, American hip-hop music diffused first to migrants living in major cities. In France, for example, some of the first hip-hop artists were African, Arab, and Spanish migrants writing about the racism they experienced in France.

The French government helped promote hip-hop artists who rapped in French. France has several policies designed to maintain French as the language of music, film, and television popular culture (see Chapter 6). In the 1990s it required that 40 percent of on-air time be in French. Of the 40 percent, half must be new artists. These policies directly benefited the French hip-hop industry. By performing in French, the new artists received quite a bit of air time on French radio.

The results of reterritorialization are seen in the ways hip-hop artists around the world compose lyrics about the real problems surrounding them and sample local music in their music. Tunisian hip-hop artist El Général's (**Fig. 4.23**) protest anthem "Rais Lebled" played a critical role in the 2011 Arab Spring. El Général was influenced by Tupac Shakur, a west coast American rapper who spoke primarily about social issues. By posting "Rais Lebled" on YouTube, El Général helped spur massive political change. He addressed the lyrics to Ben

Ali, the corrupt dictator who had ruled Tunisia for more than 30 years. "Mr. President, your people are dying / People are eating rubbish / Look at what is happening / Miseries everywhere Mr. President / I talk with no fear / Although I know I will only get troubles / I see injustice everywhere." Protestors in Tunisia and Egypt heard, memorized, and rapped his lyrics, and El Général helped inspire revolutionaries in both countries.

Replacing Old Hearths with New: Beating Out the Big Three in Popular Sports

Baseball, football, and basketball are historically the big three sports in the United States. During the 1800s and 1900s, they all benefited from advances in transportation technology, communication technology, and institutionalization. First, the railroad connected cities across the country, allowing baseball teams to compete and professional baseball to diffuse. The telegraph enabled newspapers to report baseball scores, which added to the sport's following. In the late 1880s, electric lighting made basketball a nighttime spectator sport, played inside gymnasiums. The founding of the National Football League in 1920 helped institutionalize the sport of football by creating institutions to support it, formalize it, and regulate it, with rules for the game remaining relatively unchanged since then.

During much of the twentieth century, the big three dominated sports popular culture. Figures including Mark McGwire, Michael Jordan, and Brett Favre found their way onto Wheaties boxes and reached icon status. In the last decades of the twentieth century, advertising contracts and corporate sponsorship padded and eventually surpassed the salaries of the biggest sports heroes.

Extreme Sports While the big three continued to draw millions of fans and huge crowds to their venues, a growing number of alternative sports captured the imagination of young sports fans. For example, popular films of the 1960s (including *Endless Summer*) immortalized the freedom of surfing. In the 1970s, sidewalk surfing, now known as skateboarding, diffused from its hearth in southern California. Then in the 1980s, snowboarding found a following but initially met strong resistance on ski slopes in the United States.

The debut of ESPN's X Games in 1995 and the proliferation of video games involving extreme sports propelled previously alternative sports into popular culture. Snowboarding debuted as a winter Olympic sport in 1998. Video games sparked interest in such sports, even among kids who had never tried them before. Tony Hawk, the famous skateboarder, was one of the first non–big three athletes to gain corporate sponsors, create his own brands, and sign lucrative advertising deals. He worked with Activision to create several versions of Tony Hawk's Pro Skater. Hawk, who retired from competitive skateboarding in 1999, is worth $140 million today, generating revenue through investments, sponsorships, skate tours, and sales of his skateboards, clothing lines, and video games.

FETHI BELAID/Getty Images

FIGURE 4.23 **Tunis, Tunisia.** Tunisian hip-hop artist El Général helped spark the Arab Spring with his anthem "Rais Lebled."

DAVID MCNEW/AFP/Getty Images

FIGURE 4.24 **Burbank, California.** The New York Excelsior (left) and Shanghai Dragons play during an Overwatch League match at the Blizzard Arena, which was designed to host Esport competitions.

Several forces helped drive extreme sports into popular culture. Advertisers who court the 12–34 age demographic, fans looking for athletes who are outside of major league sports, and fans who desire a sport that is different from their parents' first drove extreme sports into popular culture. These same forces are now are driving esports, or competitive video gaming, into popular culture.

Esports The advent of streaming, which enabled people to watch video content online in real time instead of downloading for later consumption, also enabled the rapid expansion of esports as the newest competitive arena in sports. Esports are watched online through streaming services like Twitch and in huge arenas designed to allows fans to see teams compete (**Fig. 4.24**). It draws more unique viewers annually than the entire regular season of the National Football League, and revenue in esports is predicted to exceed $2 billion by 2021.

Like new music or other forms of popular culture, esports are now becoming popular, mainstream, and commodified. Fan bases have formed around the best athletes in esports and around particular games. Corporate sponsors begin to tap into the new popular sport, helping it follow the same path to popular, mainstream, and commodified status. Esports are also taking positions on college campuses, where student-athletes are recruited to compete and fans gather to watch competitions.

Major video games, including League of Legends, Overwatch, and Call of Duty, have professional athletes who are outstanding at playing the game individually or on a team and who have millions of followers. Esports fans appreciate their degree of real-time access to the athletes they follow. There are different levels of access, and higher-paying fans can comment and interact with esports athletes through Twitch and other paid-streaming platforms. Esport athletes with large fan bases garner a huge share of the potential revenue streams through sponsorships, ticket sales, and product endorsements. Recent research found that a small proportion of streamers, 10 percent, account for 95 percent of viewers.

Balancing Popular Culture and Local Culture

Identity and the desire to remain at the forefront of popular culture will continue to spur the creation of new sports and innovative ways to tap into loyal followers and generate revenue. The constant creation of new products, delivery methods, and connections fills an insatiable desire for companies to make the "next thing." It is a never-ending search for what will be attractive to the younger generations who drive purchases in music, entertainment, and athletics.

When popular culture displaces or replaces local culture, it will usually be met with resistance. Concern over the loss of local distinctiveness and identity is not limited to particular cultural or socioeconomic settings. We find such concern in everything from the rise of religious fundamentalism to the establishment of semiautonomous communes in remote locations. We also find this concern in efforts to promote local languages, religions, and customs by constructing barriers to the influx of cultural influences from the popular culture. We find concern over the loss of local and national distinctiveness among political elites seeking to promote a nationalist ideology that is explicitly opposed to cultural globalization. And we find concern among social and ethnic minorities who seek greater autonomy from governments who promote acculturation or assimilation to a single national cultural norm.

Geographers realize that local cultures will interpret, choose, and reshape the influx of popular culture. People interpret individual cultural productions in very different ways, depending on the cultural context in which they view them. What people choose to adopt from popular culture, how they reterritorialize it, and what they reject help shape the character and culture of people, places, and cultural landscapes.

TC **Thinking Geographically**

What role does language play in the **diffusion** of popular culture? Think about the diffusion of hip-hop from France to former French colonies in Africa, like Tunisia. Then explain how Arabic-language hip-hop can diffuse throughout North Africa and Southwest Asia (the Middle East). Explain where South Korean Hallyu has diffused, and determine how language influences its popularity in Asia and the Americas. Finally, using Figure 6.3, explain why American and British music are popular globally and predict what the next **hearth** of popular culture may be and what language will be used.

4.4 Compare and Contrast How Local and Popular Cultures Are Reflected in Cultural Landscapes.

The tension between popular culture and local culture can be seen in **cultural landscapes**, the visible imprint of human activity on the landscape. Human imprint includes everything from how people have changed and shaped the environment to the buildings, signs, fences, and statues people erect. Cultural landscapes reflect the values, norms, and aesthetics of a culture. On major roadways in North American towns and suburbs, the landscape is a series of big-box stores, gas stations, and restaurants that reflect popular culture (**Fig. 4.25**). As you drive down one of these roadways, one place looks like the next. You drive past Chipotle, Applebee's, Walmart, Target, and McDonald's. Then, several miles down the road, you pass another cluster of the same stores with the same architecture. Geographer Edward Relph coined the word **placelessness** to describe the loss of uniqueness of place in the cultural landscape to the point that one place looks like the next.

AP® Exam Taker's Tip

Placelessness is a geographic term that could be used to help you investigate your own landscapes. First, placelessness is homogeneity. It means the landscape is homogenous. It would be difficult to tell where the photo in Figure 4.25 was taken without its description below. Why? Because almost every urban or suburban interstate highway exit in the United States looks similar. Look at your own landscape. What elements of placelessness are there? If your landscape does not have the elements of placelessness, why is that?

© Bridget Hogan Hoye

FIGURE 4.25 **Roseville, Minnesota.** A series of signs advertising national chains creates a nondescript landscape on Snelling Avenue in this St. Paul suburb. Across the street from where this photo was taken is the site of T1, the first Target store ever built, which was recently torn down and replaced with the largest Target store in the world.

Cultural Landscapes of Popular Culture

Globalization and the widespread diffusion of popular culture have led to the **convergence** of cultural landscapes worldwide. Three developments are at the heart of convergence: (1) architectural forms and planning ideas have diffused around the world; (2) individual businesses and products have become so widespread that they now leave a distinctive landscape stamp on far-flung places; and (3) the wholesale borrowing of idealized landscape images has promoted a blurring of place distinctiveness.

The global diffusion of the skyscraper provides a clear illustration of the first point. Architectural forms and planning ideas have diffused around the world, making many places look alike. In the second half of the 1800s, with advancements in steel production and improved costs and efficiencies of steel use, architects and engineers created the first skyscrapers. The fundamental difference between a skyscraper and another building is that the outside walls of the skyscraper do not bear the major load or weight of the building. Instead, the internal steel structure or skeleton of the building bears most of the load. The Home Insurance Building of Chicago is typically credited as the first building to meet these specifications.

From Singapore to Johannesburg and from Caracas to Toronto, the central business districts (CBDs) of major cities are dominated by tall buildings, many of which were designed by the same architects and engineering firms (**Fig. 4.26**). Skyscrapers require substantial land clearing in the vicinity of individual buildings, as well as the construction of wide, straight streets to promote access. Additionally, transportation systems need to be reworked around a highly centralized CBD model. The proliferation of skyscrapers in Taiwan, Malaysia, and China in the 1990s marked the integration of these economies into the major players in the world economy (**Fig. 4.27**). Today, the growth of skyscrapers in Dubai, United Arab Emirates, signals Dubai's world city status.

Reading signs is an easy way to see the second dimension of cultural landscape convergence: the far-flung stamp of global businesses on the landscape. Walking into the parking lot of the Great Wall of China, you will see a Subway restaurant. The main tourist shopping street in Prague hosts Dunkin' Donuts and McDonald's. A tourist in Munich, Germany, will wind through streets looking for the city's famed beer garden dating from 1589, the Hofbräuhaus, and will happen upon the Hard Rock Café right next door (**Fig. 4.28**). If the tourist had recently traveled to Las Vegas, he might have déjà vu. The Hofbräuhaus Las Vegas stands across the street from the Hard Rock Hotel and Casino. The storefronts in Seoul, South Korea, are filled with Starbucks, Dunkin' Donuts, and Outback Steakhouses.

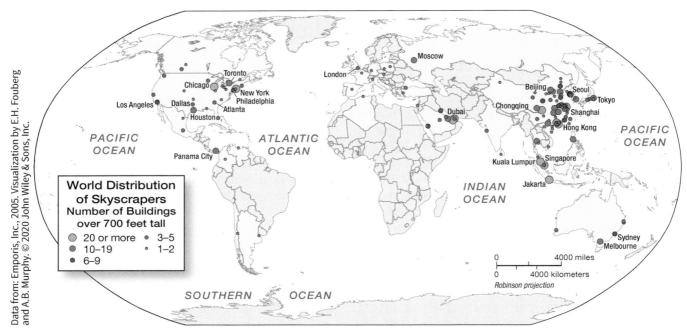

Data from: Emporis, Inc., 2005. Visualization by E.H. Fouberg and A.B. Murphy. © 2020 John Wiley & Sons, Inc.

FIGURE 4.26 **World Distribution of Skyscrapers.** The map reflects the growing importance of East Asia as a business center—particularly China. But Dubai stands out as well, a city that has staked its future on its role as an international commercial node.

Photo by A.B. Murphy. © 2020 John Wiley & Sons, Inc.

FIGURE 4.27 **Kuala Lampur, Malaysia. The Petronas Towers.** When the Petronas were completed in 1998, they were the tallest buildings in the world. They were overtaken by Taipei 101 in 2004, which in turn was dwarfed by the Burj Khalifa in Dubai in 2010.

Placeless landscapes can be found everywhere from international airports to shopping centers. Global corporations that develop spaces of commerce have wide-reaching impacts on the cultural landscape. Architectural firms often specialize in building one kind of space—performing arts centers, stadiums, medical laboratories, or international airports. Property management companies have worldwide holdings and encourage Gap, the Cheesecake Factory, and other companies to lease space in all their holdings. Facilities such as airports and college food courts begin to look the same even though they are separated by thousands of miles.

The third dimension of cultural landscape convergence is the wholesale borrowing of idealized landscape images across the world. As you study the cultural landscape, you may notice landscape features transplanted from one place to another—regardless of whether the landscape feature even "fits."

The strip in Las Vegas, Nevada, represents an extreme case of the tendency toward convergence, with various structures designed to evoke different places in the world. The popular Venetian Hotel and Casino in Las Vegas replicates the Italian city of Venice (**Fig. 4.29A and B**), including canals. In 2007 the Las Vegas Sands Corporation, a casino developer and owner, built another Venetian hotel and casino in the port city of Macao, which was once a colony of Portugal but reverted to Chinese control in 1999. The Venetian Macao resort cost $2.4 billion and is three times the size of the largest casino in Las Vegas (**Fig. 4.29C**). Gambling is illegal in mainland China, but Macao's recent incorporation into China and its special status allow gambling to flourish on the small island.

The borrowing of landscape is not confined to grand-scale projects like the Venetian. A more common borrowed

FIGURE 4.28 **Munich, Germany.** In modern-day Munich, the famed Hofbräuhaus shares a street corner with the Hard Rock Café. The juxtaposition of different cultural-commercial traditions is increasingly common.

landscape in North America is the town center. Town centers popping up in suburbia in North America have a similar look—one that is familiar if you have walked on Main Street, U.S.A., at Disneyland or Disney World, or if you have visited the centers of any number of "quaint" historic towns on the eastern seaboard. Each town center is designed to make you think of all things American and to feel immediately at home.

In less obvious ways, cultural borrowing and mixing are happening all around the world. The global–local continuum emphasizes that what happens at one scale is not independent of what happens at other scales. Human geography is not simply about documenting the differences between places; it is also about understanding the processes unfolding across scales that produce differences. What happens in an individual place is the product of interaction across scales. People in a local place mediate and alter regional, national, and global processes, in a process called glocalization. The character of place ultimately comes out of a series of dynamic interactions balancing local distinctiveness and global popular culture.

Cultural Landscapes of Local Cultures

What makes travel interesting for most people is the presence of variety in the cultural landscape. Travel beyond the tourist sites and the main roads, and one will easily find landscapes of local cultures, even in higher income countries such as the United States and Canada. By studying cultural landscapes, you can gain insight into the social structures of local cultures. In everything from the houses to the schools to the churches to the cemeteries, a local cultural landscape reveals its foundation.

Photo by A.B. Murphy. © 2020 John Wiley & Sons, Inc.

FIGURE 4.29A **Venice, Italy. UNESCO World Heritage Site.** Designation as a World Heritage Site is reserved for sites with great cultural-historical significance. But as the two photos below suggest, knock-offs of such sites are not uncommon—eroding the distinctiveness of places.

nobelIMAGES/Alamy Stock Photo

FIGURE 4.29B **The Venetian Hotel and Casino in Las Vegas, Nevada.**

siraphol/123RF

FIGURE 4.29C **The Venetian Hotel and Casino in Macau, China.**

For example, founders and early followers of the Church of Jesus Christ of Latter-day Saints created the Mormon landscape of the American West as they migrated westward under persecution and in search of a place where they could practice their religion freely. The Mormon Church began in New York, and then Joseph Smith and his followers moved westward to Independence, Missouri. From there, Mormons migrated farther west to present-day Salt Lake City, Utah. The easiest places to see the foundations of the Mormon cultural landscape are in the small towns established by Mormons throughout Utah and stretching into Arizona, Nevada, and Idaho (**Fig. 4.30**).

Geographers, including Donald Meinig, Richard Francaviglia, and Allen Noble, have studied the Mormon landscape and found the roots of the Mormon culture inscribed in the local landscape. If you drove from Chicago west to Nevada and traveled through the rural areas of Nebraska and Utah on your path, you would immediately notice one fundamental difference in the landscape: farmsteads in the plains replaced by farming villages in the west. In the Great Plains, the Homestead Act encouraged farmers to establish single farmsteads, where a farm family lived alone on their 160 acres and the nearest neighbor was down the dirt road. In the rural Mormon landscape, early settlers established farming villages with houses clustered together and croplands surrounding the outskirts of the village (**Fig. 4.31**). Such clustering allowed Mormons to protect one another, a paramount concern because the religion's followers were experiencing persecution in the East and because the settlers' fears were raised by stories of Native Americans attacking villages in the West. Equally importantly, through clustering, they sought to join together for services in each village's chapel.

Geographer Richard Francaviglia describes several factors that delimit the Mormon landscape in the western United States and Canada, including symmetrical brick houses that look more like houses on the east coast than other pioneer houses, wide streets that run due north–south and east–west, ditches for irrigation, poplar trees for shade, bishop's storehouses for storing food and necessities for the poor, and unpainted fences. Because the early Mormons were farmers and were clustered together in villages, each block in the town was quite large, allowing for one-acre city lots where a farmer could keep livestock and other farming supplies in town. The streets were wide so that farmers could easily turn a cart and horses on them.

The **urban morphology**, the size and shape of a place's buildings, streets, and infrastructure, tells us a lot, and so too can the shape and size of a local culture's housing, as the Mormon case illustrates. Distinctive housing styles are not unique to the Mormon culture. Figure 4.8 shows the distinctive housing style of

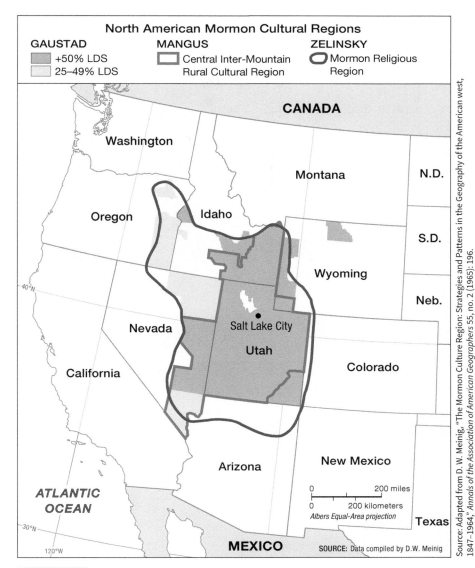

FIGURE 4.30 **The Mormon Cultural Region.** The Mormon cultural region surrounds Salt Lake City, Utah, where Mormon migrants established farms and farming communities. The religion diffused both through migration and missionary work to solidify a Mormon cultural region in North America. From this base, Mormon missionaries have diffused the religion to widespread parts of the world.

Hutterite colonies, where multiple families live in elongated housing complexes, arranged near a central common space. Amish also have a distinctive housing style, pragmatically and plainly designed to house large families. Across the world, local cultures have created housing styles that reflect their values, the materials available to them for building, and their design aesthetic.

AP® Exam Taker's Tip

Ethnocentrism is making judgments about a culture based on one's own cultural characteristics and practices. ***Cultural relativism*** is making judgments about another culture based on the characteristics and practices of the culture being studied. Which approach do you believe works best for studying and understanding cultures other than your own? Explain.

TC Thinking Geographically

Focus on the **cultural landscape** of your college campus. Think about the concept of placelessness. Determine whether your campus is a "placeless place" or whether the cultural landscape of your college reflects the unique identity of the place. Imagine you are hired to build a new student center on your campus. How could you design the building to reflect the uniqueness of your college?

Guest Field Note Cataloging the Mormon Cultural Landscape in Paragonah, Utah

Richard Francaviglia
Geo.Graphic Designs, Salem, Oregon

I took this photograph in the village of Paragonah, Utah, in 1969, and it still reminds me that fieldwork is both an art and a science. People who know the American West well may immediately recognize this as a scene from "Mormon Country," but their recognition is based primarily on their impressions of the place. "It is something about the way the scene looks," they may say, or "it feels like a Mormon village because of the way the barn and the house sit at the base of those arid bluffs." These are general impressions, but how can one prove that it is a Mormon scene? That is where the science of fieldwork comes into play. Much like a detective investigating a crime scene or a journalist writing an accurate story, the geographer looks for proof.

In this scene, we can spot several of the 10 elements that constitute the Mormon landscape. First, this farmstead is not separate from the village, but part of it—just a block off of Main Street, in fact. Next we can spot that central-hall home made out of brick; then there is that simple, unpainted gabled-roof barn; and lastly the weedy edge of a very wide street says Mormon Country. Those are just four clues suggesting that pragmatic Mormons created this cultural landscape, and other fieldwork soon confirmed that all 10 elements were present here in Paragonah. Like this 40-year-old photo, which shows some signs of age, the scene here did

© Richard Francaviglia

FIGURE 4.31 **Paragonah, Utah.** Photo taken in 1969.

not remain unchanged. In Paragonah and other Mormon villages, many old buildings have been torn down, streets paved, and the landscape "cleaned up"—a reminder that time and place (which is to say history and geography) are inseparable.

Summary

4.1 Explain Local Cultures and Global, Popular Culture.

1. A culture is a group of belief systems, norms, and values practiced by a people. We can think of cultures in terms of local culture and popular culture. A local culture is a group of people in a place who see themselves as a collective or a community and who share customs and traits. Popular culture is large, incorporates different groups of people, is typically urban, quickly changes cultural traits, and covers a larger area: national, regional, or global.

2. The values and aesthetics of a culture can be understood by studying the material culture and nonmaterial culture of a group. Material culture includes things people construct, such as art, houses, clothing, sports, dance, and foods. Nonmaterial culture includes beliefs, practices, aesthetics (what is seen as attractive), and values. The nonmaterial culture of a group is reflected in its material culture.

3. Popular culture diffuses both hierarchically and contagiously. With hierarchical diffusion, the most important and most

connected people or places learn the trait or practice first, and then it diffuses to the next most important in the hierarchy. With contagious diffusion, we see a cultural trait or practice from someone nearby us, and we adopt it.

4.2 Understand How People Sustain Local Cultures in Rural and Urban Areas.

1. Local cultures are sustained through customs. Sharing customs creates a connection among members of a local culture. Customs are passed down from generation to generation. For a local culture to sustain its customs, it must have a place to practice them. Local cultures create ethnic neighborhoods in cities and ethnic small towns in rural areas as a home base where people can practice their customs, and access the goods and services they need to maintain them.

2. During the 1800s and into the 1900s, the U.S. government had an official policy of assimilation, forcibly suppressing Native customs and replacing them with customs of the dominant culture. Through several specific programs, the U.S. government tried

to end or remove Native American customs, including sacred dances and clothing. The government also removed children from their homes, placed them in boarding schools, cut their hair, and prohibited them from speaking their Native languages.

3. A local culture that is working to reinvigorate their group and individual identities may reinstitute traditional customs and practices, teach the native language, and practice sacred ceremonies. Living in rural areas of the northern Great Plains and plains provinces of Canada has made it possible for Hutterites to live communally and maintain their identity and many cultural traits and practices.

4.3 Explain How Global, Popular Culture Is Created and Diffused.

1. At the global scale, North America, western Europe, Japan, India, and South Korea exert the greatest influence on popular culture at present. Each region acts as a major hearth for certain aspects of popular culture: North American influences are seen mainly in movies, television, music, sports, and fast food. Japan's influences are primarily in children's television programs, electronic games, and new entertainment technologies. Western Europe's are in fashion, television, art, and philosophy; South Korea's in television dramas, movies, and popular music; and India's mainly in movies.

2. Popular culture is created or manufactured. While college towns and major cities such as Nashville, Seattle, New York, Boston, and Los Angeles are still important in establishing new artists, online space is a growing way to launch artists. Corporations use big data culled from users' social media accounts and cell phones to track commonalities among celebrities' followers. Information can be used to create new trends, relaunch a celebrity, or market products.

3. Popular culture can take aspects of regional and local cultures. The hearth of hip-hop is the Bronx, New York. Hip-hop diffused

from the Bronx to include Compton (Los Angeles) in the 1980s. A third coast emerged in the South, centered on Atlanta. Around the same time, a distinct Midwest sound came out of Detroit, Chicago, and St. Louis. From its hearth in the Bronx and the three secondary hearths on the west coast, South, and Midwest, hip-hop diffused around the world, reterritorializing in each place. It took on a distinct French sound in France and then diffused from France to North Africa. In North Africa, hip-hop became a way for young people to voice their political and social concerns.

4.4 Compare and Contrast How Local and Popular Cultures Are Reflected in Cultural Landscapes.

1. The cultural landscape is the visible imprint people make on the land. Cultural landscape includes buildings, forms of cities, methods of defining land ownership, and statues and memorials. Globalization of popular culture has led to convergence. With convergence, places that are not near each other look similar. Popular culture is reflected in the cultural landscape through building types and architecture that is common across the world. For example, skyscrapers are part of popular culture architecture and can be found in every world city. Restaurant chains build structures and signage that look similar around the world.

2. Local cultures create distinct cultural landscapes. The Mormon landscape in the western United States is a good example of a local culture visible in the cultural landscape. Mormon leaders had distinct guidelines that their followers used when they built towns in Utah and surrounding states. In the rural Mormon landscape, early settlers established farming villages where houses clustered together and croplands surrounded the outskirts of the village.

Self-Test

4.1 Explain local cultures and global, popular culture.

1. Members of a local culture may work to keep out popular culture. All of the following would help people keep out popular culture except:

    a. practicing a religion unique to the local culture.

    b. celebrating festivals important to the local culture.

    c. learning to speak English and using it with one another.

    d. limiting interaction with others by living away from others.

    e. controlling access to global media.

2. Popular culture usually follows _____ diffusion, from most important people or place to the next most important.

    a. relocation

    b. hierarchical

    c. stimulus

    d. contagious

    e. relocation

3. What members of a local culture produce in terms of art, houses, clothing, sports, dance, and foods are all part of _____ culture.

    a. nonmaterial

    b. consumption

    c. material

    d. collateral

    e. ecological

4.2 Understand how people sustain local cultures in rural and urban areas.

4. When members of a local culture live together in ethnic neighborhoods or rural small towns, it helps them resist these two negative influences of popular culture:

    a. acculturation and federation

    b. customization and placelessness

    c. syncretism and stimulation

    d. immorality and greed

    e. cultural appropriation and assimilation

5. The U.S. government had an official policy of _____ toward Native Americans. Native Americans resisted and are reinvigorating their cultures by reviving their _____.

   a. customization / nonmaterial culture

   b. assimilation / customs

   c. cultural appropriation / material culture

   d. syncretism / cultural landscapes

   e. liberation / citizen rights

6. Ogallala Lakota families on Pine Ridge are building a community called Thunder Valley. Community members designed the _____, the layout of streets, houses, and community buildings, to reflect their culture.

   a. functional zonation

   b. reterritorialization

   c. urban morphology

   d. placelessness

   e. material culture

4.3 Explain how global, popular culture is created and diffused.

7. China prohibits some social networks and monitors and censors other social network sites. The government uses peoples' posts and communications to track behavior and calculate a _____ score for each Chinese person.

   a. assimilation

   b. social credit

   c. reciprocity

   d. social capital

   e. reward

8. Places in the world are not evenly connected. Innovations diffuse quickly between places that are tightly interlinked through transportation and communication technologies, creating what geographer David Harvey called:

   a. the post-modern effect.

   b. distance decay.

   c. accelerated diffusion.

   d. forward linkages.

   e. time–space compression.

9. South Korean Hallyu are waves of popular culture that diffuse from a hearth in South Korea throughout East Asia and Southeast Asia. The biggest influences of South Korean popular culture have been in all of the following except:

   a. music.

   b. video games.

   c. television.

   d. fashion.

   e. clothing.

4.4 Compare and contrast how local and popular cultures are reflected in cultural landscapes.

10. The loss of uniqueness of place in the cultural landscape happens because popular culture diffuses at the _____ scale.

   a. local

   b. national

   c. regional

   d. global

   e. micro

11. Cultural landscapes are converging, creating placelessness. Geographers have identified three developments at the heart of convergence, including all of the following except that:

   a. architectural forms and planning ideas have diffused around the world.

   b. individual businesses and products have become so widespread that they now leave a distinctive landscape stamp on far-flung places.

   c. city planners around the world follow recommendations from the United Nations Urban Planning Commission when designing cities.

   d. the wholesale borrowing of idealized landscape images has promoted a blurring of place distinctiveness.

   e. all of these answers are correct.

12. Local cultures create distinct cultural landscapes. One defining feature of the Mormon cultural landscape is:

   a. farming villages where houses are clustered together and croplands surround the outskirts of the village.

   b. single farmsteads where a farm family lives alone on their 160 acres and the nearest neighbor is down the dirt road.

   c. farming villages where houses are laid out along rivers and long lots for agriculture stretch behind each house.

   d. square sections of land where four farm families live one mile apart on each corner of the square.

   e. suburban sprawl.

CHAPTER 5

Identity: Race, Ethnicity, Gender, and Sexuality

Jerry Redfern/LightRocket/Getty Images

FIGURE 5.1 **Phnom Penh, Cambodia.** Cambodian women and men fashion rebar for a high-rise construction project. The non-profit organization CARE Cambodia estimates between 20 and 40 percent of all construction workers in Cambodia are women. Women often work the same jobs as men on construction sites but are paid less.

AP® Exam Taker's Tip

If gender is defined as the cultural assumptions about the differences between men and women, name some gender roles in your community, school, or family. Are they equal in number and/or weight of responsibility? Explain.

Cambodian women work along side men on construction sites across the country (**Fig. 5.1**). In the summer, each day starts early in hopes of getting in a full 12 hours of work before the late afternoon's monsoon rains.

After laboring all day alongside men, the women will return home with between $1 and $3 less than the men. A report from CARE Cambodia found 75 percent of Cambodian women in the construction industry are paid between $3.75 and $5 a day, which is much less than the minimum $6.25 a male construction worker earns for the same day's work. Phnom Penh's economy is growing rapidly, and construction can barely keep pace. Construction jobs, even at a lower pay rate than men, are drawing women from the country's provinces out of the rice fields and into the city.

"Education is out of reach for me now; I just have to work now to help provide for my family," a 22-year-old female construction worker explained to CARE Cambodia. The women receive few if any protections on the construction site, as most of them work at a day labor rate as part of the informal economy. While Cambodia's laws legislate a maternity leave, women in the informal economy are simply fired if their pregnancy or birth of a child prevents them from working for a day.

This chapter examines how people and society construct identities, including gender, race, ethnicity, and sexuality. We also discover how place factors into identity and how differences in power are reflected in the cultural landscapes people create.

CHAPTER OUTLINE

5.1 Define identity and explain how identities are constructed.
- Gender
- Race

5.2 Determine how place affects identity and how we can see identities in places.
- Race and Place
- Identities Across Scales
- Ethnicity and Place

5.3 Explain the role structures of power play in shaping identities.
- Identity and Space
- Counting the Work of Women
- Vulnerable Populations
- Women in Sub-Saharan Africa
- Women in India
- Shifting Structures of Power Among Ethnic Groups

5.1 Define Identity and Explain How Identities Are Constructed.

A woman pulls off a bicycle helmet and wipes her tears of joy. The voice of Serena Williams intones, "If we show emotion, we're called dramatic." A ponytail extends from under a football helmet to the middle of a jersey as a young girl tackles the running back. Williams adds, "If we want to play against men, we're nuts." Alex Morgan and teammates from the U.S. Women's National Soccer Team stand in a line for the national anthem. Williams remarks, "And if we dream of equal opportunity, we're nuts." The 90-second commercial ends with Williams urging, "If they want to call you crazy? Fine. Show them what crazy can do." Nike's "Get Crazier" advertisement campaign spoke directly to women, inspiring them to achieve athletic heights by using negative concepts of what women can and should do in sports to fuel them.

Identities are marketed through sports clothing and equipment, cars, luxury goods, club memberships, jewelry, and fundraising campaigns. Marketing campaigns give us the impression that we can buy our identity, but identity is much more personal than what we wear, drive, or belong to, or where we live. Geographer Gillian Rose (1995) defines **identity** as "how we make sense of ourselves." How do we each define ourselves? We construct our own identities through experiences, emotions, connections, and rejections. We work through derivations and delineations to find an identity that meshes with who and where we are at different points in life. An identity is a snapshot, an image of who we are at a moment. Identities are fluid, constantly changing, shifting, and becoming. Place and space are integral to our identities because our experiences in places and our perceptions of spaces help us make sense of who we are.

In addition to defining ourselves, we define others and others define us. One of the most powerful ways to construct an identity is by **identifying against** other people. To identify against, we first define the "Other," and then we define ourselves in opposing terms. Edward Said wrote thoughtfully about how Europeans, over time, constructed images of the Middle East and Asia. Europeans defined Asia as the "Orient," a place with supposedly mystical characteristics that were depicted and repeated in European art and literature.

In a similar vein, geographer James Blaut wrote perceptively about how Europeans came to define Africans and Native Americans as "savage" and "mystical." Through these images of the "Other," which developed during periods of European exploration and colonialism, Europeans defined themselves as "not mystical" or "not savage" and, therefore, as "civilized." These ideas are still part of our language (vernacular) even today, as seen in references to "the civilized world" or a time "before civilization." Phrases like these invariably carry with them a sense of superiority in opposition to an "Other."

Identities are powerful enough that governments work to construct or build national identities, often fortifying them by identifying against other countries. They do this whether they are under threat, at war, or trying to garner support for policies. State nationalism has been such a powerful force that in many contexts people think of themselves first and foremost as members of a nation: French, Japanese, Brazilian, or the like.

National identities are a product of the modern state system, which is discussed in Chapter 8. But there are all sorts of other identities that divide humanity. Alternative identities are equally and often more important to people than national identities. Language and religion are also sources of identity, and we will turn to these in Chapters 6 and 7. This chapter examines several other important foundations of identity—those based on race, gender, ethnicity, and sexuality.

Gender

Whether a culture favors males or females and how a culture sees the role of women in society are aspects of gender. Geographers Mona Domosh and Joni Seager define **gender** as "a culture's assumptions about the differences between men and women: their 'characters,' the roles they play in society, what they represent." Gender impacts everything from who is born to who eats first in a culture. Some cultures have a strong preference for males over females, and the sex ratio, the proportion of males to females, reflects that preference. In countries with a strong preference for males, females are aborted, killed, or abandoned at a higher rate than infant males, which creates a culture with many more men than women. Even in countries with balanced sex ratios, a preference for males can be seen when girls leave school at an early age to work and provide income for the family. In both lower income and higher income countries, divisions of labor and expectations of unpaid work in the home are the clearest signs of how cultures are gendered.

Factory jobs in lower income countries around the world often go to women instead of men. Factory managers report hiring women over men because they see women as an expendable labor pool. Researcher Peter Hancock (2000) studied gender relations and women's work in factories in Indonesia and reported, "Research in different global contexts suggests that factory managers employ young women because they are more easily exploited, less likely to strike or form membership organizations, are comparatively free from family responsibilities, and more adept at doing repetitive and delicate tasks associated with assembly line work."

In Southeast Asia, young women migrate from rural areas to cities and overseas to the Middle East or to larger cities in other countries in Southeast Asia to work as cooks, housekeepers, and nannies. Singapore, a higher income country in Southeast Asia, draws more than 200,000 migrant women primarily from the Philippines and Indonesia (lower income countries) to work as domestics (**Fig. 5.2**). The end goal is to earn a wage that they can send home as a **remittance** to support the schooling of their brothers and younger sisters, or to support their husbands and children. In the United States, rarely does an oldest daughter migrate to the city or another country to work so she can pay for her younger siblings' schooling. However, young women from rural areas of the United States do migrate to larger cities to work seasonally. Usually they work in the tourism industry to help financially support their children, who stay home with their father or grandparents.

Although public education in the United States is free and open to boys and girls, American society still has gendered divisions of labor. A long-standing assumption is that work requiring heavy lifting needs to be completed by men and that good-paying, unionized jobs need to go to men because men are the "heads of the household." For example, in a brick-making factory, women are hired to do tasks that require little lifting. They might glue pieces of the various types of brick to boards so that salespeople can use them as samples.

Society creates boxes in which we put people and expect them to live. These boxes are in a sense stereotypes embodying assumptions and expectations. By creating boxes, society can assign entire professions or tasks to members of certain categories. For example, we often hear of "women's work," which denotes a gendering of the division of labor. Places, like the kitchen of a home or a store in a shopping center, can also be gendered. People are constantly negotiating their personal identities, finding their ways through all the expectations placed on them by the boxes society puts around them and modifying and reinforcing the social relations that create the places where they work and live.

Race

What society typically calls a "race" is in fact a combination of physical attributes in a population. Differences in skin, eye, and hair color result from human adaptation at different latitudes. Sunlight stimulates the production of melanin, which protects skin from harmful ultraviolet rays. The more melanin in the skin, the darker the skin will be. The tropics, between 23.5°N and 23.5°S, receive consistent sunlight all 12 months of the year. According to biologists, this helps to explain why people living in the tropics, through South America, Africa, South Asia, Southeast Asia, and Australia, have darker skins.

In higher latitudes, closer to the North and South Poles, people have less melanin and less pigmentation. Higher latitudes receive little to no sunlight in winter and a lot of sunlight in summer, though at a relatively low angle. People living there have less melanin, but enough so their bodies can absorb ultraviolet light in the summer and convert it to vitamin D.

No biological basis exists for dividing the human species into four or five races based on skin color. Genes do not tell us the color of someone's skin, but genes can tell us where people's ancestors came from, geographically. **Race** is better understood as social constructions of differences among people based on skin color. Such constructions have had profound consequences on rights and opportunities.

Governments and society create and institutionalize racial categories. Think of how often we are asked to complete applications, census forms, product warranty information, surveys,

Vivek Prakash/REUTERS

FIGURE 5.2 **Singapore.** A 36-year-old woman from the Philippines works as a maid in Singapore. A survey of more than 800 domestic workers and 80 employers in Singapore found that 84 percent of workers reported working more than 12-hour days and 41 percent reported working on their one day off each week. More than a third of those surveyed reported receiving no pay.

and medical forms that ask us to check a box identifying ourselves as "white," "black," or "Asian" (**Fig. 5.3**). Such practices institutionalize and reinforce modern ways of viewing race. With each box we check, we learn to think that the categories of race on the census are natural, fixed, mutually exclusive, and comprehensive. In contrast, the more social scientists study race, the more they recognize that racial categories are constructed, fluid, overlapping, and incomplete.

Race and Class   Benedict Anderson explains that the intersection of class with race began before 1500. Wealthy French and British citizens defined themselves as superior to lower income citizens. After 1500, during European colonization, France and Great Britain claimed colonies in the Americas, Africa, and eventually Asia. In the process, lower income French and British citizens were encouraged to see themselves as superior to the people living in the colonies. The socioeconomic differences fueled a sense of superiority. As darker-skinned subjects in the colonies were easily categorized by race, racism became a method of maintaining a social, economic, and political order in which the lowest-income British and French citizens were no longer seen as the lowest class. Anderson (1982) explains:

Colonial racism was a major element in that conception of "Empire" which attempted to weld dynastic legitimacy and national community. It did so by generalizing a principle of innate, inherited superiority on which its own domestic position was (however shakily) based to the vastness of the overseas possessions, covertly (or not so covertly) conveying the idea that if, say, English lords were naturally superior to other Englishmen, no matter: these other Englishmen were no less superior to the subjected natives.

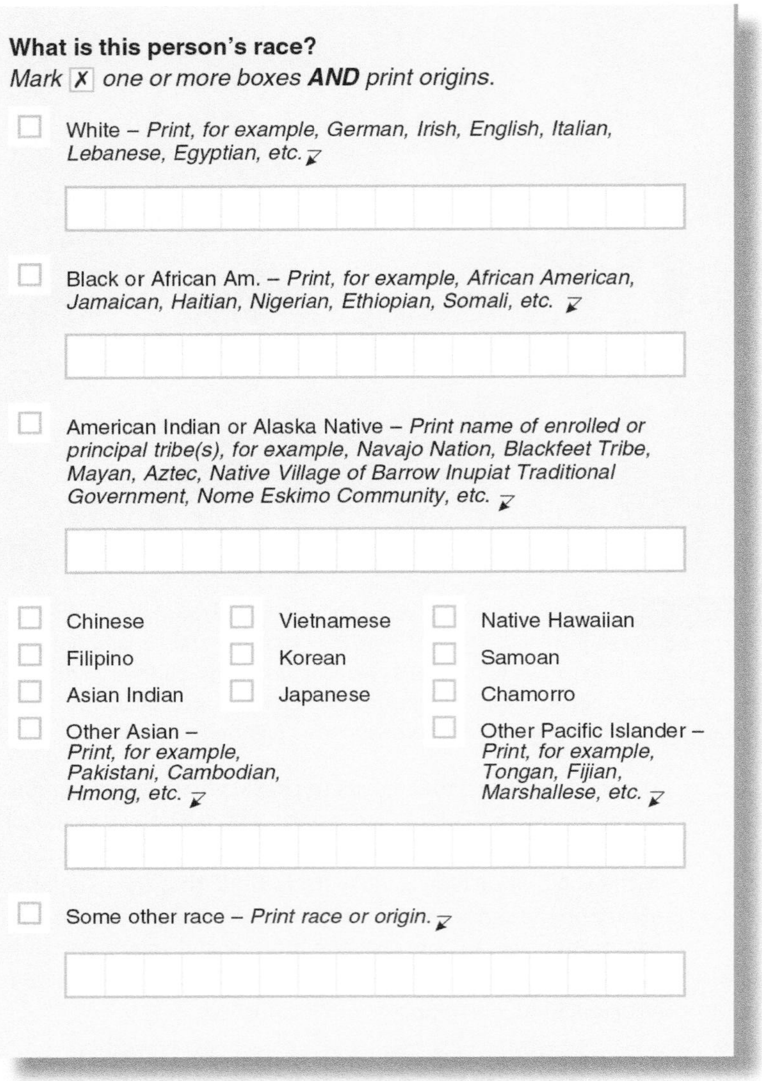

What is this person's race?

Mark X *one or more boxes* **AND** *print origins.*

☐ White – *Print, for example, German, Irish, English, Italian, Lebanese, Egyptian, etc.* ↗

☐ Black or African Am. – *Print, for example, African American, Jamaican, Haitian, Nigerian, Ethiopian, Somali, etc.* ↗

☐ American Indian or Alaska Native – *Print name of enrolled or principal tribe(s), for example, Navajo Nation, Blackfeet Tribe, Mayan, Aztec, Native Village of Barrow Inupiat Traditional Government, Nome Eskimo Community, etc.* ↗

☐ Chinese   ☐ Vietnamese   ☐ Native Hawaiian
☐ Filipino   ☐ Korean   ☐ Samoan
☐ Asian Indian   ☐ Japanese   ☐ Chamorro
☐ Other Asian –   ☐ Other Pacific Islander –
Print, for example,   *Print, for example,*
Pakistani, Cambodian,   *Tongan, Fijian,*
Hmong, etc. ↗   *Marshallese, etc.* ↗

☐ Some other race – *Print race or origin.* ↗

FIGURE 5.3 **United States Census.** Although biologically there is only one human race, we are often asked to choose race boxes for ourselves. This page of the United States Census asks the individual, "What is your race?" and directs the individual to "Mark one or more races to indicate what you consider yourself to be." The 2020 Census listed racial categories and provided a place to write in a specific race not listed on the form. Since 2000, the Census has allowed individuals to choose more than one race as their identity.

Stories that lower income British and French people heard about the "mystical" and "savage" "Others" in the colonies also fostered feelings of superiority. But since one of the easiest ways to define the "Other" is through the visible trait of skin color, differences in the color of skin became the basis for a social divide that was built on class and that defined economic places in society that privileged fair-skinned Europeans.

Racial distinctions are the product of cultural history, structures of power, and local political developments. Geographer Benjamin Forest (2001) gives us a global overview of racial distinctions:

In Britain, the term "black" refers not only to Afro Caribbeans and Africans, but also to individuals from the Indian subcontinent. In Russia, the term "black" is used to describe "Caucasians," that is, people such as Chechens from the Caucasus region. In many parts of Latin America, particularly Brazil, "racial" classification is really a kind of class placement, in which members of the wealthy upper class are generally considered as "white," members of the middle class as mixed race or Mestizo, and members of the lower class as "black." Indeed, because racial classifications are based on class standing and physical appearance rather than ancestry, "the designation of one's racial identity need not be the same as that of the parents, and siblings are often classified differently than one another."

In each of these cases, and in countless others, people have constructed racial categories to justify power, economic exploitation, and cultural oppression.

Unlike a local culture or ethnicity to which we may choose to belong, race is an identity that is more often assigned, often "imposed by a set of external social and historical constraints" (Forest 2001). In the United States, residential segregation, racialized divisions of labor, and the categories of races recorded by the United States Census reinforce race.

Definitions of race in the United States historically focused on dividing the country into "white" and "nonwhite." Influential figures in sports (Tiger Woods), politics (President Barack Obama), and music (Zendaya), who do not clearly fit into one race, are often asked by the media to choose or explain their racial identity (**Fig. 5.4**). Governments use race to justify limits on migration (see Chapter 3). In the late 1800s and early 1900s, immigration to the United States shifted from northern and western Europe to southern and eastern Europe, and the U.S. government redefined what constituted "white" so that people with olive-colored skin from the Mediterranean would count as "white."

Skin color is not a reliable indicator of genetic closeness. The indigenous peoples of southern India, New Guinea, and Australia, for example, are about as dark-skinned as native Africans, but native Africans, southern Indians, and Aboriginal Australians are not closely related genetically.

Classifying Race   Racial and ethnic classifications are arbitrary. Governments can create racial classes and institutionalize them. When Spain colonized much of the Americas, including South America, Central America, and Mexico, they created the Casta system to identify and classify different races **(Fig. 5.5)**. In each of a series of oil paintings, artists showed combinations of couples from the same and different races (mainly Spanish, indigenous, and African) with a child and designated racial labels for their children. The Casta paintings

FIGURE 5.4 **London, United Kingdom.** Actor Zendaya poses during a photo call in London. The actor has received many questions about her race. Zendaya describes her mom as having roots in Germany and Scotland, and her dad as an African American. In one interview, Zendaya answered questions about her identity saying "No one's just white and no one's just black."

rest of the text, we use the most precise description possible. Instead of a generic term like *Hispanic*, if we are talking about a group of migrants from Bolivia, we call them migrants from Bolivia. If we discuss a study about Cree Indians in Canada, we use *Cree*, not the more general term *First Nations*. In general references, we use the term *Hispanic* instead of *Latino* or *Latina*. This convention follows Census definitions and surveys of Americans who defined themselves as Hispanic or Latino. In a Pew Research survey, half of Americans who identified as Hispanic or Latino reported having no preference for either term. Among those who expressed a preference in the survey, "'Hispanic' was preferred over 'Latino' by a ratio of about 2 to 1" (Pew 2013).

In the United States, 64 percent of the Hispanic population identifies as having Mexican origin, and 9 percent of people who define themselves as Hispanic are of Puerto Rican descent. In the U.S. Census, people who identify as Hispanic can also identify a racial category. By combining race and ethnicity boxes, statisticians can separate Americans into "White, non-Hispanic" and "everyone else." Projections hold that the population of "everyone else" will surpass (in numbers) the "White, non-Hispanic" population around 2045 (**Table 5.2**).

both defined and institutionalized racial classes in Spain's colonies in the Americas.

Governments can create racial classes, and they can change racial classifications. Before 2000, the United States Census classified Hispanic as a race. A white person from Venezuela, a black person from Brazil, and a native person from Bolivia were all classified as Hispanic in the Census before 2000. Coming from Latin America overrode all other classifications or categories and made the person racially Hispanic. In 2000, the Census recognized that Hispanic is not a race and that it is better defined as an ethnicity (**Table 5.1**).

The ethnic term *Hispanic* is itself problematic. The word Hispanic means coming from a country where Spanish is the predominant language, including Spain, Mexico, and many countries in Central and South America and the Caribbean. A person from Brazil who is classified as "Hispanic" should not be under this definition. The predominant language in Brazil is Portuguese, not Spanish, which means that Brazil is not a Spanish-speaking country.

The redesignation of Hispanic as an ethnicity on the Census enables people to identify as "White, non-Hispanic," "White, Hispanic," "Black, non-Hispanic," "Black, Hispanic," and so forth. The United States Census now recognizes that "Hispanic" can be seen as excluding people who are not native Spanish speakers. The Census also recognized that some people, including U.S. Supreme Court Justice Sonia Sotomayor, prefer the term *Latina* or *Latino* to *Hispanic*. The United States Census Bureau describes Hispanic ethnicity as "Hispanic, Latino, or Spanish origin," and continues to list Hispanic as an ethnicity and not a race.

With the evolution in understanding of race and ethnicity, it is sometimes difficult to choose the right term to describe an individual or group of people. In this chapter and in the

FIGURE 5.5 **Casta Art.** When Spain colonized much of South America, Central America, and Mexico, they defined and institutionalized racial classes through a series of paintings. Casta art showed mothers and fathers of different races (Spanish, indigenous, and African) and classified the races of their children.

TABLE 5.1   **Population of the United States by Race, 2020.**

The U.S. Census projects that when looking at race alone, and not Hispanic ethnicity, whites are the majority population, followed by African Americans, Asian and Pacific Islanders, 2 or more races, and American Indians and Alaska Natives.

Source: U.S. Census 2017.

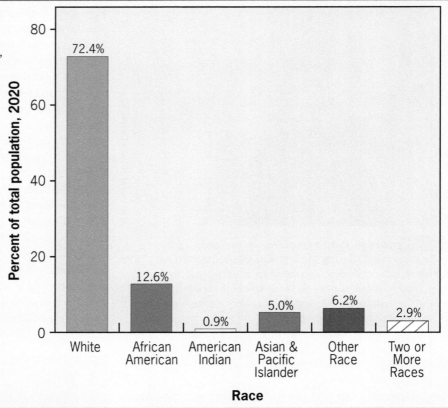

TABLE 5.2   **Estimated Percentage of United States Population by Race and Ethnicity Until 2060.**

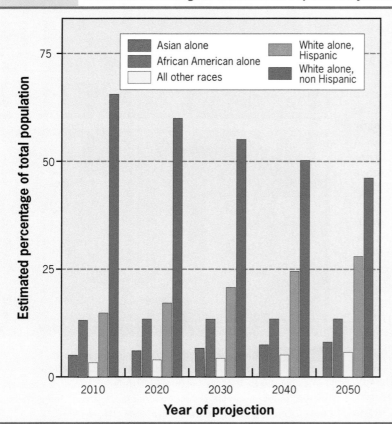

In 2000, the United States Census Bureau began to calculate race and Hispanic origin separately, allowing people to place themselves in one or more race categories plus one of two Hispanic origin categories (Hispanic or non-Hispanic). Based on projections from the U.S. Census and the Brookings Institute, the white, non-Hispanic population will no longer be the majority population in the United States after 2045.

Source: United States Census, 2017 and Brookings Institute, 2018.

TC **Thinking** **Geographically**

Think of the last time you were asked to check a box for your **race**. How does that box factor into your **identity**—how you make sense of yourself individually, locally, regionally, nationally, and globally? Does the role that race plays in your identity change at different **scales** or in different **places**?

5.2 Determine How Place Affects Identity and How We Can See Identities in Places.

The processes of constructing identities and identifying against an "Other," just like any other social or cultural process, differ from place to place and are rooted in places. When we construct identities, part of what we do is infuse place with meaning by attaching memories and experiences to it. This process of infusing a place "with meaning and feeling" is what Gillian Rose and countless other geographers refer to as "developing a sense of place." Like identity, our sense of place is fluid; it changes as the place changes and as we change.

Of particular interest to geographers is how people define themselves through places. Our sense of place becomes part of our identity, and our identity affects the ways we define and experience place. Rose (1995) explains:

> One way in which identity is connected to a particular place is by a feeling that you belong to that place. It's a place in which you feel comfortable, or at home, because part of how you define yourself is symbolized by certain qualities of that place. The geographer Relph, for example, has even gone so far as to claim that "to be human is to live in a world that is filled with significant places: to be human is to have to know your place."

The uniqueness of a place can become a part of who we are, just as who we are—individually and in communities—shapes places.

Race and Place

Racism has affected where people live throughout the history of the United States. The United States government policy of segregation ended legally in 1954, but segregation has remained at the neighborhood scale. States, cities, and towns passed laws that prevented mixing of racial groups in certain neighborhoods. The civil rights movement in the 1960s challenged the legality of neighborhood segregation, and the 1968 Fair Housing Act outlawed racial discrimination in rental and housing markets. The 1977 Community Reinvestment Act prohibited redlining in the mortgage industry, a practice that created segregated neighborhoods (see Chapter 9). Eventually, cities changed laws and ended legal segregation by neighborhood. However, many cities in the United States remain residentially segregated.

Douglas Massey and Nancy Denton defined **residential segregation** as the "degree to which two or more groups live separately from one another" within an urban area. Massey and Denton identified and measured five different kinds of residential segregation: evenness, exposure, concentrated, centralized, and clustered. Thinking of segregation along five different measurements is helpful because residential segregation is complex:

> Groups may live apart from one another and be "segregated" in a variety of ways. Minority members may be distributed so that they are over-represented in some areas and under-represented in others, varying on the characteristic of *evenness*. They may be distributed so that their *exposure* to majority members is limited by virtue of rarely sharing a neighborhood with them. They may be spatially *concentrated* within a very small area, occupying less physical space than majority members. They may be spatially *centralized*, congregating around the urban core, and occupying a more central location than the majority. Finally, areas of minority settlement may be tightly *clustered* to form one large contiguous enclave or be scattered widely around the urban area.

The methods that Massey and Denton established are used by researchers along with the United States Census to calculate segregation in the United States. Maps for the most segregated and least segregated cities can be generated using Census data. Understanding which cities are most or least segregated helps reveal where underlying structures may be entrenching residential segregation.

The roots of residential segregation in the United States are typically attributed to three factors: money, preferences, and discrimination. *Money* leads to residential segregation when only people with certain income levels can afford to live in a neighborhood. In almost all cities, race is related to class, making it difficult to afford a higher-class neighborhood that is also populated by another race. *Preference* means that people may choose to live in a neighborhood with a certain racial composition. In some of the most segregated cities, people will purposely choose to live in neighborhoods with people like themselves. Residents may choose to live in what others call a "blighted" or "rundown" neighborhood because it is their neighborhood: They have helped create it and it reflects their culture. Although discriminatory housing practices are illegal, *discrimination* in the housing market still takes place. Real estate agents and community leaders may consciously or subconsciously direct people to their "own" neighborhoods.

Residential segregation for African Americans nationwide peaked in the 1960s and 1970s. Milwaukee, Wisconsin, remains among the most residentially segregated large metropolitan areas for African Americans (**Fig. 5.6**). Phoenix-Mesa, Arizona, is the most residentially segregated metropolitan area for American Indians and Alaska Natives. Oklahoma City, Oklahoma, is the least residentially segregated. Among metropolitan areas with at least 3 percent of the population American Indian, the four least residentially segregated are all in Oklahoma. The most residentially segregated metropolitan area for Asians/Pacific Islanders is San Francisco, followed by New York and Los Angeles.

Baltimore, Maryland (**Fig. 5.7**), is one of the most residentially integrated cites in the United States for Asians as well as

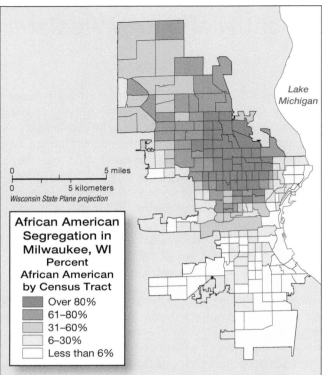

for Hispanics/Latinos. A Census report found that the cities with the highest number of Hispanic residents experience the greatest degree of residential segregation.

Entrenched Residential Segregation

Measurements of residential segregation and corresponding maps show the outcomes of a variety of stories, but they do not tell us the stories that created the patterns. Why does residential segregation persist in some places and not in others? Since 1990, overall residential segregation by race/ethnicity has been declining in the United States as a whole, but several cities have entrenched residential segregation that has not declined. Sociologists Maria Krysan and Kyle Crowder studied residential segregation in Chicago to find the underlying stories of how residential segregation has become so entrenched in the city (**Fig. 5.8**).

FIGURE 5.6 **Residential Segregation of African Americans in Milwaukee, Wisconsin.** Percent African American by Census tract. African American neighborhoods are concentrated on the north end of Milwaukee. First settled in the 1800s by Germans, northern Milwaukee became predominantly African American during the Great Migration (see Chapter 3).

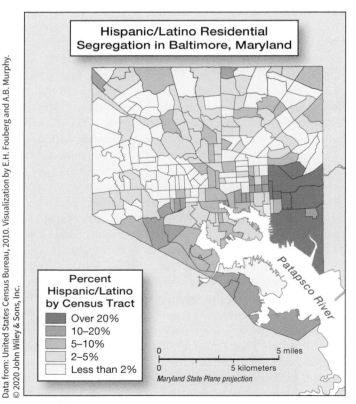

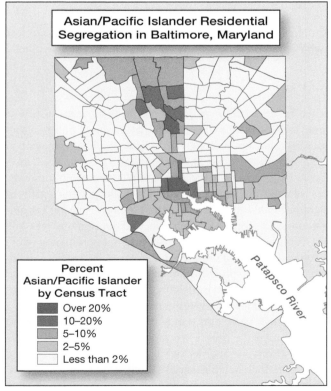

FIGURE 5.7 **Residential Segregation of Latinos and Asians/Pacific Islanders in Baltimore, Maryland.** Baltimore, Maryland, is one of the least segregated cities for Hispanics and Asians/Pacific Islanders. The Hispanic population is distributed throughout the city with some neighborhoods standing out as strongly Hispanic.

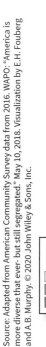

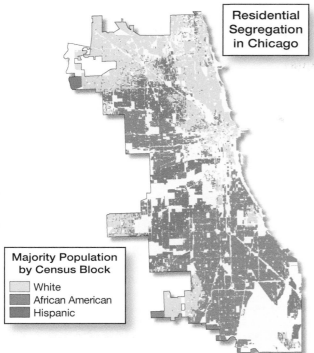

Residential Segregation in Chicago

Majority Population by Census Block
- White
- African American
- Hispanic

FIGURE 5.8 **Residential Segregation in Chicago.** Chicago is residentially segregated with clear breaks between African American neighborhoods in the south and west; white neighborhoods in the north, along Lake Michigan, and in the southwest; and Hispanic neighborhoods in the center.

The social networks, activity spaces, and lived experiences of people in Chicago perpetuate residential segregation. While Chicago is a diverse, multiracial city, people from different races have little spatial interaction in their residential neighborhoods. Social networks are divided with little overlap, and in the rounds of everyday activity, people from different racial groups do not interact much. Krysan explains that African Americans in Chicago are concerned about both explicit discrimination ("where people refuse to rent to you") and anticipated discrimination, the question of whether you will be welcomed and belong in the neighborhood. Social networks also play a role in where people choose to live.

Krysan describes the search for a residence as a three-stage process: pre-search stage, stage one, and stage two. The pre-search stage is your activity space and your social network: the places and people with which you are familiar. In stage one, you use shortcuts of what you already know to "choose which of the many possible communities you're going to search in" (Gun 2018). Then, in stage two, you look for specific attributes like cost of rent, configuration of house, or proximity to family to make your selection. Each stage helps entrench residential segregation because you start from the places with which you are familiar and then use your social networks in both stage one and stage two to select your home. As long as neighborhoods

and social networks are segregated in practice, residential segregation becomes, in Krysan's words "baked in" (Gun 2018).

Residential segregation matters, particularly in the United States, where public school districts are funded by local property taxes (**Fig. 5.9**). Being separated residentially separates groups by "educational quality and occupational opportunity," according to Crowder (Williams and Emamdjomeh 2018). In the United States school system, affluence correlates with achievement (**Fig. 5.10**). Children from families with higher incomes go to schools with higher funding and perform at grade levels above where children from families with lower incomes at lower-funded schools perform.

Identities Across Scales

The way we make sense of ourselves in an increasingly globalized world is complex. We have different identities at different scales: individual, local, regional, national, and global. At the individual scale, we may see ourselves as a daughter, a sister, a teacher, or a student. At the local scale, we may see ourselves as members of a community, leaders of a campus organization, residents of a neighborhood, or members of an ethnic group. At the regional scale, we may see ourselves as Southerners, as north Georgians, as Atlantans, as Yankees

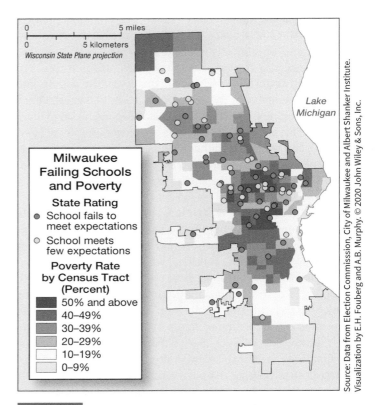

Milwaukee Failing Schools and Poverty

State Rating
- School fails to meet expectations
- School meets few expectations

Poverty Rate by Census Tract (Percent)
- 50% and above
- 40–49%
- 30–39%
- 20–29%
- 10–19%
- 0–9%

FIGURE 5.9 **School Performance and Poverty in Milwaukee, Wisconsin.** The colors on this map show the percent of people with incomes below the poverty line. The dots on the map show schools that fail or are below expectations according to a state rating of school districts.

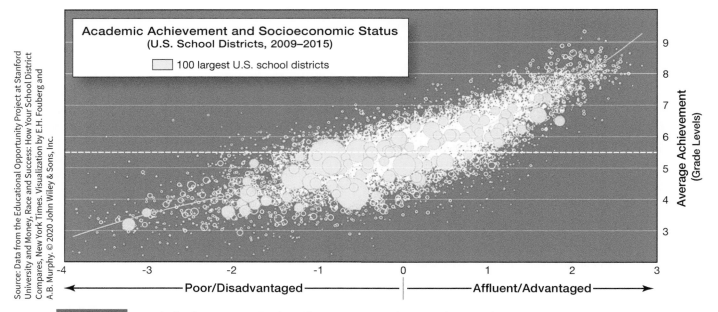

Source: Data from the Educational Opportunity Project at Stanford University and Money, Race and Success: How Your School District Compares, New York Times. Visualization by E.H. Fouberg and A.B. Murphy. © 2020 John Wiley & Sons, Inc.

FIGURE 5.10   **Correlation between Academic Achievement and Socioeconomic Status in U.S. School Districts.**   All U.S. school districts are charted on this graph, with the relative size of the student population shown in the size of each bubble. The 100 largest school districts are shown in yellow. Degrees of poverty and disadvantage and affluence and advantage are shown on the X axis and average grade level achievement is shown on the Y axis.

living in the South, or as migrants from another region of the world. At the national scale, we may see ourselves as American, as college students, or as members of a national political party. At the global scale, we may see ourselves as Western, as educated, as relatively wealthy, or as free.

One way to view an individual's various identities is to treat them as nested, one inside of the other. The appropriate identity is revealed at the appropriate scale. In this vein, each larger geographic space has its own corresponding set of identities. Today, however, geographers see identities as fluid, intertwined, and contextual rather than as neatly nested. Identities affect each other in and across scales. The ways places and peoples interact across scales simultaneously affect their identities.

The Scale of New York City   One way that scale affects identity is by helping to shape what is seen—what identity is apparent to others and to ourselves at different scales. To demonstrate this idea, we can shift our focus from residential segregation in all large metropolitan areas in North America to one enormous metropolitan area, New York City. New York has a greater number and diversity of migrants than any other city in the United States. At the scale of New York, we can see how identities change so that we are no longer simply Hispanic (as the Census enumerates us); we are Puerto Rican or Mexican or Dominican from a certain neighborhood.

The point is that the people in New York are much more diverse than the box on Census forms labeled "Hispanic" would suggest. For example, in a chapter called "Changing Latinization of New York City," geographer Inés Miyares highlights the importance of Caribbean culture to New York. The majority of New York's 2.4 million Hispanics are Puerto Rican,

Dominican, or Mexican (together accounting for over 70 percent of the city's Hispanics). The Hispanic population in New York is quite diverse, also including Ecuadorians, Colombians, and Central Americans. Each group has made its own profound imprint on New York's cultural landscape.

New migrants to a city often move to low-income areas that are being gradually abandoned by older immigrant groups. This process is called **succession**. In New York, Puerto Ricans moved into the immigrant Jewish neighborhood of East Harlem in the early twentieth century, successively assuming a dominant presence in the neighborhood. With the influx of Puerto Ricans, new names for the neighborhood developed, and today it is frequently called Spanish Harlem or El Barrio (meaning "neighborhood" in Spanish). As the Puerto Rican population grew, new storefronts appeared that catered to the Puerto Rican population, including travel agencies (specializing in flights to Puerto Rico), specialty grocery stores, and dance and music studios.

A large-scale migration from the Dominican Republic began in 1965 and resulted in a distinct neighborhood and cultural landscape. Dominican migrants landed in the Washington Heights/Inwood neighborhood of upper Manhattan, a neighborhood previously occupied by immigrant Jews, African Americans, Puerto Ricans, and Cubans. Miyares reports that although a Jewish cultural landscape persists, including a Jewish university, synagogues, and Jewish delicatessens, the cultural landscape of Washington Heights is clearly Dominican—from store signs in Spanish to the presence of the colors of the Dominican flag (**Fig. 5.11**).

New York is unique because of the sheer number and diversity of its immigrant population. The city's cultural landscape reflects its unique population. As Miyares explains:

Since the overwhelming majority of New York City's population lives in apartments as opposed to houses, it is often difficult to discern the presence of an ethnic group by looking at residential housescapes. However every neighborhood has a principal commercial street, and this is often converted into an ethnic main street. It is commonly through business signs that migrants make their presence known. Names of businesses reflect place names from the home country or key cultural artifacts. Colors of the national flag are common in store awnings, and the flags themselves and national crests abound in store décor. Key religious symbols are also common. Migrants are so prevalent and diverse that coethnic proprietors use many kinds of visual clues to attract potential customers.

Throughout the process, new migrants do not need to change the facades of apartment buildings to reflect their culture. Instead, many new migrants focus their attention on the streetscapes, offering goods and services for their community and posting signs in their language.

In New York and in specific neighborhoods like East Harlem, the word *Hispanic* does little to explain the diversity of the city. Hispanic identities in New York vary by "borough, by neighborhood, by era, and by source country and entry experience." Since 1990, the greatest growth in the Hispanic population of New York has been Mexican. The process of succession continues in New York, with Mexican migrants moving into and succeeding other Hispanic neighborhoods, sometimes producing tensions between and among the local cultures. Mexican migrants have settled in a variety of ethnic neighborhoods, living alongside new Chinese migrants in Brooklyn and Puerto Ricans in East Harlem.

Urban ethnic neighborhoods like Washington Heights and Little Italy (see Chapter 4) in New York create places where identities are rooted and reinforced. The local scale identities found in ethnic neighborhoods affect identities at larger scales including the nation.

Ethnicity and Place

Ethnicity offers a good example of how identities affect places and how places affect identities. The idea of ethnicity as an identity stems from the notion that people are closely bounded, even related, in a certain place over time. The word **ethnic** comes from the ancient Greek word *ethnos*, meaning "people" or "nation." Geographer Stuart Hall (1995) explains: "Where people share not only a culture but an ethnos, their belongingness or binding into group and place, and their sense of cultural identity, are very strongly defined." Hall makes clear that ethnic identity is "historically constructed like all cultural identities" and is often considered natural because it implies ancient relations among a people over time.

Ethnicity may sound simple, but it is not. In the United States, for example, a group of people may define their ethnicity as Swiss American. Switzerland is a country in Europe where people speak four major languages and other minor

---

Guest Field Note   Reading the Dominican Landscape in Washington Heights, New York

Inés Miyares
Hunter College of the City University of New York

It is a warm, humid September morning, and the shops along Juan Pablo Duarte Boulevard are already bustling with customers. The Dominican flag waves proudly from each corner's traffic signal. Calypso and salsa music ring through the air, as do the voices of Dominican grandmothers negotiating for the best prices on fresh mangoes and papayas. The scents of fresh empanadas de yuca and pastelitos de pollo waft from street vendor carts. The signage, the music, the language of the street are all in Spanish and call out to this Dominican community. I am not in Santo Domingo but in Washington Heights in upper Manhattan in New York City.

Whenever I exit the "A" train at 181st Street and walk toward St. Nicholas Avenue, renamed here Juan Pablo Duarte Boulevard for the founding father of the Dominican Republic, it is as if I have boarded a plane to the island. Although there are Dominicans living in most neighborhoods of New York's five boroughs, Washington Heights serves as the heart and soul of the community. Dominicans began settling in Washington Heights in 1965, replacing previous Jewish, African American, and Cuban residents through processes of invasion and succession. Over time they have established a vibrant social and economic enclave that is replenished daily by transnational connections to the residents' homeland. These transnational links are pervasive on the landscape, and include travel agencies advertising daily flights to Santo

FIGURE 5.11 **Washington Heights, New York.**

Domingo and Puerto Plata and stores handling *cargas*, *envios*, and *remesas* (material and financial remittances) found on every block, as well as *farmacias* (pharmacies) selling traditional medicines and *botanicas* selling candles, statues, and other elements needed by practitioners of Santería, a syncretistic blending of Catholicism and Yoruba beliefs practiced by many in the Spanish Caribbean.

ones. The strongest identities in Switzerland are most often at the canton level—a small geographically defined area that distinguishes cultural groups within the country. So, which Swiss are Swiss Americans? The way Swiss Americans perceive Switzerland and sense it as part of who they are may not exist in Switzerland proper (**Fig. 5.12**).

Ethnic identity is greatly affected by scale and place. The Jackson Heights neighborhood in Queens, New York, is home to speakers of 167 different languages. Half of Jackson Height's 67,000 residents identify as Hispanic, and 20 percent identify as South Asian: Indian, Pakistani, or Bangladeshi. In South Asia, the countries of Pakistan and India have a history of animosity since the British partitioned them in 1947. Pakistan and Bangladesh were one country as of 1947, but they split in 1973. However, in Jackson Heights, a world apart from India, Pakistan, and Bangladesh, many South Asians identify with one another. South Asian restaurants, grocery stores, and a theater that plays new release Bollywood movies attract Pakistanis, Indians, and Bangladeshis alike. The geographical context of Jackson Heights fosters a collective South Asian identity.

Cultural groups often invoke ethnicity when race cannot explain differences and antagonism between groups. Just as "racial conflicts" are rooted in perceptions of distinctiveness based on differences in economics, power, language, religion, lifestyle, or historical experience, so too are "ethnic conflicts." A conflict is often called ethnic when a racial distinction cannot easily be made. For example, using physical appearance and skin color, an observer cannot distinguish the ethnic groups in many of the conflicts around the world. The adversaries in post–World War II conflicts in Northern Ireland, Spain, the former Yugoslavia, Sri Lanka, Ivory Coast, or Rwanda cannot be identified racially. Thus "ethnicity" becomes the marker of difference.

In some instances, the term ethnicity is reserved for a small, cohesive, culturally linked group of people who stand apart from the surrounding culture (often as a result of migration). In other cases, ethnicity is used to describe a group that covers an entire country or world region. A map showing all recognizable ethnic areas would look like a three-dimensional jigsaw puzzle with thousands of often overlapping pieces—some no larger than a neighborhood, others as large as entire countries.

Chinatown in Mexicali

The border region between the United States and Mexico is generally seen as a cultural meeting point between Mexicans and Americans. Yet the ethnic composition of people in the border region is even more diverse.

Indigenous peoples have lived in what is now the border region for thousands of years. A treaty defined the current border between Mexico and the United States in 1848. Mexico ceded half its territory to the United States through that treaty, and the new border arbitrarily divided indigenous people. New identities were forged over time, with communities on the north side of the border becoming Native Americans and communities on the south side of the border becoming indigenous Mexicans.

Through migration, people from Germany, Russia, India, China, Japan, and many other places also live in the cities and rural areas of the United States–Mexico border region. Over time people have created distinct patterns of settlement and imprinted cultural landscapes with their ethnic identities. For example, the town of Mexicali is the capital of Baja California, located in Mexico just south of California. Not far from the central business district of Mexicali lies the largest Chinatown in Mexico, La Chinesca. Chinese migrants began arriving in 1902, brought by the Colorado River Land Company, which started growing cotton in Mexicali when diversion of the Colorado River brought water to irrigate fields in the area (Curtis 1995). Chinese in the United States were drawn to Mexicali because the American government started persecuting Chinese after passage of the Chinese Exclusion Act in 1882. Chinese settled in the town of Mexicali, and by 1919 more than 11,000 Chinese were either permanent or temporary residents of the valley. They established a thriving Chinatown in the heart of Mexicali that has served as the uncontested center of Chinese life in the region for decades (**Fig. 5.13**).

Chinese in Mexicali remained prominent players in the social and economic life of the city during the twentieth century. Chinese owned and operated restaurants, bars, retail trade establishments, commercial land developments, currency exchanges, and more. Chinese migrants also built a system of underground tunnels connecting businesses in the Chinatown area so they could avoid the hot Mexican sun by traveling and sleeping underground. The tunnels served as a refuge when anti-Chinese sentiments grew during the second Mexican Revolution, starting in 1910.

By 1989, Chinese owned nearly 500 commercial or service properties. In an effort to sustain their cultural traditions and add to the cultural life of the city, they established the China Association, which plays an active role in Mexicali's social and civic life.

Photo by E.H. Fouberg. © 2020 John Wiley & Sons, Inc.

FIGURE 5.12 New Glarus, Wisconsin. Immigrants from Switzerland established the town of New Glarus in 1845. The Maple Leaf Cheese and Chocolate Haus, across the street from the New Glarus Hotel, combines Wisconsin cheese and Swiss chocolate in one shop. The building is designed with a Swiss architecture style and flies a Swiss flag. The Swiss flag and Swiss architecture are found all over town, as a constant reminder of the pride the town has in its history and culture.

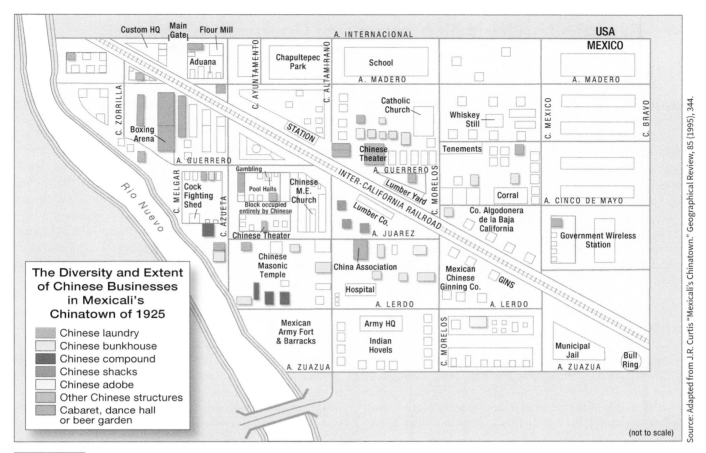

The Diversity and Extent
of Chinese Businesses
in Mexicali's
Chinatown of 1925

Chinese laundry
Chinese bunkhouse
Chinese compound
Chinese shacks
Chinese adobe
Other Chinese structures
Cabaret, dance hall
or beer garden

(not to scale)

Source: Adapted from J.R. Curtis "Mexicali's Chinatown." Geographical Review, 85 (1995), 344.

FIGURE 5.13 **Chinatown in Mexicali, Mexico.** The diversity and extent of Chinese businesses in Mexicali's Chinatown of 1925 are shown in this map.

Mexicali's Chinatown is now experiencing a transformation. Chinese residents have dispersed to the edges of the city and beyond, as many can afford to move out of town. As a result, relatively few Chinese continue to live in the city's Chinatown. Some have even moved across the border to Calexico, a city on the California side of the border, while holding on to business interests in Mexicali.

Mexicali's Chinatown continues to play an important symbolic and functional role for people with Chinese ancestry in the area who are still shaping the region's social and economic geography. The city of 1 million people is home to 300 Chinese restaurants that fuse southwestern and Mexican flavors into traditional Chinese fare (**Fig. 5.14**). Even if the ethnic population in a region is small, ethnic group identity and consciousness can have a lasting effect on the cultural landscape.

TC Thinking Geographically

Study the example of residential segregation in Milwaukee from the beginning of this section of the chapter. Hypothesize how the pattern of segregation was created and how it reflects the history of **migration** in Milwaukee (see Figure 3.11).

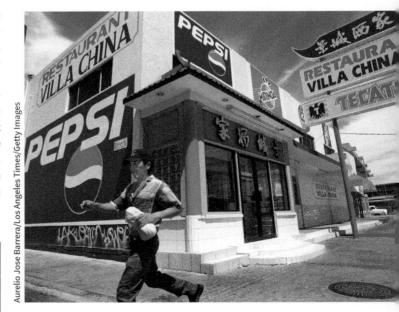

Aurelio Jose Barrera/Los Angeles Times/Getty Images

FIGURE 5.14 **Mexicali, Mexico.** The Mexican city of Mexicali still has over 300 Chinese restaurants today, including the Villa China that advertises Pepsi and Tecate, a Mexican beer.

5.3 Explain the Role Structures of Power Play in Shaping Identities.

Geographers who study identities of gender, ethnicity, race, and sexuality realize that when people make places, they do so in the context of surrounding social relationships, including structures of power. We can, for example, create places that are gendered—places seen as being appropriate for women or for men. A building can be constructed with the goal of creating gendered spaces within it, or it can become gendered by the way people make use of it. People with greater power can claim and shape spaces to match their identities. People with less power can define smaller, often informal spaces as their own and shape them to reflect their identities. The use of space is powerful in defining a place as belonging to a people.

Identity and Space

One way of thinking about place is to consider it as a cross section of space. Doreen Massey and Pat Jess (1995) define space as "social relations stretched out" and place as "particular articulations of those social relations as they have come together, over time, in that particular location." Part of the

social relations of a place are the embedded assumptions about ethnicity, gender, and sexuality. These assumptions dictate expectations about what certain groups "should" and "should not" do socially, economically, politically, and even domestically. These same assumptions also create barriers to equality and also render some groups more visible than others.

Structures of power are assumptions and relationships dictating who is in control and who has power over others. Structures of power affect identities directly, and the nature of those effects depends on the geographical context in which they are situated. Structures of power also affect cultural landscapes by determining what is seen and what is not. Massey and Jess (1995) contend that power is central to the study of place, as power controls "the contest over how the place should be seen, what meaning to give it," and power constructs the "imaginative geography, the identities of place and culture."

Structures of power do much more than shape the cultural landscape. Structures of power can also subjugate entire groups of people, enabling society to enforce ideas about the ways people should behave or where people should be welcomed or turned away. Such consequences alter the distribution of peoples. Policies created by governments can limit the access of certain groups. Jim Crow laws in the United States once separated "black" spaces from "white" spaces, right down to public drinking fountains.

Even without government support, people create places where they limit the access of other peoples. For example, in Belfast, Northern Ireland, Catholics and Protestants defined certain neighborhoods as excluding the "other" by painting murals, hanging bunting, and painting curbs (**Fig. 5.15**). In major cities in the United States, local governments do not create or enforce laws defining certain spaces as belonging to members of a certain gang, but the people themselves create these spaces, as the people of Belfast do, through graffiti, murals, and building colors.

Sexuality and Space Sexuality is part of humanity. Just as gender roles are culturally constructed, so too do cultures decide sexual norms. In their installment on "Sexuality and Space" in *Geography in America at the Dawn of the 21st Century*, geographers Glen Elder, Lawrence Knopp, and Heidi Nast contend that most social science across disciplines is written in a heteronormative way. The default

Photo by E.H. Fouberg. © 2020 John Wiley & Sons, Inc.

FIGURE 5.15 Belfast, Northern Ireland. Signs of the conflict in Northern Ireland mark the cultural landscape throughout Belfast. In the Shankhill area of Belfast, where Protestants are the majority population, a mural commemorating Stevie McKeag, member of the Ulster Defence Association, a Protestant paramilitary organization, stands in the middle of a residential neighborhood. McKeag is called "Top Gun" for killing 12 Catholics, most of whom were ordinary citizens, in the 1990s. He died in his home of a drug overdose in 2000 at the age of 30.

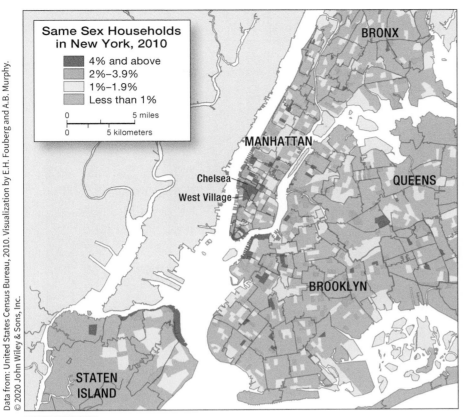

Data from: United States Census Bureau, 2010. Visualization by E.H. Fouberg and A.B. Murphy. © 2020 John Wiley & Sons, Inc.

FIGURE 5.16 **Same-Sex Households in New York.** The map shows the concentrations of same-sex households in New York, by Census tract. Chelsea and West Village, both on the west side of lower Manhattan, stand out as having a large concentration of same-sex households.

subject in the minds of the academics who write studies is heterosexual—and usually white and male as well. Elder, Knopp, Nast, and other geographers are working to find out how heteronormative ideas influence understandings of places and cultures, and how the practices of peoples who do not conform to these ideas influence the development of places.

Early research on **sexuality** by geographers focused largely on the same kinds of questions posed by those who first took up the study of race, gender, and ethnicity. Academics asked where people with shared identity live and gather, what they do to create a space for themselves, and what kinds of problems they confront. For example, early studies examining gay neighborhoods in San Francisco and London focused on how gay men created spaces and what those spaces meant to gay identities. Specific studies have looked at the role of gay pride parades in creating communities and the political struggle for access to other parades, such as St. Patrick's Day parades in some cities. Other studies examine the role that gays and lesbians play in the gentrification of neighborhoods in city centers (a topic we explore in Chapter 9).

The U.S. Census counts the number of same-sex households and same-sex marriages in the United States, which makes it possible to map their distributions. These data, by Census tract—a small area in cities and a larger area in rural America—made it possible for Gary Gates and Jason Ost to publish *The Gay and Lesbian Atlas*. Their detailed maps of major cities in the United States show concentrations of same-sex households in certain neighborhoods of cities (**Fig. 5.16**), such as Adams Morgan and DuPont

Circle in Washington, D.C., and the West Village and Chelsea in Manhattan (**Fig. 5.17**).

Demographer Gary Gates analyzed the geography of same-sex couples in the United States. He found a changing pattern, as cities with well-established gay and lesbian neighborhoods fell in the rankings of the proportion of same-sex couples, and retirement communities and smaller cities rose in the rankings. The *New York Times* reported that San Francisco fell to 28th in the rankings of communities with the top proportions of same-sex couples. Same-sex couples in the baby boomer generation are retiring and moving to cities, including Rehoboth Beach, Delaware; Palm Springs, California; and Provincetown, Massachusetts (ranked number 1).

Today, geographers studying sexuality focus not only on the distributions and experiences of people in places but also on the theories behind the experiences and the intersectionalities of LGBTQ identities. Theories explain and inform our understanding of sexuality and space. For example, many of the geographers who study sexuality are employing "queer theory" in their studies. Elder, Knopp, and Nast explain that social scientists (in geography and other disciplines) are appropriating a commonly used word with negative connotations (*queer*) and turning it in a way that "highlights the contextual nature" of opposition to the heteronormative. Use of the term *queer theory* focuses on the political engagement of queers with the heteronormative. Geographers also concentrate on extending fieldwork on sexuality and space beyond the Western world of North America and Europe to explore and explain the local contexts of political engagement in the rest of the world.

Moving beyond mapping patterns and establishing theories, geographic research on sexuality is increasingly studying intersectionality. Recognizing that much LGBT (lesbian, gay, bisexual, and transgender) research focused on white, middle-class, gay men, geographers are studying how people with intersecting identities, for example gay Muslims or black lesbians, create space and place. **Intersectionality** is the overlap or interconnection between social groups, including race, gender, class, and sexuality. The concept of intersectionality is credited to attorney Kimberlé Crenshaw, who argued black women were disadvantaged in the workplace and in labor laws because jobs were generally divided by race and by gender. Jobs designated for blacks went to black men and jobs designated for women went to white women, leaving black women underemployed. Crenshaw argues that academics need to study structures of power that create barriers to equality for less-visible social groups.

Sexuality research is also moving beyond world cities in higher income countries to smaller cities and rural areas and also to lower income countries to better understand the varying roles sexuality plays in making space and place.

Author Field Note   Parading Pride through New York, New York

"I just happened to be in New York City the weekend after the state of New York legalized same-sex marriages. I cut it close getting to the airport so I could catch the first part of the annual Pride parade. The parade, which started on the edge of the Chelsea neighborhood at 36th Street, traveled down 5th Avenue toward where I took this photograph near Union Square, and ended in the West Village. The route of the Pride parade passes by the Stonewall National Monument, the site of June 1969 riots where New York's LGBTQ community demonstrated and fought back against police raids of spaces the LGBTQ community frequented, including the bar at the Stonewall Inn. Always a boisterous, celebratory event, the Pride parade had a special feel this year as celebrants cheered what many described as one of the great civil rights victories of the current era."

– A.B. Murphy

Photo by A.B. Murphy. © 2020 John Wiley & Sons, Inc.

FIGURE 5.17   **New York, New York.**

Geographer Christopher Schroeder's study of gentrification of the Old West End neighborhood found that intersectionality played a key role in creating spaces and places for gay men and lesbian women in Toledo, Ohio. Through oral histories and archival research, Schroeder (2014) recognized 3 stages in the development of an Old West End neighborhood. As Toledo went through deindustrialization, a small group of gay men who worked as interior decorators rented and bought beautiful, architecturally interesting, older homes in the Old West End starting in the 1950s. As deindustrialization accelerated, families moved out of the neighborhood into suburbs. The neighborhood was home to 5 Methodist churches, and a minister and his wife at one church became a support system for younger, sometimes homeless and often lower income gay men, who moved into the neighborhood where rents were falling. Class, sexuality, and religion intersected to create a supportive environment for young gay men and lesbian women. Schroeder's research highlights that simply saying that gay men play an important role in gentrification of cities does not tell the whole story, and that research into change over time and the roles individuals and intersecting groups play in creating place and space better reveal the role people play in making places.

Counting the Work of Women

The statistics governments collect and report reflect the structures of power involved in defining what is valued and what is not. Think back to the Constitution of the United States prior to the Fourteenth Amendment, when the government enumerated a black person as three-fifths of a white person. Until 1924, the U.S. government also did not recognize the right of all Native Americans to vote, even though the Fifteenth Amendment guaranteed the right to vote regardless of race in 1870.

The U.S. government separated Native Americans into those who were "civilized" enough to be citizens and those who were not ("Indians not taxed") until 1924, when it recognized the citizenship of all Native Americans born in the United States. In 1920, enough states finally ratified the Nineteenth Amendment to the Constitution, which extended voting rights regardless of sex, to allow women to vote. Despite progress in counting people of all races, ethnicities, and sex, some charge that the United States Census Bureau continues to undercount minority populations (see Chapter 2).

Throughout the world, the work of women is often undervalued and uncounted. When the United States and other governments began to count the value of goods and services produced within their borders, they did so with two assumptions: (1) that the work of the household is reserved for women, and (2) that this work does not contribute to the productivity of the country's economy. The most commonly used statistic on productivity, the **gross national income (GNI)**, does not include work in the home. The GNI includes neither the unpaid labor of women in the household nor, usually, the work done by rural women in lower income countries. GNI counts only the **formal economy**, what is reported to and taxed by government, not the **informal economy**, economic activities not counted or taxed by government (**Fig. 5.18**).

AP® Exam Taker's Tip

What kinds of work that are generally done by women are not paid work or otherwise valued in the **formal economy**? Try to formulate answers at various scales, including your family, community, state, or country.

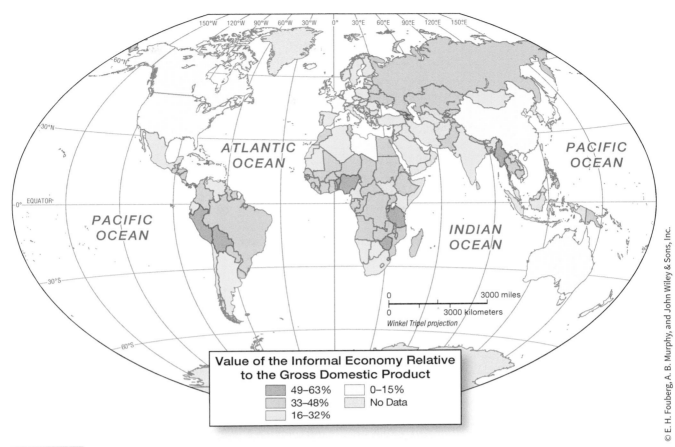

FIGURE 5.18 **Informal Economy as a Percentage of the Gross Domestic Product (GDP).** Based on economic analysis, the World Bank estimates the value of the informal economy in 162 countries as a percentage of the country's official GDP.

Scholars estimate that if women's productivity in the household alone were given a dollar value by calculating what it would cost to hire people to perform these tasks, the GNI for all countries of the world combined would grow by about one-third. In lower income countries, women produce more than half of all the food; they also build homes, dig wells, plant and harvest crops, make clothes, prepare and sell foods, and do many other things that are not recorded in official statistics as being economically productive because they are in the informal economy (**Fig. 5.19**).

The number of women working in the formal economy is rising. The United Nations reported that "women are predominantly and increasingly employed in the services sector" of the formal economy (2010). Combining paid work with work in the informal economy and unpaid domestic work, "women work longer hours than men do." The proportion of women in the labor force grew in all regions reported by the United Nations except Asia and eastern Europe. In South America, for example, the percentage of women in the labor force rose from 38 in 1990 to 59 in 2010. In North Africa, the participation of women in the labor force increased from 23 percent

Laure Siegel/Alamy Stock Photo

FIGURE 5.19 **Bangkok, Thailand.** A woman waits for a street vendor to put chocolate sauce on her coconut ice cream at a street stall. This activity is one part of the informal economy, the uncounted economy in which women play a large role. While the government does not regulate the informal economy, informal structures do. Bangkok's large informal economy includes structures of power where street vendors pay for access to certain street corners.

in 1990 to 29 percent in 2010, while over the same time period in sub-Saharan Africa, women accounted for 60 percent of the labor force.

Even though women are in the official labor force in greater proportions than ever before, they continue to be paid less and have less access to food and education than men in nearly all cultures and places around the world. Two-thirds of the 774 million illiterate adults in the world are women, and women account for 60 percent of the world's poorest citizens. The United Nations Development Program reports that "75 percent of the world's women cannot get bank loans because they have unpaid or insecure jobs and are not entitled to property ownership." As a result, women worldwide only own "one percent of the world's wealth."

The United Nations publication *The World's Women* reported regional variations in agriculture employment for women. In Africa, for example, the proportion of women employed in agriculture ranges from a low of 19 percent in countries in southern Africa to a high of 68 percent in countries in eastern, middle, and western Africa. In northern Africa, 42 percent of women are employed in agriculture and 41 percent of women are employed in services. In Asia, employment of women in agriculture ranges from 11 percent in eastern Asia, where 76 percent of women are employed in the service sector, to South Asia, with 55 percent of women working in agriculture and 28 percent in the service sector.

Although the number of women working in industries globally is small relative to the proportion of men, it is rising.

However, employment of women in the industrial sector was slowed by the global economic downturn of 2008. Simultaneously, mechanization led to job reductions and hence to layoffs of women workers. In the maquiladoras of northern Mexico (see Chapter 10), for example, many women workers lost their jobs when labor markets contracted after the 2008 financial crisis.

To provide for their family, many women engage in private, often home-based activities. They tailor, brew beer, make food products, and make soap (**Fig. 5.20**). Activities like these are not counted in the formal economy. In both long-standing neighborhoods and migrant slums on the fringes of many cities, the informal economy is the mainstay of many communities in the global periphery.

Statistics showing how much women produce and how little their work is valued are undoubtedly interesting. Yet the work that geographers who study gender have done goes far beyond the accumulation of data. Since the 1980s, geographers have asked why society talks about women and their roles in certain ways. They've asked how these ideas, heard and represented throughout our lives, affect geographic circumstances and how we understand them. For example, Ann Oberhauser (2003) and her coauthors explained that people in the West tend to think that women are employed in the textile and jewelry-making fields in poorer countries because the women in these regions are "more docile, submissive, and tradition bound" than women in more prosperous parts of the world. A geographer studying gender asks where these

---

Author Field Note   Making Pineapple Jelly in Phuket, Thailand

"The beaches are the main destination for tourists on the island of Phuket, Thailand. The western side of the island was hard hit by a major tsunami in 2004. Many hotels and restaurants were completely rebuilt after 2004. We ventured into the city of Phuket on the east side of the island to get a better sense of the island's history and older architecture. Phuket has a small Chinatown with links to Chinese laborers who migrated to Phuket to mine tin starting in the 1800s. You can get a sense of the role Phuket played on the trade route between Indian and China, and how that trade once created the heartbeat of Old Phuket. Driving across the island, we could tell it was the month of Ramadan, when Muslims fast from sunrise to sunset. Restaurants were shuttered, waiting for the evening hour of the sunset when Muslims could break their fast. North of Old Phuket, we visited a Muslim village in the Pa Klok district where several families operate a group of businesses growing rubber, pineapple, and goats. We saw the cottage industries where raw materials are processed into sheets of rubber, pineapple jelly, and goat milk soap. We watched members of a family cut pineapples, start fires in small, stone, outdoor stoves, and heat pineapple and sugar to make jelly on the patio outside their home. We each took a turn

stirring, as it took nearly an hour to stir the ingredients until they were ready to pour into small bowls made out of banana leaves to cool into jelly."

– E. H. Fouberg

Photo by E.H. Fouberg. © 2020 John Wiley & Sons, Inc.

FIGURE 5.20   **Phuket, Thailand.**

Guest Field Note   Studying Vulnerabilities of Children in Gilgit, Pakistan

Sarah J. Halvorson
University of Montana

One of the leading causes of mortality and morbidity among children under the age of 5 in developing countries is waterborne disease. My research has focused on building an understanding of the factors that contribute to the vulnerability of young children to this significant public health problem. I have conducted my research in communities located in the relatively remote Karakoram Range of northern Pakistan. Of interest to me is the microenvironment of water-related disease risk, and in particular, the factors at the household and local scale that influence the prevalence and severity of childhood illness. One of the primary methodological strategies that I employ in this research involves household microstudies, which entail in-depth interviews with family members (primarily mothers, who are the principal child health providers), child health histories, and structured observations. One of the most important findings of this research in these mountain communities, in my opinion, is that the education, social networks, and empowerment of women are all critical to breaking the cycle of disease impacts and to ensuring long-term child survival.

© Sarah J. Halvorson

FIGURE 5.21   **Gilgit, Pakistan.**

---

ideas about women come from and how they influence women's work possibilities and social positions in different places. These ideas are key elements in making places what they are.

Vulnerable Populations

Structures of power can have a fundamental impact on which populations or areas are particularly vulnerable to disease, death, injury, or famine. Geographers use mapping and spatial analysis to predict and explain what populations or people will be affected most by natural hazards such as earthquakes, volcanoes, hurricanes, and tsunamis, or by environmental policies. The study of **vulnerability** requires thinking geographically because social, political, economic, or environmental change does not affect all people and places in the same way. Rather, vulnerability is fundamentally influenced by geographically specific social and environmental circumstances.

Fieldwork is often the best way to understand how structures of power in society create vulnerable groups at the local scale. Fieldwork can reveal how vulnerable groups might be affected by particular developments. Through fieldwork and interviews, geographers can also see differences in vulnerability within groups of people.

Geographer Sarah Halvorson (2004) studied differences in the vulnerabilities of children in northern Pakistan. She examined the vulnerability of children to diarrheal diseases by paying attention to "constructions of gender, household politics, and gendered relationships that perpetuate inherent inequalities and differences between men and women and within and between social groups."

Halvorson studied 30 families, 15 of whom had a low frequency of diarrhea and dysentery and 15 of whom had a high frequency of these diseases. Through her fieldwork, Halvorson came to understand that several tangible resources, including income and housing, and several intangible resources, such as social status and position within the family structure, all influenced the vulnerability of children to diarrheal diseases in northern Pakistan. She found that people with higher incomes generally had lower disease rates, but that income was not the only relevant factor (**Fig. 5.21**). The least vulnerable children and women were those who had higher incomes and an established social network of support. In cases where income was low, if a woman had a strong social network, her children were more likely to be in the low-disease group.

Geographer Joseph Oppong recognized that the spatial analysis of a disease can reveal what populations are most vulnerable in a country. In North America and Europe, HIV/AIDS is much more prevalent among homosexual and bisexual men than among heterosexual men and women. In sub-Saharan Africa, women have much higher rates of HIV/AIDS than men. As Oppong (1998) explains, "AIDS as a global problem has unique local expressions that reflect the spatial distribution and social networks of vulnerable social groups." According to Oppong, in most of sub-Saharan Africa, HIV/AIDS rates are highest for women in urban areas and for women who work as sex workers.

However, in Ghana, HIV/AIDS rates are lower for women in the urban area of Accra. Oppong postulates that women in Accra have lower HIV/AIDS rates because they have greater access to health care than women in rural areas. Women in rural areas who were not treated for malaria had higher incidences of HIV/AIDS,

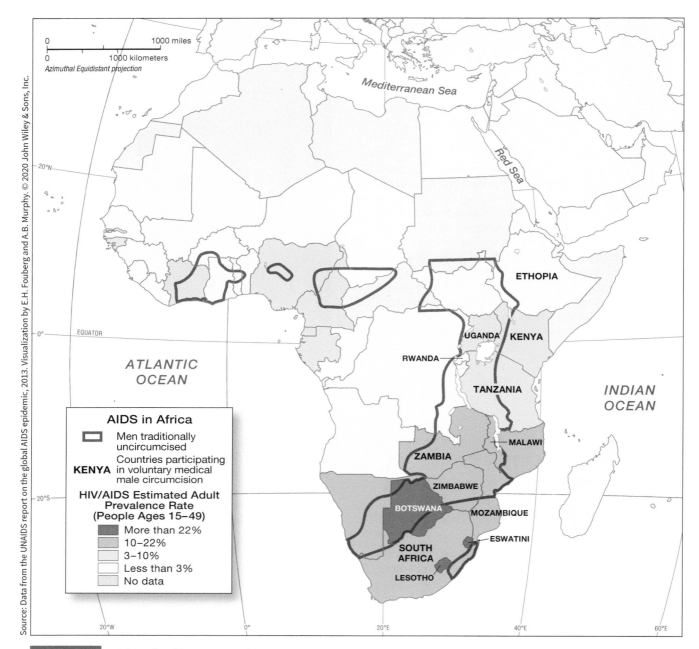

Source: Data from the UNAIDS report on the global AIDS epidemic, 2013. Visualization by E.H. Fouberg and A.B. Murphy. © 2020 John Wiley & Sons, Inc.

FIGURE 5.22 **HIV/AIDS in Africa.**   Researchers mapped HIV/AIDS adult prevalence rates and areas where males are traditionally uncircumcised to see if the two were related.

according to his research. Oppong also found that women in polygamous relationships in the Muslim part of northern Ghana had lower HIV/AIDS rates, and he offers two theories to explain this finding: First, as a matter of cultural practice, most Muslims tend to avoid sexual promiscuity, and second, Muslims in Ghana practice circumcision, which helps lower the rate of HIV/AIDS transmission in that part of the country (**Fig. 5.22**).

Fieldwork helps geographers apply vulnerability theory to understand how existing spatial structures, structures of power, and social networks affect the susceptibility of people to diseases and other hazards around the world.

Women in Sub-Saharan Africa

Migration flows, birth rates, and child mortality rates affect the gender composition of cities, states, and regions. Some regions of the world have become male-dominated, whereas other regions have become female-dominated—at least numerically.

Much of sub-Saharan Africa, especially rural areas, is dominated numerically by women. In this region of the world, most rural-to-urban migrants are men. Domosh and Seager (2001) point out that men leave rural areas to work in heavy industry and mines in the cities, "while women are left behind to tend the farms and manage the household economy. Indeed parts of rural South Africa and Zimbabwe have become feminized zones virtually depopulated of men."

In the large region of sub-Saharan Africa, women outnumber men in many rural areas. They have heavy responsibilities, coupled in many places with few rights and little say (**Fig. 5.23**). Women produce an estimated 70 percent of the region's food, almost all of it without the aid of modern technology. Their hand cultivation of corn and other staples is an endless task. As water supplies decrease, the exhausting walk to the nearest pump gets longer. Firewood is being cut at ever-greater distances from the village, and the task of hauling it home becomes more difficult every year. As men leave for the towns, sometimes to marry other wives and have other children, the women left in the villages often struggle for survival.

AP® Exam Taker's Tip

Study the **Gender Inequality Index (GII)** and Figure 5.23. What is the pattern of inequalities for women? What factors might explain the top two quintiles from the map and your knowledge of the GII?

Even though a woman in this position becomes the head of a household, if she goes to a bank for a loan, she may well be refused. Traditional banks throughout much of Africa do not lend money to rural women. Not having heard from her husband for years and having reared her children, she might apply

for title to the land she has occupied and farmed for decades, but in many places land titles are not awarded to women.

Young girls soon become trapped in the cycle of female poverty and overwork. Often there is little money for school fees; what is available first goes to pay for the boys. As soon as she can carry anything at all, the girl child goes with her mother to weed the fields, bring back firewood, or carry water. She will do so for 12 hours a day, 7 days a week, during all the years she remains capable of working. In East Africa, cash crops such as tea are sometimes called "men's crops," because the men trade in what the women produce. When the government of Kenya tried to increase productivity on the tea plantations in the 1970s and 1980s, the government handed out bonuses—not to the women who did all of the work, but to the men who owned title to the land!

Since the 1990s, women have lobbied for greater representation in governments in southern and eastern Africa. Uganda was a leader in affirmative action for women by setting up a quota or guarantee that women must hold at least 20 percent of the legislative seats. In South Africa, Apartheid, the systematic oppression of the majority black population by the minority white population, ended in 1994. The South African government established a constitution with universal suffrage (voting rights) in 1997. The constitution does not include an affirmative action policy for women's representation in the parliament. Instead, major political parties, starting with the African National Congress (ANC), reserved a certain percentage of their seats won for women.

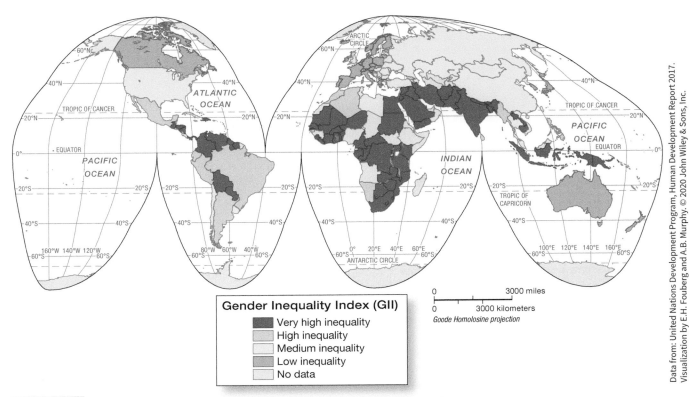

Data from: United Nations Development Program, Human Development Report 2017. Visualization by E.H. Fouberg and A.B. Murphy. © 2020 John Wiley & Sons, Inc.

FIGURE 5.23 **Gender Inequality Index (GII).**   The GII measures inequality in labor market participation, access to reproductive health, and empowerment. It measures how much achievement is lost by women as a result of inequalities in these three areas.

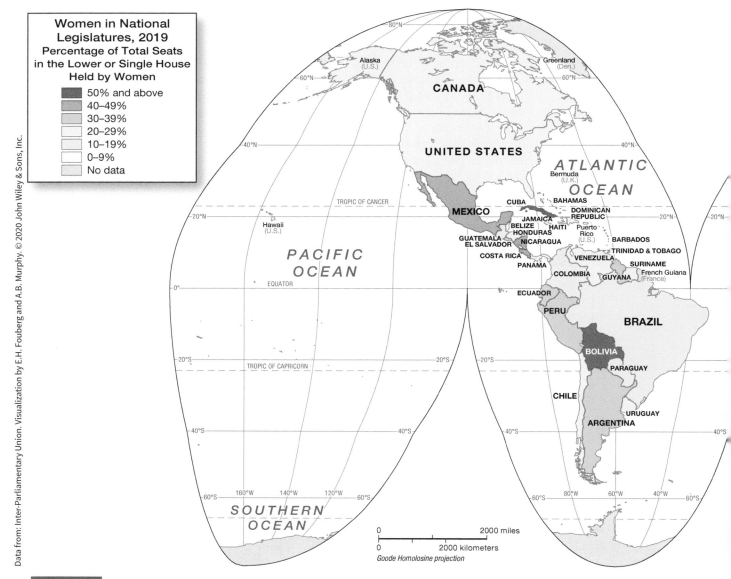

Data from: Inter-Parliamentary Union. Visualization by E.H. Fouberg and A.B. Murphy. © 2020 John Wiley & Sons, Inc.

FIGURE 5.24 **Women in National Legislatures.** Compare and contrast the pattern of the Gender Inequality Index (GII) in Figure 5.23 with this map of women in national legislatures. Several countries in sub-Saharan Africa are high on the GII, but have a large proportion of women in the national legislatures. Countries such as the United States and Australia have low gender inequality, but they do much less well when it comes to female representation in legislative bodies.

Today, the country where women hold the highest proportion of legislative seats is neither Uganda nor South Africa. Rather, another African country, Rwanda, is the first country in the world where women hold more than 50 percent of the legislative seats. Women in Rwanda passed the 50 percent mark in the 2008 election (**Fig. 5.24**). Rwanda suffered a bloody civil war in the 1990s in which over 800,000 people died (one-tenth of the population at the time), a majority of whom were men. Immediately after the war, women accounted for more than 70 percent of the population of the country. Today, women make up 55 percent of the voting-age population. The Rwandan constitution, adopted in 2003, recognizes the equality of women and set a quota of at least 30 percent women in all government decision-making bodies. Of the 80 legislative seats in Rwanda, 24 are reserved for women, and in these 24 seats,

the only candidates are women and only women can vote. In the 2013 elections, women won 26 seats in the legislature in addition to the 24 seats reserved for women, and now women hold 62.5 percent of the seats in the Rwanda legislature.

Women in India

India is a country of contrasts: the wealthiest in the world live next door to teeming slums in cities that have grown exponentially over the last 30 years. The complex relationship between culture and economy is impacting girls and women in India. Some shifts, such as a rise of love marriages, may empower women. Other shifts, such as a higher price placed on a dowry, make women and their families susceptible to extortion.

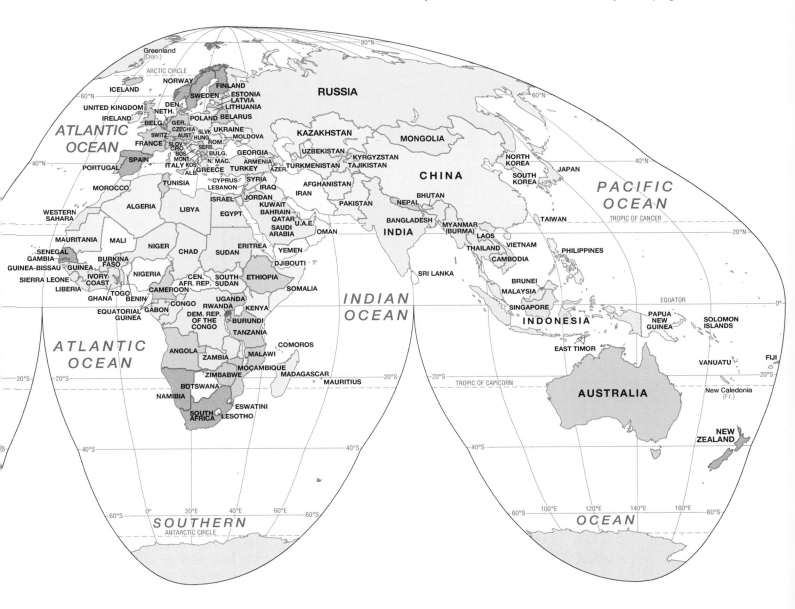

India defies the norm of economic growth leading to a more balanced **sex ratio**, the ratio of males relative to females in a population. For example, in the 1990s, South Korea had a high gender imbalance, with more boys than girls being born and living to age 4. Since the early 2000s, as South Korea's economy has grown to be one of the most competitive in the world, that gender imbalance has narrowed and is closer to normal. India has likewise undergone a massive economic change in the same time frame, but the country's gender imbalance has not been righted and is even more severe for the second- and third-born children than before the country's growth.

The cultural practice of the **dowry**, a price paid in cash and gifts by the bride's family to the groom's father, has changed over time. In the Middle Ages, the dowry was given to the bride from her family "to maintain her independence after marriage" (Pulitzer Center). Before British colonialism, marriage customs in India were diverse and the dowry was not included in all of them. During British colonialism, however, the British institutionalized the dowry and made it mandatory in India as part of a larger project to institutionalize caste and social order. The dowry practice also changed, and the dowry was now a payment to the groom's family. India gained independence from Britain in 1947, and in 1961 the Indian government outlawed the practice of dowry. The practice continues, however, and in an age of increasing demand for material goods and financial pressure on families, dowries have become exorbitant in some cases and groom's families have used dowries to extort more money even after marriage.

In the early 2000s, dowry deaths received a great deal of press globally. The bride may be brutally punished, often burned, or killed for her father's failure to fulfill a marriage agreement. Only a small fraction of India's girls are involved in dowry deaths, but the practice is not declining and reporting is increasing. According to the Indian government, in 1985 the number was 999; in 1987, 1786 women died at the hands of vengeful husbands or in-laws; in 1989, 2436 perished; in 2001, more than 7000 women died; and in 2012, it was reported that 8233 women died from dowry deaths. These figures report only confirmed dowry deaths; many more are believed to occur but are reported as suicides, kitchen accidents, or other fatal domestic incidents. Whether the number of dowry deaths is increasing as a result of the country's growing population, increased reporting by families, or another factor is not easy to discern.

The structures of power that place women below men in India cannot simply be legislated away. The government of India passed the Dowry Prohibition Act in 1961, which made it illegal to take or give a dowry. Nonetheless, the practice continues. Government entities in India have set up legal aid offices to help women who fear dowry death and seek assistance. In 1984, the national legislature passed the Family Courts Act, creating a network of "family courts" to hear domestic cases. But the judges tend to be older males, and their chief objective, according to women's support groups, is to hold the family together—that is, to force the threatened or battered woman back into the household. Indian culture attaches great importance to the family structure, and the family courts tend to operate on this principle.

India is starting to see the impact its booming economy and growing proportion of educated young women and men in well-paid jobs is having on marriage. The number of love marriages is on the rise (**Fig. 5.25**), and many couples in love marriages in India are meeting online. The number of divorces is also on the rise, with 1 in 1000 marriages ending in divorce in India today. Although this is one of the lowest divorce rates in the world, India's separation rate is three times its divorce rate. Divorce holds a stigma in India, especially for women. India's Census data showed that the number of divorced women is higher than the number of divorced men, likely because the stigma against women who are divorced makes it more difficult for them to remarry than divorced men. Changes in marriage and divorce customs will not necessarily result in fewer dowry deaths in the short run in India. An article in *The Times of India* explained that in the city of Chennai, where the information technology boom is in full swing, police reported a rise in dowry deaths. This rise was likely a result of increasing materialism among the middle class and an accompanying feeling of desperation for more goods and cash, coupled with the fact that many men in less powerful positions have begun to act out violently.

Understanding changing gender relations and structures of power in India is very difficult. Just as some statistics point to an improving place of women in Indian society, other statistics confirm that India still gives preference to males overall. India's 2011 census reported a sex ratio of 1065 males for every 1000 females, which seems to be an improvement over the 2001 sex ratio of 1080 males for every 1000 females. However, the gap between the number of boys and number of girls ages 0 to 4 is still quite wide in India, with 6.2 million more boys than girls in that age bracket alone (Denyer and Gowen 2018).

The probability of a female being born or living to age 4 in India varies by region. The northern states of India have higher gender imbalance than the southern states (**Fig. 5.26**). Pregnant women in India, especially in northern states, undergo gender-determining tests (ultrasound and amniocentesis) and may elect to have abortions when the fetus is a girl. Girls who make it to birth may suffer female infanticide because many parents fear the cost of dowries and place less social value on girls.

In India and elsewhere, directing the attention of people in far-flung places to social ills—moving the issues up in scale—has the potential to create change. Yet problems cannot really be solved unless structures of power shift at the family, local, regional, and national scales. As the number of women and men in the middle class in urban India continues to rise, love marriages will continue to rise as well. How dowry will shift as a result of India's gender imbalance remains to be seen. India has 37 million more men than women, and this imbalance "creates a surplus of bachelors and exacerbates human trafficking, both for brides and, possibly, prostitution" (Denyer and Gowen 2018). The number of girl children who are born and live to age 4, the growth of trafficking for brides, and the rate of divorces in the country will continue to fluctuate as structures of power shift across gender and scales.

Shifting Structures of Power Among Ethnic Groups

In Chapter 4, we discussed local cultures that define themselves ethnically. The presence of local ethnic cultures can be seen in the cultural landscapes of places discussed in that chapter: "Little Sweden" in Kansas and the Italian North End in Boston. In many places, more than one ethnic group lives

Photo by A.B. Murphy. © 2020 John Wiley & Sons, Inc.

FIGURE 5.25 Mumbai, India. Arranged marriages were the norm not long ago in India, and the family of the bride was expected to provide a dowry to the groom's family. Arranged marriages are still widespread in parts of rural India, but in urban areas they are rapidly giving way to love marriages following romantic courtships. Evidence of this cultural shift is not hard to find on the streets of India's major cities.

in a place. Each group creates unique cultural landscapes and reveals how structures of power factor into the ways ethnicities are constructed, revised, and solidified, where ethnic groups live, and who is subjugating whom.

Structures of Power in Alameda County
In their book *Race and Place: Equity Issues in Urban America*, three urban geographers—John Frazier, Florence Margai, and Eugene Tettey-Fio—tracked the flow of people and shifts in power among the multiple ethnic groups that have lived in Alameda County, California. Alameda County borders San Francisco and includes the cities of Berkeley and Oakland. Latinos populated the region prior to the Gold Rush. After 1850, migrants from China came to the county. The first Asian migrants were widely dispersed, but the first African Americans lived in a segregated section of the county.

Areas with multiple ethnicities often experience an ebb and flow of acceptance over time. When the economy is booming, residents are generally more accepting of each other. When the economy takes a downturn, residents often begin to resent each other and can blame the "Other" for their economic hardship. In Alameda County, much of the population resented Chinese migrants when the economy took a downturn in the 1870s. The United States government passed the first Chinese Exclusion Act, which prohibited immigration of Chinese, in 1882. Chinese exclusion efforts persisted for decades afterward in Alameda County. The exclusion resulted in the city of Oakland moving Chinatown several times.

During the 1910s, the economy of the region grew again. However, the city of Oakland limited the Chinese residents to Chinatown, using ethnic segregation to keep them apart from the rest of the population. Frazier, Margai, and Tettey-Fio (2003) described how the location and homogeneity of Oakland's Chinatown were dictated by law and not matters of choice for the Chinese:

> At a time when the Chinese were benefiting from a better economy, the "whites only" specifications of local zoning and neighborhood regulations forced separatism that segregated the Oakland Chinese into the city's Chinatown. What today is sometimes presented as an example of Chinese unity and choice was, in fact, place dictated by law.

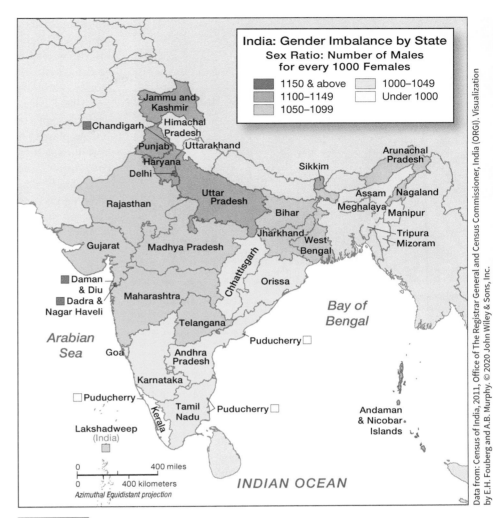

FIGURE 5.26 Gender Imbalance by State in India. The sex ratio on this map shows the number of males for every 1000 females. States in northern India have greater gender imbalance than states in southern India.

Data from: Census of India, 2011, Office of The Registrar General and Census Commissioner, India (ORGI). Visualization by E.H. Fouberg and A.B. Murphy. © 2020 John Wiley & Sons, Inc.

Chinese were segregated from the rest of Oakland's population until World War II. When the war began, residents of Alameda County focused on the Japanese population in the county. They were segregated, blamed, and interned in relocation centers, as was the case in the rest of the United States.

After World War II, the ethnic population of Asians in Alameda County became more complex. In the decade between 1980 and 1990, the Asian population alone doubled, and it also diversified to include not only Chinese, Japanese, Korean, and Indian, but also Southeast Asians, including Vietnamese, Cambodians, and Laotians. In Alameda County, the first wave of migrants from Asia (mainly from China, India, and Korea), who came to the region already educated, are not residentially segregated from the white population, as is the case in much of the rest of the United States (**Fig. 5.27**). However, the newer migrants from Asia (mainly Southeast Asia—during and following the Vietnam War) are segregated from whites residentially. More recent Asian migrants tend to earn lower incomes and reside in neighborhoods that are predominantly Hispanic or African American. Alameda County east of San Francisco and neighboring Santa

GABRIELLE LURIE/AFP/Getty Images

FIGURE 5.27 **Alameda County, California.**   An Alameda resident rides his motorcycle as part of the "Sikh Riders of America" group in the county's 4th of July parade, one of the largest Independence Day parades in the United States.

Clara county to its south are major urban/suburban counties where Asians outnumber non-Hispanic whites (31 percent Asian in Alameda and 38 percent Asian in Santa Clara).

In California and in much of the rest of the United States, the "Asian" box is drawn around a stereotype of what some call the "model minority." Frazier and his colleagues explain that this myth "paints Asians as good, hardworking people who, despite their suffering through discrimination, harassment, and exclusion, have found ways to prosper through peaceful means." Other researchers have debunked the myth by demonstrating statistically the varying levels of economic success experienced by different Asian peoples. Asian is the fastest-growing racial class in the United States, with the Asian population across the United States increasing 27.8 percent between 2010 and 2018. The most success has a tendency of going to the first wave of migrants, while lower-paying jobs go to newer migrants. Both groups are burdened by the myth that stereotypes them as the "model minority."

Structures of Power in Los Angeles   Over the

last four decades, the greatest migration flow into California and the southwestern United States has come from Latin America and the Caribbean, especially Mexico. The Census estimates the Hispanic population grew from 16 percent of the U.S. population to 18 percent of the U.S. population between 2008 and 2019. Nationwide, the U.S. Hispanic population grew from 47.8 million to 59.9 million in the same time period. Los Angeles County has over 10 million people, 49 percent of whom are Hispanic.

The area of southeastern Los Angeles County is today "home to one of the largest and highest concentrations of Latinos in Southern California," according to a study by geographer James Curtis. Four decades ago, this area of Los Angeles

was populated by working-class whites. They were segregated from the African American and Hispanic populations through discriminatory policies and practices. Until the 1960s, southeastern Los Angeles was home to corporations such as General Motors, Bethlehem Steel, and Weiser Lock. During the 1970s and 1980s, corporations began to close as the United States went through a period of deindustrialization (see Chapter 11).

As plants shut down and white laborers left the neighborhoods, a Hispanic population migrated into southeastern Los Angeles. A housing crunch followed in the 1980s, as more and more Hispanic migrants headed to this area. With a cheap labor supply now readily available in the region again, companies returned to southeastern Los Angeles, this time focusing on smaller-scale production of textiles, pharmaceuticals, furniture, and toys. In addition, the region attracted industrial toxic waste disposal and petrochemical refining facilities.

In his study of the region, Curtis records the changes to the cultural landscape in the process. He uses the term **barrioization** (derived from the Spanish word for neighborhood, *barrio*) to describe a change that saw the Hispanic population of a neighborhood jump from 4 percent in 1960 to over 90 percent in 2000. With the ethnic succession of the neighborhood moving from white to Hispanic, the cultural landscape changed to reflect the culture of the new population. The structure of the streets and the layout of the housing remained largely the same, giving the Hispanic population access to designated parks, schools, libraries, and community centers built by the previous residents and rarely found in other barrios in southern California. However, the buildings, signage, and landscape changed as "traditional Hispanic house-scape elements, including the placement of fences and yard shrines as well as the use of bright house colors," diffused through the barrios. Curtis explains that these elements were added to existing structures, houses, and buildings originally built by the white working class of southeastern Los Angeles.

The influx of new ethnic groups into a region, the replacement of one ethnic group by another within neighborhoods, the persistence of the "model minority" myth about Asian Americans, and an economic downturn can create a great deal of volatility in a city. On April 29–30, 1992, Los Angeles became engulfed in one of the worst incidents of civil unrest in United States history. During two days of rioting, 43 people died, 2383 were injured, and 16,291 arrested. Property damage was estimated at approximately $1 billion, and over 22,700 law enforcement personnel were deployed to quell the unrest.

According to the media, the main catalyst for the mass upheaval was the announcement of a "not guilty verdict in the trial of four white police officers accused of using excessive force in the arrest of Rodney King, a black motorist" (Johnson et al. 1992, 356). To the general public, the Los Angeles riots became yet another symbol for the sorry state of race relations between blacks and whites in the United States. Yet a geographic perspective on the Los Angeles riots helps us understand that they were not simply the product of localized reactions to police brutality, but reflected sweeping economic, political, and ethnic changes unfolding at regional and even global scales.

The riots took place in South Central Los Angeles. Like the region of southeast Los Angeles described above, the South Central area was once a thriving industrial region with dependable, unionized jobs employing the resident population. By the 1960s, however, the population of South Central Los Angeles was working-class African American, and the population of southeastern Los Angeles was working-class white. After 1970, South Central Los Angeles experienced a substantial decrease in the availability of high-paying, unionized manufacturing jobs when plants closed and relocated outside the city and even outside the country. The people of South Central

Los Angeles lost over 70,000 manufacturing jobs between 1978 and 1982 alone!

Geographer James Johnson and his colleagues explored the impact of economic loss on the ethnic and social geography of South Central Los Angeles. They found that the population of the area was over 90 percent African American in 1970, but by 1980 this change in population composition was accompanied by a steady influx of Korean residents and small-business owners seeking a niche in the rapidly changing urban area (**Fig. 5.28**). South Central became increasingly Hispanic after 1980 as "an influx of immigrants

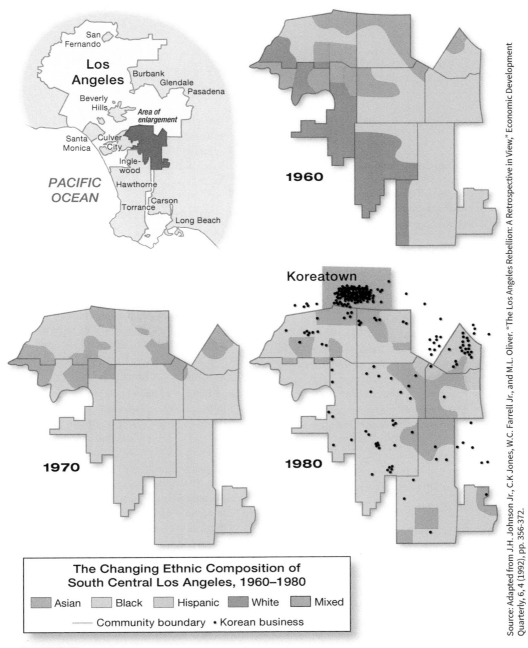

Source: Adapted from J.H. Johnson Jr., C.K Jones, W.C. Farrell Jr., and M.L. Oliver. "The Los Angeles Rebellion: A Retrospective in View," Economic Development Quarterly, 6, 4 (1992), pp. 356-372.

FIGURE 5.28 **The Changing Ethnic Composition of South Central Los Angeles, 1960–1980.** This time series of four maps shows evidence of sequent occupance, as Asian neighborhoods virtually disappeared but Korean businesses remained in 1980.

from Mexico and Central America" and an "exodus of black residents from a historically divested neighborhood" (USC 2016) combined to create a change in the racial and ethnic identity of the neighborhood. By 1990, the neighborhood was evenly split between African Americans and Hispanics. By 2000, Hispanics comprised 56.9 percent of residents, and today, two-thirds of the residents of South Central Los Angeles are Hispanic.

Johnson and his colleagues argued that the Los Angeles riots were more than a spontaneous reaction to a verdict. They were rooted in the growing despair and frustration of different ethnic groups competing for a decreasing number of jobs. Their environment of declining housing conditions and scarce public resources were aggravating factors. Johnson et al's work shows the importance of looking beyond the immediate catalysts of particular news events to the local, national, and global geographical **contexts** in which they unfold.

> **TC Thinking Geographically**
>
> Geographers who study **race**, ethnicity, **gender**, or sexuality are interested in how structures of power embedded in a **place** form and shape assumptions about "Others." Consider your own place, your campus, or your community. What structures of power are embedded in this **place**, and how can you see differences in power in the way spaces are used and claimed?

Summary

5.1 Define Identity and Explain How Identities Are Constructed.

1. Geographer Gillian Rose (1995) defines identity as "how we make sense of ourselves." We construct our own identities through our experiences. Places are important in shaping identities because we attach experiences and emotions to places. We also construct identities for others. Identities are fluid and may change based on context and scale.

2. Gender is a culture's assumptions about differences between women and men, and assumptions about what roles they should play in families and society. Some cultures have a preference for one gender, which can be seen in the sex ratio (number of males to number of females).

3. Race is socially constructed. Race includes differences assigned to people based on skin color. How cultures define races and what differences they attribute to races has a profound effect on rights and opportunities for each race. Connections between race and class found in modern society have their roots in globalization since 1500. Europeans created numerous arguments for colonization and the Atlantic slave trade based on race. People construct racial categories to justify power, economic exploitation, and cultural oppression.

5.2 Determine How Place Affects Identity and How We Can See Identities in Places.

1. Residential segregation is the degree to which two or more groups of people live separately from each other within a city. Sociologists and geographers have developed multiple ways to measure residential segregation. The roots of residential segregation in the United States are typically attributed to three factors: money, preferences, and discrimination. While overall residential segregation has declined, several cities have entrenched residential segregation that has not declined. Social networks, activity spaces, and lived experiences entrench residential segregation.

2. Ethnicities are often rooted in place. Your ethnicity may be tied to where your ancestors came from or to an ethnic neighborhood or ethnic small towns. Conflicts may be described as ethnic if the term *racial* does not fit. Ethnic conflicts, like racial conflicts, are rooted in differences in experiences.

5.3 Explain the Role Structures of Power Play in Shaping Identities.

1. How identities are shaped depends, in part, on who is in power. Structures of power are assumptions and structures about who is in control and who has power over others. Someone in power can define people of a particular race, ethnicity, or class negatively and create policies that limit their opportunities. People in power also determine what remains, what is built, and what is wiped from the cultural landscape. They also decide how to interpret the landscape and signal to others through signage what lens they should use to see a place.

2. Structures of power can have a fundamental impact on which populations or areas are particularly vulnerable to disease, death, injury, or famine. Geographers use mapping and spatial analysis to predict and explain what populations or people will be affected most by natural hazards such as earthquakes, volcanoes, hurricanes, and tsunamis, or by environmental policies. The study of vulnerability requires thinking geographically because social, political, economic, or environmental change does not affect all people and places in the same way. Rather, vulnerability is fundamentally influenced by geographically specific social and environmental circumstances.

3. Identity is a powerful concept. The way we make sense of ourselves is a personal journey that is mediated and influenced by the political, social, and cultural contexts in which we live and work. Group identities such as gender, ethnicity, race, and sexuality are constructed, both by self-realization and by identifying against and across scales. When learning about new places and different people, humans are often tempted to put places and people into boxes, into myths or stereotypes that make them easily digestible.

Self-Test

5.1 Define identity and explain how identities are constructed.

1. If a culture has a preference for one gender over another, you will be most likely to see that in all of the following except:

    a. the sex ratio.

    b. a population pyramid.

    c. the education level completed by gender.

    d. the child mortality rate by gender.

    e. life expectancy by gender.

2. The United States Census can be used as evidence that race is socially constructed. Before 2000, Hispanic was counted as a(n) _____, and since 2000, Hispanic has been counted as a(n)_____.

    a. ethnicity / race

    b. race / ethnicity

    c. race / class

    d. class / race

    e. race / language

3. TRUE OR FALSE: The intersection between race and class was entrenched through European colonization so that lower income residents of European countries began to see themselves as superior to people in their country's colonies.

5.2 Determine how place affects identity and how we can see identities in places.

4. Current residential segregation in the United States is generally attributed to all of the following except:

    a. money.

    b. preferences.

    c. discrimination.

    d. culture.

    e. government policies.

5. Entrenched residential segregation in cities like Chicago comes from all of the following except:

    a. government policies.

    b. social networks.

    c. activity spaces.

    d. lived experiences.

    e. redlining.

6. New migrants to a city often move to low-income areas that are being gradually abandoned by older immigrant groups. This process is called:

    a. segregation.

    b. succession.

    c. profiling.

    d. Apartheid.

    e. gentrification.

5.3 Explain the role structures of power play in shaping identities.

7. The work of women is often undervalued and undercounted because much of the work women do takes place in:

    a. the informal economy.

    b. the formal economy.

    c. ethnic small towns.

    d. ethnic neighborhoods.

    e. the home.

8. Halvorson's research found that intangible resources such as _____ influenced how vulnerable children are to diarrheal disease.

    a. education level and access to soap

    b. social status and position within the family structure

    c. access to health care and cleanliness of water

    d. bathrooms with flush toilets and presence of sewer systems

    e. access to clean water and household income

9. Which country has the highest proportion of women holding legislative seats?

    a. United Kingdom

    b. India

    c. France

    d. Norway

    e. Rwanda

CHAPTER 6

Language

Photo by E.H. Fouberg. © 2020 John Wiley & Sons, Inc.

FIGURE 6.1 **Dora Observatory, South Korea.** The border between North Korea and South Korea is divided by the Demilitarized Zone (DMZ), a borderland that is 160 miles (250 km) long and an average of 4 miles (2.5 km) wide. The DMZ is filled with landmines, fences, and open fields. This is the view looking from South Korea to the North Korean town of Kijong-dong.

Standing on a platform, I peered through a telescope and looked across the Demilitarized Zone (DMZ) into North Korea at the town of Kijong-dong (**Fig. 6.1**). It translates to "peace village," but South Koreans call it "propaganda village." The buildings look nice from a distance, but many appear to be shells. At night, taller buildings have lights shining out of the top windows, but no lights lower in the building, suggesting that the North Koreans mounted lights on the ceiling, but did not build any floors or walls inside the shells. The "windows" on several buildings appear to be painted facades designed to look like windows (Wharton 2018).

Maps of languages in East Asia show the Korean language being spoken across the Korean Peninsula. Both North Korea, the "hermit kingdom" that attempts to function separately from the world, and South Korea, which is deeply integrated into the global economy as the world's 11th largest economy, speak the same language. But the lack of interaction between North Koreans and South Koreans since the Korean War ended in 1953 is changing that. One linguist who studies the two Koreas reported that language divergence is already happening.

In this chapter, we question what languages are and examine the roles they play in cultures. We study the spatial distribution of the world's languages and learn how they diffuse, change, rise to dominance, and even become extinct. Finally, we examine how language contributes to making places unique.

CHAPTER OUTLINE

6.1 Define Language and Describe the Role of Language in Culture.

In an effort to prevent the creep of English words like *hashtag* and *email* into French vocabulary, the French government has created the word *#motdièse* to replace *#hashtag*. As a result, French Twitter has enjoyed poking fun at the government (**Fig. 6.2**). While some of the alternative French terms have stuck, many English terms are easier to say, are too entrenched, or are too widespread to replace.

Language is a fundamental element of local and national culture. The French government works diligently, even aggressively, to protect the French language. In 1635, it created the Académie Française, an institution charged with standardizing and protecting the French language. Since the 1970s, the diffusion of globalized terms into French, which linguists call loanwords or borrowed words, has posed an enormous challenge for the Académie Française.

With the support of many French people, the French government passed a law in 1975 banning the use of foreign words in advertisements, television, and radio broadcasts, as well as official documents, unless no French equivalent could be found. In 1992, France amended its constitution to make French the official language. In 1994, the French government passed another law to stop the use of foreign, mainly English, words in France, with a hefty fine imposed for violators. The law mandates French translations for globalized words in official communications rather than *le hashtag*, *le meeting*, *le weekend*, *le drugstore*, or *le hamburger*.

The Internet, where 45 percent of users browse in English or Chinese (**Fig. 6.3**), creates more challenges for the Académie Française. Some Académie translations are cumbersome. For example, the official translation of *email* was *courrier electronique*, but the Académie shortened it to *courriel*. Either way, *courriel* has not caught on in everyday French,

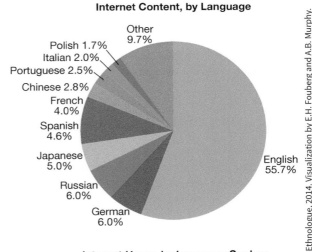

Internet Content, by Language

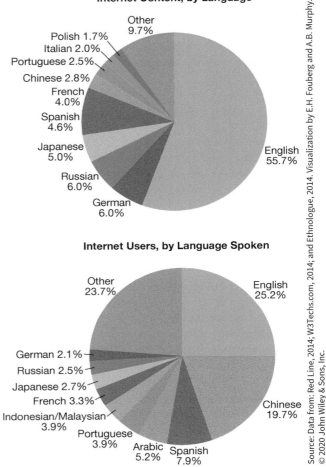

Internet Users, by Language Spoken

Source: Data from: Red Line, 2014; W3Techs.com, 2014; and Ethnologue, 2014. Visualization by E.H. Fouberg and A.B. Murphy.
© 2020 John Wiley & Sons, Inc.

FIGURE 6.3 **Internet Content and Users.** The majority of the content on the Internet is in English, but only about 25 percent of Internet users are English-speakers.

and *email* has crept into French vocabulary. The Internet has expanded the use of English as a globalized language. English is the third most spoken language globally, after Chinese and Spanish, but the majority of content on the Internet is in English (see Fig. 6.3).

Till the Cat
@TilltheCat

Follow

Avec cette histoire de #motdiese je me demande si je ne vais pas devoir me rebaptiser Gilles le chat :-/

10:52 PM - 22 Jan 2013

4 Retweets 4 Likes

💬 8   🔁 4   ♡ 4

FIGURE 6.2 French Twitter enjoyed poking fun at the Académie Française, who designated the French word *#motdièse* (translating to "sharp word") to replace the English word *#hashtag*. A French blogger who goes by @TilltheCat asked "With the story of #motdiese, I wonder if I will have to rename myself Gilles the Cat," referencing the common French name Gilles.

AP® Exam Taker's Tip

There are five verbs used on AP Human Geography FRQs: *identify, define, describe, explain,* and *compare.* The verb *identify* is the least complex, with each subsequent verb requiring more complex thinking, skill usage, and writing. FRQ answers using the explain verb must have "cause and effect" in the response. Try using the word "because" in the response when employing the more complex verbs and using an example from class.

A **language** is a set of sounds and symbols that is used for communication. But in addition to demonstrating the conflicting forces of globalized language and local or national language, the example of #*motdièse* in France reveals that language is much more than a way of communicating. Language also reflects and shapes people and places, and so it is an integral part of culture, identity, and place making. Globalization of language challenges the preservation of national languages like French. Can we have globalized social networks, food, music, and culture while preserving national and local languages?

Language and Culture

Language is one of the cornerstones of culture. It shapes our very thoughts. We can choose the perfect word from a vast vocabulary to describe new experiences, ideas, and feelings, or we can create a new word. Who we are as a culture, as a people, is reinforced and redefined through shared language. Language reflects where a culture has been, what a culture values, and even how people in a culture think, describe, and experience events.

Perhaps the easiest way to appreciate the role of language in culture is to examine people who have experienced the loss of language under pressure from others. During the colonial period, both abroad and within countries, colonizers commonly forced subjugated peoples to speak the language of the colonizer. Forced language policies continued in many places until recently and were enforced primarily through public (government) and church (mission) schools.

American, Canadian, Australian, Russian, and New Zealand governments each had policies of forced assimilation during the nineteenth and twentieth centuries, including not allowing indigenous peoples to speak Native languages. For example, the United States forced Native Americans and Alaska Natives to learn and speak English. Both mission schools and government schools enforced English-only policies to forcibly assimilate Natives into the dominant culture. Teachers punished students who spoke their native languages in schools, often with corporal (physical) punishments.

In an interview with the producers of an educational video, Clare Swan, an elder in the Kenaitze band of the Dena'ina Indians in Alaska, described the impact of language assimilation policies on identity and culture:

No one was allowed to speak the language—the Dena'ina language. They [the American government] didn't allow it in schools, and a lot of the women had married non-native men, and the men said, "You're American now so you can't speak the language." *So, we became invisible in the community. Invisible to each other.* And, then, because we couldn't speak the language—*what happens when you can't speak your own language is you have to think with someone else's words, and that's a dreadful kind of isolation* [emphases added].

Language is quite personal. Our thoughts, expressions, and dreams are articulated in our language. The assimilation policy in the United States officially ended in 1934, but teachers in federal and private boarding schools continued for decades to punish students who spoke their native languages.

Native Americans and Alaska Natives have worked to teach language and rebuild culture through schools, community centers, ceremonies, and celebrations. Shared language makes people in a culture visible to each other and to the rest of the world. Language helps cement cultural **identity**, how we make sense of ourselves (**Fig. 6.4**).

Language not only creates a shared identity; it can also reveal much about the way people and cultures view reality. For example, Irish is a Celtic language spoken mainly in western Ireland. Irish has no words for "yes" and "no." Even when speaking English, Irish people often respond to questions with phrases like, "Wouldn't that be grand?" in place of "yes," or "You think so, now?" in place of "no." Irish see "yes" and "no" as closing the door to conversation, and conversation and storytelling are arts among Irish.

Some Southeast Asian languages have no verb tenses, reflecting a less-sharp cultural distinction between then and now. Given the American culture's preoccupation with dating and timing, it is difficult for many in the United States to understand how speakers of Southeast Asian languages perceive the world.

What Is a Language?

Many geography textbooks differentiate languages based on a criterion of mutual intelligibility. **Mutual intelligibility** means that two people can understand each other when speaking. The argument goes that if two of us are speaking two different languages, say Spanish and Portuguese, we will not be able to

FIGURE 6.4 Kenai, Alaska. The Kenaitze Indian tribe built a beautiful Wellness Center that includes an integrated health center, a gym, and a wellness kitchen. The Dena'ina language and culture are embedded in the design of the building.

© 2019 Kenaitze Indian Tribe

understand each other: The languages will be mutually unintelligible. If we are speaking two dialects of one language, however, we will understand each other because the dialects are mutually intelligible. Yet linguists have rejected the criterion of mutual intelligibility as strongly as geographers have rejected environmental determinism (see discussion in Chapter 1).

First, mutual intelligibility is almost impossible to measure. Even if we used it as a criterion, many languages would fail the test. Famous linguist Max Weinreich once said that "a language is a dialect with an army." Think about it. How could we possibly see Mandarin Chinese and Cantonese Chinese as dialects of the same language, when two people speaking the language to each other cannot understand what the other is saying? Both can read the standard Chinese characters that have been developed by a strongly centralized Chinese government. Television in China has subtitles in Chinese characters so that speakers of many different dialects can read and understand the programming. The written characters have the same meaning, but the spoken dialects (Mandarin and Cantonese are two of more than 1400 dialects of Chinese) are not mutually intelligible (**Fig. 6.5**). Less than half of China's people use Mandarin Chinese as their daily language. We see Chinese as one language because of the weight of political and social institutions that lies behind it.

A further complication with the mutual intelligibility test is revealed in Scandinavia, where, for example, a Danish speaker and a Norwegian speaker (at least one from Oslo) will be able to understand what the other is saying. Yet we think of Danish and Norwegian as distinct languages. Having a Norwegian language helps Norwegians identify themselves as Norwegians rather than as Danes or Scandinavians. Other languages that are recognized as separate but are mutually intelligible in many (or nearly all) aspects are Serbian and Croatian, Hindi and Urdu, and Navajo and Apache.

Given the complexities of distinguishing languages from dialects, the actual number of languages in use in the world remains a matter of considerable debate. The most conservative calculation puts the number at about 3000. However, most linguists and linguistic geographers today recognize between 5000 and 7000 languages, including more than 700 in India and over 3000 in Africa.

Standardized Language

Language is dynamic: New discoveries, technologies, and ideas require new words. A **standard language** is published, widely distributed, and purposely taught. A government can help sustain a standard language by making it official and requiring literacy in the language for government jobs. For example, Ireland promotes the use of the Irish language by requiring all government employees to pass an Irish-language examination before they can be hired.

Who decides what the standard language will be? The answer has to do with influence and power. In France, the Académie Française chose the French spoken in and around Paris as the official, standard language during the seventeenth century. In the United Kingdom, the standard English is called "The King's English" and is the dialect spoken in and around London. In China, the government chose the Northern Mandarin Chinese heard in and around the capital, Beijing, as the official standard language.

One country may have several dialects of a language, and the standard one usually reflects who in the country had power when the standard language was chosen. The Italian spoken in Sicily is quite different from the Italian spoken north of Venice, and both dialects differ from the standard Italian spoken in Florence and Tuscany. The dialect in Florence and Tuscany became standard Italian because it was the language of the great thinkers and writers of the Italian Renaissance.

Dialects

Variants of a standard language along regional or ethnic lines are called **dialects**. Differences in vocabulary, syntax (the way words are put together to form phrases), pronunciation, cadence (the rhythm of speech), and even the pace of speech all mark a speaker's dialect. Even if the written form of a statement follows the standard language, an accent can reveal the regional home of a person who reads the statement aloud. In the United States, the words *horse* and *oil* are written the same way in New England and in the South, but to the Southerner, the New Englander may be saying "hahse," and to the New Englander, the Southerner seems to be saying "all."

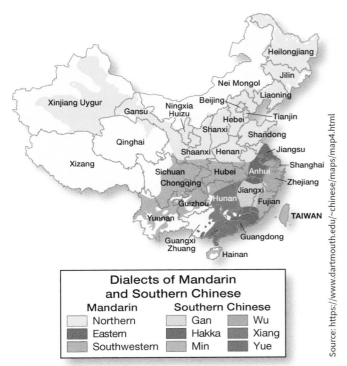

Source: https://www.dartmouth.edu/~chinese/maps/map4.html

Dialects of Mandarin and Southern Chinese

Mandarin
- Northern
- Eastern
- Southwestern

Southern Chinese
- Gan
- Hakka
- Min
- Wu
- Xiang
- Yue

FIGURE 6.5 **Major Chinese Dialects.** Mandarin dialects are in the north, and southern dialects include Yue, which is also known as Cantonese.

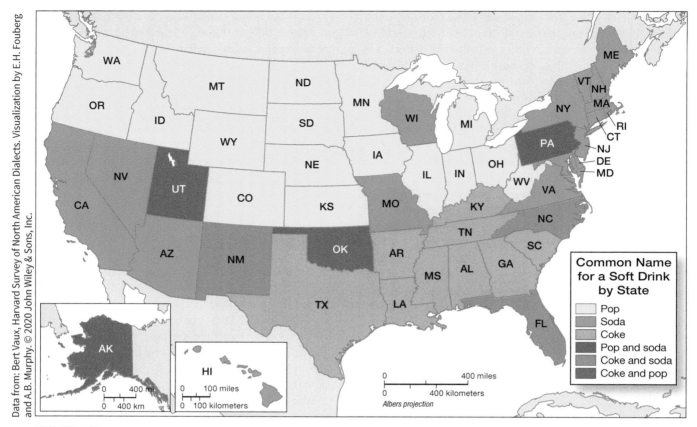

Data from: Bert Vaux, Harvard Survey of North American Dialects. Visualization by E.H. Fouberg and A.B. Murphy. © 2020 John Wiley & Sons, Inc.

FIGURE 6.6 **Common Names for a Soft Drink in the United States, by State.** The isogloss for soda and pop generally divides the coasts from the rest of the country. A north-south isogloss distinguishes where pop and coke are commonly used. For county level data and to submit the word you use, see: http://popvssoda.com/

Linguists think about dialects in terms of **dialect chains**. Dialects closest to each other geographically will be the most similar (greater spatial interaction), but as you travel farther, dialects will be increasingly different. If all of the dialects are part of one language, which dialect is the language? Language is an umbrella for a collection of dialects, and we tend to see one of these dialects as the "true" language only because it is the one we speak or because it is the one a government declares standard.

> **AP® Exam Taker's Tip**
>
> How is a **standard language** different from a **dialect**? What dialect(s) is spoken in your region? How is it different from other regions? How is an official language different from a standard language?

Dialects are often marked by actual differences in vocabulary. Linguistic geographers map the spatial distribution of words and use the map to mark isoglosses. An **isogloss** is a geographic boundary within which a particular linguistic feature occurs. In addition to the use of certain words, linguists who study dialects examine pronunciations, vocabularies, use of colloquial phrases, and syntax to determine isoglosses. While an isogloss looks like it has clear boundaries, the linguistic

feature may occur beyond the isogloss. Fuzzy isoglosses may mean that a dialect is either expanding or declining in use.

Linguistic geographer Hans Kurath published atlases of dialects in the United States, defining Northern, Southern, and Midland dialects in the eastern part of the country. In the mid-1900s, Kurath drew distinct isoglosses among the three dialects, based on pronunciation of certain sounds and words. A more recent study of American dialects by linguist Bert Vaux used a 122-question online survey to map dialects in the United States. Maps of the soda, pop, and coke question (**Fig. 6.6**) and the hero, sub, poor-boy question reveal prominent dialects. New England and the South are distinct dialects, and the fuzzy border between the two regions is what Kurath called the Midland dialect. Much of the rest of the country has a mixture of dialects with some very localized dialects.

> **TC** **Thinking Geographically**
>
> Dialects in American English have different words for common things like soft drinks and sandwiches. Think of a unique word for a common thing in your region. Where do you think the **hearth** of this word is? Study the history of your region and think about relocation **diffusion** in your answer.

6.2 | Explain How Languages Are Related and Distributed.

Linguists classify languages based on how closely related they are to one another. At the global scale, we classify languages into language families. Each **language family** includes multiple languages that have a shared but fairly distant origin. We break language families into **language subfamilies**, which are divisions within a language family that have more definitive commonalities and more recent common origins. The spatial extent of subfamilies is smaller than the extent of language families. Arranging from largest spatial extent to smallest, we classify languages into language families, language subfamilies, languages, and dialects.

AP® Exam Taker's Tip

Why are there language subfamilies? Why do languages diverge? Think about political boundaries such as North and South Korea or physical boundaries such as mountains, islands, deserts, or large jungles/rainforests.

Definition and Debate

Mapping language families at the global scale (**Fig. 6.7**) shows us how widespread some language families like Afro-Asiatic and Indo-European are and how limited the extent of other language families like Japonic are. Figure 6.7 maps the distribution of 15 major language families, but not every language fits into this list of 15. The Indo-European language family has the widest spatial distribution and claims the largest number of speakers. Its distribution is a result of both contiguous and relocation diffusion. Very early on, Indo-European languages spread from their hearth into Europe and Asia. More recently, Europeans diffused Indo-European languages to the Americas, Africa, Asia, and Australia and the Pacific through colonization.

The world map of languages shows several language families spoken by small or isolated groups. For example, languages in the Austro-Asiatic language family survive in the interior of eastern India and in Cambodia and Laos. Remoteness helps account for the remaining languages in the Amerindian language family. These languages remain strongest in areas of Middle America, the high Andes, and northern Canada.

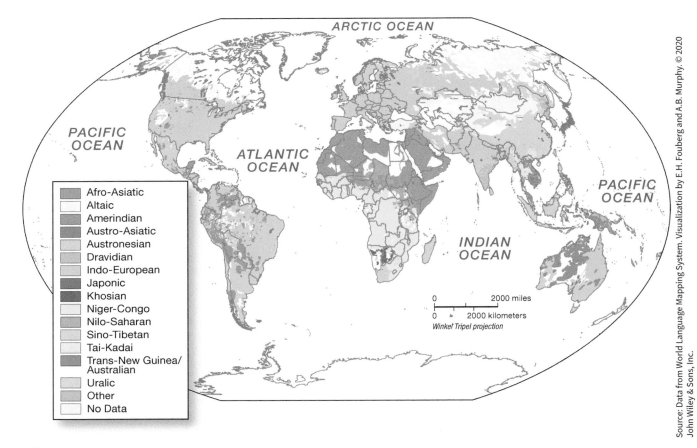

ARCTIC OCEAN

PACIFIC OCEAN

ATLANTIC OCEAN

PACIFIC OCEAN

INDIAN OCEAN

Legend:
- Afro-Asiatic
- Altaic
- Amerindian
- Austro-Asiatic
- Austronesian
- Dravidian
- Indo-European
- Japonic
- Khosian
- Niger-Congo
- Nilo-Saharan
- Sino-Tibetan
- Tai-Kadai
- Trans-New Guinea/Australian
- Uralic
- Other
- No Data

0 — 2000 miles
0 — 2000 kilometers
Winkel Tripel projection

Source: Data from World Language Mapping System. Visualization by E.H. Fouberg and A.B. Murphy. © 2020 John Wiley & Sons, Inc.

FIGURE 6.7 **Language Families of the World.** The global distribution of language families reflects centuries of spatial interaction and flows of migrants. Indo-European languages came to the Americas from Europe through relocation diffusion after 1500 during the European colonial era. Languages in Southeast Asia and Madagascar (just east of Africa) are in the Austronesian language family and are connected as a result of centuries of spatial interaction.

If you look carefully at the map of world language families, some interesting questions arise. Look at the island of Madagascar off the east coast of Africa. The primary languages people in Madagascar speak are not part of a language family found in Africa, but instead are part of the Austronesian family. Look at the spatial distribution of the Austronesian language family. Why is a language from this family spoken on an island so close to Africa? Anthropologists have found evidence that people traveled by sea from the islands of Southeast Asia across the Indian Ocean to Madagascar. At the time this happened, Africans had not sailed across the strait to Madagascar, so no African languages diffused to the island. By the time Africans arrived later in Madagascar, the Austronesian language had been well established.

Language Formation

To classify languages, linguists and linguistic geographers study relationships among languages, looking for similarities and differences. One way to find similarities among languages is to examine particular words, looking for cognates across languages. A **cognate** is a word that has the same origin, that is derived from the same word. Take the case of Italian, Spanish, and French, all of which are members of the Romance language subfamily of the Indo-European language family because they are derived from Latin. The Latin word for milk, *lacte*, became *latta* in Italian, *leche* in Spanish, and *lait* in French; all are cognates. Also, the Latin for the number eight, *oto*, became *otto*, *ocho*, and *huit*, respectively. Even if linguists did not already know that Italian, Spanish, and French were languages rooted in Latin, they could deduce a connection among the languages through the cognates.

During the nineteenth century Jakob Grimm, a scholar and a writer of fairy tales, suggested that cognates might prove the relationships between languages scientifically. He explained that related languages have similar, but not identical, consonants. He believed these consonants would change over time in a predictable way. Hard consonants, such as the *v* and *t* in the German word *vater*, softened into *vader* (Dutch) and *father* (English). Using Grimm's theory that consonants became softer over time, linguists realized that consonants would become harder as they went "backwards" toward the original hearth and original language. From Jones's notions and Grimm's ideas came the first major linguistic hypothesis. Linguists proposed the existence of an ancestral Indo-European language called Proto-Indo-European, which in turn gave rise to modern languages from Scandinavia to North Africa and from North America through parts of Asia to Australia.

Locating the Hearth of Proto-Indo-European
German linguist August Schleicher was the first to compare the world's language families to the branches of a tree (**Fig. 6.8**). In the mid-nineteenth century, he suggested that new languages form through **language divergence**, which happens when spatial interaction decreases among speakers of a language. First, the language fragments into dialects, and then dialects form discrete languages. Language divergence happened between Spanish and Portuguese and is now happening with Korean. Modern Korean may eventually diverge into two languages because of the lack of spatial interaction between North and South Koreans (see Fig. 6.1). Each new language becomes a new leaf on a tree, its branches leading back to the hearth, a major branch or even the trunk of the tree.

Through **backward reconstruction**, tracking consonants and cognates to reconstruct elements of a prior common language, linguists can provide insight into how languages fit together and where the branches were once joined. Finding the major branch of a language family is a daunting task because reconstructing even a small branch of the language tree is complicated. Languages do not change solely through divergence (the splitting of branches). They also change through convergence and extinction. If peoples with different languages have consistent spatial interaction, **language convergence** can take place, collapsing two languages into one. Instances of language convergence create special problems for researchers because the rules of reconstruction may not apply or may be unreliable.

> **AP® Exam Taker's Tip**
>
> What causes languages to converge? Be sure to think about the causes and effects of **diffusion**, such as migration patterns, conquests from outside groups (e.g., colonialism), and simple proximity. Give at least three real-world examples.

Language extinction creates branches on the tree with dead ends, representing a halt in interaction between the **extinct language** and languages that continued (**Fig. 6.9**). Languages become extinct either when all descendants perish, which can happen when an entire people succumb to disease or invaders, or when descendants use another language and abandon learning and speaking their native language. The process of language extinction does not occur overnight. It takes place across generations, with degrees of bilingualism occurring in the interim.

Tracking divergence, convergence, extinction, and spatial interaction, linguists theorize that the hearth of the Proto-Indo-European language was somewhere near the Black Sea. The hearth was most likely in Anatolia, which is present-day Turkey. Proto-Indo-European speakers moved out from the hearth, vocabularies grew, and linguistic divergence occurred, creating new languages. Analyzing the vocabulary of the Proto-Indo-European language, linguists can see the environment,

> **AP® Exam Taker's Tip**
>
> What are the external causes of language extinction? Colonialism certainly caused many languages to disappear. Why is popular culture blamed for the extinction or endangerment of many of the world's languages?

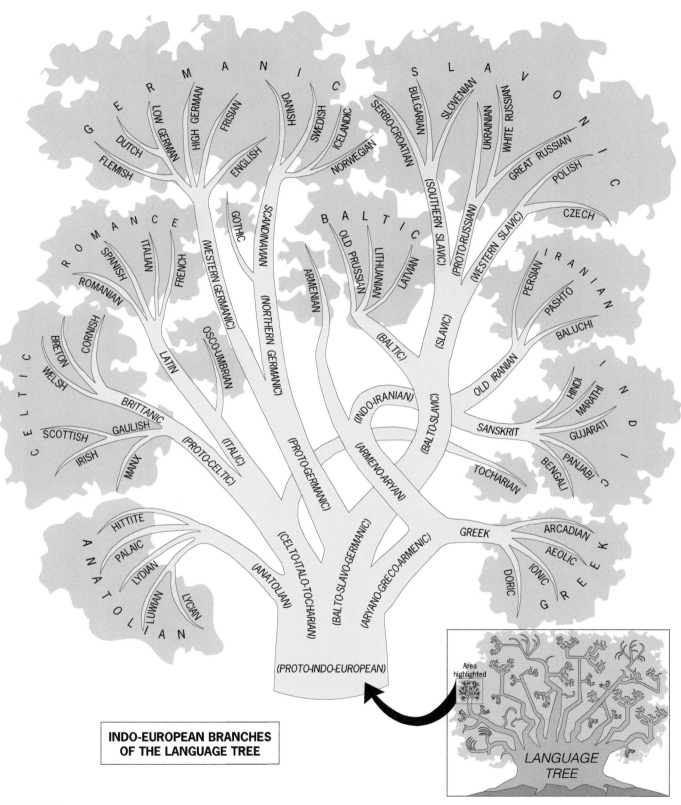

**INDO-EUROPEAN BRANCHES
OF THE LANGUAGE TREE**

Source: Adapted from T. V. Gamkrelidze and V. V. Ivanov. "The Early History of Indo-European Languages," *Scientific American*, March 1990, p. 111.

FIGURE 6.8 **Indo-European Language Tree.** The Indo-European language family is just one of more than a dozen major language families mapped in Figure 6.7. This graphic shows how the languages in the Indo-European family branched off of the same major branch, what linguists call Proto-Indo-European.

EyesWideOpen/Getty Images News/Getty Images

FIGURE 6.9 **Mahiyangana, Sri Lanka.** The Vedda people in Sri Lanka are the indigenous, aboriginal people who have lived on the island for more than 2500 years. The Vedda language is nearly extinct, as people have adopted Sinhala (an Indo-European language), which is the majority language in Sri Lanka, as their primary language. Vedda villages like this one are located in the remote interior of the country.

physical geography, culture, and economy of the language's hearth. Based on the reconstructed vocabulary of Proto-Indo-European, it looks like the language dates back to people who used horses, had the wheel, and traded goods widely.

Indo-European diffused from its hearth west into Europe and east into South Asia, including what is now Pakistan and India (**Fig. 6.10**). In Europe, the presence of Europe's oldest Indo-European language, Celtic (including Irish and Welsh), in the far west supports the idea that newer languages arrived from the east. In South Asia, evidence supports diffusion from the hearth, south to the Caspian Sea, and then east into the Indus and Ganges river basins around 3500 years ago. A second wave of Indo-European speakers moved from the hearth into present-day Iran around 2800 years ago.

How Indo-European languages took hold is another question. The **conquest theory** gives one explanation. This theory holds that early speakers of Proto-Indo-European spread from the hearth into Europe on horseback, overpowering earlier inhabitants and beginning the diffusion and differentiation of Indo-European languages. Over time Proto-Indo-European diverged into languages that are clustered today in the subfamilies of the Indo-European language family.

The **agricultural theory** gives another explanation for the spread of Proto-Indo-European. This theory holds that Proto-Indo-European spread with the diffusion of agriculture. Citing the archaeological record, Luca Cavalli-Sforza and Albert

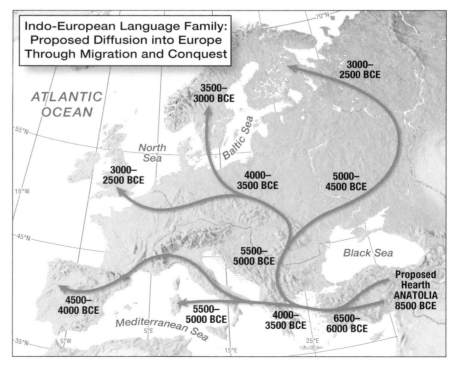

FIGURE 6.10 **Indo-European Language Family: Proposed Diffusion into Europe through Migration and Conquest.** Approximate timings and routes for the diffusion of Indo-European languages into Europe through migration and conquest.

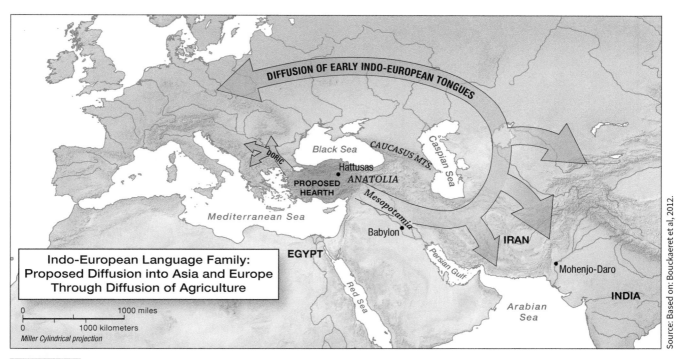

Indo-European Language Family: Proposed Diffusion into Asia and Europe Through Diffusion of Agriculture

FIGURE 6.11 **Indo-European Language Family: Proposed Diffusion into Europe and Asia through Diffusion of Agriculture.** This theory proposes that the Indo-European language family began in Anatolia and spread eastward into South Asia and westward into Europe with the diffusion of agriculture.

Ammerman proposed that for every generation (25 years), the agricultural frontier moved approximately 18 kilometers (11 mi). Farmers from the hearth of the Proto-Indo-European language moved across Europe for thousands of years. The archaeological record supports the agricultural thesis (**Fig. 6.11**). With established farming providing a more reliable food supply, population rose. A slow but steady wave of farmers moved further into Europe and mixed with nonfarming peoples. Some of the nonfarming societies in their path held out, and their languages persevered. Euskera (the Basque language) survives to this day as a probable direct link to Europe's preagricultural era.

The Languages of Europe

The map of world languages (Fig. 6.7) demonstrates how widespread the Indo-European language family is, dominating not just Europe but also significant parts of Asia (including Russia and India), North and South America, Australia, and portions of southern Africa. About half the world's people speak Indo-European languages. The Indo-European language family is broken into subfamilies such as Romance, Germanic, and Slavic. And each subfamily is broken into individual languages, such as English, German, Danish, and Norwegian within the Germanic subfamily.

The language map of Europe (**Fig. 6.12**) shows mainly Indo-European languages, with pockets of the Uralic and Altaic language families also represented. Finnish, Estonian, and Hungarian are major languages of the Uralic family, which, as Figure 6.7 shows, extends across Eurasia to the Pacific Coast. The Altaic family, to which Turkish belongs, is equally widespread and includes Turkish, Kazakh, Uigur, Kyrgyz, and Uzbek languages.

Celtic, the oldest Indo-European language in Europe, migrated into Europe around 3000 years ago. Celtic speech survives in western Ireland, Wales, Scotland, and western France. In most places, Celtic languages fell victim to subsequent migrations, and empire-building. Celtic speakers maintained their language in the most remote western margins of Europe.

The Subfamilies The Romance languages (French, Spanish, Italian, Romanian, and Portuguese) lie in the areas of Europe that were once controlled by the Roman Empire. Over time, local languages mixed with Latin, which the Roman Empire introduced to the region. The Romance languages have much in common because of their Latin connection.

The Germanic languages (English, German, Danish, Norwegian, and Swedish) reflect the expansion of peoples out of northern Europe to the west and south. Some Germanic peoples spread to the northern and northeastern edges of the Roman Empire. Other Germanic peoples spread into areas that were never part of an ancient empire (present-day Sweden, Norway, Denmark, and the northern part of the Netherlands). The Germanic character of English bears the imprint of a further migration—that of the Normans into England in 1066, which brought a Romance language to the British Isles. The essential Germanic character of English remained, but many new words were added that are Romance in origin.

Source: Based on: Bouckaeret et al, 2012.

FIGURE 6.12 **Language Subfamilies and Languages in Europe.** The Indo-European language family includes three major sub-families in Europe: Romance, Germanic, and Slavic languages. Romance languages are in the Mediterranean region. Germanic languages are found in northern Europe. Most people in eastern Europe speak Slavic languages. The distribution of language sub-families that are not part of the Indo-European language family, including Celtic, Euskera (Basque), and Finno-Ugric can be seen on this map, as well.

The Slavic languages (Russian, Polish, Czech, Slovak, Ukrainian, Slovenian, Serbo-Croatian, and Bulgarian) developed as Slavic people migrated from a base in present-day Ukraine around 2000 years ago. Slavic languages overwhelmed Latin-based languages along much of the eastern part of the old Roman Empire. One notable exception is Romanian, a Latin-based language that either survived the Slavic invasion or was reintroduced by migrants.

Relationship to the Political Pattern A comparison of Europe's linguistic and political maps shows a high correlation between the languages spoken and country borders (see Fig. 6.12). Several Romance languages have their own countries: French in France; Spanish in Spain; Portuguese in Portugal; Romanian in Romania; and Italian in Italy. The eastern border of Germany marks the transition from Germanic to Slavic languages.

In some places, linguistic and political borders do not coincide. French extends into Belgium, Switzerland, and Italy. Even inside of France, you will find Basque in the south, Dutch in the north, and Celtic in Breton in the northwest. Romanian extends into Moldavia. Figure 6.2 underscores the complex cultural pattern of eastern Europe, where borders and languages do not coincide perfectly. There are German speakers in Hungary; Hungarian speakers in Slovakia, Romania, and Yugoslavia; Romanian speakers in Greece and Moldavia; Turkish speakers in Bulgaria; and Albanian speakers in Serbia.

One language on the map of Europe stands out for two reasons: First, it covers a very small land area, and second, it is not related to any other language family in Europe. Isolated in the Andorra Mountain region between Spain and France, the Basque people and their Euskera language survived the tumultuous history of Europe for thousands of years. Euskera never blended with another language or diffused from the Andorra region. Basques have a strong identity tied to their language and independent history, an identity that was cemented by repression under fascist dictator Francisco Franco. As ruler of Spain during and after World War II, Franco banned the Basque language and placed cultural and political leaders in prisons.

The Spanish government finally recognized Basque autonomy in its 1979 constitution. Spain gave the Basque language official status and transferred (devolved) some taxation and education powers from the Spanish capital to the Basque region. The Basque region now has a parliament and its own education system. The Basque government has the right to collect taxes, which makes it possible for it to fund programs and policies passed by its parliament. For a time, a group of Basque separatists continued to demand more and waged a campaign of violence against Spanish targets and moderate Basque leaders. The main opposition organization, ETA (Euskadi Ta Azkatasuna), disarmed in 2017. Basque identity and Basque nationalism remain strong (**Fig. 6.13**).

Languages in North America

The Spanish-speaking population in the United States is growing (**Fig. 6.14**). Business owners who employ Spanish speakers advocate for Spanish-language driving tests and education to help ready Spanish speakers for the workforce. In contrast, people who are opposed to migration and who object to the growth of the Spanish language are leading movements to promote "official English" policies. Although Spanish is only one of many non-English languages spoken in the United States, it overshadows all others in terms of number of speakers and is therefore typically the focus of the official English movement (**Table 6.1**).

During the 1980s, over 30 different states considered passing laws declaring English the state's official language, and some 30 states today have declared English the official language of the state, either by statute or by amending the state constitution. A few states have passed English-plus laws, encouraging bilingualism for non-English speakers, and a few other states are officially bilingual, including Hawai'i (Hawai'ian and English), or have bilingual education, including New Mexico (Spanish and English).

Canada is officially bilingual, English and French, reflecting the country's two major colonizers: Great Britain and France. Government documents, newspapers, websites, and even scholarly journals are printed in both English and French. Most of the country's French speakers live in

Photo by E.H. Fouberg. © 2020 John Wiley & Sons, Inc.

FIGURE 6.13 **Aberdeen, South Dakota.** International students in the United States may receive a sash with their home country's colors or flag to wear at graduation. This young man from the Basque region in Spain asked his university (Northern State University) in the United States to put the Basque flag, not the Spanish flag, on his graduation sash.

the province of Quebec, and most people in Quebec speak French at home.

Since the 1970s, the Québécois (the people of Quebec) have used laws and policies to ensure that French is used in the province. In 1977, Quebec passed Law 101, which compelled all businesses in the province to demonstrate that they functioned in French. In response, many businesses and individuals moved out of the province of Quebec into neighboring Ontario. In 1993, the Quebec government passed a law requiring the use of French in advertising (**Fig. 6.15**). The Quebec law allows the inclusion of both French and English (or another language) translations on signage if the French

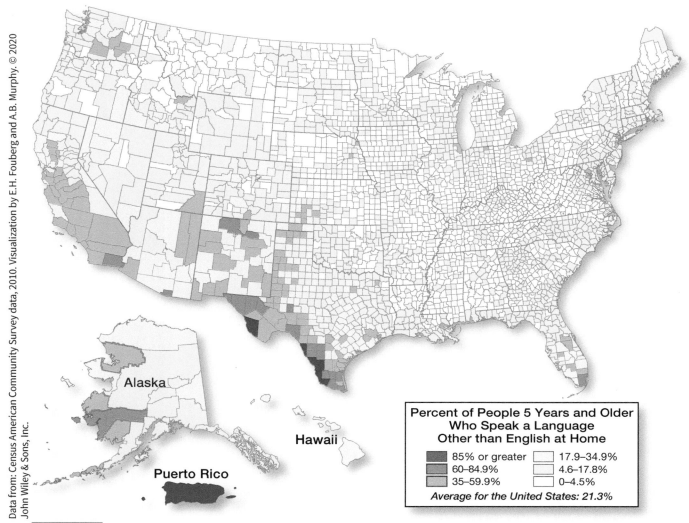

Percent of People 5 Years and Older Who Speak a Language Other than English at Home

■ 85% or greater	□ 17.9–34.9%
■ 60–84.9%	□ 4.6–17.8%
■ 35–59.9%	□ 0–4.5%

Average for the United States: 21.3%

FIGURE 6.14 **Percent of People 5 Years and Older Who Speak a Language Other than English at Home in the United States.** The data presented include all non-English languages by county, including Alaska, Hawaii, and Puerto Rico. Residents of counties in the Southwest, Florida, and Puerto Rico are predominantly Spanish speaking. Bethel County in Alaska, where most residents are Yup'ik people who speak their indigenous language, also stands out in the 60 to 84.9 percent category on the map.

letters are twice the size of the other language's letters. In 2013, the province's strict language policies made international news when an Italian restaurant was asked to provide French-language translations for menu items, including pasta. The outrage over Pastagate, as the scandal came to be known, led the provincial government to promise to respond to language compliance complaints in a more "balanced" and "measured" manner, recognizing that menus and bank statements cannot be held to the same standard as educational materials and signage.

Not all of Quebec's residents identify with the French language. Within the province, a small proportion of people speak English at home, others speak indigenous languages, and still others speak another language altogether—one associated with their country of origin. When the Quebec parliament passed several laws promoting French during the 1980s and 1990s, members of Canada's First Nations who live in Quebec, including the Crees and Mohawks, expressed a desire to remain part of Canada if Quebec ever secedes from the country. During the same period, Quebec experienced a flow of international migrants, many of whom sought residence in Quebec. New immigrants must learn French under Quebec law.

Separatist movements are strongest when the group calling for autonomy or independence is ethnically or culturally distinct, wealth is unevenly distributed, or the group is remote from the center of power (see discussion of devolution in Chapter 8). Since the vote for independence failed in 1994, calls for independence in Quebec are decreasing and the separatist political party has captured fewer seats in recent parliamentary elections in the province. But even if Québécois are happy to remain in Canada, they may still feel a connection to France. The province even has a presence in

TABLE 6.1 | Top Non-English Languages Spoken at Home by People over the Age of 5 in the United States.

Languages other than English spoken at home in the United States. Most Americans who speak these languages at home are also fluent in English.

Language	Total	Percent
1. Spanish	41,017,620	13.4
2. Chinese	3,462,091	1.1
3. Tagalog	1,746,344	0.6
4. Vietnamese	1,498,874	0.5
5. Arabic	1,227,768	0.4
6. French	1,202,060	0.4
7. Korean	1,095,161	0.4
8. Russian	936,344	0.3
9. German	917,812	0.3
10. Haitian	886,765	0.3

Source: Data from: United States Census Bureau Statistical Abstract, 2014. Visualization by E.H. Fouberg and A.B. Murphy. © 2020 John Wiley & Sons, Inc.

Paris in the Maison Quebec (House of Quebec), which functions like an embassy for Quebec in France. As people, ideas, and power flow through Quebec, change will continue. The desire of the Québécois to remain loyal to their French identity will keep the language alive.

Languages of Sub-Saharan Africa

The world map of language families does not show the extreme fragmentation of languages in parts of the world, including sub-Saharan Africa. Figure 6.7 shows six major language families in Africa, with Afro-Asiatic the most widespread in North Africa and Niger-Congo the most widespread in sub-Saharan Africa. At the scale of Africa, we can map individual languages with different color tones for different language subfamilies so you can start to see the true extent of language diversity (**Fig. 6.16**).

The oldest languages of sub-Saharan Africa are the Khoisan languages, which include "click" sounds. Although

FIGURE 6.15 **Quebec City, Quebec.** The imprint of the French-Canadian culture is evident in the cultural landscape of Rue Saint-Louis in Quebec City. Here, the architecture and store signs confirm that this region is not simply Canadian; it is French-Canadian.

Andre Jenny/Alamy Stock Photo

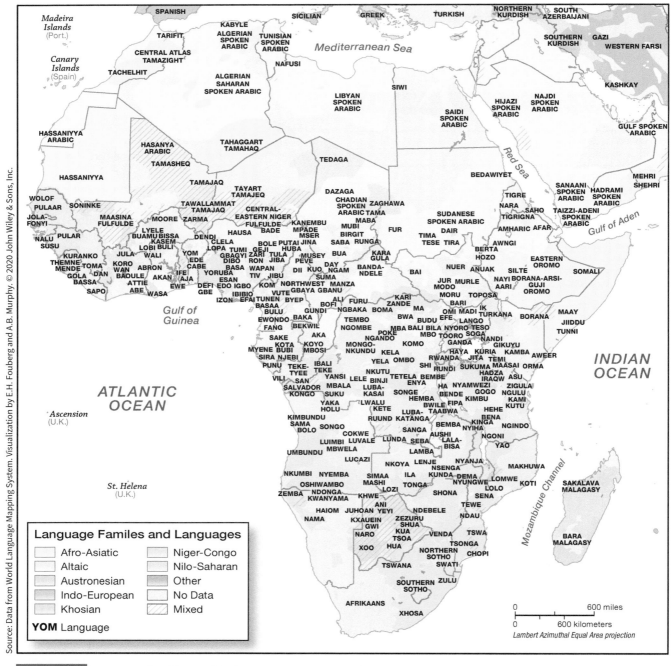

FIGURE 6.16 **Languages in Africa.** Africa has seven major language families and more than 3000 languages (not all are labeled here).

they once dominated much of the region, Khoisan languages were marginalized by the invasion of speakers of Bantu languages. Connections among languages in the Bantu subfamily can be seen through the similar prefixes and vocabularies. These similarities mean that the Bantu languages have been in sub-Saharan Africa for a shorter time. The longer a language has been in a place, the more deeply languages will have splintered.

Focusing on the country scale reveals great linguistic diversity in sub-Saharan Africa. Nigeria's 190 million people speak more than 500 different languages. The three most

prominent languages are Hausa in the north, Yoruba in the southwest, and Igbo in the southeast (**Fig. 6.17**). Of the remaining languages spoken in Nigeria, the vast majority are spoken by fewer than one million people. Indigenous languages persist because culture, community, and daily interactions are built around them.

The Nigerian government's language policy for education officially supports indigenous languages, but English is widespread even in primary school. Education in Nigeria is compulsory (required) in elementary and junior secondary school, which is a total of nine years. Primary school lasts six years and

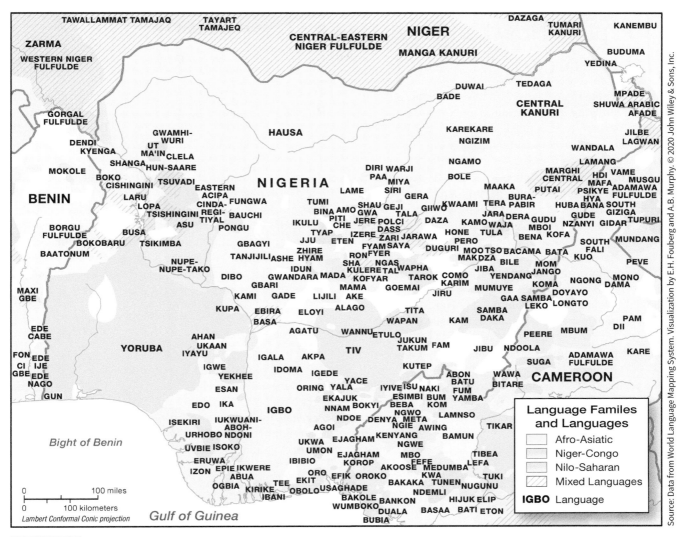

FIGURE 6.17 **Languages in Nigeria.** Nigeria has more than 500 languages (not all are labeled here). The three largest languages are Yoruba, Hausa, and Igbo. English is an official language and is used in education after early primary school.

junior secondary school lasts three years. According to Nigerian education policy, the first three years of primary school should be taught in the student's indigenous language or the "'language of his/her immediate environment,'" commonly Igbo, Hausa, or Yoruba (WENR 2018). This policy, however, is not always followed by schools. Although the law states that the first three years of primary school should be in the indigenous language, lessons are often delivered in English for all six years of primary school (WENR 2018). Reports of teachers punishing children for speaking their indigenous language are common in Nigeria.

Some Nigerian education reformers question the time and energy spent learning English because it takes away from learning other subjects. One argument is that, for many students, knowledge of English is irrelevant when they finish school. Another argument questions why the language of the colonizer is elevated over the three major indigenous languages in the school system. However, the government continues to enable

teaching in English because it sees the value of having a common language across the entire country when Nigeria has such a diversity of languages.

TC Thinking Geographically

Language is typically seen as a centripetal force that brings a **nation** together because it gives people a common way to communicate. But choosing one official language can be a centrifugal force (one that pulls a **nation** apart) because one language is elevated at the expense of other languages. Choose a country in the world and look up the diversity of languages spoken, the official language(s) of the country, and the language(s) used in primary and secondary education. Determine how the language choices made by this country help create or divide the **nation**.

6.3 Explain How Language Can Be Used as a Unifying or Dividing Force.

Languages become more fixed and stable when they are written down. Following its invention in 1440, the Gutenberg printing press stabilized language and helped spark a rise in nationalism centered on **vernacular** languages (see Chapter 8). A vernacular language is one used in everyday interaction among a group of people. Before the Renaissance and the invention of the Gutenberg press, government functions and academic conversations in western Europe were conducted in Latin, the language first of the Roman Empire and then of the Catholic Church. The choice of Latin reflected the distribution of power in western Europe at that time. However, the invention of the printing press enabled governments to claim power and reinforce that power by elevating the vernacular language over Latin. For example, the government of France could communicate to French-speaking citizens in a language shared by all citizens rather than in the language of the elite (Latin). In this way, the printing press sparked the rise of nationalism in Europe (see Chapter 8).

The printing press also sparked the Reformation in western Europe (see Chapter 7). In 1452, Gutenberg printed the first Gutenberg Bible (the sacred text for Christians), which brought the scriptures out of churches and into the hands of literate people. Before the Gutenberg Bible, the Bible was written in Latin because it was the language of the Catholic Church. The Gutenberg press made it possible to print the Bible in vernacular languages, including English, French, and German (**Fig. 6.18**). Access to the Bible in the vernacular language allowed for many interpretations of the scriptures, and printing the Bible in the vernacular also helped standardize the language. The Luther Bible played this role for German, as did the King James Bible for English. Because the ability to convey a message is politically empowering, standardizing a common language through print gave countries the opportunity to promote a common culture and a national identity. With the printing press and a standardized vernacular language, countries could distribute common histories, religious interpretations, and political thoughts.

Lingua Franca

Since 1500, globalization has brought widespread cultural, linguistic, political, and economic interaction. Trade and commerce have stimulated the formation of new, hybrid languages to facilitate this interaction. Trade encourages people who speak different languages to find ways to communicate with one another. A **lingua franca** is a language used among speakers of

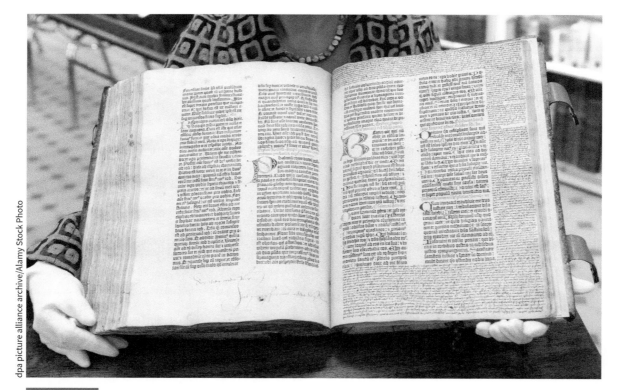

FIGURE 6.18 **Kassel, Germany.** Experts believe Gutenberg published around 180 copies of the Gutenberg Bible between 1452 and 1456. This copy was discovered in 1958 in an attic of a church in the small German town of Immenhausen and is one of 49 copies certified as part of the original printing.

different languages for the purposes of trade and commerce. It can be a single language, or it can be a mixture of two or more languages. When people speaking two or more languages are in contact and they combine parts of their languages in a simplified structure and vocabulary, we call it a **pidgin language**.

The first widely known lingua franca was a pidgin language. During the 1200s, trade in the Mediterranean Sea expanded, and traders from the ports of southern France (the Franks) revitalized the ports of the eastern Mediterranean. But the local traders did not speak the Franks's language. The language of the Franks mixed with Italian, Greek, Spanish, and Arabic and created a pidgin language that came to be known as the Frankish language. The term *lingua franca* translates to "language of the Franks," commemorating the language that served for centuries as the shared language of Mediterranean trade.

A lingua franca connects people and serves as a conduit for diffusing cultural values and systems. During the expansion of Islam, Arabic became a lingua franca that helped Arab traders establish ports and trade relationships and also furthered the diffusion of Islam. English became a lingua franca during British colonialism and became the main way British political values, including legal and governmental systems, were established in their colonies.

Creole Languages

Over time a pidgin language may gain native speakers, becoming the first language children learn in the home. When this happens, we call it a creolized or Creole language. A **Creole language** is a pidgin language that has developed a more complex structure and vocabulary, and has become the native language of a group of people. The word *Creole* stems from a pidgin language formed in the Caribbean from English, French, and Portuguese languages, mixed with the languages of enslaved Africans. The language became more complex and became the first language of people in the region, replacing African languages.

Photo by A.B. Murphy. © 2020 John Wiley & Sons, Inc.

FIGURE 6.19 **Zanzibar, Tanzania.** Locals read front pages of newspapers outside of a news stand in Zanzibar. The newspapers are printed in several languages, including Swahili.

Swahili is a pidgin language that became a Creole language and is now the lingua franca of East Africa (**Fig. 6.19**). Through centuries of trade and interaction, Swahili developed from an African Bantu language mixed with Arabic and Persian, encompassing 100 million speakers from southern Somalia to northern Mozambique, and from coastal Kenya and Tanzania to Uganda and the East African Great Lakes region. Swahili has a complex vocabulary and structure, and while millions of East Africans communicate in the language, most still learn and speak a local language as their first or primary language. Swahili has gained prominence since 2000 because of its status as the most widely used African language on the Internet. The British Broadcasting Corporation (BBC) has a Swahili language website, and *Wikipedia* offers pages of its free encyclopedia in Swahili.

AP® Exam Taker's Tip

Think about the terms **lingua franca, pidgin**, and **creole** with regard to scale. Which one is the most widely diffused? Least? In the middle? Give an example of each.

Multilingualism

More than 7000 languages are spoken in a world with fewer than 200 countries. Not a single country in the world is home to speakers of only one language. In practice, every country is multilingual, meaning that more than one language is spoken. Officially, a country can choose to recognize one official language (Indonesia), allow multiple official languages (Canada, Belgium), or not declare an official language at all (United States). Countries that have more than one official language are called *multilingual states*.

Multilingualism takes several forms. In Canada and Belgium, the two major languages are each tied to specific provinces or regions of the country. Canada recognizes two official languages at the federal level, French and English, and these languages have equal status. Each province and territory in Canada can choose its official language(s). For example, French is the official language of Quebec, and English is the official language in Nova Scotia. Canada's federal laws also protect speakers of minority languages. In Quebec, native English speakers have the right to education in their language, and in Nova Scotia, native French speakers have the right to education in their language. Several provinces officially recognize both English and French and use both languages in government and education. Indigenous languages are also recognized by some provinces and territories in Canada, especially the Inuit language in Nunavut.

Belgium has three distinct language regions. In the north, Flanders is Dutch-speaking (Flemish), and in the south, Wallonia is French-speaking. Brussels is designated as a bilingual capital region even though the city is physically surrounded by Flanders (**Fig. 6.20**). Power and decision making rest with the individual governments of Flanders and Wallonia rather than

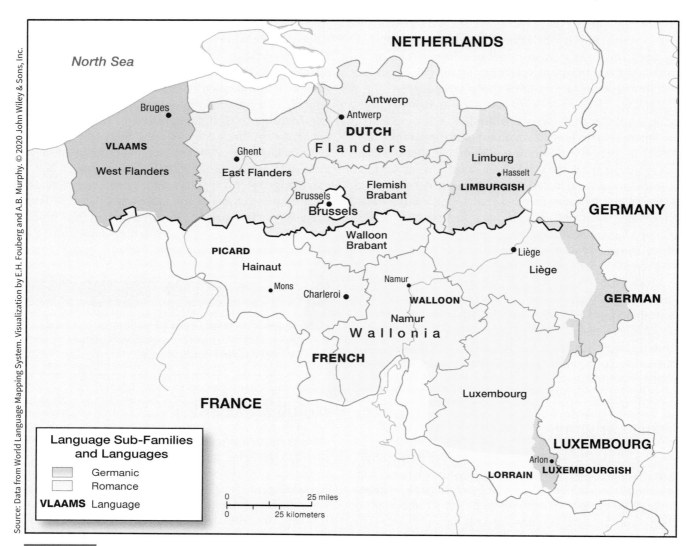

FIGURE 6.20 **Languages in Belgium.** Belgians speak French, Dutch, and German. The borders of Belgium's three regions, Wallonia, Flanders, and Brussels, and the provinces of each region, follow the pattern of language speakers. German speakers are in the east, and Brussels is officially a bilingual (French and Flemish) region.

with the national government of Belgium. No political party in Belgium operates at the national scale. Flanders and Wallonia each have their own political parties that vie for power, and each have their own source of power and government administration across their five provinces.

AP® Exam Taker's Tip

Multilingual states often times produce cultural tension that leads to separatist movements. Belgium is an example of such a state. Can you identify other multilingual countries from the reading?

Another form of multilingualism combines the language of the colonizer with one local or regional language as an official means of communication. In India and Malaysia, British colonization left the imprint of English on education and government. Choosing English as one of the official languages

acknowledged the common language spoken by the educated and politically powerful elite. During colonization, the British encouraged academically gifted Indians and Malaysians to go to college in England to become fluent in English and Western political philosophy, legal systems, and medicine. When India and Malaysia gained independence and set up parliamentary governments similar to their colonizer, each chose English as one of its official languages.

In addition to the language of their colonizer, however, India and Malaysia each chose a second official language from among the many indigenous languages spoken in the newly independent states. India selected Hindi (the first language of 26 percent of Indians and now spoken by 44 percent of Indians), and Malaysia selected Malay (now spoken as the first language by 46 percent of Malaysians). Elevating a major indigenous language that is not spoken by the majority of people in the country has caused strife in both India and Malaysia. For example, in Malaysia, the Malay ethnic group is politically

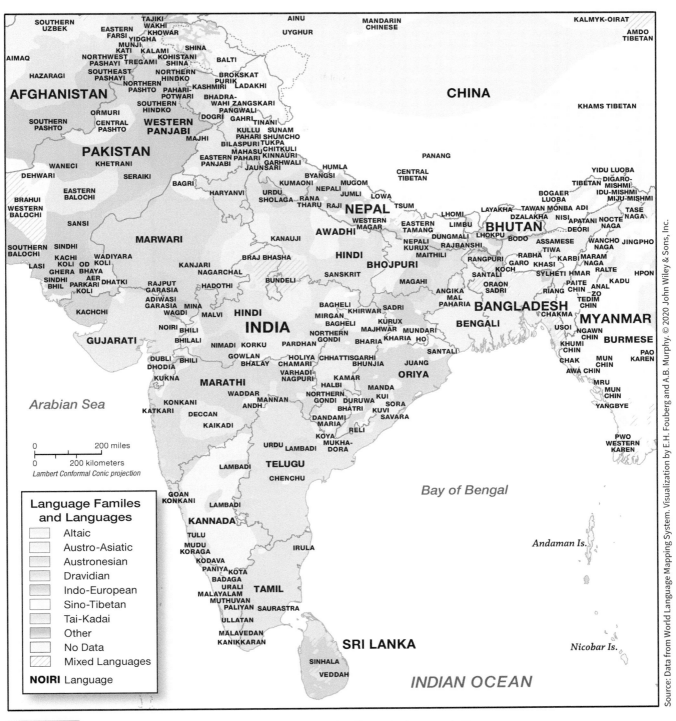

Source: Data from World Language Mapping System. Visualization by E.H. Fouberg and A.B. Murphy. © 2020 John Wiley & Sons, Inc.

FIGURE 6.21   Languages in India.   India has two major language families, Indo-European in the north and Dravidian in the south. Across the country, Indians speak more than 700 different languages (not all are labeled here).

privileged, and Malay's status reinforces this place of privilege. The Chinese ethnic group, which makes up 35 percent of Malaysia, has a great concentration of wealth and economic power, but the Malaysian government keeps the economic might of the Chinese in check by granting government jobs and seats in universities to those fluent in Malay.

In India, Hindi and English are recognized as co-official languages at the federal level. Hindi is spoken primarily in the north, in and around the capital of Delhi. It's most common among Hindus, and it was Hindu political leaders who

advocated for Hindi as an official language. However, protests came from non-Hindu groups and from political leaders and academics who spoke languages other than Hindi. Efforts to teach Hindi in secondary schools created backlash and protests in non-Hindi-speaking areas of India in the 1960s. Today, non-Hindi speakers, especially in the south, resist the imposition of the Hindi language in education.

India is very linguistically diverse, with over 700 spoken languages (**Fig. 6.21**). Because "no single language is spoken by a majority of Indians" (Wharton 2018), neither Hindi

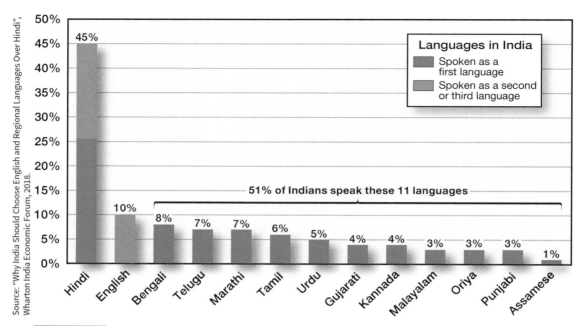

Source: "Why India Should Choose English and Regional Languages Over Hindi", Wharton India Economic Forum, 2018.

FIGURE 6.22 **Language Diversity in India.** No single language in India is spoken by a majority of people. Hindi is spoken by 45 percent of Indians, followed by English, which is spoken by 10 percent of Indians.

nor English actually binds everyone together (**Fig. 6.22**). Each Indian state can also officially recognize its own languages, with the result that across India's 29 states, 22 languages are recognized. This diversity is reflected in elections. Although India is the world's largest democracy, its extreme diversity in languages and the fact that 25 percent of the people are illiterate mean that symbols must be used in elections. The ballot in the latest vote for the Lok Sabha (lower house of parliament) and prime minister was presented in 35 symbols, including a hand, a lotus flower, and an elephant. Each symbol represented one political party, enabling voters to cast their ballots by symbol instead of by language (**Fig. 6.23**).

The Prospect of a Global Language

What will the global language map look like 50 years from now? More and more people are using English in a variety of contexts. English is now the lingua franca of international business and travel, and it is also the language of music, movies, and television in popular culture. Much of the engineering in the computer and telecommunications industries relies heavily on English. Does this mean that English is on its way to becoming a global language?

If global language means the principal language people use around the world in their day-to-day activities, English is not becoming a global language (**Fig. 6.24**). Population growth rates are generally lower in English-speaking areas than they are in other areas, and little evidence shows that people in non-English-speaking areas are willing to abandon their local or national language in favor of English. Language embodies

deeply held cultural views and is an essential part of cultural identity, so even if English diffuses broadly, many people will actively resist switching to English.

If global language means a common language of trade and commerce used around the world, the picture looks rather different. Although not always welcomed, English is a

The India Today Group/The India Today Group/Getty Images

FIGURE 6.23 **Noida, India.** Poll workers receive instructions on how to operate voting machines before the 2019 election for prime minister. Ballots displayed photos of prime minister candidates and symbols for political parties, because no one language is spoken by a majority of Indians and 25 percent of Indians are not literate.

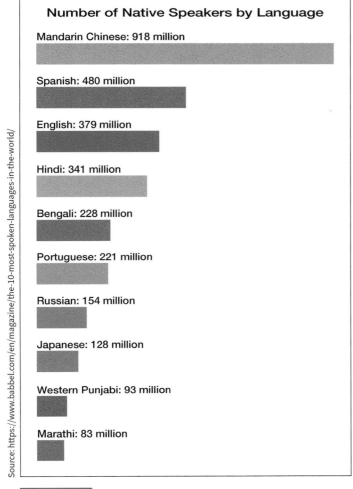

Number of Native Speakers by Language

Mandarin Chinese: 918 million

Spanish: 480 million

English: 379 million

Hindi: 341 million

Bengali: 228 million

Portuguese: 221 million

Russian: 154 million

Japanese: 128 million

Western Punjabi: 93 million

Marathi: 83 million

Source: https://www.babbel.com/en/magazine/the-10-most-spoken-languages-in-the-world/

FIGURE 6.24 **Native Speakers of World Languages.** English is a global lingua franca in business, academics, and trade, but Chinese and Spanish have many more native speakers than English.

major language of cross-cultural communication—especially in the areas of science, technology, travel, business, and education. Korean scholars are likely to communicate with their Russian counterparts in English. Japanese scientific journals are increasingly published in English. Danish tourists visiting Italy likely use English to get around. Meetings of most international financial and governmental institutions are dominated by English. Under these circumstances, the role of English as an international language will likely grow.

We must be careful in this conclusion, however. Anyone looking at the world 200 years ago would have predicted that French would be the principal language of cross-cultural communication in the future. Instead, English grew to ascendancy because Great Britain was the most powerful country in the world in the eighteenth and nineteenth centuries, and it remained on top in the twentieth century because the United States was the most powerful country in the world. Today, political geographers are looking to the rise of China as a global power. China is massively investing in much of the world through its One Belt, One Road and Maritime Silk Road initiatives (see Chapter 8), and through its development banks, which rival the International Monetary Fund (IMF) and the World Bank (see Chapter 10). We are decades away, but as China grows in power, the number of people learning Chinese will grow, making it possible for Chinese to become a global language for cross-communication in the future.

> **TC** **Thinking Geographically**
>
> What role has **globalization** played in the diffusion of some languages and the extinction of other languages around the world? How does learning to speak a global language other than your native language change your **identity** at different **scales**?

6.4 Determine the Role Language Plays in Making Places.

Geographer Yi-Fu Tuan argued that by simply *naming a place, people call that place into being*. Geographers call place-names **toponyms**. A toponym allows us to see a location as a place and imparts a certain character to a place. Tuan contrasts the examples of "Mount Prospect" and "Mount Misery" to help us understand that a name alone can color the character of a place and even the experiences of people in a place. Tuan believed that a visit to "Mount Prospect" would create different expectations and experiences than a visit to "Mount Misery."

Toponyms and History

Toponyms give us a quick glimpse into the history of places. Knowing who named a place and how the name was chosen helps us understand the uniqueness of that place. In his book, *Names on the Land: A Historical Account of Place-Naming in the United States* (1982), English professor George Stewart recognized that 10 themes are common American toponyms. He developed a classification scheme focused on 10 basic types of place-names, including *descriptive* (Rocky Mountains), *commendatory* (Paradise Valley, Arizona), and *possession* (Johnson City, Texas) (**Table 6.2**). Toponyms can be *manufactured*, like Truth or Consequences, New Mexico, where the people voted to change the town name in response to an incentive offered by a 1950s-era radio game show. Another classification of toponyms is *shift names*, which happen when migrants name a new place after their home region (Lancaster, Pennsylvania, which is named for Lancaster, England) (**Fig. 6.25**).

The 10 classes of toponyms reinforce that every toponym has a story. The stories of toponyms quite often have their roots in migration, movement, and interaction among people. When languages diffuse through migration, so too do toponyms. Toponyms brought by a group of migrants can remain

TABLE 6.2 **Toponym Classification Scheme Designed by George Stewart.**

Stewart identified ten classes of toponyms into which most place-names can be sorted.

Type of Toponym	Example
Descriptive	Rocky Mountains
Associative	Mill Valley, California
Commemorative	San Francisco, California
Commendatory	Paradise Valley, Arizona
Incidents	Battle Creek, Michigan
Possession	Johnson City, Texas
Folk	Plains, Georgia
Manufactured	Truth or Consequences, New Mexico
Mistakes	Lasker, North Carolina
Shift	Lancaster, Pennsylvania

long after the migrants move on. Clusters of Welsh toponyms in Pennsylvania, French toponyms in Louisiana, and Dutch toponyms in Michigan reveal historical migration flows.

Brazil's toponyms provide an interesting case study of the history of migration flows in one country. Most Brazilian toponyms are Portuguese, reflecting the history of Portuguese colonization. Amid the Portuguese toponyms sits a cluster of German toponyms in the southern state of Santa Catarina. Because German migrants had a fondness for the tropical flowers they saw in Brazil, the toponyms of several towns incorporate the German word for flower, *Blume*. Toponyms in Santa Catarina include Blumenau, Blumberg, Blumenhof, Blumenort,

Blumenthal, and Blumenstein. Brazilian toponyms also reflect the enormous forced migration of enslaved Africans from West Africa to Brazil during the slave trade. The Brazilian state of Bahia has several toponyms that originated in West Africa.

Changing Toponyms

Tuan explained that when people change the toponym of a place, they have the power to "wipe out the past and call forth the new." For example, people in a small town in Wales feared that the rise of English had diminished the use of the Welsh language. They also wanted to boost their local economy by attracting tourists to their town. In the mid-1800s, the people renamed their town with a Welsh word unpronounceable by others: Llanfairpwllgwyngyllgogerychwyrndrobwllllantysiliogogogoch (**Fig. 6.26**).

The toponym accurately describes the location of the town: "The Church of St. Mary in the hollow of white hazel near the rapid whirlpool by the church of St. Tysilio of the red cave." Wales has an official policy of teaching both Welsh and English in the schools in order to preserve and boost usage of the Welsh language. Saying the name of this town correctly is now a benchmark for students learning Welsh, and the residents of the town take pride in their ability to pronounce it.

Toponyms are part of the cultural landscape. Changes in place-names give us an idea of the layers of history. For example, on the Kenai Peninsula in Alaska, where Clare Swan (whom we cited earlier in this chapter) is from, the history of toponyms gives us insight into identity questions in the place. Natives in one town on the Kenai Peninsula called their home Nanwalek in the early 1800s. When the Russians came in and took over the peninsula, they changed the name to Alexandrof. Then, when Americans mapped Alaska and made it a state, they

---

Author Field Note Naming New Glarus, Wisconsin

"Driving from Chicago to Minneapolis, I decided to get off the interstate and wind my way through the hilly countryside of southwestern Wisconsin. Dairy cattle dotted the hillsides, and I knew I was not only in Wisconsin, but also nearing the site of the first Swiss cheese factory in Wisconsin. Approaching from the south, I stopped to take a photo of the Welcome to New Glarus sign. Described by a resident as 'the most typical Swiss village on Earth outside Switzerland,' New Glarus, Wisconsin was settled by 108 Swiss migrants in 1845 (Hillinger 1985). The migrants left the Glarus canton in Switzerland during a period of economic hardship and migrated first to New York and then to Wisconsin. The site for the town and its surrounding dairies and cheese factories was chosen by two scouts from the party who headed north on the Mississippi River from St. Louis and stopped in the hills of Wisconsin to found their town and name it 'New Glarus.' The first cheese factories were founded as farmer-factory cooperatives, and the idea of cooperative production persists in New Glarus. On the outskirts of town, the New Glarus Brewing Company makes Spotted Cow beer, a regional favorite sold only in Wisconsin. Started by Deb and Dan

Carey, the successful brewery owners created an employee stock ownership program that will eventually hand ownership of the privately held company to its employees."

–E. H. Fouberg

FIGURE 6.25 **New Glarus, Wisconsin.**

Photo by A.B. Murphy. © 2020 John Wiley & Sons, Inc.

FIGURE 6.26 **Llanfairpwllgwyngyllgogerychwyrndrobwllllantysiliogogogoch, Wales.** The town with the self-proclaimed longest name in the world attracts hordes of tourists each year to a place whose claim to fame is largely its name.

changed the name to English Bay. In 1991, the townspeople changed the name of their home back to Nanwalek. When you arrive in Nanwalek, you will see Native people, see signs of the Russian Orthodox religion, hear English spoken, and talk with Alaskan Natives who are reviving their Native language and culture. Each period of history is reflected in the toponyms of this one place.

Postcolonial Toponyms

Toponyms may change when power shifts hands in a place. When African colonies became independent countries, new governments immediately changed the toponyms that commemorated colonial figures and renamed several countries: Upper Volta to Burkina Faso, Gold Coast to Ghana, Nyasaland to Malawi, and Northern and Southern Rhodesia to Zambia and Zimbabwe. Leopoldville (named after a Belgian king) became Kinshasa, capital of the Congo. Salisbury, Zimbabwe, named after a British leader, became Harare. Lourenço Marques, Mozambique, commemorating a Portuguese naval hero, became Maputo.

The decision to choose a new toponym can also come years after independence. India changed *Bombay* to *Mumbai* in 1995, about 50 years after independence. *Bombay* is an Anglicized word that came from the name the Portuguese used for

the city, *Bombaim*, which meant "good bay." When a nationalist party won local elections in 1995, it renamed the city Mumbai, a toponym that both reinforces the city's Marathi identity and celebrates its patron Hindu goddess, Mumbadevi.

Postrevolution Toponyms

Independence prompts name changes, and so too do changes in power through coups and revolutions. During his reign, authoritarian dictator General Mobutu Sese Seko changed the name of the Belgian Congo in sub-Saharan Africa to Zaïre (**Fig. 6.27**). At first, other governments and international agencies did not take this move seriously, but eventually they recognized Mobutu's Zaïre. Governments and companies changed their maps and atlases to reflect Mobutu's decision. The government of Zaïre changed the name of its money from the franc to the zaïre, and it even changed the name of the Congo River to the Zaïre.

In 1997, the revolutionary leader Laurent Kabila ousted Mobutu and established his regime in the capital, Kinshasa. Almost immediately, he renamed the country. Zaïre became the Democratic Republic of the Congo (reflecting the colonial name). Again, governments and companies reacted, changing their maps and atlases to reflect Kabila's decision.

FIGURE 6.27 **Gbadolite, Congo.** The palace of former dictator Mobutu Sese Seko now stands in ruins in his hometown, Gbadolite. Once called the "Versailles of the Jungle," the palace had swimming pools, an international airport, and opulent design. It was once a five-star hotel and is now used to house soldiers and families of the armed forces of the Democratic Republic of the Congo, including the child walking through this photo.

Both the dissolution of the Soviet Union and the overthrow of Apartheid in South Africa spurred many changes in toponyms. After the Soviet Union replaced the Russian tsars, it changed many places that were named for tsars. Then, when the Soviet Union collapsed, a new round of name changes occurred, often going back to tsarist-era names. Leningrad reverted to St. Petersburg, Sverdlovsk went back to Yekaterinburg (its name under the tsars), and Stalingrad was renamed Volgograd (for the river).

South Africa experienced a major revolution that also resulted in a fundamental change in governance. Under Apartheid, black South Africans had little to no power. In post-Apartheid South Africa, however, the government restructured the country's administrative framework, creating nine provinces out of four and giving some of the new provinces African names (Mpumalanga for the new Eastern Transvaal, Gauteng for a new central province). One of the old provinces, Natal, has become Kwazulu-Natal. The government also changed some names of towns and villages, but South Africa's map still includes many names from the Apartheid period. A push to change the name of the capital from Pretoria to the more indigenous Tshwane has been challenged by white South Africans, who say the city was named Pretoria when it was founded and that the current name is therefore uniquely South African.

Disputed Toponyms The toponyms we see on a map depend in large part on who produced the map. Places claimed by two groups will have more than one name at the same time. The National Geographic Society labels some contested toponyms with the predominant name, either based on power or widespread use, and then puts the variant name in parentheses. For example, the National Geographic labels the body of water between the Korean Peninsula and Japan as the Sea of Japan (East Sea) and labels the islands of the coast of Argentina as Falkland Islands (Islas Malvinas).

The *Sea of Japan* and the *East Sea* are two names for the same body of water. Because the Japanese colonized the Korean Peninsula from the 1800s through World War II, South Koreans see the toponym *Sea of Japan* as a continued colonial influence and power grab by the Japanese, arguing that the body of water was called the "East Sea" before

Japanese colonization and should be called the "East Sea" after Japanese colonization. Japanese argue that the *East Sea* does not make sense as a toponym because the body of water is to the west of Japan, and they continue to call it the "Sea of Japan."

Argentineans refer to a small cluster (archipelago) of islands off the southeast coast of South America as Islas Malvinas, but the British call the same cluster of islands the Falkland Islands. In 1982, Argentina invaded the Malvinas, but the British forces fought back, and the islands remain under British control. British, American, and other allies call and map the islands as the Falklands, but Argentineans continue to call and map the islands as Islas Malvinas. The war ended in a matter of weeks, but the underlying dispute lingers, and so do both names.

Memorial Toponyms

People can choose a toponym to memorialize an important person or event. Hundreds of parks in the United States are named Memorial Park to commemorate a person or event. Towns or government agencies can vote to change the name of a school, a library, or a public building to memorialize people who have played a role in shaping the place or who have had an enormous influence on people in the place.

Just as certain events such as decolonization or a political revolution can spur changes in toponyms, so too can revolutions in thought and behavior. The civil rights movement of the 1960s in the United States left many lasting impressions of people and events, especially in the South, where many protests, sit-ins, and marches occurred. Geographer Derek Alderman explains that in recent decades, African Americans in the South have "taken a particularly active role in reconstructing commemorative landscapes—from calling for the removal of Confederate symbols from public places to the building of memorials and museums honoring the civil rights movement." Because so many people travel along them daily, streets are often the focal point of commemoration in the cultural landscape, serving as a constant reminder of the person or event being memorialized.

Alderman studied the practice of changing street names to memorialize Martin Luther King Jr. (MLK), the major African American leader of the civil rights movement. Although streets named after MLK are found throughout the United States, the greatest concentration of memorial streets are in the South, especially in Georgia (King's home state) and Mississippi (**Fig. 6.28**). Alderman studied the distribution of MLK streets in the South, comparing their locations with census data on race and socioeconomics. He found that although MLK streets are found in both cities and rural areas, "MLK streets are located—whether by choice or by force—in census areas that are generally poorer and with more African Americans than citywide averages" (**Fig. 6.29**). Alderman tempers this finding with a caution that not all MLK streets are in poorer areas of cities. Even when MLK streets are in depressed areas, the African American population may have purposely chosen a street because it runs through an African American neighborhood. Alderman's subsequent studies explore the scale of the city and the contested views of what kinds of streets should

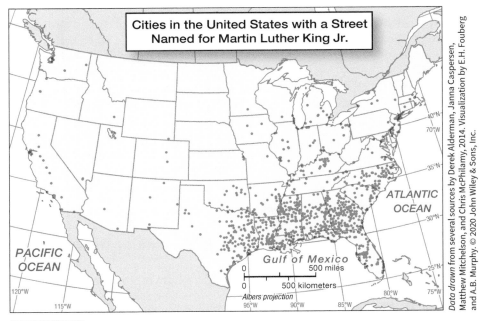

Data drawn from several sources by Derek Alderman, Janna Caspersen, Matthew Mitchelson, and Chris McPhilamy, 2014. Visualization by E.H. Fouberg and A.B. Murphy. © 2020 John Wiley & Sons, Inc.

FIGURE 6.28 **Cities in the United States with a Street Named for Martin Luther King Jr.** Streets named after Martin Luther King Jr. are concentrated in the southeastern United States (almost 70 percent of all MLK-named roads), even as such naming is a national trend. King came from Georgia, and the South was an early battleground in the civil rights movement.

Guest Field Note Commemorating Martin Luther King Jr. in Greenville, North Carolina

Derek Alderman
University of Tennessee

Greenville, North Carolina, changed West Fifth Street to Martin Luther King Jr. Drive in 1999. Originally, African American leaders wanted all of Fifth Street renamed—not just part of it—but residents and business owners on the eastern end strongly opposed the proposal. After driving and walking down the street, I quickly realized that King Drive marked an area that was predominantly black with limited commercial development, whereas East Fifth

was mostly white and more upscale. When I interviewed members of Greenville's African American community, they expressed deep frustration over the marginalization of the civil rights leader. In the words of one elected official, "The accomplishments of Dr. King were important to all Americans. A whole man deserves a whole street!" Naming streets for King is a controversial process for many cities, often exposing continued racial tensions and the potential for toponyms to function as contested social boundaries within places.

FIGURE 6.29 **Greenville, North Carolina.**

---

be named for MLK—be they residential, commercial, major thoroughfares (perhaps those that connect white and African American neighborhoods), or residential streets in largely African American neighborhoods.

The presence of streets named for civil rights leaders in the cultural landscapes of the American South creates a significant counterbalance to the numerous places of commemoration named for leaders of the Confederacy during the Civil War (see Chapter 1).

Commodification of Toponyms
The practice of commodifying (buying, selling, and trading) toponyms is growing. International media corporations bring known names to new places, drawing consumers to the place based on a corporate identity. For example, the Disney Corporation opened Tokyo Disneyland in 1983 and Disneyland Paris in 1990, both places that capitalize on the success of Disneyland and Disney World in the United States. As corporations spread their names and logos to other places, they seek to "brand" places, creating or re-creating places that consumers associate with places of the same brand.

Corporations with a global reach have been stamped on the cultural landscape through toponyms. Stadiums are especially susceptible to this form of commodification: FedEx Field, Verizon Center, TD Bank Garden, CenturyLink Field, and Coors Field are perfect examples. In 2004, the cash-strapped Metropolitan Transit Authority (MTA) in New York City proposed renaming the metro stops, bridges, and tunnels after corporate sponsors. The plan was approved in 2013, and metro riders have been assured the name changes will not elicit confusion. Corporate sponsors are only eligible to buy naming rights provided they have "a unique or iconic geographic, historic or other connection" to a particular MTA facility "that would readily be apparent to typical MTA customers."

TC Thinking Geographically

The **toponym** of this place was first chosen by Gabrielino Indians. In 1769, Spanish Franciscan priests **migrated** to the place and gave it a new toponym. In 1850, English speakers renamed the place. Do not use the Internet to help you. Use only maps in this book or in atlases to help you deduce what this place is. Maps of European exploration and colonialism will help you the most. Look at the end of the chapter self-test for the answer.

Summary

Define Language and Describe the Role of Language in Culture.

1. A language is a set of sounds and symbols that is used for communication. Language is a fundamental element of local and national culture. The diffusion of global languages, including English, challenges the preservation of national languages. Some countries, including France, are working diligently to preserve national and local languages, while social networks, food, music, and popular culture are becoming more globalized.

2. Language is an essential part of culture because we think in our language and communicate our thoughts and feelings in a language. Language also makes members of a certain culture visible to each other through communication. Language even reflects how a culture views the world in terms of time and possibilities.

3. A standard language is published, widely distributed, and purposely taught. Governments often support standard languages. For example, the Chinese government standardized characters so that speakers of different Chinese dialects can read the same text. The Académie Française keeps the standard for the French language in France. And the government of Ireland helps support a standard Irish language by requiring public employees and officials to pass a test in the language. Variants of a standard language along regional or ethnic lines are called dialects. Differences in vocabulary, syntax (the way words are put together to form phrases), pronunciation, cadence (the rhythm of speech), and even the pace of speech all mark a speaker's dialect.

Explain How Languages Are Related and Distributed.

1. Linguists classify languages based on how closely related they are to one another. At the global scale, we classify languages into language families. Each language family includes multiple languages that have a shared but fairly distant origin. We break language families into language subfamilies, which are divisions within a language family that have more definitive commonalities and more recent common origins. Subfamilies have a smaller spatial extent than language families. Arranging from largest spatial extent to smallest, we classify languages into language families, language subfamilies, languages, and dialects.

2. The world map of language families shows 15 major language families, but not all languages spoken worldwide fit into those 15 families. Indo-European languages encompass most of Europe and the Americas. They are also spoken in northern Asia (especially Russia), southern Asia (especially India), and the Pacific (including Australia and New Zealand). Indo-European languages diffused into the Americas, Australia, and New Zealand during European colonization from the 1500s to the 1900s CE.

3. Linguists use several tools to understand how languages are related historically. Languages diverge when speakers of one language decrease spatial interaction to the point that the languages drift apart. Through backward reconstruction, or tracking consonants and cognates back to reconstruct elements of a prior common language, linguists can provide insight into how languages fit together and where the branches were once joined.

4. Indo-European languages are related historically to one language called Proto-Indo-European. Linguists generally agree that the original language began somewhere near the Black Sea in present-day Turkey. Linguists offer several theories of how Proto-Indo-European diffused from its hearth, including the two most common: the conquest theory and the agriculture theory.

Explain How Language Can Be Used as a Unifying or Dividing Force.

1. The Gutenberg printing press was invented in 1440 and helped unify speakers of vernacular languages by standardizing the languages, and printing political communications and also literature in the vernacular language. In 1452 Gutenberg printed the Bible in the vernacular language. The Reformation, a reform movement in the Catholic Church, was possible in part because the Gutenberg press made it possible to publish the Bible in local, vernacular languages, including English, French, and German, instead of the church's official language, Latin.

2. A lingua franca is a language used among speakers of different languages for the purposes of trade and commerce. It can be a single language or a mixture of two or more languages. When people speaking two or more languages are in contact and they combine parts of their languages in a simplified structure and vocabulary, we call it a pidgin language.

3. More than 7000 languages are spoken in a world with fewer than 200 countries. Not a single country in the world is home to speakers of only one language. In practice, every country is multilingual, meaning that more than one language is spoken. Officially, a country can choose to recognize one official language (Indonesia), support multiple official languages (Canada, Belgium), or not declare an official language at all (United States). Countries that have more than one official language are called multilingual states.

Determine the Role Language Plays in Making Places.

1. One way we express the identity of a place is through toponyms, or place-names. Geographers have studied toponyms and found that they can be descriptive, possessive, manufactured, or otherwise derived. A toponym can give insight into the layers of history in a place, often including stories of migrants who established and named a town or place. People may choose to change a toponym to commemorate a person or event. For example, many streets in the United States have been renamed Martin Luther King Jr. Street in honor of the civil rights leader.

2. Toponyms can be disputed. Maps produced by two different people or nations may have different place-names for the same feature or place. For example, the body of water between the Korean Peninsula and Japan is called the East Sea by Koreans and the Sea of Japan by Japanese. Koreans see the name Sea of Japan as a remnant of the Japanese colonization of Korea in the late 1800s and early 1900s. As another example, the islands off the east coast of Argentina are called Islas Malvinas by Argentinians and the Falklands by the British. In 1982, a war broke out between Argentina and Britain over the islands. The war ended, but the dispute over what to call the islands continues.

Self-Test

Define language and describe the role of language in culture.

1. Globally, the two most commonly used languages by Internet browsers are:
   a. French and English.
   b. English and German.
   c. Spanish and English.
   d. Arabic and English.
   e. English and Chinese.

2. Language is an essential part of culture because:
   a. a shared language makes people in a culture visible to one another.
   b. language helps cement cultural identity.
   c. thoughts and feelings are explained through language.
   d. language can be used to help sustain local culture.
   e. all of the answers are correct.

3. True or False: The Irish (Celtic) language has no words for "yes" and "no."

4. The number of languages spoken worldwide is difficult to pinpoint primarily because:
   a. it is difficult to distinguish between languages and dialects.
   b. not all languages are registered with the Académie Française.
   c. European Union policies have led to the extinction of hundreds of languages.
   d. the United Nations only keep statistics on the number of speakers of five major world languages.
   e. there are too many languages to track effectively.

Explain how languages are related and distributed.

5. From largest spatial extent to smallest, languages are classified as:
   a. dialects, languages, language subfamilies, language families.
   b. language subfamilies, dialects, language families, languages.
   c. language families, language subfamilies, languages, dialects.
   d. languages, language families, dialects, language subfamilies.
   e. extinct, isolated, endangered, vigorous.

6. Indo-European languages diffused across the world primarily through:
   a. expansion of the Roman Empire between 400 BCE and 400 CE.
   b. European colonization between the 1500s and 1900s CE.
   c. the invention and expansion of the Internet from the 1990s to the present.
   d. efforts of Queen Victoria to expand the number of English speakers during the 1800s.
   e. warriors on horseback.

7. Linguists understand that when spatial interaction decreases significantly among speakers of one language (e.g., Korean today), the language can _____ and two new languages can be created from one.
   a. converge
   b. conflate
   c. deflate
   d. diverge
   e. assimilate

8. Canada is officially a bilingual country with official languages of _____. The Canadian province of Quebec identifies as _____.
   a. English and German / English
   b. French and German / German
   c. English and French / French
   d. English and Irish / French
   e. English and Celtic / Gaelic

Explain how language can be used as a unifying or dividing force.

9. The Gutenberg printing press was significant because:
   a. it helped spark a rise in nationalism centered on vernacular languages.
   b. it helped standardize English and make it the major language used in government communications in England and its colonies around the world.
   c. it helped spark the Reformation because Christians could read the Bible in their vernacular language.
   d. it help diffuse ideas more rapidly over space.
   e. All of the answers are correct.

10. A language used for purposes of trade and communication among speakers of different languages is called a(n):
    a. pidgin language.
    b. Creole language.
    c. lingua franca.
    d. vernacular language.
    e. official language.

11. Swahili is a good example of a Creole language because it:
    a. began as a pidgin language and eventually developed a more complex vocabulary and syntax, and became the native language of a group of people.
    b. began as a lingua franca and eventually became a pidgin language.
    c. has been institutionalized by the government of Kenya.
    d. has been adopted by the United Nations as an official language.
    e. all of the above.

12. True or False: Not a single country in the world is home to speakers of only one language.

13. In India, at the federal level, Hindi and English are recognized as co-official languages. However:

    a. neither language is spoken by a majority of Indians.

    b. Hindi is spoken by 90 percent of Indians and English is only spoken by 10 percent of Indians.

    c. English is spoken by 90 percent of Indians and Hindi is only spoken by 10 percent of Indians.

    d. the majority of Indians speak both Hindi and English.

    e. the majority of Indians speak Hindi.

Determine the role language plays in making places.

14. Toponyms that diffuse through migration, such as when migrants from Lancaster, England, brought the place-name *Lancaster* to Pennsylvania, follow _____ diffusion:

    a. contagious

    b. hierarchical

    c. relocation

    d. stimulus

    e. nodal

15. After decolonization, a newly independent country may choose to change toponyms to:

    a. remove colonial place-names.

    b. recognize locally significant people, cultural traits, and events.

    c. help create a new national identity.

    d. symbolize the end of the colonial era.

    e. all of the answer choices are correct.

16. Two people or two countries can call the same place different toponyms. Koreans call the body of water between the Korean Peninsula and Japan:

    a. the East Sea.   d. the Sea of Korea.

    b. the West Sea.   e. the Great Sea.

    c. the Sea of Japan.

17. Geographer Derek Alderman studied the location of MLK Jr. streets in the United States and found that most are located:

    a. in poorer areas of cities where more African Americans live.

    b. in wealthier areas of cities where fewer African Americans live.

    c. on main streets.

    d. in industrial areas.

    e. in the Northeastern United States.

Answer to final Thinking Geographically question: Los Angeles, California.

CHAPTER 7

Religion

What the burqa or niqabi means to Muslim women and how it is perceived varies across Europe. While much of Europe's history, art, and architecture is religious, church attendance is low and the role of religion in society is declining as the region has become increasingly secular. Migrants from North Africa and Southwest Asia who were invited into Europe as guest workers after World War II brought Islam to cities in northern and western Europe through relocation diffusion.

While Muslims comprise less than 5 percent of the population of Europe and Muslims who wear the burqa or niqabi are a fraction of that, several countries in the European Union have passed laws banning traditional face coverings in public places. The main targets are burqas or niqabi worn by observant Muslim women (**Fig. 7.1**). France banned the burqa in 2011 when an estimated 1900 French Muslim women covered their face, accounting for less than 0.0003 percent of the population of France at the time (some argue the number was even lower).

The bans have sparked debate in Europe about religious liberty and its limits. This debate reminds us that religion can unite and divide. In this chapter, we study the origins, diffusions, and transformations of the world's great religions, their regional patterns and cultural landscapes. Even when secularism is rising, appreciating the role of religion in culture is essential to understanding human geography.

FIGURE 7.1 **Frankfurt, Germany.** Only a small percentage of traditional-minded Islamic women in the Middle East cover their faces. In Europe the percentage is even smaller—far less than 1 percent of the total Islamic population in Europe. Nonetheless, the presence of niqabs and burqas have generated controversy in some European countries.

Michael Gottschalk/Photothek/Getty Images

CHAPTER OUTLINE

7.1 Describe the Nature of Religion and Its Cultural Significance.

Religion and language lie at the foundation of culture: Both shape and reflect identity. Every hearth of urbanization (see Chapter 9) developed with a religion and a language. Like languages (Chapter 6), religions constantly change as a result of diffusion, evolving practices, and mixing with other religions and philosophies. Religion and language often diffuse together. Romance languages from Europe, including Spanish and Portuguese, diffused to South America and Central America with Roman Catholicism during colonization (**Fig. 7.2**). Arabic diffused with Islam to Southeast Asia during the spice trade. The Hindi language diffused with Indian migrants to east Africa, as did the Hindu religion.

Geographers Robert Stoddard and Carolyn Prorak define **religion** as "a system of beliefs and practices that attempts to order life in terms of culturally perceived ultimate priorities." Stoddard and Prorak explain that the idea of "perceived ultimate priorities" is often expressed in terms of "should." People explain and justify how they and others "should" behave based on their religious beliefs. From eating habits to dress codes, religions set standards for followers' behaviors (**Fig. 7.3**). The idea

David Wall/Alamy Stock Photo

FIGURE 7.2 Cuzco, Peru. The Cuzco Cathedral and the Church de Compania de Jesus stand in the central square. Cuzco was the historic capital of the Inca Empire. Spanish colonizers brought the Catholic Church to this square, which was a plaza during Incan times. Cuzco served as a secondary hearth for Catholicism. From here, the Spanish brought the Catholic Church to its colonies in South America.

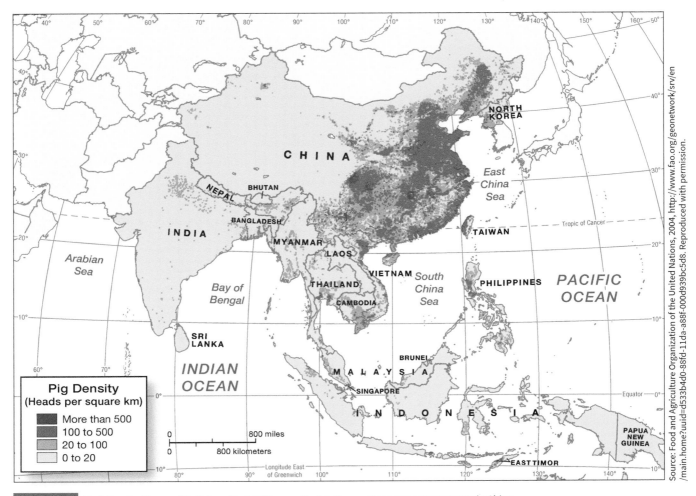

Source: Food and Agriculture Organization of the United Nations, 2004, http://www.fao.org/geonetwork/srv/en/main.home?uuid=d533b4d0-88fd-11da-a88f-000d939bc5d8. Reproduced with permission.

Pig Density (Heads per square km)
- More than 500
- 100 to 500
- 20 to 100
- 0 to 20

FIGURE 7.3 Pork Production and Religious Prohibitions. Pork is the most common meat source in China, but pork production is slim to none in predominantly Muslim countries, including Bangladesh and Indonesia and in the predominantly Hindu country of India, where pork consumption is prohibited for religious reasons.

Photo by A.B. Murphy. © 2020 John Wiley & Sons, Inc.

FIGURE 7.4 **Agra, India.** Many of the world's best known buildings have religious significance. The Taj Mahal is one of these, a white-marble mausoleum and mosque built in the seventeenth century to house the tomb of a Mughal emperor's wife.

that a "good" life has rewards and that "bad" behavior risks punishment has enormous influence on cultures and on how people behave and view the behavior of others.

Cultural landscapes are marked by religion, including churches, synagogues, temples and mosques, cemeteries and shrines, statues, symbols, and mausoleums (**Fig. 7.4**). Other more subtle markers of religion dot the cultural landscape. Residents of Catholic neighborhoods may have statues of the Virgin Mary in their gardens or front yards. In India, small altars with statues or icons of Hindu gods often stand in front of homes or along roadsides. In Buddhist Thailand, spirit houses are built in auspicious locations in front of homes and businesses to attract good spirits to the place who will in turn keep out bad spirits (**Fig. 7.5**). Stores, including restaurants with Kosher foods (Judaism) or halal butcher shops that prepare meat according to religious law (Islam), signal religion in the cultural landscape. Cultural landscapes can also signal religion by the absence of certain features. The absence of stores selling alcohol or of works of art with people in them is typical of Islamic areas, where drinking alcohol and drawing images of the human form are generally forbidden. Religion is also embedded in physical landscapes. We can see religion in the worship of ancestors, who are thought to inhabit mountains, animals, or trees.

Religious practices such as ritual and prayer are found in most religions. Religious rituals mark important events in people's lives: birth and death, becoming an adult, or marriage. Many rituals occur at regular intervals: in the days of rest in Christianity and Judaism, at certain times of the day in Islam, or during astronomical events in Judaism, Hinduism, Islam, and Christianity. A common ritual is prayer at mealtime, at sunrise and sundown, at night upon retiring, or when waking in the morning (**Fig. 7.6**).

In some places, formal religion has become less significant. **Secularism** refers to the indifference to or rejection of formal religion. The most secular countries are found in Europe. A 2018 Pew study focused on a decade's worth of surveys in more than 100 countries to explore how important religion is in people's lives (**Figure 7.7**). Among the wealthiest countries surveyed, the United States had the highest level of religiosity, with 53 percent of Americans surveyed saying that religion is very important in their lives. Only 11 percent of people

Photo by E.H. Fouberg. © 2020 John Wiley & Sons, Inc.

FIGURE 7.5 **Bangkok, Thailand.** Religion can be seen in large spaces, like the Taj Mahal, and also in small spaces, like spirit houses that stand in front of homes and businesses in Southeast Asia.

surveyed in France, 10 percent in Sweden, and 7 percent in the Czechia said the same thing. Survey respondents in sub-Saharan Africa, North Africa, Southwest Asia, South Asia, and South America more strongly agreed that religion is very important in their lives: 98 percent in Senegal, 80 percent in Bangladesh, 93 percent in Indonesia, 90 percent in Honduras, and 72 percent in Brazil.

Survey respondents in Europe largely did not see religion as very important in their lives, but religion certainly played a critical role in European history. During the Middle Ages and into the colonial period, the Christian Church was a dominant force politically, economically, and culturally, and much of the art, architecture, history, customs, and cultural norms derive from Christianity. Even in secular societies, what people eat (e.g., pork or no pork), when they rest (e.g., on Friday, Saturday, or Sunday), and what they regard as proper behavior (e.g., males taking multiple wives or not) are influenced by religion.

TASS/ITAR-TASS News Agency/Alamy Stock Photo

FIGURE 7.6 **New York, New York.** A Muslim man takes a break from serving food off a vendor cart to pray on a busy Manhattan street.

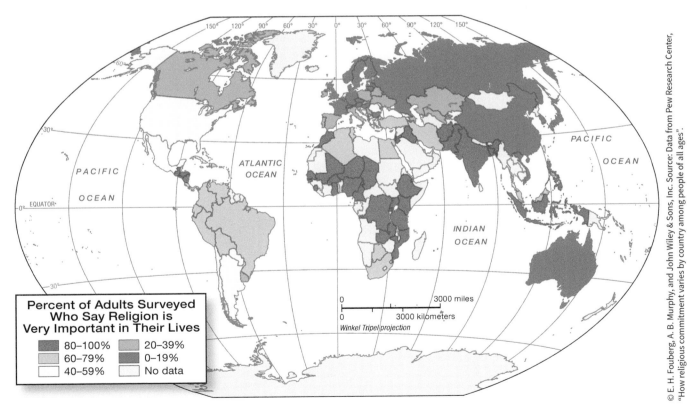

Percent of Adults Surveyed Who Say Religion is Very Important in Their Lives

- 80–100%
- 60–79%
- 40–59%
- 20–39%
- 0–19%
- No data

Winkel Tripel projection

© E. H. Fouberg, A. B. Murphy, and John Wiley & Sons, Inc. Source: Data from Pew Research Center, "How religious commitment varies by country among people of all ages".

FIGURE 7.7 **Percent of Adults Surveyed Who Say Religion is Very Important in their Lives.** Using surveys from countries across the world, this map shows the percent of people surveyed in each country who said religion is very important in their lives. The countries reporting the highest percentage of people who see religion as very important in their lives are in South Asia and Africa. The countries with the lowest percentages are in Europe and East Asia.

The larger point is that organized religion is a powerful force in shaping human societies, beliefs, and behaviors. Religion has been a major force in combating social ills, helping the poor, promoting the arts, educating the disadvantaged, and advancing medical knowledge. However, religion has also blocked scientific study, encouraged the oppression of parts of society, supported colonialism, and condemned women to inferior roles. Religion can help create harmony or division.

TC Thinking Geographically

Examine figures 7.4 and 7.5. Religion can be seen in large features on the **cultural landscape**, like the Taj Mahal, and in small features on the landscape, like spirit houses. Think about your own neighborhood or town. Describe and explain the patterns of large and small religious features in the cultural landscape of your neighborhood.

7.2 Describe the Distribution of Major Religions and the Factors That Shaped Their Diffusion.

Religions are commonly grouped into three broad categories based on the number and form of deities. Followers of **monotheistic religions** worship a single deity. Believers in **polytheistic religions** worship more than one deity. **Animistic religions** are centered on the belief that inanimate (nonliving) objects, such as mountains, boulders, rivers, and trees, possess spirits and should be revered.

Almost all religions were animistic, polytheistic, or both throughout most of human history. Around 3500 years ago, a monotheistic religion developed in Southwest Asia called Zoroastrianism. Some scholars think that the monotheism of Judaism, Christianity, and Islam can be traced to Zoroastrian influences. Others believe that Judaism was the first monotheistic religion. Whichever the case, the eventual diffusion of Christianity and Islam spread monotheistic ideas across the world. This marked a major theological shift from the long dominance of polytheistic and animist beliefs in most places.

By 500 BCE (Before the Common Era), four major hearths of religion and philosophy had developed (**Fig. 7.8**).

A **hearth** of Greek philosophy developed along the northern shores of the Mediterranean Sea. Hinduism came from a hearth in South Asia, along the Indus River Valley. Judaism originated along the eastern Mediterranean; and Chinese philosophy took root in the Huang He Valley. These early established religious and philosophical hearths profoundly influenced other religions and places, as the arrows in Figure 7.8 show. Greek philosophy and Judaism together influenced Christianity. By 500 BCE, four hearths of religious and philosophical thought that still influence culture today were well established: Chinese philosophy, Hinduism, Judaism, and Greek philosophy. Philosophies and religions diffused from these hearths, affecting one another and giving rise to new religions. The two religions with the greatest number of adherents today, Christianity and Islam, are both called Abrahamic faiths because they go back to Judaism, which was founded on a covenant between Abraham and God. Judaism, Christianity, and Islam all recognize Abraham as their first prophet.

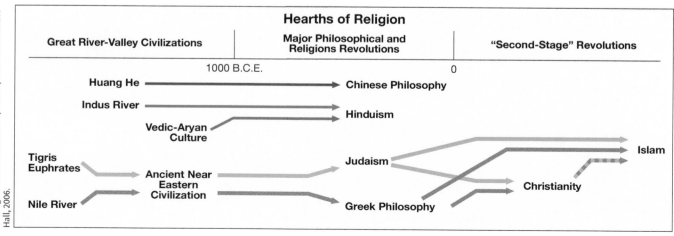

FIGURE 7.8 Hearths of Major World Religions. By 500 BCE, Chinese philosophy, Hinduism, Judaism, and Greek philosophy were established.

The World Map of Religions Today

Figure 7.9 shows the distribution of the major religions. Many factors help explain the distributions shown on the map, but all of the widespread religions share one characteristic: They are all universalizing religions. **Universalizing religions** actively seek converts because they view themselves as offering belief systems that are universal—appropriate for everyone. Christianity, Islam, and Buddhism all fall within this category, and their universalizing character helps explain their widespread distribution.

Universalizing religions are relatively few in number and of recent origin. Throughout human history, most religions have not actively sought converts. Rather, each culture or ethnic group had its own religion. In an **ethnic religion**, followers are born into the faith from a given group, while conversion may be possible, converts are not actively sought. Ethnic religions tend to be spatially clustered—as with traditional religions in Africa and South America (250 million followers). The principal exception is Judaism (14.5 million adherents), an ethnic religion whose followers are widely scattered as a result of forced and voluntary migrations.

A global scale map of religions, like Figure 7.9, is a generalization, and caution must be used when interpreting it. First, the shadings show the major religion in an area and so mask minority religions, many of which have a significant number of followers. India, for example, is depicted as a Hindu region (except in the northwest), but Islam and Sikhism attract millions of adherents there. Of the 1.2 billion people in India, upwards of 172 million are Muslims, which makes India the third largest Muslim country behind Indonesia and Pakistan.

Second, some of the regions shown as belonging to a particular religion are places where faiths have arrived relatively recently. In 1900, neither Christianity nor Islam had many followers in sub-Saharan Africa, though Islam had many followers in North Africa. By 2010, the number of Muslims in sub-Saharan Africa had grown from 11 million to 234 million, and the number of Christians had grown from 7 million to 470 million.

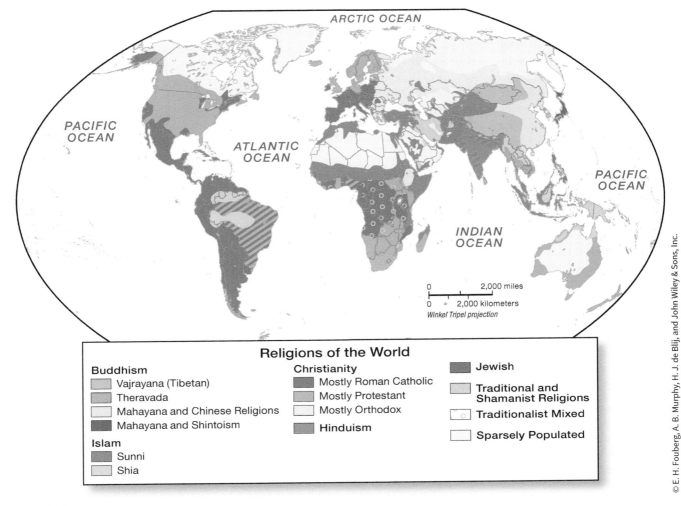

FIGURE 7.9 **World Religions.** The most widespread world religions are universalizing religions, including Christianity, Islam, and Buddhism. Christianity diffused globally through European colonization. Islam diffused early on through conquest and later through trade. Buddhism diffused and mixed with local cultures, creating different regional forms.

In these places traditional religious ideas influence the practice of the dominant faith. Many self-declared Christian and Muslim Africans, for example, continue to believe in traditional powers. A 2010 Pew Research survey of 25,000 people in 19 African countries found that "large numbers of Africans actively participate in Christianity or Islam yet also believe in witchcraft, evil spirits, sacrifices to ancestors, traditional religious healers, reincarnation and other elements of traditional African religions." The survey found that 25 percent of the Christian Africans and 30 percent of the Muslim Africans they interviewed believed in the protective power of sacrifices to spirits or ancestors. The country with the highest percentage of respondents who agreed with this statement was Tanzania with 60 percent, and the lowest was Rwanda with 5 percent.

In Cameroon, 42 percent of those surveyed believed in the protective power of sacrifices to spirits or ancestors. For example, the Bamileke tribe in Cameroon lives in an area colonized by the French, who brought Catholicism to the region. The Bamileke are largely Christian today, but they also continue to practice aspects of their traditional animist religion. Ancestors are still very important, and many believe that ancestors decide everything for them. It is common to place the skull of a deceased male tribal member in the basement of the home of the family's oldest living male. Birth practices also reflect traditional religious practices. The Bamileke bury the umbilical cord in the ground outside their home so that the baby remembers where he or she came from. Members of the Bamileke tribe also commonly have two weddings today: a Christian ceremony in the church and a traditional tribal ceremony.

Finally, Figure 7.9 fails to capture the growth of secularism, especially in Europe. In some areas many people have moved away from organized religion entirely. France appears on the map as a Roman Catholic country, yet many people in France profess adherence to no particular faith, and only 11 percent of French people say religion is very important in their lives.

Despite these limitations, the map of world religions illustrates important aspects of human geography. The map shows how far Christian religions have diffused (2.3 billion adherents worldwide, according to a 2015 Pew study), the extent of the diffusion of Islam (1.8 billion), the connection between Hinduism (1.1 billion adherents) and India, and the continued importance of Buddhism (500 million followers) in much of Asia.

AP® Exam Taker's Tip

When studying religion in AP Human Geography, it is important to focus on the *who*, *where*, and *how many* questions with regard to understanding Chapter 7's religious terms and concepts. These include being able to identify and explain that **universalizing religions** such as Christianity, Islam, Buddhism, and Sikhism are spread through **expansion** and **relocation diffusion**. The same is true for **ethnic religions**, which can explain why Hinduism and Judaism are found generally near the **hearth** or spread through **relocation diffusion**. As one example, relocation diffusion might explain why you might have a Hindu, Sikh, or Buddhist temple in an American city.

From the Hearth of South Asia

Hinduism

Hinduism is the third largest religion after Christianity and Islam, in terms of number of followers. It is one of the oldest religions, dating back over 4000 years. Its roots are in the Indus River Valley of what is today part of Pakistan.

Hinduism is unique in several ways. The religion does not have a single founder, a single theology, or a single origin story. The common account of the history of Hinduism holds that the religion arose in the Indus River cities, including Mohenjo-Daro and Harappa. Ancient practices included ritual bathing and belief in reincarnation, or at least a long journey after death. Aryans from the northwest invaded (some say migrated) into the Indus region and gave the name *Hinduism* to the diverse religious practices of those who lived along the Indus River.

Despite uncertainties about its beginnings, Hinduism is no longer associated with its hearth in Pakistan. Pakistanis are primarily Muslim and, as Figure 7.9 demonstrates, Indians are primarily Hindu. Archaeologists think that flooding along the Indus may have led to migration of early Hindus eastward to the Ganges River. The Ganges is Hinduism's sacred river. Hindus regard its ceaseless flow and spiritual healing power as earthly manifestations of God.

Hinduism defies the western classifications of monotheistic vs. polytheistic and of ethnic vs. universalizing. Hinduism looks to be polytheistic because of the presence of many gods. However, many Hindus see their religion as monotheistic. Hindus often believe in a supreme god who is represented by multiple gods. How the supreme god is seen in Hinduism varies regionally, just like all other aspects of Hinduism. Different regions and people of India are tied to different gods. Groups within cities and villages hold festivals for gods who have been important or popular in their region. Who celebrates a certain festival varies, too; it may be a group of women or men, and they may be from a lower caste or higher caste.

Western academics usually define Hinduism today as an ethnic religion because Hindus do not actively seek converts. Yet historical evidence shows Hindus migrating into Southeast Asia and diffusing their religion, as a universalizing religion would, before Buddhism and Islam took root there (**Fig. 7.10**). Although Hinduism is now more of an ethnic religion, it has millions of followers in South Asia, extending beyond India to Bangladesh, Myanmar, Sri Lanka, and Nepal.

Hinduism does not have a prophet or a single book of scriptures, although most Hindus recognize the sacredness of the Vedas, four original texts with later additions that make up Hinduism's "Books of Knowledge." Hinduism is a conglomeration of beliefs characterized by a great diversity of forms and practices.

At the root of Hinduism is *karma*, the idea that the collective impact of physical and mental actions shapes what happens. According to Hindu thought, all beings have souls and are arranged in a hierarchy. The ideal is to move upward in the hierarchy and then escape from the eternal cycle of *reincarnation* through union with Brahman (the universal soul). A soul moves upward or downward according to an individual's

Photo by E.H. Fouberg. © 2020 John Wiley & Sons, Inc.

FIGURE 7.10 **Siem Reap, Cambodia.** The extensive number of temples in and around Ankgor Wat, Cambodia, include both Hindu and Buddhist symbols. The Bayon temple, shown here, was built with 54 towers, each with 2, 3, or 4 faces like these, to represent a *bodhisattva* (person on the path to enlightenment) known as Avalokiteshvara. A later king converted the empire back to Hinduism and altered the Bayon temple and others by adding Hindu symbols.

behavior during his or her life. Good deeds and adherence to the faith lead to a higher level in the next life, whereas bad behavior leads to demotion to a lower level. All souls, those of animals as well as humans, participate in this process. The principle of reincarnation is thus a cornerstone of Hinduism.

Hinduism's doctrines are closely bound to India's caste system, for castes are steps on the universal ladder. The **caste system** locks people into particular social classes and imposes many restrictions, especially in the lowest castes and in those considered beneath the caste system, Dalits. Until a generation ago, Dalits could not enter temples, were excluded from certain schools, and were restricted to performing the most unpleasant tasks. The coming of other religions to India, the work of the famous spiritual and political leader Mahatma Gandhi, affirmative action policies of the Indian government, the expansion of higher education, and the growth of India's economy have helped loosen the social barriers of the caste system. Through affirmative action policies, seats in universities and jobs in government are reserved for peoples belonging to lower castes and to Dalits.

Diffusion of Hinduism   Hinduism began in its hearth along the Indus River in modern-day Pakistan and diffused first to the Ganges River and then throughout South Asia and into Southeast Asia. Hinduism first attached itself to traditional faiths and then slowly replaced them. Later, when Islam

and Christianity diffused into Hindu areas, Hindu thinkers attempted to integrate some Islamic and Christian teachings into their own. For example, elements of the Sermon on the Mount (Jesus's sermon in which he described God's love for the poor and the peacemakers) now form part of Hindu preaching, and Christian teachings contributed to the weakening of caste barriers. In other instances, the confrontation between Hinduism and other faiths created faiths bearing elements of each: a **syncretic** religion. The interaction between Hinduism and Islam gave rise to Sikhism, whose followers disapprove of the worship of idols and dislike the caste system, but who retain the concepts of reincarnation and karma.

> ### AP® Exam Taker's Tip
>
> When studying religion in AP Human Geography, it is important to focus on the who, where, and how many questions with regard to understanding religion terms and concepts. How have they borrowed from each other? How can historical **diffusion** patterns explain these syncretic characteristics? Think about how **acculturation**, **assimilation**, and **multiculturalism** play a role in syncretism.

Given its current character as an ethnic religion, it is not surprising that Hinduism's geographical extent is somewhat limited. Indeed, throughout most of Southeast Asia,

Photo by A.B. Murphy. © 2020 John Wiley & Sons, Inc.

FIGURE 7.11 **Bali, Indonesia.** The town of Ubud in central Bali is dotted with Hindu temples. Hinduism arrived in Southeast Asia some 2000 years ago. It was gradually replaced by Buddhism, and then Islam came to the southern parts of the region. Bali became a refuge for believers in Hinduism. It is the one place in Indonesia where Hinduism continues to dominate today.

Buddhism and Islam overtook the places where Hinduism had diffused during its universalizing period. In overwhelmingly Muslim Indonesia, the island of Bali remains a Hindu outpost (**Fig. 7.11**). Bali became a refuge for Hindu holy men, nobles, and intellectuals during the sixteenth century, when Islam diffused through neighboring Java, which now retains only architectural remnants of its Hindu age. Since then, the Balinese have developed a unique faith, still based on Hindu principles but mixed with elements of Buddhism, animism, and ancestor worship. Religion is extremely important in Bali. Temples and shrines dominate the cultural landscape, and participation in worship, festivals, and other ceremonies is almost universal.

Outside South Asia and Bali, Hinduism's presence is relatively minor. Migrants from India have brought Hinduism to pockets around the world through relocation diffusion. During colonialism, the British forcibly migrated indentured laborers from their colony in India to their colonies in eastern Africa, Southeast Asia, and Caribbean America (**Fig. 7.12**). More recently, significant numbers of Indian Hindus have voluntarily migrated to Europe and North America, primarily for work in medicine or technology. Because Hinduism is not a universalizing religion today, relocation diffusion has produced pockets rather than regions of Hinduism.

Buddhism **Buddhism** splintered from Hinduism over 2500 years ago, when it developed in a hearth in northern India as a reaction to questions about Hinduism's teachings. For example, reformers questioned Hinduism's strict social hierarchy that protected the privileged. Prince Siddhartha Gautama, heir to a wealthy kingdom in what is now Nepal, was profoundly shaken by the misery he saw around him, which contrasted sharply with the splendor and wealth in which he had been raised. Siddhartha came to be known as Buddha, the enlightened one, and he founded Buddhism. He may have been the first prominent Indian religious leader to speak out against Hinduism's caste system. Salvation, he preached, could be attained by anyone, no matter what his or her caste. Enlightenment would come through the Eightfold Path, including right view, right thought, right speech, right action, right livelihood, right efforts, right mindfulness, and right samadhi (concentration or absorption through meditation).

After Buddha's death in 487 at the age of 80, the faith grew rather slowly until the middle of the third century BCE, when the Emperor Ashoka became a convert. Ashoka was the leader of a large and powerful Indian empire that extended from the Punjab to Bengal and from the Himalayan foothills to Mysore. He ruled his country in accordance with Buddhism and also sent missionaries to carry Buddha's teachings to distant peoples (**Fig. 7.13**).

Over a span of about 10 centuries, Buddhism spread as far south as Sri Lanka and later advanced north into Tibet and east into China, Korea, Japan, Vietnam, and Indonesia. Although Buddhism diffused to distant lands, it began to decline in its hearth in northern India. During Ashoka's rule, there may have been more Buddhists than Hindus in India, but later Hinduism gained ground. Today Buddhism is practiced by relatively few in India, but it thrives in Sri Lanka, Southeast Asia, Nepal, Tibet, and Korea. Along with other faiths, Buddhism is part of Japanese culture.

Like Christianity and Islam, Buddhism changed as it grew and diffused. Its branches have some 500 million adherents, with Mahayana Buddhism and Theravada Buddhism being the largest branches. *Theravada* Buddhism translates as "the way of the elders." It spread first to Sri Lanka, and from there to Myanmar (Burma), Thailand, Laos, and Cambodia. Theravada Buddhism holds that salvation is a personal matter, achieved through good behavior and religious activities, including periods of service as a monk or nun. Theravada Buddhists tie their teachings to the historical Buddha; they see themselves as followers of true Buddhism.

FIGURE 7.12 **Singapore.** The city-state was a British colony, but in the 19th and early 20th centuries, many Indians came from South Asia to work for the British, and millions of Chinese moved to Singapore as well. The city's landscape bears witness to this migration history. Not far from this Hindu temple is a major Buddhist temple, and churches are found throughout the city as well.

Mahayana Buddhism was the second form of Buddhism established in northern India, and it diffused into China, Vietnam, Korea, and Japan. Mahayana Buddhism translates as "the greater vehicle," and the idea is that more people can achieve enlightenment through its teachings than through the strict teachings of Theravada Buddhism. The Buddha is regarded as a divine savior, and other great Buddhists are regarded as *bodhisattvas* (those who have reached enlightenment) and are worshipped along with the Buddha. Mahayana Buddhists do not serve as monks, but they spend much time

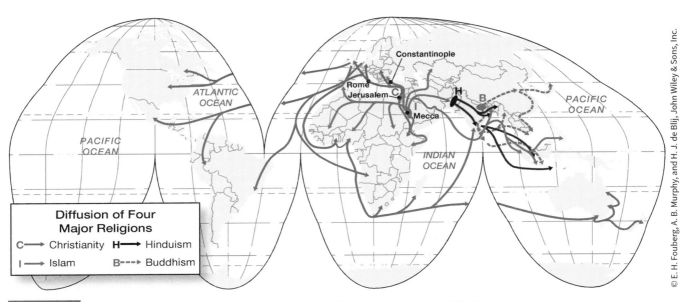

FIGURE 7.13 **Diffusion of Four Major World Religions.** The hearths and major routes of diffusion are shown on this map. It does not show smaller diffusion streams: Islam and Buddhism, for example, are gaining strength in North America, although their numbers are still comparatively small.

FIGURE 7.14 **Kyoto, Japan.** A tori marking the transition from this world into a sacred space, leads to the Fushimi Inari Taisha shrine, which is part of a shrine complex that dates to 711. The shrine draws several million worshippers over the Japanese New Year.

in personal meditation and worship, believing that achieving enlightenment helps all beings on Earth. Mahayana Buddhism was influenced by indigenous Chinese and Japanese religions, including Taoism and Shintoism.

The third largest branch of Buddhism is *Vajrayana* (Tibetan), which emphasizes the role of the guru or lama as religious and political leader. Vajrayana Buddhism was the last branch to be established, diffusing north from India into Tibet and Mongolia. Gurus in Vajrayana Buddhism use mantras, tantras, and meditation to help followers achieve enlightenment faster than the bodhisattva approach in Mahayana Buddhism, which can take several lifetimes.

Buddhism has become a global religion over the last two centuries, diffusing to many areas of the world, but not always peacefully. Governments have attacked the religion in Cambodia, Mongolia, and Vietnam. Militant Buddhists in Burma (Myanmar) and Thailand have used violence to advance political causes.

Shintoism

Buddhism mixed with a local religion in Japan, producing a new ethnic and syncretic religion, **Shintoism**, that includes nature and ancestor worship (**Fig. 7.14**). The Japanese emperor made Shintoism the state religion in the nineteenth century, giving himself the status of divine-right monarch. At the end of World War II, Japan separated Shintoism from the emperor, taking away the state sanctioning of the religion. At the same time, the role of the emperor in Japan was diminished and given more of a ceremonial status. Some 100 million Japanese are Shinto adherents. Most Japanese observe both Buddhism and Shintoism.

From the Hearth of the Huang He Valley

Taoism

While the Buddha's teachings were gaining converts in India, two major schools of Chinese philosophy,

Taoism and Confucianism, were forming. The beginnings of **Taoism** are unclear, but scholars trace the religion to an older contemporary of Confucius, Lao-Tsu, who published a volume titled *Tao te ching*, or "Book of the Way." Lao-Tsu focused on the proper form of political rule and on the oneness of humanity and nature. People, he said, should learn to live in harmony with nature. This emphasis gave rise to **Feng Shui**—the art and science of organizing settlements, buildings, or living spaces to channel the natural life forces in favorable ways. According to tradition, nothing should be done to nature without consulting the *geomancers*, people who know the desires of the powerful spirits of ancestors, dragons, tigers, and other beings that occupy the natural world and can give advice on Feng Shui.

Among the Taoist virtues are simplicity, spontaneity, tenderness, and tranquility. Competition, possession, and even the pursuit of knowledge are discouraged. War, punishment, taxation, and ceremonial ostentation are viewed as evils. The best government, according to Lao-Tsu, is the least government. Thousands of people began to follow Taoism. Taoist temples include statues of deities who teach specific lessons, along with the yin-yang symbol to remind followers of the duality of life, and swords to remind adherents that struggle is part of life.

Confucianism

Confucius lived from 551 to 479 BCE. His followers used his teachings to construct a blueprint for Chinese civilization in philosophy, government, and education. In religion, Confucius questioned some traditional Chinese beliefs, among them the belief in heaven and the existence of the soul, ancestor worship, sacrificial rites, and shamanism. The real meaning of life lay in the present, not in some future abstract existence, and service to people should supersede service to spirits.

Confucianism is mainly a philosophy of life. Like Taoism, it had great and lasting impacts on Chinese life. Appalled at the suffering of ordinary people at the hands of feudal lords, Confucius urged the poor to assert themselves. He was not a prophet who dealt in promises of heaven and threats of hell. He denied the divine ancestry of China's aristocratic rulers, educated the landless and the weak, disliked supernatural mysticism, and argued that human virtues and abilities, not heritage, should determine a person's position and responsibilities in society.

Confucius came to be revered as a spiritual leader after his death in 479 BCE, and his teachings diffused widely throughout East and Southeast Asia. Followers built temples in his honor all over China. From his writings and sayings emerged the Confucian Classics, 13 texts that became the focus of education in China for 2000 years. Over the centuries, Confucianism (with its Taoist and Buddhist ingredients) became China's state ethic, although the Chinese emperors modified Confucian ideals over time. For example, one emperor made worship of and obedience to the emperor part of Confucianism. In government, law, literature, religion, morality, and many other realms, the Confucian Classics were the guide for Chinese civilization.

Diffusion of Chinese Religions   Confucianism diffused early into the Korean Peninsula, Japan, and Southeast Asia, where it has long influenced the practice of Buddhism. More recently, Chinese immigrants brought Chinese religions to parts of Southeast Asia and helped to introduce their principles in Europe, North America, and beyond.

The diffusion of Chinese religions even within China has been tempered by the Chinese government's efforts to suppress religion. The communist government that took control of China in 1949 attempted to ban religion from public practice. But after guiding all aspects of Chinese education, culture, and society for 2000 years, Confucianism did not fade easily from the Chinese consciousness.

Feng Shui is also still a powerful force today, even in burial traditions. Where Chinese who follow Feng Shui have the means to buy large burial plots, entire cemeteries and individual burial plots are aligned with Feng Shui teachings (**Fig. 7.15**). Even in more densely populated places with large Chinese populations, like Hong Kong and Singapore, burial practices follow Feng Shui. Geographer Elizabeth Teather studied the rise of cremation and columbaria (resting places for ashes) in Hong Kong. She investigated the impact Feng Shui has had on city structures and the continued influence of Chinese religious beliefs on burial practices. Traditional Chinese beliefs favor a coffin and burial plot aligned with Feng Shui teachings. However, with the growth of China's population, the government has encouraged cremation in recent decades. Burial plots in cities like Hong Kong are scarce and their costs are high.

Teather explains that although cremation is on the rise in Hong Kong, traditional Chinese beliefs are dictating the final resting places of ashes. Most Chinese people have a "cultural need to keep ancestral remains appropriately stored and in a single place." In North America and Europe, many families scatter the ashes of a loved one, but a Chinese family tends to keep the ashes together in a single identifiable space so that family members can visit the ancestor during annual commemoration periods. Teather describes how Feng Shui masters are consulted in the building of columbaria and how Feng Shui helps dictate the price placed on the niches for sale in the columbaria, with the lowest prices for the niches near the "grime of the floor."

From the Hearth of the Eastern Mediterranean

Judaism   Judaism grew out of the belief system of the ancient Hebrews living in Southwest Asia about 4000 years ago. The roots of the Jewish religious tradition lie in the teachings of Abraham (from Ur), who is credited with uniting his people to worship only one god. According to Jewish teaching, Abraham and God had a covenant in which Jews agreed to worship only one God and God agreed to protect Abraham and his Hebrew tribe, the Jews. Judaism teaches rituals including daily prayer,

observance of the Sabbath, and dietary practices. Judaism instructs followers to love their neighbor, pursue justice, and to give to charity.

Moses led the Jews from Egypt, where they had been enslaved, to Canaan. Over time, Jews built a central place of life and worship in and around Jerusalem, but then fell victim to a series of foreign powers. The Romans destroyed their holy city in 70 CE and drove the Jews out of Jerusalem and the holy land. Jews retained only a small presence in the holy land until the late nineteenth century.

Our map shows that because of centuries of migration and persecution, Judaism is not limited to contiguous territories (**Fig. 7.16**). Followers of Judaism are distributed throughout parts of the Middle East and North Africa, Russia, Ukraine, Europe, and parts of North and South America (Fig. 7.9). According to *The Atlas of Religion*, of all the world's 14.5 million Jews, 39.3 percent live in the United States, 44.5 percent live in Israel, and then in rank order, less than 5 percent live in France, Canada, the United Kingdom, Argentina, and Russia. Judaism is one of the world's most influential religions, although it claims only 14.5 million adherents.

During the nineteenth century, a Reform movement developed to adjust Judaism and its practices to current times. However, many, fearing that reform would cause a loss of identity and cohesion, became part of an Orthodox movement that

Aliaksandr Mazurkevich/Alamy Stock Photo

FIGURE 7.15   **Kanchanaburi Province, Thailand.**   This Chinese cemetery follows the principles of Feng Shui. The shape of the graves, the mountains in the background, and the way the grass is maintained are following principles of Feng Shui.

Kumar Sriskandan/Alamy Stock Photo

FIGURE 7.16 **Prague, Czechia.** The Pinkas Synagogue was built in 1535 and founded by a prominent Jewish family in Prague. The Jewish quarter in Prague was part of a vibrant ethnic neighborhood with thousands of families that worshiped in several synagogues. After the Holocaust, the Pinkas Synagogue was transformed into a memorial for 80,000 Jews from the area who were killed during the Holocaust. Names of the victims line the walls of the interior of the Pinkas.

the Ashkenazim and the Sephardim were persecuted, denied citizenship, driven into ghettos, and massacred.

In the face of constant threats, Jews were sustained by extraordinary efforts to maintain a sense of community, a focus on the Torah, and a desire to return to the Holy Land. The desire for a homeland for the Jewish people in the Holy Land developed into the ideology of **Zionism**, a movement that began in the nineteenth century.

The horrors of the Nazi campaign against Jews from the 1930s through World War II, when the Nazis killed some 6 million Jews, persuaded many Jews to adopt Zionism. Jews from all over the world concluded that their only hope of survival was to establish a strongly defended country in the holy land between the Mediterranean Sea and the Jordan River. Aided by sympathetic members of the international community, the Zionist goal of a Jewish state became a reality in 1948. The United Nations passed a resolution carving out two states, Israel and Palestine, along the eastern shores of the Mediterranean.

sought to retain traditional practices and ideas (**Fig. 7.17**). Between those two poles is a sector that is less strictly orthodox, but not as liberal as that of the reformers. It is known as the Conservative movement. Significant differences in ideas and practices are associated with these three branches, but Judaism is united by a strong sense of ethno-cultural distinctiveness.

Diffusion of Judaism The large-scale migration of Jews after the Roman destruction of Jerusalem is known as the **diaspora**—a term that now signifies the spatial dispersion of any ethnic group. The Jews who went north into central Europe came to be known as *Ashkenazim*, and the Jews who traveled across North Africa and into the Iberian Peninsula (Spain and Portugal) are called *Sephardim*. For centuries, both

While adherents to Judaism live across the world, many Jews have moved to Israel since its establishment in 1948. The Israeli government passed the Law of Return in 1950, which recognizes the rights of every Jew to immigrate to Israel. Since the fall of communism in the former Soviet Union in 1989, more than 1 million people have migrated from the former Soviet Union to Israel. Jewish migration to Israel continues. In 2018, nearly 30,000 Jews migrated to Israel, including 10,500 from Russia, 6500 from Ukraine, and 3500 from the United States and Canada.

Author Field Note   Eating Kosher in Long Beach, New York

"The Orthodox Jewish community in Long Beach, New York, is large enough that the Dunkin Donuts on Beech Street is kosher. Supervised by a rabbi, kosher-prepared foods follow strict requirements of what foods can be eaten, what can be eaten together, how animals are slaughtered, and how foods are prepared. In addition to the kosher Dunkin Donuts, another sign of the large Orthodox Jewish community in Long Beach is the Eruv, a line encircling the town that distinguishes private space from public space. The Eruv is not noticeable, unless you are looking for it, as it generally follows utility lines and the boardwalk. But the Eruv creates a private space that allows Orthodox Jews to carry keys, foods, and even babies on the Sabbath."

– E. H. Fouberg

Photo by E.H. Fouberg. © 2020 John Wiley & Sons, Inc.

FIGURE 7.17 **Long Beach, New York.**

Christianity

Christianity began in the same hearth in the Mediterranean as Judaism; indeed, it was an offshoot of Judaism. Like Judaism, Christianity is a monotheistic religion that stems from a single founder, in this case, Jesus. Jesus of Nazareth was born in Bethlehem and traveled through the holy land preaching, performing miracles, and gaining followers. Christian teachings hold that Jesus is the son of God, placed on Earth to teach people how to live according to God's plan. Christians celebrate Easter as the day Jesus rose from the dead after being crucified three days prior (Good Friday). According to Christian teaching, the crucifixion of Jesus fulfilled an ancient prophecy and gave Jesus's followers the promise of eternal life.

Christianity took root in various cities, most importantly Rome and Byzantium (later Constantinople, now Istanbul in Turkey). At the end of the third century, the Roman Emperor Diocletian attempted to keep the empire together by dividing it for purposes of government. Then, when the Roman Empire collapsed, western Europe, centered on Rome, transitioned into the Middle Ages, while eastern Europe became the new focus of the Byzantine Empire (**Fig. 7.18**).

The split into west and east at the end of the Roman Empire became a cultural fault line over time. It was formally recognized in 1054 CE when the **Roman Catholic Church** formally separated from the **Eastern Orthodox Christian Church**.

Today, the Eastern Orthodox Church is one of the three major branches of Christianity. It suffered historical blows, however, first when the Ottoman Turks expanded into southeastern Europe in the late fourteenth century and took Constantinople in 1453, and then when the Soviet Union suppressed Eastern Orthodox churches in the twentieth century. During the Soviet period, many churches were torn down, and most others were either boarded up or converted to practical uses such as storage sheds and even livestock barns.

After the Soviet Union collapsed in 1991, however, the Russian Orthodox Church revived, and many churches were rebuilt and reopened. Within 10 years, Vladimir Putin rose to power in part by forging a close alliance with leaders of the Russian Orthodox Church. Putin regularly refers to the importance of the Orthodox Church to Russian society.

The Roman Catholic Church claims the most adherents of all Christian denominations (more than 1 billion). Centered in Rome, Catholic theology teaches the leadership of the pope in interpreting Jesus's teachings and in navigating through the modern world. The power of the Roman Church peaked in the Middle Ages, when the church controlled sources of knowledge and worked with monarchs to rule much of western Europe.

During the Middle Ages, Roman Catholic authorities often wielded their power autocratically and distanced themselves from the masses. Moreover, the widespread diffusion of the Black Death caused many Europeans to question the role of religion. The Roman Catholic Church also experienced divisions within its hierarchy, as evidenced by the Western Schism during the early 1300s, which at one point resulted in three people claiming to be the pope.

During the fifteenth and sixteenth centuries, John Huss, Martin Luther, John Calvin, and others challenged fundamental teachings of Roman Catholicism, leading to the Protestant Reformation—*protesting* the power of the church's leader and seeking to *reform* the teachings of the church. **Protestant** denominations, including the Lutheran church, the Church of England, and the Methodist church, compose the third major branch of Christianity. Like Buddhism's challenge to Hinduism, the Protestant Reformation affected Roman Catholicism, which answered some of the challenges to its theology and political structures in the Counter-Reformation.

Christianity is the largest and most widely dispersed religion. Christian churches claim more than 2.3 billion adherents, including some 565 million in Europe and Russia, 804 million in the Americas, 516 million in sub-Saharan Africa, and 285 million in Asia. Christians thus account for nearly 40 percent of the members of the world's major religions.

Roman Catholicism continues to have the largest number of followers. Figure 7.9 reveals the strength of Roman Catholicism in parts of Europe and North America, as well as throughout much of Middle and South America. By contrast, Protestant churches dominate in significant parts of North America, Australia, New Zealand, and South Africa. Eastern Orthodoxy attracts as many as 250 million adherents—mostly in Europe, Russia, and its neighboring states, but it has some presence in Africa (where a major cluster exists in Ethiopia) and North America.

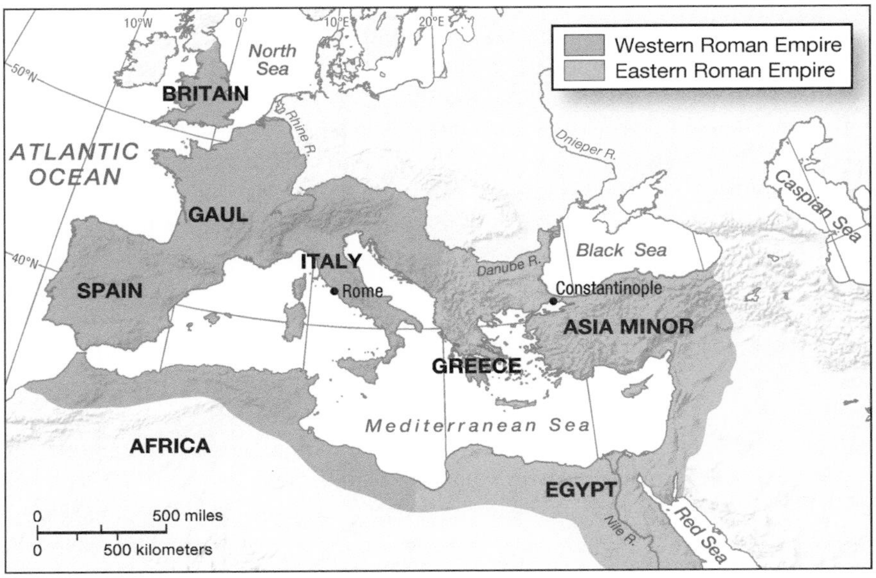

© E. H. Fouberg, A. B. Murphy, and John Wiley & Sons, Inc.

FIGURE 7.18 **The Roman Empire, Divided into West and East.** This map reflects the split in the empire, with the western empire focusing on Rome and the eastern empire focusing on Constantinople.

Author Field Note   Hearing Familiar Hymns in Vaitape, Bora Bora

"I found myself on the tiny South Pacific island of Bora Bora on a Sunday morning. As I strolled around the island's largest city, Vaitape, I heard Christian hymns being sung by a congregation—sounds that transported me back to places halfway around the world. Rounding a bend, I came upon this church, built by French missionaries about 10,000 miles (16,000 km) from their homeland. The impact missionaries had on this and many other South Pacific islands has been profound and long lasting."

– A. B. Murphy

Photo by A.B. Murphy. © 2020 John Wiley & Sons, Inc.

FIGURE 7.19   **Vaitape, Bora Bora.**

Diffusion of Christianity   Christianity spread through contagious, hierarchical, stimulus, and relocation diffusion. In western Europe, Paul of Tarsus brought Christianity through his travels, creating secondary hearths. From those new hearths in Europe, Christianity diffused contagiously. As Christianity diffused to more remote locations over time, stimulus diffusion occurred when Christianity mixed with local religions and re-adopted sacred sites as Christian in places like Ireland. Later still, European colonization brought Christianity to the Americas with migration, spurring relocation diffusion.

In the case of the Eastern Orthodox faith, contagious diffusion took place from Constantinople to the north and northeast. The Protestant branch of Christianity began in several parts of western Europe and expanded to some degree through contagious diffusion. Much of its spread in northern and central Europe, however, was through hierarchical diffusion. First, political leaders would convert—sometimes to escape control from Rome—and then the population would gradually come to accept the new state religion.

The worldwide diffusion of Christianity (Fig. 7.10) occurred during the era of European colonialism beginning in the sixteenth century—often through relocation diffusion. Spain invaded and colonized Middle and South America, bringing the Catholic faith to those areas. Protestant refugees, especially those oppressed for their beliefs, came to North America in large numbers.

The Christian faith today has over 33,000 denominations. Hundreds of these proselytize (purposefully spread religious teachings) around the world. This effort creates a complex geographical distribution of Christians within the spaces that Figure 7.9 shows as Christian. Christian missionaries created an almost worldwide network of missionaries during the colonial period that endures and continues to expand today (**Fig. 7.19**).

Islam   Like Christianity, **Islam**, the youngest of the major religions, also had a single founder—in this case Muhammad, who was born in Mecca in 571 CE. According to Muslim belief, Muhammad received the truth directly from Allah (God) in a series of revelations that began when the Prophet was about 42 years old. During these revelations, Muhammad spoke the verses of the Qur'an (Koran), the Islamic holy book.

Muhammad admired the monotheism of Judaism and Christianity; he believed that Allah had already revealed himself through other prophets, including Judaism's Abraham and Christianity's Jesus. However, Muhammad came to be viewed as the one true prophet among Muslims.

After his visions, Muhammad doubted that he was chosen to be a prophet, but was convinced by further revelations and subsequently devoted his life to fulfilling the divine commands. In those days the eastern Mediterranean and the Arabian Peninsula were in religious and social disarray, with Christianity and Judaism coexisting with polytheistic religions. As Muhammad's opponents began to combat his efforts, the Prophet was forced to flee Mecca, where he had been raised, for Medina, and he continued his work from this new base.

Many principles of Islam are revisions of Judaic and Christian beliefs and traditions. The central principle is that there is one god, who occasionally reveals himself through prophets, such as Abraham, Jesus, and Muhammad. Another is that earthly matters are profane (not sacred); only Allah is pure. Allah's will is absolute; he is omnipotent and omniscient. Muslims believe that all humans live in a world that was created for them, but only until the final judgment day.

Muslims observe the "five pillars" of Islam (repeated expressions of the basic creed, frequent prayer, a month of daytime fasting, almsgiving, and, if possible, at least one pilgrimage to Mecca in one's lifetime). The faith dictates behavior in other spheres of life as well. Islam forbids alcohol, smoking, and gambling. In Islamic settlements, people build mosques to observe the Friday prayer (Friday being the holy day); mosques also serve as social gathering places (**Fig. 7.20**).

Islam, like all other major religions, divided over time—most obviously into **Sunni** and **Shi'ite** (Shiah)branches. The Sunni branch is much larger and includes various subgroups; the smaller Shi'ite branch is concentrated in Iran and surrounding areas. Smaller sects of Islam include Wahhabis, Sufis, Salafists, Alawites, Alevis, and Yazeedis.

The division between Sunni and Shi'ite occurred almost immediately after Muhammad's death and was associated with conflict over his succession. Muhammad died in 632 CE. To some, the rightful heir to the Prophet's caliphate (area of influence) was Muhammad's son-in-law, Ali. Others preferred different candidates who were not necessarily related to Muhammad. The ensuing conflict was marked by great upheaval and lasting doctrinal disagreements. The Sunni Muslims eventually prevailed in many places, but the Shi'ite Muslims, the followers of Ali, survived in some areas.

Early in the sixteenth century, an Iranian (Persian) ruling dynasty made Shi'ite Islam the only legitimate faith of that empire—which extended into what is now southern Azerbaijan, southeastern Iraq, and western Afghanistan and Pakistan. This gave the Shi'ite branch unprecedented strength and created the foundations of its modern-day culture region centered on the state of Iran.

Shi'ite veneration of the descendants of Muhammad has contributed to a much more centralized and hierarchical clergy than in the Sunni world. In Shi'ite areas, the religious leaders are called imams. Shi'ites treated the early imams as the sole source of true knowledge, and their successors continue to have great social and political authority. Sunni Islam is less centralized; an imam is simply a religious leader or scholar. Nonetheless, the Sunni branch has given rise to stricter, in some cases radically conservative, offshoots of the religion.

Diffusion of Islam   By the time of Muhammad's death in 632 CE, Muhammad and his followers had converted kings on the Arabian Peninsula to Islam. The kings then used their missionaries, traders, and armies to spread the faith across the Arabian Peninsula through

conversion and conquest. Moving west, Islam diffused across North Africa and beyond.

By the early ninth century, the Muslim world included emirates extending from Egypt to Morocco, a caliphate occupying most of Spain and Portugal, and a unified realm encompassing Arabia, the Middle East, Iran, and most of what is today Pakistan. Ultimately, the Muslim realm extended from Morocco to India and from Turkey to Ethiopia. Later, as Muslim traders settled trading ports in Southeast Asia (**Fig. 7.21**), they established new secondary hearths of Islam, from which the religion spread through contagious diffusion. Recent diffusion of Islam into Europe (beyond Spain and Portugal), South Africa, and the Americas has largely been from migration and relocation diffusion.

Today, Islam, with more than 1.8 billion followers, ranks second to Christianity in global number of adherents. It is the fastest growing of the world's major religions, dominating in northern Africa and Southwest Asia, extending into Central Asia, the former Soviet Union, and China, and including clusters in Indonesia, Bangladesh, and the southern Philippines. Islam is strongly represented in India, with over 172 million adherents, and in North Africa, where nearly two-thirds of the population is Muslim. Islam has followers in Bosnia and Albania, and it has substantial numbers of adherents in the United States and western Europe (**Fig. 7.22**).

The largest Muslim country is actually outside of the Middle East: Indonesia (in Southeast Asia), where more than 87 percent of the population is Muslim. In fact, of Islam's 1.8 billion followers, more than half live outside Southwest Asia and North Africa.

Photo by A.B. Murphy. © 2020 John Wiley & Sons, Inc.

FIGURE 7.20   **Kuala Lampur, Malaysia.**   The sprawling National Mosque serves as a landscape reminder of Islam's dominant religious role in the country.

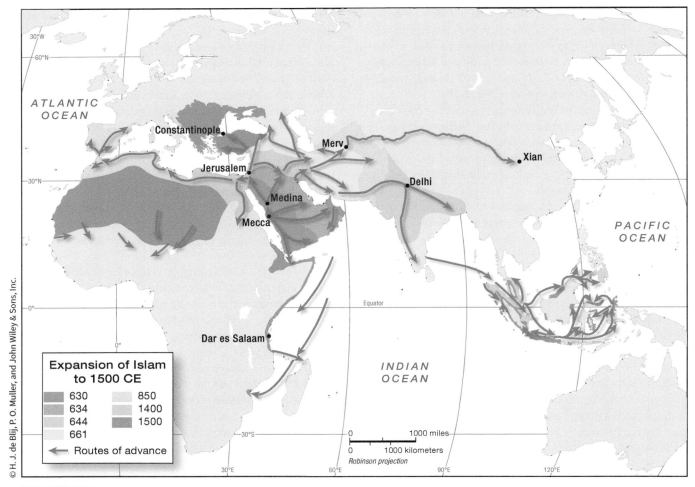

© H. J. de Blij, P. O. Muller, and John Wiley & Sons, Inc.

FIGURE 7.21   Diffusion of Islam.   The map shows the diffusion of Islam from 600 CE to 1500 CE. The hearth of Islam was established by 630. By 644, Islam diffused into Egypt and the Levant. By 900, Islam reached Spain, North Africa, and Central Asia. By 1400, Islam reached Indonesia through trade. Islam diffused into Southeast Europe, South Asia, and North Africa by 1500.

Photo by A.B. Murphy. © 2020 John Wiley & Sons, Inc.

FIGURE 7.22   London, England.   This mosque in East London serves the United Kingdom's largest Muslim community. It attests to the scale of Islamic migration to the United Kingdom since World War II. Global religions are not grouped into neat geographical spaces; they are now found side by side all over the world.

Beyond the Major Religious Hearths

Indigenous and Shamanist Religions
Figure 7.9 identifies large areas in Africa and several other parts of the world as "Indigenous and Shamanist." **Indigenous religions** are local in scope (they are ethnic religions), they typically treat nature as having divine properties, and they are passed down through family units and groups (tribes) of indigenous peoples. We do not group indigenous religions together because they share a common belief system, but because they share the same pressures from the diffusion of global religions—and they have survived (**Fig. 7.23**).

Shamanism is a faith in which a community places great trust in a shaman—a religious leader, teacher, healer, and visionary. Shamans have appeared at various times in Africa, Native America, Central Asia, Southeast Asia, and East Asia, and these appearances had similar effects on the cultures of widely scattered peoples. Unlike Christianity or Islam, shamanist faiths are small and comparatively isolated, most likely because they have not developed elaborate bureaucracies and do not send representatives abroad.

Shamanism is a traditional religion, an intimate part of a local culture and society, but not all traditional religions are shamanist. Many traditional African religions involve beliefs in a god as creator and provider, in divinities both superhuman and human, in spirits, and in a life hereafter. Christianity and Islam have converted some followers of traditional religions, but as the map indicates, indigenous religions still dominate in significant areas (Fig. 7.9).

The Rise of Secularism

A world map of religion can be misleading because many people in areas shown as Christian or Buddhist do not in fact follow those faiths. Even the most careful analysis of religious membership produces about 4 billion followers of major religions—in a global population of over 7 billion. Hundreds of millions of peoples are not counted in this figure because they practice traditional religions. But even when they are taken into account, additional hundreds of millions do not practice a religion at all.

Even church membership figures do not accurately reflect the number of active members of a church. When polled about their churchgoing activities, fewer than 10 percent in Scandinavia reported frequent attendance. In France and Great Britain, around 10 percent of the population reported attending church at least once a month. The lack of active members underscores the rise of secularism—indifference to or rejection of organized religious affiliations and ideas.

The level of secularism throughout much of the Christian and Buddhist worlds varies from country to country, as it does regionally within countries. In North America, for instance, a survey published in 2018 asked whether people felt religion was very important to them. Only 27 percent of Canadians agreed with this statement, whereas 53 percent of Americans did.

The French government recently banned the wearing of overt religious symbols in public schools. The stated goal was to remove the "disruption" of Muslim girls wearing hijabs (head scarves), Jewish boys wearing yarmulke (skullcaps), and Christian students wearing large crosses to school. The French government stated that banning all religious symbols was the only egalitarian approach. In other cases, however, the state targets a more specific population. That was the case in 2009 when the Swiss voted to ban the construction of new minarets.

Polls showing responses to questions about the importance of religion do not give us the complete picture. The 27 percent of Canadians who state that religion is very important to them would be much lower if we removed recent or second-generation immigrants from the tally. Immigrants often hold on to their religions more intensely, in part to help them ease into a new place and to link to a community in their new home. Thus, Buddhists and Hindus on Canada's west coast and Muslims in the eastern part of Canada have a higher rate of adherence to their religion than many long-term residents.

Author Field Note   Climbing Uluru, Australia

"Arriving at the foot of erosion-carved Uluru just before sunrise, I do not find it surprising that this giant monolith, towering over the Australian desert, is a sacred place to local Aboriginal peoples. Throughout the day, the changing sun angle alters its colors until, toward sunset, it turns a fiery red that yields to a bright orange. At night it looms against the moonlit, starry sky, silent sentinel of the gods. Just two years before this, my first visit in 1987, the Australian government had returned Ayers Rock (named by European settlers after a South Australian political leader) to Aboriginal ownership and reclaimed its original name, Uluru. Visitors continued to be allowed to climb to the 1100 feet (335 m) to the top, from where the view over the desert is awesome.

My day had begun eventfully when a three-foot lizard emerged from under my motel-room bed, but the chain-assisted climb was no minor challenge either. At the base, you are warned to be 'in good shape' and some would-be climbers don't make it, but the rewards of persisting are dramatic. Uluru's iron-rich sandstone strata have been sculpted into gullies and caves, the latter containing Aboriginal carvings and paintings, and on the broad summit there are plenty of places where you can sit quietly to contemplate historic, religious, and cultural significance of a place that mattered thousands of years before globalization reached Australia."

– H. J. de Blij

© H. J. de Blij

FIGURE 7.23 **Uluru, Australia.**

Photo by A.B. Murphy. © 2020 John Wiley & Sons, Inc.

FIGURE 7.24 **Leeds, England.** A couple of decades ago, the building shown here was a functioning church. As the congregation shrank, it could no longer stay open. The building was still in good shape and its location near a major university inspired an entrepreneur to turn it into a club. Since its purchase in 2005, the former church has been home to two nightclubs: first Halo and now Church.

In some countries, antireligious ideologies have contributed to the decline of organized religion. Maoist China's drive against Confucianism had sweeping effects, and China continues to suppress organized religious practices, as reports of religious persecution continue to emanate from the country. As we have seen, the case of the Soviet Union is different; despite decades of religious suppression there, church membership rebounded after the collapse of communist rule.

Other forces have led to the decline in organized religion in many of the areas labeled as Catholic and Protestant in Figure 7.9. From North America to western Europe to Australia, congregations have shrunk (**Fig. 7.24**). Even if people continue to be members of a church, their participation in church activities has declined.

The growth of secularism is more muted in strongly Catholic areas outside North America and Europe. The Catholic Church remains strong in the South and Middle America, although it has lost some followers in response to its teachings on restricting birth control and the church's sexual abuse scandals. While some of those who have left the Catholic Church have become more secular, many others are turning toward evangelical Christian denominations.

Traditions associated with religion are also weakening throughout much of the Christian world. For example, there was a time when almost all shops and businesses were closed on Sundays, preserving the day for sermons, rest, and introspection. Today, shopping centers are mostly open as usual, and Sunday is increasingly devoted to business and personal affairs. To witness the rise of secularism among Christians in America firsthand, explore your town, city, or suburb on a Sunday morning: How many people are wearing casual clothes and hanging out at the coffee shop reading newspapers, and how many people are attending church services?

Even as secularism is on the rise in the United States, many people remain deeply rooted in their religious beliefs—sometimes more fervently than ever. Religious traditions are stronger in some cultural regions of the United States than in others. Sunday observance continues at a high level, for example, in the Mormon culture area. Even though mainline churches are closing churches in some parts of the United States and western Europe, many evangelical and other alternative churches are growing rapidly. Entire industries, such as Christian music and Christian publications, depend on the growing commitment of many Americans and Europeans to their religion.

The trend toward secularism is not confined to the Christian world. Secularism is also growing in South Korea, where half of the population does not profess adherence to any particular religion. But although major faiths are experiencing an overall decline in followers, several smaller religions are growing in importance, including Baha'i, Cao Dai, Jainism, and the Spiritual Church of Brazil.

TC **Thinking Geographically**

Religions can spread through contagious, hierarchical, stimulus, and relocation **diffusion**. Think about Chapter 2 and the **population pyramids** of Europe. Determine how the aging of Europe is impacting Christianity in the region. Then, consider how modern forces of contagious, hierarchical, stimulus, and relocation diffusion are impacting patterns of religions and secularism in Europe.

7.3 Explain How the Cultural Landscape Reflects Religious Ideas and Practices.

Religion has a clear presence in the cultural landscape—in houses of worship such as churches, mosques, synagogues, and temples; cemeteries dotted with religious symbols and icons; and stores designated for sales of religious goods. When adherents voluntarily travel to a sacred site to pay respects or participate in a ritual, the travel is called a **pilgrimage**. Pilgrimage routes are evident in the cultural landscape. Geographers who study religion are interested in pilgrimage and its impacts on place, people, religion, culture, and environment.

Sacred Sites

Sacred sites are places or spaces that people infuse with religious meaning. Members of a religious group may define a space or place as sacred out of either reverence or fear. If a sacred site is revered, adherents may make a pilgrimage to the site for rejuvenation, reflection, healing, or fulfillment of a religious commitment.

In ancient history, physical geographic landscape features such as buttes, mountain peaks, and rivers were often chosen as sacred sites. As universalizing religions diffused across the world, many sacred sites were abandoned or altered. Geographer Mary Lee Nolan studied Irish sacred sites and observed that many of the remote physical geographic features of the Irish landscape were sacred to the Celtic people (**Fig. 7.25**). When Roman Catholicism diffused to Ireland, however, the Catholic Church usurped many of these features, infusing them with Christian meaning. Nolan described the marriage of Celtic sacred sites and Christian meaning:

> The early Celtic Church was a unique institution, more open to syncretism of old and new religious traditions than was the case in many other parts of Europe. Old holy places, often in remote areas, were "baptized" in the new religion or given new meaning through their historical, or more often legendary, association with Celtic saints. Such places were characterized by sacred site features such as heights, insularity, or the presence of holy water sources, trees, or stones.

Nolan contrasted Irish sacred sites with those in continental Europe, where sacred sites were typically built in urban, accessible areas. In continental Europe, Nolan found that the bones of saints or images were typically brought to a place to give it religious meaning.

In many societies, special features in the physical landscape remain sacred to religious groups. Yet access to these features varies depending on ownership, environmental regulations, and the need or desire to control the flow of visitors. Geographer Kari Forbes-Boyte (1999) studied Bear Butte, a site sacred to members of the Lakota and Cheyenne people in the northern Great Plains of the United States. The site became a state park in the 1960s. Today both Lakota and Cheyenne people use Bear Butte in religious ceremonies, but it is also a popular recreational site. Nearby Devils Tower, a national

---

Guest Field Note Tying Cloth Offerings from Ireland to India to Eastern Russia

Mary Lee Nolan
Oregon State University

At St. Declan's Holy Well in Ireland, I found a barbed wire fence substituting for the more traditional thorn tree as a place to hang scraps of clothing as offerings. This tradition, which died out long ago in most parts of Continental Europe, was one of many aspects of Irish pilgrimage that led me to speculate on 'Galway-to-the-Ganges' survival of very old religious customs on the extreme margins of an ancient Indo-European cultural realm. My subsequent fieldwork focused on contemporary European pilgrimage, but my curiosity about the geographical extent of certain ancient pilgrimage themes lingered. While traveling in Asia, I found many similarities among sacred sites across religions. Each religion has formation stories, explanations of how particular sites, whether Buddhist monasteries or Irish wells, were recognized as sacred. Many of these stories have similar elements. And, in 1998, I traveled across Russia from the remote Kamchatka Peninsula to St. Petersburg. Imagine my surprise to find the tradition of hanging rag offerings on trees alive and well all the way across the Russian Far East and Siberia, at least as far as Olkon Island in Lake Baikal.

© Mary Lee Nolan

FIGURE 7.25 Ardmore, Ireland.

Photo by A.B. Murphy. © 2020 John Wiley & Sons, Inc.

FIGURE 7.26 **Jerusalem, Israel.** The Western Wall (foreground, right), which is sacred to Jews, stands right next to the Dome of the Rock (background, left), which is sacred to Muslims.

monument, experiences the same pull between religious use by American Indians and recreational use by tourists.

Places such as Bear Butte and Devils Tower become sites of contention when one group sees the sites as sacred and another group does not. In other places, sacred sites may become contentious when adherents of more than one religious faith see them as significant. How a common sacred site is shared or debated depends on the larger geographical and historical context of political, economic and social connections between the groups. Voltура Peak in Rajgir (northeastern India), for example, is holy to Buddhists because it is the site where Buddha first proclaimed the Heart Sutra, a very important canon of Buddhism. Hindus and Jains also consider the site holy because they hold Buddha to be a god or prophet. The site has created little discord among religious groups, and pilgrims of all faiths peacefully congregate in the place year after year.

> **AP® Exam Taker's Tip**
>
> What shared religious and cultural practices, attitudes, and behaviors make a site sacred? What geographic components of the sacred site are there (e.g., pilgrimages, rituals performed on site, sacred directions)?

Sacred Sites of Jerusalem
The ancient city of Jerusalem is sacred to Jews, Christians, and Muslims. Jews saw Jerusalem as sacred and they maintained control over the site from 1200 BCE to the time of the diaspora. After the diaspora, Jerusalem remained sacred to Jews even though they did not control it. The Zionist movement recognized the sacredness of Jerusalem and sought a return of Jews to the Holy Land.

The most important sacred site for Jews is the Western Wall, at the edge of the Temple Mount in Jerusalem (**Fig. 7.26**). The

Temple Mount occupies the top of a modest hill where, according to the Torah (the sacred book of Judaism that is also part of the Old Testament of Christianity's sacred book, the Bible), Abraham almost sacrificed his son Isaac. On this hill, Jews built two temples, both destroyed by invaders. The Western Wall is all that remains of the second temple, and Jews gather there to remember the story of Abraham and the destruction of the temples, and to offer prayers. Both men and women pray at the site, but they do so separately, and the area reserved for women is fairly small. Beyond personal prayer, the sacred site is a place to mourn and recognize the suffering of Jews over time.

For Christians, Jerusalem is sacred both because of the sacrifice Abraham was willing to make of his son at the Temple Mount and because Jesus's crucifixion took place just outside the city's walls. Jesus was then buried in a tomb that Roman emperor Constantine later marked with a basilica that is now the Church of the Holy Sepulchre (**Fig. 7.27**). Christians believe that Jesus rose from that tomb on the day marked by the Easter celebration. For centuries the Roman, and then the Byzantine, Empires controlled the city and protected the sacred site.

In the seventh century, Muslim armies took control of Jerusalem from the Byzantine Empire. Muslims constructed a mosque

Mazur Travel/Shutterstock.com

FIGURE 7.27 **Jerusalem, Israel.** The Church of the Holy Sepulchre is sacred to Christians, who believe it is the site where Jesus Christ was resurrected. This structure inside the church is the tomb of Jesus.

called the Dome of the Rock adjacent to the Western Wall to mark the site where Muslims believe Muhammad visited heaven on his Night Journey in 621 (**Fig. 7.26**). The site Jews call Temple Mount is called al-Haram al-Sharif (the Noble Sanctuary) by Muslims.

In the Middle Ages, Christians and Muslims fought the Crusades over the question of who should control the sacred land of Jerusalem. Between 1095 and 1199, European political and religious leaders organized a series of Crusades to retake the holy land. The first Christian crusaders captured Jerusalem in 1099, and Christians then ruled the city for almost 100 years. As the first crusaders traveled across what is modern-day Turkey on their way to Jerusalem, they also left conquests in their wake—laying claim to the city of Antioch and other strategically important sites. Some of the crusaders returned to western Europe, but many settled, mingled, and intermarried with the local people.

Muslims ultimately retook Jerusalem in 1187, and later Christian crusaders were unable to conquer it again. The Crusades helped strengthen a commitment by Christians to protect the Church of the Holy Sepulchre, even as they cemented a commitment by Muslims to protect the Dome of the Rock. Zionism represented a commitment by Jews to protect the Western Wall. The commitment by three major religions to protect and control their sacred sites has led to political turmoil that echoes far beyond Jerusalem, as we will see in the next major section of this chapter.

Landscapes of Hinduism and Buddhism

Traditional Hinduism is more than a faith; it is a way of life. Pilgrimages follow prescribed routes, and millions of people attend rituals. Festivals and feasts are frequent, colorful, and noisy. Hindus believe that the erection of a temple, whether modest or elaborate, bestows merit on the builder and will be rewarded. As a result, the Hindu cultural landscape—urban as well as rural—is dotted with countless shrines, ranging from small village temples to structures so large and elaborate that they are virtually holy cities.

Photo by A.B. Murphy. © 2020 John Wiley & Sons, Inc.

FIGURE 7.28 Varanasi, India. Hindus perform morning rituals in the Ganges River at one of Hinduism's most sacred places, the city of Varanasi, known as the city of Lord Shiva. For Hindus, the river itself is a sacred site.

The location of shrines is important because Hindus believe that holy places should not greatly disrupt the natural landscape. Whenever possible, a Hindu temple is located in a "comfortable" position, for example, under a large, shady tree. Hindus also tend to locate their temples near water because they believe that many gods will not venture far from water and because water serves the holy function of ritual bathing (**Fig. 7.28**). A village temple should face the village from a prominent position, and followers must make offerings frequently. Small offerings of fruit and flowers lie before the sanctuary of the deity honored by the shrine.

The cultural landscape of Hinduism is closely associated with that of India as a whole. As one travels through India, the Hindu faith is a visual as well as an emotional experience. Temples and shrines, holy animals by the tens of millions, distinctively garbed holy men, and the sights and sounds of long processions and rituals all contribute to a religious atmosphere (**Fig. 7.29**).

Author Field Note   Celebrating the Bonalu Festival in Hyderabad, India

"In the summer of 2007, the newer, HITEC (high tech) city area of Hyderabad, India, was under construction. Migrant workers built new roads, apartment houses, and office buildings throughout the city. Beautiful homes reflected the wealth accrued by many. In front of the new homes, I saw Hinduism in the cultural landscape where owners built temples for their favorite Hindu god. In the older part of the city, I visited Golconda Fort, built more than 1500 years ago. On the day I was there, Hindu women participated in the Bonalu Festival as an act of honoring Mother Goddess. The women climbed nearly 400 steps to the top of the fort, carrying with them offerings of food. A the top, I was welcomed into the temple. I took off my shoes and took in a festival that began in the mid-1800s, when Hindu women began the festival to ward off the anger of the gods, as the city stood under the siege of the bubonic plague."

– E. H. Fouberg

Photo by E.H. Fouberg. © 2020 John Wiley & Sons, Inc.

FIGURE 7.29 Hyderabad, India.

When Buddha received enlightenment, he sat under a large tree, the Bodhi (enlightenment) tree, at Bodh Gaya in India. The Bodhi tree now growing on the site is believed to be a descendant of the original tree. It has a thick, banyan-like trunk and a wide canopy of leafy branches. Because of its association with the Buddha, the tree is revered and protected. Buddhists make pilgrimages to Bodh Gaya and other places where Buddha may have taught beneath Bodhi branches. Along with Buddhism, the Bodhi tree diffused as far as China and Japan, its purposeful planting marking the cultural landscape of numerous villages and towns.

Buddhism's architecture includes some magnificent achievements, especially the famed structures at Borobudur in central Java (Indonesia). Buddhist shrines include stupas, bell-shaped structures that protect burial mounds. Buddhists also construct temples that enshrine an image of Buddha in his familiar cross-legged pose, as well as large monasteries that tower over the local landscape. The pagoda is perhaps Buddhism's most familiar structure. Its shape is derived from the relic (often funeral) mounds of old. Every fragment of its construction is a meaningful representation of Buddhist philosophy (**Fig. 7.30**).

We can also see evidence of religion in the cultural landscapes of the dead. Traditionally, Hindus, and more recently Buddhists and Shintoists, cremate their dead. Thus, crematoriums are found wherever a large group of Hindus, Buddhists, or Shintoists live. The Hindu crematorium in Kenya stands in stark contrast to much of the cultural landscape and signals the presence of a large Hindu population (see **Fig. 7.31**).

The cultural landscapes of Hinduism and Buddhism extend into Southeast Asia. Later, Islam replaced the South Asian religions in many of these places, and even later Christian missionaries gained adherents in Southeast Asia when Christian governments encouraged the migration of their people and their religion to their colonies. Today, we can stand in a city such as Singapore, study the cultural landscape, and see the influences of Christianity, Buddhism, Hinduism, and Islam.

Photo by A.B. Murphy. © 2020 John Wiley & Sons, Inc.

FIGURE 7.30 **Yangon, Myanmar.** In the heart of the city, the Shwedagon Pagoda is one of Southeast Asia's most spectacular Buddhist shrines. Its religious importance is striking: Eight hairs of the Buddha are preserved here. Vast amounts of gold went into the creation of the Shwedagon Pagoda; local rulers often gave the monks their weight in gold—or more. Today, the pagoda draws millions of visitors—both faithful Buddhists and tourists.

Author Field Note   Seeing Hinduism in the Cultural Landscape of Mombasa, Kenya

"Each religion approaches the disposition of the deceased in its own way, and cultural landscapes reflect religious traditions. In largely Christian, Western religions, the deceased are buried in cemeteries. The Hindu faith, which is predominantly found in India, requires cremation of the deceased. When the British colonized both India and Kenya in the late nineteenth and early twentieth centuries, they brought Indians to Kenya as 'bonded laborers' to lay the Kenya-Uganda railroad (Bhowmick 2008). The number of Indians in Kenya peaked at 175,000 in 1962 and is approximately 100,000 today, large enough to need a crematorium, the equivalent of a Hindu funeral home."

– H. J. de Blij

© H. J. de Blij

FIGURE 7.31 **Mombasa, Kenya**

FIGURE 7.32 **Antwerp, Belgium.** The cathedral in Antwerp was built beginning in 1352 and still dominates the central part of town.

Landscapes of Christianity

The cultural landscapes of Christianity's branches reflect the changes the faith has undergone over the centuries. In medieval Europe the cathedral, church, or monastery was the focus of life. Other buildings clustered around the tower, steeple, and spire of the church, which could be seen (and whose bells could be heard) for miles (**Fig. 7.32**). In the square or plaza in front of the church, crowds gathered for ceremonies and festivals, and the church was always present—even if the event was not primarily religious. Good harvests, military victories, public announcements, and much else took place under the symbol of religious authority. Then in the colonial era, Europeans exported the ornate architecture of European Christian churches wherever they settled (**Fig. 7.33**).

The Reformation, the rise of secularism, and the decline of organized religion are reflected in the cultural landscape as well. Some of the ornate churches in the town squares of medieval cities now function as museums instead of serving active congregations. Other churches in secular regions are closing

FIGURE 7.33 **Mombasa, Kenya.** Built at the end of the nineteenth century, the neo-gothic Holy Ghost Cathedral reflects the European colonial imprint on the city. The sign in the street next to the cathedral serves as a reminder of a more recent external cultural influence—this time from China. The number of Chinese in the city is not large, but Chinese immigrants have found niches in the restaurant business and as purveyors of Chinese traditional medicine.

their doors or significantly reducing the number of religious services offered. However, not all of Europe's sacred sites have become secularized. Famous cathedrals continue to hold services while tourists marvel at the architecture and art. Moreover, other sacred sites of Christianity, such as churches for specific saints, places where significant events occurred, and Vatican City in Rome, are still major pilgrimage sites. When in Rome, the pope holds an outdoor service for pilgrims to Vatican City, attracting thousands of followers to St. Peter's Square each week (**Fig. 7.34**).

FIGURE 7.34 **Vatican City.** Pope Francis waves to pilgrims as he arrives in the Popemobile at St. Peter's Square for his weekly audience. Thousands gather each week to see the pope and hear him greet visitors in multiple languages.

Cities in Europe are also home to centuries-old Christian cemeteries. Traditionally, Christians bury, rather than cremate, their dead, and in Christian-dominated cities, cemeteries are often crowded with tombstones. Outside of European cities and in North America, Christian cemeteries can resemble large parks. They often reflect class differences, with some graves marked by simple tombstones and others by elaborate structures. With rising land-use pressures and the associated costs of burial, cremation is becoming increasingly common among Christians—particularly in North America and western Europe.

Christian Landscapes in the United States   The
United States, a predominantly Christian country, demonstrates considerable diversity in its religious cultural landscapes. In *The Cultural Geography of the United States*, geographer Wilbur Zelinsky constructed a map identifying religious regions in the country. **Figure 7.35** is a modified version of Zelinsky's map.

The New England region is strongly Catholic; the South's leading denomination is Baptist; the Upper Midwest has many Lutherans; and the Southwest is predominantly Spanish Catholic. The broad midland region from the Middle Atlantic to the Mormon region (in the western United States) has a mixture of denominations in which no single church dominates; this is also true of the West. As Figure 7.35 shows, some regions represent local clustering, such as the French Catholic area centered in New Orleans and the mixed denominations of peninsular Florida, where a large Spanish Catholic cluster has emerged in metropolitan Miami.

In a 2008 study, geographers Barney Warf and Mort Winsberg used data on religious adherents by U.S. county to discern which regions have the most and the least religious diversity. One way the authors mapped religious diversity is presented in **Figure 7.36**, a map showing counties with the least religious diversity in the darkest colors. In these areas, one religion accounts for 64 percent or more of all religious adherents

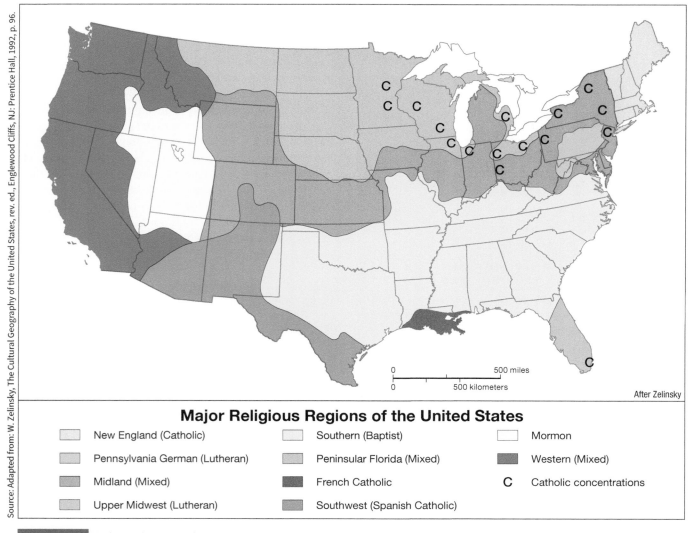

Source: Adapted from: W. Zelinsky, The Cultural Geography of the United States, rev. ed., Englewood Cliffs, NJ: Prentice Hall, 1992, p. 96.

After Zelinsky

Major Religious Regions of the United States

- New England (Catholic)
- Pennsylvania German (Lutheran)
- Midland (Mixed)
- Upper Midwest (Lutheran)
- Southern (Baptist)
- Peninsular Florida (Mixed)
- French Catholic
- Southwest (Spanish Catholic)
- Mormon
- Western (Mixed)
- C   Catholic concentrations

FIGURE 7.35   **Major Religious Regions of the United States.**   A generalized map of the religious regions of the United States shows patterns and concentrations of the major religions.

in the county. In comparing Figure 7.35 to Figure 7.36, we can see that the Mormon region in Utah and southern Idaho, the Southern Baptist region in the South, and the Catholic region of the Northeast are some of the least diverse regions. There you can see the imprint of one major religion throughout the cultural landscape. By contrast, many lightly colored counties have a rich religious mix.

The plain white churches of the South and Lutheran Upper Midwest coincide with the Protestant Church's pragmatic spending of church money—not on art and architecture (**Fig. 7.37**). Conversely, many Catholic churches in the Northeast, Chicago, and other immigrant-magnet cities were built by migrants who spent their own money and used their building skills to construct ornate churches and dozens of cathedrals that tied them back to their countries of origin (**Fig. 7.38**).

The modern cultural landscape also bears witness to the rapid growth of evangelical Protestant dominations. Even in modest-sized cities, large evangelical churches with congregations over 10,000 people have sprung up in suburbs around cities (**Fig. 7.39**). And some large cities have evangelical churches that can accommodate services attended by thousands of followers. These churches are particularly widespread in the central and southern parts of the United States.

Landscapes of Islam

Elaborate, sometimes magnificently designed mosques whose balconied **minarets** rise above the townscape dominate Islamic cities, towns, and villages. Often the mosque is the town's most imposing and most carefully maintained building. Five times every day, from the towering minarets, the faithful are called to prayer. The sounds emanating from the minarets fill the streets as the faithful converge on the holy place to pray facing Mecca.

At the height of Islam's expansion into eastern North Africa and southern Europe, Muslim architects incorporated earlier Roman models into their designs. The results included some of the world's greatest architectural masterpieces, such as the Alhambra Palace in Granada and the Great Mosque of Cordoba in Spain. Islam's prohibition against depicting the human form led to the wide use of geometric designs and calligraphy—the intricacy of which is truly astounding (**Fig. 7.40**). During the eleventh century, Muslim builders began glazing the tiles of domes and roofs. To the beautiful arcades and arched courtyards, they added the exquisite beauty of glass-like, perfectly symmetrical cupolas. Muslim architecture represents the unifying concept of Islamic monotheism: the perfection and vastness of the spirit of Allah.

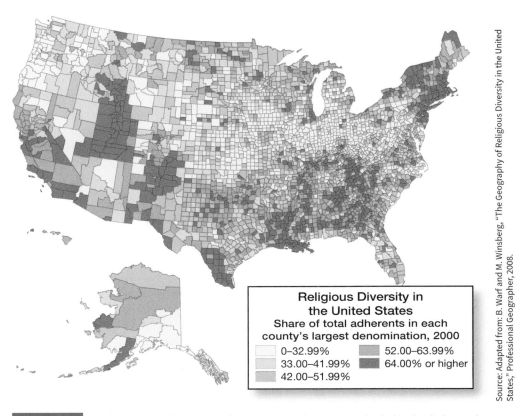

Source: Adapted from: B. Warf and M. Winsberg, "The Geography of Religious Diversity in the United States," Professional Geographer, 2008.

Religious Diversity in the United States
Share of total adherents in each county's largest denomination, 2000

0–32.99%	52.00–63.99%
33.00–41.99%	64.00% or higher
42.00–51.99%	

FIGURE 7.36 **Religious Diversity in the United States.** The counties shaded in the darkest color have the least diversity in religions. The counties shaded in the lightest color have the most diversity within them. Compare and contrast with Figure 7.35 to explain which major religions in the United States are the dominant religions in counties with low religious diversity.

Photo by E.H. Fouberg. © 2020 John Wiley & Sons, Inc.

FIGURE 7.37   Brown County, South Dakota.   The Scandinavian Lutheran Church was founded by immigrants from northern Europe. The simple architecture of the church is commonly found in Protestant churches in the Great Plains.

Photo by E.H. Fouberg. © 2020 John Wiley & Sons, Inc.

FIGURE 7.38   Zell, South Dakota.   St. Mary's Catholic Church was built by nuns in 1875 to serve Catholic immigrants and Native Americans. The more ornate architecture and stained glass of St. Mary's Church is commonly found in Catholic churches in the Great Plains.

Islam achieved its greatest artistic expression, its most distinctive visible element, in architecture. Even in the smallest town, the community helps build and maintain its mosque. The mosque symbolizes the power of the faith and its role in the community. Its importance in the cultural landscape confirms the degree to which, in much of the Muslim world, religion and culture are one.

The physical landscape of Mecca, Islam's holiest city, bears witness to one the best-known pilgrimages in the modern world, the **hajj**. The hajj is one of the five pillars of Islam. Each year, over 2 million Muslims from outside of Saudi Arabia and over 1 million from inside the country make the pilgrimage to Mecca (**Fig. 7.41**). The hajj requires the faithful to follow certain steps of reverence in a certain order and within a certain time frame. As a result, the pilgrims move from Mecca through the steps of the hajj en masse.

In 2015, over 4000 pilgrims were trampled to death as hordes of people followed the steps of the pilgrimage. The Saudi government now restricts the number of visas granted each year to Muslims from outside the country. Yet the number of pilgrims continues to climb, and the services needed for Muslim pilgrims now employ four times as many people in Saudi Arabia as the oil industry does. The landscape around Mecca reflects the growing number of pilgrims year-round, as towers of apartment buildings and hotels encircle the sacred city.

Timothy Fadek/Corbis News/Getty Images

FIGURE 7.39   Houston, Texas.   Pastor Joel Osteen's Lakewood Church in Houston is one of the biggest mega churches in the United States. Mega churches are defined as non-Catholic churches with at least 2000 weekly attendants. Estimates of weekly attendance at Lakewood church are as high as 50,000 people.

Photo by A.B. Murphy. © 2020 John Wiley & Sons, Inc.

AP Images/AMEL EMRIC

FIGURE 7.41 **Mecca, Saudi Arabia.** Pilgrims circle the holy Kaaba in the Grand Mosque in Mecca during the hajj.

FIGURE 7.40 **Isfahan, Iran.** The dome of this mosque demonstrates the geometric art evident in Muslim architecture. The towers to the right of the dome are minarets from which the call to prayer is broadcast.

> **TC Thinking Geographically**
>
> Choose a pilgrimage site, such as Mecca, Vatican City, or the Western Wall, and describe how the act of pilgrimage (in some cases by millions of people) alters this place's **cultural landscape** and environment.

7.4 Identify and Describe the Role Religion Plays in Political Conflicts.

Religious beliefs and histories can bitterly divide peoples who speak the same language, have the same ethnic background, and make their living in similar ways. Such divisions are not only between followers of different major religions (like Muslims and Christians in the former Yugoslavia). They sometimes emerge among believers of the same overarching religion. Indeed, some of the most destructive conflicts have pitted Christian against Christian and Muslim against Muslim.

Religious conflicts usually involve more than differences in spiritual practices and beliefs. Religion serves as a symbol of a wider set of cultural and political differences. The "religious" conflict in Northern Ireland is not just about different views of Christianity, and the conflict between Hindus and Muslims in India has a strong political dimension. Nevertheless, in these and other cases, religion serves as the principal symbol separating competing groups.

Conflicts Along Religious Borders

A comparison between Figure 7.9 and a world political map reveals that some countries lie entirely within the realms of individual world religions and others straddle **interfaith**

boundaries (the boundaries between the world's major faiths). Many countries that straddle interfaith boundaries have experienced divisive cultural forces—particularly when the people see their religious differences as a primary source of social identity. This is the case in several African countries straddling the Christian–Muslim interfaith boundary (**Fig. 7.42**). In India, where Hindu nationalism is deeply rooted, close to 200 million Muslims live in a state that resulted from the 1947 partition of South Asia into largely Hindu (India) and Muslim (East and West Pakistan[1]). Other countries with major religious disputes straddle **intrafaith boundaries**, the boundaries within a single major faith. Intrafaith boundaries include divisions between Christian Protestants and Catholics (Northern Ireland), divisions between Muslim Sunnis and Shi'ites (Iraq).

Israel/Palestine and Nigeria provide examples of interfaith conflicts, whereas Northern Ireland is an example of an intrafaith conflict. In each case, religious difference is not the only factor driving the conflict, but it plays a powerful symbolic role. Interface areas, where interfaith and intrafaith boundaries occur, may be peaceful, or they can play host to violent political conflict.

[1]East Pakistan is now Bangladesh.

FIGURE 7.42 **African Transition Zone.** The divide shown on the map marks interfaith boundaries between religions. Considerable conflict has occurred in the transition zone.

© H. J. de Blij, P. O. Muller, and John Wiley & Sons, Inc.

AP® Exam Taker's Tip

Name three real-world examples where migration has caused or exacerbated conflict between groups. See Chapter 3 to review possible examples.

Israel and Palestine

Earlier in this chapter, we discussed the history of the conflict over the sacred space of Jerusalem. Israel and Palestine are home to one of the most contentious religious conflicts today.

After World War I, European colonialism came to a region that had previously been controlled and fought over by Jews, Romans, Christians, Muslims, and Ottomans. A newly formed League of Nations (a precursor to the United Nations) recognized British control of the land, calling the territorial mandate Palestine. At that point, the vast majority of people living in the land were Muslim Palestinians.

The goal of the British government was to meet Zionist goals and to create, in Palestine, a national homeland for the Jewish people (who had already begun to migrate to the area). The British explicitly assured the world that the religious and civil rights of existing non-Jewish peoples in Palestine would be protected.

The British policy did not produce a peaceful result, however. Civil disturbances erupted almost immediately, and they became much worse after the Holocaust and World War II, when many more Jews migrated to flee persecution and concentration camps in Europe. Between 1914 and 1946, the Jewish population of Palestine grew from around 60,000 to over 528,000.

In 1948, the British mandate ended, shortly after the newly formed United Nations voted to partition Palestine. The Zionist dream of a State of Israel was realized when the United Nations created two independent, noncontiguous states: Israel and Palestine (see Fig. 3.26). Even before the partition, Palestinians and surrounding Arabs opposed the large-scale migration of Jews to the area. Arabs rejected the UN plan, citing the UN Charter's Article 1(2) that recognizes the right to self-determination of peoples. After the British ended their mandate, Israel declared independence, using the borders designed by the United Nations. Immediately, Arabs fought against the Israeli state, and Israel won lands between 1948 and 1949.

During two wars in 1967 and 1973, Israel decisively won military victories and expanded Israeli territory. In the course of these wars, Palestinians lost their lands, farms, and villages, and many migrated or fled to refugee camps in neighboring Arab states. In the 1967 Six-Day War, Egypt, Jordan, Syria, and Lebanon attacked Israel, and Israel fought back, gaining control of the Gaza Strip and Sinai from Egypt, the West Bank and Jerusalem from Jordan, and the Golan Heights from Syria. In the Yom Kippur War in 1973, Syria and Egypt launched surprise attacks on Israel on an Israeli high holy day, and Israel won the war.

The international community calls the lands Israel gained through the 1967 and 1973 wars the Occupied Territories. The primary concern of Palestinians and Arab countries since 1973 has been the growing presence of Israelis in the West Bank and East Jerusalem. The Israeli government has built **settlements** for Israelis across the West Bank, which has increased tensions on the ground as Palestinians continue to lose land and control. Settlements include housing developments enclosed in walls that are patrolled by the Israeli military, along with streets, sewer and water extended to each settlement.

Through the settlement policy, Israel has extended control over Jerusalem, expanding the city into the West Bank and razing Palestinian houses along the way. At the same time, the Israeli government has restricted new building by Palestinians in Jerusalem and the West Bank. The situation has produced considerable conflict, with Palestinians claiming oppression and violence by Israel and Israelis claiming a right to recover their historic homeland and to defend themselves from Palestinians who are hostile to their presence.

Efforts at peace between Israel and Palestine have often been led by U.S. presidents, though with few successes. In 1978, a peace accord agreed to by Israeli Prime Minister Menachem Begin and Egyptian President Anwar Sadat and negotiated by U.S. President Jimmy Carter lowered tensions between Israel and Egypt. In what became known as the Camp David Accords, Israel returned the Sinai Peninsula to Egypt and Egypt recognized Israel as an independent country. The peace was short-lived. Palestinians spontaneously launched what

FIGURE 7.43 **Erez Crossing, Gaza Strip.** The Israeli Army withdrew from the Gaza Strip in 2005, after occupying the territory for 38 years. Israeli troops demolished the Israeli Army liaison offices on September 9, 2005, in preparation for completing the Israeli retreat from the Gaza Strip on September 11, 2005.

became known as the first intifada, including boycotts, demonstrations, and attacks on Israelis, in the 1980s.

In 1993, Prime Minister Yitzhak Rabin of Israel and Yasser Arafat of the Palestine Liberation Organization agreed to the Oslo Accords, facilitated by U.S. President Bill Clinton. The Palestinian Authority was recognized and allowed to practice limited self-government over the Occupied Territories of the West Bank (including East Jerusalem) and the Gaza Strip. The second intifada began in the 2000s when peace negotiations broke down. Both sides blame each other for the breakout in violence in the second intifada. Violence in the second intifada escalated to individual Palestinians and Palestinian terrorist organizations like Hamas using suicide bombings and sniper attacks and the Israeli military using force (defined by Palestinians as excessive) and cracking down on movement of Palestinians in response to Palestinian demonstrations. Nearly 5000 Palestinians died, including over 1200 children. Over 1100 Israelis died and thousands more were wounded.

In 2005, Israel withdrew from the Gaza Strip and Palestine took control of 223 square miles (360 square kilometers). Israel evacuated the settlements that had been built there, burned down the buildings that remained (**Fig. 7.43**), and in 2007 granted autonomy to Gaza. The Palestinians living in the Gaza Strip rejoiced—visiting the beaches that were previously open only to Israeli settlers and traveling across the border into Egypt to purchase goods. Their joy was short-lived, however. Gaza became economically isolated, the standard of living dropped, and continued conflict with Israel made the situation worse. The Israeli government now tightly controls the flow of Palestinians and goods into and out of the Gaza Strip. Gaza is surrounded by fences, and in some places a wall—with landmines in certain areas.

In the face of these developments, Palestinians have dug dozens of tunnels between Egypt and Gaza to bring arms, fuel, and goods to the Hamas government in Gaza. But in 2014, Egypt followed Israel's lead and declared Hamas to be a terrorist organization. Egypt then moved to shut down the flow of goods through the tunnels. This did little to ease conflict along the Gaza-Israel border, however. In recent years Palestinians in Gaza have periodically fired missiles into Israeli territory, and Israel has responded with deadly force. In 2018, 52 Palestinians were killed and thousands were injured during demonstrations along the border against the plan to move the U.S. embassy from Tel Aviv to Jerusalem.

The situation in the West Bank is different. Palestinian lands in the West Bank are not contiguous, and for years Israel has been constructing a barrier that does not follow the 1947 border between the West Bank and Israel (Fig. 7.37). Instead, areas with significant Israeli settler populations in the West Bank are on Israel's side of the fence. The patchwork geography of Palestinian control in the West Bank means that movement of Palestinian people there can, and often is, restricted. In a particularly controversial move, a road constructed and controlled by Israelis, Route 4370, gives Jewish settlers in the West Bank easier access to Jerusalem than their Palestinian counterparts. Israeli officials argue that security concerns justify this approach, but it also helps to fuel Palestinian resentment.

The situation in Israel and Palestine today is not the product of a conflict along a simple interfaith boundary. The tiny region has a multitude of interfaith boundaries, especially in the West Bank (see **Fig. 7.44**), where the settlements have produced many miles of interfaith boundaries within a small political territory. The prospects for peace between Israel and Palestine are greatly complicated by the fact that each side feels it has a historic right to the land and by the violence inflicted on each side by the other.

Nigeria

Like other countries in West Africa, Nigeria is predominantly Muslim in the north and Christian and animist in the south. These groups converge in the middle part of the country in a region called the Middle Belt or North Central Zone, where Muslim, Christian, and animist communities now live side by side. With over 168 million people, Nigeria is Africa's most populous country. Since 1999, when the country emerged from years of military rule, Nigeria has witnessed persistent violence along the interfaith boundary between these communities, which has cost hundreds of thousands of lives.

As with many such conflicts, the causes of north–south violence in Nigeria cannot be attributed solely to different religious beliefs. Because of differences in climates, many people engage in cattle herding in northern Nigeria, whereas in the south, most rural peoples are farmers. As land has become scarcer, the fertile grasslands of central Nigeria have become coveted by both cattle herders and farmers. Land that was once reserved for grazing has been gradually replaced by agriculture, and violence against herders is often justified as retaliation for acts of trespassing on planted fields and crop destruction by cattle.

The north and south of Nigeria differ in other respects as well (**Fig. 7.45**). The rich oil economy and jobs tied to it are concentrated in the south. As a result, southern Nigeria has a higher per capita GDP and greater concentration of wealth than northern Nigeria. In addition, while northern Nigeria is dominated by the Hausa-Fulani ethnic group, the south is more diverse. Western-style education is more accepted in the south than in the north, and the south has higher female literacy rates. Finally, access to health care, as reflected in the percentage of 1-year-olds who have received all the basic vaccinations, is higher in the south than the north.

AP® Exam Taker's Tip

Nigeria provides rich examples for many AP Human Geography concepts and vocabulary. Nigeria straddles a major religious dividing line (Fig. 7.42), which has been the focus of many conflicts. Figure 7.45 provides more examples from Nigeria of human development and natural resources. Look for examples throughout the text to give you a background for answering an FRQ on the exam.

Since 2009, the worst violence in Nigeria has taken place in the northern half of the country, along the interfaith boundary and in the northeast, where the extremist Muslim group, Boko Haram, operates. Mohammed Yusuf began the organization in 2002 in Maiduguri, Nigeria, with the goal of pushing Western-style education out of northern Nigeria. The words *Boko Haram* roughly translate to "Western education is forbidden" in the Hausa language. Yusuf built an Islamic school, which drew mainly students from the Kanuri ethnic group, and then used the school to recruit members to Boko Haram. The group, like many other religious organizations in the north, received funding from local politicians seeking to disrupt elections in 2003 and 2007. As its support ran out, Boko Haram turned to other forms of criminality for funding, including bank robberies, extortion, and kidnapping for ransom.

As the influence of Boko Haram grew, state authorities sought to undermine it. In 2009, Nigerian police publicly executed the founder of Boko Haram on a street in Maiduguri. In response, members armed themselves, found a new leader, and turned increasingly to violence. At first, the group focused attacks on police and military as vengeance for the killing of its leader, but in 2012, Boko Haram began attacking schools. In 2014, northern Nigeria made global news when members

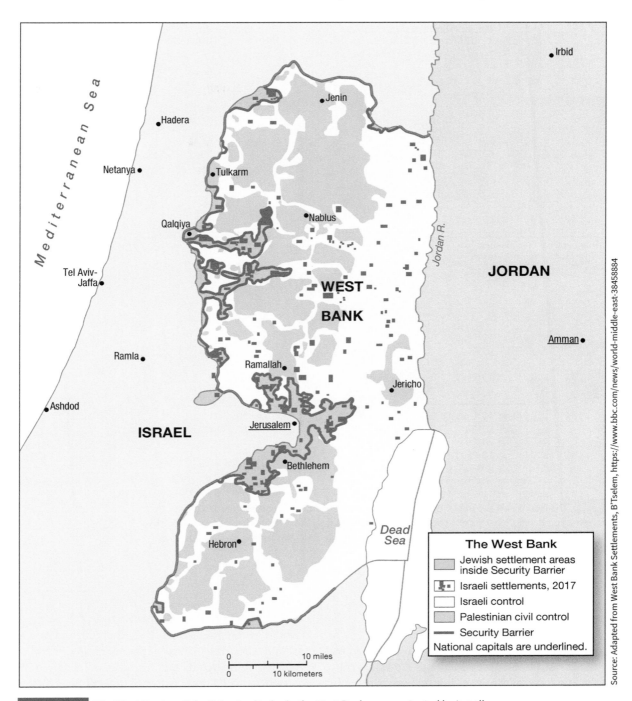

FIGURE 7.44 **The West Bank.** Palestinian territories in the West Bank are punctuated by Israeli settlements. The security fence surrounds the West Bank, and in several places it juts into the West Bank to separate Israeli settlements from Palestinian areas.

Source: Adapted from West Bank Settlements, B'Tselem, https://www.bbc.com/news/world-middle-east-38458884

of the terrorist organization kidnapped 250 teenage girls from their school in Chibok (**Fig. 7.46**).

In recent years, Boko Haram has aligned itself with the Islamic State in Iraq and Syria (ISIS) and has committed itself fully to overthrowing the Western-aligned Nigerian government in favor of a system based on fundamentalist Islam (Shari'a law). It has not succeeded; in 2019, Nigeria reelected Muhammadu Buhari, a moderate Fulani Muslim from the far north. Still, in the leadup to the presidential election, hundreds died as Boko Haram insisted that participating in the election amounted to apostasy.

The violence may have its roots in the struggle for access to land, political power, and resources, but religion has served as a key marker of difference. Violence along the interfaith Christian–Muslim boundary reinforces the perceptual importance of the boundary and promotes a sense—whether right or wrong—that religious differences represent the most important obstacle to social cohesion in Nigeria. And Nigeria is not the only northern African country experiencing violence along this interfaith boundary. Cote d'Ivoire (Ivory Coast), Sudan, and other countries face this problem as well.

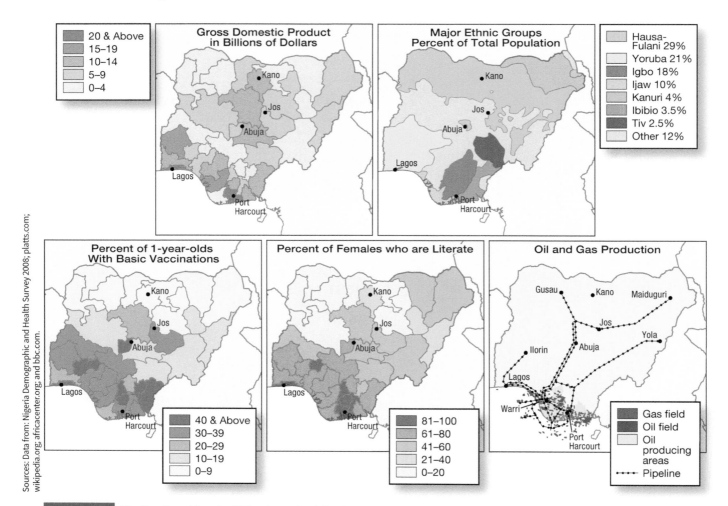

Sources: Data from: Nigeria Demographic and Health Survey 2008; platts.com; wikipedia.org; africacenter.org; and bbc.com.

FIGURE 7.45 **The North and South of Nigeria.** Nigeria's oil resources are concentrated in the south. Northern Nigeria has lower GPD per capita rates, lower levels of female literacy, and less access to health care than southern Nigeria. The extremist group Boko Haram has grown in the context of lower levels of wealth and female literacy in the north.

Northern Ireland

A number of western European countries, as well as Canada and the United States, have large Catholic and Protestant communities. Over the past century, the split between these two sects of Christianity has not been a source of violent confrontation. The most notable exception is Northern Ireland.

Northern Ireland and Great Britain (which includes England, Scotland, and Wales) form the United Kingdom of Great Britain and Northern Ireland (the UK). For centuries, the island of Ireland was free from outside control. It was divided into kingdoms and its people followed a mix of Celtic and Western Christian religious practices. As early as the 1200s, however, the English began to infiltrate Ireland. Colonization began in the sixteenth century, and by 1700 Britain controlled the entire island.

During the 1700s, Protestants from Great Britain (primarily Scotland) migrated to Ireland to take advantage of the political and economic power granted to them in the colony. During the 1800s, migrants were drawn principally to northeastern Ireland, where industrial jobs and opportunities were greatest and where the Irish colony produced industrial wealth for Britain in its shipyards. During the colonial period, the British treated the Irish Catholics harshly, taking away their lands and depriving them of their legal right to own property or participate in government.

In the late 1800s, the Irish began reviving older Celtic and Irish traditions, thus strengthening their identity. This led to ever greater resentment against the British, and in the early 1900s, a major rebellion began. The rebellion was successful throughout most of the island, which was predominantly Catholic, leading to the creation of the Republic of Ireland.

The conflict was settled in 1922. Britain retained control of six counties in the northeast, where significant concentrations of Protestant migrants from Britain lived. These counties constituted Northern Ireland, which became part of the United Kingdom. The substantial Catholic minority in Northern Ireland, however, did not want to be part of the

FIGURE 7.46 **Abuja, Nigeria.** Malala Yousafzai, a Pakistani who was attacked by the Taliban while on a school bus in her home country at the age of 15 in 2012, holds a picture of kidnapped schoolgirl Sarah Samuel with her mother Rebecca Samuel, during a visit to Abuja, Nigeria, Sunday July 13, 2014. Malala Yousafzai traveled to Abuja in Nigeria to meet the relatives of 250 schoolgirls who were kidnapped by Boko Haram in northern Nigeria.

United Kingdom (**Fig. 7.47**)—particularly since the Protestant majority, constituting about two-thirds of the total population (about 1.6 million) of Northern Ireland, possessed most of the economic and political power.

As time went on, economic stagnation for both populations worsened. The Catholics in particular felt they were being repressed. Terrorist acts by the Irish Republican Army (IRA), an organization dedicated to ending British control over all of Ireland by violent means if necessary, led to increased British military presence in the area in 1968. The Republic of Ireland was sensitive to the plight of Catholics in the north, but it was in no position to offer official help.

In the face of the worsening conflict—called the Troubles—Catholics and Protestants in Northern Ireland increasingly distanced their lives and homes from one another. The cultural landscape bears witness to the religious conflict, as each group clusters in its own neighborhoods and celebrates special Catholic or Protestant events. Irish geographer Frederick Boal wrote a groundbreaking work in 1969 on the Northern Irish in one area of Belfast. Boal used fieldwork to mark Catholic and Protestant neighborhoods on a map, and he interviewed over 400 Protestants and Catholics in their homes. Boal used the concept of **activity space** to demonstrate how Protestants and Catholics had each chosen to separate themselves as they went about their daily activities.

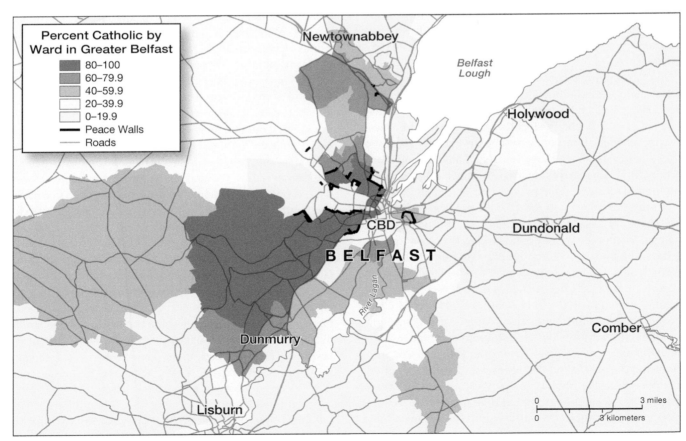

FIGURE 7.47 **Religious Affiliation and Peace Lines in Belfast, Northern Ireland.** Catholic neighborhoods are clustered west of the central business district (CBD) and west of the River Lagan. Protestant neighborhoods are separated from Catholic neighborhoods by Peace Walls in West Belfast.

Author Field Note   Listening to Laughter in Belfast, Northern Ireland

"I felt uneasy as I stood in the Clonnard Martyrs Memorial Garden. Built to honor Catholics who had fallen during the Troubles between Catholics and Protestants, the gardens were more of a brick patio with brick walls than a garden. A 40-foot-tall peace wall towered behind the gardens, and next to the garden stretching along the wall was a row of houses settled by Catholics. On the other side of the peace wall was the Protestant Shankhill neighborhood, where I had been 10 minutes earlier. My sense of unease came from a sound that I typically find comforting, a child laughing. I looked over the brick wall of the memorial gardens to see the child. It was a scene I could see in my backyard on a summer evening, a child jumping on a trampoline, but I did not see trees, grass, swing sets, barbeques, or the other familiarities of backyards in my neighborhood. The peace wall loomed behind the trampoline. The back side of the child's house was shielded by a rather large cage. I looked up at the wall again and realized the cage was there to protect the back door and windows from anything flung over the wall from the Protestant Shankhill neighborhood into the Catholic Falls neighborhood."

– E. H. Fouberg

Photo by E.H. Fouberg. © 2020 John Wiley & Sons, Inc.

FIGURE 7.48 **Belfast, Northern Ireland.**

Although religion is the tag line we use to describe the Troubles, the conflict has much more to do with nationalism, economics, oppression, access to opportunities, terror, civil rights, and political influence. Nonetheless, religion and religious history have long demarcated opposing sides; as such, churches and cathedrals have become symbols of strife rather than peace.

Belfast now has 99 peace lines, or peace walls, separating Catholic and Protestant neighborhoods (**Figure 7.48**). In the 1990s, Boal updated his study of Northern Ireland and found hope for a resolution in the fact that religious identities were actually becoming less intense among the younger generation and among the more educated. He found Catholics and Protestants intermixing in spaces such as downtown clubs, shopping centers, and college campuses.

As interaction increased, so did the political commitment to bring the Troubles to an end. In April 1998, the parties signed an Anglo-Irish peace agreement. The Good Friday Agreement (Belfast Agreement) raised hopes of a new period of peace in Northern Ireland. Those hopes have been realized in part. The two sides have made major strides toward reconciliation in recent years. Although the conflict remains unresolved, violent encounters are all but nonexistent. Moreover, mixing across Christian faiths is growing, though more commonly among the better educated and less segregated. Still, in a 2006 study, Madeleine Leonard found that teens who grew up in Catholic or Protestant neighborhoods rarely interacted with the "Other" and that "some children restricted their movements" to local neighborhoods. Moreover, Catholic and Protestant celebrations continue to generate tensions between the communities, and uncertainties about the status of the Ireland–Northern Ireland border in the wake of the United Kingdom's Brexit could open old wounds.

Conflicts in the Face of Migration

Religion can also provoke conflict when it is tied to a socially contentious migration stream. Europe is perhaps the best example of this phenomenon in today's world. So-called guest workers began arriving in Europe in the 1950s and 1960s—often at the invitation of European governments with high demands for workers. Most of the guest workers came from Southwest Asia and North Africa, and most were Muslims.

In its early stages, this migration was not controversial. In the 1970s, it became more contentious as migration continued apace while the European economy slipped into recession. Two things have happened to make the migration more contentious in recent decades: (1) Migration has grown significantly as instability, conflict, and economic hardship have gripped North Africa and Southwest Asia, and (2) Terrorist incidents with roots in that region have stoked fear among many Europeans.

Muslims who have migrated to Europe come from places with widely different customs, practices, and languages. Their faith hardly makes them all the same, but opponents of migration have tended to lump them together because of their affiliation with Islam. This tendency to group all migrants together has made religion a central symbolic feature of the conflict over migration. Anti-immigration extremists began speaking of an Islamic invasion. Even in more moderate circles, concerns were expressed about how recent migrants did not integrate into European societies, with Islamic practices trotted out as supporting evidence.

It was not just traditional Europeans who were lumping peoples of diverse backgrounds and beliefs under one religious label. Islamic extremists such as Osama bin Laden were doing the same thing—calling for all Muslims to put aside their differences and create a unified, powerful Islamic world.

Moreover, the rhetoric coming from some radical mosques in Europe encouraged an us-them way of thinking based on broad religious-cultural differences. Whatever its source, the growing presence of Islam in Europe has clearly been a source of conflict—with anti-Islamic pronouncements and harassment of Muslims found at one end of the spectrum, and calls for uprisings and even terrorist bombings at the other end.

As we saw in Chapter 3, migration can lead to social conflict without religion being a significant issue, as is the case with the migration stream from Mexico and Central America into the United States or of central Europeans into western Europe. The arrival of migrants in Europe from North Africa and Southwest Asia reminds us, however, that tensions can intensify when migrants of one religion move to a place where different religious traditions dominate. That tendency serves as clear evidence of the strong link between religion and cultural identity.

Religious Fundamentalism and Extremism

The drive toward **religious fundamentalism** often comes from a sense of powerlessness. Often people are frustrated over the perceived breakdown of society's morals and values and obstacles to economic advancement. There is a perceived loss of local control and a focus on the failure of governmental institutions. Regardless of the religion, members of fundamentalist groups then see their religious beliefs as nonnegotiable and beyond question.

People in one society often fear fundamentalism in other societies without recognizing it in their own. What many call fundamentalism is sometimes better defined as extremism. **Religious extremism** is fundamentalism carried to an (often violent) extreme. The attacks on the United States in September 2001 reinforced the tendency of some Americans to associate extremism with Islam. Yet Christian extremism is also a potent force. In the United States, religious zealots have killed physicians who perform legal abortions, and have detonate bombs, as Timothy McVeigh did in Oklahoma City in 1995. Although fundamentalists can be extremists, by no means are all fundamentalists extremists.

Today the forces of globalization affect religions. Education, radio, television, and travel spread ideas about individual liberties, sexual equality, and freedom of choice—but also consumerism and secularism. Some Christian churches have allowed women and members of the LGBTQ community to serve as religious leaders and same-sex partners to marry. Others have reaffirmed fundamental or literalist interpretations of religious texts and tried to block what they see as morally corrupting influences and external cultural interference.

Christian Fundamentalism   The Roman Catholic Church has long resisted innovations deemed incompatible with the fundamentals of the faith. Among the disputed issues are birth control and the role of women in the religious hierarchy. The major religions tend to be male-dominated, and few women have gained high positions. In the Roman Catholic Church, women are not allowed to serve as priests. The Roman Catholic Church has over 1 billion adherents and has a global diplomatic and political presence, influencing policies in numerous places and on many topics.

In the United States, a few branches of the Catholic Church continue to hold Mass in Latin and are much more fundamentalist than the rest of the church. Some of these branches are recognized parts of the Catholic Church, but others stand apart; they do not recognize the authority of the pope, nor does the Vatican sanction them. For example, actor and director Mel Gibson belongs to the Holy Family Church, which fits this description. Gibson's church is most closely associated with the Traditionalist Catholic Movement, a fundamentalist movement that believes that the Mass should still be conducted in Latin and that most modern religious leaders are not following the traditional theology and practices of the church.

In the United States, some branches of Protestantism are fundamentalist. Preaching a doctrine of strict adherence to the literal precepts of the Bible, many Protestant Christian fundamentalists believe that the entire character of contemporary society needs to be brought into alignment with biblical principles. Fundamentalist Protestant churches range from tiny churches to enormous warehouse-style churches with thousands of members (see Fig. 7.32).

Regardless of the size of the congregation, fundamentalist Protestant churches have become increasingly active in political and social affairs—promoting prayer in public schools, the teaching of creationism in science courses, and a strict ban on abortion. In the process, they have gained considerable influence, both in local politics (school boards and city councils) and at the national level (in think tanks and issue-focused research institutes).

Judaic Fundamentalism   Like all other major religions, Judaism has fundamentalist sects. The most conservative of the three major branches of Judaism is Orthodox, though Orthodoxy takes many forms. Indeed, Orthodox Jews embrace different schools of thought, and they have diverging views on Israel, education, and interaction with non-Orthodox Jews. More fundamentalist Orthodox Jews who have migrated to Israel tend to vote for more conservative candidates in Israeli elections, affecting election outcomes. Similarly, many of the more fundamentalist Jews in Europe or North America send money to politicians who support conservative Israeli policy positions.

Judaism also has its extremist elements—people whom the majority of Jews denounce and whom the government of Israel has even banned from the country. Among these are the two groups Kach and Kahane Chai—followers of the late American-born Israeli rabbi, Meir Kahane. Rabbi Kahane espoused anti-Arabism in his teachings, and his followers (Kahane Chai) continue to do so. Members of Kach and Kahane Chai are suspected in several terrorist acts in Israel.

Islamic Fundamentalism   The growth of a fundamentalist movement in Afghanistan (the Taliban) provided a particularly striking example of how quickly a fundamentalist movement can use extremism to change a place once it comes to power. The Taliban regime seized control of much of the country during the 1990s and asserted the strictest fundamentalist regime in the contemporary world. The leadership imposed a wide range of religious restrictions, sought to destroy all statues depicting human forms, required followers of Hinduism to wear identifying markers, and forbade women to appear in public with their head exposed.

The Taliban in Afghanistan also provided a haven for the activities of Islamic extremists who sought to promote an Islamic holy war, or **jihad**, against the West in general and the United States in particular. One of the key figures in the Islamic extremist movement of the past decade, Osama bin Laden, helped finance and mastermind a variety of terrorist activities conducted against the United States. These activities including the destruction of the World Trade Towers, the attack on the Pentagon, and the downing of Flight 93 on September 11, 2001.

Bin Laden is now dead, but those following in his footsteps are a product of a fundamentalist revolutionary Islamic movement that views the West as a great enemy and that opposes many of the changes associated with modernization and globalization. These beliefs are certainly not representative of Islam as a whole, but they are religious beliefs. Indeed, they can be traced to a form of Islam, known as Wahhabi Islam, that developed in the eighteenth century in opposition to what was seen as the sacrilegious practices of Ottoman rulers. Its champions called for a return to a pure variant of Islam from centuries earlier. The Saudi Arabian state is the hearth of Wahhabi Islam today. The Saudi royal family has championed Wahhabi Islam since the 1800s, and Saudis fund Wahhabi Islamic schools, called madrassas, around the world.

A variety of forces have fueled the violent path of the Wahhabi extremist movement, but some of these forces are decidedly geographic. Perhaps the most important is the widely held view among movement followers that "infidels" have invaded the Islamic holy land over the past 80 years. Islamic extremists are particularly concerned about the presence of American military and business interests in the Arabian Peninsula, the establishment of the state of Israel, and the support that European and American governments have given Israel. A principal goal is to bring an end to what are seen as improper external influences on the Islamic world. A second, geographically related, concern is the diffusion of modern culture and technology into the Islamic world and its impact on traditional lifestyles and spiritual practices. Ridding the Islamic world of such influences is thus a major goal.

Extremist Islamic fundamentalists have resorted to violence in pursuit of their cause. They are relatively small in number, however. Indeed, most Muslims in the Middle East oppose Islamic extremism. A 2014 Pew Research study found that a considerable majority of those surveyed in 14 Islamic countries have a negative opinion of al-Qaeda; most people surveyed in Pakistan oppose the Taliban; most Palestinians hold unfavorable views of Hezbollah and Hamas; and most Nigerians are concerned about Boko Haram.

TC Thinking Geographically

Jerusalem is a sacred **site** for 3 major religions: Judaism, Christianity, and Islam. Both Hinduism and Buddhism have sacred **sites** near the Ganges River in India. Hypothesize why some sacred sites are surrounded by political conflict and others are not. Study Figures 7.13 and 7.9 to look at **hearths**, paths of **diffusion**, and current locations of major religions to help you formulate your answer. Thinking about sacred sites, and pilgrimages, hypothesize why followers of some religions are in political conflict and others are not.

Summary

7.1 Describe the Nature of Religion and Its Cultural Significance.

1. Organized religion has a powerful effect on most human societies. It has been a major force in combating social ills, sustaining the poor, promoting the arts, educating the disadvantaged, and advancing medical knowledge. However, religion has also blocked scientific study, encouraged the oppression of parts of society, supported colonialism, and condemned women to inferior roles.

2. The cultural landscape is marked by religion—most obviously by churches, synagogues, temples, and mosques, and by cemeteries, shrines, statues, and religious symbols. More subtle landscape markers of religion exist as well, for example, the lack of stores selling alcoholic beverages in traditional Islamic areas.

7.2 Describe the Distribution of Major Religions and the Factors That Shaped Their Diffusion.

1. Universalizing religions actively seek converts because their belief systems are deemed to be appropriate for everyone (i.e., universal). Christianity, Islam, and Buddhism are all universalizing religions. Their universalizing character helps explain why they are the most widespread religions on Earth.

2. Ethnic religions tend to be more spatially concentrated because followers are born into the faith of a given group, and no efforts are made to convert others. Judaism is an exception because, even though it is an ethnic religion, its followers have scattered widely over the past two millennia as a result of forced and voluntary migrations.

3. Religions reflect and influence social arrangements. Hinduism is closely associated with India's caste system. Buddhism adopted

elements of traditional Asian philosophical perspectives. Christianity spread around the world as a result of European colonialism and imperialism.

4. In some places, secularism (indifference to or rejection of formal religion) has grown rapidly in recent decades. The most secular countries in the world today are found in Europe, but secularism is growing elsewhere, particularly in urbanized areas in countries with a high level of economic development.

7.3 Explain How Cultural Landscapes Reflects Religious Ideas and Practices.

1. Religion has a clear presence in the cultural landscape. Sacred sites are places or spaces to which people attach religious meaning. Jerusalem has sites that are sacred to Jews, Christians, and Muslims alike.

2. Each of the world's major religions has developed a distinctive architectural style and set of landscape practices associated with its belief system. Hindus and Buddhists build shrines and temples. Christians build churches. Muslims build mosques.

3. Christianity is the dominant religion in the United States, but there is significant diversity from region to region in the variant of Christianity that dominates. In recent decades, the United States has seen the growth of evangelicalism in some places and secularism in others.

7.4 Identify and Describe the Role Religion Plays in Political Conflicts.

1. Religious beliefs and histories can bitterly divide people. Significant conflicts exist at the borders between major religions (interfaith boundaries) and at the borders between variants of faiths (intrafaith boundaries).

2. Religion has played an important symbolic role in the Israeli-Palestinian conflict and the conflict between Protestants and Catholics in Northern Ireland. In both cases, however, the conflicts are less about religious beliefs than they are about the competing territorial agendas of ethno-nationalist groups.

3. Recent migration streams into Europe from Southwest Asia and North Africa have brought a substantial number of Muslims into Europe. Resulting tensions have often had a religious dimension.

4. In some places religious fundamentalism has led to a form of religious extremism that encourages followers to resort to violence. Terrorist attacks undertaken in the name of religious extremism have become increasingly common—in the process fueling tensions between societies in the name of religion.

Self-Test

7.1 Describe the nature of religion and its cultural significance.

1. Religions spread through:
   a. expansion diffusion.
   b. relocation diffusion.
   c. contagious diffusion.
   d. conquest.
   e. all of the above.

2. True or False: Religion played a major role in the historical development of culture, but aside from churches, temples, and synagogues, it has little impact on culture today.

3. Secularism has gained the most ground in:
   a. Europe.
   b. South America.
   c. sub-Saharan Africa.
   d. South Asia.
   e. East Asia

7.2 Describe the distribution of major religions and the factors that shaped their diffusion.

4. True or False: The hearth of each of the four major world religions is in the Eastern Hemisphere.

5. Which type of religion is most likely to diffuse over a wide area?
   a. an ethnic religion
   b. a universalizing religion
   c. an animistic religion
   d. a syncretic religion
   e. a folk religion

6. Theravada Buddhism is found principally in:
   a. South Asia.
   b. Southeast Asia.
   c. Mongolia and Tibet.
   d. eastern China and Japan.
   e. India

7. The term *diaspora* refers to:
   a. the spatial dispersion of members of an ethnic or religious group.
   b. the conversion of people to a particular religion.
   c. the ways in which religions change when they move into new areas.
   d. the religious hierarchy that tends to develop in ethnic religions.
   e. all of the above.

8. The country with the largest Muslim population in the world is:
   a. Saudi Arabia.
   b. Egypt.
   c. Afghanistan
   d. Pakistan.
   e. Indonesia.

7.3 Explain how cultural landscapes reflects religious ideas and practices.

9. Jerusalem has sites that are sacred to:

   a. Jews, Christians, and Muslims.

   b. Jews, Christians, and Hindus.

   c. Jews and Christians only.

   d. Jews and Muslims only.

   e. Jews only.

10. The practice of making pilgrimages to visit sacred sites is associated with:

    a. Christianity and Hinduism, but not Islam.

    b. Christianity and Islam, but not Hinduism.

    c. Hinduism and Islam, but not Christianity.

    d. Christianity, Islam, and Hinduism.

    e. Islam and Sikhism only.

11. A minaret is an architectural feature of:

    a. Hindu temples.

    b. Christian cathedrals

    c. Buddhist temples.

    d. Shinto shrines.

    e. Muslim mosques.

7.4 Identify and describe the role religion plays in political conflicts.

12. In _____, the most significant religious conflict is intrafaith (as opposed to interfaith).

    a. Israel/Palestine

    b. Nigeria

    c. Northern Ireland

    d. Cyprus

    e. None of the above.

13. True or False: In most cases of religious conflict, the central point of contention is not differences in religious practices. Instead, it is rooted in ethno-national differences and/or competition over access to political power and economic opportunity.

14. Migration is sometimes strongly associated with religious conflict. In which of the following examples is that not the case?

    a. migration from North Africa and Southwest Asia into Europe over the last 60 years

    b. migration from Europe into Israel after 1947

    c. migration from Mexico and Central America into the United States over the last 30 years

    d. migration from Great Britain into Northern Ireland during the eighteenth century

    e. internally displaced persons in Columbia.

CHAPTER 8

Political Geography

In December 2010, an anti-government movement began in Tunisia in North Africa when Tunisian street vendor Mohammed Bouazizi set himself on fire to protest police harassment and corruption. Tunisian rapper El Général's anthem "Rais Lebled" (see Chapter 4) became a protest song against corrupt dictators. As news of the revolution in Tunisia diffused, Libyans, Egyptians, and Syrians, among others, protested corrupt dictators. As winter turned to the spring of 2011, protests became so widespread and influential that commentators began speaking of the series of uprisings as the Arab Spring.

The uprisings of the Arab Spring had a larger impact on countries with authoritarian dictatorships than countries with absolute monarchies. Many of the monarchies in the Middle East have oil resources that they can use to invest in public resources like infrastructure, education, and hospitals. In 2010, just before the Arab Spring, I visited Oman and Egypt. The differences between how governments were using revenues was stark (**Fig. 8.1**).

Revolutions like the Arab Spring do not have the same impact in each country. In Tunisia, Libya, and Egypt, protesters toppled governments. In Oman and other Persian Gulf monarchies, governments stayed in place. Understanding how revolutions develop or fizzle out requires a deeper understanding of context.

In this chapter, we examine how geographers study politics. Political geographers study the spatial assumptions and structures underlying politics, the ways people organize space, and the role territory plays in politics.

FIGURE 8.1 **Cairo, Egypt, (top) and Muscat, Oman (bottom)** The Arab Spring is often presented as a backlash against authoritarian governments. But, authoritarian governments run by dictators, including Egypt (top photo), were more prone to protests in the Arab Spring than governments run by absolute monarchies, including Oman (bottom photo).

CHAPTER OUTLINE

8.1 Compare and contrast states, nations, and nation-states.
- The Birth of the Modern State Idea
- Nations, States, and Nation-States
- Multistate Nations, Multinational States, and State-less Nations
- European Colonialism and the Diffusion of the Nation-State Model

8.2 Determine how the modern political map evolved.
- Construction of the Capitalist World Economy
- Territory and Political Power in an Unequal World
- Internal Organization of States
- Electoral Geography

8.3 Explain the nature and significance of international boundaries.
- Establishing Boundaries Between States

- Types of Boundaries
- Boundary Disputes
- How the Significance of International Borders Is Changing

8.4 Explain classical and critical geopolitics.
- Classical Geopolitics
- Influence of Geopoliticians on Politics
- Critical Geopolitics
- Geopolitical World Orders
- Challenges to Traditional Political-Territorial
- Arrangements

8.5 Compare and contrast supranational organizations and states.
- From League of Nations to United Nations
- Regional Supranational Organizations

Compare and Contrast States, Nations, and Nation-States.

Political geography is the study of the political organization of the world. Political geographers study politically significant spaces at various scales: how they come into being and how they influence what happens. At the global scale, the most influential political spaces are individual countries, officially called states under international law. A **state** is a politically organized territory with a permanent population, a defined territory, and a government. To be a state, a politically organized area must be recognized as one by other states.

The present-day division of the world into states resulted from endless encounters between and among people and places. The political map of states is the most common cartographic representation of our world. That map hangs in the front of our classrooms, appears in our textbooks, and has become so normal looking to us that we begin to think it is natural.

Yet the world map of states is anything but natural. The map represents a way of politically organizing space that is only a few hundred years old. Just as people create places, shaping their landscapes and culture, people make states. States and state boundaries are constructed and refined by people, their ideas and actions, and their interactions.

Territory is central to states. The boundaries of states are the result of efforts to stake out territorial claims—of human **territoriality**. In a book published in 1986, geographer Robert Sack defined human territoriality as "the attempt by an individual or group to affect, influence, or control people, phenomena, and relationships, by delimiting and asserting control over a geographic area." Sack sees human territoriality as a key ingredient in the making of social and political spaces—including states. Human territoriality can take place at different scales, from the home and local to the state and global. The development and global diffusion of states as a way of organizing our world entrenched or institutionalized the idea of territoriality at the scale of the state.

The Birth of the Modern State Idea

The modern state idea can be traced back to seventeenth century Europe. Europeans were by no means the only ones who behaved territorially. For example, Native American tribes behaved territorially but not necessarily exclusively. Plains tribes shared hunting grounds with neighboring tribes that were friendly, and fought over hunting grounds with neighboring tribes that were unfriendly. Plains tribes also held territory communally, so that individual tribal members did not "own" land. In both Southeast Asia and Africa, state-like political entities existed and were used as a meaningful way to politically organize space. In all of these places, rulers had a say over people, but there was no collective agreement among political units in the Americas, Africa, Europe, and Asia about how territory would be organized or what rulers could do within their territory.

The emergence of the modern state idea began in western Europe at the end of the Middle Ages. In what is now the heart of England, France, and Spain, individual rulers gradually centralized power over former feudal domains. At the same time, increasingly independent cities emerged in northern Italy and at the northwestern edge of the European mainland. There, urban elites became prosperous enough through commerce and trade to free themselves from feudal obligations. Influential scholars and political figures called for a political order rooted in fixed political spaces governed by sovereign rulers. Those calls were inspired by ideas about property rights that developed in ancient Greece and Rome. The new political units helped develop what geographer Stuart Elden has called the modern concept of territory: a system of political units with fixed, distinct boundaries and at least quasi-independent governments.

The larger-scale political-territorial units that developed in western Europe coexisted with a complicated patchwork of state-like entities to the east and south. Political units included the Republic of Venice, Brandenburg, the Papal States of central Italy, the Kingdom of Hungary, and a large number of minor German states—many with poorly defined borders (**Fig. 8.2**). German territories were dragged into a decades-long conflict over religion in the early seventeenth century called the Thirty Years War. With no clear victor and all sides exhausted, they entered into a peace agreement that marks the formal beginning of the modern state system: the **Peace of Westphalia** (1648).

The treaties that were part of this peace put an end to Europe's internal struggle over how to define political space. The treaties recognized the rights of rulers within defined territories. The language of the treaties laid the foundations for a Europe made up of mutually recognized, exclusive, territorial states that at least claimed to respect one another's sovereignty. **Sovereignty** refers to a government's legal right to control its own territory, both politically and militarily. Sovereign states legally have the last say, over what happens in their territories. When the international community recognizes an area as a state, it also recognizes that it is officially sovereign and has the right to defend its **territorial integrity** when threatened by other states.

The rise of the Westphalian state system marked a major change in the relationship between people and territory. In previous eras, *where* a society lived constituted its territory. In the Westphalian system, the territory defined the society. Before Westphalia, French people defined the territory of France. After Westphalia, the territory of France defined who was French. Territory came to be seen as a fixed element of political identification, with states occupying exclusive, non-overlapping territories.

The Peace of Westphalia brought stability to Europe for a time, and it enhanced the power of rulers by giving a base for both colonialism and mercantilism. Through **colonialism**, states took over territories across the world and ruled them for their benefit. Through **mercantilism**, government controlled trade and colonies and protected home industries. Mercantilism and colonialism promoted rivalry and competition among European states.

During the later seventeenth and eighteenth centuries, an increasingly wealthy middle class developed in some places

FIGURE 8.2 **European Political Fragmentation in 1648.** At the time the treaty known as the Peace of Westphalia was agreed to in 1648, Europe was divided into a few larger territories and dozens of small principalities. With the treaty, territories and principalities became sovereign states.

through the income generated by mercantilism and colonialism. In some places, ruling class became more isolated and out of touch with their subjects. Both developments were the undoing of absolutism in parts of western Europe. City-based merchants gained money, influence, and prestige, while the power of the monarchy and the nobility were increasingly challenged.

In the late eighteenth century, upheavals began that changed the continent, most notably the French Revolution of 1789. The revolution brought a new era into being in which the foundations for political authority came to be seen as resting with a state's citizenry, not with a hereditary monarch.

Nations, States, and Nation-States

The popular media and press often use the words *nation*, *state*, and *country* interchangeably. Political geographers use *state* and *country* interchangeably (often preferring *state*), but they recognize that the word *nation* is distinct. *State* is a legal term in international law, and the international political community agrees a state is a political unit with a defined territory, a people, a government and recognition by other states. **Nation** refers to a group of people with a sense of cultural connection and a shared identity that is attached to a territory, but not necessarily to a state. A nation is a group of people with a shared past and common future who relate to each other and share a political goal. Nations can be groups of people, including the Kurds, the Palestinians, and indigenous peoples, who

share a common identity and political goals. Nations can also be constructed by governments who work to create nations out of all of the people living within a state's borders. For example, the government of France may want everyone in France to see themselves as part of the French nation.

AP® Exam Taker's Tip

A common mistake by geography students is not understanding that a state is a country and a nation is not a country. Remember, **state** = country and **nation** = group of people.

A nation is a group of people who see themselves as one based on a sense of shared culture and history. Different types of cultural communities could fit that definition. A nation could be knit together by a common religion, a shared language, or a collective sense of ethnic identity. One of the most widely read scholars on nationalism today, Benedict Anderson, defined the nation as an "**imagined community.**" It is imagined because one will never meet all of the people in the nation, and it is a community because individuals see themselves as part of the larger nation.

All nations are ultimately mixtures of different peoples. The French are often considered the classic example of a nation. However, the most French-feeling person in France today came from a melding together of many cultural groups over time: Celts, ancient Romans, Franks, Goths, and many more. If most inhabitants of modern France belong to the French nation, it is because during the formation of the French territorial state, the people came to think of themselves as French—not because the French nation existed as a distinctive group throughout history.

People in a *nation* tend to look to their past and think, "We have been through much together," and when they look to their future they often think, "Whatever happens, we will go through it together." It follows, then, that the term is an appropriate one when referring to groups such as the Kurds and Palestinians. But why is the term also used to refer to all peoples living within a given state? After all, rarely does a nation's geographical extent correspond precisely with state borders, and many countries have multiple nations within their borders. The answer lies in the growing influence of the nation-state idea.

The Nation-State Idea In the French Revolution of 1789 the French people overthrew the monarchy, drawing from and invigorating a sense of French national identity. The revolution promoted the idea that the people are the ultimate sovereign—that is, the people, the nation, have the final say over what happens within the state. Each nation, it was argued, should have its own sovereign territory.

The ideal of the nation, the people, being the sovereign led to a growing number of independence movements in Europe that were launched in the name of culturally defined nations. The Age of Nationalism brought unity within some long-established states, such as in France or Portugal. In other cases, nationalism became a rallying cry for creating states out of nations. Italy and Germany were both the product of nineteenth century unification movements that sought to bring together people who shared historical or cultural similarities. In yet other cases, people who saw themselves as separate nations within states or colonial empires launched successful separatist movements. Ireland, Norway, and Poland all serve as examples of successful separatist movements sparked by nationalism.

The common denominator was the **nation-state** idea— the idea that the map of states should align with the map of nations. The result was the emergence of a modern European political map that was less fragmented than its seventeenth-century counterpart (see Fig. 8.2). Of course, bringing that map of nation-states into being required ignoring complicated eth-nocultural distributions, incorporating smaller entities into larger states, and resolving conflicts by force as well as by negotiation. Not all states on the map were comprised of nations. Belgium and Switzerland, for example, have multiple identities tied to the languages spoken within their borders. States promoted nationalist feelings through education (e.g., developing a common curriculum for teaching national history), the use of national symbols (flags, patriotic songs, and writings), and the staging of political events championing the glories of the nation.

States also encourage people to identify with the dominant national ideal by providing security, infrastructure, and goods and services. Governments support education, health care, a civil service, and a military in the name of preserving the state. Some European states even used the colonization of Africa and Asia in the late 1800s and early 1900s as a way to promote nationalism. People could take pride in their nation's vast colonial empire. People could identify themselves with their nation, be it French, Dutch, or British, by contrasting themselves with the people in the colonies, whom they defined as mystical or savage. By defining themselves in relation to an "Other," the state and the people helped identify the supposed "traits" of their nation. In so doing, they reinforced the nation-state idea.

With time the sovereign nation-state was seen as the ultimate form of political-territorial organization for achieving stability. And given that Europe had carved up much of the rest of the world into colonies, the European political-territorial order became the template for the larger global system of states that emerged in the twentieth century (**Fig. 8.3**). No matter how complicated underlying cultural patterns might be in terms of religions, languages, or ethnicities, independence movements were mounted in the name of the people who lived in particular colonies (such as Burma, Indonesia, and Nigeria). And nation-building efforts in longer-standing countries were aimed at forging a sense of common national purpose.

To this day, major players in international relations seek solutions to complex political conflicts by trying to redraw the political map to bring political and national borders into closer correspondence. Faced with the disintegration of the former Yugoslavia or the complex problems of Israel/Palestine, for example, they propose new boundaries around nations, with the goal of making the nation and state fit one another in geographical space. Even when it is all but impossible to draw neat boundaries, alternative approaches are rarely considered (e.g., creating spaces of shared sovereignty). Instead, the European-derived nation-state idea has become so ingrained that few people even stop to think about what it means to treat *nation* and *state* as essentially synonymous terms.

The fundamental problem, of course, is that then the nation-state idea assumes there is, or can be, a world made up of reasonably well-defined, stable nations living together within separate and exclusive territorial states. Yet very few places come even close to fitting this model. Countries such as Iceland, Poland, and Japan come close, but they are the exception, not the rule. Moreover, efforts to create nation-states often lead to conflict and instability. Some states seek to define their nation around one ethnic group at the expense of others, with serious consequences for minority groups. Other states champion a single history and culture that they hope will be seen as a common denominator for all inhabitants, but that some do not embrace. The goal of these efforts is to suppress identities that might challenge a sense of nationalism. The world map of nations and the map of states are not the same. Few, if any, countries are nation-states, but the goal of creating nation-states fuels unity through nation-building and division through separatist movements.

Multistate Nations, Multinational States, and Stateless Nations

Despite the widespread use of the term *nation-state* to describe the territories that appear on a world political map, the underlying reality is much more complicated. Nearly every

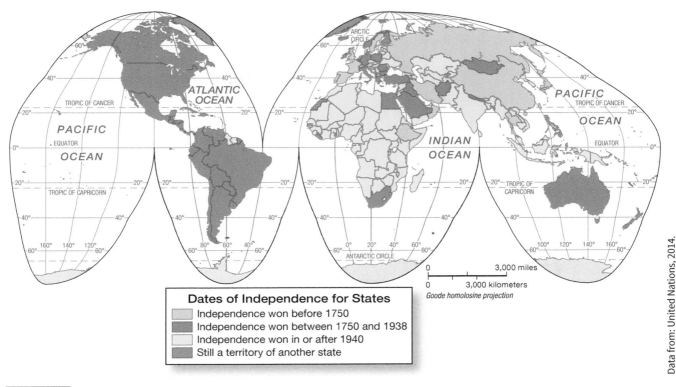

Dates of Independence for States

- Independence won before 1750
- Independence won between 1750 and 1938
- Independence won in or after 1940
- Still a territory of another state

Data from: United Nations, 2014.

FIGURE 8.3 **Dates of Independence for States.** States (countries) that became independent before 1938 are largely in the Americas, Europe, and Asia. States that won independence after 1940 are mainly in Africa and Asia.

state contains more than one nation. A nation of people may reside in more than one state, and many nations do not have a state at all (**Fig. 8.4**).

AP® Exam Taker's Tip

Learning the definition of **states, nations, nation-states, stateless nations, multinational states, multistate nations,** and **autonomous** and **semiautonomous regions** is important. But it is more important to be able to *change scales* as you work with these different terms. Figure 8.4 might help you better see the complexities when analyzing issues at the state scale and then changing to scales below the state level.

Nearly every state in the world is a **multinational state,** a state with more than one nation inside its borders. Millions of people who were citizens of Yugoslavia never had a Yugoslav national identity but instead identified themselves as Slovenes, Croats, Serbs, or members of other nations or ethnic groups. Yugoslavia was a state that comprised more than one nation, and it eventually collapsed.

When a nation with a state of its own also stretches across borders into other states, the nation is called a **multistate nation.** Political geographer George White studied the states of Romania and Hungary and their overlapping nations (**Fig. 8.5**). As he has noted, the territory of Transylvania is currently in the middle of the state of Romania, but it has not always been that way. For two centuries, Hungary's borders stretched far enough

east to encompass Transylvania. The Transylvanian region today is populated by Romanians and by Hungarians, and places within Transylvania are seen as pivotal to the histories of both Hungary and Romania. In keeping with the nation-state ideal, it is not surprising that both Romania and Hungary have interests in Transylvania, and some Hungarians continue to look upon the region as a territory that was wrongfully taken from them.

White explains how important territory is to a nation: "The control and maintenance of territory is as crucial as the control and maintenance of a national language, religion, or a particular way of life. Indeed, a language, religion or way of life is difficult to maintain without control over territory." In a world in which the nation-state is treated as the ideal, when multiple nations or states claim attachments to the same piece of territory, the potential for conflict is significant.

Another complication that arises from the lack of fit between nations and states is that some nations do not have a state; they are **stateless nations.** The Kurds are a stateless nation. They are a group of 25 to 35 million people living in an area called Kurdistan that covers parts of six states (**Fig. 8.6**). In the aftermath of the 1991 Gulf War, the United Nations established a Kurdish Security Zone north of the 36th parallel in Iraq, and that area continues to have significant autonomy in present-day Iraq.

Kurds in Iraq are joined by Kurds in Syria, Turkey, and Iran. The Kurds in northern Syria played a major role in the fight against ISIS, in the process garnering some international support for a Kurdish state. Kurds form the largest minority in Turkey, where Diyarbakir is the unofficial Kurdish capital of

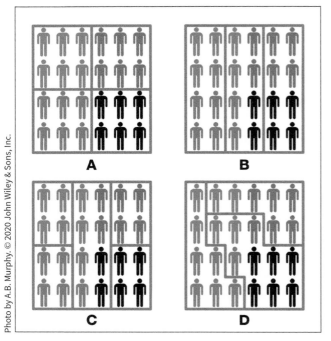

FIGURE 8.4 **Nation-States (A), Multinational States (B), Multistate Nations (C), and Stateless Nations (D).** In this figure, distinct nations are shown by different colors. In reality, nations are not neatly segregated, as this diagram suggests. But simplifying things is useful when trying to understand the different types of relationships that exist between the pattern of states and the pattern of nations. It is often said that we live in a world of nation-states, but something close to the pattern shown in the upper left (A) is found in very few places. Instead, B, C, and D are the norm.

Turkey. Relations between the 10 million Kurds in Turkey and the Turkish government in Ankara have been volatile. The Kurds in Iran live in a state that casts itself as the nation-state of the Iranian/Persian people; so, the Iranian government gives little recognition of the rights or political ambitions of Kurds and other national minorities.

European Colonialism and the Diffusion of the Nation-State Ideal

Europe exported its concepts of state, sovereignty, and the nation-state ideal to much of the rest of the world through two waves of **colonialism** (**Fig. 8.7**). In the sixteenth century, Spain and Portugal drew from a period of internal political stability to explore and eventually colonize the Americas. Britain, France, and the Netherlands joined the **first wave of colonialism**, which extended from South America through Central America and the Caribbean, North America, and the coasts of Africa. The world economy was based on agriculture, and colonizers established large scale plantation agriculture and the Atlantic slave trade to generate production of crops. Sugar was the most valuable commodity, and Europeans forcibly migrated millions of enslaved Africans to grow, harvest, and process sugar.

Independence movements in the Americas during the late 1700s and early 1800s brought an end to most formal colonialism in Central and South America, but by the late 1880s a second wave of colonialism was well under way. In the **second wave of colonialism**, the major colonizers were Britain, France, the Netherlands, Belgium, Germany, and Italy. The colonizing parties met for the Berlin Conference in 1884–1885 and arbitrarily divided Africa into colonies without

---

Guest Field Note Tracing Roots in Transylvania, Romania

George White
South Dakota State University

To Hungarians, Transylvania is significant because it was an important part of the Hungarian Kingdom for a thousand years. Many of their great leaders were born and buried there, and many of their great churches, colleges, and architectural achievements are located there too. For example, in the city of Cluj-Napoca (Kolozsvár in Hungarian) is St. Michael's Cathedral, and next to it is the statue of King Matthias, one of Hungary's greatest kings. Romanians have long lived in the territory too, tracing their roots back to the Roman Empire. To Romanian nationalists, the existence of Roman ruins in Transylvania is proof of their Roman ancestry and their right to govern Transylvania because their ancestors lived in Transylvania before those of the Hungarians. When archaeologists found Roman ruins around St. Michael's Cathedral and King Matthias's statue, they immediately began excavating them, which in turn aggravated the ethnic Hungarians. Traveling in Transylvania made me very aware of how important places are to peoples and how contested they can be.

© George White

FIGURE 8.5 **Cluj-Napoca, Romania.**

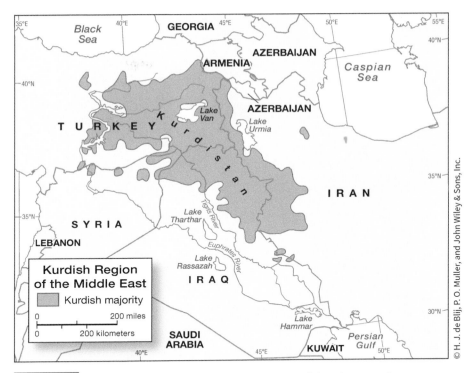

© H. J. de Blij; P. O. Muller, and John Wiley & Sons, Inc.

FIGURE 8.6 **Kurdish Region of the Middle East.** The Kurdish nation extends across several states in the Middle East, and because the Kurds do not have a state, they are considered a stateless nation.

reference to indigenous cultural patterns and political relationships. Driven by motives ranging from economic profit to national pride to the desire to bring Christianity to the rest of the world, colonialism projected European power and diffused a European approach to organizing political space across the world (**Fig. 8.8**).

AP® Exam Taker's Tip

Be able to provide at least three examples of stateless nations. Hint: Figure 8.6 provides your first example. Now, consider Native American tribal lands in the United States or Nunavut in Canada. Where do these two examples fit in this discussion?

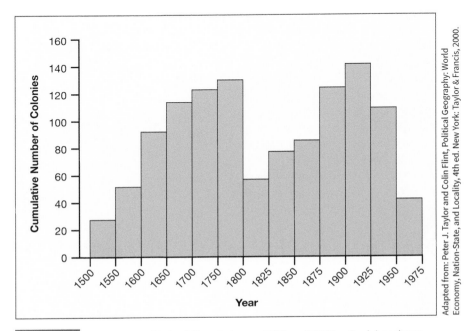

Adapted from: Peter J. Taylor and Colin Flint, Political Geography: World Economy, Nation-State, and Locality, 4th ed. New York: Taylor & Francis, 2000.

FIGURE 8.7 **Two Waves of Colonialism Between 1500 and 1975.** Each bar shows the total number of colonies around the world. When the total number drops from one period to the next, for example from 1800 to 1825, the drop reflects the number of colonies that became independent between those two dates.

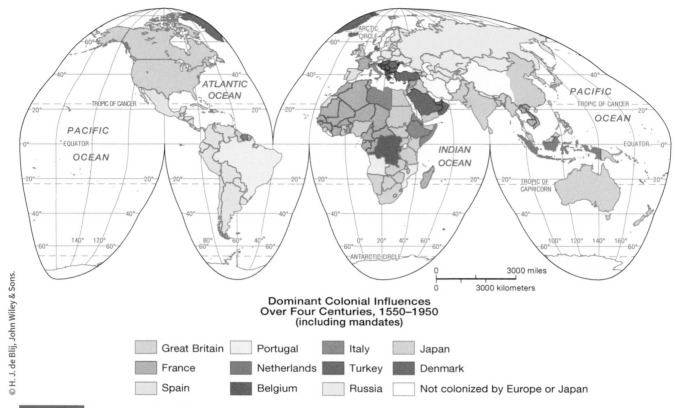

**Dominant Colonial Influences
Over Four Centuries, 1550–1950
(including mandates)**

Great Britain	Portugal	Italy	Japan
France	Netherlands	Turkey	Denmark
Spain	Belgium	Russia	Not colonized by Europe or Japan

FIGURE 8.8 **Dominant Colonial Influences, 1550–1950.** The map shows the dominant European or Japanese colonial influence in each country over four centuries.

During both waves of colonialism, colonizers often exercised ruthless control over the colonies and organized them for maximum economic exploitation. The ability to install the infrastructure necessary for such efficient profiteering is itself evidence of the structures of power involved. Colonizers organized the flows of raw materials for their own benefit. The tangible evidence of that organization (plantations, ports, mines, and railroads) is present in the cultural landscape to this day.

European colonialism is largely behind us, but Europeans laid the ground rules for the current international state system. Both the borders drawn around colonies and the exploitative economic systems established are still very much with us. Most of the former colonies are now independent states, but their economies are anything but independent. In many cases, raw material flows are as great as they were before the colonial era ended.

Today in Gabon, Africa, for example, the railroad goes from the interior forest, which is logged for plywood, to the major port and capital city, Libreville. Meanwhile, the second largest city, Port Gentil, is located to the south of Libreville and lacks transportation infrastructure to connect it with other parts of the country. Port Gentil is, however, tied to the global oil economy, with global oil corporations responsible for building much of the city and employing many of its people. The city is designed to extract and export oil. In fact, Port Gentil has no roads that connect it to Libreville.

TC **Thinking Geographically**

Imagine you are the leader of a newly independent **state** at the end of the second wave of colonialism. What can your government do to build a **nation** within your state? What roles do education, government, military, and cultural programs play in building a **nation-state**?

8.2 | Determine How the Modern Political Map Evolved.

States vary widely in size—from ones that extend across continents to small units that are no larger than cities. Some have extensive resources, while others do not. Some states have long coastlines, and others are landlocked.

Different state territorial characteristics can carry potential advantages and disadvantages; even the shape of a state can influence its potential. Thailand, for example, has struggled at times to integrate its far southern portion, which is connected to the central part of the state by a long, thin corridor. But it is important not to assume that state power and stability are simply functions of territorial size, resource endowment, or geographic situation. Switzerland is a small, landlocked state with limited resources. The Democratic Republic of the Congo is one of the largest states in Africa with many valuable resources and a territory that encompasses much of the water basin of Central Africa's most important river: the Congo. Yet by any measurement, Switzerland is the more globally influential, stable state.

When thinking about the relationship between territory and power, then, it is important not to focus solely on the characteristics of the units making up the world political map. Historical and geographical circumstances matter as well. Chief among these is the global economic order that developed through European colonialism, in which the European states and those areas dominated by European migrants emerged as the major centers of capitalism and political influence. Through colonialism, Europeans extracted wealth from colonies and put colonized peoples in a subservient position (see Fig. 12.2).

Of course, not all Europeans profited equally from colonialism, nor were European powers the only ones trying to expand their influence. Enormous poverty persisted within even the most powerful European states. Moreover, sustaining control over colonies was costly. In the late seventeenth century, the high cost of maintaining the large Spanish colonial empire took such a toll on Spain's economy that it lost control of its colonies in the Americas in the early nineteenth century. But the concentration of wealth that colonialism brought to Europe and to parts of the world dominated by European settlers, including the United States, Canada, and Australia, is at the heart of the highly uneven global distribution of power that continues today.

Construction of the Capitalist World Economy

Colonialism knit together the economies of widely separated areas, giving birth to a world economy. Wealth is unevenly distributed in the world economy, as can be seen in statistics on per capita gross national income (GNI): Bangladesh's GNI is only $1470, whereas Norway's GNI is $75990 (and the divide has increased in recent years). To understand why wealth is distributed unevenly, we cannot simply study each country, its resources, and its production of goods. Rather, we need to understand where countries fit in the larger global political-economic picture.

Think of the magnificent work of nineteenth-century French painter Georges Pierre Seurat, *Sunday Afternoon on the Island of La Grande Jatte* (**Fig. 8.9**). The pointillist painting hangs in the Art Institute of Chicago. If you stand close enough, you will see Seurat's post-Impressionist method of painting millions of points or dots—single, tiny brush strokes, each a single color. When you step back again, you can see how each dot fits into the picture as a whole.[1]

---

[1]We give credit to former student Kelsey Lynd, who came up with this metaphor for world-systems theory in a political geography class at the University of Mary Washington in 1999.

AP® Exam Taker's Tip

Read the text on page 233 comparing Seurat's pointillist painting in Figure 8.9 and world-systems theory. This is a great example of learning how to use scale by seeing the individual parts of the painting (or countries) as points/dots, sets of characters or scenery (or regions), and the whole painting (the global economy). Now, we might try to see this as the periphery, semiperiphery, and the core. Change scales yet again and understand that there are peripheries within a core and cores within the periphery! For example, wealthy countries like the United States also have very poor areas that function as economic peripheries and poor countries will have core areas within their boundaries.

In the last few decades, social scientists have sought to understand how each dot, how each country and each locality, fit into the picture of the world. If you focus on a single dot or even each dot one at a time, you miss the whole. Even if you study every single dot and add them together, you still miss the whole. You need to step back and see the whole, as well as the individual dots, studying how one affects the other. This is one of the ways geographers think about scale.

A concern with scale led some political geographers to take note of one sociologist's theory of the world economy and add much to it. Building on the work of Immanuel Wallerstein, proponents of **world-systems theory** view the world as much more than the sum total of the world's states. Much like a pointillist painting, world-systems theorists argue that to understand any state, we must also understand its position within the global economy.

Wallerstein's publications number in the hundreds, and the political and economic geography publications tied to world-systems theory number in the thousands. To simplify, there are three basic tenets of world-systems theory:

1. The world economy has one market and a global division of labor.

2. Although the world has multiple states, almost everything takes place within the context of the world economy.

3. The world economy has a three-tier structure (core, semi-periphery, and periphery).

FIGURE 8.9 Chicago, Illinois. Sunday Afternoon on the Island of La Grande Jatte, by Georges Pierre Seurat, hangs in the Art Institute of Chicago.

World History Archive/Alamy Stock Photo

According to Wallerstein, the development of a world economy began with the mercantilist activities of early modern European states. Mercantilism set the stage for the rise of an increasingly far-reaching capitalist economic order that encompassed the globe by 1900. **Capitalism** refers to a system in which individuals, corporations, and states own land and produce goods and services that are exchanged for profit. To generate a profit, producers seek the cheapest production and costs. For example, when labor (including salaries and benefits) became the most expensive component of production costs, corporations sought to move production from North Carolina to Mexico, and then to China and Southeast Asia to take advantage of lower cost labor.

In addition to taking advantage of the world labor supply, producers gain profit by commodifying whatever they can. **Commodification** is the process of placing a price on a good, service, or idea and then buying, selling, and trading that item. Companies create new products, generate new twists on old products, and create demand for the products through marketing. As children, neither of the authors of this book could have imagined buying a bottle of water. Now, the sale of water in bottles is commonplace.

When colonies became independent, gaining the legal status for sovereign states was relatively easy. The United Nations Charter even set up a committee to help colonies do so after World War II. But gaining true economic independence is all but impossible because the economies of the world are tied together, generating intended and unintended consequences that no one place can control.

Lastly, world-systems theorists see the world economy as a three-tiered structure comprising a core, a periphery, and a semiperiphery, based on how goods are produced. **Core** production methods include higher levels of education, higher salaries, and more technology—processes that generate wealth in the world economy. **Periphery** production methods incorporate lower levels of education, lower salaries, and less sophisticated technology—processes associated with a more marginal position in the world economy. But core and periphery do not exist independently of one another. Instead, their socioeconomic characteristics are shaped by their relationship to one another.

Figure 8.10 presents one way of dividing up the world in world-systems terms. The map designates some states as part of the **semiperiphery**—places where core and periphery processes are both occurring. The semiperiphery acts as a buffer between the core and periphery, preventing the polarization of the world into two extremes.

Political geographers, economic geographers, and other academics continue to debate world-systems theory. Detractors argue that it overemphasizes economic factors and does not fully account for how places move from one category to another. Nonetheless, Wallerstein's work has encouraged many to see the world political map as a system of interlinked parts that need to be understood in relation to one another and as a whole. Since the impact of world-systems theory has been considerable, geographers now often refer to the kinds of core–periphery distinctions suggested by world-systems theory.

Most obviously, world-systems theory helps explain how colonial powers were able to amass and sustain great concentrations of wealth. During the first wave of colonialism, colonizers extracted goods from the Americas and the Caribbean and exploited Africa for slave labor, amassing wealth through sugar, coffee, fruit, and cotton production. During that same period,

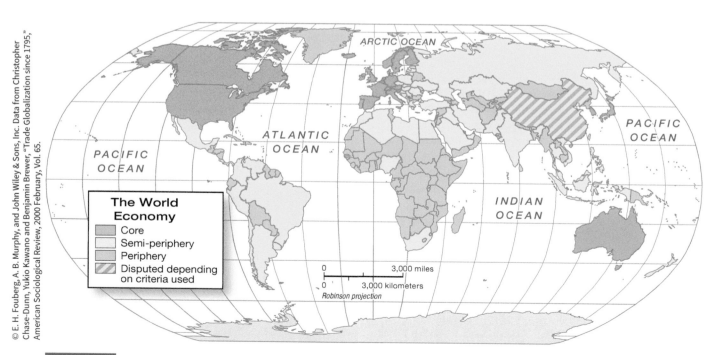

© E. H. Fouberg, A. B. Murphy, and John Wiley & Sons, Inc. Data from Christopher Chase-Dunn, Yukio Kawano and Benjamin Brewer, "Trade Globalization since 1795," American Sociological Review, 2000 February, Vol. 65.

FIGURE 8.10 **The World Economy.** One representation of core, periphery, and semiperiphery places North America, Europe, Japan, South Korea, and Australia in the core. China leans toward core in some ways and semiperiphery in others.

Russia expanded over land rather than overseas, profiting from the seizure of territory and the subjugation of indigenous peoples. The United States did the same in the late eighteenth and nineteenth centuries.

During the second wave of colonialism, which happened after the Industrial Revolution, colonizers set their sights on industrial labor, raw materials, and large-scale agricultural plantations. Their reach expanded inward in Africa, Southeast Asia, and elsewhere, creating an increasingly globalized world economy. Even countries such as China and Iran that were never formally colonized could not escape and were forced into signing unequal treaties giving concessions to European powers. And then Japan, inspired by the European example, developed its own colonial empire, ultimately controlling Korea and other parts of East and Southeast Asia as well as many Pacific islands until its defeat in World War II.

The result was a global system of structures of power characterized by extraordinary inequalities between core and periphery. Not all core countries in the world today were colonial powers, however. Countries such as Switzerland, Singapore, and Australia have substantial global influence even though they were never classic colonial powers. Their influence is tied either to their relationship with traditional colonial powers or their ability to tap into a global economy dominated by the core. They gained their core positions through access to networks of production, consumption, and exchange in the wealthiest parts of the world and through their ability to take advantage of that access.

Territory and Political Power in an Unequal World

Political power is not simply a function of sovereignty. Each state is theoretically sovereign, but not all states have the same ability to influence others or achieve their political goals. Economic power and political power are not necessarily one and the same, but economic power can bring political power. Having wealth helps leaders amass political power. For instance, a higher income country can establish a powerful military. But political influence is not simply a function of hard (military) power; it is also diplomatic. A country's economic might can aid its diplomatic efforts, which gives it greater political power.

World-systems theory helps us understand how colonizing powers politically reorganized the world. When colonialism ended in Africa and Asia, the newly independent states continued to follow the European model of politically organizing into states. The arbitrarily drawn colonial borders of Africa, dating from the Berlin Conference of 1884–1885, became the boundaries of the newly independent states. On the map, former colonies became new states and colonial administrative borders transformed into international boundaries. In most cases, colonial administrative towns became capitals. The greatest political challenge facing the states of Africa since independence has been building stable states out of incredibly diverse (sometimes antagonistic) peoples.

Internal Organization of States

Territory's influence on power is not solely a function of a state's position in the world economy. How states organize the territory within their boundaries matters as well. In the 1950s, political geographer Richard Hartshorne described the forces within a state that encourage unity as **centripetal** and the forces that divide them as **centrifugal**. Whether a state thrives, according to Hartshorne, depends on the balance between centripetal and centrifugal forces.

Many political geographers have debated Hartshorne's theory, and most have concluded that we cannot select a given circumstance and simply define it as centrifugal or centripetal. A war with an outside power can pull a state together for a short time and then divide the state over the long term. Timing, scale, interaction, and perspective factor into unification and division at any given point, as does a state's position in the world economy. Whatever their circumstances, governments attempt to unify states by structuring themselves to encourage buy-in across the territory, by defining and defending boundaries, and by exerting control over all of the territory within those boundaries.

Focusing attention on how different governments have tried to unify peoples and territories within their domains reminds us of how important geography is. Governance does not take place in a vacuum. The particular spatial strategies pursued by governments interact with the characteristics of places to solve or worsen problems.

Unitary and Federal States   Until the mid-twentieth century, most states were highly centralized, with the capital city serving as the focus of power. Few states sought to accommodate minorities (such as Bretons in France or Basques in Spain) or outlying regions where identification with the state was weaker. Political geographers call these highly centralized states **unitary** states. Their administrative framework is designed to ensure the central government's authority over all parts of the state. The French government divided the state into more than 90 départements, but their representatives came to Paris not just to express regional concerns but also to implement central government decisions back home.

One way of governing a state with significant ethnocultural differences is to construct a federal system. This divides the territory into regions, substates, provinces, or cantons that exercise significant control over their own affairs. In a strong federal system, the regions or states have substantial authority over such matters as education, land use, and infrastructure planning. In the United States, for example, there are significant differences from state to state in the approach to such matters as penalties for crimes, property taxes, access to alcohol (**Fig. 8.11**), and the right to carry concealed weapons.

AP® Exam Taker's Tip

Given your knowledge of the definitions of **unitary** and **federal** states, which type of state (unitary or federal) is likely to be larger with regard to territory? Explain why this is so.

Paul T. Gray, Jr.
Russellville High School

In most states in the United States, a "dry county" might cause one to think of a place where there is very little rain. But in the South, there are many dry counties—counties with laws forbidding the sale of packaged alcohol. In the late 1800s and early 1900s, keeping counties dry was much easier than it is today. A hundred years ago, it took up a to a day to travel to the next town or city on very poor roads. Today, with cars traveling 70 mph on an interstate, the same trip takes a matter of minutes. Why would counties continue to ban alcohol sales today? Many of the reasons are cultural. Of the Arkansas residents who attend church, most are Baptists or other Protestant denominations. Many of these churches prohibit consumption of alcoholic beverages. The Arkansas legislature supports dry counties by requiring counties that want to sell packaged liquor to get 38 percent of the voters in the last election to sign a petition. It only takes 10 percent of that voter pool to get any other issue on the ballot. Today, however, many dry counties in Arkansas are known as "damp." Damp counties are those where restaurants, country clubs, and social organizations can apply and receive a license to serve alcohol by the drink. This arrangement seems

FIGURE 8.11 **Blackwell, Arkansas.**

counterintuitive to the idea of a dry county. But business and economic development authorities want damp counties to encourage investment and growth in the local economy.

Giving control over certain policy areas (especially cultural policies) to smaller-scale governments is one strategy for keeping the state as a whole together. Federalism functions differently depending on the context, however. In Nigeria, each of the 36 states chooses its own judicial system. In the Muslim north, 12 states have Shari'a laws (legal systems based on traditional Islamic laws), whereas in the Christian and animist south, Shari'a law plays no role (**Fig. 8.12**). Shari'a law in the northern states of Nigeria is only applied to Muslims, not to Christians and animists. The move to Shari'a law in the north came at the same time as democracy swept Nigeria in 2000. Nigerians in the north hoped that

stricter laws would help root out corruption among politicians, although they have failed to do so. Supporters of the Shari'a tradition also cite the need to curb rampant crime, prostitution, and gambling.

Some northerners seek to expand Shari'a law to other states. That idea is a motivating force for the Islamic fundamentalist group Boko Haram, which uses violence in an effort to overthrow the existing government and bring into being an Islamic state. The movement has used bombings, assassinations, and abductions to advance its agenda. The Nigerian government has declared a state of emergency in the country's northeast and has devoted significant resources to fighting the militant group, but with limited success. Many Nigerians, in the north as well as the south, oppose Boko Haram's tactics, but chronic poverty, widespread corruption, and north-south tensions play into the organization's hands.

Federalism accommodates regional interests by vesting primary power in substate units over all matters except those explicitly given to the central government. The Australian geographer K. W. Robinson described a federation as "the most geographically expressive of all political systems, based as it is on the existence and accommodation of regional differences… federation does not create unity out of diversity; rather, it enables the two to coexist."

Choosing a federal system does not always quell nationalist sentiment. After all, the multinational states of the Soviet Union, Yugoslavia, and Czechoslovakia fell apart, despite their federalist systems, and the future of states such as Belgium and Iraq is in some doubt.

Source: Data from Legit, Sharia law in Nigerian constitution.

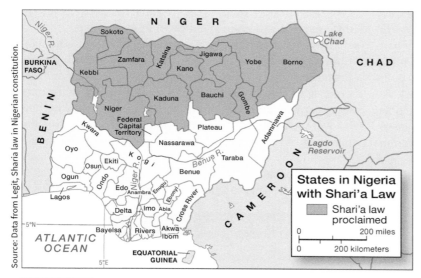

FIGURE 8.12 **States in Nigeria with Shari'a Law** Only Muslims in the northern states of Nigeria are subject to Shari'a law.

Devolution   Devolution is the transfer of power "downwards" from the central government to regional governments within a state. Sometimes devolution happens when a constitution is revised to establish a federal system that recognizes the status of the regional governments, as Spain has done. In other places, governments devolve power without altering constitutions. A parliamentary body in the United Kingdom, the Northern Ireland Assembly, was the product of devolution. Devolutionary forces can emerge in all kinds of states, old and young, large and small. These forces arise from several sources of internal division: ethnocultural, economic, and territorial.

Many of Europe's devolutionary pressures are the result of groups within states seeing themselves as ethnically, linguistically, or religiously distinct from the majority, and identifying as a nation (**Fig. 8.13**). In some cases, state governments keep these pressures under control devolving power to the regions. The goal of devolving power to nationalist regions led the United Kingdom in 1997 to grant Scotland the right to establish its own parliament, a body that had last met in 1707. The 129 members of the modern Scottish Parliament swear allegiance to the Queen of England, but they dictate how a variety of issues in Scotland are handled today, including education, health, housing, and police. Devolution was

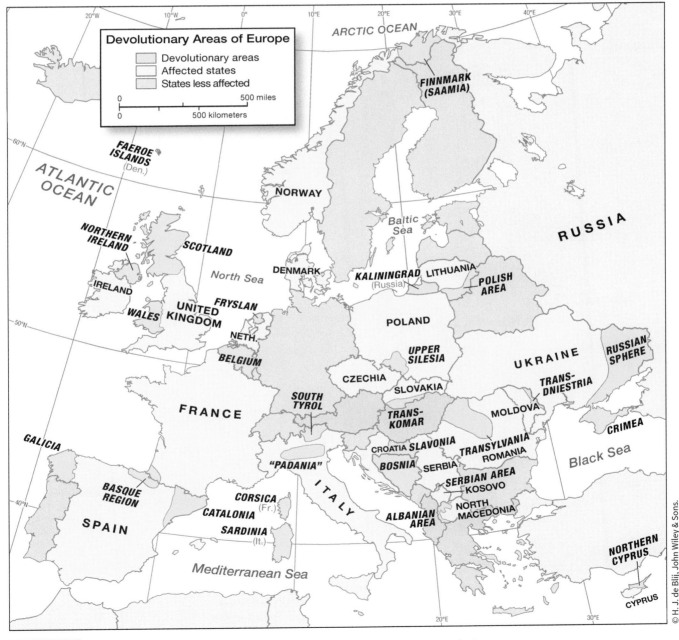

FIGURE 8.13   Europe: Foci of Devolutionary Pressures, 2019.   Devolutionary movements in Europe are found where a nation with a shared history has the political goal of greater autonomy, unification with the rest of their nation, or independence.

not enough to head off a referendum on independence in September 2014 (ultimately unsuccessful), but devolution makes it more difficult for the champions of independence to argue that independence is the only way that Scotland can gain control over its own affairs. Parliaments were also established in Wales and Northern Ireland in the late 1990s, but their powers are more limited.

In two eastern European cases, devolutionary pressure has led to the disintegration of states: Yugoslavia and Czechoslovakia. Division in Yugoslavia led to a civil war that tore the country apart in the early 1990s. In Czechoslovakia, disintegration occurred without significant violence: Czechs and Slovaks agreed to divide their country, creating a new international boundary in 1992. As **Figure 8.14** shows, however, one of the two new states, Slovakia, is not homogeneous. About 11 percent of Slovakians are Hungarian, and that minority is concentrated along the border between Slovakia and Hungary. The Hungarian minority, concerned about linguistic and cultural discrimination, has at times demanded greater autonomy to protect its heritage.

Source: Adapted from George Hoffma, ed., Europe in the 1990s: A Geographical Analysis, 6th rev. ed., p.551

FIGURE 8.14 Ethnicities in Eastern Europe.   The ethnic groups in this map are largely based on language. The presence of Russians in Ukraine, Belarus, and Latvia is a result of the policy of Russification, where Russians were moved throughout the region to help spread the Russian culture and establish a Soviet national identity based on Russian culture. The central part of Romania, where there is a concentration of Hungarians, is Transylvania, a land important to both Hungarians and Romanians.

Elsewhere, devolutionary pressures associated with ethnocultural differences have produced devastating wars. Sri Lanka (South Asia) is a prime example, where conflict raged from the 1980s to 2009 between the Sinhalese (Buddhist) majority and the Tamil (Hindu) minority, which sought an independent state. The Sinhalese ultimately prevailed, but at an incredible cost in human life.

Devolutionary forces based on ethnocultural claims are gaining ground in places that have long looked stable from the outside. The central government of China has pragmatically, and often relatively successfully, integrated 56 ethnic nations into the state of China. China has acknowledged the precarious place of the minority nations within the larger Han-dominated state by extending rights to minorities, including the right to have two children during the period when the one-child policy was in effect.

Some nations within China continue to challenge the state, however. In China's far west, Tibetan and Uyghur separatist movements have become more visible, but the Chinese government's firm control on its territory has increased over time. Through heavy policing, the encouragement of in-migration by Han Chinese, and economic incentives, the Chinese have sought to suppress these movements. They nonetheless persist, and China's increasingly extreme measures against them have spurred reactions among locals and attracted growing international attention.

Regional economic inequalities often play a role in the development of devolutionary movements. In Catalonia, a region of Spain with a large population that sees itself as ethnoculturally distinct, the Catalan language is different from Spanish, and much of the region's historical development differed from that of the rest of Spain. Catalonia constitutes 8 percent of Spain's territory and just 16 percent of its population, yet it produces some 35 percent of all Spanish exports by value and 54 percent of its high-tech exports. What is more, nearly 70 percent of all Spanish exports pass through the region (**Fig. 8.15**). Pro-independence groups in Catalonia held a referendum in October 2017 seeking a vote for independence. The vote passed, but the Spanish central government did not endorse either the referendum or the result (many did not vote). Instead, the government dissolved the Catalan parliament and charged leaders of the separatist movement with a host of crimes, from misappropriation of funds to rebellion. For now, Catalonia remains part of Spain, but the devolutionary forces continue to frustrate efforts of the central government to maintain the territorial integrity of Spain.

Economic forces have also played into devolutionary pressures in Italy. Demands for autonomy for Sardinia are rooted in the island's economic circumstances, with accusations of neglect by the government in Rome high on the list of grievances. Italy also faces serious devolutionary pressures on its mainland peninsula because of north–south differences. The Mezzogiorno region lies to the south, below sthe Ancona Line (an imaginary border extending from Rome to the Adriatic coast at Ancona). The higher income north

contrasts with the lower income south. Despite the large subsidies granted to the Mezzogiorno, the development gap between the north, part of the European core, and the south, part of the European periphery, has been widening. Some Italian politicians have exploited widespread impatience with the situation by forming organizations to promote northern interests, including devolution. One of these organizations, the Northern League, has raised the prospect of an independent state called Padania in the northern part of Italy centered on the Po River. After a surge of enthusiasm, the Padania campaign faltered, but it pushed the Italian government to focus more attention on regional inequalities.

Brazil also exemplifies the interconnections between devolutionary movements and economics. As in northern Italy, a separatist movement emerged in the 1990s in a better-off

Photo by A.B. Murphy. © 2020 John Wiley & Sons, Inc.

FIGURE 8.15 **Barcelona, Spain.** Barcelona's long-standing economic and political significance is indelibly imprinted in the urban landscape. Once the heart of a far-flung Mediterranean empire, Barcelona went on to become a center of commerce and banking as the Iberian Peninsula industrialized. In the process, the city became a center of architectural innovation where major streets are lined with impressive buildings—many with intricate stone façades.

Author Field Note   Waving the Flag for Devolution in Honolulu, Hawai'i

"As I drove along a main road through a Honolulu suburb, I noticed that numerous houses had the Hawai'i state flag flying upside down. I knocked on the door of this house and asked the home-owner why he was treating the state flag this way. He invited me in and we talked for more than an hour. 'This is 1993,' he said, 'and we native Hawai'ians are letting the state government and the country know that we haven't forgotten the annexation by the United States of our kingdom. I don't accept it, and we want our territory to plant our flag and keep the traditions alive. Why don't you drive past the royal palace, and you'll see that we mean it.' He was right. The Iolani Palace, where the Hawai'ians' last monarch, Queen Lil-iuokalani, reigned until she was deposed by a group of American businessmen in 1893, was draped in black for all of Honolulu to see. Here was devolutionary stress on American soil."

– H. J. de Blij

© H. J. de Blij

FIGURE 8.16 **Honolulu, Hawai'i.**

region in the south that includes the three southernmost states of Rio Grande do Sul, Santa Catarina, and Parana. Southerners complained that the government was misspending their tax money on assistance to Amazonia in northern and interior Brazil. The southerners found a leader, manufactured a flag, and demanded independence for their Republic of the Pampas. The Brazilian government outlawed the separatists' political party, but the economic differences between north and south continue, and devolution pressures will certainly arise again.

Devolutionary events have at least one feature in common: They most often occur on the margins of states. Most of the devolution-affected areas shown in Figure 8.13 are on a coast or on a border. Distance, remoteness, and marginal location frequently strengthen devolutionary tendencies. The regions most likely to seek devolution are those far from the national capital. Many are separated from the center of power and adjoin neighbors that may support separatist objectives.

Many islands are subject to devolutionary processes: Corsica (France), Sardinia (Italy), Taiwan (China), Hong Kong (China), Zanzibar (Tanzania), Jolo (Philippines), Puerto Rico (United States), Mayotte (Comoros), and East Timor (Indonesia) are notable examples. Some of these islands became independent states. Not surprisingly, the United States faces its most serious devolutionary pressures on the islands of Hawai'i (**Fig. 8.16**). The year 1993 marked the hundred-year anniversary of the United States' annexation of Hawai'i. In that year, a vocal minority of native Hawai'ians and their sympathizers demanded the return of rights lost during the "occupation." These demands included the right to reestablish an independent state called Hawai'i (before its annexation Hawai'i was a Polynesian kingdom) on several of the smaller islands. Their hope is that ultimately the island of Kauai, or at least a significant part of that island, which is considered ancestral land, will become a component of the

independent Hawai'ian state. At present, the native Hawai'ian separatists do not have the numbers, resources, or influence to achieve their aims. The potential for some form of separation between Hawai'i and the mainland United States does, however, exist.

Electoral Geography

Another important aspect of the internal political geography of states is the division of state territory into electoral districts. Electoral geographers examine how and where these electoral districts emerge and then consider how the voting patterns in particular elections reflect and influence social and political affairs. Various countries use different voting systems to elect their governments, with impacts on who is represented and who is not. For example, in the 1994 South African election, government leaders introduced a system of majority rule while awarding some power to each of nine newly formed regions. The overall effect was to protect, to some extent, the rights of minorities in those regions.

The geographic study of voting behavior is especially interesting because it helps us assess whether people's voting tendencies are influenced by their geographic situation. Maps of voting patterns often produce surprises that can be explained by other maps, and geographic information systems (GIS) have raised districting analysis to new levels. Political geographers study church affiliation, income level, ethnic background, education attainment, and numerous other social and economic factors to learn why voters in a certain region might vote the way they do.

Electoral geographers can have the most influence in the drawing of electoral districts. In a **democracy** where representatives are elected by district, the spatial organization of electoral districts determines whose voice is heard in a given place.

For example, the United States Constitution establishes a system of territorial representation. In the Senate, each major territorial unit (state) gets two representatives. The 435 members of the House of Representatives are elected from territorially defined districts that have similar-sized populations.

The Constitution requires a Census every 10 years in order to reapportion the House of Representatives. **Reapportionment** is the process by which districts are changed according to population shifts. For example, after the 2010 Census, several states in the so-called Rust Belt, including Pennsylvania, Ohio, and Michigan, lost representatives as a result of population decline (each district is supposed to encompass approximately the same number of people). Because of the same Census, the Sun Belt states of Georgia, South Carolina, and Florida, along with the southwestern states of Arizona, Nevada, and Utah (all of which gained population), gained representatives.

In the United States, once reapportionment numbers are established, individual states go through the process of territorial redistricting, with each state following its own rules. The criteria involved in territorial redistricting are numerous, but the most important is equal representation. To achieve that end, districts are supposed to have approximately the same populations. In addition, the Supreme Court has established a preference for compact, contiguous districts that keep political units (such as counties) intact. Finally, the courts have repeatedly called for representational equality of racial and linguistic groups.

Even after the U.S. civil rights movement of the 1950s and 1960s, minorities were denied voting rights in some places. County registrars would close their doors when African Americans came to register to vote, and intimidation kept many away from voting. Even where minorities were allowed to register and vote, it was nearly impossible for the election of a minority to occur. The parties drawing the voting districts or choosing the electoral system purposefully chose systems to disadvantage minorities. For example, if a government has to draw 10 districts in a state that is 60 percent white, 30 percent African American, and 10 percent Hispanic, it can easily weaken the impact of minority voters by **splitting** them among multiple districts, ensuring that the white population holds the majority in each district.

In 1982, the United States Congress amended the 1965 Voting Rights Act by outlawing districts that result in weakened minority voting power. In a series of decisions, the courts interpreted this amendment to mean that states needed to redistrict in a way that would ensure minority representation. This criterion was used in the redistricting that followed the 1990 Census. As a result, states increased the number of **majority–minority districts** in the House of Representatives from 27 to 52. Majority–minority districts are packed districts in which a majority of the population is from the minority. In the hypothetical state described before, a redistricting following this criterion could have the goal of creating at least three majority–minority districts and a fourth where minorities had a sizable enough population to influence the outcome of the election.

Ideally, majority–minority districts would be compact and contiguous and follow existing political units. Political geographers Jonathan Leib and Gerald Webster have researched the court cases that have resulted from trying to balance these often-conflicting criteria. To include minorities who do not live compactly and contiguously, states have drawn bizarrely shaped districts. These sometimes connect minority populations with meandering corridors or follow major highways to connect urban areas that have large minority populations (**Fig. 8.17**).

Strange-looking districts constructed to attain certain political ends are nothing new in American politics. In 1812, Governor Elbridge Gerry of Massachusetts signed into law a district designed to give an advantage to his party—a district that looked so odd to artist Gilbert Stuart that he drew it with a head, wings, and claws. Stuart called it the "salamander district," but a colleague immortalized it by naming it a gerrymander (after the governor). Ever since, the term **gerrymandering** has been used to describe "redistricting for advantage." Many of the districts now on the United States electoral map may be seen as gerrymanders. However, some provide representation to minorities who, without it, would not be represented as effectively in the House of Representatives. Despite this well-intentioned goal, others argue that the packing of minorities into majority–minority districts simply concentrates minority votes, creating a countrywide government that is less responsive to minority concerns.

The larger point is that the spatial organization of voting districts is a fundamentally geographical phenomenon, and it can have profound impacts on who is represented and who is not—as well as on peoples' sense of fairness. Recognition of these issues grew after the highly partisan approach to redistricting took place in some states after the 2010 Census. In states ranging from North Carolina to Texas, state legislatures drew new electoral district maps that clearly favored the party in power (the Republicans in those two places). This led to a number of legal challenges (a few extreme examples were struck down by the courts) and a growing movement to place the redistricting process in the hands of independent, nonpartisan bodies. The map of electoral districts can greatly influence political outcomes, and so the drawing of electoral districts will almost certainly be a continuing source of tension.

TC **Thinking Geographically**

Choose an example of a devolutionary movement. Look at the territory claimed by the movement and find evidence of how it serves as a functional **region** currently. Study the culture of the people in the territory and determine how their group **identity** is formed and how it is different from others'. Finally, thinking at the **scale** of the country in which the territory is located, predict what circumstances may lead to this territory seceding and becoming its own state.

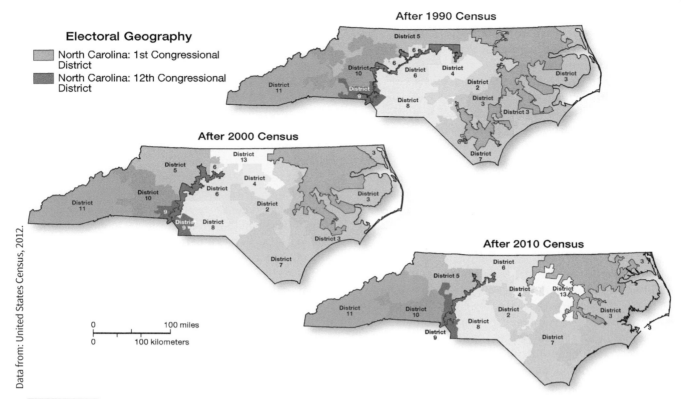

Electoral Geography
- North Carolina: 1st Congressional District
- North Carolina: 12th Congressional District

Data from: United States Census, 2012.

FIGURE 8.17 **Electoral Geography.** North Carolina's congressional districts in 1992, 2002, and 2012. In 1992, North Carolina concentrated minorities into majority–minority districts. In 2002, North Carolina made its districts more compact and explained they were based on criteria other than race, in accordance with Supreme Court decisions during the 1990s. Using the same criteria, North Carolina redistricted again after the 2010 Census, shaping districts that once again prioritized concentrating minorities while trying to achieve compactness and contiguity.

8.3 Explain the Nature and Significance of International Boundaries.

The territories of individual states are separated by international boundaries, referred to as borders when crossing them. Boundaries may appear on maps as straight lines, or they may twist and turn to conform to rivers, hills, and valleys. But a **boundary** is more than a line on the ground. The lines are actually markers of a vertical plane that cuts through the rocks below (the subsoil) and the airspace above, dividing one state from another (**Fig. 8.18**). Only where the vertical plane intersects Earth's surface (on land or at sea) does it form the line we see on the ground.

Many boundaries were established on the world map before the extent or significance of subsoil resources was known. As a result, coal seams and aquifers cross boundaries, and oil and gas reserves are split between states. Europe's main coal reserves extend from Belgium underneath the Netherlands and on into the Ruhr area of Germany. Soon after mining began in the mid-nineteenth century, these three neighbors began to accuse each other of mining coal that did not lie directly below their own national territories. The underground surveys available at the time were too inaccurate to pinpoint the ownership of each coal seam.

During the 1950s and 1960s, Germany and the Netherlands argued over a gas reserve that lies in the subsoil across their boundary. The Germans claimed that the Dutch were withdrawing so much natural gas that the gas was flowing from beneath German land to the Dutch side of the boundary. They wanted compensation for the gas they felt they lost.

As another example, a major issue between Iraq and Kuwait, which in part led to Iraq's invasion of Kuwait in 1990, was the oil in the Rumaylah reserve that lies underneath the desert and crosses the border between the two states. The Iraqis asserted that the Kuwaitis were drilling too many wells and draining the reserve too quickly, as well as drilling oblique boreholes to penetrate the vertical plane extending downward along the boundary. At the time the Iraq–Kuwait boundary was established, however, no one knew that this giant oil reserve lay in the subsoil or that it would contribute to an international crisis (**Fig. 8.19**).

Above the ground, too, the interpretation of boundaries as vertical planes has serious implications. A state's "airspace" is defined by the atmosphere above its land area as marked by its boundaries. But how high does the airspace extend? Most states insist on controlling the airline traffic over their territories, but states do not yet control the paths of satellite orbits.

Establishing Boundaries Between States

States typically *define* their boundaries in a treaty-like legal document in which actual points in the landscape or points of latitude and longitude are described. Cartographers *delimit* the boundary on maps. If either or both of the states so desire, they can *demarcate* where the boundary exists by using steel posts, concrete pillars, fences, or walls.

By no means are all boundaries on the world map demarcated. Demarcating a lengthy boundary is expensive, and it is hardly worth the effort in high mountains, vast deserts, frigid polar lands, or other places with few permanent settlements. Demarcating boundaries is part of state efforts to determine how the borders will be maintained and which goods and people may cross them. But how a border is administered can change dramatically over time (**Fig. 8.20**).

AP® Exam Taker's Tip

Define, **delimit**, and **demarcate** are the steps that establish a boundary. But the contesting or disputing of boundaries is what causes many regional conflicts. Explain the issues behind the Jammu and Kashmir boundary dispute. Explain at least three other boundary disputes in the world.

Types of Boundaries

Boundaries come into being in a variety of ways. When boundaries are drawn using grid systems such as latitude and longitude or township and range, they are called **geometric boundaries**. The United States and Canada used a single line of latitude west of the Great Lakes to define their boundary. During the 1884–1885 Berlin Conference, colonial powers used arbitrary reference points and drew straight lines to establish the boundaries in much of Africa.

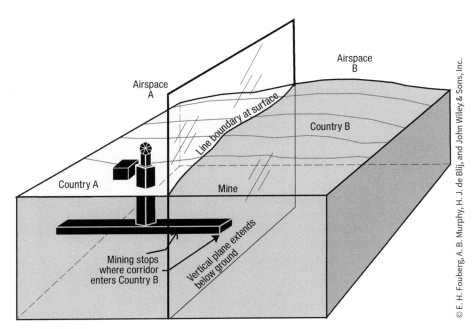

FIGURE 8.18 **The Vertical Plane of an International Boundary.** Boundaries between states divide territory at the surface, below the surface, and in the airspace above the surface.

© E. H. Fouberg, A. B. Murphy, H. J. de Blij, and John Wiley & Sons, Inc.

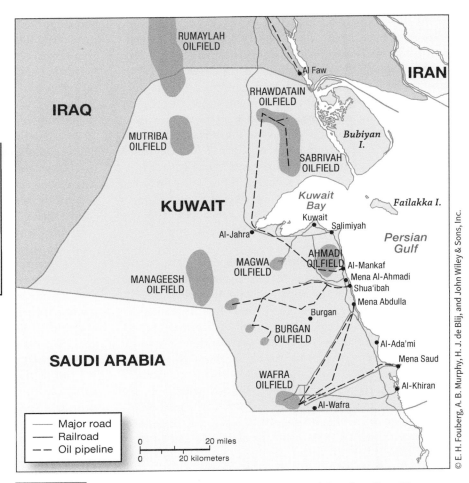

FIGURE 8.19 **The International Boundary Between Iraq and Kuwait.** Kuwait's northern boundary was defined and delimited by a United Nations boundary commission; it was demarcated by a series of concrete pillars 1.24 miles (2 km) apart.

© E. H. Fouberg, A. B. Murphy, H. J. de Blij, and John Wiley & Sons, Inc.

Author Field Note   Stradling the Border between Italy and Slovenia

"Seeing the border between Italy and Slovenia marked by a plaque on the ground reminded me of crossing this border with my family as a teenager. The year was 1973, and after waiting in a long line, we finally reached the place where we showed our passports to the authorities. They asked us many questions and they looked through the luggage in our trunk. Now that Slovenia is part of the European Union and has signed the Schengen Accord eliminating border controls between countries, crossing that same border today is literally like a walk in the park."

– A. B. Murphy

Photo by A.B. Murphy. © 2020 John Wiley & Sons, Inc.

FIGURE 8.20 **Piazza della Transalpina.**

At different times, political geographers and other academics have advocated natural boundaries over geometric boundaries because they are visible as physical geographic features. **Physical-political boundaries** (also called natural-political boundaries) follow an agreed-upon feature in the natural landscape, such as the center point of a river or the crest of a mountain range. The Rio Grande is an important physical-political boundary between the United States and Mexico. Another physical-political boundary follows the crest lines of the Pyrenees separating Spain and France. Lakes sometimes serve as boundaries as well; four of the five Great Lakes of North America are boundaries between the United States and Canada, and several of the Great Lakes of East Africa are boundaries between the Democratic Republic of the Congo and its eastern neighbors.

Physical features sometimes make convenient political boundaries, but topographic features are not static. Rivers change course, volcanoes erupt, and mountains slowly erode. People perceive physical-political boundaries as stable, but many states have entered into territorial conflicts over borders based on physical features that change over time. Moreover, physical boundaries do not necessarily stop the flow of people or goods across boundaries, leading some states to reinforce physical boundaries with human-built obstacles (e.g., the United States on the Rio Grande). The stability of boundaries has as much or more to do with historical and geographical circumstances than with the character of the boundary itself.

Maritime Boundaries
Boundaries do not exist solely on land; for coastal states, they also extend outward into the sea or ocean. Before World War II, there was wide acceptance that states should have sovereign control over a zone extending three nautical miles outward from their coastlines.[2] In the post–World War II era, however, states began demanding larger zones of control—at least over the resources (mostly fish) that lay farther away from their coastline, if not over all activities taking place in those zones.

In the face of growing uncertainty and threats of conflict, the United Nations organized a set of conferences that, by the early 1980s, led to the adoption of a third United Nations Convention on the Law of the Seas (UNCLOS) that came into force in 1994. UNCLOS establishes basic principles that are reflected in zones with varying levels of state control **(Fig. 8.21)**. (1) States have complete sovereign control over *territorial seas* that extend out 12 nautical miles (NM) from their coastlines. (2) States have the right to control fiscal transactions, immigration, and sanitation in the *contiguous zone* that extends an additional 12 NM beyond their territorial seas. (3) States have control over all resources found in the *exclusive economic zone (EEZ)* that extend out 200 NM from their coastlines. (4) States have complete control over resources found in their continental shelves, which are defined by distance instead of by geology. (5) *International waters*, which are considered the common heritage of humankind, to be used by all, start at the end of the EEZs and include vast areas of oceans.

Not all countries signed UNCLOS (the United States did not), but its basic principles are widely accepted as part of international law. States often disagree over what counts as a coastline and who owns islands because a state's EEZ starts at the end of its coastline and can also extend around each island. Claiming an EEZ can be quite valuable when there are vast fish resources. States also disagree over maritime boundaries between them, which creates overlapping state claims to territorial seas,

[2]1 nautical mile = 1.15 mile.

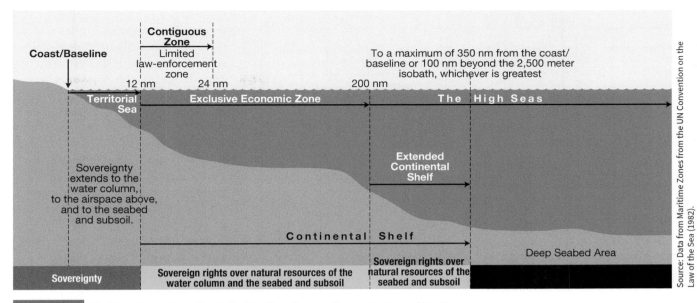

Source: Data from Maritime Zones from the UN Convention on the Law of the Sea (1982).

FIGURE 8.21 **Maritime Zones from the United Nations Convention on the Law of the Sea (UNCLOS).** The relationship among territorial sea, contiguous zone, and exclusive economic zone are clear on this graphic that marks each of them as well as the continental shelf.

contiguous zones, and EEZs. Where any of the zones overlap with the zones of another state or states, UNCLOS calls for boundaries to lie at midpoints between the coastlines of affected states.

The Spratly Islands in the South China Sea are hotly contested. Several countries, including China, Vietnam, the Philippines, Taiwan, Malaysia, and Brunei, have EEZs that come together in the middle of the South China Sea, where the Spratly Islands sit. The South China Sea is valuable because it holds 10 percent of the world's fish resources and billions of barrels of oil. Also, much of the world's shipping travels through the South China Sea.

The Spratly Islands are mostly uninhabited, but by claiming the islands, a country can claim the territorial seas, contiguous zones, and EEZs around them, thus creating disputes with the EEZs of the surrounding countries (**Fig. 8.22**). China claims a large area of the South China Sea based on an historical claim called the nine dash line, which extends from Hainan, China around the Spratly Islands. Vietnam, the Philippines, Taiwan, Malaysia, and Brunei also claim islands in the Spratlys. China has built up at least seven islands that were under the surface to establish above-surface islands and claimed them. They have also established seaports and airbases on the islands, and have recently installed coastal defense missile systems on the Spratlys.

AP® Exam Taker's Tip

States make claims of **sovereignty** over adjacent seas. Some states are making claims of **maritime** areas that are not adjacent to that state. Most of these claims are over resources. But some are about **national identity** and future influence of that area. Use Figure 8.22 and explain China's claims to the Spratly Islands. Do China's claims match the **United Nations Law of the Sea** rules? Explain.

Boundary Disputes

Clashes over maritime boundaries are just one example of boundary disputes. A boundary line on a map is the product of complex legal steps that begin with a written description of the boundary. Sometimes that legal description is old and imprecise. Some land boundaries imposed by a stronger power produced a long-standing grievance in a neighboring country. In other cases, the geography of the borderland has changed; the river that marked the boundary changed course, or a portion of it was cut off. Resources lying across a boundary can also lead to conflict. In short, states often argue about both their land and maritime boundaries.

Boundary disputes take four principal forms: definitional, locational, operational, and allocational.

- *Definitional boundary disputes* focus on the legal language of the boundary agreement. A boundary definition may stipulate that the median line of a river will mark the boundary. That would seem clear enough, but the water levels of rivers vary. If the valley is asymmetrical, the median line will move back and forth between low-water and high-water stages of the stream. This may involve hundreds of meters of movement—not very much, but enough to cause serious argument, especially if there are resources in the river. The solution is to refine the definition to suit both parties.

- *Locational boundary disputes* center on differences over where the boundary should actually be placed. The definition is not in dispute, but its fairness or implementation is contested. Disputes reflect different views over the criteria or process that led to the demarcation, or how much the boundary conforms to specified criteria. In a few instances, locational disputes arise because no

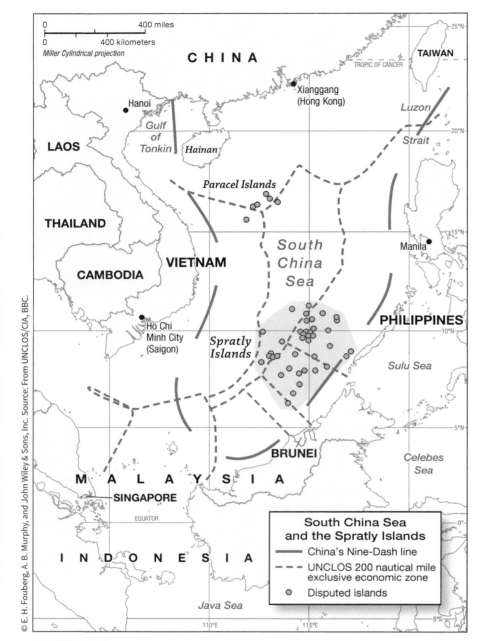

FIGURE 8.22 **South China Sea and the Spratly Islands.** The EEZs of several countries meet in the middle of the South China Sea. Countries that claim ownership of the Spratly Islands, including China and Vietnam, the Philippines, Taiwan, Malaysia, and Brunei, also claim maritime zones around the islands, which then overlap with the EEZs of the countries surrounding the South China Sea. The nine dash line in red on this map is China's claim to the South China Sea.

- *Operational boundary disputes* involve neighboring states that differ over the way their border should function. When two adjoining countries agree on how cross-border migration should be controlled, the border functions satisfactorily. However, if one state wants to limit migration while the other does not, a dispute may arise. Similarly, efforts to prevent smuggling across borders sometimes lead to operational disputes—especially when one state's efforts are not matched (or are possibly even sabotaged) by its neighbor. And in areas where nomadic ways of life still prevail, the movement of people and their livestock across international borders can lead to conflict.

- *Allocational boundary disputes* are the kind of disputes described earlier between the Netherlands and Germany over natural gas or Iraq and Kuwait over oil. Today many such disputes involve international boundaries at sea. Oil reserves under the seafloor below coastal waters sometimes lie where exact boundary delimitation is subject to debate. Disputes can also arise over water supplies: The Tigris, Nile, Colorado, and other rivers are subject to such disputes. When a river crosses an international boundary, the rights of the upstream and downstream users of the river often come into conflict.

Beyond these categories, some boundary conflicts are simply the product of the raw exercise of brute force by a powerful country. A case in point is the Russian annexation of Crimea in 2014. Crimea has been part of Ukraine since 1954, when the Soviet Union transferred it from the Russian Republic to the Ukrainian Republic. Crimea's population is predominantly Russian, but for more than half a century, it was universally understood to be part of Ukraine, and Russia had signed agreements guaranteeing Ukraine's territorial integrity. Nonetheless, under the pretext of protecting the Russian population in Crimea, Russia forceably annexed the territory in 2014. The annexation was condemned as a violation of international law by world leaders around the globe and Russia was suspended from the Group of Eight (G8; now the G7), a powerful inter-governmental political forum. Russia is fully in control of Crimea, but its control its deeply contested not just by Ukraine, but by most other countries—a status reflected in our maps, which show it as contested territory.

definition of the boundary exists at all. That was long the case for the Saudi Arabia–Yemen boundary—an oil-rich boundary area. That boundary was finally demarcated in 2000, but the demarcation was not accepted by all parties and violence persists. Locational boundary disputes are also common in the maritime arena, and with sea levels on the rise, such disputes may well intensify in the face of increasingly dramatic, and contestable, shoreline changes (the baselines from which zones of control are measured).

How the Significance of International Borders Is Changing

The world political map is neatly divided into around 200 states separated by clear, distinct lines. The reality is much more complex—and not just because many of these lines are contested. Globalization and the cybercommunication revolution have changed the role of borders. Moreover, the movement of people and goods globally challenges the strength of borders.

States have responded to these pressures in different ways. One response is to build walls or fences and increase policing around borders. But border fortification has also extended far beyond the lines shown on the world political map. For example, the European Union sends ships into the Mediterranean and along the northwest coast of Africa to reduce the flow of undocumented immigrants and illicit goods into Europe. The United States' Immigration and Customs Enforcement agency (ICE) seeks to enforce immigration laws in towns and cities that are located far from the border. ICE was founded after September 11, 2001, and is entirely distinct from the United States Border Patrol.

The previous examples help explain why political geographers no longer focus only on the lines on maps. Instead, they look at the broader range of borders and border activities and study how different border arrangements reflect and shape human geographic patterns, whether they lie along the border or far from it.

In the face of globalization and the cybercommunications revolution, borders are increasingly losing their ability to constrain economic activities and social interactions. This raises fundamental questions, including whether the territorial state will continue to be the basic building block of the political map. The future is uncertain, but concerns about states' loss of control over their territories have led some governments to view borders as important lines of defense, not just against unwanted people and goods, but also against the in-flow of unwanted information and ideas.

For example, crossing the border from Hong Kong to mainland China does not simply involve showing your passport and paying customs duties on nonexempt goods. On the Hong Kong side of the border, you can access Gmail, read the *New York Times* online, and look at Facebook. As soon as you step into mainland China, however, none of these are available. Of course, some Chinese use virtual private networks to get around Internet restrictions, but the Chinese government has moved quickly to shut many of these down. And China is not alone. As **Figure 8.23** shows, many countries place restrictions on the Internet, particularly in parts of Asia and the Middle East.

States are also anxious to protect their own ideas and innovations. To do that, they develop and seek to enforce *intellectual property* (IP) laws and try to combat IP theft beyond their borders. They also restrict the export of domestic technologies

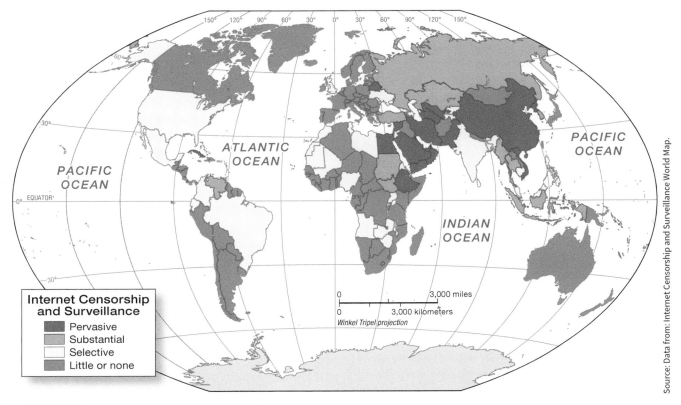

Source: Data from: Internet Censorship and Surveillance World Map.

FIGURE 8.23 **Internet Censorship and Surveillance.** The number of countries placing restrictions on Internet access has grown in recent years, but the effectiveness of these restrictions varies widely from country to country.

and research ideas that might compromise national security or give other countries an unfair advantage in an economically competitive sector. These examples remind us that borders are about more than dividing one governmental system from another and restricting the free movement of people and goods. They also influence how information and ideas move around and what people do or do not know about the world around them.

TC **Thinking Geographically**

Find a recent news story on the Spratly Islands and explain what China is doing to strengthen their claims to them (see Fig. 8.22). Using Figure 8.21, explain how territorial seas and EEZs operate as functional **regions**. Hypothesize how the **mental maps** of the South China Sea for Chinese, Philippine, and Vietnamese leaders differ and how their varying perceptions of the region may lead to conflict.

8.4 Explain Classical and Critical Geopolitics.

Geopolitics is concerned with how geographical circumstances influence international relations and the distribution of power. It focuses on the impact of location, environment, territorial arrangements, and influential geographical ideas on foreign affairs.

Classical Geopolitics

Classical geopolitics began in the late nineteenth and early twentieth centuries—a time of heightened state nationalism and interstate competition. Geopoliticians generally fit into one of two camps: the German school or the British/American school. The *German school* sought to explain why and how certain states became powerful. The *British/American school* sought to offer political advice by identifying places and regions that were particularly strategic for maintaining and projecting power. A few geopoliticians tried blending the two schools, but most classical geopoliticians today are in the British/American school. They offer geostrategic perspectives on the world.

The German School Why are certain states powerful, and how do states become powerful? The first political geographer who studied these issues was the German professor Friedrich Ratzel (1844–1904). Influenced by the writings of Charles Darwin, Ratzel postulated that the state resembles a biological organism whose life cycle extends from birth through maturity and, ultimately, decline and death. To prolong its existence, the state requires nourishment, just as an organism needs food. Such nourishment is provided by acquiring territories that provide adequate space for the members of the state's dominant nation to prosper. Ratzel called this *Lebensraum*—literally life space. If a state is confined within permanent and static boundaries and deprived of overseas domains, Ratzel argued, it can become weak. Territory is thus seen as the state's essential, life-giving force.

Ratzel based his theory on observations of states in the nineteenth century, including the United States. It was so speculative that it might have been forgotten if some of Ratzel's German followers in the 1930s had not resurfaced his abstract

writings. These were turned into policy recommendations that ultimately were used to justify Nazi expansionism.

The British/American School Not long after the publication of Ratzel's initial ideas, other geographers began looking at the overall organization of power in the world. They began studying the physical geographic map with a view toward determining the locations of the most strategic places on Earth. Prominent among them was the Oxford University geographer Sir Halford J. Mackinder (1861–1947). In 1904 he published an article titled "The Geographical Pivot of History" in the Royal Geographical Society's *Geographical Journal*. That article became one of the most intensely debated geographic publications of all time.

In the nineteenth century, Britain built a global empire through its domination of the seas. To many of Mackinder's contemporaries, the oceans—the paths to colonies and trade—were the key to continued British primacy, but Mackinder disagreed. He concluded that a land-based power, not a sea power, would ultimately rule the world. He assessed the largest and most populous landmass: Eurasia (Europe and Asia together). At the heart of Eurasia lay a hard-to-attack, resource-rich "Pivot Area" extending from eastern Europe to eastern Siberia (**Fig. 8.24**). Mackinder argued that if this Pivot Area became unified, a great empire could be formed.

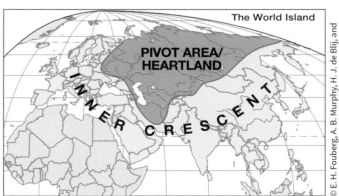

FIGURE 8.24 **The Heartland Theory.** The Pivot Area/Heartland, the Inner Crescent/Rimland, and the World Island, following the descriptions of Halford Mackinder.

Mackinder later renamed his Pivot Area the Heartland. In his book *Democratic Ideals and Reality* (1919), Mackinder (calling Eurasia "the World Island") summarized his theory as follows:

> Who rules East Europe commands the Heartland
> Who rules the Heartland commands the World Island
> Who rules the World Island commands the World

When Mackinder proposed his **heartland theory**, there was little to foretell the rise of a superpower in the heartland. Russia was largely a poor peasant society, having recently lost a war against Japan (1905), and was facing revolution. Eastern Europe was fractured. Germany, not Russia, was gaining power. But when the Soviet Union emerged and Moscow came to control much of eastern Europe by the middle of the twentieth century, the heartland theory attracted renewed attention.

In 1943, Mackinder wrote a final warning expressing concern that the Soviet Union, under Stalin, would seek to control eastern Europe. He offered strategies for keeping the Soviets in check, including resisting the expansion of the Heartland into the Inner Crescent (Fig. 8.22) and creating an alliance around the North Atlantic to join the forces of land and sea powers against the Heartland. His ideas were not embraced by many at the time, but within 10 years of his book's publication, the United States began its containment policy to stop the expansion of the Soviet Union. The United States, Canada, and western Europe formed an alliance called the North Atlantic Treaty Organization (NATO). Even after the Soviet Union collapsed, Mackinder's theories influenced Russian foreign policy circles.

Influence of Geopoliticians on Politics

Ratzel and Mackinder are only two of many geopoliticians who influenced international relations. Their writings were grounded in history, current events, and physical geography. They sounded logical and influenced many politicians, and in some ways they still do. NATO still exists and has not invited Russia to join the military alliance. Instead, it has extended membership to 28 states since the end of the Cold War, including those that were once part of the Soviet bloc. NATO also has a working partnership with some former republics of the Soviet Union. However, the war between Russia and Georgia in 2008 and Russia's 2014 seizure of Crimea brought NATO's eastward expansion to a halt.

Despite the staying power of classical geopolitical theories, geopolitics declined as a formal area of study after World War II. Because of the influence Ratzel's theory had on another geopolitician, Karl Haushofer, and then on Hitler, the term *geopolitics* acquired a distinctly negative meaning. For decades after World War II, the term was in such disrepute that few political geographers would identify themselves as students of geopolitics, even those studying structures of power. Time, along with more balanced perspectives, has reinstated geopolitics as a significant field of study.

Critical Geopolitics

Many current students of geopolitics focus on the underlying geographical assumptions and perspectives of international actors. Political geographers Gearoid O'Tuathail and John Agnew refer to those actors (presidents, prime ministers, foreign policy advisors, influential academics, and journalists) as "intellectuals of statecraft." The basic concept is that intellectuals of statecraft construct ideas about geographical circumstances and places that influence and reinforce their political behaviors and policy choices. Those behaviors and choices in turn affect what happens and how most people interpret what happens. Therefore, understanding international relations requires understanding where geopolitical ideas come from (what ideas and assumptions they reflect) and how they influence policies.

In his early writings, O'Tuathail focused on how several American leaders often spatialize politics into a world of "us" and "them." Political leaders and the media can influence how their constituents see places and organize international space in their minds. By drawing on American cultural logic and certain representations of America, O'Tuathail argued that the shapers of foreign policy have repeatedly divided the world into an "us" that is prodemocracy, independent, self-sufficient, and free, and a "them" that is in some way against all of these things.

During the Cold War, President Ronald Reagan coined the term *Evil Empire* for the Soviet Union and represented the United States as "the shining city on a hill." During subsequent presidencies, terrorism replaced the Soviet Union as the "they." Sounding remarkably similar, Democratic President Bill Clinton and Republican President George W. Bush justified military actions against terrorists by invoking "us-them" arguments that were both about people (terrorists) and places (areas where radical Islam was strong). In 1998, President Clinton justified American military action in Sudan and Afghanistan as a response to terrorist plans by Osama bin Laden by noting that the terrorists "come from diverse places but share a hatred for democracy, a fanatical glorification of violence, and a horrible distortion of their religion, to justify the murder of innocents. They have made the United States their adversary precisely because of what we stand for and what we stand against." Immediately after September 11, President George W. Bush argued that "they [the terrorists] stand against us because we stand in their way." In 2002, President Bush again explained, "I've said in the past that nations are either with us or against us in the war on terror." Statements such as these are rooted in a particular geopolitical perspective on the world—one that divides the globe into opposing camps and competing places.

Critical geopolitics explores the spatial ideas and understandings at the heart of geopolitical perspectives, and political geographers seek to shed light on how these ideas influence policy approaches. One of the most powerful geopolitical ideas since the end of the Cold War in 1989 came from Samuel Huntington (1996), who argued that conflicts will increasingly reflect major religious-civilizational divides. His emphasis on the importance of the "Islamic World" helped to shape responses to the September 11, 2001, attacks on the United States. The U.S. government, concerned about al-Qaeda's influence, justified military involvement in Iraq and Afghanistan based on the threat of a volatile "Islamic world." That idea was picked up and amplified by countless policy analysts, news commentators, and bloggers.

Critical geopolitics does not simply aim to identify geopolitical ideas, however; it also often critiques them. Commentators began to point out that the "Islamic world" is tremendously diverse, culturally and religiously. In fact, some of the most serious conflicts of recent times have been fought within the Islamic world, not between Muslims and others. Belief in the geopolitical significance of a unified "Islamic world" is not any more rational than belief in a geopolitically unified "Judeo-Christian world"—hardly a given when one considers recent conflicts between Russia and Ukraine, for example. Regardless, if geopolitical ideas are believed, they shape the policies that are pursued, and they become the narratives through which we perceive what happens. Geographers, then, seek to understand the ideological roots and implications of different geopolitical conceptions.

Geopolitical World Orders

A geopolitical world order describes a general consensus about the geographical character of international relations during a given period. For example, during the Cold War the geopolitical world order was thought to be bipolar: the Soviet Union and its Warsaw Pact satellites versus the United States and its close allies in western Europe. After the Soviet Union collapsed in 1991, the world entered a transition period, again opening up different geopolitical possibilities. Some politicians spoke optimistically about a new geopolitical world order reflecting the forces that connect nations and states, including supranational organizations such as the European Union and the promise of multilateral military action should any state violate international rules of conduct. The risks of nuclear war would diminish, it was hoped, and negotiation would replace confrontation. Then in 1991, when a United Nations coalition drove Iraq out of Kuwait, the framework of a new world order seemed to be taking shape. The Soviet Union, the United States' principal geopolitical rival, endorsed the operation. Arab as well as non-Arab forces helped repel the Iraqi invaders.

Soon, however, uncertainties began to cloud hopes for a mutually cooperative world order. National self-interest still acted as a powerful force. Nations wanted to become states, and the number of United Nations members increased from 159 in 1990 to 184 by 1993 and 193 as of 2011, when South Sudan seceded from Sudan. At the same time, organizations not tied to specific territories posed a new challenge to the territorially defined state.

Moreover, with the United States emerging from the Cold War as the dominant power, some U.S. commentators championed a geopolitical world order based on **unilateralism**, with the United States assuming a position of dominance. They argued that any other course of action would risk global instability. The fact that the U.S. military budget is almost as large as all the military budgets of all other states in the world combined puts it in a position to play a significant international role.

Recent events have brought into question whether military dominance can achieve the ends that unilateralists hope to achieve. The United States' controversial invasion of Iraq in 2003 significantly undermined its influence. A divide developed between the United States and some European countries, and anti-Americanism surged. More recently, trade disputes between the United States and other countries, together with a strong nationalist agenda in the United States, have fueled anti-Americanism in many places. And China's increasing power and influence suggest that the twenty-first century will not be one of unchecked U.S. geopolitical dominance.

China's growing international economic and political significance is no better illustrated than in its Belt and Road Initiative (BRI)—an umbrella term encompassing both its "One Belt, One Road" initiative and its "21st Century Maritime Silk Road" initiative. The BRI is a grand strategy aimed at massive infrastructure development and investment in more than 125 countries, linked together by roads and railroads over land and by well-developed sea routes (**Fig. 8.25**). The Chinese say the project will bring economic benefits to China and the other countries that are involved. Critics from outside China, however, see it as a push for geopolitical dominance. Whatever the merits of the latter claim, the BRI carries with it greater Chinese influence in the world.

Nuclear weapons further complicate the geopolitical picture, as they give even small states the ability to inflict massive damage on large and distant adversaries. Combined with missile technology, nuclear bombs may be one of the most serious dangers the world faces. Some states publicize their nuclear weapons programs, whereas other nuclear states have never formally acknowledged that they possess nuclear weapons. There's much potential for a hostile state or group to gain the power with which to threaten the world. North Korea's nuclear weapons are viewed with great anxiety, and Iran's nuclear intentions have been seriously questioned. Vigorous international efforts are under way to control the spread of nuclear materials and nuclear technology because of potential threats.

Russia's new assertiveness, first in Georgia in 2008 and then in Ukraine in 2014, raises the possibility of a return to Cold War geopolitical realities. Concerns over that possibility have ramped up in the wake of Russian interference in elections in western Europe and the United States. However, Russia is no longer widely seen as the champion of a political-economic system with broad appeal, and it is a less formidable military power than was the Soviet Union at its height. Hence, many believe that Russia's rift with its Western neighbors will simply be one dimension of a rapidly evolving geopolitical order characterized by several influential powers (including the United States, Germany, China, India, and Russia) seeking to exert influence over regional or global affairs.

Challenges to Traditional Political-Territorial Arrangements

Many of the geopolitical scenarios already discussed revolve around shifting structures of power among and between states. Yet a variety of developments are challenging the traditional

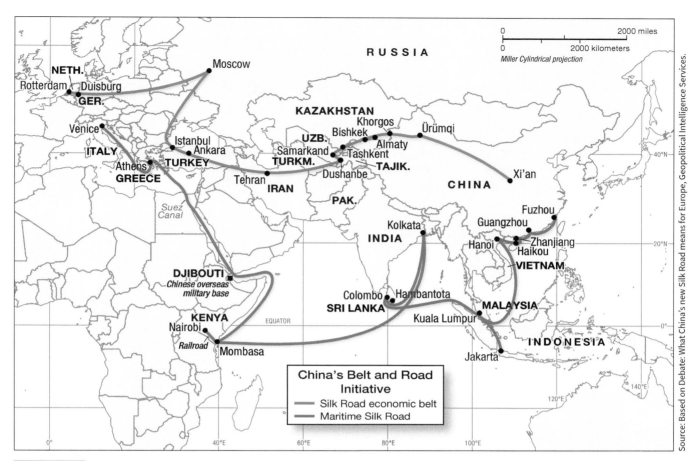

FIGURE 8.25 **China's Belt and Road Initiative.** The initiative has become a central tenet of China's foreign policy. It has led to a substantial increase in Chinese investment along the routes shown on the map—in some cases spurring economic development, but also raising concerns about China's growing global influence and its geopolitical intentions.

Source: Based on Debate: What China's new Silk Road means for Europe, Geopolitical Intelligence Services.

powers of the state. Such challenges raise questions about whether states will continue to be central to twenty-first-century geopolitics. Globalization has fostered many economic and social interconnections that are not tied to states. Moreover, recent decades have seen the rise of increasingly powerful nonstate or extrastate groups with political agendas. These developments point to a **deterritorialization** trend characterized by structures of power that are less tied to the traditional territorial state.

Of course, states continue to provide the territorial foundation from which producers and consumers operate. They still exert considerable regulatory powers. But globalization makes it more difficult for states to control what happens within their borders. States are responding to this situation in a variety of ways, with some giving up traditional areas of governmental control and others seeking to insulate themselves from the forces of globalization. Even states pursuing the latter strategy must compete with other forces in the international arena.

The state's traditional position is being further challenged by the globalization of social and cultural relations. Networks of interaction are being constructed in ways that do not correspond to the map of states. Scholars and researchers in different countries commonly work together in teams. Increased mobility has brought individuals from far-flung places into much closer contact than before. Paralleling all this change is

the spread of popular culture in ways that make national borders virtually meaningless. Ariana Grande is listened to from Iceland to Australia; fashions developed in northern Italy are hot items among Japanese tourists visiting South Korea; Thai restaurants are found in towns and cities across the United States; Russians hurry home to watch the next episode of soap operas made in Mexico; and movies produced in Hollywood are seen on screens from Bangkok to Santiago.

The rise of fundamentalist religious movements with geopolitical goals represents another global phenomenon with potentially significant implications. In Chapter 7, we noted that fundamental religious movements sometimes turn to violent extremism. Violence by extremists challenges the state—whether undertaken by individuals at the local scale or by widely dispersed groups. A state's effort to combat religious extremism can produce greater unity in the short term, but its inability to defeat extremist attacks may weaken the state in the long term.

Terrorist attacks have been threatened or carried out by religious extremists from a variety of different faiths, but the wave of terrorism that began in the 1980s in the name of Islam has dominated the international scene over the past several decades. The attacks of September 11, 2001, the invasions of Iraq and Afghanistan that followed, and the rise of the Islamic State of Iraq and the Levant (ISIS) moved terrorism to the geopolitical center stage. Other high-profile terrorist attacks in Madrid, Moscow, Mombasa, Mumbai, and several cities in Sri Lanka have helped to keep it there, as have terrorist attacks against Muslims (e.g., the deadly attack that occurred in Christchurch, New Zealand, in 2019). Almost daily, newspapers report on terrorist incidents in cities around the world. The University of Maryland's Global Terrorism Database tracked some 180,000 terrorist-related bombings, assassinations, and kidnappings from 1970 to 2017.

All of these developments are occurring outside the framework of the map of states. Nonetheless, nationalism continues to be a fundamental social force. Indeed, many states are solidifying control over their territory through **reterritorialization**—initiatives that enhance the power of traditional political-territorial arrangements. For example, in response to concerns over undocumented immigration, some state borders are becoming more heavily fortified, and moving across those borders is becoming more difficult.

Populist appeals to state nationalism are fueling the turn toward reterritorialization. Populist leaders have come to power all over the world based on calls to roll back the forces of globalization and reassert national power. It is hard to know where this will lead. Just over a hundred years ago, a geopolitical order characterized by intense competition among states pursuing strong state-nationalist agendas led to one of the most destructive conflicts the world had seen: World War I. We are not necessarily headed toward something similar today because the world is much more interconnected now. But as state nationalism becomes increasingly entrenched, the potential for conflict rises.

The tension between deterritorialization and reterritorialization will likely play an important role as the twenty-first century continues to unfold. Given the continuing power of state nationalism, there are few signs that competition among individual states will slow. Yet it is also increasingly clear that the spatial distribution of power is more complex than the traditional map of states would suggest. Analyzing the relationship between traditional territorial structures and new spatial power arrangements will be a challenge for geographers and others for decades to come.

TC **Thinking Geographically**

Examine the map of China's Belt and Road Initiative (Fig. 8.25). Study the **sites** where China is building or investing in ports. Describe the **situation** of these ports relative to China's larger Belt and Road Initiative (BRI). Hypothesize how China is using **development** strategies in the countries where it is investing through the BRI as a larger geopolitical strategy.

8.5 Compare and Contrast Supranational Organizations and States.

Few countries exist today that are not involved in some **supranational organization**. A supranational organization is an institution created by three or more states to promote cooperation. The twentieth century witnessed the establishment of numerous supranational associations in political, economic, cultural, and military spheres.

Today, states have formed over 60 major supranational organizations (such as NATO and the EU), many of which have subsidiaries that bring the total to more than 100 (**Fig. 8.26**). The more states participate in such multilateral associations, the less likely they are to act alone in pursuit of a self-interest that might put them at odds with other association members. And in most cases, participation in a supranational entity is advantageous to the partners, while being left out can have negative consequences.

From League of Nations to United Nations

The modern beginnings of the supranational movement can be traced to conferences following World War I. Woodrow Wilson, president of the United States, proposed an international organization that would include all the states of the world (fewer than 75 states existed at that time). That idea took on concrete form with the founding of the League of Nations in 1919. Nevertheless, the United States was among the countries that did not join the organization because isolationists in the U.S. Senate opposed membership. In all, 63 states participated in the League, although the total membership at any single time never reached that number. Costa Rica and Brazil left the League before 1930; Germany departed in 1933, shortly before the Soviet Union joined in 1934. The League later expelled the Soviet Union in 1939 for invading Finland.

The failure of the United States to join dealt the organization a severe blow. In the mid-1930s, the League had a major opportunity when Ethiopia's Haile Selassie appealed for help in the face of an invasion by Italy, a member state until 1937. The League failed to take action and in the chaos leading up to World War II, the organization collapsed.

Even though the League of Nations ceased functioning, it gave rise to other supranational organizations. Between World War I and World War II, many states came together to create the Permanent Court of International Justice, which was charged with adjudicating legal issues between states, such as boundary disputes and fishing rights. The League of Nations also initiated international negotiations on maritime boundaries and related aspects of the law of the sea. The conferences organized by the League laid the groundwork for the final resolution of the extent of territorial seas decades later.

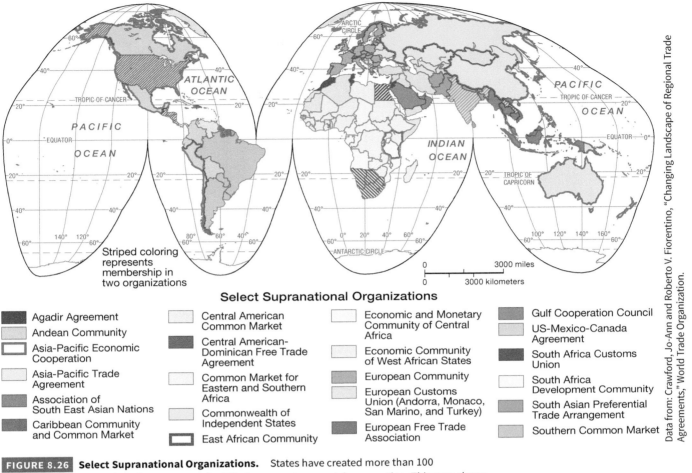

Data from: Crawford, Jo-Ann and Roberto V. Fiorentino, "Changing Landscape of Regional Trade Agreements," World Trade Organization.

Select Supranational Organizations

- Agadir Agreement
- Andean Community
- Asia-Pacific Economic Cooperation
- Asia-Pacific Trade Agreement
- Association of South East Asian Nations
- Caribbean Community and Common Market

- Central American Common Market
- Central American-Dominican Free Trade Agreement
- Common Market for Eastern and Southern Africa
- Commonwealth of Independent States
- East African Community

- Economic and Monetary Community of Central Africa
- Economic Community of West African States
- European Community
- European Customs Union (Andorra, Monaco, San Marino, and Turkey)
- European Free Trade Association

- Gulf Cooperation Council
- US-Mexico-Canada Agreement
- South Africa Customs Union
- South Africa Development Community
- South Asian Preferential Trade Arrangement
- Southern Common Market

Striped coloring represents membership in two organizations

FIGURE 8.26 **Select Supranational Organizations.** States have created more than 100 supranational organizations for purposes of political, economic, or social cooperation. This map shows major supranational organizations centered on trade.

After World War II, a new organization was founded to promote international security and cooperation: the United Nations (UN). Membership in the UN has grown significantly since its inception in 1947 (**Fig. 8.27**). A handful of states still do not belong to the organization, but with the most recent addition in 2011, it now has 193 member states. Additionally, the organization allows permanent observers, including the nonmember states of Palestine and Vatican City, and several supranational and nongovernmental organizations participate in the UN General Assembly. The UN organization includes numerous less visible but significant subsidiaries, including the FAO (Food and Agriculture Organization), UNESCO (United Nations Educational, Scientific and Cultural Organization), and WHO (World Health Organization). Not all UN members participate in every subsidiary, but many people around the world have benefited from their work.

We can find evidence of the United Nations' work in almost any discussion of global events. UN peacekeeping troops have helped maintain stability in some of the most contentious regions. The United Nations High Commissioner on Refugees is called upon to aid refugees in countries around the world. UN documents on human rights standards, such as the Universal Declaration on Human Rights, the Covenant on Civil and Political

Rights, and the Covenant on Economic and Social Rights, laid the groundwork for countless human rights groups working today.

By participating in the United Nations, states agree to internationally approved standards of behavior. Many states still violate the standards embodied in the United Nations Charter, but such violations can lead to collective action, such as economic sanctions or Security Council–supported military action. The UN's aid, refugee, and peacekeeping efforts in South Africa during the transition away from Apartheid are an example of UN success.

Nonetheless, the organization has its critics. Some point to the composition of its Security Council, which reflects the world of 1950 more than the world of today. All five permanent members of the Council—the victors of World War II: the United States, United Kingdom, France, China, and Russia (formerly the Soviet Union)—wield veto power over Council resolutions and use the veto regularly, often making the UN ineffective during times of crisis. The Syrian civil war showcased Security Council tensions as Russia and China forcefully vetoed resolutions aimed at greater UN involvement to curb violence directed at civilians. Those who seek UN reform say the Permanent Five with their veto power destroy UN credibility and reinforce outdated power arrangements. Other UN critics express concern

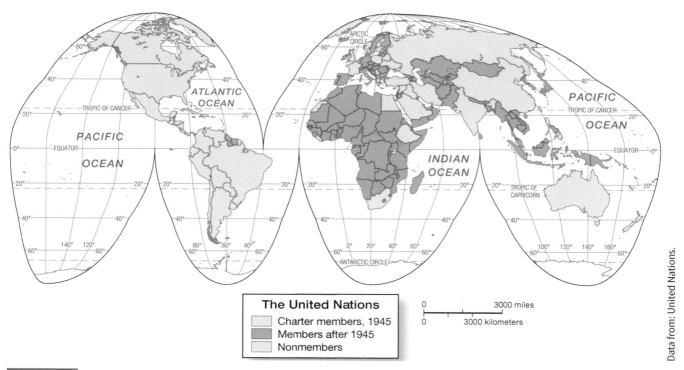

FIGURE 8.27 **Member States of the United Nations.** The charter members of the United Nations are differentiated from states that joined the United Nations after 1945. A few states are nonmembers of the United Nations.

about power being vested in an organization that is not directly responsible to voters and that provides little room for nonstate interests. Still others note that states with troubled human rights records, such as China and Cuba, sit on the organization's Human Rights Council. For all its weaknesses, however, the United Nations represents the only truly international forum for addressing many significant global problems.

Regional Supranational Organizations

The League of Nations and the United Nations are global examples of something that is also found at the regional level. States organize supranational organizations at the regional scale to advance economic and political agendas. Examples include the United States-Mexico-Canada Agreement (USMCA, formerly the North American Free Trade Agreement, NAFTA), the Asia-Pacific Economic Council (APEC), and the Commonwealth of Independent States (CIS). At the heart of most of these organizations are efforts to reduce tariffs and import restrictions to ease the flow of commerce in different parts of the world. Not all of these alliances are successful, but economic supranationalism is a sign of the times.

Belgium, the Netherlands, and Luxembourg undertook the first major modern experiment in regional economic cooperation. The three countries have much in common culturally and complement one another economically. Dutch farm products are sold in Belgian markets, and Belgian industrial goods go to the Netherlands and Luxembourg. During World War II, representatives of the three countries decided to remove tariffs among them and eliminate import licenses and quotas. In

1944, even before the end of the war, the three governments met in London to sign an agreement of cooperation, creating the Benelux (Belgium, the Netherlands, and Luxembourg) region.

Following World War II, U.S. Secretary of State George Marshall proposed that the United States finance a European recovery program. A committee representing 16 western European states plus then-West Germany presented the U.S. Congress with a joint program for economic rehabilitation, which Congress approved. From 1948 to 1952, the United States gave Europe some $12 billion under the Marshall Plan, the largest foreign aid program in history. This investment revived European national economies and spurred a movement toward European cooperation. That movement was also driven by the rise of an increasingly integrated and potentially threatening Soviet bloc to the east and the desire to create a framework that could help break the historical pattern of European conflict.

The European Union   From the European states' involvement in the Marshall Plan came the Organization for European Economic Cooperation (OEEC), which gave rise to other cooperative organizations. Soon after Europe established the OEEC, France proposed the creation of a European Coal and Steel Community (ECSC) to lift the restrictions and obstacles that impeded the flow of coal, iron ore, and steel among the mainland's six primary producers: France, West Germany, Italy, and the three Benelux countries. The six states entered the ECSC and gradually, through negotiations and agreement, enlarged their sphere of cooperation to include reductions and even eliminations of certain tariffs and a freer flow of labor, capital, and commodities beyond steel. This led, in 1958, to the creation of the European Economic Community (EEC).

The success of the EEC induced other countries to apply for membership. Denmark, Ireland, and the United Kingdom joined in 1973, Greece in 1981, and Spain and Portugal in 1986. The organization became known as the European Community (EC) because it began to address issues beyond economics. By the late 1980s, the EC had 12 members: the three giants (Germany, France, and the United Kingdom); the four southern countries (Italy, Spain, Portugal, and Greece); and five smaller states (the Netherlands, Belgium, Luxembourg, Denmark, and Ireland). These 12 members initiated a program of cooperation and unification that led to the formal establishment of a European Union (EU) in 1992. In the mid-1990s, Austria,

Sweden, and Finland joined the EU, bringing the total number of members to 15 (**Fig. 8.28**).

In the late 1990s, the EU began preparing for the establishment of a single currency—the euro. First, all electronic financial transactions were denominated in euros, and on January 1, 2002, the EU introduced euro coins and notes. Not all EU member states are currently a part of the euro zone, but the euro has emerged as a significant global currency.

The integration of 10 eastern European and Mediterranean island states into the European Union in 2004, two more in 2007, and one more in 2014 represented a large expansion over a relatively short period. Integration is a difficult process and

Data from: The European Union, www.europa.eu.int © H. J. de Blij, P.O.Muller, and John Wiley & Sons, Inc.

FIGURE 8.28 **European Supranationalism.** The European Union started with six countries and expanded over time. Not all countries in Europe are members of the European Union. Switzerland and Norway voted not to join the European Union, and the United Kingdom voted to leave the European Union. Countries in the common currency zone, the Eurozone, are also shown on this map.

often requires painful adjustments because of the diversity of the states involved. For example, some general policy must govern the widely varying agricultural policies throughout the EU. Individual states have found these adjustments difficult at times, and the EU has had to devise policies to accommodate regional contrasts and delays in implementation.

The European Union recognizes 24 official languages and offers simultaneous translation among the official languages to any member state that requests it. The EU only produces legislation and policy documents of "major public importance" in all of its official languages; other documents are translated only into the languages relevant to each document.

Translation is just one of the significant expenditures associated with integration. Under the rules of the EU, the richer countries must subsidize (provide financial support to) the poorer ones; therefore, the entry of eastern European states adds to the financial burden on the wealthier western and northern European members. A major economic downturn at the end of the first decade of the twenty-first century and associated financial crises in Greece, Ireland, Spain, and Portugal, put the EU under unprecedented pressure. The citizens of wealthier countries such as Germany began to question why they should foot the bill for countries that have not (at least in German eyes) managed their finances responsibly.

AP® Exam Taker's Tip

What are some advantages of supranational organizations for states? What are some disadvantages? Explain why supranational organizations, such as the EU and the United States-Mexico-Canada Agreement (formerly NAFTA), are under pressure today. The Brexit situation (see Fig. 8.29) is a good example of a supranational organization under pressure.

The EU is a patchwork of states with many different ethnic traditions and histories of conflict and competition, and concerns have grown in parts of Europe over losing local control over economic, social, and political matters. Economic success and growing well-being have worked against these concerns, but in the face of difficult economic or social times, divisive forces can, and have, reasserted themselves. Moreover, as the EU has gotten bigger, it has become increasingly difficult for individual states (even powerful ones) to shape its direction. And some

citizens in smaller states such as Denmark and Sweden worry about getting lost in the mix. As a result, challenges to the legitimacy of an increasingly powerful EU have grown.

Those challenges came to a head in the United Kingdom in 2016, when a narrow majority of the British public voted in a special referendum in favor of leaving the EU (a process referred to as Brexit—British exit from the EU). The referendum exposed deep divides. Whereas a considerable majority of voters in some economically depressed parts of England voted to leave, most of those living in the London metropolitan area, in Scotland, and in Northern Ireland voted to remain (**Fig. 8.29**). The "remain" vote was strong enough in

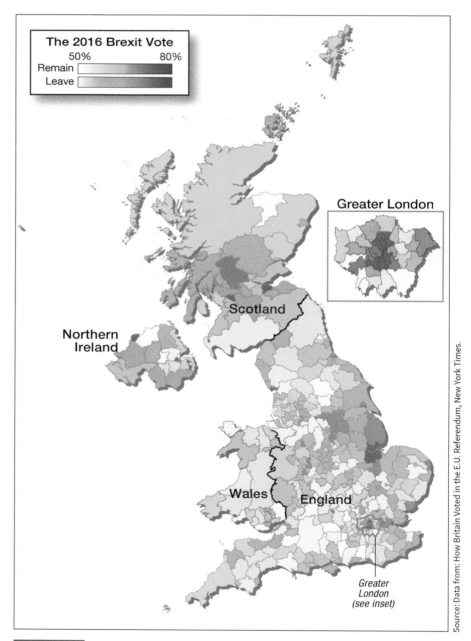

FIGURE 8.29 **The 2016 Brexit Vote.** The vote to leave the EU was strongest in areas in England that have suffered economically in recent decades. The remain vote was strongest in the London metropolitan area, Scotland, and the parts of Northern Ireland that border on the Republic of Ireland.

Source: Data from: How Britain Voted in the E.U. Referendum, New York Times.

FIGURE 8.30 **Brussels, Belgium.** A woman with a European Union umbrella shops in the flower market in the Grande Place of Brussels. On their website, the European Union states that the number of stars on the flag has no official meaning and that the circle of stars represents "unity, solidarity and harmony among the peoples of Europe."

Scotland to raise fears that Brexit would reinvigorate calls for independence.

After the referendum, some commentators claimed that the leave campaign misrepresented the consequences of Brexit, and many voters did not appear to have much understanding of the EU or what it does. Nonetheless, the vote revealed the depth of negative feeling about the EU in parts of the UK, as well as a frustration over where the country was headed due to declining economic circumstances in some areas and concerns about the growing number of immigrants. As such, there are parallels between the Brexit vote and elections that have brought to power populist leaders who have championed state-nationalist agendas.

Once the vote went in favor of leaving the EU, the government of the UK had no choice but to begin the process of working out a deal that would take the UK out of the EU. The difficulties of that process soon became apparent, however, as no approach to handling Brexit was able to gain majority support. Some wanted a complete break with the EU, others thought the referendum was flawed and needed to be redone, and yet others thought it important to retain some kind of customs agreement with the EU. Further complicating matters, in the absence of at least a customs agreement between the UK and the EU, the open status of the border between Northern Ireland (part of the UK) and the Republic of Ireland

would be threatened (it would become an external border of the EU)—threatening the 1998 Good Friday Agreement that guaranteed an open border (see Chapter 7). As a result of these complications, the Brexit process dragged on much longer than initially expected, and the full range of consequences of the Brexit vote will not become clear for some years to come.

Brexit is symptomatic of larger challenges the EU is facing in the wake of growing anti-EU populist movements that play on anti-establishment and anti-immigrant sentiments. From the Netherlands to Italy to Hungary, such movements target EU policies facilitating the flow of refugees and workers across borders and promoting regulatory harmonization—arguing that such policies are undermining the ability of states to advance their own interests. Whatever the challenges, the EU is a supranational organization unlike any other. It is not a state, nor is it simply an organization of states. It has taken on a life of its own—with a multifaceted government structure, three capital cities, and billions of euros flowing through its coffers.

The European Union's reach extends into foreign relations, domestic affairs, and military policies. Those living in some parts of Europe have come to identify with the EU (**Fig. 8.30**), and it is almost impossible to imagine two EU countries going to war with one another (a remarkable achievement given the long history of conflict between, for example, France and Germany, which culminated in two world wars during the twentieth century). The EU, then, represents the world's boldest attempt to move beyond a political order dominated by states, but it is facing serious challenges that remind us of the continuing power of the state as an international actor and focus of identity.

TC Thinking Geographically

What impact do supranational organizations have on devolutionary movements? Study the Brexit votes of Scotland, Northern Ireland, and Wales (Fig. 8.29). At what **scales** were each of these voters identifying when they voted on Brexit? What does their Brexit vote say about their **identity** relative to their region, the United Kingdom, and the European Union?

Summary

8.1 Compare and Contrast States, Nations, and Nation-States.

1. The modern state idea can be traced back to the Europe of the 1600s. It called for a world divided into discrete territorial units, each of which has the right to control affairs within its own territory (sovereignty).

2. The term *nation* originally referred to a group with a sense of common culture that seeks control over its own affairs (an ethnocultural nation). The *nation-state* idea is based on the notion that each ethnocultural nation should have its own state. The world political order does not match this idea, however. Instead, we live a world that is primarily made up of *multinational states* (states that encompass more than one ethnocultural nation). There are also many *multistate nations* (ethnocultural nations that span across different states) and *stateless nations* (ethnocultural nations that want a state of their own, but do not have it).

3. The European state idea diffused to much of the rest of the world through two periods of European colonialism. As a result, most state leaders throughout the world embrace the nation-state ideal and claim to represent their nation, even when the states encompass multiple ethnocultural nations.

8.2 Determine How the Modern Political Map Evolved.

1. Different state territorial characteristics (e.g., territorial size, resource endowment, geographic situation) can carry potential advantages and disadvantages, but state power and stability are not simply the result of these characteristics. Historical and geographical circumstances often play a more important role—especially a country's role in the world economy.

2. World-systems theory draws attention to the position of states within the world economy. It is based on the idea that the world political map is a system of interlinked parts that need to be understood in relation to one another. Colonizing powers politically reorganized the world, giving rise to a global political-economic order that gives some states (*core* states) great power and leaves other states (*periphery* states) in a weakened position. Between these two are semiperiphery states.

3. The internal territorial integrity of states is affected by *centrifugal* forces (forces that tend to pull a state apart) and *centripetal* forces (forces that promote unity). The factors that can have centrifugal or centripetal tendencies include the spatial organization of power within states, the presence or absence of regionally concentrated ethno-national minorities, and in democracies, the geographical configuration of electoral districts. The impacts these factors have on the territorial integrity of states depend on the circumstances present in a given state.

8.3 Explain the Nature and Significance of International Boundaries.

1. Boundaries are more than straight lines on the ground; they are vertical planes that extend from deep below Earth's surface to high up in the atmosphere. Boundaries also extend out to sea for countries with coastlines, allowing them sovereign control for 12 nautical miles beyond their coastline, control over resources in the water column for 200 nautical miles, and control over resources in their continental shelves for up to 200 nautical miles.

2. There are different types of boundaries: geometric boundaries (boundaries drawn using a grid system) and physical-political boundaries (boundaries that follow an agreed-upon feature in the natural landscape).

3. Boundary disputes between countries are common. They reflect disagreements over the definition and location of boundaries and the way boundaries function.

4. Boundaries are changing in the modern world as a result of globalization, increased migration, and technological advances in telecommunications. Nonetheless, many governments are working actively to secure their boundaries.

8.4 Explain Classical and Critical Geopolitics.

1. Geopolitics is concerned with how geographical circumstances influence international relations and the distribution of power on Earth's surface. Classic geopolitics began in the late nineteenth century and focused attention on the advantages and disadvantages of controlling different parts of Earth's surface. The ideas of classical geopoliticians such as Halford Mackinder and Friedrich Ratzel ended up having a significant influence on foreign policy during the Cold War era and in Germany during the period when Nazism was on the rise.

2. Geographers interested in geopolitics have increasingly turned their attention to the underlying geographical assumptions and perspectives of international actors—an approach known as critical geopolitics. Critical geopolitics focuses on the ideas and geographical assumptions that shape the political behaviors and policy choices of those who influence statecraft.

3. There are competing ideas about how the world is organized geopolitically today. One of the challenges facing contemporary geopolitical theorists is to understand how the competing forces of *deterritorialization* (the move away from states serving as the primary locus of power) and *reterritorialization* (trends in the opposite direction) affect geopolitical arrangements and understandings.

8.5 Compare and Contrast Supranational Organizations and States.

1. Almost all countries today participate in multiple supranational organizations. These range from the United Nations to regional organizations, many of which are focused on promoting economic interaction among member countries.

2. The European Union is the most far-reaching regional supranational organization in the world today. It has brought peace and stability to an area long wracked by conflict, but it is facing serious challenges from those who believe that the transfer of power away from states is undermining the ability of the inhabitants of individual states to control their own affairs. The 2016 vote in the United Kingdom to leave the EU (Brexit) reflected the growing influence of the latter way of thinking.

Self-Test

8.1 Compare and contrast states, nations, and nation-states.

1. The Peace of Westphalia (1648) is associated with which of the following principles underlying the modern state system?

   a. sovereignty

   b. nationalism

   c. the nation-state idea

   d. colonialism

   e. Imperialism

2. Which of the following countries is the best example of a "nation-state" in the original meaning of the term?

   a. Switzerland

   b. Indonesia

   c. Japan

   d. Nigeria

   e. Russia

3. The Kurds today are an example of a:

   a. nation-state.

   b. multinational state.

   c. a multi-ethnic state.

   d. multistate nation.

   e. a stateless nation.

4. Which of the following statements about European colonialism is accurate?

   a. European colonialism took off around 1500, and by 1650 most of the world was colonized.

   b. European colonialism took off around 1500 and unfolded in two major waves, one between 1500 and 1800 and another between 1850 and 1950.

   c. European colonialism unfolded slowly beginning around 1700 and affected only a few regions until the late nineteenth century.

   d. European colonialism began in the early nineteenth century, and by the end of the century most of the world was colonized.

   e. European colonialism began in 1400, and by 1800 most of the world was colonized.

8.2 Determine how the modern political map evolved.

5. True or False: Territorial size is directly correlated with power (i.e., almost all larger states are more powerful than smaller states).

6. World-systems theory draws attention to:

   a. the degree of ethnocultural diversity within states.

   b. the role that resources play in the power of states.

   c. the role that sovereignty plays in protecting state autonomy.

   d. The role supra-national organizations play globally.

   e. The power relations at play in the international state system.

7. The term *devolution* refers to:

   a. the decline and fall of a political regime.

   b. the transfer of power from one ruler to the next based on hereditary connections.

   c. the transfer of power "downwards" from the center to regions within a state.

   d. the surrender of sovereign powers to outsiders in exchange for economic benefits.

   e. The failure of a state to govern effectively.

8. Separatist movements are active in each of the following states except:

   a. the United Kingdom.   d. Sweden.

   b. Spain.   e. Democratic Republic of the Congo

   c. China.

9. Gerrymandering refers to:

   a. the drawing of odd-shaped electoral districts to ensure fairness across ethnic and political affiliation lines.

   b. the drawing of odd-shaped electoral districts to favor certain ethnic groups or political parties.

   c. the drawing of odd-shaped electoral districts to promote political participation by a broad range of people.

   d. the drawing of odd-shaped electoral districts to take into account the impacts of topography on population distributions.

   e. The drawing of regular shaped electoral districts to promote a just voting process.

8.3 Explain the nature and significance of international boundaries.

10. True or False: Boundaries are not just lines on the ground, but vertical planes that descend down into the subsoil and upwards into the air.

11. Geometric boundaries are common:

a. in sub-Saharan Africa as a result of boundary drawing by Europeans at the 1884–1885 Berlin Conference.

b. in Southeast Asia as a result of the gradual penetration of European powers into the region.

c. in South America as a result of the need to draw boundaries that correspond to topography.

d. in Europe as a result of the influence of Greek and Roman mathematical ideas on the development of states.

e. In Northern Eurasia as a result of the large landmass.

12. An exclusive economic zone gives coastal states the right to control the resources in the waters off their coasts up to:

a. 3 nautical miles from their coastlines.

b. 12 nautical miles from their coastlines.

c. 50 nautical miles from their coastlines.

d. 100 nautical miles from their coastlines

e. 200 nautical miles from their coastlines.

13. A dispute over how much water a state has the right to extract from an aquifer that straddles a boundary is known as:

a. a definitional boundary dispute.

b. a locational boundary dispute.

c. an operational boundary dispute.

d. an allocational boundary dispute.

e. a resource boundary dispute.

8.4 Explain classical and critical geopolitics.

14. Which of the following was not a major concern of classical geopolitics?

a. understanding why and how certain states became powerful

b. understanding which parts of Earth's surface are particularly strategic to control

c. understanding the geographical assumptions underlying foreign policy decisions

d. understanding how physical geography can influence the projection of power

e. All of the above are correct

15. Which geopolitical concept or theory was championed by Halford Mackinder?

a. World Systems Theory

b. *Lebensraum*

c. critical geopolitics

d. Clash of Civilizations

e. Heartland

16. Which of the following is an example of deterritorialization?

a. efforts by ethno-national minorities to have greater representation in state government

b. governments building border walls to reduce undocumented migration

c. transnational networks that give corporations powers that are beyond the control of states

d. populist leaders making impassioned nationalistic pleas

e. Changing colonial toponyms to reflect the end of the colonial era

8.5 Compare and contrast supranational organizations and states.

17. True or False: Most countries in Europe and North America participate in supranational organizations, but in other parts of the world such participation is not common.

18. Which of the following supranational organizations or agreements has had the greatest impact on the sovereignty of individual member states?

a. the United Nations

b. the North Atlantic Treaty Organization

c. the European Union

d. the US-Mexico-Canada Agreement, formerly the North American Free Trade Agreement (NAFTA)

e. The League of Nations

19. The Brexit vote was a response to all of the following EXCEPT:

a. declining economic circumstances in some parts of Britain.

b. concerns about the growth in the number of migrants coming to Britain.

c. worries over Britain's limited ability to influence what was happening in the EU.

d. concerns that Scotland would leave the UK if Brexit did not happen.

e. concerns about trade tariffs and global economic competition.

CHAPTER 9

Urban Geography

PA Images/Alamy Stock Photo

FIGURE 9.1 **Dublin, Ireland.** Dublin residents organized a Take Back the City demonstration to protest the city's housing crisis. Take Back the City is a conglomeration of 15 housing groups whose members are concerned about the cost and availability of housing for the city's residents. Each flat and house a developer buys to lease through home-sharing platforms is another residence not available for locals to rent or buy.

Protesters walk the streets of Dublin, Ireland, with a sign reading, "Take back the city" (**Fig. 9.1**). In Barcelona, Spain, a protester's sign reads, "Tourist flats displace families." And in Paris, France, a sign reads, "Homes. Not hotels." The protesters believe that Airbnb and other home-sharing platforms are destroying their cities by undermining their sense of community, driving up housing prices, compressing housing stock, and crowding tourist destinations.

The number of tourists in a city used to be somewhat regulated by the number of beds in hotels. But with home-sharing platforms, every building can become a short-term hotel, and the number of tourists in a city at one time is swelling beyond the city's capacity, making it difficult for the people who live there to get around or enjoy their city.

The first people to live in cities clustered together for community, security, and innovation. For a city to flourish, people need to live in community and be invested in the place and one another. Tourists darting through a town do not vote for candidates or run in elections, serve on community boards and councils, or teach or send their children to the local school. Protesters argue that a city not populated by residents is basically a museum.

Urban geographer Edward Soja sees the city as a force in society. Concentrate millions of people in a close-knit city, and the very act of being so close and sharing space makes the city a catalyst for innovation. If Soja is right, home sharing can fundamentally shift the role cities play in society. His theory assumes that everyone in a city is invested in a place and identifies with that place.

In our study of urban geography in this chapter, we look at the city spatially, examining the forms of cities around the world, the role of people in building and shaping cities, and the changes that cities have undergone over space and time.

CHAPTER OUTLINE

9.1 Describe the Sites and Situations of Cities.

More people now live in cities than at any point in human history. A **city** is an agglomeration of people and buildings clustered together to serve as a center of politics, culture, and economics. It is a large settlement of people with an extensive built environment. At the global scale, most people live in cities. In Japan, the United States, Canada, and western Europe, four out of five people now live in cities or towns. China is mostly urban, with a little over 50 percent of Chinese living in cities, but India is mostly rural, with 70 percent of Indians living in rural areas.

The large concentration of people in cities gives people access to goods, services, and opportunities not available in rural areas. Cities also have governments that can levy taxes and then use the funds to build massive infrastructure systems, including webs of subway systems (**Fig. 9.2**) and bridges that

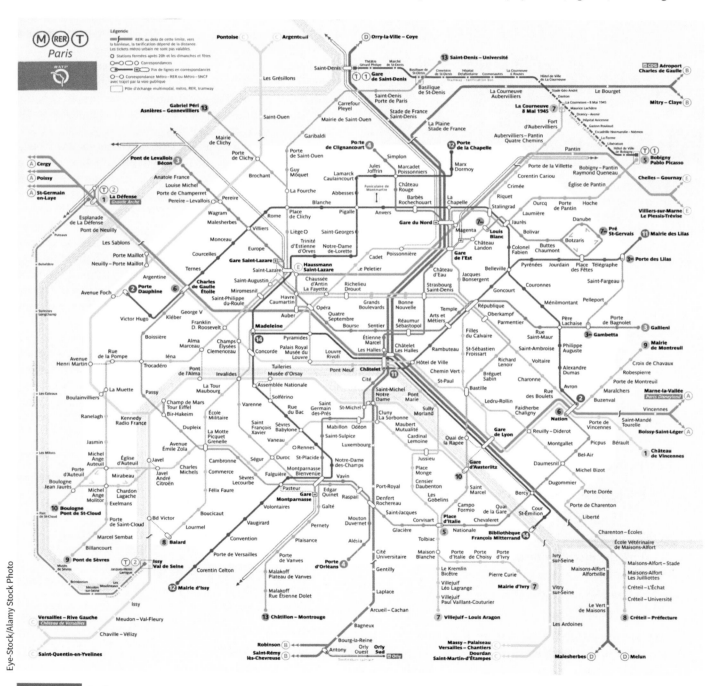

FIGURE 9.2   Paris Metro Map.   Construction of the Paris Metro began in 1898. The first line opened for travelers in 1900. This map shows the more than 130 miles (214 km) of metro lines connecting the city today. Cities collect taxes, which makes it possible for them to build large infrastructure projects like subways.

FIGURE 9.3 **Sydney, Australia.** The Gladesville bridge spans over the Parramatta River, connecting passengers with the Sydney central business district (CBD) in the background.

are works of art (**Fig. 9.3**). Cities are centers of political and economic power, higher education and technological innovation, artistic achievement and historical records, and research and medical advances. News and information are collected in cities and broadcast around the world. Enormous entertainment and sports complexes draw famous people to perform, teams to compete, and fans to watch them.

> ### AP® Exam Taker's Tip
>
> Understanding the common site characteristics of the hearths of urbanization is very important. What role does agriculture play in early urbanization?

The Hearths of Urbanization

A city can seemingly pop up on the landscape overnight. In 1979, the Chinese government designated the small fishing village of Shenzhen, located next to Hong Kong, as a special economic zone (SEZ). The designation propelled investment from foreign companies, and many industries moved from Hong Kong to Shenzhen to take advantage of lower labor costs. Shenzhen grew from 30,000 people to 12 million people in just over 40 years. Skyscrapers now tower where thatch houses, rice paddies, and duck ponds once stood (**Fig. 9.4**).

Unlike today, it took thousands of years for the first **hearths**, or centers, of urbanization to form in Mesopotamia, the Nile River Valley, the Indus River Valley, the Huang He and Wei River valleys, Mesoamerica, and Peru. Urbanization began when hunters and gatherers first clustered in permanent settlements to defend themselves and their leaders, grow crops, develop

new arts and industries, cluster around sacred sites, and build places that aligned with their understanding of the universe.

The First Urban Revolution

The first permanent settlements were small agricultural villages. In these villages, everyone worked in agriculture and people were relatively equal in status. As cities formed, this situation changed. In a city, people engage in many economic activities besides agriculture and stratify into classes as they generate personal, material wealth.

Some cities grew out of agricultural villages, and others grew in places previously unoccupied. The first formation of cities is called the **first urban revolution**, and it occurred independently in six separate hearths[1] (**Fig. 9.5**). In each of the urban hearths, people became engaged in various economic

[1]Some scholars argue that there are fewer than six hearths and attribute some early centers of urbanization to diffusion.

FIGURE 9.4 **Shenzhen, China.** When Shenzhen became the first special economic zone (SEZ) in China in 1979, the town had approximately 30,000 residents. Chinese banks and foreign investors flooded money into the city, building a network of transportation, utilities, and buildings. In just four decades, the city grew at an unprecedented rate to more than 12 million people.

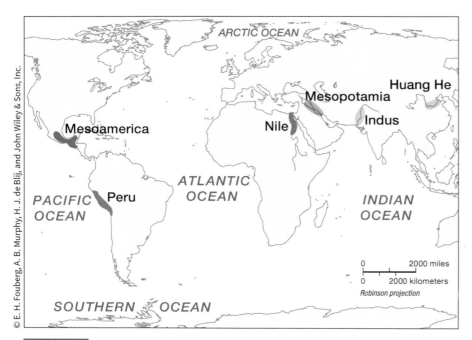

© E. H. Fouberg, A. B. Murphy, H. J. de Blij, and John Wiley & Sons, Inc.

FIGURE 9.5 **Six Hearths of Urbanization.** From these hearths, urbanization diffused around the world.

activities beyond agriculture, including specialty crafts, the military, trade, and government.

The six urban hearths were closely tied to the first hearths or centers of agriculture. The first hearth of agriculture, the Fertile Crescent, is the first place archaeologists find evidence of cities, dating to about 3500 BCE. This urban hearth, called **Mesopotamia**, included the cities of Ur and Babylon, located near the Tigris and Euphrates rivers. The social classes in Mesopotamian cities are seen in the different sizes of houses and their varying ornamentation. Cities in Mesopotamia had palaces, temples, and walls, all built with taxes and tribute collected by the priest-kings from farmers and workers.

The second hearth of urbanization, the **Nile River Valley**, dates to 3200 BCE. Irrigation distinguished the Nile from other urban hearths. The different social classes of the Nile civilization are evidenced by the great pyramids, tombs, and statues built by slaves and laborers. One distinct feature of Nile cities is the lack of walls, which was likely an environmental decision. Walls on the Nile side would have blocked access to the river, which was needed for irrigation. Walls on the side away from the river were unnecessary because just a few miles away from the Nile stretches a vast desert. The Nile flooded annually, and the river left rich sediment behind on the floodplain when the river receded. Walls would have blocked the river from flooding and annually nourishing the agricultural fields. The lack of walls may also have been a political decision. Settlements along the Nile were part of the same civilization; so they would not have had to protect themselves from each other.

The third urban hearth, dating to 2900 BCE, was the **Indus River Valley**, another place where agriculture likely diffused from the Fertile Crescent. The cities of Harappa and

Mohenjo-Daro are distinct from every other urban hearth because they do not show signs of social classes. The intricate planning of the cities points to the existence of a leadership class, but the built landscape does not indicate who was in charge. The houses are equal in size and have access to the same infrastructure. Cities in the Indus River Valley did not have palaces or monuments, but they did have thick walls. The discovery of coins from as far away as the Mediterranean points to significant trade over long distances.

The fourth urban hearth arose around the **Huang He (Yellow) and Wei valleys** of China, dating to 1500 BCE. Cities were planned to coincide with the cardinal directions and reflected the Chinese understanding of astronomy. The typical city had a vertical structure in the middle, surrounded by temples and palaces and encircled with an inner wall. Cities also had outer walls. Some workers lived inside the outer wall and some lived outside it. Leaders advertised their power by building enormous structures, including the Great Wall and the tomb of the emperor Qin Xi Huang. An estimated 700,000 laborers worked for over 40 years to craft an army of over 7000 terracotta warriors who stand guard over the emperor's burial place, complete with detailed facial expressions and weapons, horses, and chariots (**Fig. 9.6**).

The fifth urban hearth, found in **Mesoamerica**, dates to 1100 BCE. The ancient cities of Mesoamerica were religious centers. The Olmec built cities, including San Lorenzo, on the Gulf Coast of Mexico. They carved large stone monuments, and archaeologists believe they moved the volcanic stones for these monuments 50 miles from the interior of Mexico to the coast. The Olmec civilization died out, but based on Olmec cultural teachings, the Maya built cities in the same region that were also centered on religious temples, including Tikal, Chichén Itzá, Uxmal, and Copán (**Fig. 9.7**).

Recent archaeological evidence establishes **Peru** as the sixth urban hearth, where people built cities dating to 900 BCE. The largest settlement, Chavín, was sited at an elevation of 10,530 feet in the Andean highlands.

Urban Morphology and Functional Zonation

Other cities were built after the establishment of these sixth hearths. In each time and place that people formed new cities, civilizations left their own mark on the cultural landscape. Cities reflect the power and economic structures of the time they were built and of later periods as well. The religious buildings, monuments, organization, and architecture of cities all show what people value.

Two concepts in urban geography create the overall picture of any city we study: urban morphology and functional

O. Louis Mazzatenta/National Geographic Image Collection/Getty Images

FIGURE 9.6   **Xi'an, China.**   Terracotta warriors guard the tomb of the Chinese Emperor Qin Xi Huang. An estimated 700,000 laborers worked for over 40 years, around 200 BCE, to craft more than 7000 terracotta warriors who stand guard over the emperor's tomb.

zonation. The **urban morphology** of a city is its layout, including the sizes and shapes of buildings and the pathways of infrastructure. The **functional zonation** is the division of a city into different regions (e.g., residential or industrial) by use or purpose (e.g., housing or manufacturing). Understanding the zones in a city and the functions of each zone helps us imagine how power and wealth were distributed in ancient cities and also gives us insight into what people in power value in modern cities.

We can use cities in the Indus Civilization to understand functional zonation and urban morphology. The Indus Civilization flourished from 2900 BCE to 1900 BCE. Archaeologists cannot find enough writing from this civilization to decipher the language and interpret the writing they have found. The best clues of what the Indus Civilization was like are in the city's urban morphology and functional zonation. The Indus city Mohenjo-Daro (in present-day Pakistan) has an urban morphology and functional zonation that give archaeologists clues about how the civilization was structured. The city does not have any temples or palaces, which leads us to believe that whoever oversaw the city did not display their leadership through wealth. Streets crossed at right angles, and the city had a system to get fresh water to the residents (**Fig. 9.8A**). Houses were about the same size, and each house had access to a covered sewer system (**Fig. 9.8B**). The city also had an older area built around the Great Bath, which had watertight brickwork and a slope designed to drain the bath. It appears that everyone had access to this Great Bath (**Fig. 9.9**).

Archaeologists believe the Great Bath was used for ablutions because ritual bathing is still important in Hinduism, the religion whose hearth was in this area (see Chapter 7).

We can also use urban morphology and functional zonation to study a modern city. The urban morphology of

Mardoz Lule/123RF

FIGURE 9.7   **Chichén Itzá, Mexico.**   The Mayans built the famous El Castillo (castle) pyramid between the 9th and 12th centuries CE. El Castillo demonstrates the incredible astronomical skills of the Mayans and their intricate knowledge of earth-sun geometry. The pyramid has 91 stair steps on each side with a platform connecting them on the top, making for 365 total steps. The Mayans designed it so the sun casts a serpent-shaped shadow over the pyramid on the spring and fall equinoxes.

Source: Google LLC

Werner Forman Archive/Shutterstock.com

FIGURE 9.8A AND B **Mohenjo-Daro, Pakistan.** **A)** Satellite view of Mohenjo-Daro. From this perspective, the Mound of the Great Bath is in the center top of the image. The round structure on the upper right is a Buddhist stupa, build around 200 CE, to the east of the Great Bath. **B)** Residential district of Mohenjo-Daro. Archaeologists believe the city housed around 5000 people. Houses were similar sizes, and each house had access to water and sewer. Each residential block had one or more circular wells where residents could draw fresh water.

Nadeem Khawar/Moment Open/Getty Images

FIGURE 9.9 **Mohenjo-Daro, Pakistan.** The Great Bath is located at the highest point in the ancient city. Measuring 39 feet by 23 feet (12 m by 7 m), the Great Bath is the most important part of the city because it is at the highest point and streets lead to it. A Buddhist stupa built around 200 BCE stands in the background of this photo. When Buddhists built this stupa more than 1500 years after the original residents abandoned Mohenjo-Daro, they also chose the highest point to build their sacred place.

Washington, D.C., includes the sizes and shapes of buildings and the layout of the streets. Urban planner Pierre L'Enfant designed the city in 1791 (**Fig. 9.10**), building diagonal streets that are reminiscent of the grand boulevards of Paris. Figure 9.10 shows that the streets all radiate like the spokes in a wheel from the

hub of the U.S. Capitol building. The placement of the government buildings also has a historical foundation. The U.S. Constitution set up three branches of government: legislative (the Capitol), judicial (the Supreme Court), and executive (the White House). The U.S. Constitution establishes the legislative branch first, in Article I, and so L'Enfant gave the U.S. Capitol a central location and marked it with 0° longitude. The White House is noticeable to the west and a bit north of the Capitol. The Supreme Court is not visible on the map because it was housed in the U.S. Capitol at the time. Today, the Supreme Court is located directly east of the U.S. Capitol.

A modern tourist map of Washington, D.C., reveals the functional zonation of the city (**Fig. 9.11**). The central Mall stretches east-west from the U.S. Capitol to the Lincoln Monument. The Arlington Bridge connects the city to Virginia and the Arlington National Cemetery. Memorials to presidents and civil rights leaders, as well as museums housing the heritage and art of the country, encircle the Mall. The U.S. Capitol and U.S. Supreme Court are still central on the tourist map, but they are nearly off the page on the right side of Figure 9.11. The Washington Monument, built between 1848 and 1884, stands in the center of the map and is the tallest structure in the city. The White House is to the north of the

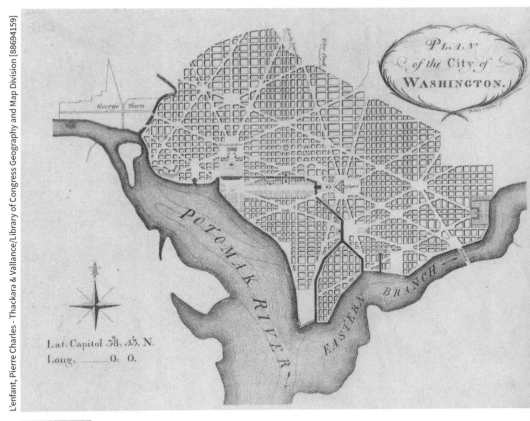

L'enfant, Pierre Charles - Thackara & Vallance/Library of Congress Geography and Map Division [88694159]

FIGURE 9.10 **L'Enfant Plan for Washington, D.C.** President George Washington employed Frenchman Pierre L'Enfant to design the District of Columbia (D.C.). The center of the city is the U.S. Capitol, with streets radiating out from its hub. L'Enfant also marked the site of the U.S. Capitol as 0° longitude in his plan.

Washington Monument, even more centrally located on the map. The top left of the map draws your eye to the Washington National Cathedral, which was built between 1907 and 1990. The U.S. Constitution established a separation between church and state, and this separation is apparent in the city's functional zonation because the cathedral is not located in the same zone as government buildings and museums (**Fig. 9.12**).

AP® Exam Taker's Tip

Governments and societies determine the layout of cities – how cities are laid out (*urban morphology*) and where factories are located versus housing (*functional zoning*). Explain how Washington D.C.'s layout was determined.

Site and Situation

The **site** of a city is its absolute location: its precise position on Earth. A site is often chosen for its advantages in trade or defense, or as a center for religious practice. It may be chosen because it is a good port in a natural bay or a high point that works well for defense. City sites chosen for trade may be at the confluence of rivers, where two or more rivers come together

(such as Pittsburgh, Pennsylvania), or at the fall line of rivers, where the river is no longer navigable by boat.

The fall line on the east coast of the United States marks where the continent's bedrock changes (**Fig. 9.13**). To the west of the fall line, the continent is at a higher elevation and the bedrock is more resistant to erosion. East of the fall line, the rock is more easily eroded and the coastal plains extend to the Atlantic Ocean. At the time the east coast city sites were chosen, boats could travel from the Atlantic Ocean into the interior by river to the point of the fall line. At the fall line, navigators encountered falls and a changes in elevation. Cities sited along the fall line became major centers for trade, connecting traffic from the ocean to traffic from the interior. Goods brought up river from the ocean were transported by horse and buggy to the higher elevation and were traded further into the interior by horse or by barge on the rivers.

The **situation** of a city is its relative location, its place in the region and the world around it. The situation of each city in Figure 9.13 changed multiple ways from colonial to modern times. For example, Fredericksburg, Virginia, was first a trading post in the Virginia colony where enslaved Africans were auctioned and from which the cotton they produced in the interior was shipped. In the mid-1700s, Mary Ball Washington, mother of George Washington, moved to Fredericksburg. When Washington became president, he reportedly visited Mary at her home

FIGURE 9.11 **Washington, D.C.** Tourist maps show the urban morphology and functional zonation of cities. On this trolley map from Washington, D.C., you can see the zone of museums and memorials along the Mall between the Lincoln Memorial and the U.S. Capitol. You can also see the zone of government buildings around the Mall, including the U.S. Capitol, and how it is separated from the Washington National Cathedral on the top left of the map.

Westend61 GmbH/Alamy Stock Photo

FIGURE 9.12 **Washington, D.C.** From base to top, the Washington National Cathedral is not as tall as the Washington Monument (in the background of this photo). However, the Washington National Cathedral sits on the city's tallest hill.

Within a city itself, certain sites are chosen for specific functions. With the hilly topography of Greece, every city had its **acropolis** (*acro* means high point; *polis* means city) where temples were sited. The rocky hilltop of Athens is home to the Parthenon, a temple dedicated to the goddess Athena (**Fig. 9.14A**). Open, spacious squares, often in a low part of town with steps leading down to them, served as the site of the agora, or market (**Fig. 9.14B**). The agora became the focus of commercial activity and also served as a space where Athenians could debate, socialize, and make political decisions.

Roman urban planners adeptly chose favorable sites for cities and thought about each site and its role in the larger situation of the Roman Empire (**Fig. 9.15**). Rome was situated amid small villages and large cities that were all part of this empire. The Romans linked places in their empire with an extensive transportation network that included hundreds of miles of roads, well-established sea routes, and trading ports along the roads, sea, and rivers.

As with Fredericksburg, Virginia, the situation of Rome changed over time. For example, Rome was at first the center and focal point of the Roman Empire. When the Roman Empire dissolved, Rome became the center of the Roman Catholic Church, a role it still plays today. During the Renaissance, when Florence flourished, and during the Industrial Revolution, when Naples and points north of Rome grew economically, the situation of Rome within Italy shifted so that it no longer was the scientific and economic focal point of the country.

before his inauguration to receive her approval. Decades later, during the Civil War, the situation of Fredericksburg changed because it was halfway between the capital of the North, Washington, D.C., and the capital of the South, Richmond, Virginia. Several Civil War battles, including the Battle of Fredericksburg, took place in and around the city. After the Civil War, Fredericksburg functioned as part of the South, oppressing African Americans through segregation. Segregation did not end in the local schools until five African American students went to Spotsylvania High School in 1960, six years after the Supreme Court ruled that segregation was unconstitutional in *Brown v. Board of Education*.

Site and Situation in Europe and Africa Before 1500
How civilizations chose sites for their cities tells us something about what the people valued and how the civilization operated. Ancient Greece encompassed a network of more than 500 cities and towns, not only on the mainland but also on the many Greek islands. The Greeks chose islands and coastal ports for the sites of their major cities and then connected the cities with trade routes across the Mediterranean. Athens and Sparta, which often vied with each other for power, were Greece's leading cities. Both were sited on mountainous peninsulas, which served them well for defense and trade.

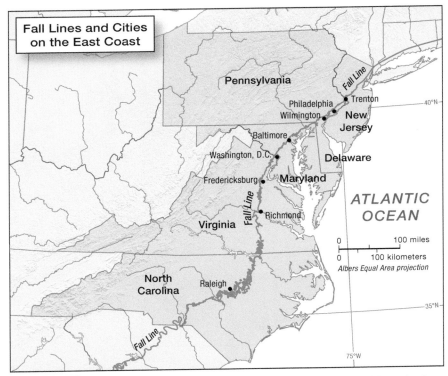

FIGURE 9.13 **Fall lines and cities on the east coast.** On the east coast of the United States, several cities, including Raleigh, Richmond, Washington, D.C., and Philadelphia, are sited on the fall line.

© H.J. de Blij

© H.J. de Blij

FIGURE 9.14A AND B **A) Athens, Greece; the Acropolis.** The rocky hilltop of Athens is home to the Acropolis (*acro* means high point). The Athens Acropolis is still crowned by the great Parthenon. The Parthenon has stood through nearly 2500 years of wars, erosion, vandalism, and environmental impact.

B) Athens, Greece; the Agora. Looking down from the Acropolis, you can see the agora, the ancient trade and market area, which is surrounded by new urban buildings. The situation of the agora in Athens has changed from a central gathering space to an area preserved from the urbanization growing around it.

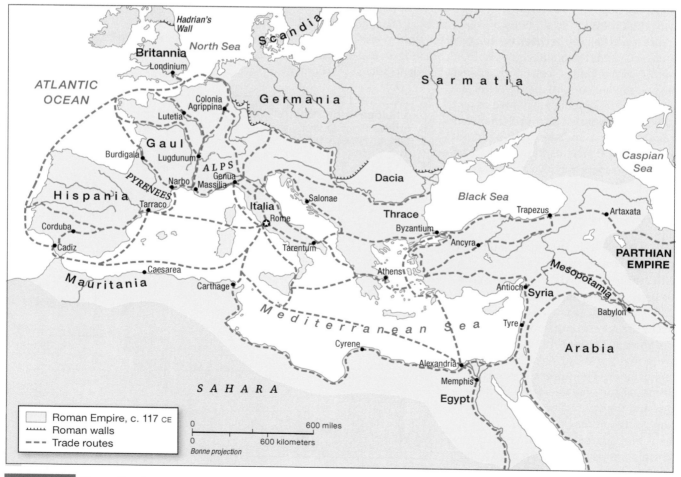

FIGURE 9.15 **Roman Empire Trade Routes c. 117 CE.** The Romans established a system of cities linked by a network of land and sea routes. Many of the Roman cities have grown into modern cities.

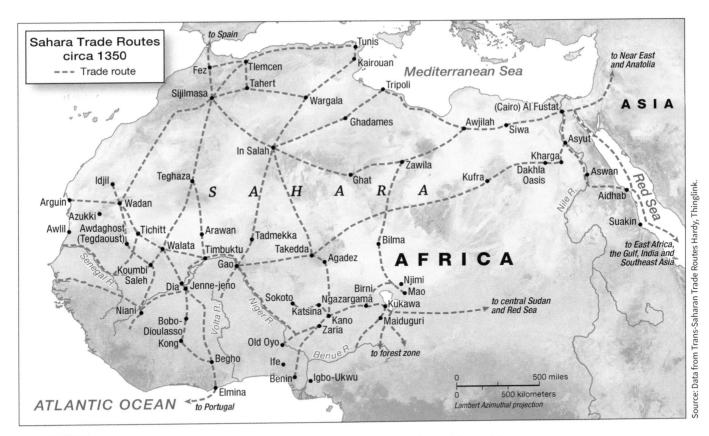

FIGURE 9.16 **Saharan Trade Routes pre-1500.** Before European colonization, African cities mainly looked inland. Trade routes connected the region across the Sahara Desert.

Before 1500 in West Africa, trading cities developed along the southern margin of the Sahara (**Fig. 9.16**). By 1350, Timbuktu (part of Mali today) was a major city: a seat of government, a university town, a market, and a religious center. Other cities included Niani (Guinea), Gao (Mali), Zaria (Nigeria), Kano (Nigeria), and Maiduguri (Nigeria). Here, cross-desert caravan traffic met boat traffic on the Niger River (where "camel met canoe"), and people exchanged goods from northern deserts for goods from coastal forests.

Site and Situation During European Colonization

Before European exploration, most cities in the world were sited on trade routes in the interiors of continents, whether in Africa, Asia, or the Americas. Interior trade routes such as the Silk Route and the caravan routes of West Africa sustained inland cities and helped them prosper. The relative importance of interior trade routes changed, however, when European exploration and colonization expanded from 1500 on. Cities like Basel (Switzerland) and Xi'an (China) changed from being crucial nodes on interior trading routes to being peripheral to ocean-oriented trade.

Cities sited on coasts gained prominence as the situation changed with global sea trade and European colonization after 1500. In Asia, coastal cities such as Bombay (now Mumbai, India), Madras (Chennai, India), Malacca (Malaysia), Batavia (Jakarta, Indonesia), and Tokyo (Japan) grew in economic and political importance. Exploration and trade also altered the situations of cities in West Africa. Coastal ports became the leading markets and centers of power, and the African cities of the interior began a long decline. European colonizers set up ports and railroads to extract resources from the interior and ship them globally (**Fig. 9.17**).

TC Thinking Geographically

Focus on Africa and compare cities in the Nile civilization, cities in the Sahara region before 1500, and cities after European colonization. Explain how changes in transportation, communication, trade, and **globalization** influenced urbanization in Africa over time. Be sure to incorporate the geographic concepts **site** and **situation**.

AP® Exam Taker's Tip

Remember to use Unit 1 terminology throughout the course and in your answers to free-response questions on the exam. For example, a *trade area* is a great example of a **functional region**.

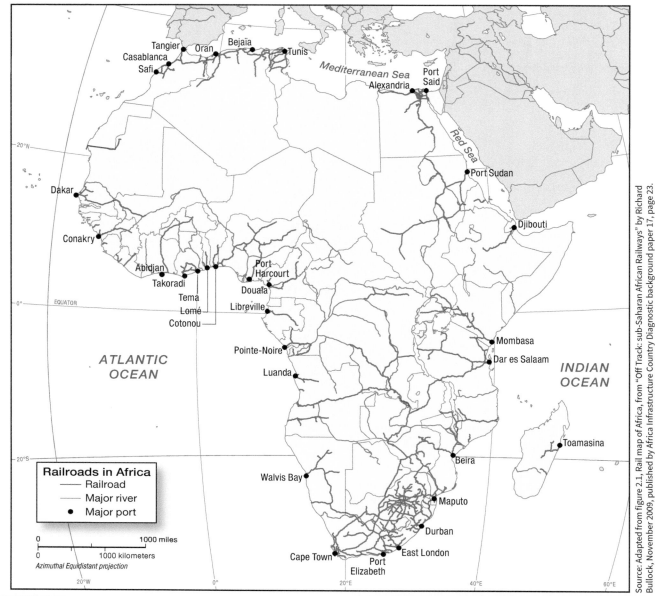

Source: Adapted from figure 2.1, Rail map of Africa, from "Off Track: sub-Saharan African Railways" by Richard Bullock, November 2009, published by Africa Infrastructure Country Diagnostic background paper 17, page 23.

FIGURE 9.17 **Railroads in Africa.** European colonizers built railroads to extract resources from the interior of the continent. Railroads ended in ports, and resources from Africa were shipped around the world from these ports. This map shows where railroads in Africa are located today. Nearly all of these railroads were built before 1960, during European colonialism.

AP® Exam Taker's Tip

Figure 9.18 illustrates *commuter flows* (and their associated services/goods exchanges), which is another excellent example of a **functional region**.

9.2 | Analyze the Distribution of Cities and Their Relative Size.

If you look at a map of cities with symbols displaying the relative population of each city, you may notice that cities appear to be distributed in a predictable way. Every city has a dominant trade area that acts like a force of gravity to the communities around it. People are drawn to the major city in the trade area to work, shop, receive medical care, or find entertainment (**Fig. 9.18**). If you zoom in on one area on Figure 9.18, you can see a hierarchy to the trade areas. The largest city has a large trade area, and then nested within that trade area are smaller cities, each with its own trade area (**Fig. 9.19**).

The goods and services provided within a large city's trade area will be different from those provided within a smaller city's trade area. People within the trade area of a small city likely travel to the small city to purchase milk and bread, have a beer at a bar, order breakfast at a café, or fill a tank of gas. The same consumers will travel to the larger city, whose larger trade area they are also in, to purchase a car, stock up at a big-box store like Target or Costco, visit a doctor, or go to a concert.

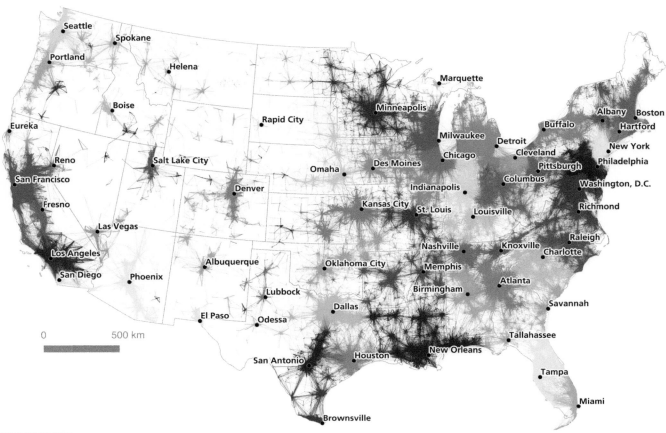

Source: Dash Nelson G, Rae A (2016) An Economic Geography of the United States: From Commutes to Megaregions. PLoS ONE 11(11): e0166083. https://doi.org/10.1371/journal.pone.0166083.

FIGURE 9.18 **Trade Areas of the United States.** Using data from more than 4,000,000 commuter flows, geographers identified megaregions centered on major cities in the United States. Each megaregion can be thought of like a trade area – not only commuters but also consumers may travel to the major city for the kinds of goods and services only available in large cities (e.g. doctors with certain specialties).

The Rank-Size Rule and Primate Cities

Urban geographers have created several ways to measure the hierarchy, relative size, and spacing of cities. The **rank-size rule** states that the population of a city will be inversely proportional to its rank in the hierarchy. The second largest city in an area is half the population of the largest city, and the third largest city will have one-third the population of the largest city. For example, if the largest city has 12 million people, the second largest will have about 6 million; the third largest city will have 4 million; the fourth largest city 3 million; and so on. The difference in population between the sizes of cities decreases as you go down the hierarchy. The biggest difference is between the first and second largest cities. In this example, where the largest city is 12 million, the ninth largest city would have 1.33 million people and the tenth largest city would have 1.2 million people.

German scholar Felix Auerbach suggested the rank-size rule in 1913, and linguist George Zipf is credited with recognizing the mathematical equation for the rank-size rule in 1941. Scholars across various disciplines have tested the rule and questioned when it applies and when it does not. Belgium is a good modern example of the rank-size rule (**Fig. 9.20**). The largest city, Brussels, has 1.78 million people. The second largest, Antwerp, has 940,000 people (should be closer to

890,000 to better follow the rank-size rule). The third, Liege, has 633,000 (the rank-size rule would say 587,000); the fourth, Ghent, has 416,000 (425,000).

Studies in 1966, 1980, and again in 2002 found that most countries had populations with more even distributions than the rank-size rule would predict. Other recent studies have questioned why the rank-size rule fits the countries where it does fit, and answers have included random growth (chance) and economies of scale (efficiency). One major reason the rank-size rule "works" is that the relationship between rank and size is inherently negative, so as rank goes down (closer to 1), size goes up (population), or as rank goes up (farther from 1), size goes down (population).

The size and rank of cities can be disproportionate, however, and in the case of a country with a primate city, one city is quite large and is surrounded by many relatively small cities. In 1939 geographer Mark Jefferson defined a **primate city** as "a country's leading city, always disproportionately large and exceptionally expressive of national capacity and feeling." Governments often help to create primate cities when they focus economic development and infrastructure projects in one city, such as the capital. Focused investment in one place bolsters that city and its population above the rest of the cities. The primate city is the largest and most economically and politically influential, while the remaining cities are all relatively small and lacking in influence.

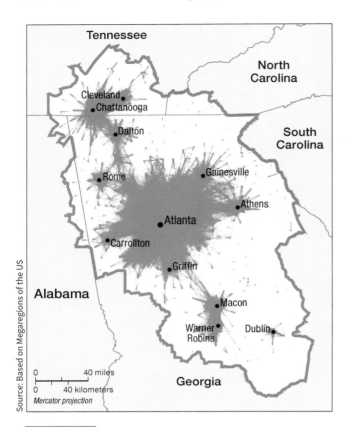

Source: Based on Megaregions of the US

FIGURE 9.19 **Nested Trade Areas of Atlanta, Georgia.** Using the same commuter flow data from Figure 9.18, geographers mapped the commuter shed of each major city. Atlanta's commuter shed is a good estimate of its trade area. Smaller cities that are part of the Atlanta megaregion, or trade area, each have their own smaller trade areas.

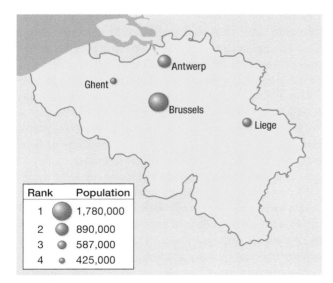

Rank	Population
1	1,780,000
2	890,000
3	587,000
4	425,000

FIGURE 9.20 **Rank-Size Rule in Belgium.** Belgium is a great example of the rank-size rule, which says cities' sizes will vary with their rank. The sizes of the circles on this map are proportional to each city's population. The largest city, Brussels, is twice as large as the second largest city, Antwerp.

fazon1/Deposit Photos

FIGURE 9.21 **Manila, the Philippines.** Manila is a primate city in the Philippines. The city is much bigger than all other cities in the country. This image shows how large the footprint of the city is, as it stretches it all directions.

In 1961, geographer Brian Berry studied 37 populations of countries and found that the rank-size rule worked in 13 countries and the primate city pattern was more evident in 15 countries, while the remaining 9 countries followed neither pattern.

Many former colonies have primate cities because colonizers ruled from one city and concentrated economic and political activities in that place. Examples of primate cities in former colonies include Mexico City, Mexico, and Manila, the Philippines (**Fig. 9.21**). In the noncolonial context, London and Paris serve as examples of primate cities in the United Kingdom and France, respectively.

Central Place Theory

Walter Christaller wrote a classic urban geography study to explain where cities, towns, and villages are likely to be located. In his book *The Central Places in Southern Germany* (1933), Christaller laid the groundwork for **central place theory**. His goal was to predict where central places in the urban hierarchy (hamlets, villages, towns, and cities) would be located. Christaller believed that the urban hierarchy was nested. The largest central place, a city, would provide the greatest number of functions to a large trade area, a **hinterland**. Within that trade area, a series of towns would provide functions to smaller villages. The smaller villages would then provide fewer central functions to hamlets.

Christaller's theory makes several assumptions. First, the surface of the ideal region would be flat and have no physical barriers. Second, soil fertility would be the same everywhere. Third, population and purchasing power would be evenly distributed. Fourth, the region would have a uniform transportation network to permit direct travel from each settlement to the other. Finally, from any given city, a good or service could be sold in all directions as far from the city as might be profitable.

Christaller believed that cities would be regularly spaced so that cities that sold the same product at the same price would be located a standard distance apart. He reasoned that a person would not travel 11 miles to one place to buy an item if he or she could travel 9 miles to buy the same product at the same price. With rationally behaving consumers, each city, each central place, would have an exclusive trade area where it had a monopoly on certain goods.

Hexagonal Hinterlands

A series of cities with distinct trade areas spaced regularly from each other could be envisioned as a set of similarly shaped circles distributed evenly across a map. However, Christaller reasoned that circular trade areas would be inefficient because they would overlap one another or would leave out some places that would be unserved. Instead of circles, Christaller chose perfectly fitted hexagons as the shapes of the trade areas (**Fig. 9.22**).

Urban geographers were divided on the relevance of Christaller's model. Some saw hexagons everywhere, and others saw none. In China, both the North China Plain and the Sichuan Basin display the seemingly uninterrupted flatness assumed by Christaller's model. Geographer G. William Skinner examined the distribution of cities, towns, and villages in China in 1964 and found regularly spaced cities and trade areas that followed Christaller's model. Studies in the U.S. Midwest also found that the flatness and relative sparsity of population followed Christaller's theory.

Christaller recognized that not all his assumptions would be met in reality; physical barriers, uneven resource distributions, and other factors all modify Christaller's hexagons. However, Christaller's theories confirm that the distribution of cities, towns, and villages in a region is not an accident but is tied to trade areas, population size, and distance. Christaller's theory has illuminated hierarchies of urban places, nesting of smaller towns with smaller trade areas inside of the trade areas of larger cities, and the relatively regular spacing of large cities.

Thinking Geographically

Look up the populations of the 10 largest cities and towns in your state and type them into a spreadsheet in order of largest to smallest. Determine whether the cities in your state follow the rank-size rule or the primate city model better. Play around with the data on your spreadsheet and look at a map of your state to see where the cities are located. Create a new rule or model of how cities are sized and distributed in your state. Justify your rule or model by considering how much has changed in lifestyles, economies, and communications since the rank-size rule and primate city model were developed.

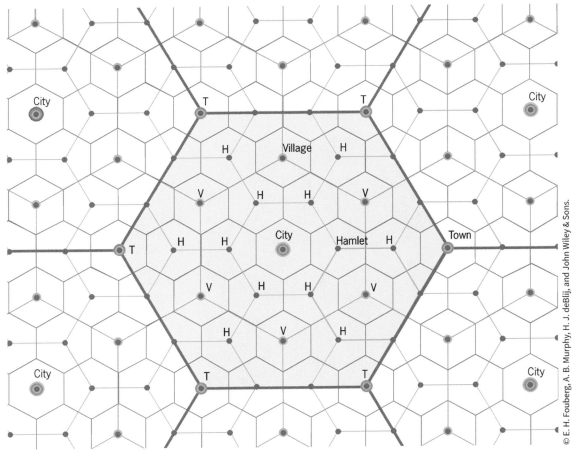

© E. H. Fouberg, A. B. Murphy, H. J. deBlij, and John Wiley & Sons.

FIGURE 9.22   Christaller's Hierarchy of Settlements and Their Service Areas.   In this model: C = city, T = town, V = village, H = hamlet. Each city, town, village, and hamlet has its own hexagonal trade area. The trade areas are nested so the city's much larger trade area includes the trade areas of several villages and hamlets.

9.3 Explain the Internal Structure of Cities and Compare Urban Models.

A city teeming with millions of people may look chaotic, but it functions because the local people understand the organization behind the chaos. The sights, smells, sounds, and movement can be sensory overload to the tourist, but it's just another day for the city's residents (**Fig. 9.23**). What a tourist sees as chaotic, local people see as predictable. They understand how the city is laid out and how each zone functions independently and in concert with other zones.

Urban geographers have studied, charted, and mapped cities to create models that describe the layout of major cities in world regions. City models reveal the structures of the city and describe where functions take place, including trade, education, transportation, manufacturing, and governance. City models also show the combination of historic, spatial, economic, cultural, and political processes that have shaped cities in each world region. Regardless of the region or city, we recognize that models show us a product of many forces that have shaped cities over time. Each model focuses on its author's main interests, reflects his or her perceptions, and leaves out part of the story. Each city is a dynamic place, and its residents are currently reshaping and changing the use of spaces. These models offer a snapshot in time but also help us understand the role people play in making cities around the world.

Zones in Cities

Each model of the city, regardless of the region, is a study in functional zonation—the division of the city into certain regions (zones) for certain purposes (functions). Models of cities give us context for understanding the history and geography of regions and the major cities within them. Studying the location and interplay of zones within cities and cities' changing cultural landscapes helps us grasp the interplay of local and global forces that shape urban development.

Before examining specific models of urban space, we must define some terms commonly used in referring to parts of the city. Each zone is named with a descriptor that indicates the purpose that area of the city serves, such as an industrial zone or a residential zone. The key economic zone of the city is the **central business district** (CBD). The **central city** is the older part of the city surrounding or near the CBD. A **suburb** is an outlying, primarily residential area on the outskirts of a city. The oldest suburbs are typically close to the central city, and the newest suburbs are farther away. **Suburbanization** happens when lands once outside the urban area—often farmland or small towns—are transformed into urban areas.

The European City Model

The founding date of a European city gives some idea of how the city will be laid out. Cities built during the Roman Empire are often sited on prime trade locations like rivers or ports. Streets in the central city are narrow and winding, with paths leading to the trade center. Cities built during the Middle Ages typically have town centers with an elaborate church (built as a Catholic church) on one end, a town hall on the other end, and shops around the square. Residential zones near the central city usually demand high rents and are desirable for their proximity to amenities.

Surrounding the close-in residential zones is a preindustrial periphery that, in earlier times, housed people with lower incomes. This part of the city was significantly impacted by the development of railroads and factories during the Industrial Revolution. Beyond the preindustrial core lies a ring of industrial and postindustrial suburbs that are often \the product of urban planning. Suburbs of European cities may be centers of commerce, residential zones that primarily house immigrants and guest workers (see Chapter 3), or bedroom communities for commuters.

FIGURE 9.23 **Dhaka, Bangladesh.** A traffic jam on a crowded street corner in Dhaka includes cars, rickshaws, auto-rickshaws, and pedestrians trying to merge into an already choked main road.

MissRuby/Shutterstock.com

The North American City Model

Athens, Greece, is 5000 years old. Beijing, China, is 3000 years old. Quebec City, Canada, and Boston, United States, are around 400 years old. North American cities have fewer layers of history than cities in Europe and Asia. However, North America's oldest cities look and feel a bit like Europe because they were built by European migrants.

Models of North American cities developed and changed over the twentieth century as access to cars expanded, city planning increased, migration flows shifted, and functions of the central city diffused. One of the first models of North American cities was drawn by sociologist Ernest Burgess, who studied Chicago in the 1920s and divided the city into five **concentric zones**, all defined by their function (**Fig. 9.24**). At the center is the CBD (1), which is itself subdivided into several subdistricts (financial, retail, theater). The zone of transition (2) is characterized by residential deterioration and encroachment by business and light manufacturing. Zone 3 is a ring of closely spaced, modest homes occupied by factory workers. Zone 4 is middle-class residences, and Zone 5 is the suburban ring. Burgess described his model as dynamic: As the city grew, inner zones encroached on outer ones, so that CBD functions invaded Zone 2 and the problems of Zone 2 affected the inner margins of Zone 3.

In the late 1930s, Homer Hoyt published his **sector model**, partly as an answer to the limitations of the Burgess model (see Fig. 9.24). Hoyt focused on residential patterns, explaining where the wealthy in a city chose to live. He argued that the city grows outward from the center, so that a low-rent area could extend all the way from the CBD to the city's outer edge, creating zones that are shaped like a piece of pie. Hoyt found that the pie-shaped pieces include the high-rent residential, intermediate-rent residential, low-rent residential, education and recreation, transportation, and industrial sectors.

Researchers studied both theories, and in the mid-twentieth century Chauncy Harris and Edward Ullman argued that neither the concentric rings nor the sector model adequately reflected city structure. In the 1940s, they proposed the **multiple nuclei model** (see Fig. 9.24). This model recognizes that the CBD was losing its dominant position as the single nucleus of the urban area. Several of the urban regions shown in Figure 9.24 have their own nuclei.

Access to personal cars and the construction of ring roads and interstates after World War II led to rapid suburbanization, especially around transportation corridors. Suburban downtowns emerged near transportation intersections to serve residents in the suburbs. They attracted large shopping centers, industrial parks, office complexes, hotels, restaurants,

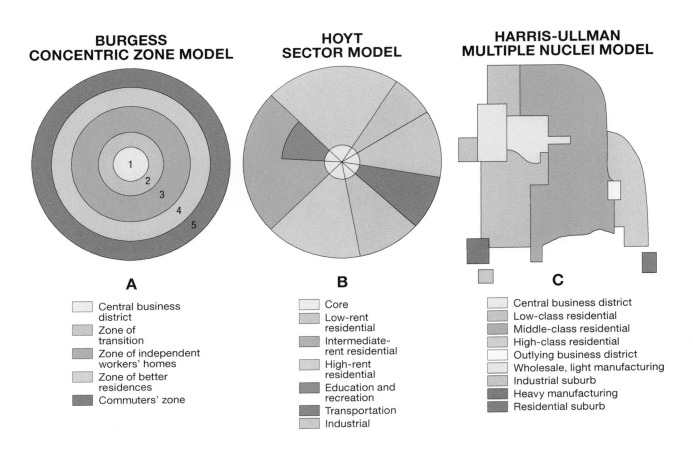

BURGESS CONCENTRIC ZONE MODEL

A

- Central business district
- Zone of transition
- Zone of independent workers' homes
- Zone of better residences
- Commuters' zone

HOYT SECTOR MODEL

B

- Core
- Low-rent residential
- Intermediate-rent residential
- High-rent residential
- Education and recreation
- Transportation
- Industrial

HARRIS-ULLMAN MULTIPLE NUCLEI MODEL

C

- Central business district
- Low-class residential
- Middle-class residential
- High-class residential
- Outlying business district
- Wholesale, light manufacturing
- Industrial suburb
- Heavy manufacturing
- Residential suburb

FIGURE 9.24 **North American City Models.** The Burgess concentric zone model (left) was the first model of a North American city. The Hoyt sector model and Harris-Ullman multiple nuclei model followed, each tweaking zones laid out in Burgess's original model to fit zones the authors thought the Burgess model missed and the ways the authors saw the growth of North American cities.

The Washington Post/Getty Images

FIGURE 9.25 **Tysons Corner, Virginia.** In the suburbs of Washington, D.C., on Interstate 495, Tysons Corner has developed as a major edge city, with offices, retail, and commercial services.

and Irvine, California (outside Los Angeles), are classic edge cities. Edge cities offer suburbanites office space, shopping opportunities, leisure activities, and all the other elements of a complete urban environment, making trips into the central city less necessary (**Fig. 9.25**).

Present-day Los Angeles and Toronto are prime examples of what is sometimes called a **galactic city**—a complex urban area where functions of the city are not centered in one place (**Fig. 9.26**). Cities with post-industrial economies often follow the galactic city model. The CBD has high rises and businesses and is surrounded by a less densely populated central city. The central city plays the role of a festival or recreational area, while around the city, industrial parks, shopping centers, high-tech centers, and edge-city downtowns each serve as centers of economic activity. The city often has a ring road or highway surrounding it and radial roads reaching out from the CBD. Suburbs create distant nuclei near the ring and radial roads. Suburban residents can

entertainment facilities, and even sports stadiums. Geographers call such large urban areas with extensive space for offices and retail businesses on the outskirts of major cities **edge cities**. Tysons Corner, Virginia (outside Washington, D.C.), find the goods and services they need in the suburbs, which reduces the volume and level of interaction between the CBD and suburbs. Thus the galactic city is a decentered urban area with multiple nuclei that serve different functions.

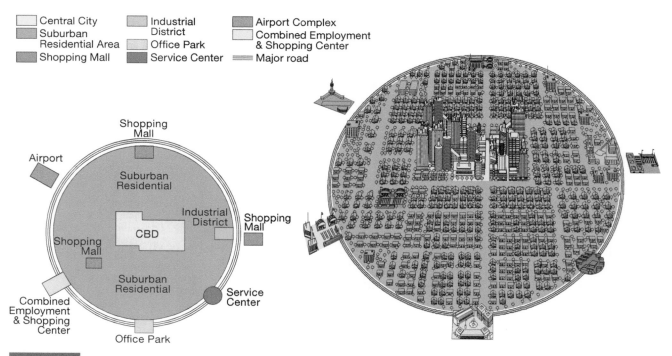

Legend:
- Central City
- Suburban Residential Area
- Shopping Mall
- Industrial District
- Office Park
- Service Center
- Airport Complex
- Combined Employment & Shopping Center
- Major road

FIGURE 9.26 **The Galactic City Model.** Several North American cities, including Detroit, Atlanta, Los Angeles, and Toronto follow the galactic city model. The CBD has high rises and businesses. Suburban downtowns grow from the ring road, encircling the city, and radial highways stretch out from the CBD.

The Latin American City Model

Geographers Ernst Griffin and Larry Ford created a model of South American cities that combined radial sectors and concentric zones. The **Latin American city model**, also called the Griffin–Ford model, blends traditional elements of South American culture with the influences of the global economy. When building cities in the Americas, Spanish colonizers followed the Laws of the Indies, which dictated how wide streets should be and specified that each city should be built around a central plaza. Over time the central plaza became a central business district (CBD).

The Latin American city model (the Griffin–Ford model) is anchored around a thriving CBD, which remains the city's primary business, employment, and entertainment focus. The CBD is divided into a traditional market sector and a more modern high-rise sector. Reaching out from the CBD are three radial sectors: the commercial spine and two zones of squatter settlements. The two radial sectors of squatter settlements are the oldest low-income neighborhoods (called favelas or barrios), with the oldest slums built closest to the CBD. The commercial spine includes offices, shopping areas, high-quality housing for the upper and upper-middle classes, restaurants, theaters, and amenities such as parks, zoos, and golf courses. The commercial spine is surrounded by the elite residential sector.

Surrounding the CBD are three concentric zones of residential areas. The zone of maturity is the closest to the CBD and has the oldest housing and the best transportation links to the CBD. The zone of in situ accretion is marked by constant building and rebuilding and is mainly a middle-class residential zone. A ring around the outside of the city is the zone of peripheral squatter settlements where more recent migrants from rural areas live (**Fig. 9.27**). The Griffin–Ford model also displays two smaller sectors: an industrial park, where industrial activity is concentrated, and a gentrification zone, where middle-class and wealthier residents are remodeling and rebuilding older homes close to the CBD.

A structural element common to many South American cities is the **disamenity sector**, the very poorest areas that may not be connected to regular city services and may be controlled by gangs or drug lords who run the informal economy in the sectors. Neighborhoods in the disamenity sector are known as *barrios* or *favelas* (**Fig. 9.28**). Favelas can be tucked in close to the CBD, as seen in the "squatter settlement" zones radiating from the CBD in the Griffin–Ford model. Residents of the closer-in favelas have lived there for generations. Many are descendants of enslaved Africans who migrated to the city from farming areas after Brazil became the last country in the Americas to abolish slavery in 1888. Favelas that encircle the outskirts of the city, near the ring highways or *periféricos*, are typically home to more recent migrants from rural areas who are drawn to the city for work.

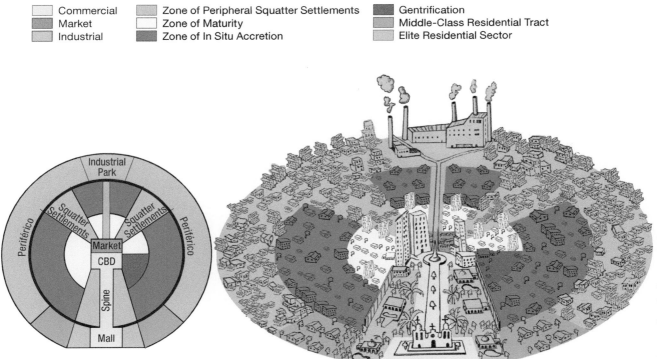

☐ Commercial	☐ Zone of Peripheral Squatter Settlements	■ Gentrification
■ Market	☐ Zone of Maturity	■ Middle-Class Residential Tract
☐ Industrial	■ Zone of In Situ Accretion	☐ Elite Residential Sector

Source: Adapted with permission from: T. G. McGee, The Southeast Asian City, London: Bell, 1967, p. 128

FIGURE 9.27 **Latin American City Model.** This model includes both the zones created in the original Griffin–Ford model and the new Ford model of the South American city.

Author Field Note   Winding Through the Hillside Favelas of Rio de Janeiro, Brazil

"Thanks to a Brazilian colleague, I spent a day in two of Rio de Janeiro's hill-slope favelas, an eight-hour walk through one into the other. Here live millions of the city's poor, in areas often ruled by drug lords and their gangs, with minimal or no public services, amid squalor and stench, in discomfort and danger. And yet life in the older favelas has become more comfortable as shacks are replaced by more permanent structures, electricity is sometimes available, water supply, however haphazard, is improved, and an informal economy brings goods and services to the residents. I stood in the doorway of a resident's single-room dwelling for this overview of an urban landscape in transition: Satellite television dishes symbolize the change going on here. The often-blue cisterns catch rainwater; walls are made of rough brick and roofs of corrugated iron or asbestos sheeting. There are no roads or automobile access, so people walk to the nearest road at the bottom of the hill. In preparation for the 2014 World Cup, the city of Rio and government of Brazil demolished several favelas and spent millions of dollars working to provide services to remaining favelas in the path of the public eye."

– H.J. de Blij

FIGURE 9.28 **Rio de Janeiro, Brazil.** Approximately 25 percent of people in Rio de Janeiro live in favelas. This favela is one of more than 1,000 in the city.

The African City Model

African cities predate European colonialism and include Timbuktu (Mali), home to the oldest university in the world. Geographer H.J. de Blij created the **African city model**, or the de Blij model, to show how colonial cities were often built around African cities. In the model, the central city often consists of three CBDs (**Fig. 9.29**): a traditional CBD where commerce is conducted on streets, in stalls, and behind storefronts; an informal and sometimes periodic market zone, and a colonial

☐ Traditional CBD	☐ Zone of Slums and Squatter Settlements	☐ Market Zone
☐ Colonial CBD	☐ Zone of Lower to Middle Income Residential	☐ Mining and Manufacturing

Major Road
—— Local Street

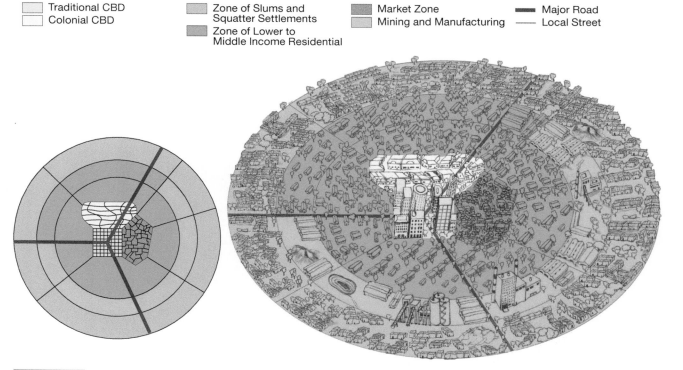

FIGURE 9.29 **African City Model.** The de Blij model of the African city includes a colonial CBD, a traditional CBD, and a market zone.

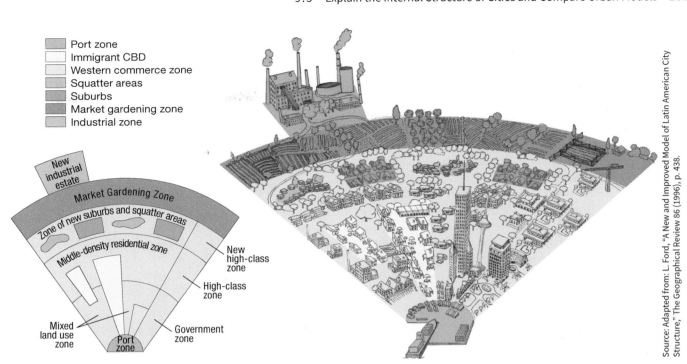

Legend:
- Port zone
- Immigrant CBD
- Western commerce zone
- Squatter areas
- Suburbs
- Market gardening zone
- Industrial zone

New industrial estate

Market Gardening Zone

Zone of new suburbs and squatter areas

Middle-density residential zone

New high-class zone

High-class zone

Mixed land use zone

Government zone

Port zone

Source: Adapted from: L. Ford, "A New and Improved Model of Latin American City Structure," The Geographical Review 86 (1996), p. 438.

FIGURE 9.30 **Southeast Asian City Model.** A model of land use in the Southeast Asian city includes sectors and zones within each sector.

CBD. High-rise buildings are mainly found in the colonial CBD. The traditional CBD is usually a zone of single-story buildings with some traditional architecture. The market zone tends to be an open-air sector for the informal economy.

Around the CBDs, residential zones include lower-, middle-, and high-income housing. Ethnic neighborhoods are common and are populated by descendants of European colonizers, descendants of migrants from India who came over during the European colonial era, longtime African residents, and new migrants from rural areas who may be from neighboring countries. Mining operations may still take place in the African cities that developed first as mining towns. Factories are often found in and around mining areas, too, for proximity to workers. Much like Latin American cities, African cities often have rings of slums that are home to the most recent rural-to-urban migrants.

The Southeast Asian City Model

In 1967, urban geographer T. G. McGee studied medium-sized cities of Southeast Asia and found that they exhibit similar land-use patterns. He created a model referred to as the **Southeast Asian City Model** or the McGee model (**Fig. 9.30**). The focal point of the city is the old colonial port zone, which is combined with the largely commercial district that surrounds it. McGee found no formal CBD. Instead, he found that the elements of the CBD are present as separate clusters surrounding the old colonial port zone: the government zone; the Western commercial zone

(WC on the model); and the immigrant CBD settled by Chinese merchants whose residences are attached to their places of business. The other nonresidential areas are the market-gardening zone at the outskirts of the urban area and, still farther from the city, a recently built industrial zone (or "estate").

The residential zones in the Southeast Asian city model include a higher-income residential zone radiating out from the port just beyond the government zone, and a new higher-income residential zone beyond that. On the left side of the diagram in Figure 9.30, a mixed land-use zone stretches from the port and is interspersed with the immigrant CBDs (IC in the model). Beyond that, a middle-density residential zone is followed by new suburbs and newer slums (A and B in the model). The outskirts of the city include a market-gardening zone.

Thinking Geographically

Employing the concepts defined in this section of the chapter, compare and contrast the Latin American city model with either the African city or Southeast Asian city model. What is similar? Can you see influences of colonialism in each model? Are the lowest income residential areas located on the outskirts of the city? Where are the highest income residential areas located relative to manufacturing zones?

9.4   Analyze How Political and Economic Policies Shape Cities.

Individuals, governments, corporations, developers, financial lenders, and realtors all play a role in shaping cities. Government planning agencies can directly affect the layout of cities by restricting the kinds of development allowed in certain regions or zones. People also shape cities by choosing to live in certain neighborhoods and by opening stores, houses of worship, and even stadiums that reflect the values of their culture.

Zoning laws divide up the city and designate the kinds of development allowed in each zone. Portland, Oregon, is often described as the best-planned city in North America because it is built around free transportation in the central city to discourage the use of cars. Office buildings and residential zones are in close proximity to encourage walking, biking, and public transportation. In contrast, Houston, Texas, is the only large city that does not have zoning laws on the books. Houstonites voted against the creation of zoning laws three different times (most recently in 1993).

Cities in the global economic periphery, or the lower income parts of the world, generally lack enforceable zoning laws. Without zoning laws, people live anywhere there is space in cities in the periphery. For example, in cities such as Hyderabad, India (and in other cities in India), open space between new buildings is often occupied by squatter settlements (**Fig. 9.31**). In Accra, Ghana, slums like Nima are located between two high-income neighborhoods. In Manila, the Philippines, thousands of families live on and around garbage dumps and millions scavenge to find materials to sell and food to eat (**Fig. 9.32**). Over time, such living conditions may change,

Photo by E.H. Fouberg. © 2020 John Wiley & Sons, Inc.

FIGURE 9.31   Hyderabad, India.   Homes made from corrugated steel, sticks, and blue tarps are tucked between building projects near an information technology park. The migrants who live here built their homes to withstand the rain of the summer monsoon.

as rising land values and greater demand for enforced zoning regulations are transforming the central cities of East Asia. But in South Asia, sub-Saharan Africa, Southwest Asia, North Africa, and Middle and South America, unregulated growth continues.

Guest Field Note   Scavenging a Living in Manila, the Philippines

Johnathan Walker
James Madison University

"I passed through cargo shipping piers in Manila, the Philippines, and encountered row after row of hand-built squatter houses. I was struck by the scale of the settlements and the sheer number of people who inhabit them. I was shocked at the level of squalor in people's living conditions. The people scavenging garbage in this picture wore cotton gloves and held prods to dig through the trash for items they can use, trade, or sell. Poorer residents live in settlements like this throughout the city because the city does not have enough housing and the housing available is not affordable. Still, thousands from rural areas and smaller cities migrate to Manila, recognizing that working in the informal economy and even scavenging garbage offer more opportunity than life in the rural provinces."

© Jonathan Walker

FIGURE 9.32   Manila, the Philippines.   Garbage scavengers in Manila look for materials to recycle and sell, and many also look for food to consume or sell.

Redlining, Blockbusting, and White Flight

The goals people have in establishing cities have changed over time. People constantly remake the cities where they live, reinventing neighborhoods or altering layouts to reflect changing goals and aesthetics. During the segregation era in the United States, realtors, financial lenders, and city governments defined and segregated spaces in urban environments. For example, before the civil rights movement of the 1960s, a federal agency (the Home Owners' Loan Corporation) and banks engaged in **redlining**. The federal agency assessed the risk of real estate investments in major cities in the United States, using 4 categories. They drew red lines on a map around neighborhoods they considered to be "hazardous" or "risky" (**Fig. 9.33**). The main criteria they used to assess risk was race, and they placed predominantly black neighborhoods within red lines. Banks refused to offer mortgage loans to anyone purchasing a house in the redlined neighborhoods.

Redlining, which became illegal with the 1968 Fair Housing Act, worked against those living in the "hazardous" neighborhoods that were redlined. Not being able to secure a mortgage meant that black residents of redlined neighborhoods could not easily buy homes. Those who did buy homes saw little to no increase in the value of their houses. These factors grew the wealth gap between blacks and whites because equity gained through home ownership is a major generator of household wealth in the United States. The impacts of redlining persist today. A report by the real estate company Zillow in 2018 found that across the United States, the median housing value of homes in redlined neighborhoods is 85 percent of the median value in surrounding, non-redlined neighborhoods.

Also before the Fair Housing Act, realtors could purposely sell a house in a white neighborhood at a very low price to a black buyer. In a practice called **blockbusting**, realtors would then solicit white residents of the neighborhood to sell their homes under the guise that the neighborhood was "going downhill" because a black person or family had moved in. This practice produced what urban geographers and sociologists call **white flight**—movement of whites from the city and adjacent neighborhoods to the outlying suburbs. Blockbusting led to significant turnover in housing, which of course benefited real estate agents because of the commissions they earned as representatives of buyers and sellers. Blockbusting also prompted landowners to sell their properties at low prices to get out of the neighborhood quickly, which in turn allowed developers to subdivide lots and build tenements. Typically, developers did not maintain tenements well, dropping the property values even further.

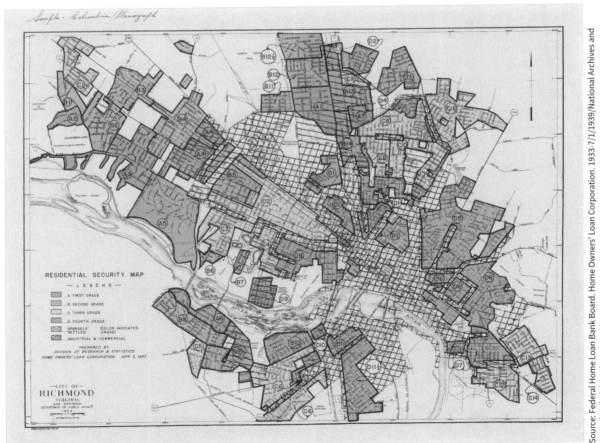

Source: Federal Home Loan Bank Board. Home Owners' Loan Corporation. 1933-7/1/1939/National Archives and Records Administration

FIGURE 9.33 **Richmond, Virginia.** The Federal Home Loan Bank Board and the Home Owners' Loan Corporation mapped four zones of the City of Richmond, Virginia in 1933. The areas colored in red on the map were deemed "hazardous" and banks denied mortgage loans to residents in redlined areas. The Home Owners' Loan Corporation drew red lines around predominantly black neighborhoods.

Gentrification

Developers and governments are also important actors in shaping cities. In cities of the global core that have experienced high levels of suburbanization, people have left the city proper for the suburbs in search of single-family homes, yards, better schools, and safety. As a result, city governments lose tax revenue, as middle- and upper-class taxpayers leave the city and pay taxes in the suburbs instead. To counter the suburbanization trend, city governments are encouraging commercialization of the CBD and gentrification of neighborhoods in and around that district.

The plans that city governments develop to revive central cities usually involve cleaning streets, sidewalks, and buildings; tearing down old, abandoned buildings; and building up commercial offerings and residences. City governments have often created programs to encourage the commercialization of CBDs, which entails transforming the CBD into an area attractive to residents and tourists alike. Several cities, including Miami, New York, and Baltimore, have created waterfront "theme" areas to attract visitors. These areas include festival marketplaces, parks with exotic sculptures and play areas, and amusement zones occupying former industrial sites. Cities such as Detroit and Minneapolis commercialize their CBDs by building or using tax incentives to attract professional sports stadiums to the central areas in the city. Such ventures have been successful in attracting tourists and in generating business, but they alone cannot revive downtowns because they cannot attract what the core of the city needs most: permanent residents with a stake in its future.

Newly commercialized downtowns often stand apart from the rest of the central city. Beginning in the 1960s, low-income central-city neighborhoods located conveniently close to CBDs began to attract buyers who were willing to move back into the city to renovate rundown houses and live in central-city neighborhoods. A process called **gentrification**, the renewal or rebuilding of lower-income neighborhoods into middle- to upper-class neighborhoods, took hold near the centers of many cities.

In the United States, gentrification began in cities with a tight housing market and defined central-city neighborhoods, including San Francisco, Portland, and Chicago. Gentrification slowed in the 1990s, but it is growing again as city governments encourage beautification programs and give significant tax breaks to people who buy up abandoned or dilapidated housing. The growing interest in central-city housing has resulted in part from the changing character of American society: The proportion of childless couples (heterosexual and homosexual) is growing, as is the number of single people in the population. Childless couples and singles often choose to live in cities because features of the suburbs, including excellent school districts and large back yards, do not have the same draw. Gentrified central-city neighborhoods attract residents who want to live within walking distance of their workplace and close to cultural, entertainment, and recreational amenities, nightlife, and restaurants (**Fig. 9.34**).

One consequence of gentrification is increased housing prices in central-city neighborhoods. Gentrification usually displaces lower-income residents because property taxes rise as land values rise, and the cost of goods and services in the neighborhood, from parking to restaurants, rises as well. For urbanites displaced by gentrification, the consequences can be serious. Rising housing costs associated with gentrification have played a key role in the growing number of homeless in American cities.

Gentrification in Suburbs

Suburbs are not immune to gentrification. In suburbs that are close to the city or directly connected by commuter rail, people purchase smaller or older homes with the intention of tearing the house down and building a much larger home. The homes intended for

---

Author Field Note   Tracking Gentrification over Three Decades in Fort Worth, Texas

"In 2008, downtown Fort Worth, Texas, looked quite different than it did when I first visited in 1997. In that 11-year period, business leaders in the city of Fort Worth gentrified the downtown. The Bass family, who has a great deal of wealth from oil holdings and who now owns about 40 blocks of downtown Fort Worth, was instrumental in the city's gentrification. In the 1970s and 1980s, members of the Bass family looked at empty, stark, downtown Fort Worth and sought a way to revitalize the downtown. They worked with the Tandy family to build and revitalize the spaces of the city, which took off in the late 1990s and into the present century. The crown jewel in the gentrified Fort Worth is the beautiful cultural center called the Bass Performance Hall, named for Nancy Lee and Perry R. Bass, which opened in 1998. I returned to Fort Worth in 2016, and found public spaces where families were watching movies outdoors at night, new restaurants, and a vibrant retail district. The city's gentrification, however, is pushing out low-income residents and access to affordable housing is lacking. People without homes have built tent-cities in Fort Worth. Churches and coalitions provide shelters and other services to a growing number of homeless."

–E.H. Fouberg

Photo by E.H. Fouberg. © 2020 John Wiley & Sons, Inc.

FIGURE 9.34 Fort Worth, Texas.

FIGURE 9.35 Hinsdale, Illinois. In this upscale suburb of Chicago, a new McMansion stands in the place where a smaller house (similar in size to the one still standing in the right of the photo) used to stand. One historic preservation consultant estimated half of the houses in Hinsdale were torn down and replaced, usually with much larger houses, since the 1990s.

suburban demolition are called **teardowns**. In their place, suburbanites build newer homes that often are supersized and stretch to the outer limits of the lot. New supersized mansions are sometimes called **McMansions** (**Fig. 9.35**).

Like gentrification in the city, the teardown phenomenon changes the landscape and increases average housing values, tax revenue for the suburb, and the average household income of the neighborhood. Unlike with central-city gentrification, with teardowns the original houses are destroyed instead of preserved. Teardowns often occur in middle-class and wealthy suburbs such as Greenwich, Connecticut, and Hinsdale, Illinois.

Greenwich, a high-end neighborhood in Fairfield County, Connecticut, just outside of New York City, issued 138 permits for teardowns in 2004 (56 more than it did the year before). The collapse of the housing market brought a decline in the number of teardowns in Fairfield County starting in 2007. The number of teardowns annually rose again after 2010 but has ticked down as the area has reached an oversupply in multimillion-dollar homes.

The teardown phenomenon may have hit saturation, as desire for enormous houses is declining in neighborhoods like Hinsdale and Greenwich. Owners often overestimate the value of their larger, newer homes and have found it more difficult to sell the homes than they expected because of the oversupply. Realtors are speculating that as teardowns decline in

popularity in high-end neighborhoods, they may increase in popularity in middle-income suburbs where tract homes were built quickly following World War II. The number of new lots within reasonable commuting distance is limited, and if incomes continue to rise, new areas of cities will be looked toward for teardowns.

Those in favor of teardowns argue that the phenomenon slows urban sprawl by replacing existing homes with new homes, rather than converting farmland to residential lots. Those opposed to teardowns see the houses as too large for their lots, dwarfing the neighboring houses and destroying the character of the street by demolishing the older homes on it.

Urban Sprawl and New Urbanism

As populations have grown in certain areas of the United States, such as the Sun Belt and the West, urban areas have experienced **urban sprawl**—unrestricted growth of housing, commercial developments, and roads over large expanses of land, with little concern for urban planning. Urban sprawl is easy to spot as you drive down major roadways in any urbanized part of the country. You will see strip malls, big-box stores, chain restaurants, huge intersections, and numerous housing developments, all spread out over many acres (**Fig. 9.36**).

Sprawl is a phenomenon of the automobile era. Cities that expanded before the automobile typically grew "up" instead of "out." For instance, Boston grew around the marketplace and port, but it grew before the automobile, resulting in development over smaller areas. When you go through the central city of Boston today, you can walk where you need to go or take the T (metro). Places are built up vertically, and curving, narrow streets and commercial developments with a flavor of the old city (Quincy Market) give the city a cozy, intimate feel.

FIGURE 9.36 Henderson, Nevada. Henderson is the largest suburb of Las Vegas, and it was also the fastest-growing urban settlement in the United States between 1990 and 2000. Many of the houses in this photograph are empty today, as Las Vegas is experiencing high vacancy rates.

Does population growth explain which cities experience the most urban sprawl? In a study of sprawl from 1960 through the 1990s, Leon Kolankiewicz and Roy Beck (two anti-sprawl writers) used United States Census data on urbanized areas and found that urban sprawl happened even in urban areas without significant population growth. In the United States, urban sprawl is more common in the Sun Belt of the South (Atlanta) and in the West (Houston) in urban areas where population is rapidly growing (**Table 9.1**). Yet, even in cities such as Detroit and Pittsburgh, where urban populations fell between 1960 and 1990—by 7 percent in Detroit and 9 percent in Pittsburgh—urban sprawl increased the urbanized areas of the cities by 28 percent and 30 percent, respectively. When urban sprawl happens, farmlands and old industrial sites are razed, roads are built or widened, strip malls are erected, and housing developments come to monopolize the horizon.

To counter urban sprawl, a group of architects, urban planners, and developers (now numbering over 2000 in more than 20 countries) proposed an urban design vision they call new urbanism. Forming the Congress for the New Urbanism in 1993, the group defines **new urbanism** as development, urban revitalization, and suburban reforms that create walkable neighborhoods with a diversity of housing and jobs. On their website, the Congress for the New Urbanism explains that "New Urbanists support regional planning for open space, appropriate architecture and planning, and the balanced development of jobs and housing. They believe these strategies are the best way to reduce how long people spend in traffic, to increase the supply of affordable housing, and to rein in urban sprawl." New urbanists want to create neighborhoods that promote a sense of community and a sense of place.

TABLE 9.1	Most Sprawling Metro Areas with a Population Over 1 Million in the United States

Smart Growth America created an index to measure urban sprawl based on development density, land-use mix, activity centering, and street accessibility. These ten major metro areas have the lowest density over a wide space, creating urban sprawl.

Most Sprawling Large Metro Areas, 2014	
Cities with a population of more than one million	**State**
1. Atlanta-Sandy Springs/Marietta	GA
2. Nashville/Davidson/Murfreesboro/Franklin	TN
3. Riverside-San Bernardino/Ontario	CA
4. Warren/Troy/Farmington Hills	MI
5. Charlotte/Gastonia-Rock Hill	NC/SC
6. Memphis	TN/MS/AR
7. Birmingham-Hoover	AL
8. Rochester	NY
9. Richmond	VA
10. Houston/Sugar Land/Baytown	TX

Source: *Data from*: R. Ewing, Rolf Pendall, and Don Chen. *Measuring Sprawl and Its Impact*. Volume 1. Smart Growth America. http://www.smartgrowthamerica.org/documents/MeasuringSprawlTechnical.pdf.

The most famous new urbanist projects are cities that new urbanists designed from the ground up, including Seaside, Florida (featured in the movie *The Truman Show*), West Laguna, California, and Kentlands, Maryland. When new urbanists build a town, the design is reminiscent of Christaller over a much smaller area. The planners choose the central shopping areas and open spaces and develop the neighborhoods around them, with housing clustered around the central space so that people can walk to the shopping area within five minutes. One goal of new urbanist designs is to build housing more densely, taking up less space. In addition, making shopping and other amenities walkable decreases dependency on the automobile, which in the process helps improve sustainability.

Although some see new urbanist designs as manufactured communities and feel disconnected in a new urbanist space, others see these designs as an important antidote to sprawl. Celebration, Florida, is a remarkable new urbanist space: It is adjacent to Walt Disney's theme parks, was envisioned by Walt Disney himself, and was originally owned by the Disney Company (**Fig. 9.37**). Built in 1994, Celebration is centered on Market Street, a shopping district with restaurants (including a 1950s-style diner and a pizza place), a town hall, banks, a post office, and a movie theater with a nostalgic marquee (**Fig. 9.38**). The town includes schools, a health center, a fitness center, and churches. The Disney Company chose certain architectural styles for the houses in Celebration, and builders initially offered homes and townhouses in a price range from $300,000 to over $1 million. To meet the new urbanist goal of incorporating diverse people in a community, Celebration includes apartments for rent and condominiums for sale.

For geographers, new urbanism marks a redefinition of space in the city. Public spaces, they say, become privatized for the enjoyment of the few (the residents of the neighborhood). Geographers Stuart Aitken, Don Mitchell, and Lynn Staeheli note that as new urbanism strives to turn neighborhoods back in time, "spaces and social functions historically deemed public (such as parks, neighborhood centers, shopping districts)" are privatized. The houses with porches that encourage neighbors to talk and the parks that are within walking distance for the residents create "mythic landscapes that are ingratiating for those who can afford them and exclusionary for those who cannot."

Noted geographer David Harvey offers one of the strongest critiques of new urbanism, explaining first that most new urbanist designs are "greenfield" projects designed for the affluent to make suburban areas more livable. This fact is evidence, Harvey argues, that the new urbanism movement is a kind of "spatial determinism" that does not recognize that "the fundamental difficulty with modernism was its persistent habit of privileging spatial forms over social processes." Harvey, and others who critique new urbanism, claim that new urbanism does nothing to break down the social conditions that privilege some while disadvantaging others; that new urbanist projects take away much of the grittiness and character of the city; and that the "communities" that new urbanists form through their projects are exclusionary communities that deepen racial segregation.

Despite the critiques against new urbanism, developments in the new urbanist tradition are attracting a growing

Author Field Note   Embracing Nostalgia in New Urbanism in Celebration, Florida

"When I visited Celebration, Florida, in 1997, one year after residents moved into the first houses in the community, I felt like I was walking onto a movie or television set. The architecture in the Walt Disney-designed new urbanist development looked like a quintessential American town. Each house has a porch, but on the day I was there, the porches sat empty—waiting to welcome the arrival of their owners at the end of the work day. We walked through town, past the 50s-style movie marquee, and ate lunch at a 50s-style diner. At that point, Celebration was still growing. Across the street from the 'Bank of Celebration' stood a sign marking the future home of the 'Church in Celebration.'

I recently returned to Celebration, and I spent the day walking the same streets. The 'Church in Celebration,' a Presbyterian community church, was built, and the main street through the town square was hosting an arts festival focused on dogs. The city had grown to 11,000 residents, suffered its first murder, and was experiencing a higher rate of foreclosures than the rest of Florida. The movie theater still stood but no longer showed movies. A Starbucks took up a main corner in town, standing next door to a Morgan Stanley office and an Irish pub. Disney no longer owns the town, but the influence of the Disney vision still stands, with architectural covenants allowing only certain house styles, a few pastel house colors, and hiding the trash and cars in alleys."

–E.H. Fouberg

FIGURE 9.37   Celebration, Florida.

FIGURE 9.38   **Celebration, Florida.**   Opened in 1996 with two screens and operated by AMC, the Celebration Cinema closed in 2010. The spires remain landmarks in the town.

Photo by E.H. Fouberg. © 2020 John Wiley & Sons, Inc.

number of people, and when they are situated within cities, they can work against urban sprawl.

Gated Communities

As you drive through urban spaces in the United States, suburban and central city alike, you will note more and more neighborhoods being developed or redesigned to align with new urbanist principles. In your inventory of landscapes, even more overwhelming will be the proliferation of gated communities. Gated communities are fenced-in neighborhoods with controlled access gates for people and automobiles. Often gated communities have security cameras and security forces (privatized police) keeping watch over the community, as the main objective is to create a space of safety within the uncertain urban world. A secondary objective is to maintain or increase housing values in the neighborhood through enforcement of the neighborhood association's bylaws, which control everything from the color of houses to the character and size of additions.

During the late 1980s and early 1990s, developers in the United States began building gated communities in urban areas around the country. In a 2001 American Housing Survey, the United States government reported that 16 million people, or about 6 percent of Americans, live in gated communities. Recent surveys have not gathered the same statistics; so, it's difficult to estimate what percent of U.S. residents live in gated communities today, but the demand for homes in gated communities is increasing. Gated communities in the U.S. are quite popular in the Sun Belt and have diffused both across the U.S. and around the globe at record speed. Gated communities are now found in Europe, Asia, Africa, and Latin America.

In countries in the global periphery, where cities are divided between wealthy and poor, between haves and have-nots, gated communities provide another layer of comfort for the city's wealthy. In the large cities of Latin America and Africa, you commonly see walls around individual houses belonging to wealthy and middle-class families, enclosing yards and pools and keeping out crime. Barbed wire or shards of glass are often fixed to the top of walls to discourage intruders from scaling them.

Walled houses and gated communities in wealthy suburbs north of Johannesburg, South Africa, are threatening to undo the desegregation of this post-Apartheid city. White, wealthy residents fear crime in the city, which, along with neighboring Pretoria, has a murder rate of 5000 per year (in an area with about 5 million people). In response to their fear of crime, by 2004 people in the suburbs of Johannesburg had blocked off over 2500 streets and posted guards to control access to the streets. Today, more than 15 percent of housing in Johannesburg is enclosed in gated communities. Many see the gated communities as a new form of segregation. Since the vast majority of crimes occur in lower income, primarily black communities or in the central city,

the concern is that gated community developments are a new means of creating racial segregation.

Gated communities have taken off in China as well, with communities now crossing socioeconomic classes and assuming a prominent place in the urban landscape (**Fig. 9.39**). Like the gated communities in Europe and North America, the gated communities of China privatize spaces and exclude outsiders with gates, security cameras, and restricted access. However, China's gated communities are 5 to 10 times more densely populated than Europe's and North America's. Geographer Youqin Huang has found other differences between gated communities in China and those in North America and Europe. China has a long history of gated communities, dating back to the first Chinese cities and persisting since. Huang argues that the "collectivism-oriented culture and tight political control" in China explain why the Chinese government built gated communities during the socialist period and why privately developed gated communities have proliferated since China's 1998 housing reform promoted individual home ownership.

In Europe and North America, gated communities are not only for the wealthy and privileged; the middle and lower classes also have a growing desire to feel safe at home. Some urban planners have encouraged governments to recast low-income housing as small communities, gated from each other, to reduce the flowthrough traffic and associated crime. Cities have sometimes torn down enormous high rises, typically ridden with crime and referred to as "the projects," including Cabrini-Green in Chicago and Pruitt-Igoe in St. Louis, in an effort to make the lower income spaces more livable.

Champions of middle-income and low-income neighborhoods seek to create a sense of community and make the spaces "defensible" from undesired activities such as drug dealing and prostitution. One of the best-documented cases of gating a middle-income community is the Five Oaks district of Dayton, Ohio, a neighborhood that is about 50 percent African American and 50 percent white and has a high rate of rentals. Urban planner Oscar Newman encouraged planners in Dayton to divide the

Photo by A.B. Murphy. © 2020 John Wiley & Sons, Inc.

FIGURE 9.39 **Guangzhou, China.** This gated housing community just outside the city is much more serene than the teeming metropolis next door.

FIGURE 9.40 **Beijing, China.** The artificial intelligence company Megvii developed real-time facial recognition software. It claims that once a face is in their system, it can recognize them anywhere. The Chinese government, which uses real-time facial recognition software to track and control who is moving in and around the country, is a major investor in Megvii.

2000 households in the Five Oaks district into 10 smaller, gated communities with restricted access. The city turned most of the residential streets in each of these mini-neighborhoods into cul-de-sacs. It has experienced a serious reduction in crime, along with an increase in housing sales and housing values.

Urban Geopolitics

Geographer Stephen Graham coined the term **urban geopolitics** to draw attention to the impact of global geopolitical developments on the character of cities. Urban areas play a central role in twenty-first-century geopolitics. Global surveillance networks and advanced weaponry have transformed how countries control people, especially in cities. With each terrorist attack since 9/11, whether in London or Mumbai, countries and cities have built concrete barricades, jersey barriers, and bollards around government facilities, embassies, and high-profile buildings. In some cases, fixtures close off entire blocks of sidewalks and bike lanes in the name of safety and security. In other cities, local governments have redirected the flow of traffic in the city center, even closing some streets off to vehicular traffic altogether.

Artificial intelligence surveillance systems shape contemporary urban landscapes, perhaps nowhere more so than in China. The government of China and Chinese technology companies are using facial recognition software to control movement around major cities, including Beijing and Shanghai, through surveillance (**Fig. 9.40**). The Chinese government tracks people's movement across public spaces officially in the name of public safety, but more so for government control. Since he took office in 2014, China's president Xi Jinping has used systems of control to quell any contrary opinions. A minority group of Sunni Muslims in China, the Uighurs, are under constant surveillance through facial recognition and checkpoints because the government wants to track minorities that it fears may protest the country's authoritarian control and crackdowns on religious practices.

TC Thinking Geographically

Analyze the map of redlined neighborhoods in Richmond, Virginia (**Fig. 9.33**). Go online and find a recent map of the distribution of **races** in Richmond, Virginia. You can use the Racial Dot Map at: https://demographics.virginia.edu/DotMap/index.html. Compare and contrast the map you find with the map of redlined neighborhoods. Explain how and why redlining has long-lasting impacts on neighborhoods as **places** and **identities** of people.

9.5 Explain What World Cities Are and Describe How They Shape and Reflect Globalization.

Globalization, as we defined the term in the first chapter, is a set of processes that are heightening interactions, increasing interdependence, and deepening relations across country borders. Through globalization, cities are taking over in ways we barely understand. Most data about economic activity are collected by countries and reported as one statistic representing an entire country. For example, gross national income (GNI) and total fertility rates (TFR) give one number for each country. Neither tells us about differences within countries, such as how cities are faring compared to rural areas. While we have little data about differences within countries, many of the most important processes of globalization happen among and between world cities, not between countries. The very way we collect data masks the integral role world cities play in globalization. World cities function at the global scale, beyond the reach of state borders, as nodes in the world economy.

Arguing that models and hierarchies of cities do not reflect the reality of what is happening with the city, geographers Peter Taylor and Robert Lang (2004) argued that the city has become "something else." The city cannot be understood as a CBD tied into a hierarchy of other cities within a country. The world city is a node in globalization, reflecting processes that have "redrawn the limits on spatial interaction" (Felsenstein et al. 2002). A **node** is a place where action and interaction occur. As nodes, world cities are connected to other world cities, and through these connections, they act as forces shaping globalization.

Geographers Jon Beaverstock and Peter J. Taylor and their Globalization and World Cities Study Group and Network have produced over 400 research papers, chapters, and books on the geography of world cities. They have collected data for each city on producer services in the areas of banking, law, advertising, and accounting. Using the data, the geographers have established an inventory and a classification of world cities into Alpha, Beta, and Gamma world cities (**Fig. 9.41**). Comparing the top Alpha world cities in 2000 to the top Alpha cities in 2018 demonstrates the remarkable rise of China in the world economy over the last two decades (**Fig. 9.42**). Alpha cities are categorized as Alpha++, Alpha+, and Alpha, based on the level of global impact they have. All three categories of Alpha world cities have the global capacity to provide services in the world economy.

The two Alpha++ world cities, New York and London, are the most important nodes. These two cities have remained at the top in terms of influence in the world economy since the Globalization and World Cities group began collecting data. However,

FIGURE 9.41 **World Cities: Alpha, Beta, and Gamma.** Alpha world cities are labeled with city names on the map.

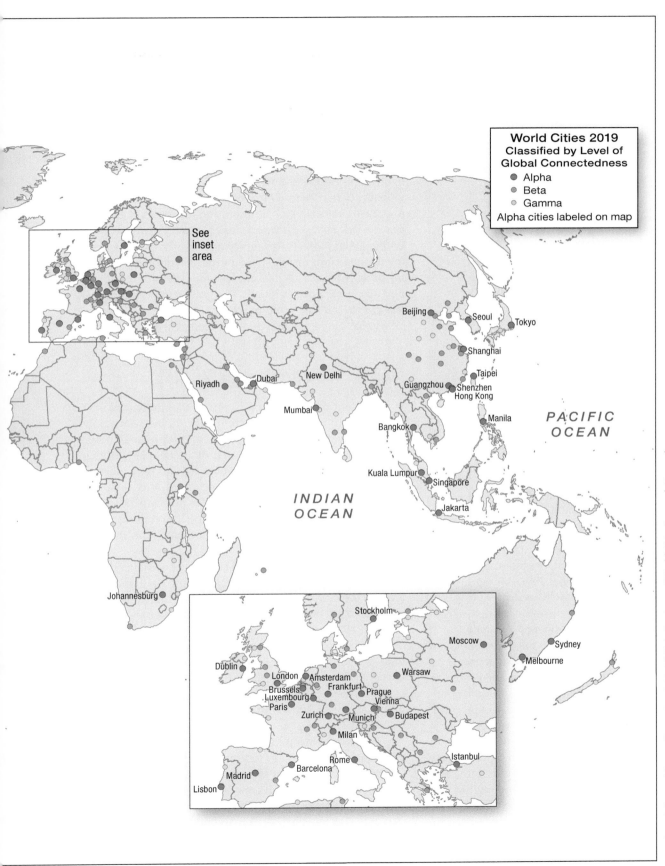

Data from: "The World According to GaWC 2018," Globalization and World Cities Research Network, https://www.lboro.ac.uk/gawc/world2018t.html.

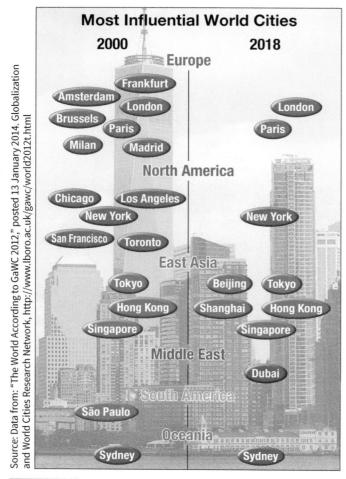

Source: Data from: "The World According to GaWC 2012," posted 13 January 2014. Globalization and World Cities Research Network, http://www.lboro.ac.uk/gawc/world2012.html

FIGURE 9.42 **Shifting Alpha World Cities.** The rise of China's global influence since 2000 is evident when comparing locations of Alpha++ and Alpha+ world cities in 2000 to 2018.

whether they will remain so is to be seen. The three largest banks in the world as of 2019 are all located in China. Moreover, both the United States and the United Kingdom are experiencing conservative movements that are pulling them back from their central role in the world economy: The presidency of Donald Trump in the United States and the Brexit vote in the United Kingdom (see Chapter 8) both signal a movement toward isolationism.

In addition to being major players in the world economy, world cities play a huge role in the economies of their countries. World cities like London and Paris are also capital cities. Governments help concentrate development and encourage interconnections between their capital cities and the rest of the world. The United States has several world cities that are both connected to each other within the United States and are also connected to world cities in other world regions. For example, data from the Globalization and World Cities project indicate that Washington, D.C., is most overconnected to Chicago (meaning the data show the cities are more interlinked than distance would predict) and to other world cities in the United States (**Fig. 9.43**).

Beijing, the capital of China, is also most overconnected to another city in China, in this case Guangzhou. **Figure 9.44**

shows the other cities that are linked to Beijing. Not as regionally confined as the cities linked to Washington, D.C., the world cities linked to Beijing are in Southeast Asia, Europe, Africa, and the Americas. Beijing plays a central role in China's One Belt, One Road, and Maritime Silk Road initiatives (see Chapter 8). Through these initiatives, China's global investments extend to over 70 countries.

The world cities listed as over linkage, mainly in Asia, Southeast Asia, and Europe, are most connected to Beijing, China. The world cities listed as under linkages are least connected. Connections among world cities reveal the pulses of globalization across country borders (Fig. 9.45). World cities operate as nodes in globalization, and the forces of globalization are pulsing across world cities without regard to country borders (**Fig. 9.45**). By inventorying world cities and generating data on cities instead of countries, geographers are helping us see how world cities are reshaping the map of political and economic power globally. Geographers have uncovered the globalized flows and processes occurring across world cities, mapping them and bringing them to light.

Megacities and Global Slums

Whereas world cities are measured by their influence in the world economy, megacities are measured by their number of residents. A **megacity** is a large city with over 10 million people. Providing services to that many people is difficult in the global core (wealthier countries) and only increases in difficulty in the global semiperiphery and periphery. Megacities act as centers of gravity for migrants (see Chapter 3), who are attracted by the prospect of finding work in the formal economy or finding opportunities in the informal economy.

Megacities often have large slum developments that are tucked into and around the city center and that create rings around the city where the permanent buildings end. If you stand on a hill outside Lima (Peru), overlook the Cape Flats near Cape Town (South Africa), or fly a drone camera over a city, you see an unchanging panorama of makeshift slums built of every conceivable material, vying for every foot of space, and extending to the horizon (**Fig. 9.46**). Photos of slums and tent cities reveal few, if any, trees and narrow footpaths leading to a few unpaved streets that go into the central city.

The number of people living in slum developments is uncertain, but the United Nations has estimated the proportion of each country living in slums (**Fig. 9.47**). In Rio de Janeiro (Brazil), the migrants build their dwellings on dangerous, landslide-prone slopes; in Port Moresby (Papua New Guinea), the migrants sink stilts in the mud and build out over the water, risking wind and waves. In Kolkata (formerly Calcutta, India), thousands of migrants do not even try to erect shelters. There and in many other cities, people live in the streets, under bridges, and even in storm drains. City governments do not have the resources to adequately educate, medicate, or police

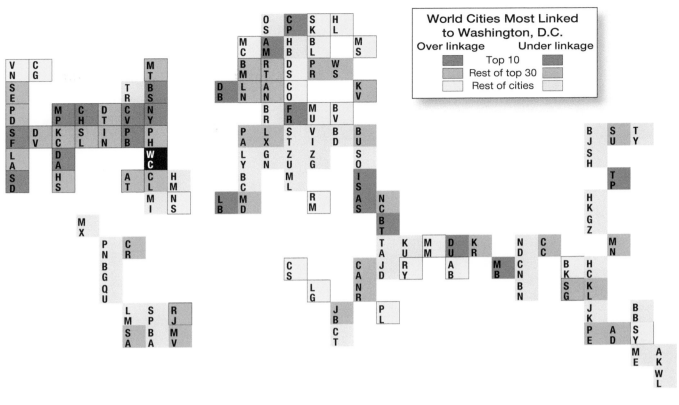

World Cities Most Linked to Washington, D.C.

	Over linkage	Under linkage
Top 10		
Rest of top 30		
Rest of cities		

AB Abu Dhabi	**BV** Bratislava	**GZ** Guangzhou	**LG** Lagos	**NR** Nairobi	**SG** Singapore
AD Adelaide	**CA** Cairo	**HB** Hamburg	**LM** Lima	**NS** Nassau	**SH** Shanghai
AK Auckland	**CC** Calcutta	**HC** Ho Chi Minh City	**LN** London	**NY** New York	**SK** Stockholm
AM Amsterdam	**CG** Calgary		**LX** Luxembourg	**OS** Oslo	**SL** St Louis
AN Antwerp	**CH** Chicago	**HK** Hong Kong	**LY** Lyon	**PA** Paris	**SO** Sofia
AS Athens	**CL** Charlotte	**HL** Helsinki	**MB** Mumbai	**PB** Pittsburgh	**SP** São Paulo
AT Atlanta	**CN** Chennai	**HM** Hamilton (Bermuda)	**MC** Manchester	**PD** Portland	**ST** Stuttgart
BA Buenos Aires	**CO** Cologne		**MD** Madrid	**PE** Perth	**SU** Seoul
BB Brisbane	**CP** Copenhagen	**HS** Houston	**ME** Melbourne	**PH** Philadelphia	**SY** Sydney
BC Barcelona	**CR** Caracas	**IN** Indianapolis	**MI** Miami	**PL** Port Louis	**TA** Tel Aviv
BD Budapest	**CS** Casablanca	**IS** Istanbul	**ML** Milan	**PN** Panama City	**TP** Taipei
BG Bogotá	**CT** Cape Town	**JB** Johannesburg	**MM** Manama	**PR** Prague	**TR** Toronto
BJ Beijing	**CV** Cleveland	**JD** Jeddah	**MN** Manila	**QU** Quito	**TY** Tokyo
BK Bangkok	**DA** Dallas	**JK** Jakarta	**MP** Minneapolis	**RJ** Rio de Janeiro	**VI** Vienna
BL Berlin	**DB** Dublin	**KC** Kansas City	**MS** Moscow	**RM** Rome	**VN** Vancouver
BM Birmingham	**DS** Düsseldorf	**KL** Kuala Lumpur	**MT** Montréal	**RT** Rotterdam	**WC** Washington, DC
BN Bangalore	**DT** Detroit	**KR** Karachi	**MU** Munich	**RY** Riyadh	**WL** Wellington
BR Brussels	**DU** Dubai	**KU** Kuwait	**MV** Montevideo	**SA** Santiago	**WS** Warsaw
BS Boston	**DV** Denver	**KV** Kiev	**MX** Mexico City	**SD** San Diego	**ZG** Zagreb
BT Beirut	**FR** Frankfurt	**LA** Los Angeles	**NC** Nicosia	**SE** Seattle	**ZU** Zurich
BU Bucharest	**GN** Geneva	**LB** Lisbon	**ND** New Delhi	**SF** San Francisco	

FIGURE 9.43 **World cities most linked to Washington, D.C.** The world cities listed as over linkage, mostly in North America, are most connected to Washington, D.C. The world cities listed as under linkages are least connected.

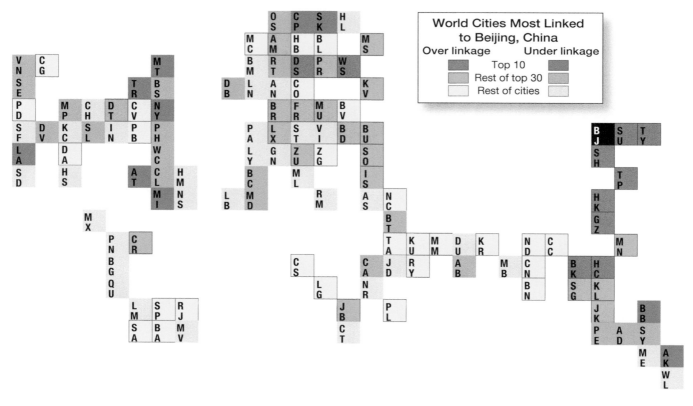

AB	Abu Dhabi	
AD	Adelaide	
AK	Auckland	
AM	Amsterdam	
AN	Antwerp	
AS	Athens	
AT	Atlanta	
BA	Buenos Aires	
BB	Brisbane	
BC	Barcelona	
BD	Budapest	
BG	Bogotá	
BJ	Beijing	
BK	Bangkok	
BL	Berlin	
BM	Birmingham	
BN	Bangalore	
BR	Brussels	
BS	Boston	
BT	Beirut	
BU	Bucharest	
BV	Bratislava	
CA	Cairo	
CC	Calcutta	
CG	Calgary	
CH	Chicago	
CL	Charlotte	
CN	Chennai	
CO	Cologne	
CP	Copenhagen	
CR	Caracas	
CS	Casablanca	
CT	Cape Town	
CV	Cleveland	
DA	Dallas	
DB	Dublin	
DS	Düsseldorf	
DT	Detroit	
DU	Dubai	
DV	Denver	
FR	Frankfurt	
GN	Geneva	
GZ	Guangzhou	
HB	Hamburg	
HC	Ho Chi Minh City	
HK	Hong Kong	
HL	Helsinki	
HM	Hamilton (Bermuda)	
HS	Houston	
IN	Indianapolis	
IS	Istanbul	
JB	Johannesburg	
JD	Jeddah	
JK	Jakarta	
KC	Kansas City	
KL	Kuala Lumpur	
KR	Karachi	
KU	Kuwait	
KV	Kiev	
LA	Los Angeles	
LB	Lisbon	
LG	Lagos	
LM	Lima	
LN	London	
LX	Luxembourg	
LY	Lyon	
MB	Mumbai	
MC	Manchester	
MD	Madrid	
ME	Melbourne	
MI	Miami	
ML	Milan	
MM	Manama	
MN	Manila	
MP	Minneapolis	
MS	Moscow	
MT	Montréal	
MU	Munich	
MV	Montevideo	
MX	Mexico City	
NC	Nicosia	
ND	New Delhi	
NR	Nairobi	
NS	Nassau	
NY	New York	
OS	Oslo	
PA	Paris	
PB	Pittsburgh	
PD	Portland	
PE	Perth	
PH	Philadelphia	
PL	Port Louis	
PN	Panama City	
PR	Prague	
QU	Quito	
RJ	Rio de Janeiro	
RM	Rome	
RT	Rotterdam	
RY	Riyadh	
SA	Santiago	
SD	San Diego	
SE	Seattle	
SF	San Francisco	
SG	Singapore	
SH	Shanghai	
SK	Stockholm	
SL	St Louis	
SO	Sofia	
SP	São Paulo	
ST	Stuttgart	
SU	Seoul	
SY	Sydney	
TA	Tel Aviv	
TP	Taipei	
TR	Toronto	
TY	Tokyo	
VI	Vienna	
VN	Vancouver	
WC	Washington, DC	
WL	Wellington	
WS	Warsaw	
ZG	Zagreb	
ZU	Zurich	

Source: Data from Atlas of Hinterworlds: Beijing

FIGURE 9.44 **Beijing, China.** The world cities listed as over linkage, mostly in Asia, Southeast Asia, and Europe are most connected to Beijing. The world cities listed as under linkages are least connected.

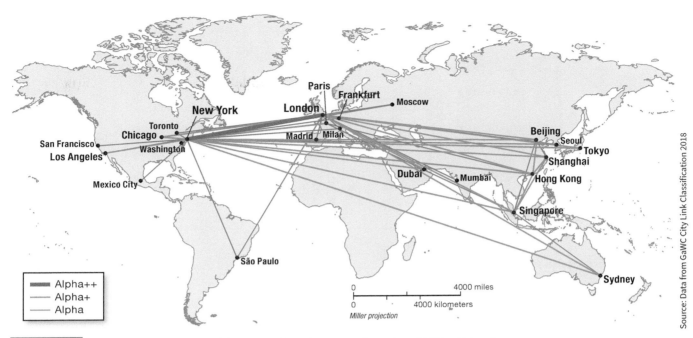

Source: Data from GaWC City Link Classification 2018

FIGURE 9.45 **Networks of Alpha world cities.**   Data from the Geography and World Cities Network shows the extent of connections among Alpha++, Alpha+, and Alpha world cities.

the growing populations, let alone provide even minimal housing for most.

People living in most shanty settlements are not really squatters—they pay rent. When settlements expand outward from the central city, they occupy land owned by previous residents, families who farmed what were once the rural areas beyond the city's edge. Some of the farming families were favored by the former colonial administration; they moved into the cities but continued to own the lands their farms were on. As shanty developments encroached on their lands, the landowners began to charge people rent for living in the dilapidated housing the new residents built on the land. After establishing an owner-tenant relationship, the landowners steadily raise rents, threatening to destroy the flimsy shacks if residents fail to pay.

Media Drum World/Alamy Stock Photo

FIGURE 9.46   **Mumbai, India.**   This bird's-eye view of Mumbai shows the stark contrast between wealthy neighborhoods in the background and tent settlements and slums in the foreground.

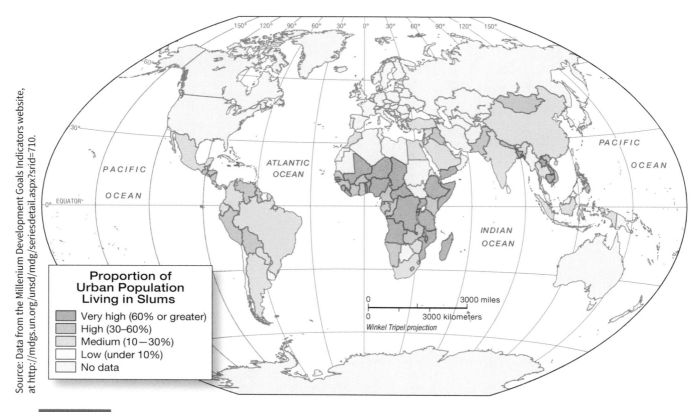

Source: Data from the Millenium Development Goals Indicators website, at http://mdgs.un.org/unsd/mdg/seriesdetail.aspx?srid=710.

Proportion of Urban Population Living in Slums

- Very high (60% or greater)
- High (30–60%)
- Medium (10—30%)
- Low (under 10%)
- No data

0   3000 miles
0   3000 kilometers
Winkel Tripel projection

FIGURE 9.47 **Urban Population Living in Slums by Country.** Sub-Saharan Africa and Southeast Asia have the highest proportion of city-dwellers living in slums.

In this way, powerful long-term inhabitants of the city exploit the weaker, more recent arrivals.

In the vast slums, barrios, and favelas, residents are not idle. Everywhere you look, people are at work, inside or in front of their modest habitats, fixing things, repairing broken items for sale, sorting through piles of garbage for salvageable items, or trading and selling goods from makeshift stands. **Hutment factories** are centers of entrepreneurship where slum residents sew clothing, recycle plastic and cardboard, build products, and provide services (**Fig. 9.48**). Dharavi, a slum in Mumbai, India, is home to 20,000 hutment factories, where according to one hutment owner, "Every unit, big or small, has workers coming from all over the country" (*Guardian* 2014). He continued that the workers "have nothing in mind but work. All they think of is of working the whole day and night to earn livelihood for their family back home. All they require is a small space to work and sleep and a television set in the corner of the room" (*Guardian* 2014).

AP® Exam Taker's Tip

Can you name some of the many other names for a slum area? Barrios, favelas, shantytowns, bidenvilles, and bustees are just a few examples of names of slum areas around the world.

While the fabric garments and leather belts and bags sewn in hutment factories are sold in name-brand stores around the world, the hutment factories are part of the informal economy of India. If you have heard the statistic that 3 billion people live on less than $2.50 a day, you have probably wondered how. The answer is the informal economy. The **informal economy** is not taxed and is not counted toward a country's gross national income (GNI). Work in the informal economy fills the gap between the job that is hoped for in the formal economy and the reality of providing for yourself and your family.

Tent cities and temporary housing are not confined to countries in the global periphery and semi-periphery. The high cost of housing in Silicon Valley, California, and the large number of jobs available in the region have created a class of working poor who cannot afford housing. The streets of Palo Alto, California are lined with RVs (recreational vehicles) that are either owned by the residents or owned by landlords who rent the RVs to low-income residents. The Palo Alto police have tried to crack down on RVs being parked for too long on streets, but landlords who are renting RVs worry less about residents being towed or ejected and more about earning rent.

Other cities in the United States are starting to look more like pockets of Mumbai. These are not large slums like Dharavi, but greenscapes on boulevards, between neighborhoods, and

FIGURE 9.48   **Dharavi, Mumbai, India.**   Workers operate sewing machines and sew by hand in one of 20,000 hutment factories in the Dharavi slum.

FIGURE 9.49   **Honolulu, Hawai'i.**   Tent settlements like this one in the Kakaako district of Honolulu are increasingly common in cities in the global core because of the high cost of housing. Hawaii News Now reports that Hawai'i has the largest gap between cost of rent and average salary in the country. The average renter wage is $15.64, but the average hourly wage needed to rent a two-bedroom apartment in Oahu is $32.50.

near bridges where residents put up tents for dwellings. San Francisco, Los Angeles, Washington, D.C., and Honolulu have housing prices that make living in the cities unaffordable to low-income residents. As a result, tent settlements are dotting these landscapes (**Fig. 9.49**).

Thinking Geographically

Think through the challenges to the state presented in Chapter 8 and predict whether and under what circumstances world cities might replace states as the basic and most powerful form of political organization in the world. What arguments can be made for and against this proposition?

Summary

9.1 Describe the Sites and Situations of Cities.

1. At the global scale, most people live in cities. In Japan, the United States, Canada, and western Europe, four out of five people now live in cities or towns. China is mostly urban, with a little over 50 percent of Chinese living in cities, but India is mostly rural, with 70 percent of Indians living in rural areas.

2. The idea of living together in cities originated in six different hearths and diffused globally from there. The six hearths include, in chronological order: Mesopotamia, Nile River Valley, Indus River Valley, Huang He and Wei valleys, Mesoamerica, and Peru.

3. Two concepts in urban geography help us get the overall picture of any city we study: urban morphology and functional zonation. The urban morphology of a city is the layout of the city, including the sizes and shapes of buildings and the pathways of infrastructure. The functional zonation is the division of a city into different regions (e.g., residential or industrial) by use or purpose (e.g., housing or manufacturing). Understanding the zones in a city and the functions of each zone helps us imagine how power and wealth were distributed in ancient cities and gives us insight into what people in power value in modern cities.

4. Sites are the unique descriptors that explain where a city is located. For example, several major cities on the east coast of the United States are located on the fall line, where rivers are no longer navigable. The cities were natural locations for trade involving river-transported goods and land-transported goods. Situation is the relative location of a place based on its context in the larger region around it. The situation of a place changes over time. For example, Fredericksburg, Virginia, is sited on the fall line of the Rappahannock River. The situation of Fredericksburg has changed. During the Civil War, it was located halfway between the capital of the North and the capital of the South. Today, it is one of the farthest southern suburbs of Washington, D.C., or the farthest northern suburbs of Richmond, Virginia.

9.2 Analyze the Distribution of Cities and Their Relative Size.

1. Every city has a trade area. The largest city has a large trade area, and then nested within that trade area are next smaller cities with their own trade areas. Urban geographers have created several ways to measure the hierarchy, relative size, and spacing of cities. The rank-size rule says the population of each city in a rank will be lower than the one above it in a predictably proportional way. When a country has a primate city, one city is quite large and all the other cities are much smaller in comparison.

2. Walter Christaller's central place theory predicts that cities will be distributed in an urban hierarchy. The smallest units are hamlets; then come villages, then towns, and finally cities. Each city will have a hexagonal hinterland, or trade area. Towns, villages, and hamlets will be nested inside each hexagon in a regularly spaced pattern.

9.3 Explain the Internal Structure of Cities and Models.

1. Urban geographers have developed models of cities to explain the historic, spatial, economic, cultural, and political processes that shaped cities in each world region. Models show us a snapshot after the fact, after the city has gone through growth and distinct areas have developed. Models are not great at predicting change, but they do give us a lens to understanding the history of change in a city.

2. Models of North American cities include the Burgess concentric zone model, the Hoyt sector model, and the Harris–Ullman multiple nuclei model. Access to personal cars and construction of ring roads and interstates after World War II led to rapid suburbanization, especially around transportation corridors. Suburban downtowns called edge cities developed with more office and retail space than housing. Edge cities offer suburbanites office space, shopping areas, leisure activities, and all the other elements of a complete urban environment, making trips into the central city less necessary. Models of North American cities drawn after World War II, including the multiple nuclei and galactic city models, account for suburbs and edge cities.

3. Geographers have created models for cities in different world regions. The Latin American city model, also known as the Griffin-Ford model, highlights a commercial sector stretching out from a central business district (CBD). Another notable feature is a zone of peripheral squatter settlements that rings the outskirts of the city. In Latin America, this zone is often home to newer migrants from rural areas. The African city model, created by geographer H. J. de Blij, has a distinct colonial CBD surrounded by a traditional CBD and a market zone. The Southeast Asian city model, known as the McGee model, is centered on a port zone that is flanked by a western commercial core.

9.4 Analyze How Political and Economic Policies Shape Cities.

1. Governments shape cities through zoning laws that designate what kinds of buildings and businesses can be built and what functions those buildings can have in different parts of the city. Cities may have strict or loose zoning laws. How strictly a city enforces zoning laws varies in part based on the resources the city designates to enforcement.

2. In the United States, cities have a history of racial segregation. Before the civil rights movement of the 1960s, banks engaged in redlining. They would draw red lines on a map around neighborhoods they considered to be "risky"—often predominantly black neighborhoods—and refuse to offer loans to anyone purchasing a house in those neighborhoods. Demand for housing in the redlined areas fell, and housing values fell, which made it difficult for homeowners to access loans or tap into equity to upkeep homes.

3. Gentrification is the renewal or rebuilding of lower-income neighborhoods into middle- to upper-class neighborhoods.

Gentrification began in the 1960s and slowed in the 1990s but is increasing again. Changing family structures in the United States, where couples are choosing not to have children or have only one child, are making living near the central city in a gentrified neighborhood more attractive.

9.5 Explain What World Cities Are and Describe How They Shape and Reflect Globalization.

1. Through globalization, cities are taking over in ways we barely understand. Most data about economic activity are collected by countries and reported as one statistic representing an entire country. Some of the most important processes in globalization happen between cities and are difficult to track. Geographers created the Globalization and World City network to create, gather, and analyze data about world cities.

2. The two Alpha++ world cities are the most important nodes in the world economy: New York and London. These two cities have remained at the top in terms of influence in the world economy since the Globalization and World Cities group began collecting data. The three largest banks in the world as of 2019 are all located in China, and the number of Chinese world cities that have attained Alpha+ status has grown significantly since 2000.

Self-Test

9.1 Describe the sites and situations of cities.

1. The majority of people live in cities in all of the following countries except:

 a. France.

 b. China.

 c. United States.

 d. United Kingdom.

 e. India.

2. Before the first urban revolution, people lived in agricultural villages. One defining characteristic of agricultural villages that made them different from cities was that:

 a. the leadership class was female.

 b. the government did not tax or charge tribute.

 c. everyone was employed in agriculture or agricultural trades.

 d. irrigation had not been invented.

 e. economic diversity.

3. Unlike in Mesopotamia, cities in the Nile River civilization did not have walls for all of the following reasons except:

 a. walls would have blocked access to the river, which was needed for irrigation.

 b. walls on the sides of cities away from the river were unnecessary because of the vast desert.

 c. cities along the Nile were all controlled by the same leader, so they did not need to protect themselves from each other.

 d. cities on the Nile were not really cities; they were agricultural villages, so they did not need walls.

 e. walls were an environmental decision.

4. When Europeans colonized Africa, they built railroad lines primarily to:

 a. connect cities with one another.

 b. build up existing towns on trade routes in the interior.

 c. transport passengers.

 d. enable market produce to make it from the ports to the interior.

 e. transport resources from the interior to ports.

9.2 Analyze the distribution of cities and their relative size.

5. The populations of the four largest cities in Belgium are: 1) Brussels 1.78 million people; 2) Antwerp 940,000 people; 3) Liege 633,000 people; 4) Ghent 416,000 people. This pattern best follows which theory of urban hierarchy?

 a. primate city

 b. rank-size rule

 c. central place

 d. urban morphology

 e. hexagonal hinterlands

6. Central place theory was developed by _____, who believed that cities, towns, villages, and hamlets would:

 a. Christaller / each have their own trade area, with cities having the largest and hamlets the smallest.

 b. Christaller / each have their own trade area, with cities having the smallest and hamlets the largest.

 c. Harris / each have hexagonal trade areas nested inside each other.

 d. Harris / each have circular trade areas nested inside each other.

 e. Burgess / be divided into five concentric zones.

7. One of the shortcomings of central place theory is that the author made several assumptions. All of the following are assumptions behind central place theory except:

 a. people will travel the shortest possible distance to get a product.

 b. the landscape is relatively flat with no physical barriers.

 c. each city has an exclusive trade area in which it has a monopoly on the sale of certain goods.

 d. trade areas of cities will overlap.

 e. the urban hierarchy is nested.

9.3 Explain the internal structure of cities and models.

8. Suburbanization happens when lands once outside the urban area become urbanized. Thinking geographically, you can infer that one outcome of suburbanization will be:

    a. gentrification of the central business district.

    b. removal of farmland around the outskirts of a city from production.

    c. an increase in the population density of the city.

    d. a rise in the average age of people living in the city.

    e. greater population density.

9. The Burgess model of the North American city is best known for having:

    a. edge cities.

    b. sectors.

    c. multiple nuclei.

    d. concentric zones.

    e. hexagonal hinterlands.

10. The Latin American city model, also known as the Griffin–Ford model, includes a commercial sector stretching out from the central business district. Both sides of the commercial sector are lined by:

    a. an elite residential sector.

    b. the zone of peripheral squatter settlement.

    c. a zone of maturity.

    d. an industrial zone.

    e. green space.

9.4 Analyze how political and economic policies shape cities.

11. Portland, Oregon, is considered the best-planned city in the United States for all of the following reasons except that it:

    a. offers free transportation in the central city to discourage the use of cars.

    b. is a compact city with office buildings and residential zones in close proximity.

    c. has designated bike lanes throughout the city to encourage biking.

    d. has wealthy residential zones located next to industrial zones.

    e. has zoning laws.

12. In the United States before the civil rights movement, banks practiced redlining in cities. Major consequences of redlining included all of the following except:

    a. lower demand for houses in redlined areas.

    b. lower housing values in redlined areas.

    c. lower investment in redlined areas.

    d. increasing racial segregation in the city.

    e. gentrification of redlined areas.

13. One major consequence of gentrification is:

    a. displacement of lower-income residents from the gentrified neighborhood.

    b. decreased housing values in the gentrified neighborhood.

    c. lower property taxes in the gentrified neighborhood.

    d. decreased cost of goods and services provided in the gentrified neighborhood.

    e. creating more affordable housing for residents in the gentrified neighborhood.

9.5 Explain what world cities are and describe how they shape and reflect globalization.

14. Many of the most important processes of globalization take place between world cities. The two most influential world cities are:

    a. New York and Los Angeles.   **d.** Paris and London.

    b. Paris and Shanghai.   **e.** Tokyo and New York.

    c. New York and London.

15. Megacities are large cities with populations over 10 million. People migrate to megacities in hopes of finding work. Work that is not taxed by government is considered part of the:

    a. formal economy.

    b. informal economy.

    c. trade economy.

    d. barter economy.

    e. gift economy.

16. People live in tents and recreational vehicles in cities in the core when:

    a. the cost of housing is unaffordable.

    b. they are snowbirds.

    c. the city is growing too fast.

    d. gentrification has been banned.

    e. the economy is in recession.

CHAPTER **10**

Development

FIGURE 10.1 **Central Square, Timbuktu, Mali.** Sited along the Niger River on the edge of the Sahara Desert, Timbuktu was once a major trade center. Goods from the north, carried on camels, were traded with goods from the south brought in on boats. But in the sixteenth century, the development of sea trade routes on the west coast of Africa allowed traders to circumvent Timbuktu, and the city's central trade role declined.

Photo by A.B. Murphy. © 2020 John Wiley & Sons, Inc.

Why does the name *Timbuktu* sound familiar? One reason is that centuries ago, the city was a well-known intellectual, spiritual, and economic center. Yet the contemporary urban landscape of Timbuktu provides few clues of its former glory (**Fig. 10.1**). What happened?

The city's wealth many centuries ago came from its strategic position along a major route across the Sahara desert used by traders of gold, salt, and other valuable commodities. With European exploration, colonization, and exploitation of Africa, trade patterns shifted. Port cities gained in importance with the development of sea trade routes established to ship enslaved Africans and gold from coastal Africa. Timbuktu lost its strategic position and a long period of decline began.

Timbuktu's story serves as a reminder that *where* a place is located can affect its economic fortunes—its development. But the "where" factor is not a simple one. Sometimes the presence of valuable raw materials can produce wealth. More often development prospects are shaped by a place's strategic position relative to other places and innovations, its relationship with other places, its political and economic past, and its access to capital. Development also takes place in the context of the capitalist world economy where structures and relationships help create high levels of uneven development.

In this chapter, we discuss some of the major theories of development. We also examine how geography affects development, considering the influence of structural features of the world economy and local circumstances. We also look at the geographical barriers to and costs of development within countries, and we consider why uneven development occurs not just across the globe but also within countries.

CHAPTER OUTLINE

10.1 Explain how development is defined and measured.
- Gross National Income
- Alternative Measures of Development

10. 2 Describe the nature and limitations of development models.
- Traditional Models
- Alternative Approaches to Modeling Development

10. 3 Explain major influences on development.
- Economic Arrangements

- Aid and International Financial Institutions
- Social Conditions
- Political Corruption and Instability
- Costs of Economic Development

10. 4 Evaluate how political and economic institutions influence uneven development within states.
- The Role of Governments
- Islands of Development
- Creating Growth in the Periphery of the Periphery

10.1 | Explain How Development Is Defined and Measured.

The economic and social geography of the modern world is a patchwork of contrasts. On some fields in equatorial America and in African forests, farmers practice **shifting cultivation** to grow root crops using ancient methods and hand tools. On the Great Plains of North America, in Ukraine, and in eastern Australia, farmers use expensive, modern machines to plow the land, plant seeds, and harvest grains. Farmers in Uzbekistan harvest cotton by hand on soil left salinized by over-irrigation in arid Central Asia. On the other hand, factory workers in Japan and South Korea work with high-tech robots to produce automobiles by the shipload for distribution to markets thousands of miles away.

Most people use the term *developed* to describe Japan and South Korea, in contrast to Uzbekistan. That notion of development originated with the **Industrial Revolution** and the idea that technology can improve the lives of people. Through advances in technology, people produce more food, create new products, and accrue material wealth. But these things do not necessarily bring happiness (see Chapter 14), social stability, or environmental sustainability. Development can be a narrow, sometimes controversial, indicator of the human condition.

Whatever the complexities, development has a great influence on places and people. It is therefore important to understand the different approaches taken to measuring development and assessing its advantages and disadvantages.

Gross National Income

Most measures of development focus on one of three factors: economic well-being, technology and production, or social welfare. Beginning in the 1960s, the most common way to measure economic well-being was to use the index economists created to compare countries: gross national product. **Gross national product** (GNP) is a measure of the total value of the officially recorded goods and services produced by residents of a country in a given year. It includes goods and services made both inside and outside a country's territory. It is therefore broader than **gross domestic product** (GDP), which includes only goods and services produced within a country during a given year.

Economists have increasingly turned to **gross national income** (GNI) as a measure of development. The GNI is a calculation of the monetary value of what is produced within a country, plus income received from investments outside the country, minus income payments to other countries around the world. GNI is seen as a more accurate way of measuring a country's wealth because it accounts for wealth generated by investments outside a country's borders.

In order to compare GNI across countries, economists must standardize the data. The most common way to standardize GNI data is to divide it by the population of the country, which yields a **per capita GNI** figure. In Japan the per capita GNI in U.S. dollars in 2017 was $38,550. In the United States it was $58,270. In Norway it was $75,990. But in India it was $1870, in

Nigeria it was $2160, and in Indonesia, the world's fourth most populous country, it was $3540. This enormous range in per capita GNI reflects the wide gap between rich and poor.

Using GNI to measure wealth has several shortcomings. First, it includes only transactions in the **formal economy**, the legal economy that governments tax and monitor. Quite a few countries have a per capita GNI of less than $1000 per year—a figure so low it seems impossible that people could survive. A key component of survival in these countries is the **informal economy**, the uncounted or underground economy that governments do not tax and keep track of, including everything from a garden plot in a yard to the illegal drug trade. The informal economy is a significant element in the economies of many countries, but GNI statistics omit the informal economy entirely (see Fig. 5.18).

GNI per capita also tells us nothing about the distribution of wealth across the world or within a country (**Fig. 10.2**). The Middle Eastern oil countries of Kuwait and the United Arab Emirates (UAE) have per capita GNIs of $31,440 and $39,130 respectively, both ahead of Spain and New Zealand in 2017. However, these figures give us no hint of what proportion of the population participates in the country's economy, the average citizen's standard of living, or gaps between genders or among regions. The wealth generated by the formal economy in the UAE is not distributed evenly across the seven emirates that make up the country. Billionaires in the UAE own more than 40 percent of the economy, but there are only 6.5 of them per million people. Abu Dhabi, the emirate that dominates the banking and financial sector and the petroleum industry, generated roughly 14 percent of the country's GDP in 2017. Dubai, the next largest emirate, generated about 26 percent of the GDP. The Sharjah emirate accounted for 7.6 percent of the GPD, and the Qaywayn emirate generated less than 1 percent of the country's gross GDP.

Another limitation of GNI per capita is that it measures only outputs (i.e., production). It does not take into account the nonmonetary costs of production, which take a toll on the environment through resource depletion and pollution of air and water. Per capita GNI may even treat such matters as a plus. An example is the sale of cigarettes, which augments GNI. When cigarette use leads to sickness and hospitalization, the GNI figure grows further. Conversely, quitting smoking improves health and saves lives, but reduces money spent on cigarettes and health care, thus reducing the total production and the GNI in a country.

AP® Exam Taker's Tip

Measuring Development – Be able to apply **measures of development** such as **GNI, GDP,** and **GNP.** More important, know and be able to apply the limitations of these measures. Change **scale** and the development measures may change. **Formal** and **informal** economies must be accounted for.

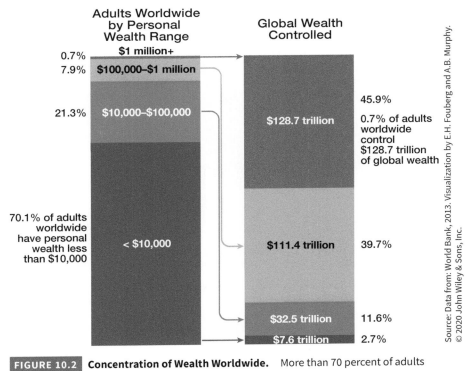

Adults Worldwide
by Personal
Wealth Range

Global Wealth
Controlled

Source: Data from: World Bank, 2013. Visualization by E.H. Fouberg and A.B. Murphy.
© 2020 John Wiley & Sons, Inc.

FIGURE 10.2 **Concentration of Wealth Worldwide.** More than 70 percent of adults worldwide have personal wealth less than $10,000, and they control less than 3 percent of global wealth. Less than 1 percent of adults worldwide have personal wealth more than $1 million, and they control more than 45 percent of global wealth.

Alternative Measures of Development

The limitations of GNI have prompted analysts to look for alternative measures of economic development, ways of measuring the roles that technology, production, transportation, and communications play in an economy. To measure the use of technology, we can look at the number of workers relative to the amount of production in a given sector. For example, in the 2017–2018 growing season, the United States produced roughly 1.7 times the amount of corn that China did. At the same time, it employed only about 1.63 percent of its labor force in the agriculture sector in 2018, whereas China employed about 16.45 percent of its labor force in agriculture. The large proportion of the labor force employed in agriculture shows that China still relies significantly on labor-intensive rather technologically intensive production methods.

In conventional development terms, a country with a high percentage of laborers engaged in the production of agriculture is less developed than one in which a high percentage of workers are involved in high-tech industries. Productivity per worker is examined by summing production over the course of a year and dividing it by the total number of persons in the labor force. The World Bank reported that, in the agricultural, forestry, and fishing sector, productivity per worker in the United States was $83,735 in 2016, whereas China's productivity per worker in that sector was $5325 the same year. A more

productive workforce usually suggests a higher level of mechanization in production.

One good measure of access to technology is access to railways, roads, airports, telephones, radios, televisions, and so forth. **Figure 10.3** highlights some of the extraordinary differences in communications access, including access to the Internet, mobile cellular subscriptions, and telephone landlines around the world. The world average for Internet and mobile access is increasing, while the world average for landline access is declining.

Nonprofit and nongovernmental development agencies, including one called Living Cities, have called the mobile phone "the great equalizer." Yet evidence is mixed. In a 2014 study, analysts at Pew Research Center surveyed residents of 24 middle-income countries, including Turkey, Venezuela, Kenya, Brazil, and Nigeria. They found that while cell phones "are almost omnipresent in many nations," most people are still offline (Pew 2014). A high degree of correlation between income and Internet access (**Fig. 10.4**) means that instead of mobile phones equalizing Internet access for higher and lower income countries, the technology can either reinforce or exacerbate the **digital divide** between rich and poor. The Pew survey data also confirmed that people with college educations are more likely to have smartphones and thus mobile access to the Internet.

Another way to measure development is to compare the size of the working-age population with the number of older

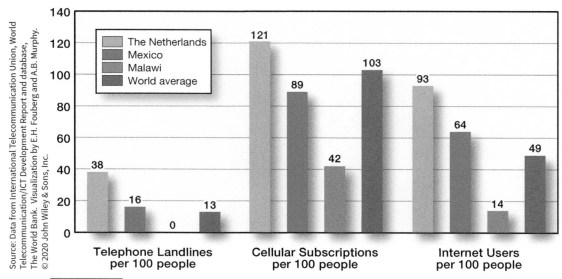

Source: Data from International Telecommunication Union, World Telecommunication/ICT Development Report and database, The World Bank. Visualization by E.H. Fouberg and A.B. Murphy. © 2020 John Wiley & Sons, Inc.

FIGURE 10.3 **Differences in Communications Connectivity.** While connection to telephone land lines may not be as important in the era of cellular phones, the pattern of differences is the same in all three forms of communication access.

or younger people in the society who are not contributing to the country's economy. The resulting **dependency ratio** measures the proportion of dependents in the population relative to every 100 people of working age.

The overall dependency ratio of young and old relative to the working-age population can be divided into an *older person dependency ratio* (population over the age of 64 relative to the working-age population) and a *younger person dependency ratio* (population ages birth to 14 relative to the working-age population). The older person dependency ratio (proportion of the population over age 64) is highest in Japan at 45, meaning that every group of 100 working-age adults (ages 15 to 64) is paying taxes to support 45 people over the age of 64 (**Fig. 10.5A**). Just behind Japan are several European countries, including Italy, Finland, and Portugal. The countries with high older person dependency ratios generally have high per capita GNIs, but the larger proportion of older adults in society can be a financial strain on the country. Aging populations in Japan and Europe require greater investments in health care, housing for the elderly, and retirement welfare (similar to Social Security in the United States).

Another way to look at dependency is to measure the percentage of young people, ages birth to 14, relative to the working-age population. The World Bank reports these data as the younger person dependency ratio. Niger has the highest

ratio, with 106 young people for every 100 working-age adults. All of the 10 countries with the highest younger person dependency ratio are in sub-Saharan Africa (**Fig. 10.5B**). Having a large proportion of young people in a country can also be a financial strain if countries invest in childcare, public education, immunization programs, and health care for children.

In addition to access to technology and dependency ratios, we can use many other statistics to measure social welfare, including literacy rates, infant mortality (Fig. 2.17), life expectancy (Fig. 2.20), undernourishment (Fig. 1.2), percentage of family income spent on food, and amount of savings per capita.

The United Nations calculates the Human Development Index (**Fig. 10.6**) to incorporate the "three basic dimensions of

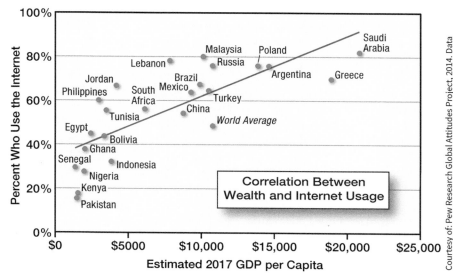

Courtesy of: Pew Research Global Attitudes Project, 2014. Data from GDP per capita 2017, and percent of population using the internet 2017. Visualization by E.H. Fouberg and A.B. Murphy. © 2020 John Wiley & Sons, Inc.

FIGURE 10.4 **Correlation Between Income and Internet Access.** The correlation between income and Internet access is positive and relatively high, with higher income countries having greater access to the Internet.

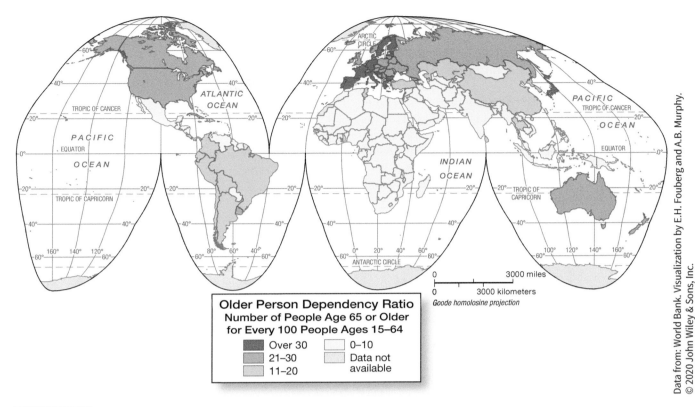

Data from: World Bank. Visualization by E.H. Fouberg and A.B. Murphy.
© 2020 John Wiley & Sons, Inc.

FIGURE 10.5A **Older Person Dependency Ratio.** The older person dependency ratio is a measure of the number of people 65 and older relative to 100 working-age adults, between 15 and 64. The working-age adults in the formal economy contribute to a country's tax base, thereby supporting the older population of a country.

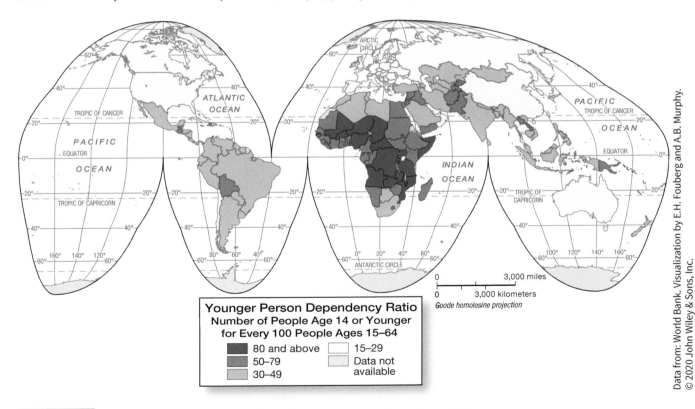

Data from: World Bank. Visualization by E.H. Fouberg and A.B. Murphy.
© 2020 John Wiley & Sons, Inc.

FIGURE 10.5B **Younger Person Dependency Ratio.** The younger person dependency ratio is a measure of the number of people birth to age 14 relative to 100 working-age adults, between 15 and 64. The working-age adults in the formal economy contribute to a country's tax base, thereby supporting the younger population of a country.

human development: a long and healthy life, knowledge and a decent standard of living." Several statistics, including per capita GDP, literacy rates, school enrollment rates, and life expectancy at birth, are included in the calculation of the Human Development Index.

In 2015, the United Nations held a high-profile summit during which more than 150 world leaders adopted the Agenda for Sustainable Development. The goal is to improve the condition of the people in the countries with the lowest standards of human development. At the summit, world leaders recognized the principal barriers to economic development and identified key development goals to be achieved by the year 2030. They were:

1. No poverty

2. Zero hunger

3. Good health and well-being

4. Quality education

5. Gender equality

6. Clean water and sanitation

7. Affordable and clean energy

8. Decent work and economic growth

9. Industry, innovation, and infrastructure

10. Reduced inequalities

11. Sustainable cities and communities

12. Responsible consumption and production

13. Climate action

14. Life below water

15. Life on land

16. Peace, justice, and strong institutions

17. Partnership for the goals

These **Sustainable Development Goals** represent a fairly high degree of consensus about the conditions that need to be changed to achieve economic development.

In 2018 the United Nations reported that progress had been made toward reducing undernourishment, but the degree of progress varied by world region. Reducing undernourishment is a goal the United Nations originally set in 2000 with its Millennium Development Goals. **Figure 10.7** plots the progress made toward that goal as of 2016. Progress has also been made in expanding access to clean water and education, but inequality is a worsening problem in many places. As for the goal of gender equality, the UN reported progress in the proportion of women in legislatures, but a lack of progress in the number of hours women spend on unpaid domestic labor. The UN reports that, "based on data between 2000 and 2016 from about 90 countries, women spend roughly three times as many hours in unpaid domestic and care work as men."

Looking across all of the maps showing different measures of development, it is clear that many countries come out in approximately the same position, no matter which measure

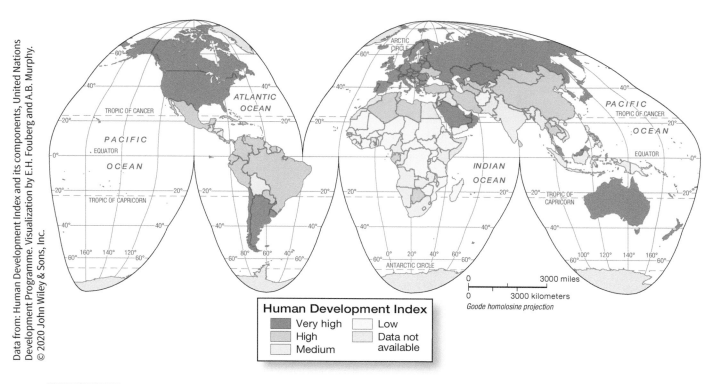

Data from: Human Development Index and its components, United Nations Development Programme. Visualization by E.H. Fouberg and A.B. Murphy. © 2020 John Wiley & Sons, Inc.

Human Development Index

- Very high
- High
- Medium
- Low
- Data not available

Goode homolosine projection

FIGURE 10.6 **Human Development Index.** The Human Development Index measures development beyond GNI or GDP by taking into account literacy, school enrollment, and other factors that contribute toward quality of life in a country.

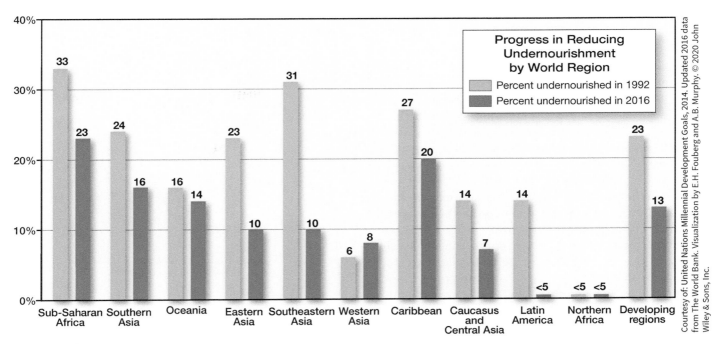

FIGURE 10.7 **Progress in Reducing Undernourishment by Region.** The United Nations Millennium Development Goals sought to reduce undernourishment in each world region. According to these data, these goals were achieved in every region except Western Asia, where undernourishment actually rose between 1992 and 2016, from unrest in the region, including the war and ongoing conflict in Iraq and the civil war in Syria.

is used. And all the maps and statistics share one fundamental limitation: They do not capture differences in development within countries, an issue we consider later in this chapter.

TC **Thinking Geographically**

To what degree is economic **development** a Western concept? How do Western notions of development affect what happens in world **regions** outside Europe and North America? If you addressed development at different **scales** from local to national to world regional, how would development goals and ideas for solutions vary?

AP® Exam Taker's Tip

Development Theories/Models – Now apply your knowledge of these models/theories. Look up the Hans Rosling video called *The Joy of Stats* and answer these questions:

1. What are the basic assumptions of each model?
2. Based on the data you see in the video, compare 2–3 reasons how the models are different from each other. Compare 2–3 reasons how the models are similar.

10.2 Describe the Nature and Limitations of Development Models.

Governments, nongovernmental organizations, and international financial institutions (including the World Bank, the World Trade Organization, and the International Monetary Fund) use a variety of development models to understand how and why countries develop. The models, which seek to explain how countries move along a path to development, have influenced development policies around the world. But most of them have

a Western bias. They assume that development occurs when the strategies that led to development in Europe and North America are pursued elsewhere. However, Western-inspired measures do not always have positive effects. Some measures designed to improve development in lower income countries, such as attracting industry and mechanizing agriculture, can lead to worsened social and environmental conditions for many people.

Traditional Models

The most influential classic development model is economist Walt Rostow's **modernization model**. Many theories of development grew out of the major decolonization movements of the 1960s. Motivated by a concern with how the dozens of newly independent countries in Africa and Asia would survive economically, Rostow looked at how the countries that were already economically powerful in the 1960s had gotten where they were.

Rostow's model assumes that all countries follow a similar path to development or modernization, advancing through five stages of development. In the first stage, the society is *traditional* and the dominant activity is subsistence farming. The social structure is rigid and technology is slow to change. The second stage brings the *preconditions of takeoff*. New leadership moves the country toward greater flexibility, openness, and diversification. These changes, in turn, lead to the third stage, *takeoff.* Now the country experiences something akin to an industrial revolution, and sustained growth takes hold. Urbanization increases, industrialization proceeds, and technological and mass-production break-throughs occur.

Next, the economy enters the fourth stage, the *drive to maturity*. Technologies diffuse, industrial specialization occurs, and international trade expands. Modernization is evident in key areas of the country and population growth slows. Finally, some countries reach the final stage in Rostow's model, *high mass consumption*, which is marked by high incomes and widespread production of many goods and services. During this stage, a majority of workers enter the service sector of the economy.

Another name for Rostow's model (and other models derived from it) is the ladder of development. Visually, we can see his five stages of development as rungs on a ladder (**Fig. 10.8**), with each country climbing the ladder one rung at a time. The major limitation of Rostow's model is that it provides no larger context for development. Is a climb up the ladder largely dependent on what happens within one country? Or do we need to take into account all of the other countries, their places on the ladder, and how their actions and global forces affect an individual country's movement on the ladder? The theory also misses the particular conditions that can influence development decisions within an individual country, with no consideration of the role that cultural or political differences might play.

As these questions suggest, Rostow's development model does not pay much attention to the different geographical and historical circumstances that can affect what happens to places. Instead it treats countries as individual, autonomous units that simply move through the process of development at different times and at different speeds. It fails to consider the ability of some countries to influence what happens in other countries or the different positions countries occupy in the world economy. Japan moved from a rural, agrarian state to an urbanized, industrial one in a particular way during the

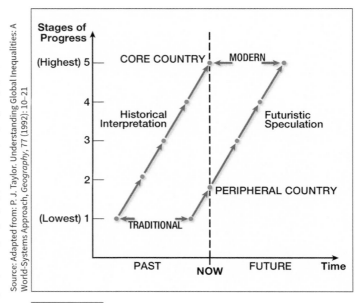

Source: Adapted from: P. J. Taylor. Understanding Global Inequalities: A World-Systems Approach, *Geography*, 77 (1992): 10–21

FIGURE 10.8 **Rostow's Ladder of Development.** This ladder assumes that all countries can reach the same level of development and that all will follow a similar path.

twentieth century. However, that does not mean that Mali will go through the same transition today, that it will do so in the same way.

Rostow's model also led many people to think of the world as divided into two basic economic realms: "developed" and "less developed." Those countries moving from the second to the first category were termed *developing*, and that term came to be used more widely in the late 1960s and 1970s as some lower income countries began to advance economically. Before long, all countries that were not viewed as developed were called "developing." Using the term *developing*, however, implies that countries are improving along each indicator of development: increasing per capita GNI, increasing productivity per worker, improving access to communications and technology, improving access to health care and clean water, and improving literacy rates for males and females.

Rostow's model is still influential, despite all its limitations. Even calling higher income countries "industrialized" and saying that lower income countries need to "industrialize" implies stages of development. It suggests that economic development can be achieved only by climbing the same ladder of development that the higher income countries have already climbed. Yet if a lower income country quickly industrialized today through foreign investment, it might not reap much economic benefit. In fact, it could experience severe environmental consequences. The higher income countries we call "industrial" today are really "postindustrial." Declining transportation costs and new approaches to production have moved the manufacturing of goods to other parts of the world. Many of the highest income countries have economies built on the service sector, not the industrial sector (see Chapter 12).

Alternative Approaches to Modeling Development

Development happens in **context**. To understand why some countries are poor and others are wealthy, we need to consider the role played by geographical context: the spatial organization, character, and history of a place and its interactions with the broader world.

Historically, ideas about government and economics diffused from Europe through the world as a result of colonialism, global trade, and the rise of capitalism. The Industrial Revolution and colonialism made colonies dependent on the colonizers. This relationship brought wealth to the colonizers. Even after colonialism ended, the economic, political, and social networks created through colonialism persisted. Goods and capital continued to flow from colonies to their former colonizers. The continuation of colonial relationships after formal colonialism ends is called **neocolonialism**. The term draws attention to the continuing ability of former colonial powers to control the economies of the lower income independent countries.

Development scholars have produced a number of alternative theories to explain the barriers to development under neocolonialism. These theories are called structuralist theories. A **structuralist theory** holds that difficult-to-change, large-scale economic arrangements shape what is possible for a country's development in fundamental ways. The world economy has a set of structural circumstances that make it very difficult for lower income countries to improve their economic situation. Such circumstances include the concentration of wealth in certain areas and unequal relations among places. Structuralists argue that less well-off countries face a very different set of development circumstances and different contexts than those faced by the countries of western Europe that were described in Rostow's model. Some even question whether it is possible for all countries to develop at the same time or whether structural circumstances require that some countries be on the bottom in order for others to remain on top.

Dependency Theory   Structuralists have developed a major body of development theory called **dependency theory**, which holds that the political and economic relationships between countries and regions of the world control and limit the economic development possibilities of lower income areas. Dependency theorists note, for example, that colonialism created political and economic structures that caused the colonies to become dependent on the colonial powers. They further argue that such dependency helps sustain wealth in developed regions and poverty in other areas, even after decolonization occurs.

Dependency theory is based on the idea that economic prosperity is difficult to achieve in regions and countries that have traditionally been dominated by external powers because a dependency relationship continues after independence. For example, 14 countries in Africa have used the CFA franc as their currency since 1945. They long tied the value of their currency to the value of the French franc, and they now tie it to the European Monetary Union's euro (France switched to using the euro in 2002). The economies of these 14 African countries are thus tied to the economy of the European Union—they rise and fall together. The CFA franc was set up before African countries gained independence starting in the 1950s and 1960s, and the former colonies (12 of the 14 were colonies of France) continue to use the CFA franc because their economies are based on the currency. Moreover, the countries are dependent on France in other ways because the French treasury and French parliament set policies that directly affect their economies.

Other types of dependency are important as well. Although the United States did not colonize Central and South America, several countries in the region now recognize that their economy is dependent on the United States and explicitly link their economy to the U.S. dollar. Indeed, more than 40 countries around the world peg the value of their currency to the U.S dollar, and ten countries have abandoned their currency and completely adopted the U.S. dollar. The process of adopting the U.S. dollar as a country's currency is called **dollarization**.

For the people of El Salvador, dollarization made sense because the economy of El Salvador depends on the economy of the United States (**Fig. 10.9**). Over 1.42 million Salvadorians live in the United States, and in 2016 they sent $4.6 billion in remittances to El Salvador. Because of this flow of American dollars to El Salvador, many transactions occurred in dollars

YURI CORTEZ/AFP/Getty Images

FIGURE 10.9   **San Salvador, El Salvador.**   A bank employee loads an automatic teller machine (ATM) with U.S. currency in El Salvador, a country that underwent dollarization in 2001.

long before the official switch. The United Nations Development Program estimates that 22.3 percent of families in El Salvador receive remittances. In addition, over 40 percent of El Salvador's exports go to the United States. When the Federal Reserve Board in the United States controls the supply of dollars by altering the interest rates or when the U.S. economy enters a recession, the consequences are felt directly in El Salvador. The greatest disadvantage of dollarization is that it involves surrendering to the United States aspects of policymaking that affect the local economy. The biggest advantage of dollarization is stabilization of the country's currency because of the stability of the U.S. dollar.

Like modernization theory, dependency theory is based on generalizations about economic change that do not pay much attention to geographical differences in culture, politics, and society. Not every country is in the same situation at the same time, so countries cannot all follow the same path of development, as modernization theory would have it. Likewise, not every country is affected by a dependent relationship in the same way. Pegging a currency to or adopting the currency of a higher income country may be beneficial for one country but not for another.

World-Systems Theory
Development models—even dependency theory—tend to underplay geographical, historical, and political context. In reaction to that tendency, some geographers have embraced a development theory we have already encountered (see Chapter 8): Immanuel Wallerstein's **world-systems theory**. This theory incorporates attention to the role that space (geography) and time (history) play in the power relationships that exist in the world economy.

Wallerstein divided the world into a **three-tier structure:** core, periphery, and semiperiphery. The division helps explain the interconnections among places in the global economy. Recall that **core** processes generate wealth in a place because they require higher levels of education, more sophisticated technologies, and higher wages and benefits. When core processes are embedded in a place (such as the Telecom corridor in Richardson-Plano, Texas), wealth is generated for the people in that place. **Peripheral** processes, on the other hand, require little education, lower technologies, and lower wages and benefits. Producing agriculture by hand using little technology may generate a stable food supply in a place, but it does not have a significant impact on the larger formal economy.

Core regions are those in which core processes are grouped together. Core regions have achieved high levels of economic prosperity and are dominant players in the world economy. When peripheral processes are found in a place, the processes often generate little wealth for the people in that place. Periphery regions are areas where peripheral processes are concentrated. They are lower income regions that are dependent in significant ways on the core and do not have as much control over their own affairs, economically or politically. The **semiperiphery** exhibits both core and peripheral processes, with semiperipheral places serving as a buffer between the core and periphery in the world economy. Countries of the semiperiphery exert more power than peripheral regions but remain heavily influenced by core regions.

Dividing the world into cores, semiperipheries, and peripheries might seem to do little more than replace *developed*, *developing*, and *underdeveloped* with a new set of terms. But the core–periphery model is different from the modernization model because it holds that not all places can be equally wealthy in the capitalist world economy. World-systems theory also makes the power relations among places explicit and does not assume that socioeconomic change will occur in the same way in all places. It is thus sensitive to geographical context, at least in economic terms.

Geographer Peter J. Taylor uses the analogy of a school of tadpoles to demonstrate these ideas. He envisions different places in the world as tadpoles and explains that not all tadpoles can survive to develop into toads. Rather, those that dominate survive and the others perish. World-systems theorists see domination (exploitation) as a function of the capitalist drive for profit in the global economy. Thus, capitalists can move production from one place to another around the globe to enhance profits, but places that lose a production facility can suffer. Moreover, their coping capacity can be small if, as is often the case, they abandon traditional ways and shift to an export economy once external investment arrives.

Another benefit of Wallerstein's three-tier structure is that it focuses on *how* a good is produced instead of *what* is produced. Rostow looked at what is produced. He argued that in order to develop, a country needs to move from traditional agricultural production to industrial production. Wallerstein disagreed—arguing that a country can produce agriculture using core processes and gain wealth while another country can produce the very same agricultural product with peripheral processes and gain almost no wealth from it.

Generating wealth is not determined by *what is produced*; it depends on *how something is produced*. Farmers can grow cotton with simple tools or with $700,000 module-making cotton pickers. Using the $700,000 cotton picker produces more wealth because of all that went into it: Educated engineers designed it, laborers manufactured it, marketing professionals and salespeople sold it, the John Deere dealership received $700,000 for it, and the educated farmer employs the picker to increase productivity per worker.

Another reason why some geographers are drawn to world-systems theory is its potential applicability at multiple scales. For example, Los Angeles can be described as the core of the Southern California region; the Johannesburg area can be seen as the core of southern Africa; or the central business district can be studied as the core of São Paulo, Brazil.

TC **Thinking Geographically**

Compare and contrast Rostow's ladder of development, dependency theory, and Wallerstein's three-tier structure of the world economy. Describe the **commodity chain** of a specific good. How do differences in core and peripheral processes in the production of this good create **unequal exchange**?

10.3 Explain Major Influences on Development.

Regardless of which development theory you find the most persuasive, most of the theories accept that structures shape the world economy. These structures help to sustain the concentration of power in core states and entrenched poverty in peripheral states.

Economic Arrangements

The concentration of wealth and power in the global economic core that resulted from colonialism and early industrialization put economic actors in those places in the driver's seat. Increasingly powerful corporations developed with a global reach—transnational corporations—that had the ability to shape patterns of development through their investment strategies. Huge banana companies such as Chiquita, Del Monte, Dole, and Noboa could come into a country such as Ecuador, promote the development of vast banana plantations, and ultimately create an economy that was heavily dependent on a single commodity—meaning that development prospects were hostage to the ups and downs of the global banana market.

Manufacturing-oriented transnational corporations also influence development through the globe-spanning production networks they establish. To understand how the production of goods creates wealth in some areas but not in others, it is useful to understand the concept of a commodity chain and the role that places play in the chain of production. A **commodity chain** is a series of links connecting the many places of production and distribution that are involved in the creation of a final product that is bought and sold on the market. Consider an automobile sold in your hometown. It was likely assembled elsewhere using component parts that were made in dozens of different countries around the world. The component parts were most likely made using raw materials from yet other countries. And transport networks knit all of these places together. Each link along the car's commodity chain added value, producing differing levels of wealth for different places and people at each step in production.

In earlier times, what Timbuktu had to offer was the ability to coordinate and facilitate trade based on a geographic site where the Niger River turned north at the edge of the Sahara Desert. The river was the last major water source for those crossing the Sahara from south to north across what is now Mali and Algeria. Timbuktu was a **break-of-bulk** location, where goods traded on one mode of transport, camel, were transported to another mode of transport, boat. The points along the chain where materials and goods are traded change over time, directly impacting the prosperity of places.

Commodity chains today span the globe, and break-of-bulk locations are only one of many nodes along the chain.

Places occupy different niches along commodity chains, and they do not all benefit equally from the production of a good. The generation of wealth depends on how production occurs at each step and who reaps most of the economic benefits from production. Sophisticated technology, high skill levels, extensive research and development, and high salaries tend to be associated with the segments of global commodity chains located in the core. The segments located in the periphery, by contrast, tend to be associated with low technology, less education, little research and development, and lower wages.

Aid and International Financial Institutions

A number of countries in the global economic core offer aid to lower income countries. **Figure 10.10** provides an overview of the geography of development assistance. The major donor countries are in North America, Europe, and East Asia, and they also include Australia and New Zealand. The main recipient countries are in Africa, southern Asia, Central America, and South America. China and the United States are the largest donors of foreign aid when measured by total dollars, but they are not among the top 10 donor countries when contributions are measured as a percentage of GNI (Fig. 10.10).

Foreign aid can serve as a catalyst for development, as was dramatically illustrated when the United States pumped $12 billion (some $100 billion in today's money) into western Europe after World War II in an effort to help the devastated region get back on its feet (the Marshall Plan). Aid initiatives, however, are rarely driven solely by concern for the well-being of others (altruism). Aid programs they also reflect the interests of donor countries. The Marshall Plan was not just about helping Europe recover from war. The United States wanted to build a strong transatlantic alliance and help Europe resist expanding Soviet influence.

Development assistance may be given to stop problems in the receiving country from impacting the donor country. For example, a donor country may give aid to stabilize a neighboring country with the hope of stopping or slowing the flow of migrants into the donor country. Donor countries may give development aid to gain access to markets in the receiving country or to exert political control over their government. Some donor countries approach development aid altruistically. They may believe all countries do better when the situation of lower income, struggling countries improves.

The interests of donor countries are the prime drivers in development aid, and donor countries may make aid decisions that harm recipient countries. For example, if a donor country ships food or clothing regularly, the steady supply of goods from the donor country will undermine domestic production. Agriculture and textile industries in the receiving country will have fewer customers and less incentive for production.

Source: Data from World Development Indicators: Aid dependency, The World Bank and Indicator 17.2.1: Net official development assistance (ODA) as a percentage of OECD-DAC donors' GNI, by donor countries (percent), United Nations. Visualization by E.H. Fouberg and A.B. Murphy. © 2020 John Wiley & Sons, Inc.

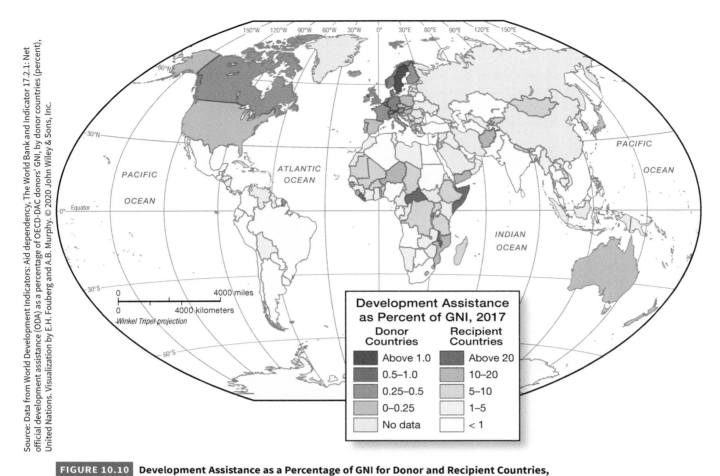

FIGURE 10.10 **Development Assistance as a Percentage of GNI for Donor and Recipient Countries, 2017.** Two sets of data are represented on the map. Donor countries are shown in the purple shades, with color intensity reflecting the percentage of GNI devoted to foreign aid. Recipient countries are shown in orange shades, with darker tones reflecting higher levels of aid relative to their GNIs.

International Financial Institutions: Western

International financial institutions create the assumptions, guidelines, policies, and structures for development. As World War II was winding down, the allied powers met in Bretton Woods (New Hampshire) to draw up a plan for the postwar economic world. Out of that conference came the World Bank and the International Monetary Fund (IMF)—international financial institutions aimed at promoting economic reconstruction, free trade, and stability in the global financial system. The World Bank initially focused on rebuilding Europe and has become a major source of development funds for lower income countries. The IMF is tasked with monitoring currency exchange rates and balance of payments in trade to create financial stability in global markets.

The United States and Europe are the dominant donors and influencers of the World Bank and IMF. The president of the World Bank is always an American, and the president of the IMF is always a European. The IMF and World Bank loaned substantial amounts of money to newly independent countries in Africa and Asia after World War II. Loans have typically been earmarked for large infrastructure projects like dams, highways, and airports.

Countries receiving loans were generally able to repay them until the world economy took a downward turn in the 1970s. The price of oil rose, and by the early 1980s commodity prices dropped. Rising oil prices make the production of goods more expensive, and falling commodity prices make it difficult to repay loans as the value of exports declines. The Third World Debt Crisis began as export revenue declined, the cost of oil increased, and state-run companies created in the 1960s and 1970s were found to be both inefficient and a drain on government funds.

The World Bank and the International Monetary Fund stepped in to lend more money to help borrower countries out of the Third World Debt Crisis. These loans came with conditions. Borrower countries had to agree to implement economic and governmental reforms, including privatizing government entities, opening themselves to foreign trade, reducing tariffs, and encouraging foreign direct investment. These loans are known as **structural adjustment loans**. By the early 1990s, the set of policies associated with them came to be known as the **Washington Consensus**.

Opponents of the Washington Consensus argue that such policies support and protect core country economies at the expense of peripheral and semiperipheral economies. Countries had limited options to reject structural adjustment loans because the cost of servicing debts (repayments plus interest) often exceeded revenues from the export of goods and services (**Fig. 10.11**). Borrower countries also needed to demonstrate that they were repaying their debts as well as restructuring their economies. The intention was to attract multinational corporations that could offer employment to their people and investment in their economies.

Structural adjustment loans were part of a larger trend toward **neoliberalism** in the late twentieth century. Neoliberalism is a variant of the neoclassical economic idea that government intervention into markets is both inefficient and undesirable. Neoliberals resist government intervention wherever possible. That way of thinking was at the heart of the structural adjustment conditions that were attached to loans and refinancing programs. Neoliberal ideas spurred a trend toward transferring economic control from states to the private sector. As a result, the size of the public sector in a number of countries shrank. Corporate control expanded, and state and regional governments had less control over their economic destinies.

High debt obligations and related neoliberal reforms contributed to the economic and political crisis in Argentina at the end of 2001 and beginning of 2002. Argentina privatized some government activities in the 1990s and took out loans, which led to short-term economic growth in the 1990s. In 1999, however, a recession hit Argentina, and by 2000 the country had a debt equal to 50 percent of its GDP (Blustein 2003) (**Fig. 10.12**). The IMF extended emergency loans in 2000 and again in 2001.

Coupled with unchecked government spending and corruption, Argentina's economy experienced a meltdown, and the country defaulted on its debt in 2002. More than half the population of 38 million ended up in poverty (McCarthy 2007).

By 2005, internal economic growth and aid from Venezuela put Argentina in a position to work out a complex debt restructuring plan that pulled the country back from the brink. Argentina's agricultural economy bounced back in 2010 with the rise of corn and soy prices. Its struggles with loans are far from over, however. In 2018, Argentina requested $50 billion from the IMF to help manage a worsening inflation crisis amid serious doubts about its ability to pay back debt. Countries in Argentina's position find themselves in a severely disadvantaged position when it comes to attracting future external investment. If a substantial number of countries were to default at the same time, a global economic crisis could ensue that would work to the disadvantage of almost everyone.

International Financial Institutions: Chinese

In recent years, the World Bank and the IMF have backed away from some of their more controversial lending practices—showing a greater concern for the social and environmental implications of development funds. But with the rise of China, development finance is no longer primarily a Western game. In 1994, the China Development Bank was established under Chinese governmental control. Since then, a variety of

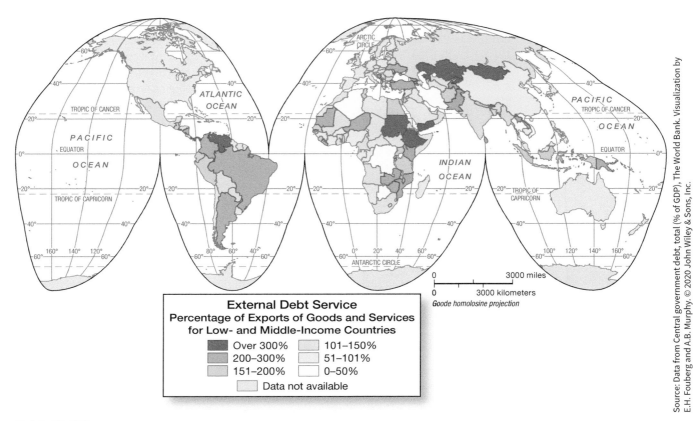

External Debt Service
Percentage of Exports of Goods and Services
for Low- and Middle-Income Countries

Over 300%	101–150%
200–300%	51–101%
151–200%	0–50%
Data not available	

Source: Data from Central government debt, total (% of GDP), The World Bank. Visualization by E.H. Fouberg and A.B. Murphy. © 2020 John Wiley & Sons, Inc.

FIGURE 10.11 **External Debt Service as a Percentage of Exports of Goods.** Repaying loans, let alone paying the interest on the loans, is more difficult for countries with large debt and low income from exports. Exports create revenue for a country that can help them pay back loans.

| Author Field Note | Watching the Upheaval of the Economy in Buenos Aires, Argentina. |

"Arriving in Argentina during the political and economic upheavals that had begun in 2001, I saw signs of dislocation and trouble everywhere. People asking for money pursued pedestrians on the once-fashionable Avenida Florida. Banks had installed protective shutters against angry crowds demanding return of their frozen and devalued deposits. A bus trip on the Patagonian Highway turned into an adventure when masked protesters carrying rocks and burning rags stopped vehicles and threatened their occupants. Newspapers carried reports of starvation in Tucumán Province – in a country capable of producing seven times the food its population needs."

– H. J. de Blij

FIGURE 10.12 Buenos Aires, Argentina.

other Chinese banks with international reach have come on the scene, turning China into a major player in the international development arena. Indeed, the four largest banks in the world, as measured by total assets, are Chinese. The biggest bank in the world is ICBC (Industrial and Commercial Bank of China), followed by China Construction Bank, Agricultural Bank of China, and the Bank of China. These banks are called the "Big Four" and are all owned by a holding company that is owned by the government of China. The Big Four banks have locations all over the world (**Fig. 10.13**). In addition to these enormous financial institutions, the China Development Bank and the

Export-Import Bank of China now provide as much development financing to less developed countries as the World Bank does.

China's development funding is appealing to many countries because they see the loans as having no strings attached—loans do not require governments to follow structural adjustments. While Chinese development funding is helping to meet the infrastructure needs of many countries, a heavy emphasis on large infrastructure and energy projects (coal-burning power plants and large dams designed to produce hydroelectricity) means that Chinese development assistance carries with it serious environmental costs. In Bangladesh, for example, Chinese-financed coal plants have worsened air pollution and created health problems (to say nothing of their contribution to global climate change). And large Chinese-financed hydroelectric plants along the Mekong River have reduced fish stocks and threatened people's livelihoods.

While Chinese development loans come without strings attached in terms of having to change government operations, they come with serious financial and political consequences when borrowers become trapped in debt and cannot repay loans. Each investment in China's Belt and Road Initiative (BRI, see Chapter 8, Fig. 8.25) benefits Chinese financial lenders (including the Big Four banks), Chinese development companies (including China Development Bank and the Export-Import Bank of China), Chinese infrastructure and construction companies (including China Harbor Engineering Company—also owned by the Chinese government), and even Chinese workers who are transported temporarily to work on major construction projects. Because Chinese companies build the projects, they hire the workers, and they hire Chinese workers instead of locals, depriving locals of construction jobs.

When countries cannot repay loans from BRI projects, the government of China steps in and takes ownership. The President of Sri Lanka, Mahinda Rajapaska, took enormous loans from Chinese lenders and the China Harbor Engineering Company to build a state-of-the-art port in Sri Lanka during his 2005–2015

FIGURE 10.13 **Hong Kong.** This scene shows both the global financial role Hong Kong plays and the history of the place. The Bank of China tower is on the left. The Cheng Kong Centre in the middle back houses a major Hong Kong-based multinational conglomerate. The HSBC Bank building, housing a UK bank that first entered Hong Kong in 1865, is on the right. In the foreground is the Legislative Building, built during the British colonial era.

term in office. When the president was voted out in 2015, the new Sri Lankan government inherited an unpayable debt. The Sri Lankan government negotiated with the Chinese and the end result was handing over the brand-new, Chinese-funded port to China. China now owns Sri Lanka's port , which sits on 15,000 acres of land, for the next 99 years. While the agreement to hand over the port "erased roughly $1 billion in debt for the port project," Sri Lanka continues to accrue debt to China as they take additional loans with high interest rates (*New York Times* 2018).

While the Chinese loans do not have official strings constraining governments, Chinese investors have worked to influence election outcomes in borrower countries. In Sri Lanka, Chinese financial institutions contributed at least $7.6 million to Rajapaska's 2015 campaign. An internal investigation in Sri Lanka found that checks from an account controlled by the Chinese port development project paid for gifts to voters and supporters as well as "two checks totaling $1.7 million," which were delivered by volunteers to Rajapaska's home (*New York Times* 2018). Rajapaska lost the 2015 election but became politically active again, along with his brother, in 2018. Chinese investment ratcheted up almost immediately, with Ritz Carlton and JW Marriott hotels, financed by Chinese companies, going up next to the port (**Fig. 10.14**).

China's BRI projects, the global influence of Chinese banks, and Chinese development organizations are changing the structures and face of global economic development. The impacts of development financing—whether from Chinese or Western sources—will not be the same everywhere. Conditions within countries also matter. Lack of education, poverty, corrupt leadership, political instability, and disease can all hamper development. It is possible to get into the chicken-or-egg debate here: Did the interconnections that characterize the world economy create these conditions, or do these conditions help create the structures of the world economy? Many people think that neither argument can stand alone, but understanding both structures and conditions is important.

Social Conditions

Across the global periphery, as much as half the population is 15 years old or younger (see Fig. 10.5B), making the supply of adult, taxpaying laborers low relative to the number of dependents. Low life expectancies and high infant and child mortality rates stem from inadequate nutrition. Despite the UN's efforts to achieve the Sustainable Development Goals, just under one in four children worldwide had stunted growth in 2017; they do not receive enough calories to grow as tall as they should be for their age.

Peripheral countries have little access to public sewage systems, clean drinking water, and health care making economic development all the more difficult. According to the United Nations, 159 million people still rely on unsafe drinking water from rivers, ponds, and unprotected wells and springs, and close to 900 million people still practiced "open defecation" in 2018. Open defecation spreads disease and is found most often in South Asia, Oceania, and sub-Saharan Africa (UN 2014).

FIGURE 10.14 **Colombo, Sri Lanka.** The Colombo deep sea port is a project in the Chinese Belt and Road Initiative. Sri Lanka handed ownership of the port over to China in 2015 when they could not repay the debt. The government continues to take loans from China and as of 2019, owes Chinese financial institutions an estimated $5 billion for the port, a new airport, and a new railroad, with interest growing each year. The new buildings going up are Ritz Carlton and JW Marriott hotels, which are projects financed by Chinese investors.

Lack of access to education is also a major problem in the periphery. However, the number of children in the periphery enrolled in primary school, both boys and girls, has increased since 2000, thanks to governmental efforts to extend education. For example, the government of Rwanda eliminated fees for primary education in 2003. Doing so guaranteed six years of primary and three years of secondary school for all children. Then two years later, the government started distributing funds to schools based on the number of students they were educating. Rwanda successfully increased the proportion of students attending school through grade 6, reporting a 95 percent enrollment rate (Republic of Rwanda 2014). Growing education so quickly makes it difficult to establish quality education, however. The United Nations Development Program reported in 2014 that only 5 percent of Rwandan students met or exceeded reading goals and that a majority did not meet numeracy goals. Nevertheless, Rwandan officials continue to work to improve access to education, and recently they supported a 5 percent increase in money allocated to education.

Governments have used innovative policies to promote education, including financial incentives for families to enroll and send their children to school. Historically, children would drop out of primary school or have low attendance so they could help their family by working in farms and factories, or providing child or elderly care at home. Children in peripheral countries often have to pay a fee for attending school, and in some places girls drop out of school to earn wages to pay school fees for their brothers. Cash transfer policies seek to undermine this practice by providing a financial incentive to enroll in school and attend regularly. Yet the problem persists—particularly in rural areas, where girls from lower income families are the least likely to attend primary school (United Nations 2014).

Mario Tama/Getty Images News/Getty Images

FIGURE 10.15 **Rio De Janeiro, Brazil.** The parents of the children in this photograph credit Bolsa Familia with assisting them in purchasing a new home after their previous home was condemned. Bolsa Familia has reduced extreme poverty in Brazil from 13 percent of the population to 7 percent of the population.

Brazil's Bolsa Familia conditional cash transfer program is a particular success. It began in the 1990s, and former president Lula da Silva expanded the scope of the program in 2003. Bolsa Familia pays families in cash under the condition that their children enroll and attend school (children cannot miss more than 15 percent of classes) and that they receive medical checkups. One fourth of Brazil's families, 11.1 million families (46 million people) are enrolled in the program. Brazil credits the program with bringing "36 million Brazilians out of extreme poverty" (Barnes 2013).

Bolsa Familia is held up as a model for economic development, as it gives people with lower incomes the ability to choose how to spend their financial assistance instead of living within the constraints of separate programs designed to address different aspects of poverty (**Fig. 10.15**). Conditional cash transfer programs have the added benefit of increasing school attendance for girls and boys. However, in the wake of the 2018 election of Jair Bolsonaro as Brazil's president, Bolsa Familia was targeted for budget cuts based on the argument that it encourages overdependence on the government. The program operates in all 5570 municipalities in Brazil, so Bolsonaro will need to weigh his targeted budget cuts with how extensive a network the Bolsa Familia program has woven.

South Africa's conditional cash transfer program has led to an increase in the number of children receiving primary education. However, many of the schools are in poor condition, and the quality of education is below par. Data from South Africa's national literacy and numeracy tests reveal that "only 15 percent of 12-year-olds (sixth graders) scored at or above the minimum proficiency on the language test," and in math, only 12 percent were proficient (*The Economist*, South Africa 2012). At the end of 2016, the South African government lowered the passing grade for math to 20 percent to make it easier for students to continue their education, despite evidence that the system as a whole poorly served students. Although South Africa needs 25,000 new qualified teachers each year, less than half that number enter the system. The South African economy in turn suffers because schools do not produce enough graduates to fill the jobs that require education.

Lack of education for girls is made worse by the assumption that girls should only leave their homes (and communities) when they marry and contribute to their husband's family. These types of assumptions, when taken to an extreme, feed into the human **trafficking** of girls and young women, who are seen as less important than boys and are treated as financial drains because of the assumption that their earning potential is limited. Mike Dottridge, a modern antislavery activist, explains that tracking happens when "adults and children fleeing poverty or seeking better prospects are manipulated, deceived, and bullied into working in conditions that they would not choose."

Trafficking is not usually considered slavery because the family does not sell a child. Instead, the family sends the child away with a recruiter in the hopes that the child will earn money to send home. Trafficked children are often taken to neighboring or nearby countries that are wealthier and where demand for domestic servants is high. Dottridge explains that the majority of trafficked children are girls and that the majority of girls are "employed as domestic servants or street vendors," but some are trafficked into the commercial sex trade (see Chapter 3).

Political Corruption and Instability

Political corruption and instability can greatly impede economic development. In peripheral countries, a wide divide often exists between the very wealthy and the poorest of the poor. In Kenya, for example, the wealthiest 0.1 percent have more wealth than the bottom 99.9 percent. The disenfranchisement of the poor and the competition among the rich for control of the government can lead to extreme political instability within a state. Kenya experienced this problem in 2007–2008, when roughly 1300 people died as a result of violence around a presidential election. Kenya's presidential election in 2017 proved less violent, but it was still controversial. After high courts found irregularities in the vote, a new election went forward. The incumbent president, who had lost in the earlier annulled vote, ended up retaining the presidency only after his opponent withdrew.

Many countries in the periphery and semiperiphery have struggled to establish and maintain democracies in the wake of decolonization. The governments that emerged often reflected the political and social hierarchies of the colonial period. Some failed, some were overthrown by military coups, and some saw power fall into the hands of a dictatorial strongman. Many countries in the periphery and semiperiphery have alternated repeatedly between quasi-democratic and military governments. Some argue that without considerable wealth, maintaining a liberal democracy is all but impossible.

Looking at international news on any given day will reveal a story somewhere that demonstrates the link between economic stability and political stability. In Afghanistan, economic woes represent one of the greatest threats to the stability of the U.S.-supported government in Kabul. More than half of the population is impoverished. The government also lacks the funds to invest in development. Foreign aid has provided some help, but the flow of aid has been variable and the amount is insufficient to address the country's searing economic problems. Many analysts see this as a key impediment to achieving stability in Afghanistan. As *The Economist* once noted, "poverty helps the Taliban."

In places where poverty is rampant, politicians often become corrupt, misusing aid and exacerbating the plight of the families with lower incomes. In Zimbabwe, the year 2002 left many people starving, as poor weather conditions created a meager harvest. The country's ruling party, ZANU-PF, headed by Robert Mugabe, demanded that Zimbabweans who registered for the "food for work" program had cards demonstrating membership in the ZANU-PF political party. As conditions worsened in subsequent years, the Mugabe government faced increasing resistance. A potential challenger, Morgan Tsvangirai, emerged in 2008, but members of his opposition party were killed and the challenger was harassed. And after a contested election that many believe Tsvangirai won, a power-sharing agreement came into effect that kept Mugabe as president and made Tsvangirai the prime minister. Some stability returned, but not for long. In late 2017 Mugabe faced impeachment and ceded power to his hand-picked vice president, Emmerson Mnangagwa. Mnangagwa was declared the winner of a contested election in 2018, and Mugabe died in 2019. Zimbabwe faces enormous political and economic challenges going forward.

The Zimbabwe case shows that in low income countries, compromised leaders can stay in power for decades. Circumstances and timing need to work together to allow a new government to come to power. When governments become excessively corrupt, other countries and nongovernmental organizations sometimes withdraw development aid to the country. Yet when this happens, everyday people often bear the brunt of hardship. And even when aid is provided, it is sometimes mismanaged, and it is almost never sufficient to meet basic needs or reverse a trajectory of hardship.

Costs of Economic Development

Economic development changes a place. To increase productivity, whether industrial or agricultural, people transform the environment. As countries industrialize, air and water often become more polluted. And pollution is not confined to industry. The pesticides and herbicides that are used in intensive agriculture have negative impacts on soil and groundwater. Tourism can be just as difficult on the environment because it taxes the existing infrastructure beyond its capacities. The costs of tourism often stretch far beyond the environment, affecting ways of life and fundamentally altering the cultural landscape.

AP® Exam Taker's Tip

Costs of Economic Development – Name the negative effects of **economic development**. Identify examples of natural-resource depletion, mass consumption, effects of pollution, and the impact on the climate from economic development.

Costs of Industrialization   In their efforts to attract new industries, many governments in the periphery and semiperiphery have set up special manufacturing export zones

called export processing zones (EPZs) or special economic zones (SEZs). These zones offer favorable tax, regulatory, and trade arrangements to foreign firms. By 2006, 130 countries had established 3500 such zones, and many of these had become major manufacturing centers (Engman et al. 2007). Two of the best known of these zones are the Mexican maquiladoras and the special economic zones of China (discussed in Chapter 9). Governments locate such zones in places with easy access to export markets. **Maquiladora** zones in Mexico are mainly sited directly across the border from the United States, and the special economic zones of China are located near major ports (**Fig. 10.16**). These zones typically attract a mix of manufacturing operations, depending on the skill levels of the labor force and the available infrastructure.

The maquiladora program started in 1965 when the Mexican government designated the region of northern Mexico as a maquiladora district. It became a place where raw materials could be shipped into Mexico, manufactured into goods, and then sent back to the United States free of import tariffs. U.S. corporations relocated manufacturing plants to Mexico to take advantage of the program. Although the maquiladora phenomenon started in 1965, it did not really take off until the 1980s, when American companies recognized the expanding wage and benefit differences between U.S. and Mexican workers and began relocating to the maquiladora district in northern Mexico. Competition from other parts of the world has since led to the closing of some plants. However, some 3000 maquiladoras continue to function. They employ more than 1 million workers and account for 50 percent of Mexico's exports.

Mexican maquiladora plants produce goods such as electronic equipment, electrical appliances, automobiles, textiles, plastics, and furniture. The plants are controversial in both Mexico and the United States. Corporations that have relocated there avoid the employment and environmental regulations that are in force just a few miles to the north. Many maquiladora factories hire young women and men for low pay and few, if any benefits. They work in repetitive jobs, sometimes in environmentally questionable conditions.

In 1992, the United States, Mexico, and Canada established the North American Free Trade Agreement (NAFTA), which prompted further industrialization of the border region. NAFTA took effect January 1, 1994. In addition to manufacturing plants, it facilitated the movement of service industries from the United States to Mexico, including data-processing operations. Most of the new plants are located in two districts: Tijuana on the Pacific Coast—linked to San Diego across the border—and Ciudad Juarez on the Rio Grande across from El Paso, Texas.

In 2018, the United States-Mexico-Canada Agreement (USMCA) replaced NAFTA, but not much has changed. Violent crime remains a serious problem in Ciudad Juarez, even as El Paso remains comparatively safe. The slums of Tijuana are a world apart from much of San Diego. In both Ciudad Juarez and Tijuana, Mexican drug cartels compete for control (see Fig. 11.32), creating instability in northern Mexico. Instability makes economic development more difficult. In response, Mexicans continue to migrate to the United States, despite the tightly controlled border.

Data from: International Labor Organization. Visualization by E.H. Fouberg and A.B. Murphy. © 2020 John Wiley & Sons, Inc.

FIGURE 10.16 **Special Economic Zones.** Manufacturing in China is centered on Special Economic Zones (SEZs). Exports per province are highest in the east, in and around SEZs, and lowest in western China.

Costs of Agricultural Intensification In peripheral countries, agriculture typically focuses on personal consumption or on production for a large agricultural conglomerate. Where zones of larger-scale, modernized agriculture have developed in the periphery, foodstuffs are produced for the foreign market and often have minimal impact on the impoverished conditions of surrounding areas. Little is produced for the local marketplace because distribution systems are poorly organized and many locals are unable to pay for foodstuffs.

A turn to commercial agriculture can have multiple economic, social, and ecological effects. Most traditional farmers work small, fragmented plots of land, and what they produce does not generate much income. Even on larger plots of land, many farmers only have access to simple tools and equipment. They tend to grow grains, root crops, and fruits and vegetables. Yields per unit area are low, and subsistence modes of life prevail.

The introduction of large-scale commercial agriculture into this mix can make it more difficult for small-scale farmers to compete in the sale of their products. They do not often have access to the fertilizers and pesticides used in commercial agriculture. Social relations are often strained as well. There are major wealth disparities between the few who benefit from agricultural modernization and the many who do not. Moreover, the combination of expanding land devoted to commercial agriculture and worsening economic conditions for traditional farmers can push these farmers into ever more marginal lands.

The ecological effects of the latter tendency can be severe. Soil erosion is commonplace in many peripheral areas. Severe soil erosion in places with dry or semiarid climates around deserts results in extreme degradation of the land and the spread of the desert into these lands. Although the expansion and contraction of deserts can occur naturally and cyclically, the

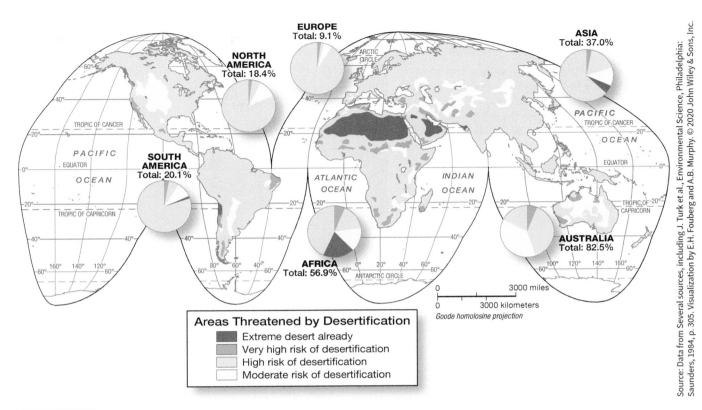

Source: Data from Several sources, including: J. Turk et al., Environmental Science, Philadelphia: Saunders, 1984, p. 305. Visualization by E.H. Fouberg and A.B. Murphy. © 2020 John Wiley & Sons, Inc.

FIGURE 10.17 **Areas Threatened by Desertification.** Deserts expand and contract cyclically, but nature's cycles can be distorted by human intervention. This map shows areas threatened or affected by desertification.

process of **desertification** often results from humans destroying native vegetation and eroding soils through the overuse of lands for livestock grazing or crop production.

Desertification has hit Africa harder than any of the other continents (**Fig. 10.17**). In sub-Saharan Africa over the last 50 years, more than 270,000 square miles (700,000 km²) of farming and grazing land have become desert, extending the Sahara Desert to the south. Some of the African desertification is partly a result of climate change (Chapter 13), but human factors matter as well. The problem comes not only from traditional farmers and ranchers turning marginal, semiarid lands into farm and ranch lands. Lands that are available for farming or ranching are also being turned over to intensive agricultural production. The result is further degradation of the land, out-migration, and in some cases conflict.

Costs of Tourism

All development strategies have pros and cons, as is well illustrated by the case of tourism. Peripheral island countries in the Caribbean region and in Oceania have become leading destinations for millions of tourists from richer states. Tourism is now one of the major industries in the world and has surpassed oil in overall economic value (see Chapter 12). While tourism can bring employment to peripheral countries, it can also have serious negative effects on cultures and environments.

To develop tourism, the "host" country must make substantial investments in infrastructure, including airports, cruise ports, roads, and communication systems. High-end hotels, swimming pools, and man-made waterfalls are typically owned by large

multinational corporations, not locals. The multinational corporations earn enormous profits, most of which are sent back to owners, shareholders, and executives outside of the country. Tourism can create local jobs, but they are often low paying, and most do not offer job security. In tourist zones, employees sometimes work two or three jobs to break even.

Tourism frequently strains the fabric of local communities as well. The invasion of lower-income communities by wealthier visitors can lead to resentment. Tourism can also have the effect of altering, and even debasing, local culture (see Chapter 4), which is adapted to suit the tastes of visitors.

In many instances, tourism fosters a "demonstration effect" among locals that encourages them to behave in ways that may please or interest visitors, but that is viewed negatively by the local community. Tourists build expectations of what they will see and how they will experience local cultures, which creates ideas of authenticity that may or may not exist. Local cultures constantly change, and communities and people within a culture may behave differently or have different values than the authentic ideal created and reinforced by tourism. Some tourism workers consider employment in the tourist industry degrading because it demands performances of culture to meet tourist expectations and displays of servitude to tourists that locals find offensive.

A flood of affluent tourists may be appealing to the government of a lower-income country whose elite have a financial stake in the hotels where they can share the pleasures of the wealthy. But local entrepreneurs have difficulty tapping into tourist

---

"Walking by a group of tent shelters put up by locals lacking brick and mortar homes, I was struck by the contrast with the palace in the background at the top of the hill, which once housed a royal family. The palace in the background was acquired by the Taj Hotel franchise, which is part of one of India's largest business conglomerates: The Tata Group. It has been turned into one of the finest, most luxurious hotels in India—attracting a wealthy clientele from around the world. The cost of spending a single night in the hotel must be more than the families living in the foreground can make in a year, if not more."

– A. B. Murphy

Photo by A.B. Murphy. © 2020 John Wiley & Sons, Inc.

FIGURE 10.18   **Jodhpur, India.**

---

revenues. Powerful multinational corporations and national governments limit the opportunities of local, small-scale operators. Instead, they favor mass, prearranged tourist destinations that isolate tourists from the local cultures and communities.

Overreliance on tourism can also leave an economy vulnerable if shifting economic circumstances cause a sharp decline in the number of tourists, or if natural disasters hit. Because many tourist destinations in lower-income countries are beach attractions, natural hazards such as the 2017 hurricane that swept across the Caribbean island of St. Maarten can destroy the linchpin of a country's economy. The country must deal with the after effects and cope with rebuilding tourist destinations while the flow of tourist-related income has stopped.

Growing recognition of the cultural and environmental impacts of tourism has led to the rapid growth of *ecotourism*. Ecotourism focuses primarily on fragile natural areas; the goal is to organize small-scale tourist experiences that involve minimal environmental disruption and that are sensitive to the well-being of local people. In the words of the International Ecotourism Society, the goal is to "build environmental and cultural awareness and respect." Many people see ecotourism as a positive alternative to mass tourism. Nonetheless, ecotourism does not avoid all the environmental and social costs of mass tourism. Most ecotourism operations are foreign owned, there are environmental costs to bringing people to remote areas and showing them around, and the presence of outsiders inevitably influences the lives of local people.

Whatever form tourism takes, the associated cultural landscape is frequently a study in harsh contrasts (**Fig. 10.18**). Gleaming hotels tower over modest, often poor housing; luxury liners glide past poverty-stricken villages; opulent meals are served in hotels while, down the street, children suffer from malnutrition. If the tourist industry offered real prospects for sustained economic progress in low-income countries, such circumstances might be viewed as temporary, unfortunate byproducts. However, in many cases the evidence points in the other direction.

TC **Thinking Geographically**

Reading back through Chapter 4 on local cultures and the section on **tourism** in this part of the chapter, explain why tourism can be problematic for the sustainability of local cultures. Specifically, consider how **authenticity** undermines the sustainability of local cultures.

10.4 Evaluate How Political and Economic Institutions Influence Uneven Development Within States.

Poverty is not confined to the periphery. Core countries have regions and peoples that are markedly poorer than others. On the Pine Ridge Indian Reservation in the northern Great Plains of the United States, unemployment hovers at 80 percent, and American Indians on the reservation live in poverty, with a per capita income of under $8000. Other countries of the core have similar regions where peoples' economic lives do not improve when the country's economy grows. In Europe, areas of isolation and stagnation persist—particularly in the east. At the same time, some areas within peripheral countries are experiencing rapid economic growth. In each of these cases, local conditions differ markedly from those found in surrounding areas.

Regional contrasts in income are a reminder that per capita GNI does not capture important aspects of economic development. Any statistic that is derived for an entire country hides economic variations within the country. Peripheral countries are marked by severe regional disparities. In Chapter 9, we discussed the stark contrasts between higher income and lower income within the cities of Central and South America and of Africa. When viewed at the scale of the state, major cities (particularly capitals) and their surroundings often look like islands of prosperity. Modern buildings, factories on the outskirts, and modern farms tend to be nearby. In some cases, roads and rails lead to a bustling port, where luxury automobiles are unloaded for use by the privileged elite, and raw materials or agricultural products from the country are exported to points around the world. In these core areas within peripheral countries, the rush of "progress" may be evident. If you travel a few miles into the countryside or into a different neighborhood, however, you will see a very different picture.

The Role of Governments

The contrasts between rich and poor areas are not simply the result of differences in the economic endowment of places. Government policy affects development patterns as well. Governments influence the geography of wealth through tariffs, trade agreements, taxation arrangements, land ownership rules, environmental regulations, and more. Government policies shape patterns of development within states—between urban and rural areas and also among different sectors of the economy. Governments alone do not determine patterns of wealth and poverty, but they are usually part of the picture.

Consider the case of the Ninth Ward in New Orleans, which was devastated by Hurricane Katrina in 2005. On its surface, what happened to the Ninth Ward was the result of a natural disaster. But the flooding of that part of New Orleans was also a consequence of government decisions made decades ago to build levees and settle flood-prone areas. The concentration of people living there also resulted from policies affecting housing, the construction of businesses, and the like. Once the hurricane hit, many looked to government to rebuild the devastated section of the city, but rebuilding was slow and spotty (**Fig. 10.19**).

Every government policy has a geographical expression, meaning that some regions are favored whereas others are not. When policies come together to favor some regions over others, uneven development is the result. Moreover, uneven development often becomes worse over time as wealthy areas grow wealthier and poorer areas stagnate.

Consider the contrasting outcomes of U.S. agricultural policy in parts of rural Wisconsin and rural Appalachia. In rural Wisconsin, farmers typically hold college degrees, usually from land-grant universities, in plant and animal sciences and in agribusiness. A farmer may run a highly mechanized dairy farm in which each cow has a barcode that is used to record a range of data about that particular cow. The data include any medical attention the cow has needed, how much milk the cow is producing, and when the cow last calved. The farmer feeds the cow a diet geared toward improving or maintaining milk production. When the cow ambles over to the trough to feed,

---

Author Field Note   **Reconstructing the Ninth Ward in New Orleans, Louisiana**

"As I walked through the Lower Ninth Ward of New Orleans more than two years after Hurricane Katrina, it seemed as if the natural disaster had just happened. Street after street of devastated, vacant buildings was all the eye could behold—many still bearing the markings of the emergency crews that had moved through the neighborhood in the wake of the hurricane, showing whether anyone had died inside. It struck me that reconstruction would require a public commitment on the order of what occurred in Europe after World War II, when cities reduced to rubble by bombing were rebuilt almost from scratch. No such commitment ever materialized, but some progress has been made in recent years. Census data shows a city that is slightly smaller and slightly wealthier than the pre-Katrina city, with a somewhat reduced African American population and a modestly expanding number of Hispanics."

– A. B. Murphy

Photo by A.B. Murphy. © 2020 John Wiley & Sons, Inc.

FIGURE 10.19   **Lower Ninth Ward, New Orleans.**

a sensor reads the cow's barcode and automatically mixes the correct balance of proteins, carbohydrates, and nutrients for the cow, dispensing them into the trough for the cow to eat. If the cow has already eaten that day, the computer dispenses nothing into the trough, and the cow is left to amble away.

In parts of rural Appalachia, by contrast, hardscrabble farming is the norm. Farmers have limited education, and there is little mechanization. In short, life in some of the lowest income parts of rural Appalachia is a world apart from life on a modern Wisconsin dairy farm. Locational and economic facts influence those differences, but so do government policies: subsidies for particular agricultural pursuits, funding to promote the development of particular technologies, and the like. Wisconsin supports its $26 billion dairy industry, and the University of Wisconsin receives major grants and corporate funding to improve dairy farming.

Government policy can also help reduce uneven development. In the case of Appalachia, the United States Congress created an Appalachian Regional Commission in 1965 to address poverty in the region. The Commission put together a program of government investment in roads, schools, health-care facilities, and water and sewer systems that promoted development in parts of the region. Significant areas benefited from these policies, although pockets of deep poverty remain.

Returning to a consideration of commodity chains can also help us understand the role governments play in uneven development—both within and between states. Though written more than 15 years ago, economist Pietra Rivoli's 2005 book *The Travels of a T-Shirt in the Global Economy* still offers relevant insight into the influence governments have on the distribution of wealth between and within states. Rivoli grabs a T-shirt out of a bin at a Walgreens in Florida, buys it, and then traces its production back through the commodity chain to see how it ends up in her hands. The cotton for her T-shirt was grown in West Texas, where the cotton lobby (the political arm of America's cotton producers) effectively politicked for governmental labor programs and price supports that help the industry grow cotton and sell it at predictable prices. From West Texas, the cotton bale reaches China by ship. There it is spun into thread and woven into fabric. Women from rural China work in state-owned factories set up in regions that are slated for economic development—cutting and sewing T-shirts and keeping the textile machines in good repair. The women are considered cheap labor, earning about $100 per month.

The T-shirts are then shipped to the United States for sale. In an attempt to protect T-shirts produced in America with higher labor costs from those produced in China, the United States government has established quotas on how many items from various clothing categories can be imported into the United States from China and other countries. An unintended consequence of the quota system has been a "quota market" that allows countries to buy and sell their U.S. quota numbers to producers in other countries (an illegal but common practice). Instead of trading in quotas, some production facilities have moved to places where quotas and cheap labor are available—places such as Sri Lanka, Poland, and Lesotho. Rivoli describes how one producer of cotton shirts has moved around the world:

> The Esquel Corporation, today the world's largest producer of cotton shirts, started in Hong Kong in the late 1970s, but, unable to obtain quota to sell to the United States, shifted production to mainland China. When the United States tightened Chinese shirt quotas in the early 1980s, Esquel moved production to Malaysia. When Malaysian quota also became difficult to obtain, Esquel moved yet again, this time to Sri Lanka. The globe hopping continued, with the Chinese shirt producer setting up operations in Mauritius and Maldives.

The point is that quota laws, like other policies made by governments, as well as international financial institutions such as the World Trade Organization and the International Labor Organization, affect whether and how regions can produce and exchange goods on the world market.

Islands of Development

In both periphery and core, governments often invest heavily in expanding the economy of the capital city so that it can act as a showcase for the country. Capital cities are home to government buildings and jobs. They often house universities, museums, heritage centers, convention centers, and the headquarters of large corporations. After gaining independence, many former colonial states spent lavishly on their capitals. Such spending was not essential to political or economic success, but the money was spent because the states wanted to showcase their independence and future potential. They wanted to create a national treasure. European colonizers provided the model that had been followed elsewhere, having themselves already directed significant wealth in earlier times to building grand capital cities: The United Kingdom's London, France's Paris, and the Netherlands' Amsterdam.

In many countries of the global economic periphery and semiperiphery, the capital cities are by far the largest and most economically influential cities in the state (i.e., primate cities, discussed in Chapter 9). Some newly independent states have built new capital cities away from the colonial headquarters to separate themselves from their colonizers. Their cities are meant to bring together diverse groups and to reflect their common culture. Economic development might begin to extend into the interior of the state, or help establish control over a region with a population whose loyalties to the state might be in question.

Nigeria moved its capital from Yoruba-dominated Lagos along the coast to an ethnically neutral territory in the center of the state: Abuja. Malawi moved its capital from Zomba, deep in the south, to more central Lilongwe. Pakistan moved the capital from the colonial headquarters of Karachi to

Islamabad in the far north. The move symbolized the country's reorientation toward its historically important interior and north. Brazil moved its capital from coastal Rio de Janeiro to centrally located Brasília to direct attention to the huge, sparsely populated, yet poorly integrated interior. More recently, Kazakhstan moved its capital from Almaty in the south to Astana in the north, partly to be closer to Russia and the center of the possibly restless Russian population. Malaysia has also recently moved its capital from the colonial capital of Kuala Lumpur to a completely new center called Putrajaya, about 25 miles (40 km) to the south. The Malaysian government decided to build a new, ultramodern seat of government to symbolize the country's rapid economic growth (**Fig. 10.20**).

Corporations can also make cities focal points of development by concentrating corporate activities in a particular place. Often, corporations build up the cities near the resources they are extracting or near manufacturing centers they have built. Multinational oil companies create subsidiaries in countries of the periphery and semiperiphery, creating or expanding cities near oil reserves. For example, Elf and Shell, two oil companies based in Europe but with major operations in Gabon, run ElfGabon and ShellGabon in the Central African country. The oil companies took the small colonial town of Port Gentil and turned it into a city that the locals call "oil city." The oil companies built housing, roads, and stores, and provide much of the employment in the town (**Fig. 10.21**).

When a government or corporation builds up and concentrates economic development in a certain city or small region, geographers call that place an **island of development**. In Chapter 3, we identified islands of development in the periphery and semiperiphery, and discussed why people migrate to these places from lower income areas. The hope for jobs drives many migrants to move to these islands of comparative prosperity (see Fig. 3.8).

EXTREME-PHOTOGRAPHER/E+/Getty Images

FIGURE 10.20 **Putrajaya, Malaysia.** Putrajaya is the newly built capital of Malaysia, replacing Kuala Lumpur.

Creating Growth in the Periphery of the Periphery

One of the greatest challenges to development is creating development opportunities outside of islands of development. In the most rural, impoverished regions of lower income countries, some nongovernmental organizations try to improve the plight of people. **Nongovernmental organizations (NGOs)** are not run by state or local governments. Rather, NGOs operate independently, and the term is usually reserved for entities that operate as nonprofits. Thousands of NGOs operate in the world today, from churches to charities such as Heifer International. Each NGO has its own set of goals, depending on the primary concerns outlined by its founders and financiers (**Fig. 10.22**).

Some countries have so many NGOs operating within them that they serve as what *The Economist* (1998) calls "a parallel state, financed by foreigners and accountable to nobody." For example,

---

Author Field Note **Building an Island of Development in Port Gentil, Gabon**

"Before the 1970s, Gabon's principal exports were manganese, hardwoods, and uranium ores. The discovery of oil off the Gabonese coast changed all that. This oil storage tank at the edge of Port Gentil is but one reminder of a development that has transformed Gabon's major port city –and the economy of the country as a whole. Oil now accounts for 80 percent of Gabon's export earnings, and that figure is climbing as oil prices rise and new discoveries are made. But how much the average citizen of Gabon is benefiting from the oil economy remains an open question. Even as health care and infrastructure needs remain unmet, the French publication *L'Autre Afrique* listed Gabon's recently deceased ruler as the African leader with the largest real estate holdings in Paris."

– A. B. Murphy

Photo by A.B. Murphy. © 2020 John Wiley & Sons, Inc.

FIGURE 10.21 **Port Gentil, Gabon**

Guest Field Note   Interviewing Female Guest Workers in Sukabumi, Indonesia

Rachel Silvey
University of Toronto

My own research is based on fieldwork in Indonesia as well as ongoing engagement with students in the United States. The women pictured here collaborated with me on a research/activism project for migrant women workers in Indonesia. The woman on the left ("Rina") had returned from working in Saudi Arabia as a domestic worker for two years. She wanted to return to Saudi Arabia for another contract to earn more money for herself and her family, but she was concerned about her rights and her safety. She had been employed by a person she considered fair and reasonable, but she had heard from friends and neighbors that many migrants had experienced serious abuses while abroad. The woman pictured on the right ("Sorani") is an Indonesian activist who works in support of migrant rights. She discussed with Rina and me her strategies for mobilizing political change, and she helped us to see possibilities for building transnational alliances among American and Indonesian workers, students, and activists.

FIGURE 10.22 **Sukabumi, West Java, Indonesia**

Based on these interviews, as well as many years of working with migrant women working in factories in Indonesia, my own research has increasingly sought to understand the ways in which we in the United States, as scholars, students, workers, and consumers, can better serve global justice.

thousands of NGOs operate within the country of Bangladesh at any time, focusing mainly on the rural areas and villages of the state. But the NGO phenomenon can mask the depth of problems some places face. In the wake of the 2010 earthquake in Haiti, one respected British newspaper, *The Guardian*, reported that there was approximately one NGO per 1000 people in Haiti, but that much of the money funneled through these NGOs never reached the people most affected by the earthquake.

One type of NGO program that has found some success in less prosperous countries is the microcredit program. The idea behind a microcredit program is to give loans to people with low incomes, particularly women, to encourage the development of small businesses. Programs either have women in the village guarantee each other's credit, or they make future lending to others contingent on repayment by the first borrowers. With repayment rates hovering at 98 percent, **microcredit programs** can finance themselves, and many NGOs offer such programs (**Fig. 10.23**).

FIGURE 10.23 **Bwindi, Uganda.** Women walk by a microcredit agency that works to facilitate economic development in the town.

AP® Exam Taker's Tip

Microcredit – Small-scale credit is the loaning of small amounts of money - usually for small businesses. Most microcredit loans are given to women in developing areas. Investigate microcredit and give examples where it has been successful and where it has not been successful.

Microcredit programs have been less successful in places with high mortality rates from diseases such as AIDS. If the borrower is unable to work or if the family has medical and funeral bills, the borrower is much more likely to default on a microcredit loan. People in the poorest parts of the periphery experience a multitude of challenges. These include, but are not limited to, disease, corrupt governments, high mortality rates, high fertility rates, and disruptions from natural hazards. When people in the periphery experience one or more of these challenges, the goal of economic development takes a back seat to daily survival.

By providing microcredit to women, NGOs can alter the gender balance in a region, giving more fiscal power to women. Some microcredit programs are credited with lowering birth rates in parts of developing countries and altering the social fabric of cultures by empowering women. Successful microcredit programs also help reduce malnourishment, as women with incomes can feed themselves and their children.

TC Thinking Geographically

Define islands of **development**. Using **site** and **situation**, explain where islands of development are located in Africa and why they are located there (see Fig. 3.8). Explain the role islands of development play in **migration** within world regions.

Summary

10.1 Explain How Development Is Defined and Measured.

1. Levels of development are often determined by looking at a country's *gross national product* (the total value of the officially recorded goods and services produced and sold in the country in a given year). *Gross national income* (GNI) is a more meaningful indicator, because it includes income received from investments outside the country, minus income payments to other countries around the world. Measures of this sort are most meaningful when they are looked at on a per capita basis. Their value is limited by the fact that they only capture what is happening in the formal economy.

2. A variety of alternative measures of development are increasingly popular. These measures capture such factors as access to technology, the size of the working-age population in relation to the total population, health, education, and levels of inequality.

3. The United Nations has promulgated a set of 17 Sustainable Development Goals. These represent a fairly high degree of consensus about the conditions that need to be changed to achieve economic development, and they are increasingly influencing development initiatives.

10.2 Describe the Nature and Limitations of Development Models.

1. Walt Rostow's *modernization model* has had a significant influence on thinking about development. It assumes that all countries follow a similar path to development or modernization, advancing through five stages of development.

2. Rostow's model led many people to think of the world as divided into two basic economic realms: developed and less developed (originally underdeveloped). More recent approaches to development proceed from the idea that not all states can or will move through stages of development in the same way. The argument is that development prospects are shaped by the political-economic context within which individual states find themselves, and those contextual circumstances will affect how and whether development takes places. This way of thinking led to structuralist theories of development, including *dependency theory* and *world-systems theory*.

10.3 Explain Major Influences on Development.

1. The economic niche a country occupies in the world economy has an important influence on development. Economic arrangements influence that niche, including commodity chains (the links connecting places of production and distribution that are involved in the creation of a final product). So do the initiatives of governments and government-supported international institutions, which together have a significant influence on international investment, foreign aid, and development financing.

2. Governments influence development through the investments they make, the alliances they form, the trade deals they negotiate, and the purchases they make. They also influence development through development assistance and support for international financial institutions and investment banks. Development assistance sometimes can have positive effects in lower-income countries (that is not always the case), but the assistance that is offered usually reflects the interests of donor countries. Countries in North America and western/central Europe long dominated the development assistance landscape, but China has recently become a major player.

3. Many countries struggle to promote development in the face of high levels of public debt. The public debt of many lower-income countries comes from structural adjustment loans made by organizations such as the World Bank. When countries are not in a position to repay their debt, the terms of repayment are renegotiated. In most cases, countries are obliged to undertake reforms that reflect the turn toward neoliberalism in the late twentieth century. Neoliberalism is based on the idea that government intervention into markets is both inefficient and undesirable, and should be resisted wherever possible. There are growing critiques of this way of thinking, but it is still quite influential.

4. The social conditions within countries greatly influence development prospects. Among the most important factors are access to health and clean water, the presence or absence of political corruption, and the educational opportunities that are available to a country's inhabitants, including girls and women.

5. Economic development changes places, in some cases for the worse. It can bring environmental pollution, it can produce greater inequalities, and it can undermine traditional cultural practices and values.

10.4 Evaluate How Political and Economic Institutions Influence Uneven Development Within States.

1. Poverty is not confined to the periphery. Core countries have some regions and peoples that have markedly lower income than others. Governments influence patterns of wealth through such mechanisms as taxation arrangements, land ownership rules, and environmental regulations.

2. Governments often invest heavily in expanding the economy and infrastructure of the capital city so that it can act as a showcase for the country. These cities can serve as islands of development, as can strategic investment in other places within a country.

3. Nongovernmental organizations (NGOs) play a significant role in development. Through initiatives such as microcredit programs, NGOs bypass state governments in the effort to promote development. Some of these initiatives have promoted development, but NGO involvement can sometimes mask the depth of problems certain places face.

Self-Test

10.1 Explain how development is defined and measured.

1. Gross national product (GNP) is a measure of:

    a. the value of officially recorded goods and services that are produced and exchanged within a country.

    b. the income earned from goods and services produced inside a county, plus external investments.

    c. the total economic value of all goods and services produced and exchanged within a country, including the informal economy.

    d. the value of all goods produced in a country.

    e. All of the above.

2. The *digital divide* refers to:

    a. the generational divide between younger people who grew up with smartphones and computers and older people who did not.

    b. the divide between those with access to widely available technologies (e.g., smartphones) and those with access to high-end technologies (e.g., supercomputers).

    c. the unequal access to telecommunication technologies by people with higher incomes and lower incomes.

    d. the divide between those who use technology developed in the United States and those who use technology developed in China.

    e. the divide between rural and urban areas in terms of access to technology.

3. Which of the following statements is true regarding the progress that has been made toward achieving the United Nations' Sustainable Development Goals?

    a. Substantial progress has been made in reducing the number of hours women spend on unpaid domestic labor.

    b. Little progress has been made in expanding access to clean water.

    c. Substantial progress has been made in reducing extreme poverty.

    d. Substantial progress has been made in reducing inequality.

    e. Little progress has been made in raising years of schooling for girls and women.

10.2 Describe the nature and limitations of development models.

4. Rostow's modernization model assumes that:

    a. former colonies will experience different development challenges than countries that were never colonized.

    b. all countries follow a similar path to development.

    c. modernization is most likely to happen in countries that have weakly developed agricultural sectors.

    d. the power relations between countries have a significant impact on development potential.

    e. gaps in development remain constant over time.

5. True or False: Many of the higher income countries we call "industrial" today are really "postindustrial."

6. _____ is based on the idea that the world is divided into a three-tier structure (core, periphery, and semiperiphery) that influences development prospects.

    a. The UN Sustainable Development Agenda

    b. The Washington Consensus

    c. Dependency theory

    d. Ravenstein's theory

    e. World-systems theory

7. Which of the following countries is typically thought to be part of the semiperiphery?

    a. Japan

    b. Australia

    c. Mexico

    d. Rwanda

    e. Bangladesh

10.3 Explain major influences on development.

8. Which of the following statements about Western-dominated development financing is true?

    a. It is largely driven by altruism.

    b. It is largely driven by neoliberal ideas.

    c. It is largely driven by a desire to insulate Western economies from the wider world.

    d. It is largely driven by a desire to counteract Chinese influence.

    e. It is largely driven by a desire to reduce uneven development globally.

9. The largest donors of foreign development assistance in the world, as measured by total dollars spent, are:

    a. the United States and Japan.

    b. the United States and Germany.

    c. China and the United States.

    d. China and Australia.

    e. the European Union and the United States.

10. Maquiladora zones in Mexico are mainly sited:

    a. directly across the border from the United States.

    b. near Pacific ports with access to shipping coming from Asia.

    c. in and around Mexico City (the capital).

    d. in the south across the border from Guatemala.

    e. near the Yucatan peninsula.

11. True or False: Unlike agricultural intensification and the development of special manufacturing export zones, tourism represents a development strategy with little environmental impact.

10.4 Evaluate how political and economic institutions influence uneven development within states.

12. Uneven development is influenced by:

    a. taxation rates.

    b. land ownership rules.

    c. tariffs.

    d. non-tariff trade regulations.

    e. all of the above.

13. True or False: Commodity chains are one of the few products of economic globalization that are largely unaffected by governmental regulation.

14. Which of the following is an example of an "island of development"?

    a. A microcredit program created by an NGO in a rural community

    b. A production facility established by a transnational corporation in a new place

    c. A new capital city established in a central location

    d. A levy constructed to protect an area from flooding and associated economic ruin

    e. An island nation that benefits greatly from its modern ports

Agriculture

FIGURE 11.1 **Hong Dong, Thailand.** Hmong farmers practice shifting cultivation high on this hillside in the mountainous region of northern Thailand.

We left our hotel inside the walls of the old city of Chiang Mai early in the morning and drove west into a forested area and up a mountain to a Hmong village to a visitor site frequented by tourists. Heading into the forest on a planned six-hour hike that was described as "easy to moderate," I was happy to have two Hmong guides, two Thai hiking guides, and our two tour guides to lead our group of 20 through the forest. We quickly learned that the hike was not at all "easy," though one of our Thai hiking guides, who was in his 50s, wore flip-flops.

After a long hike up the mountain, we had a lunch of fried rice served out of banana leaves and then headed deeper into the forest toward our destination, a more remote Hmong village. We happened first upon a small cluster of about five or so houses and a dog that kept watch. Within a half-mile of the houses, we saw small plots of sugarcane, an avocado tree, and a pepper tree. We rounded a bend and looked up the hillside to where the residents of the houses were farming in the hot afternoon sun, bent over with short-handle hoes on a field readied for crop production (**Fig. 11.1**). Forest surrounded the field. Looking around, we could see a former field sitting fallow where trees were shorter than the rest of the forest. Hmong migrated to Thailand from China in the 1800s and settled in the northern hills to practice shifting cultivation, a system of crop production that has sustained them for generations and continues to do so.

In this chapter, we examine the origins of agriculture and trace the geography of changes in the production of food and the raising of livestock, from the earliest domestication of plants to contemporary developments, including genetic modification and commercial agribusiness.

AP® Exam Taker's Tip

Are the farming practices in Figure 11.1 more likely **intensive** or **extensive** agriculture? Be sure you can support your answer.

11.1   Compare and Contrast the Three Agricultural Revolutions.

Before the beginning of agriculture, people hunted, gathered, and fished for food. Then, during the First Agricultural Revolution, which occurred 10,000 years ago, farmers successfully planted and grew crops and domesticated animals. This was the beginning of agriculture. Domesticating plants and animals required effort, observation, and resiliency as early farmers learned which wild plants they could grow and what animals they could tame.

During the Second Agricultural Revolution, between the eighteenth and twentieth centuries, both population and agricultural yields increased dramatically. The Third Agricultural Revolution is better known as the Green Revolution, which focuses on genetically modifying seeds and changing land-use techniques to increase yields for a global population that is quickly multiplying.

Hunting, Gathering, and Fishing

The size of hunting and gathering clans varied according to climate, seasonal shifts, and resource availability. Communities were adept at tracking the migration cycles of fish and land animals. Using tools and fire, hunter-gatherers altered their environments to establish more reliable food supplies.

What people hunted or gathered depended on where they lived. Native Americans in the Pacific Northwest, the Ainu of Japan and coastal East Asia, and communities in coastal western Europe caught salmon as they swam up rivers and negotiated rapids and falls. Archaeologists have found huge accumulations

FIGURE 11.3 **Aleutian Islands.** This island is part of the Aleutian volcanic island chain off the coast of Alaska. Archaeologists and anthropologists are finding evidence the ancient Aleuts used the abundance of birds on the islands for food, fire kindling, and tools. The rocky islands are still covered with birds.

Maximilian Buzun/Alamy Stock Photo

of fish bones at Native American sites near salmon runs. In the Great Plains, Native Americans hunted bison and developed cultural festivals and rituals around the hunt. Archaeologists have found evidence of Lakotas running bison herds off cliffs called buffalo jumps. Hunters worked together to run the bison off a cliff so that they fell to their deaths (**Fig. 11.2**).

In the colder climates of North America, Native Americans followed the migrations of the caribou herds. Archaeologists have found hunting structures thousands of years old that First Nations in Canada used to hunt caribou. Farther north, in the coastal zone stretching from present-day Alaska to Russia, the Aleut developed specialized techniques for fishing cod and salmon and hunting whales, walrus, and seal. Archaeologists found evidence that the Aleut, whose Aleutian islands are rocky and not well-suited for agriculture, lived not only on sea life, but also on the bird populations on the islands, including puffins and gulls (**Fig. 11.3**). Aleut ate duck eggs, hunted certain species in winter, made spoons and brooms from bones, and used downy feathers for kindling in fires. (Rudebusch 2018).

Hunter-gatherers migrated to take advantage of cyclical movements of animals and to avoid exhausting the supply of edible plants in any one area. In the Pacific Northwest, after the summer salmon runs, Native Americans hunted deer during the fall and again in the spring, taking advantage of seasonal movements to trap deer where they crossed rivers or in narrow valleys. During the winter, people lived off dried meat and other stored foods. In addition to hunting game on land, hunter-gatherers harvested shellfish, trapped fish by cutting off small patches of standing water from the open sea, and invented tools to catch fish, including harpoons, hooks, and baskets.

Before developing agriculture, hunter-gatherers worked on perfecting tools, controlling fires, and adapting environments to their needs. The first tools used in hunting were simple clubs, tree limbs that were thin at one end and thick and heavy at the other. Over time, hunter-gatherers used bone

© Molly Richter

FIGURE 11.2 **Deadwood, South Dakota.** Tatanka buffalo site commemorates how Lakota hunters used buffalo jumps. Lakota hunters rode on horseback to herd buffalo across the prairie and drove them off of cliffs.

and stone and developed spears, which made hunting far more effective. By fashioning stone into hand axes and, later, handle axes, hunters could skin their prey and cut the meat. Hunter-gatherers used axes to cut down trees and build better shelters and tools.

Early human communities also became adept at using fire for controlled burns. The first opportunities to control fire were offered by natural conditions like lightning. Archaeological digs of ancient settlement sites suggest that people captured a fire caused naturally and worked to keep the fire burning continuously. Later, people learned to spark fire by rapidly rotating a wooden stick in a small hole surrounded by dry tinder and fanned by oxygen. Fire became the focal point of settlements and a tool both for cooking food and for driving hunted animals off a cliff or into a ravine to be killed.

The First Agricultural Revolution: Origins and Diffusion of Agriculture

The idea to move from hunting and gathering to domesticating plants and animals developed independently in different **hearths** (areas of innovation). **Agriculture** is purposefully growing crops and raising livestock to produce food, feed, and fiber. The transition from hunting and gathering to farming marks the beginning of the **First Agricultural Revolution**.

Geographers have debated how and why farming began. Did early agriculture begin out of *necessity*, because there was too little food to hunt and gather, or out of *luxury*, because the food made available through hunting and gathering gave people the time to experiment with growing crops? Jared Diamond believes that scarcity forced people into farming, that competition forced people to become resourceful and grow their own food. Cultural geographer Carl Sauer believed that luxury was more likely, that a reliable food supply created the opportunity for people to experiment with raising plants or invest the time to domesticate animals.

Plant Domestication   Growing seed crops involves seed selection, sowing, watering, and well-timed harvesting. The innovation of seed crop agriculture developed in more than one hearth and at different times. The first hearth for plant cultivation was the **Fertile Crescent**, which includes the lands between the Tigris and Euphrates rivers in present-day Iraq and extends west to Syria. **Figure 11.4** shows the Fertile Crescent and the Nile River Valley, which is considered another hearth of agriculture.

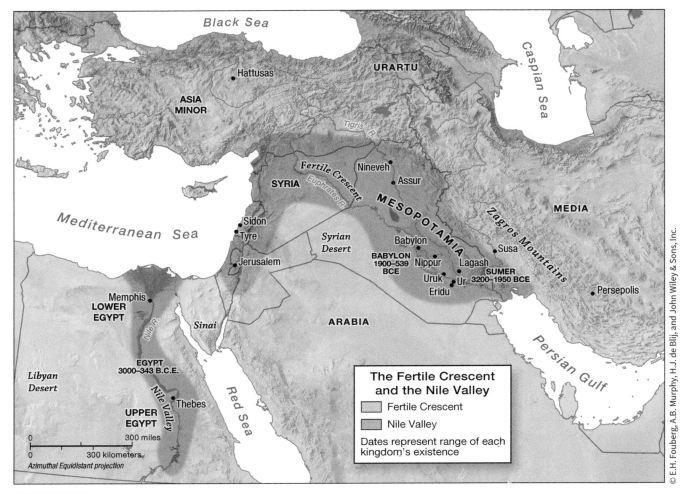

FIGURE 11.4   **The Fertile Crescent and Nile River Valley.**   The Fertile Crescent and Nile River Valley were two hearths of the First Agricultural Revolution. Modern political boundaries are shown for reference.

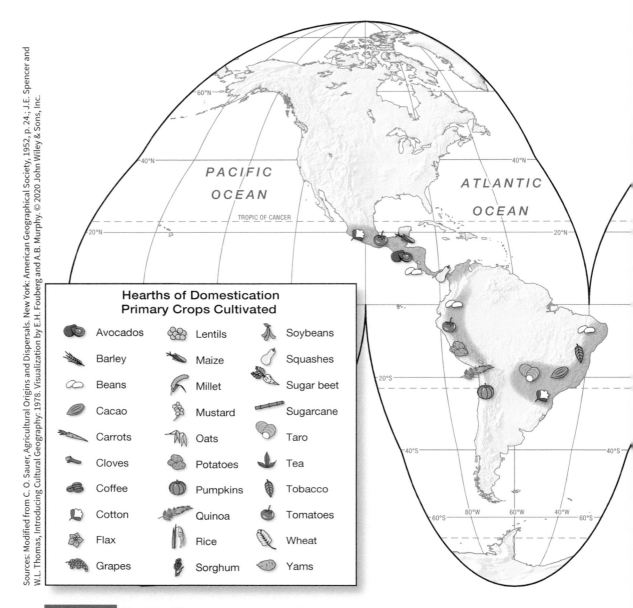

Sources: Modified from C. O. Sauer, Agricultural Origins and Dispersals. New York: American Geographical Society, 1952, p. 24.; J.E. Spencer and W.L. Thomas, Introducing Cultural Geography: 1978. Visualization by E.H. Fouberg and A.B. Murphy. © 2020 John Wiley & Sons, Inc.

FIGURE 11.5 **Hearths of Early Domestication.** The domestication of plants and animals occurred around the world. Each hearth of agriculture focused on domesticating certain crops that are shown on this map as well as animals not shown on this map. For example, the Fertile Crescent was the hearth for the domestication of goats and sheep as well as oats and lentils. Mesoamerica was the hearth of domestication for maize (corn), tomatoes, avocados, and the turkey.

Plant domestication changed the plants themselves. Farmers chose seeds from the largest, hardiest plants to save for planting the next year. Over time, domesticated plants grew larger than their counterparts in the wild. By analyzing seeds, archaeologists can determine which plants grew in abundance and the dates when they were commonly grown. Farmers in the Fertile Crescent grew wheat and barley.

Farming began in more than one hearth. **Figure 11.5** maps the major agricultural hearths and the primary crops each cultivated. Farmers domesticated several crops, including yams and rice, independently, each experimenting with spreading seeds and growing crops. For example, Southeast Asians domesticated rice, yams, beans, and sugarcane. The Indus Civilization grew wheat, barley, and mustard. Farmers in Central America grew avocados, tomatoes, and cotton. Archaeological research on agriculture is ongoing, and scientists revise the timeline of what crops were grown, where they were first grown, and when. Researchers debate whether agriculture developed independently in each hearth or if crop domestication diffused from certain hearths to others.

Agriculture increased food security and changed civilizations. Growing enough grain to store a surplus enabled people to settle permanently in one place and create villages and towns. People could do jobs other than farming, including working as artisans, metalworkers, soldiers, shamans, and leaders. Trade of surpluses, handmade goods, and resources grew among agricultural hearths. Civilizations grew and built great structures, from the Egyptian pyramids in the Nile to Angkor Wat in Southeast Asia.

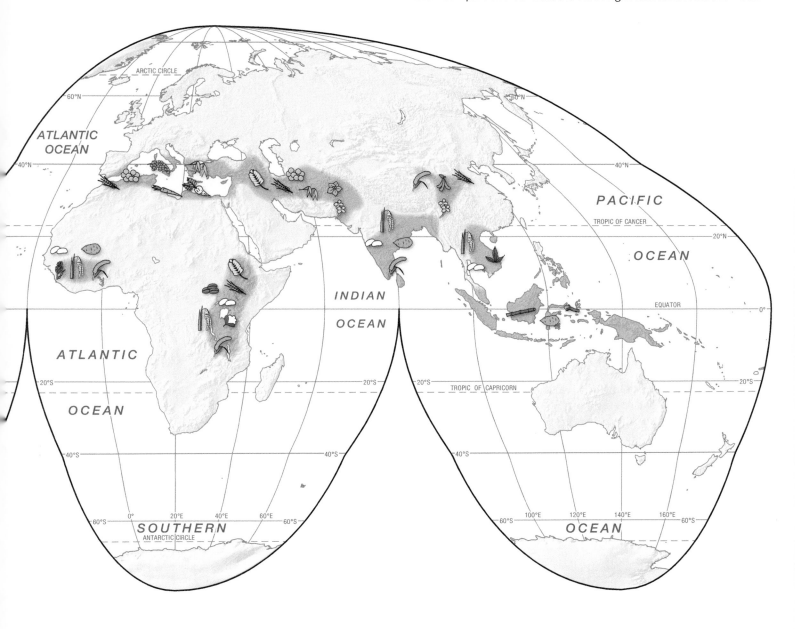

Animal Domestication

Domestication of animals, or adapting wild animals for human use, began around 10,000 years ago, also in the Fertile Crescent. Archaeologists study bone fragments and tools to identify where domestication of animals began. Researchers have found, for example, that goat bones became smaller over time as farmers domesticated goats. In the Fertile Crescent, farmers first domesticated goats in the Zagros Mountains around 8000 BCE (in present-day Iran), followed by sheep in Anatolia (present-day Turkey) around 7500 BCE. Soon after, people in the same region domesticated pigs and cattle.

Around the same time, farmers domesticated chickens in Southeast Asia. Southeast Asians also domesticated several kinds of pigs, the water buffalo, and some waterfowl (ducks and geese). In South Asia (eastern India and western Burma), farmers domesticated cattle. In Central Asia, farmers domesticated yaks, horses, some species of goats, and sheep. In the Andean highlands, early Americans domesticated the llama and alpaca, along with a species of pig and the turkey.

Some species of animals may have been domesticated almost simultaneously in different places. The water buffalo, for example, was probably domesticated in both Southeast and South Asia during the same period. Camels were domesticated in both western and eastern ends of Southwest Asia. The pig was domesticated in numerous areas. Different species of cattle were domesticated in regions other than South Asia. Dogs and cats attached themselves to human settlements very early (they may have been the first animals to be

Author Field Note   Domesticating Eland in Nairobi, Kenya

"At Hunter's Lodge on the Nairobi-Mombasa road, we met an agricultural officer who told us an animal domestication experiment station was not far into the bush, just 10 miles south. On his invitation, we spent the next day observing his work. In some herds, domestic animals (goats) were combined with wild gazelles, all penned together in a large enclosure. This was not working well; all day the gazelles sought to escape. By comparison, the eland in this photo were docile, manageable, and in good health. Importantly, they also were reproducing in captivity. Here, our host describes the program."

– H. J. de Blij

FIGURE 11.6   **Nairobi, Kenya.**

domesticated) and in widely separated regions. Single, specific hearths can be pinpointed for only a few animals, including the llama and the alpaca, the yak, the turkey, and the reindeer.

Humans used the relatively small animals they domesticated first for milk, eggs, meat, and hides. They used larger animals as beasts of burden, or as sources of meat or providers of milk. The integrated use of domesticated plants and domesticated animals eased the work burden for early farmers. Animal waste fertilized crops, animals pulled plows, and crops fed animals. The advantages of animal domestication stimulated the rapid diffusion of livestock raising among places linked by trade.

Through domestication and in captivity, animals changed from their wild state. In early animal domestication, people chose the more docile, often smaller goats, pigs, and cattle to breed. Quite possibly, the first domesticated animals attached themselves to human settlements either to scavenge for food by foraging through garbage or to seek protection from predators. Interaction with relatively calm or easily calmed wild animals likely helped humans think they could keep, corral, and tame the animals.

Archaeological research indicates that when animals such as wild cattle were penned in a corral, they physically changed. In the wild, physically strong animals survived. In corrals, animals were protected from predators, enabling calmer, more docile, and sometimes weaker animals to survive. Animals that successfully bred in corrals lived longer than those that did not.

Across the world, only about 40 species of animals have ever been domesticated—and most of these were domesticated long ago. Humans looked for four traits in the animals they domesticated: diet, temperament, growth rate, and size. Herbivores, or animals who graze on grass, are the easiest animals to domesticate. Domesticating omnivores and meat eaters makes less sense, because you have to raise animals just to be eaten by other animals. Animals with docile temperaments and herd mentality like cattle are easier to domesticate than aggressive, independent animals like tigers. Domesticating

animals that grow quickly also makes more sense than investing decades into animals that take several years to reach adulthood, like elephants. Animals for domestication were also chosen for their size so they would produce enough meat to make the work of domestication worthwhile.

Jared Diamond, author of *Guns, Germs, and Steel*, explains that 148 animals in the wild meet these four criteria (diet, temperament, growth rate, and size). Humans have successfully domesticated 14 of the 148 animals, and each of the 14 was domesticated at least 4500 years ago.

Modern attempts at animal domestication have failed because of problems with the animal's diet, growth rate, breeding, disposition, or social structure. For example, several experimental stations in the savanna are trying to find ways to domesticate Africa's wildlife. In East Africa, farmers are attempting to domesticate the eland to make it serve as a source of meat and a stable protein source (**Fig. 11.6**).

Subsistence Agriculture
Growing only enough food to survive, or practicing **subsistence agriculture**, was the norm throughout most of human history. Subsistence farmers held land in common and shared any surplus among the members of the community. In subsistence farming communities, accumulation of personal wealth was generally restricted. Traditions and festivals were often created to redistribute surplus from families who had bountiful production to those who did not.

Traditional subsistence agriculture declined with European colonization. As Europeans colonized other lands and settler populations expanded, they used treaties and force to acquire lands owned by subsistence agricultural communities. Colonizers and eventually the countries that replaced them (including the United States and Canada) legally changed land ownership from communal to individual. This shift from large areas of land owned communally to particular plots of land owned by individuals undermined the economic system of subsistence agriculture and left lasting consequences that are still felt in communities today (**Fig. 11.7**).

A return to subsistence agriculture has taken hold in parts of the world where farmers feel that production for the global market has not benefited them financially or culturally. For example, indigenous people in the southern Mexican states of Oaxaca, Chiapas, and Guerrero have largely returned to subsistence agriculture. *The Nation* reported in 2010 that Zapatista farmers have "in effect chosen to withdraw from the national economy, some weaning themselves off expensive chemical fertilizers and subsisting on corn they can grow, harvest, and barter."

Shifting Cultivation

In tropical climates where vegetation, sunlight, and rainfall are plentiful, farmers engage in a form of subsistence agriculture called shifting cultivation. Also called swidden or slash-and-burn agriculture, **shifting cultivation** is the process of clearing and burning a plot of land, farming it for 2 to 10 years, and then moving on to a new field while leaving the plot to regenerate. Shifting cultivation is most common in tropical and subtropical climate regions where soils stay fertile for a few years after vegetation is cut down and burned. Once stripped of their natural vegetative cover and deprived of the constant input of nutrients from decaying vegetative matter on the forest floor, soils in these regions can quickly lose their nutrients as rainwater leaches out organic matter. When this happens, farmers leave the field to regenerate and move to another parcel of land.

Shifting cultivation is a sustainable form of agriculture in places where land is abundant and the population is relatively sparse. The term *slash and burn* suggests that farmers are drivers of deforestation in the tropics, but that is not the case. In the tropical forest regions of Africa, farmers allow fields to sit fallow for 30 years so they can be replenished before they are farmed again. In South America and Southeast Asia, farmers leave fields fallow for 10 to 20 years before farming them again. If the population of a village practicing shifting cultivation grows too large or the distance to usable land becomes too great, part of the village's population may establish a new settlement in another part of the forest.

For indigenous peoples of the Amazon Basin, sedentary farmers of Africa's savanna areas, villagers in much of India, and peasants in Indonesia, subsistence is not only a way of life, but a state of mind. Experience has taught farmers and their families that subsistence farming is often precarious and that times of comparative plenty will be followed by times of scarcity.

Author Field Note   Persevering on the Lake Traverse Reservation, South Dakota

"The U.S. government used the Dawes Act in 1887 to change ownership on Native American reservations. The Sisseton-Wahpeton Sioux Oyate communally owned the Lake Traverse Reservation. In 1891, the U.S. government passed a congressional act to allot the reservation lands and then open "surplus" lands to non-Indians. The U.S. government counted the number of tribal members and surveyed the land using the township and range system. It allotted 160 acres to each tribal member and divided the reservation's 918,779 acres into 309,914 acres allotted to tribal members and 608,866 acres opened for non-Indians. On April 15, 1892, non-Indians perched on horseback around the reservation, waiting for the reservation to officially open. They quickly snapped up the glacially rich land. The allotment of the reservation had no regard for where the tribe's historical burial grounds or sacred places were. It completely disrupted the economic system by moving individuals apart on small acreages. And it had no thought for the future of the tribe. Within a generation, each 160-acre plot of land would be divided among the allotee's descendants. And each of those plots would be divided again within a generation. Today, land ownership on the reservation is checkerboarded. After generations of splitting the inheritance, tribal members who have land often have tiny plots too small to farm. Despite allotment and assimilation, Native Americans persevered, and the Sisseton-Wahpeton Sioux Oyate tribal government has created new job opportunities at tribally-owned businesses, including

Photo by E.H. Fouberg. © 2020 John Wiley & Sons, Inc.

FIGURE 11.7   Lake Traverse Reservation, South Dakota.

gas stations, casinos, and a manufacturing plant called Dakota Western, which produces plastic and biodegradable trash can liners and garbage bags."

– E. H. Fouberg

With shifting cultivation, farmers avoid **monoculture**, which is more taxing on the soil and makes it more difficult for a community to build a nutrient-rich diet. Instead, farmers plant a diversity of crops, both for self-consumption and for trade in local markets (**Fig. 11.8**). In northern Thailand, hill tribes such as the Hmong, Lisu, Yao, Khamu, and Karen plant rice, sticky rice, maize, beans, gourds, eggplants, sugarcane, taro, yams, sesame, and chili peppers (see Fig. 11.1). In Africa, shifting cultivators plant yams, cassava, bananas, oil palm, maize, and other crops. In the Amazon in South America, shifting cultivators plant trees such as acai palms and avocado trees, as well as crops such as cassava, plantains, maize, and sweet potatoes.

AP® Exam Taker's Tip

Many colonial powers forced their subjects to farm particular items. Long after the end of colonial rule, those products are still a primary source of the economy for many of these countries. What are examples of modern-day agricultural **monocultures** that trace back to colonialism?

The Second Agricultural Revolution: Mechanization of Agriculture

To fuel the industrialization and urbanization that occurred from the 1700s on, people needed to create a Second Agricultural Revolution, moving beyond subsistence farming to generating the surpluses needed to feed thousands of people working in factories instead of on agricultural fields. Like the Industrial Revolution (see Chapter 12), the **Second Agricultural Revolution** included a series of innovations, improvements, and techniques developed in different places at different times, which together significantly improved the production of crops and livestock.

FIGURE 11.8 **Mopti, Mali.** Farmers who produce a variety of crops using shifting cultivation, also called swidden agriculture, sell their produce at the market on a Saturday morning.

FIGURE 11.9 **Great Britain.** The seed drill helped farmers improve yields. By planting crops in clear rows, farmers could tell the difference between crops and weeds.

In the 1700s, the British and the Dutch invented the seed drill, improved livestock breeding methods, consolidated land into larger farms, and began using new crop rotation systems. The seed drill enabled farmers to avoid wasting seeds and to plant in rows, making it simpler to distinguish weeds from crops (**Fig. 11.9**). In addition, governments encouraged land consolidation to increase the scale of production. Great Britain's Enclosure Act encouraged consolidation of fields into large, single-owner holdings. Farmers increased the size of their farms, pieced together more contiguous parcels of land, fenced in their land, and instituted crop rotation. They also improved their methods of soil preparation, fertilization, crop care, and harvesting.

Mechanization and Advances in Breeding

Successful innovation fueled more advancements. By the 1830s, European farmers were using new fertilizers on crops and giving artificial feeds to livestock. Increased agricultural output in the primary economic sector made it possible to feed much larger urban populations, enabling the growth of the secondary economic sector (manufacturing). In 1831, Cyrus McCormick, a farmer in Lexington, Virginia, perfected his father's design for a mechanical reaper (**Fig. 11.10**). At the time, farmers were limited in their production not by what they could sow (plant), but by what they could reap (harvest) because harvesting required much more time and labor than planting. Harvesting involved laborers cutting grain with a scythe, followed by more laborers who bundled the grain into bales. McCormick's mechanical reaper was pulled by horses and both cut and bundled grain. His invention diffused quickly during the 1840s, reportedly increasing yields of individual farmers by at least 10 times. McCormick's company eventually became International Harvester and is now Case IH, one of the largest agricultural implement companies in the world today.

Advances in breeding livestock enabled farmers to develop new breeds that were either strong milk producers or good for beef. The most common breeds of dairy cattle found in North America today trace their lineage back to the Second Agricultural Revolution in Europe. In the 1700s and 1800s, European farmers bred dairy cattle to adapt to different climates and topography.

FIGURE 11.10 **Midwest, United States.** Pioneers used the mechanical reaper designed by Cyrus McCormick to cut and bundle grain on the prairie. Pulled by horses, the mechanical reaper sped up harvesting and diffused around the world.

For example, the black-and-white Holstein dairy cow came from the Netherlands and is well suited to graze on grass and produce high quantities of milk. Scottish Highland cattle were bred for their meat (**Fig. 11.11**) and are raised in the United States as American Highland cattle. Scottish farmers also bred the red-and-white Ayrshire dairy cattle to produce milk well suited for butter and cheese. Both Scottish cattle breeds forage for food in rough, rocky topography, which makes them well suited for similar topographies and climates in the Americas.

Innovations in machinery that occurred with the Industrial Revolution in the late 1800s and early 1900s helped sustain the Second Agricultural Revolution. The railroad helped move agriculture into new regions, including the Great Plains. Geographer John Hudson traced the major role that railroads and agriculture played in changing the landscape of that region from Native American communal hunting and agricultural lands to individual, homesteaded farms. Railroad companies advertised in Europe to attract immigrants to the Great Plains region, and the railroads took the new migrants to railroad-built towns.

The Columbian Exchange

The **Columbian Exchange** was the movement of goods, people, and diseases between Europe, Africa, and the Americas across the Atlantic Ocean that began with Spanish and Portuguese exploration in the late fifteenth century. This trade pattern, called the triangular trade network, brought new seeds and livestock to each continent. Through the Columbian Exchange, new crops came into Europe from trade with Africa and the Americas. The diffusion of crops and seeds was greatly accelerated by the worldwide trade and communications networks established with the development of European exploration and colonization (**Fig. 11.12**).

Places known today for growing certain crops, like Idaho and Ireland for potatoes, Hawai'i for pineapples, and Colombia for coffee, are not the places the crops originated. The corn grown in the American Corn Belt diffused from Central America. During the Colombian Exchange, Portuguese traders carried corn across the Atlantic and into Africa and Europe, where it became a staple in some regions. The white potato we associate with Ireland and Idaho came originally from the Andean highlands. It was brought to Europe in the 1600s, where it became a staple in Ireland and the North European Plain. Likewise, the banana we associate with Central America came from Southeast Asia, as did a variety of yam.

The Columbian Exchange brought many new crops to places with similar climates, soils, and topography. Farmers found crops that could grow in places that previously did not support agriculture, bringing new lands that were previously defined as marginal into cultivation. The system of trade did not only include seeds. Europeans also forcibly enslaved Africans and moved them across the Atlantic to labor on plantations in the Americas. European migrants brought diseases to the Americas, infecting and killing millions of indigenous people, overturning civilizations, and dispossessing Natives of their land.

The Columbian Exchange not only changed the landscape of crops among Europe, Africa, South America, and North America, but it also set up a system of unequal exchange that is foundational to globalization. **Unequal exchange** is the idea that global trade is set up to structurally benefit some more than others, creating an unevenness in wealth in the capitalist world economy. Those who produce the food, first enslaved

FIGURE 11.11 **Edinburgh, Scotland.** Scottish Highland cattle have fluffy coats with heavy undercoats that make them well suited for living in colder climates. Farmers bred and named Scottish Highland cattle during the agricultural revolution that led up to the Industrial Revolution.

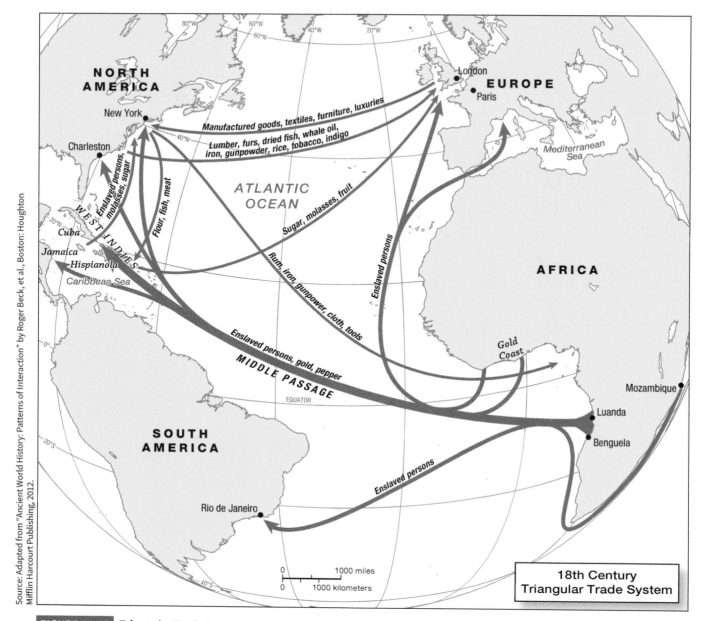

Source: Adapted from "Ancient World History: Patterns of Interaction" by Roger Beck, et al., Boston: Houghton Mifflin Harcourt Publishing, 2012.

FIGURE 11.12 **Triangular Trade System.** The eighteenth-century triangular trade system among Europe, Africa, and the Americas helped establish the foundations of the capitalist world economy.

Africans and now farm workers, receive little income compared to those who process food into products and trade it globally. For example, a coffee farmer may sell beans for $1.50 a pound, but by the time you buy a pound of coffee at Target, it is $9 a pound. Large coffee companies buy the beans, roast them, brand them, and sell them to retail outlets that mark the price up for consumers. This system of unequal exchange dates back to European colonialism and the beginnings of the capitalist world economy.

The Impact of the Rise of States on Agriculture

In the process of colonizing much of the world between the sixteenth and twentieth centuries, Europeans divided the world into states or countries (see Chapter 8). Under international law, states are territories with defined borders. The meaning of land and its ownership changed with the rise of the state system. Land became a system of control and power.

This change has greatly impacted hunter-gatherers and subsistence farmers. The relatively small groups of hunter-gatherers who migrate cyclically often move across country borders and are experiencing pressures to change their livelihoods. In many cases, the state pressures hunter-gatherers to settle in one place and farm. Some nongovernmental organizations encourage settlement by digging wells or building medical buildings, permanent houses, or schools for hunter-gatherers. Even hunter-gatherers who continue to use their knowledge of seeds, roots, fruits, berries, insects, and animals to gather and trap the goods they need for survival do so in the context of a highly interconnected economic world (**Fig. 11.13**).

From 1500 to 1950, European powers sought to "modernize" the economies of their colonies by ending subsistence farming and integrating farmers into colonial systems of production and exchange. Their methods included both taking land and implementing tax systems to force farming. By demanding that farmers pay taxes, they forced subsistence farmers to sell some of their produce to raise cash to pay taxes.

Colonial powers also compelled many subsistence farmers to devote some land to a crop such as cotton that would be sold on the world market, thus bringing them into the commercial economy. They encouraged commercial farming by conducting soil surveys, building irrigation systems, and establishing lending agencies that provided loans to farmers. Because it was difficult to squeeze sellable quantities of surplus from subsistence farming areas, colonizers also designed forced cropping schemes. If farmers in a subsistence area cultivated a certain acreage of food crops, they were required to grow a specified acreage of a cash crops as well. Whether this crop would be grown on old land or newly cleared land was the farmers' decision. If no new lands were available, the farmers would have to give up food crops for the compulsory cash crops. In many areas, severe famines resulted and local economies were disrupted from the push for cash crop production.

Subsistence land use continues to give way to more intensive farming and cash cropping—even to mechanized farming in which equipment does much of the actual work. Societies from South America to Southeast Asia are being profoundly affected. Land that was once held communally is being parceled out to individuals for cash cropping. In the process, small landowners are often squeezed out, leaving the land in the hands of wealthier farmers and the owners of commercialized farming operations.

For too long, governments have focused on how "to tempt [subsistence farmers] into wanting cash by the availability of suitable consumer goods," as A.N. Duckham and G.B. Masefield wrote in *Farming Systems of the World* in 1970. In the interests of "progress" and "modernization," subsistence farmers have been pushed away from their traditional modes of livelihood, even though many aspects of subsistence farming may be worth preserving. Regions with shifting cultivation may not have neat rows of plants, carefully turned soil, or precisely laid-out fields. Yet shifting cultivation conserves both forest and soil; its harvests are often substantial, given environmental limitations; and it requires better organization than one might assume. It also requires substantially less energy than more modern techniques of farming. It is no surprise, then, that shifting cultivation has been a sustained method of farming for thousands of years.

The Third Agricultural Revolution: The Green Revolution

World population grew rapidly in the 1900s, and agricultural companies, researchers, and farmers created new technologies designed to expand agricultural production to feed the growing population. The goal was not necessarily to expand the amount of arable land, but to find ways to increase productivity

FIGURE 11.13 **Lake Eyasi, Tanzania.** A Hadza man practices archery on land his ancestors have lived on for thousands of years. The Hadza people live in the Rift Valley in east Africa and have hunting grounds that stretch into the Serengeti plain.

on the land that existed and to create seeds that grow in more marginal lands. The **Green Revolution** is the use of biotechnology to create disease-resistant, fast-growing, high-yield seeds, as well as fertilizers and pesticides, and the result has been a large increase in crop production, especially in staple crops like rice, corn, and wheat. Because of the fundamental ways biotechnology has changed agriculture, the Green Revolution is also called the **Third Agricultural Revolution**.

Agricultural scientist Donald Baker suggests that we can think about the three agricultural revolutions by considering the "critical factor" that spurred each revolution. The First Agricultural Revolution depended on a change in human effort. The Second Agricultural Revolution hinged on improving technology with innovations like the seed drill. The Third Agricultural Revolution focuses on engineering the seed and the land. With the Third Agricultural Revolution, farmers genetically engineer seeds to grow in certain circumstances (wind and drought), intensively use technology and irrigation, and expand the use of land, either by not leaving it fallow or by farming marginal land.

Origins of the Green Revolution
The Green Revolution began in North America in the 1930s, when agricultural scientists in the Midwest experimented with technologically manipulated seed varieties to increase crop yields. Then, in the 1940s, American philanthropists interested in combating hunger funded research on crops in Mexico, trying to find hybrid seeds that would grow better. American agricultural scientist Norman Borlaug developed a wheat grain that was resistant to a fungus common in Mexico (**Fig. 11.14**). This disease-resistant wheat grew on a tall stalk, which made it topple before it fully grew. Borlaug then crossed the disease-resistant wheat with a Japanese dwarf wheat to create a dwarf wheat that grew so dependably in Mexico that Mexico became self-sufficient in grain production.

Photo by E.H. Fouberg. © 2020 John Wiley & Sons, Inc.

FIGURE 11.14 **St. Cresco, Iowa.** Norman Borlaug's home has been preserved and is a destination for tourists interested in agriculture and the Green Revolution.

Realizing that technology could help combat global hunger, the Ford Foundation and Rockefeller Foundation funded research into additional staple grains, including rice. In the 1960s, the focal point of the Green Revolution shifted to India, when scientists at a research institution in the Philippines crossed a dwarf Chinese variety of rice with an Indonesian variety and produced IR8. This new rice plant had several desirable properties, including developing more grains of rice on each head and growing a stronger stem that did not collapse under the added weight of the bigger head.

Building on the success of IR8, in 1982 scientists produced IR36, bred from 13 parents to achieve genetic resistance against 15 pests. With a growing cycle of 110 days under warm conditions, farmers could grow three crops per year in some places. By 1992, IR36 was the most widely grown crop on Earth, and in September 1994, scientists developed a strain of rice that was even more productive than IR36. The Green Revolution also brought new high-yield varieties of wheat and corn from the United States to other parts of the world, particularly South and Southeast Asia. India became self-sufficient in grain production by the 1980s, and Asia saw a two-thirds increase in rice production between 1970 and 1995. These drastic increases in production stemmed not only from new seed varieties, but also from the use of fertilizers, pesticides, irrigation, and significant capital improvements.

Outcomes of the Green Revolution
The Green Revolution has had both positive and negative outcomes. The promise of increasing food production in a world in which more than 800 million people are undernourished has led many people to view the Green Revolution only in positive terms. Others worry about social changes, health risks, and environmental hazards. The large-scale monocropping that is often part of Green Revolution agriculture can make farms vulnerable to changes in climate or the infestation of pests. In addition, the higher inputs of chemical fertilizers, herbicides, and pesticides that go along with Green Revolution agriculture can lead to reduced organic matter in the soil and to groundwater pollution.

The Green Revolution has also worked against the interest of many small-scale farmers who lack the resources to acquire genetically enhanced seeds and the necessary chemical inputs to grow them. One particularly vocal opponent of the Green Revolution in India, Vandana Shiva, argues that the Green Revolution has been a failure. It has led to reduced genetic diversity, increased vulnerability to pests, soil erosion, water shortages, reduced soil fertility, micronutrient deficiencies, soil contamination, reduced availability of nutritious food crops for the local population, the displacement of vast numbers of small farmers from their land, rural impoverishment, and increased tensions and conflicts. The beneficiaries have been the agrochemical industry, large petrochemical companies, manufacturers of agricultural machinery, dam builders, and large landowners.

It is no easy matter to weigh the enormous increases in food production that have occurred in places that have adopted Green Revolution approaches against the types of social and environmental issues highlighted by Shiva.

A 2005 report in *Scientific American* contends that many small farmers have not benefited from the Green Revolution: "The supply-driven strategies of the Green Revolution . . . may not help subsistence farmers, who must play to their strengths to compete in the global marketplace. The average size of a family farm is less than four acres in India, 1.8 acres in Bangladesh and about half an acre in China." Smaller farmers are in a poor competitive position, and their position is further undermined by the fact that a few large corporations with the seed patents for biotechnologically altered grains and a virtual monopoly of the needed chemical inputs can have tremendous power over the agricultural production process. In addition, the need for capital from the West to implement Green Revolution technologies has led to a shift away from production for local consumers toward export agriculture. In the process, local places become subject to the changing circumstances of the global economy, and a downward fluctuation in the price of a given crop can create enormous problems for places dependent on the sale of that crop.

Despite the negative impacts of the Green Revolution, proponents question why anyone would argue against reducing famine and starvation and feeding the ever-growing world population. Researchers at the International Rice Research Institute, with help from an $18 billion grant from the Bill and Melinda Gates Foundation, bred a genetically modified "Green Super Rice" that does not have to be transplanted as seedlings, but can be seeded directly in the paddy soil. The charting of the genome of rice (the 12 chromosomes that carry all of the plant's characteristics) is making it possible to transform rice genetically so that it will continuously acquire more new properties that could make it resistant to a wider spectrum of diseases and pests. Dozens of Green Super Rice varieties are being planted in several countries, and new varieties are in development.

Genetically Modified Organisms

Agricultural scientists alter the chemical makeup of crops and modify the genes of plants to create genetically engineered (GE) seeds and genetically modified organisms (GMOs). Farmers have been experimenting with hybrid crops and crossbreeding livestock ever since the First Agricultural Revolution. What is different today is that genetic modification involves splicing together genes from different species to create new plants.

According to the Grocery Manufacturers of America, GMOs are now found in 75 percent of all processed foods in the United States. The United States leads the world in the production of genetically engineered crops (**Fig. 11.15**). Since 1996, the percentage of planted acres that are genetically engineered to be herbicide tolerant or insect resistant has grown from below 20 percent to over 80 percent.

Genetically engineered seeds are planted on 88 percent of corn acres (up from 25 percent in 2000), 93 percent of soybean acres (up from 54 percent in 2000), and 85 percent of cotton acres in the United States (**Fig. 11.16**).

A major debate has developed around GMOs. Proponents argue that GMOs can help feed an expanding world population and that hard evidence of negative consequences to their use is lacking. Opponents contend that GMO companies are releasing organisms into the environment without adequate understanding of their environmental, health, or socioeconomic consequences. Another concern is the impact of pollen dispersal from GMOs on other organisms and the potential for disease-resistant plants to spur the evolution of superpests.

Some regions have embraced genetically engineered crops, whereas others have banned them. The United States has largely been in the former camp, though there is a growing movement to require labeling of products containing GMOs and a growing demand for organic products. The expansion of organic agriculture in the United States has been, in part, a reaction to the growth of GMOs. Ideological resistance to genetically engineered foods is strong in western Europe. Agricultural officials in most western European countries have declared GMOs to be safe, but labeling is required, and there is strong public reaction against GMOs based on combined concerns about health and taste.

In lower income regions, seeds are a cultural commodity, reflecting agricultural lessons learned over generations. Farmers resist the invasion of foreign, genetically engineered crops. But in their search for new markets, major GMO companies promote their products in the global periphery and semiperiphery.

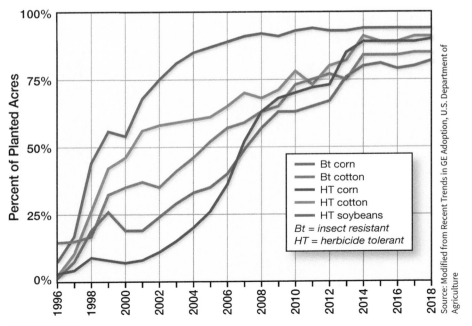

Source: Modified from Recent Trends in GE Adoption, U.S. Department of Agriculture

FIGURE 11.15 **Adoption of Genetically Engineered Crops in the United States, 1996–2018.** HT varieties are herbicide tolerant. Roundup Ready seeds produced by Monsanto are an example of herbicide tolerant seeds.

Impacts on Women   Shifting from subsistence agriculture to commercial agriculture in the Third Agricultural Revolution has had dramatic impacts on rural areas. Land-use patterns, land ownership arrangements, and agricultural labor conditions have all changed as rural residents cope with shifting economic, political, and environmental conditions. In Latin America, dramatic increases in the production of cash crops (export crops such as fruits and coffee) have occurred at the expense of crop production for local consumption. In the process, subsistence farming has been pushed to ever more marginal lands. In Asia, where the Green Revolution has had the greatest impact, the production of cereal crops (grains such as rice and wheat) has increased for both foreign and domestic markets. In sub-Saharan Africa, total commercialized agriculture has increased, but African farms have remained relatively small and dependent on extensive manual labor.

What this regional-scale analysis does not tell us is how these changes have affected rural communities. These changes can be environmental, economic, and social. A recent study in the small country of Gambia (West Africa) by Judith Carney has shown how changing agricultural practices have altered not only the rural environment and economy, but also relations between men and women (**Fig. 11.17**). Over the last 30 years, international developmental assistance to Gambia has led to ambitious projects designed to convert wetlands to irrigated agricultural lands, making possible year-round production of rice. By the late 1980s, virtually all of the country's suitable wetlands had been converted to year-round rice production. This transformation created tensions within rural households because lands women traditionally used for family subsistence were converted into commercialized farming plots. In addition, when rice production was turned into a year-round occupation, women found themselves with less time for other activities crucial for household maintenance.

Author Field Note   Expanding Acreage of Roundup Ready Soybeans in Presho, South Dakota

"Driving across the semiarid ranchlands of western South Dakota, I noticed the presence of a crop in the landscape that was recently found only in the eastern, more humid region of the state: soybeans. I called a colleague who works in agriculture at South Dakota State University to ask, 'When did the cattle ranchers of western South Dakota start growing soybeans?' He replied, 'When the soy biodiesel plants started popping up in Nebraska and Kansas and when genetically modified soybeans made it possible to grow the crop here.' He explained the development of Roundup Ready soybeans, a particular genetically modified soybean that can grow in more arid regions of the country. First you plant the soybean; then you use an airplane to spray Roundup, a common weed killer that is manufactured by the company that produces the Roundup Ready soybeans, over the field. The application of Roundup over the entire field saves a lot of time and energy for the farmers because the genetically modified soybeans are resistant to the Roundup, but the weeds are killed. Monsanto, the company that produces Roundup, has developed soybeans, corn, cotton, and other crops that are resistant to Roundup."

– E. H. Fouberg

Photo by E.H. Fouberg. © 2020 John Wiley & Sons, Inc.

FIGURE 11.16 **Presho, South Dakota.**

Guest Field Note   Growing Rice and Gender Disparity in Gambia

Judith Carney
University of California, Los Angeles

I am interested in women and rural development in sub-Saharan Africa. In 1983, I went to Gambia to study an irrigated rice project that was being implemented to improve the availability of rice, the dietary staple. What grabbed my attention? The donors' assurance that the project would benefit women, the country's traditional rice growers. Imagine my surprise a few months after project implementation when I encountered hundreds of angry women refusing to work because they received nothing for their labor from the first harvest.

In registering women's traditional rice plots as "family" land, project officials effectively sabotaged the equity objectives of the donors. Control now was concentrated under male heads of household who reaped the income produced by female labor. Contemporary economic strategies for Africa depend increasingly upon labor intensification. But whose labor? Human geography provides a way of seeing the significance of gender in the power relations that mediate culture, environment, and economic development.

© Judith Carney

FIGURE 11.17 **Gambia.**

This situation underscores the fact that in Africa, as in much of the periphery, agricultural work is overwhelmingly carried out by women. In sub-Saharan Africa and South Asia, 60 percent of all employed females work in the agriculture sector. A geographical perspective helps to shed light on how changes in agricultural practices throughout the world not only alter rural landscapes, but also affect family and community relationships.

TC Thinking Geographically

Many arguments have been raised about the impacts of the **Green Revolution**, both pro and con. How might the **scale** at which the Green Revolution is examined affect the arguments that are made about it? What types of factors are likely to be considered if the question is "Has the Green Revolution been good for Asia?" as opposed to "Has the Green Revolution been good for a village or a particular agricultural community in India?"

11.2   Describe the Spatial Patterns of Agriculture.

Whatever the time period or process involved, agriculture leaves a distinct imprint on the cultural landscape, from land surveys to land ownership to land use. Globalization has made an imprint on landscapes and agribusiness. What is produced where is not simply a product of the environment and locally available plants; the modern geography of agriculture depends on factors ranging from climate and government regulation to technology and shifting global consumption patterns.

National Land Survey Methods

Flying from the west coast of the United States to the east coast, if you have a window seat, you will see the major imprint

agriculture makes on the cultural landscape. The green circles standing out in the grain belts of the country are places where center pivot irrigation systems rotate to provide irrigation to a circle of crops. The checkerboard pattern on the landscape reflects the system used in most of the country (**Fig. 11.18**). The pattern of land ownership seen in the landscape reflects the **cadastral system**—the method of land survey through which land ownership and property lines are defined. Cadastral systems were adopted in places where settlement could be regulated by law, and they impose a remarkable uniformity across the land.

The prevailing survey system used throughout much of the United States, the one that appears as checkerboards across agricultural fields, is the federal rectangular survey system,

NNehring/E+/Getty Images

FIGURE 11.18 **Great Plains, United States.** The square pattern of land ownership found in the township and range land survey system marks farmland and towns as you fly over the Great Plains. The circles are from center-pivot irrigation systems.

also known as the **township and range system**, with farms spaced by sections, half sections, or quarter sections (**Fig. 11.19**). The U.S. government adopted the rectangular survey system after the American Revolution. Designed to facilitate the settlement of non-Indians in the farmlands of the interior of the United States, the system imposed a rigid checkerboard pattern on the land (**Fig. 11.20**). The imprint of the rectangular survey system is evident in Canada as well, where the government adopted a similar cadastral system as it sought to allocate land in the Prairie provinces.

Portions of the United States and Canada have different cadastral patterns, reflecting different ideas of how land should be divided and used. Among the most significant is the **metes-and-bounds** survey approach adopted along the east coast, which uses natural features like rivers and trees to demarcate irregular parcels of land (see **Fig. 11.20**).

One of the most distinctive regional approaches to land division can be found in the Canadian Maritimes and in parts of Quebec, Louisiana, and Texas, where a **long-lot survey** system was implemented. This system divided land into narrow parcels stretching back from rivers, roads, or canals. The long-lot survey system spread from France through relocation diffusion with French migrants to Quebec and then Louisiana (**Fig. 11.21**).

Many parts of the world do not have cadastral systems, so field patterns are irregular. But whether regular or irregular, societies with property ownership have parcels of land divided into neat, clearly demarcated segments. The size and order of those parcels are heavily influenced not just by land partition schemes, but also by rules about property inheritance. In systems where one child inherits all of the land—such as those associated with the traditional Germanic practice of **primogeniture**, in which all land passes to the eldest son—parcels tend to be larger and farmers work a single plot of land. This is the norm in northern Europe and in the principal areas of northern European colonization—the Americas, South Africa, Australia, and New Zealand.

In areas where land is divided among heirs, however, considerable fragmentation can occur over time. This is the norm throughout much of Asia, Africa, and southern Europe, as well as most of the allotted Indian reservations in the United States (see Fig. 11.7). Farmers in these areas tend a variety of scattered small plots of land. In some places, land reform initiatives have consolidated landholdings to a degree, but fragmentation is still common in many parts of the world.

Spatial Layout of Agriculture Around Towns and Cities

Once agricultural goods are produced, they need to be transported from fields to consumers. Agricultural goods such as milk, fresh meat, and produce are **perishable**, susceptible to spoiling in transit. As patterns of production emerged around cities and towns, goods that were heavy to transport and highly perishable were produced within a short drive of the city center. Social scientists noticed geographical patterns of land use based on the perishability of products and the cost of transportation.

Craig Aurness/Corbis/VCG/Getty Images

FIGURE 11.19 **Garden City, Iowa.** Small towns and cities were initially laid out following the one-mile square sections of the township and range land survey system.

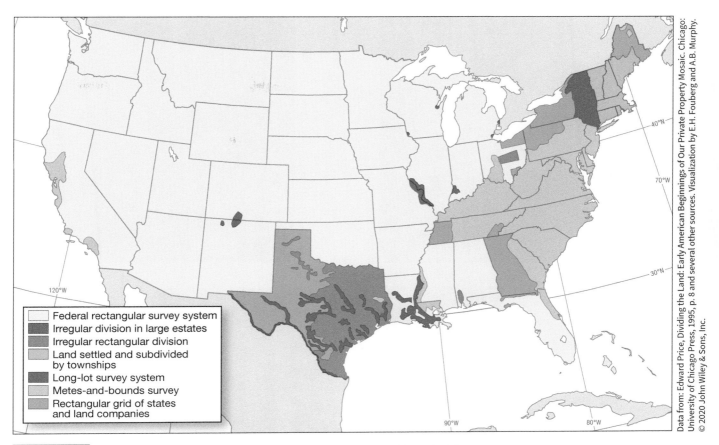

Legend:
- Federal rectangular survey system
- Irregular division in large estates
- Irregular rectangular division
- Land settled and subdivided by townships
- Long-lot survey system
- Metes-and-bounds survey
- Rectangular grid of states and land companies

FIGURE 11.20 **Dominant Land Survey System in the United States.** Most of the United States uses the federal rectangular survey system, which is also known as township and range. Small areas influenced by French settlers use long-lots, and the east coast uses metes-and-bounds.

von Thünen In the 1800s, one German farmer, Johann Heinrich von Thünen (1783–1850), experienced the Second Agricultural Revolution firsthand: He farmed an estate not far from the town of Rostock, in northeast Germany. Studying the spatial patterns of land use around his town and similar towns, von Thünen noted that as he moved away from a town, one commodity or crop gave way to another. He also noticed that this process occurred without any visible change in soil, climate, or terrain. When he mapped the patterns, he found that each town was surrounded by a set of concentric rings within which agricultural goods were grown.

Closest to the town, farmers generally produced commodities that were perishable and commanded high prices, such as dairy products and strawberries. In this zone, much effort would go into production, in part because of the value of the land closer to the city. In von Thünen's time, the town was still surrounded by a belt of forest that provided wood for fuel and building, but immediately beyond the forest, the ringlike pattern of agriculture continued. In the next ring, crops were less perishable and bulkier, including wheat and other grains. Still farther out, farmers raised livestock for meat, hides, and other products.

Von Thünen used his observations to build a model of the spatial distribution of agricultural activities around settlements (**Fig. 11.22**). As with all models, he had to make several assumptions. He assumed that the terrain was flat, that soils and other

environmental conditions were the same everywhere, and that there were no barriers for transportation to market. Von Thünen assumed that the cost of transportation would be greater at distances farther from the market and that the cost of transportation would be added to the cost of producing a crop or commodity. With these assumptions, transportation costs and accessibility would determine how farmers used land.

The **von Thünen model** (including the ring of forest) is often described as the first effort to analyze the spatial character of economic activity. Agricultural production that matches von Thünen's model is not solely the result of distance and transportation cost, however, and some of von Thünen's assumptions only rarely hold true. Around any given city, you can find differences in climate, precipitation patterns, access to transportation, topography, and soil quality that farmers factor into the goods they produce.

Even if von Thünen's model does not always work, the general pattern makes intuitive sense, and you can find support for it at certain scales and even in certain cities. If you drive east out of Denver on a major highway, you cannot miss a certain zonation that puts dairying and market gardening nearest the city (**Fig. 11.23**), cash grains such as corn and soybeans in the next zone, more extensive grain farming and livestock raising beyond, and cattle ranching in the outermost zone. This pattern does not work in all directions. It is truncated by the Rocky Mountains to the west and other urban areas of Colorado to the north and south. Thus von Thünen's model is a general

Andia/Alamy Stock Photo

A

Russ Heinl/All Canada Photos/Alamy Stock Photo

B

Matthew D White/Photolibrary/Getty Images

C

FIGURE 11.21A, B, AND C The French long-lot land survey system diffused from **A)** France to **B)** Quebec and then to **C)** Louisiana with French migrants and settlers.

Source: Based on Von Thünen Model from PennState College of Earth and Mineral Sciences. Visualization by E.H. Fouberg and A.B. Murphy. © 2020 John Wiley & Sons, Inc.

Grazing

Grains and field crops

Forestry

City

Market gardening and dairy

City

FIGURE 11.22 **von Thünen Model.** The key influence on land use in the von Thünen model is the cost of transporting goods to market. Perishable, high-priced goods like milk and produce are farmed closest to the city. Being close to the city allows transportation systems to get milk and produce to market quickly and frequently.

FIGURE 11.23 **Aurora, Colorado.** Several dairy farms and dairies are located within the suburbs of the Denver metropolitan area.

guideline, but is not consistently confirmed because how and where people live often differ from the assumptions of his model.

Even when agricultural production does not conform to the concentric rings of von Thünen's model, his underlying concern with the interplay of land use and transportation costs

still explains many agricultural patterns. Fresh flowers grown in the Caribbean for sale in New York City could be viewed as the application of the von Thünen model on a larger scale, for it is less expensive to grow flowers in the Caribbean and ship them to New York City than it is to grow them in other locations.

Agricultural Villages

Although the twentieth century has witnessed unprecedented urban growth throughout the world, half of the world's people still reside in villages and rural areas. In China, 43 percent of the 1.4 billion people live in rural areas. In India, with a population of over 1.3 billion, between 60 and 70 percent of the people live in places the government defines as non-urban. Small rural settlements are home to most of the inhabitants of Indonesia, Bangladesh, Pakistan, and other countries of the global economic periphery, including those in Africa. Agricultural villages remain one of the most common forms of settlement.

In core regions of the world economy, by contrast, agriculture has taken on a very different form, and true farming villages, in which farming or providing services for farmers are the dominant activities, are disappearing. In the United States, where farming once was the leading economic activity, less than 2 percent of the labor force remains engaged in agriculture, and the population of most rural villages and towns is a mix of farmers and people who commute to work in urban areas.

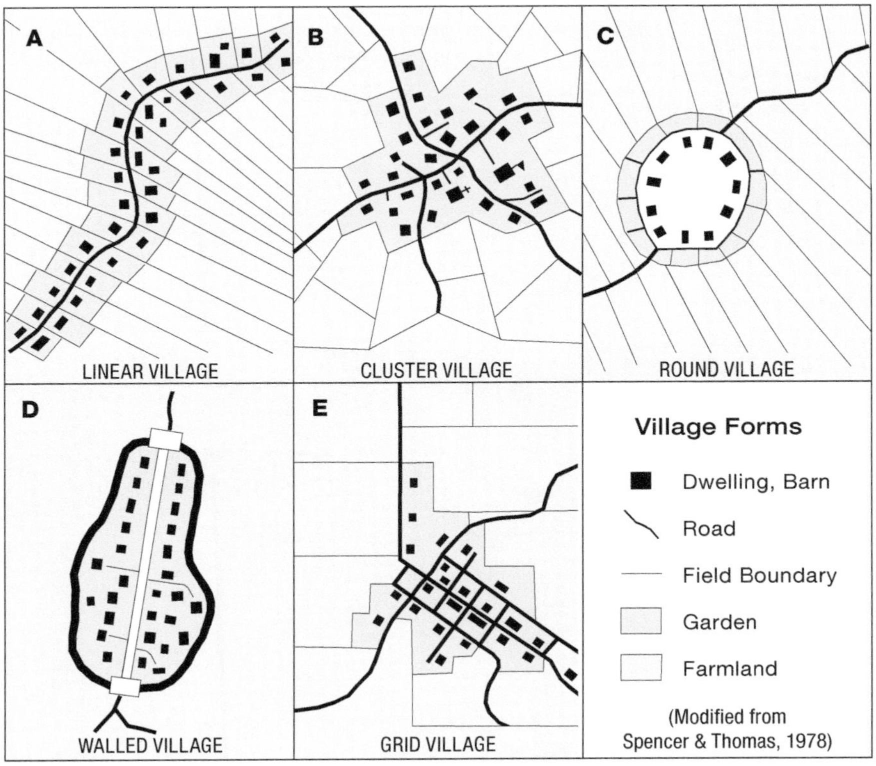

Types of Agricultural Villages
Traditionally, people who lived in villages either farmed the surrounding land or provided services to those who did the farming. They were closely connected to the land, and most of their livelihoods depended, directly or indirectly, on the cultivation of cultivating nearby farmland. Geographers have derived a classification of agricultural villages based on their layout that gives us an idea of what the people who built villages valued (**Fig. 11.24**). All the patterns in Figure 11.24 are examples of nucleated villages, or villages clustered around a central point, or nucleus.

Nucleated settlement is by far the most prevalent rural residential pattern in agricultural areas around the world (**Fig. 11.25**). When houses are grouped together in tiny clusters or hamlets, or in slightly larger clusters we call villages, their spatial arrangement also has significance. Houses in Japanese farming villages, for example, are so tightly packed together that only the

A LINEAR VILLAGE

B CLUSTER VILLAGE

C ROUND VILLAGE

D WALLED VILLAGE

E GRID VILLAGE

Village Forms
- ■ Dwelling, Barn
- ＼ Road
- — Field Boundary
- ▨ Garden
- ▢ Farmland

(Modified from Spencer & Thomas, 1978)

FIGURE 11.24 **Village Forms.** Five different representative nucleated village layouts are shown here. Compare Figure 11.21 to these five village layouts and note how apparent the linear village is in Quebec.

© Barbara A. Weightman

FIGURE 11.25 **Aquitaine, France.** The agricultural village of Aquitaine demonstrates three features of rural France: people living in nucleated villages, a highly fragmented land ownership pattern, and land divided according to the French long-lot system.

narrowest passageways remain between them. This village form reflects the pressure to allocate every possible square foot of land to farming. Villages are nucleated so people do not use land where crops could grow. In the populous Indonesian island of Java, villages are located every half mile or so along rural roads, and settlement there is also defined as nucleated.

In the hilly regions of Europe, villages frequently are clustered on hills, leaving the level land for farming. Often an old castle sits atop the hill, so in earlier times, the site offered protection as well as land conservation. In many low-lying areas of western Europe, villages are located on dikes and levees, so that they often take on linear characteristics (Fig. 11.24A). Villages oriented along roads or rivers also have this characteristic. Where there is space, a house and outbuildings may be surrounded by a small garden; with farms and pasturelands just beyond.

In other cases, a village may take on the characteristics of a cluster (Fig. 11.24B). It may have begun as a small hamlet at the intersection of two roads and then developed by accretion. The European version of the East African circular village, with its central cattle corral, is the round village or rundling (Fig. 11.24C). This layout was first used by Slavic farmer-herdsmen in eastern Europe and was later modified by Germanic settlers.

In many parts of the world, farm villages were fortified to protect their inhabitants against marauders. Ten thousand years ago, the first farmers in the Fertile Crescent faced attacks from the horsemen of Asia's steppes and clustered together to ward off this danger. In Nigeria's Yorubaland, the farmers would go out into the surrounding fields by day, but retreat to the protection of walled villages at night. Villages, as well as larger towns and cities in Europe, were frequently walled and

surrounded by moats. When the population became so large that people had to build houses outside the original wall, a new wall would be built to protect them as well. Walled villages (Fig. 11.24D) still exist in rural areas of many countries—reminders of a turbulent past.

More modern villages, notably planned rural settlements, may be arranged on a grid pattern (Fig. 11.24E). Grid patterns are not, however, a twentieth-century invention. Ancient Rome, ancient Greece, Indus cities such as Mohenjo-Daro and Harappa, ancient cities in central Mexico, and early cities in China all had streets laid out in grid patterns.

Functional Differentiation Within Agricultural Villages

Villages everywhere display certain common qualities, including evidence of social stratification and differentiation of buildings. The range in size and quality of houses, representing their owners' wealth and standing in the community, reflects social stratification. Material well-being is the chief determinant of stratification in Western commercial agricultural regions, where it translates into more elaborate homes. In Africa, as in most other places, a higher social position in the community is associated with a more impressive house. The house of the chief or headman may not only be more elaborate than others, but may also be in a more prominent location. In India, caste still strongly influences daily life, including village housing; the manors of landlords, often comprising large walled compounds, stand in striking contrast to the modest houses of domestic workers, farm workers, carpenters, and craftspeople. The poorest people of the lowest castes live in small, one-room, wattle- and thatch dwellings. In Cambodia, the buildings in stilt villages built throughout the Mekong Basin look similar (**Fig. 11.26**).

© Barbara A. Weightman

FIGURE 11.26 **Siem Reap, Cambodia.** A stilt village in the rural countryside of Cambodia. In the dry fall and winter, the stilts of the houses are exposed. In the wet spring and summer, as shown in this photo, monsoon rains inundate the village, covering the stilts with water.

The functional differentiation of buildings within farm villages (like the functional zonation of cities—where different areas of the city play different roles and function differently) is more elaborate in some societies than in others. Protection of livestock and storage of harvested crops are primary functions of farm villages, and in many villages where subsistence farming is the prevailing way of life, the storage place for grains and other food is constructed with as much care as the best-built house. Moisture and vermin must be kept away from stored food; containers of grain often stand on stilts under a carefully thatched roof or behind walls made of carefully maintained sun-dried mud. In India's villages, the paddy-bin made of mud (in which rice is stored) often stands inside the house. Similarly, livestock pens are often attached to houses, or, as in Africa, dwellings are built in a circle surrounding the corral.

The functional differentiation of buildings is greatest in Western cultures, where a single farmstead may contain as many buildings as an entire hamlet elsewhere in the world. A prosperous North American farm is likely to include a two-story farmhouse, a stable, a barn, and various outbuildings, including shops to store farm implements and tools, and silos for grain storage (**Fig. 11.27**). The space these structures occupy can exceed that used by entire villages in Japan and other agrarian regions where space is at a greater premium.

Aerial Archives/Alamy Stock Photo

FIGURE 11.27 **Southern Illinois.** The modern American farm typically has a two-story farmhouse surrounded by several outbuildings that include shops for storing implements and tools and silos for grain storage.

TC **Thinking Geographically**

Think of an agricultural **region** where you have visited or lived. Describe the imprint of agriculture on the landscape, and consider what the **cultural landscape** tells you about how agriculture is produced in this region or how production has changed over time.

11.3 Explain the Map of Global Agricultural Production.

Understanding global agricultural patterns requires looking at more than market location, land use, and transportation costs—the factors analyzed by von Thünen. We must also consider the effects of different climate and soil conditions, variations in farming methods and technology, the role of governments and social norms, and the lasting impacts of history.

Commercial farming has come to dominate in the world's economic core, as well as some places in the semiperiphery and periphery. Commercial farming is the agriculture of large-scale grain producers and cattle ranches, mechanized equipment, and factory-type labor forces. It is a world apart from the traditional farms of Asia and Africa.

The spatial expansion of modern commercial agriculture began in the eighteenth and nineteenth centuries when Europe became a market for agricultural products from around the world. Moreover, European countries manufactured and sold in their colonies the finished products made from imported raw materials. Thus, cotton grown in Egypt, Sudan, India, and other countries colonized by Europe was bought cheaply, imported to European factories, and made into clothes—many of which were then exported and sold, often in the very colonies where the cotton had been grown in the first place.

Major changes in transportation and food storage, especially refrigeration, further intertwined agricultural production and food-processing regions around the world. The beef industry of Argentina, for example, secured a world market when the invention of refrigerated ships made it possible to transport a highly perishable commodity over long distances. More than 80 percent of the fruits and vegetables sold in U.S. supermarkets arrive through the **cold chain**, a system of harvesting produce that is not quite ripe and ripening it by controlling temperature from the fields to the grocery store (**Fig. 11.28**).

European colonial powers required farmers in their colonies to cultivate specific crops. One major impact of colonial agriculture was the establishment of **monoculture** (dependence on a single agricultural commodity) throughout much of the colonial world. Colonies became known for certain crops, and colonizers came to rely on those crops. Farmers in Ghana still raise cacao; those in Mozambique still grow cotton; and Sri Lankans still produce tea.

Nature Picture Library/Alamy Stock Photo

FIGURE 11.28 **Hong Kong.** Thousands of pounds of produce sit in cold storage, waiting to be shipped via cold chain across the world.

The World Map of Climates

Before we can study the distribution of agriculture in the world today, we need to examine **Figure 11.29**, the distribution of climate zones. All of the elements of weather—absorption of the sun's energy, rotation of the Earth, circulation of the oceans, movement of weather systems, and the jet stream—produce a pattern of climates represented in the map, and those climate patterns have a profound impact on what can be grown where. Rice and oil palm are grown in tropical latitudes. Soybeans, sunflowers, and corn are grown at the mid-latitudes. Wheat is grown on the poleward side of the mid-latitudes both north and south of the equator.

Figure 11.29 provides one means of understanding the distribution of climatic regions (areas with similar climatic characteristics) across the planet.

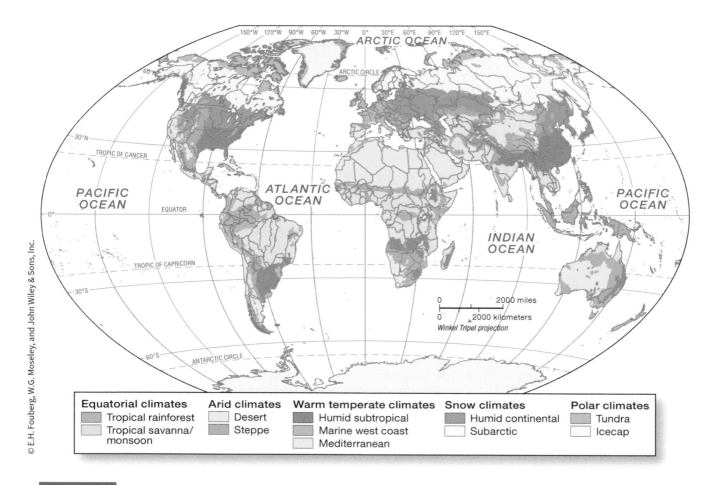

© E.H. Fouberg, W.G. Moseley, and John Wiley & Sons, Inc.

FIGURE 11.29 **World Climates.** Climates generally follow lines of latitude because the amount of incoming solar radiation varies by latitude. Climates are shaped further by the presence of mountains (as is seen in western North and South America), by the proximity to warm or cold ocean currents, and by proximity to and migration of high and low pressure belts.

- **Equatorial climates** are hot or very warm and generally humid. Equatorial rainforests have no dry season. Tropical savanna and tropical monsoon are grouped because they both have a distinct dry season and a distinct wet season. Both climate zones are wet when the subsolar point (the sun's direct rays) are nearby and dry when the subsolar point is in the opposite hemisphere.

- **Arid climates** include true desert and steppe or semi-arid. True deserts receive almost no precipitation, and semi-arid regions receive very little precipitation. Semi-arid regions are found next to deserts.

- **Warm temperate climates** include the humid subtropical. If you know the local climate in Atlanta or Nashville or Jacksonville, you understand why this climate is called humid. It is moist and generally warm because it just outside the tropics. Marine west coast and Mediterranean climates are along coasts and are found next to each other because they are created by the same conditions. Both marine west coast and Mediterranean climates experience wet winters and dry, hot summers.

- **Snow climates** are found closer to the poles, and include humid continental and subarctic. Humid continental climates are found in the U.S. upper Midwest, southern

Canada, and western Russia. Humid continental climate areas are in the middle of continents. Land heats and cools more quickly that water, so temperatures are more extreme in humid continental regions than other parts of the world. Winters are quite cold and summers can get quite hot. Subarctic climates are found poleward of humid continental regions.

- **Polar climates** include tundra and icecap climates and are found poleward of snow climates or at very high elevations. The polar location means temperatures are cold throughout the year. As a result, plant life does not break down and nourish the soil during the year, and a layer of permafrost (frozen ground) exists year-round.

The World Map of Agriculture

When comparing the world map of agriculture (**Fig. 11.30**) with the distribution of climate types across the world (Fig. 11.29), we can see the correlation between climate and agriculture. For example, drier lands rely on livestock ranching, whereas moister climates are characterized by grain production. Understanding the major agricultural regions shown in Figure 11.30 requires looking at both environmental and social variables.

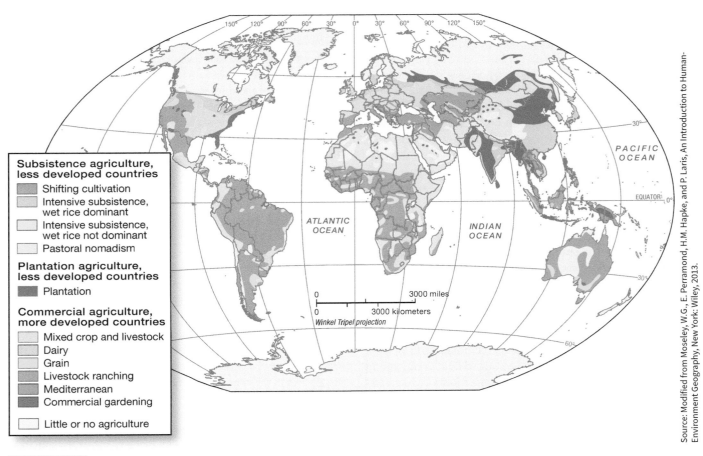

Source: Modified from Moseley, W.G., E. Perramond, H.M. Hapke, and P. Laris, An Introduction to Human-Environment Geography, New York: Wiley, 2013.

FIGURE 11.30 **World Agriculture.** The type of agriculture practiced varies with climate. Compare this map with Figure 11.29. Livestock raising is common in semiarid and savanna climate zones. Crop farming and commercial grain farming are found in places that receive higher rainfall. Dairy production generally occurs where climates are cooler. In addition to climate, land ownership patterns factor into the type of agricultural production globally. Where parcels of land are small, farmers generally focus on subsistence production.

Plantation Agriculture Colonialism profoundly shaped nonsubsistence farming in many lower income countries. Colonial powers implemented agriculture systems to benefit their needs, a practice that has tended to lock lower income countries into production of one or two cash crops. Cash crop farming has the benefit of providing cash to the periphery, even if the conditions of sale to the core are unfavorable. In the Caribbean whole national economies depend on sugar, which was introduced by the European colonizers in the 1600s. Caribbean countries want to sell the sugar at the highest possible price, but they are not in a position to dictate prices because sugar is produced by many countries around the world, as well as by farmers in the global economic core. Governments in the core place quotas on imports of agricultural products, including sugar, and subsidize domestic production of the same commodities within their own countries.

Occasionally, producing countries consider forming a cartel to present a united front to the importing countries and to gain a better price, as oil-producing countries did during the 1970s. Such collective action is difficult to coordinate, as the wealthy importing countries can buy products from countries that are not members of the cartel.

Also, if a group of countries controls exports of a good, non-producing countries may create incentives for their own production of the good. For example, although cane sugar accounts for 75 percent of the commercial world sugar crop each year, farmers in the United States, Europe, and Russia also produce sugar from sugar beets. Sugar beets already yield 25 percent of the annual world sugar harvest, and core countries could incentivize higher production.

When cash crops are grown on large estates, we use the term **plantation agriculture** to describe the production system. Plantations are colonial legacies that persist in peripheral, primarily tropical, countries along with subsistence farming. Figure 11.30 shows that plantation agriculture continues in South and Southeast Asia and China. Laid out to produce bananas, sugar, coffee, and cocoa in Middle and South America, rubber, cocoa, and tea in West and East Africa, tea in South Asia, and rubber in Southeast Asia, plantations have outlasted the period of decolonization and continue to provide specialized crops to wealthier markets. Many of the most productive plantations are owned by European or American individuals or corporations.

Multinational corporations have tenaciously protected their economic interests in plantations. In the 1940s and 1950s, the Guatemalan government began an agrarian reform program that entailed renting unused land from foreign corporations to landless citizens at a low appraised value. The United Fruit Company, an American firm with extensive holdings in the country, was greatly concerned by this turn of events. The company had close ties to powerful individuals in the American government, including Secretary of State John Foster Dulles, CIA Director Allen Dulles (the two were brothers), and Assistant Secretary of State for Inter-American Affairs John Moors Cabot. In 1954, the United States supported the overthrow of the government of Guatemala because of stated concerns about the spread of communism. This ended all land reform initiatives, but led many commentators to question the degree to which the United Fruit Company was behind the coup. Indeed, except for President Dwight Eisenhower, every individual involved in the decision to help topple Guatemala's government had ties to the company. This example illustrates the inextricable links between economics and political motivations—and it raises questions about the degree to which multinational corporations based in wealthy countries influence decisions about politics, agriculture, and land reform in other parts of the world.

Commercial Agriculture As Figure 11.30 shows, by far the largest areas of commercial agriculture lie outside the tropics. Dairying is widespread at the northern margins of the midlatitudes—particularly in the northeastern United States and in northwestern Europe. Commercial gardening is found in the eastern and southeastern United States and in widely dispersed in small areas where environments are favorable.

Only one form of agriculture mentioned in the legend of Figure 11.30 refers to a particular climatic zone: Mediterranean agriculture. As the map shows, this kind of specialized farming occurs only in areas where the dry summer Mediterranean climate prevails (Fig. 11.29): along the shores of the Mediterranean Sea, in parts of California and Oregon, in central Chile, at South Africa's Cape, and in parts of southwestern and southern Australia. Farmers here grow a special combination of crops: grapes, olives, citrus fruits, figs, certain vegetables, dates, and others. From these areas come many wines. These and other commodities are exported to distant markets because Mediterranean products tend to be popular and command high prices.

Mixed crop and livestock farming is widespread in the more humid parts of the midlatitudes, including much of the eastern United States, western Europe, and western Russia, but it is also found in South America and South Africa. Commercial grain farming prevails in the drier parts of the midlatitudes, including the southern Prairie Provinces of Canada, in the Dakotas and Montana in the United States, as well as in Nebraska, Kansas, and adjacent areas. Spring wheat (planted in the spring and harvested in the summer) grows in the northern zone, and winter wheat (planted in the autumn and harvested in the spring of the following year) is used in the southern area. An even larger belt of wheat farming extends from Ukraine through Russia into Kazakhstan. The Argentinean and Australian wheat zones are smaller in area, but their exports are an important component of world trade.

Even a cursory glance at Figure 11.30 reveals the wide distribution of livestock ranching, the raising of domesticated animals to produce meat and byproducts such as leather and wool. In addition to the large cattle-ranching areas in the United States, Canada, and Mexico, much of eastern Brazil and Argentina is devoted to ranching, along with large tracts of Australia and New Zealand, as well as South Africa. You may see a Thünian pattern here: livestock ranching on the periphery and consumers in the cities. Refrigeration has overcome the problem of perishability, and high volume has lowered the unit cost of transporting beef, lamb, and other animal products.

Subsistence Agriculture The map of world agriculture labels four types of subsistence agriculture: shifting cultivation, intensive subsistence—wet rice dominant, intensive subsistence—wet rice not dominant, and pastoral nomadism. In some regions that are labeled as subsistence, that label does not tell the whole story (**Fig. 11.31**). For example, in Southeast Asia, rice is grown on small plots and with a lot of labor, so that subsistence and export production occur side by side. Despite the region's significant rice exports, most Southeast Asian farmers are subsistence farmers. Thus, Southeast Asia appears on the map as primarily a subsistence grain-growing area.

AP® Exam Taker's Tip

Knowing the definition of **subsistence agriculture** is important. Be able to understand how processes like land ownership, agribusiness, and political factors have limited or made subsistence agriculture extinct in some areas. For example, how did **colonialism** create losses in agricultural practices for indigenous peoples?

Drug Agriculture   Certain important agricultural activities cannot easily be mapped at the global scale and therefore do not appear in Figure 11.30. One of those activities is the cultivation of crops that are turned into illegal drugs. Because of the high demand for drugs—particularly in the global economic core—farmers in the periphery often find it more profitable to cultivate poppy, coca, or marijuana plants than to grow standard food crops. Cultivation of these plants has increased steadily over the past several decades, and they

now constitute an important source of revenue for parts of the global economic periphery. Coca, the source plant of cocaine, is grown widely in Colombia, Peru, and Bolivia. Over half of the world's cultivation of coca occurs in Colombia alone.

Heroin and opium are derived from opium poppy plants, grown predominantly in Southeast and South Asia, especially in Afghanistan and Myanmar. In the 2013 World Drug Report, the United Nations reported that 74 percent of the world's opium production took place in Afghanistan. The U.S.-led overthrow of the Taliban in Afghanistan in 2001 created a power vacuum in the country and an opportunity for illegal drug production to quickly rebound (the austere Taliban government had virtually eradicated opium production in Afghanistan by 2001). Most opium production in Afghanistan today occurs in five unstable southern provinces.

U.S. government policies have affected production of illegal drugs in Latin America. During the 1980s and 1990s, the U.S. government worked with local authorities to crack down on coca production in Colombia. As a result, much of the drug production and trafficking moved north to northern Mexico. In June 2005, *The Economist* quoted one American official as reporting that "Mexican criminal gangs 'exert more influence over drug trafficking in the U.S. than any other group.' Mexicans now control 11 of the 13 largest drug markets in the United States." Marijuana and opium production in Mexico is on the rise, and the United States Drug Enforcement Agency (DEA) is concerned about the high potency of marijuana coming out of Mexico and Canada. Despite Afghanistan's dominance as a heroin producer, most heroin (which is derived from opium)

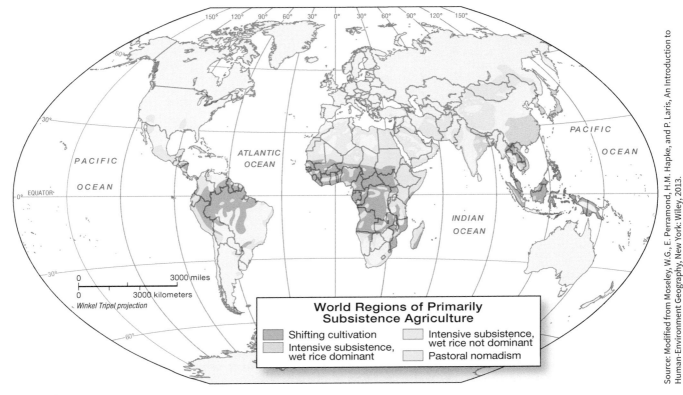

Source: Modified from Moseley, W.G., E. Perramond, H.M. Hapke, and P. Laris, An Introduction to Human-Environment Geography, New York: Wiley, 2013.

FIGURE 11.31 **World Regions of Primarily Subsistence Agriculture.** Areas of subsistence agriculture include parts of South America, Africa, and Asia.

consumed in the western United States comes from opium grown in Mexico, whereas the heroin consumed in the eastern United States comes from opium grown in Colombia.

Drug cartels that oversee the drug trade have brought crime and violence to the places where they hold sway (**Fig. 11.32**). There are areas in Rio de Janeiro where the official police have little control, and drug lords have imposed reigns of terror over swaths of the countryside in parts of Central and South America, Southwest Asia, Southeast Asia, and elsewhere. The drug trade depends on the voracious appetite for mind-altering substances in North America and Europe in particular.

The supply of marijuana in the United States traditionally came from Mexico and Canada, as the DEA has reported. But an increasing amount of marijuana consumed in the United States is grown in the United States. Since 1996, a total of 16 states — mostly in the West—have legalized marijuana for medicinal purposes, and in 2013 Colorado and Washington legalized it entirely (though they forbid consumption in public places and have placed additional restrictions on cultivation for personal use and the amount of marijuana people can purchase). An April 2011 article in *The New York Times* valued marijuana production at $40 billion, "with California, Tennessee, Kentucky, Hawaii and Washington the top five production states," despite the fact that medicinal marijuana is not legal in Tennessee or Kentucky.

Marijuana production has more than a monetary impact. Marijuana grown indoors consumes massive amounts of electricity. The cost of indoor production includes grow lamps that are the kinds used in operating rooms, dehumidifiers, air conditioners, electric generators, water pumps, heaters, carbon dioxide generators, ventilation systems, and electrical control systems. Studies estimate that the energy used to produce marijuana in the United States costs about $6 billion a year (around 1 percent of all power consumed in the United States). Marijuana grown outdoors has much lower energy costs than marijuana grown indoors. Growers may plant crops on public lands using only energy from sunlight, especially in the West, because the remote location of public lands makes detection less likely. Also, the land is public and therefore not owned by any one person to whom a crop could be traced.

TC **Thinking Geographically**

Analyze the world agriculture map and the world climate map. Find an agricultural type that does not seem to correspond with a certain climate **region**. Hypothesize why the two do not overlap and what variables in addition to climate need to be considered to understand the location of this agricultural type.

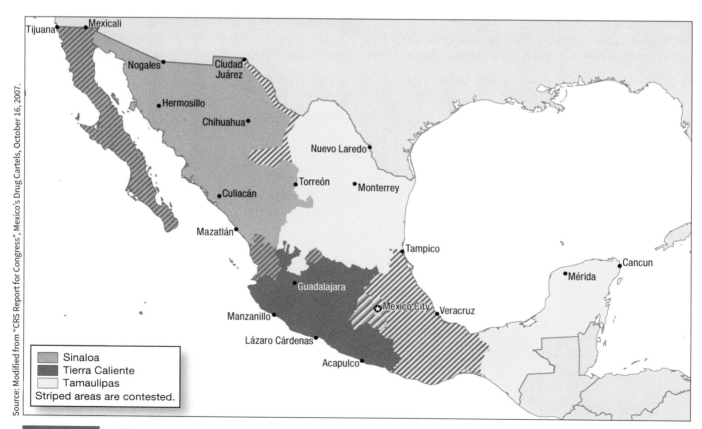

Source: Modified from "CRS Report for Congress", Mexico's Drug Cartels, October 16, 2007.

Sinaloa
Tierra Caliente
Tamaulipas
Striped areas are contested.

FIGURE 11.32 **Mexican Drug Cartel Regions of Influence in Mexico.** Mexican drug cartels claim swaths of the country and fight with each other for control of territory. Control of territory is important in order to move cocaine, methamphetamine, and marijuana into the United States. The cartels involved and their territorial control have changed as the Mexican government has worked to disrupt the control of the cartels since its war on drugs began in 2006.

11.4 | Analyze How Commercial Agriculture Operates.

With modern agriculture and food production, it is possible for many people to put farming largely out of their minds. As a result of the industrialization of agriculture and improvements in transportation, consumers come in contact with farmers much less frequently than in previous generations. On a freezing cold winter day in Cincinnati, Ohio, they can purchase fresh strawberries grown in Chile. Consumers can also purchase highly processed foods with long shelf lives and forget where the item was purchased, much less think of the farm work that went into the ingredients.

The commodity chains involved in agricultural production and delivery are increasingly complicated and interconnected. The label on your strawberries may say "grown in Chile," but imagining exactly how your strawberries are produced, whether in a field, in a greenhouse, in an urban farm, is increasingly difficult in a system of globalized, commercial agriculture.

Farms and Farmers

Examining the proportion of people employed in agriculture gives us an idea of whether agriculture is more commercial (intensive) or subsistence (extensive) in a country (**Fig. 11.33**). India is the second largest agricultural producer in the world (after China), with its agricultural goods valued at $358,905

million and 42.74 percent of its labor force employed in agriculture. The United States is the third largest agricultural producer in the world, with its agricultural goods valued at more than $32.7 billion. The share of the U.S. labor force employed in agriculture is much smaller, though, at only 1.66 percent. The same amount of agricultural production requires much more labor in India than it does in the United States, pointing to a more commercial (intensive) approach to agriculture in the United States.

AP® Exam Taker's Tip

Having less than 10 percent of the labor force working in agriculture is a characteristic of a core country. Countries with over 40 to 50 percent of the labor force in agriculture are usually in the periphery. Use Figure 11.33 and Figure 8.10 (p. 234) to make connections between labor force in agriculture to cores, peripheries, and semiperipheries.

Two other countries with similar total production have similar differences in how labor intensive their agricultural production is. The agricultural goods produced in the United Kingdom are valued at $24.6 billion, and those produced in

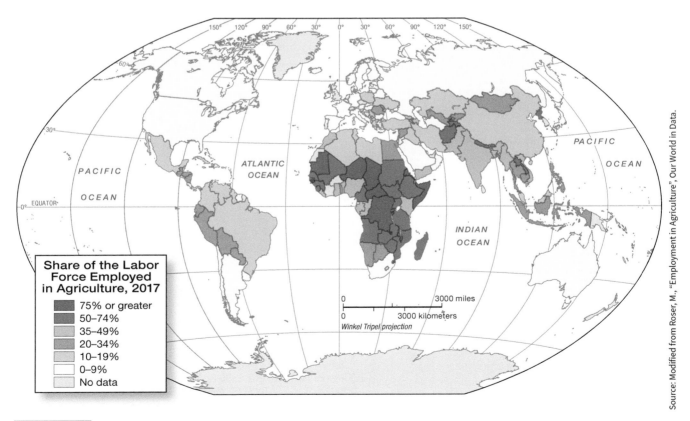

Source: Modified from Roser, M., "Employment in Agriculture", Our World in Data.

Share of the Labor Force Employed in Agriculture, 2017

- 75% or greater
- 50–74%
- 35–49%
- 20–34%
- 10–19%
- 0–9%
- No data

FIGURE 11.33 **Share of Labor Force Employed in Agriculture.** The proportion of the labor force employed in agriculture varies by country. Countries in Africa have the highest proportion of their labor forced employed in agriculture. Countries in North America and western Europe have 9 percent or less of their labor force employed in agriculture.

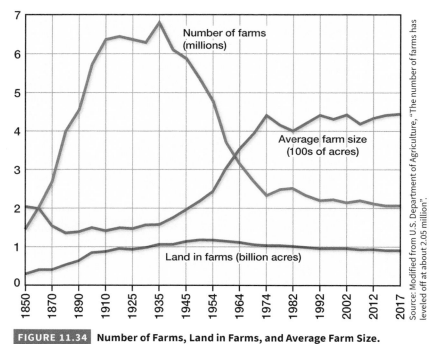

Source: Modified from U.S. Department of Agriculture, "The number of farms has leveled off at about 2.05 million".

FIGURE 11.34   **Number of Farms, Land in Farms, and Average Farm Size.** The amount of land in farms has stayed relatively steady while the number of farms has fallen since the Great Depression and the average size of farms has grown.

The mechanization of agriculture goes beyond machinery such as combines and harvesters. New technologies include hybrid seeds and genetically engineered crops, pesticides, and herbicides, all of which are designed to increase yields.

The drive toward economic efficiency has meant that between 1910 and 2017, the number of farms in the United States has fallen and then tapered off, while the amount of land in agriculture has stayed relatively consistent. As a result of these two trends, the average size of farms (acres in production) in the United States has risen (**Fig. 11.34**). The United States currently has about 2.05 million farms in operation with an average size of 444 acres (compared to 135 acres in 1935) (USDA). Of the 2.05 million farms, 2.8 percent are classified as large and produce 39 percent of all agricultural goods, and 88.8 percent are classified as small and produce 25.8 percent of all agricultural goods. While we tend to think of farms as family farms or corporate farms, most corporate farms are owned by families. Nonfamily farms account for 2.2 percent of all farms and produce 12.6 percent of all agricultural goods (**Fig. 11.35**).

Malaysia are valued at $23.6 billion. Figure 11.33 reveals the difference in labor, with 1.1 percent of the United Kingdom and 11.01 percent of the Malaysian labor force employed in the agriculture. In this case, the United Kingdom is using more commercial methods of agricultural production than Malaysia.

The data on labor force in agriculture are even more interesting if you look at the definition provided by the World Bank: "share of persons of working age who were engaged in any activity to produce goods or provide services for pay or profit in the agricultural sector (agriculture, hunting, forestry and fishing)" (2018). The 1.1 percent of the United Kingdom's labor force employed in agriculture includes those who "provide services" to producers. Many of these workers include research scientists for universities, workers for seed companies, or workers for producers of chemicals (antibiotics, pesticides, and herbicides). Lobbyists for industry groups such as wheat producers and cattle ranchers, as well as engineers who design, sell, and repair farm implements, are also part of the agricultural labor force.

In the United States, total agricultural production is at an all-time high, but the proportion of the labor force in agriculture is at an all-time low. Mechanization and efficiencies created by new technologies have led to a significant decrease in the number of workers needed in agricultural production. In 1950, one farmer produced enough to feed 27 people; today, one farmer in the United States produces enough to feed 144 people.

Bid Rent Theory

Another way of thinking about production of agricultural products around towns and cities is to consider the cost of land. Land values are generally higher closer to the central city and lower farther away from the city. The cost of land affects what farmers produce because where land values are high, farmers want to grow valuable crops like market produce that will help them pay for the rent on their land. Where land values are low,

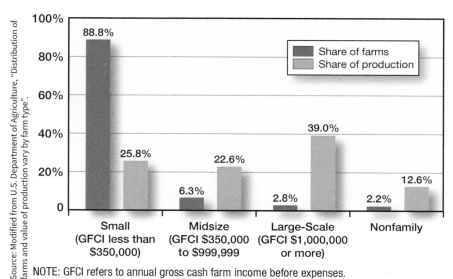

Source: Modified from U.S. Department of Agriculture, "Distribution of farms and value of production vary by farm type".

NOTE: GFCI refers to annual gross cash farm income before expenses.

FIGURE 11.35   **Farms and Their Value of Production by USDA Farm Type.**   Small farms make up the largest proportion of farms in the United States, but large-scale farms generate the largest share of production.

farmers grow more common crops that need a lot of space to grow, like grain.

The **bid rent theory** holds that the price and demand for land will go up the closer it is to the central city. Agriculture, retail, manufacturing, and residential will all compete for the land closest to the central city, driving up its cost. In agriculture, the bid rent theory helps us understand whether farmers will use intensive agricultural practices or extensive agricultural practices. Intensive agricultural practices use a great deal of capital relative to the land area farmed, whereas extensive agricultural practices use less capital.

Intensive agricultural practices include applying fertilizers, insecticides, and high-cost inputs to achieve the highest yields possible. They often occur closer to the city where land values are high. With the rapid growth of world cities and the expansion of big data and artificial intelligence, intensive agriculture is rapidly growing near major cities. One form is **indoor vertical farms**, also known as plant factories, which rely on growing produce hydroponically, without soil (**Fig. 11.36**). Sensors throughout the building constantly collect data and gather it into the Cloud. Companies like Microsoft are developing artificial intelligence systems to help farmers analyze data and change conditions for optimal crop yields. These plant factories are located close to city centers, use space efficiently, and require serious technology investments. The next step is automation, which will use robotics to harvest fresh produce from indoor vertical farms and deliver it to a customer in the city the same day.

Extensive agricultural practices use less capital and larger areas of land to cultivate what has traditionally been a lower yield. Applying bid rent theory, extensive agriculture takes place farther from the city center, where land values are low relative to labor and capital. Crops grown extensively include grains like wheat and rice and tubers like yams, taro, cassava, and potatoes.

Modern agriculture, especially in large agricultural countries like the United States and Canada, challenges the traditional conception of extensive agriculture. Farmers who put millions of dollars into seeds, fertilizers, GPS-guided combines, drones, and data are using a combination of intensive practices, including high technology and high capital, and extensive practices, including more remote, expansive fields. The result is a high yield, often even in adverse conditions like drought.

Organic Agriculture: Consumer Demand

Organic agriculture, the production of crops without the use of synthetic or industrially produced pesticides and fertilizers, is growing globally in terms of land devoted to organic farming (69.8 million hectares), number of organic farmers (2.9 million), and the market value of organic food ($97 billion). Organic foods are sold at the highest rates in the United States,

FIGURE 11.36 Tokyo, Japan. Farmers grow market produce using vertical farming and other high-tech methods to save space.

AzmanL/E+/Getty Images

Germany, France, and China. Australia, Argentina, and China have the most land in organic production.

Comparing the number of hectares in organic production to the number of organic producers gives an idea of whether organic production is intensive or extensive. India has the most organic producers (835,200) but only has 1.78 million hectares of land in organic production. Indian organic farmers are producing on small plots, using a lot of labor and not a lot of technology. India has 0.46 organic producers per hectare of organic farmland. The United States has fewer organic producers (14,217) and more land (2.03 million hectares) in organic production. American organic producers are producing on larger plots, using less labor and more technology. The United States has 0.007 organic producers per hectare of organic farmland.

Sales of organic food in the United States went from under $200 million in 1980 to $8 billion by 2000 and $40 billion in 2017 (**Table 11.1**). In 2000, the sales of organic food reached a tipping point, where more organic food was purchased in supermarkets than in health food stores. Organic foods are sold in three out of four conventional grocery stores and approximately 20,000 natural food stores in the United States, with increasing demands for organic animal products such as meats and dairy.

Organic foods are now 5.7 percent of all food sales in the United States, up from 3.4 percent in 2010. The growth rate is so strong that some predict organic sales will approach 10 percent of total U.S. food sales within a decade. Denmark already hit double digits with 13.3 percent of total food sales in organic. Sweden, Switzerland, and Austria follow with 9.1, 9.0, and 8.6 percent of total food sales in organic, respectively. Farmers who can gain organic certification from a government or an internationally recognized third party are increasingly at a competitive advantage (**Fig. 11.37**).

Organic farming has helped some farmers extract themselves from major corporate farming interests. However, the largest organic food seller in the United States, WhiteWave Foods, is a subsidiary of Danone, which is ranked 24 on the list

TABLE 11.1 Organic Sales per Year from 2000 to 2017 for United States, India, and World.

Organic Sales per Year, 2000–2017 Retail Sales, Millions of Euros			
Year	United States	India	World
2000	8000		15,156
2001	8000		16,355
2002	8514		18,798
2003	8510		19,615
2004	8945		20,938
2005	10,658	39	23,560
2006	12,447		27,958
2007	13,271		31,754
2008	13,865	8	34,137
2009	15,247	13	36,945
2010	17,320	20	41,282
2011	18,066	31	43,916
2012	21,766	51	49,584
2013	23,626	70	54,863
2014	26,420	101	61,344
2015	35,156	144	75,317
2016	38,402	172	84,459
2017	40,011	186	92,062

Source: Data from: https://statistics.fibl.org/

of the largest food producers in the country. The second largest organic food producer, Hain Celestial Group, stands at 64 on the list of largest producers overall. The third largest organic producer is General Mills, which is likely a familiar brand for their cereals, and is ranked 10 on the list.

The organic movement has some clear environmental benefits, particularly in reducing the levels of synthetic chemicals in soil and water. The putative health and taste advantages of organic produce help ensure the continued growth of the organic movement.

Ethanol and Biodiesel: Government Impacts

Grains, other plant life, vegetable oils, and animal fats can be converted into fuel, either ethanol or biodiesel. **Ethanol** is a renewable fuel made from plant materials called biomass. Ethanol is added to about 98 percent of all gasoline sold in the United States. **Biodiesel** is also a renewable fuel, and it is made from vegetable oils, animal fats, or recycled restaurant grease. Ethanol is used more frequently in colder climates because it has properties that prevent it and the gasoline it's mixed with from freezing in cold temperatures. Biodiesel is

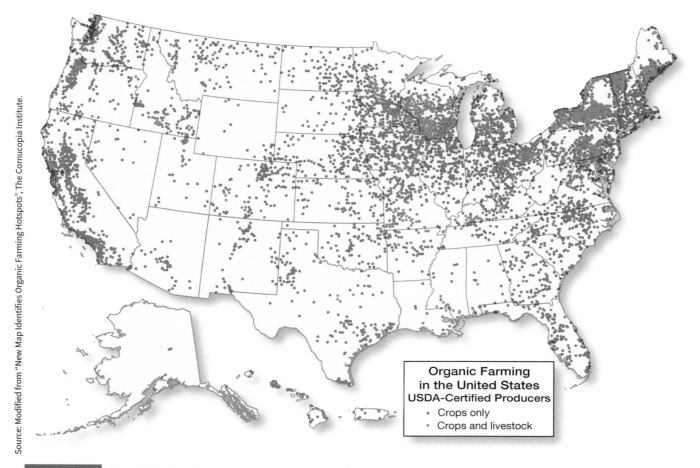

Source: Modified from "New Map Identifies Organic Farming Hotspots," The Cornucopia Institute.

Organic Farming in the United States
USDA-Certified Producers
- Crops only
- Crops and livestock

FIGURE 11.37 **Organic Farming in the United States.** Organic farming is widespread in the United States and is found in all 50 states. Organic livestock production coincides well with the map of dairy production in the United States (see Fig. 11.30).

used in warmer climates because its components can freeze and crystalize in cold weather.

Much of the corn produced in the United States and the sugar produced in Brazil is converted into ethanol and used for fuel. The two countries account for 85 percent of the ethanol produced worldwide. In 2018, 38 percent of all corn produced in the United States was processed into fuel instead of food or feed. Ethanol production took off in both Brazil and the United States in the 1970s when the price of oil rose and the price of corn and sugar dropped. In the 1980s, when the price of oil fell again, federal and state governments subsidized ethanol production. The current federal ethanol subsidy in the United States gives ethanol blenders a tax credit of $0.45 for every gallon of ethanol they blend with gasoline, at a cost to taxpayers in taxes not paid of $5.7 billion annually.

While ethanol and biodiesel are renewable fuels that burn cleaner than gasoline, each comes with several environmental concerns. The chief concern is that not all products used to create the fuels are efficient. The efficiency by acre of ethanol and biodiesel depends on the product used to create the fuel (**Fig. 11.38**). The biggest source of ethanol in the United States is corn (maize), but the number of gallons per acre from corn is much lower (401 gallons/acre) than for switchgrass (1150 gallons/acre). Most biodiesel in the United States is derived from soybeans, which yield 59 gallons of biodiesel per acre, while microalgae produce 5020 gallons of biodiesel per acre.

Scientists do not agree on the net energy savings or cost of ethanol or biodiesel over hydrocarbons like oil. Dozens of variables that are difficult to quantify go into the calculations of energy and water use for production. Land use is the first variable. A field of corn can be a carbon dioxide sink because the plants use carbon dioxide to grow through photosynthesis. But the actual production and then burning of the corn release carbon dioxide. Because ethanol is plant based, burning ethanol still creates carbon dioxide, but most studies agree that burning ethanol releases less carbon dioxide than burning hydrocarbons does. Another concern with biofuel is that ethanol burns less efficiently than gasoline. Gasoline produces more miles per gallon than ethanol. It takes energy to refine both fuels, but it takes less energy to create biodiesel than it does to create ethanol.

How much more water is used for ethanol and biodiesel production depends on where the corn or soybeans are planted. If they are planted in a rain-fed cornfield, they do little to deplete aquifers or divert rivers. If they are planted in irrigated fields, switching land use to more corn and soybeans to meet demands for biofuels leads to much higher water consumption rates. Consumptive water use is a measurement of the gallons of water needed to refine gallons of fuel. In rank order from least to most, it requires 1.0 gallon of water to produce 3.0 gallons of soy biodiesel, 1.5 gallons of water to produce 3.0 gallons of oil, and 3.0 gallons of water to produce 4.0 gallons of ethanol (NAP 2008).

Ethanol refineries are generally located close to areas of corn production, which helps reduce the cost of transporting biomass from cornfields to refineries (**Fig. 11.39**). The counties that produce the most corn stover (remnants of corn plants after harvesting) are concentrated in the **Corn Belt**, stretching from North Dakota, South Dakota, and Nebraska east through Minnesota and Iowa to Wisconsin, Illinois, and Indiana.

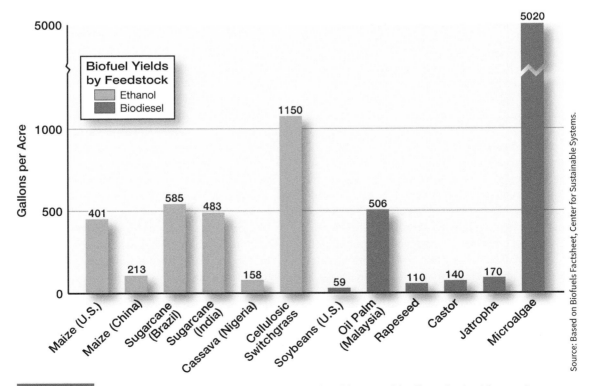

Source: Based on Biofuels Factsheet, Center for Sustainable Systems.

FIGURE 11.38 **Biofuel Yields by Feedstock.** Grains, other plant life, vegetable oils, and animal fats can be converted into fuel, either ethanol or biodiesel. The efficiency by acre of ethanol and biodiesel depends on the product used to create the fuel. The y-axis shows the gallons of ethanol produced by acre, and the x-axis lists different sources for ethanol and biodiesel.

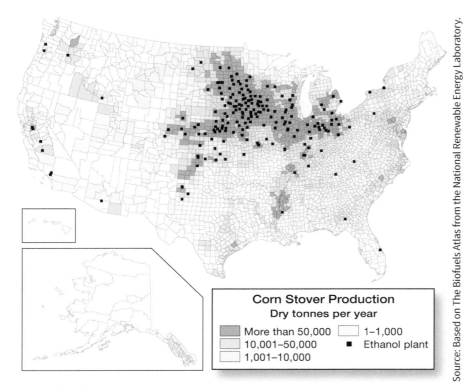

Corn Stover Production
Dry tonnes per year

More than 50,000 ☐ 1–1,000
10,001–50,000 ■ Ethanol plant
1,001–10,000

Source: Based on The Biofuels Atlas from the National Renewable Energy Laboratory.

FIGURE 11.39 **Corn Stover Production.** Corn stover is the remnants of corn plants after harvesting the ears of corn. It is the stalks, leaves, and cobs that remain in a field after harvest. Farmers can harvest that biomass and sell it for ethanol production.

AP® Exam Taker's Tip

A map very similar to Figure 11.39 was used on an FRQ in the 2010 APHG exam. Look up this 2010 exam question (https://secure-media.collegeboard.org/apc/ap10_frq_human_geo.pdf) and try to answer it. Think about studying the many maps and tables in the text and formulating possible FRQs for some of these.

Biodiesel refineries are located close to high soybean-production counties in several cases in the Great Plains, Midwest, and Mississippi River region, because 57 percent of biodiesel in the United States comes from soybean oil (**Fig. 11.40**). However, soybean production areas do not explain the location of all of the biodiesel refineries on the map. Biodiesel refineries on the west coast and east coast are located close to population centers, where plenty of used cooking oil is available for producing biodiesel. Some locations on the map are close to livestock production centers, including hog production in the Carolinas and Virginia and chicken production in the South and Delmarva Peninsula, because animal fats are also used to produce biodiesel.

Coffee: Fair Trade

Agriculture is also affected by social and cultural factors. As incomes rise, many people start consuming more meat and processed foods, seek out better-quality fruits and vegetables, or demand fresh produce year-round. Consider the case of coffee, one the most important luxury crops in the modern world. Coffee was first domesticated in present-day Ethiopia, but today it is grown primarily in Middle and South America, where approximately 70 percent of the world's annual production is harvested.

In the early eighteenth century, coffee was virtually unknown in most of the world. Yet after petroleum, coffee is now the second most valuable legally traded commodity in the world. The United States buys more than half of all the coffee sold on world markets annually, and western Europe imports most of the rest. A well-known image of coffee production in North America is Juan Valdez, portrayed as a simple yet proud Colombian peasant who handpicks beans by day and enjoys a cup of his own coffee by night. This image is quite contrary to the reality of much coffee production in Latin America. In most cases, coffee is produced on enormous, foreign-owned plantations, where it is picked by local laborers who are hired at very low wage rates. Most coffee is sent abroad, and if the coffee pickers drink coffee, it is probably of the imported and instant variety.

In the past few decades, however, coffee production has undergone changes as more consumers demand fair trade coffee and more coffee producers seek fair trade certification.

The aim of fair trade is to raise the income of certified producers by reducing the number of actors in the supply chain. Coffee producers form democratically run cooperatives that, if certified, can be registered on the International Fair Trade Coffee Register. Coffee importers then purchase the fair trade coffee directly from the registered cooperatives. Being registered guarantees coffee producers a "fair trade price" of $1.40 per pound of coffee (plus bonuses of $0.30 per pound for organic).

When organic agriculture bears a fair trade certification, some producers in the periphery and semiperiphery benefit substantially, though they also have to abide by rules established in the core. Over 1.3 million farmers and workers in 70 countries, mainly in the periphery and semiperiphery, are connected to the 1150 fair trade–certified producer organizations worldwide (**Fig. 11.41**). The fair trade campaign pressured Starbucks into selling fair trade coffee, and Starbucks now buys around 20 million pounds of fair trade coffee each year. That amounts to just 5 percent of its total purchases, but it is the largest purchaser of fair trade coffee in the world. Other retailers have followed suit; for example, all espresso sold at Dunkin' Donuts in North America and Europe is fair trade certified. Fair trade coffee is available at large retail outlets and under

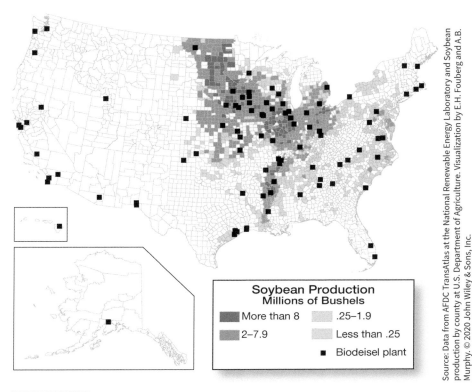

Source: Data from AFDC TransAtlas at the National Renewable Energy Laboratory and Soybean production by county at U.S. Department of Agriculture. Visualization by E.H. Fouberg and A.B. Murphy. © 2020 John Wiley & Sons, Inc.

Soybean Production
Millions of Bushels

More than 8   .25–1.9

2–7.9   Less than .25

■ Biodeisel plant

FIGURE 11.40 **Biodiesel Plants in the United States.** Biodiesel plants are located in soybean production zones or close to major population centers.

Early in the twentieth century, poultry production in the United States was highly disaggregated, with many farmers raising a few chickens as part of a multifaceted farming operation. Over the past 50 years, however, poultry production has changed. Today, the farmers on the Delmarva Peninsula east of Washington, D.C., account for 8 percent of poultry production in the United States, and they do so by contracting and working directly with four major poultry companies. In an article on modern agriculture, David Lanegran summarized the impact of this transformation as follows:

Today, chickens are produced by large agribusiness companies operating hatcheries, feed mills, and processing plants. They supply chicks and feed to the farmers. The farmers are responsible for building a house and maintaining proper temperature and water supply. Once a week the companies fill the feed bins for the farmers, and guarantee them a price for the birds. The companies even collect market ready birds and take them away for processing and marketing. Most of the nation's poultry supply is handled by a half dozen very large corporations that control the process from chicks to chicken pieces in stores.

corporate brands at Target, Walmart, and Sam's Club. The corporate embrace of fair trade coffee has boosted the movement considerably, though it has also raised concerns about corporate co-optation of fair trade standards.

The push for fair trade production shows how social movements can influence agriculture. And fair trade goes beyond coffee. Dozens of commodities and products, ranging from tea, bananas, fresh-cut flowers, and chocolate to soccer balls, can be certified fair trade. According to Fair Trade International, consumers spent more than $6.5 billion on fair trade–certified products in 2012.

Poultry and Hogs: Agribusiness

The commercialization of crop production and new agricultural technologies have changed how agricultural goods are grown and have sparked the rapid growth of *agribusiness*: the businesses that provide a vast array of goods and services to support the agricultural industry. As part of a networks of agribusiness, farmers are tied to an extensive web of production and consumption. Agribusiness also helps concentrate agricultural industries because fewer farmers produce more to take advantage of economies of scale in order to compete in agribusiness. Both trends are revealed in the development of the poultry industry in the United States.

© Lindsay Naylor

FIGURE 11.41 **Los Altos, Chiapas, Mexico.** A Mayan farmer picks ripe coffee beans for sale to North American customers as fair trade coffee.

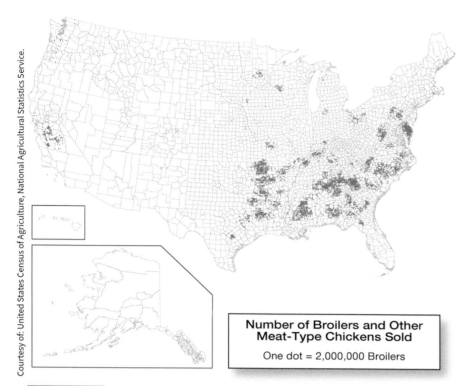

Number of Broilers and Other Meat-Type Chickens Sold

One dot = 2,000,000 Broilers

FIGURE 11.42 **Broiler Chicken Sales in the United States.** Broiler chickens are grown for meat, which means they will be processed and consumed once sold. Farmers typically sell broiler chickens to one of 40 large processing companies, including Tyson and Purdue. Ninety-five percent of broiler chickens in the United States are produced by farmers who are under contract with a large processing firm and are required to follow their standards and use their feed from hatched egg to table.

farms. John Fraser Hart and Chris Mayda described the quick change with statistics. In 1992, the U.S. Census of Agriculture counted just over 31,000 hogs marketed in Texas County, Oklahoma, and just four years later "the panhandle was plastered with proliferating pork places, and Texas County alone produced 2 million hogs. It was the epicenter of an area that produced 4 million hogs, 4 percent of the national total and one-seventh as many finished hogs as the entire state of Iowa." The availability of both inexpensive water and natural gas on the Oklahoma panhandle was enticing for corporate hog farms, which require both. Hart and Mayda explain that the "reasonable" price of land and the accessibility to "growing metropolitan markets of the South and the West" also made the region attractive for hog production. As in poultry production, a corporation built a processing plant, and production (both by farms owned by the corporation and those owned privately) increased to meet the demand (**Fig. 11.43**).

Because of agribusiness, the shelves of urban supermarkets in the United States, with their range and variety of products, are a world apart from the constant quest in some areas for sufficient, nutritionally

Lanegran goes on to show how selective breeding has produced faster-growing, bigger chickens, which are housed in enormous broiler houses that are largely mechanized.

Broiler houses are concentrated in northwestern Arkansas, northern Georgia, the Delmarva Peninsula (Delaware, Maryland, and Virginia), the Piedmont areas of North Carolina, and the Shenandoah Valley of Virginia (**Fig. 11.42**). Lanegran shows that the "farmers" who manage these operations are involved in manufacturing as much as in farming. They are as likely spend their time talking to bank officers, overseeing the repair of equipment, and negotiating with vendors as they are to tending their animals. Thus, they symbolize the blending of the rural and the urban in wealthier parts of the world—as well as the interconnections between rural places and distant markets.

The poultry example is not unusual. During the 1990s, hog production on the Oklahoma and Texas panhandles increased rapidly with the arrival of corporate hog

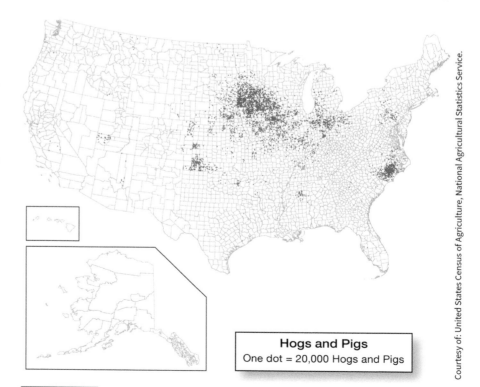

Hogs and Pigs

One dot = 20,000 Hogs and Pigs

FIGURE 11.43 **Hogs and Pigs in the United States.** Hog and pig production is concentrated in the Corn Belt in and around Iowa and also in North Carolina. The earliest stages of hog production are done inside buildings using systems designed to reduce the possibility of disease spreading among the livestock.

balanced food. A global network of farm production is oriented to one-fifth of the world's population that is highly urbanized, wealthy, and powerful. Few farmers in distant lands have real control over land-use decisions, for the higher income people in the global economic core play a disproportionate role in deciding what will be bought at what price. The colonial era may have come to an end, but as the map of agricultural regions reminds us, its imprint remains strong.

> **TC** **Thinking Geographically**
>
> Compare and contrast the **pattern** of commercial and subsistence agriculture on the world map. If a community wanted to abandon commercial agriculture and return to subsistence agriculture, what steps would it need to take in terms of land ownership, agricultural goods produced, and land use to be successful?

11.5 | Examine the Challenges of Feeding Everyone.

Currently, enough food is produced worldwide to feed Earth's population, but in the face of inadequate distribution systems and widespread poverty, food security looms as a significant issue for the twenty-first century.

The United Nations (UN) World Food Program defines **hunger** as living on less than the daily recommended 2100 calories the average person needs to live a healthy life. While news stories focus on starving populations in the wake of wars and natural disasters, acute emergencies account for less than 8 percent of the global hungry. Chronic undernourishment is a much greater problem, impeding childhood development, weakening immune systems, and undermining the social fabric of communities. Globally, 11 percent of the population, or around 815 million people, went hungry in 2016, according to the UN Food and Agricultural Organization. Undernourishment is a key factor in the deaths of 45 percent of children worldwide who do not live to age 5.

In response to widespread undernourishment and famine, in 1985 the U.S. Agency for International Development created the Famine Early Warning System, which collaborates with other organizations worldwide to monitor food stores and predict food insecurity. Many governments and nongovernmental organizations provide food aid to populations in need. The UN World Food Program is the largest source of food aid in the world. It delivers food that is tailored to meet nutritional needs based on the population in a certain location. A typical food basket includes a staple food such as wheat flour or rice; a protein (often lentils or other legumes); vegetable oil; sugar; and salt.

Despite these initiatives, the battle against hunger and undernourishment is far from won. The World Food Program identifies several causes of hunger globally:

- Poverty trap: People who cannot afford food become weaker, which makes it more difficult to find or keep a job, creating a cycle of poverty and hunger.
- Lack of investment in agriculture infrastructure: Countries that lack infrastructure to keep produce cold at the point of harvest until it can be shipped globally by cold chain, and countries that lack infrastructure such as roads to move food are at a disadvantage in production and consumption.

- Climate and weather: Natural disasters have longer-lasting impacts in peripheral countries. Climate change is creating extended droughts, exacerbating threats from new pests, and altering growing conditions for traditional crops.
- War and displacement: Conflict disrupts agriculture. Refugees and internally displaced peoples from farming areas no longer live on their farms and cannot produce crops.
- Unstable markets: Fluctuating and unpredictable food prices make it difficult to access healthy foods consistently.
- Food wastage: About one-third of all food produced globally is never consumed.

These six factors help explain why people go hungry in a world with enough food for everyone.

Finding your way out of food insecurity and undernourishment is not easy. Undernourished people rarely have the **agency**, the capacity to make independent choices and act intentionally to affect change, to combat the poverty and the political and social issues at the root of undernutrition and famine. In their landmark work on **vulnerability**, geographers Michael Watts and Hans Bohl found three interrelated causes of food insecurity:

1. Declining control over local food resources
2. Lack of political power
3. Political-economic structures

Farmers in vulnerable agricultural areas, like South Asia and sub-Saharan Africa, have less say over local food production and hand over decision making to agribusiness, including seed and fertilizer suppliers. Politically, farmers have little agency if their governments are corrupt or the political system has institutional inefficiencies. Governments that actively create policies to disempower or disadvantage certain groups as a means of control set the stage for food insecurity and famine.

According to the World Health Organization, **malnutrition** has several forms, including "undernutrition (wasting, stunting, underweight), inadequate vitamins or minerals, overweight, obesity, and resulting diet-related noncommunicable diseases." Worldwide, 462 million adults are underweight and 224 million children under age 5 are underweight. Of the children under age 5 who are underweight, 17 million are severely wasted, 52 million are wasted, and 155 million are stunted. Also worldwide, 1.9 billion adults and 41 million children are overweight or obese.

Conversion of Farmland to Nonfarm Use

As the world population increases and the footprints of cities continue to grow, developers are converting fertile, productive farmlands to housing, retail, offices, and infrastructure (**Fig. 11.44**). In the 1800s and early 1900s, cities near productive farmlands often grew because farmers could supply food to the residents (see discussion of von Thünen). Rapid suburban growth after World War II and urban sprawl since the 1980s have converted farmland to urban development. A recent report by American Farmland Trust found that "over 70 percent of urban development and about 54 percent of low-density residential development occurred on agricultural land" between 1992 and 2012. The authors of the study mapped lands by their PVR value (productivity, versatility, and resiliency), and found that land with high PVR value was more likely to be developed (**Fig. 11.45**). In that time period, 11 million acres of productive farmland in the United States, a size equivalent to 47 percent of the state of Indiana, were converted to nonagricultural use.

The conversion of farmlands into housing developments is not confined to areas close to major cities that could become suburbs. Expendable wealth and the desire to have a place to "get away from it all" have led highly productive commercial agricultural areas to be converted into regions for second homes. On the Delmarva (Delaware, Maryland, Virginia) Peninsula in the United States, for example, where poultry production is concentrated, the price of land rose as city-dwellers from Pennsylvania, Washington, D.C., Maryland, and New York bought land on the Eastern Shore to build second homes. Once the new residents settled on the peninsula, they demanded higher environmental standards. But rising land prices and stricter environmental standards impact the cost of chicken production. As the urban population continues to grow and expendable wealth increases, more agricultural lands will be converted to second homes, especially on coastlines or idyllic country landscapes.

Conversion of productive farmland to urban, suburban, and rural residential, retail, and office use and infrastructure is not confined to the United States. The European Environmental Administration reported that when agricultural lands have been converted to artificial surfaces, it is often for housing.

Even though productivity on remaining agricultural land has risen because of technology, irrigation, pesticides, fertilizers, and engineered seeds, the loss of productive farmland will have a ripple effect on land use, especially forests. Because of the combination of pressure on agricultural land and climate change, more forestlands are being converted to agricultural lands. The results of this trend are not ideal. Cutting and burning forestland both removes a carbon dioxide sink and releases large quantities of carbon dioxide into the atmosphere. Moreover, because soils in forests are different from soils in productive farmlands, planting in newly converted forestlands may require more pesticides, fertilizers, and irrigation, which create additional strains on the global water supply.

Aerial Archives/Alamy Stock Photo

FIGURE 11.44 **Davis, California.** As suburbs spread from urban areas into productive farmlands, the number of borders between farming and residential zones multiplies.

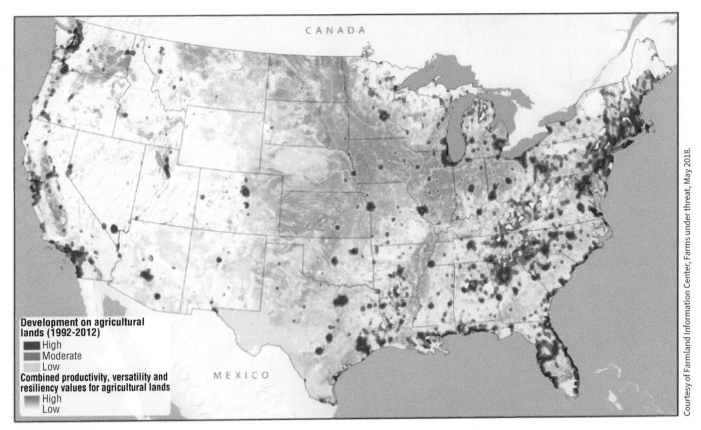

Development on agricultural
lands (1992-2012)
◼ High
◼ Moderate
◻ Low
Combined productivity, versatility and
resiliency values for agricultural lands
◼ High
◻ Low

Courtesy of Farmland Information Center, Farms under threat, May 2018.

FIGURE 11.45 **Farms Under Threat: Conversion of Agricultural Land to Urban and Low-Density Residential Development.** This map from American Farmland Trust, whose charge is to preserve farmland, highlights where development on agricultural lands in the contiguous United States took place over two decades. Urban areas are shown in gray on the map (look at Atlanta and Minneapolis to see the gray centers of cities) and are often encircled by high rates of development on agricultural land.

Food Security

The National Research Council identifies four major issues that affect food security worldwide:

1. varying abilities to balance production and consumption across regions and countries,

2. accelerating conversions of agricultural land to urban uses,

3. increasingly energy-intensive food production methods in a world of shrinking fossil fuel resources, and

4. expanding use of food crops for biofuel production.

The first issue highlights the fact that where agricultural goods are produced does not overlap with where goods are consumed. The second and fourth issues both point to how we use agricultural lands. Converting farmland to suburbs and using productive farmland to grow crops like soybeans that are destined for biofuels reduces the amount of productive land that is available for growing food for people and feed for livestock.

The third issue points to the fluctuating price factors that producers weigh. Each price factor impacts farmers' bottom line and their ability to maintain their operation, whether they are using hydrocarbons (fossil fuels) to run implements and irrigation systems; buying farm insurance; taking out loans for operations, equipment, or land; taking out a bridge loan to stay afloat; selecting an expensive drought-resistant seed or a less-expensive seed; selecting and applying fertilizers and pesticides; or buying or renting land.

Food Deserts

Malnourishment in the form of obesity or undernourishment can be linked to living in a **food desert**, a small region or area with limited access to fresh, nutrient-rich foods. Urban food deserts are typically found in low-income neighborhoods where medium-size and large grocery stores are largely absent. The only grocery stores within easy reach are convenience stores offering processed, energy-dense but nutrient-poor food. Rural food deserts can cover large expanses. Rural areas often lack local grocery stores or public transportation to major towns with stores. A White House Task Force on Childhood Obesity, led by former First Lady Michelle Obama reported that 23.5 million Americans live in food deserts, including 6.5 million children.

Consumers in urban food deserts are more likely to purchase unhealthy foods like chips, sugary cereals, and snack cakes, because they are cheaper than fresh fruits and vegetables. The USDA created a Food Access Research Atlas at the scale of the United States that is accessible online. You can zoom into certain cities or states and map food deserts in rural and urban areas. The atlas maps the distance to a grocery store at different increments, creating zones of 0.5 and 1.0 miles for urban areas and zones of 10 or 20 miles for rural areas. It also maps low-income Census tracts, and Census tracts where more than 100 households do not have a vehicle. Food deserts in both rural and urban areas overlap frequently with race, because disadvantaged minorities often have lower incomes. A comparison of **Figure 11.46A** with **Figure 11.46B** shows that the Census tracts of Birmingham, Alabama, where most people are African American, are also the Census tracts classified as food deserts.

Walgreens, a major drugstore chain in the United States, recognized in 2011 that 45 percent of its stores are "located in areas that don't have access to fresh food." So Walgreens committed to turning at least 1000 of its stores into **food** oasis stores, locations where fresh fruits and vegetables, whole grains, and lean, fresh meats are available at affordable prices. Walgreens opened its first store in Chicago and has its headquarters in a Chicago suburb. Building on this history, Walgreens opened its first 10 food oasis stores in food deserts in Chicago. The most recent reports show that Walgreens is falling far behind its goal of opening 1000 food oasis stores. While Walgreens has a larger percentage of grocery sales in the U.S. than Trader Joes or Natural Abundance, most groceries sold at Walgreens are packaged foods and not fresh foods.

Geographers Akihiko Michimi and Michael Wimberly found that rural food deserts lack not only larger grocery stores, but also public transportation to reach larger grocery stores (**Fig. 11.47**). In their study of food deserts and access to fruits and vegetables, the geographers found that since the 1980s, in rural areas of the United States a "restructuring of food retail industries has occurred such that local grocery stores that once served small rural communities have been closed" and replaced with larger national chains in regional trade centers. The geographers found one major difference

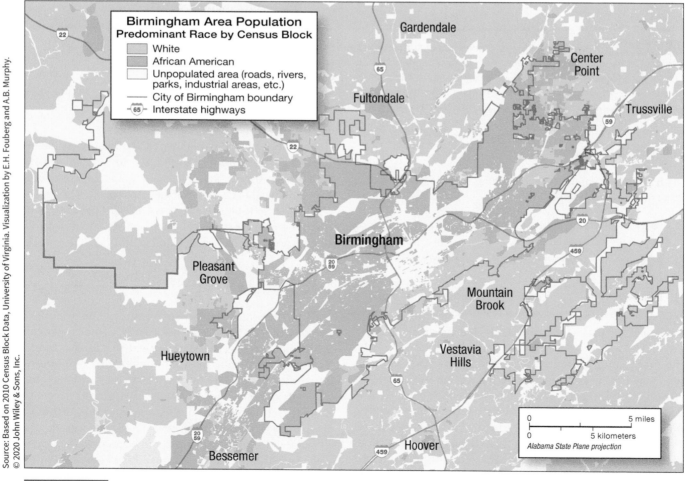

Source: Based on 2010 Census Block Data, University of Virginia. Visualization by E.H. Fouberg and A.B. Murphy. © 2020 John Wiley & Sons, Inc.

FIGURE 11.46A **Birmingham, Alabama.** Predominantly African American and predominantly white neighborhoods are separated from each other in and around Birmingham.

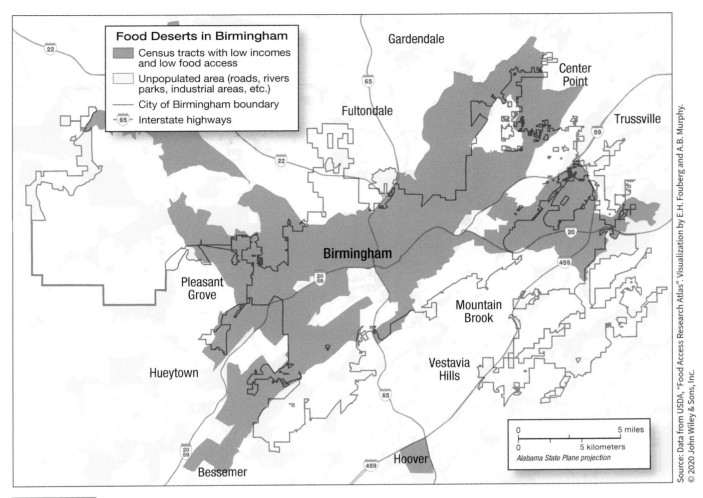

FIGURE 11.46B   Birmingham, Alabama.   Food deserts are mapped in blue and designated by census tracts that have low incomes and low access to food. Compare 11.46A and 11.46B to see how race correlates with food deserts in Birmingham.

between food deserts in urban and rural areas. In urban food deserts, obesity rates increased and the rate of fruit and vegetable consumption decreased with increasing distance from grocery stores. Rural areas did not have similar correlations between distance and obesity rates and fruit and vegetable consumption. Rural residents may have access to fresh fruits and vegetables in their personal or neighbors' gardens. This diet combines with manual labor in support of the agricultural economy to keep obesity rates lower than expected in rural food deserts.

Urban Agriculture

Globally, billions of people cultivate small plots of land in and around their homes for self-consumption or informal trade. While not captured by formal agricultural statistics or maps, food grown this way plays a vital role in the lives of billions of people. Even city-dwellers in many parts of the world are involved in **urban agriculture**. By cultivating land or raising livestock in small plots near their homes, in rooftop gardens, or in community gardens on converted brownfields or abandoned residential areas, urban farmers are increasing agricultural production in food deserts (**Fig. 11.48**).

Sustainability of Agriculture

Commercial agriculture produces significant environmental changes. For example, the growing demand for protein-rich foods and more efficient technologies is leading to overfishing in many regions of the world, and in many places, fish stocks are declining at an alarming rate. From midcentury to the late 1980s, the fish harvest from oceans and seas increased fivefold, and there seemed to be no limit to it. Countries quarreled over fishing rights, poorer countries leased fishing grounds to richer ones, and fleets of trawlers plied the oceans. International attempts to regulate fishing industries failed. Then in the

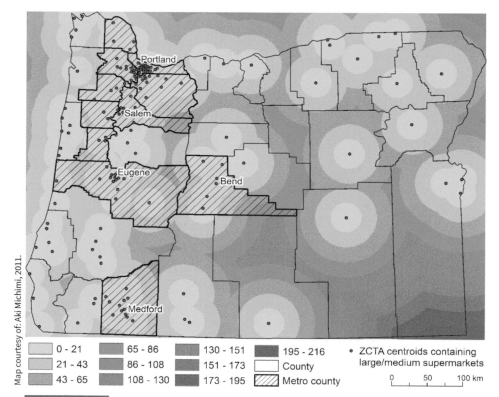

Map courtesy of: Aki Michimi, 2011.

0 - 21		65 - 86		130 - 151		195 - 216	• ZCTA centroids containing large/medium supermarkets
21 - 43		86 - 108		151 - 173		County	
43 - 65		108 - 130		173 - 195		Metro county	0 50 100 km

FIGURE 11.47 **Food Deserts in Oregon.** Mean distance (km) from population-weighted ZIP Code Tabulation Area (ZCTA) centroids containing large or medium supermarkets in Oregon. The yellow circles around centroids are areas within 13 miles (21 km) of a supermarket and have higher access to food.

Alison Hancock/Shutterstock.com

FIGURE 11.48 **Toronto, Canada.** Urban agriculture takes place on rooftops like this one, in brownfields that used to be industrial zones, or on lots where homes have been abandoned and torn down. Urban agriculture can also be indoor and vertical in densely populated cities (see Fig. 11.36).

1970s and 1980s, overfishing began destroying fish stocks. The cod fisheries on Canada's Grand Banks off Newfoundland collapsed. In 1975, biologists estimated the Atlantic bluefin tuna population at 250,000; today the western stock is listed as critically endangered, and the stock in the Mediterranean is listed as endangered. From ocean perch and king crabs off Alaska to rock lobsters and roughies off New Zealand, fish and shellfish populations are depleted. The total annual catch is also declining and may already be beyond the point of recovery. Much of the damage has already been done, and fishing industries in many parts of the world have reported dwindling harvests and missing species.

On land as well, the industrialization and commercialization of agriculture have accelerated the pace and extent of agriculture's impact on the environment. If you travel to Mediterranean Europe today, you will see a landscape that reflects the clearing of forests in ancient times to facilitate agriculture and trade, as well as evidence of terraces cut into the hills many centuries ago. In recent times, more land has been cleared, and the land that is under cultivation is ever more intensively used.

Significant agriculturally driven changes to the environment go far beyond the simple clearing of land. They range from soil erosion to changes in the organic content of soils to the presence of chemicals in soils and groundwater (herbicides, pesticides, and even antibiotics and growth hormones from livestock feces). In places where large commercial crop farms dominate, the greatest concerns often center on the introduction of chemical fertilizers and pesticides into the environment—as well as soil erosion. And, as we have seen, the movement toward genetically modified crops carries with it another set of environmental concerns.

The growth of organic farming and the move toward the use of local foods in some communities can benefit the environment. Yet such initiatives have had only modest impacts on the majority of the world's peoples and places. A telling sign is that the organic movement has had little effect on the production of the staple foods on which billions of people depend. Moreover, large corporate entities are playing an increasingly prominent role in the organic movement—raising concerns about standards and rendering illusory the ideal of an independent organic farmer engaged in "sustainable" agriculture. Smaller farmers argue that they are priced out of the market by subsidies favoring large farms and by the failure of most agribusinesses to incorporate the environmental and health costs of large-scale, intensive farming into their production costs.

The environmental impacts of large-scale intensive agriculture can be particularly severe when agriculture moves into marginal environments, as has happened with the expansion of livestock herding into arid or semiarid areas (see the map of world climates, Fig. 11.28). The natural vegetation in these areas cannot always sustain the herds, especially during prolonged droughts. As a result, ecological degradation and, in some areas, desertification are the result.

In recent decades, the popularity of fast food chains that serve hamburgers has led to the deforestation of wooded areas in order to open additional pastures for beef cattle, notably in Central and South America. But livestock ranching is an extremely land-, water-, and energy-intensive process. Significant land must be turned over to the cultivation of cattle feed, and the animals themselves need extensive grazing areas. In addition, by stripping away vegetation, the animals can promote the erosion of riverbanks, with implications for everything from water quality to wildlife habitat.

Agricultural production has changed drastically since the First Agricultural Revolution. Today, agricultural products, even perishable ones, are shipped around the world. Agriculture has industrialized, and large-scale agribusiness has replaced small family farms to produce most of our food. A major commonality between ancient agriculture and modern agriculture remains: the need to change. Trial and error were the norms of early plant and animal domestication; those same processes are at play in the biotechnology-driven agriculture of the contemporary era.

TC Thinking Geographically

Spend some time clicking around your city or home town on the USDA Food Access Research Atlas at https://www.ers.usda.gov/data-products/food-access-research-atlas.aspx. Aside from income, hypothesize what other factors overlap with the locations of food deserts in your area. Imagine how the **cultural landscapes** of food deserts looks different than areas where fresh foods are readily available. Look for maps or news articles about food deserts in your area to confirm your hypothesis.

Summary

11.1 Compare and Contrast the Three Agricultural Revolutions.

1. Before the First Agricultural Revolution, people hunted, gathered, and fished for food. The First Agricultural Revolution began around 10,000 years ago in the Fertile Crescent. Whether the first farmers successfully domesticated plants in a time of scarcity or a time of luxury is debated. Plant domestication occurred in multiple hearths, including Southeast Asia, the Indus River Civilization, and Central America. Animal domestication also began in the Fertile Crescent around the same time as plant domestication.

2. The Second Agricultural Revolution, like the Industrial Revolution, was a series of innovations that happened in different places over the eighteenth to twentieth centuries to mechanize agriculture and improve yields. Rather than sow seeds by casting them over the ground and seeing which ones took root, farmers began planting crops in rows using seed drills, improving plowing techniques, creating better breeding systems for livestock, experimenting with new seed hybrids, and expanding irrigation.

3. The Third Agricultural Revolution is better known as the Green Revolution, and it took place in the twentieth century. The hearth of the Green Revolution was the United States, where agricultural scientists set the goal of reducing hunger and ending famine. In the 1940s, agricultural researcher Norman Borlaug bred a strain of disease-resistant dwarf wheat that thrived in Mexico. By 1960, Mexico was independently producing enough wheat to no longer import it. The Green Revolution diffused to India in the 1960s and continues to expand today.

11.2   Describe the Spatial Patterns of Agriculture.

1. A cadastral system is a method of surveying land. Several land survey systems are found in the United States. The major ones include metes and bounds, township and range, and longlot. Metes and bounds is an early survey system in which objects in the environment, such as trees and fence posts are used to define a plot of land. Township and range is an orderly, checkerboard system in which land is surveyed into 1 mile by 1 mile sections. The long-lot system was developed in France and is designed to give multiple farmers access to important waterways and roads.

2. The goods farmers produce vary based on the distance between field and market, the amount of labor required for production, the value of the good, and the perishability of the product. von Thünen studied the spatial pattern of agricultural production around cities and towns and found that distance was the most important factor. Each town is surrounded by a set of concentric rings in which specific agricultural goods are grown.

3. Half of the world's people still reside in villages and rural areas. Geographers classify agricultural villages based on how they are laid out. The five types of agricultural villages are cluster, linear, round, grid, and walled.

11.3   Explain the Map of Global Agricultural Production.

1. On the global map of climates, many climate regions extend west to east because the amount of sunlight places receive depends on their latitude. The world map of agriculture and the global climate map correlate in many cases. Drier climates are likely to be areas of livestock raising. Moister climates are likely to be areas of grain production.

2. Several types of commercial agriculture are practiced. Plantation agriculture is a form of commercial agriculture that is typically left over from colonialism. The colonizers practiced monoculture; they consolidated and took ownership of land and then used enslaved Africans to produce a single crop, such as coffee, bananas, sugar, or cocoa.

3. Subsistence agriculture is different from commercial agriculture because landholdings are generally smaller and production is not monoculture. Subsistence farmers produce a variety of agricultural goods, from fruit trees to grains to market produce. They produce enough for self-consumption and to sell in local markets.

11.4   Analyze How Commercial Agriculture Operates.

1. The drive toward economic efficiency has meant that between 1910 and 2017, the number of farms in the United States has fallen and then tapered off while the amount of land in agriculture has stayed relatively consistent. The result is that the average size of farms (acres in production) in the United States is rising.

2. The bid rent theory says that what farmers produce depends on the cost of the land used for production. Intensive farming includes applying fertilizers, insecticides, and high-cost inputs to achieve the highest yields possible. It often occurs closer to the city, where land values are high. Extensive agricultural practices use less labor and capital and larger areas of land to cultivate what has traditionally been a lower yield. Applying bid rent theory, extensive agriculture takes place farther from the city center, where land values are low relative to labor and capital.

3. The proliferation of GMOs in the United States has resulted in two opposing movements: one moving toward non-GMO alternatives and the other leading to expansion of GMO production. Organic agriculture is a response to demand from consumers for non-GMO agricultural products. The amount of land dedicated to organic agriculture is growing globally. At the same time, increasing demand for ethanol and biodiesel has led to the expansion of GMO corn and soybean production.

11.5   Examine the Challenges of Feeding Everyone.

1. As the world population is growing and cities and towns are expanding, productive agricultural land near cities and towns is under greater pressure. Even though productivity on remaining agricultural land has risen through use of technology, irrigation, pesticides, fertilizers, and engineered seeds, the loss of productive farmland will have a ripple effect on land use, especially forests. Because of the combination of pressure on agricultural land and climate change, more forestlands are being converted to agricultural lands.

2. Malnourishment in the form of obesity or undernourishment can be linked to living in a food desert, a small region or area with limited access to fresh, nutrient-rich foods. Urban food deserts are typically found in low-income neighborhoods where medium-size and large grocery stores are largely absent and the only grocery stores within easy reach are convenience stores offering processed, energy-dense but nutrient-poor food. Rural food deserts can cover a large expanse and lack local grocery stores and public transportation to major towns with stores.

Self-Test

11.1 Compare and contrast the three agricultural revolutions.

1. The agricultural hearth where both plants and animals were first successfully domesticated was:
   a. the Indus Civilization.
   b. Southeast Asia.
   c. the Fertile Crescent.
   d. Central America.
   e. East Asia

2. The U.S. government destabilized the traditional subsistence agriculture practice by Native American tribes by changing land from:
   a. communal ownership to individual ownership.
   b. individual ownership to communal ownership.
   c. hunting to farming.
   d. farming to hunting.
   e. pastoral nomadism to agriculture.

3. The Columbian Exchange moved goods, people, and ideas across the Atlantic Ocean through trade. All of the following are impacts of the Columbian Exchange except:
   a. Crops well suited for certain climates, soils, and topographies took root in new locations.
   b. European diseases brought to the Americas infected and killed millions of indigenous people.
   c. Enslaved Africans were forcibly migrated from Africa to the Americas to labor on plantations.
   d. Genetically engineered wheat from Mexico diffused to Africa.
   e. all of the above are correct.

4. The hearth of the Green Revolution was _____, which is also the country that has the highest rates of genetically modified organisms (GMOs) in the food supply today.
   a. the United Kingdom
   b. France
   c. China
   d. Russia
   e. the United States

11.2 Describe the spatial patterns of agriculture.

5. Which of the following pairs of land survey systems and locations is incorrect?
   a. township and range and Great Plains
   b. metes and bounds and east coast
   c. progressive cadastral and California
   d. longlot and Louisiana
   e. township and range and Northeastern United States

6. In the von Thünen model of agricultural land use, the biggest factor in what agricultural goods are produced where is:
   a. time.
   b. connectivity.
   c. distance.
   d. diffusion.
   e. climate.

7. An agricultural village where houses are grouped together in tiny clusters or hamlets is classified as:
   a. cluster.
   b. linear.
   c. round.
   d. grid.
   e. zone.

8. In a place that was surveyed using the township-and-range system, agricultural villages are most likely to be:
   a. cluster.
   b. linear.
   c. round.
   d. grid.
   e. sparse.

11.3 Explain the map of global agricultural production.

9. Agricultural products transported in controlled temperatures from field to grocery store are transported using what system?
   a. cold chain
   b. commodity chain
   c. barge
   d. just-in-time
   e. bulk weight

10. On the world climate map, several climate regions extend west to east because ____ varies by _____.
    a. cloud cover/latitude
    b. cloud cover/longitude
    c. sunlight/latitude
    d. sunlight/longitude
    e. weather/longitude

11. When comparing the world climate map and the world agricultural map, all of the following are connections you can see except:
    a. drier climates and livestock ranching.
    b. moister climates and grain production.
    c. polar climates and commercial dairy farming.
    d. tropical climates and subsistence agriculture.
    e. all of the above are identifiable.

11.4 Analyze how commercial agriculture operates.

12. The value of agricultural products in India is higher than in the United States. India also uses more:

- **a.** GMOs.
- **b.** labor.
- **c.** refrigeration.
- **d.** von Thünen methods.
- **e.** intensive agriculture.

13. In the United States, most ethanol is made from ___ and most biodiesel is made from ____.

- **a.** switchgrass/sugar
- **b.** sugar/switchgrass
- **c.** beets/soybeans
- **d.** soybeans/corn
- **e.** corn/soybeans

14. Growing demand for organic agricultural products in the United States is in part a response to the expansion of:

- **a.** government subsidies.
- **b.** GMOs.
- **c.** school lunch programs.
- **d.** fair trade.
- **e.** consumer awareness.

11.5 Examine the challenges of feeding everyone.

15. With climate change, more forests may be converted to agricultural land because:

- **a.** cities are expanding into productive agricultural land.
- **b.** deforestation is a common way to combat climate change.
- **c.** forest soils are nutrient rich and can sustain agriculture well.
- **d.** groundwater supplies are abundant under forests.
- **e.** desertification is affecting existing agricultural lands.

16. Malnourishment in food deserts is common because consumers lack access to:

- **a.** snack foods.
- **b.** milk and eggs.
- **c.** fresh produce.
- **d.** fortified grains.
- **e.** organic products.

17. Walgreens is trying to combat food deserts by building:

- **a.** food oases.
- **b.** food rivers.
- **c.** food pantries.
- **d.** food cupboards.
- **e.** food shacks.

CHAPTER 12

Industry and Services

FIGURE 12.1 **Regensburg, Germany.** Robots work on the chassis of Bayerische Motoren Werke AG (BMW) automobiles.

Entering the main part of the BMW automobile plant near Regensburg, Germany, I felt like I was stepping onto the set of a science fiction movie. I saw rows of giant orange-colored machines making jerky motions as they assembled the parts of engines that would be placed into car bodies (**Fig. 12.1**). A few people walked the factory floor, but not many—and they were not working on the cars themselves; instead, they were maintaining the machines and making sure everything ran smoothly.

Decades ago, an automobile plant such as this would have employed thousands of workers—many engaged in low-skill tasks. Now, the workforce at most plants of this sort is dramatically smaller, and much of the work is highly skilled, requiring advanced training in electrical engineering, computer programming, and the like. What I was witnessing was one example of a massive economic transformation of the last few decades, one that raises fundamental questions about the changing nature of manufacturing and the future of work.

There is no simple answer to such questions because what is happening in the manufacturing and employment sectors differs greatly from place to place. A few months earlier, I had visited a garment factory in Pacific Asia where I saw people cutting cloth by hand and sewing it with traditional sewing machines (see Fig. 12.15). The contrasts with the German automobile plant show why any attempt to make sense of the evolving character of the industrial and service sectors must take geographical circumstances into account.

In this chapter, we begin by looking at the origin and diffusion of industrial production. Next, we explore how industrialization has changed in recent decades. We examine concepts including flexible production and the global division of labor. Then, we consider how the expanding service economy is altering employment and shaping economic geography.

CHAPTER OUTLINE

12.1 Describe the hearth and diffusion of the Industrial Revolution.

- The Industrial Revolution
- Diffusion of the Industrial Revolution to Mainland Europe
- Diffusion of the Industrial Revolution Beyond Europe

12.2 Examine how and why the geography of industrial production has changed.

- Fordist Production
- Classical Location Theory
- The Impact of Transportation Innovations
- Flexible Production and Product Life Cycle
- The Globalization of Production

- Multinational Corporations, Outsourcing, and Global Production Networks

12.3 Explain global patterns of industrial production.

- The Regulatory Environment
- The Energy Picture
- The Growing Role of Skilled Labor
- Contemporary Centers of Industrial Activity
- Do Places Still Matter?

12.4 Determine how deindustrialization and the rise of service industries have changed the economic geography of trade.

- Geographical Dimensions of the Service Economy
- New Patterns of Economic Activity
- Place Vulnerabilities in a Service Economy

12.1 | Describe the Hearth and Diffusion of the Industrial Revolution.

Manufacturing began long before the Industrial Revolution. In **cottage industries**, families in a community worked together out of their homes, each creating a component of a finished good or making the good itself. For example, in a small town in England, a few families would receive a shipment of wool from a merchant and then prepare the wool and pass it on to families who would spin the wool into yarn. Those families then passed the yarn to weavers who made blankets and other wool products. Typically, this work was done over the winter, after harvest and before planting the next year's crop. In the spring before planting, the merchants returned to pick up the finished products and pay for the production. Merchants then shipped the goods around the world.

In the 1700s, as global trade grew and faster ships came into use, iron, gold, silver, and brass goods produced in cottage industries in India were in demand wherever they could be bought. India's textiles, made on individual spinning wheels and hand looms, were considered the best in the world. They were so finely made that British textile makers rioted in 1721, demanding legislative protection against imports from India. China and Japan also possessed substantial cottage industries long before the Industrial Revolution.

The transition from cottage industries to the Industrial Revolution happened as Europeans sought to generate greater profit by producing larger quantities of the goods in high demand. They looked for ways to take advantage of **economies of scale**—increasing the quantity of goods produced to decrease the average cost of production for each item.

European manufacturing operations, from the textile makers of Flanders and Britain to the iron smelters of Thüringen, grew during the 1700s. However, Europe's products could not match the price or quality of those in other parts of the world. European companies worked to gain control of overseas industries. For example, the Dutch and British East India Companies targeted local industries in Indonesia and India, respectively, in the 1700s and 1800s.

Both the Dutch and British companies were privately owned and operated companies. Each company recruited and established battalions of soldiers to help them take control of production in Southeast and South Asia. Their presence created political chaos, which they took advantage of by pitting local factions against one another. British merchants exported tons of raw fiber from India to expand textile industries in northern England, including Liverpool and Manchester.

The Industrial Revolution

The wealth brought into the Netherlands and England through trade (**Fig. 12.2**) funded technological innovations in manufacturing that enabled European factories to produce more products at lower prices. The resulting **Industrial Revolution** gave rise to the mass production of goods using machines, not just human labor. Europe flooded global markets with inexpensive products, burying cottage industries at home and abroad. Colonies were no longer merely sites of valuable cottage production; they became providers of essential raw materials and generators of revenue that fueled rapid industrial expansion in Europe.

The first steps in industrialization occurred in the mid-1700s in northern England, where cotton from America and India was shipped to the port of Liverpool. Textile factories in the British Midlands, south of Manchester, took advantage of rivers flowing downhill from the Pennines (a range of mountains and hills in north-central England) to power cotton spinning machines.

Wealth brought to Europe through trade funded improvements such as the spinning jenny and the steam engine. James Watt improved the steam engine by creating a separate chamber to house the steam and by perfecting the pistons that are driven by steam pressure. The invention did not happen overnight. A series of attempts over a few decades finally worked when Watt partnered with toymaker and metalworker Matthew Boulton, who inherited great wealth from his wife (her father had amassed wealth as a global cloth trader). Boulton paid for the final trials and errors that made the Boulton & Watt steam engine work. Coal powered the steam engine, which came to be used in water pumps, trains, looms, and eventually ships.

A pre-Industrial Revolution in iron working enabled iron to be used in many inventions of the Industrial Revolution. In Coalbrookdale, England, in 1709, ironworker Abraham Darby found a way to *smelt* iron. He found that by burning coal in a vacuum-like environment, he could remove impurities, leaving behind coke, the high-carbon portion of coal that burns at a high temperature. Darby put iron ore and coke in a blast furnace and then pushed air into the furnace. Smelting iron ore with coke made it possible for ironworkers to melt the ore and pour it into molds (instead of shaping it by hammering against anvils). The use of molds allowed inventors to make the same product over and over again, thus increasing production. As the **toponym** indicates, the residents of Ironbridge, a town near Coalbrookdale, still take pride in their town's bridge, the first to be constructed entirely from cast iron in 1779 (**Fig. 12.3**).

During the early Industrial Revolution, before the railroad connected industrial sites and reduced the transportation costs of coal, manufacturing had to be located close to coal fields. In Britain, densely populated and heavily urbanized industrial regions developed near coal fields (**Fig. 12.4**). The two largest centers of British industry were an ironworking region in the Midlands, where Birmingham is located, and a textile production region in the Northwest, where Liverpool and Manchester developed as important cities.

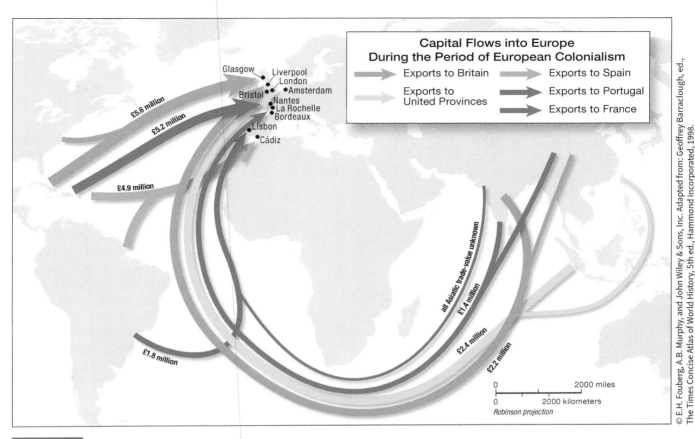

© E.H. Fouberg, A.B. Murphy, and John Wiley & Sons, Inc. Adapted from: Geoffrey Barraclough, ed., The Times Concise Atlas of World History, 5th ed., Hammond Incorporated, 1998.

FIGURE 12.2   **Capital Flows into Europe During the Period of European Colonialism.**   This map shows the major flows of capital into Europe from Europe's colonies. The capital helped fuel Europe's Industrial Revolution at the end of the 1700s and into the 1800s.

Manufacturing plants also needed to be connected to ports, where raw materials could arrive and finished products could depart. In the first decades of the Industrial Revolution, manufacturers used boats and barges traveling down canals and rivers to move raw materials to industrial zones and finished products to ports.

The steam engine helped concentrate even more industrial production in the British Midlands and Northwest. Industrialists used the steam engine to pump water out of coal mines, making it possible for coal workers to reach deeper coal seams. In the textile industry, the steam engine powered spinning wheels that spun over 100 spools of thread at a time and powered dozens of looms in a factory all at once. Steam engines also fueled the newest modes of transportation: locomotives on railroads and steamships on the oceans.

The first commercial railway connected Manchester, a center of textile manufacturing, along 35 miles of track to the port of Liverpool in 1830. Sited where the River Mersey flows into the Irish Sea, Liverpool faced west—toward the Atlantic Ocean and British colonies in North America. Cotton and tobacco from the colonies arrived in Liverpool and was transported by rail or canal to factories in Manchester. Coal from Leeds, northeast of Manchester, was transported to Manchester to fuel steam engines. The coal, cotton, and textile factories were located close to each other, helping the area become the hearth of textile manufacturing in the Industrial Revolution.

The rail network expanded as thousands of miles of iron and then steel track were laid. Railroads made it possible to move larger quantities of products faster over land. The steam engine also made its mark on ocean transportation. The first

John Robertson/Alamy Stock Photo

FIGURE 12.3   **Ironbridge, England.**   The world's first bridge made entirely of cast iron was constructed in the late eighteenth century near Coalbrookdale, England, reflecting the resources, technology, and available skills in this area at the time.

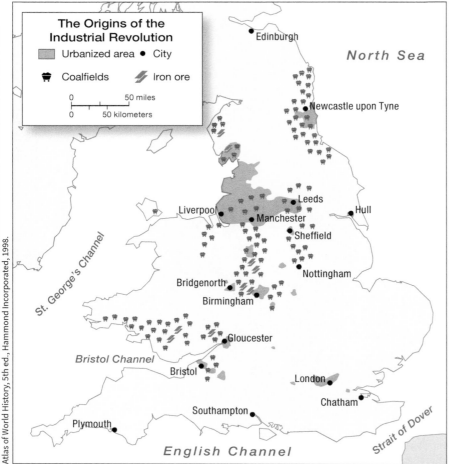

FIGURE 12.4 **The Hearth of the Industrial Revolution.** The areas of Great Britain that industrialized earliest were those closest to the resources needed for industrialization: coal, iron ore, and capital. Large areas of urbanization grew near industrial zones and in the port cities where materials came in and from which industrialized products went out.

Diffusion of the Industrial Revolution to Mainland Europe

In the early 1800s, the innovations of Britain's Industrial Revolution diffused into mainland Europe. Once there, the same set of locational criteria for industrial zones applied. Sites needed to be close to resources and connected to ports by water. Coal and iron ore were heavy, and transportation of both resources was costly. The first manufacturing belts in continental Europe were therefore located close to coal fields. They were also connected by water to a port so that raw materials could be imported from the Americas and Asia and finished products could be exported.

A belt of major coal fields extends from west to east through mainland Europe, across northern France and southern Belgium, the Netherlands, the German Rühr Valley, western Bohemia in Czechia, and Silesia in Poland. Colonial empires gave access to the necessary capital and raw materials to fuel industrialization, benefiting France, Britain, Belgium, the Netherlands, and eventually Germany. Iron ore is found along a similar belt. The map outlining the diffusion of the Industrial Revolution into Europe shows that industrial production was concentrated along the coal and iron ore belt through the middle of mainland Europe (**Fig. 12.6**).

steam-powered ship crossed the Atlantic Ocean in 1819, shrinking the time it took sailing ships to travel across seas. Soon after, shipbuilders designed larger steamships that could transport more goods (**Fig. 12.5**).

With the development of the railroad and steamship, Great Britain expanded its economic advantages over the rest of the world. British investors and business leaders held a near-monopoly over many products. The British perfected coal smelting, cast iron, the steam engine, and the steam locomotive. The systems Britain set during the Industrial Revolution became institutionalized and helped entrench British economic power. For example, the railroad pioneer George Stephenson, who led the building of the railway between Manchester and Liverpool, set the standard gauge (the distance between the two railroad tracks) that is still used for 60 percent of the world's railroads today. The Industrial Revolution increased Britain's global influence. The British capitalized on their manufacturing monopolies, resources in their colonies, and wealth generated through colonialism and trade to become the world's dominant economic and political power in both the eighteenth and nineteenth centuries.

When industries developed in one area, economic growth had a spillover effect on the port cities to which they were linked by river, canal, or rail. One of the largest industrial centers in continental Europe was the Rühr area of present-day Germany (Germany did not become a single country until the 1870s). The Rühr is connected to the port of Rotterdam, the Netherlands, by the Rhine River. Each port has a **hinterland**, or an area from which goods can be produced, delivered to the port, and then exported. A port also serves its hinterland by importing the raw materials that are delivered to manufacturing sites for production. In other words, Rotterdam is the port, and its hinterland includes the region along the Rhine, including the Rühr in Germany.

Rotterdam grew to be the most important port in Europe. Over the last 200 years, the Dutch have radically altered the port, expanding it from the mouth of the Rhine delta west to the coast of the North Sea. As production and transportation innovations took hold, Rotterdam built new facilities to accommodate them. For example, in the 1950s, Rotterdam Municipal Port Management recognized the growth in the use of oil and built the Europoort. They extended pipelines to the port and dug a deep canal to enable oil imports. Rotterdam became the distributor for oil throughout the port's hinterland.

In the 1980s, Rotterdam saw an opportunity to connect the port with the interior of continental Europe by railroad. It extended the port further west and built the Betuweroute rail line, which connects Rotterdam with Emmerich, Germany. Rotterdam is both the starting and end point for goods along the corridor. It continues to expand to meet the changing **situation** of the global economy. In the process, it has solidified its position as one of the most important hubs of global commerce.

Once railroads were well established in Great Britain and continental Europe, companies could locate manufacturing plants away from coal and iron ore and in (or close to) major cities such as London and Paris. Cities could import raw materials, produce goods drawing from their large labor supply, and sell the goods to the many consumers living in cities. Until the railway expanded throughout Great Britain, industrialization was slow to reach London because it lacked easy access to coal and iron ore. But when the railroad arrived, London became a particularly attractive site for industry. Its port location on the Thames River was an advantage. More importantly, it was the nerve center of the British Empire. By choosing a **site** in London, a manufacturing company could put itself at the heart of Britain's global **network** of influence.

Paris was already continental Europe's greatest city, but like London, it did not have coal or iron deposits in its immediate vicinity. However, when a railroad system was added to the existing network of road and waterway connections to Paris, the city became the largest local market for manufactured products for hundreds of miles around and attracted major industries. The city had long been a center for the manufacture of luxury items, including jewelry, perfumes, and fashions, and it now experienced substantial growth in metallurgy and chemical manufacturing. Paris had a ready labor force, the presence of governmental agencies, a nearby ocean port (Le Havre), and France's largest domestic market.

London and Paris became, and remain, important industrial centers because of their commercial and political connections with the rest of the world (**Fig. 12.7**). Germany still ranks among the world's leading producers of both coal and

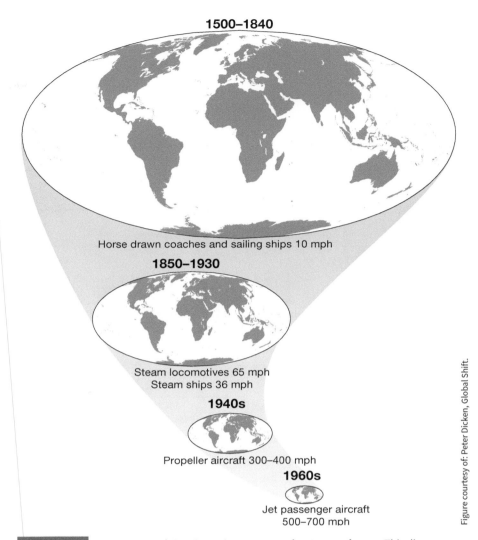

1500–1840

Horse drawn coaches and sailing ships 10 mph

1850–1930

Steam locomotives 65 mph
Steam ships 36 mph

1940s

Propeller aircraft 300–400 mph

1960s

Jet passenger aircraft
500–700 mph

Figure courtesy of: Peter Dicken, Global Shift.

FIGURE 12.5 **The World Shrinks Through Transportation Innovations.** This diagram helpfully illuminates how much more quickly goods and people could move over land and sea after 1960 compared to 1850. The maps are slightly misleading, though, because new transportation technologies do not connect every single place on Earth. Places close to airports and seaports are more connected to each other than places away from transportation nodes. Time–space compression tells us the world is shrinking, but unevenly, as some places are closer and some are as far or farther away than they have ever been.

steel, and remains Europe's most important industrial power. By the early twentieth century, industry began to diffuse far from the original European hearth to northern Italy (now one of Europe's major industrial regions), Catalonia (anchored by Barcelona) and northern Spain, southern Sweden, and southern Finland.

Diffusion of the Industrial Revolution Beyond Europe

Western Europe's early industrialization gave it an enormous economic head start, known as a **first mover advantage**. The region was positioned at the center of a quickly growing

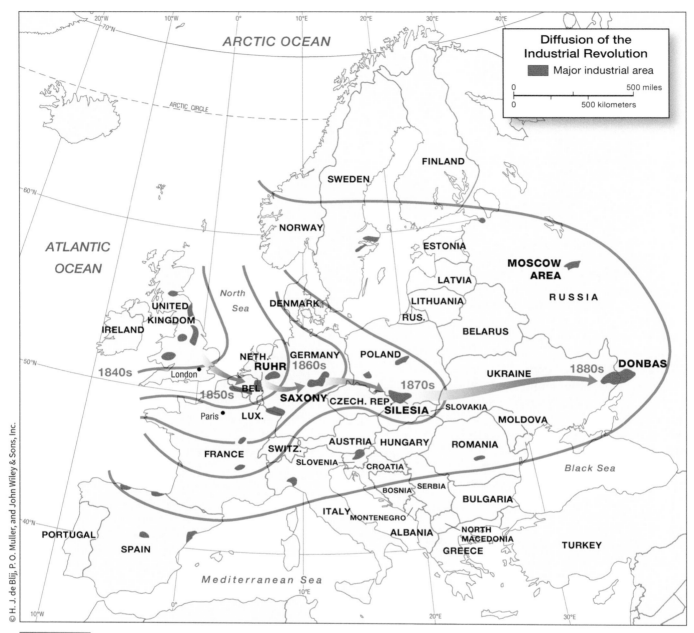

FIGURE 12.6 **Diffusion of the Industrial Revolution.** The eastward diffusion of the Industrial Revolution occurred during the second half of the nineteenth century.

world economy in the nineteenth century, when industrialization began to diffuse from Europe to the Americas and Asia. **Secondary hearths** of industrialization developed in eastern North America, western Russia and Ukraine, and East Asia. The primary industrial regions established by the 1950s were close to coal, the major energy source, and were connected by water or railroad to ports (**Fig. 12.8**). These regions were targets of heavy investment, bringing prosperity to the regions and great wealth to the investors.

North America By the beginning of the twentieth century, there was only one serious rival to Europe. It was a territory settled predominantly by Europeans and with particularly

close links to Britain, which provided links to the capital and innovations that fueled industrialization there: North America. Manufacturing in North America began in New England during the colonial period. Although the northeastern states were not especially rich in mineral resources, American companies could acquire needed raw materials from overseas sources.

Industries developed along the Great Lakes, where goods could be moved in and out of industrial centers by canals, rivers, and lakes. A ready supply of coal fueled industrialization, and there was never any threat of a coal shortage. U.S. coal reserves are among the world's largest and are widely distributed, from Appalachian Pennsylvania to the northwestern Great Plains (**Fig. 12.9**).

Author Field Note   Viewing Industrial History in Paris, France

"When the Eiffel Tower was built in 1887, it served as a symbol of the Industrial Age. Viewing it against the backdrop of the sprawling metropolitan area of Paris (photo taken from the top of the only skyscraper in Paris proper, Montparnasse) reminds me that the Paris basin is the industrial as well as agricultural heart of France. The city and region are served by the Seine River, along which lies a string of ports from Le Havre at the mouth to Rouen at the fall line. A district of high-rise buildings has sprung up just outside Paris proper (behind the Eiffel Tower in this photo), and nearby lies a major industrial complex including power plants, petrochemical plants, and oil installations."

– A. B. Murphy

Photo by A.B. Murphy. © 2020 John Wiley & Sons, Inc.

FIGURE 12.7   **Paris, France.**

Russia and Ukraine   The St. Petersburg region is one of Russia's oldest manufacturing centers. Tsar Peter the Great planned and built the city to serve both as Russia's capital and as the country's industrial core. He encouraged western European artisans with skills and specializations to migrate to the region and imported high-quality machine-building equipment to help fuel industrialization. St. Petersburg developed manufacturing based on shipbuilding, chemical production, food processing, and textile making.

After World War I, the newly formed Soviet Union annexed Ukraine and took control of its agricultural lands, rich resources, and industrial potential, especially the coal-rich

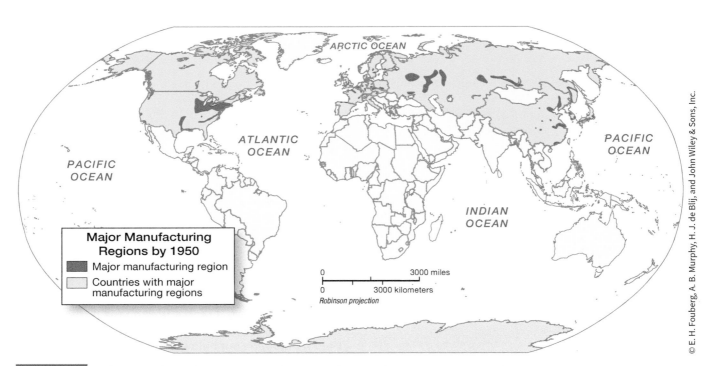

Major Manufacturing Regions by 1950
- Major manufacturing region
- Countries with major manufacturing regions

0   3000 miles
0   3000 kilometers
Robinson projection

© E. H. Fouberg, A. B. Murphy, H. J. de Blij, and John Wiley & Sons, Inc.

FIGURE 12.8   **Major Industrial Regions of the World in 1950.**   This map shows the major industrial districts of Europe, North America, Russia, and East Asia in approximately 1950.

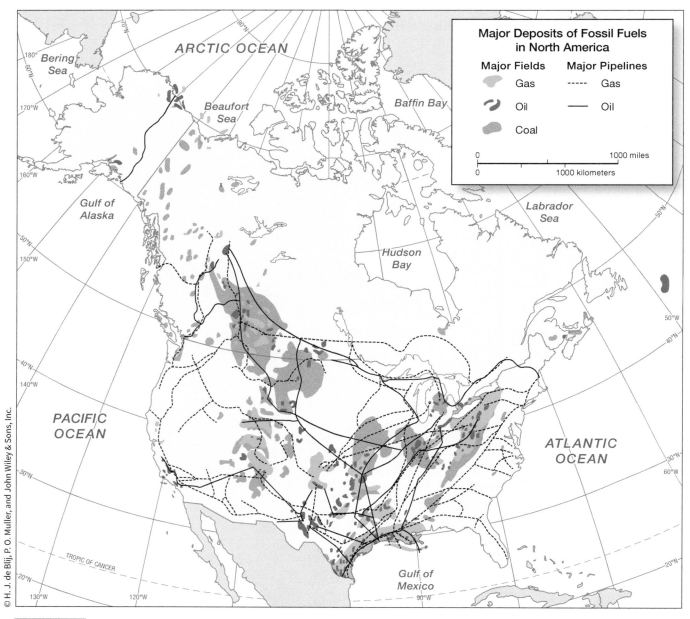

© H. J. de Blij, P. O. Muller, and John Wiley & Sons, Inc.

FIGURE 12.9 **Major Deposits of Fossil Fuels in North America.** North America is one of the world's largest energy consumers, and the continent is also endowed with substantial energy sources.

Donbas region. The Soviet Union was resource rich, as is Russia today. Soviet leaders tapped into resources in Ukraine and also directed an economic plan to industrialize areas closer to Moscow to develop a large industrial belt. They developed industries in Nizhni Novgorod, a river port located at the confluence of the Volga and Oka rivers, 270 miles southeast of Moscow. Following the Volga River, goods can be imported or exported from Nizhni Novgorod to the Black Sea or the Caspian Sea.

East Asia
During the 1700s and much of the 1800s, Japan's government chose to be economically isolated from most of the world economy. Japan opened its economy

through a change in government policy in 1868. Soon after, the Industrial Revolution diffused to Japan. Japan encouraged young men to study sciences in universities abroad so they could take their knowledge back to Japan and create industries. With limited natural resources, Japan depended on raw materials imported from other parts of the world for manufacturing.

Early Japanese industrialization focused heavily on the military sector. In the late 1800s and early 1900s, Japan used its modernized military to colonize Korea, Taiwan, and portions of mainland China. These places provided resources for Japan's further industrialization and imperial expansion. Japan's dominant region of industrialization and urbanization is the Kanto Plain (see Fig. 12.8), which contains about one-third of the nation's population and includes the Tokyo–Yokohama–Kawasaki metropolitan area. Japan's second largest industrial complex extends from the eastern end of the Seto Inland Sea to the Nagoya area and includes the Kobe–Kyoto–Osaka triangle.

TC Thinking Geographically

Compare and contrast the **site** and **situation** of industrial production early on in the Industrial Revolution and today. Consider the chapter opener about the BMW plant in Germany. What resources does a manufacturing company now need to produce goods, and how does the situation of the current world economy influence the sites companies choose for manufacturing?

12.2 Explain How and Why the Geography of Industrial Production Has Changed.

So far, globalization has helped us understand many human geographic developments, including local and popular cultures, identities, language loss, colonialism, political disputes, and of development. We turn now to globalization's impact on the geography of manufacturing and service industries since World War II.

Globalization includes the processes that are increasing interactions, deepening relationships, and heightening interdependence across country borders. It is also the outcomes of these processes, which are unevenly distributed and look different from place to place. Globalization could not have happened without improvements in transportation and communication technologies. Improved sailing ships and navigation methods helped establish global trade routes and the first wave of colonialism. The invention of the steamship, the diffusion of railroads, and the diffusion of the telegraph and then the telephone quickened global trade and created the context for the second wave of colonialism. Major technological developments that expanded or were invented after World War II, including jet airplanes, container ships, telephones, and the Internet, furthered globalization.

Fordist Production

The manufacturing boom of the twentieth century began with early innovations in the production process. Perhaps the most significant was the mass-production assembly line pioneered by Henry Ford, which allowed the inexpensive production of consumer goods at a single site on a previously unknown scale. Ford's idea was so important that the dominant mode of mass production came to be known as **Fordist**.

Fordist production also gave rise to political-economic and financial arrangements that supported mass production by corporations. Global manufacturing operated under Bretton Woods financial order, a series of agreements made at a 1944 conference in Bretton Woods, New Hampshire. Countries who signed the Bretton Woods accords agreed to peg the value of their currency to the U.S. dollar, which was pegged to gold (the U.S. later stopped pegging its currency to gold in 1971). In the uncertainty after WWII, Bretton Woods created the stability in international exchange that was needed to encourage the mass production of goods on a global scale.

The 1900s were marked by a surge in both production and consumption. Workers found employment on assembly lines. Ford paid his workers a good wage, and droves of job seekers migrated to the Detroit area to work in the automobile industry. Ford's goal was to mass-produce goods at a price point where his workers could afford to purchase them.

Ford's River Rouge plant in Dearborn, Michigan (**Fig. 12.10**), used the **vertical integration** of production common during the Fordist period. Ford imported coal, rubber, and steel from

Everett Collection Inc/Alamy Stock Photo

FIGURE 12.10 Dearborn, Michigan.   The industrial complex of the Ford River Rouge plant as it stood in the 1940s. The corporation imported raw materials, bringing them by barge and rail to the plant. The complex included a power plant and facilities for producing steel and the component parts of automobiles. Nearly everything Ford needed to produce an automobile was brought together at the factory complex, where up to 100,000 employees (at its peak in the 1930s) manufactured components and assembled automobiles.

around the world and brought them to his River Rouge plant in Dearborn, just west of Detroit. The massive Ford River Rouge was an industrial complex of 93 buildings with over 120 miles of conveyor belts that covered an area 1 × 1.5 miles. The Henry Ford Foundation states that "Henry Ford's ultimate goal was to achieve total self-sufficiency by owning, operating and coordinating all the resources needed to produce complete automobiles." The Rouge complex included a power plant, boat docks, and a railroad. Up to 100,000 people worked there. It even included a fire station and a police department, prompting the Henry Ford Museum to describe it as "a city without residents."

Following the Fordist example, industries moved toward sites with available labor, resources, developed infrastructure, and proximity to consumers. Furniture manufacturing shifted from Boston in 1875 to Cincinnati by 1890 and then to Grand Rapids, Michigan, by 1910. It also took off in High Point, North Carolina, where entrepreneurs built manufacturing plants in the early 1900s to take advantage of the "abundance of lumber, low-cost labor combined with Reconstruction era wood-working skills and attitudes" (Walcott 2011). Furniture manufacturers were also drawn to High Point for the presence of infrastructure, proximity to customers, and a humid climate, which kept wood from cracking. High Point and other furniture centers agglomerated, or clustered together, to take advantage of nearby forests and available services and infrastructure.

AP® Exam Taker's Tip

The terms **Fordist** and **post-Fordist production** are all-important, and they are linked together in the **post-Fordist** system. The ability to apply a term or concept means you truly understand. List three applications and/or examples of each of these terms: **multiplier effects, economies of scale, agglomeration, just-in-time delivery,** and the **emergence of service sectors, high-technology industries,** and **growth poles.**

Classical Location Theory

The North Carolina furniture example illustrates some of the locational influences on industry. Efforts to develop generalizations about locational influences gave rise to classical **location theory**, often credited to British economist Alfred Marshall (1842–1924). Marshall argued that similar industries tend to cluster in an area. He called this process localization, and later theorists called it **agglomeration**. Marshall held that clustered industries could attract workers with industry-specific skills, share information, and attract support services specific to the industry.

Whereas Marshall explained *why* industries would cluster together, German economic geographer Alfred Weber (1868–1958) explained *where* industries would cluster. In *Theory of the Location of Industries* (1909), Weber examined the factors that pull industry to specific locations. His **least cost theory** focused on a factory owner's desire to minimize three

categories of costs. The first and most important (at the time) was transportation. Weber suggested that it is least expensive to bring raw materials to the point of production and to distribute finished products where transportation costs are lowest. The **friction of distance** is the increase in time and cost that comes with increased distance over which commodities must travel. If a heavy raw material is shipped thousands of miles to a factory, the friction of distance increases. Friction of distance long prompted manufacturers to locate their plants close to raw materials—particularly if needed raw materials, such as coal and iron ore, were heavy.

AP® Exam Taker's Tip

Understanding Weber's **least cost theory** can help you connect many geographic concepts together. If you understand the locational relationships between transportation, labor, and agglomeration (from **location theory**) in locating industry, you can apply terms like **friction of distance, distance decay, scale,** and many others. See Figure 12.11 to help you visualize this theory.

The second cost was labor. Higher labor costs tend to reduce the margin of profit, so a factory farther away from raw materials and markets can do better if cheap labor compensates for the added transport costs.

The third factor in Weber's model was similar to Marshall's theory of localization in that Weber described the advantages of agglomeration. When many companies that produce the same or similar goods cluster in one area, as with furniture manufacturing in North Carolina, they can share talents, services, and facilities. For example, all furniture companies need access to lumber, textiles, ports, and skilled employees. By clustering together in the High Point region, the furniture manufacturers can also share infrastructure improvements. Moreover, they all have access to the accountants and lawyers in the area who specialize in contracts and trade. In 2012, local governments in the High Point region invested in a system of wireless Internet access. Now the 75,000 furniture buyers who go to High Point twice a year can use the wireless system on their iPads and tablets as they seal deals. Finally, agglomeration can make a location more attractive by potentially overcoming higher transportation or labor costs.

Considering these three factors together—transportation, labor, and localization (agglomeration)—Weber determined that the least cost location for a manufacturing plant could be determined by a location triangle (**Fig. 12.11**). Economic geographer Jean-Paul Rodrigue (2014) explains that "solving Weber's location model often implies three stages; finding the least transport cost location, and adjusting this location to consider labor costs and agglomeration economies." Weber reasoned that industry will be located close to raw materials to lower transportation costs, but that labor availability (either skilled or cheap) and agglomeration of industry can "pull" industries toward sites where these other two factors are advantageous.

WEBER'S LOCATION TRIANGLE

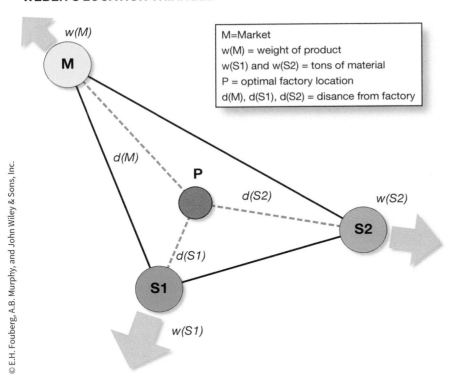

M=Market
w(M) = weight of product
w(S1) and w(S2) = tons of material
P = optimal factory location
d(M), d(S1), d(S2) = disance from factory

© E.H. Fouberg, A.B. Murphy, and John Wiley & Sons, Inc.

FIGURE 12.11   **Weber's Location Triangle.**   Weber assumed that the cost of transporting goods was the same in all directions and increased at an equal rate in all directions. He also assumed that water was available everywhere, but that labor was available only in certain population centers.

The Impact of Transportation Innovations

Weber's theory of location was written over a century ago, when the cost of transportation accounted for over 50 percent of the final price of a good traveling over significant distances. Hence, he emphasized transport costs as the most important variable in industrial location. But transportation now accounts for 5 percent or less of the cost of most goods. In an era of vastly improved infrastructure, relatively cheap oil, and container ships, widely dispersed production systems can be cost effective.

Efficient transportation systems enable manufacturers to buy raw materials from distant sources and distribute finished products to consumers in distant locations. Since World War II, major developments in transportation have improved **intermodal** connections, places where two or more modes of transportation meet (including air, road, rail, barge, and ship), in order to ease the flow of goods and reduce the costs of transportation. Manufacturers also look to develop alternative transportation options in the event of emergencies (e.g., truck routes when rail service is interrupted).

The high volume of resources and goods shipped around the globe over the past few decades could not have happened without the invention of the container system. Goods are now packed in standard-sized containers that are picked up by

special mechanized cranes at an intermodal connection and placed on ships. At the next destination, they are moved to semitrailer trucks, barges, or railroad cars (**Fig. 12.12**). The container system has lowered costs and increased flexibility, permitting many manufacturers to pay less attention to transportation costs in their location decisions. Refrigerated containers also ease the shipment of perishable goods around the globe (see Chapter 13).

The container ship has dramatically changed the economic geography of the world economy since the first one sailed in 1956. Before containers, a ship would arrive at port with various, odd-sized crates and boxes. Hundreds of longshoremen would flock to the dock to unload goods by hand. With containerization, ports now have relatively few employees, who operate high-tech cranes, moving standard-sized containers from ship to dock or dock to ship with precision. A massive container ship can be unloaded within 24 hours of reaching a port.

Nearly 90 percent of long-distance cargo is now shipped in containers. With a volume in excess of 2250 cubic feet (more than 65 m³), a standard container can accommodate goods worth millions of dollars. Steel containers are structurally sound and can be stacked and moved from truck to rail to ship without worrying about how fragile the contents of the containers are (Fig. 12.12).

The largest of today's container ships are enormous—more than four American football fields long and over 60 yards wide. Most container ships are designed to fit through the Suez Canal and the Panama Canal, the latter of which was widened in 2016 to accommodate all but the largest of the new container ships.

Containerization has even changed the map of major port cities. Ports have become intermodal hubs, and port authorities and managers are constantly expanding and improving their infrastructure and systems to attract more cargo. Ports do not solely attract cargo, as the cruise ship in the background of Figure 12.12 demonstrates.

Container ships have changed the layout and size of many ports. Ports such as San Francisco have declined because their piers are not well suited to loading and unloading containers. Others have boomed. Nearby Oakland has capitalized on a container-friendly port retrofit that made it one of the more important shipping centers along the west coast. The growth in global consumption of goods has helped small ports located near consumers, such as Busan, South Korea, to expand dramatically. And previously nonexistent ports such as Tanjun Pelepas, Malaysia, have emerged as significant port cities because containerization has made it economical to produce goods in Southeast Asia that are sold as far away as New York, London, and Buenos Aires.

Photo by A.B. Murphy. © 2020 John Wiley & Sons, Inc.

FIGURE 12.12 **Copenhagen, Denmark.** Cranes and container ships are found at every major port around the world. Unlike railroad gauges that are not standard globally, containers are a standard size. Container ships keep getting larger, though, and ports change their design and infrastructure to keep pace.

in different places around the globe and then brought together for assembly. The term **flexible production** is used because firms can pick and choose among many suppliers and production strategies all over the world. Then they can quickly shift where they manufacture or assemble their products in response to adjustments in production costs or consumer demand. These systems respond to consumers who want the newest, best, or greatest offering, and enable manufacturers to lower the cost of production by moving around the world.

Capitalism persists as an economic system not only because people consume, but also because producers create and respond to consumer demand. Companies adapt to changing consumer preferences. Through the process of **commodification**, goods that were not previously bought, sold, and traded gain a monetary value and are bought, sold, and traded on the market. A new good, such as a virtual assistant (e.g., Alexa or Echo), starts at a high price and becomes somewhat of a status symbol because of its high cost. The longer the virtual assistant is on the market and the greater the number of firms producing virtual assistants, the lower the price drops. To compete, companies eventually move the production of virtual assistants to lower the cost of production.

The production of a good changes over time. For example, the production of televisions moved through four stages: introduction, growth, maturity, and decline. Commercial production of television sets began after World War II. A variety of small and medium-sized firms in Europe, Asia, and North America were involved in production during this stage. Firms in the United States, including Zenith, were the dominant producers until the 1970s. The cost of manufacturing televisions was high in the introductory stage because the company had invested a great deal in developing the technology, but had not sold enough units to lower the cost.

During the 1970s and 1980s, television production hit the growth stage, when a dramatic shift occurred. A small number of large Asian producers—particularly in Japan—seized a much larger percentage of the market and a few European firms increased their position as well. The increased sales and profits during this stage encouraged companies to produce and sell large numbers of televisions.

During the 1970s, major firms moved the manufacture of components and the assembly of televisions out of their home countries. U.S. firms moved these functions to the maquiladoras of Mexico (discussed in Chapter 10) and the special economic zones of China (described in Chapter 9). Japanese firms moved component manufacturing and assembly to Taiwan, Singapore,

Belgian geographer Jacques Charlier has studied how containerization has increased trade in the Benelux (Belgium, the Netherlands, and Luxembourg) seaport system. He explains the locational advantage of Rotterdam is that it is no more than six hours by rail or truck from 85 percent of the population of western Europe. The container system and the growth in shipping at Rotterdam and other Benelux ports have combined to foster the development of other industries, helping to make the region, in Charlier's words, a "warehouse for Europe." The Netherlands is now home to more than 1800 U.S. firms, including call centers, distribution centers, and production centers, especially for food. Over 50 percent of all goods entering the European Union pass through Rotterdam or Amsterdam (also in the Netherlands).

Flexible Production and Product Life Cycle

Fordist production was based on both mass production and mass consumption. Money flowed through the world economy as consumers bought goods manufactured in large-scale complexes. As the global economy became more integrated and transportation costs decreased, the advantages of concentrating production in large-scale complexes declined. As a result, in the latter third of the twentieth century, many enterprises began moving toward a post-Fordist, flexible production model.

In the post-Fordist model, production processes are driven by customer demand, and the components of goods are made

Malaysia, and South Korea. The assembly stage was the most labor intensive, so television manufacturers tapped into the global labor market and located assembly plants not just in Mexico, China, and Southeast Asia, but also in India and Brazil.

In the maturity stage, a few manufacturers continued to make small changes to the product and invested in marketing to secure their market share. Manufacturing of televisions became more mechanized. More technology lowered wage costs, and companies moved production closer to consumers. By 1990, 10 large firms were responsible for 80 percent of the world's color television sets. Of those 10, eight were Japanese and two were European. Only one firm in the United States, Zenith, remained, and its share of the global market was relatively small.

In the decline stage, fewer consumers were demanding the product. In response, manufacturers began shifting to research and development of new goods or production of other, higher-demand goods. In the twenty-first century, electronics companies like Samsung and Panasonic have invested in research and development of high-definition and plasma televisions, and these high-end televisions are now produced in Japan—and more recently China and South Korea. These investments began a new product development cycle for high-definition electronics.

The Globalization of Production

The various innovations described above have led to an increasingly globalized landscape of production. Tracing the production of conventional television sets throughout the world over time helps us see how this happened and how it has given rise to a **global division of labor** (also called the new international division of labor), which refers to the late-twentieth-century tendency for production facilities to be concentrated in the global economic periphery and semiperiphery to take advantage of lower labor costs. Then research and development operations can continue to be located in the core. The global division of labor is still with us. However, the recent trend toward flexible production has meant that production can and does move to take advantage of infrastructure, skilled labor, and accessible markets as products and methods of assembly change.

Geographically, the term **time–space compression**, coined by geographer David Harvey, captures the dramatic changes taking place in the contemporary global economy. This is the idea that developments in communication and transportation technologies have accelerated the speed at which things happen so that the distance between places has become less significant (see Chapter 4). Harvey argues that modern capitalism has so accelerated the pace of life and the relationship between places that "the world seems to collapse inwards upon us." Fluctuations in the Tokyo stock market affect New York minutes later. Overnight, marketing campaigns can turn a product innovation into a fad around the world. Kiwis picked in New Zealand yesterday can be in the lunch boxes of children in Canada tomorrow. And decisions made in London

can make or break a fast-developing deal over a transport link between Kenya and Tanzania.

Time–space compression shapes the global division of labor. When the world was less interconnected, most goods were produced not just close to raw materials, but also close to consumers. Thus, the major industrial belt in the United States was in the Northeast, both because there was readily available coal and other raw materials and because most of the population was there. This has changed with **just-in-time delivery**. Rather than keeping a large inventory of components or products, companies keep just what they need for short-term production and new parts are shipped to them quickly when needed.

Advances in information technologies and shipping coupled with the global division of labor make it possible for companies to move production from one site to another. The movements are based on the "new place-based cost advantages." David Harvey has called this decision process a **spatial fix**. In choosing a production site, location is only one consideration. "Distance is neither determinate nor insignificant as a factor in production location decisions" today (Walcott 2011).

Major global economic players take advantage of low transportation costs, favorable governmental regulations, and expanding information technology to construct vast economic networks in which different parts of the production process are carried out in different places to benefit from the advantages of specific locations. Examples of companies that have created such networks include General Motors, Philips, Union Carbide, and Exxon.

One way to grow profits is to cut costs, and labor (wages, benefits, insurance) makes up a sizable proportion of production costs. Most multinational corporations have moved labor-intensive manufacturing to peripheral countries that have low cost labor, few regulations, and low tax rates. The manufacturing that remains in the core is usually highly mechanized. Technologically sophisticated manufacturing also tends to be sited in the core or semiperiphery because the expertise, infrastructure, and research and development are there.

Nike We can use Weber's location theory to consider the site for a factory producing lightweight consumer goods, including textiles and shoes, during the first half of the twentieth century. In the triangle of factors, the most important for lightweight consumer goods is a ready supply of low-cost labor. Being close to the raw materials is less of a concern because shipping low-weight components is relatively inexpensive. Agglomeration is also a draw, so producers of component parts locate nearby and serve more than one company.

In the shoe business, companies that made shoelaces used to locate close to shoe manufacturers. In the 1920s, towns near Boston, Massachusetts—great "shoe towns" such as Haverhill, Brockton, and Lynn—were home to factories specializing in both men's and women's shoes. About 300 shoe factories had sales offices "within a few blocks of each other in Boston" (Smith 1925), and in a leather district close to the city, tanneries prepared hides imported from around the world.

Economic geographer J. Russell Smith (1925) described the economic landscape of the shoe factory town of Lynn:

> Walking the streets of Lynn one realizes what concentration an industry can have; the signs upon the places of business read—heels, welts, insoles, uppers, eyelets, thread, etc., etc. It is an astonishing proof of the degree to which even a simple commodity like a shoe, so long made by one man, can be subdivided and become the work of scores of industries and thousands of people.

Shoe salespeople periodically went to shoe company headquarters in Boston to learn about the company's newest offerings. Then they would fill their suitcases with samples to show their clients as they made the rounds of their sales territories.

With flexible production systems and container ships, lightweight consumer goods still need to be located close to low-cost labor, but connectedness to an intermodal port is vital as well. Not surprisingly, the production of shoes is no longer concentrated in a handful of shoe towns on the east coast. Nike demonstrates how selecting manufacturing sites for components and products has changed with just-in-time production and the globalization of production.

The transformation from making shoes in a few shoe towns to having them pass through an elaborate global network of international manufacturing and sales did not happen overnight. University of Oregon track coach Bill Bowerman and one of his former runners, Phil Knight, founded Nike in 1961. Knight designed a trademark waffle sole that would create more traction for runners, and Nike sold $8000 in footwear in its first year. The company established headquarters in Beaverton, Oregon, a suburb of Portland.

Nike began production in the 1960s by contracting with an Asian firm to manufacture its shoes. In 1974, Nike set up its first domestic shoe manufacturing plant in the small town of Exeter, New Hampshire, just 46 miles from Lynn, Massachusetts. By the end of that year, Nike's workforce was still modest in number. Nike employees in Oregon concentrated on running the company and expanding sales, while employees who worked directly for Nike in New Hampshire and Asia produced shoes.

Nike grew to become the world's leading manufacturer of athletic shoes, with global sales of over $36 billion in fiscal year 2018 and a worldwide labor force of over 70,000 people in 44 countries (**Fig. 12.13**). As its sales skyrocketed, Nike established new manufacturing plants in Asia and beyond. Although several thousand people work today for Nike in Beaverton, not a single individual in Oregon is directly involved in putting a shoe together. Employees at Nike headquarters are designers, planners, financial administrators, marketing and sales specialists, information technology directors, computer technicians, lawyers, and support personnel. They work to orchestrate the production and sale of Nike products through

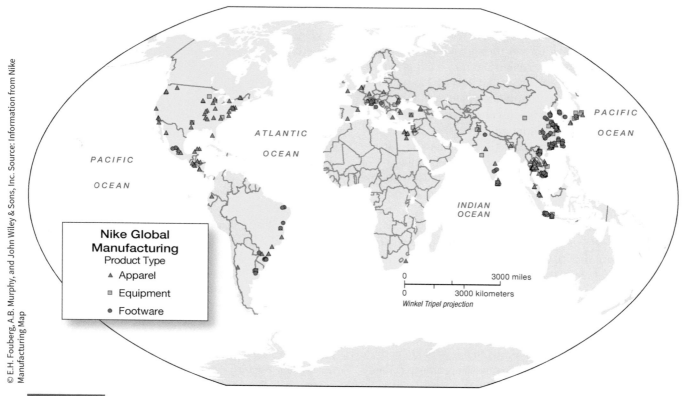

FIGURE 12.13 **Nike Production Facilities and Contract Factories.** Nike uses flexible production to manufacture shoes and apparel in hundreds of contract factories around the world. It plans short- and long-range contracts with factories, constantly assessing the best possible places to manufacture shoes, apparel, and equipment.

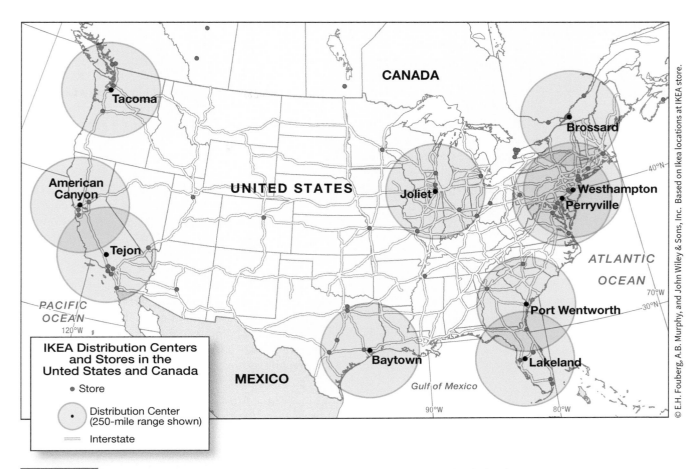

IKEA Distribution Centers and Stores in the Unted States and Canada

- Store
- Distribution Center (250-mile range shown)
- Interstate

FIGURE 12.14 **Ikea Distribution Center and Store Map.**   Ikea recently opened the Lakeland, Florida distribution center, designed specifically to deliver Internet orders in Florida and the southeastern states.

a **network** in which each **node**, or connection point, makes some contribution. Then it, in turn, is influenced by the niche it occupies in the network. Nike's Beaverton employees do this from a place that bears little resemblance to what one might have found in a town housing an important shoe company in the early twentieth century.

Ikea

The largest producer, distributor, and seller of furniture in the world today is based in Sweden. Ingvar Kamprad founded the company in 1943 at the age of 17. Kamprad, a born entrepreneur, first sold matches from door to door in his neighborhood in Sweden. He expanded his offerings to pens, Christmas decorations, and greeting cards during his teenage years. Pens were one of the main offerings in Ikea when he founded the company in 1943. Kamprad first produced and sold furniture in 1948, using wood from Sweden's sizable forests. The company has expanded in product offerings and locations since, focusing on producing modern and classic furniture at an affordable price point.

Ikea has created its own **commodity chain**. It designs the furniture, but draws on nearly 1000 suppliers located in 50 countries (Krewson 2010). The company's volume of production and sales is so high that it chooses the sites for its distribution centers with an eye on where stores are and where store expansion will occur.

Ikea has ten distribution centers scattered around the United States (**Fig. 12.14**). Opening a distribution center in Savannah, Georgia (Port Wentworth), allowed it to reduce the transportation time and cost of distribution to its stores in Orlando, Tampa, and Atlanta. The Savannah distribution center also enabled Ikea to open more locations in Florida and elsewhere in the southeast. Growth in the demand for Ikea products in the southeast led to the company opening its most recent distribution center in Lakeland, Florida. Ikea's newest distribution centers are models of efficiency. Computerized robotic cranes move products into the distribution center and then pull goods out for distribution to stores. The crane is never empty-handed; the same crane that loads goods into the distribution center from a ship also finds and loads goods onto trucks and railroad cars for transport to stores.

Developing and controlling a large proportion of its commodity chain allows Ikea to operate at incredibly high volume with low prices, generating small profits for the company along each step in the commodity chain, but large profits overall. Ikea invests in distribution infrastructure to keep transportation costs as low as possible. The company has reorganized its distribution center structure so that low-flow products (products that do not turn over in stores quickly) are stored in central distribution centers, and high-flow products are stored closer to stores so they can quickly replenish supply.

The system is efficient, but there are environmental costs to building multiple facilities and transporting items across significant distances. Ikea is aware of these costs and so has embraced green technologies. For example, the company has moved aggressively to adopt renewable energy sources for the heating and cooling of its buildings. It has also worked with the United Nations High Commissioner on Refugees (UNHCR) to create new, more durable, housing units for refugees, including a solar panel that generates enough energy to power one light and a USB charging port. These environmental and social initiatives are examples of the ways some transnational corporations seek to demonstrate their responsibility to a sometimes-skeptical public.

Multinational Corporations, Outsourcing, and Global Production Networks

A large part of business decision making today focuses on outsourcing and global sourcing—on where to extend contracts to complete projects and where to have component parts produced and assembled. Economic geographers originally used the term **outsourcing** to describe a company in a core country moving production or services abroad (**Fig.12.15**). In the 1990s and into the twenty-first century, outsourcing implied taking work that would normally be done in the global economic core and moving it to the semiperiphery or periphery. Media coverage often focused on the outsourcing of manufacturing jobs to China and the outsourcing of call centers to India.

But *outsourcing* suggests a one-way movement of economic activities—from core to periphery—that is overly simplistic in today's globalized economy. Growing **connectivity** and the rise of major Chinese and Indian companies have deepened globalization. *Outsourcing* has thus become an umbrella term for the use of global production networks to manufacture goods and provide services globally.

Outsourcing has been driven in part by the growth of Indian companies that specialize in completing projects and fulfilling contracts by becoming experts in outsourcing themselves. Imagine that a global company, headquartered in the United States, produces and sells accounting software. A major regulatory change in the United States might require the company to reprogram the software to account for the

---

Author Field Note   Sewing Textiles in the Pearl River Delta, China

"Humen is one of the Pearl River Delta cities that has been transformed by outsourcing to China. The small textile factory I visited provided insights into the opportunities and challenges that are confronting China today. The 40 or so employees were mostly young, but there were a few older folks. They were making women's clothes for the French market. Most of them made the clothes from start to finish. Into each of the items of clothing was sewn a label with a fancy-sounding Italian name. The clothes were sold in Humen for the equivalent of $1.50–$2.50 each, but most of them were destined for France, where they would be sold for 20 times that amount.

The employees work under a contract that stipulates a nine-hour day and a base wage of about $275/month plus basic room and board. They can work more hours, however, and are

FIGURE 12.15 **Humen, China.**

Photo by A.B. Murphy. © 2020 John Wiley & Sons, Inc.

compensated based on how much they produce during the extra hours. Apparently, almost all employees choose to work extra hours—typically seven days a week, with breaks only on Sunday evenings and one day at the beginning of each month. If they work that hard, they can earn the equivalent of close to $500/month. The main workroom has decent lighting and ventilation. The manager told me there had been significant upward pressure on the wages of employees in the last few years, making it harder for him to earn much of a profit. He worried about factories relocating to lower-wage countries. In addition, he said that he was having an increasingly hard time recruiting employees. He also noted with some mixture of amusement and annoyance that the people who had made out the best in his part of the city were the former farmers, who either had received substantial compensation (in the form of apartments) for being displaced or were getting some share of rent for buildings constructed on the land they used to farm."

– A. B. Murphy

complexities of the new regulation. The company can hire an Indian company like Tata or Infosys or Wipro that specializes in what is called business process outsourcing (BPO). The ball is then in the Indian company's court. It has to produce a finished product by a contractually agreed-upon date to get paid, and it can do whatever it sees fit to get the job done. In many cases, the Indian company outsources the work itself, keeping tabs on and testing the product before delivering it to the company in the United States. BPO also happens when certain business functions (call centers, human resources, accounting, software engineering, and the like) are turned over to an Indian firm to manage.

As the BPO software example suggests, maximizing profits when producing goods is no longer as simple as moving from core to periphery to take advantage of lower labor costs. Indeed, China has capitalized on the desire of companies to produce goods globally by becoming the world leader in **global sourcing**. Say you are daydreaming and you think of a great new product, like sunglasses with windshield wipers on them. You no longer need to figure out where to make your product. You can mock up a prototype and take it to a global sourcing fair in Las Vegas, Mexico City, Johannesburg, or São Paulo, and meet with dozens of Chinese global sourcing firms. They will give you a bid on what it will cost to produce your awesome new product, and they will tell you when it can be done. You sign a contract, and you receive shipment of your product without ever having set foot in China.

The Chinese global sourcing firm you have signed up with likely has connections to manufacturers throughout Asia, Africa, and the Americas. Your windshield wiper sunglasses may be stickered "Made in Mexico" when you receive them. If your product flies off the shelf and you order another shipment, your Chinese global sourcing company may ship the next order with stickers saying "Made in China." The global sourcing firm is connected and nimble, so you do not have to be. It controls a larger part of the commodity chain and can generate more wealth for itself by making the lowest-cost production decisions.

BPO and global sourcing both fall under the umbrella of outsourcing. Both move a segment of the commodity chain to another country, and place full responsibility for that segment in the contracted company's hands. BPO typically involves tertiary, quaternary, and quinary economic activities (i.e., service activities). Global sourcing, by contrast, typically concerns the secondary, or manufacturing, sector of the economy. However, global sourcing also includes quite a bit of service work, because the Chinese sourcing company develops the relations with the manufacturers, uses its knowledge of trade regulations, and manages a large sector of the product's commodity chain.

Given the complex geographically dispersed networks that now are part of the creation of many goods and services, economic geographers increasingly argue that the commodity chain model is too simplistic. Instead, we should be thinking about **global production networks**—networks that encompass the wide variety of activities, arrangements, and transactions that are involved in the production, distribution, and consumption of goods and services. The concept draws attention to the wide variety of arrangements and relationships that knit together people and places and define the world economy today.

Made in America or Designed in America? ABC World News features a segment called "Made in America," In one season of episodes, journalists knocked on doors and challenged homeowners to look at every item in their home for the "made in" sticker. The news crew then helped families move all goods not "Made in America" onto the street so the family could get a sense of how much of what is in their home is manufactured in the United States and how much is manufactured elsewhere in the world. The ABC World News crew then, according to their website, "took on the challenge of trying to fill three rooms in a home entirely with 100 percent American-made products."

Would an iPhone or AirPods get to stay in the house redesigned by ABC World News? When you open a box with an Apple product, the typed words "designed by Apple in California" greet you. Analyzing the commodity chain of an iPhone shows the product is made in several countries, including Italy, Taiwan, Germany, Japan, South Korea, and the United States (**Fig. 12.16**). The iPhone is not made solely in the U.S., but few products, especially technology products, are produced solely within one country.

Does the fact that the entire iPhone is not produced in the U.S. mean the iPhone does not benefit the U.S. economy? The research and development that went into the iPhone and other innovative components took place in the United States, and great benefits flow to U.S.-based Apple, which employs many Americans and whose stockholders have benefited from the product. Apple also captures much of the financial benefit from the sale of iPhones around the world, and the invention of the iPhone has led to the development of related products and services, many of which are based in the United States and contribute to the country's economy.

When considering how American a "Made in America" product is, it is also important to think about the social and environment impacts of its creation and use. For any product or service that is tied to a global production network—and most higher-value products are—the impacts do not stay within individual countries. What happens during the production process gets most of the attention, but consumption matters as well.

Consumption, while an end point of a global production network, is the beginning of a product's afterlife—and the afterlife impacts of a product created and designed by an American firm can extend far beyond a country's boundaries. What happens when people discard their old iPhones? Corporations such as Apple work to reduce consumer waste by recycling iPhones and computers, and by offering discounts to consumers who recycle their old iPhones. Nonetheless, there is a growing problem with the electronic waste that comes

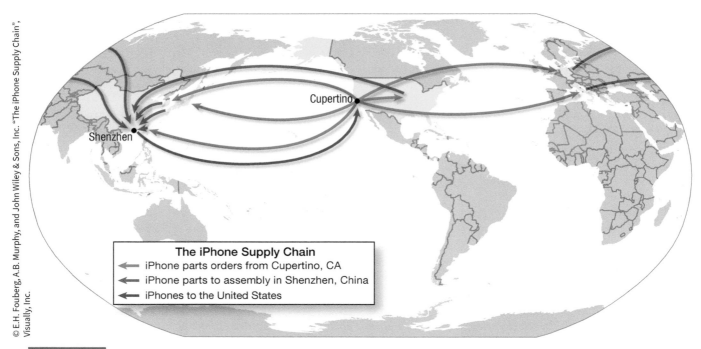

FIGURE 12.16 **Inside an iPhone.** The countries that produce the component parts of the iPhone are mapped along with the major companies involved in production.

from discarded iPhones and other computer products. Much of the waste ends up in hazardous dumps. In many global cities in the periphery, adults and children work with toxic materials to recover valuable copper wire and other components of computers and related electronic devices made by Apple and its competitors.

The jobs created by industry in one place can cause environmental damage and social effects in another. Consumption, or purchasing an item, is the end point in a global production network that affects places in different ways. Studying the geography of these networks sheds light on the origins and life cycles of products and helps explain how production and consumption affect places and peoples that are part of the network.

TC **Thinking Geographically**

Think about a cutting-edge, high-technology product that was recently commodified and is still quite expensive to purchase, and not yet broadly used (perhaps something you have read about, but not even seen). Using the Internet, determine where this product is manufactured and assess why the product is manufactured there. Hypothesize why this location is the **site** of production and how the **situation** for the product in the larger world economy has to change to shift production in the future. Think about how long it might take for production costs (and the price of the product) to decrease substantially if the location of production changes.

12.3 Explain Global Patterns of Industrial Production.

Industrial production encompasses a broad range of manufacturing activities, not just the steel mills and chemical plants that we tend to associate with the word *industry*. The world map of industrial production today (**Fig. 12.17**) is more complicated than its 1950s predecessor (Fig. 12.8). Some older centers of industrial production have declined or shifted to different kinds of production, and many new centers have sprung up. These changes are tied to the forces we have examined in this chapter: transportation innovations, the global division of labor, flexible production, and increasingly complex global production networks.

Outside of a narrow range of products that rely on heavy raw materials, Weber's location theory no longer works to explain the

spatial organization of industrial production. In an increasingly integrated network of global cities, industrial location is influenced not just by labor costs, transportation, and market access (as Weber suggested). Now it is also driven by the regulatory environment, the changing energy picture, and access to skilled labor.

The Regulatory Environment

Governments regularly enter into agreements with one another that affect production and imports. Over the past 70 years, production has also been affected by the proliferation of regional trade associations and related agreements, including the Association of Southeast Asian Nations (ASEAN), the United States-Mexico-Canada Agreement (USMCA), the European Union (EU), and many more. Regional trade agreements are similar to bilateral agreements between two countries, but they involve more than two countries. They can result in the movement of production within a region and can diminish (or remove) trade quotas and tariffs among member countries to promote trade.

Most state governments (164 as of 2019) are also members of the World Trade Organization (WTO), which develops rules of trade among the member states. The WTO generally seeks to promote freer trade by encouraging member states to sign agreements. It also works against import quota systems and discourages protection by a country of its domestically produced goods. It is, in short, an organization that promotes globalization and has advanced the diffusion of industrial production.

Agreements negotiated under the auspices of the WTO often come into force in stages in order to avoid major economic shocks. In 2001, when Europe and the United States agreed to allow China to become a member of the WTO, they also agreed to remove the quota system that restricts the import of Chinese goods into Europe and the United States. Soon after these quotas were eliminated, both the United States and the European Union issued "safeguard quotas" against certain Chinese imports to buffer the impact of Chinese goods on domestic producers.

The buffering helped for a while, but the rapid expansion of Chinese exports over the last two decades has been a source of tension. The United States and Europe argue that Chinese subsidies give their industries an unfair advantage and that China imposes unfair requirements on foreign companies doing business there. China rejects these claims. It argues that it has the right to control certain aspects of its economy, given that it is still a relative newcomer to the global economic game. Additionally, China claims that under any circumstances, its exports boost North American and European economies. The resulting tug-of-war is behind the prolonged negotiations and battles over tariffs that have plagued relations between China and Western countries—particularly the United States.

Regulations at the state and local scales also matter. Environmental regulations, safety requirements, minimum wage laws, and much more affect the cost of production. These make the cost of production higher—sometimes prompting companies to move to different locations with weaker regulatory requirements. That can boost the company's profit, but it can also have negative implications for both the place being abandoned and the new place of business. The former has to deal with job loss, whereas the latter may face environmental challenges and a job market dominated by businesses that offer limited benefits for locals.

Regulations at the state and local levels can also be used to attract businesses. Governments often seek to recruit manufacturers through incentives that include tax breaks, subsidies, and other forms of support. Export processing zones such as the maquiladoras, discussed in Chapter 10, provide a case in point. Many hundreds of such zones around the world are now shaping the global geography of industry.

The Energy Picture

Earlier in the chapter, we explained that at the start of the Industrial Revolution, manufacturing plants were established on or near coal fields. During the mid-twentieth century, the use of coal as an energy source in industry increasingly gave

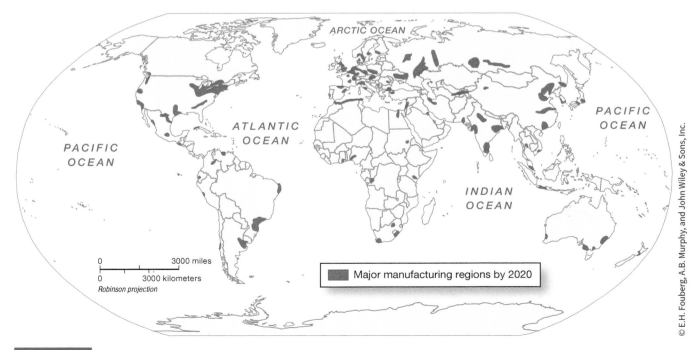

© E.H. Fouberg, A.B. Murphy, and John Wiley & Sons, Inc.

Major manufacturing regions by 2020

0   3000 miles
0   3000 kilometers
Robinson projection

FIGURE 12.17 **Major Concentrations of Industrial Production Today.** Manufacturing is global, and production networks make it possible for components of goods to be produced in many places.

way to oil and gas. Today, energy-intensive major industrial complexes are not confined to areas near oil fields. Instead, a huge system of pipelines and tankers delivers oil and natural gas to manufacturing regions throughout the world.

Even though energy supply has become a less significant factor in industrial location, having a secure energy supply is a priority for states—in part to ensure that the state's industrial potential is not threatened. This is certainly true in the United States. U.S. consumption of petroleum and natural gas today is about 20 percent of the annual world total. The United States requires around 20.5 million barrels of petroleum per day to keep its power plants, machinery, vehicles, aircraft, ships, buildings, and homes functioning. More so than many countries, the United States taps the oil that it has (**Fig. 12.18**).

Even with this level of production, the United States remains somewhat dependent on foreign oil supplies. Concerns over that state of affairs are behind the push for the United States to expand offshore oil drilling. Besides drilling for oil, the United States also undertakes large-scale fracking of oil and natural gas shale (the high-pressure injection of fluid into well bores to release petroleum and natural gas). Opposition to these activities has grown. Opponents of offshore drilling point to the risks of oil spills, as happened on a large scale in the Gulf of Mexico in 2010 (the BP oil spill). As for fracking, opponents argue that it causes air and water pollution and can trigger earthquakes. Nonetheless, contesting these projects is difficults given the combination of state interest in promoting

energy security and corporate interest in enhancing profits. Such projects can, however, be slowed when they are no longer very profitable due to declining oil and natural gas prices, as happened in the second half of the 2010s.

The expanding use of natural gas since World War II has also weakened the link between where energy resources are found and where industrial production takes place. That's because the development of natural gas has led to the construction of vast numbers of pipelines that carry natural gas across enormous distances. In the United States alone, 2.4 million miles (over 4 million km) of pipelines had been constructed by 2018, 2.1 million miles of which are dedicated to distributing natural gas.

The long-standing reliance on oil and gas in industrial production throughout much of the world has had a profound impact on countries with extensive oil and gas reserves: Saudi Arabia, Kuwait, Iraq, Russia, and others (**Table 12.1**). None of these countries except Russia is a major industrial power, but they all played a key role in the industrial boom of the twentieth century. While oil brought great wealth to some in these countries, it has also ensured that outside powers, including the United States and Great Britain, were anxious to ensure that they would not lose access to their energy resources. This set of circumstances put these countries in the geopolitical spotlight (Chapter 8). It also left them vulnerable to global fluctuations in the price of oil and gas—a continuing issue today. Looking forward, states dependent on oil and gas production are facing questions about what happens when the oil and

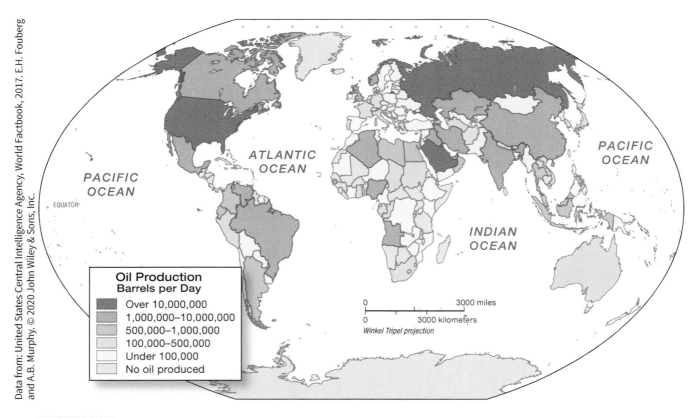

Data from: United States Central Intelligence Agency, World Factbook, 2017. E.H. Fouberg and A.B. Murphy. © 2020 John Wiley & Sons, Inc.

FIGURE 12.18 **Oil Production by Country, 2017.** Saudi Arabia, the United States, and Russia each produce more than 10 million barrels of oil per day.

TABLE 12.1 **World's Largest Oil Producers**

Top Oil Producers (Barrels per Day)			
1. United States	17,886,000	12. Nigeria	2,057,000
2. Saudi Arabia	12,419,000	13. Kazakhstan	1,959,000
3. Russia	11,401,000	14. Qatar	1,943,000
4. Canada	5,295,000	15. Norway	1,864,000
5. China	4,816,000	16. Angola	1,655,000
6. Iraq	4,616,000	17. Algeria	1,577,000
7. Iran	4,468,000	18. Venezuela	1,527,000
8. United Arab Emirates	3,791,000	19. United Kingdom	1,163,000
9. Brazil	3,428,000	20. Libya	1,074,000
10. Kuwait	2,870,000	21. India	1,012,000
11. Mexico	2,084,000	22. Oman	988,000

gas runs out, or when the growth in alternative energy sources weakens the oil and gas market.

New sources of energy have been developed over the past 70 years to supplement oil and gas, furthering the spatial decoupling of industrial production from natural resource reserves. The use of nuclear power expanded rapidly in the 1960s and 1970s, with many plants coming on line in widely dispersed locations. More recently, the combination of several high-profile accidents (e.g., Chernobyl, Three Mile Island, and Fukushima) and concerns over the disposal of nuclear waste have prompted some countries to turn away from nuclear power. Nonetheless, nuclear power still accounts for some 14 percent of global energy production (over 50 percent in some countries, with France leading the way at 75 percent). And the geographic dispersal of these plants makes it possible for manufacturing facilities to locate in a wide range of places.

The growing use of renewable alternative energy sources represents another recent energy-related development that has facilitated the spatial diffusion of manufacturing. Even earlier in the industrial era, hydropower was a renewable source of energy that allowed some industries to move away from coal-producing regions. For example, it takes enormous amounts of energy to turn copper into usable products, prompting manufacturers to locate their plants near electricity-producing dams that provided relatively cheap energy.

The newer story, though, is the growth in alternative energy. Plants producing solar and wind energy have sprung up far from the traditional places where coal is found—taking advantage of abundant sunshine in some places and steady winds in others. Although alternative energy still represents only a fraction of the total energy used in manufacturing, and will likely remain that way for many years, its contribution is growing (Chapter 13). Many believe that alternative energy technologies will serve as major catalysts of future economic growth. Europe and East Asia in particular are investing heavily in these technologies, and as they become more widespread, industrial locational flexibility will grow.

The Growing Role of Skilled Labor

Over the past half-century, mechanization has revolutionized the industrial production of many goods. Factories that once employed thousands of people now operate with only a few hundred employees who maintain the machines that do much of the work once done by human hands. Moreover, the complex global production networks that are part of the life cycle of many products demand a workforce that is more focused on business management than on mechanical tasks. And the increasingly complex regulatory environment surrounding industrial production in many places requires individuals who know how to navigate that environment.

These developments make it important for a growing number of industries to locate in places with access to skilled labor. To be sure, many industries still employ substantial numbers of people performing lower-skilled jobs. However, the balance between those jobs and the ones requiring more advanced computer, business, and human resource skills has shifted. The result is that places with substantial pools of high-skilled individuals can help attract certain types of manufacturing. Examples are capital cities and cities with universities and research institutes. That helps to explain why Figure 12.17 shows industrial agglomerations located close to major urban centers in a variety of world regions.

Contemporary Centers of Industrial Activity

As a result of various forces that have altered the nature of industrial production over the past half-century, many older manufacturing regions have experienced deindustrialization. Companies move industrial jobs to other regions, leaving the newly deindustrialized region to work through a period of high unemployment. If possible, these regions switch to a service economy (see the last major section of this chapter). Nonetheless, most of them still show up on the modern map of industrial production (Fig. 12.17), either because some older industries have held on or (more likely) because new types of manufacturing have sprung up. The newer manufacturing operations may be located a modest distance away from the older industrial concerns, but at the scale of a world map, those moves are not very visible.

Take the case of the central part of Germany—one of the most important centers of heavy industrial production in the early twentieth century. Much of the former industrial base is gone, and individual places suffered greatly. But not too far away (when viewed at the global scale), newer highly mechanized factories have sprung up, making a variety of sophisticated machines. As a result, the central part of Germany continues to show up on Figure 12.17 as a place of significant industrial production.

The same can be said of many other centers of industrial production that were already on the 1950 map (Fig. 12.8). The biggest change from that map is the emergence of a much more geographically dispersed pattern of industrial production. We have seen the basic ingredients that gave rise to that pattern: the declining cost of transportation, the draw of low-cost labor, flexible production, and changes associated with the regulatory environment, the changing energy picture, and the growing need for high-skilled labor.

The pattern also reflects developments that unfolded in particular world regions that have changed the world economy. In particular, East Asia has become an important new region of industrialization. The islands, countries, provinces, and cities fronting the Pacific Ocean have made the geographic term *Pacific Rim* synonymous with manufacturing.

The Rise of East Asia   Throughout most of the twentieth century, Japan was the only global economic power in East Asia, and its regional dominance seemed beyond doubt. Other nodes of manufacturing existed, but these were no threat, and certainly no match, for Japan's industrial might. In the 1960s and 1970s, the picture began to change with the rise of the so-called Four Tigers of East and Southeast Asia: South Korea, Taiwan, Hong Kong, and Singapore. The benefits were threefold: Labor-intensive industries shifted to areas with lower labor costs, government made efforts to protect developing industry, and governments invested in education and training. From these benefits, the tigers emerged as **newly industrializing countries (NICs)**.

South Korea developed significant manufacturing districts exporting products ranging from automobiles and grand pianos to calculators and computers. One of these districts is centered on the capital, Seoul. The city can boast some 10 million inhabitants in the city proper and over 25 million in the metropolitan area. The two other districts lie at the southern end of the peninsula, anchored by Pusan and Kwangju. Taiwan's economic planners promoted high-technology industries such as personal computers, telecommunications equipment, precision electronic instruments, and other high-tech products. More recently, the South Koreans have moved in a similar direction.

Just a trading colony seven decades ago, Hong Kong started producing textiles and light manufactures in the 1950s. The success of these industries was based on plentiful, cheap labor. Next came expanded production of electrical equipment, appliances, and other household products. Hong Kong's geographical situation contributed enormously to its economic fortunes. The colony became mainland China's gateway to the world, a bustling port, financial center, and **break-of-bulk point**, where goods are transferred from one mode of transport to another (**Fig. 12.19**).

In 1997, China took over the government of Hong Kong from the British. Consequently, a showplace of capitalism came under nominal control of the quasi-communist Chinese central government. However, there was a guarantee that it could maintain much of its autonomy for 50 years. Hong Kong is a special administrative region (SAR) of China under the principle of one country, two systems.

The industrial growth of Singapore also was influenced by its geographical setting and the changing global economic division of labor. Strategically located at the tip of the Malay Peninsula, Singapore is a small island inhabited by a little over 4 million people, mostly ethnic Chinese, but with Malay and Indian minorities. Fifty years ago, Singapore was mainly an entrepôt (transshipment point) for such products as rubber, timber, and oil. Today, the bulk of its foreign revenues comes from exports of manufactured goods and, increasingly, high-technology products. Singapore is also a center for quaternary industries, selling services and expertise to a global market.

Rapid economic growth brings with it risks. In 1997, risky lending practices and government investment decisions caused Thailand's currency to collapse. Its stock market then followed; banks closed and bankruptcies were filed. Soon Malaysia and Indonesia were affected. By early 1998, one of the Four Tigers, South Korea, required a massive infusion of dollars (provided by the International Monetary Fund, an international financial institution), to prevent economic chaos. However, the reforms that allowed the region to overcome these economic troubles served to strengthen East and Southeast Asia's economies. The Four Tigers continue to exert a powerful regional—and international—economic role.

The Chinese Juggernaut   China's major industrial expansion took place during the communist period. Some industrial growth occurred during the period of European colonial influence and later during the Japanese occupation. But when communists took over in 1949, one of their leading priorities was to develop China's resources and industries as rapidly as possible.

China is a vast country with a substantial resource base. The quality of some of its coal is good, the quantity enormous, and many of the deposits are near the surface and easily

Photo by A.B. Murphy. © 2020 John Wiley & Sons, Inc.

FIGURE 12.19 **Hong Kong.** The urban skyline of Hong Kong today is one of the most dramatic on the planet.

extracted. China's iron ores are not as productive and are generally of lower grade, but new finds are regularly being made.

Until the early 1960s, Soviet planners helped promote China's industrial development. China was constrained by the low level of development before the 1949 communist takeover. At the time, China had a poorly developed transport network. Moreover, its major resource deposits lay far from the areas where most people lived. Like their Soviet allies, China's rulers were determined to speed up the industrialization of the economy, and their decisions led to the creation of several major and lesser industrial districts.

Under state planning rules, the Northeast district (formerly called Manchuria and now Dongbei) became China's industrial heartland. The region's coal and iron deposits located in the basin of the Liao River supported the development of a heavy industry complex. Shenyang became the "Chinese Pittsburgh," with metallurgical, machine making, engineering, and other large industries. Anshan, to the south, emerged as China's leading iron and steel-producing center. Harbin to the north (China's northern-most large city, with more than 5 million inhabitants) produced textiles, farm equipment, and light manufactures of many kinds.

The second largest industrial region in China, the Shanghai and the Chang Jiang district, developed in and around the country's biggest city, Shanghai. The Chang Jiang district contains both Shanghai and Wuhan. It rose to prominence and, by some measures, eventually exceeded the Northeast as a contributor to the national economy. Another industrial complex that developed farther upstream, along the Chang Jiang River, focused on the city of Chongqing.

Political and economic reforms starting in the 1980s led to a tremendous surge in the Chinese economy. The state embraced aspects of capitalism and opened itself to foreign investment, while retaining strong state overall control. For many years thereafter, China had the fastest-growing economy in the world. In traditional industrial sectors, the Chang Jiang district became a pacesetter for Chinese industrial growth—both in terms of iron and steel production, and also in terms of its diversified production. Railroad cars, ships, books, foods, chemicals—an endless variety of products—come from the Chang Jiang district. China also moved aggressively into high-tech manufacturing. Then the making of new consumer products led to a diffusion of manufacturing to a wide variety of cities. Those within striking distance of Hong Kong benefited the most.

In Chinese cities, bulldozers are sweeping away the vestiges of the old China; cottages with porches and tile roofs on the outskirts of the expanding cities make way for new buildings. Decaying remnants of the old cities stand amid the glass-encased towers that symbolize the new economic order (**Fig. 12.20**). Modern skyscrapers now dominate the skyline of the cities at the top of the Chinese urban-economic and administrative hierarchy—including Beijing, Shanghai, and cities in special economic zones (SEZs). China's major cities now play host to gleaming new airports, daring architecture, spectacular pubiic projects, and the termini of efficient high-speed railroads (**Fig. 12.21**).

Photo by A.B. Murphy. © 2020 John Wiley & Sons, Inc.

FIGURE 12.20   **Shanghai, China.**   Remnants of the old city remain, but they are rapidly losing ground to high-rise apartment and office buildings.

At the same time, the Northeast has become China's "Rust Belt." Many of its state-run factories have been sold or closed, or are operating below capacity. Eventually, the Northeast is likely to recover because of its resources and its favorable

Photo by A.B. Murphy. © 2020 John Wiley & Sons, Inc.

FIGURE 12.21   **Shenzhen, China.**   Shenzhen was not even incorporated as a city until 1979, but today it is a city of some 12 million people. The futuristic landscape of the central city reflects its role as a technology and trading hub.

Photo by A.B. Murphy. © 2020 John Wiley & Sons, Inc.

FIGURE 12.22 **Mumbai, India.** Cotton products made in factories in the Mumbai metropolitan area are readily available in the city's markets. The cotton industry has been a major part of Mumbai's economy since the first cotton mill in India was built there in 1854.

geographic site. But under the state's new economic policies, the dynamic eastern and southern provinces have grown into major manufacturing belts and have changed the map of this part of the Pacific Rim.

Today, the Chinese government is pushing industrialization into the country's interior. New investment is flowing into poorer parts of the central and western portions of the country. China is also looking to take advantage of its proximity to South and Southeast Asia through efforts to deepen transnational economic cooperation. From a global perspective, what is particularly striking is the magnitude and influence of the Chinese economic juggernaut. On August 15, 2010, China officially surpassed Japan as the world's second largest economy. China has become the world's largest exporter, and its energy and raw material demands are now affecting the global supply of key resources. More passenger vehicles are purchased in China each year than in the United States, and China invests more domestically than any other country in the world (see the discussion of the Belt and Road Initiative in Chapters 8 and 10).

Nonetheless, China's economy still depends heavily on exports and foreign investment. China's gross national income (GNI) per capita, while on the rise, is three times smaller than Japan's and almost four times smaller than that of the United States. Moreover, there are potentially destabilizing social and environmental costs to China's rapid rise. With labor costs growing in China relative to Southeast Asia, China's economic growth is slowing. China may well find itself facing some of the very forces that gave it an advantage over other places not long ago.

The Wider World Other newly industrializing countries have become increasingly significant global nodes of production. Over the past decade, manufacturing has surged in world cities of South and Southeast Asia, in South Africa, and in parts of Central and South America. Brazil, Russia, India, China, and South Africa are sometimes grouped under the acronym BRICS (each letter standing for one of these countries), because these countries demonstrate a shift in global economic power away from the traditional economic core. India has become the world's sixth largest economy. Although industrial production in India is modest when compared to the country's huge size and enormous population, major industrial complexes have developed around Kolkata (the Eastern district, with engineering, chemical, cotton, and jute industries, plus iron and steel based on the Chota Nagpur reserves), Mumbai (the Western district, where cheap electricity helps the cotton and chemical industries), and Chennai (the Southern district, with an emphasis on light engineering and textiles) (**Fig. 12.22**).

India has no major oil reserves, so it spends heavily on oil energy. But the country has a great deal of hydroelectric potential and access to ample coal. Its Bihar and Karnataka iron ore reserves may be among the largest in the world. With a large labor force, a growing middle class, and a location midway between Europe and the Pacific Rim, India's economic influence is on the rise.

Do Places Still Matter?

The diffusion of manufacturing activity to the semiperiphery and periphery, coupled with time–space compression, has led some commentators to suggest that we are entering an era characterized by the "end of geography." By this they mean an era characterized by so much fast, easy connectivity that where something happens does not matter much. Alvin Toffler first suggested this idea in his *Future Shock* (1970). More recently, Richard O'Brien advanced a similar idea in *Global Financial Integration: The End of Geography* (1992), and Thomas Friedman suggested something similar in *The World Is Flat* (2005). Each author argues that technological changes and developments in the global economy have reduced the significance of location and made place differences increasingly insignificant.

Geographers who study industrial production recognize that the nature and meaning of location and place have changed greatly in recent times. However, they also note that these changes do not create a geographically undifferentiated world. Local influences continue to matter a great deal; they just matter in different ways than they did in the past. So it is important to understand how places have changed as a result of new production methods, new corporate structures, and new patterns of industry. Then it is necessary to cultivate an awareness of how the relationship between global processes and local places creates opportunities and constraints for different parts of the planet.

TC **Thinking Geographically**

What steps have been taken by your community to attract new business? Tax breaks? Promises to provide infrastructure? Research what debates have developed over promises to attract new business in your community. What assumptions about **development** and **globalization** are made by those arguing for and against those promises?

12.4 Determine How Deindustrialization and the Rise of Service Industries Have Changed the Economic Geography of Trade.

Service industries—tertiary, quaternary, and quinary sectors—produce ideas, advice, innovations, and assistance to businesses and individuals. Tertiary services involve a broad range of actions that aid people and businesses, including personal services such as cutting hair and giving massages, as well as entertainment, transportation, and retail. Quaternary industries are those involved with the collection, processing, and manipulation of information and capital. These include the realms of finance, administration, insurance, legal services, and computer services. Quinary industries aid complex decision making and the advancement of human capacities. Think of scientific research, higher education, and high-level management when considering quinary industries.

Distinguishing among types of services is useful, given the growth in the size and complexity of the service sector. In the global economic core, service industries employ more workers than the primary and secondary industries combined. Yet these service industries range from small-scale retailing to tourism services to research on the causes of cancer. Placing all of these activities in a single category is not very helpful.

Distinguishing among different types of service industries is also useful in highlighting particular phases in the development of the service sector. Early in the twentieth century, the domestic and quasi-domestic tertiary industries experienced rapid growth in the industrialized world. With the approach of World War II, the quaternary sector began expanding rapidly, and this expansion continued after the war. During the last three decades, both the quaternary and quinary sectors have experienced very rapid growth, giving greater meaning to the term *postindustrial*.

The expanding service sector in the core economies is only one aspect of the changing global economy. Accompanying, and in some cases driving, this expansion are several other developments that have already been mentioned: the increasing mechanization of production, particularly in manufacturing enterprises operating in the core; the growth of large multinational corporations; and the scattering of the production process across geographic space.

Not all services contribute equally to an economy. You can pay $20 for a haircut and $20,000 for a surgery, but both are part of the service industry. You can also think about services in terms of *low cost, low benefit* versus *high cost, high benefit*. When you pay $20 for a haircut, the money goes to the person who cuts your hair, and the stylist in turn uses some of the money to pay rent to the salon owner and some of the money to buy groceries. The impact of the fraction devoted to rent multiplies, as the owner devotes a portion of it to the utility companies that serve the salon and the beauty companies that supply the salon with the products it uses.

With the $20,000 surgery, you are paying part of the incomes of the surgeon, the anesthesiologist, and the nurses. You are also paying the hospital, which in turn purchases utilities and all kinds of medical products. For each service you purchase, think about the persons being paid as having a wake (like that caused by a boat) behind them. The stylist can pay for only a small part of the rent and a couple of groceries from your $20—low cost, low benefit to the economy. The surgeon can pay part of a child's private school tuition, part of a vacation, and an entire month's worth of groceries—high cost, high benefit to the economy.

Geographical Dimensions of the Service Economy

Deindustrialization and the growth of the service economy unfolded in a world economy already characterized by wide socioeconomic disparities. Only areas that had industry could deindustrialize. At the global scale, the wealthier industrial regions were the most successful in establishing a postindustrial service economy. Deindustrialization did little to change the basic disparities between core and periphery that have long characterized the global economy. Even in the manufacturing realm, a few key resources were necessary to allow the core industrial regions to retain their dominance. Such resources included the availability of capital, access to technology and infrastructure, and innovative production strategies. Today, eastern Asia, western Russia and Ukraine, western Europe, and North America still account for well over 75 percent of the world's total output of manufactured goods.

Despite its continued dominance in the manufacturing arena, the core has experienced wrenching changes associated with the economic shifts of the past 70 years. Anyone who has spent time in Detroit, Michigan, the British Midlands, or Silesia (southern Poland and northeastern Czech Republic) knows there are pockets of significant hardship in relatively prosperous countries. These are the result of large-scale deindustrialization.

In the United Kingdom, the major industrial zones of Newcastle, Liverpool, and Manchester lost much of their industrial base during the 1960s and 1970s. The industrial zone of the northeastern United States (around the Great Lakes) did too, with steel manufacturing jobs moving to areas of the world

FIGURE 12.23 **Major Manufacturing Regions of North America.** North American manufacturing has dispersed to the Sun Belt, and deindustrialization has taken hold in parts of the American Manufacturing Belt, now known as the Rust Belt. But new industries have sprung up there as well.

with lower wages. This region of the United States, which used to be called the Manufacturing Belt, came to be called the **Rust Belt**, evoking the image of long-abandoned, rusted-out steel factories (**Fig. 12.23**). Then the global economic downturn that began in 2008 resulted in job losses in communities dependent on both secondary and tertiary industries. These examples remind us that not all deindustrialized regions find their niche easily in the new service economy. It also posits that a tertiary economy, once established, does not necessarily buffer places from recessionary trends.

Nonetheless, some parts of the Rust Belt have revived significantly in recent years. Moreover, a number of secondary industrial regions have transitioned to a viable service economy fairly successfully. The **Sun Belt** is found in the southern part of the United States, stretching through the Southeast to the Southwest (Fig. 12.23). Both the population and economy of this region have grown over the last few decades. Service-sector businesses have chosen to locate in places such as Atlanta and Dallas, where the climate is warm and local laws favor business interests. The eastern part of the Sun Belt served as an early industrial region. Birmingham developed an iron and steel economy and Atlanta an industrial economy around cotton, tobacco, and furniture. In recent decades,

high-tech and financial industries have changed the economy and landscape of the Sun Belt, as can be seen in the names of its sports stadiums: TIAA Bank Field in Jacksonville, Florida; Bank of America Stadium in Charlotte, North Carolina; and the AT&T Stadium in Arlington, Texas.

New Patterns of Economic Activity

Most service industries are not tied to raw materials and do not need large amounts of energy. Market accessibility is more relevant, but advances in telecommunications have rendered even that factor less important for some types of service industries.

To understand the influences that shape the location of services, it is useful to review the distinction among tertiary, quaternary, and quinary industries. Tertiary services related to transportation and communication are closely tied to population patterns and to the location of primary and secondary industries. Other tertiary services, such as food service and retail, are influenced mainly by market considerations. If they are located far from their consumers, they are unlikely to succeed.

Geographers can use technologies like GIS to model the best locations for new businesses, office complexes, government centers, and transportation connections. Major retailers do not just shape the landscapes of the places where they choose to put stores. They also change the economic prospects and physical landscapes of the places where their headquarters are located.

Walmart's headquarters in Bentonville, Arkansas, provide a particularly striking example. If producers of consumer products want to sell their goods in Walmart stores, they must travel to Bentonville to negotiate deals with Walmart. In order to provide low prices to consumers, Walmart negotiates low prices with major producers. To create lower-priced products, companies have moved production abroad, and to create good relationships with the world's number one retailer (with sales of over $500 billion in fiscal year 2019), a variety of companies have moved into Arkansas (**Fig. 12.24**). Those companies, along with an array of other businesses supporting their activities (hotels, restaurants, copy centers, delivery services), have fundamentally transformed the state.

The locational influences on quaternary services are more diverse. These are high-level services aimed at the collection, processing, and manipulation of information and capital. Some are strongly tied to particular locations. Retail banking and various types of administrative services require a high level of personal contact, so those services tend to be located near the businesses they are serving.

Other types of quaternary services can operate almost anywhere as long as they have access to digital processing equipment and telecommunications. When you send in your credit card bill, it is unlikely to go to the city where the headquarters of the issuing bank is located. Instead, it will go to North Dakota, South Dakota, Nebraska, or Colorado. Similarly, many "back-office" tasks related to insurance are performed in places such as Des Moines, Iowa, not Chicago or Hartford.

Many quaternary service activities are spread across the globe. If you go in for an MRI at a North American hospital late in the day, the image that is produced may well be evaluated in India (when it is night in the United States, it is daytime in India). Many of the call centers for technical help for computers and related industries (software, hardware) are located in India and the Philippines. Given the relatively high levels of college education and the large numbers of English speakers in these places, as well as the ease of routing phones through the Internet, "help desks" need not be located down the hall or even down the street. These locational curiosities occur because technological advances in the telecommunications sector have allowed all sorts of quaternary industries to be located far away from either producers or consumers. What matters most is infrastructure, a workforce that is sufficiently skilled but not too expensive, and favorable tax rates.

Those who work in the quinary sector can be widely dispersed. However, many concentrate close to seats of government, universities, and corporate headquarters. Corporate headquarters tend to be located in large metropolitan areas, whereas seats of government and universities can be found in places that were chosen long ago as appropriate sites for administrative or educational activities based on cultural values or political compromises. The American ideal of the "university town" (which originated in Germany) led to the establishment of many universities in modest-sized towns

---

Guest Field Note   Watching Walmart Grow in Fayetteville, Arkansas

Fiona M. Davidson
University of Arkansas

For most geographers, the simple act of daily observation of the world around them becomes a profoundly satisfying habit. The rapidly changing urban/economic landscape of northwest Arkansas is one of the fastest growing metropolitan areas in the United States. Walmart originated in Bentonville, Arkansas, and as it became increasingly successful, it remained committed to its home in this affordable, rural corner of the mid-South. By the early 1990s, the company's growth had fueled the growth of other service industries and had contributed to the retention of several other major corporations. A decision to require Walmart suppliers to locate offices in the region similarly boosted growth in the area. Procter & Gamble put its office in Fayetteville, only 25 miles from Walmart's home in Bentonville. Dozens of other major corporations have a presence in the region as well. The results have been both positive and negative. Property prices have risen, with rising tax revenues and better public service provision, and the corporations have proven to be generous philanthropists. However, sprawl, congestion, overcrowded schools, and serious waste disposal

FIGURE 12.24 **Fayetteville, Arkansas**

issues also followed, This once-rural corner of America has become a metropolitan growth pole, complete with national coffee shops, rush hour congestion, and sprawling golf course subdivisions of 6000-square-foot "European" mansions.

such as Champaign-Urbana, Illinois; Norman, Oklahoma; and Eugene, Oregon, rather than in major commercial centers. Political compromises led to the establishment of major seats of government in small towns. Ottawa, Canada, and Canberra, Australia, are examples. The point is that historical location decisions influence the geography of the quinary sector. It is not just university professors and government officials who are affected. All sorts of high-level research and development activities are located on the fringes of universities, and a host of specialized consultants tend to concentrate around governmental centers. These then become major nodes of quinary activity.

High-Technology Corridors

A **high-technology corridor** is an area designated by local or state government to benefit from lower taxes and high-technology infrastructure. These areas provide high-technology jobs to the local population and attract designers of computers, semiconductors, telecommunication infrastructure, sophisticated medical equipment, and the like.

California's Silicon Valley is a well-known example of a high-technology corridor. Several decades ago, a number of innovative technology companies located their research and development activities near the University of California, Berkeley, and Stanford University. Both universities are near San Francisco. These companies were attracted by the prospect of developing links with existing research communities and the availability of a highly educated workforce. Once some high-technology businesses located in the Silicon Valley, others were drawn to the area as well, creating what geographers call a *growth pole* that spurred economic development in the surrounding area.

Today, Silicon Valley is home to dozens of computer companies (such as Cisco Systems, Adobe, Hewlett-Packard, Intel, and IBM). Manuel Castells, Peter Hall, and John Hutriyk call

such a concentration a *technopole*, an area where agglomeration is based on a synergy among technological companies. A similar sort of technopole developed outside Boston near Harvard University, the Massachusetts Institute of Technology, and many other universities, creating the "Route 128 high-technology corridor." This corridor has been largely supported by the federal government rather than the local government, which supports many other technopoles.

Technopoles can be found in western Europe, East Asia, North America, and Australia. Few are on the scale of Silicon Valley, but they are visible elements of the economic landscape. Many have sprung up on the edges of good-sized cities, particularly near airports. In Brussels (Belgium), for example, the route into the city from the airport passes buildings occupied by computer, communication, and electronics firms. In Washington, D.C., the route from Dulles International Airport (located in the Virginia suburbs) to the city passes the headquarters of companies such as AOL, MCI, and Orbital Sciences (the Dulles Corridor). In the Telecom Corridor of Plano-Richardson (just outside of Dallas, Texas), telecom companies such as Nortel and Ericsson have taken root, but so too have numerous high-technology companies that are not telecom related (**Fig. 12.25**). In each of these technopoles, major multinational companies attract other startup companies hoping to become major companies, to provide services to major companies, or to be acquired by major companies.

Many of the technology firms are multinationals. Like their counterparts in other countries, they function in a globalized information environment and market their products all over the world. Being near raw materials or even a particular market is unimportant. What matters is being close to major transportation and communication networks.

High-technology industries have become such an important symbol of the postindustrial world that local, regional, and national governments often pursue aggressive policies to attract firms in this sector. Bidding wars sometimes develop between localities seeking to attract such industries. Although high-technology industries often bring economic benefits, they have some drawbacks. Communities that have attracted production facilities find that the manufacture of computer chips, semiconductors, and the like requires toxic chemicals and large quantities of water. And even more research-oriented establishments sometimes have negative environmental impacts in that land must be cleared and buildings constructed to house them. But the high-technology sector is clearly here to stay, and areas that can tap into it usually are in an advantageous economic position.

Michael Vi/Alamy Stock Photo

FIGURE 12.25 Plano-Richardson, Texas. The Plano-Richardson Telecom Corridor is located just north of Dallas and is home to Diodes, a semi-conductor company with its headquarters in Plano, Texas and offices in Silicon Valley, Shanghai, Taipei, Shenzhen, Tokyo, Seoul, and Munich.

AP® Exam Taker's Tip

Can you connect **high-technology corridors** to models and theories in AP Human Geography? High-technology corridors are areas of agglomeration which are primary components of both location theory and least cost theory. Think about high-technology corridors like Silicon Valley in California or high-tech areas of Austin, Texas. Why do like businesses cluster in these corridors?

Tourism Services   Every service industry has its own locational characteristics. However, tourism is almost in a class by itself due to its geographical extent and economic significance. Once a relatively small activity confined to selected locations, tourism is now the world's largest service-sector industry.

Tourism grew dramatically in the global economic core during the second half of the twentieth century, when incomes and leisure time increased for many people. Over the past three decades, the number of East and Southeast Asian tourists has risen much faster than the global average, reflecting the economic boom in many Pacific Rim countries. A weakening global economy and concerns over political stability caused a noticeable dip in travel around 2010, but absent a major economic or geopolitical crisis, tourism is likely to continue to expand.

In Chapter 10, we looked at the social and cultural impacts of tourism, but tourism is a major service industry as well. Communities all over the world have worked hard to promote tourism, and many economies now rely on tourist receipts. The tourist industry has transformed downtowns, ports, hinterlands, parks, and waterfronts. High-rise, ultramodern hotels dominate urban skylines from Boston to Brisbane. The Port of Miami and Fort Lauderdale's Port Everglades have been reconstructed to serve the cruise industry. Many ports from Tokyo to Tampa have added cruise terminals complete with shopping malls and restaurants. Theme parks such as Disney's establishments near Orlando, Paris, Tokyo, Hong Kong, Shanghai, and Los Angeles draw millions of visitors and directly or indirectly employ thousands of workers. Dubai has constructed an indoor ski run in the Mall of the Emirates to attract more visitors. Once-remote wildlife parks and nature reserves in East Africa and South Asia currently receive thousands of visitors. They now require expanded facilities, and the increase in visitors can cause ecological damage. Many formerly isolated beaches are now lined by high-rise hotels and resorts. In the Caribbean and the Pacific, some entire islands have been taken over by tour operators.

The economic impacts of tourist-related development are far reaching. The monetary value of goods and services associated with tourism now exceeds $8 trillion. If spillover effects are considered, the figure is even larger. With a growing middle class in China and India, and with increases in average life expectancy, that figure is likely to continue to grow. That growth will then affect places all over the world.

Place Vulnerabilities in a Service Economy

Places are subject to vulnerabilities in any type of economy. In the early stages of industrialization, the economic fortunes of places were tied to their manufacturing operations. As a result, such places were vulnerable when demand shifted for the goods produced by local manufacturers. They were also

Photo by A.B. Murphy. © 2020 John Wiley & Sons, Inc.

FIGURE 12.26   **Duisburg, Germany.**   The old industrial canal corridor has been converted to a pedestrian district to attract businesses, shops, and restaurants.

threatened by the changing costs of transportation, or decisions by business owners to downscale or shift production elsewhere. Many older industrial areas in the United States and Europe experienced such adjustments, and their best hope for rebuilding often lay in the service economy. For example, in Duisburg—a city at the heart of Germany's Ruhr Valley—abandoned steel mills were turned into tourist attractions and warehouses were converted into retail establishments, restaurants, and offices (**Fig. 12.26**).

AP® Exam Taker's Tip

Repurposing of old industrial landscapes into **festival landscapes** (connect these landscapes to the **galactic city model** in Chapter 9) is part of the shift to the **service sector.** Figure 12.26 shows an old industrial canal that is being converted to a pedestrian path. What similar conversions do you see in your local area? Your local repurposed landscapes can make great examples to use when answering a free-response question.

Service economies create their own vulnerabilities. Tourism can fall off in the face of economic downturns or natural hazards, and office work can be outsourced to distant places. We usually think of manufacturing jobs being affected by mechanization, but service jobs are vulnerable as well. In recent decades, countless jobs in the travel planning industry have been lost to the Internet. Similarly, scanning machines in supermarkets have reduced the need for employees, and automated answering services have taken the place of live voices in many businesses. Such changes can create the same sorts of hardships and pressures for economic readjustment faced by communities that rely on secondary industries.

In our globalized world, a disruption in a city or region with which a service-oriented place is linked can have serious consequences for that place that are beyond the control of anyone there. When the Arab Spring broke out in Cairo, the economy of Luxor (some 400 miles south of Cairo) took a major hit because international tourism stopped.

Some globalized economic developments can also negatively affect local places. For example, the financial service industry expanded rapidly over the past few decades because of increasingly innovative products and arrangements. Some people made spectacular amounts of money, but some financial instruments and procedures were based on unrealistic assumptions. Banks made loans they should not have made, and mortgages were issued to people who were unlikely to meet their payments. These practices contributed to the dramatic economic downturn of 2008, when a housing slump led to many defaults on so-called subprime mortgages. A banking crisis followed that rippled throughout the economy and, in our interconnected world, affected the fortunes of places near and far.

The 2008 crisis reminds us of the continuing vulnerabilities of places in a service economy, even if there is no direct challenge to the specific service industries on which the local economy is based. It also raises a key question with a geographical foundation: What are the consequences of divorcing the development of wealth in a knowledge economy from the fate of individual places, regions, or countries?

TC **Thinking Geographically**

How do the service industries in a country change in response to changes in **population pyramids**? When a country like Japan has an aging population, how can it use technological innovation or **migration** of workers to help provide health-care services to older residents? Using reputable news sources and working to find sources from multiple countries, determine how Japan is addressing the shortage of workers in the health care service industry.

Summary

12.1 Describe the Hearth and Diffusion of the Industrial Revolution.

1. The transition from cottage industries to the Industrial Revolution happened as Europeans sought to generate greater profit by producing more of the goods in high demand. To do this, they looked for ways to take advantage of economies of scale—increasing the quantity of goods being produced in an effort to decrease the average cost of producing each item.

2. The Industrial Revolution began in northern England in the mid-eighteenth century. It was characterized by the mechanization of production and the use of hydropower and coal as sources of energy. Because of the high cost of moving heavy raw materials, factories initially concentrated close to the location of energy resources. With the invention of the railroad in the late eighteenth century, production facilities could start moving closer to where consumers lived.

3. Industrialization diffused to continental Europe starting in the early 1800s. The first manufacturing belts in continental Europe were located close to coal fields in northern France, southern Belgium, and northwestern Germany. Early industrialization led to the growth of port cities, notably Rotterdam. Rotterdam is still Europe's most important port city.

4. By the mid-nineteenth century, industrialization diffused outside western Europe—principally to North America and parts of eastern Europe. Japan also began to industrialize in the late nineteenth century after the country opened up to the outside world after a change in government in 1868.

12.2 Examine How and Why the Geography of Industrial Production Has Changed.

1. In the early twentieth century, larger-scale industrial concerns adopted Fordist production techniques, especially mass-production assembly lines. The Fordist period was marked by a surge in both production and consumption. Fordist production led to changes in the location of industry toward sites with good access to available labor, resources, infrastructure, and consumers.

2. Efforts to develop generalizations about the influences on industrial location gave rise to classical location theory. The most influential classical location theory was Weber's least cost theory, which focused on the importance of three factors: transportation costs, labor costs, and the advantages that come with industrial clustering or agglomeration.

3. The costs associated with Weber's three factors have shifted over time. Transportation innovations such as containerization have greatly reduced the cost. Labor costs have increased, particularly in the global economic core. These shifts have altered the spatial organization of production. They have also ushered in an era of flexible production, in which the components of goods are made in different places around the globe and then brought together for assembly in response to customer demand.

4. Flexible production and the growth in labor costs in the global economic core gave to a global division of labor. Production facilities making everyday goods came to be increasingly concentrated in the global economic periphery and semiperiphery, while research and development operations remained in the

core. Developments in communication and transportation technologies accelerated the speed with which things happened and made the distance between places less significant. The term *time–space compression* describes this situation.

5. Industrial production in the contemporary world is dominated by multinational corporations. These corporations obtain component parts for the goods they produce from around the world (global sourcing), and many of them acquire the businesses they deal with (vertical integration). Large-scale industrial production today takes place in what are called global production networks, which encompass the activities, arrangements, and transactions involved in the production, distribution, and consumption of goods and service.

12.3 Explain Global Patterns of Industrial Production.

1. Industrial location today is influenced not just by labor costs, transportation, and market access, but also by regulatory constraints, the changing energy picture, and access to skilled labor. Government regulation can attract or discourage business. The shift from coal to oil, and more recently to nuclear power and alternative energy sources, makes it easier for industrial production to be more spatially disaggregated. The emergence of centers of education and research in major cities around the world have furthered this trend.

2. Centers of industrial production are now found all over the world. Many older industrial zones have experienced deindustrialization, but most still show up on the modern map of industrial production either because some older industries have held on or because new types of manufacturing have sprung up near older industrial sites. East Asia has emerged as the greatest new center of industrialization over the past 50 years, with China taking the lead after political and economic reforms were instituted in 1989.

3. Recently industrializing countries have become increasingly significant global nodes of production. Over the past decade,

manufacturing has surged in the urban cores of South and Southeast Asia, in South Africa, and in parts of Central and South America.

4. Despite the diffusion of industrial production and the shrinking of the world through time–space compression, local influences still matter. A plan to develop an industrial operation in two different places will play out differently because those places are not alike.

12.4 Determine How Deindustrialization and the Rise of Service Industries Have Changed the Economic Geography of Trade.

1. In the global economic core, service industries employ more workers than primary and secondary industries combined. The growth of the service sector reflects the changing nature of the world economy, the increasing mechanization of production in manufacturing enterprises operating in the core, the growth of large multinational corporations, and the scattering of the production process across geographic space.

2. Deindustrialization in the global economic core has led to wrenching changes in some places. The so-called Rust Belt in the United States was hard hit, as were parts of northern England in the United Kingdom and the early-to-industrialize regions in continental Europe.

3. Factors affecting the location of service industries include access to markets and the availability of skilled labor. The latter has a particular influence on high-level services (quaternary and quinary sectors of the economy). A combination of skilled labor, tax incentives, and infrastructure has led to the development of high-technology corridors, which are now centers of wealth and are influential economic nodes.

4. Tourism has emerged as a major service industry. It has brought considerable wealth to some areas, but it can also leave places vulnerable to larger economic shifts or events that discourage people from traveling. Vulnerabilities exist in places dependent on other service industries as well.

Self-Test

12.1 Describe the hearth and diffusion of the Industrial Revolution.

1. The Industrial Revolution began in the mid-eighteenth century:

   a. in the London metropolitan area where major banks were located.

   b. in northern England near accessible coalfields.

   c. in the Paris metropolitan area where migrants had congregated.

   d. in parts of China where cottage industries were strong.

   e. in Germany near navigable rivers.

2. In the wake of the Industrial Revolution, _____ grew to be the most important port in Europe.

   a. London

   b. Paris

   c. Rotterdam

   d. Rome

   e. Liverpool

3. Which of the following inventions helps to explain the emergence of London and Paris as major industrial centers in the nineteenth century?

   a. The factory

   b. The water wheel

   c. The steamship

   d. The automobile

   e. The railroad

4. By the first half of the twentieth century, major industrial complexes had sprung up in each of the following regions except:

    a. the Kanto region around Tokyo, Japan.

    b. the Great Lakes region of the United States.

    c. the Rühr River Valley of Germany.

    d. the Ganges River Valley of northern India.

    e. Rotterdam in the Netherlands.

12.2 Examine how and why the geography of industrial production has changed.

5. Fordist production is characterized by:

    a. assembly-line production.

    b. just-in-time delivery systems.

    c. flexible production.

    d. containerization.

    e. cheap labor.

6. Which of the following was not taken into consideration in Weber's least cost theory of industrial location?

    a. transportation costs

    b. labor costs

    c. the skill of the labor force

    d. agglomeration

    e. none of the above

7. The fact that kiwis picked in New Zealand yesterday can be in the lunch boxes of children in Canada tomorrow is an example of:

    a. the global division of labor.

    b. outsourcing.

    c. flexible production.

    d. time–space compression.

    e. distance decay.

8. True or False: Global outsourcing is common in the secondary sector, but not in the tertiary sector.

12.3 Explain global patterns of industrial production.

9. Which of the following has had a significant influence on industrial location in recent decades?

    a. government regulation

    b. the geography of agricultural production

    c. access to capital at places where an industrial operation might be built

    d. the location of oil fields

    e. environmental concerns

10. The expansion of alternative energy will likely:

    a. eclipse traditional energy sources in a few years.

    b. lead to greater flexibility in industrial location.

    c. advantage North America over Europe and East Asia.

    d. slow the turn toward the mechanization of industrial production.

    e. produce little change for existing systems.

11. True or False: Industrial production is more spatially concentrated today than it was in the 1950s.

12. Which of the following countries was one of East/Southeast Asia's newly industrializing countries (one of the region's "Four Tigers") in the 1960s and 1970s?

    a. China

    b. Japan

    c. Korea

    d. Vietnam

    e. Cambodia

12.4 Determine how deindustrialization and the rise of service industries have changed the economic geography of trade.

13. The provision of legal services is an example of a:

    a. secondary economic activity.

    b. tertiary economic activity.

    c. quaternary economic activity.

    d. quinary economic activity.

    e. primary economic activity.

14. Areas that have experienced deindustrialization over the past few decades are primarily concentrated in:

    a. the global economic core.

    b. the global economic semiperiphery.

    c. the global economic periphery.

    d. no one of the foregoing more than another.

    e. all areas of the global economy.

15. Technopoles tend to emerge:

    a. in and around industrial manufacturing zones.

    b. in small towns where environmental regulations are weak.

    c. close to ports served by large container ships.

    d. close to research universities.

    e. in areas lacking universities.

16. True or False: Tourism is the world's largest service-sector business.

CHAPTER 13

The Humanized Environment

Lou Linwei/Alamy Stock Photo

FIGURE 13.1 **Shanghai, China.** This residence hall at Shanghai University is typical for Chinese students. Chinese universities have different living conditions for Chinese and international students. Chinese students generally live in older halls with with limited access to electricity and in more crowded conditions, with 4 to 8 per room. International students studying in China typically live in newer halls with 2 people per room.

"That's the hall where I lived, and over there is the facility where I showered," the Chinese student explained as she toured me around her home campus (**Fig. 13.1**). I paused before asking a question. She had studied in the United States the year before and taken my geography course, so she was used to my questions. I wanted to know about access to hot water. "Can you tell me about the shower facility?" I asked.

"Oh yes. We can shower in our dorms, but it's cold water and the lights turn off at 11 P.M." She then explained that they can access hot water in the shower facilities on certain hours and days of the week.

Earlier that day, I had been thinking how remarkable the Shanghai subway system is. The underground tunnels and trains are gleamingly clean, and the route map is expanding each year. China's economy is growing quickly, and the central government has invested more than $60 billion in the Shanghai subway system alone since it began construction in 1993. The seven longest subway systems in the world are in cities in China, and all have been built since the 1980s.

But while China is building a world-class infrastructure system, it is still struggling with the same water and electricity shortages that much of the world is facing. Dutch scientists estimate that 4 billion people worldwide already experience a water shortage at least 1 month a year (Mekonnen and Hoekstra 2016). Growth in population and wealth are driving global consumption and increasing the human impact on the environment, but not without consequences.

CHAPTER OUTLINE

13.1 **Explain what natural hazards are and how natural hazards can become natural disasters.**

- Tectonic Hazards and Disasters
- Hydrological Hazards and Disasters
- Meteorological and Climatological Hazards and Disasters

13.2 **Identify the ways that humans impact Earth through land use, water use, and resource extraction.**

- Land Use
- Water Use
- Resource Extraction

13.3 **Explain how climate change is impacting human–environment interactions.**

- Hurricanes
- Water Scarcity

13.4 **Explain How Human Consumption Is Changing the Scale of Human Impact and Challenging Sustainability.**

- Global Patterns of Consumption
- Sustainability
- Waste Disposal

13.1 Explain What Natural Hazards Are and How Natural Hazards Can Become Natural Disasters.

Earth is dynamic and ever changing. The lithosphere, or crust and upper mantle, is broken into tectonic plates that are constantly in motion. The water that covers more than 70 percent of Earth moves through oceans, rivers, and lakes into soil and plants, and is treated and used by humans. Changing winds and weather systems are shaped by the uneven heating of Earth and its atmosphere. The constant motion of these three processes—tectonic, hydrological, and meteorological or climatological—creates **natural hazards**, naturally occurring physical phenomena that produce change.

How much damage a natural hazard causes depends on its proximity to people and property. If a volcano erupts on an island with no people and no property, it is a natural hazard, but not a natural disaster. When a volcano erupts on an island that is populated with people and property, it becomes a **natural disaster**, a naturally occurring physical phenomenon that causes damage and loss of life. Kilauea is the largest of several active volcanoes on the Big Island of Hawai'i. It has erupted continuously since 1983, but in April 2018, the eruption was large enough to collapse the crater, transform the landscape, and destroy 700 homes (Andrews 2018). Previous eruptions of Kilauea were natural hazards, but the lava flow in 2018 created a natural disaster. A fissure that appeared in May sent lava flowing into the Leilani Estates subdivision (**Fig. 13.2**). Hawai'i Volcanoes National Park remained closed until near the end of September 2018, which amplified the economic cost of the natural disaster. The closed park and active

eruptions meant fewer tourists and less revenue for the people in the area.

A natural disaster map highlights the places in the world most susceptible to natural disasters, whether caused by tectonic activity (earthquakes, volcanoes, and tsunamis), hydrological hazards (floods or landslides), or meteorological and climatological hazards (cyclones and droughts) (**Fig. 13.3**). Comparing the map of mortality risk with the map of total economic loss risk shows that when a natural disaster hits an area with higher incomes, the area is likely to be hit financially, whereas an area with lower incomes is likely to be hit by both financial loss and the loss of lives. For example, when a devastating earthquake hit the Kobe region in Japan in 1995, it caused enormous property damage, but fewer than 6500 people died. When an earthquake of a similar magnitude struck Haiti in 2010, well over 100,000 people lost their lives.

AP® Exam Taker's Tip

A key concept in human geography deals with human-environmental interactions. Can you list the ways in which the **environment** impacts people?

Tectonic Hazards and Disasters

Earth's **lithosphere** (crust and upper mantle) is broken into approximately 15 major plates and several minor plates (**Fig. 13.4**). These plates are in constant motion, with most movement happening where plates meet, along plate boundaries. Tectonic plates **diverge** (spread apart), **converge** (come together), or **transform** (slide past one another). Where plates are diverging, as at the Mid-Atlantic Ridge, magma moves to the surface from the upper mantle, creating new crust and volcanic activity in a process called **seafloor spreading**. The newest oceanic crust in the Atlantic is found just adjacent to either side of the Mid-Atlantic Ridge. The age of the ocean floor increases as you move out to the east and west, in parallel bands from the ridge. The oldest oceanic crust in the Atlantic is found close to the North American and Eurasian plates (**Fig. 13.5**).

While new crust is formed where plates diverge, old crust is pushed down into the upper mantle and recycled in what are called **subduction zones**, areas where an oceanic and a continental plate converge or meet. The oceanic plates, which are denser, subduct underneath the less-dense continental plates (**Fig. 13.6**). The Pacific plate, an enormous oceanic plate surrounded by several continental plates, forms subduction zones where it converges with continental plates. When the edge of an oceanic plate subducts under a continental plate, it melts under the heat and pressure of subduction and becomes magma. Magma can then rise to the surface and create

FIGURE 13.2 **Big Island, Hawai'i.** A pyroclastic lava flow from the Kilauea volcanic eruption moves toward a subdivision along Hookapu Street in the Leilani Estates subdivision. The eruption destroyed homes and forced evacuations on the Big Island.

USGS/Alamy Stock Photo

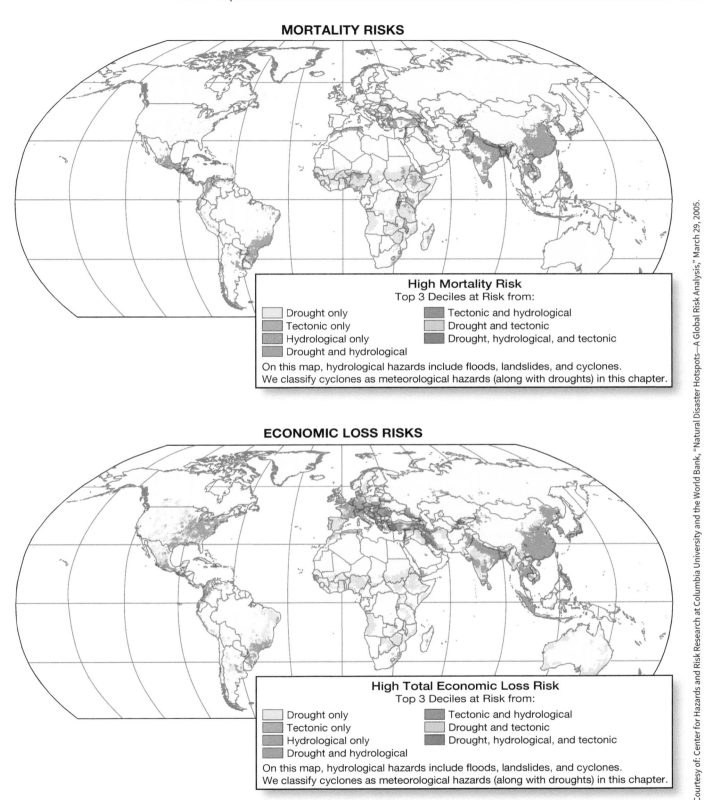

MORTALITY RISKS

High Mortality Risk
Top 3 Deciles at Risk from:

- Drought only
- Tectonic only
- Hydrological only
- Drought and hydrological
- Tectonic and hydrological
- Drought and tectonic
- Drought, hydrological, and tectonic

On this map, hydrological hazards include floods, landslides, and cyclones.
We classify cyclones as meteorological hazards (along with droughts) in this chapter.

ECONOMIC LOSS RISKS

High Total Economic Loss Risk
Top 3 Deciles at Risk from:

- Drought only
- Tectonic only
- Hydrological only
- Drought and hydrological
- Tectonic and hydrological
- Drought and tectonic
- Drought, hydrological, and tectonic

On this map, hydrological hazards include floods, landslides, and cyclones.
We classify cyclones as meteorological hazards (along with droughts) in this chapter.

Courtesy of: Center for Hazards and Risk Research at Columbia University and the World Bank, "Natural Disaster Hotspots—A Global Risk Analysis," March 29, 2005.

FIGURE 13.3 **Mortality and Economic Risks in Natural Disaster Hot Spots.** The top map shows the potential mortality risks and the bottom map shows economic risks if major natural disasters occur in natural disaster hot spots.

a **volcanic arc**, a chain of volcanoes that parallels the subduction zone. **Trenches** are long, narrow, deep features that mark the place where an oceanic plate is subducting under a continental plate.

The tectonically active region of volcanoes and earthquakes on plate boundaries around the Pacific is called the **Ring of Fire** (**Fig. 13.7**). The map of this area shows volcanic arcs (e.g., the Aleutian Islands in Alaska and the islands

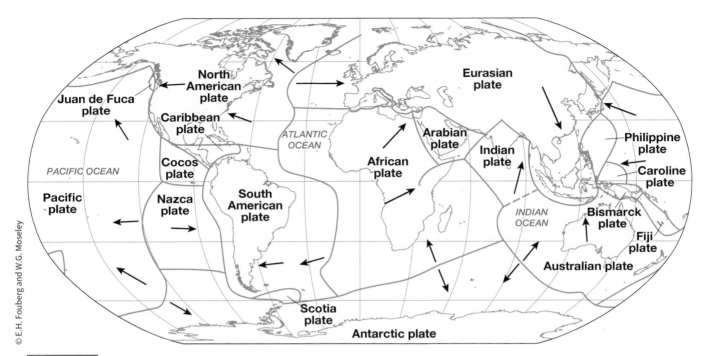

FIGURE 13.4 **Tectonic Plates.** Earth's lithosphere (crust and upper mantle) is broken into approximately 15 major plates, composed of either oceanic or continental crust, and several minor plates.

of Japan) on the continental side of the plate boundaries. Trenches form along plate boundaries in subduction zones. Eruptions on the volcanic arcs and movement of the plates along the plate boundaries are natural hazards.

Tsunamis   **Tsunamis** are seismic sea waves that result from underwater earthquakes or volcanoes. Not all underwater earthquakes create tsunamis. The size of a tsunami depends on the location of the earthquake or volcano, the magnitude

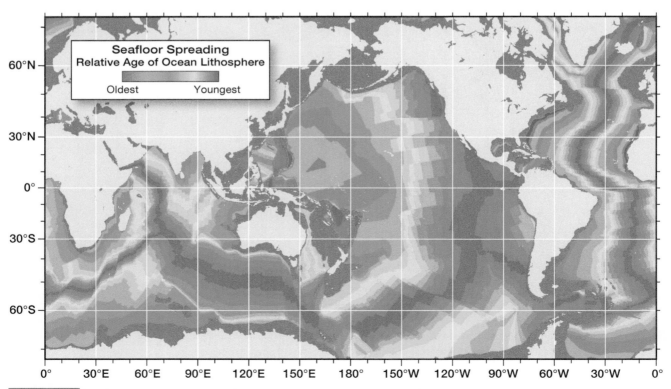

FIGURE 13.5 **Seafloor Spreading.** The seafloor in the middle of the Atlantic Ocean is spreading along a divergent plate boundary. Where plates are spreading, molten rock is rising and cooling along both sides of the Mid-Atlantic Ridge.

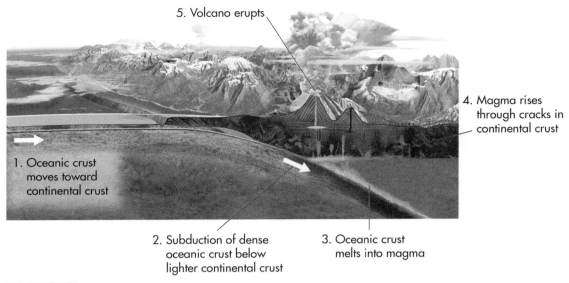

5. Volcano erupts

4. Magma rises through cracks in continental crust

1. Oceanic crust moves toward continental crust

2. Subduction of dense oceanic crust below lighter continental crust

3. Oceanic crust melts into magma

FIGURE 13.6   **Subduction Zone.**   A subduction zone forms where a denser oceanic plate descends under less dense continental plate.

of the tectonic activity, and its proximity to inhabited areas. Large displacements along a subduction zone can generate massive tsunamis.

In a tsunami, the movement of crust sets the ocean water in motion, creating huge waves. If you were on a cruise ship in the middle of the ocean, nothing catastrophic would mark the passing of a tsunami. Your ship would be lifted and lowered, but it would not overturn. On shore, however, a tsunami wave can be catastrophic. As the tsunami moves to shore, the amount of space beneath it, the distance between the ocean surface and the ocean floor, shallows (**Fig. 13.8**), and the

energy in the moving water rises, creating a wall of waves that crash onshore and destroys people and property.

Whether a tsunami, earthquake, or volcano becomes a natural disaster depends on the magnitude of the tectonic events, the proximity of the events to people and property, and the preparedness of the region impacted. The 2004 Indian Ocean tsunami began with a violent earthquake measuring more than 9.1 on the (10-point) Richter scale that happened in a subduction zone off the west coast of the island of Sumatra, Indonesia. The tsunami waves hit Sumatra and Phuket, Thailand, on the east and Sri Lanka on the west. The coasts of

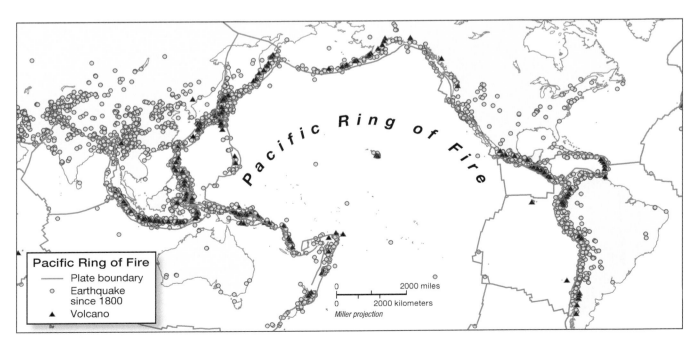

Pacific Ring of Fire

— Plate boundary
○ Earthquake since 1800
▲ Volcano

Pacific Ring of Fire

0   2000 miles
0   2000 kilometers
Miller projection

FIGURE 13.7   **Pacific Ring of Fire.**   Active volcanoes and earthquakes surround the Pacific plate and are found primarily along subduction zones where oceanic plate is subducting under continental plate.

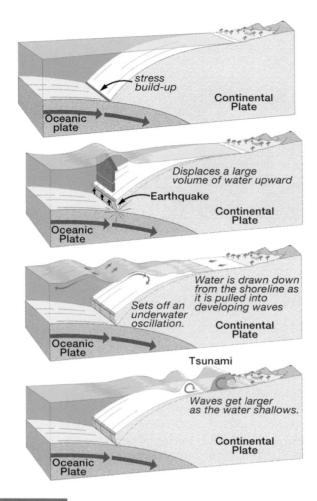

FIGURE 13.8 **Tsunami.** Earthquakes and volcanoes that occur underwater generate seismic sea waves called tsunamis. Water is displaced, which sets off an oscillation. Seismic waves form and get larger as the ocean shallows.

FIGURE 13.9 **Ishinomaki, Japan.** The 3/11 tsunami leveled large parts of Ishinomaki, Japan, as seen in this photograph. Few houses stand in an area that was heavily populated before the tsunami.

Sumatra and Phuket are densely populated, and the beaches attract many tourists. With no warning that the earthquake had occurred and a tsunami was coming, more than 230,000 people died when the tsunami waves hit.

On March 11, 2011, an earthquake registering 9.0 on the Richter scale occurred along a subduction zone off the east coast of Japan. The earthquake generated tsunami waves that reached heights up to 128 feet (39 m) when they hit the coast (**Fig. 13.9**). Japan has a tsunami warning system, but the subduction zone is so close to the coast of Japan that the people in Sendai (in northern Japan) only had about 8 to 10 minutes of warning. What came to be known as the 3/11 tsunami killed more than 15,000 people. The tsunami leveled property, destroying about 120,000 buildings and partially destroying hundreds of thousands more. More than 150,000 Japanese lost their homes. The World Bank estimated the total economic impact of the 3/11 tsunami at $235 billion.

Both the 2004 Indian Ocean tsunami and the 3/11 tsunami in Japan were natural hazards that created natural disasters. Both tsunamis hit densely populated coasts. With no warning system, the Indian Ocean tsunami killed more than 230,000 people. With a warning system that gave people 8 to 10 minutes to move to higher ground and farther inland, the 3/11 tsunami killed more than 15,000 people. The Indian Ocean tsunami caused approximately $10 billion in damages, and the 3/11 tsunami caused $235 billion in damages. Japan, a higher income country, was more susceptible to monetary damage from the tsunami, and Indonesia, a lower income country, was more susceptible to loss of life.

Hydrological Hazards and Disasters

More than 70 percent of Earth is covered by water that cycles through soil, plants, humans, animals, freshwater lakes and rivers, oceans, and the atmosphere. The amount of water on Earth has not changed, but its distribution has changed over long periods of geologic history. During periods of **glaciation**, more water is in the form of ice in glaciers at higher latitudes and elevations. During warming periods, more of Earth's water is in liquid form in oceans, rivers, and lakes.

About 97.5 percent of Earth's water is saltwater and the rest is freshwater. In the current era, almost 69 percent of freshwater is in glaciers and ice caps, another 30.1 percent is in groundwater, and about 1.2 percent is surface or other freshwater found in rivers, lakes, and reservoirs. Of the small portion of freshwater that is surface water, 69 percent is ground ice and permafrost, 20.9 percent is in lakes, 3.8 percent is soil moisture, 3 percent is in the atmosphere, and the rest is in living things, rivers, swamps, and marshes. The entire Earth has 332,500,000 cubic miles (1,386,000,000 cubic km) of water, and of that, only 22,339 cubic miles (93,113 cubic km) is in rivers and lakes. These numbers mean that only 0.006 percent of all water on Earth is in the rivers and lakes

Robert Timoney/Alamy Stock Photo

FIGURE 13.10 **Bristol, United Kingdom.**   Flash flooding in Bristol filled lower-elevation roads with enough floodwater that they looked like rivers. Impervious surfaces in cities, like roads that may also be at lower elevations, often flood after large rainfalls.

that provide freshwater for human and animal consumption and serve as a source of irrigation for crops.

It is difficult to believe that such a small portion of all the water on Earth is in rivers and lakes when flooding of these rivers and lakes can create large-scale damage to people and property. However, when they meander from side to side, rivers carve **floodplains**, flat areas adjacent to river channels that are designed to flood. At flood stage, river water flows over its banks and into the floodplain, depositing sediment as it slows down. After the river recedes to its channels and water evaporates off the floodplain, this nutrient-rich sediment is left behind. Farmers around the world are drawn to floodplains to grow crops in these nutrient-rich soils, and people concentrate cities and settlements near freshwater sources, whether rivers or lakes. Because of this concentration of people, property, and cropland, flooding often creates natural disasters.

AP Images/Nati Harnik

FIGURE 13.11 **Bellevue, Nebraska.**   The Missouri River flooded and low spots in fields around the region also flooded when heavy rains in March fell on frozen ground. This photo was taken in May, two months after the rains.

Flash Floods   A **flash flood** happens when excessive rain or meltwater from snow overflows rivers, fills dry riverbeds, and causes a rapid rise in water levels. People try to prevent such floods by building dams and levees to control the flow of rivers and to keep river water in stream channels and off floodplains. But they also build **impervious surfaces**, including concrete and asphalt surfaces and buildings, that prevent rain dumped by large storms from percolating into soil and down into groundwater. When large rainstorms land on impervious surfaces that either purposefully or inadvertently direct floodwaters, flash flooding can result (**Fig. 13.10**).

In spring 2019, Nebraska, Iowa, and parts of South Dakota and Minnesota experienced widespread flooding when inches of rain fell on melting snow that was underlain by frozen ground (**Fig. 13.11**). The cold, snowy winter meant that soil was still frozen

-/AFP/Getty Images

FIGURE 13.12 **Kerala, India.** Volunteers and rescue personnel evacuate locals in a boat in a residential area after heavy monsoon rains flooded villages.

when rain started falling in March. The rainwater was warm enough to help speed the snowmelt, and all the water from rain and snowmelt flowed quickly over frozen ground. "The flat, frozen land, unable to soak in much of the water, spread it fast and furious, the way liquid would spread across a tiled floor. And the runoff quickly filled many rivers and streams to overflowing" (Hassan 2019). Rivers quickly breached dams and levees.

Floodwater stood on croplands for months, creating a natural disaster for farmers and residents of floodplains. In Nebraska, the cause was a snowy winter followed by rainfall amounts that were higher in March than in previous years. With climate change, "a warmer atmosphere can hold more water," which increases the likelihood of high rainfall, snowfall, and snowmelt (Hassan 2018). The devastating floods in the U.S. Midwest in 2019 created $1.3 billion in damages in Nebraska alone, which included "$449 million in damages to roads, levees and other infrastructure; $440 million in crop losses; and $400 million in cattle losses" (Schwartz 2019).

Meteorological and Climatological Hazards and Disasters

Meteorological hazards are created by the uneven heating of the Earth and Earth's atmosphere. This uneven heating generates winds that rebalance energy in the atmosphere, moving heat from the hotter equatorial area to the colder poles. The water vapor that is in the atmosphere is not evenly distributed spatially or seasonally. Because warm air can hold more water vapor than cold air, places near the equator that receive constant heating from the sun and have higher temperatures can evaporate more, hold more moisture, and produce more condensation

and precipitation. Evaporation of ocean water adds more moisture to the atmosphere. When both the ocean and the air above the ocean are warmer, the resulting high evaporation rates fuel storms, including hurricanes. That is why hurricanes happen at tropical latitudes where oceans are warmer, and from August to October when ocean temperatures and evaporation rates are highest.

Monsoons The uneven heating of Earth also creates high- and low-pressure systems and seasonal precipitation in climate regions. A **monsoon** is a prevailing wind coming from one direction for a long period of time. The monsoon climate region, which is located on either side of the equator in coastal areas, has a wet monsoon and a dry monsoon. During the wet monsoon, the prevailing wind flows from a high-pressure system over the ocean to a low-pressure system over land, pulling warm, moist air from the ocean onto the land. During the dry monsoon, the prevailing wind flows from a high-pressure system over land to a low-pressure system over the ocean, pulling cool, dry air across the land.

Monsoons are regularly occurring climate phenomena that do not generally pose a natural hazard or create natural disasters. Instead, the rains are welcomed each summer because they regenerate rivers and flood the fields where rice is grown. However, increasing temperatures in the oceans are creating more intense wet monsoons in India. A recent study of the Indian monsoon found that "extreme wet and dry spells within the monsoon period have increased since 1980" (Ogburn 2014). Such changing monsoon intensities impact people, property, and agriculture in India. In 2018, the southern state of Kerala experienced the "worst monsoon flooding in a century, with more than one million people displaced, and more than 400 reported deaths" (Taylor 2018). The intense monsoon rains caused flooding and landslides that displaced approximately 800,000 people (**Fig. 13.12**). When the monsoon, which is a climatological event that is predictable and desirable, becomes unreliable and unpredictable, it can become a natural hazard or even a natural disaster.

TC **Thinking Geographically**

Tourism is a major focus of **development** efforts in lower income tropical countries with beautiful coastlines, like Indonesia. Explain how developing tourism on coastlines impacts the vulnerability of countries to natural hazards and natural disasters.

13.2 Identify the Ways That Humans Impact Earth Through Land Use, Water Use, and Resource Extraction.

Early societies had relatively small populations, and their impacts on the physical environment were limited in both duration and intensity. With the development of agriculture and settlement in agricultural villages, people increasingly altered the physical environment, but the effects of these early activities were still limited in scale. Even the beginning of urbanization and the development of cities, which concentrated large numbers of people in certain places, had relatively limited global effects. However, the current era includes large-scale industrialization, intensification of agriculture, the growth of megacities, massive consumption and waste generation, and global trade. For the first time in history, the combined impacts of humanity's destructive and exploitative actions are producing environmental changes at a global scale.

The natural environment is being modified and stressed by human activity in many obvious and some less-obvious ways. Some environmental stress is more obvious because it takes place around human habitats, such as that caused by cutting forests and emitting pollutants into the atmosphere. Less-obvious environmental stress takes place away from dense concentrations of humans, including that caused by mining mountaintops, burying toxic wastes that contaminate groundwater supplies, and dumping vast amounts of garbage into waterways and the world's oceans. Humans have terraced mountains to grow rice, built miles of aqueducts and qanats to move water, and dammed enormous rivers to make places livable for larger numbers of people.

Over the last 500 years, both the rate and the scale at which people modify Earth have increased dramatically. Particularly during the last half-century, every place on Earth has been transformed, either directly or indirectly, by people. The twentieth-century surge in the size of the human population, combined with a rapid escalation in consumption, magnifies humanity's impact on Earth in unprecedented ways. Earth is predicted to reach 9.9 billion people by 2050. Because people across the world do not consume or pollute in the same ways, we cannot make a simple chart showing that each additional person born on Earth results in a certain amount of consumption or generates a specific amount of pollution or waste. Nonetheless, a greater number of people on Earth coupled with current levels of human consumption necessarily translates into greater environmental change (**Fig. 13.13**).

Recognizing the rapid growth of human population and the incredible role humans play in shaping Earth's environment,

scientists report that we have entered a new geologic epoch, the **Anthropocene**. The Anthropocene is the current geologic time period when humans are the dominant influence on climate and environment. *Anthropo* means "human" and *cene* is a term used by geologists to denote time periods in Earth's history.

Land Use

As the number of people on Earth increases, so too does the strain on land. People clear forests and burn grasses to plant crops. People flatten mountains to build transportation systems and mine resources. Cities grow at remarkable rates and sprawl into productive farmland. **Land use** refers to the ways people use land resources for specific purposes. For example, agriculture is a land use. **Land cover** refers to what is on the ground, such as grasses, trees, or pavement (Coffey 2013). What people choose to do with the land—land use—changes over time, and these choices impact land cover. If we choose to deforest a swath

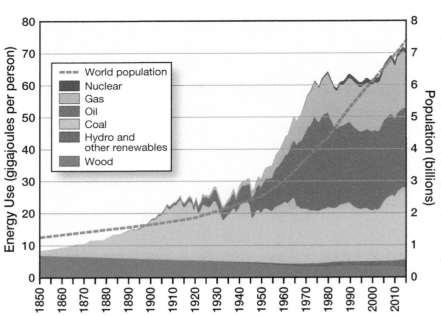

FIGURE 13.13   **Human Population and Energy Consumption since 1850.**   As the number of people on Earth has quickly risen, energy consumption has grown markedly. Energy sources have also diversified.

Source: Data from Curriculum and Population Information, Population Education. Visualization by E.H. Fouberg and A.B. Murphy. © 2020 John Wiley & Sons, Inc

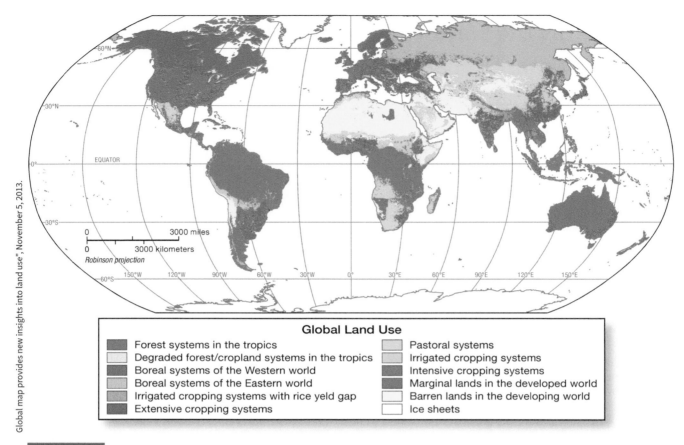

Global Land Use

- Forest systems in the tropics
- Degraded forest/cropland systems in the tropics
- Boreal systems of the Western world
- Boreal systems of the Eastern world
- Irrigated cropping systems with rice yield gap
- Extensive cropping systems

- Pastoral systems
- Irrigated cropping systems
- Intensive cropping systems
- Marginal lands in the developed world
- Barren lands in the developing world
- Ice sheets

FIGURE 13.14 **Global Land Use.** A group of European scientists created this map of 12 land system archetypes (LSAs) based on intensity of land use, environmental and climate conditions, and socio-economic factors. Regardless of the factors going into global land use maps, land use varies by latitude and elevation and correlates strongly with climates.

of land to grow crops, we change the *land use* from forest to agriculture. At the same time, our choice impacts the *land cover*, switching it from forest to row crops.

Geographers map land cover using both remote sensing and GIS (geographic information systems). Mapping land use requires millions of data points and a classification system to organize the data. A global land use map based on land use data and population density gives us an idea of how people extract productivity from land (**Fig. 13.14**).

Instead of simply mapping land cover, such as crops, a land use map shows differences in farming methods, including areas of extensive agriculture and intensive agriculture. **Extensive agriculture** uses little fertilizer, pesticides, and machinery to farm the land, while **intensive agriculture** uses significant capital investments, including in fertilizer, pesticides, and machinery, relative to the amount of land farmed. The yield, or amount of crop grown per acre, is typically less with extensive agriculture than with intensive, but extensive agriculture may have less impact on waterways because of less runoff from fertilizers and pesticides. However, farmers who practice intensive agriculture have little interest in wasting fertilizers and pesticides because each has a cost. A great deal of research and technology goes into helping farmers in intensive agriculture decide when and where to spray pesticides or apply fertilizer, and what seeds to plant in different conditions.

Deforestation and Palm Oil Plantations A land use map also differentiates forest systems. High-latitude, boreal forests in the Western world are differentiated from those in the Eastern world. Forest systems in the tropics are differentiated from degraded forests in the tropics.

Forests play a critical role in the oxygen cycle. Through photosynthesis, plants take in carbon dioxide from the air, water, and sunlight, and produce oxygen, which humans need to breathe. The destruction of vast tracts of forest, typically caused by clearing forestland for agriculture or livestock use, is called **deforestation**. Deforestation impacts the carbon cycle because it removes a major sink of carbon dioxide from Earth. In addition, burning trees to clear a forest releases massive amounts of carbon dioxide into the atmosphere. Between 2000 and 2013, 10 percent of all anthropogenic (human-caused) greenhouse gases released into Earth's atmosphere came from tropical deforestation (Vijay et al. 2016). Indonesia had so much deforestation in 2015 that it outpaced the United States as the biggest emitter of greenhouse gases that year.

A major motivator for deforestation in Indonesia is the production of palm oil, which is now the most widely used vegetable oil in the world. Around 50 percent of the products in a grocery store, from snack food to shampoo, include palm oil. Palm oil is also used as a biofuel in the United States and the European Union. When the United States and Europe passed laws mandating the

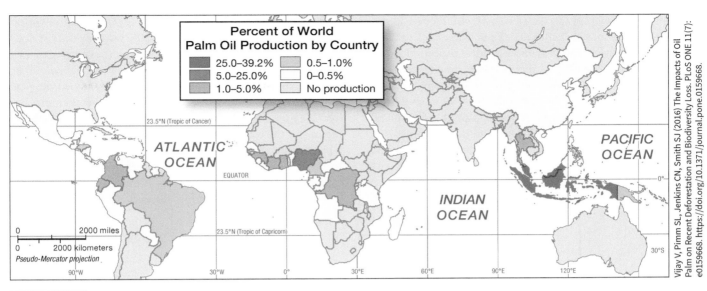

Vijay V, Pimm SL, Jenkins CN, Smith SJ (2016) The Impacts of Oil Palm on Recent Deforestation and Biodiversity Loss. PLoS ONE 11(7): e0159668. https://doi.org/10.1371/journal.pone.0159668.

FIGURE 13.15 **Palm Oil Production.** Palm oil is produced in the tropics, along the equator (between the Tropic of Cancer and the Tropic of Capricorn), with highest production levels in Indonesia and Malaysia.

increased use of biofuels in the early 2000s, cropland needed to be expanded, and it has been at the expense of forests:

> Lawmakers never anticipated that their well-intentioned plan—to help the climate by helping American farmers—might instead transform Indonesia and present one of the greatest threats to the planet's tropical rain forests. But as Indonesian palm oil began to flood Western markets, that is exactly what began to happen. (Lustgarten 2018)

Agricultural production had already spread to nearly all marginal land, including semiarid lands in the western United States. To create a bigger supply of vegetable oils to meet the demand for biofuels the law created, the United States had to look toward imports. In this way, a policy intended to decrease dependence on foreign oil and the burning of fossil fuels contributed more greenhouse gases to the atmosphere than all of Europe did in 2015. Because forests have carbon trapped in the trees and soils, clearing and burning "the existing forests to make way for oil-palm cultivation had a perverse effect: It released more carbon. A lot more carbon" (Lustgarten 2018).

Palm oil production is having the biggest impact on Indonesia and Malaysia (**Fig. 13.15**). The two countries produce 90 percent of all palm oil, and they are also home to 90 percent of the world's orangutans. Biodiversity is directly impacted by crop production. When you clear a complex rainforest ecosystem and plant rows of palm oil trees, habitat is directly lost. The ecosystem of a palm oil plantation is nothing remotely like the ecosystem of a naturally occurring rainforest (**Fig. 13.16**). The population of orangutans on the island of Borneo (which is shared by Indonesia and Malaysia) has declined by 50 percent since 1999 (Gibbens 2017).

The demand for palm oil continues to climb because it can be used in so many products and because its yield is much higher per acre than that of soybean oil or coconut oil. The massive deforestation effort across the tropical zone to rachet up production of palm oil is directly impacting indigenous

people and small landholders. More than 700 conflicts between large palm oil corporations and indigenous people or small landholders have been reported in Indonesia alone. The Indonesian government has generally fallen on the side of the palm oil producers, though under international pressure, it recently passed legislation placing a moratorium on oil palm permits.

Water Use

Resources that are replenished even as they are being used are **renewable resources**, and resources that are present in finite quantities are **nonrenewable resources**. Water, essential to life, is a renewable resource. The volume of precipitation in the

Rich Carey/Shutterstock.com

FIGURE 13.16 **Malaysia.** The border is sharp between a palm oil plantation at the bottom of the photo and tropical rainforest at the top of the photo. Rainforests have great biodiversity that is threatened by turning forest land into palm oil plantations.

world is enormous; spread out evenly, it would cover Earth's land area with about 33 inches (83 cm) of water each year. But the available supply of freshwater is not distributed evenly across the globe. Figure 1.22 shows the world distribution of precipitation, with the largest totals recorded along the equator and in the tropics. While the amount of water on Earth is plentiful, the global supply of freshwater is anything but plentiful. Chronic water shortages afflict rural and urban areas.

We learn to think of water as a constant whose distribution is sustained through the **hydrologic cycle**, in which water from oceans, lakes, soil, rivers, and vegetation evaporates, condenses, and then falls as precipitation on land. Precipitation infiltrates and recharges groundwater or runs off into lakes, rivers, and oceans. However, physical geographer Jamie Linton questions the utility of any model of the water cycle that does not consider the role of humans and culture, suggesting that by "representing water as a constant, cyclical flow, the hydrologic cycle establishes a norm that is at odds with the hydrological reality of much of the world" (Linton 2008). For example, the hydrologic cycle does not consider the norms of water in arid regions of the world, and it also assumes that water cycles in a predictable, linear fashion. But the amount of water cycling through the Earth is not a constant. For instance, changes in land cover affect how much water is in the cycle. The **global water system** better accounts for human water use and the built environment (**Fig. 13.17**).

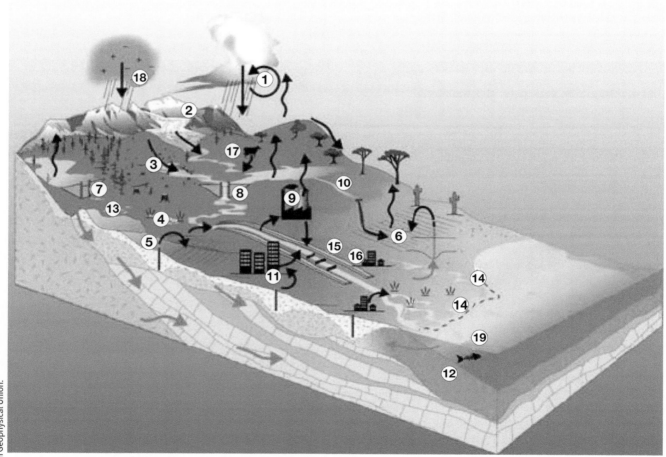

Source: Adapted from American Geophysical Union.

1. Hydrological cycle accelerated
2. Mountain snow and ice lost
3. Tree removal increases runoff, reduces transpiration, affects water table and landscape salinity
4. Wetlands dried up or drained
5,6. Ground- and surface water used for irrigated agriculture

7,8. Dams alter flow and reservoirs increase evaporation
9. Industrial water coolers release water vapor
10. Water transfers between basins
11. Urban, mining, and construction areas alter water flows and quality
12. Coastal saltwater intrudes inland

13. Impoundments reduce flows
14. Siltation, erosion, and nutrient flows change coastlines and affect water quality
15. Levees and locks modify flows and channels
16. Settlements alter floodplain landscapes
17. Grazing affects runoff and water quality
18. Industry causes acid rain
19. Coastal waters polluted and species lost

FIGURE 13.17 **The Global Water System.** Unlike the traditional diagram of the hydrologic cycle (water cycle), the human imprint is reflected in this diagram of the global water system.

A Plastic Ocean Earth is often called the Blue Planet because more than 70 percent of its surface is covered by water and views from space are dominated by blue hues and swirls of white clouds. Oceans are essential to life. First, they produce oxygen through photosynthesis of phytoplankton and other plants. Oxygen is essential to human, animal, and plant survival. Oceans also absorb enormous quantities of carbon dioxide (CO_2). Ocean currents redistribute energy from the tropics to the polar regions. Oceans also provide resources, including fish stocks, and are homes for fish farms. Oil companies extract billions of barrels of oil from the continental shelf under oceans.

With oceans covering 70 percent of Earth, it would seem that Earth's 7.6 billion people would not impact the entire ocean, but we do. About 10 percent of the plastic used by humans ends up in the ocean each year, and the amount is compounding quickly as the amount of plastic waste ratchets up each year (**Fig. 13.18**). Of the 8.3 billion metric tons of plastic that has been produced, 6.3 billion metric tons has been discarded as waste. Plastic recycling bins are everywhere, but little plastic is recycled. Only 9 percent of the 6.3 billion metric tons of waste is recycled. Another 12 percent is incinerated, and 79 percent is "accumulated in landfills or the natural environment" (Geyer et al. 2017).

Human use of plastic and fascination with it are relatively recent. The first plastics were made in the 1920s and were used primarily in the military. After World War II, less expensive, synthetic plastics were created and the use of plastics exploded. The diffusion of the automobile, the growth of suburbs, and growing numbers of people in the workforce after World War II all helped create demand for convenience. Plastics are used in household appliances like toasters and goods like hairbrushes, but their most widespread use is in packaging. Think of the number of premade meals in your grocery store, whether in the freezer section or the hot food case at the deli. Each one is encased in plastic. Now imagine the number of grocery stores in the world (one estimate is 40,000 grocery stores in the United States alone) and you start to realize how ubiquitous single-use plastic packaging is.

Human use of plastic impacts the environment from the point of production. Plastics are synthetic polymers made up of monomers, which are carbon-based compounds derived from oil. Chemists can create a broad range of plastics in the lab, and large-scale production of goods is made simple because plastics are easily shaped into everything from a toy car to a toilet bowl brush to a computer keyboard. The moldability of plastics is what makes them so attractive for producing consumer goods and packaging.

Plastics do not easily decay. Once created, used, and disposed of, plastics break down slowly over time but do not biodegrade. Plastics are either directly disposed of in the ocean or find their way there from beaches, through waterways that empty into the ocean, through improper disposal or incineration, or through natural hazards like tsunamis that demolish the built environment and carry waste into the ocean (**Fig. 13.19**). In the ocean, sunlight and waves break plastics down into millions of smaller pieces called **microplastics** that not only float on the surface but also are carried to depths by marine invertebrates (Parker 2017). The presence of microplastics is directly impacting marine life and humans. The smallest animals in the food chain, foraging fish like anchovies, eat plastic in the ocean. Larger fish eat the smaller fish, and humans ingest the toxicity of the plastic when they consume the larger fish.

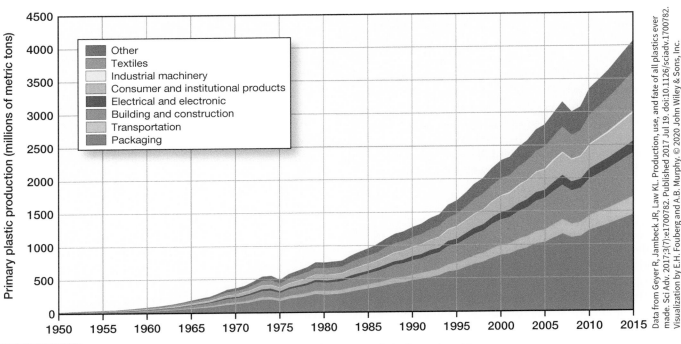

Data from Geyer R, Jambeck JR, Law KL. Production, use, and fate of all plastics ever made. Sci Adv. 2017;3(7):e1700782. Published 2017 Jul 19. doi:10.1126/sciadv.1700782. Visualization by E.H. Fouberg and A.B. Murphy. © 2020 John Wiley & Sons, Inc.

FIGURE 13.18 **Plastic Production Since 1950.** The growth in the amount of plastic produced for packaging has ramped up at a faster rate than other uses.

Rich Carey/Shutterstock.com

FIGURE 13.19 **Semporna, Malaysia.** Much of the plastic we produce ends up in oceans and washes onto beaches, following currents and wave patterns.

Ocean waves deposit microplastics and even larger pieces of plastic on beaches, and ocean currents circling around high-pressure systems gather plastic dumped into the ocean into huge gyres. The **Great Pacific Garbage Patch** is the biggest of the garbage gyres and forms around the high-pressure cell in the northern Pacific Ocean. More plastic swirls through this gyre than through others because plastic is produced, consumed, and dumped at alarming rates around the North Pacific, which is flanked by Asia on the west and North America on the east. As the high-pressure cell moves, the gyre of plastic moves with it. Scientists can reach the Great Pacific Garbage Patch, but removing the plastics would have more consequences for the ocean. Right now, the only way to remove the microplastics is by using fine-mesh nets, which would also skim the ocean phytoplankton, the base of the ocean's food chain and source for atmospheric oxygen.

Resource Extraction

Since the Industrial Revolution began in the late 1700s, humans have increasingly turned to technology to solve problems, improve productivity, protect against disease, and create new products. But technologies come at a cost. Resource extraction, including drilling for oil and natural gas, mining for elements, and logging, have fundamentally changed economic, political, and environmental systems. The products humans have created and the multitude of ways we have innovated to produce

and ship goods are truly remarkable. However, there are by products, including hazardous toxins, pollution, and health problems, that we are only now beginning to recognize.

Human ingenuity has enabled both population and life expectancies to grow but has also led to degradation of the oceans (oil and gas exploitation and spills, pollution dumping, and massive overfishing), land surfaces (open-pit and mountaintop mining, dams, and irrigation projects), the biosphere (deforestation, vegetation loss), and the atmosphere (air pollution).

As the first parts of the planet to industrialize, western Europe and North America long led the world in industrial-related pollution. Now attention is turning to China, which rapidly industrialized in the late 1900s and early 2000s. China is extending industrial production through its One Belt, One Road and Maritime Silk Road initiatives to around 100 countries worldwide (see Chapter 8 and Chapter 10).

Hydrocarbons Oil is a nonrenewable resource. It is not a question of whether the world's oil supply will run out but when. Because discoveries of new reserves continue to be made, and because the extraction of hydrocarbons is becoming ever more efficient, it is difficult to predict exactly how much longer oil will remain a viable energy source. Many suggest that the current level of oil consumption can be sustained for up to 100 years, although you can find as many arguments for much shorter or much longer time frames. Despite the range of calculations, most scientists believe that by the middle of

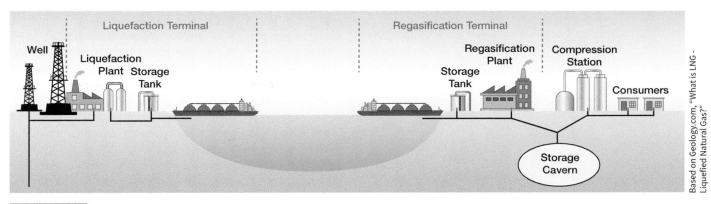

Based on Geology.com, "What is LNG - Liquefied Natural Gas?"

FIGURE 13.20 **Liquification and Regasification of Natural Gas.**   Transporting liquid is easier than transporting gas. Scientists created a method to liquefy natural gas at its source location, ship it long distances, and regasify it at its destination.

this century, alternative sources will have to play a much more significant role than they do now.

The widespread technological change that has happened since the beginning of the Industrial Revolution has been built on burning **hydrocarbons**: organic compounds made of hydrogen and carbon. Because hydrocarbons can be burned when in the presence of oxygen, they can be used as fuel. The Industrial Revolution was built on burning coal to power steam engines. We still use coal as a fuel, especially in power plants. And you see the ubiquitous use of oil in gas pumps across the country.

In recent decades, natural gas has emerged as an increasingly common alternative to oil. Natural gas can be extracted from the oil refinement process. Major subsurface reservoirs of natural gas also exist, and we use fracking and other methods to extract natural gas from the subsoil. Like oil, natural gas is a hydrocarbon that releases carbon dioxide when it is burned, but it burns somewhat more cleanly than oil.

Despite its advantages, natural gas is difficult to store and transport. To address this problem, scientists have figured out how to condense natural gas at a very low temperature to create liquefied natural gas (LNG). The process is expensive, and LNG is highly flammable, but demand for LNG is increasing. The largest exporters of LNG are Qatar, Australia, Indonesia, and the United States. As part of a nation-wide fuel switching program, China has rapidly increased its demand for LNG. Most of China's power is created through burning dirty coal (power plants that do not using air scrubbers), and to reduce air pollution, the government has instituted a fuel-switching plan to cleaner-burning natural gas. A great deal of engineering is needed to liquify and then regasify natural gas (**Fig. 13.20**).

Natural gas deposits are not always easy to reach. Hydraulic fracturing, or fracking, is one method used to reach these deposits in shale (**Fig. 13.21**). Hydraulic fracturing requires injecting a high-pressure fluid—water mixed with sand and a proprietary blend of chemicals—into deep shale

rock formations to create small fissures and release natural gas. The gas is captured and transported via pipeline to compression stations or liquification terminals.

Hydraulic fracturing comes at a potentially high environmental cost. First, it uses a lot of water. In addition, the chemicals added to the water may contaminate groundwater. Residents who live near fracking operations have reported unclean or even flammable water coming out of their faucets. Second, fracking can also create seismic activity. Some earthquakes are too small to be easily detectable, but scientists do not know what the long-term consequences may be. Finally, removing oil and gas from shale also emits greenhouse gases, especially methane.

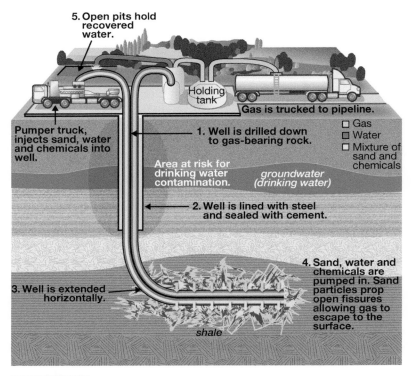

FIGURE 13.21 **How Hydraulic Fracturing (Fracking) Works.**   First, deep wells are drilled and then chemicals and water are pumped into the wells to force natural gas out of shale and toward the surface.

Photo by E.H. Fouberg. © 2020 John Wiley & Sons, Inc.

FIGURE 13.22 **Lake Benton, Minnesota.** The wind park near Lake Benton, Minnesota, was developed beginning in 1994 and now includes more than 600 wind turbines.

Rare Earth Elements

One advantage of alternative energies is that their production creates fewer emissions of carbon dioxide and other greenhouse gases. However, the production of alternative energy still requires resources and infrastructure. A single wind turbine (**Fig. 13.22**) is made of fiberglass, weighs hundreds of metric tons, stands 90 meters (196 ft) high, and "fundamentally relies on roughly 300 kilograms of soft, silvery metal known as neodymium," a rare earth element (Biello 2010, 16). Neodymium is used for the powerful magnets in a wind turbine that generate electricity. It is one of 17 elements on the periodic table that are considered rare earth elements.

Rare earth elements are in demand because they are used not only in wind turbines, but also in alternative energy cars, computers, screens, compact fluorescent light bulbs, cell phones, MRI scanners, and advanced weapons systems (Biello 2010). They are found in rock, and 97 percent of the rare earth elements mined today come from China. Mining is only the first step in their exploitation, because making them usable requires separating elements that are bound together in rock. Once the rocks are mined, Chinese companies intensively boil them in acid to separate the neodymium from other rare earth elements, repeating the process "thousands of times because the elements are so chemically similar" (Biello 2010, 17).

The chemical processing of rare earth elements uses electricity and water—leaving behind chemicals and residuals, including thorium (a radioactive metal) and salt. The environmental consequences of rare earth element mining have historically been costly enough that production stopped at the one mine in the United States in 2002, in part because of the cost of complying with environmental laws.

Looser environmental laws and lower labor costs have increased the production of rare earth elements in China during the last decade (**Fig. 13.23**). In Inner Mongolia, China,

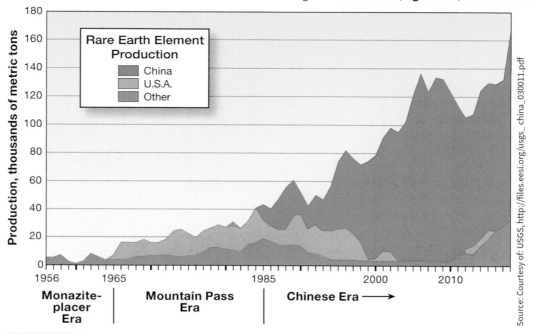

Source: Courtesy of: USGS, http://files.eesi.org/usgs_china_030011.pdf

FIGURE 13.23 **Rare Earth Element Production Since 1956.** Rare earth elements are produced primarily in China because of the environmental impacts of extraction and refinement. Technological devices like cell phones are increasingly recycled to extract and reuse the rare earth elements in them.

FIGURE 13.24 **Inner Mongolia, China.** Satellite imagery of the Bayan Obo mine shows two large open-pit, circular mines near the center top of the image. The leaf-shaped features to the right and left of the mines are tailings (ground rocks) piles.

the extraction of rare earth elements at the Bayan Obo mine alone accounts for 40 percent of the world's supply. China closed off access to the mine to all outsiders, but the mine's enormous pits and waste ponds can still be viewed from space and are even visible using Google Earth (**Fig.13.24**).

China will likely remain the leading producer of rare earth elements in the near term. However, recycling rare earth elements from discarded devices and new mining efforts in the United States, Australia, and Vietnam will likely improve the availability of rare earth elements from sources outside of China in years to come.

> **TC** **Thinking Geographically**
>
> Coal fuels most power plants in Ohio. Look at this website to understand where most coal is produced in the United States: https://www.eia.gov/energyexplained/coal/where-our-coal-comes-from.php. Think through how coal is transported to Ohio's power plants. If Ohio changed its fuel source to renewable energy (wind, solar), how would that create new **development** opportunities, including technologies, businesses, and employment opportunities in and around Ohio? How would it impact the coal-producing states?

13.3 Explain How Climate Change Is Impacting Human–Environment Interactions.

The sun emits shortwave radiation that travels over 94 million miles through the atmosphere to reach Earth's surface. Earth absorbs the shortwave radiation and then emits longwave radiation, creating **sensible heat**, the temperature we feel around us. This process of absorption and emission happens every place on Earth that receives the sun's energy.

This description is not the complete picture, though. The atmosphere is a layer of gases surrounding Earth. The shortwave energy from the sun travels through the atmosphere to reach the surface, and the longwave radiation from Earth travels through the atmosphere as it rises. Naturally occurring greenhouse gases cluster at the top of the troposphere (about 8 to 11 miles above Earth's surface). These **greenhouse gases** absorb some longwave energy emitted from Earth and act like a "lid," reradiating it back to the surface. This naturally occurring greenhouse effect keeps Earth about 59°F (15°C) warmer than it would be without greenhouse gases (**Fig. 13.25**).

The basic premise of climate change science is that humans are burning hydrocarbons, which releases greenhouse gases that intensify the greenhouse effect. Since the Industrial Revolution, the amount of greenhouse gases in the atmosphere has increased at an alarming rate. Automobiles, steel mills, power plants, oil and natural gas refineries, and chemical plants account for much of this increase. An overwhelming majority of climate scientists have concluded that the increase in greenhouse gases from anthropogenic (human) sources is causing

the Earth to retain more energy. Energy is the driver of climate, ocean currents, winds, and storms. Adding more energy into Earth's atmosphere has consequences, and like other global processes, those consequences are uneven and often unintended.

The average temperature of Earth has risen 1.1°F (0.6°C) since 1980. In the same time frame, the amount of carbon dioxide in the atmosphere has risen from 336 to 441 parts per million (**Fig. 13.26**). Because the average temperature of Earth is increasing, climate change is sometimes called global warming, but *climate change* is a more accurate term because it's not as simple as a cozy blanket warming us up "just a bit." The temperature alone is not the story; the added energy in Earth's atmosphere is what matters. Energy fuels Earth processes, and entire systems are changing.

Sea-level rise is one aspect of climate change. Low-lying islands in the Indian Ocean and the South Pacific are already experiencing this effect. Tuvalu is an average of 6.5 feet (2m) above sea level (**Fig. 13.27**), and current predictions mean that the Pacific Ocean will inundate Tuvalu by 2050. Change has already reached the island. Rainfall is less predictable, saltwater is flowing into coastal freshwater supplies, and storms are intensifying. Media reports often call Tuvaluans "climate change refugees." Locals reject the term *refugees*, however, because it suggests they are passive victims (Farbotko). Tuvaluans are actively choosing migration to cope with the impact of climate change (see Chapter 3).

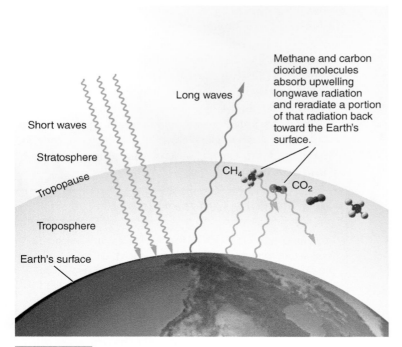

FIGURE 13.25 **Greenhouse Effect.** Incoming solar radiation (insolation) is relatively short wave. Earth absorbs the energy and emits energy at longer wavelengths. The long wave energy moves up through the troposphere and hits greenhouse gases, where some of the energy is absorbed, some makes it through to the stratosphere, and some is reradiated to Earth. The energy reradiated to Earth creates a warming effect called the greenhouse effect.

AP® Exam Taker's Tip

Human behavior is changing the natural environment. Can you describe the ways that humans have changed the environment and the impact it is having across the globe?

Hurricanes

With higher temperatures and more energy in the atmosphere, the rates of evaporation—through which liquid water turns to water vapor—increase. Energy must be added in the form of latent heat to transform liquid water to water vapor. In a storm, this water vapor is condensed into liquid water, and in the process of condensation, latent heat is released. Because energy fuels evaporation and is released through condensation, higher temperatures and warmer oceans mean that more energy goes into storms, whether hurricanes or midlatitude cyclones.

Today greater energy is fueling more intense hurricanes. For example, Hurricane Harvey dumped 60 inches of rain on Houston, Texas, in fall 2017 (**Fig. 13.28**). Scientists found that "the amount of energy Harvey pulled from the ocean in the form of rising water vapor" was equal to the "the amount of energy it

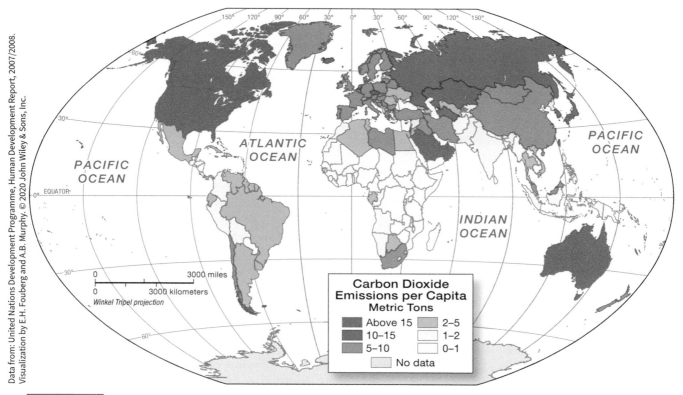

Data from: United Nations Development Programme, Human Development Report, 2007/2008. Visualization by E.H. Fouberg and A.B. Murphy. © 2020 John Wiley & Sons, Inc.

FIGURE 13.26 **Carbon Dioxide Emissions per Capita.** China's total carbon dioxide emissions exceed those of the United States. However, in per capita emissions of carbon dioxide, mapped here, the United States, Canada, Saudi Arabia, and Australia are among the highest.

FIGURE 13.27 **Tuvalu.** The country of Tuvalu has an average elevation of 6.5 feet and the highest elevation is 15 feet above sea level. Much of the Pacific island country is barely above sea level.

dropped over land in the form of rain." In other words, the energy that went into evaporation was released through condensation. And because climate change led to warmer oceans and warmer air, the amount of energy in the hurricane system increased. Scientists estimate that "climate change caused Harvey's rainfall to be 15 to 38 percent greater than it would have been otherwise" (Fischeti 2018).

Water Scarcity

One-fifth of the world's population lives in regions confronting **water scarcity**, the lack of enough water to meet demand. Remarkably, geographers have found that countries facing growing water concerns tend toward cooperation instead of political violence. Cooperation usually takes the form of transboundary or multilateral treaties governing the use and protection of water resources. Between 1948 and 1999, countries entered into more than 150 agreements over water. From the Mekong to the Ganges to the Indus to the Niger, treaties have helped to promote the equitable management of river waters.

Geographers Shira Yoffe, Aaron T. Wolf, and Mark Giordano created the *Basins at Risk* project to monitor changes in river flows and cooperation levels between countries. The researchers integrated socioeconomic, political, and physical variables into a geographic information system (GIS). Tying the data to specific countries and river basins, they tested how well the data predicted historical disputes and cooperation between countries over international river basins (2001). Their research found that no single indicator, including per capita GDP, population density, dependence on water for agriculture, or government type, predicted conflict over water. Between 1948 and 1999, cooperation over water "far outweighed overall conflict over water and violent conflict in particular" (2001, 72). Their findings dispelled

many statements coming from academics in international relations and environmental security research that arid places fight more over water than nonarid places. Yoffe, Wolf, and Giordano found that "arid regions were not . . . substantially less cooperative than other climate zones" (2001, 89). Their map of current conflicts, protests over water, and indicators of conflict by river basin reveals no clear connection between arid climate regions and water conflict (**Fig. 13.29**).

However, not all agreements over water will be able to handle the extremes of drought and flooding that are more likely with climate change. It takes cooperation to reach a water treaty or agreement, and cooperation needs to continue over monitoring and enforcement. Water stress is rising in basins where the extremes of drought and flooding from climate change are challenging the agreements.

People cope with water stress by moving. People may migrate to another place, or those with livestock may move herds to more dependable freshwater sources. Migration and movement spurred by growing extremes in water variability are occurring both across country borders and within countries. A 2018 World Bank study predicts that a growing number of people will move within their country in response to water stress, either flooding or drought. Specifically, the World Bank predicts 143 million internal migrants by 2050. This will be in addition to a growing number of migrants crossing borders.

Human-Induced Water Scarcity in the Aral Sea

In addition to being caused by extreme fluctuations caused by climate change, water scarcity can be created by humans. As human populations have expanded, people have increasingly settled in arid regions. One of the great ecological disasters of the twentieth century occurred in Kazakhstan and Uzbekistan, whose common boundary runs through the Aral Sea. Streams that feed this large body of water were diverted to irrigate the surrounding desert, mainly for commercial cotton production.

Both Kazakhstan and Uzbekistan were part of the Soviet Union (USSR) when it controlled much of Eurasia between

FIGURE 13.28 **Houston, Texas.** Hurricane Harvey caused record flooding in Houston in 2017.

Source: Based on Yoffe, S., Wolf, Aaron T. and Giordano, M., "Chapter 4 Conflict and Cooperation over International Freshwater Resources: Indicators and Findings of the Basins at Risk Project", Oregon State University.

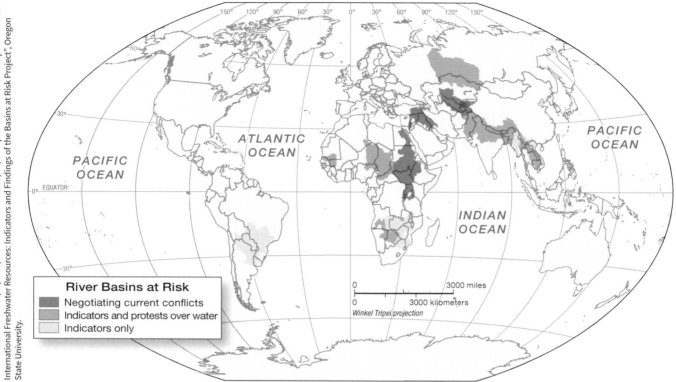

River Basins at Risk

- Negotiating current conflicts
- Indicators and protests over water
- Indicators only

FIGURE 13.29 **River Basins at Risk.** Geographers at Oregon State University created a database of conflicts and protests in and around river basins globally. Through their research, they found water scarcity did not correlate with protests and conflicts over river use.

1924 and 1991. Under the Soviet policy of centralized planning, the countries were required to produce a certain amount of cotton each year. Cotton is a water-intensive crop. To produce it in an arid climate, farmers diverted water from the two rivers that fed the Aral Sea. Over a short time, between the 1960s and the 1990s, the Aral Sea lost more than three-quarters of its total surface area (**Fig. 13.30**).

In 2001, the Kazakhstan government, with a loan from the World Bank, began work to restore the lake. A dam was completed in 2005, and leaky irrigation canals have been fixed. As a result,

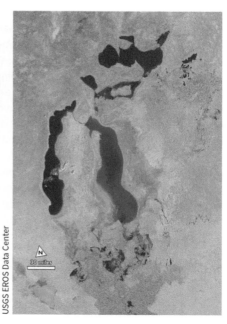

FIGURE 13.30 **The Aral Sea.** The Aral Sea on the border of Kazakhstan and Uzbekistan has shrunk significantly. The image on the left is from 1977, and the one in the middle is from 1998. The image on the right from 2010 reflects a loss of three-quarters of its surface area and more than 90 percent of its volume.

the northern end of the lake is capturing more water from the Syr Darya River and the fishing industry has rebounded slightly. The southern part of the Aral Sea is not rebounding as well as the northern. The independent Uzbekistan government continues to set cotton production quotas for farmers and imposes a system of forced "volunteer" labor, pulling people out of their regular work and into cotton fields to help harvest by hand each year. In both countries, overuse of the land has created salty, parched soils. Because of overuse, pesticides have leached into the groundwater and created an additional environmental impact in the region.

TC Thinking Geographically

Study the map of flooding caused by Hurricane Harvey in Houston in 2017: https://www.air-worldwide.com/Models/Tropical-Cyclone/Hurricane-Harvey-s-Lasting-Legacy--Flood/. Describe the **pattern** of flooding, paying particular attention to rivers, streams, and coastlines. Then determine how impervious surfaces in Houston impacted flooding both during Hurricane Harvey and in flooding events that have happened since.

13.4   Explain How Human Consumption Is Changing the Scale of Human Impact and Challenging Sustainability.

We can map the forces of globalization, from container ships to instant global communication to the movement of electronic money. We can see which places are most connected and which are most remote. What we cannot see are cause and effect. In a globalized world, every policy and every action has unintended consequences. A decision made in one place has outcomes halfway around the world. Think for a minute about the example of the secondhand clothing trade discussed in Chapter 10. You donate a shirt in your hometown, and it gets bundled into bales with hundreds of other pieces of clothing, stuffed into containers, and shipped to Africa. The intention is to help someone who needs clothing. The unintended consequence is supporting an entire industry of secondhand clothing, using fossil fuels to propel a container ship across the Atlantic, and undermining the textile industry in Africa, whether in Senegal or Zambia.

Living in a world where we cannot see or even imagine the outcomes of our actions makes it perhaps easier to ignore them. But one problem we need to be aware of is **human consumption**, which is increasing rapidly with growing populations and rising levels of income, and which has both intended and unintended consequences. You purchase a gift for a friend on an Etsy store to support a creative person's small business. Eventually, that gift reaches the end of its life cycle and your friend disposes of it. At that point, the gift could end up anywhere in the world as part of the global system of waste disposal. The scale of human consumption today and the consumption predicted for 30 years from now creates a range of problems that need to be addressed. Being conscious of this problem, whether as consumers or producers of goods, is a first step.

Global Patterns of Consumption

Humans rely on Earth's resources for survival. At the most basic level, we consume water, oxygen, and organic and mineral materials. Over time we have developed increasingly complex ways of using resources to intensify agricultural and industrial production. Our **pattern** of consumption has shifted from all of our needs coming from a small, concentrated area, to our needs being imported from dozens of countries, some of which are

halfway around the world. To examine patterns, geographers look at how things are distributed and then analyze whether they are clustered, dispersed, or follow some other pattern. Ancient hunter-gatherers subsisted, on average, on the resources found within an area of about 26 square kilometers (10 sq mi) (Simmons 1996). Today, we consume resources at a level and rate that far exceed basic subsistence needs.

Nongovernmental organizations such as the Global Footprint Network and the World Wildlife Fund create scales to measure the amount of resources needed to support individuals and countries today. The **ecological footprint** is the impact a person or country has on the environment. It is measured by how much land is required to sustain the person's or country's use of natural resources and to dispose of the waste produced. The current average ecological footprint of a person today is 6.8 global hectares, which is "four times the resources and wastes that our planet can regenerate and absorb into the atmosphere" (Global Footprint Network 2018). The two most populated countries, China and India, have high total footprints, coming in at first and third, respectively. The ecological footprints of the United States (second), Russia (fourth), and Brazil (fifth) are quite high for countries with much smaller populations than China and India.

Most of us living in the global economic core draw on resources from places scattered all over the world. The **pattern** of our consumption is widespread. In any room in a house, goods are imported from all parts of the world. The countries with the highest per capita ecological imprint are small or arid countries that typically import foodstuffs and even water, making their imprint larger (**Fig. 13.31**). In rank order, the top five countries in terms of per capita ecological footprint are Qatar, Luxembourg, United Arab Emirates, Bahrain, and Kuwait. The United States and Canada rank seventh and eighth behind Trinidad and Tobago.

AP® Exam Taker's Tip

Figure 13.31 looks at the ecological footprint. A possible free-response question on the AP exam could ask you to define ecological footprint and explain why it is higher in some countries than others. How would you construct an answer?

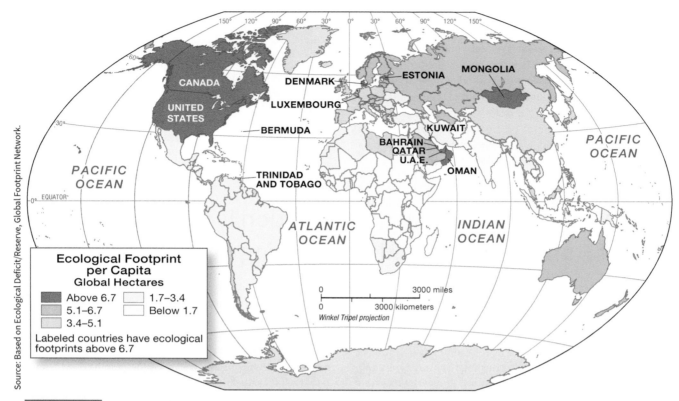

Source: Based on Ecological Deficit/Reserve, Global Footprint Network.

Ecological Footprint per Capita
Global Hectares

■ Above 6.7	☐ 1.7–3.4
■ 5.1–6.7	☐ Below 1.7
☐ 3.4–5.1	

Labeled countries have ecological
footprints above 6.7

FIGURE 13.31 **Ecological Footprint per Capita.** Countries with the highest ecological footprint per capita (those that are labeled on the map) are dispersed across the world. Both small and large countries can have high ecological footprints per capita.

Countries with higher incomes account for a relatively small proportion of the world population (Chapter 2), but they make far greater demands on Earth's resources (per capita) than do their counterparts in lower income countries. It has been estimated that a baby born in the United States during the first decade of the twenty-first century, at current rates, consumes about 250 times as much energy over a lifetime as a baby born in Bangladesh over the same lifetime. In food, housing and its components, metals, paper (and thus trees), and many other materials, the consumption of individuals in affluent countries far exceeds that of people in countries with lower incomes.

Impervious Surfaces The ecological footprint helps us think geographically about human impacts on the natural world. People living in the global economic periphery tend to affect their immediate environment, putting pressure on soil, natural vegetation, and water supplies, and polluting the local air with the smoke from fires. The environmental impact of the global economic core is much greater. Consumers in the core have access to a vast array of goods with few limits on what they can get and when they can get it. They purchase fruits that ripen at a time different from the local growing season by importing them from across the world. When purchasing goods online, consumers may not know how far products will travel before they reach them. The demand for low-cost meat for hamburgers in the United States has led to deforestation in Central and South America to make way for pastures and cattle herds. In the process, water demand has increased in such areas (**Table 13.1**). This example shows just one of the many ways in

which the American (and Canadian, European, Japanese, and Australian) consumer has an impact on distant environments.

TABLE 13.1 **Estimated Liters of Water Required to Produce 1 Kilogram of Food**

Estimated Liters of Water Required to Produce 1 Kilogram of Food

Food	Liters
Chocolate	17,196
Beef	15,415
Chicken meat	4,325
Rice	2,497
Bread	1,608
Potatoes	287

© John Wiley & Sons, Inc.

Determining environmental impact when people consume widely distributed resources that are produced halfway around the world is difficult. Mapping mines, factories, forests, and farms may help calculate where resources are produced, but it does not tell us where they are consumed. However, geographic tools can help create global measurements of human consumption using remotely sensed data. Geographer Paul Sutton and a team of researchers mapped locations of human consumption by measuring impervious surfaces using remote sensing and GIS. They stated that the impervious surfaces people construct for "shelter, transportation, and commerce" are "one of the primary anthropogenic modifications of the environment" (Sutton et al.

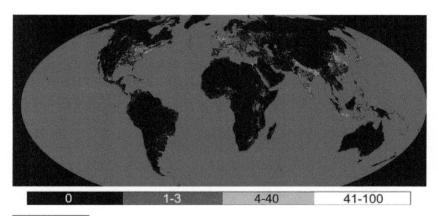

| 0 | 1-3 | 4-40 | 41-100 |

FIGURE 13.32 **Global Impervious Surfaces.** Using satellite data and other data layers, scientists measured the amount of impervious surfaces globally. The lighter the color on the map, the more impervious surfaces.

Source: Paul C. Sutton, Sharolyn J. Anderson, Christopher D. Elvidge, Benjamin T. Tuttle and Tilottama Ghosh, "Paving the planet: impervious surface as proxy measure of the human ecological footprint", Progress in Physical Geography 2009; 33; 510. DOI: 10.1177/0309133309346649

2009, 513). Using statistical analysis, several layers of data from satellite images, and population data, the researchers derived estimates of impervious surfaces for the entire world. They created a measurement of constructed area per person that can be used as a proxy measure for resource consumption (**Fig. 13.32**).

Growing Consumption in China
The growing wealth over the last two decades in the semiperiphery, especially in the world's most populated countries—China and India— has significantly increased the overall global consumption of consumer goods. As recently as the 1980s, China's GDP was smaller than Spain's. Over the past few decades, however, the

Chinese economy has surged forward. In 2010 China surpassed Japan to become the world's second largest economy, and in 2013, it became the world's second biggest consumer country.

Overall consumer spending in the United States still significantly outpaces that in China, but China is gaining ground, and because of the size of its population, it surpasses the United States as a consumer in some areas. In 2010 China became the world's biggest consumer of energy, and it has led the world in the consumption of coal for many years. China has also emerged as one of the world's leading consumers of a wide variety of raw materials, from logs to iron ore to grains.

As global consumption of consumer goods increases, the market for luxury goods has similarly expanded. Luxury handbags by European designers (Louis Vuitton, Hermes, Gucci, and Chanel) have become a status symbol in China. Chinese nationals purchase 32 percent of luxury handbags globally (**Fig. 13.33**), and Chinese tourists often purchase goods in Japan, South Korea, Hong Kong, Thailand, or the United States.

AP® Exam Taker's Tip

Using Table 13.1 and Figure 13.33, could you create your own free-response question about consumption patterns? Being able to construct free-response questions is an effective approach to prepare for the AP exam.

Author Field Note   Consuming Luxury Goods in Bangkok, Thailand

"I led a group of college students and my family through Cambodia and Thailand over 12 days. We had taken in everything from the killing fields of the Cambodian genocide to the temples of Angkor Wat, to a local Buddhist festival with thousands of worshipers in Chiang Mai. Our last night in Bangkok fell on my son's birthday, and I asked him what he wanted to do that night. He looked at me and said 'Cheeseburger. Cheeseburger with ranch.' The Midwesterner in him was craving ranch dressing, which he normally uses to dip his fries, burgers, and chicken, as well as on salad. I realized to find not only a burger but ranch that would meet his standards, we were going to need to go to the Hard Rock Cafe in Bangkok. We jumped in a cab to the district of the city with luxury malls, including the Paragon and the Gaysorn. After a meal that passed his test, even though the ranch was only a 2 on his 10-point scale, we walked through the malls. From Supreme to Louis Vuitton to Commes des Garçon to Gucci, every brand he had ever seen posted by a social medial influencer filled the floors of the mall. He kept looking at me, asking, 'Are these knock-offs?' They were not. The luxury stores are clustered in Bangkok to serve tourists, lately especially Chinese tourists. Chinese are over 10 million of the 28 million tourists in Thailand. The number of Chinese tourists has taken off since 2014, and everyone from luxury stores to stalls in the city's night market rely on their consumption."

– E. H. Fouberg

SubstanceTproductions/Shutterstock.com

FIGURE 13.33 **Bangkok, Thailand.** Chinese tourists queue in line to shop for luxury handbags at a Louis Vuitton store in the Gaysorn Village mall, which is down the street from another luxury mall, the Paragon.

Japan and Hong Kong have the greatest market share of luxury handbag sales in the region. In Hong Kong, a local moneylender even allows women to hand over their designer bags as collateral to receive loans of up to 80 percent of the bag's value.

To meet the growing demand for natural resources, China has greatly expanded its overseas investments. From Africa to South America to other parts of Asia, Chinese firms are increasingly in evidence—extracting resources and shipping them back home. As a result, China's role in consumption-related environmental change now rivals that of the United States and the European Union. China's new international economic clout also carries with it predictable social consequences. In some places, Chinese investment is seen as a boost to the local economy and is welcomed. But there is growing concern that China is acting as a neocolonial power, altering environmental and social systems while returning relatively little to the local economy.

Sustainability

The idea of sustainability is often dated to the United Nations World Commission on Environment and Development. The commission issued its findings in the 1987 Brundtland Report, which was named after the Norwegian prime minister, Gro Harlem Brundtland, who chaired the group. The commission asked the central question of how humanity can improve the condition of developing countries without degrading the environment when Earth has limited resources (Kuhlman and Farrington 2010). The Brundtland Report answered the question by defining the concept of **sustainable development** as "development that meets the needs of the present without compromising the ability of future generations to meet their own needs."

Since the Brundtland Report, sustainable development has become the goal of thousands of programs enacted by both governments and nongovernmental organizations. Policymakers often look at three pillars or goals: social, economic, and environmental. Not all scholars support the idea of three pillars, but they are useful to think about because economic development may be at the expense of social or environmental development. The hope is that considering all three pillars will make work toward development more comprehensive and sustainable.

Planning for sustainability in development, industry, agriculture, or any other realm is difficult because it requires policymakers to think about long-term goals while ensuring short-term welfare. We tend to worry more about the immediate problem than the long term. To help gauge what is possible within a certain realm, policymakers have turned to the concept of **carrying capacity**, a measure of how much can be produced on a certain amount of land without causing environmental degradation. This concept ties into the original concept of sustainability better than it does the modern concept of sustainable development. Sustainability was originally applied to the use of renewable resources, and forestry provided the first application: One should not harvest more trees than there are new-growth trees. In this case, sustainable practice could be easily measured.

Carrying capacity is also often perceived as measurable because the term was first used to describe how much cargo a ship could hold. Over time, policymakers and scholars began using it as a measure of how much productivity land could handle. However, ecologists have largely dismissed the concept because land is not the same everywhere, species vary, conditions are in flux, and technology changes. Because it is intuitively logical, however, carrying capacity may still be a meaningful way to talk about sustainable development. It pushes humans to think about how much of something Earth can handle and perhaps plan for longer-term preservation of resources instead of immediate consumption.

Political Ecology   Creating sustainable development at the local scale requires fieldwork because assumptions about human behavior and development at the global scale may not be true at local and regional scales. Starting in the 1960s and 1970s, geographers began using scale to study human–environment interaction. The field of **political ecology** approaches the study of human–environment interactions in the context of political, economic, and historical conditions operating at different scales, and its practitioners are interested in how political, economic, social, and ecological circumstances shape environmental issues like sustainable agriculture in a specific place.

Political ecologists work to understand whether the global assumptions we have about environmental issues play out at the local scale and how people in a local place negotiate experiences and understandings at different scales to make environmental decisions. For example, development experts assumed that globally, the poorest farmers do the least to conserve soil and therefore cause more soil degradation than wealthier farmers. Political ecologists such as geographer William Moseley dispelled this myth through fieldwork (**Fig. 13.34**).

Moseley studied the conservation behaviors of farmers in southern Mali. Through extensive fieldwork, interviews, and soil surveys, he found that poorer farmers in southern Mali were more likely to use organic materials to preserve topsoil, whereas wealthier farmers were more likely to use inorganic fertilizers and pesticides. Thus the poorest farmers caused the least soil degradation. The explanation for this outcome lies in the policies and power relationships at play in southern Mali. The government agricultural extension service in Mali singled out the wealthiest households for cotton farming, which "helped these households become even wealthier in the short term" (Moseley). Wealthier farmers who could afford inorganic fertilizers increased their usage when they faced an increasingly competitive global cotton market.

The work of political ecologists is important in solving environmental problems because the factors involved in a human-environment interaction vary by scale. Solving a global problem like climate change may require millions of individual accomplishments at local, national, and regional scales. To do so, we must question our assumptions and use fieldwork to understand the decisions people make in their environments.

> **AP® Exam Taker's Tip**
>
> **Political ecology** is an important concept to understand because government policies or lack of policies impact human actions and consumption patterns. Can you find an example of this in the text?

Guest Field Note   Approaching Agriculture Through Political Ecology in Try, Mali

William Moseley
Macalester College

In this photo, a young man brings home the cotton harvest in the village of Try in southern Mali. Prior to my graduate studies in geography, I spent a number of years as an international development worker concerned with tropical agriculture—both on the ground in Africa and as a policy wonk in Washington, D.C. I drew at least two important lessons from these experiences. First, well-intentioned work at the grassroots level would always be limited if it were not supported by broader-scale policies and economics. Second, the people making the policies were often out of touch with the real impacts their decisions were having in the field. As such, geography, and the subfield of political ecology, were appealing to me because of its explicit attention to processes operating at multiple scales, its tradition of fieldwork, and its longstanding attention to human–environment interactions. I employed a political ecology approach during fieldwork for my dissertation in 1999–2000. Here, I sought to test the notion that poor farmers are more likely to degrade soils than their wealthier counterparts (a concept widely proclaimed in the development policy literature of the 1990s). Not only did I interview rich and poor farmers about their management practices, but I tested their soils and questioned policymakers at the provincial, national, and international levels. My findings (and those of others) have led to a questioning of the poverty–environmental degradation paradigm.

© William Moseley

FIGURE 13.34   **Try, Mali.**

Biodiversity

The expanding ecological footprint of humans is resulting in a decline in biodiversity. Maintaining biodiversity is often a goal in sustainable development. Combining the words *biological* and *diversity*, **biodiversity** is the variety of plants and animals on Earth or in a specific area. Human encroachment on species habitat through logging, agriculture, and expansion of urban areas is dramatically increasing the natural rate of species extinction. Knowing the exact rate of species extinction is difficult because we do not know how many species Earth has. Scientists have recorded 1.9 million animal species, including everything from large mammals to small insects, and 450,000 plant species. Using recorded rates of disappearance for known species, scientists estimate that humans have caused species extinction rates 1000 times higher than in prehuman times (Dell'Amore 2014).

Because of the rapid expansion of smartphones, organizations can tap into citizen scientists and use crowdsourcing to record data and map locations. With millions of citizen scientists taking photos and uploading them with the geolocation of their phones to an app such as iNaturalist, we are gaining more data on the number and diversity of species and their range. Whether a species is threatened with extinction depends on the range of the species, its scarcity, and its geographic concentration. If a species with a small range, a high degree of scarcity, and a small geographic concentration has its habitat threatened, extinction can follow. Because most species have small ranges, human-created changes like draining a wetland, killing off coral, or damming a river in one place can affect a species. Conservationists work to preserve species by preserving species habitat. Using geographic data collected on apps, through drone images, and from satellite data, conservationists can better manage species habitat.

Waste Disposal

If anything has grown faster than population itself, it is the waste that households, communities, and industries generate. The level of socioeconomic well-being and solid waste production have a strong, positive correlation (**Fig. 13.35**). Globally, we generated 2.01 billion tons of municipal solid waste in 2016, according to a World Bank report. That same report predicted a global production of 3.4 billion tons annually by 2050. The United States is one of the largest producers of solid waste, debris, and garbage discarded by people, industries, mines, and agriculture. It produces about 4.87 pounds (2.21 kg) of solid waste per person per day, which adds up to more than 284 million tons (258 million metric tons) per year. The kind of waste varies by region. More than half of the waste produced in countries classified as low to middle income is organic, made up of food and green waste. Countries classified as higher income produce much more nonorganic waste, especially plastics from packaging.

AP® Exam Taker's Tip

Practice makes perfect. Use the many charts, graphs, and data from the text to prepare for the AP exam. Use Figure 13.35 to describe possible patterns in the data. The caption helps summarize the pattern. Try this task without using the caption.

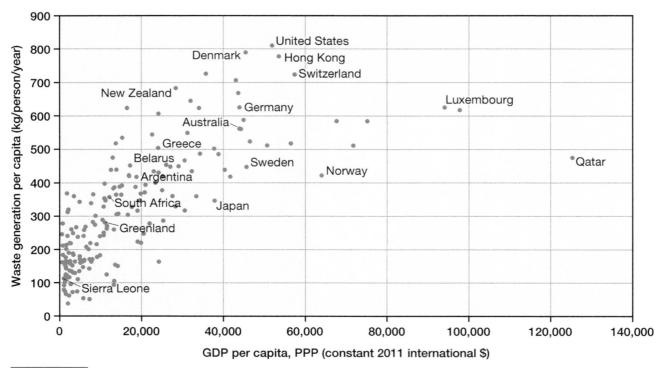

FIGURE 13.35 **GDP and Solid Waste.** Countries with higher gross domestic products (GDPs) generally produce larger amounts of solid waste, creating a positive correlation between GDP and solid waste.

After production, waste is collected and disposed. Collection happens in cities and towns, where waste is either collected door to door or dropped off at a central location. Waste collection rates are close to 100 percent in countries with higher incomes. In countries considered middle income, waste collection rates are 51 percent, and in countries classified as lower income, waste collection rates are only 39 percent (World Bank 2018). Across all country income levels, waste disposal rates are higher in cities than in rural areas.

Cities are expected to solve their own waste disposal, but disposal has become global. The growing volume of waste must be put somewhere, but space near cities is expensive and difficult to find. In lower income countries, over 90 percent of waste is deposited in open dumps, which are often located near housing in major cities. Decomposition sends methane gas into the air, rain and waste liquids carry contaminants into the groundwater below, and fires pollute the surrounding atmosphere. Breathing the gas and being constantly exposed to bacteria deteriorate the health of people who live on or near garbage dumps. In addition, dumps that receive trash beyond their capacity can create landslides that can cover homes and kill residents. In 2017, 113 people died in Addis Ababa, Ethiopia, from a landslide at a garbage dump, and in the same year, 19 died from a similar landslide in Colombo, Sri Lanka (**Fig. 13.36**).

In countries that can afford it, waste is placed in sanitary landfills. The city digs a hole, sets a floor of materials to treat seeping liquids, and then mixes layers of soil over compacted layers of waste. The number of suitable sites for sanitary landfills is decreasing, and it is increasingly difficult to design new sites. About a dozen states in the United States, mostly on the east coast, have reached capacity in their sanitary landfills. States

truck or send garbage by rail to distant landfills, which is expensive and can be dangerous. If the transported waste is hazardous, a truck or train accident can have disastrous consequences.

Exporting Waste Globally, wealthier countries such as the United States, those in the European Union, and Japan export solid waste, including hazardous waste and industrial waste, to East Asia, Central and South America, the Middle East, and Africa. Accepting waste for disposal generates income, but it comes at a cost if the country does not have the capacity to treat and dispose of the waste properly. In the late 1980s, exporting waste to countries with lower incomes created controversy. Countries negotiated the Basel Convention in 1989, a treaty designed to regulate global waste export. The treaty does not prohibit exportation of hazardous waste, but it regulates the export of hazardous waste from countries with higher incomes to countries with lower incomes. The convention also sets goals to regulate the toxicity of waste close to the site of waste production. One hundred eighty-seven countries have ratified the Basel convention. The United States is the only country that has not signed it.

Until 2018, China imported more than 50 percent of the world's waste. As part of a program to reduce air pollution in China, the government officially banned the import of 24 types of waste, including plastic, in 2018 (**Fig. 13.37**). The plastic waste that Europe, the United States, and Canada sent to China was often slated for recycling but would end up being burned or dumped. One scientist explained that the wealthier countries exported "their mixed toxic plastic wastes to developing Asian countries claiming it would be recycled in the receiving country. Instead, much of this contaminated mixed waste

FIGURE 13.36   **Colombo, Sri Lanka.**   Sri Lanka has both sanitary landfills and garbage dumps, and there is a world of difference between them. Sanitary landfills are dug and fully lined to keep dangerous waste from contaminating the water table and soil. On the other hand, garbage dumps like the Meethotamulla garbage dump in the background of this photo are unstable and toxic. This dump caught fire, collapsed, destroyed more than 140 houses, and killed 19 people in 2017.

toxicity from burning plastic is now polluting the atmosphere above Southeast Asia instead of above China.

Waste Disposal on Everest

Humans are impacting even the most remote places on Earth. By the 1920s, the Himalayas included several of the last mountains that humans had not ascended. Over 30 years, 10 parties of mountaineers attempted to reach and scale Mt. Everest at 29,029 feet (8848m). The first people to scale Mt. Everest were Tenzing Norgay and Edmund Hillary, who were part of a British-led expedition in 1953. Norgay was the most experienced Himalayan mountaineer in the British-led group and was part of a Swiss team that in 1952 had reached 28,210 feet (8598m). Norgay took part in six other expeditions of Everest before the successful climb to the summit. Hillary was a New Zealand explorer and beekeeper who had attempted three Himalayan expeditions in the two years leading up to the successful scaling of Everest.

cannot be recycled and is instead dumped or burned, or finds its way into the ocean" (DM 2019).

In response to China's waste ban, countries who are signatories to the Basel Convention met and created a legally binding framework to reduce plastic waste. Germany immediately banned plastic bags and joined a new international waste alliance called Prevent, which included 30 countries working with major industries that use plastics in packaging, including Nestlé and Coca Cola, and major universities (DM 2019). The aims are to prevent the production of waste and to reduce waste as much as possible.

China's plastic waste ban had immediate impacts on where European plastic waste is sent (**Fig. 13.38**). China announced the ban in 2017 and began it in 2018. Europe responded by reducing plastic exports to China and increasing exports to Vietnam, Malaysia, and Turkey. While no longer importing plastic waste, China is still creating revenue from the plastic waste trade. Instead of importing the plastic into China, Chinese have built facilities across Southeast Asia, especially in Vietnam and Malaysia, where they process plastic waste. Chinese-owned plastic waste facilities are popping up across Southeast Asia, and the

FIGURE 13.37   **Guiyu, China.**   Before 2018, China imported plastic trash from around the world and burned it along with other globally imported garbage at sites like this one.

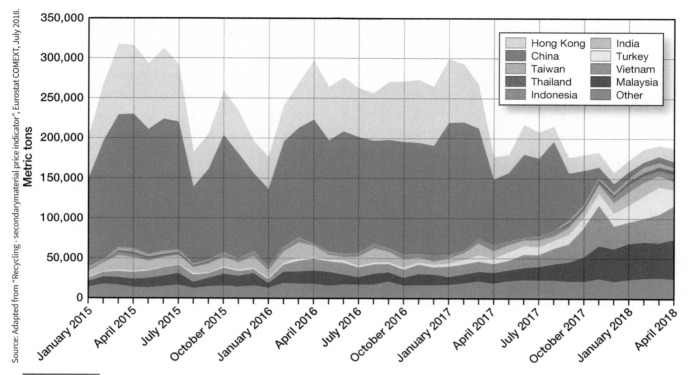

Source: Adapted from "Recycling - secondary material price indicator", Eurostat COMEXT, July 2018.

FIGURE 13.38 **Export of Plastic Waste for Recycling from the European Union.** Until China banned importation of plastic waste, European Union (EU) countries primarily exported plastic waste to China and Hong Kong for recycling. Since the ban went into effect in 2018, the EU sends more plastic waste to Vietnam and Malaysia.

Norgay had lived his life at higher elevations. He was born in Tibet and then migrated to Nepal and married a Sherpa woman. Sherpas are an ethnic group who live in Nepal at a high elevation near Everest Base Camp 1. Since the first parties attempted to reach the summit, Sherpas have fueled the climbing economy on Everest. They meet climbers at base camp and do high-altitude work to carry oxygen tanks and camping and hiking materials up Mt. Everest. A "river of money" is flowing through Sherpa communities as more and more people attempt the summit or trek to Base Camp 1. Nepal's Department of Tourism records show that as of 2019, 5891 people have reached the summit of Everest, and the pace is quickening (**Fig. 13.39**). Nepal's records show that 563 people reached the summit in 2018; 302 of the 563 were Nepali workers, including Sherpas, who had permits to work as high-altitude guides.

Human impact on Everest is increasing as the number of people with the means to hire Sherpas, pay deposits, invest in travel insurance, and buy high-tech climbing and hiking equipment is growing. In addition to those climbing the summit or attempting to do so, many more are trekking in Nepal. Tourism agencies advertise six-day treks to Everest Base Camp 1 at 5364 meters, and while hundreds are making that trek, no report gives the exact number. But the trekkers create waste, both solid and fecal. Solid waste includes plastic, wrappers, cans, glass, paper, gear, and equipment. Parties attempting to reach the summit of Everest pay a $4000 deposit on waste removal. About half the parties get their deposit back, which happens if each member

AP Images/Rizza Alee

FIGURE 13.39 **Mt. Everest.** The number of climbers attempting to ascend the summit of Mt. Everest is growing quickly. On this day in May 2019, a line of climbers waited to ascend. Overcrowding makes climbing Everest dangerous for climbers and Sherpas.

carries 18 pounds (8 kilos) of waste down the mountain. The government of Nepal hires porters to ascend to each basecamp and carry trash off the mountain.

Human waste is another matter. Fecal material is collected in bags and barrels and carried to central locations in Sherpa villages. The Nepali government pays climbers to carry waste from base camps and off the mountain (**Fig. 13.40**). The fecal material is either dumped into pits or thrown into ravines. When monsoon rains fall in the summer and water flows through the ravines, human waste is carried downstream. The waste is significantly impacting water quality for locals. Two mountaineers are developing a biogas solution that would use microorganisms to digest waste, leaving behind fertilizer and methane gas that could be captured and used for fuel.

TC Thinking Geographically

Why is Mt. Everest getting so crowded? Think about **globalization** and how climbing Mt. Everest has changed from a feat of human exploration to an expression of human **identity**. What has made this shift possible and how can you see the shift in the **cultural landscape** of Mt. Everest?

NAMGYAL SHERPA/AFP/Getty Images

FIGURE 13.40 **Everest Base Camp, Nepal.** Nepalese climbers pose after collecting garbage from the Everest clean-up expedition. 20 Nepali climbers collected 4,000 pounds (1,800 kg) of garbage in a risky expedition to clean up Everest.

Summary

13.1 Explain What Natural Hazards Are and How Natural Hazards Can Become Natural Disasters.

1. Natural hazards and natural disasters are both naturally occurring physical phenomena that create change. The difference between them is whether they cause loss of life and destruction of property. If a natural hazard, like a volcano erupting, happens close to a populated area, killing people and damaging infrastructure and houses, it is a natural disaster. Natural hazards are created by Earth processes, including tectonic change, hydrological change, and meteorological or climatological change.

2. Earth's lithosphere, or upper mantle and crust, is divided into more than 15 plates. Tectonic natural hazards most often happen along boundaries between plates. Plates can diverge, converge, or transform. When two plates of different densities converge, they form a subduction zone. The oceanic plate is denser and goes under the continental plate at the converging plate boundary. Subduction zones create massive earthquakes under the ocean, which generate destructive seismic sea waves called tsunamis. How much damage a natural disaster like a tsunami causes in terms of human lives and property damage depends on the country and whether it has a tsunami warning system. The Indian Ocean tsunami in 2004 killed 230,000 people and did more than $10 billion in damage to coasts of Indonesia and Thailand. The 3/11 tsunami in Japan in 2011 killed 15,000 people and did an estimated $235 billion in damages.

3. A flash flood happens when excessive rain or meltwater from snow overflows rivers, fills dry riverbeds, and causes a rapid rise in water levels in a short time. Flash floods are increasingly common because climate change has warmed oceans, which makes evaporation rates higher. Flash floods often happen in cities near

infrastructure and buildings because impervious surfaces do not absorb rainwater, creating conditions for flooding if the storm drainage system is not well built or cannot handle the quantity and frequency of rainwater.

4. Monsoons are predictable patterns of winds coming from a certain direction for an extended period. Monsoon rains are welcome because they flood rice fields and regenerate rivers. However, climate change is making monsoon rains less predictable and more extreme. A monsoon is a climatological norm and not a natural hazard, but it can become a natural disaster if extremes bring widespread flooding or drought.

13.2 Identify the Ways That Humans Impact Earth Through Land Use, Water Use, and Resource Extraction.

1. Recognizing the rapid growth of human population and the incredible role humans play in shaping Earth's environment, scientists report we have entered a new geologic epoch, the Anthropocene. As the number of people on Earth continues to rise to a predicted 9.9 billion by 2050, people create greater strain on land by clearing forests, building infrastructure, mining minerals, growing crops, raising livestock, and creating sprawling cities at accelerated rates. Geographers differentiate between land use, which is how people use the land, and land cover, which is what is physically on the land.

2. Palm oil is an inexpensive oil derived from oil palm trees. It is used in everything from snack foods to shampoo and is found in an estimated 50 percent of items in a grocery store. Tropical forests are being deforested at greater rates and land is cleared through burning to plant oil palm plantations. Indonesia and

Malaysia produce about 90 percent of the world's palm oil. Deforestation of tropical forests removes a carbon dioxide sink, releases more carbon dioxide into the air, and creates conflict between large palm oil companies and indigenous and small landholders.

3. Over the last century, humans invented and began using plastic in millions of goods and products. Once created, used, and disposed of, plastics break down slowly over time but do not biodegrade. They are either directly disposed of in the ocean or find their way there from beaches, through waterways that empty into the ocean, through improper disposal or incineration, or through natural hazards like tsunamis that demolish the built environment and carry waste into the ocean. Plastics have entered the food chain, which is dangerous for sea life and humans.

4. Since the Industrial Revolution, humans have relied on hydrocarbons as a source of fuel. Coal first powered steam engines in factories, trains, and ships. The advent of the automobile created demand for oil. Indoor heating and cooling systems create demand for energy, and power plants are often fueled by coal. Natural gas burns cleaner than oil, and demand for natural gas is increasing. Extracting natural gas through fracking has consequences, including pollution of groundwater from the chemicals pumped into the ground to release and extract the natural gas.

13.3 Explain How Climate Change Is Impacting Human–Environment Interactions.

1. The greenhouse effect is a naturally occurring process in Earth's atmosphere. The sun emits shortwave radiation, which Earth absorbs. Earth emits longwave radiation that creates sensible heat (the heat we feel in temperature). Some of the longwave radiation from Earth travels toward the top of the troposphere (the lowest layer of Earth's atmosphere). Greenhouse gases at the top of the troposphere absorb some of the longwave radiation from Earth and counter-radiate it back to Earth's surface. This naturally occurring process keeps Earth at a livable temperature for humans. The basic premise of climate change science is that humans are burning hydrocarbons, which release excess greenhouse gases that intensify the greenhouse effect and trap more energy in Earth's atmosphere than would be trapped naturally. These human-created greenhouse gases are a major concern of climate change scientists.

2. With higher temperatures and more energy in the atmosphere, evaporation rates increase. Through evaporation, liquid water turns to water vapor. Energy must be added in the form of latent heat to transform liquid water to water vapor. In a storm, water vapor is condensed into liquid water, and in the process of condensation, latent heat is released. Because energy fuels evaporation and is released through condensation, higher temperatures and warmer oceans mean that more energy goes into storms, whether hurricanes or midlatitude cyclones.

3. Geographers use GIS to help understand and solve environmental problems, including water scarcity. They have studied conflict between countries within river basins and have found that water stress does not generally compound conflict. Instead, under water stress, countries are more likely to agree to solutions for equitable water use.

13.4 Explain How Human Consumption Is Changing the Scale of Human Impact and Challenging Sustainability.

1. Human consumption is increasing rapidly with growing populations and rising levels of income. At the most basic level, we consume water, oxygen, and organic and mineral materials. Over time we have developed increasingly complex ways of using resources in pursuit of intensified agricultural and industrial production. Consequently, many societies now consume resources at a level and rate that far exceed basic subsistence needs. The ecological footprint is the impact a person or country has on the environment. It is measured by how much land is required to sustain a person's or country's use of natural resources and to dispose of the waste produced.

2. The Brundtland Report defined the concept of sustainable development as "development that meets the needs of the present without compromising the ability of future generations to meet their own needs." Sustainable development is often considered according to three pillars: social, economic, and environmental.

3. Socioeconomic well-being and solid waste production have a strong, positive correlation. Rising middle and upper classes globally and especially in the two most populated countries in the world, China and India, are creating higher levels of consumption globally. Greater consumption means greater waste production. The United States, Canada, and Europe used to export waste to China. In 2018, China stopped the import of 24 kinds of waste, including plastic. In response, 187 countries, not including the United States, met to extend the Basel Convention, creating a legally binding framework to reduce plastic waste. Chinese businesses continue to profit off waste production and are building plastic waste disposal sites in Southeast Asia, especially in Malaysia and Vietnam. Europe shifted export of plastic waste from China to Malaysia, Vietnam, and Turkey after China instituted its ban.

Self-Test

13.1 Explain what natural hazards are and how natural hazards can become natural disasters.

1. Natural disasters cause:
   a. damage to property and permanent changes in landscape.
   b. permanent changes in landscape and loss of human life.
   c. damage to property and loss of human life.
   d. loss of human and animal life.
   e. environmental damage.

2. When a natural disaster hits an area with higher incomes, damages will likely be:
   a. higher in terms of property loss than loss of lives.
   b. higher in terms of loss of lives than property loss.
   c. higher in terms of landscape changes than loss of lives.

d. higher in terms of loss of lives than landscape changes.

e. higher in terms of incidence of disease than property loss.

3. The Mid-Atlantic Ridge is a good example of a _____ plate boundary.

a. converging

b. subduction

c. transforming

d. submerging

e. diverging

4. When you study a map of the Ring of Fire and look at the plate boundaries around the Pacific plate, you can tell that many of the plate boundaries (especially near Alaska and Japan) are _____ because of the presence of _____.

a. transforming / earthquakes

b. subducting / trenches

c. diverging / volcanoes

d. converging / mountains

e. colliding / multiple plates

13.2 Identify the ways that humans impact Earth through land use, water use, and resource extraction.

5. The current geologic era is often called the _____ because of the rate of human impact on the environment.

a. Amorphous

b. Manmade

c. Pleistocene

d. Anthropocene

e. Ecumene

6. If you look at a map of land cover, you can tell if an area is agricultural or forest. If you look at land use, you can tell differences in:

a. farming methods, such as intensive versus extensive.

b. how long the land has been used for agriculture.

c. the amount and frequency of pesticide use.

d. the presence or absence of irrigation systems.

e. the amount of fertilizer use.

7. Growing demand for palm oil, which is now used in about 50 percent of products in grocery stores, has led to tropical deforestation, especially in Malaysia and Indonesia. Tropical deforestation is problematic for all of the following reasons except:

a. tropical forests are a major sink (user) of carbon dioxide from the atmosphere.

b. burning trees to clear a tropical forest releases carbon dioxide into the atmosphere.

c. clearing tropical forests creates conflict between large palm oil companies and indigenous and small landholders.

d. clearing tropical forests creates conflicts between countries that compete for large palm oil company investments.

e. all of the above are reasons why deforestation is problematic.

8. True or False: Once created, used, and disposed of, plastics break down slowly over time but do not biodegrade.

13.3 Explain how climate change is impacting human–environment interactions.

9. The greenhouse effect is naturally occurring and creates an atmosphere that is _____ than/as Earth's atmosphere would be without it.

a. warmer

b. colder

c. about the same

d. wetter

e. drier

10. With climate change, the atmosphere has higher rates of evaporation because:

a. warm air can hold more water vapor than cold air.

b. cold air can hold more water vapor than warm air.

c. warm air has a higher specific heat capacity than cold air.

d. cold air has a higher specific heat capacity than warm air.

e. vapor in warm air evaporates more quickly.

11. Geographers who study international conflict over river basins have found that water scarcity generally:

a. leads to higher conflict between countries in a river basin.

b. leads to higher cooperation between countries in a river basin.

c. is caused by anthropogenic overuse of water.

d. is caused by climate change.

e. is caused by over irrigation.

12. The Aral Sea in Central Asia dried up significantly in a relatively short time primarily because:

a. climate change created drought.

b. farmers diverted water to grow cotton.

c. Uzbekistan built a dam that diverted water from reaching the sea.

d. Kazakhstan added salt to the Aral Sea to build fish farms.

e. it is located in a desert region.

13.4 Explain how human consumption is changing the scale of human impact and challenging sustainability.

13. The countries with the overall highest ecological footprint are China, the United States, and India. When measuring ecological footprint per capita, the top five countries in terms of impact are primarily:

a. wealthy.   b. poor.   c. frigid.   d. humid.   e. arid.

14. Using remote sensing and GIS, a team of geographers found that impervious surfaces are a good proxy (substitute) measurement of:

a. resource extraction.

b. resource consumption.

c. lower precipitation from climate change.

d. higher precipitation from climate change.

e. sustainable development.

15. Since the 1980s, China has been the primary importer of waste generated by the United States, Canada, and Europe. In 2018, China banned importation of 24 types of waste, including plastic. Starting in 2018, Europe shifted exportation of plastic waste to _____v, where Chinese businesses set up plastic disposal sites.

a. Australia and New Zealand

b. Chile and Argentina

c. Kenya and Uganda

d. Malaysia and Vietnam

e. Cambodia and Thailand

CHAPTER 14

Globalization and the Geography of Networks

imageBROKER/Alamy Stock Photo

FIGURE 14.1 **Bangkok, Thailand.** This storefront in Bangkok has a sign for Manchester United in the foreground and one for Liverpool in the back ground. Supporters for both British football (soccer) clubs are found in Bangkok and also in much more remote Hat Yai, where I saw Manchester United fans cheering against Liverpool.

Shortly after arriving in Hat Yai to meet with a graduate student doing research in southern Thailand, we went to a simple outdoor restaurant serving delicious food. Our attention was soon drawn to a crowd focused intently on a television. Wandering over, we discovered they were watching a football (soccer) match between rivals Manchester United and Liverpool (**Fig. 14.1**).

Hat Yai is more than 6000 miles (10,000 km) from Manchester, England. It lies in a socioeconomically disadvantaged region with a substantial Malay-Muslim population. Members of an insurgent group in Hat Yai have recently taken responsibility for bombings that, have driven away visitors and depressed outside investment. Hat Yai, then, would seem to be an unlikely place for Premier League football to attract passionate followers.

Yet passionate followers there are. It is impossible to explain this seeming oddity without considering the networks that connect different parts of the world to one another—and the impacts of those networks on people's identities. A Premier League club such as Manchester United uses corporate and telecommunications networks to advertise its brand broadly. It develops links with media organizations in many different places and promotes its players, matches, and gear on social media.

Understanding why people in Hat Yai are loyal fans of Manchester United requires understanding the networks created through globalization. In this chapter, we examine these networks and consider what they tell us about how the world works today.

CHAPTER OUTLINE

14.1 Describe How Identities Are Changing in a Globalized World.

Gillian Rose defines **identity** as "how we make sense of ourselves." She explains that we have identities at different scales: local, national, regional, and global identities. At each scale, place factors into our identities. We infuse places with meaning and emotions based on our experiences in those places. Globally, relatively few people are world travelers who have visited several countries overseas. And many of those who have traveled have missed out on the uniqueness of places. Tourists often visit only world cities and tourist destinations. Some tourists stay in all-inclusive resorts and never encounter the local place, except on the drive between the airport and resort. Business travelers often go only to world cities, visiting airports, office buildings, conference centers, and hotels. How, then, can a person have a global identity if he or she has not experienced the globe?

Globalization links us with other people and places, and the flow of information technology is part of that linkage. We constantly receive information about other places, whether it's North Korea testing a nuclear device, economic instability in Venezuela, or trade negotiations with China. We may be overwhelmed by the flow of information and choose to ignore it. Even if we ignore or do not comprehend much of what we hear about the world, our sense of self and our place in the world is affected by globalization. We define ourselves by identifying with or against others at different scales, including the global scale.

In 1995, an article in *National Geographic* discussed the future of the digital age. The author argued that, as a result of technological advances and the Internet, face-to-face interaction was declining. At the same time, he claimed that people would continue to have "a need for skin," a need to interact with other humans in person (Swerdlow 1995). As evidence, the author cited the many visitors to malls who were not there to purchase anything. Online shopping has made malls less of a destination than when the article was written. But coffee shops, restaurants, sports arenas, and performance spaces continue to draw in people.

Swerdlow's discussion of the pull between a faceless Internet and the "need for skin" took place nine years before Mark Zuckerberg created Facebook in 2004. People with Facebook or Twitter accounts can feel connected by posting a quip or thought, and friends around the world can respond to that post immediately. But these platforms may be contributing to declining human interaction. Service organizations and clubs, like Lions Club, Rotary International, and Junior League, used to be a major way for members of a community to connect, but their membership numbers are declining.

In the early days of the digital revolution, psychologists predicted that people would have poorer social skills because of the lack of personal or face-to-face interaction. We can certainly see evidence of this in our daily lives. People often answer phone calls or text messages when they are in the middle of in-person conversations, and some students text or multitask on laptops during geography lectures (not you, we're sure).

Today, however, psychologists also recognize that the **networks** created through digital technology can enable greater personal interaction and opportunities for empathy, such as when people share personal experiences and ideas on Twitter, Tumblr, or a blog. Someone with medical problems or a family member can post a journal on a site such as Caring Bridge, and hundreds can follow the person's recovery and offer words of support. A young boy with a medical condition that makes it difficult to leave home can post lip-synched videos on YouTube, develop followers around the world, and end up with recording artists stopping by to lip-sync with him. Social networks are one way individuals develop a sense of belonging and a feeling of personal connectedness to others in our global, digital age.

Personal Connectedness and the Making of Places

Twenty-one years before hundreds of millions around the world watched a live feed of the wedding of British Prince Harry and American actress Meghan Markle, the news broke that Prince Harry's mother, Princess Diana, had died. That news traveled quickly around the world. Many felt the need to mourn for a princess they had never met in a place they had never visited. Some wanted to leave a token offering for the princess: a rose, a note, a candle, a photograph. Impromptu shrines to Princess Diana cropped up at British embassies and consulates around the world. People in Britain left more than 1 million bouquets of flowers at Kensington palace in London, where Princess Diana lived (**Fig. 14.2**).

What made people feel connected to a woman who was a royal, a member of a family that presides over a modest-sized country? Why do we relate to someone from an elite group of people of wealth and privilege? What made people want to see how her sons turned out? Why did they want to "get to know" the person Prince Harry was marrying 21 years later? Millions of people watched programs and read stories about Meghan Markle, but why?

The idea that people who do not personally know each other are linked by shared reactions to events draws from Benedict Anderson's concept of the nation as an **imagined community** (see Chapter 8). When high-profile tragedies occur, such as the 2019 terrorist attack in New Zealand, devastating wildfires that ripped through the U.S. west coast, or the fire that ravaged Paris' Notre Dame Cathedral in 2019, people often talk about someone they knew who was in the place (or had been at some point),

FIGURE 14.2 **London, United Kingdom.** Mourners gathered at Kensington Palace, Princess Diana's residence, two days after her funeral in 1997. More than 1 million bouquets were left in her memory. Notice the difference in public mourning between now and then. How many cell phones can you find in the photo?

someone who died (even those they did not know but heard about in the news), or an act of bravery or triumph that occurred in the midst of tragedy. The desire to personalize, to localize, a tragedy or even a joyous event feeds off the sense that we are all part of a community that extends far beyond where we live. The process of personalizing and localizing distant events reminds us of our shared humanity.

We live in a world where things like global superhighways of information transcend place. Even so, people continue to focus attention on territories and create places. When a death or a tragedy occurs, how do people choose a local space in which to express a personal or global sorrow? In the case of Princess Diana's death, people created hundreds of spaces to mourn the loss of a seemingly generous, if troubled, person whose life was cut short. In the case of September 11, people transformed homes, schools, public spaces, and houses of worship into spaces of reflection by creating human chains, participating in moments of silence, or holding prayer vigils for the victims.

In his book *Shadowed Ground: America's Landscapes of Violence and Tragedy*, geographer Kenneth Foote examined the "spontaneous shrines" created at places where loss occurred and at places that represents loss. He described these spontaneous shrines as a "first stage in the commemoration of a

disaster." Foote drew from extensive fieldwork that he conducted while visiting hundreds of landscapes of tragedy and violence in the United States. His goal was to show how people mark or do not mark tragedy, both immediately with spontaneous shrines and later with permanent memorials (**Fig. 14.3**). He examined the struggles over whether and how to memorialize places of loss and tragedy in the United States. After tracing and following the stories of hundreds of people and places, Foote concluded that "the debate over what, why, when, and where to build" a permanent memorial for a person or event is "best considered a part of the grieving process."

Foote's work shows that the creation of a permanent memorial (or not) in a particular place depends on whether funding is available, what kind of memorial is to be built, who or what is being remembered, whether a site is socially contested, and how people think about the site. In recent American history, major terrorist attacks have been memorialized, often with the word *closure* being used. Oklahoma City memorialized the site of a terrorist attack at the Murrah Federal Building on the five-year anniversary of the tragedy. Other tragedies, such as that experienced at the World Trade Center in New York City on September 11, 2001, take longer to memorialize. Millions of people feel a personal connection to the World Trade Center site, and choosing a design and building a memorial took longer (**Fig. 14.4**).

The intensity of recent debates over Confederate monuments in the United States shows that memorials are not just impersonal reminders of events. They are bound with how people think about themselves and the places they inhabit. For some, a Confederate monument honors a particular sense of place and history that, they argue, should not be forgotten.

Guest Field Note   Creating a Sense of Common Purpose in Columbine, Colorado

Kenneth E. Foote
University of Connecticut

I took this photo at the dedication ceremony for the memorial to the victims of the Columbine High School shooting of April 20, 1999. Columbine is located near Littleton, Colorado, in Denver's southern suburbs. The memorial, dedicated on September 21, 2007, provides a quiet place for meditation and reflection in a public park adjacent to the school. Hundreds came to the ceremony to honor those killed and wounded in the attack, one of the deadliest school shootings in U.S. history. After tragedies like the Columbine shootings, creating a memorial often helps to rebuild a sense of community. Public ceremonies like this can set an example for survivors who may otherwise have difficulty facing their loss in private. A group memorial helps to acknowledge the magnitude of the community's loss and, by so doing, helps assure families and survivors that the victims did not suffer alone—that their deaths and wounds are grieved by the entire community. Memorials are important too because they can serve as a focus for remembrance and commemoration long into the future, even after all other evidence of a tragedy has disappeared.

In my research for *Shadowed Ground*, I have visited hundreds of such places in the United States and Europe. I am still surprised by the power of such places and the fact that shrines and memorials resulting from similar tragedies are tended lovingly for decades, generations, and centuries. They produce strong emotions and sometimes leave visitors—including me—in tears. But by allowing individuals to share loss, tragedy, and sorrow with others, they create a sense of common purpose.

© Kenneth E. Foote

FIGURE 14.3 **Columbine, Colorado.**

For others, these monuments serve to honor the terrible practice of slavery and a dark period in American history. And the debate does not just take place among locals; people far and wide are drawn into the debate through networks that make them feel as if they have a personal stake in the outcome.

The mass of information coming our way each day is often overwhelming. As people filter through or ignore the flow of information, they may personalize the information and either make a connection or differentiate themselves from particular people or places. In the end, many people's identities reflect developments unfolding at the global scale. Engaging daily with global events was not possible before the age of modern telecommunications. But distant people and places may now be more present in our minds and lives. Globalization modifies how we interact with one another and how we make sense of ourselves in our world, our state, our region, and our locality.

TC **Thinking Geographically**

Select a memorial site that is significant locally, nationally, or globally. Describe the **site** of the memorial and explain how tragedy is represented in the memorial. Look at the photos of the memorial online and then look at a map of where the memorial is located. Zoom in and out on the map. Thinking across **scales**, explain the larger **context** of the memorial.

"The 9/11 Memorial commemorates those who died in the terrorist attacks on the World Trade Center on September 11, 2001. The wall includes the names of those who died in each tower, the first responders, those who died at the Pentagon, and those who died on each flight involved in that day's attacks. I had given a talk in the World Trade Center just a few years earlier, and it seemed almost impossible that the great buildings crowning lower Manhattan were no longer there. But what really hit close to home was the knowledge that among the dead was Bob LeBlanc—a retired geography professor at the University of New Hampshire who had taught in the summer program at my university. His name is among the 2983 names etched into the walls around the memorial pools of the North and South Towers, the footprints of the former buildings. Beyond those who died during the 2001 attack on the World Trade Center, the memorial incudes the victims of a bomb detonated in the parking garage of the North Tower on February 26, 1993. I took a photo of

Robert LeBlanc's name, and I was reminded of Ken Foote's research. I, like so many others, related to this tragedy not only by my own experience but through someone like me – a geography professor whom I knew and admired."

– A. B. Murphy

FIGURE 14.4 New York, New York.

Clarence Holmes Photography/Alamy Stock Photo

14.2 Identify Networks and Explain Their Role in Globalization.

Whether you are in favor of or opposed to globalization, we all must recognize that globalization is "neither an inevitable nor an irreversible set of processes," as John O'Loughlin, Lynn Staeheli, and Edward Greenberg put it. Andrew Kirby explains that globalization is "not proceeding according to any particular playbook. It is not a smoothly evolving state of capitalist development." Rather, globalization is fragmented, and its flows are "chaotic in terms of origins and destinations."

Globalization is a "chaotic" set of processes and outcomes created by people. These people might be corporate CEOs, university administrators, bloggers, electrical engineers, and protesters at a trade meeting. The processes of globalization and the connectedness created through globalization occur across scales and across networks, regardless of country borders.

The original backbone of economic globalization was trade. Trade across vast distances has taken place for centuries, and many debates over globalization continue to focus on trade. To visualize how trade fosters globalization, examine a map of shipping routes (**Fig. 14.5**). The density of the networks

on the map tells us how extensively connected the world really is. But what are the consequences of those connections? The arguments in favor of globalization were explained by economist Keith Maskus (2004), who noted that "free trade raises the well-being of all countries by inducing them to specialize their resources in those goods they produce relatively most efficiently" in order to lower production costs. He concluded that "competition through trade raises a country's long-term growth rate by expanding access to global technologies and promoting innovation."

The view that free trade raises the wealth of all countries underpins a set of neoliberal policies that together form the **Washington Consensus** (Chapter 10). Western international financial institutions, including the World Bank, the International Monetary Fund, the World Trade Organization, and investment banks are all part of the Washington Consensus. Together these institutions created a set of policies, including structural adjustment loans, that encouraged neoliberalism. Not everyone has accepted this "consensus." Leaders in both lower income and higher income countries have questioned

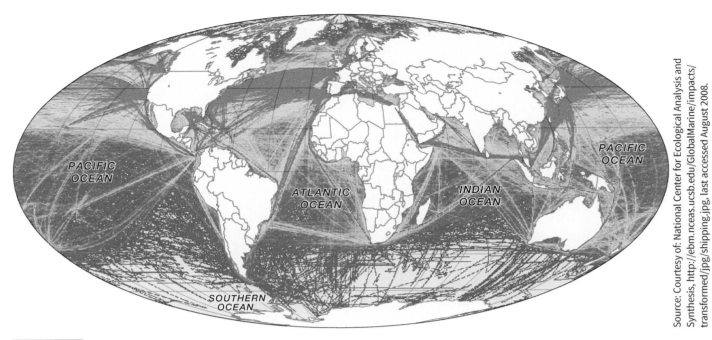

Source: Courtesy of: National Center for Ecological Analysis and Synthesis, http://ebm.nceas.ucsb.edu/GlobalMarine/impacts/transformed/jpg/shipping.jpg, last accessed August 2008.

FIGURE 14.5 **Global Shipping Lanes.** The map traces over 3000 shipping routes used by commercial and government vessels. The red lines mark the most frequently used shipping lanes.

the underlying assumptions of the Washington Consensus—both from the left and from the right.

Critics on the left view the Washington Consensus as part of a Western-dominated effort to get the rest of the world to privatize state-owned entities, to open financial markets, to liberalize trade by removing restrictions on the flow of goods, and to encourage foreign direct investment (**Fig. 14.6**). They argue that the countries of the global economic core protect their own economies while forcing the semiperiphery and periphery to open their economies. These countries are then left vulnerable to control by the core. According to Maskus, the rules negotiated for the World Trade Organization "inevitably reflect the economic interest of powerful lobbyists" in places such as the United States and the European Union. They have heightened wealth differences between more and less prosperous regions, and they have deepened the inequalities of the global system.

The traditional right long supported the Washington Consensus. However, a form of right-wing populism that is hostile to globalization and has protectionist instincts has recently gained ground. People in this camp argue that globalization has made people and places more economically vulnerable, undermining the ability of countries to control what happens within their territories, and undermining traditional national/cultural (and for some racial) norms. This perspective on globalization has increasingly entered the political mainstream. Right-wing populist parties have been winning national elections, or at least gaining support, in Europe, North America, Asia, and elsewhere. They push for stronger borders, a my-country-first approach to trade, and the reduction in influence of international organizations.

Wherever you stand on these debates, there is general agreement that globalization has intensified over the last few decades.

This means that people's lives are increasingly tied to interconnections that exist on an unprecedented scale. In Andrew Kirby's words, we are living "not so much in a world without boundaries, or in a world without geography—but more literally in a world, as opposed to a neighborhood or a region." Some want to embrace this reality and others want to resist it, but understanding its geographical character and impact is clearly one of the great challenges of our time. To do that, we have to take seriously the networks around which globalization is built.

Networks

Manuel Castells defines **networks** as "interconnected nodes" without a center. A nonhierarchical network is horizontally structured, with power shared among all participants and ideas flowing in all directions. A multitude of networks exist in the world: financial, transportation, communication, kinship, corporate, nongovernment, trade, government, media, education, social, and dozens of other networks. These networks create a higher degree of interaction and interdependence among people than ever before. Deeply entrenched hierarchies in networks knit together the contemporary world and affect the character of different places and the interactions among them.

AP® Exam Taker's Tip

Review **functional regions** from Chapter 1. Try to imagine functional regions at various scales: personal, family, corporate, city, regional, state, national, and global. Reference all of the examples listed here. Think about what functional regions you use and of which you are a part. This can help you better apply these concepts throughout the AP exam.

Author Field Note   Protesting Globalization in Frankfurt, Germany

"Walking near the headquarters of the European Central Bank, I came across a modest-sized encampment of people staging an anti-globalization protest. A couple of the protesters told me this was a part of the larger 'Occupy' movement that started after the global financial crisis of 2008 and a follow-on debt crisis in Europe. The movement sought to draw attention to the social and economic inequalities produced by economic globalization. It turned out to be a harbinger of things to come.

Reactions to the negative impacts of globalization can be seen in everything from the rising influence of populist movements with nationalist agendas to the Brexit vote in the United Kingdom. The protesters set up their encampment at the European Central Bank because the bank manages the common currency of the European Union (EU), the euro, and sets interest rates for money it lends to commercial banks in the EU euro zone."

– A.B. Murphy

Photo by A.B. Murphy. © 2020 John Wiley & Sons, Inc.

FIGURE 14.6 **Frankfurt, Germany.**

While networks have always existed, Castells argues that they have fundamentally changed since 1995. The diffusion of information technology has created links between places in a global, yet uneven, way. Through information technology networks, Castells argues that globalization has proceeded by "linking up all that, according to dominant interests, has value anywhere in the planet, and discarding anything (people, firms, territories, resources) which has no value or becomes devalued." Some places are linked more than others, helping to create the spatial unevenness of globalization flows and outcomes.

Time–Space Compression

Access (or lack of access) to information technology networks creates time–space compression (Chapter 12). It is sometimes shocking to realize how quickly technology has changed and diffused. In 1992, the highest-income countries had on average

only 10 cellular subscribers and 2.5 Internet users per 1000 people. Now, these technologies have reached the vast majority of people in the global economic core (see Fig. 10.3). Castells (2000) argues that the age of information technology is more revolutionary than the advent of the printing press or the Industrial Revolution. It is shrinking both time and space. He claims that we are just at the beginning of this age "as the Internet becomes a universal tool of interactive communication, as we shift from computer-centered technologies to network-diffused technologies, (and) as we make progress in nanotechnology (and thus in the diffusion capacity of information devices)."

The impacts of time–space compression vary among places, creating some places with great access to technology and others with little access to technology, typically along income lines. The **digital divide**, the difference between those who have access to technology and those who do not, both reinforces the flows of globalization and manifests in the uneven outcomes of globalization. The International Telecommunications Union (ITU) collects data on the levels of digital access for different world regions. In 2018, the ITU reported that developed (high income) countries had on average 128 mobile cellular subscriptions and 81 Internet users for every 100 people. On average, developing (low and middle income) countries had 102 mobile cellular connections and 45 Internet users for every 100 people. These figures show less of a divide than existed a decade earlier, but they still speak to the existence of a significant digital divide along socioeconomic lines. That divide looks even more dramatic if you change the scale to a more fine-grained one, such as by looking at the differences between remote parts of interior West Africa and world cities near coastal West Africa.

> ### TC Thinking Geographically
>
> Castells claims that the age of informational technology is more revolutionary than either the advent of the printing press or the Industrial Revolution. Explain how revolutions in information technology have made **globalization** possible. Identify one **network** in trade, migration, or politics, and determine how that network helps create **time-space compression**. Which places are more linked through the network you chose, and which places are farther apart as a result of the network?

14.3 Explain How Social, Information, and Economic Networks Operate in a Globalized World.

In this section, we examine three types of influential networks: those designed to promote a social end, those concerned with the development and spread of information, and those that promote economic exchange. Because networks are not just global, we consider each type of network at more than one scale. People have created their own local or regional networks, often in response to a network operating at the global scale.

Social Networks

Between 2014 and 2017, the fight against the Islamic State of Iraq and Syria (ISIS) rocked the Middle East. In both Syria and Iraq, Kurdish forces fought against ISIS, in the process freeing significant areas from Islamic State control. As we saw in Chapter 8, the Kurds are a stateless nation distributed across four different states. The conflict with ISIS helped to bring Kurds together throughout the region. In Iran, Kurds organized a major demonstration in 2014 in solidarity with their ethnic kin in Syria during the siege of Kobani (a city just south of the border with Turkey). And Iraqi Kurdistan's 2017 independence referendum was celebrated by Kurds all over the region.

Without **social networks**, it would have been impossible for Kurds to organize the kind of demonstration they did in 2014 because of state control of the formal media in Iran. Moreover, social networks played a major role in spreading news of Iraqi Kurdistan's independence referendum. Social networks did not simply promote the exchange of information. They helped to create a sense of common cause across Kurdish lands and promoted identification with Kurdistan as an imagined, if not actual political space.

Social networks, especially Facebook and Twitter, were also credited with making uprisings possible in connection with the Arab Spring (Chapter 8). In Egypt, a Google employee anonymously created a Facebook page titled "We are all Khaled Said" in honor of a young Egyptian businessman who was beaten and killed by two police officers. The page attracted 473,000 supporters, and it "helped spread the word

about the demonstrations in Egypt, which were ignited after a revolt in neighboring Tunisia toppled the government there" (Preston 2011, 1).

Rap or hip-hop music diffused among protesters who shared the Arabic language (Chapter 4). Because Islam, the predominant religion in the region, instructs followers to learn the Arabic language, most people there can speak Arabic (Chapters 6 and 7). El Général's raps, spoken in Arabic, were readily understood by Arabic speakers around the region. He rapped, "My president, your country is dead/People eat garbage/Look at what is happening/Misery everywhere/Nowhere to sleep/I'm speaking for the people who suffer/Ground under feet." The accessibility of social media helped a low-cost video of a Tunisian rapper diffuse quickly and widely.

Social media has also played a major role in the #MeToo movement, which is aimed at combating sexual harassment and assault. Starting from a relatively narrow base, the movement spread like wildfire as a hashtag on social media. Hundreds, then thousands, then millions of women, as well as some men, began sharing their stories on social media, giving rise to a movement that spread around the world. Within one year of the first tweet, 19 million tweets included #MeToo. As a result, discussions of sexual harassment and assault have entered the mainstream, from the United States, to Russia, to South Africa, to Australia.

There is, of course, a dark side to the explosion in networking through social media. Social media can also serve as a platform for spreading messages of hatred and racism, for planning terrorist attacks, and for spreading false information. The threat is not simply abstract. Platforms such as YouTube, Facebook, and Twitter are easy to access and inexpensive. Extremist groups have used them to recruit new members and plan attacks, ranging from attacks carried out by Islamic extremists in and around Paris in 2015 to the mass murder of Muslims in Christchurch, New Zealand, in 2019. In response to the 2019 attack, Facebook, Twitter, Google, Microsoft, and Amazon signed a pledge to combat online extremism. Some critics believe such pledges amount to censorship, but others think there need to be some checks on how, and for what purposes, social media is used.

Before leaving the topic, it is important to note that even though social media serves as a connector, it also can produce isolation. Increasing studies show that feelings of loneliness have grown, particularly among young people who spend a great deal of time on social media. There is an irony here—one with significant geographical consequences. While social media networks can connect individuals with the wider world and promote identification with larger-scale regional and global events, they can also work against connectedness and attachment to the local scale—the places where people live.

The Impacts of Social Networks on Development Initiatives

For all the downsides of social networks, they unquestionably help in addressing the way society deals with issues and challenges. Efforts to address development challenges provide a case in point. The sizable community of nongovernmental organizations (NGOs) focused on development has created a web of global networks that give them considerable influence on the development landscape. And NGO development networks often counterbalance the concentration of power in governments, international financial institutions, and corporations. After the devastating 2019 earthquake in the Bahamas, NGOs from around the world cooperated to respond to the crisis. In many cases, they intervened more efficiently than the government of the Bahamas. Social media networks played a major role in making that cooperation possible.

The stated goal of many development-oriented NGOs is to include the voices of the poor and those directly affected by development. They seek to amplify the voices of those they are trying to help. To be sure, some NGOs have been criticized for falling far short of this goal. Leroi Henry, Giles Mohan, and Helen Yanacopulos (2004) argue that power relationships exist both within and between networks—often privileging the views of NGOs headquartered in the core as opposed to those in the periphery. Nonetheless, development networks now make it possible for NGOs in different parts of the world to bypass political and economic power centers. They can then work together to reach a consensus on how to achieve economic development and respond to crises. These networks also help open the door to local voices in development discussions.

Interest is growing in **participatory development**—incorporating the ideas and interests of locals in the creation of development plans. Stuart Corbridge has studied how the global push for participatory development has encouraged the government of India to enact participatory development programs. Corbridge and his colleague Sanjay Kumar describe the goal as giving the people who are directly affected by policies and programs a voice in making those policies and programs—to use local networks to structure development projects to meet local goals. Kumar and Corbridge found that "there can be no doubting the sincerity of" participatory development programs "to engage the rural poor" in India. However, they also found that local politics influence the distribution of poverty reduction schemes. Wealthier farmers and elites in rural areas tend to be the people who are most involved with development programs and hence seek to protect their interests.

Information Networks

As we discussed in Chapter 4, the diffusion of products and ideas associated with popular culture depends largely on globalized media and retail store networks, as well as associated advertising practices. Today's media encompass much more than print, radio, and television. With technological advances, media include streaming entertainment and music sites, video games, smartphone apps, and social networks.

Through mergers and consolidations, much of the global media has come to be controlled by a few globe-spanning corporations: Alphabet (Google), Comcast, Walt Disney, AT&T Entertainment Group, New Corp, Sony, Facebook, Bertelsmann, Viacom, and a few others. These media corporations are masters of **vertical integration**. A vertically integrated corporation owns all or most of the points along the commodity chain (global production chain)—from the supply of raw materials to consumption.

Media companies compete for three things: content, delivery, and consumers (Pereira 2003). Through consolidation and mergers, vertically integrated global media companies such as the Walt Disney Company (**Table 14.1**) control content and delivery. Their ownership of production companies, radio shows, television stations, film producers, and publishers allows them to create a range of content. Then they deliver that content through ownership of streaming platforms, radio, television stations, magazines, music, video games, apps, and movies. Delivery of content also includes technological infrastructure—the technologies used for creating and sharing digital media.

Vertical integration also helps media giants attract and maintain customers through **synergy**, or the cross-promotion of vertically integrated goods. For example, you can visit Disney World's Animal Kingdom to catch the Festival of the Lion King, which is based on the Disney theatrical production, which was based on the Disney picture that had been previously released. And while you are waiting in line to see the theatrical version of a former Disney picture, you can play the Disney app "Where's My Water?" on your smartphone.

Vertical integration of media changes the flow of ideas around the globe by limiting the ultimate number of **gatekeepers**, people or corporations with control over access to information. A gatekeeper can choose not to tell a story, which in turn makes the story less likely to be heard. Concern is mounting that the consolidation of media gives more and more power to fewer and fewer gatekeepers. The big media conglomerates, in this view, have become the ultimate gatekeepers.

Countering this trend is the proliferation of podcasts, online publications, and platforms that allow individuals to share their stories with millions without the endorsement of a major media company (e.g., YouTube, Reddit, etc.). These platforms reduce the control of large gatekeepers in the world today. The diversity of media outlets has the same effect, including television channels that are geared to specific populations (or markets).

TABLE 14.1

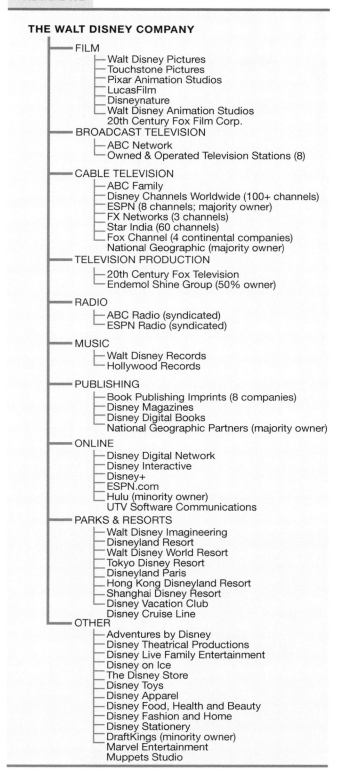

THE WALT DISNEY COMPANY

FILM
- Walt Disney Pictures
- Touchstone Pictures
- Pixar Animation Studios
- LucasFilm
- Disneynature
- Walt Disney Animation Studios
- 20th Century Fox Film Corp.

BROADCAST TELEVISION
- ABC Network
- Owned & Operated Television Stations (8)

CABLE TELEVISION
- ABC Family
- Disney Channels Worldwide (100+ channels)
- ESPN (8 channels; majority owner)
- FX Networks (3 channels)
- Star India (60 channels)
- Fox Channel (4 continental companies)
- National Geographic (majority owner)

TELEVISION PRODUCTION
- 20th Century Fox Television
- Endemol Shine Group (50% owner)

RADIO
- ABC Radio (syndicated)
- ESPN Radio (syndicated)

MUSIC
- Walt Disney Records
- Hollywood Records

PUBLISHING
- Book Publishing Imprints (8 companies)
- Disney Magazines
- Disney Digital Books
- National Geographic Partners (majority owner)

ONLINE
- Disney Digital Network
- Disney Interactive
- Disney+
- ESPN.com
- Hulu (minority owner)
- UTV Software Communications

PARKS & RESORTS
- Walt Disney Imagineering
- Disneyland Resort
- Walt Disney World Resort
- Tokyo Disney Resort
- Disneyland Paris
- Hong Kong Disneyland Resort
- Shanghai Disney Resort
- Disney Vacation Club
- Disney Cruise Line

OTHER
- Adventures by Disney
- Disney Theatrical Productions
- Disney Live Family Entertainment
- Disney on Ice
- The Disney Store
- Disney Toys
- Disney Apparel
- Disney Food, Health and Beauty
- Disney Fashion and Home
- Disney Stationery
- DraftKings (minority owner)
- Marvel Entertainment
- Muppets Studio

Microblogs   A microblog allows individuals to post thoughts, photographs, and experiences without cost, albeit in a limited number of characters. Despite the character cap, people can spread word about a cause or a concern through hashtags. The person or organization behind each account can represent, or claim to represent, actors and networks at local, regional, national, or global scales. As a result, microblogs have experienced extraordinary growth, including Twitter, Qzone, and Weibo. Well over 400 Chinese use Weibo, the largest microblog in the country, and many millions use Twitter, even though it is formally blocked in China. This trend can make tight gatekeeping more difficult, though the Chinese authorities keep a close eye on what happens on these microblogs.

Despite censorship in some places, microblogs can challenge the dominant informational spin given to stories. This is a particularly significant factor in countries without a free press, where governments and journalists can be strong gatekeepers by choosing what stories to release or tell. For example, in July 2014, a Malaysian airliner was shot down by a surface-to-air missile by Russian separatists in eastern Ukraine. Russian television reported that Ukrainian nationalists shot down the plane because they suspected President Putin was on board. However, Ukrainian and American intelligence revealed that a Russian separatist leader, who was in communication with Russian President Putin, openly stated that separatists were responsible for shooting down the plane (*The Economist* 2014). Microbloggers helped to spread the word of this finding, which undercut the official Russian description of the event.

Just like social media, microblogging has its downsides—particularly political polarization (echo chambers where people read only material that supports their own worldview) and the spread of false information (e.g. Earth is not flat despite what you may see on YouTube). Thomas Jefferson famously argued for the need to "educate and inform the whole mass of the people . . . [t]hey are the only sure reliance for the preservation of our liberty." But educate and inform people about what? The answer is complicated given the many different interpretations of facts circulating on microblogs and elsewhere. Nonetheless, the recent growth in the number of stories that are unambiguously wrong represents a challenge. In response, there is growing awareness of the importance of fact-checking the content of microblogs and related platforms.

Economic Networks

Unlike traditional vertically integrated media, many economic networks are horizontally integrated. A horizontally integrated corporation is one that acquires ownership of other corporations engaged in similar activities. The retail industry may appear to be a large number of different companies. However, many retail companies bearing different names are in fact owned by the same horizontally integrated parent corporation.

Horizontal integration is common in clothing companies and housewares. Athleta, Old Navy, Gap, and Banana Republic are separate stores in a mall, but they are all owned by the same parent company, Gap, Inc. Likewise, Facebook, Instagram, and WhatsApp are different apps available for download, but they are all owned by Facebook, Inc. The incentive for horizontal integration is that a company that is successful in producing one good can replicate its success, share costs (such as websites), and increase profits selling at different price points or by developing slightly different varieties of the same good.

CSAs in the Contiguous
United States

Source: Courtesy of: Local Harvest.org.

FIGURE 14.7 **CSAs in the Contiguous United States.** Researchers found that CSAs are more likely to be found in urban or suburban areas where people have higher levels of education and are actively involved in discussing politics.

The Agricultural Sector

We often think of economic networks primarily in relation to manufacturing and service industries, but they play a role in the agricultural sector as well. Over the better part of the last century, these networks promoted the industrialization of agriculture (Chapter 11), which increased the distance between farmers and consumers. Container ships and refrigerated trucking and shipping allowed consumers in cold regions in winter months to purchase fresh fruits and vegetables grown thousands of miles away in warmer climates.

In some places, the pendulum is swinging back from large-scale industrial agriculture, however, and economic networks are playing a role in that shift. In the United States, around 2 million people act as the principal operators of farms—a figure that is as large as it is because of **community-supported agriculture** groups, known as CSAs (**Fig. 14.7**). CSAs began in Japan in the 1960s when a group of women, "dissatisfied with imported, processed, and pesticide-laden food, made arrangements directly with farmers to provide natural, organic, local food for their tables" (Schnell 2007). From its hearth in Japan, CSAs diffused to Europe and then to the United States, where the first CSA was in the Berkshire Mountains of Massachusetts. By 2017, the number of CSAs in the United States had risen to over 4000, according to Local Harvest, an organization that maps CSAs to help consumers and farmers connect (**Fig. 14.8**).

Through a CSA, a farmer and consumers create a network where both assume risk. Consumers pay for a share of the farmer's harvest, typically fruits and vegetables, before the growing season begins. Farmers use the cash to purchase

AP Images/Angela Major

FIGURE 14.8 **Elkhorn, Wisconsin.** Two workers wash lettuce in a tub at LotFotL, which stands for living off the fat of the land, a CSA farm. Subscribers can pay for their share or work on the farm to earn their share.

seeds and then plant, harvest, and deliver goods to consumers over a period of weeks during the growing season. Many CSA farmers use organic growing standards, but not all take the time to certify their land or label their products as such. With the growth in demand for organic products, however, the incentives for moving to certified organic farming are growing (Chapter 11).

The Service Sector
Modern transportation and communication networks are at the heart of economic globalization. These networks make global production networks possible, and they allow for innovations and ideas to spread rapidly. They play a fundamental role in time–space compression, and they link together the fortunes of distant places.

Consider, for example, global financial networks. Globalized financial systems that influence international flows of capital, patterns of investment, and trade financing. Financial networks are so closely linked that a significant shift in the financial markets on Wall Street in New York can have almost immediate impacts in London, Tokyo, and beyond. Shifts in Chinese financial institutions and financial markets are increasingly impacting countries tied directly to China's economy through China's development loans and projects (Chapter 10).

The most important nodes in these networks are **world cities**. Indeed, one of the signal features of economic globalization is the network of highly linked world cities. In Chapter 9, we discussed the growth of world cities in the core, semiperiphery, and periphery, and the deepening of their connectedness. We considered how network analysis is used to examine levels of connectivity among world cities, based on such factors as air travel between cities and the extent of the financial and advertising networks connecting cities. Another study of world cities, produced by the Brookings Institution, identified 123 world cities and mapped them according to seven categories (**Fig. 14.9**).

Drawing on dozens of economic indicators that speak to the influence of world cities on networks, the Brookings Institution study identified a few so-called global giants in the United States (New York and Los Angeles), Japan (Tokyo and Osaka-Kobe), the United Kingdom (London), and France (Paris). Instead of developing a single hierarchy of cities below those giants (the usual approach), the Brookings study looks at different ways cities can exert broad influence. They can be centers of innovative quinary economic activity (knowledge capitals), emerging gateways, or regionally important cities. The resulting picture provides another insight into the role world cities play in global, regional, and national economic networks.

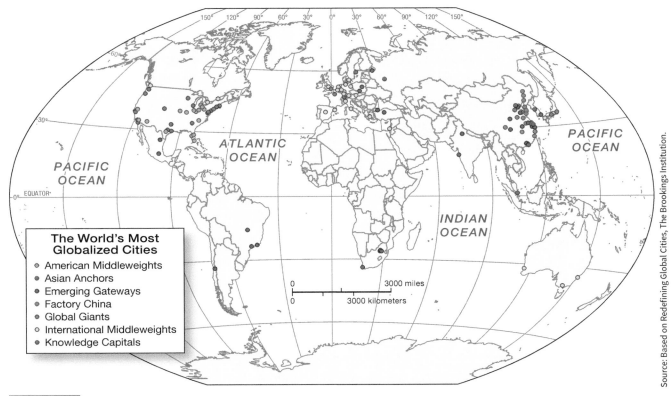

The World's Most Globalized Cities
- American Middleweights
- Asian Anchors
- Emerging Gateways
- Factory China
- Global Giants
- International Middleweights
- Knowledge Capitals

Source: Based on Redefining Global Cities, The Brookings Institution.

FIGURE 14.9 **The World's Most Globalized Cities.** The Brookings Institution used a variety of metropolitan-level economic characteristics, data on industrial structure, and indicators of competitiveness (trade, infrastructure, innovation, talent) to classify large cities into the seven categories shown on the map.

Focusing on world cities is important because they are the drivers of the networks that underpin and sustain globalization. The linkages among these cities tell us much about the spatial character of globalization (see Fig. 9.43 and 9.44). Those linkages influence not just the evolution of the world economy, but also the flow of ideas—in the process, shaping how people think about and make sense of the world around them.

The Larger View

No one can understand all the complexities that govern life on Earth. But the ideas and perspectives set forth in this text can give you insights into what it means to think geographically. That type of thinking is critical if you are to raise the types of questions that go beyond the generalizations that work against deeper understanding. Authors can treat complex issues with simplistic, often alarmist book titles like *The World is Flat* (Thomas Friedman) or *The Post-American World* (Fareed Zakaria). Books like these often start with an interesting observation and find evidence to support it, but they overlook complexities that do not support their theses.

Understanding complexities and diversity of experiences is essential to challenging simplistic stereotypes and developing a deeper understanding of how the world works.

It is important to identify the major trends that are shaping our world, but we also need to recognize the uniqueness of places. Then we might begin to understand the influence that particular uniqueness has on how major trends unfold and what they mean. Our hope is that this text has helped you think through these matters and, in the process, enhanced your awareness and appreciation of the world we call home.

TC **Thinking Geographically**

Think about the news you see each day on the Internet and social media. Go to the global media bias chart at: https://www.adfontesmedia.com/

Open the chart and analyze it – look for any media sources you use regularly for information. Go to Columbia Journalism Review's website, Who Owns What https://www.cjr.org/resources/?c=disney

Pick a media company and analyze their **network** of companies. Determine how many gatekeepers control the information you use to make decisions and understand your world, and analyze the bias of the sources in your information network.

Summary

14.1 Describe How Identities Are Changing in a Globalized World.

1. People have identities that reflect their relationships to people and events at different scales. In the wake of globalization, the global scale has increasingly become a focus of identity. We are constantly made aware of what is happening at the global scale, and the global scale affects our lives in multiple ways.

2. Despite the emergence of communication networks that transcend places, people continue to focus attention on territories and create specific places—in their minds and in tangible ways. For example, in the face of death or tragedy, people often construct memorials that reflect their thoughts about what happened and its significance. Different views of these matters can lead to conflicts over where memorials should be located and what they should look like.

14.2 Explain Networks and Their Role in Globalization.

1. Over the past 70 years, globalization has been advanced by the so-called Washington Consensus, which championed neoliberal policies designed to promote free trade. The consensus is increasingly being challenged. The challenge from the left comes from those who see it as part of a Western-dominated effort to get the rest of the world to privatize state-owned entities, open financial markets, liberalize trade by removing restrictions on the flow of goods, and encourage foreign direct investment—with the primary benefits flowing to the global economic core. The challenge from the right is based on the idea that globalization has weakened the ability of states to control what happens inside their borders and has undermined traditional national/cultural (and for some racial) norms.

2. At the heart of globalization are a wide variety of networks. Because these networks have become so widespread and are having such an enormous impact on people and places, some argue that they are bringing about changes that are even greater than the changes that occurred following the invention of the printing press or the arrival of the Industrial Revolution.

3. A major divide in access to information technology—called the digital divide—is a product of the proliferation of cyberspace networks. These networks link some places more than others, helping to create the uneven outcomes of globalization.

14.3 Explain How Social, Information, and Economic Networks Operate in a Globalized World.

1. Social networks play a major role in the organization of sociopolitical events (e.g., protests), the coordination of responses to disasters, the implementation of development initiatives, and the dissemination of information about important developments and causes. These networks can also make it easier to spread messages of hatred and racism, to plan terrorist attacks, and to spread false information (fake news). Ironically, even though they

connect people, there is growing evidence that they also lead to feeling of isolation and loneliness.

2. Information networks influence what people hear about and how different circumstances and events are described. Mergers and consolidations of media giants through vertical integration have reduced the number of information gatekeepers, leading to concern that more and more power rests with fewer and fewer gatekeepers. Microblogs represent a counter-trend, and these now play an important role in the information environment. But microblogs can also be platforms for spreading false or misleading information, and they can promote ideological and political polarization.

3. Economic networks are at the heart of globalization. They affect the agricultural sector as well as the manufacturing and service sectors. Global cities play an important role in these networks, giving them disproportionate economic influence and power in the contemporary world.

Self-Test

14.1 Describe how identities are changing in a globalized world.

1. True or False: The development of digital communications is rapidly displacing the desire for face-to-face interaction.

2. A tragic event that draws people together from distant places is an example of:

    a. an imagined community.

    b. participatory development.

    c. vertical integration.

    d. horizontal integration.

    e. social cohesion.

3. Each of the following was primarily a product of the modern telecommunications revolution except:

    a. the embrace of a more global identity by an increasing number of people.

    b. the personalization of events occurring in faraway places.

    c. the development of strong attachments to the places where people live.

    d. the growth in awareness of events occurring in distant places.

    e. all of the above are correct.

14.2 Explain networks and their role in globalization.

4. The roots of globalization can be traced to:

    a. trade over substantial distances.

    b. conflicts between world regions.

    c. the invention of the telephone.

    d. the rise of e-commerce.

    e. the industrial revolution.

5. The Washington Consensus refers to a Western-dominated effort:

    a. to restrict the flow of goods to benefit Western interests.

    b. to reduce the digital divide among peoples around the world.

    c. to promote a global trading network with the United States as its central node.

    d. to promote the global privatization of state-owned entities and liberalize trade.

    e. to spread democracy globally.

6. Which of the following is an example of time–space compression in the modern world?

    a. a migrant caravan moving north from Central America to the United States

    b. a website making it possible to order products and have them delivered the next day

    c. an intensification of flooding along a coast in response to sea-level rise

    d. a switch from gasoline-powered to hybrid automobiles

    e. the location of dairy farms in rural areas.

14.3 Explain how social, information, and economic networks operate in a globalized world.

7. The involvement of nongovernmental organizations (NGOs) in development initiatives:

    a. usually means that core–periphery power relations are removed from the picture.

    b. typically means that international financial institutions are also part of the picture.

    c. in many cases helps to foster participatory development.

    d. usually occurs only when governments have already taken steps to address problems.

    e. usually leads to their failure.

8. True or False: Many major media organizations have become more vertically integrated.

9. The most important nodes in global service networks are:

    a. microbloggers.

    b. seats of government (capitals).

    c. transport hubs.

    d. centers of secondary economic activity.

    e. global cities.

AP® Exam Taker's Prep Guide

Your exploration through AP® Human Geography (APHG) is almost complete. The final goal is to take the AP® exam. The APHG Exam consists of 60 multiple-choice questions (MCQ) and three free-response questions (FRQ). This section will examine the structure of MCQs and FRQs, as well as strategies needed to be successful in taking the APHG Exam.

In the preface of the book, general information about the structure of the class and the AP® exam was highlighted. In this section, specific tips for succeeding on the exam will be provided.

This section will explore the following topics:

1. The APHG Exam at a Glance
2. Understanding the MCQ Portion of the APHG Exam
3. Understanding the FRQ Portion of the APHG Exam

1. The APHG Exam at a Glance

The purpose of the APHG Exam is to assess how well you have mastered the content and skills of the course. Understanding the basic framework of the exam is extremely important to success on the exam.

The exam is 2 hours and 15 minutes and has 2 main components: 60 multiple-choice questions followed by 3 free-response questions. Please note that there is a break in between the multiple-choice portion and the free-response portion.

Section	Question Type	Number of Questions	Exam Weight	Time
1	Multiple-choice	60	50%	60 minutes
2	Free-response	3	50%	75 minutes

Section I—60 MCQs—Exam Time: 60 minutes

- The MCQ portion of the exam consists of 60 MCQs.
- Each MCQ has a *stem*, which is the question itself.

- Each MCQ has four *distractors*, which are answer choices that are not correct. (Note: Some distractors can be marginally or somewhat correct but are NOT the best answer.)
- Each MCQ has a *key*, or the most correct answer.
- Forty to sixty percent of MCQs will be in *sets*. A set is a group of 2–3 MCQs that are linked together by a common topic, theme, group of data, graphic, or so forth.
- Each MCQ point is linked to a specific *learning objective*.
- Each MCQ point is linked to a specific *Course and Exam Description (CED) skill*.
- The MCQ section is weighted at 50 percent of the exam.

Section II—Three FRQs—Exam Time: 75 minutes

- The FRQ portion of the exam consists of three FRQs.
- Each FRQ will usually have seven prompts labeled A, B, C, D, E, F, and G.
- All FRQs will be worth 7 points.
- Five task verbs will be used on FRQs: identify, define, describe, explain, compare.
- Each FRQ point is linked to a specific *learning objective*.
- Each FRQ point is linked to a specific *CED skill*.
- There is intentional scaffolding as each FRQ progresses through items A–G.
- The FRQ section is weighted at 50 percent of the exam.

Quick Tips for Students

- There are 60 minutes to answer all 60 multiple-choice questions. That leaves you with an average of one minute to answer each question. The best way to practice these skills is to take timed assessments.
- There are 75 minutes to answer three FRQs. Make sure you take no longer than 25 minutes for any one FRQ.
- If you finish the three FRQs and there is time remaining, go back to the question(s) or section(s) you were not sure about and add to your FRQ answer(s).

2. Understanding the MCQ Portion of the APHG Exam

Multiple-choice questions (MCQs) test you on two key elements of the course: knowledge and skills. In addition, there are other aspects of the structure of MCQs that you need to know. We will cover the following concepts regarding the MCQ portion of the APHG Exam:

- A. Knowledge Breadth in MCQs
- B. Skill Development in MCQs
- C. Multiple-Choice Question Sets
- D. Stimulus Material in MCQs
- E. Final Advice on MCQs

A. Knowledge Breadth in MCQs

These 60 questions examine the breadth of your knowledge—in other words, knowledge from *all* units of the course. For example, a multiple-choice question (MCQ) may focus on one particular APHG topic that you studied in the beginning of the first semester of or from your last day in class. Or, an MCQ may test your combined knowledge of population, culture, and economics all at the same time. Therefore, it is important to prepare for all units of the course, especially those early units where concepts might be a bit hazy.

The weightings for each unit of MCQ exam are as follows:

Unit 1: Thinking Geographically	8–10%
Unit 2: Population and Migration Patterns and Processes	12–17%
Unit 3: Cultural Patterns and Processes	12–17%
Unit 4: Political Patterns and Processes	12–17%
Unit 5: Agriculture and Rural Land-Use Patterns and Processes	12–17%
Unit 6: Cities and Urban Land-Use Patterns and Processes	12–17%
Unit 7: Industrial and Economic Development Patterns and Processes	12–17%

Do You Have the Essential Knowledge (EK)?

The College Board provides access to all teachers and students to the essential knowledge that you need to learn to be successful on the exam in a document called the Course and Exam Description (CED). In the CED, every unit is broken down into units and then further subdivided into subunit learning targets.

The essential knowledge, or EK, is a statement that describes the knowledge required to perform an APHG learning objective(s). Learning objectives are the sets of explicit knowledge and skills that must be learned to be proficient in APHG. EKs are what is tested explicitly in the APHG Exam

(both MCQs and FRQs). Your teacher uses the EKs in daily classroom instruction. But you can take a look at them as well in the CED. You can focus some of your study and exam preparation by learning and being able to apply each EK. The bottom line: Exam items are made from EKs. Know and understand the EKs, and you will be ready for the MCQs. For access to the CED, google "AP® Human Geography CED" or visit AP® Central.

In closing, the key to doing well on the MCQ portion of the exam is demonstrating proficiency in applying the wide base of knowledge presented in the APHG course. Reviewing all the essential knowledge targets from the College Board is one way to ensure you are ready for the exam.

B. Skill Development in MCQs

In addition to a strong knowledge base, MCQs will also test skills particular to APHG. What skills might you employ as you answer an MCQ? A deeper look at the APHG skills will follow below. The extent to which each of the APHG skill categories will be assessed are indicated in the following:

1. Concepts and Processes (25–36%)—This skill asks you to analyze geographic theories, concepts, or processes in theory or applied to a given context.
2. Spatial Relationships (16–25%)—With these questions you will be asked to analyze patterns, relationships, and outcomes in geographic contexts.
3. Data Analysis (13–20%)—You will need to be comfortable analyzing quantitative data represented in a variety of ways, including but not limited to maps, graphs, and tables.
4. Source Analysis (13–20%)—These questions will ask you to analyze and interpret qualitative information represented in a variety of ways, including but not limited to maps, images, and photographs.
5. Scale Analysis (13–20%)—Like Skill Category 1, you will need to analyze geographic concepts and processes but for these questions you will need to apply that analysis across geographic scales.

Verbs in MCQs Skill Development A more comprehensive view of the APHG course skills explains exactly what you need to think about when answering MCQs. Notice how each skill category is broken down into four to six skills. Further, notice how each skill begins with a *task verb*. For example, in Skill Category 5 there are sub-skills that require you to *identify, explain, and compare* different components of a given question that will help you demonstrate a clear understanding of Skill Category 5. It is essential that you understand what level of thinking (and writing on the FRQs) each task verb requires you to do. For more information on task verbs, see the FRQ section later in this chapter.

Using the APHG Skills in MCQs

All of the skills are embedded in the APHG Exam. In fact, all of the skills will be used on the exam at least once. Therefore, it is important to have a good handle on what the skills are. Stimulus material will be a major part of utilizing skills in MCQs. Here is a quick look at the information on how MCQs may or may not have stimulus material by category:

Skill Categories 1 and 2 *may use* stimulus material.

Skill Categories 3 and 4 *will have* stimulus material.

Skill Category 5 *does not have to have* stimulus material (but it could).

Be sure to study the skill information that the College Board provides. For further information and explanation of the APHG skills, see pages 143–151 of the CED.

Summary of Knowledge and Skills on MCQs

Study the EKs and skills from the CED. Remember, all MCQs are based on the EKs and skills. Here are some helpful guidelines:

- The number of MCQs in Unit 1 will average 5–6 MCQs.
- The number of MCQs in Units 2–7 will average 7–10 MCQs each.
- The number of MCQs for Skill 1 will average 15–21 MCQs.
- The number of MCQs for Skill 2 will average 10–15 MCQs.
- The number of MCQs for Skills 3–5 will average 8–12 MCQs.

C. Multiple-Choice Question Sets

Another important aspect of the MCQ portion of the exam is question sets. A *question set* is a combination of two to three MCQs that are linked together by stimulus material, topic(s), or other common content. Here are some important points to understand about MCQ sets:

- There will be six to eight sets in the 60 MCQs.
- That means approximately 40–60 percent of the APHG Exam MCQs will be presented in question sets.
- Many of these sets will include stimulus material such as maps, charts, data sets, diagrams, reading passages, photographs, or a combination of these.
- A question set will be intentionally scaffolded—meaning each MCQ in the set gets a little more complicated from questions 1 to 2 and 2 to 3.
- Therefore, the verbs will change in the MCQ sets—in other words, there will not be two questions with the very identify in the same set.

D. Stimulus Material in MCQs

Another important aspect of the MCQ portion centers on stimulus materials. *Stimulus materials* are items that accompany and/or are the focus of the MCQ. These might include maps, charts, diagrams, data sets/tables, photographs, images, infographics, and landscapes. These stimulus materials will be divided roughly in half between quantitative and qualitative sources.

Quantitative Data (Skill 3)—empirical and measurable data that has amounts, ranges, and quantities. Examples in the APHG Exam may include tables, charts, population pyramids, and so forth.

Qualitative Data (Skill 4)—data collected by observation, photographs, or interviews. Examples in APHG Exam may include photos, text excerpts, imagery, quotes, and so forth.

Stimulus material will be used in a minimum of 30 to 40 percent of MCQs. The percentage of stimulus material in MCQs can be as high as 40 to 60 percent, as the stimulus material in sets combined with MCQs with stimulus material could increase the percentage over 40 percent.

E. Final Advice on MCQs

There is no penalty for guessing on MCQs. In other words, do NOT leave any MCQ answer blank. Always read all of the answers on an MCQ before choosing your final answers. All MCQs have a *best* answer. This means one of the choices is the best among all of the potential answers. It also means that one of the distractors might also be somewhat correct. But that somewhat correct distractor is not the *most* correct, or *best* answer. This is why it is essential that you read all of the potential answers before you choose your answer.

Finally, the stem of an MCQ *may* provide information that will assist you in answering the question. This means you should use the text (and any stimulus material) that is provided. The information provided in the stem is not meant to trick you in any way. That information is there to frame and drive the question.

| **What might information in an MCQ stem look like?** |

EXAMPLE: An MCQ stem might look something like this: "Sugarcane is a global commodity that is demanded for several industries and products. Brazil produces over 725,000 TMT (thousand metric tons) of sugarcane each year." With that information, the MCQ will continue into the multiple-choice answers.

| **What do we need to learn here?** |

Brazil is among the top three producers of sugarcane each year. You did not need to memorize that fact to be successful on an MCQ that starts with that information. The point is that you did not need to memorize the top 10 countries of sugarcane production or the amount they produce. But you do need to be able to recognize the data being presented to you in an MCQ and be prepared to use those data to select the correct answer.

The MCQ might be testing your knowledge that sugarcane is grown in subtropical and equatorial climates. Or the correct answer could have been that sugarcane is grown mainly by plantation agriculture. Or the MCQ could have tested your understanding that sugarcane is a luxury crop with colonial roots. All of these potential answers are geographic knowledge that you need to supply. The MCQ stem has information that helps you frame the question so you can supply the correct answer.

Further Practice For further practice, ask your teacher to let you use the practice MCQs from the College Board. AP® Classroom is a way to use practice questions online through the College Board. Your teacher has the ability to access these questions and set up practice exams for you. Ask your teacher about AP® Classroom resources.

In addition, use the practice MCQ exam located on pages 160–166 in the CED. It provides 15 sample MCQs. Sample questions can help you learn what the individual MCQs look like, as well as what the MCQ sets are like. These MCQs also provide valuable practice and have a set of answer keys located on page 170. The key page also provides the intended skill for each question, as well as its respective learning objective.

Understanding the FRQ Portion of the APHG Exam

As with the MCQs, FRQs will assess both knowledge and skills. All three FRQs will have seven prompts. A prompt is a portion of an FRQ. All FRQs will have 7 points labeled as A, B, C, D, E, F, and G. Each point is weighted equally. The FRQ portion of the exam occurs after you have completed the 60 MCQ portion of the test. You will have 75 minutes to answer all three FRQs.

We will cover the following concepts regarding the FRQ portion of the APHG Exam:

    A. Knowledge Depth in FRQs

    B. Skill Development in FRQs

    C. Task Verbs in FRQs

    D. Stimulus Material in FRQs

    E. Changing Scale(s) in FRQs

    F. Models in FRQs

    G. General Tips for the FRQ Portion of the Exam

A. Knowledge Depth in FRQs

While both MCQs and FRQs address knowledge, FRQs tend to test the *depth* of your knowledge in APHG, more so than MCQs. Since there are only three questions, FRQs are not designed to cover all the material in APHG. Instead, you must provide specific details and demonstrate a deeper understanding of concepts from the course. In addition, FRQs will not be solely on one topic but will test on your ability to connect multiple parts of the course together with an in-depth analysis. Most

likely, an FRQ will test your ability to integrate several parts of the course (e.g., urban, culture, political) into a comprehensive response.

One way to understand the amount of depth necessary to answer FRQs is to think of each FRQ as writing a 25-minute answer to one question. This requires a depth of knowledge to do so correctly.

B. Skill Development in FRQs

As with the MCQs, FRQs will also test the same APHG skills. The extent to which each of the APHG skill categories will be assessed are indicated in the following chart:

Skill Category	Exam Weighting
1. Concepts and Processes	23–29%
2. Spatial Relationships	33–43%
3. Data Analysis	10–19%
4. Source Analysis	10–19%
5. Scale Analysis	10–14%

C. Task Verbs in FRQs

There are five *task verbs* used in the FRQs. In alphabetical order, the task verbs are *compare, define, describe, explain,* and *identify*. You must understand that all verbs are not created equally. It is essential to be able to apply the verb that is utilized in a question properly. In fact, the verb used in an FRQ prompt determines how much you need to write and what to do. Therefore, the order of the verbs with regard to complexity and amount of writing needed for a sufficient answer go in this order (from least complex to most complex): *identify, define, describe, explain,* and *compare*.

It is also essential to understand that there is intentional scaffolding as the FRQ proceeds from beginning to end. What that means is parts A, B, C, and maybe even D are designed to use verbs like *identify, define,* and *describe*. The *explain* and *compare* verbs would more likely be used in the latter part of the question in E, F, and G. Having said that, each FRQ is designed to get more complicated as the FRQ progresses. Translation? Expect the lower-level task verbs in the beginning of the FRQ and the higher-level task verbs nearer to the end of the FRQ. In the end, there is no specific order prescribed for verb use in FRQs. Simply use the verb in the way it should be used no matter where it appears in an FRQ.

FRQ Verb Mechanics

The task verbs are listed in a scaffolded order from the lower-order verbs to the higher-order verbs. Understand that *identify* and *define* are both equally lower-level verbs. Let's take a look at each verb and its definition according to page 159 of the College Board CED:

- Identify – indicate or provide information about a specific topic, without elaboration or explanation
- Define – provide a specific meaning for a word or concept
- Describe – provide the relevant characteristics of a specified topic
- Explain – provide information about how or why a relationship, process, pattern, position, or outcome occurs, using evidence and/or reasoning
- Compare – provide a description or explanation of similarities and/or differences

If the task verb is *identify*, then you should write one complete sentence. Do not write using bullet points and/or incomplete sentences. One full sentence should easily answer an identify prompt.

If the task verb is *define* or *describe*, several detailed sentences are necessary in order to answer the prompt. Defining tends to more general, whereas describing tends to be more specific.

Explain and *compare* are the most challenging task verbs and need some detailed explanation for each, because both have some "hidden" tasks that need to have light shone upon them:

Explain
Explain actually means you must state a term, concept, fact, situation, or so forth followed by *because* and then continue to account for the factors that show the sources or origins of what is being explained. If you use the word *because* between your two thoughts, you are much more likely to receive credit.

OR

Explain is to show cause and effect. That is, you write a *cause* that you are prompted by the question and then write the *effect* of that *cause*. Conversely, you might give the *effect* first and then give the *cause* or *causes*.

OR

Explain is to write the answer to the prompt, followed by your *demonstrating the results* of the first sentence of your answer. This means you would identify a term, concept, fact, situation, or so forth followed by you laying out the results.

The bottom line is that both *explain* and *compare* must have *two parts* to get the one point that is available for that part of the question.

Compare
Compare is a description or explanation of *similarities and/or differences*. Look carefully and you will see two of the other APHG task verbs (*describe* and *explain*) in the definition. That means your answer to an FRQ with *compare* in it means you must *describe* or *explain* the differences and/or

similarities posed in the prompt. Your task may be to compare the differences or similarities in a particular prompt. You are more likely to be asked to compare *both* the differences *and* similarities of a particular term, concept, data set, scenario, or so forth.

Finally, *compare* means the FRQ prompt will have two separate items to compare. This does *not* mean two options. It means there will be two or more items to be compared within the prompt.

Task Verb Number 6: The Hidden Task Verb

Wait, I thought there were only five task verbs. Well, there is actually a clandestine sixth task verb concealed in the APHG skills. Look at Skills 2E and 6D listed below (p. 14 of the CED):

> 2E: *Explain the degree* to which a geographic concept, process, model, or theory effectively explains geographic effects in different contexts and regions of the world.
>
> AND
>
> 6D: *Explain the degree* to which a geographic concept, process, model, or theory effectively explains geographic effects across various geographic scales.

The clandestine task verb is *explain the degree* of something. It is not that this is really a sixth task verb but an extension of the verb *explain*. *Explain the degree* actually means you need to explain the span, spectrum, or range of what is being asked in the prompt. Further, remember the *explain* verb needs a two-part answer. Think of it like this: Explain the degree might be like you trying to explain what made you angry *and then* the level of anger that you have. Or, let's use a real human geography situation. An FRQ prompt might ask the following:

Explain the degree to which the von Thünen model from 1826 is still viable in modern agriculture.

A possible *explain the degree* might be:

> **The classic von Thünen model has been antiquated in many ways due to agribusiness practices such as canning, refrigeration, freezing, containerized shipping, and other methods to keep food fresh. However, the von Thünen model continues to be very relevant through many *locavore* and *community-supported agriculture* movements. There are significant numbers of people who want fresh food from local and relatively nearby areas. The large increase in the sales of organic, specialty, local, and low carbon-footprint foods are examples. These movements have made the von Thünen model continue to be relevant.**

Do you recognize how the answer "stretches" the *explain* verb by saying the von Thünen model is perhaps more relevant today with regard to some issues in modern agriculture? This example is a good model for how the *explain the degree* idea of something works.

D. Stimulus Material in the FRQs

There will be stimulus material in two of the three FRQs on the APHG Exam. According to the College Board's Course and Exam Description (CED), stimulus material refers to the following: maps, tables, charts, graphs, images, infographics, and/or landscapes.

Here is the formula for FRQ stimulus material:

1. FRQ #1: No stimulus material
2. FRQ #2: One stimulus (data, map, or image)
3. FRQ #3: Two stimuli (data, images, and/or maps)

Important: All stimulus is analytical, not contextual, which means you need to analyze what is in front of you. Do not try to infer meanings that may not be there. Just use the data that are presented to you and answer the prompt(s). Specifically, being analytical means you use the data from what is presented. Contextualizing something is an attempt to draw conclusions or deductions that simply may not be there. Therefore, do not try to "see" something in a stimulus-based question that is not there.

There will be data in some of the stimulus material in FRQs. Make sure you can *explain* the data via the course terms and concepts you have been taught. This means you cannot simply restate those data presented in the FRQ. This is one of the most common mistakes students make: answering FRQs with data or data sets. The skill or skills being tested in this circumstance is your ability to explain how the data work or how they might be relevant to the situation or scenario posed in the FRQ. Remember, *explain* means you must make a point or take a position *and then* give the results, effects, consequences, or other outcomes from the point/position you introduced.

E. Changing Scale(s) in FRQs

According to the CED, "At least two of the three FRQs will assess students' ability to analyze across geographic scales." What this means is that you must be able to recognize and respond to a change of scale *within* a question. It is important to understand that it is likely you will *not* be prompted to change scales in the question(s). Therefore, you must be ready to recognize the shift in scale and answer accordingly.

Let's imagine what a change of scale in an FRQ might look like:

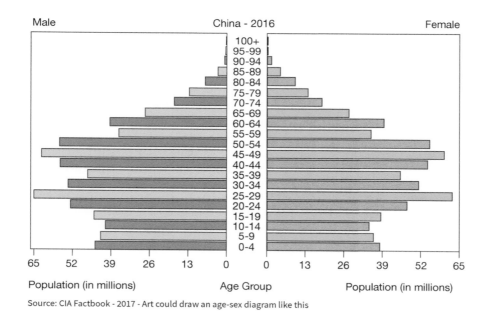

Source: CIA Factbook - 2017 - Art could draw an age-sex diagram like this

A. Identify the age cohort(s) where the population begins to drop significantly.
B. Explain the primary cause of the general drop in fertility in China.
C. Based on your understanding of China's demographics, compare how a population pyramid would look in a rural region and an urban region.

Parts A and B start off referring to the population pyramid specifically.

Part A asks you to *identify* a particular part of the population pyramid. This task is very targeted, uses a low-level verb, and asks for you to be able to read the diagram.

Part B asks you to provide an explanation for the decrease in fertility. You are operating at the country-level scale of the population pyramid. So, the population pyramid is being addressed indirectly in this part. Remember that the *explain* verb requires you to show cause and effect or state something and then provide the "because."

Part C changes the scale. The assumption in Part B is that you would address the One Child Only policy somewhere in your explanation. Part C asks you to imagine what population pyramids would look like in an urban setting and a rural setting based on the implementation of the One Child Policy. This is not an easy task. You have to think about all the political, economic, and social factors operating at a local scale. In addition, you must consider the infrastructure in place. The goal here is to understand that a population pyramid at a country-level scale looks different than a local scale.

F.   Models in FRQs

First, models are just models. You can't fly over a city and see Burgess's urban concentric zones. But via data application and using the geographic skills, you can apply those concentric zones. The geographic models are used to construct ways of thinking spatially about particular spaces and processes. Second, the models are not meant to be static. Models should be applied by the user to think about change or understand that no change has taken place in part of what the model has proposed.

Many students (and teachers) make a critical error when using models. Mentioning a model in an FRQ response is not usually helpful. Applying the model, or suggesting how change that might be explained by the model has occurred, is what will score points on an FRQ.

A really good example of a misused model is the demographic transition model (DTM). Many students believe the DTM is static in that you just plug in a country somewhere on the model and voilà! We are done. In actuality, you should be thinking about the processes that have placed the country where it is *and* think about where it is going on the model (and how fast or slow this will be).

G.   General Tips for the FRQ Portion of the Exam

Hopefully, you have practiced FRQs and MCQs throughout the year. Use strategies you have learned in the textbook and in class when writing FRQs.

Some General Tips for FRQs

- Listen to the proctor and read the FRQ instructions. There is valuable information in there!

- An example of what you might miss by not reading/listening to the instructions: You may not write in bullets. They are not scored. More details on this later.

- Remember, FRQs require a more deliberate approach than the MCQs because FRQs have more moving parts and variables.

Outlining and Writing the FRQs

- Create a plan of attack for the 75 minutes you have to answer the three questions in this section.

- Once the 75-minute clock begins, outline the three FRQs for a maximum of five minutes.

- IMPORTANT NOTE: Be sure that any outline notes you create are transferred to the FRQ pages where you write. Why? Because nothing you write on your outline is scored unless it is moved over.

- Finally, determine which FRQ you believe is the least difficult and the most difficult.

- Now, let's begin writing the answers to the FRQs.

Writing the FRQs

- Allow up to 15 minutes to answer the question you believe to be the least difficult.

- Then, answer the FRQs in the order you have determined from least difficult to most difficult.

- Allow up to 20 minutes to answer the second most difficult question.

- Finally, allow up to 25 minutes to answer the most difficult question.

- If you follow the time limits to their maximums, you will still have 10 minutes left to go back over your answers and make any last-minute changes.

- This process allows you to start quickly and accurately. As you write, your confidence will increase.

- And, as you write, more geographic knowledge is likely to come to you, making the more difficult FRQs more accessible as you go through this process.

Helpful Hints in Writing the FRQs

- Put a *square* around the verbs. This will help you stay focused and remember that the verbs tell you exactly how much to write.

- Put a *circle/oval* around conjunctions (e.g., and, or, unless) and prepositions (e.g., around, between, within, across) and numbers (e.g. one example of supranationalism, two luxury crops). Circling conjunctions and prepositions will help you stay focused on the connections and extensions you need to make in your answers. Circling the numbers will keep you focused on the exact quantity required to answer the question properly.

- Underline the *geography terms*, *concepts*, or other *key words* in the FRQ. This will keep your focus on exactly what topic(s) the prompt is about. For example, make sure to underline the human geography words such as diffusion, regional, migration, Berlin Conference, new urbanism, periphery, and so forth. Again, this helps you stay focused on what the question is asking you to write about.

- Many of the FRQ prompts and stimuli will have a great deal of information in them—especially in the opening stem of the FRQ. You should use this information to help answer the question prompts.

  - For example, an FRQ stem might list the top 10 countries with regard to population. A prompt in the FRQ might ask you to compare the growth of a couple of those countries. Look back at the list of countries and use that information along with your geographic knowledge and thinking to answer the question.

- One of the most common mistakes students make is trying to answer an FRQ all at one time. Stay focused on one task at a time on an FRQ. You really do need to use a tunnel-visioned approach and literally tackle a prompt, finish it, and then move to the next one and do the same thing again.

- While using good grammar and spelling is always a plus, the FRQs are a timed exercise and you are under some pressure. Understand that grammar and spelling are NOT scored on the FRQs. So relax and focus on writing the best geographic answer you can provide.

- Do *not* ever write in bullets. Why? Because the exam instructions say not to. And bullets will lead you to writing incomplete thoughts. Plus, bulleted items are not scored. Read the instructions!

- Do not simply repeat the stem/prompt in an FRQ as your answer. This is a *very* common error students make. Answer what the stem/prompt is asking.

- Another major error students make is not answering the question that is actually in front of them. Many students answer the question they want to answer or think they have been asked.

Let's imagine the following FRQ prompt example.

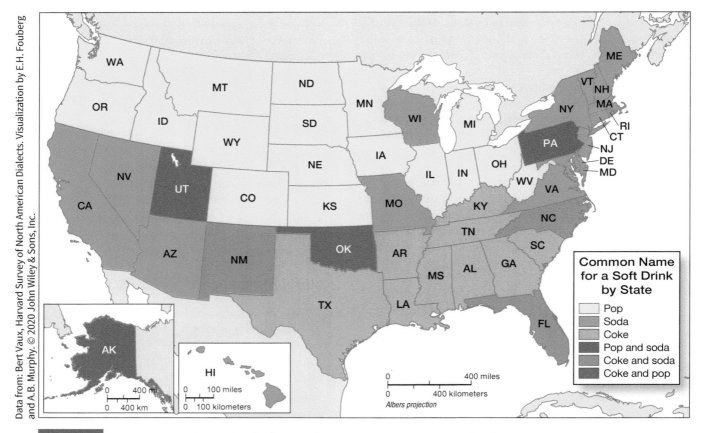

Common Name for a Soft Drink by State
- Pop
- Soda
- Coke
- Pop and soda
- Coke and soda
- Coke and pop

FIGURE 6.6 **Common Names for a Soft Drink in the United States, by State.** The isogloss for soda and pop generally divides the coasts from the rest of the country. A north-south isogloss distinguishes where pop and coke are commonly used. For county level data and to submit the word you use, see: http://popvssoda.com/

Pop, Soda, and Coke are all different terms associated with carbonated beverages in the United States.

A. Describe how these terms spread through contagious diffusion.

- Make sure you read the task correctly.
- A student would not receive credit for merely stating the definition of contagious diffusion.
- The prompt did not ask for the students to define the terms. It asked the writer to describe how these terms diffuse spatially.
- This is an excellent example of how many students tend to answer the question they wanted to answer—not the question that was actually posed.

Believe it or not, students lose valuable points in FRQs because they do not read the data on the map. Take a look at this example below.

A. Identify the prominent ranges of Crude Death Rates in Western and Eastern Europe.

- Many students simply do not attempt an answer on a prompt like this, or will write a definition of crude birth rate. Neither of these will give the student points.
- Part A was supposed to be the easiest part of the question—read the map and any data, and use it to answer the prompt.
- All a student needs to do on this question is read the key on the map and address the differences in Western Europe and Eastern Europe like this. "In Western Europe crude death rates are lower than Eastern Europe. In Western European, crude death rates range from 8–14 for the most part; whereas, Eastern European ranges are from 10–15 or more."

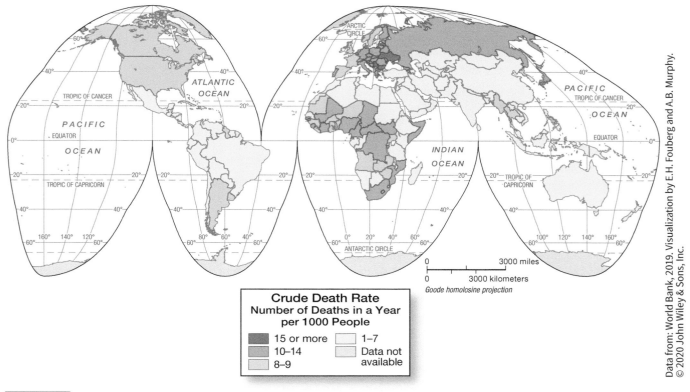

Data from: World Bank, 2019. Visualization by E.H. Fouberg and A.B. Murphy.
© 2020 John Wiley & Sons, Inc.

FIGURE 2.8 **Crude Death Rate: Number of Deaths in a Year per 1000 People.**   The death rate has declined globally as countries have transitioned into the third stage of the demographic transition and beyond. A few countries in the global north have relatively high death rates, including Russia and a number of eastern European countries.

Other Dos and Dont's on the FRQs

- **Numbers of examples**—If a prompt asks you to name two examples of something, understand that only the first two you give will be scored (this is part of the general exam instructions). For example, let's say the question

asks for two examples of supranationalism; your answer is "MERCOSUR, Walmart, and the African Union." You gave three answers, and the question asked for two. MERCOSUR and the African Union are supranational organizations; Walmart is not. Your answer would get credit for MERCOSUR, and no points would be awarded for Walmart. The answer of African Union would not be scored even though it is correct.

- **Striking out an answer**—Let's say you write an example or sentence that you suddenly believe to be a wrong answer. You strike through that example, sentence, or even paragraph. If you strike through or in any way "line out" an answer or part thereof, it will not be scored. Even if the answer you had was correct and the reader can clearly see it, that portion will not be scored. So be careful.

- **Time frames**—No, the APHG Exam is certainly not a history test. However, many questions will ask about geographic issues framed in a particular time. For example, the exam might ask about nation-states in the "late twentieth century" or about technology "developed in the past 10 years." Be sure your answer addresses only the geographic issues in that time frame.

- **Know your A, B, Cs**—Answer the FRQ prompts by labeling each response in ABCDEFG format. If you organize your answers in a coherent way, you are much more likely to write an answer that will achieve a higher score. In other words, clearly label each answer with the appropriate letter. Again, it keeps you organized, but it also allows the reader to find your answer easily and give you the credit you earned.

- **Do not use stereotypes**—The use of stereotypes is a common mistake made by many APHG students on the exam. Stay away from using stereotypes when answering FRQs. Many students might incorrectly write, "Everyone in Africa is poor." Or students use stereotypes like: "Poor women are all uneducated and have many babies." Not only are these kinds of answers wrong—they are hurtful stereotypes that show no geographic thought or understanding. This is especially true when stereotypes are used at the regional level. Be a geographer and provide real analysis—not stereotypes.

- *Always* and *lots*—Avoid using words like *always, lots, never, bunches*, and so forth when answering FRQs. Superlatives like *never* and *always* are just not found much in the real world. It stands to reason that they do not make good FRQ answers. Words like *lots* and *a bunch* do not provide specificity or quantity sufficient to adequately answer an FRQ prompt.

Final General Tips for Thinking About and Preparing for the APHG Exam

Here are some general tips that are not in the preceding suggestions and tips. These final tips are meant to help you understand some of the issues of the exam such as scoring and approaches to the exam.

- **Scoring a 5, 4, or 3**—You do not have the ace the APHG Exam. Earning a score of 5, 4, or 3 on the exam does not correlate to scoring 90 percent on an exam in your classroom. That is not how AP® scoring works. To get a 5, 4, or 3 on the exam, you really need to be somewhere around 55 percent. Why?

- **Be above the mean**—The answer to the previous why is being above the mean score. In other standardized exams like the ACT or SAT, you are essentially competing against the exam. In AP® exams, you are competing against the other exam takers. The APHG Exam uses a scaled score. That means everyone's exam receives a rank. Your rank goes in with everyone else's who took the exam. Therefore, you need to carefully try to collect as many points as you can during the exam. If you are above the mean score of the entire exam, you will get at least a 3. Yes, you can make a 51 percent on the APHG Exam and get a score of 3.

- **Use good geography vocabulary, and terminology**—Use the vocabulary you learned during the year (e.g., diffusion, regions, scale) in your FRQ answers. Also use geographic terminology (e.g., adjacent, node, nested, nucleated, agglomerated, dispersed, zones) in your answers. Thinking and writing geographically always pays off.

- **Write an opening and closing paragraph?**—No. These are not helpful and only cost you time. Just begin writing. It might be helpful to restate the FRQ prompt in the form of a statement. That is, take the FRQ prompt and turn it into a statement to begin your answer. For example, if the prompt says, "Describe the migration pattern between the United States and Mexico since 1950," you might begin your answer by stating, "The migration pattern between the United States and Mexico since 1950 . . ." and then add your answer. This helps you maintain focus on what the prompt is asking you to do.

- **More or less**—You are not penalized for writing too much. And you are not penalized for being wrong as you write. You are scored on the *correct information you provide*. So if you are not sure you have answered the question and have more to say—write it. It usually cannot hurt you, unless you directly contradict what you have previously written in an answer.

- **Current events on the exam?**—There are no current events on the exam. Something that happens in the world a few months before the exam will not be there. It takes a year or two from when they are written for new items to appear on the exam. However, you *can* use current events as examples or references to answer FRQ prompts. Current events can be very useful in FRQ answers.

- **Accommodations**—If you need accommodations (e.g., extra time on exams, use of keyboard), make sure you talk to your teacher and counselor as soon as your course begins. Any accommodations for an AP® exam must be approved long before the exam is given. It takes time and must go through a process.

Activities and Strategies to Help You Score Well on the APHG Exam

- **Pretests and posttests**—Personalize your pretest and posttest data. If your teacher gives you a pre- and posttest, ask to record how many you missed and in what kind (e.g., population, agriculture, economic) of question. This can help you target your studying as you prepare for the AP® exam.

- **You know what I meant!**—Have you ever said or heard someone say, "You know what I meant!"? Sometimes, teachers read FRQs and know that the student knows something. But the student never really addressed what the FRQ prompt actually asked. When you write an FRQ answer, try to write like you are explaining your answer to someone who knows nothing about APHG. Write clearly in plain language like you were talking to your grandparents or parents. If you follow this advice (while still following what has been taught above), you are likely to make clear statements with relevant examples. This provides a good way to make sure you do not leave out details you should have included.

- **Write your own FRQs and rubrics**—Writing FRQs and rubrics is a great way to study. Try writing an FRQ with a rubric—but write the rubric first. The rubric provides the answers. If you can write down some answers, then you can frame FRQ prompts that ask those things. Once you write a question about something in APHG, you will know it.

- **Practice FRQs**—This textbook has an online practice test with three FRQs. This would be a great way to practice your skills.

Maps

The geographer's greatest ally is the map. Maps can present enormous amounts of information efficiently and effectively, and can be used to establish theories and solve problems. Furthermore, maps often are fascinating, revealing things no other medium can. It has been said that if a picture is worth a thousand words, then a map is worth a million.

Maps can be fascinating, but they often do not get the attention they deserve. You may spend 20 minutes carefully reading a page of text, but how often have you spent 20 minutes with a page-size map, studying what it reveals? It is difficult to summarize every pattern a map shows in a caption or paragraph of text. Readers should actively read maps by looking for patterns and themes. For example, in Chapter 2 we study several maps that depict health and population by country, including birth and death rates, infant mortality, mothers' index, and life expectancy. In the text, we can refer only to highlights (and low points) on those maps. But make a point of looking beyond the main issue to get a sense of the global distributions these maps represent. It is part of an intangible but important process: to enhance your mental map of the world.

While on the topic of maps, we should remind ourselves that a map—any map—is an incomplete representation of reality. In the first place, a map is smaller than the real world it represents. Second, it must depict the curved surface of our world on a flat plane. And third, it contains symbols to convey the information that must be transmitted to the reader. These are the three fundamental properties of all maps: scale, projection, and symbols.

Understanding these basics helps us interpret maps while avoiding their pitfalls. Some maps look so convincing that we may not question them as we would a paragraph of text. Yet maps, as representatives of the world, all distort reality to some extent. Most of the time, such distortion is necessary and does not invalidate the map's message. But some maps are drawn deliberately to mislead. Propaganda maps, for example, may exaggerate or distort reality to promote political aims. We should be alert to cartographic mistakes when we read maps. The proper use of scale, projection, and symbolization ensures that a map is as accurate as it can be made.

Map Scale

The scale of a map reveals how much the real world has been reduced to fit on the page or screen on which it appears. It is the ratio between an actual distance on the ground and the length given to that distance on the map, using the same units of measurement. This ratio is often represented as a fraction (e.g., 1:10,000 or 1/10,000). This means that one unit on the map represents 10,000 such units in the real world. If the unit is 1 inch, then an inch on the map represents 10,000 inches on the ground, or slightly more than 833 feet. The metric system certainly makes things easier. One centimeter on the map would actually represent 10,000 cm, or 100 meters. Such a scale would be useful when mapping a city's downtown area, but it would be much too large for the map of an entire state.

As the real-world area we want to map gets larger, we must make our map scale smaller. As small as the fraction 1/10,000 seems, it still is 10 times as large as 1/100,000, and 100 times as large as 1/1,000,000. If the world maps in this book had fractional scales, they would be even smaller. A large-scale map can contain much more detail and be far more representative of the real world than a small-scale map. Look at it this way: When we devote a half page of this book to a map of a major city (**Fig. A.1**), we are able to represent the layout of that city in considerable detail. But if the entire country in which that city is located must be represented on a single page, the city becomes just a large dot on that small-scale map, and the detail is lost in favor of larger-area coverage (**Fig. A.2**). The selection of scale depends on the objective of the map.

When you examine the maps in this book, you will note that most, if not all, of them have scales that are given in graphic form, not ratios or fractions. This method of representing map scale is convenient from several viewpoints. Using the edge of a piece of paper and marking the scale bar's length, you can quickly—without calculation—determine approximate distances. And if a map is enlarged or reduced in reproduction, the scale bar is enlarged or reduced with it and remains accurate. That is not true of a ratio or fractional scale. Graphic scales, therefore, are most common in this book.

Map Projections

For centuries cartographers have faced the challenge of creating map projections, ways of representing the spherical Earth, or part of it, on a flat surface. To get the job done, there had to be a frame of reference on the globe itself, a grid system that could be transferred to the flat page. Any modern globe shows that system: a set of horizontal lines, usually at 10-degree intervals north and south from the equator, called parallels, and another set of vertical lines, converging on the poles,

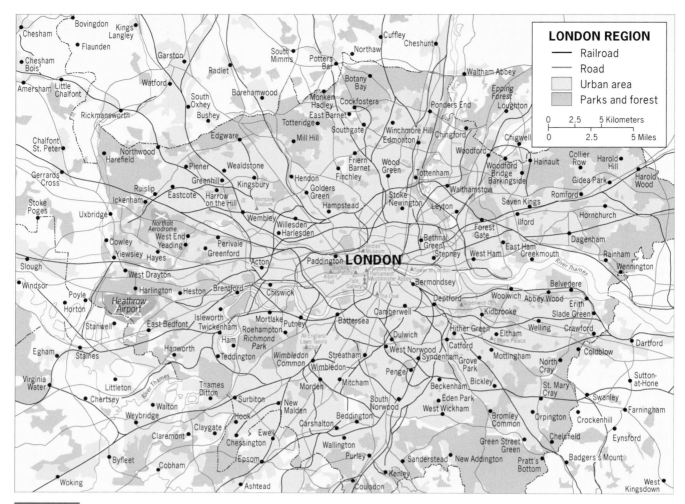

FIGURE A.1 **London, United Kingdom.** The layout of London, including neighborhoods, city parks, and forests, can be shown in considerable detail at this large scale. In cartographic terms, a large scale map shows a small area, in this case London.

often shown at 15-degree intervals and called meridians. On the spherical globe, parallels and meridians intersect at right angles (**Fig. A.3**).

Ancient cartographers had to determine how to number lines of latitude and longitude. For the (horizontal) latitude lines, that was easy. The equator, which bisects the Earth midway between the poles, was designated as 0° latitude, and all parallels north and south of the equator were designated by their angular position (see Fig. A.3). The poles are at 90° from the equator, making the North Pole 90° north and the South Pole a point that is 90° south. The parallel midway between the equator and the poles is 45° north latitude in the northern hemisphere and 45° south latitude in the southern hemisphere.

The (vertical) longitude lines do not have a natural break. Each line of longitude is the same length, and each one of them divides Earth into equal halves. During the second half of the nineteenth century, maps with conflicting locations for 0° longitude multiplied, and it was clear that a solution was needed. The most powerful country at the time was Britain and in 1884,

countries reached an international agreement. The meridian that ran through the Royal Observatory in Greenwich, England, was designated the prime meridian, 0° longitude. All meridians east and west of the prime meridian could now be designated by number, from 0° to 180° east and west longitude.

All of the lines of longitude intersect at the North Pole and at the South Pole. The lines of longitude cannot intersect when you put the Earth on a flat piece of paper. In 1569, cartographer Gerardus Mercator designed a map projection that made the lines of longitude parallels. On the Mercator projection, lines of latitude and longitude intersect at right angles. The amount of distortion on a Mercator projection varies. The area along the Equator (where the cylinder touches Earth, see Fig. A.6) is relatively accurate. The amount of distortion grows with every degree of latitude until, in the northern and southern higher latitudes, the continents appear not only stretched out, but also misshapen (**Fig. A.4**). Because lines of longitude are parallel on the Mercator projection, Antarctica looks like a giant, globe-girdling landmass.

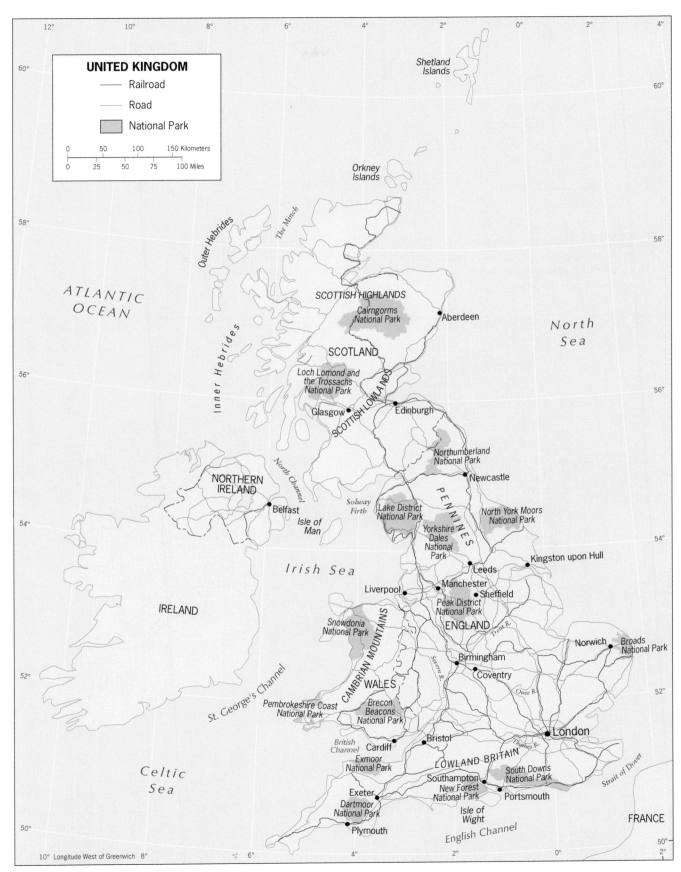

FIGURE A.2 **United Kingdom.** At this smaller scale, national parks in the United Kingdom are shown, as the map allows the display of a larger area. Notice this smaller scale map shows less local detail. City parks, rail lines, and roads within London are not visible at this scale, but they are visible in Fig. A.1.

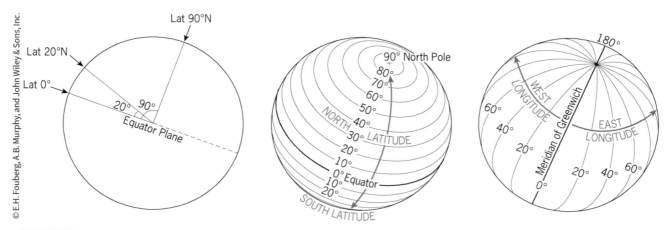

FIGURE A.3 **Latitude and Longitude.** The Equator is half way between the North Pole and South Pole and is the longest line of latitude. Lines of latitude get shorter until they become points at the poles. Lines of longitude are all the same length, as each intersects both the North Pole and South Pole and divides Earth in half with a great circle.

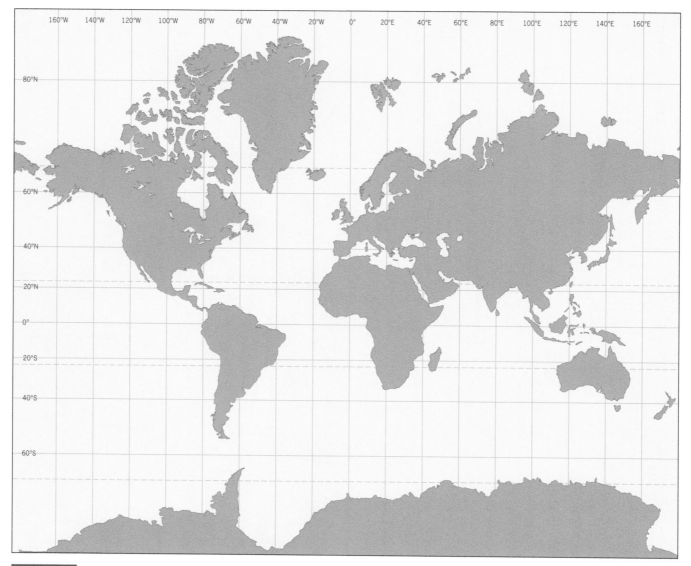

FIGURE A.4 **Mercator Projection.** Mercator's projection greatly exaggerates the size and shape of higher-latitude landmasses, but direction is true everywhere on this map. On the Mercator projection, Africa and Greenland look to be about the same size, but in reality, Africa is 14 times larger than Greenland.

The Mercator projection does not preserve size or shape of continents, but it does preserve direction, which makes it useful for navigation. The Mercator projection enables navigators to maintain an accurate course at sea simply by adhering to compass directions and plotting straight lines. The Mercator projection is used for navigation still today.

The spatial distortion of the Mercator projection serves to remind us that scale and projection are interconnected. On the Mercator projection, a scale that is accurate at the equator is quite inaccurate at higher latitudes. One might imagine that the spatial distortion of the Mercator projection is so obvious that no one would use it to represent the world's countries. But in fact, many popular atlas maps (Mercator also introduced the term atlas to describe a collection of maps) and wall maps still use a Mercator projection to map the countries of the world.

The National Geographic Society published its world maps on a Mercator projection until 1988, when it finally abandoned the practice in favor of a projection developed by the American cartographer Arthur Robinson (**Fig. A.5**). During the news conference at which the change was announced, a questioner rose to pursue a point: Why had the Society waited so long to make this change? Was it because the distortion inherent in the Mercator projection made American and European middle-latitude countries large, compared to tropical countries in Africa and elsewhere? Although that was not the goal of the National Geographic Society, the questioner clearly understood how misleading map projections can be.

The Mercator projection is one of a group of projections called cylindrical projections. Imagine the globe's lines of latitude and longitude represented by a wire grid, at the center of which we place a bright light. Wrap a piece of photographic paper around the wire grid, extending it well beyond the north and south poles, turn on the bulb, and the photographic image will be that of a Mercator projection (**Fig. A.6**).

We can also create map projections using cones instead of cylinders by placing a cone-shaped paper over each hemisphere, touching the grid, say, at the 40th parallel north; the result would be a conic projection (**Fig. A.7**). If we wanted a map of North America or Europe, a conic projection would be appropriate. On a conic projection, lines of longitude approach each other toward the poles (unlike the Mercator projection), and there is much less shape and size distortion.

We can also use a piece of paper, a plane, to create a map projection. For example, if we need a map of Arctic and Antarctic regions, we would place a paper as a flat sheet against the North and South Poles. The planar projection would show a set of diverging lines, because the longitude lines diverge from each pole, and the parallels would appear as circles (**Fig. A.8**). A planar projection is a good choice for a map of the Arctic Ocean or the Antarctic continent.

No projection is accurate. Every projection distorts size, shape, distance, or direction. The best projection to choose depends on the purpose of a map. Just as the Mercator is appropriate for navigation because direction is true, other projections are designed to preserve size (equal area),

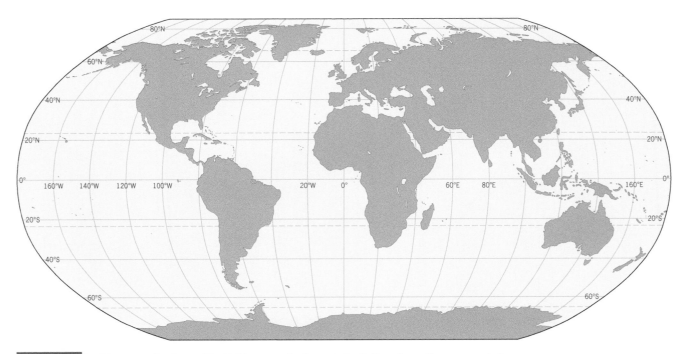

FIGURE A.5   **Robinson Projection.**   The Robinson projection substantially reduces the exaggerated size of polar landmasses because the lines of longitude curve toward each other in the polar regions. The Robinson projection better approximates shape, but it lacks the directional utility of the Mercator projection.

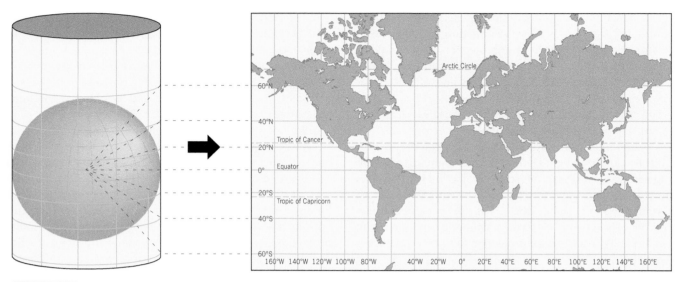

FIGURE A.6 **Cylindrical Projection.** A cylindrical projection is created by encircling Earth with a cylinder. The most accurate part of the map projection is where the cylinder touches Earth (usually the Equator). The projection decreases in accuracy toward the poles. The Mercator projection is a cylindrical projection.

distance, or shape of landmasses and countries. Many maps in this book show the global distribution of a geographic phenomena. For example, a world population map shows the pattern of where people live. A world climate map shows the patterns of where different climate times are found. World maps that show global distributions on land should be made

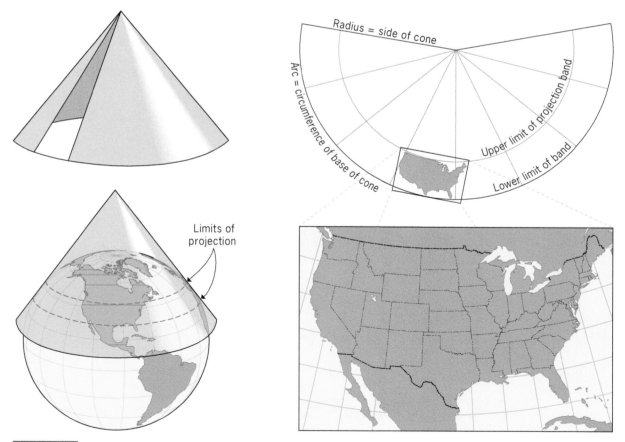

FIGURE A.7 **Conic Projection.** A conic projection is constructed by covering part of Earth with a cone. The most accurate part of the map projection is where the cone touches Earth (usually a line of latitude).

of distortion. And for a city map—even of a large city such as Chicago—the projection problem virtually disappears. The problem of how to represent the round Earth on a flat surface has been attacked for centuries, and there is no single best solution.

Map Symbols

Symbols are used on maps to represent features in the real world. Anyone who has used an atlas map is familiar with some of these symbols: dots (perhaps black or red) for cities; a large dot with a circle around it, or a star, for capitals; red lines for roads, double lines for four-lane highways, black lines for railroads; and patterns or colors for areas of water, forest, or farmland. Notice that these symbols respectively represent points, lines, and areas on the ground.

Point symbols are used to show individual features or places. On a large-scale map of a city, dots can represent individual houses or locations of businesses. A dot map shows a spatial distribution, such as the distribution of Starbucks coffee shops in Washington, D.C. (**Fig. A.9**). Starbucks shops are clustered around federal and corporate buildings downtown and in northwest neighborhoods, where incomes are higher (see Fig. 1.20). Lower income neighborhoods in Maryland suburbs to the east and west of D.C. have few Starbucks retail outlets.

Line symbols include not only roads and railroads, but also political and administrative boundaries, rivers, and other linear features. Again, scale plays a crucial role: On a large-scale map, it is possible to represent the fenced boundaries of a single farm, but on a small-scale map, such detail cannot be shown.

Some lines on maps do not actually exist on the ground. When physical geographers do their field work, they use contour maps, lines that represent a certain consistent height above mean sea level (**Fig. A.10**). All points on a contour line are the same elevation. The spacing between contour lines reveals the local topography (the shape of the land surface). When the contour lines are spaced closely together, the slope of the ground is steep. When they are widely separated, the land surface slopes gently.

Contour lines cannot be found in the real world, and neither can the lines drawn on weather maps. On a weather map, lines connect points of equal pressure (isobars) or equal temperature (isotherms), and show the development of weather systems. Note that the letters *iso* (meaning "the same") appear in these terms. Invisible lines of this kind are collectively known as isolines, lines of equal or constant value.

Area symbols take many forms, and you will see some of them on the maps in this book. Area symbols are used to represent distributions and magnitudes. Distribution maps use symbols, including points, lines, and areas, to show patterns of physical or human geographic phenomena. A clustered

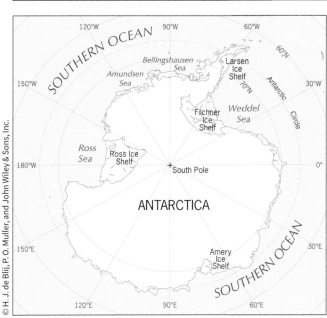

© H. J. de Blij, P. O. Muller, and John Wiley & Sons, Inc.

FIGURE A.8 **Planar Projection.** Planar projections are created by setting a plane (flat paper) on Earth. The most accurate part of the map projection is the point where the plane touches Earth.

on map projections that preserve accuracy of continents at the expense of the oceans. A Goode's projection interrupts the oceans, taking out slices of ocean to preserve accuracy of land.

Choosing the wrong projection may weaken the effectiveness of a map and may lead to erroneous interpretations. Of course, the problem diminishes when the area to be mapped is smaller and the scale larger. We may consider various alternatives when it comes to a map of all of North America, but a map of a single state presents far fewer potential problems

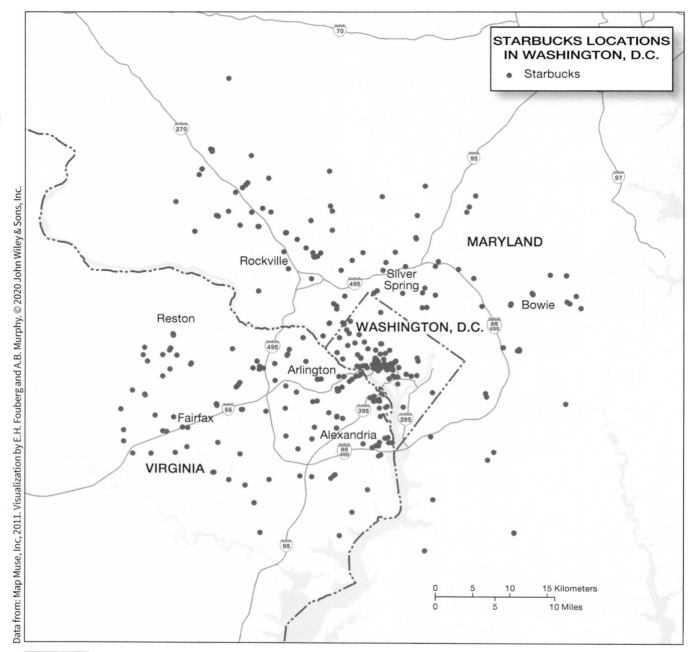

FIGURE A.9 **Starbucks Locations in Washington, D.C.** This map uses dot symbols to indicate the locations of Starbucks stores in the Washington, D.C. area.

pattern shows a concentration of phenomena in distinct places and a lack of the phenomena in other areas. Choropleth maps show magnitudes of a phenomena by area. Choropleth maps show how much of a phenomenon prevails in one unit (e.g., country) on the map, compared to others. The maps of population attributes (e.g. Total Fertility Rate, Dependency Ratio) in Chapter 2 are examples of choropleth maps. Chropleth maps show higher magnitude with darker colors and lower magnitude with lighter colors.

Whether an interest in maps drew you to the study of geography or studying geography drew you into thinking about maps, being able to read and understand maps is essential to thinking geographically. With each map you read in the book, as yourself "What is the story this map is telling?" Read the map title. Read the legend. Then, think again about the story the map is telling. Next, look for the pattern on the map. Is there a clear distribution of where symbols on the map are and are not? Is there a clear pattern to which areas have

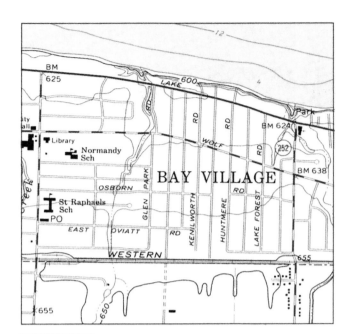

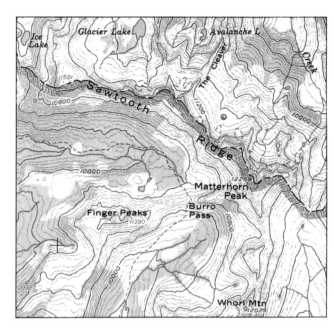

FIGURE A.10 **Contour Lines.**   The map at left is part of the U.S.G.S. North Olmstead Quadrangle, Ohio, and the contour lines are far apart, showing the area is relatively flat and slopes are gentle. The map at right is part of the U.S.G.S. Matterhorn Peak Quadrangle, California, and the contour lines are close to each other, showing the area is hilly and slopes are steep.

the highest magnitude and which have the lowest magnitude of what is being mapped? Once you can see the pattern, ask yourself why. Find where in the text the map is referenced, and read that paragraph of text again. Tie the map and the text together in your mind. Use the text to explain the map and the map to confirm or explain the text. Take a deliberate, reflective approach to reading the maps in this book, and you will strengthen your ability to think geographically.

Area and Demographic Data

Country	Land Area (sq km)	Land Area (sq mile)	Arable Land (sq km)	Total Population 2017 (millions)	Population Growth (percent)	Projected Population 2030 (millions)	Arithmetic Population Density (sq km)	Physiologic Population Density (sq km)	Total Fertility Rate (TFR)	Life Expectancy Female	Life Expectancy Male	Infant Mortality (per 1000 live births)	Rate of Natural Increase (percent)	Net Migration 2017 (thousands)	Urban Population (percent)	GINI Index (0-100)	Human Development Index	Corruption Index	GNI per Capita	CO2 Emissions per Capita
Afghanistan	6,52,860	2,52,071	3,79,100	35.5	2.5	49.1	54.42	93.72	4.6	65	62	51.5	2.6	-300	25	n/a	0.498	16	560	25.3
Albania	27,400	10,579	11,743	2.9	-0.1	2.8	104.87	244.70	1.7	80	76	7.8	0.4	-40	59	29	0.785	36	4,320	59.4
Algeria	23,81,741	9,19,595	4,14,564	41.3	1.7	51.8	17.35	99.67	2.8	77	75	20.6	1.8	-50	72	27.6	0.754	35	3,940	72.1
Andorra	470	181	188	0.1	-0.4	0.1	163.76	409.39	n/a	n/a	n/a	3.2	0.5	n/a	88	n/a	0.858	n/a	n/a	88.2
Angola	12,46,700	4,81,353	5,91,900	29.8	3.3	45.8	23.89	50.32	5.7	64	59	53.8	3.3	0	65	42.7	0.581	19	3,570	64.8
Antigua and Barbuda	440	170	90	0.1	1.0	0.1	231.85	1,133.47	2.1	79	74	5.4	1.0	0	25	n/a	0.78	n/a	13,810	24.7
Argentina	27,36,690	10,56,641	14,87,000	44.3	1.0	50.2	16.18	29.77	2.3	80	73	9.2	1.0	24	92	42.7	0.825	40	13,030	91.7
Armenia	28,470	10,992	16,764	2.9	0.2	3.0	102.93	174.81	1.6	78	71	11.3	0.4	-25	63	32.4	0.755	35	3,990	63.1
Australia	76,82,300	29,66,151	36,59,130	24.6	1.6	30.2	3.20	6.72	1.8	85	81	3.0	0.6	850	86	34.7	0.939	77	51,360	85.9
Austria	82,523	31,862	27,185	8.8	0.8	9.8	106.75	324.05	1.5	83	79	2.9	0.1	100	58	30.5	0.908	76	45,440	58.1
Azerbaijan	82,663	31,916	47,698	9.9	1.1	11.3	119.31	206.77	1.9	75	69	20.5	1.1	0	55	31.8	0.757	25	4,080	55.3
Bahamas, The	10,010	3,865	140	0.4	1.0	0.5	39.50	2,824.01	1.8	79	73	5.8	0.8	5	83	n/a	0.807	65	29,170	82.9
Bahrain	771	298	86	1.5	4.6	2.7	1,935.91	17,355.63	2.0	78	76	6.3	1.2	235	89	n/a	0.846	36	21,150	89.2
Bangladesh	1,30,170	50,259	91,942	164.7	1.0	188.7	1,265.04	1,791.02	2.1	74	71	26.9	1.4	-2350	36	32.1	0.608	26	1,470	35.9
Barbados	430	166	140	0.3	0.3	0.3	664.46	2,040.85	1.8	78	73	11.5	0.1	2	31	n/a	0.8	68	15,270	31.2
Belarus	2,02,910	78,344	85,820	9.5	0.1	9.6	46.86	110.79	1.7	79	69	2.8	0.0	10	78	26.7	0.808	44	5,280	78.1
Belgium	30,280	11,691	13,280	11.4	0.4	11.9	375.56	856.33	1.7	83	79	3.1	0.1	240	98	28.1	0.916	75	41,790	98.0
Belize	22,810	8,807	1,600	0.4	2.1	0.5	16.43	234.18	2.5	73	68	12.2	1.7	7	46	53.3	0.708	n/a	4,390	45.6
Benin	1,12,760	43,537	37,500	11.2	2.8	16.0	99.11	298.02	5.0	62	59	63.5	2.8	-10	47	47.8	0.515	40	800	46.8
Bhutan	38,117	14,717	5,256	0.8	1.2	0.9	21.19	153.65	2.1	70	70	25.6	1.2	0	40	38.8	0.612	68	2,660	40.2
Bolivia	10,83,300	4,18,264	3,77,045	11.1	1.5	13.4	10.20	29.31	2.9	72	67	28.0	1.6	-50	69	45.8	0.693	29	3,130	69.1
Bosnia and Herzegovina	51,200	19,768	21,830	3.5	-0.3	3.4	68.50	160.65	1.4	79	74	4.9	-0.2	-3	48	33.8	0.768	38	4,910	47.9
Botswana	5,66,730	2,18,816	2,60,010	2.3	1.8	2.9	4.04	8.81	2.7	70	64	30.8	1.7	15	69	60.5	0.717	61	6,730	68.7
Brazil	83,58,140	32,27,095	28,25,890	209.3	0.8	231.8	25.04	74.06	1.7	79	72	13.2	0.8	30	86	51.3	0.759	35	8,600	86.3
Brunei	5,270	2,035	144	0.4	1.3	0.5	81.35	2,977.06	1.9	79	76	9.0	1.2	2	77	n/a	0.853	63	29,600	77.3
Bulgaria	1,08,560	41,915	50,119	7.1	-0.7	6.4	65.18	141.18	1.5	78	71	6.3	-0.6	-24	75	37.4	0.813	42	7,860	74.7
Burkina Faso	2,73,600	1,05,638	1,21,000	19.2	2.9	27.9	70.15	158.62	5.4	61	60	51.2	3.0	-125	29	35.3	0.423	41	590	28.7
Burundi	25,680	9,915	20,320	10.9	3.2	16.4	423.06	534.66	5.7	59	56	42.5	3.1	20	13	39.2	0.417	17	280	12.7
Cabo Verde	4,030	1,556	790	0.5	1.3	0.6	135.58	691.63	2.3	75	71	15.0	1.5	-7	65	47.2	0.654	57	3,030	65.3
Cambodia	1,76,520	68,155	54,550	16.0	1.5	19.5	90.67	293.41	2.6	71	67	25.1	1.7	-150	23	n/a	0.582	20	1,230	23.0
Cameroon	4,72,710	1,82,514	97,500	24.1	2.6	33.7	50.88	246.70	4.7	59	57	55.1	2.6	-24	56	46.5	0.556	25	1,370	55.8
Canada	90,93,510	35,11,022	6,26,562	36.7	1.2	43.0	4.04	58.59	1.6	84	80	4.5	0.3	1100	81	34	0.926	81	42,870	81.4
Central African Republic	6,22,980	2,40,534	50,800	4.7	1.4	5.6	7.48	91.71	4.9	54	50	87.6	2.2	-150	41	56.2	0.367	26	390	41.0
Chad	12,59,200	4,86,180	4,99,350	14.9	3.0	22.1	11.83	29.84	5.9	54	52	73.4	3.0	10	23	43.3	0.404	19	640	22.9
Chile	7,43,532	2,87,079	1,57,850	18.1	0.8	20.0	24.28	114.38	1.8	82	77	6.3	0.7	85	87	47.7	0.843	67	13,610	87.5
China	93,88,211	36,24,807	52,78,330	1,386.4	0.6	1,490.9	147.67	262.66	1.6	78	75	8.0	0.5	-1625	58	42.2	0.752	39	8,690	58.0

Country	Land Area (sq km)	Land Area (sq mile)	Arable Land (sq km)	Total Population 2017 (millions)	Population Growth (percent)	Projected Population 2030 (millions)	Arithmetic Population Density (sq km)	Physiologic Population Density (sq km)	Total Fertility Rate (TFR)	Life Expectancy Female	Life Expectancy Male	Infant Mortality (per 1000 live births)	Rate of Natural Increase (percent)	Net Migration 2017 (thousands)	Urban Population (percent)	GINI Index (0-100)	Human Development Index	Corruption Index	GNI Capita	CO_2 Emissions per Capita
Colombia	11,09,500	4,28,380	4,46,656	49.1	0.8	54.8	44.22	109.85	1.9	78	71	12.7	0.9	-147	80	51.1	0.747	36	5,890	80.4
Comoros	1,861	719	1,330	0.8	2.3	1.1	437.35	611.96	4.3	65	62	52.2	2.5	-10	29	45	0.503	27	1,280	28.8
Congo, Dem. Rep.	22,67,050	8,75,313	2,62,000	81.3	3.3	124.2	35.88	310.46	6.1	61	58	70.0	3.2	119	44	42.1	0.457	20	460	43.9
Congo, Rep.	3,41,500	1,31,854	1,06,270	5.3	2.6	7.4	15.40	49.50	4.7	66	63	34.7	2.7	-20	66	48.9	0.606	19	1,430	66.5
Costa Rica	51,060	19,714	18,110	4.9	1.0	5.6	96.08	270.89	1.8	82	77	7.8	0.9	16	79	48.2	0.794	56	11,120	78.6
Cote d'Ivoire	3,18,000	1,22,780	2,06,000	24.3	2.5	33.6	76.40	117.94	4.9	55	52	64.2	2.5	30	50	41.7	0.492	35	1,580	50.3
Croatia	55,960	21,606	15,376	4.1	-1.2	3.5	73.73	268.32	1.4	81	75	3.9	-0.3	-40	57	32.2	0.831	48	12,570	56.7
Cuba	1,04,020	40,162	62,403	11.5	0.1	11.6	110.41	184.04	1.7	82	78	4.1	0.3	-110	77	n/a	0.777	47	n/a	77.0
Curacao	444	171	44	0.2	0.8	0.2	362.64	3,659.41	1.7	81	75	n/a	0.2	3	89	n/a	n/a	n/a	n/a	89.2
Cyprus	9,240	3,568	1,272	1.2	0.8	1.3	127.66	927.32	1.3	83	78	2.1	0.4	25	67	35.6	0.869	59	23,720	66.8
Czech Republic	77,210	29,811	42,130	10.6	0.2	10.9	137.18	251.40	1.6	81	76	2.6	0.1	60	74	25.9	0.888	59	18,160	73.7
Denmark	42,262	16,317	26,110	5.8	0.7	6.3	136.52	220.97	1.7	83	79	3.7	0.2	76	88	28.5	0.929	88	55,220	87.8
Djibouti	23,180	8,950	17,020	1.0	1.5	1.2	41.28	56.23	2.8	64	61	51.5	1.5	5	78	44.1	0.476	31	1,880	77.6
Dominica	750	290	250	0.1	0.5	0.1	98.57	295.70	n/a	n/a	n/a	31.5	0.0	n/a	70	n/a	0.715	57	6,590	70.2
Dominican Republic	48,310	18,653	23,520	10.8	1.1	12.4	222.87	457.78	2.4	77	71	25.0	1.4	-151	80	44.9	0.736	30	6,630	80.3
Ecuador	2,48,360	95,892	57,884	16.6	1.5	20.1	66.94	287.21	2.5	79	74	12.5	1.5	-31	64	46.5	0.752	34	5,920	63.7
Egypt, Arab Rep.	9,95,450	3,84,345	38,202	97.6	1.9	125.4	98.00	2,553.61	3.3	74	69	18.8	2.1	-275	43	31.8	0.696	35	3,010	42.7
El Salvador	20,720	8,000	16,020	6.4	0.5	6.8	307.81	398.12	2.1	78	69	12.5	1.2	-203	71	40.8	0.674	35	3,560	71.3
Equatorial Guinea	28,050	10,830	2,840	1.3	3.7	2.1	45.19	446.37	4.7	59	56	65.3	2.4	80	72	n/a	0.591	16	7,050	71.6
Eritrea	1,01,000	38,996	75,920	4.5	n/a	n/a	44.30	58.94	4.1	67	63	32.1	2.5	-50	n/a	n/a	0.44	24	n/a	n/a
Estonia	42,390	16,367	9,936	1.3	0.0	1.3	31.03	132.40	1.6	83	73	2.1	-0.1	-5	69	34.6	0.871	73	18,190	68.7
Eswatini	17,200	6,641	12,220	1.4	1.8	1.7	79.49	111.89	3.1	61	54	40.8	1.9	-10	24	51.5	0.588	38	2,950	23.6
Ethiopia	10,00,000	3,86,102	3,62,590	105.0	2.5	144.6	104.96	289.47	4.2	67	64	41.0	2.5	-60	20	33.2	0.463	34	740	20.3
Faroe Islands	1,396	539	30	0.0	0.4	0.1	35.31	1,643.00	2.6	85	80	n/a	0.6	n/a	42	n/a	n/a	n/a	n/a	41.9
Fiji	18,270	7,054	4,250	0.9	0.7	1.0	49.56	213.06	2.5	73	67	21.4	1.2	-20	56	36.4	0.741	n/a	4,970	55.7
Finland	3,03,890	1,17,333	22,734	5.5	0.3	5.7	18.14	242.43	1.7	85	79	1.9	0.0	70	85	26.8	0.92	85	44,580	85.3
France	5,47,557	2,11,413	2,87,269	67.1	0.4	70.6	122.58	233.64	2.0	86	79	3.5	0.3	400	80	32.3	0.901	72	37,970	80.2
French Polynesia	3,660	1,413	455	0.3	1.0	0.3	77.32	621.99	2.0	79	75	n/a	1.0	-1	62	n/a	n/a	n/a	n/a	61.8
Gabon	2,57,670	99,487	51,600	2.0	2.3	2.7	7.86	39.25	3.8	68	65	35.1	2.2	5	89	42.2	0.702	31	6,650	89.0
Gambia, The	10,120	3,907	6,050	2.1	3.0	3.1	207.57	347.20	5.4	63	60	41.4	3.1	-13	61	47.3	0.46	37	680	60.6
Georgia	69,490	26,830	25,484	3.7	-0.1	3.7	53.49	145.86	2.0	77	69	9.7	0.0	-50	58	38.5	0.78	58	3,780	58.2
Germany	3,48,900	1,34,711	1,67,310	82.7	0.4	87.3	237.02	494.26	1.5	83	78	3.1	-0.2	1850	77	31.4	0.936	80	43,490	77.3
Ghana	2,27,540	87,854	1,57,000	28.8	2.2	38.4	126.72	183.65	4.0	64	62	35.7	2.3	-100	55	42.2	0.592	41	1,880	55.4
Greece	1,28,900	49,769	77,830	10.8	-0.1	10.6	83.48	138.26	1.3	84	79	4.3	-0.2	50	79	35.8	0.87	45	18,090	78.7

Country	Land Area (sq mile)	Land Area (sq km)	Arable Land (sq km)	Total Population 2017 (millions)	Population Growth (percent)	Projected Population 2030 (millions)	Arithmetic Population Density (sq km)	Physiologic Population Density (sq km)	Total Fertility Rate (TFR)	Life Expectancy Female	Life Expectancy Male	Infant Mortality (per 1000 live births)	Rate of Natural Increase (percent)	Net Migration 2017 (thousands)	Urban Population (percent)	GINI Index (0–100)	Human Development Index	Corruption Index	GNI per Capita	CO₂ Emissions per Capita
Greenland	4,10,450	1,58,476	2,359	0.1	0.0	0.1	0.14	23.81	2.0	n/a	n/a	n/a	0.6	n/a	87	n/a	n/a	n/a	n/a	86.6
Grenada	340	131	80	0.1	0.5	0.1	317.13	1,347.81	2.1	76	71	15.3	1.2	-3	36	n/a	0.772	52	9,180	36.2
Guatemala	1,07,160	41,375	37,938	16.9	2.0	21.9	157.83	445.82	3.0	77	70	23.1	2.0	-46	51	48.7	0.65	27	4,060	50.7
Guinea	2,45,720	94,873	1,45,000	12.7	2.6	17.7	51.75	87.70	4.9	61	59	56.4	2.7	-50	36	33.7	0.459	28	790	35.8
Guinea-Bissau	28,120	10,857	16,300	1.9	2.5	2.6	66.19	114.19	4.6	59	56	55.6	2.6	-10	43	50.7	0.455	n/a	660	42.9
Guyana	1,96,850	76,004	16,800	0.8	0.6	0.8	3.95	46.30	2.5	69	64	26.0	1.2	-25	27	44.5	0.654	37	4,500	26.5
Haiti	27,560	10,641	18,400	11.0	1.2	12.9	398.45	596.81	2.9	66	61	53.9	1.6	-175	54	40.9	0.498	20	760	54.3
Honduras	1,11,890	43,201	32,350	9.3	1.7	11.5	82.81	286.40	2.5	76	71	15.6	1.7	-14	56	50.1	0.617	29	2,250	56.5
Hong Kong SAR, China	1,050	405	51	7.4	0.7	8.1	7,039.71	1,44,935.29	1.2	87	81	n/a	0.2	147	100	n/a	0.933	76	46,310	100.0
Hungary	90,530	34,954	53,470	9.8	-0.3	9.4	108.04	182.93	1.5	79	72	3.8	-0.3	30	71	30.9	0.838	46	12,870	71.1
Iceland	1,00,250	38,707	18,720	0.3	1.7	0.4	3.40	18.23	1.8	84	81	1.6	0.5	2	94	25.6	0.935	76	60,830	93.8
India	29,73,190	11,47,955	17,97,210	1,339.2	1.1	1,550.5	450.42	745.14	2.3	70	67	32.0	1.2	-2450	34	35.2	0.64	41	1,800	33.6
Indonesia	18,11,570	6,99,451	5,70,000	264.0	1.1	304.4	145.73	463.14	2.4	71	67	21.4	1.2	-825	55	39.5	0.694	38	3,540	54.7
Iran, Islamic Rep.	16,28,760	6,28,867	4,59,532	81.2	1.1	93.6	49.83	176.62	1.7	77	75	12.8	1.2	-275	74	38.8	0.798	28	5,430	74.4
Iraq	4,34,320	1,67,692	92,690	38.3	2.8	55.4	88.13	412.93	4.4	72	68	25.3	2.8	39	70	29.5	0.685	18	4,630	70.3
Ireland	68,890	26,599	44,300	4.8	1.2	5.6	69.87	108.66	1.9	83	80	3.0	0.7	23	63	31.9	0.938	73	55,290	62.9
Israel	21,640	8,355	5,339	8.7	1.9	11.2	402.61	1,631.84	3.1	84	81	2.9	1.6	50	92	41.4	0.903	61	37,270	92.3
Italy	2,94,140	1,13,568	1,29,450	60.6	-0.1	59.6	205.86	467.76	1.4	85	80	2.9	-0.2	350	70	34.7	0.88	52	31,020	70.1
Jamaica	10,830	4,181	4,440	2.9	0.3	3.0	266.88	650.97	2.0	78	74	13.1	1.0	-93	55	45.5	0.732	44	4,760	55.4
Japan	3,64,560	1,40,757	44,960	126.8	-0.2	124.1	347.78	2,819.97	1.4	87	81	1.9	-0.3	250	92	32.1	0.909	73	38,550	91.5
Jordan	88,780	34,278	10,566	9.7	2.6	13.6	109.29	918.26	3.4	76	73	14.6	2.3	0	91	33.7	0.735	49	3,980	90.7
Kazakhstan	26,99,700	10,42,360	21,69,920	18.0	1.4	21.5	6.68	8.31	2.7	77	68	8.9	1.5	0	57	26.5	0.8	31	7,970	57.3
Kenya	5,69,140	2,19,746	2,76,300	49.7	2.5	69.0	87.32	179.88	3.9	69	65	33.6	2.6	-50	27	48.5	0.59	27	1,460	26.6
Kiribati	810	313	340	0.1	1.7	0.1	143.70	342.35	3.7	70	63	42.7	2.1	-2	53	37	0.612	n/a	3,010	53.3
Korea, Dem. People's Rep.	1,20,410	46,491	26,300	25.5	0.5	27.1	211.70	969.24	1.9	75	68	14.4	0.5	-10	62	n/a	n/a	n/a	n/a	61.7
Korea, Rep.	97,480	37,637	17,360	51.5	0.4	54.4	527.97	2,964.64	1.2	85	79	2.8	0.2	200	82	n/a	0.903	57	28,380	81.5
Kosovo	10,887	4,203	5,700	1.8	0.8	2.0	168.15	321.18	2.1	74	70	n/a	1.0	n/a	n/a	n/a	n/a	37	3,900	n/a
Kuwait	17,820	6,880	1,494	4.1	2.1	5.4	232.13	2,768.76	2.0	76	74	6.9	1.4	100	100	n/a	0.803	41	31,430	100.0
Kyrgyz Republic	1,91,800	74,054	1,05,571	6.2	2.0	8.0	32.33	58.74	3.1	75	67	17.9	2.1	-100	36	29	0.672	29	1,130	36.1
Lao PDR	2,30,800	89,112	23,690	6.9	1.5	8.3	29.71	289.50	2.7	68	65	48.6	1.7	-74	34	36.4	0.601	n/a	2,270	34.4
Latvia	62,180	24,008	18,845	1.9	-1.0	1.7	31.21	102.98	1.7	80	70	3.6	-0.3	-50	68	35.1	0.847	58	14,740	68.1
Lebanon	10,230	3,950	6,580	6.1	1.3	7.2	594.56	924.37	1.7	81	78	6.7	1.1	-150	88	31.8	0.757	28	8,400	88.4
Lesotho	30,360	11,722	22,773	2.2	1.3	2.7	73.56	98.07	3.1	56	52	66.5	1.5	-20	28	54.2	0.52	41	1,210	27.7
Liberia	96,320	37,189	27,000	4.7	2.5	6.6	49.13	175.26	4.6	63	62	55.9	2.6	-25	51	33.2	0.435	32	620	50.7
Libya	17,59,540	6,79,362	1,53,500	6.4	1.3	7.5	3.62	41.53	2.3	75	69	10.6	1.4	-10	80	n/a	0.706	17	5,500	79.8
Liechtenstein	160	62	52	0.0	0.7	0.0	237.01	729.27	1.4	85	81	n/a	0.3	n/a	14	n/a	0.916	n/a	n/a	14.3

Country	Land Area (sq km)	Land Area (sq mile)	Arable Land (sq km)	Total Population 2017 (millions)	Population Growth (percent)	Projected Population 2030 (millions)	Arithmetic Population Density (sq km)	Physiologic Population Density (sq km)	Total Fertility Rate (TFR)	Life Expectancy Female	Life Expectancy Male	Infant Mortality (per 1000 live births)	Rate of Natural Increase (percent)	Net Migration 2017 (thousands)	Urban Population (percent)	GINI Index (0-100)	Human Development Index	Corruption Index	GNI per Capita	CO_2 Emissions per Capita
Lithuania	62,650	24,189	30,060	2.8	-1.4	2.4	45.14	94.07	1.7	80	69	3.4	-0.4	-25	68	37.7	0.858	59	15,200	67.5
Luxembourg	2,590	1,000	1,313	0.6	3.0	0.9	231.45	456.55	1.5	85	80	2.1	0.4	25	91	31.2	0.904	81	70,260	90.7
Macedonia, North	25,220	9,737	12,630	2.1	0.1	2.1	82.60	164.94	1.5	78	74	12.0	0.1	-5	58	35.6	0.757	37	4,880	57.7
Madagascar	5,81,800	2,24,634	4,14,150	25.6	2.7	36.2	43.95	61.74	4.2	68	64	32.7	2.7	-8	37	42.7	0.519	25	400	36.5
Malawi	94,280	36,402	57,900	18.6	2.9	27.1	197.52	321.63	4.6	66	61	38.5	2.9	-60	17	46.1	0.477	32	320	16.7
Malaysia	3,28,550	1,26,854	78,390	31.6	1.4	37.9	96.25	403.42	2.0	78	73	6.7	1.2	250	75	46.3	0.802	47	9,650	75.4
Maldives	300	116	79	0.4	2.0	0.6	1,454.43	5,523.16	2.1	78	76	6.8	1.5	10	39	n/a	0.717	31	9,760	39.4
Mali	12,20,190	4,71,118	4,12,010	18.5	3.0	27.4	15.20	45.00	6.1	59	57	65.8	3.2	-200	42	33	0.427	32	770	41.6
Malta	320	124	102	0.5	2.2	0.6	1,454.04	4,561.69	1.5	84	80	5.6	0.3	5	95	n/a	0.878	54	24,080	94.5
Marshall Islands	180	69	115	0.1	0.1	0.1	295.15	461.97	n/a	n/a	n/a	28.0	0.0	n/a	77	n/a	0.708	n/a	4,840	76.6
Mauritania	10,30,700	3,97,955	3,97,110	4.4	2.7	6.3	4.29	11.13	4.7	65	62	53.3	2.6	26	53	32.4	0.52	27	1,100	52.8
Mauritius	2,030	784	850	1.3	0.1	1.3	622.96	1,487.78	1.4	78	71	11.6	0.2	0	41	35.8	0.79	51	10,130	40.8
Mexico	19,43,950	7,50,563	10,67,050	129.2	1.3	152.2	66.44	121.05	2.2	80	75	11.5	1.3	-300	80	48.2	0.774	28	8,610	79.9
Moldova	32,870	12,691	24,589	3.5	-0.1	3.5	107.99	144.36	1.2	76	67	13.3	-0.1	-14	43	27	0.7	33	2,200	42.6
Monaco	2	1	1	0.0	0.5	0.0	19,347.50	38,695.00	n/a	n/a	n/a	2.7	0.0	n/a	100	n/a	n/a	n/a	n/a	100.0
Mongolia	15,53,560	5,99,833	11,29,035	3.1	1.6	3.8	1.98	2.72	2.8	74	65	14.8	1.8	-15	68	32	0.741	37	3,270	68.4
Montenegro	13,450	5,193	2,314	0.6	0.0	0.6	46.28	269.00	1.7	79	75	3.2	0.2	-2	66	31.9	0.814	45	7,400	66.5
Morocco	4,46,300	1,72,317	3,05,915	35.7	1.3	42.3	80.08	116.83	2.5	77	75	20.0	1.5	-257	62	40.7	0.667	43	2,860	61.9
Mozambique	7,86,380	3,03,623	4,99,500	29.7	2.9	43.1	37.73	59.40	5.2	60	56	53.3	2.9	-25	35	45.6	0.437	23	420	35.5
Myanmar	6,53,080	2,52,155	1,27,350	53.4	0.9	60.1	81.72	419.09	2.2	69	64	38.5	1.0	-100	30	38.1	0.578	29	1,210	30.3
Namibia	8,23,290	3,17,874	3,88,090	2.5	2.2	3.4	3.08	6.53	3.4	67	61	31.8	2.2	-2	49	61	0.647	53	4,570	49.0
Nauru	20	8	4	0.0	4.5	0.0	682.45	3,412.25	n/a	n/a	n/a	27.3	0.0	n/a	100	n/a	n/a	n/a	10,220	100.0
Nepal	1,43,350	55,348	41,210	29.3	1.1	33.8	204.43	711.11	2.1	72	69	27.8	1.3	-350	19	32.8	0.574	31	800	19.3
Netherlands	33,690	13,008	18,370	17.1	0.6	18.5	508.54	932.65	1.7	83	80	3.3	0.1	80	91	28.6	0.931	82	46,180	91.1
New Caledonia	18,280	7,058	1,842	0.3	1.4	0.3	15.34	152.26	2.1	80	74	n/a	1.0	6	70	n/a	n/a	n/a	n/a	70.3
New Zealand	2,63,310	1,01,665	1,11,160	4.8	2.1	6.3	18.21	43.13	1.9	83	80	4.4	0.6	74	86	n/a	0.917	87	38,970	86.5
Nicaragua	1,20,340	46,464	50,650	6.2	1.1	7.2	51.67	122.76	2.2	78	72	14.8	1.5	-106	58	46.6	0.658	25	2,130	58.3
Niger	12,66,700	4,89,075	4,56,820	21.5	3.8	35.3	16.96	47.01	7.2	61	59	48.3	3.8	-28	16	34	0.354	34	360	16.4
Nigeria	9,10,770	3,51,650	7,08,000	190.9	2.6	267.6	209.59	269.61	5.5	54	53	64.6	2.6	-300	50	43	0.532	27	2,100	49.5
Northern Mariana Islands	460	178	30	0.1	0.2	0.1	119.88	1,838.13	n/a	n/a	n/a	n/a	0.0	n/a	92	n/a	n/a	n/a	n/a	91.5
Norway	3,65,245	1,41,022	9,861	5.3	0.9	5.9	14.46	535.67	1.7	84	81	2.1	0.3	140	82	26.8	0.953	84	75,990	81.9
Oman	3,09,500	1,19,499	14,688	4.6	4.7	8.5	14.98	315.65	2.7	79	75	9.7	1.6	605	84	n/a	0.821	52	14,440	83.6
Pakistan	7,70,880	2,97,638	3,62,520	197.0	2.0	254.0	255.57	543.46	3.5	68	66	61.2	2.1	-1072	36	30.7	0.562	33	1,580	36.4

Country	Land Area (sq km)	Land Area (sq mile)	Arable Land (sq km)	Total Population 2017 (millions)	Population Growth (percent)	Projected Population 2030 (millions)	Arithmetic Population Density (sq km)	Physiologic Population Density (sq km)	Total Fertility Rate (TFR)	Life Expectancy Female	Life Expectancy Male	Infant Mortality (per 1000 live births)	Rate of Natural Increase (percent)	Net Migration 2017 (thousands)	Urban Population (percent)	GINI Index (0-100)	Human Development Index	Corruption Index	GNI per Capita	CO_2 Emissions per Capita
Palau	460	178	50	0.0	1.0	0.0	47.24	434.58	n/a	n/a	n/a	13.2	0.2	n/a	79	n/a	0.798	n/a	12,700	79.4
Panama	74,340	28,703	22,570	4.1	1.6	5.0	55.13	181.59	2.5	81	75	13.9	1.5	31	67	51	0.789	37	13,280	67.4
Papua New Guinea	4,52,860	1,74,850	11,900	8.3	2.0	10.7	18.22	693.37	3.7	68	63	41.8	2.0	-1	13	41.8	0.544	28	2,340	13.1
Paraguay	3,97,300	1,53,398	2,18,850	6.8	1.3	8.0	17.14	31.12	2.5	75	71	17.9	1.5	-82	61	48	0.702	29	5,470	61.3
Peru	12,80,000	4,94,211	2,43,306	32.2	1.2	37.7	25.13	132.20	2.4	78	72	11.6	1.4	-180	78	44.3	0.75	35	5,960	77.7
Philippines	2,98,170	1,15,124	1,24,400	104.9	1.5	128.1	351.87	843.39	2.9	73	66	22.2	1.7	-650	47	40.1	0.699	36	3,660	46.7
Poland	3,06,190	1,18,221	1,43,710	38.0	0.0	38.1	124.03	264.25	1.3	82	74	4.0	0.0	-50	60	32.1	0.865	60	12,730	60.1
Portugal	91,605	35,369	37,000	10.3	-0.3	9.9	112.37	278.21	1.3	84	78	3.1	-0.2	-30	65	35.6	0.847	64	19,820	64.7
Qatar	11,610	4,483	656	2.6	2.7	3.7	227.32	4,023.19	1.9	80	77	6.5	0.9	200	99	n/a	0.856	62	60,510	99.1
Romania	2,30,080	88,834	1,38,350	19.6	-0.6	18.1	85.13	141.57	1.6	79	72	6.6	-0.3	-150	54	27.5	0.811	47	10,000	53.9
Russian Federation	1,63,76,870	63,23,142	21,77,218	144.5	0.1	146.5	8.82	66.37	1.8	77	67	6.5	0.0	800	74	37.7	0.816	28	9,230	74.3
Rwanda	24,670	9,525	18,117	12.2	2.4	16.7	494.87	673.86	3.9	69	65	28.9	2.5	-45	17	50.4	0.524	56	720	17.1
Samoa	2,830	1,093	350	0.2	0.7	0.2	69.41	561.26	4.0	78	72	14.2	2.0	-13	18	42	0.713	n/a	4,090	18.5
San Marino	60	23	10	0.0	0.6	0.0	556.67	3,340.00	n/a	n/a	n/a	2.0	0.0	n/a	97	n/a	n/a	n/a	n/a	97.1
Sao Tome and Principe	960	371	487	0.2	2.2	0.3	212.84	419.56	4.5	69	64	25.2	2.7	-5	72	30.8	0.589	46	1,770	72.0
Saudi Arabia	21,49,690	8,30,000	17,36,472	32.9	2.0	42.9	15.32	18.97	2.5	76	73	6.3	1.6	590	84	n/a	0.853	49	20,090	83.6
Senegal	1,92,530	74,336	88,680	15.9	2.8	22.8	82.33	178.74	4.8	69	65	32.7	3.0	-100	47	40.3	0.505	45	1,240	46.7
Serbia	87,460	33,768	34,685	7.0	-0.5	6.6	80.29	202.46	1.5	78	73	5.0	-0.5	-50	56	29.1	0.787	39	5,180	55.9
Seychelles	460	178	16	0.1	1.2	0.1	208.35	5,990.19	2.8	80	69	12.2	1.0	-1	56	46.8	0.797	66	14,170	56.3
Sierra Leone	72,180	27,869	39,490	7.6	2.2	10.0	104.70	191.37	4.5	52	51	81.7	2.2	-21	42	34	0.419	30	510	41.6
Singapore	709	274	7	5.6	0.1	5.7	7,915.73	8,01,750.43	1.2	85	81	2.2	0.5	298	100	n/a	0.932	85	54,530	100.0
Slovak Republic	48,086	18,566	19,216	5.4	0.2	5.6	113.13	283.09	1.4	80	73	4.6	0.1	5	54	26.1	0.855	50	16,610	53.8
Slovenia	20,140	7,776	6,166	2.1	0.1	2.1	102.62	335.18	1.6	84	78	1.7	0.0	6	54	25.7	0.896	60	22,000	54.3
Solomon Islands	27,990	10,807	1,080	0.6	2.0	0.8	21.84	566.06	3.9	72	69	17.6	2.4	-12	23	37	0.546	44	1,920	23.3
Somalia	6,27,340	2,42,217	4,41,250	14.7	2.9	21.6	23.50	33.41	6.3	58	55	79.7	3.2	-200	44	n/a	n/a	10	n/a	44.4
South Africa	12,13,090	4,68,376	9,68,410	56.7	1.2	66.7	46.75	58.57	2.5	66	59	28.8	1.1	300	66	63.4	0.699	43	5,430	65.9
South Sudan	n/a	0	2,85,332	12.6	2.8	18.1	n/a	44.07	4.9	58	56	62.5	2.5	150	19	n/a	0.388	13	n/a	19.3
Spain	5,00,210	1,93,132	2,62,660	46.6	0.2	47.7	93.10	177.31	1.3	86	80	2.6	0.0	200	80	36	0.891	58	27,180	80.1
Sri Lanka	62,710	24,212	27,400	21.4	1.1	24.8	341.96	782.63	2.0	79	72	7.5	0.8	-450	18	39.2	0.77	38	3,850	18.4
St. Kitts and Nevis	260	100	60	0.1	1.0	0.1	212.87	922.42	n/a	n/a	n/a	11.6	0.0	n/a	31	n/a	0.778	n/a	16,240	30.8
St. Lucia	610	236	106	0.2	0.5	0.2	293.19	1,687.21	1.5	78	73	14.9	0.5	0	19	42.6	0.747	55	8,830	18.6
St. Vincent and the Grenadines	390	151	100	0.1	0.2	0.1	281.79	1,098.97	1.9	75	71	14.9	0.8	-3	52	n/a	0.723	58	7,390	51.8

Country	Land Area (sq km)	Land Area (sq mile)	Arable Land (sq km)	Total Population 2017 (millions)	Population Growth (percent)	Projected Population 2030 (millions)	Arithmetic Population Density (sq km)	Physiologic Population Density (sq km)	Total Fertility Rate (TFR)	Life Expectancy Female	Life Expectancy Male	Infant Mortality (per 1000 live births)	Rate of Natural Increase (percent)	Net Migration 2017 (thousands)	Urban Population (percent)	GINI Index (0–100)	Human Development Index	Corruption Index	GNI per Capita	CO_2 Emissions per Capita
Sudan	23,76,000	9,17,378	6,81,862	40.5	2.4	55.3	17.06	59.45	4.5	66	63	43.7	2.5	-250	34	35.4	0.502	16	2,380	34.4
Suriname	1,56,000	60,232	882	0.6	0.9	0.6	3.61	638.78	2.4	75	68	17.5	1.1	-5	66	57.6	0.72	43	5,150	66.0
Sweden	4,07,310	1,57,263	30,398	10.1	1.4	12.2	24.72	331.20	1.9	84	80	2.3	0.3	200	87	27.2	0.933	85	52,590	87.1
Switzerland	39,516	15,257	15,088	8.5	1.1	9.8	214.24	561.11	1.5	85	81	3.7	0.3	250	74	32.5	0.944	85	80,560	73.8
Syrian Arab Republic	1,83,630	70,900	1,39,210	18.3	-0.9	16.3	99.49	131.24	2.9	77	65	14.0	1.6	-1240	54	35.8	0.536	13	n/a	53.5
Tajikistan	1,38,786	53,586	47,450	8.9	2.1	11.7	64.28	188.02	3.4	74	68	29.4	2.4	-100	27	34	0.65	25	990	27.0
Tanzania	8,85,800	3,42,009	3,96,500	57.3	3.1	85.5	64.70	144.54	5.0	67	64	38.3	3.1	-200	33	37.8	0.538	36	910	33.1
Thailand	5,10,890	1,97,256	2,21,100	69.0	0.3	71.3	135.13	312.25	1.5	79	72	8.2	0.2	97	49	37.8	0.755	36	5,950	49.2
Timor-Leste	14,870	5,741	3,800	1.3	2.2	1.7	87.18	341.13	5.5	71	67	40.8	3.0	-50	30	30.3	0.625	35	1,790	30.2
Togo	54,390	21,000	38,200	7.8	2.5	10.8	143.37	204.13	4.5	61	59	49.2	2.5	-10	41	43	0.503	30	610	41.2
Tonga	720	278	330	0.1	0.8	0.1	150.03	327.33	3.6	76	70	13.7	1.8	-5	23	37.5	0.726	n/a	4,010	23.2
Trinidad and Tobago	5,130	1,981	540	1.4	0.3	1.4	266.89	2,535.42	1.8	74	67	23.1	0.4	-4	53	40.3	0.784	41	15,340	53.2
Tunisia	1,55,360	59,985	1,00,730	11.5	1.1	13.3	74.23	114.49	2.2	78	74	11.2	1.2	-20	69	35.8	0.735	43	3,490	68.6
Turkey	7,69,630	2,97,156	3,85,460	80.7	1.5	98.6	104.91	209.48	2.1	79	72	10.0	1.0	1525	75	41.2	0.791	41	10,940	74.6
Turkmenistan	4,69,930	1,81,441	3,38,380	5.8	1.7	7.2	12.25	17.02	2.9	71	64	40.6	1.8	-25	51	40.8	0.706	20	6,380	51.2
Turks and Caicos Islands	950	367	10	0.0	1.6	0.0	37.31	3,544.60	n/a	n/a	n/a	n/a	0.0	n/a	93	n/a	n/a	n/a	n/a	92.8
Tuvalu	30	12	18	0.0	0.9	0.0	373.07	621.78	n/a	n/a	n/a	21.0	0.0	n/a	62	39.1	n/a	n/a	4,970	61.5
Uganda	2,00,520	77,421	1,44,150	42.9	3.3	65.5	213.76	297.35	5.6	62	58	35.4	3.3	-150	23	41	0.516	26	600	23.2
Ukraine	5,79,290	2,23,665	4,12,748	44.8	-0.4	42.6	77.39	108.62	1.5	76	67	7.5	-0.4	-100	69	25.5	0.751	32	2,390	69.2
United Arab Emirates	83,600	32,278	3,823	9.4	1.7	11.3	112.44	2,458.84	1.7	79	77	7.8	0.8	301	86	n/a	0.863	70	39,130	86.2
United Kingdom	2,41,930	93,410	1,71,380	66.0	0.6	71.8	272.90	385.24	1.8	83	79	3.7	0.3	900	83	34.1	0.922	80	40,530	83.1
United States	91,47,420	35,31,837	40,58,625	325.7	0.7	357.3	35.61	80.25	1.8	81	76	5.7	0.4	4500	82	41	0.924	n/a	58,270	82.1
Uruguay	1,75,020	67,576	1,44,496	3.5	0.4	3.6	19.75	23.92	2.0	81	74	7.0	0.5	-15	95	41.7	0.804	70	15,250	95.2
Uzbekistan	4,25,400	1,64,248	2,67,700	32.4	1.7	40.3	76.13	120.98	2.5	74	69	20.0	1.8	-44	51	35.3	0.71	23	2,000	50.6
Vanuatu	12,190	4,707	1,870	0.3	2.1	0.4	22.66	147.72	3.3	74	70	22.6	2.1	1	25	37.3	0.603	46	2,920	25.2
Venezuela, RB	8,82,050	3,40,561	2,16,000	32.0	1.3	37.8	36.25	148.04	2.3	79	71	25.7	1.3	-60	88	46.9	0.761	18	n/a	88.2
Vietnam	3,10,070	1,19,719	1,17,100	95.5	1.0	109.1	308.13	815.89	2.0	81	72	16.7	1.1	-200	35	34.8	0.694	33	2,160	35.2
West Bank and Gaza	6,020	2,324	2,980	4.7	2.9	6.8	778.20	1,572.07	4.0	75	72	17.9	2.8	-33	76	n/a	0.686	n/a	3,180	75.9
Yemen, Rep.	5,27,970	2,03,850	2,35,460	28.3	2.4	38.5	53.51	119.98	4.0	66	64	43.2	2.5	-150	36	36.7	0.452	14	n/a	36.0
Zambia	7,43,390	2,87,024	2,38,360	17.1	3.0	25.2	22.99	71.72	5.0	64	59	41.5	3.0	-40	43	57.1	0.588	35	1,290	43.0
Zimbabwe	3,86,850	1,49,364	1,62,000	16.5	2.3	22.4	42.73	102.04	3.8	63	59	36.5	2.5	-100	43	43.2	0.535	32	1,170	32.2

Sources: Land area, World Bank 2018. Arable land, World Bank's measure of agricultural land 2016. Total population, World Bank 2017. Population growth, World Bank 2017. Projected 2030 population, produced by authors based on 2017 population measure and 2018 land area measure from the World Bank. Physiologic density, produced by authors based on 2017 population and 2016 agricultural land area measures from the World Bank. Total fertility rate, World Bank 2016. Life expectancy for females, World Bank 2016. Life expectancy for males, World Bank 2016. Infant mortality, World Bank 2016. Rate of natural increase, produced with birth and death rates from the World Bank 2016. Net migration, calculated by the World Bank using five-year aggregate estimates 2017. Urban population, World Bank 2017. GINI value, World Bank 1995–2015 (GINI was originally calculated on a scale from 0 to 1, but it is increasingly formatted as 0 to 100, so we've used that scale here). Human development index, United Nations Development Programme 2017. Corruption index, Transparency International 2018. GNI per capita, World Bank 2017. CO_2 emissions, World Bank 2017.

Appendix C

Answers to Self-Tests

Chapter 1

1. Answer: e
2. Answer: c
3. Answer: False
4. Answer: a
5. Answer: b
6. Answer: c
7. Answer: b
8. Answer: e
9. Answer: b
10. Answer: a
11. Answer: False
12. Answer: d

Chapter 2

1. Answer: c
2. Answer: a
3. Answer: e
4. Answer: b
5. Answer: b
6. Answer: e
7. Answer: c
8. Answer: a
9. Answer: False
10. Answer: c
11. Answer: d
12. Answer: c
13. Answer: b
14. Answer: c
15. Answer: True

Chapter 3

1. Answer: c
2. Answer: b
3. Answer: True
4. Answer: e
5. Answer: d
6. Answer: c
7. Answer: b
8. Answer: c
9. Answer: a
10. Answer: b
11. Answer: e
12. Answer: True

13. Answer: c
14. Answer: d
15. Answer: c
16. Answer: b

Chapter 4

1. Answer: c
2. Answer: b
3. Answer: c
4. Answer: e
5. Answer: b
6. Answer: c
7. Answer: b
8. Answer: e
9. Answer: b
10. Answer: d
11. Answer: c
12. Answer: a

Chapter 5

1. Answer: e
2. Answer: b
3. Answer: True
4. Answer: e
5. Answer: a
6. Answer: b
7. Answer: a
8. Answer: b
9. Answer: e

Chapter 6

1. Answer: e
2. Answer: e
3. Answer: True
4. Answer: a
5. Answer: c
6. Answer: b
7. Answer: d
8. Answer: c
9. Answer: e
10. Answer: c
11. Answer: a
12. Answer: True
13. Answer: a
14. Answer: c
15. Answer: e

16. Answer: a
17. Answer: a

Chapter 7

1. Answer: e
2. Answer: False
3. Answer: a
4. Answer: True
5. Answer: b
6. Answer: b
7. Answer: a
8. Answer: e
9. Answer: a
10. Answer: d
11. Answer: e
12. Answer: c
13. Answer: True
14. Answer: c

Chapter 8

1. Answer: a
2. Answer: c
3. Answer: e
4. Answer: b
5. Answer: False
6. Answer: e
7. Answer: c
8. Answer: d
9. Answer: b
10. Answer: True
11. Answer: a
12. Answer: e
13. Answer: d
14. Answer: c
15. Answer: e
16. Answer: c
17. Answer: False
18. Answer: c
19. Answer: d

Chapter 9

1. Answer: e
2. Answer: c
3. Answer: d
4. Answer: e
5. Answer: b
6. Answer: a

7. Answer: d
8. Answer: b
9. Answer: d
10. Answer: a
11. Answer: d
12. Answer: e
13. Answer: a
14. Answer: c
15. Answer: b
16. Answer: a

Chapter 10

1. Answer: e
2. Answer: c
3. Answer: c
4. Answer: b
5. Answer: True
6. Answer: e
7. Answer: c
8. Answer: b
9. Answer: c
10. Answer: a
11. Answer: False
12. Answer: e
13. Answer: False
14. Answer: c

Chapter 11

1. Answer: c
2. Answer: a
3. Answer: d
4. Answer: e
5. Answer: c
6. Answer: c
7. Answer: a
8. Answer: d
9. Answer: a
10. Answer: c
11. Answer: d
12. Answer: b
13. Answer: e
14. Answer: b
15. Answer: a
16. Answer: c
17. Answer: a

Chapter 12

1. Answer: b
2. Answer: c
3. Answer: e
4. Answer: d
5. Answer: a
6. Answer: c
7. Answer: d
8. Answer: False
9. Answer: a
10. Answer: b
11. Answer: False
12. Answer: e
13. Answer: c
14. Answer: a
15. Answer: d
16. Answer: True

Chapter 13

1. Answer: c
2. Answer: a
3. Answer: e
4. Answer: b
5. Answer: d
6. Answer: a
7. Answer: c
8. Answer: True
9. Answer: a
10. Answer: a
11. Answer: b
12. Answer: b
13. Answer: e
14. Answer: b
15. Answer: d

Chapter 14

1. Answer: False
2. Answer: a
3. Answer: c
4. Answer: a
5. Answer: d
6. Answer: b
7. Answer: c
8. Answer: True
9. Answer: e

Glossary

Absolute location   Precise location of a place, usually defined by latitude and longitude.

Accessibility   Ease of flow between two places.

Acropolis   The upper, fortified part of an ancient Greek city. Commonly a religious site.

Activity (action) spaces   Places within the rounds of daily activity.

Africa city model (de Blij model)   Model of African cities showing how colonial cities were often built around African cities. The central city has three CBDs: traditional, informal, and colonial. Designed to help see the layers of history in cities in Africa.

Agency   The belief an individual has in their ability to affect change in their life.

Agglomeration   Cost advantages created when similar businesses cluster in the same location. For example, car manufacturers cluster in a city or region to tap into a skilled labor force and access infrastructure, services, and technology.

Agricultural theory   The theory that the Proto-Indo-European language spread with the diffusion of agriculture.

Agriculture   Purposefully growing crops and raising livestock to produce food (for humans), feed (for livestock), and fiber (for textiles).

Animistic religion   Traditional or indigenous religion where animals or objects are significant.

Anthropocene   Current geologic epoch in which humans play a major role in shaping Earth's environment.

Arithmetic population density   Number of people per unit area of land. To calculate: Divide the population of an area by the amount of land (in sq miles or sq km).

Assimilation   When a minority group loses distinct cultural traits, such as dress, food, or speech, and adopts the customs of the dominant culture. Can happen voluntarily or by force.

Asylum-seeker   Migrant who claims the right to protection as a refugee in a country other than their home country.

Authenticity   The idea that one place or experience is the true, actual one.

Backward reconstruction   Tracking **sound shifts** and hardening consonants backward to uncover an original **language**.

Barrioization   Dramatic increase in Hispanic population in a neighborhood; referring to *barrio*, the Spanish word for neighborhood (defined by geographer James Curtis).

Bid rent theory   The premise that the price and demand for land will go up the closer it is to the central city.

Biodiesel   Renewable fuel made from vegetable oils, animal fats, or recycled restaurant grease.

Biodiversity   Variety of plants and animals in an area.

Blockbusting   Rapidly changing racial or class composition of a neighborhood that occurs when real estate agents persuade residents to sell homes because of fear that another race or class of people is moving into the neighborhood. Real estate agents profit through the rapid buying and selling of properties.

Boundary   A plane that stretches beneath the subsoil and into the airspace that legally divides two countries.

Bracero Program   Laws and agreements passed in the U.S. and Mexico in 1942 to encourage Mexicans to migrate to the United States to work in agriculture.

Break-of-bulk   A place where goods are transferred from one form of transport to another. For example, in a port, containers are unloaded from ships and put on trains, trucks, or riverboats for inland distribution.

Break-of-bulk point   A place where goods are transferred from one form of transport to another. For example, in a port, cargoes of ships are unloaded and put on trains, trucks, or riverboats for inland distribution.

Buddhism   Religion based on the belief that humans can reach enlightenment by following the middle path. Buddhism splintered from **Hinduism** in the 6th century BCE. Hearth in Lumbini and Sarnath (present-day Nepal/India).

Cadastral system   Method of land survey through which land ownership and property lines are defined.

Capitalism   Economic system where people, corporations, and **states** produce goods and services and trade them on the world market with the goal of making a profit.

Carrying capacity   The idea that land can hold a measurable amount of plant and animal life.

Cartography   The art and science of making maps.

Caste system   Social structure of South Asian society dating to the Indus civilization (2500-1800 BCE) where people are born into their place in society.

Census   An official count of a population.

Central Business District (CBD)   The zone of a city where businesses cluster and around which a city and its infrastructure are typically built.

Central city   Urban area that is not suburban. Generally, the older or original **city** that is surrounded by **suburbs**.

Central place theory   Walter Christaller's theory that the size and locations of cities, towns, and villages are logically and regularly distributed.

Centrifugal   In nationalism, attributes of a nation that can be activated or manipulated to divide the nation, such as unequal distribution of wealth, or religious, linguistic, ethnic, and ideological differences.

Centripetal   In nationalism, attributes of a nation that can be activated or manipulated to unite the nation, such as national iconography, patriotism, shared culture and history, or common religion or ideology.

Chain migration   Permanent movement from one place to another that follows kinship links. For example, a group of migrants settles in a place and then communicates with family and friends at their former location to encourage migration along the same path.

Child dependency ratio   Number of people between the ages of 0 and 14 for every 100 people between the ages of 15-64 (working age population).

Child mortality rate   Probability per 1000 live births that a child will die before reaching age 5 years.

Christianity   Religion based on the belief that Jesus was born as the son of God, was crucified, and was resurrected to atone for peoples' sins. Developed out of **Judaism** in 1st century CE. Hearth in Bethlehem and Jerusalem (present-day Palestine/Israel).

Chronic (or degenerative) diseases   Generally long-lasting afflictions, now more common because of longer life expectancies.

City   A large settlement of people with an extensive built environment that functions as a center of politics, culture, and economics.

Cognate   A word in one language that shares its origin with a word in another language. Cognates have similar meanings and spellings and show shared origins and connections among languages.

Cold chain System of harvesting produce that is not quite ripe and ripening it by controlling temperature from the fields to the grocery store.

Columbian Exchange Movement of plants, animals, people, diseases, and ideas among Africa, Europe, and the Americas across the Atlantic.

Colonialism Physically taking over a territory and people and controlling the economy and government.

Commodification Transformation of goods and services into products that can be bought, sold, or traded.

Commodity chain Steps in the production of a good from its design and raw materials to its production, marketing, and distribution.

Community-supported agriculture (CSA) Direct link between producers and consumers where individuals invest in the harvest of a specific farmer and receive a weekly share of the farmer's output.

Concentric zones model Urban model that explains the distribution of social groups around a central business district (CBD) using 5 concentric zones with the newest built on the outskirts. Created by Ernest Burgess in 1925 based on Chicago, United States.

Confucianism Political philosophy that values benevolence, loyalty, and diligence within the structure of the family and the government. Developed from the writings of Confucius in 6th to 5th centuries BCE. Hearth in China and traditionally thought of as one of the core elements of Asian culture.

Connectivity Position of a place or area relative to others in a network.

Conquest theory Idea that early speakers of Proto-Indo-European left the hearth area and moved westward on horseback, overpowering earlier inhabitants and beginning the **diffusion** and differentiation of Indo-European tongues.

Contagious diffusion Spread of an idea or innovation from one person or place to another person or place based on proximity. Specific type of expansion diffusion.

Containerization System of intermodal transportation (ships, trucks, barges, and railroads) that each hold and move freight shipping containers.

Context The physical and human geographies creating the place, environment, and space in which events occur and people act.

Contraceptive prevalence rate Percent of women who are currently using or have a sexual partner who is using a method of contraception.

Converge A plate boundary where Earth's tectonic plates are coming together. If different densities (one oceanic, one continental), the denser plate subducts. If similar densities, the plates lift upward, forming mountains.

Convergence Merging of cultural landscapes that happens with broad diffusion of landscape traits.

Core Places in the world economy where core processes dominate.

Corn Belt Region stretching from North Dakota to Indiana that, since the 1800s, has been the focus of corn production in the United States.

Cottage industries Production of goods in a home or small workshop, typically by hand or with low technology.

Creole language A language that began as a **pidgin language** and was later adopted as the mother tongue of a people.

Critical geopolitics Deconstruction and explanation of underlying spatial assumptions and territorial perspectives of politicians.

Crude Birth Rate (CBR) Number of live births per 1000 people among a population in an area in a year.

Crude Death Rate (CDR) Number of deaths per 1000 people among a population in an area in a year.

Cultural appropriation When one culture adopts customs and knowledge from another culture and uses them for its own benefit.

Cultural ecology Study of the historical interaction between humans and environment in a place, including ways humans have modified and adapted to environment.

Cultural homogenization Sharing of cultural traits through globalization that results in a reduction in the diversity of cultures.

Cultural landscape The visible human imprint on the landscape.

Cultural trait A learned belief, norm, or value passed down through generations in a culture.

Culture complex A group of interrelated **cultural traits**, such as prevailing dress codes and cooking and eating utensils.

Culture Group of belief systems, norms, and values practiced by a people.

Custom Common practice or routine way of doing things in a culture.

Cyclic movement Regular journey that begins at a home base and returns to the exact same place. A form of movement.

Deforestation Clearing forests without replanting or giving time for land to regenerate. Commonly done for urban development or agriculture.

Deindustrialization Decline in industry in a region or economy. Happens when companies move industry to other regions or mechanize production.

Democracy Government by the people where the people are sovereign and have the final say over what happens within a state.

Demographic transition Observation that a country's birth rate and death rate change in predictable ways over stages of economic development. Model is based on population change in western Europe.

Dependency theory Andre Gunder Frank's theory that wealthy countries set up exploitative economic relations whereby lower income countries became dependent on wealthy countries, who in turn benefit economically.

Dependency ratio Number of people not working age (0-14 and over 65) relative to number of people working age (15 to 64).

Desertification Spread of desert like conditions to semiarid lands due to overuse or misuse of land and water resources.

Deterritorialization Movement of economic, social, and cultural processes out of the hands of states (countries).

Development Improvement in the economy and well-being of a place relative to another place. Improved wealth or progress in other socioeconomic variables, including education and health.

Devolution Transfer of power from central government to regional or local government within a state (country).

Dialect chains A group of contiguous dialects where the dialects nearest to each other geographically are the most similar and the dialects farther apart are least similar.

Dialects Variants of a standard language along regional or ethic lines.

Diaspora Dispersal of a people from their homeland to a new place, either voluntarily or by force.

Diffusion Spread of an idea, innovation, or technology from its hearth to other people and places. See also **contagious, expansion, hierarchical, relocation**, and **stimulus diffusion**.

Digital divide Growing gap in access to Internet and communication technologies between connected and remote places.

Disamenity sector Residential zone where lowest income residents in the city live, especially in the Latin American city model. Often built on unstable or undesirable land.

Distance decay Decreasing likelihood of diffusion with greater distance from the hearth.

Diverge A plate boundary where Earth's tectonic plates are splitting apart. Forms a rift valley on land or a mid-oceanic ridge under water.

Dollarization When one country abandons their local currency and officially adopts the currency of another country.

Dot map Thematic map where individual symbols represent a certain number of cases of a phenomenon. For example, a map where one dot represents 100,000 people.

Doubling time Time required for a population to double in size.

Dowry Price paid in cash and gifts through marriage. Generally given by the bride's family to the groom's father.

Eastern Orthodox Church   One of three major branches of Christianity (together with Roman Catholic and Protestant).

Ecological footprint   The impact of a person on environment in terms of resources used and waste produced, with special focus on carbon production.

Economies of scale   Savings in cost of production that comes from increasing production of a good.

Edge cities   Large urban areas on the outskirts of major cities, typically found on major roads. Edge cities are characterized by extensive space for offices and retail, and few residential areas.

Emigrant   A person who permanently moves out of their home country.

Endemic   Disease found among people in a certain location or region.

Environmental determinism   Set of theories that use environmental differences to explain everything from intelligence to wealth.

Epidemic   Widespread, rapid diffusion of disease among a people in a particular location or region at a particular time.

Epidemiological transition   Change in the pattern of mortality in a society from high mortality among infants (including malnutrition and diarrheal disease) and periods of widespread famine to high mortality from degenerative diseases which coincide with longer life expectancies.

Ethanol   Renewable fuel made from plat materials called biomass.

Ethnic   identity shared by a group of people who have a common culture, generally based on cultural traits (religion, language), national origin, or race.

Ethnic neighborhood   Area within an urban area where a relatively large group of people from one ethnic group or local culture lives.

Ethnic religion   A religion into which people are born and whose followers do not actively seek converts.

Eugenic population policies   Government policies designed to limit population growth among a certain group of people.

Expansion diffusion   The spread of an idea or innovation from its hearth across space without the aid of people moving.

Expansive population policies   Government policies designed to encourage large families and raise the rate of population growth.

Extensive agriculture   Production of agricultural goods primarily by hand with low use of fertilizers and high use of human labor.

Extinct language   Language without any native speakers.

Federal government   A system with a central government and several states that retain independence on internal affairs.

Feng Shui   Chinese art and science of placement and orientation of tombs, dwellings, buildings, and cities. Structures and objects are positioned to channel flow of *sheng-chi* ("life-breath") in favorable ways.

Fertile Crescent   Region in Mesopotamia and Anatolia where agriculture began.

Fieldwork   Observations researchers make of physical and cultural landscapes with a focus on seeing similarities and differences.

First Agricultural Revolution   The transformation of societies from hunting and gathering to purposeful raising of food, feed, and fiber.

First mover advantage   Benefit a service or product receives by being the first to market.

First Urban Revolution   The transformation of societies from agriculture villages to permanently settled cities, which occurred independently in five separate **hearths**.

First wave of colonialism   From the late 1400s to 1850s, when Europeans colonized the Americas and coastal Africa.

Flash flood   Excessive rain or meltwater from snow that overflows rivers, fills dry riverbeds, and causes a rapid rise in water levels.

Flexible production   Method of manufacturing designed to adapt quickly to changes in demand, labor, and resources.

Floodplains   areas of low-lying ground adjacent to rivers that flood when a river overflows its banks.

Folk culture   Small, homogenous population that is typically rural and cohesive in cultural traits that are passed down from generation to generation.

Food desert   Area characterized by a lack of availability of affordable, fresh, and nutritious food.

Food oasis   Convenience stores located in food deserts where fresh fruits and vegetables, whole grains, and lean, fresh meats are available at affordable prices.

Fordist   Manufacturing system in which raw materials are brought into a central location and component parts and the final product are produced at the same location and then shipped globally.

Formal economy   Economic productivity in agriculture, mining, industry, and services that is counted or taxed by government. Trade is through formal channels, often using credit.

Formal region   Area of land with common cultural or physical traits.

Friction of distance   Difficulty in time and cost that usually comes with increasing **distance**.

Functional region   Area of land defined as sharing a common purpose in society.

Functional zonation   Division of a city into different regions (e.g., residential or industrial) by use or purpose (e.g., housing or manufacturing).

Galactic city   Modern city in which the old downtown plays the role of a festival or recreational area, and widely dispersed industrial parks, shopping centers, high-tech industrial spaces, edge-city downtowns, and industrial suburbs are the new centers of economic activity.

Gated communities   residential neighborhoods where access is controlled in order to define exclusive space and deter movement of people and traffic through the neighborhood.

Gatekeepers   Individuals or corporations who control access to information.

Gender   Socially constructed ideas of roles, behaviors, and activities that are appropriate for men and women.

Genetic or inherited diseases   Diseases caused by variation or mutation of a gene or group of genes in humans.

Gentrification   Renewal or rebuilding of a lower income neighborhood into a middle- to upper-class neighborhood, which results in driving up property values and rents and the dispossession of lower income residents.

Geographic concepts   Mental categories used to organize and analyze the world spatially.

Geographic Information Systems (GIS)   A system of computer hardware and software designed to show, analyze, and represent geographic data (data that have locations).

Geometric boundaries   Political boundaries **defined** and **delimited** (and occasionally **demarcated**) as a straight line or an arc.

Geography   The spatial study of people, place, space, and environment.

Gerrymandering   Manipulating electoral districts to give one political party unfair advantage.

Glaciation   A period of global cooling during which continental ice sheets and mountain glaciers expand.

Global division of labor   The ability of corporations to employ labor from around the world, made possible by the compression of time and space through innovations in communication and transportation systems.

Global Positioning System (GPS)   Satellite-based system for determining the **absolute location** of **places** or geographic features.

Global Production Networks   Pattern of flows from raw material to global product to disposal or reuse of products that shows all the places connected through production.

Global sourcing   Tapping into companies that specialize in production around the world to manufacture goods.

Global water system   Cycle of water through Earth that accounts for human water use and the built environment.

Globalization   Processes heightening interactions, increasing interdependence, and deepening relations across country borders.

Gravity model Urban geography model that mathematically predicts the degree of interaction and probability of migration (and other flows) between two places.

Great Pacific Garbage Patch A cluster of plastics and trash in the northern Pacific Ocean that move in a gyre around a high-pressure system.

Green Revolution Intensified agriculture that uses engineered seeds, fertilizers, and irrigation to increase intensive agricultural practices.

Greenhouse gases Naturally occurring and human-produced gases that cluster in the upper troposphere, where they absorb long-wave energy emitted by Earth and reradiate it back to the surface, trapping energy and keeping Earth's temperature warmer than it would be without the gases.

Griffin-Ford model Model of Latin American cities showing a blend of traditional elements of Latin American culture with the modern world-economy. Developed by geographers Ernst Griffin and Larry Ford.

Gross Domestic Product (GDP) A measurement of a country's wealth that includes the total value of all goods and services produced within a country in a year.

Gross National Income (GNI) A measurement of a country's wealth that includes the total value of all goods and services produced within the borders of a country, plus income received from investments outside of the country in a year.

Gross National Product (GNP) A measurement of a country's wealth that includes the total value of all goods and services produced by residents of a country, including domestic and foreign production, in a year.

Guest worker Migrants who are invited into a country to work temporarily, are granted work visa status, and are expected to return to their home country at the end of the visa.

Gulags Forced labor or prison labor camps. Most often associated with authoritarian countries.

Hajj Muslim **pilgrimage** to Mecca, the birthplace of Muhammad.

Hallyu South Korean waves of popular culture, especially in music, television, and movies.

Hearth Area or place where an idea, innovation, or technology originates.

Heartland theory British geographer Halford Mackinder's theory that a political power based in the heart of Eurasia could gain enough strength to eventually dominate the world. "Who controls Eastern Europe controls the Heartland; Who controls the Heartland controls the World Island; Who controls the World Island controls the world."

Hierarchical diffusion Spread of an idea or innovation from one person or place to another person or place based on a hierarchy of connectedness. Specific type of expansion diffusion.

High-technology corridor Areas along or near major transportation corridors that are devoted to the research, development, and sale of high-technology products.

Hinduism Religion based on a range of beliefs, including karma and reincarnation. Hinduism began around 2000 BCE and does not have a single founder. Hearth in Indus Valley (present-day Pakistan).

Hinterland An area of economic production that is located inland and is connected to the world by a port.

Horizontal integration Common ownership of multiple companies that compete at the same point on a **commodity chain**.

Huang He (Yellow) and Wei River valleys Region in China where the first urban revolution occurred around 1500 BCE.

Human consumption Goods used by people, including food, water, consumer goods, and fossil fuels, along with the resources needed to produce them.

Human geography One of the two major divisions of **geography**; the spatial analysis of human phenomena, including population, cultures, activities, and landscapes.

Human trafficking A form of forced migration where people are involuntary sold and traded for manual labor or as workers in the commercial sex trade.

Human-environment Reciprocal relationship between humans and environment (one of the five themes of geography).

Hunger Living on less than the daily recommended 2100 calories the average person needs to live a healthy life.

Hutment factories Manufacturing conducted in slums, typically relying on intensive hand labor and low-cost machines.

Hydrocarbons Chemical components of oil and natural gas.

Hydrologic cycle Continual circulation of water among the atmosphere, oceans, and above and below the land surface.

Identifying against Constructing an **identity** by first defining an "other" and then defining self "not the other."

Identity How people make sense of themselves and how they see themselves at different scales.

Imagined community A socially constructed identity that is imagined because the people in the group will never meet each other and simply believe they have a similarity and shared connection.

Immigrant A person who permanently moves into a new country.

Impervious surfaces Land coverings (including concrete and asphalt) that prevent rain from percolating into soil and down into groundwater.

Independent invention When an innovation is realized in more than one hearth independent of each other.

Indigenous religions Belief systems and philosophies practiced and traditionally passed from generation to generation among peoples within an indigenous tribe or group.

Indigenous local culture People who see themselves as a community (see local culture) and also identify as indigenous, or original, to a place.

Indoor vertical farms Factories where produce is grown hydroponically without soil.

Indus River Valley Region in South Asia where the first urban revolution occurred around 2200 BCE.

Industrial Revolution Cluster of inventions and innovations that brought large-scale economic changes in agriculture, commerce- and manufacturing in late eighteenth century Europe.

Infant Mortality Rate (IMR) Probability per 1000 live births that a child will die before reaching age 1 year.

Infectious diseases Diseases that are spread by bacteria, viruses, or parasites. Infectious diseases diffuse directly or indirectly from human to human.

Informal economy Portion of the economy that is not taxed or regulated by government. Goods and services are exchanged based on barter or cash systems, and earnings are not reported to government.

Intensive agriculture Production of agricultural goods using fertilizers, insecticides, and high-cost inputs to achieve the highest yields possible.

Interfaith boundaries Boundaries between the world's major faiths.

Intermodal Where two or more modes of transportation meet (including air, road, rail, barge, and ship).

Internal migration Purposeful movement of people within a country from one location to another with a degree of permanence or intent to stay.

Internally displaced persons (IDPs) People who have been displaced within their home country and do not cross international boundaries.

International migration Purposeful movement of people from one country to another with a degree of permanence or intent to stay.

Intersectionality interconnection and overlap between social categories (e.g. race, sexuality, class, gender).

Intervening opportunity Presence of an opportunity near a migrant's current location that greatly diminishes the attractiveness of migrating to a site farther away.

Intrafaith boundaries Boundaries between sects within a single major faith.

Islam Religion based on the belief in one God who revealed himself to the prophet

Muhammad. Islam dates to the 7th century CE. Hearth in Mecca and Medina in present-day Saudi Arabia.

Island of development   Cities in developing regions where foreign investment is concentrated and to which rural migrants are drawn.

Isogloss   A geographic boundary where linguistic features occur.

Jihad   Commonly translated as "Holy War," jihad represents either a personal or collective struggle on the part of Muslims to live up to the religious standards set by the *Qu'ran*.

Judaism   Religion based on the belief in one God who revealed himself to and entered a covenant with Abraham. Judaism dates to 2000 BCE. Hearth in present-day Israel.

Just-in-time delivery   Production system in which parts are delivered as needed to the assembly line so that parts are not warehoused, stored, or overproduced.

Land cover   What is on the ground, such as grasses, trees, or pavement.

Land use   Ways people use land resources for specific purposes, such as agriculture or industry.

Landscape   The overall appearance of an area. Most landscapes are a combination of natural and human-induced influences.

Language   A set of sounds and symbols that are used for communication.

Language convergence   Process where two languages collapse into one language. Happens when people speaking two languages have frequent and consistent spatial interaction with each other; the opposite of language divergence.

Language divergence   Process where discrete, new languages are eventually formed from one language. Happens when people speaking two dialects of a language are relatively isolated from each other and have little spatial interaction; the opposite of language convergence.

Language family   Group of languages with a shared but distant origin.

Language Subfamilies   Divisions within a language family where commonalities are more definite and the origin is more recent.

Latin American city model (Griffin-Ford model)   Model of Latin American cities showing central plazas and wide streets commonly designed by Spanish colonizers. Designed to help see the layers of history built in cities in Latin America.

Least Cost Theory   Determining the location of manufacturing based on minimizing three critical expenses: labor, transportation, and agglomeration. Model developed by Alfred Weber.

Lingua franca   Language used for trade or cultural interaction among people who speak different languages.

Lithosphere   Earth's upper mantle and crust

Local culture   People who see themselves as a collective or a community, share experiences, customs, and traits, and work to preserve their traits and customs in a place.

Location   Position on Earth, including both absolute location and relative location (one of the five themes of geography).

Location theory   Understanding the distribution of cities, industries, services, or consumers with the goal of explaining why places are chosen as sites of production or consumption. The von Thünen model is an example.

Locavore   A person who seeks to eat a diet of locally-sourced foods for reasons including avoiding pesticide and genetically-modified food use, reducing carbon footprints, and other industrial farming practices.

Long-lot survey   Land survey system that divides Earth into narrow parcels stretching back from rivers, roads, or canals. Commonly found in France or places of French settlement, including Quebec and Louisiana.

Majority-minority districts   Electoral district where the majority of the people in the district are from a minority group.

Malaria   Vectored disease spread by a certain type of mosquitoes.

Malnutrition   Undernutrition, inadequate vitamins, or obesity resulting from diet.

Maquiladora   Foreign-owned factories in Mexico where low-wage workers assemble imported components and raw materials into finished products for export.

Material culture   Physical aspects of culture, including art, tools, buildings, and clothing that are made by people.

McMansions   Large homes often built in place of tear-downs in American suburbs.

Megacity   A large city with more than 10 million people.

Megalopolis   An urban agglomeration that stretches from Washington, DC in the south to Boston, Massachusetts in the north.

Mental maps   Maps of an area made from memory or experience by individuals or groups (also known as cognitive maps).

Mercantilism   An early form of capitalism based on trading large quantities of goods, using gold and silver as currencies.

Mesoamerica   Region in central America where the first urban revolution occurred around 200 BCE.

Mesopotamia   Region in southwest Asia where the first urban revolution occurred around 2200 BCE.

Metes-and-bounds system   Land survey system that relies on descriptions of land ownership and natural features such as streams or

trees. Commonly found on the east coast of the United States.

Microcredit programs   Practice of giving small loans to individuals, who operate within a community of other borrowers, to start businesses and cottage enterprises.

Microplastics   Smaller pieces of plastic that are broken down in the ocean.

Migration   Purposeful movement from a home location to a new place with a degree of permanence or intent to stay in the new place.

Minaret   Tall, thin tower on or near a mosque. Traditionally, a muezzin stands on the balcony of a minaret to call Muslims to prayer.

Modernization model   Theory that countries follow the same path along stages of development. Developed by economist Walter Rostow.

Monoculture   dependence on production of a single agricultural commodity

Monotheistic religion   Belief in one god.

Monsoon   Predictable patterns of winds coming from a certain direction for an extended period.

Movement   Mobility of people, goods, and services across Earth (one of the five themes of geography).

Multinational state   State (country) with more than one nation (people).

Multiple nuclei model   Layout of American cities, including a central business district (CBD) and suburban business districts that each serve as nuclei around which businesses and residences cluster.

Multistate nation   Nation (people) that stretches across states (countries).

Music festival   Concert event featuring multiple performers and additional entertainment that often lasts more than one day.

Mutual intelligibility   Ability of two people to understand each other when speaking.

Nation   A group of people with a shared past and common future who relate to each other and share a common political goal.

Nation-state   A nation (people) and a state (country) who share the same borders.

Natural disaster   Earth processes, including tectonic, hydrological, and meteorological, that cause serious damage to human lives and property.

Natural hazards   Earth processes, including tectonic, hydrological, and meteorological, that have the potential to impact human lives and property.

Natural population increase   Difference between number of births and deaths in a year. Positive if births exceed deaths and negative if deaths exceed births. Does not include emigration and immigration.

Neocolonialism   Economic and financial policies that give higher income countries and organizations control over lower income countries.

Neoliberalism Policies based on the economic theory that government should not intervene in markets.

Neolocalism Conscious effort to define a sense of place for local or regional culture. Often used by local businesses, such as microbreweries, to identify local products with local or regional culture.

Net migration Difference between the number of immigrants (those coming into a country) and the number of emigrants (those leaving a country).

Networks A set of interconnected nodes without a center.

Newly industrializing countries States with growing industrial and service economies and an increasing presence in global trade.

Nile River Valley Region along the Nile River in North Africa where the first urban revolution occurred 3200 BCE.

Node Connection point in a network, where goods and ideas flow in, out, and through the network.

Nongovernmental organizations (NGOs) Privately funded institutions that aid in development and relief work.

Nonmaterial culture Non physical aspects of culture, including beliefs, practices, aesthetics, and values that are defined by people.

Nonrenewable resources Resources that are present in finite quantities because they are not self-replenishing or take an extraordinarily long time to replenish.

Old-age dependency ratio Number of people 65 years of age or older for every 100 people between the ages of 15-64 (working age population).

One-child policy Antinatalist policy instituted by China in 1979 to slow population growth.

Organic agriculture Approach to farming and ranching that avoids the use of herbicides, pesticides, growth hormones, and other similar synthetic inputs.

Outsourcing Hiring employees outside the home country of a company in order to reduce the cost of labor inputs for the good or service.

Pandemic An outbreak of a disease that spreads worldwide.

Participatory development Projects designed to incorporate local knowledge, input, and solutions with the goal of enabling locals to decide what development means for them and how it should be achieved.

Pastoralism a type of cyclic movement when herders move livestock through the year to continually find fresh water and green pastures.

Patterns Description of the spatial distribution of a human or physical phenomenon (e.g., scattered or concentrated).

Peace of Westphalia Treaties negotiated in 1648 that formally recognized the sovereignty of states.

Per capita GNI The Gross National Income (GNI) of a given country divided by its population.

Perceptions of places How a place is envisioned.

Perceptual regions Area of land that an individual perceives as being similar.

Periphery Places in the world economy where periphery processes dominate.

Perishable Agricultural products that are susceptible to spoiling in transit.

Peru Region in South America where first urban revolution occurred around 900 BCE.

Physical geography One of the two major divisions of geography; the spatial analysis of physical phenomena, including climate, environmental hazards, weather systems, animals, and topography.

Physical-political boundary Political boundary defined by a prominent physical feature in the physical landscape, such as a riverbank or the crest of a mountain range.

Physiologic population density Number of people per unit area of arable land. To calculate: Divide the population of an area by the amount of arable land (in sq miles or sq km).

Pidgin language Combination of two or more languages in a simplified structure and vocabulary.

Pilgrimage Purposeful travel to a sacred site for religious reasons.

Place Uniqueness of a location (one of the five themes of geography).

Placelessness Loss of uniqueness of a location so that one place looks like the next.

Plantation agriculture Production system based on a large estate owned by an individual, family, or corporation, and organized to produce a cash crop.

Political ecology An approach to studying human-environment interactions in the context of political, economic, and historical conditions operating at multiple scales.

Polytheistic religion Belief in many gods.

Popular culture Cultural traits such as dress, diet, and music that identify and are part of today's changeable, urban-based, media-influenced, global society.

Population composition Structure of a population in terms of age, sex, and other properties such as marital status and education.

Population density Number of people per unit area of land.

Population distribution Description of spatial distribution of people, including where large numbers of people live closely together and where few people live.

Population pyramid A graphic representation of the age and sex composition of a population.

Possibilism Theory in geography that humans, not environment, shape culture.

Primate city The lead city in a country in terms of size and influence.

Primogeniture land ownership inheritance practice where land is passed down to the eldest son.

Protestant One of three major branches of Christianity (together with Eastern Orthodox and Roman Catholic).

Pull factors Circumstances a migrant considers when deciding where to migrate.

Push factors Circumstances a migrant considers when deciding to leave the home country.

Race Social constructions of differences among humans based on skin color that have had profound consequences on rights and opportunities.

Rank-size rule Observed statistical relationship that the population of a city will be inversely proportional to its rank in the hierarchy. For example, second largest city is half the population of largest city.

Reapportionment Redistribution of representatives based on population change. For example, seats in the U.S. House of Representatives are reapportioned across states after each census before each state redistricts.

Redlining Discriminatory real estate practice (now illegal) that prevents minorities from getting loans to purchase homes or property in predominantly white neighborhoods. The practice derived its name from the red lines drawn on cadastral maps used by real estate agents and developers.

Reference maps Maps showing absolute location of places and geographic features.

Refugees Migrants who flee their country because of political persecution and seek asylum in another country.

Region Area of Earth identified as sharing a formal, functional, or perceptual commonality that makes it different from regions around it (one of the five themes of geography).

Relative location The location of a place or attribute in reference to another place or attribute.

Religion System of beliefs that order life in terms of ultimate priorities and direct behavior and practices in reference to achieving the ultimate priorities.

Religious extremism Religious fundamentalism carried to the point of violence.

Religious fundamentalism Religious movement whose objectives are to return to the foundations of the faith and to influence state policy.

Relocation diffusion Spread of an idea or innovation from its hearth by the act of people moving and taking the idea or innovation with them.

Remittance Money that migrants send back to families and friends in their home countries, often in cash, forming an important part of the economy in many lower income (peripheral) countries.

Remote sensing A method of collecting data or information through the use of instruments (e.g., satellites) that are physically distant from the area of study.

Renewable resources Resources that can regenerate as they are exploited.

Repatriation A refugee or group of refugees returning to their home country, usually with the assistance of government or a non governmental organization.

Rescale Changing the geographical scope at which a problem is addressed by engaging decision makers and gatekeepers at another scale.

Residential segregation Degree to which two or more groups live separately from one another, in different parts of an urban environment.

Restrictive population policies Government policies designed to reduce the rate of natural population increase (also called antinatalist).

Reterritorialization When a local culture shapes an aspect of popular culture as their own, adopting the popular culture to their local culture.

Reverse remittances Money flowing from home countries to migrants in their destination countries.

Ring of Fire Tectonically active region of earthquakes and volcanoes surrounding the Pacific Ocean.

Roman Catholic Church One of three major branches of Christianity (together with the Eastern Orthodox and Protestant).

Rust Belt A region in the northeastern United States that once had an extensive manufacturing industry but has been deindustrialized during the post-Fordist era.

Sacred sites A place infused with religious or spiritual meaning.

Scale Geographical scope (local, national, or global) in which we analyze and understand a phenomenon.

Seafloor spreading Formation of new oceanic crust on both sides of a diverging plate boundary where magma comes to the surface.

Sea-floor spreading A diverging plate boundary under water, where new oceanic crust is being formed along the plate boundary.

Second Agricultural Revolution A cluster of advances in breeding livestock, agricultural technology, and seed production to increase food, feed, and livestock production that took place in Europe in the 1700s and 1800s.

Second wave of colonialism From the 1850s to 1960s, when Europeans colonized Africa and Asia in the context of the industrial revolution.

Secondary hearth Area to which an innovation diffuses and from which the innovation diffuses more broadly.

Sector model A structural model of the American city centered on a central business district with distinct areas of manufacturing and residences extending in wedge-shaped zones from the CBD (like pieces of pie).

Secularism Indifference to or rejection of religion.

Semiperiphery Places where core and periphery processes are both occurring; places that are exploited by the core but in turn exploit the periphery.

Sense of place Infusing a place with meaning as a result of experiences in a place.

Sensible heat The heat we feel in air temperature.

Sequent occupance imprints left on the cultural landscape by a series of successive societies. Each society contributed to the cumulative cultural landscape.

Settlements places where a group of people reside and have established permanent community.

Sexuality sexual orientation or preference identified by a person

sex ratio number of males relative to number of females in a population

Shi'ite Sect of Islam that believes Muhammad's successor needed to be a blood relative of Muhammad. Found commonly in and around Iran.

Shifting cultivation Agricultural practice based on clearing and farming land for a time before moving on to a new parcel and allowing the first to fill in with native vegetation.

Shintoism Religion located in Japan and related to Buddhism. Shintoism focuses particularly on nature and ancestor worship.

Site Physical attributes of the location of a human settlement – for example, at the head of navigation of a river or at a certain elevation.

Situation The position of a city or place relative to its surrounding environment or context.

Snowbirds Retired or semiretired people who live in cold states and Canada for most of the year and move to warm states for the winter.

Social networks Interconnections among individuals that foster social interaction.

Southeast Asian city model (McGee model) Model of Southeast Asian cities showing a city with an old colonial port zone surrounded by a large commercial district and no formal CBD. Designed to help see the layers of history built in cities in Southeast Asia.

Sovereignty The legal authority to have the last say over a territory. Under international law, states are sovereign.

Spatial distribution Physical locations of geographic phenomena, usually shown on a map.

Spatial fix The movement of production from one site to another based on the place-based cost advantages of the new site.

Spatial interaction Degree of connectedness or contact among people or places.

Spatial perspective Looking at where things occur, why they occur where they do, and how places are interconnected.

Splitting A redistricting practice where a minority population is divided across districts to ensure the majority population controls each district (also called dilution).

Standard language The variant of a language that a country's political and intellectual elite seek to promote as the norm for use in schools, government, the media, and other aspects of public life.

State A sovereign territory, recognized as a country by other states under international law. A state has a defined territory, a permanent population, a government, and is recognized by other states.

Stateless nation A nation that does not have a state.

Stimulus diffusion A process of diffusion where two cultural traits blend to create a distinct trait.

Structural adjustment loans A set of requirements to open markets, privatize industries, and allow foreign direct investment in developing countries in exchange for loans from international financial institutions.

Structuralist theory Theories based on the idea that difficult-to-change, large-scale economic arrangements shape what is possible for a country.

Structures of power Assumptions and relationships dictating who is in control and who has power over others.

Subduction zones A converging plate boundary where the denser oceanic plate descends under the less dense continental plate.

Subsistence agriculture Self-sufficient agriculture that is small scale and low technology and emphasizes food production for local consumption, not for trade.

Suburb A built-up residential and shopping district connected to a central city by major transportation routes.

Suburbanization Transformation of farmland and small towns outside of an urban area into suburbs.

Succession Process by which new immigrants move to a city and take over areas or neighborhoods occupied by older immigrant groups.

Sun Belt Region of economic growth with an expanding technology-based service sector and a stable manufacturing sector that stretches along the southern United States from Virginia to California.

Sunni Sect of Islam that believes Muhammad's successor did not need to be a blood relative of Muhammad.

Supranational organization An organization of three or more states involving formal political, economic, and/or cultural cooperation to promote shared objectives. For example, the European Union is one such organization.

Sustainable development Economic development that meets the needs of the present while preserving environment and resources for future use.

Sustainable Development Goals Agenda agreed to by member countries of the United Nations to improve peoples' lives across several human conditions, including education, environment, political liberty, poverty, and inequality.

Syncretic A blend of religious beliefs and traditions, often forming a new religion.

Synergy Cross-promotion of vertically integrated goods.

Taoism Religion believed to have been founded by Lao-Tsu and based upon his book entitled "Tao-te-ching," or "Book of the Way." Lao-Tsu focused on the proper form of political rule and on the oneness of humanity and nature.

Teardowns Homes bought in suburbs with the intent of tearing them down and replacing them with much larger homes, often referred to as McMansions.

Terra incognita Areas on maps that are not well defined because they are off limits or unknown to the map maker.

Territorial integrity Right of a state to defend sovereign territory against incursion from other states.

Territoriality Sense of ownership and attachment to a specific territory.

Thematic maps A map that tells a story, typically showing the degree of some attribute or the movement of a geographic phenomenon using map symbols.

Third Agricultural Revolution see Green Revolution.

Three-tier structure Division of the world economy into the core, periphery, and semi-periphery according to Immanuel Wallerstein's world-systems theory.

Threshold Concepts Concepts in geography, which once learned, help students think like geographers. For example, cultural landscapes. Threshold concepts are transformative because they change how students' see something; irreversible because once students see them, they cannot unsee them; integrative because they help students make connections among concepts; bounded because they often belong to

one discipline; and, troublesome because they require tenacity and persistence for students to understand them.

Time-distance decay The likelihood of a trait or innovation diffusing decreases the farther away in time or distance it moves from the origin (hearth).

Time-space compression Increasing connectedness between world cities from improved communication and transportation networks.

Toponym Place name.

Total Fertility Rate (TFR) The average number of children born to a woman of child-bearing age.

Township and range system Land survey system that divides Earth into square parcels called townships (6 miles by 6 miles), each of which has 36 sections (1 mile by 1 mile). Commonly found west of the Appalachian Mountains.

Trafficking A form of forced migration in which organized criminal elements move people illegally from one place to another, typically either to work as involuntary laborers or to participate in the commercial sex trade.

Transform A plate boundary where one of Earth's tectonic plates slides past another tectonic plate.

Transhumance Migration pattern in which livestock are led to highlands during summer months and lowlands during winter months to graze.

Trenches Steep depressions in the ocean floor that typically form along subduction zones.

Tsunami Seismic sea wave.

Unauthorized migrants Migrants who do not have legal permission to stay in the country where they live. Unauthorized migrants can be those who enter a country legally, as authorized migrants with a visa, and then stay when the visa expires. They can also enter a country without permission by crossing a border without legal approval.

Unequal exchange Uneven relationship between low labor costs and high-value products.

Unilateralism World order in which one state is in a position of global dominance.

Unitary A state that has a centralized government and administration that exercises power equally over all parts of the state.

Universalizing religions A religion believed by its followers to have universal application and to which followers actively seek converts.

Urban agriculture Cultivating land or raising livestock in small plots in cities, generally on converted brownfields or on rooftops.

Urban geopolitics How cities shape and are shaped by geopolitical processes at national, regional and global scales.

Urban morphology The layout of a city, including the sizes and shapes of buildings and the pathways of infrastructure.

Urban sprawl the expansion of low density urban areas around a city. New urbanism a modern approach to planning and developing cities and communities that values walkability, attracting diverse incomes, and access to public spaces.

Vernacular A language used in everyday interaction among a group of people in a local area.

Vertical integration The merging of businesses that serve different steps in one commodity chain.

Volcanic arc Chain of volcanoes that forms along the continental side of a subduction zone.

von Thünen Model A model that explains the location of agricultural activities in a spatial pattern of rings around a central market city, with profit-earning capability the determining where a crop or good is produced in reference to the market.

Vulnerability Probability of destruction of life or property from a hazard or crisis.

Washington Consensus Agreement among international financial institutions that policies opening markets in lower income countries would lead to economic development.

Water scarcity Lack of water resources needed to meet usage for personal consumption, irrigation, and industrial consumption in a region.

White flight Movement of whites from the city and adjacent neighborhoods to outlying suburbs in response to a growth in the number of residents who are a different race. Common in U.S. cities in response to **blockbusting**.

world cities highly connected cities that function as nodes in global networks.

World-systems theory Theory originated by Immanuel Wallerstein and illuminated by his **three-tier structure**, proposing that social change in and economic wealth in the periphery is inextricably linked to the core.

Zero population growth A state in which a population is maintained at a constant level because the number of deaths is exactly offset by the number of births.

Zionism Movement for the establishment of a national homeland for Jews in the land between the Mediterranean Sea and the Jordan River.

Zoning laws Legal restrictions on land use that determine what types of building and economic activities are allowed.